Introduction to

Robotics

ELECTRONIC SYSTEMS ENGINEERING SERIES

Consulting Editor **E L Dagless**
University of Bristol

OTHER TITLES IN THE SERIES

Introduction to
Robotics

Phillip John McKerrow
University of Wollongong
Australia

ADDISON-WESLEY PUBLISHING COMPANY

Sydney · Wokingham, England · Reading, Massachusetts
Menlo Park, California · New York · Don Mills, Ontario
Amsterdam · Bonn · Singapore · Tokyo · Madrid · San Juan

Cover designed by Hybert Design and Type, Maidenhead based on a two-dimensional sonar map produced by Alberto Elfes at CMU Robotics Institute. See Figure 8.23 on page 444.
Typeset by Colset Private Limited, Singapore.
Printed in Singapore.

First printed 1991.

British Library Cataloguing in Publication Data
McKerrow, P. J.
  Introduction to Robotics
  1. Robotics   I. Series
628.8'92
ISBN 0–201–18240–8

Library of Congress Cataloging in Publication Data
McKerrow, P. J.
  Introduction to Robotics
     p.   cm.
  Includes bibliographic references
  ISBN 0–201–18240–8
  1. Robotics   I. Title   II. Series
QA76.6.Z56   1990
628.8'92

90–317
CIP

Preface

Goals

The rapid advance of robotics during the last five years has made it an exciting field to work in. During that time, we have witnessed an explosion in knowledge. Some areas of robotics have matured and now have generally agreed upon sets of principles and techniques, whilst others still require considerable research. Following the ferment in research has been an increasing variety of applications.

This growth in the science of robotics has led to the establishment of robotics courses in universities and institutes of technology. Because robotics involves several disciplines, these courses are taught by different departments in different universities. From an *ad hoc* collection of topics, courses have settled into two main groups. First, there are courses that teach mechanics and control in depth. Second there are courses that cover many topics at a fairly shallow level. The former courses are criticized because of their narrow view of robotics; the latter courses are criticized because they tend to give a user's view of robotics.

The main aim of this book is to bridge the gap between these two approaches by covering the whole of robotics at sufficient technical depth for the student to feel confident enough to engage in further independent study in any area. Thus, I have sought a balance between breadth and depth. To do this, I treat some topics from an algorithmic understanding point of view, and others from a rigorous mathematical point of view, depending upon their maturity and whether or not they are fundamental to the whole discipline. I have also sought to place understanding before techniques, but without sacrificing accuracy. Also, the coverage is intended to be sufficiently up to date to provide a research resource for practitioners.

In order to achieve this goal, I had to decide what constitutes the discipline of robotics (McKerrow, 1986). Then I had to integrate an

v

apparently *ad hoc* collection of topics from several disciplines into a coherent whole. Finally, I had to determine the level at which each topic should be presented.

Trade offs

The achievement of this goal required several significant trade offs. Each chapter in this book could be expanded into a book on its own, as evidenced by the range of books on the market. Thus, the first and most difficult trade-off was the balance between technical depth and breadth of coverage. The balance that I have tried to strike is to cover fundamental topics, such as kinematics, at considerable depth with mathematical rigour, and other topics from an algorithmic standpoint. For this reason, the approach and level of content varies through the book, with major changes occuring at Chapter 3 and in Chapter 8.

The second trade off is that between the desires of lecturers and the desires of students in a text book. Many lecturers like a cryptic coverage of a topic that can be used as a quick reference, because they are educated in the field and can insert the intermediate steps into problem solutions. In contrast, many students desire a text that gives an overview of each topic and where it fits in the scheme of things, step-by-step development of solutions to problems, and plenty of worked examples. Students learn the technical details more quickly if first they understand their purpose. I have leaned toward the students' perspective, as they are the ones who require an aid to learning.

One aim in taking the student's view has been to make robotics accessible to undergraduate students, by providing a simpler introduction to each topic than is generally found in rigorous texts. I have sought to simplify the analysis of manipulators, without loss of rigor, by emphasizing two-link manipulators. The principles are the same, but the mathematics is much simpler.

Third is the trade off between the amount of background material required by students from different disciplines. This trade off is a direct consequence of the multi-disciplinary nature of robotics. For example, mechanical engineering students can be expected to have considerable background in dynamics but not computer science students: all students will lack background in some topics. For each topic, I have attempted to help the weaker student (weaker in the discipline that that topic is derived from) with a descriptive introduction and background information in windows. I have shifted some background information to windows to reduce the tedium for the reader who is familiar with the topic.

Finally, I have tried to maintain a balance between research oriented analytical techniques and practical empirical techniques. In many areas, the results of research are still to be applied in practice.

Course structure

As a consequence of the explosion of knowledge in robotics, there is sufficient material in this book for a one year course at graduate or senior undergraduate level. In a department that is offering a stream of robotics courses, this introductory course could be followed by in-depth courses in specific topics, such as mechanics and vision.

However, many departments only have enough space in a crowded curriculum to offer a half year course. The range of material in this text allows the lecturer the flexibility to focus his course to comply with the theme of his department. To aid in focusing courses, I have laid out a suggested subject matrix in Table 1. This matrix includes themes for the four main disciplines involved in robotics: computer science, electrical engineering, production engineering, and mechanical engineering.

I have laid out the matrix for a 14-week course of two lectures per week, with individual lectures ranging from 1 to 2 hours. The number of lectures allocated to each topic indicates the importance of the topic within that theme and the depth to which it should be covered. When only one

Table 1 Subject matrix of suggested course structures, based on two lectures per week for 14 weeks during half a year. Lecture times may range from 1 to 2 hours. The lectures allocated to *Other* may be used to expand a topic and for discussing laboratory work.

Course Duration	Half year				Full year
Discipline	Computer Science	Electrical Engineering	Production Engineering	Mechanical Engineering	All
Focus	Perception Planning Programming	Sensors Interfaces Control	Manufacturing Applications Programming	Mechanisms Mechanics Control	Robotics
Chapter topic	Number of lectures				
1. Introduction	1	1	2	1	2
1.5 Applications	1	2	3	1	3
2. Components	1	2	2	3	4
3. Object Location	2	2	2	2	2
4. Arm Position	4	4	4	3	4
5. Arm Motion	0	2	0	2	4
6. Statics	0	0	0	2	3
6.4 Arm Statics	0	1	0	1	1
7. Arm Dynamics	0	0	0	2	4
8. Mobile robots	3	0	1	0	4
9. Task Planning	3	0	3	0	4
10. Sensors	2	4	2	2	4
10.8 Vision	4	2	2	2	4
11. Control	1	4	1	3	4
12. Programming	2	0	0	0	2
12.4 Languages	2	2	4	2	3
Other	2	2	2	2	4

lecture is allocated to a topic, it is meant to be an introductory overview. The lectures allocated to *Other* allow the lecturer the flexibility to include videos, demonstrations, tutorials, and so on.

To run an effective robotics course requires access to a laboratory for hands-on experience. A laboratory configuration containing the right hardware can be constructed from low-cost equipment for less than the price of an industrial robot. An industrial robot will provide a greater range of practical experience, but the students will require more detailed supervision, as safety issues have to be considered.

Content

The ordering of the chapters follows the traditional bottom-up approach of acquainting students with the physical mechanisms of robotics before moving to the higher level issues of modelling, planning, control, and programming. This approach moves the student from the concrete to the abstract, from the known to the unknown. In contrast, the design of a robot system should be top down, from task requirements to physical detail.

Chapter 1 includes sections on the history, philosophy and applications of robotics. It sets the stage for the rest of the book and includes a system design example to show how the parts fit to form a coherent whole. A brief introduction is given to several important applications. Manufacturers and research institutions have video tapes which give a good insight into applications. Many of these are available for a small fee.

The section on the philosophy has been included for a number of reasons. First, I set out to cover the field, and social issues are an important aspect of the development of technology. Second, there is increasing concern about the impact of technology on society and the environment. The attitude, 'that if we can do it then we should do it' is not accepted by many thinking people. Third, when we lecture to a class we present our values along with the subject material. There is no such thing as value-neutral education. If we are honest about our values, then students can evaluate what we teach in the light of that knowledge. Finally, this section is meant to provide a springboard for discussion, which the lecturer and student can choose to use or ignore, as they desire.

Chapter 2 covers the subsystems and physical components used to construct a robot. Chapters 3 to 7 cover the mathematical modelling of manipulator position, motion, and force using vectors and homogeneous matrices. The notation used in these chapters (Figure 3.1) is an amalgam of the notations found in robotics books. Classroom experience with this notation indicates that it is easy to comprehend.

Chapters 3 and 4 have had more classroom testing than the rest of the book. They contain fundamental modelling concepts. The main difficulty people have when modelling the world with coordinate frames is their lack of goemetric reasoning skills, particularly the ability to visualize spatial relationships. Setting assignments similar to the worked examples in Chapter 3 will help develop these skills.

From Chapter 8 onwards, the style of presentation is more descriptive treatment than the earlier part of the book. These chapters have a heavy concentration on algorithmic solutions to problems. Mobile robots are treated in Chapter 8 because the algorithms used for planning are simpler than those used for manipulators. Also, the sections on mobile robot kinematics and dynamics align closely with the previous chapters.

The task planning hierarchy developed in Chapter 9 is fleshed out in the following chapters; hence the order of treatment. Programming is dealt with last because the software is the ingredient that turns a set of subsystems into an integrated robot.

Acknowledgements

During the writing of this book, I have interacted with many people. Each has had some influence on the final product. Some I have enjoyed meeting in person; others I have only met in papers and books. I particularly want to thank the students at Wollongong University and Carnegie-Mellon University on whom I tried out much of this material, and who graciously pointed out difficulties and errors.

During a sabbatical year at Carnegie-Mellon University, I collected much of the material in a preliminary form and worked out how to fit it together. Professors Raj Reddy and Art Sanderson provided considerable practical support during that time. The discussions between members of the robotics interest group co-ordinated by Marc Raibert and Mat Mason contributed greatly to my understanding of the science of robotics.

This book has improved vastly through the constructive, and at times critical, comments made by the reviewers and the editorial staff at Addison-Wesley. Thank you to all the reviewers, particularly those who took the trouble to anotate the manuscript.

Professor Greg Doherty, head of The Department of Computing Science at The University of Wollongong, supported me in numerous practical ways. I have greatly appreciated the excellent typing and editing performed for me by Priscilla Kendle, the departmental secretary.

Finally, I want to thank my wife, Ann, and my children, Rochelle, Daniel, Owen, and Joel, for their love, support and encouragement. The credit for this work belongs to the Lord Jesus Christ who does all things well.

Phillip McKerrow
Wollongong,
September 1990

Publisher's Acknowledgements

The author and publisher wish to thank the following for permission to use photographs and drawings in figures throughout the text.

Chapter 1

Figure 1.1 is reproduced courtesy of Robot/X™ News. Figure 1.2 is reproduced courtesy of General Electric (U.S.A.) Research and Development Center. Figure 1.3 is reproduced courtesy of Burden Neurological Institute. Figure 1.4 is reproduced courtesy of SRI International. Figure 1.6 is reproduced courtesy of Robot Defense Systems, Inc. Figure 1.7 is reproduced courtesy of Ewell Parker Industrial Trucks. Figures 1.9, 1.10(a) and 1.10(b) are reproduced courtesy of Hobart Brothers. Figure 1.13 is reproduced courtesy of The Robotics Institute, Carnegie-Mellon University. Figure 1.14 is reproduced courtesy of Oldelft. Figure 1.15 is reproduced by courtesy of Adept. Figure 1.18 is reproduced courtesy of Cochlea Corp. Figure 1.19 is reproduced courtesy of The Robotics Institute, Carnegie-Mellon University. Figure 1.21 is reproduced courtesy of Zymark Corporation. Figure 1.22 is reproduced courtesy of The Robotics Institute, Carnegie-Mellon University. Figure 1.25 is reproduced courtesy of University of Missouri-Rolla. Figure 1.26 is reproduced courtesy of Eshed Robotec. Figure 1.27 is reproduced courtesy of R. B. Robot.

Chapter 2

Figure 2.3 is reproduced courtesy of Shigeo Hirose Department of Physical Engineering, University of Tokyo. Figures 2.5, 2.6, 2.8, 2.9, 2.10 and 2.12 are reproduced courtesy of The Robotics Institute, Carnegie-Mellon University. Figure 2.13 is reproduced courtesy of International Robotic Engineering Inc. Figures 2.14 and 2.15 are reproduced courtesy of Marc Raibert. Figures 2.16, 2.17 and 2.18 are reproduced courtesy of Isao Shimogama, Department of Mechanical Engineering, University of Tokyo. Figure 2.19 is reproduced courtesy of Shigeo Hirose, Department of Physical Engineering, University of Tokyo. Figure 2.21 is reproduced courtesy of Odetics Inc. Figure 2.22 is reproduced courtesy of The Robotics Institute, Carnegie-Mellon University. Figure 2.24 is reproduced courtesy of Robomatix. Figure 2.27 is reproduced courtesy of Hobart Brothers. Figure 2.29 is reproduced courtesy of the Central Office of Information, Crown Copyright reserved. Figure 2.32 is reproduced courtesy of Hobart Brothers. Figure 2.37 is reproduced courtesy of the DiVilbiss Company. Figure 2.39 is reproduced courtesy of EOA Systems. Figure 2.40 is reproduced courtesy of AT&T Bell Laboratories: R. A. Boie: mechanical design; M. J. Sibilia: fabrication and testing; G. L. Miller: finger position sensors; M. K. Brown: control algorithms. Figure 2.41 is reproduced courtesy of the University of Utah. Photograph by M. Milocek. Figure 2.42 is reproduced courtesy of Martonair. Figure 2.43 is reproduced courtesy of Moog. Figures 2.45, 2.47 and 2.50 are reproduced courtesy of PMI Motors, a division of Kollmorgan Corporation. Figure 2.52 is reproduced courtesy of Emhart. Figure 2.53 is reproduced courtesy of The Robotics Institute, Carnegie-Mellon University. Figure 2.54 is reproduced courtesy of Helical Products Co. Figure 2.55 is reproduced courtesy of IKO. Figure 2.56 is reproduced courtesy of Hobart Brothers. Figure 2.57 is reproduced courtesy of Robot Defense Systems, Denver CO.

Chapter 6

Figures 6.2, 6.3, 6.4, 6.5 and 6.14 are reproduced courtesy of The Robotics Institute, Carnegie-Mellon University.

Chapter 7

Figures 7.10 and 7.12 are reproduced courtesy of The Robotics Institute, Carnegie-Mellon University.

Chapter 8

Figure 8.1 is reproduced courtesy of Flexible Manufacturing Systems Inc. Figures 8.12, 8.13, 8.14 and 8.15 are reproduced courtesy of Marc Raibert. Figures 8.21 and 8.23 are reproduced courtesy of The Robotics Institute, Carnegie-Mellon University. Figure 8.31 is reproduced courtesy of SRI International.

Chapter 9

Figure 9.3 is reproduced courtesy of SRI International. Figure 9.5 is reproduced courtesy of McDonnell Douglas. Figure 9.9 is reproduced courtesy of

The Robotics Institute, Carnegie-Mellon University. Figure 9.11 is reproduced courtesy of McDonnell Douglas.

Chapter 10

Figure 10.9 is reproduced courtesy of Dr Johannes Heidenhain. Figure 10.10 is reproduced courtesy of The Robotics Institute, Carnegie-Mellon University. Figure 10.27 is reproduced courtesy of Lord Corporation. Figure 10.24 is reproduced courtesy of Shigeo Hirose, Department of Physical Engineering, University of Tokyo. Figures 10.25 and 10.26 are reproduced courtesy of Tactile Robotic Systems. Figures 10.39(c) and 10.41 are reproduced courtesy of The Robotics Institute, Carnegie-Mellon University. Figure 10.46 is reproduced courtesy of Dr Susumu Tachi, Mechanical Engineering Laboratory, Tsukuba Science City. Figure 10.52 is reproduced courtesy of General Electric (U.S.A.) Research and Development Center.

Chapter 11

Figure 11.16 is reproduced courtesy of Stephen Young.

Chapter 12

Figure 12.22 is reproduced courtesy of Stephen Young.

Contents

1 · *Introduction*

You end up with a tremendous respect for a human being if you're a roboticist

Joseph Engelberger (Bortz, 1985)

Objectives

In this chapter, we introduce the field of robotics, raise questions about social issues for discussion, and look briefly at some applications. Our objective is to provide a context for the detailed analysis of robots in subsequent chapters. This background material includes the following topics:

- a brief history of robotics,
- some definitions of robotics,
- a system design example to illustrate how the pieces fit together,
- a review of social issues from a Christian perspective, and
- a short description of several applications.

1

1.1 History

For centuries, people have built mechanisms to imitate parts of the human body. The ancient Egyptians attached mechanical arms to the statues of their gods. These arms were operated by priests, who claimed to be acting under inspiration from the gods. The Greeks built hydraulically operated statues, originally to illustrate the science of hydraulics. These too found their way into temples, where they were used to fascinate worshippers (Hillier, 1978).

During the eighteenth century, intricate mechanical puppets, **automata**, were built in Europe. These enacted convincing imitations of human and animal actions and were a tremendous success with the public. They included accurate models of people with arms, lips and other parts driven by linkages and cams controlled by rotating drum selectors. Some could write, some could draw, and a famous one, a shepherd, could play a flute (Williams, 1978). Art and technology had advanced to the point where the designer, Jacques de Vaucanson, was able to make rubber lips move into the correct shape to control the flow of air into the flute to produce musical notes, in the same way that a musician does. By making finger motions over the holes of the flute, this android could play a repertoire of twelve tunes. Each automaton was mechanically programmed to carry out one task, but it could not execute a different task without complete rebuilding. They did not respond to their environment in any way.

Until the middle of the twentieth century, programmable automata were used solely for entertainment. However, prior to this, considerable advances were made in programmable machines for specific industrial processes, starting with the Jacquard loom in 1801. Developments in technology; including the modern electronic computer, feedback control of actuators, power transmission through gears, and sensor technology were required before programmable automata were sufficiently flexible to be of any practical use in manufacturing.

Several factors contributed to the development of robots during the latter half of the twentieth century. Artificial intelligence researchers developed ways to emulate human information processing with electronic computers and invented a variety of mechanisms to test their theories. The capital cost of hard automation, particularly in the car industry, spurred industrial interest in flexible automation. Safety problems in the nuclear industry led to the development of teleoperators for remote handling of radioactive material. The problems of placing people in other remote and hostile environments led to the development of undersea vehicles and space robotics. Many scientists were gripped by a desire to understand the control and perception processes in people; creative engineers were challenged by the possibility of building programmable machines and the deeply felt human needs of the physically disabled stimulated work in prosthetic devices and improvements to wheelchairs.

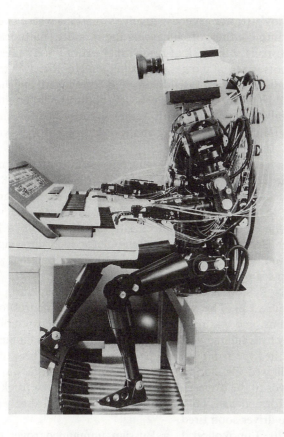

Figure 1.1
The Wasubot — a humanoid musician at Tsukuba Expo' 85. It can sight-read music, recognize a limited set of voice commands, respond in a synthesized voice, and play a wide range of music. Sixty-seven microprocessors are used.

Robot is a Slavic word for worker. In 1921, it was popularized in the play *RUR* (Rossum's Universal Robots) written by the Czechoslovakian playwright, Karel Kapek. The machines in his play revolted, killed their human masters and took over the world. These machines resembled people, but worked twice as hard. In 1926, the first movie involving robots, *Metropolis*, was released in Germany. In 1939, Electro, a walking robot, and his dog Sparko were displayed at the New York World's Fair. In 1950, Isaac Asimov published his book *I Robot*, which revolves around intelligent humanoid robots designed according to a set of laws:

1. A robot may not injure a human being, or through inaction allow a human being to come to harm.

2. A robot must obey the orders given it by human beings, except where such orders would conflict with the first law.

3. A robot must protect its own esistence as long as such protection does not conflict with the first or second law.

Consequently, Asimov's robots are all obedient servants of humans, representing a totally different attitude to advanced technology to that of

Kapek. Asimov's stories generally involve situations where two of the laws are brought into conflict, often causing the robot to malfunction. Human robot specialists have the task of resolving the conflict. The response of the public to robots in recent movies, for example, 'Number 5' in the film *Short Circuit*, has been one of fascination with 'intelligent' mechanisms. The reader should be aware that popular beliefs about the capabilities of robots are considerably out of line with actual practice. Unfortunately, many efforts to stimulate interest in robotics reinforce these wrong images (Figure 1.1).

Goertz is credited with developing **teleoperators** (remote manipulators under human control (Martin and Hamel, 1984)). In 1948, he built a bilateral mechanical master-slave manipulator at Argonne National Laboratory. In the same year, General Mills manufactured a unilateral manipulator based on electric motors with switch control. In 1954, Goertz built another electric master-slave manipulator incorporating servos and force reflection, and in 1956, a General Mills manipulator was fitted for manned deep-sea operation.

In 1968, R.S. Mosher at General Electric built a quadrupedal walking machine (Figure 1.2). This walking truck was over 3 metres long, weighed 1 400 kilograms, and was powered by a 68 kilowatt petrol motor. Each leg was driven by hydraulic servos, and was controlled by the human driver. The driver controlled the front legs of the truck by moving his arms, while the back legs followed the motion of his legs. Force feedback was reflected by the joint servos to the driver, allowing him to control the truck by feel. The machine performed well, but driving it required an extremely high level of skill, and the driver soon tired.

In 1970, Lunokohod 1, a Russian unmanned rover explored the surface of the moon under remote control from earth (Moore, 1972). During the 1960s, work started on the design of **prostheses** to replace lost human limbs (Whitney, 1969). While there is considerable contention as to whether or not teleoperators and prostheses constitute robots, there is no doubt that their development contributed significantly to the development of robots, and that the basic technology is applicable in all three fields (Bejczy, 1980).

The first robots which could be programmed to respond to external sensory information without direct human intervention were built in artificial intelligence laboratories to test theories in cognition and vision. In the late 1940s, Claude Shannon built a maze-solving mouse (Sutherland, 1969). His maze was a 5×5 array of squares, which could be configured with removable aluminium walls. A motorized carriage underneath the maze provided power to the mouse through magnetic coupling. Simple relay circuits provided logic for exploring the maze and memory for recording a solution.

A 2-bit relay memory was allocated to each of the 25 squares. This memory recorded the direction the mouse travelled last time it left a square. Shannon used a simple learning algorithm: when the mouse entered a square,

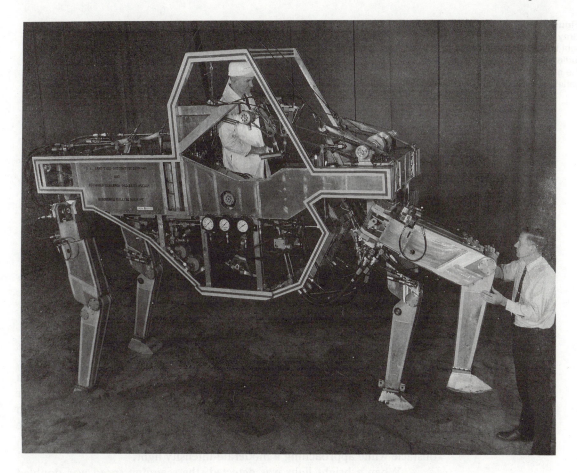

Figure 1.2
Mosher's walking truck: a
research prototype of a four-
legged quadruped built at
General Electric Research
and Development Centre.

it tried to leave the square 90° to the left of the path it took last time it exited
that square, as recorded by the 2-bit relay memory. If the mouse ran into a
wall, it returned to the centre of the square, turned a further 90° to the left
and tried again, often leaving in the direction it entered the square.
Eventually, the mouse reached the cheese, and its solution to the maze was
recorded in the relay memories.

Grey Walter (1953) used a tortoise (Figure 1.3) in his cybernetic
research. The tortoise was oval in shape, driven by one electric motor, and
steered by another under the control of a sophisticated two-valve circuit.
This circuit was controlled by signals from two sensors: a bump detector and
a light detector. The tortoise was placed in a dark room with one or more
point sources of light. The light detector was mounted on the steering
column, so that it always faced in the same direction as the single front driving wheel. In the dark, the steering wheel rotated continuously, so that the

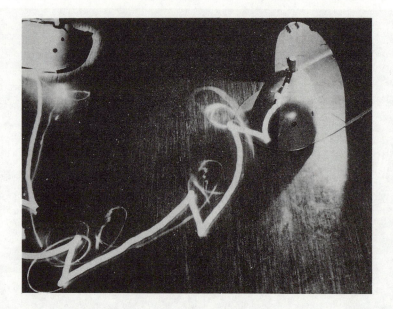

light detector scanned steadily. When a moderately intense light was detected, the scanning stopped and the tortoise moved towards the light. When it ran into an obstacle, a bump detector attached to the oval shell sent a signal to the electronic circuit. In response, the circuit alternated power between the two motors to produce a turn-and-push manoeuvre, an action which continued until the obstacle was cleared. This sensory response overrode the light-sensing mechanism, allowing the tortoise to avoid an obstacle while approaching a moderate-intensity light.

When a bright light was detected, the scanning speed was doubled while the light was visible to the detector, effectively causing the tortoise to back away from the light. When the tortoise's batteries were almost flat, the electronic circuit switched, causing a bright light to be perceived as a moderate light. A bright light was placed in the tortoise's hutch together with a battery charger, so that when its battery was flat, the tortoise would seek its hutch, enter it and recharge its battery. When the battery was charged, the circuit switched again, causing the tortoise to back away from the light to continue its search of the room.

In 1969, a more sophisticated mobile robot was built at Stanford Research Institute to carry out experiments in using vision to control action (Nilsson, 1984). This robot was called Shakey (Figure 1.4) because of its shakey mechanical construction. Shakey was set simple tasks to solve: recognize an object using vision; find its way to the object, and then perform some action on the object, for example, push it over.

In 1952, the first **numerically controlled machine** was built at Massachusetts Institute of Technology (Dorf, 1983). In 1954 George Devol

ANTENNA FOR
RADIO LINK

TELEVISION
CAMERA

RANGE
FINDER

ON-BOARD
LOGIC

CAMERA
CONTROL
UNIT

BUMP
DETECTOR

CASTER
WHEEL

DRIVE
MOTOR

DRIVE
WHEEL

Figure 1.4
Shakey: a robot developed
at Stanford Research
Institute. It was the first
mobile robot controlled by
vision.

designed the first programmable robot, a device he called a 'programmed articulated transfer device'. Joseph Engelberger, often called the father of the industrial robot, started Unimation, bought the rights to Devol's device, and developed the robot further. In 1962, General Motors installed its first Unimation robot. In 1976, the first robot arm in space was used by NASA's Viking probe to collect samples of Martian soil for analysis.

1.2 Robotics

The emphasis of this book is on planning tasks, programming, sensing the environment, and the design of robots. In this chapter we will, obtain an overview of the field, examine some of the human factors in robotics and look at the great variety of applications to which robots are being applied. There is currently no generally accepted definition for a robot. The Japanese have defined a robot as 'any device which replaces human labour' (Sosoka, 1985), and the Japanese Industrial Robot Association has classified robots into six categories from manual manipulators to intelligent robots (Schlussel, 1985). The Robot Institute of America has a more restricted definition:

> A programmable multi-function manipulator designed to move material, parts, or specialized devices through variable programmed motions for the performance of a variety of tasks.
>
> (Schlussel, 1985)

These definitions restrict robots to industrial applications and, indeed, some people believe that robotics should be a branch of manufacturing technology. Many current applications involve integrating robots into existing manufacturing processes, and engineers are building plants for automated manufacture where robots play a central role. However, the results of the research going on in laboratories throughout the world is leading both to hard automation being replaced by flexible machines and to robots that have no role in manufacturing processes. As a result, the use of hard automation will gradually reduce to high volume manufacturing plants, where flexibility is not required and the high cost of fixed automation can be justified. In comparison, robotics technology will make low volume production by small firms competitive. A better definition is:

> A Robot is a machine which can be programmed to do a variety of tasks, in the same way that a computer is an electronic circuit which can be programmed to do a variety of tasks.
>
> (McKerrow, 1986)

A narrow view of this definition excludes numerically controlled machines, because they can be programmed for variations within only one task. Teleoperators are not considered to be robots, because a human is the controlling element during operation. They provide an extension of human capabilities, not a replacement of them. Teleoperation is often the first stage of robot development. Prostheses provide replacements for impaired human limbs and thus are not robots either.

This definition is very narrow, but it can be widened out if desired. All four classes of mechanism share a common technological base, consequently the distinction is one of function, not one of technology. A numerically controlled machine could be classed as a specialized robot; teleoperators and prostheses can also be included, if one considers that they are programmed in real time by the operator. In other words, by expanding and restricting the scope of the words 'variety' and 'programming', the defintion can be as narrow or as broad as desired. Continued development in each of these areas will bring them closer together, justifying a broad definition. The study of robots is called **robotics**. One definition of robotics is:

> Robotics is the intelligent connection of perception to action.
>
> (Brady, 1985)

From a different perspective (McKerrow, 1986):

> Robotics is the discipline which involves:
>
> (a) the design, manufacture, control, and programming of robots;
>
> (b) the use of robots to solve problems;
>
> (c) the study of the control processes, sensors, and algorithms used in humans, animals, and machines; and
>
> (d) the application of these control processes and algorithms to the design of robots.

A clear distinction must be made between robotics engineering and the science of robotics. Robotics engineering is concerned with the design, construction, and application of robots. While robots are built during the course of scientific research, the goal of robotics science is not the development of machines, but to understand the physical and information processes underlying perception and action. Once basic principles are established, they can be used in the design of robots.

In this book, I have deliberately separated human beings from animals and machines. While some consider people to be no more than machines, and others consider people to be animals, many consider people to possess traits which distinguish them from animals and machines (MacKay, 1979). Alfred North Whitehead (1925) pointed out that there is a radical inconsistency at the basis of modern thought:

> A scientific realism, based on mechanism, is conjoined with an unwavering belief in the world of men and of the higher animals as being composed of self-determining organisms.

Our concept of what a person is, is based on religious truth, rather than on abstract scientific truth. To ignore this would be to suggest that truth can be found only through science and not in other areas of human endeavour. For example, a scientific description of water differs greatly from the non-scientific description a farmer would give. The scientist describes water as a molecule of oxygen atoms and hydrogen atoms, and the farmer describes water as essential to the growth of his plants. Both descriptions are true, but not exclusive; one describes the composition of water; the other, one of its functions. In addition, our scientific understanding of human intelligence, emotions, personality, relationships, biomechanics, and faith is so limited at present that science is not in a position to make such a definitive statement. Future research may arrive at this position, if it is within the realm of science, or, as has often happened in the past, may demonstrate how limited our knowledge is.

1.3 Overview

Robotics is a broad discipline, with significant content from the disciplines of physics, mathematics, electrical engineering, mechanical engineering, and computer science. As a result of considerable research during the late 1970s and 1980s, the volume of knowledge that constitutes robotics is large. To see how the components from other disciplines integrate into robotics, and to gain an overview of this book, we will look at the design of a system for an industrial application (Figure 1.5).

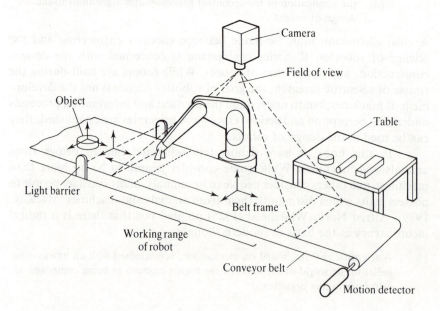

Figure 1.5
Robot system for picking objects off a moving conveyor belt.

System design progresses in a series of steps, each of which refines the results of the previous step. These steps are the specification of the task, decomposition of the task into actions, selection of components to achieve these actions, and evaluation of the design against performance criteria. Often these steps interact, and the overall process is repeated until a design is achieved which meets the desired compromise between cost, performance, and human impact.

In the task specification step, the designer specifies the task the system is to perform and spells out the performance criteria by which it will be evaluated. The task considered here is the task of picking objects off a moving conveyor belt and placing them on a table in a specified order and orientation. The conveyor belt will deliver the parts in an unknown order at a variable rate, although the speed of the conveyor belt is constant.

A robot is usually part of a larger system, so a task specification for the robot has to be extracted from the overall task specification. We will assume that the following process removes the objects from the table, faster than the robot places them there. In practice, the interaction between these two processes is a very important design consideration. In addition, we will assume that both manual and hard automation systems have been designed previously and that those designs are available for comparison.

Once the task is specified precisely, the designer can begin the process of decomposing the task into actions. The process of task planning is discussed in Chapter 9. All good design methodologies start by defining the output from the system. Given the task specification, what must the system do in order to perform the task and meet the desired performance goals? Once that question is answered, the designer can determine the actions required to produce that output. Finally, he or she can specify the inputs required to perform those actions.

In contrast to computing, which is concerned with the transformation of information from input to output, robotics is concerned with the transformation of the physical world from an input state to an output state. This transformation is achieved by manipulating real objects. From the definition of robotics as the intelligent connection of perception to action, we can decompose this physical transformation into a sequence of processes. These processes are: measurement, modelling, perception, planning and action. We will call this composition a **perception model** of robotics, because it describes the information processing required to perceive the current state of the world and respond accordingly.

When developing a system to achieve this transformation the designer works from the outputs (action) to the inputs (measurement). The actions of the robot effect the desired change in the physical state of the system. For our example, the following decomposition is obtained:

- **Action** The robot is to pick objects off the conveyor belt and place them on the table. To do this, it must detect each object, locate its position and orientation on the conveyor belt, grasp the object without damaging it, and place it on the table. Also, the robot must return to the start position before the next object arrives. To perform this task, the robot must move the gripper at constant velocity in a straight line along the conveyor. In order to get into the grasping position, the robot must be faster than the conveyor, and it must have sufficient reach to track the conveyor for long enough to grasp the object. Finally, the gripper must be designed to grasp the expected array of objects securely.

From the specification of the above actions, the designer should be able to specify the type of robot and its performance characteristics (speed, reach, and so on). Fixed-arm robots and mobile robots are discussed in Chapter 2. The design of grippers and other mechanisms used in robots are also discussed in Chapter 2. To achieve accurate path following, the motion of the joints of the robot arm must be controlled; servo control of robot motion is discussed in Chapter 11.

- **Planning** By examining the task, the designer has decomposed it into a repetitive sequence of actions: move to the start position, detect the object, move the gripper to the object, track the object, grasp the object, lift the object off the conveyor, and place the object on the table. Once these actions have been planned in detail, the designer can decompose them into sequences of robot motions.

  Planning trajectories to follow desired paths and planning grasping motions are discussed in Chapter 9. As part of the planning, we must consider the grasping forces, and the effect of minor errors in grasping position on the object. Interaction forces and the use of compliance to correct for minor errors are analysed in Chapter 6.

- **Perception** To perform the desired actions, decisions have to be made by the supervisory control program. For example, the objects on the table in Figure 1.5 have different shapes, and hence have different grasping positions. Using information from sensors, the system must perceive which object is on the conveyor, and select the appropriate grasping position.

- **Modelling** To achieve this task, numerous models are required. The information from the sensors must be fused into a task model (Chapter 10), which the robot uses to recognise which object is on the conveyor and to calculate the motion of the grasp point. To model objects in space we use coordinate frames, and to model the relationships between objects we use transformations. These are discussed in Chapter 3.

  To model this task, the designer places a belt frame on the centre of the belt, at the midpoint of the working range of the robot. This frame is fixed in space and the belt moves in relation to it. When an object is detected, an instantaneous frame is attached to it. This frame moves with the object. When the type, orientation, and lateral position of the object are determined, the instantaneous frame is modified to specify the grasp point. Thus, the equation which describes the motion of the instantaneous frame (task model) is:

$$I_{frame}(\text{time}) = - \text{ the distance from the belt frame to the light barrier}$$
$$+ \text{ a function of the motion of the conveyor}$$
$$+ \text{ a function of the type of the object} \qquad (1.1)$$
$$+ \text{ a function of the orientation of the object}$$
$$+ \text{ a function of the lateral position of the object}$$

To control the manipulator to track the object, the designer must model the manipulator. The modelling of the kinematics of manipulator position is discussed in Chapter 4, and the modelling of the kinematics of manipulator motion is discussed in Chapter 6. As the robot has mass, he or she must also model the dynamics of the robot if he or she is to achieve precise control (Chapter 7).

- **Measurement**   The robot obtains the parameters of the task model by measurement. It detects the object with a light barrier and uses a vision system to recognize the type of the object, and to calculate its orientation and lateral position. Conveyor motion is measured with an optical pulse generator. Also, to control its position and motion, the robot measures the joint angles and velocities with optical pulse generators. In addition, the robot confirms that the object is grasped with a touch sensor. All these sensors are discussed in Chapter 10. An important part of the design is the placement of these sensors, so that they obtain the correct information.

Having completed the design process, the designer can now select a suitable robot and sensors. During the selection, he or she has to consider one further thing. Will the programming language provided with the robot support each of the above transformation stages? Programming languages are discussed in Chapter 12. Once the components are selected, the cost of the system can be calculated.

Now the designer is in a position to compare the robotic system to manual operation and to hard automation. The first criterion he or she considers is performance. Does the robot provide the desired (or better) performance? The second criterion is cost. Is the robot system cost effective? The third criterion is human issues. Will management support this level of technology? Will the workforce accept it? What happens to displaced staff? Does the company have the infrastructure to service the equipment? What safety hazards are involved? What social and ethical problems are involved? Increasing public awareness of the impact of technology on people's lives and on the environment demands that engineers must take responsibility for the consequences of the equipment they design. These human issues are briefly discussed in the next section.

1.4 Philosophy

In this section, we will turn aside from a purely technical discussion to look at some of the human consequences of robotics. Each of us is faced with moral decisions with respect to the use of the technology we design. We are better equipped to make these decisions if we understand our own beliefs and their implications. What we think is grounded in what we believe. Many of the early scientists (for example, Newton, Pascal, Faraday, and Maxwell) never thought of science as being isolated from Christian beliefs (Trevelyan, 1942; Schaefer, 1976). Alfred North Whitehead (1925) made the following criticism of science:

> It has never cared to justify its faith or to explain its meanings . . . If science is not to degenerate into a medley of *ad hoc* hypotheses, it must become philosophical and must enter upon a thorough criticism of its foundations.

Robotics as a discipline in currently an *ad hoc* collection of topics. For these topics to be brought together into a unified body of knowledge, each of us has to think through the philosophical basis of our discipline. In the following sections, we will look at a number of topics in order to highlight the issues involved in working in robotics.

1.4.1 Axioms

Historically, science developed in the Christian civilization of western Europe, rather than other cultures with similar, highly developed, mathematical systems, owing to the character of the God they believed in (Whitehead, 1925). The Chinese, for example, had an early knowledge of the world but lost interest in science because:

> there was no confidence that the code of nature's laws could ever be unveiled or read . . . there was no assurance that a divine being, even more rational than ourselves, had ever formulated such a code capable of being read
>
> (Needham, 1969).

The sixteenth and seventeenth century European scientists rejected the world view of Aristotle in favour of a Christian world view (Schaefer, 1976). They believed that the universe was created by a God of order and purpose. Consequently, nature must also be ordered, and therefore, able to be studied and described in an ordered manner. From this world view, the following basic presuppositions of science were developed (Rhodes, 1965):

- a belief in an orderly, regular, rational, universe,
- a belief that this orderliness of the natural world is intelligible to the scientist,

- a belief in the reliability of human reason,
- a belief in the broad principle of causality,
- a belief in the personal integrity of the scientist.

On these presuppositions, the method of inductive and empirical enquiry, the process of observation, experimentation, and hypothesis, has its foundation. Hypothesis formulation involves the abstraction of certain elements from the total range of human experience. Thus, the scientific method is only one of a set of methods of describing human experience.

A Christian world view considers that the world can be explained only in terms of a personal creator God, and that truth is based upon revelation, and thus is absolute. The rationalist philosophers of the eighteenth century sought to develop a closed philosophical system based solely on man without reference to God. This was found to be impossible. However, instead of questioning their basic axiom, Hegel suggested a redefinition of truth – that truth no longer consisted of thesis (a true statement) and antithesis (the opposite of truth – a false statement), but was to to found in a synthesis of the two. This thinking leads to a general relativism where there are no absolutes, and no one is sure what is true. Faced with this, Søren Kierkegaard, a Danish philosopher, suggested that one could not arrive at synthesis by reason, but one achieved everything of real importance by a leap of faith, providing the basis for modern existential thought (Schaeffer, 1968).

The influence of existential philosophy on modern thought leaves many scientists in the position of having a set of axioms which are based upon a world view that they no longer accept. Some suggest that the practice of science is sufficient to validate its axioms. However, the truth of one's axioms cannot be validated from within one's axiomatic system. Many scientists accept these axioms as a valid research framework, without thinking about their basis. Along with other sciences, robotics accepts the above axioms. By a careful study of robotics-research papers, we can discern the axioms on which people are basing their research. Their axioms reflect the above general axioms, and are a refinement of them. They include:

- Nature consists of order not chaos, and is therefore worthy of study.
- The methods used by people to carry out tasks are ordered, and can thus be described using heuristics and algorithms. In current industrial practice, emphasis is not on human problem-solving skills, but rather on the methods used to execute a task once the problem is solved. The extent to which robots will be able to emulate human problem-solving skills is a matter for considerable research in artifical intelligence.
- Through careful study, scientists can understand the designs and algorithms used in creation.
- Engineers can emulate these designs and algorithms in the machines they develop.

- Scientists can derive basic principles from the designs in creation, principles which engineers can apply to the design of robots and robotic applications.
- By building machines to simulate the designs and algorithms found in biological systems, scientists can gain insight into the operation of these systems.
- Researchers can invent new solutions to problems and new designs which may show little resemblance to those found in nature.

1.4.2 Artificial intelligence

Artificial intelligence must have a central role in robotics if the connection of perception to action is to be intelligent (Brady, 1985). While artificial intelligence research gave birth to robotics, current industrial use of robotics involves little application of artificial intelligence (Joseph Engelberger in Bortz, 1985). The state of the art is for intelligent people to find solutions to robotics problems, which they implement with robotics technology. This is partly because much of the artificial intelligence research currently being carried out involves artificial problems in abstract domains (artificial in the sense that they are contrived to allow study of a particular concept), whereas robotics involves practical problems in a real physical world. Artificial intelligence is called upon to tackle the problems of how to represent knowledge (in particular, sensory data), how to perceive crucial aspects of the world which impact on the problem at hand, how to use knowledge in problem solving, and how to act on that knowledge in the robot's current situation.

In his book *Godel, Escher, Bach: an Eternal Golden Braid*, (Basic Books, 1979), Douglas Hofstadter makes the following comments on artificial intelligence:

> No one knows where the borderline between non-intelligent behavior and intelligent behavior lies; in fact, to suggest that a sharp borderline exists is probably silly. But essential abilities for intelligence are certainly:
>
> - to respond to situations very flexibly;
> - to take advantage of fortuitous circumstances;
> - to make sense out of ambiguous or contradictory messages;
> - to recognize the relative importance of different elements of a situation;
> - to find similarities between situations despite differences which may separate them;
> - to draw distinctions between situations despite similarities which may link them;
> - to synthesize new concepts by taking old concepts and putting them together in new ways;
> - to come up with ideas which are novel.
>
> Here one runs up against a seeming paradox. Computers by their very nature are the most inflexible, desireless, rule-following beasts. Fast though

they may be, they are nonetheless the epitome of unconsciousness. How, then, can intelligent behavior be programmed? Isn't this the most blatant contradiction in terms? One of the major theses of this book is that it is not a contradiction at all.

In the rest of his book, Hofstadter argues that intelligent behaviour can be obtained with many sets of rules at different levels, where rules at one level may be modified by rules at a higher level using recursion. Other researchers dispute this claim, because brain research has shown that the human brain changes its 'architecture' as well as its 'programming' and its 'data'. At its very core, artificial intelligence is struggling with two closely related problems: 'what is intelligence?', and, 'is it possible to make a machine intelligent?'.

In robotics, researchers are studying, and trying to copy, the human capabilities of mobility, dexterity, intelligence and sensory perception. The result may well be a highly dextrous, very intelligent, sensor-packed social misfit. The 'higher' characteristics of humans; such as personality, insight, empathy, the appreciation of beauty, and the ability to engage in meaningful personal relationships; and the 'nobler' attributes of people; such as trust, love, hope, faith, and dignity bear no relationship to a person's physical ability or intelligence. The simplest person can enter into a loving relationship, while the most intelligent can have a very boring personality. These characteristics and attributes are certainly influenced by our physical and intellectual abilities, but they are moulded to a greater extent by the emotional crises of life, which often call upon resources derived from aspects of our personalities of which we were previously unaware.

1.4.3   Evolution

Evolution is a popular topic in robotics literature. The idea of people evolving into robots has become quite popular in science fiction, and many articles are being written by scientists on the possible outcomes of robot evolution (for example, Scheckley, 1985). A number of writers are claiming that the evolution of people into robots is inevitable. One researcher (Moravec, 1985) bases his research methodology on the theory of evolution. If we base our ideas for the development of robots on one of the current theories of origins then we should be aware of the shortcomings of that theory, and the impact that changes in it will have on our hypotheses.

Evolution is one of a number of theories proposed to explain the origin of the human race and it is the most popular theory in the scientific community. Since the mid-nineteenth century, it has changed several times in response to new discoveries, particularly the failure to discover the intermediate links hypothesized by Darwin (1859). Each of the theories of evolution holds that the current species have common ancestors, and that some mechanism of selection plays an important part in the process (Stebbins and

Ayala, 1985). They differ in their attempts to provide a mechanism by which natural selection could work. Many mechanisms have been proposed only to be rejected later (Punnett, 1938). Some scientists seek an answer in the stars (Hoyle and Wickeramasinghe, 1981). From time to time, the theory of evolution is challenged by people who hold that the available evidence supports an alternative theory better (Anderson and Coffin, 1977). The proponents of the various theories agree that many species have disappeared from the earth, that variation has occurred within species, but they disagree on the possibility of the formation of new, more complex species.

All take the same limited set of facts, apply the same set of scientific methods, and end up with different theories because their axioms are different. Many evolutionists now assume evolution as a scientific axiom, to be accepted without question. Stephen J. Gould (in Adler and Carey, 1982) put it his way: 'Evolution is a fact, like apples falling out of trees . . .'. They are faced with the problem of proving their axioms from within their axiomatic system.

Robotics involves evolution in the sense of gradual development guided by intelligent researchers, not evolution in the sense of natural selection by a mechanism of chance, fundamental to some biological theories of evolution. All technological design involves intelligent creativity, and consequently, the evolution of humans to robots is not inevitable, as suggested by some, but we have the power to decide what we will use robots for (de Garis, 1989). Fundamental to all this is the value we place on people. If people are considered to be unique and valuable, scientists will design robots to serve humans, not to replace them.

1.4.4 Social impact

> Given resistance, whatever its focus, it may be time for the industrial roboticist to take a moral and ethical stance
>
> (Clapp, 1982)

The introduction of technology is often justified on the basis that a net gain in productivity will benefit society as a whole, even if, in the process, a (comparatively) few people suffer the loss of employment and dignity (Minsky, 1985). This argument holds up well until you are the person to be replaced, then you suffer the crisis of being unwanted, and your self-esteem as well as your income drops dramatically. Too often, the only people to benefit are the owners of the business, who make more profit. Any benefit to society is often offset by the economic and social costs of unemployment (Cooley, 1981). For robotics to benefit all, a balance must be sought between making profit and caring for people.

The introduction of computer and robotic technology makes possible greater skill, more creative work, and a more autonomous work environment. All of these potential benefits should lead to enriched occupations and increased job satisfaction. Unfortunately, rather than realizing the exceptional potential of computer technology, the reality is moving in a direction of increased authority in industrial production, where technology is used to monitor and discipline workers. A direction that frequently degrades the quality of life on the job, and ironically, can throttle rather than increase worker productivity (Shaiken, 1986).

Technological advance is not a bad thing in itself, but the inventors of the technology must take some responsibility for the consequences of it, by ensuring that safeguards are set up to protect those who could be hurt by it.

> Will our children be able to live with the world we are here and now
> constructing?
>
> (Weizebaum, 1983)

Proponents of robotics often suggest that the introduction of robots will increase both the wealth and leisure of people. We should aim for a society where the wealth is evenly spread among the people and not concentrated in the hands of a few investors, or in the State as is the case with a socialist system. Only then will robotics benefit each individual.

A second factor forcing the introduction of new technology is the fierce competition between the industrialized nations, each striving to maintain a share of a world market that is already oversupplied by highly productive industries. During the first half of the 1980s, the steel industry went through a slump, resulting in massive unemployment in the USA and Australia, as a result of oversupply on the world market, particularly from the more productive Asian manufacturers. To cut production costs, many companies turn to labour-saving technology. However, the factors contributing to the cost of production in a broad range of manufacturing companies have been found to be (roughly): materials, 55 per cent; overhead, 35 per cent; and direct labour, 10 per cent. There is some additional labour cost in materials and overhead, but it is obvious from these figures that more can be saved by cutting the cost of materials or overhead than by cutting the cost of labour.

In terms of robotics Frank Pitman, assistant director of the Carnegie–Mellon University Robotics Institute, commented:

> People displacement because of robotics is not as great as one would think.
> The need to change a plant's capabilities has had a greater impact on
> labour than robotics. Management and labour now realize that without
> making improvements in processes, they quickly find themselves in a non-
> competitive situation, like what happened to the U.S. automakers
>
> (in Cichowicz, 1985)

Manufacturers often justify the introduction of robots on the basis that they perform consistently. They believe that if a robot does a job incorrectly, it will do it incorrectly every time; and if a robot does a job correctly, it will do it correctly every time. This statement is true while the environment of the robot doesn't change. Electronics manufacturers thought that using robots to mount components on printed circuit boards would reduce the number of defects to zero. What has happened is that a robot produces defects where people didn't. A human assembler will produce a defect through carelessness. A robot produces defects because it is not flexible enough to correct for exceptions. For example, when a lead on a component is bent a person will straighten it before inserting the component into a printed circuit board; in contrast a robot may not recognize that the lead is bent and try to insert the component, resulting in a bad connection with the lead crunched up on top of the board. The most difficult task faced by robot programmers is the detection and correction of errors, because of uncertainty about the state of the process (Section 12.4.7). In many applications, a conscientious person will do a better job every time.

Neale Clapp (1982) has proposed three basic laws which might govern industrial robot installations:

- Organizations may not install robots to the economic, social or physical detriment of workers or management.
- Organizations may not install robots through devious or closed strategies which reflect distrust or disregard for the workforce, for surely they will fulfill their own prophecy.
- Organizations may only install robots on those tasks which, while currently performed by men, are tasks where the man is like a robot, not the robot like a man.

1.4.5 Machines of war

Asimov's laws of robotics precluded robots harming people, instead they were to sacrifice themselves to save people. Modern military planners have no such ideals, instead robots are seen as making a significant contribution to future arsenals (Fulsang, 1985). Currently the main military use of robotics is in remote defusing of bombs, and undersea mine hunting (Adam, 1985). Much of the research into remotely controlled vehicles has the goal of removing people from the front lines. This research is based on the following premise (Grahman, 1972):

By every measure, Remotely Manned Vehicles (RMVs) will prove more versatile, more accurate and much less costly than conventionally operated tactical aircraft . . . In comparison with manned aircraft, tactical RMVs have the following advantages, they:

- can attack much closer in.
- present much less area to defending anti-aircraft artillery and surface-to-air missiles.
- withstand much greater maneuvering forces.
- delay weapon release until very close (and very sure).
- do not risk pilot injury or capture.
- can use all existing ordnance in highly lethal environments.

- cost much less per target kill.
- need fewer sorties to make any strike successful.

These optimistic predictions have not been validated, however, because the problems encountered in development are more difficult than first thought (Townsend, 1985). For example, much more computing power is required than expected, and signal jamming continues to be a problem. However, the cruise missile is one outcome of such thinking. Based on this premise, research is being conducted into autonomous military robots. The idea that robotic warfare will lead to less injury to people may be a double-edged sword, because in the minds of some it makes the option of armed combat more viable.

The Prowler (Figure 1.6) can patrol a designated perimeter with or without human supervision. In the latter case, it follows a preprogrammed path, using sensory information to correct tracking errors. Audio and visual links are used for remote manual control. It can be equipped with a sophisticated array of sensors: including day and night video cameras, laser range finders, directional microphones, battlefield surveillance doppler radar, electromagnetic motion detectors, seismic monitors for detecting ground vibrations caused by men and vehicles, and infrared scanners. It can be equipped with lethal weapons including machine guns, grenade launchers, missiles, and flame throwers and with non-lethal weapons such as shotguns with rubber bullets.

Figure 1.6
RDS Prowler from Robot Defence Systems: an autonomous perimeter surveillance robot that can be equipped with a variety of sensors and weapons.

The development of weapons systems raises a number of ethical problems requiring moral decisions on the part of society. In the theory of 'just' war, war is considered to be a necessary evil, required as a police action to keep militant nations in line, and to protect freedom. This view is contradicted when indiscriminate weapons are developed whose destructiveness cannot be limited to military targets (for example, the neuron bomb). Thus, according to proponents of this theory, indiscriminate weapons should not be made. Autonomous robot weapons may become a moral 'cop out', because their use could be an excuse to remove the responsibility for the destruction of war from people and place it on machines. Finally, at least one false alert indicating a probable nuclear attack has been traced to the failure of an electronic circuit: dare we trust our future to autonomous machines under the control of a malicious despot?

1.4.6 Goals

One more question needs to be discussed: 'What should the goals of robotics be?'.

> Bacon . . . saw science as the notation of a universal language to be learn't by the scientist in the service of God for the benefit of man.
>
> (Purver, 1967)

The second charter of the Royal Society includes the following comments about its members

> . . . whose studies are to be applied to further promoting by the authority of experiments the sciences of natural things and useful arts, to the glory of God the Creator, and the advantage of the human race . . .

A paper by Robert Hooke (1663) spelt out the implications of these goals with particular emphasis on the principle that no hypothesis would be accepted until all opinions had been discussed and appropriate experiments conducted (in Lyons, 1968).

Much current scientific research is the result of economic and technological push. The momentum originally generated by Christian ideals is now being fuelled by the consumer society and the military–industrial complex. Some researchers see the ultimate goal of robotics to be to create a machine in the image of man (Asimov and Frenkel, 1985). Others see robots merely as cheap labour in the factories of the future, so that more profit can be made, and often don't address the social consequences. Still others predict future societies where robots will be the servants of people, just as the peasants, and slaves, were in the feudal societies of the past. What is the place of people in a roboticised society? What part does compassion for our fellow humans play in our application of technology?

In his keynote speech to the 1985 IEEE conference on decision and control, Harley Shaiken concluded with this challenge to technologists:

> To use computer technology in a human way – to realise its extraordinary potential to enrich jobs and provide increased productivity for the society – requires a careful, thorough exploration of the alternatives, and the placing of human beings as the central point of the equation rather than as an afterthought.
>
> (Shaiken, 1986)

1.5 Applications

Robots are used in many diverse applications, from turtle robots in school classrooms, to welding robots in car manufacturing factories, to the teleoperated arm on the space shuttle. Each application has its own set of problems, and consequently, its own set of robotics requirements. Many new industries have arisen as a result, and we are likely to see more in the future, as new concepts are developed in research laboratories. While many of the consumer-oriented robots are of more novelty value than practical use, the introduction of robots into factories has already had a considerable impact on manufacturing processes.

The automobile industry has been largely responsible for the development of industrial robots. Traditional production lines were designed for one car model only, and had to be redesigned and rebuilt before a new model could be manufactured. Also, manual welding was subject to considerable variability because the spot welding guns were heavy and difficult to handle. It was not uncommon for a plant to have one chassis welding line going at full production unable to meet the demand for a new model, while a second line was on reduced operation because of low demand for another model. Thus, capital intensive plant was idle at a time when the company could not produce enough cars to meet its orders.

Introducing robot technology into these factories solved these problems. A robot welding line can be changed from one car model to another simply by reprogramming the welding pattern performed by the robots. Consequently, it is possible to mix models on the one line, and to customize models for a particular order. Also, the quality of the welds is more consistent, because the robots don't suffer from the same fatigue problems the human operators were subject to. Thus, the new lines are more flexible, produce a higher quality product, represent a better investment of capital, and enable tailoring of the product. However, if all robot applications result in a similar reduction in labour, we will have considerable unemployment and social dislocation. For example, during the last decade, the number of people employed by large capital-intensive companies in the

American manufacturing sector has decreased, while the number of people employed by small, high-technology companies has increased by a greater amount (Drucker, 1984).

Robotics technology can contribute to employment in small factories, because of the increased flexibility it gives to small-volume, batch-oriented manufacturing. This flexibility allows the company to manufacture a wider range of products with less equipment – one flexible machine replaces several inflexible ones – resulting in a reduction in capital outlay for the company, and less idle time for the equipment it has. Thus, correctly applied, robotics has the potential for making a small family business competitive with a large corporation, resulting in increased employment and decentralized industry. An example of this is the shift of the film processing and printing industry from a few, large, highly-automated factories to shops in many city suburbs as a result of the development of low-cost developing and printing machines. These shops provide shorter turn around time than the large film manufacturers did. The result is local employment and wealth distribution.

Initially, many companies approached robotics by buying a robot to see what they could do with it. This approach is being replaced with a more traditional engineering approach now that the management and unions are more familiar with the technology. The result is that many robot manufacturers are offering integrated solutions to manufacturing problems, and systems houses have sprung up to deal with new applications. The first step in attaining an integrated solution is to define the application clearly, and to specify the goals to be achieved. Then a number of solutions, involving both robotics and hard automation, can be studied. If you decide to use a robot, be prepared to redesign completely the manufacturing process. Also, the manufacturing techniques evolved during manual production are often unsuitable when using robots, as current robots lack the sensory and dexterity capabilities of humans.

Industrial experience has shown that employees are much more likely to accept robotics technology if their managers are honest about their intentions. Companies who hide their robotics development in the corner are only creating future industrial problems for themselves. Managers who try to deceive their staff in this way clearly indicate by their attitude that they consider profit to be more important than employee welfare. A person who has been doing a job for a period of time develops skills that enable him to fulfill an aim, whether it be high volume, high accuracy, or consistent quality. If that person is happily involved in the installation of a robotics system, then he or she will willingly contribute process knowledge that cannot be obtained easily in any other way. In contrast if he or she is opposed to the introduction of robotics technology then he or she can make the installation fail.

1.5.1 Industry

Robots are used in a wide range of industrial applications. The earliest applications were in materials handling, spot welding, and spray painting (Hartley, 1983). Robots were initially applied to jobs that were hot, heavy, and hazardous such as die casting, forging, and spot welding. One problem in these industries is finding people who are willing to work with the poor equipment and under the poor conditions which exist in some factories. For example, in die casting and forging a lot of existing plant is so old that it will have to be replaced before robots can be used.

Spot welding in car assembly plants is currently the largest single application of robots. The car chassis is fixed to a remotely piloted vehicle (RPV), which carries it through the factory (Figure 1.7). When the RPV arrives at the welding station, clamps hold the parts to be welded in place, while the robots move through a preprogrammed sequence of welds. The parts must be positioned accurately, because the robots currently used for welding have no sensors to detect misalignment.

Figure 1.7
Artist's impression of an Elwell Parker Automated Guided Vehicle carrying a die.

Owing to the inhalation of fumes, spray painting has always been a hazardous job. People can be removed from this hostile environment by using a robot arm. All spray-painting robots are 'taught' by an expert painter holding the spray gun and moving it through the correct sequence of motions. The motion sequence is recorded, and when the robot is to spray the object it simply follows this sequence. Thus, spray-painting robots must have joints that can be back driven easily by a human spray painter since deriving the sequence of spray gun motions from a solid model of the object to be sprayed and a knowledge of the mechanics of spraying is beyond current technology. One of the problems in spray painting is getting into the areas of motor cars that are obstructed by doors. This can sometimes be overcome by having a second robot to open and shut the doors, bonnet, and boot. This application has led to the development of 'elephant trunk' arms for greater flexibility (Figure 1.8).

Robots are used in many other applications, for example: grinding, deburring, tending machine tools, molding in the plastics industry, applying sealants to motor car windscreens, and picking items up off conveyors and packing them on to fork lift pallets. These applications, and the problems involved, are reported in numerous conference proceedings. Innovative new applications include laser-beam welding (Kehoe, 1984) and water-jet cutting. In the following sections, three industrial applications that are in various stages of research are examined.

1.5.1.1 Arc welding

Most arc welding is currently done manually. However, productivity is low because of the physical demands placed on the welder when manipulating the

Figure 1.8
Spline robot demonstrating its car-painting technique.

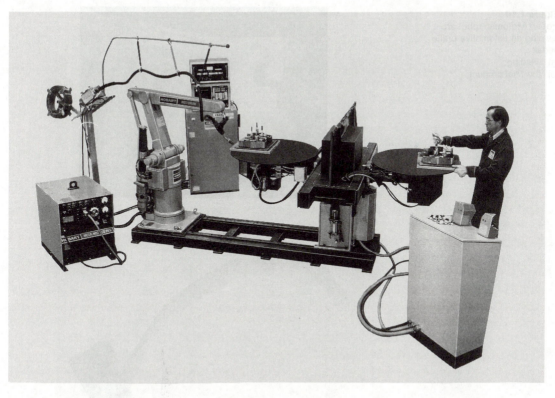

Figure 1.9
Hobart Motoman robot arc
welding system, including
robot, welder, and work
positioner. A human operator
positions workpieces for the
robot to weld.

torch, and the harsh environment resulting from the fumes and heat generated by the process. Arc welding, which is potentially a large application for robots, places high demands on the technology.

Unlike spot welding, where the weld has to be placed at a fixed spot, an arc weld has to be placed along a joint between two pieces of metal. Commercial arc welding systems (Figure 1.9) rely on people to fix the parts to be welded accurately, and then the robot goes through a programmed welding sequence (Figure 1.10). The only advantage this has over manual welding is the consistent quality of the weld. The human operator is now left with the tedious job of fixing. Productivity is speeded up by having rotating fixture tables, so that the operator can be fixing one set of parts while the robot is welding another. This system works well for short welds on accurately aligned parts. However, there are always part fit problems due to manufacturing tolerances (parts might not be cut accurately resulting in varying weld gaps), part warpage, and designs which call for joins that follow non-uniformly curved paths (Figure 1.11). All of these make accurate fixing difficult, particularly on large, flimsy (at least before they are welded), sheet–metal assemblies. In addition, the seam to be welded may not be accessible to the torch, because it is obscured by the workpiece. Manual

Figure 1.10
Hobart Motoman robot arc
welding an automotive brake
pedal:
(a) welding;
(b) the final product.

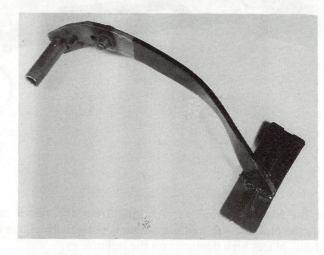

welders have difficulty handling the wide variety of joints and workpiece positions. Recent research has focused on methods of seam tracking, with the aim of reducing the need for accurate fixing, and hence cutting the cost of welding, while improving the quality.

For all types of joints, a minimum requirement for arc weld sensors is that they are capable of indicating the proper tracking position (Cook, 1983). Further requirements are that the weld is placed accurately, and is of the required size and shape. To achieve these conditions, the robot must hold the electrode at the correct orientation to the seam, at the correct distance from the seam, and move at a constant velocity so that a constant amount of material flows into the joint. These problems are more complex on three-dimensional objects than on flat plates, and often require geometric modelling to plan the robot motion.

In the gas-metal arc welding (GMAW) process, the volume of molten material in the weld bead is proportional to the heat input (Tomizuke *et al.*,

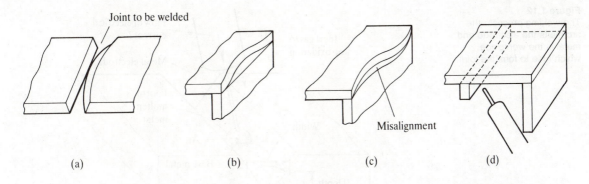

Joint to be welded

Misalignment

(a)   (b)   (c)   (d)

Figure 1.11
Problems that occur during arc welding:
(a) inaccurate cutting of parts leaves gaps at joint;
(b) buckle of top plate;
(c) alignment problems with complex curves and thin metal;
(d) occlusion causes accessibility problems.

1980). Heat from the arc melts the electrode material (feed wire) and the base metal (penetration into the workpiece). It is lost by heat transfer into the base metal (Figure 1.12). Thus, the cross-sectional area of the weld bead (width×penetration depth of the weld) is controlled by the heat input. The heat input H_{net} to the workpiece is determined by the arc voltage E, arc current I, torch velocity v_t, and the heat transfer efficiency η (70–80 per cent for mild steel) (Equation 1.2).

$$H_{net} = \frac{\eta E I}{v_t} \text{ J/mm} \tag{1.2}$$

Arc voltage is proportional to arc length, and arc current is proportional to the rate at which wire is fed into the arc. If these are constant, heat input is a function of torch speed. To achieve a constant weld bead cross-section, both torch velocity and arc current must be controlled.

Several types of weld tracking sensors are under investigation (Prinz and Gunnarsson, 1984). The most promising are **preview sensing, through-the-arc sensing**, and **direct-arc sensing**. Variants of these are available commercially (Hanright, 1984).

Through-the-arc sensing is the most prevalent form of joint tracking in use today. During the welding cycle, the welding head is moved in a weaving pattern from one side of the joint to the other, and the arc voltage and welding current are continuously monitored, as these are proportional to the distance between the electrode and the work piece (Cook, 1983). From variations in either of these arc parameters, the surface profile of the joint can be estimated and the weaving pattern controlled to constrain the weld to be within the joint, effectively tracking the seam. For this system to work, there must be a measureable difference between the seam and the surrounding metal. Because of this, through-the-arc sensing does not work well with thin-walled seams, such as those in sheet metal constructions. A second problem is that the welding arc must be established before the seam can be tracked, thus, through-the-arc sensing can not be used to find or start the

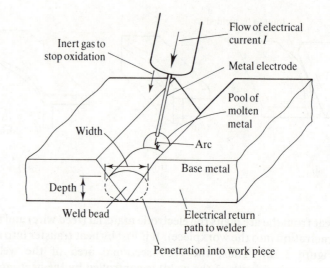

weld. In a number of systems, the robot searches for the weld seam using the
tip of the torch as a touch sensor.

Preview sensing is a technique that collects information about the
joint before it is welded. Contact sensors, for example, a simple **linear
voltage displacement transducer** (LVDT), can be used to follow the seam,
but they provide no information about the fit between the pieces to be
welded, can jam, and cannot be used in some weld geometrics such as tight
corners. However, LVDTs can provide useful information on part location,
and, due to their simplicity, they reduce the time to find the seam. Consequently, they may be used in conjunction with a more sophisticated sensor to
speed up the task of finding and starting the weld.

The majority of research into seam tracking focuses on non-contact
sensors. The most promising sensing method is optical triangulation (Figure
1.13), where a rotating mirror scans a thin beam of light across the objects to
be welded. A second mirror, which rotates with the first, directs the reflected
spot on to a line detector (Oomen and Verbeck, 1983). At any moment the
position of the reflected spot on the photo detector is proportional to
the distance to the object (Figure 1.14). From the position of the spot on the
detector, the sensor calculates the angle of the returning beam and
determines the distance to the object by triangulation (Section 10.6.3). By
recording the changing position of the spot on the line detector during a
sweep of the beam, the sensor obtains the geometry of the surface from
which it identifies the location of the seam.

As all preview sensors are mounted on the welding torch, they restrict
access of the torch to certain locations – for example, walls and corners. In
addition, movement of the object to be welded during the welding cycle will
result in faulty tracking because the sensor is looking at the seam some

Figure 1.13
Oldelft Seampilot: a three-
dimensional, laser-based
optical seam tracking sensor
mounted on an arc welding
torch.

distance ahead of the weld pool. Also, the sensor has to be shielded from the welding process to protect physically the sensor from heat and weld spatter and to reduce the optical noise entering the sensor from the arc. Some commercially available systems overcome the noise problem by executing the welding cycle in two passes over the object. Information about the seam is obtained during the first pass, and used for control during the second pass, when the weld is made. Considerable computation is required to filter and process the incoming signals, increasing the cost of these sensors. Unfortunately, a two-pass process takes longer to make the weld.

Direct arc sensing systems sense characteristics of the weld pool in order to provide information for both real-time seam tracking and weld pool control. These sensors look directly at the weld pool and the area immediately in front of the weld pool. This eliminates the transport delay

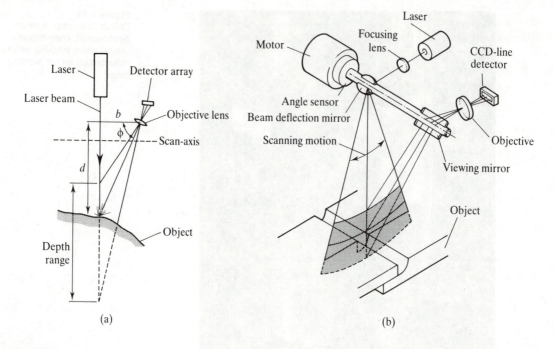

Figure 1.14
Principle of operation of scanning laser used in Oldelft seampilot sensor:
(a) Distance to object is measured by sensing the position of the reflected spot on a linear detector array;
(b) Operation of scanning laser.

between sensing and control, enabling real-time response to any changes in the weld environment which affect the weld parameters. In an attempt to overcome the problems associated with preview sensors, some direct arc sensors are integrated into the welding torches.

Optical direct-arc sensors must be able to separate the desired information from the light produced by the arc. The weld pool emits visible radiation, but at a much lower intensity than the arc. Halogen lamps are used to illuminate the weld pool because the intensity of the light from the welding arc is minimal in the frequency range of the light emitted by halogen lamps. Also, the weld pool is capable of specular reflection, and can show a sharp edge under diffuse illumination. Researchers are investigating the measurement and use of the following parameters: arc length, electrode-to-object distance, arc shape, weld pool shape, weld pool height, seam geometry forward of the weld pool, brightness of the weld pool, and the shape of the surface bead behind the weld pool. Prior knowledge of the expected joint geometry, the reflectivity of the object surface, and possible variations in the arc intensity, are all used to help filter out noise in sensor signals.

1.5.1.2 Assembly

One long-term goal of manufacturing technology is the totally automated factory, where a design is conceived at a computer graphics terminal and no further human intervention is required to manufacture the article. Manufacturing in a totally automated environment would include the following steps: product conception, high level specification, product design (all done interactively by human designers), materials ordering, generation of machine tool commands, generation of parts flow strategies through the factory, control of parts transfer and machine tools, automatic assembly and inspection (all done automatically using robotics technology).

The achievements of such a manufacturing environment requires a considerable commitment to research and development over the next few years (Nevins and Whitney, 1977). Many of the components of such a system are available now, particularly for high-level design and low-level parts processing. One of the major hurdles is linking these processing stages together. Another is the need for methods to generate descriptions of procedures from computer models of the product. For example, the automatic generation of the sequence in which parts are put together in an assembly (Section 9.2.2.1).

Today, there are two examples of highly automated factories where very few people are employed. One is the processing of film by photographic companies, and the other is the machine tool centre operated by Fujitsu-Fanuc. Both are examples of successful hard automation with very few robots. The automation of photographic processing is possible because it is a high-volume, single-task process. The machine centre consists of numerical controlled machines, combined with robots and conveyor belts for tool changing and parts transfer.

A major potential application for robots is the automation of assembly (Figure 1.15), This is currently a very labour intensive process and

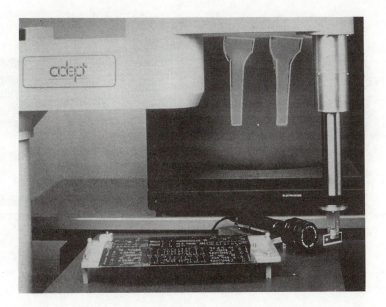

Figure 1.15
Adept robot assembling printed circuit boards: a vision system is used to determine the position of the pins on the component.

much more difficult than it appears at first sight. For example, take a simple hand torch and pull it apart (Figure 1.16). How many parts are there? How many ways can you assemble it? Can you assemble it with only one hand? Can you assemble it with your eyes closed as well? Now you are approaching the limits of robotics, except you still have five fingers with sophisticated tactile sensing. Try using only your forefinger and your thumb. The development of sensors and their integration into robots is of fundamental importance in the application of robotics to assembly (Sanderson and Perry, 1983). A torch is a simple object, yet to assemble it we must obtain all the parts, find the position and orientation of each part, pick up the first part and place it in a fixing device, pick up the other parts in the correct order and attach them to the parts already assembled in the fixing device (Section 9.2.2.1).

Attachment involves many different processes, inserting one part into another, placing one part over another, tightening up a nut, driving a screw, snapping a fastener into place, or applying glue. In its simplest form, assembly means bringing two parts into contact in the correct position, in the correct orientation, and in the correct sequence, so that they stay together. What if the two parts are not fixed together, but are fixed by a third part, for example when you change the wheel on a car you have to hold the wheel in place on the hub while you thread the nut? How do you ensure that the parts stay in the correct position while you obtain and attach the fixing part? Is there anything to be gained by assembling several modules and then assembling the modules to form the final product?

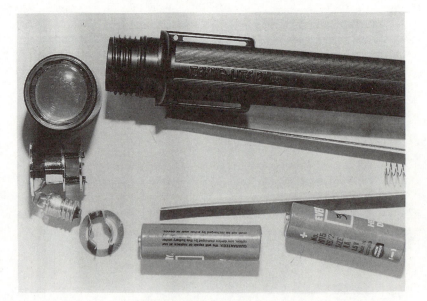

Figure 1.16
A torch in pieces.

Once the assembly sequence is established, two significant problems remain. First, the parts have to be brought to the assembly station and the completed assemblies removed. Design decisions to be made at this point are:

- Should the parts arrive with known positions and orientations?
- Should the parts arrive individually from different sources, or should they be in kits?
- If the parts arrive in random orientations, should special machines be used to orient them, or should sensors be used to determine their position and orientation?

Using sensors to determine part orientation is more flexible than using special orienting machines, but is usually more costly. An obvious way to reduce the cost of assembly is to maintain the parts in known positions and orientations, once the best way of presenting them has been determined. This is one of the major advantages of kitting.

Some parts (for example, resistors) come already oriented by their carrying device. However, it is probable that, at some stage, the position and orientation of the parts is unknown. In many, current, automated assembly lines such as in watch manufacture, special hard automation is used to position and orient parts. Usually the parts are placed in a bowl feeder and a series of mechanical and pneumatic limits and orientation devices are used to move the parts into the correct orientation (Figure 1.17). A major disadvantage of these feeders is that once they are set up for one part, they have to be modified considerably to handle another part of different shape. One

Figure 1.17
Bowl feeder: hard automation used to present parts.

development in robotics technology has been the design of flexible parts feeders (Figure 1.18), where sensors are used to determine the orientation of the part, the type of the part (these can handle multiple parts), and the quality of the part.

The second significant problem is the programming of the robot to carry out the task (Chapter 12). The robot must check that the parts are available, and if sensor-based orientation is used, determine their orientation. It must pick up the parts in the correct sequence, and obtain tools as needed. It must then place the parts on to the assembly, and fix them in place. Finally, the assembly must be inspected. Every robot motion has to be controlled to avoid collision with any object in the environment, and damage to sensitive components. If two arms are involved, their motion must be coordinated so that they do not interfere with each other. Currently, such a task is programmed either manually, by moving the robot through the correct sequence of motions, or by programming each motion in terms of Cartesian coordinate descriptions. Programming languages that can take high-level task descriptions (for example, pick up nut and place it on bolt) are not generally available; those that are available are limited to specific problem domains, and are usually found in research projects into the design of languages.

Unfortunately, many products designed for human assembly cannot

Figure 1.18
The Inspector General from Cochlea Corporation: a programmable small-part handler that uses acoustic sensing to obtain an image of a part which is compared to a previously recorded image of a correctly oriented part.

be assembled automatically. Considerable research effort is being expended in developing the concept of design for manufacture (Lund and Kahler, 1984; Boothroyd *et al.*, 1982). An immediate impact of this is the realization that we can significantly increase the productivity of manual assembly by redesigning the product. For example, the IBM Proprinter, which was designed for automatic assembly, can be assembled manually from 30 parts (Figure 1.19) and tested in less than five minutes. Many products have been designed without thought for the work involved in assembling them. A common-sense decision to use only one size of screw through the whole assembly rather than a dozen different screws in different locations can simplify and speed up the assembly process. Design for assembly leads to designs which use fewer parts, complex moldings, sub-assemblies which allow a hierarchical approach to assembly, fixers that don't require special tools and techniques, and, unfortunately, assemblies that are often difficult to diassemble because of the types of fixers used.

Design for manufacture results in the design of factories for robots (Pierson, 1985; Winter, 1985). Factories originally designed for people often have to be redesigned before robots can be used. Part manufacture involves many different processes, all of which have to be automated before an automated factory can be built. In the next section, we will examine some of the problems involved in automated machining. The integration of the stages in a manufacturing process requires the congregation of like tasks into manufacturing cells and the integration of cells into factories. Every area involves knowledge data bases, and programs to take the knowledge at one level and convert it into a form suitable for use at the next lower level. Each level requires its own programming languages and user interfaces.

Figure 1.19
Designed for assembly, the IBM Proprinter can be manually assembled from these modules and tested in less than five minutes.

1.5.1.3 Machining metals

> The more you attempt untended machining, the more you appreciate the
> human operator.
>
> Richard Kegg (in Raia, 1985)

Mass production was made possible by the ability to machine parts to the
designer's specification repeatedly. There are eight basic ways of machining
metals: drilling, milling, grinding, turning and boring, shaping, planing, and
slotting (Feirer and Tatro, 1961).

Drilling is the operation of producing holes in solid metal, usually
with a rotating drill called a **twist drill** (Figure 1.20). A **lathe** is used for
turning and boring. **Turning** is the operation of cutting or removing metal
from a revolving workpiece with a cutting tool, which is fed into or along the
workpiece. **Boring** is the operation of enlarging a hole that has been drilled or
cast into the workpiece, by feeding the cutting tool into the workpiece as it
revolves.

Milling is the operation of removing metal with a rotating cutting tool,
which may have two or more cutting edges. The workpiece moves under the
cutting tool, as a result, flat cuts are made in it. **Grinding** is the operation of
removing metal by means of an abrasive wheel, to produce an accurate

Figure 1.20
Basic ways of machining
metals: (a) drilling; (b)
grinding; (c) boring; (d)
planing; (e) milling; (f)
turning; (g) shaping; (h)
slotting.

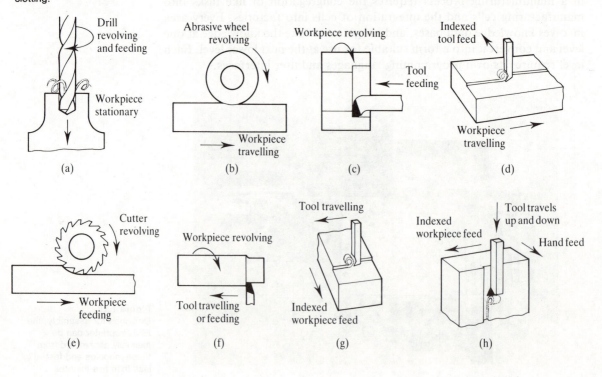

smooth surface. If the workpiece is round, it is rotated as it is fed against the turning wheel. If the workpiece is flat, it is passed back and forth under the turning wheel.

Shaping, **planing** and **slotting** produce flat surfaces by moving the tool over the workpiece. On a shaper, the cutting tool moves back and forth over the stationary workpiece. After each pass, the workpiece is indexed (fed) across the path of the cutting tool in preparation for the next cut, which is parallel to the previous one. On a planer, the workpiece moves back and forth under the cutting tool. After each pass, the tool is indexed across the path of the workpiece in preparation for the next parallel cut. A slotting machine is really a vertical shaper, with the cutting tool moving up and down. Machine tools come in various shapes and sizes, but each can be classified as performing tasks that can be fitted into one of these categories.

As a large capital investment is required to set up a machine shop, the owners demand high productivity from the machines. While most machines are capable of continuous operation, in practice they are used for about 6 per cent of the available time (Raia, 1985). The rest of the time is used to set up for new jobs. This huge proportion of set up time occurs because approximately 75 per cent of all machined parts are produced in batches of less than 50. Machining the first part from a batch will often take longer than the rest, because the machinist has to determine and check the machining strategy.

A number of problems, routinely handled by human operators, have to be solved before manufacturers can confidently run machine tools unmanned. At the top level, as part of research into the development of rule-based machinist systems (Section 9.2.2.2), observation of expert machinists has revealed that the process of deciding how to machine a part involves a complex set of heuristics. These heuristics are acquired over a lifetime, and vary from machinist to machinist. Problems solved by a machinist include deciding if it is possible to machine the part, determining in what order the various cuts should be made, and consequently, determining in what order the machines and tools are to be used. These problems raise the issues of design for machining (a little understood field), optimum tool use, tool selection, avoidance of collisions between tools and sections of the part not to be removed (for example, when undercutting), and reduction of both wastage and machine time by appropriate selection of the block to be machined.

Automated machines, including robots, are used to transfer parts between machines, and to change tools. Machine shops are being redesigned to group dissimilar machines into cells in order to simplify parts transfer, to allow one robot to service several machines, and to allow one machinist to tend several machines (Cutkosky *et al.*, 1984). Automated parts transfer and tool-changing programs are developed from detailed descriptions of the sequence in which the machining operations are to be carried out. High utilization of the cell will be achieved only if machines aren't waiting around for parts. A research robot, developed at the MIT AI Laboratory, to study the design of highly 'stiff' robots, has been found to be stiff enough to carry out a number of machining tasks, including milling. It might be possible to develop flexible machining robots that can perform a variety of machining tasks, analogous to the multipurpose machines currently sold to hobbyists.

Machine designers quickly get bogged down in a myriad of little problems that human operators handle with apparently little thought. As the machine removes metal, shavings are produced and these have to be cleared away. Long shavings can wrap around the part or tool causing damage. Tool wear has to be compensated for if the correct amount of metal is to be removed, and worn tools removed before they break or become inefficient. Undetected tool breakage can result in considerable damage if no one is around to intervene. Experienced machinists can detect that a tool is nearing the end of its life from sparks, unusual noises, vibration, and poor surface finish. Finally, the finished parts have to be inspected for tolerance and surface finish. Each of these problems requires the development of process models and sophisticated sensors (Livingston, 1985) before automated solutions will be viable. As machining processes produce refuse, and tool tips are often obscured, sensing is not easy.

1.5.2 Laboratories

Robots are finding an increasing number of applications in laboratories. They are good at carrying out repetitive tasks, such as placing test tubes into measuring intruments, relieving the laboratory technician of much tedious work. At this stage of their development, robots are used to perform manual procedures automatically. A typical sample-preparation system (Figure 1.21) consists of a robot and laboratory stations such as balancers, dispensers, centrifuges, and test tube racks. Samples are moved from laboratory station to laboratory station by the robot under the control user-programmed procedures.

Manufacturers of these systems claim they have three advantages over manual operation: increased productivity, improved quality control, and reduced exposure of humans to harmful chemicals. Successful applications include measuring pH, viscosity, and the percentage of solids in polymer emulsions; preparing samples of human plasma for assays; heating, pouring, weighing, and dissolving samples for presentation to spectrometers (Hawk and Strimaitis, 1984). Some laboratories have found that sample preparation methods developed in a research laboratory are easier to apply in regular production if a robot is used to transfer material between the various processing stages. Thus, the use of robots speeds up the transfer of technology from the laboratory to the production line.

Figure 1.21
Zymark Laboratory robot used for automating sample preparation.

1.5.3 Kinestatic manipulators

Robotics technology found its first application in the nuclear industry with the development of teleoperators to handle radioactive material (Martin and Hamel, 1984). More recently robots have been used for remote welding and pipe inspection in high-radiation areas. The accident at the Three Mile Island nuclear power plant in Pennsylvania in 1979 has spurred the development and application of robots to the nuclear industry (Moore, 1984). The Number 2 reactor (TMI-2) lost coolant, resulting in destruction of much of the reactor core, leaving large areas of the reactor containment building inaccessible to humans. Owing to the high level of radiation, some of the clean-up jobs could only be done remotely.

Several robots and remotely controlled vehicles have been used at Three Mile Island. SISI (system in-service inspection), a mini-mover-5 arm mounted on a track driven base, took photographs and measured radition in areas surrounding the water purification system. Fred, a six-wheeled remotely-controlled vehicle, decontaminated the walls and floor of a cubicle in the basement of the auxiliary building with a high-pressure water spray. Louie, a mobile vehicle which carries radiation-hardened television cameras, monitored radiation levels during the decontamination of the water purification system.

Rover (or RRV), a remote reconnaissance vehicle developed at Carnegie-Mellon University (Figure 1.22), was used to inspect the basement of the reactor containment buildings, to obtain concrete core samples from the walls, and to remove the top layer of concrete from floors in parts of the reactor building using a pneumatically powered scabbing machine and

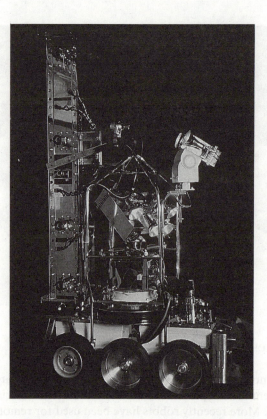

vacuum cleaner. While the water has been pumped out of the basement, a radioactive sludge remains, making steering difficult. This vehicle was designed to carry different equipment into the basement on each trip. Consequently, the robot must be decontaminated using water sprays, after it is removed from the basement, and before technicians commence working on it.

Rosa (Remotely Operated Service Arm), a manipulator arm which can operate under water, is used to inspect and repair steam generator tubes for some utility companies. Rosa is mounted on the generator by service personnel. It is proposed to use Rosa to defuel the TMI-2 reactor core.

1.5.4 Agriculture

To many, the idea of a robot planting corn or riding the range is science fiction, yet serious research is being conducted into the application of robots to agriculture. One of the most successful projects so far has been the development of a sheep-shearing robot in Australia (Figure 1.23). The trajectory of the cutting shears over the body of the sheep is planned using a

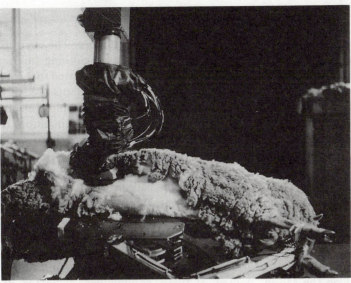

Figure 1.23
Australian sheep-shearing robot built by James Trevelyan at the University of Western Australia.

geometric model of a sheep. To compensate for variations in the size of a sheep from the model, and for its changing shape as it breathes, data from sensors mounted on the cutter is used to modify the trajectory in real-time, as the wool is removed. Over 200 sheep have been shorn (though not completely) with fewer injuries to the sheep than occur with human shearers (Trevelyan *et al.*, 1984). Whether this technology will ever be implemented in union-controlled shearing sheds is debatable.

An Australian robotics system developed in response to a shortage of workers is a machine for the automatic break-up of pork carcasses (Clarke, 1985). Meat processing is labour intensive, and many tasks are dangerous, requiring people to work with little protection in close proximity to band-saws and shears. Even though most tasks are repetitive, many operations require high levels of hand/eye coordination to compensate for the biological variations between animals. The prototype system can break a full carcass into eight pieces in less than 30 seconds. The carcass is measured with respect to a datum point (the base of the pelvis), placed on its back in a cradle arrangement consisting of four sets of support clamps with two degrees of freedom, positioned accurately under the saws, and cut into pieces. Because of the combination of measurement with adjustable clamps, the machine can handle pigs varying in weight from 20 to 70 kg and in spinal length from 800 to 1 100 m.

Other experimental applications of robots in agriculture include transplanting of seedlings (Hwang and Sisttle, 1985), pruning grapevines in France (Sevila, 1985), and picking apples (D' Enson, 1985). All these systems are in experimental stages, but they have each demonstrated their potential.

1.5.5 Space

Space exploration poses special problems for robotics. The environment is hostile to humans, who require expensive protective clothing and Earth-like environments. Many astronautical engineers have suggested that robots, not people, should be sent into space. As autonomous robots are still in their technical infancy, they cannot yet be used to replace people. Teleoperators, which combine human intelligence with mechanical manipulation, require a person in the loop. This has been achieved with the space shuttle arm, where the two are in close proximity, but the delay when sending a command from Earth to another planet is so long that it makes remote teleoperation very difficult, if not impossible. Future applications of robots in space include planetary rovers with manipulator arms, free-flying general purpose robots within space stations, satellite maintenance robots, manipulator arms for space manufacturing, and construction robots for the construction of space stations and space ships (Korf, 1982).

In November 1970, Lunokhod 1, the Russian unmanned lunar rover, landed on the Moon. A crew of five – commander, navigator, engineer, radio operator, and a driver – controlled the vehicle from the Earth using sensor information from television cameras. An on-board computer operated Lunokhod's subsystems through a series of preprogrammed activities in response to commands from earth. These commands could be automatically overridden if signals from tilt sensors indicated that tilt limits had been exceeded. Lunokhod 1 explored a path about 2 kilometres long and 150 metres wide (Deutsch and Heer, 1972).

In July 1976, Viking 1 landed on Mars. It carried a robot arm, which was used to dig a small trench in the Martian soil and to scoop up soil samples for analysis. After a soil sample was screened, a miniature conveyor carried it to a highly sophisticated biological laboratory, where a number of tests were carried out for signs of life on Mars. In addition, the craft photographed its immediate environment, and monitored the atmospheric conditions. Each of these operations was carried out automatically in response to commands from earth.

In March 1982 the teleoperator arm (RMS: Remote Manipulatory System) on board the space shuttle Columbia was first used to move scientific payloads out of the hold into space. This arm, which is fifteen metres long, enables astronauts to handle cargo from the environmental safety of the shuttle's cabin using information from television cameras, one located in the wrist and one in the elbow. Images from the wrist camera can be analysed by computer for automatic control of the arm. The grasp point on any object to be manipulated is a knob with four white dots painted on it. From images of these dots, the position and motion of the end effector relative to the grasp point can be calculated (Section 11.7). The end effector is a three-wire snare. This snare is slipped over the grasp point, and the wires are pulled to tighten the snare around the knob.

1.5.6 Submersible vehicles

Two events during the summer (in the northern hemisphere) of 1985 increased the public's awareness of undersea applications of robotics. In the first – the crash of an Air India jumbo jet into the Atlantic Ocean off the coast of Ireland – a remotely guided submersible robot, normally used for cable laying, was used to find and recover the black boxes from the jetliner. The second was the discovery of the Titanic at the bottom of a canyon, where it had settled after hitting an iceberg in 1912, four kilometres below the surface. A remotely controlled submersible vechile was used to find, explore, and film the wreck.

In addition to undersea searching, unmanned vehicles are used in the inspection and maintenance of offshore oil-wells, in laying and inspecting communications cables, and in geological and geophysical surveys of the ocean floor. A potential new application is mining on the ocean floor. Most submersible robots are equipped with manipulators and television cameras. Some have high power cutters, simple claws, magnetographic testing instruments, ultrasonic inspection devices, and other tools and sensors (Adam, 1985).

Tethered remotely operated vehicles are the workhorses of many offshore industries, particularly the oil industry. While tethers minimize the problems of communicating to the vehicles and solve the problems of supplying power to the vehicles, they limit the range of the vehicles and can become snagged. Consequently, a number of groups are developing free-swimming vehicles which carry their own power supply, have some degree of intelligence, and roam unhindered by a tether. Unfortunately, they easily get lost.

Seawater is opaque to all but very low-frequency radio signals and to the blue-green portion of the visible light spectrum, creating problems for high-bandwidth communication, such as television. Some researchers are exploring the use of pulsed blue-green laser beams as a communications medium. The main method of communication to free-swimming vehicles involves acoustics in which transducers convert eletrical energy into sound waves. Practical systems can communicate from 600 to 6 000 m using frequencies from 8 to 40 kHz.

1.5.7 Education

Robots are appearing in the classroom in three distinct forms. First, educational programs using simulation of robot control as a teaching medium. The programming language Karel the Robot, a subset of Pascal, is used as an introductory programming language (Pattis, 1981). Karel has the control structures and syntax of Pascal, but variables have been replaced by a robot, objects for the robot to manipulate, and a grid-based environment. The student writes programs to define the environment (positions of walls and locations of beepers), and to control the robot to search the environment and pick up the beepers. Robot Odyssey is an adventure game for teaching logic design (Dewdney, 1985). The player has to escape from Robotropolis, past hostile robots, with the aid of three friendly robots. At any time, he can return to the workshop to modify the operation of the robots by changing the design of their logic circuits. The hazards that have to be avoided increase in difficulty as the game progresses, requiring increasingly complex logic designs.

The second, and currently most common, use of robots in education is the use of turtle robots (Figure 1.24) in conjunction with the LOGO language to teach computer awareness. LOGO was intended to create an environment where learning mathematics would be natural and fun (Pappert, 1980). The turtle is an object to think with and to be used to draw geometric patterns (Abelson and di Sessa, 1981). While LOGO is used for this purpose, the language has been so well human engineered, from an educational point of view, that it provides a natural environment for a child's first excursions into programming.

The third use is in the robotics classroom. A range of low cost manipulators (Figure 1.25), mobile robots, and complete systems (Figure 1.26) have been developed for use in robotics educational laboratories (Stelzer and Moss, 1985). Owing to their low cost, many of these systems suffer from poor mechanical reliability, low accuracy, non existent sensors, and inadequate software (McKerrow and Zelinsky, 1985).

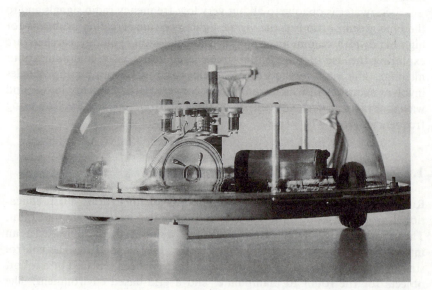

Figure 1.24
Tasman turtle robot used in schools.

Figure 1.25
Three-joint robot used in
teaching built from a
Fischertechnik model kit at
the University of Missouri-
Rolla.

Home robotics is currently a solution looking for a problem. During the first half of the 1980s, a number of home robots were marketed (Figure 1.27), but all lacked the sensing technology to do more than follow a carefully taught routine (Bell, 1985). Many found applications in education, and some are used to attract people to sales booths at exhibitions. Another significant problem is that reliable low cost manipulators are not available for use with these robots.

1.5.8   Assisting the handicapped

Potential robotics aids for the disabled range from automatic wheelchairs, which carry the occupant around a hospital in response to voice commands, to robots which feed severely handicapped people. The overriding goal of this research is to make machines which restore some of the autonomy the user lost when he or she lost the use of his bodily functions. Developers of these systems face severe economic restrains. The market for products for

Figure 1.26
Scorbot robotics training
system from Esched
Robotic.

Figure 1.27
RB5X Personal Robot.

the disabled is small, and often the disabled cannot afford to pay high prices. Thus, there is very little incentive from the point of view of capitalist economics to do this kind of research. Currently, most of the development work is government sponsored, or done by volunteers.

The technological problems are difficult. As a person is intimately involved with the machine, Asimov's laws must work or someone will be seriously injured and the developer will be the target of legal proceedings. Having a person in the loop allows the use of teleoperation, but methods of controlling the teleoperator appropriate to the level of the user's disability are needed. One promising application is the use of robots to perform reasonably complex tasks by people with limited disability. This will enable some people to obtain useful employment, significantly boosting their self esteem.

Constructing robots for use by people with significant disability places much greater demands on technology. Sensor technology is pushed to its limits to protect the user, and to perform the desired tasks in an unstructured environment. How does a quadriplegic tell a robot to put the spoon in his mouth? How does the robot find the quadriplegic's mouth? Once the spoon is in, how does the robot know when to remove it? How does a mobile robot avoid collisions with other mobile robots and people as it navigates its way down a hospital corridor carrying a disabled person?

1.6 Future directions

The writings of some researchers look more like science fiction than the reality that is to be found in research laboratories. Most of the futuristic predictions of androids are unlikely to be achieved in the near future. The complexity of the human brain is such that monitoring many of its activities is beyond current technology. Researchers investigate small sections of the brain in detail to try and pinpoint which areas perform which functions. At present, we don't understand the sensory process of hearing and interpreting speech, which involves the analysis of a single analogue signal. Our knowledge of the brain is similar to that of a person who, when looking at a printed circuit board, can draw a map of the connections between the integrated circuits, but has little understanding of what operations are performed inside the integrated circuits and even less idea of how the circuits interact to perform their overall function.

At a more practical level, one of the significant problems in robotics is communication between computers, sensors, and robots. Lack of common communications standards (both hardware networks and software protocols) creates real problems when integrating robots and sensors into a work cell. To overcome these problems, some manufacturers have adopted the Manufacturing Automation Protocol (MAP) standard developed by

General Motors for factory networks (Jurgen, 1986). A number of current problems will only be solved when a significant amount of research is devoted to the development of new robot languages (and associated programming tools) that handle sensor interaction, world modeling, high-level task descriptions and communication between robots.

Another desirable development is low cost, small, high performance, manipulators for use in applications where the expense of current robots can not be justified. The development of new sensors, and their integration into robotics systems will continue to be a high priority. As will methods for teaching tasks to robots. As each new level in robot control is achieved, there will continue to be the choice between programming the task using a language or teaching the system. 'Teach' systems will continue to be easier for shop floor personnel to use than programming, as they require less training. More complex robots will require increasingly inventive teaching systems, designed to keep the human interface simple.

Robotics is in its infancy. In the laboratories, basic research into the science of robotics will contribute to maturing robotics technology. Models of the physical processes that robots are to execute, ranging from theoretical models of grasping to models of grinding, have to be developed and refined. Many problems in kinematics, in particular, collision avoidance, still have to be solved. The dynamics of motion and balance, the control of articulated fingers, perception of the environment from sensory information, hybrid control of manipulators, general solutions for inverse kinematics, control of robot dynamics, navigation in unstructured environments, three dimensional vision, and the control of highly flexible robot links are a few of the problems where considerable theoretical research has to be done.

The question of the social impact of robotics has yet to be adequately addressed. One way in which robotics may create jobs, and distribute wealth is through the development of small scale appropriate technology. It will soon be possible to make low cost systems that will interactively control the manufacture of a product from design to production. These systems will be flexible enough to make small volume and batch production economical. With this technology, small companies will be able to compete with large corporations. An example of where this has already happened is in the photofinishing industry, where the development of small scale film processing and printing machines has spawned a host of small shops in competition with the large photographic companies.

Key points

- The study of robotics is motivated by our fascination with mechanisms which imitate intelligent behaviour, by our desire for more productive manufacturing equipment, and by our need for intelligent autonomous systems to work in hazardous environments.

- A robot is a machine which can be programmed to do a variety of tasks, in the same way that a computer is an electronic circuit which can be programmed to do a variety of tasks.

- From the perspective of classical artificial intelligence, robotics is the intelligent connection of perception to action.

- System design requires a mechanism for decomposing a task into a set of smaller tasks. With a perception model we can decompose robotics into five processes: measurement, modelling, perception, planning, and action.

- Scientific research is carried out within the framework provided by a set of axioms: axioms that we accept as true because of our beliefs.

- Social issues lie at the intersection of technology and belief systems, because what we do is based on what we think, and what we think is grounded in what we believe.

- The key to applying robot technology is to understand the algorithms and processes involved in successfully executing the task.

Exercises

■ *Essay questions*

1.1. Find a simple commercially made item, and

(a) list the parts it is made of
(b) list the sequence of steps to make it
(c) lay out a factory to make it
(d) specify one or more robots required to carry out the task.

1.2. Write a short paper on a current robot application giving particular emphasis to the skills required by the robots. Include in your discussion the process model and the algorithms used in this application.

1.3. Carry out a case study on a local robot installation. Include a discussion of the reasons for using the robot, the results of using the robot, the social impact of the robot on the workplace, and the process redesign that was required before the robot could be used.

1.4. Design a robot system for a particular application using the steps in Section 1.3. Suitable applications include fitting strings in a tennis racquet, assembling a mechanical clock, or casting a model car.

1.5. Read the paper: Artificial Intelligence and Robotics by Michael Brady (1985). Write a short paper about one of the topics he discusses.

■ *Practical questions*

1.1. Construct a simple model using large blocks (wooden blocks or Lego). Pull the model to pieces and design an assembly sequence. Program the laboratory robotics system to construct the model, using a pick and place procedure with the blocks in known positions.

1.2. Change the experiment to use a simple conveyor to present the parts to the robot. Use a photo cell to detect the presence of the parts at the end of the conveyor, and to stop the conveyor upon part detection. A simple conveyor can be built from some construction kits (such as Fischertechnik), or one can be bought from any educational robotics supplier.

1.3. Modify the experiment to disassemble the model and place the parts back on the conveyor (reverse the direction of the conveyor) so that the construction/disassembly sequence can run continuously.

2 · Components and Subsystems

The hand is an exquisite machine. The same basic structure can be trained for use by a weight lifter or to perform extraordinarily delicate tasks, as evidenced by the microvascular surgeon who is able to sew minute arteries and nerves together.

(David Thompson, 1981)

Objectives

In this chapter, we view a robot as a set of integrated subsystems. These are: mechanical, electrical, sensor, software, process, planning, and control. Our objective is to examine the physical components used in the mechanical subsystem. This descriptive material includes the following topics:

- the mechanical structure of wheeled and legged vehicles,

- the geometry of manipulator arms,

- the mechanical design of wrists,

- the mechanical design of end effectors,

- the characteristics of electric, hydraulic, and pneumatic actuators,

- the transmission elements used to transfer power through the robot, and

- the materials used in robot fabrication.

A robot can be viewed at different levels of sophistication, depending on the viewer's perspective. A maintenance technician may see a robot as a collection of mechanical and electronic components where as a systems engineer may think of a robot as a collection of interrelated subsystems. To a programmer, a robot is a machine to be programmed but to a manufacturing engineer it is a machine able to perform a certain task. In contrast, a research scientist may think of a robot as a mechanism which he builds to test a hypothesis.

A robot can be decomposed into a set of functional subsystems (Figure 2.1): process, planning, control, sensor, electrical, and mechanical. The **software subsystem** (Chapter 12) is not referred to explicitly in Figure 2.1 because it is an implicit part of the sensing, planning, and control subsystems. It knits them together into an integrated system. Today, many of the functions in these subsystems are performed off-line, or manually, but future research will lead to their automation.

The **process subsystem** includes the task the robot performs, the environment in which it is placed, and the interaction between it and the environment. This is the domain of the applications engineer. Before a robot can perform a task, the task must be refined into a sequence of steps that the robot can execute. Task refinement is carried out in the **planning subsystem**,

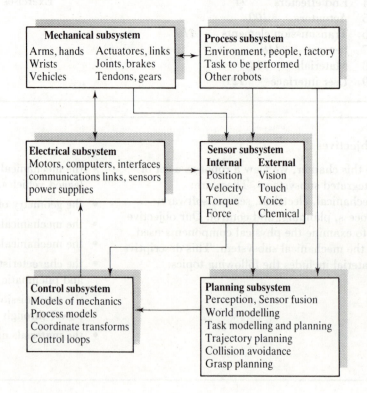

Figure 2.1
Robot subsystems. Process subsystem is external to the robot but other subsystems are all functionally part of the robot, and may be physically distributed.

Figure 2.2
Physical parts of a robot.

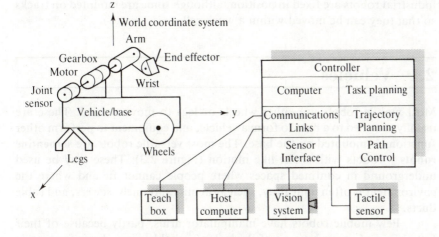

which includes the 'intelligent' processes of modelling, perception, and planning. In the modelling process, data from a variety of sensors is fused with mathematical models of the task to form a model of the world. Using this world model, the perception process selects strategies to execute the task. These strategies are converted into robot control programs during the planning process (Chapter 9).

These programs are executed by the **control subsystem**. In this subsystem, high-level commands are converted into references for physical actuators, feedback values are compared to these references, and control algorithms stabilize the motion of the physical elements (Chapter 11). To perform these tasks, the mechanisms are modelled, the process is modelled, control loop gains may be adapted, and measured values are used to update the process and mechanism models.

Actuator references from the control subsystem are fed to the **electrical subsystem** which includes all the electrically controlled actuators. Hydraulic and pneumatic actuators are usually driven by electrically controlled valves. Also, this subsystem contains computers, interfaces, and power supplies. These actuators drive the mechanisms in the **mechanical subsystem** to operate on the environment, and thus, perform the given task. Parameters within the robot and in the environment are monitored by the **sensor subsystem** (Chapter 10). This sensory information is used as feedback by the control loops to detect potentially hazardous situations, to verify that the task has been performed correctly, and to construct a world model.

In this chapter, we will examine the physical components used in these subsystems (Figure 2.2). These physical components include a base (which may be mobile); a manipulator arm (Section 2.2), including a wrist (Section 2.3) to which a gripper is attached (Section 2.4); actuators (Section 2.5); sensors (Chapter 10); a human interface such as a 'teach box' (Section 2.9); and computer-based controllers. Some robots do not have all of these. Most industrial robots are fixed in position, although some are mounted on tracks so that they can be moved within a work cell.

2.1 Vehicles

Most mobile robots use either wheels or legs to move around. These are usually attached to a base to form a vehicle, and equipment to perform other functions is mounted on the base. The most versatile robots are **serpentine robots** – robots with snake-like motion (Figure 2.3). These may be used underground in confined spaces where people cannot fit and where the environment is often unhealthy, such as in mines, tunnels, sewers, and cable ducts.

Few mobile robots have manipulator arms, partly because of their function, and partly because of the lack of suitable arms. Arms for mobile robots have to be small, strong, reliable, and cheap – constraints which are in conflict. A second major problem faced by all mobile robot designers is the generation and storage of power: umbilical cords restrict motion while providing unlimited power. In contrast free roaming robots are restricted by the amount of energy they can carry and require wireless communication links.

As robots become more sophisticated, they will be applied to a greater range of applications, many of which will require mobility. In some industrial applications, the need for mobility is eliminated by building work cells around the robot, so that a fixed robot can service several machines. In these **flexible manufacturing systems** (FMSs) parts are carried from one work cell

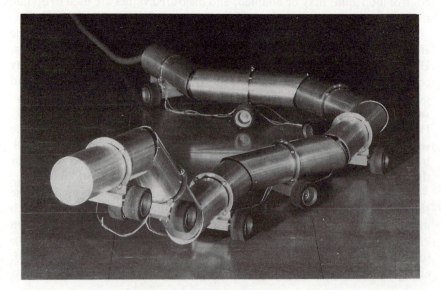

Figure 2.3
Serpentine Robot built by
Shigeo Hirose at the Tokyo
Institute of Technology.

to another by conveyors or by **automated guided vehicles** (AGVs). In some work cells, limited mobility is given to the robot by mounting it on tracks.

People are able to work in unstructured environments with a complex array of tools, but current robots require structured environments, largely due to their lack of sensing capabilities. A company which installs a flexible system must invest a lot of time and money in redesigning manual procedures into procedures that a robot can perform. In many factories, some of these problems can be solved only by the physical separation of people and robots.

Mobility is usually achieved with wheels, tracks, or legs. This is discussed further in Chapter 8. Legged robots can handle rougher terrain than wheeled robots can, but the control problems encountered are more difficult. Robots can also achieve mobility by flying. Some glide slightly above the ground on air bearings; others use magnetic levitation, requiring specially prepared surfaces. Robots designed for use in space are not constrained by gravity, eliminating the problems of levitation, but increasing the problems of control and stability.

2.1.1   Wheeled vehicles

While people and many animals walk on legs, most mobile machines roll on wheels. Wheels are simpler to control, pose fewer stability problems, use less energy per unit distance of motion, and can go faster than legs. Stability is maintained by ensuring that the centre of gravity of the vehicle is always within a triangle formed by three points touching the ground. Wheeled vehicles are reasonably manœuvrable, some are able to turn in their own length, and some can move sideways. However, wheels are only usable on relatively smooth, solid terrain; on soft ground they can slip and get bogged down. In order to scale rough terrain, wheels have to be larger than the obstacles they encounter.

The most familiar wheel layout for a vehicle is that used by the family car (see Figure 2.49). Four wheels are placed at the corners of a rectangle. Normally the rear two are used for driving and the forward two for steering. Alternative arrangements include front-wheel drive, four-wheel drive, and four-wheel steering allowing some limited sideways motion. Most four-wheeled vehicles have limited manoeuvrability because they have to move in a forward direction in order to turn. Also, a wheel suspension system is required to ensure that the wheels are in contact with the ground at all times. When moving in a straight line, all wheels rotate by the same amount. When turning corners, the inside wheels rotate slower than the outside wheels, to avoid 'scrubbing' because the contact distance travelled by the inside wheels is shorter. In a mobile robot, these requirements are met by good mechanical design and by controlling the speed of the drive wheels independently.

One way to reduce the problems of four-wheeled vehicles is to replace the coupled steering wheels with one wheel, as in a three-wheeled car. The

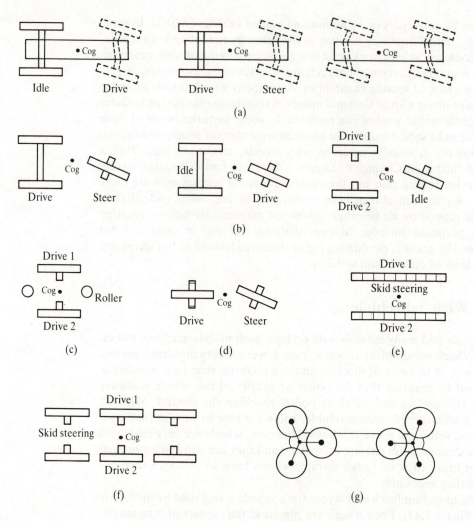

Figure 2.4
Possible wheel
arrangements for mobile
robots (cog equals centre of
gravity): (a) four-wheeled
vehicles; (b) three-wheeled
vehicles; (c) turtle; (d)
bicycle; (e) tracked vehicle;
(f) six-wheeled vehicle; (g)
stair-climbing vehicle.

problem still remains that, for accurate control of turning, the two drive
wheels must rotate at slightly different speeds. Three-wheeled vehicles have
the advantage that wheel-to-ground contact can be maintained on all wheels
without a suspension system. The centre of a three-wheeled vehicle is the
centre of the circle defined by the ground contact points of the three wheels.

Other variants of the three-wheeled vehicle configuration are found in
practice. In one, the single wheel is the drive wheel as well as the steering
wheel, enabling the other wheels to idle (Figure 2.5). Combining drive and
steering mechanisms in one wheel results in a more complex mechanical
design, and small tolerances can result in noticeable steering errors over a
distance of a few metres. The kinematics of this robot are analysed in Section
8.4.2.

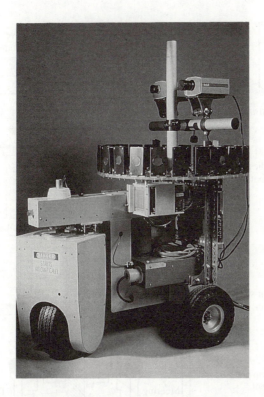

Figure 2.5
Neptune mobile robot with
Denning sonar ring and
stereo cameras built by
Chuck Thorpe and Greg
Podnar at Carnegie-Mellon
University.

One ambitious design (Figure 2.6), took this concept further and had all three wheels operate as both drive and steering wheels, using motors on concentric shafts. The three wheels are mounted 120 degrees apart on a circle, and all turn when steering. As they are all driven, they have to rotate at different speeds when turning. The kinematics of this machine have proved to be so complex that two eight-bit microprocessors cannot control one wheel in real time.

Some mobile robots have three wheels controlled by a **synchronous drive system** (Figure 2.7). All wheels are used for driving and steering. However, in this case, the wheels are coupled with a belt drive or gears, so that they can be steered by the one motor (Holland, 1986). The body of the robot always maintains a fixed orientation to the external world, and a sensor platform above the body always points in the direction of motion. Also, the wheels are driven by a single motor.

In other three-wheeled vehicles, two wheels are driven independently and the third idles. Steering is accomplished by driving the wheels at different speeds. For the robot to follow straight lines and curves accurately, motor speeds must be controlled precisely. However, inaccuracies in achieving the desired trajectory can be caused by mechanical factors such as wheel slip, bent drive shafts, and misaligned wheels. In this design, the vehicle turns around a point along the axis between the driven wheels. If this

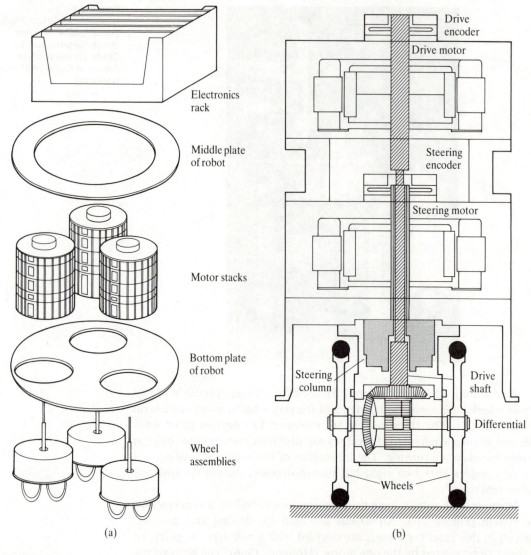

Figure 2.6
Pluto mobile robot built by
Hans Moravec at Carnegie-
Mellon University.
(a) Sub assemblies;
(b) wheel assembly.

axis passes through the centre of the vehicle then the centre of gravity has to be offset towards the idle wheel to maintain stability.

Turtle robots overcome this stability problem by having two idling castors, or skids, on an axis perpendicular to the axis of the drive wheels. Unless the castors are supported by a suspension system, the turtle arrangement is suitable only for flat or slowly varying surfaces. On rapidly varying surfaces, one of the wheels can lose contact with the surface, and hence lose traction and control. Two-wheeled vehicles, like bicycles, have stability problems, and thus have not been used in robotics.

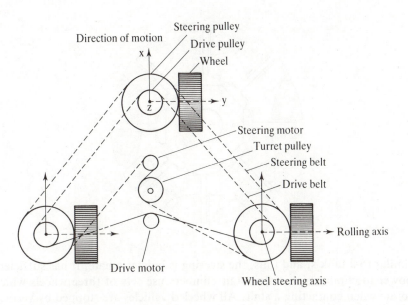

Direction of motion

Steering pulley
Drive pulley
Wheel

x
z
y

Steering motor
Turret pulley
Steering belt

Drive belt

Rolling axis

Drive motor

Wheel steering axis

Figure 2.7
Synchronous drive system using timing belts to synchronize the motion of the wheels – similar to drives used in Cybermation K2A and Denning Sentry™ Robots. The body of the robot maintains a fixed orientation with respect to the environment, as changes in the direction of motion are achieved by turning all the wheels.

Several designs are used for robots that traverse rough terrain. Tracked vehicles, like bulldozers, handle rough terrain very well, but can damage the environment, particularly when turning. The **terragator** (Figure 2.8) has six wheels, three on each side, all driven. It turns with a skid turn

Figure 2.8
Terragator mobile robot at Carnegie-Mellon University.

Figure 2.9
Stanford omni-directional
wheel.

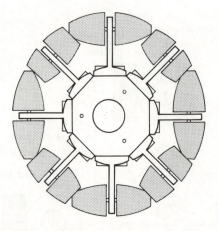

similar to a tank's, and thus, the steering is indeterminate. It has sufficient power to climb stairs. Other stair climbers use sets of three wheels which rotate when contacting a stair. All wheeled vehicles are stopped by vertical walls greater than a certain height, and cannot cross trenches with steep sides.

Some wheeled vehicles are capable of sideways motion. They use wheels which consist of a circular hub surrounded by rollers. On the **Stanford wheel**, the rollers are perpendicular to the axis of the hub (Figure 2.9), and on the **Illanator wheel**, the rollers are at 45 degrees to the axis of the hub (Figure 2.10). In both cases, the hub is driven, and the rollers idle.

A robot built at Stanford with the Stanford wheel uses three wheels, one at each corner of an equilateral triangle, aligned so that their axes intersect at the centre of the robot (Carlisle, 1983). This arrangement does not require a suspension system, but has less resistance to tipping than a four-wheel system. A second problem with a three-wheel arrangement of this nature is that if one roller jams the robot is immobilized. Due to the small diameter of the rollers, they have difficulty traversing obstacles lying parallel to their axis of rotation. During this type of motion, the robot might wobble when the point of roller contact shifts from one roller to the next as the hub turns. A single wheel has two modes of motion: rotation about the axis of the hub with the rollers remaining still, and translation in the direction of the hub axis with the roller in contact with the floor spinning and the hub fixed. Motion in other directions involves a combination of hub rotation and roller rotation.

When the wheels of the robot turn, they apply a force to the ground (f_n), tangential to the circle described by the contact points of the three wheels. The forces applied by the three wheels sum to form a force vector (f) (Figure 2.11), which determines the direction of motion of the robot (Window 2.1). The resultant motion vector can be decomposed into a **translation** of the centre of the robot and a rotation about the centre of the

Figure 2.10
The Illanator wheel.

robot. If the force vector passes through the centre of the robot, pure translation results. For example, to translate along a hub axis, the wheel on that axis is held still while the other two wheels are driven at the same speed in the opposite directions (with respect to their axes). In contrast, if the magnitudes of the force vectors sum to zero, with indeterminate direction, then pure **rotation** occurs. Pure rotation can be accomplished by driving all wheels in the same direction at the same speed, assuming no slippage and accurate wheel alignment. The **angular velocity** of rotation is the linear peripheral speed of the wheels (v_n) divided by the radius of the robot ($d/2$).

An Illanator wheel (Daniel *et al.*, 1985), as used on the Carnegie-Mellon robot Uranus, can rotate about the hub with the rollers still, or move at 45° with the hub still and the roller in contact with the ground spinning. Left-handed and right-handed arrangements of the wheel are possible, where

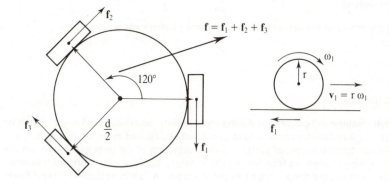

Figure 2.11
Force relationships in a three-wheeled vehicle using Stanford omni-directional wheels.

Window 2.1   Forces acting on a wheeled vehicle (Walker, 1978)

A vehicle moving on flat ground is opposed by two forces: rolling friction F_r and air drag F_d. To accelerate the vehicle, an acceleration force F_a must be applied to overcome inertia. When the vehicle climbs a hill, a grade force F_g must be applied to overcome a component of vehicle weight. The total **traction force** is therefore:

$$F_t = F_a + F_r + F_d + F_g \text{ Newton}$$

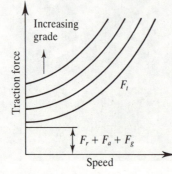

The **power** required to drive an electric powered vehicle is:

$$P_t = \frac{F_t v}{\eta} \text{ watts}$$

where

v is vehicle speed (m/sec) and
η is transmission efficiency (90%)

Motor torque (T_m) is a function of the required power and the required motor velocity, expressed as:

$$T_m = \frac{P_t}{2\pi \, v_m} \text{ Newton-metres}$$

where

Motor velocity $= v_m = vR_g/(\pi D_t)$ revolutions per second,

D_t is the tyre diameter (metres), and
R_g is the gear ratio (dimensionless).

If a battery is used to supply power in the drive system, the required **battery energy** is:

$$E = F_t d \text{ watt-seconds}$$

where

d is the distance travelled (metres)

Frequent acceleration or hill climbing will exhaust the battery more rapidly, and the desired range will not be achieveable. Also the battery may add significantly to the weight of the vehicle, further reducing its range.

Rolling friction is the resistance to motion caused partly by the deformation of the tyres as they contact the road surface. The magnitude of the rolling friction is a function of vehicle weight, speed, and tyre pressure. Because vehicle weight contributes to rolling friction, reducing it improves performance. A lighter vehicle will travel faster and further than a heavier vehicle with the same motor and transmission.

Rolling friction $= F_r = C_t W$ Newton

where

C_t is the coefficient of tyre friction (dimensionless) – 0.12 for a properly inflated tyre, and
W is the weight of the vehicle (kg).

The coefficient of tyre friction changes with inflation and vehicle speed. If the tyre is badly under inflated, the coefficient of tyre friction is significantly higher; conversely it reduces for over-inflated tyres. As the speed of the vehicle increases, the coefficient of tyre friction increases.

Air drag is the force exerted on a body as it moves through air. The magnitude of the drag force is a function of body size, relative speed, and body shape or streamlining.

Drag force $= F_d = S_g C_d A v^2$ Newton

where

A is the maximimum cross-sectional area of the vehicle facing the direction of motion (metre^2).
$S_g = 0.00071$ (specific gravity of air in kilograms/metre^3).
C_d is the drag coefficent (dimensionless).

The drag coefficients for, some common, shapes are given in the following table.

Drag coefficient for various shapes (moving along centre axis)

Shape	Rectangular solid	Cylindrical solid	Hemisphere	Sphere	Car
C_d	1.4	0.9	0.4	0.3	0.35–0.6

The drag coefficient depends on the amount of streamlining of the body. A poorly designed profile can have twice the air drag of a similarly sized streamlined vehicle. The cross-sectional area of the vehicle is the product of the height and width, neglecting the clearance between the vehicle and the ground.

When a vehicle climbs a slope, it is opposed by gravity, or **grade force**, requiring additional traction to maintain a constant speed. Grade force is independent of vehicle speed.

Grade force $= F_g = W \sin\theta = Ws$ Newton

where

θ is the slope angle (degrees)
s is the % slope (rise/run)

To accelerate the vehicle an **acceleration force** must be applied to overcome the vehicle's inertia.

Acceleration force $= F_a = Wa/g$

where

a is the required acceleration in m/s^2
$g = 9.824$ m/s^2 (acceleration due to gravity).

Normally, a vehicle is accelerated for only a short period of time, after which it runs at constant velocity. An acceleration of 4 m/s^2 will reach a velocity of 20 m/s in five seconds. Faster acceleration rates will draw excessive current from the batteries powering an electric drive system, reducing the range of the vehicle.

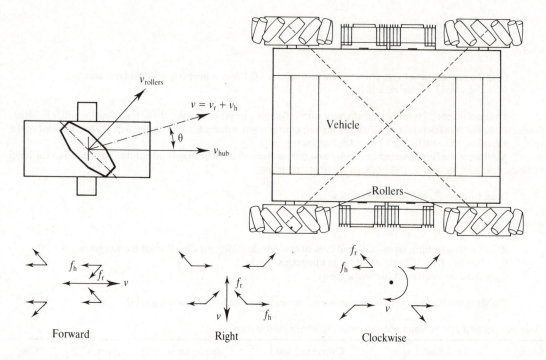

Forward   Right   Clockwise

Figure 2.12
Force and velocity relationships of a four-wheeled robot using Illanator wheels. Uranus was built by Greg Podnar at Carnegie-Mellon University.

left or right is the direction the wheel will move with only the rollers spinning. Motion in other directions involves rotation of both the rollers and the hub. The velocity of the wheel can be resolved into two components (Figure 2.12), one perpendicular to the axis of the wheel ($\theta=0°$), and one perpendicular to the axis of the rollers ($\theta=45°$). Similarly, the force applied to the ground by the wheel can also be resolved into components.

Uranus uses four wheels, two left-handed and two right-handed, and requires a suspension system. The wheels are arranged so that the diagonal lines through the wheel contact points intersect at the centre of the vehicle. Thus, the wheel contact points form a square. With these wheels, the vehicle can still move forwards or backwards if a roller jams. A disadvantage of Illanator wheels is that drive efficiency is poor when moving in a lateral direction, because vehicle movement is at 90° to the direction of rotation of the hubs.

Uranus moves forward and backward in the conventional manner, with the hubs rotating and the rollers still. To move laterally, diagonal pairs of wheels are driven in opposite directions. The robot can move at 45° to the forward direction, by driving one pair of diagonal wheels and holding the other pair still. The vehicle is omni-directional and can translate in any direction. If the magnitudes of the wheel velocities are equal and the pair of wheels on the right side of the robot rotate in the opposite direction to the pair on the left side then the robot spins around its centre. Other combinations of wheel speeds result in circular trajectories – the natural trajectory for this platform. Many trajections rely on friction to cause the rollers to rotate, otherwise the rollers would have to slide laterally on the ground. Again, the forces applied to the ground by the wheels sum to produce a force vector which determines the motion of the robot (Figure 2.12). As the platform has three degrees of freedom, only three of the four wheel velocities can be assigned independently.

2.1.2 Legged vehicles

There are many places on the surface of the earth where wheeled and tracked vehicles cannot go, but people and animals can. **Legged vehicles** are more difficult to construct and control than wheeled vehicles, however, in principle, they have a number of advantages:

- Legged vehicles can step over obstacles.
- They can walk up and down stairs.
- They can step over trenches, and walk on extremely broken ground.
- They can give a smooth ride over rough ground by varying the effective length of their legs to match the surface undulations.
- Legs are less likely to sink into the ground and cause damage (Window 2.2).

These potential advantages, coupled with scientific curiosity, are the justification for research into, and development of, legged vehicles. So far, only one legged vehicle is used regularly in a practical application (Figure 2.13); all others are used in research projects. The RM3 was developed for marine applications, such as video inspection of ship hulls, underwater hull cleaning, and weld inspection. A team of marine robots can clean the submerged hull of a ship while it is unloading freight. Regular brushing of the hull prevents the build up of the slime layer on which barnacles and algae grow, eliminating the need for hull scraping. The makers of RM3, Nordmed Shipyards of France, claim that regular cleaning of the hull of a ship can reduce fuel usage by up to 20 per cent. Also, RM3 can be used for land-based applications, including deburring, painting, shot blasting, high pressure washing, and gamma ray inspection of structural welds.

RM3 has two legs, each with three feet arranged in a triangle. One leg is fixed to the body of the robot, and one leg is moveable with respect to the body of the robot. These legs are moved by hydraulic actuators. With electromagnetic cups for feet, RM3 can walk up a vertical steel plate. When walking on non-magnetic surfaces, vacuum cups are used for feet (for example, on aircraft wings). Sure footing on curved surfaces is guaranteed with feedback from sensors in the feet of the robot. RM3 walks by attaching the body leg to the surface, raising the movable leg, moving it forward,

Window 2.2   Soil mechanics (Todd, 1985)

When a vehicle moves, it reacts with the ground at the points of contact between it and the ground. On hard ground, a solid wheel sits on the surface and does not sink in. The frictional force acting between a towed wheel and the ground causes the wheel to turn. A small amount of energy is lost in the bearing that connects the wheel to its shaft. When the wheel is driven, the driving force turns the wheel, with some energy loss in the transmission. The driving force, which accelerates the wheel, is opposed by the frictional force between the wheel and the ground. If the driving force exceeds the frictional force, the wheel may slip on the ground and energy is lost. The frictional force limits the rate of acceleration of the vehicle. A leg reacts with hard ground in a similar way, except that it pivots around the joint which connects it to the body.

Hard ground

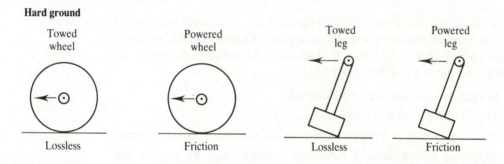

On soft ground, wheels and legs sink into the ground. As a wheel moves forward it compacts the ground in front of it. When towing a wheel, the vehicle uses energy to overcome the compaction resistance. If the wheel is driven, it has to expend energy compacting the soil before it can move. A towed leg sinks into the soil. A driven leg compacts the soil behind the foot as it drives the body forward, reducing the effective step length. In soft soil, legs have the advantage that they only have to overcome compaction forces at the point of contact, whereas wheels are continually opposed by compaction forces. If the frictional force is low, a wheel may not be able to generate enough driving force before slippage to overcome the compaction resistance, and will spin. In contrast, a leg uses the compaction force to aid motion, and thus, a legged vehicle can move over a surface with a low friction.

Soft ground

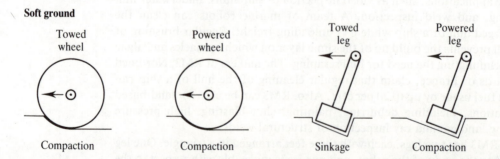

Two properties of soil determine the degree to which a wheel sinks, and hence the compaction resistance: cohesion and friction. Dry sand has mainly frictional properties, whereas clay supports large cohesive forces. When soil is cohesive, it may stick to a wheel and break away from the ground, placing an additional load on the wheel. In the case of a leg sinking into cohesive soil, additional energy may have to be expended to raise the foot at the start of the next step. When soil is viscous (mud) a wheel is opposed by an additional force: the bulldozing force which is required to push the soil aside.

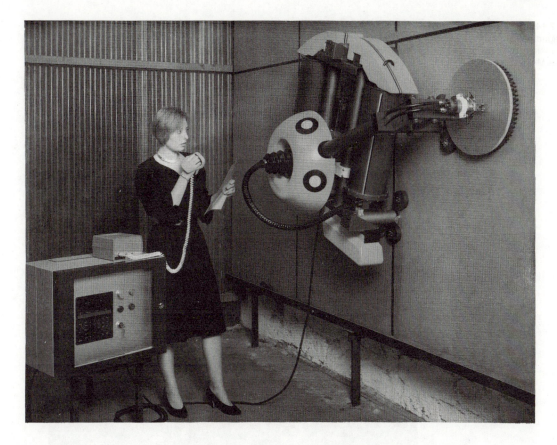

attaching it to the surface, detaching the body and lifting it with the movable leg, and finally moving the body forward with respect to the movable leg. The process is then repeated. The robot has a two-degree-of-freedom arm to which a variety of tools can be attached.

Legged robots are grouped into two classes: dynamically and statically stable systems. For **static stability**, at least three feet must be firmly placed on the ground and the centre of gravity of the vehicle must be within the triangle formed by the feet contact points. **Dynamic stability** is essential for vehicles with less than three feet, and useful for multi-legged vehicles. It is achieved by moving either the body or the feet to maintain the centre of gravity within the area described by the contact points between the feet and the ground.

Marc Raibert and others (Raibert *et al.*, 1984) are building hopping robots for research into the dynamics of locomotion. They developed a theory of dynamic stability, and built hopping machines to test and extend their theory. The study of kangaroos prompted their research approach. The mechanisms involved will be examined in this section and a discussion of the

Figure 2.13
RM3 legged robot from International Robotic Engineering for use in marine applications.

Figure 2.14
One-legged hopping robot –
built by Marc Raibert at
Carnegie-Mellon University.

Figure 2.14
One-legged hopping robot –
built by Marc Raibert at
Carnegie-Mellon University.

theories of locomotion is left to Chapter 8. Their first machine moved in two
dimensions on an inclined plane. This machine revealed fundamental
problems in the original theory. They re-thought the theory, and used the
new theory as the basis for control of one, two, and four legged hopping
machines.

The **one-legged hopping machine** consists of a circular body with a
cylindrical leg under the center of the body (Figure 2.14). The leg and
body are connected by a gimbal joint that forms a hip. A pair of linear
hydraulic actuators control the angles between the body and the leg. Sensors
and interface electronics are mounted in the body. Pneumatic power,
hydraulic power, and control information are carried to the machine

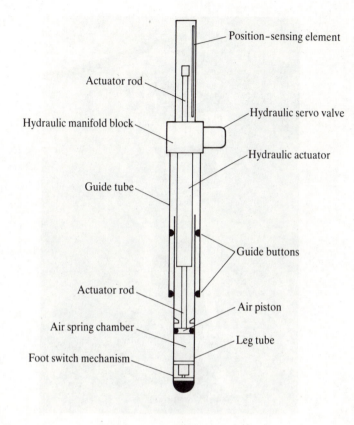

Position–sensing element

Actuator rod

Hydraulic manifold block

Hydraulic servo valve

Hydraulic actuator

Guide tube

Guide buttons

Actuator rod

Air piston

Air spring chamber

Leg tube

Foot switch mechanism

Figure 2.15
Schematic diagram of a leg
used in the four-legged
hopping robot.

through an umbilical cord. Motion is imparted to the robot by a pneumatic
cylinder acting in the vertical direction, which drives the foot down causing
the body to hop. The timing of pressure and exhaust are chosen to excite the
spring-mass oscillator formed by the leg and body.

The single-legged robot hops high enough for the leg to swing freely to
its new position before landing. The ratio of the moment of inertia of the
body to that of the leg is high enough to ensure that movement of the leg
during flight does not severely disturb the attitude of the body. The upper
chamber of the pneumatic cylinder in the leg forms an air spring, which
absorbs energy when the leg shortens as the machine settles on its foot, and
supplies energy when the leg lengthens at the start of a hop. It is the storage
and recovery of energy in this air spring that transfers kinetic energy from
one hop to the next, thereby reducing energy consumption during continuous hopping. This robot has run at speeds up to 2.2 m/s, with strides of up
to 0.79 m. Hopping heights of up to 0.5 m, and hopping frequencies up to
three per second have been achieved.

In his **multi-legged hopping robots**, Raibert used a different leg design
(Figure 2.15). Moving legs have to retract while swinging to new positions,

Figure 2.16
BIPER-3, a stilt type robot
built by Isao Shimoyama at
the University of Tokyo.

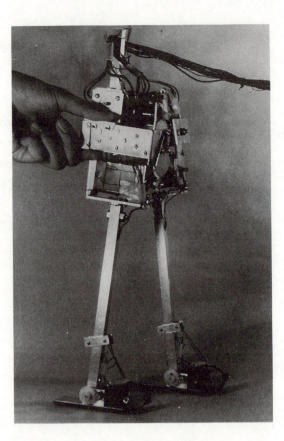

because for many multi-legged gaits some legs are planted firmly on the ground while the others move. The length of this leg is controlled with a hydraulic cylinder located inside the leg. Using the same theory of dynamic stability, he can control a four legged machine running with a trotting gait: a gait where diagonal pairs of legs move in unison. His two-legged machine can run at high speed in a circular path. The path is dictated by a support boom which is used to give the machine lateral stability, and thus, constrains the problem of controlling stability to one dimension.

A second research group (Miura and Shimoyama, 1984) have taken a different approach to studying dynamic stability. Dynamic walk is considered to be a series of **inverted-pendulum motions** with appropriate co-ordination between the legs. They developed a series of progressively more complex machines to model the human torso/leg system. All of them are statically unstable, but they can perform a dynamically stable walk with suitable control. BIPER-1 and 2 can walk only sideways. BIPER-3 is a stilt-type robot, with feet that contact the ground at a point, which can walk side-ways, backwards, and forward (Figure 2.16). The legs of BIPER-4 have

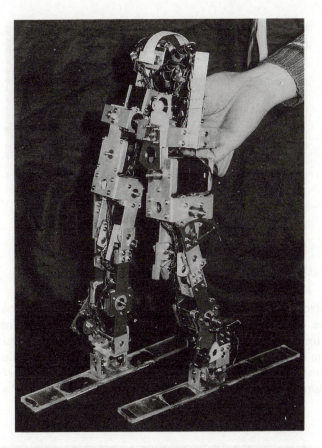

Figure 2.17
BIPER-4, a robot with the
degrees of freedom of a
human leg, built by Isao
Shimoyama at the University
of Tokyo.

nearly the same degrees of freedom as human legs (Figure 2.17). BIPER-5 is similar to BIPER-3, but all the control apparatus is mounted on it.

These robots use direct current motors for actuators. BIPER-3 has four motors located at the hip; two control roll and two control pitch. As it has no ankle torque and the foot contacts the ground at a point, it falls over if both feet are kept in contact with the ground. Thus, BIPER-3 must step continuously to maintain balance. Postural balance is monitored with signals from potentiometers attached to each joint. When an imbalance is detected, the control system drives the joint motors to cause the robot to take a step which will correct the balance. BIPER-4 uses eight motors, two to control the roll of the hip and six to move the legs about the pitch axis. Miura *et al.* (1984) are extending this work to study quadrupeds (Figure 2.18).

Researchers have built a number of vehicles to study statically stable locomotion, with particular emphasis on gait (Section 8.2.1). In recent years, they have proposed **adaptive gaits** for handling situations like climbing stairs (Hirose, 1984). PV11 and TITAN III were built to test theories of adaptive

Figure 2.18
COLLIE-1, an experimental
quadruped built by Isao
Shimoyama at the University
of Tokyo.

gait control in a variety of terrains (Figure 2.19). These robots have a
pantomec leg mechanism (three-dimensional Cartesian-coordinate pantograph), touch sensors in each foot, and a posture sensor consisting of a
pendulum in an oil damper and a pair of electrodes. PV11 uses simple touch
sensors on the soles and sides of each foot. TITAN III (Hirose *et al.*, 1984)
uses a more sophisticated whisker-touch sensor (Figure 10.24).

Figure 2.19
Quadruped walking vehicle
TITAN III built by Shigeo
Hirose at Tokyo Institute of
Technology.

To be autonomous, a walking vehicle must use energy efficiently, because it must carry all its driving and control units inside its body. Energy efficiency in walking motion is hard to achieve, because both body-support and propulsive forces are delivered by the joint actuators. An appropriate measure of the energy efficiency of a locomotion system is specific resistance (Window 2.3).

Energy efficiency is significantly increased by transfering energy from one stride to the next. On the basis of energy flow, actuator action can be classified into three modes:

- the **positive work mode**, when the actuator supplies a force or torque to produce motion,

- the **isometric mode**, when the actuator supplies a force or torque but no motion is produced,

- the **negative work mode**, when the actuator supplies a braking force or torque.

An actuator that consumes energy during all work modes, is the least efficient – for example, a muscle. Actuators which can recover energy during

---

Window 2.3   Energy efficiency of locomotion (Hirose, 1984)

A walking vehicle must have high **energy efficiency**, because it has to carry all its driving and control units in addition to its body if it is to be autonomous. Energy efficiency in walking motion is hard to achieve, because both body-support forces and propulsive forces are delivered by the joint actuators. An appropriate measure of the energy efficiency of a locomotion system is the specific resistance:

$$\rho = \frac{E}{(W \times L)}$$

where

E is the energy consumed during locomotion,
W is the weight of the vehicle, and
L is the distance traveled

When the vehicle is moving vertically, the specific resistance is 1. A perfectly efficient vehicle moving horizontally at a constant velocity on a frictionless surface has a specific resistance of 0. For a foot sliding on a surface, the specific resistance is the coefficient of friction. Human walking at normal speed has a specific resistance of 0.3 to 0.4.

The above definition contains some ambiguities associated with the definition of weight and energy consumption. As well as meaning total weight and total energy used, these parameters can also mean payload and the energy used in locomotion. The latter definition is more appropriate for locomotion studies because it gives a measure of payload in terms of the energy required to move the payload. The former definition gives a measure of the overall efficiency of the vehicle.

Combinations of these definitions provide useful measures in certain circumstances. The efficiency of a vehicle for transporting a load can be calculated using the payload and the total energy consumption. When studying animal physiology, total weight and locomotion energy gives a measure of the efficiency of moving the animal's body around.

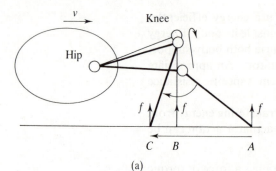

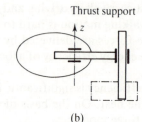

(a)

(b)

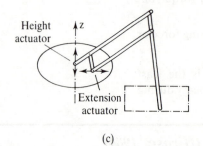

(c)

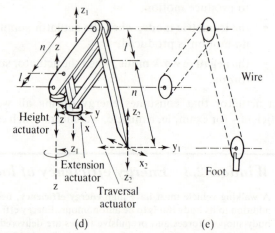

(d)

(e)

Figure 2.20
Saving energy by decoupling thrust and support motions with a three degree of freedom pantograph mechanism.
(a) As the body moves to the right, the motion of the upper leg reverses, consuming considerable energy.
(b) Reducing energy consumption by decoupling the thrust and support motions.
(c) Two-dimensional pantograph mechanism.
(d) Three-dimensional Cartesian coordinate pantograph mechanism.
(e) Ankle control mechanisms.

the negative mode for use during a following positive mode are the most efficient. An example of this is the air spring on Raibert's hopping machines. Most walking machines use actuators in the positive mode and brakes in the negative mode – the negative mode merely dissipates energy already in the system.

The leg motion of a walking vehicle is shown in Figure 2.20(a), with the position of the leg changing from A to B to C as the vehicle moves to the right. As the body moves toward the foot, the motion of the upper leg reverses, consuming considerable energy. The reaction force at the foot (f) produces a counter-clockwise torque at the hip joint, which the actuator must oppose with clockwise torque. During the motion from A to B, the upper leg moves in a counter-clockwise direction about the hip, placing the hip actuator in negative work mode. At position B, the motion of the upper leg changes direction, placing the hip actuator in positive work mode during the traversal from B to C. At the knee joint, the situation is reversed, with the knee actuator in positive work mode from A to B and the negative work mode from B to C. If actuators that cannot recover energy during the negative work mode are used, this system will consume considerable energy.

A simple solution to this problem is to decouple the thrust and support mechanisms using a leg geometry such as that shown in Figure 2.20(b). In this configuration, one actuator is locked while the other moves. Thus, energy is consumed only in the positive work mode. This type of actuator system is refered to as a **gravitationally decoupled actuator** because the actuators are geometrically decoupled between its gravitational direction and its perpendicular direction. A leg design which exhibits gravitational decoupling is a **pantograph mechanism** (Figure 2.20(c)). This mechanism magnifies the horizontal and vertical motion of its linear actuators. The horizontal actuator controls the extension of the leg and the vertical actuator controls the height of the body above the foot. Furthermore, the pantograph mechanism permits a wide area of reach with the lightweight leg structures desirable for walking.

In order to achieve a flexible gait, a third degree of freedom is introduced by allowing the whole mechanism to rotate about a vertical axis through the height actuator. If a rotary actuator is used, the foot moves in a circle centred on the height actuator. However, if a linear traversal actuator is connected to the same point as the extension actuator, and the extension actuator is free to move in the traverse direction only (Figure 2.20(d)), then a horizontal pantograph is formed causing the leg to extend automatically as it traverses, and the foot to move in a straight line. As the basic motion of walking is more easily described in Cartesian coordinates than in cylindrical co-ordinates, this design is more desirable from the standpoint of controllability. One problem experienced with this design is that control of traversal motion is lost if the axes z and z_1 line up (form a singularity).

The results of simulation studies indicate that the pantomec leg reduces energy loss by up to 80 per cent at slow speeds. At high speeds, losses in kinetic energy become significant, and a means of energy transfer from one stride to the next is essential. In addition to the pantomec, each leg includes a parallelogram mechanism to maintain vertical orientation at the ankles (Figure 2.20(e)). The ankle-control mechanism consists of three pulleys connected by two wire loops. The pulley at the hip is fixed to the body and the pulley at the ankle is fixed to the foot, while the pulley at the knee joint is free to rotate. Rotation of the hip joint will cause an opposing rotation of the ankle joint, keeping the foot in a horizontal attitude.

With its science fiction-like appearance, a spherical transparent dome surmounting a cylindrical body with insect-like legs, Odex 1 (Figure 2.21) is possibly the most publicized walking vehicle around (Russell, 1983). Six legs are distributed symmetrically around its body, and it walks with an alternating tripod gait. The legs are so flexible that the robot can assume a tall thin profile or a short squat profile, tuck its feed underneath it in a sitting position, and raise its feet high enough to climb into a truck. The robot is also a remarkable breakthrough in strength-to-weight ratio – it can lift almost five times its own (168 kg) weight. Also, it can carry objects by using a leg as a manipulator.

Each leg is driven by three d.c. motors under the control of one microprocessor. Vertical motion and extension are accomplished with linear

Figure 2.21
Odex 1 climbs out of a truck.

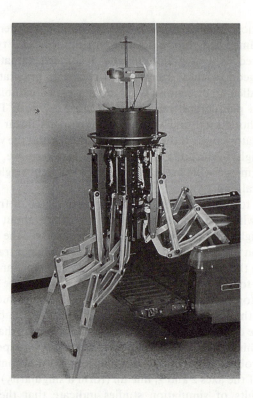

actuators, and traversal (called swing) with a rotary actuator. Odex 1 carries its own battery power, with enough capacity to operate for one hour of normal walking. Vertical and lateral contact between the feet and other objects is detected with sensors in the lower legs. Compliance in the ground is detected with force sensors. In combination with a self stabilization system, this sensory information is used to adjust leg height to compensate for variations in the terrain. For example, Odex 1 can climb up and down stairs using sensory information only.

2.2   Manipulator arms

Anthropomorphic descriptions abound in robotics. The common industrial manipulator is often referred to as a robot arm, with links and joints described in similar terms. Manipulators which emulate the characteristics of a human arm are called **articulated arms**. All their joints are rotary (or revolute joints). A common articulated manipulator is Unimation's Puma robot (Figure 2.22). An articulated arm consists of three links (Figure 2.25(d)). The first, which is oriented vertically, performs the function of the human torso and rotates around the waist joint. The second link, the upper

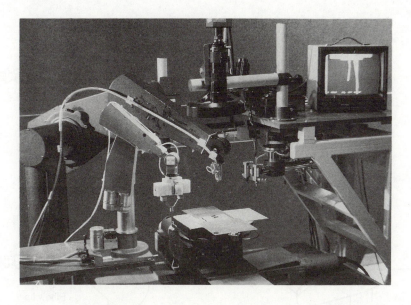

Figure 2.22
Two Unimation Puma articulated robot arms in an experimental electronic assembly cell at Carnegie-Mellon University.

arm, is connected to the torso by the shoulder joint. The third link, the forearm, is connected to the upper arm by the elbow joint. Attached to the forearm is a three-jointed wrist and a hand.

The motion of articulated robot arms differs from the motion of the human arm. While robot joints have fewer degrees of freedom, they can move through greater angles. For example, the elbow of an articulated robot can bend up or down (Figure 2.23(a)), whereas a person can only bend their elbow in one direction with respect to the straight arm position. Also, the shoulder of the Puma robot is offset from the axis of the waist, like a human arm. Consequently, the robot can move from a right-arm configuration to a left-arm configuration simply by turning both waist and shoulder joints through 180° (Figure 2.23(b)). Thus, the greater range of motion available to joints in robot arms gives them greater flexibility than human arms, but, as will be shown later, this increased flexibility increases the complexity of the models used to control the arm.

Many applications do not require arms with articulated (or revolute) geometries. Simpler geometries involving **prismatic** or **sliding** joints are often adequate. Prismatic and revolute joints represent the opposite extremes of a universal screw. In a revolute joint, the screw pitch is zero, constraining the joint to pure rotation. In a prismatic joint, the pitch is infinite, constraining the joint to pure sliding motion. Revolute joints are often preferred because of the strength, low friction and reliability of ball bearings. Joints that allow a combination of translation and rotation (such as lead screws) are not normally used to join the links of robot arms.

Figure 2.23
Flexible motion of an
articulated manipulator due
to the large operating range
of the joints.
(a) Articulated robot
reaching a location in space
with elbow-down and elbow-
up configurations;
(b) Articulated robot
reaching the same location in
space with right-arm
configuration;
(c) Three-axis wrist in same
orientation with two different
joint configurations.

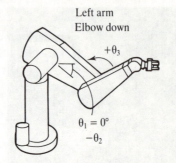

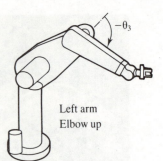

Left arm
Elbow down

$+\theta_3$

$\theta_1 = 0°$
$-\theta_2$

$-\theta_3$

Left arm
Elbow up

(a)

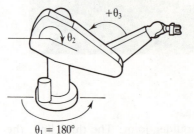
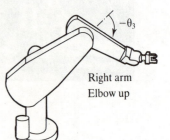

Right arm
Elbow down

$+\theta_3$

θ_2

$-\theta_3$

Right arm
Elbow up

$\theta_1 = 180°$

(b)

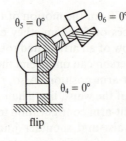
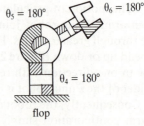

$\theta_5 = 0°$ $\theta_6 = 0°$

$\theta_5 = 180°$ $\theta_6 = 180°$

$\theta_4 = 0°$

$\theta_4 = 180°$

flip

flop

(c)

One exception is the **doverential** (Figure 2.24), which converts the rotary motions of two drive motors into a combination of translation and rotation. This joint has been designed for use in situations where both translation and rotation are required with respect to the same axis. For example, when driving a screw, or when turning a part to avoid collision while lowering it into an assembly. If both drive gears are rotated at the same speed and in the same direction, then the resultant motion is purely rotary, and the output angular velocity is the same as the input angular velocity. If both drive gears are rotated at the same speed but in opposite directions then the

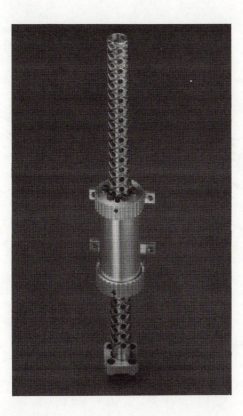

Figure 2.24
Doverential from Robomatix:
a belt-driven joint that
converts two input rotary
motions into a combination
of rotation and translation at
the output.

resultant motion is purely translational, and the output linear velocity is the product of the input angular velocity and the pitch of the doverential screw. By varying the input angular velocities between these extremes, any desired combination of rotation and translation can be achieved.

Manipulators are grouped into classes according to the combination of joints used in their construction (Figure 2.25). A **Cartesian geometry** arm (sometimes called a **gantry crane**) uses only prismatic joints, and can reach any position in its rectangular workspace by Cartesian motions of the links. By replacing the waist joint of a Cartesian arm with a revolute joint, a **cylindrical geometry** arm is formed. This arm can reach any point in its cylindrical workspace (a thick-shelled cylinder) by a combination of rotation and translation. If the shoulder joint is also replaced by a revolute joint, an arm with a **polar geometry** is formed. The workspace of this arm is half a thick spherical shell, and end effector positions are best described with polar coordinates. Finally, replacing the elbow joint with a revolute joint results in a **revolute geometry,** or articulated arm. The workspace of an articulated arm is a rather complex thick walled spherical shell (Figure 2.26). The outside of the shell is a single sphere, but the inside is a set of intersecting spheres.

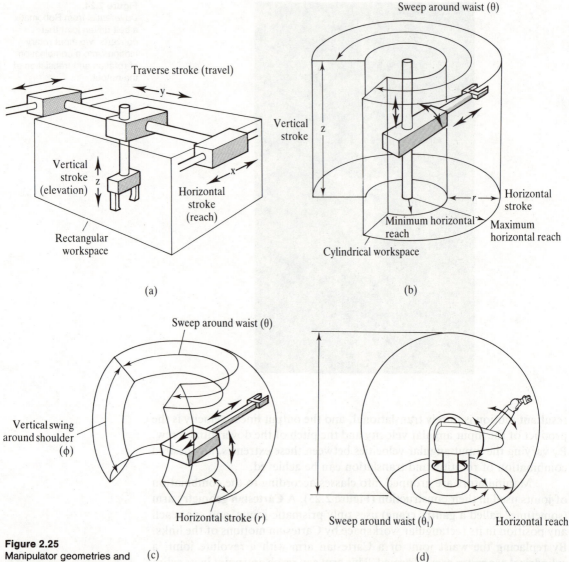

Figure 2.25
Manipulator geometries and
their associated workspace.
(a) Cartesian geometry
robot: achieves *x, y, z*
motion with 3 prismatic
joints;
(b) Cylindrical geometry
robot with revolute waist
joint;
(c) Polar (spherical)
geometry robot with revolute
waist and shoulder;
(d) Revolute geometry
robot – articulated arm.

Workspace considerations, particularly reach and collision avoidance, play an important part in the selection of a robot for an application
(Table 2.1). All manufacturers give detailed specifications of the work space
of their robots and associated equipment (Figure 2.27). Calculating the
position of the end of the arm in Cartesian coordinates (x, y, z) from the
positions of the joints is easiest with a Cartesian geometry arm, where joint
positions are already in Cartesian coordinates. The complexity of this
calculation increases as the number of revolute joints increases. Simpler

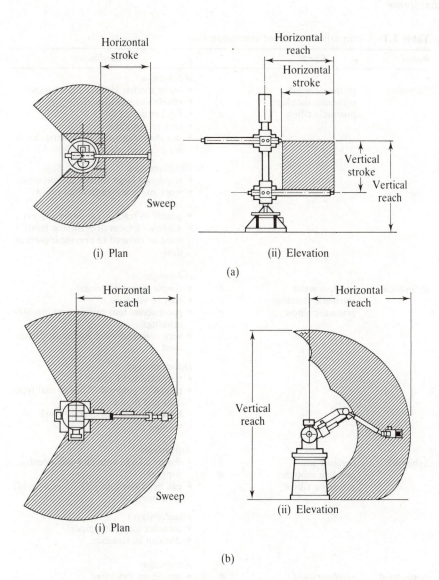

Figure 2.26
Workspace of cylindrical and revolute robots.
(a) Work envelope of a cylindrical robot: elevation is the same as for a Cartesian robot, plan is the same as for a spherical robot;
(b) Work envelope for a revolute robot: the complex elevation is a set of intersecting spheres defined by the rotation of the links about the joints.

equations result in simpler control systems, thus, more complex revolute geometries should be used only where their greater flexibility is needed. For example, articulated arms can reach around an object to positions that a Cartesian arm cannot reach, without colliding with the object.

Consideration of the motions involved in assembly has led to the development of a simpler arm geometry for use in assembly applications, known as the SCARA (Selective Compliance Automatic Robot Arm) geometry. While all SCARA robots have the same geometry (Figure 2.28), the name SCARA does not have a geometric basis. It is derived from a

Table 2.1 Comparison of robot configurations.

Robot	Joints		Coordinates
Cartesian	prismatic waist	x	*Advantages* • linear motion in three dimensions • simple kinematic model • rigid structure • easy to visualize • can use inexpensive pneumatic drives for pick and place operation
	prismatic shoulder	y	
	prismatic elbow	z	
			Disadvantages • requires a large volume to operate in • work space is smaller than robot volume • unable to reach areas under objects • guiding surfaces of prismatic joints must be covered to prevent ingress of dust
Cylindrical	revolute waist	θ	*Advantages* • simple kinematic model • easy to visualize • good access into cavities and machine openings • very powerful when hydraulic drives used
	prismatic shoulder	z	
	prismatic elbow	r	
			Disadvantages • restricted work space • prismatic guides difficult to seal from dust and liquids • back of robot can overlap work volume
Spherical	revolute waist	θ	*Advantages* • covers a large volume from a central support • can bend down to pick objects up off the floor
	revolute shoulder	ϕ	
	prismatic elbow	r	
			Disadvantages • complex kinematic model • difficult to visualize
Articulated	revolute waist	θ_1	*Advantages* • maximum flexibility • covers a large work space relative to volume of robots • revolute joints are easy to seal • suits electric motors • can reach over and under objects
	revolute shoulder	θ_2	
	revolute elbow	θ_3	
			Disadvantages • complex kinematics • difficult to visualize • control of linear motion is difficult • structure not very rigid at full reach

DIMENSIONS

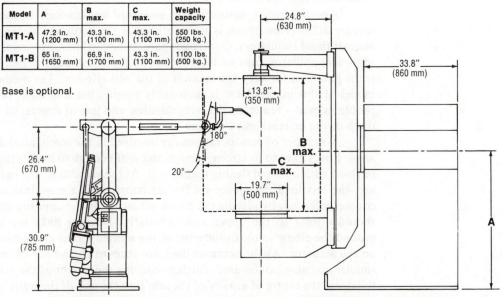

Model	A	B max.	C max.	Weight capacity
MT1-A	47.2 in. (1200 mm)	43.3 in. (1100 mm)	43.3 in. (1100 mm)	550 lbs. (250 kg.)
MT1-B	65 in. (1650 mm)	66.9 in. (1700 mm)	43.3 in. (1100 mm)	1100 lbs. (500 kg.)

Base is optional.

24.8″ (630 mm)

33.8″ (860 mm)

13.8″ (350 mm)

180°

26.4″ (670 mm)

20°

19.7″ (500 mm)

30.9″ (785 mm)

B max.

C max.

A

Hobart MT1-A TURN-OVER shown with Hobart Motoman L-10W Manipulator (data sheet 553-J).

desirable property for arms used in assembly: **compliance**, the flexing of an arm to accommodate the small errors in position that occur when one object is brought into contact with another. Most assembly operations involve building up the assembly by placing parts on top of a partially complete assembly. A SCARA arm has two revolute joints in the horizontal plane, allowing it to reach any point within a horizontal planar workspace defined by two concentric circles. At the end of the arm is a vertical link which can translate in the vertical direction, allowing parts to be raised from a tray and

Figure 2.27
Workspace specifications for the Hobart Motoman arc-welding robot and turn-over work positioner.

Three revolute joints

Prismatic joint

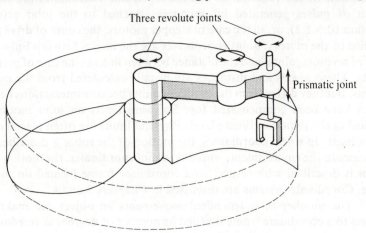

Figure 2.28
Workspace of a SCARA robot is a thick flat cylinder.

placed on to the assembly. A gripper placed at the end of this link may be able to rotate about the vertical axis of this link, facilitating control of part orientation in a horizontal plane.

Another robot designed for assembly applications is the Gadfly (Figure 2.29). This design is an inversion of the actuation system used in aircraft flight simulators. Gadfly has parallel acting links, not serial as in the other manupulator arms we have looked at. One advantage of parallel links is the potential for very fast motion of the end effector. The mathematical model of this manipulator is reasonably simple, but a number of control problems exist – redundancies, singularities, and loss of degrees of freedom towards the extremities of motion.

A number of considerations are involved in the mechanical design of arms. Links have to be strong enough and stiff enough to handle the desired payload with minimal flexing under load. At the same time, the lighter they are, the less load they place on the actuators. Upper arm links are often counterbalanced, by placing the elbow actuators on the opposite side of the shoulder joint to the upper arm. Similarly, forearm links are balanced around the elbow joint. Counterbalancing minimizes the gravitational load on the actuator. As the actuator does not support the weight of the link, a smaller actuator can be used, further reducing the weight of the arm. Also, the closer the centre of gravity of the arm is to the axis of the waist joint, the less lateral stress is placed on that joint. Arms designed to be mounted upright on the floor might not work mounted upside down on the ceiling, or mounted sideways on a wall. The capacity of the bearings to handle axial loads as well as normal torques will determine the robot's ability to handle these situations.

The motion of a robot arm can be described in four different **frames of reference**, where the current reference frame is commonly referred to as the **coordinate system** of the robot. Each coordinate system relates to a different physical measurement point on the robot, and to a different level of description of the function of the robot. **Motor coordinates** are the raw count of pulses generated by encoders attached to the joint actuators (Section 10.5.1.2), or, in the case ot stepper motors, the count of drive pulses applied to the motors. **Joint coordinates** are the angles between links in the case of revolute joints, and the distance between links in the case of prismatic joints. These angles and distances are usually calculated from the encoder counts, but they differ from the encoder counts because interactions between joints have been compensated for. Software limits on joint motion are applied at the joint coordinate level. Physical limits are often placed on the robot itself. In **world coordinates**, the motion of the robot is described with reference to the environment, where as in **tool coordinates**, the motion of the robot is described with respect to a coordinate frame located on the tool plate. Coordinate systems are discussed in Chapters 3 and 4.

The number of independent movements an object can make with respect to a coordinate frame is called its number of **degrees of freedom**. An

Figure 2.29
The Gadfly robot from GEC
Electrical Products writing on
an egg.

unconstrained object can translate in three directions along the axes of a
world coordinate frame, and rotate about each of those axes, giving it six
degrees of freedom. The motion of any object can be decomposed into these
six independent motions. If the object is constrained to sit on the surface of a
table, one degree of translation is lost (movement in the vertical direction),

and up to two degrees of rotation may be lost, depending on the shape of the object. Thus, a cube lying on a table has three degrees of freedom, a cylinder lying on its side had four degrees of freedom, and a sphere has five degrees of freedom.

A robot is expected to move its end effector to a given position and orientation in three-dimensional space, requiring six degrees of freedom in the absence of constraints. A SCARA robot has only four degrees of freedom: three translational and one rotational about the vertical axis of the end effector. Thus, to orient a part at the side of an assembly, it must use a special tool. Some tools can be used with a robot with less than six degrees of freedom and the total system still have six degrees of freedom. For example, the rotation of the bit of an electric drill provides one degree of freedom. Adding extra degrees of freedom to a robot costs money. However, a designer can reduce the cost of a robot by matching the number of degrees of freedom of the robot to that required by the task, if the task requires less than six degrees of freedom.

The number of degrees of freedom a robot has is often incorrectly determined by counting the number of joints. This can lead to errors, because two joints may result in the same motion. For example, a camera tripod has several sliding joints in each leg, but all the joints in one leg contribute to the same degree of freedom. The count of joints is best described as the number of **degrees of mobility** (Coiffet and Chirouze, 1982). A robot can have a maximum of six independent degrees of freedom, and an unlimited number of degrees of mobility. Mounting a hand with three degrees of freedom on a six degree of freedom arm results in a manipulator with six-degrees-of-freedom, and probably nine degrees of mobility.

2.3   Wrists

In most robot manipulators, the three proximal links form the arm and the distal links form a wrist. Typically the arm controls the position of the end effector in space, and the wrist controls the final orientation. The functions of position and orientation cannot be fully decoupled to be separate operations of the arm and the wrist. The arm geometries we studied in the previous section all have three degrees of freedom. Thus, to obtain a six degree of freedom robot, we need a three degree of freedom wrist. The rotations of a typical three degree of freedom robot wrist are the same as that of the human hand, commonly described by the nautical terms **roll**, **pitch**, and **yaw** (Figure 2.30). Prismatic joints are not normally found in wrists.

Owing to the complexity of wrist design, many low cost robots have wrists with only two degrees of freedom. Typical two degree of freedom wrists consist of a bevel gear arrangement (Figure 2.31). If the two drive gears are rotated in opposite directions at the same speed the end effector

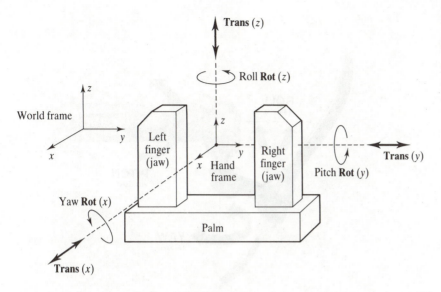

Figure 2.30
Six motions – three of
rotation and three of
translation – are required to
position and orient a gripper
at any point in space with
any orientation.

rolls, and if both drive gears are rotated in the same direction at the same
speed the end effector pitches. An infinite variety of combined roll and pitch
motions can be obtained by controlling the speed and direction of the drive
gears. In this wrist design, the joint motions have to be decoupled in
software, because of the mechanical coupling between the joints. In response
to more demanding tasks, two degree of freedom wrists on some industrial

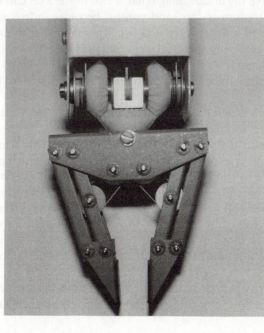

Figure 2.31
Two-degree-of-freedom wrist
on the Mini-Mover 5 robot
arm.

Figure 2.32
Two degree of freedom wrist
upgraded to a three degree
of freedom wrist on a Hobart
Motoman robot.

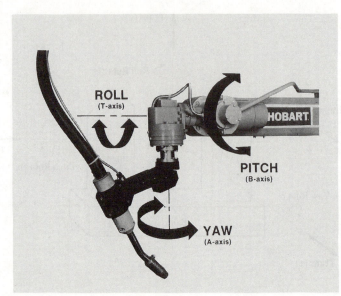

robots have been modified to become three degree of freedom wrists
(Figure 2.32).

A wrist where the three axes of rotation intersect is called a *spherical
wrist*. These have the advantage that the mathematical model used to
calculate the wrist joint angles from their position and orientation in space is
soluble. They have the disadvantage that if two of the axes can line up then
one degree of freedom is lost, and control becomes indeterminate. This
condition is termed a **degeneracy** and is discussed further in Section 4.11.
One problem in achieving spherical wrist design is the physical difficulty of
fitting all the components into the available space. The size of the human
wrist is small because the muscles which power it are located in the forearm,
not in the wrist.

The motors which drive the wrist on the IBM 7565 Cartesian robot
(Figure 2.33) are located in the wrist. This wrist achieves a spherical
configuration, with the joints physically spread out. This wrist has been
designed for use in precision assembly applications where high power is not
needed. When the roll and yaw axes line up, one degree of freedom is lost, as
both effectively control roll. Technically it is more correct to refer to this
wrist as a **roll-pitch-roll wrist**. The roll and yaw axes can be differentiated by
recognizing that roll causes the wrist to rotate around the z axis and yaw
cause the z axis to move in space. At first, this may seem opposite to the
human wrist, but it is consistent with the mathematical description given in
Figure 2.30.

The motors which drive the wrist on the Puma 560 are located on the
other side of the elbow joint (Figure 2.34), effectively balancing the forearm

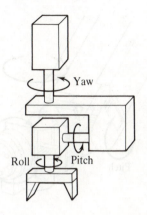

Figure 2.33
Structure of the IBM 7665 wrist.

Yaw

Roll   Pitch

and removing the drive mechanism from the wrist. Roll and pitch are controlled through separate gears. But motion of the pitch drive also causes the roll joint to move. Consequently, pitch and roll motions have to be decoupled in software. Yaw is achieved by rotating the whole wrist assembly about the axis of the forearm. Pitch and yaw are coupled through the structure of the wrist, and constitute a *yaw-or-the-other* as called a bisection wrist configuration.

Many other wrist designs occur. Figure 2.34 (Rosselson, 1982). The wrist on the Unimation Mini on Robot (Figure 2.34) effectively decouples pitch, yaw, and roll acting on the wrist has several features. The available motors are mounted at the joints. The wrist is more powerful (Figure 2.36) is compact and rugged, but it can not be checked if drive power is supplied to the joints through a coordinate shaft system. Three series comp roll. Double preloaded bearings are used throughout the wrist, helping to make it extremely precise, with little lost motion, though they add to its bulk with roll. Also, it has an internal space to be pressurized air to power and effector, eliminating outgassing. Also the tool plate is very close to the intersection of the three axes, the axis of the wrist is shortened. The upper hemispherical half of the wrist; the lower hemispherical half in a plane at 45° to the axis of the arm. Gimbal configuration is lost when the first and last axes align.

The last axis uses a set of heavy circular redundant gimbal rings connected together. Each gimbal is a groved angle set as two axis perpendicular to this axis with roll of it in one gimbal to the next. In other declines bevel gears, or master cogs, or ball and socket joints are used instead of the friction simplified dc hydraulic actuators are connected to the first gimbal with links, as shown in Figure 2.30, these linkages both act on one side of the gimbal, roughly 90° apart. If the actuators both extend the same amount, the first gimbal rotates around a horizontal axis, carrying the second gimbal/shell to move in a counter-clockwise direction. This shell is coupled to the third shell, which moves in

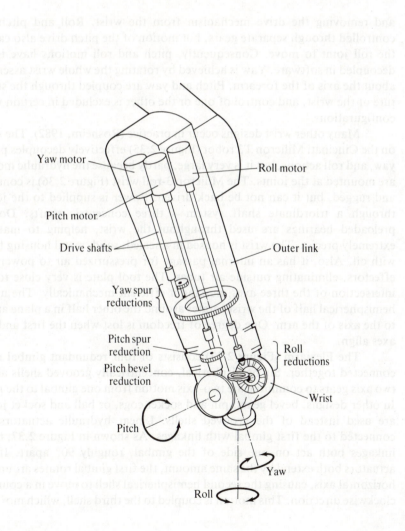

Yaw motor

Roll motor

Pitch motor

Drive shafts

Outer link

Yaw spur reductions

Pitch spur reduction

Pitch bevel reduction

Roll reductions

Wrist

Pitch

Yaw

Roll

Figure 2.34
Unimation Puma 3-axis wrist.

Figure 2.35
Cincinnati Milacron T3 wrist.

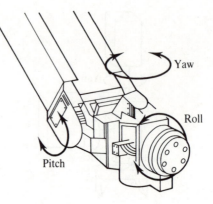

and removing the drive mechanism from the wrist. Roll and pitch are controlled through separate gears, but motion of the pitch drive also causes the roll joint to move. Consequently, pitch and roll motions have to be decoupled in software. Yaw is achieved by rotating the whole wrist assembly about the axis of the forearm. Pitch and yaw are coupled through the structure of the wrist, and control of one or the other is excluded in certain wrist configurations.

Many other wrist designs occur in practice (Rosheim, 1982). The wrist on the Cincinati Milicron T3 robot (Figure 2.35) effectively decouples pitch, yaw, and roll actions, but it is very large, partly because the hydraulic motors are mounted at the joints. The Milicron 3-roll wrist (Figure 2.36) is compact and rugged, but it can not be back driven. Power is supplied to the joints through a triordinate shaft system – three concentric shafts. Double preloaded bearings are used throughout the wrist, helping to make it extremely precise. The wrist is housed in a sealed, solid, metal housing filled with oil. Also, it has an internal passage for pressurized air to power end effectors, eliminating outside air tubes. The tool plate is very close to the intersection of the three axes, making it efficient mechanically. The upper hemispherical half of the wrist rotates around the other half in a plane at 45° to the axis of the arm. One degree of freedom is lost when the first and last axes align.

The Flexiarm (Figure 2.37) consists of four redundant gimbal rings connected together. Six hemispherical, concentrically grooved shells act as two axis gears to communicate two-axis motion from one gimbal to the next. In other designs, bevel gears, pin and socket cogs, or ball and socket joints are used instead of the grooved shells. Linear hydraulic actuators are connected to the first gimbal with linkages. As shown in Figure 2.37, these linkages both act on one side of the gimbal, roughly 90° apart. If the actuators both extend by the same amount, the first gimbal rotates around its horizontal axis, causing the second hemispherical shell to move in a counter-clockwise direction. This motion is coupled to the third shell, which moves in

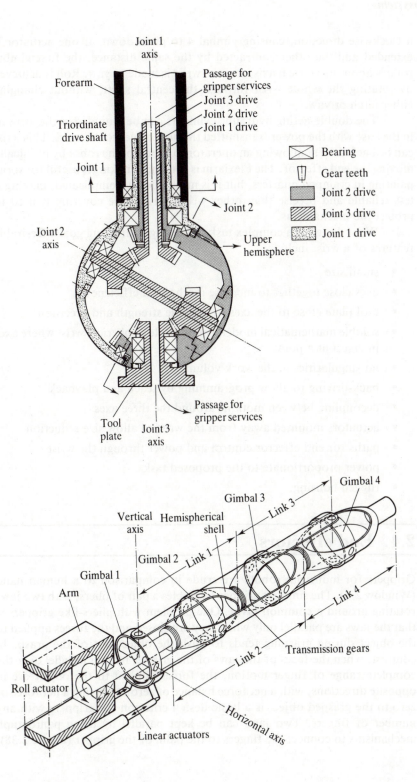

Figure 2.36
Cincinnati Milacron 3-Roll
wrist.

Joint 1
axis

Forearm

Passage for
gripper services
Joint 3 drive
Joint 2 drive
Joint 1 drive

Triordinate
drive shaft

Joint 1

Joint 2

Joint 2
axis

Upper
hemisphere

Tool
plate

Joint 3
axis

Passage for
gripper services

⊠ Bearing
▯ Gear teeth
▨ Joint 2 drive
▨ Joint 3 drive
▨ Joint 1 drive

Gimbal 4

Gimbal 3

Link 3

Vertical
axis

Hemispherical
shell

Gimbal 2

Link 1

Gimbal 1

Arm

Link 4

Roll actuator

Link 2

Transmission gears

Horizontal axis

Linear actuators

Figure 2.37
Flexiarm wrist used in
DeVilbiss spray-painting
robots.

a clockwise direction, causing gimbal 4 to pitch down. If one actuator is extended and the other contracted by the same distance, the first gimbal rotates about its vertical axis, and the wrist is made to yaw. Roll is achieved by rotating the whole wrist through the central shaft, without changing either pitch or yaw.

The double-acting hydraulic cylinders can be mounted in the arm, or in the base with the power transmitted through cables to the wrist. This wrist can be back driven, allowing an operator to program the robot by physically moving the end effector. The Flexiarm is compact, making it useful for spray painting in cramped quarters, but it is mechanically complicated, making it less reliable and precise than other wrists. A flexible covering is used to protect the mechanisms.

Wrist design is a complex task, involving conflicting goals. Desirable features of a wrist include:

- small size
- axes close together to increase mechanical efficiency
- tool plate close to the axes to increase strength and precision
- soluble mathematical model, for example a spherical wrist where axes intersect at a point
- no singularities in the work volume
- back-driving to allow programming by teach and playback
- decoupling between motions around the three axes
- actuators mounted away from the wrist to allow size reduction
- paths for end effector control and power through the wrist
- power proportionate to the proposed task
- rugged housing.

2.4 End effectors

Grippers for industrial robots are crude in comparison to a human hand (Window 2.4). The simplest gripper resembles a pair of pliers, with two jaws rotating around a common pivot. One problem with pliers-like grippers is that the jaws are parallel only when they are closed and the forces applied to the object during grasping tends to push the object out of the grasp. In contrast, when the faces of the jaws of the gripper remain parallel over the complete range of finger motion, the forces applied to the object are in opposite directions, with a net force balance of zero. Applying a net force of zero to the grasped object is a basic design criterion for grippers with any number of fingers. Two jaws can be kept parallel by using pantograph mechanisms to connect the fingers to the palm of the gripper (Figure 2.38).

Window 2.4   The human hand (Thompson, 1981)

Human muscles can only apply force by contracting. They can not extend by their own effort, and thus, they can not push. Muscles are extended by the contraction of other muscles. Two sets of muscles act on the hand: **extrinsics** which are located in the forearm, and the less powerful **intrinsics** which are located within the hand itself. Most of the dexterity and flexibility of the hand can be attributed to the action of the intrinsic muscles. Some muscles act directly on the bones, and others act through tendons. Flexors are used to close the fingers to grip an object, and extensors are used to open the hand again.

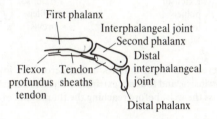

First phalanx
Interphalangeal joint
Second phalanx
Distal
interphalangeal
joint
Flexor   Tendon
profundus sheaths
tendon
Distal phalanx

A simplified drawing of a flexor tendon acting through sheaths and across joints.

A **flexor tendon** connects the distal phalanx (bone at the tip of the finger) to a muscle, and it transmits the force and excursion produced by the muscle to the finger. This tendon is held close to the intermediate bones by sheaths, which maintain the position of the tendon relative to the phalanges, and thus to the line of action of the finger. The sheaths are responsible for the smooth, gliding action of the tendon. The articular surfaces of joints and sheaths that surround tendons have some of the lowest coefficients of friction known. At each point where the tendon crosses a joint space, it acts as a moment couple tending to flex that joint. The shortest distance between the centre of the joint and the centre of the tendon is called the moment arm. The further the tendon is from the effective centre of the joint, the greater its moment arm, or mechanical advantage, at that joint.

At every joint traversed by a tendon, changes in the joint's position use up some of the potential excursion of the muscle. If a muscle acts across many joints, it must be capable of a large range of motion. The larger the moment arm of the tendon at a joint, the greater the required excursion. Thus a weak muscle acting with a large moment arm can exert a significant torque, but if the joint moves, the muscle must be able to maintain its force over the large contractions necessary. A stronger muscle could exert the same torque over a short moment arm with less extension.

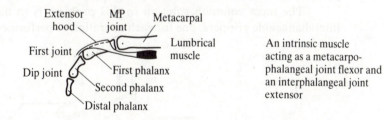

Extensor   MP
hood   joint   Metacarpal
Lumbrical
muscle
First joint
Dip joint
First phalanx
Second phalanx
Distal phalanx

An intrinsic muscle acting as a metacarpo-phalangeal joint flexor and an interphalangeal joint extensor

The human hand has been optimized for strength in flexion (gripping) not extension. Consequently, it contains more flexors than extensors. Extensors and their tendons are more compact and less powerful than flexors, and are very cleverly designed. They are used to extend the fingers, to control the impedence of the fingers, and for applying small forces to objects. Some muscles act as both flexors and extensors. For example, the lumbrical muscle flexes the metacarpophalangeal joint and extends the interphalangeal joint.

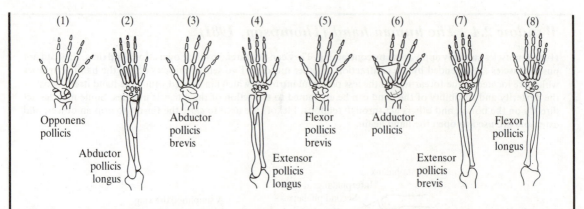

(1)   (2)   (3)   (4)   (5)   (6)   (7)   (8)

Opponens
pollicis

Abductor
pollicis
longus

Abductor
pollicis
brevis

Flexor
pollicis
brevis

Adductor
pollicis

Flexor
pollicis
longus

Extensor
pollicis
longus

Extensor
pollicis
brevis

The great flexibility of the thumb is achieved with eight muscles acting across the joint at its base (the carpometacarpal thumb joint). Four of these are intrinsics, and four are extrinsics. The extrinsics individually act on the joint by means of long tendons, which must cross the wrist before reaching the thumb. Six of the muscles act on the more distal joints of the thumb.

Gippers with two or three parallel jaws can only grasp a limited number of objects. They lack the flexibility required for manipulation of complete objects. In many applications, a robot does not use a gripper, but instead, a tool is attached directly to the end plate. Flexible grippers are not required for tasks such as spot welding or spray painting, where the robot continuously performs the same operation and never has to change end effectors. But, during assembly operations or when tending machine tools, a robot has to grasp a variety of dissimilar objects, a requirement which is difficult to achieve with a parallel-jaw gripper.

The most common solution to this problem is to have a range of interchangeable grippers, one for each operation to performed by the robot.

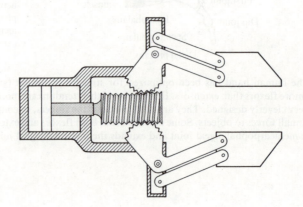

Figure 2.38
Rack and pinion parallel-jaw
gripper.

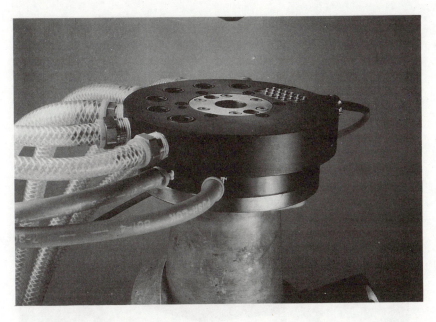

Figure 2.39
Flexible tooling connector
from EOA Systems.

Manual changing of grippers reduces the cost effectiveness of the robot, so automatic changing with a flexible tooling connector is preferable (Figure 2.39). Services such as air and electrical signals have to be turned off before the gripper is changed. Hydraulic connections pose even greater problems. The disadvantages of interchangeable grippers are the cost of maintaining an inventory of grippers, the time required to switch between them, and the difficulty of making connections for sensors and actuators. In fact, a large part of the time taken up in the design of a robot system for a new application is spent designing specialized grippers.

These disadvantages can be avoided by using more flexible grippers. Flexibility is achieved by changing the fingers on a gripper, by permanently mounting several gripers on the tool plate, and by using human-like grippers. Some assembly tasks can be achieved with parallel-jaw grippers if the fingers can be changed rapidly between sequential operations. Typically, a special set of fingers is designed for each stage of the operation. These are placed on a tooling rack within the reach of the robot, and between operations, the robot returns one set of fingers and picks up another. The design of fingers for automatic pick up and release is difficult. The fingers have to fit snugly on the jaws of the gripper so that they do not move during operation, but they must also be easy to remove at the end of the operation. In addition, any sensors in the fingers must be simple to connect and disconnect. Some researchers are experimenting with infrared communication links to transfer multi-bit tactile information from removable fingers to the robot controller.

One solution to the disconnect problem is to mount multiple grippers on the tool plate, each with special fingers. When a gripper is required it is

Figure 2.40
Bell Laboratories controlled impedance gripper built by R.A. Boie, M.J. Sibilia, G.L. Miller and M.K. Brown.

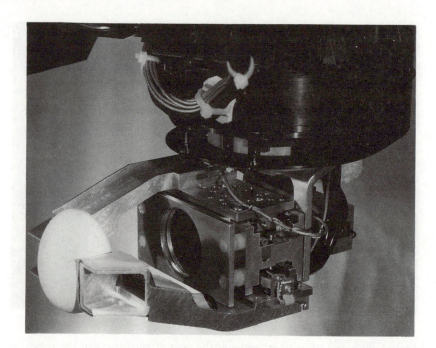

indexed into the operating position and becomes the operating gripper. This system works well with small grippers, provided none of the grippers snags on the assembly. As the volume occupied by the several grippers attached to the tool plate is considerably larger than the volume of a single gripper, the possibility of a collision is much greater.

The most versatile gripper known is the human hand (Window 2.4). While many robot applications can be accomplished with specially designed tools and grippers, a truly flexible industrial robot will require grippers with a flexibility approaching that of a human hand. Two characteristics of human hands that are achievable are controlled impedance and variable finger movement. The fingers of one controlled-impedance gripper (Figure 2.40) are mounted on linear slides and driven independently by two direct current servomotors through a rack and two pinions (Brown, 1984). Due to the low internal friction of this gearing, this mechanism is mechanically back drivable, meaning that a force applied to a finger will cause the motor to move. Under computer control, this feature allows the motor drive mechanism to function as a mechanical impedance applying all the appropriate effects of mass, damping, and compliance directly to the fingers.

With normal grippers, problems can occur when the object to be grasped is not midway between the fingers. When the jaws are closed, one finger will strike the object first and the object will be pushed toward the other finger. If the object is fixed so that it can not slip, the compliance of the

Figure 2.41
Utah/MIT dextrous hand.

manipulator must compensate for the positional error or the object will be damaged. Whatever happens, excessive force is applied to the object. In contrast, with a controlled-impedance gripper, when the object is off centre, the first finger to touch the object stops while the other continues to move. When both fingers touch the object, a pre-determined force is applied to the object to ensure a stable grasp. The grasping force is measured with capacitive tactile sensors located in the jaws of the gripper. To achieve controlled impedance, the stiffness of the fingers is low during the approach phase so that they offer low impedance to contact forces, and, the stiffness is increased to hold the object firmly as soon as the grasp is established. Also, this gripper includes an ultrasonic sensor in the palm to detect the object before it is grasped.

A second important characteristic of human fingers is their ability to conform to the shape of the object they are grasping. This feature is because of the compliant nature of flesh and skin, and because each finger has three bones and three joints. The Omnigripper (Scott, 1985) is a two-jaw gripper, with an array of 8×16 closely spaced pins on each finger. As the gripper is lowered on to an object, these pins are pushed up into the palm of the gripper. When the gripper is in the grasping position, the jaws are closed and the object is grasped by the pins. If sensors are attached to the pins, a low resolution image of the object can be obtained.

Moulding fingers around an object is best achieved with multi-jointed fingers (Figure 2.41). Also, with human fingers, stiffness control can be achieved independently of the grasping force, because the contraction and extension of the fingers are achieved with counteracting tendon actuators, as in human fingers. For low stiffness, these counteracting forces are small, and for high stiffness they are large. The grasping force is the difference between the counteracting extension and contraction forces, hence it is independent of stiffness. However, human-like grippers are likely to remain a subject of research for a long time to come. The mechanical problems of packing all the actuator hardware in a small enough space to fit in a robot linkage, and the routing of tendons through three degree of freedom wrists still have to be solved. Also, current models of grasping are inadequate for control.

2.5 Actuators

Power for robot motion is provided by **electrical**, **hydraulic**, and **penumatic actuators**. Current robotic actuators are refinements of industrial actuators, with the main difference being the requirement of high a power-to-size ratio. Many newer actuators include built-in position and velocity sensors. One non-traditional method of actuation, used only experimentally, is the application of heat and cold to 'memory-metal' wire causing it to expand and contract to provide actuation force (Kuribayashi, 1986). As in other industrial applications, each actuator type has its own advantages and disadvantages (Table 2.2): Environmental conditions have to be considered as well as differences in mechanical capabilities. For example, electric actuators require special cases before they can be used in environments which include explosive gases. Consequently, in these environments, hydraulic actuators are often preferred. On the other hand, hydraulic actuators use oil, and create a mess when a pipe leaks, so in environments where a high degree of cleanliness is required, pneumatic actuators may be preferred.

The most common application of pneumatic actuators is the opening and closing of grippers. Also, linear pneumatic cylinders are used in simple pick-and-place robots, where no path control is required (Figure 2.42). Cylinders are either extended or retracted, with the extension and retraction positions being controlled by mechanical stops, resulting in 'bang-bang' control of motion. Some actuators achieve limited rotary motion by using the linear actuator to turn a shaft with a rack and pinion gearing system, or with a chain. Rotary air motors, such as those used in pneumatic tools, have found little application in robotics as yet.

Gas is compressible, and thus, it can store large quantities of energy per unit mass (typically an order of magnitude more than a battery). For this reason, it is ideal for powering prosthetic arms. However, the compressibility of gas makes servocontrol of pneumatic actuators complex. To move a load a small distance with a cylinder at reasonable speed, a high differential pressure is required between the chambers in the cylinder. To

Table 2.2 Comparison of pneumatic, hydraulic, and electric actuators.

Pneumatic actuators

Advantages

- Relatively inexpensive
- High speed
- Do not pollute work area with fluids
- Can be used in laboratory work
- No return line required
- Common energy source in industry
- Suits modular robot designs
- Actuator can stall without damage

Disadvantages

- Compressibility of air limits control and accuracy aspects
- Noise pollution from exhausts
- Leakage of air can be of concern
- Additional drying/filtering may be required
- Difficulties with control of speeds, take up of loads, and exhausting of lines

Hydraulic actuators

Advantages

- Large lift capacity
- High power to weight ratio
- Moderate speeds
- Oil is incompressible, hence once positioned joints can be locked to a stiff structure
- Very good servo control can be achieved
- Self lubricating and self cooling
- Operate in stalled condition with no damage
- Fast response
- Intrinsically safe in flammable and explosive atmospheres
- Smooth operation at low speeds

Disadvantages

- Hydraulic systems are expensive
- Maintenance problems with seals causing leakage
- Not suitable for high speed cycling
- Need for a return line
- Hard to miniaturize because high pressures and flow rates
- Need for remote power source which uses floor space
- Cannot back drive links against valves

Electric actuators (DC motors and stepper motors)

Advantages

- Actuators are fast and accurate
- Possible to apply sophisticated control techniques to motion
- Relatively inexpensive
- Very fast development times for new models
- New rare earth motors have high torques, reduced weight, and fast response times

Disadvantages

- Inherently high speed with low torque, hence gear trains or other power transmission units are needed
- Gear backlash limits precision
- Electrical arcing may be a consideration in flammable atmospheres
- Problems of overheating in stalled condition
- Brakes are needed to lock them in position

Figure 2.42
Pneumatic pick-and-place
robot from Martonair.

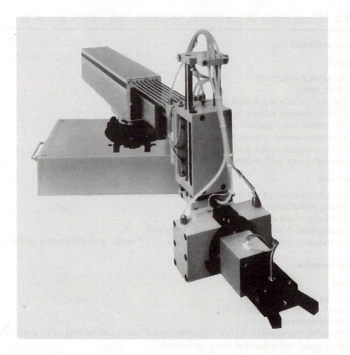

achieve this pressure, more air must be let into the chamber than will fill the
resultant change in volume of the chamber. Before the piston has travelled
the required distance, the air in the chamber must be expelled to atmosphere,
and air let into the other chamber to decelerate the piston. Once the piston
has stopped, this air must also be vented which means that considerable
energy is wasted. Also, as a consequence of the compressibility of air, the
process is difficult to model and thus to control, accurately.

In comparison, fluids are incompressible, giving hydraulic actuators
different properties from pneumatic actuators. Hydraulic fluid cannot be
used for energy storage, so another power source must be used to create
pressure in the oil. Also, hydraulic oil cannot be vented into the atmosphere
so a return path must be provided for the used oil. The extension of a linear
hydraulic cylinder is controlled by controlling the differential pressure
between the two chambers. While a differential pressure exists, the cylinder
shaft moves. As the hydraulic fluid is incompressible, a very high pressure is
achieved by letting a small amount of fluid into the chamber. The volume of
oil let into the chamber controls the distance the cylinder moves. Overshoot
is damped by an increase in pressure in the other chamber, causing the piston
to stop in the position where the chamber pressures equalize. Absolute
pressure is used to control the stiffness of the system, while differential
pressure is used to control position. Thus, hyraulic actuators are easily
controlled using feedback of position, and are fast with minimum overshoot
and controllable stiffness.

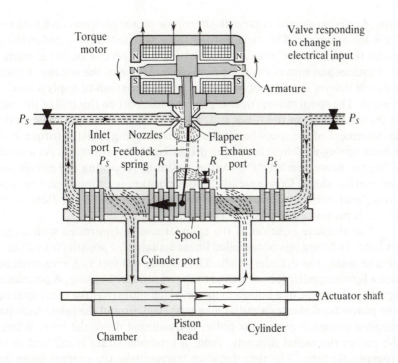

Figure 2.43
Moog hydraulic Servovalve.

Oil flow into and out of the two chambers is usually controlled with a spool valve (Figure 2.43). Moving the valve lets oil into one chamber and out of the other. The pressure on the two parts of the spool is almost equally balanced, so it is easy to move the spool back and forth to control the flow of high pressure oil into the chambers of the cylinder. The spool is controlled electromechanically: a marriage of electrical and hydraulic technologies. Information can be more easily processed electrically, while delivery of power at high speeds can be accomplished best with a hydraulic actuator. Two methods of spool control are in common use: 'bang-bang' control, and servocontrol. In bang-bang control, the spool is held centrally by opposing springs, one at each end, and solenoids are located at each end of the spool. When energized, a solenoid moves the spool to one end, allowing oil to flow into one chamber and out of the other. Control of absolute cylinder displacement is difficult with this method of control because either full or zero pressure is applied to the chamber.

Servovalves were developed to allow fast, precise control of hydraulic actuators. They control the rate of flow of oil into the cylinders by controlling the size of the openings, and thus provide proportional control. When the spool valve is central, all cylinder ports are closed, and oil flows through the nozzles to the drain. Moving the spool valve in one direction opens the inlet port for the chamber on that side and the exhaust port for the chamber on the other side, allowing oil to flow, and hence moving the cylinder. Spool valve position is controlled by a flapper driven by a torque motor. Applying electric current to the torque motor coils sets up a magnetic field in the armature. This field distorts the magnetic fields created in the air gaps by the permanent magnets, impressing a net torque on the armature, which rotates and moves the flapper to close off one of the nozzles. Closing the nozzle diverts the flow of oil to that end of the spool to apply a force to the spool. The spool moves, opening the exhaust port on this end of the valve and the entry port on the other end, allowing oil to flow into the cylinder. The movement of the spool bends the feedback spring until the torque in the feedback spring matches the torque produced by the armature. As a result, the flapper moves back to the central position, reopening the nozzle, and spool motion stops. Consequently, spool position is proportional to input current, and with a constant hydraulic supply pressure, oil flow to the cylinder is proportional to spool position.

The absolute position of the cylinder can be controlled with a feedback loop. In Moog servocontrolled linear actuators, a position transducer is mounted inside the cylinder shaft. The sensing element is a wire stretched inside a ferromagnetic tube attached to the transducer housing. A permanent magnet (in the shape of a hollow cylinder which slides over the tube) attached to the piston head creates a radial magnetic field around the tube. A crystal-controlled sequence of current pulses is trasmitted down the wire. When a pulse passes the radial magnetic field, a torsional strain is induced in the ferromagnetic tube. The time between transmitting the current pulse and sensing the torsional strain is proportional to the extension of the cylinder.

Parallel connection of hydraulic actuators causes the actuators to share load forces equally because the oil pressure is equal in each of the actuators. The motion of individual actuators depends on the external constraints imposed on them. This feature was used in the control of the legs of a six-legged walking robot (Sutherland and Ullner, 1984) to automatically compensate for variations in terrain height.

Rotary hydraulic servodrives are often used in robotics (Window 2.5). Well-designed actuators include oil paths through the actuator shafts, so that oil can flow through the actuators from one link to the next, eliminating external hydraulic cables. Servodrives are also controlled by a servovalve, but the output is rotational, requiring a different drive mechanism from linear actuators and a rotary velocity transducer. A typical hydraulic motor uses nine pistons to apply force to a *swash plate* (Figure 2.44). A swash plate is a circular plate, concentric with the shaft, but attached at an angle to it. Oil is released into a piston when the swash plate is closest to the end of the piston. As each piston extends, it applies a force to the plate causing it to turn to reduce the force by moving the swash plate away from the cylinder, allowing the cylinder to extend. Flow of oil into the cylinders is controlled by a **distributor** – a set of tubes which rotate with the shaft. The distributor connects two groups of four sequential pistons to the inlet and outlet servovalve ports. As the shaft rotates, pistons move from one control port to the other depending upon whether they are extending or contracting. The

Window 2.5   Hydraulic servomotor model (Clark, 1969)

The **ideal hydraulic motor** provides output shaft torque proportional to servovalve differential pressure and speed proportional to servovalve flow.

$$\text{Ideal shaft torque} = T_m = \frac{D_m \Delta P_l}{2\pi} \text{ Newton meter}$$

where

D_m = servomotor volumetric displacement (metre^3/revolution), and
ΔP_1 = servovalve load differential pressure (Newtons/metre^2)

$$\text{Shaft speed} = \omega_m = \frac{2\pi\, Q_l}{D_m} \text{ radians/second}$$

where

Q_l = servovalve load flow (metre^3/second)

For an ideal motor, the output power is equal to the input power:

$$\text{Power}_{\text{ideal}} = T_m \omega_m = Q_l \Delta P_l$$

The flow and differential pressure to the servomotor are supplied from a constant pressure hydraulic supply through an electrohydraulic servovalve. The mathematical relation between load flow and load pressure is parabolic, because the second stage of the servovalve controls load pressure by throttling load flow across sharp-edged orifices.

$$\frac{Q_l}{Q_{nl}} = \frac{i_v}{i_r} \sqrt{1 - \frac{\Delta P_l}{P_s}}$$

where

Q_{nl} = no-load servovalve flow (metre^3/second)
P_s = hydraulic supply pressure (Newtons metre^2)
i_v = torque motor current (milliamp)
i_r = rated servovalve current (milliamp)

From the above equation, for a constant load differential pressure, load flow is linearly proportional to the current in the servovalve torque motor coils. Also, for a constant coil current, load flow is related to the square root of load pressure. When the load pressure reaches the supply pressure, the load flow will be zero (the load is stalled). No-load flow occurs when the load differential pressure is zero. In this case, all of the supply pressure is lost across the valve orifices and no torque is available at the motor shaft.

These ideal properties are sufficient for valve and motor selection, if a 10–20 per cent margin is allowed on system pressure to compensate for hydraulic line losses, leakage, and viscous friction losses in the motor. However, a number of non-ideal properties must be considered in designing a closed loop control system using a servodrive, particularly if smooth control is required over a wide dynamic range (1000:1). These, non-ideal properties include:

- Variation of motor displacement with shaft angle.
- Motor leakage, both constant and shaft angle dependent.
- Breakout and running fiction of the motor and the load.
- Servovalve null shift, threshold, and hysteresis.
- Oil compressibility effects (load resonance).

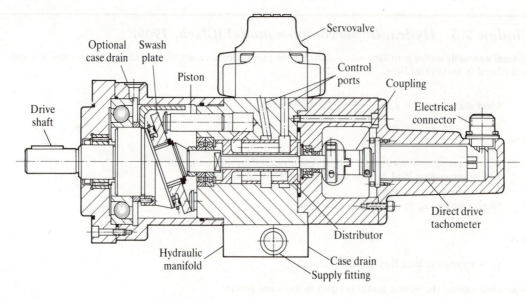

Figure 2.44
Moog-Donzelli rotary
hydraulic servodrive.

ninth piston is always in transition between one control port and the other.

Users of hydraulic drives must install a hydraulic power supply, maintain the system regularly, and be prepared to handle oil leakages. Hydraulics manufacturers cite the following advantages of electrohydraulic drives over conventional electric drives:

- They have substantially higher power-to-weight ratios resulting in higher machine frame resonant frequencies.

- They are much stiffer, resulting in higher loop gains, greater accuracy, and better response.

- They give smoother performance at low speeds, and have a wide speed range without special control circuits.

- They are self-cooling, and can operate in a stalled condition without overheating.

Despite these advantages, many robot manufacturers choose to use electric motors. Two types of electric motors are in use: **stepper motors** and **direct current (d.c.) motors**. Stepper motors (Figure 2.45) are driven by a train of electrical pulses. The stator (fixed part) is wound as two separate coils, which produce magnetic fields offset angularly by half a rotor pole. These coils are pulsed alternately to produce a rotating magnetic field (Figure 2.46). The rotor (rotating part), which is polarized with alternating north and south poles, aligns itself with this field, and rotates with it. Each pulse turns the rotor through a fixed angle (one step) and consequently, angular position change is proportional to the number of pulses. Accurate

Figure 2.45
Cutaway view of a PMI
stepper motor.

open-loop control of the rotational velocity is achieved by controlling the pulse rate. Stepper motors can slip during rapid acceleration of high inertia loads, thus, for accurate open loop control, the pulse frequency has to be varied during times of acceleration. Feedback control is used with stepper motors in situations where accuracy is required. Stepper motors can oscillate around the stopped position and overshoot when driving light loads. Some form of damping is required to eliminate vibrations and to suppress overshoot. If power is applied to one phase only, the motor is held firmly in place by the magnetic field.

Stepper motors are classified according to the material of which the rotor is made. **Variable reluctance steppers** have a toothed soft iron rotor. They have low torque, low inertia, medium step angles (5° to 15°), and rapid acceleration (high slew rate). **Permanent magnet steppers** have a permanent magnet rotor. They are more economical, but have slower step rates, and lower torques. They also provide a detent-holding torque when the power is off. The shape of rotors in permanent magnet stepper motors has changed

Figure 2.46
Motion of a stepper motor as
current pulses are alternately
applied to the two stator
coils.

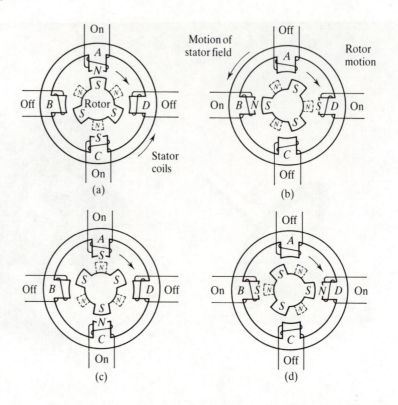

from a cylinder to a thin disk by using samarium cobolt magnets, with up to
fifty pole pairs around the circumference of the disk. To accommodate this
change in geometry, the stator has been redesigned to provide an axial
magnetic field (Figure 2.45). These motors have a tenth of the inertia, a third
of the mechanical time constant, and about seven times the theoretical
acceleration of the conventional steppers. **Hybrid steppers** have a variable
reluctance motor with a permanent magnet inserted in it. They have high
torque, high inertia, small step angles (0.5° to 15°), and high accuracy.

   Direct current motors are more common in industrial robots. The
rotational velocity of a shunt motor is proportional to the applied voltage,
and the output torque is proportional to the armature current.

V (voltage) $= E + IR$ where IR = current × armature resistance   **(2.1)**

E (back emf) $= k\phi\omega$ $\approx$ constant × angular velocity   **(2.2)**

T (torque) $= k\phi I$ $\approx$ constant × armature current   **(2.3)**

Feedback is required if positioning is to be controlled accurately, as there is
no position term in the above equations. Typical d.c. servomotors include
integrated position and velocity sensors (Figure 2.47) Complex electronic

Figure 2.47
Cutaway view of a PMI d.c.
servomotor, integral
tachometer and optical
encoder.

circuits and power amplifiers are required to control them. Large motors
have a wound stator, while small motors have a permanent magnet stator.
High power-to-weight ratios (similar to hydraulic motors) have been
achieved by using samarium cobolt magnets. The rotor is wound, and a commutator connects the windings to the power supply brushes (Figure 2.48). A
commutator is a cylinder with copper contacts placed around the periphery.
Carbon brushes connect the power source to the commutator to energize one
rotor winding at a time. The magnetic field produced by the rotor winding
distorts the magnetic field produced by the stator. The resultant torque turns
the rotor. As the rotor turns, the commutator turns under the carbon
brushes, disconnecting the current rotor winding and connecting the next.
This commutation of the rotor windings has the effect of permanently dis-
placing the resultant rotor field with respect to the stator field, and rotary
motion is maintained.

    Brushless d.c. motors have the same torque-speed characteristics as
conventional d.c. motors, but their operation is more complex. There are no
electrical connections to the rotor because the rotor is made of permanent
magnets. Samarium cobolt magnets are often used because they provide
higher torque than alnico magnets. A rotating magnetic field is produced by
electronically commutating the stator field windings. The proper stator
winding polarities (at each instant) are derived from shaft position, as read
by an optical encoder, and the desired direction of rotation. Velocity control
is accomplished either by adjusting stator current, or by adjusting the

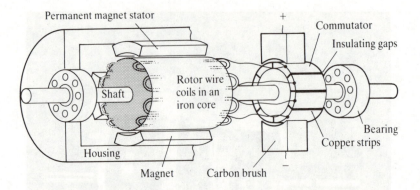

Figure 2.48
Cut-away view of a
permanent magnet d.c.
motor.

current duty cycle with pulse-width-modulated control. Reversal of the direction of rotation is achieved by reversing the sequence in which the stator windings are powered. A number of practical advantages accrue from the removal of the commutator: brush wear and sparking are eliminated, and cooling is easier because heat-generating sources are removed from the rotor (Muir and Neuman, 1985). Also, power transistors operating in switching mode are more efficient than the analogue power amplifiers used with conventional motors.

2.6   Transmission elements

Power has to be transmitted from an actuator to the object it is moving, for example, from an electric motor to a linkage. Typical transmission devices are **gears**, **tendons**, and **linkages**. Which transmission device is choosen depends on the power requirements, the nature of the desired motion, and the placement of the power source with respect to the joint. The primary considerations in transmission design are cost, stiffness, efficiency, geometry, compactness, and simplicity. Drive mechanisms with high static friction are not very efficient at low power levels. High static friction often results from attempts to maximize stiffness or minimize backlash. The complex adjustment and setup procedures used to achieve this significantly increase the cost of the robot, and decrease its reliability. Gear backlash is controlled by adjusting the distance between gear centres. Tendon setup requires the adjustment of tension idlers or *centre* distances.

    Tendons are made from wires, chains (Figure 2.49), and timing belts. They are used when the designer wants the actuator to be remote from the application. This allows joints to be smaller, and reduces the load applied to the actuators of previous joints. When tendons are used, actuators are often mounted in the base of the robot, allowing the overall bulk of the robot to be reduced, improving the power-to-weight ratio. Tendons provide smooth

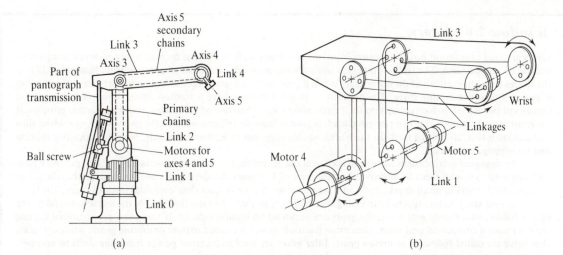

(a)   (b)

Figure 2.49
Using chains and linkages to
transmit power from
actuators in the trunk to
joints 4 and 5 of robot
manipulators.
(a) Chain transmission in
Yaskamor Motoman robot;
(b) Linkage transmission in
the ASEA IRB Robot.

control at low speeds, however, they can stretch, reducing control accuracy. Also, if the tendon has to travel around a number of joints in the manipulator, the movement of those joints may change the distance the tendon has to travel. This cross coupling between joints is usually compensated for by software in the controller. Chains must be preloaded to minimize the droop caused by the weight of the chain. Drive stiffness in tendon drives is a function of the materials used in the tendon.

Some robots use **linkages** to transmit power to the joints, because linkages do not suffer from inaccuracies due to stretching and wear (Figure 2.49). Even though linkages are stiff, transmission stiffness is limited by the bearings and shafts that connect the linkages. Power is often transmitted in robots through torsion shafts or weight-saving torque tubes. Shaft diameter can be minimised by transmitting power at high angular velocities, but fatigue life may be reduced, particularly with aluminum shafts.

Gears are the most common transmission elements used in robots (Window 2.6). When designing gears, factors to consider are tooth shape, material, material surface treatment, and manufacturing precision (Savage, 1984). Gear stiffness increases with gear diameter, and is limited by the stiffness of the teeth. When designing a geared transmission, the designer has to consider gear type, gear ratio, shaft support, lubrication, and ways to minimize backlash. Several types of gearing are in common use: rack and pinions, ball screws, gear boxes, and harmonic drives. Gear boxes are often integrated into electric servomotors (Figure 2.50). Rack and pinion drives and ball screws are used in prismatic joints, where linear motion is required. Ball screws are also used to move transmission linkages (Figure 2.51). They are efficient, moderately stiff, very accurate, and have a large mechanical advantage, but they are difficult to back drive. Inaccuracies and backlash

Window 2.6   Gears

Gears are used to transmit positive motion from one revolving shaft to another by means of a series of wheels with accurately shaped teeth. The teeth of one gear must always mesh with the teeth of another gear, fiting exactly into the spaces between the teeth of the other gear. When a gear turns, the gear it meshes with must turn also. This is what is meant by **positive motion drive**. The opposite to positive motion drive is **friction drive**. A simple friction drive consists of two wheels, which contact on their circumferences. When one wheel rotates, the other rotates also, but if the resistance to rotation, due to an external load, is greater than the friction between the two wheels, one wheel slips and motion is lost. By cutting teeth on the wheels so that they mesh together accurately, we obtain positive motion and no slippage can occur.

Several gear tooth designs have been used over the centuries. During the industrial revolution, pin teeth were replaced with cycloidal teeth to improve the dynamics of the gears. Modern gears use involute teeth, which can tolerate small errors in mesh depth, and can transmit a much greater load than cycloidal teeth (Savage, 1984).

A **gear train** is constructed by meshing several gears, so that when the first gear in the sequence rotates, the others follow. In a simple gear train, the gears are mounted on separate shafts. If two gears are mounted on one shaft we have a compound gear train. Gears that transmit power are called **drivers** or **driving gears**, while the gears they drive are called **followers** or **driven gears**. **Idler gears** are used to transmit power from one shaft to another, when the distance between shafts is to large to be covered by only two gears.

Gear size is measured by counting the number of teeth around the circumference of the gear. Two gears in mesh having the same number of teeth will rotate at the same speed in opposite directions. **Gear speed ratio** is the inverse of the ratio of counts of gear teeth (size ratio). A 2:1 speed ratio means that the input shaft rotates twice to produce one rotation of the output shaft. On most gear trains the input shaft and the output shaft can be swapped depending on whether you want to step the speed up or down.

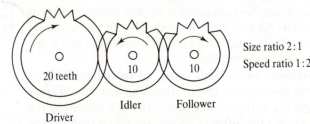

Size ratio 2:1
Speed ratio 1:2

Spur gears transmit power between parallel shafts. The teeth on spur gears are cut straight across the face of the gear, parallel to the shaft the gear is mounted on. A **rack and pinion** consists of a flat piece of metal or wood with gear teeth cut in it – the rack – meshed with a spur gear – the pinion. When the pinion rotates, the rack moves in a straight line, effectively changing rotary motion into linear motion.

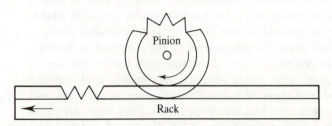

Bevel gears are used to transmit power between shafts that are at an angle to each other. A bevel gear is a slice of a cone, with teeth cut across the angular face formed by the surface of the cone. When the gears are of equal size and the shafts are at 90° to each other, a bevel gear is called a **mitre gear**. A straight-tooth bevel gear has the teeth cut straight across the face of the gear. A spiral-tooth bevel gear has the teeth cut at an angle across the face of the gear. Spiral-tooth bevel gears give a smoother and quieter drive than straight-tooth bevel gears.

Helical (spiral) **gears** are like spur gears, except that the teeth are cut at an angle across the face of the gear. They can be used to transmit power between parallel shafts but they can also be used to transmit power between shafts which cross one another at an angle without intersecting. The angle of intersection depends upon the angle of the gear teeth. **Herringbone gears** are double helical gears, where the teeth are cut in a V shape across the face of the gear. This shape gives a smoother and quieter drive for high-speed gear trains where a large speed reduction is required.

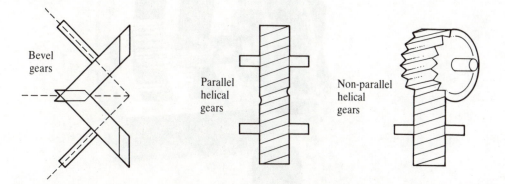

A **worm and worm-gear** drive consists of a worm, which looks like a screw thread (the driver), and a worm–gear, which looks similar to a helical gear (the follower). When the worm rotates, the worm gear turns at a much slower speed: the worm gear turns the angle of one tooth for every rotation of the worm. Worm gear drives can be used to transmit power between perpendicular shafts, and to obtain large speed-reduction ratios. They have the disadvantage that they can not be back driven. Some worm gears are called **worm nuts** because they are the shape of a metal nut surrounding the worm. When the worm turns, the nut moves linearly along the axis of the worm. These gears convert rotary motion into linear motion, and are often used to drive slides.

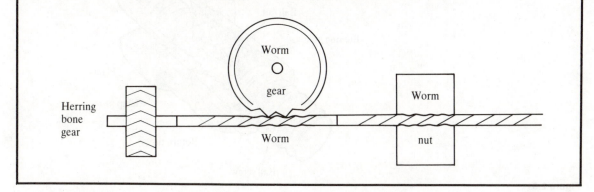

can be eliminated by preloading the nuts and shimming the screws, and nonuniformities are absorbed through elastic deformation of system components.

Harmonic drives (Figure 2.52) are commonly used with revolute joints. These drives have in-line parallel shafts, very high gear ratios, high mechanical advantage, compact packages, and, with proper parts matching, near zero backlash. They suffer from high static friction and cyclic frictional torque variations called **cogging**. A harmonic drive consists of three

Figure 2.50
Cut-away view of a PMI d.c.
servomotor and gearbox.

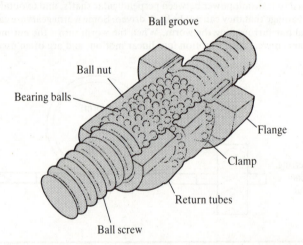

Ball groove

Ball nut

Bearing balls

Flange

Clamp

Return tubes

Ball screw

(a)

Figure 2.51
Warner electric brake and
clutch ball screw
transmission.
(a) Arrangement of ball-
bearing screw.
(b) Drive motor rotates
screw and the nut travels
along the screw, for
example, the control of the
shoulder joint in the
Motoman robot (Figure
2.49).

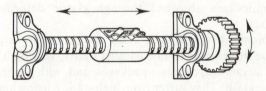

(b)

(a)

Circular Spline
A rigid, internal
gear

Wave Generator
An elliptical ball-
bearing assembly

Flexspline
A nonrigid, external
gear

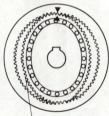

Flexspline teeth are fully
disengaged at minor axis

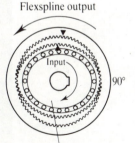

Flexspline output

Input

90°

Eliptical wave generator
deflects flexspline to engage
teeth at the major axis

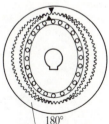

180°

Fixed circular spline

(b)

concentric components: an inner elliptical wave generator, a flexspline, and an outer rigid circular spline. The teeth of the nonrigid flexspline and the rigid circular spline are in continuous engagement at the apogees of the ellipse, but are disengaged at the perigees, where they are misaligned by half a tooth (90°). The flexspline has two less teeth than the circular spline. When the elliptical wave generator is turned through one revolution, the flexspline moves relative to the circular spline by a distance of two teeth. With the circular spline rotationally fixed, the flexspline will rotate in the opposite direction to the input, with a reduction equal to half the flexspline tooth count. Normally, the flexspline is used as the output but any of the drive elements can be input, output, or fixed, depending on whether speed reduction, speed multiplication, or differential operation is required.

All transmission elements have the following problems (Asada and Kanade, 1981):

- Dynamic response is poor because of the heavy weight and/or high compliance of the transmission.

- Fine movements and pure torque control are difficult because of the relatively large friction and backlash at the transmission.

- Additional complicated mechanisms for minimizing the backlash are necessary and they need careful adjustment and regular maintenance.

Transmission elements can be eliminated by directly coupling a joint axis to the rotor of a rare earth magnet d.c. torque motor. **Direct drive systems** have no backlash, low friction, low compliance, high reliability, and fast dynamic

Figure 2.52
Emhart Harmonic Drive.
(a) Cut-away view of Emhart harmonic drive;
(b) Operation of harmonic drive mechanism.

Figure 2.53
CMU direct-drive arm II.

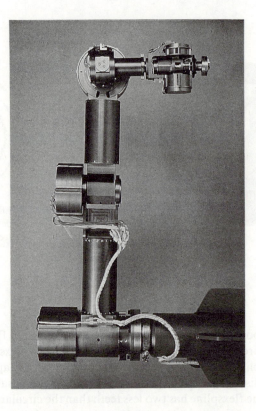

response, but are more difficult to control, because changing dynamics and other nonlinear effects are no longer suppressed by high gear ratios. Experimental direct drive arms have been built at the MIT Artificial Intelligence Laboratory and the CMU Robotics Institute (Figure 2.53). The first commercially available arm using direct drive technology was the Adept One arm.

Figure 2.54
Flexible couplings from
Helical Products Co.

Figure 2.55
IKO Bearings.

Flexible couplings (Figure 2.54) are often placed between motors and drive shafts. These minimize the loads placed on the motor bearings due to misalignment of the motor shaft and the drive shaft. **Roller bearings**, sometimes with alternately crossed rollers (Figure 2.55), can withstand axial loads as well as loads perpendicular to the shaft. **Torque-limiting clutches** are used in some robots to protect the robot from damage caused by the high torques produced when the robot collides with an object. Clutches are also used to disconnect actuators, so that a robot can be back driven. Damage to drive mechanisms can be limited by using **shock absorbers** rather than solid mechanical limits at the limits of travel. When the power fails, an arm might collapse and damage the object the robot was manipulating. In the event of a power failure, an **electromechanical brake** will freeze the robot arm in its current position. When electric power is lost, the brake coil de-energizes, releasing a spring–loaded pressure plate, which pushes against the shaft, locking it in position.

2.7 Sensors

Sensors are grouped into two classes: **internal** and **external sensors**. **Internal** sensors measure variables within the robot – for example, joint angle, wrist force, and platform velocity. **External sensors** measure the environment – for example range, vision, and voice. Sensor installation poses a number of problems for the robot designer. Often sensors have to be mounted in awkward positions, such as on the fingers of a gripper, where they have to be protected from impact, dust, and moisture. The more data they produce, the larger the cable loom, and thus, the more complex the routing problems.

The range and resolution requirements of the application often push sensor technology to its limits. A joint supporting a manipulator linkage 1 m long turns through an angle of 0.00573° to move the end of the linkage 0.1 mm. If the joint can rotate through 360°, the sensor must have a range of 62,832 bit in order to measure an angle this small, that is, sixteen-bit binary. For this reason, optical shaft encoders with a resolution of 500 bit per revolution, are mounted on the motor shaft and not on the joint shaft. However, if backlash is larger than the angle to be measured, the robot cannot achieve the desired accuracy of control.

Sensors are discussed in detail in Chapter 10.

2.8 Materials

Robots must be made from light but strong, rigid materials. As component wear can affect the accuracy of the whole mechanism, gears and slides have to be made out of hard materials. Some applications place additional requirements on the materials – undersea robots, for example, require materials that resist corrosion. The material used in linkages should be light so that its weight adds little to the forces on the other components. Flexing of linkages results in inaccurate position control and so they must to be rigid.

The commonest **structural materials** are steel and aluminium (Window 2.7). Other materials such as titanium and beryllium are used but titanium is expensive and beryllium is toxic. Many alloys are available, each tailored for a specific application. While steel and aluminium rods of the same weight and length have similar tensile stiffness, they have different resistance to bending. Aluminium rod will resist bending far better, because

Window 2.7   Properties of materials (courtesy A. Russell)

Two important structural properties of materials are **stress** and **strain**. Stress in a material under load is the force per unit area at a given cross section. It can be thought of as an internal pressure. Strain is proportional to the change in the dimension of the material as a result of the applied force. When tensile stress is applied to an object it gets longer and thinner. The relationship between increase in length and decrease in width of a material when it is stretched is called **Poisson's ratio**.

$$\text{Poissons's rotio: } \rho = \frac{\text{lateral strain}}{\text{longitudinal strain}}$$

In many materials, the amount of internal (or tensile) stress is proportional to the strain. This ratio is known as **Young's Modulus**.

$$\text{Young's modulus: } E = \frac{\text{Stress}}{\text{Strain}} \text{ (provided that the yield stress is not exceeded)}$$

Above the **yield stress**, the material deforms permanently: ductile materials will stretch and brittle materials crack and break. **Isotropic materials** have a constant grain structure in all directions, i.e. their microscopic structure does not vary much with direction. In these materials, Young's modulus is constant throughout the material. In **non-isotropic materials**, such as wood, Young's modulus is very dependent on direction. The higher the Young's modulus of a material, the stiffer the material – a larger force is required to produce the same deformation.

When selecting materials for robots, the ratio of the stiffness of the material to its weight is important

$$\frac{\text{Stiffness}}{\text{Weight}} = \frac{\text{Young's modulus}}{\text{Density}} = (\text{Speed of sound in the material})^2$$

Robot linkages must be light in weight and very stiff. The higher the stiffness to weight ratio, the more suitable the material. Materials with these characteristics also have the advantage of good dynamic response. Dynamic response is proportional to the speed of sound in the material. The speed of sound in steel, aluminium, and titanium is similar, indicating that they are equally suitable for use in robots. But, because aluminium is lighter than steel, an aluminium rod of the same weight as a steel rod will be thicker, and hence will be more resistant to bending. Titanium is also lighter than steel, but it is expensive to fabricate.

Material	Density (tonne/metre^2)	Young's Modulus (kilopascals$\times 10^6$)	Speed of Sound (metres/second)
Aluminum alloy (diecast)	2.7	71.0164	1 554
Steel alloys	7.7	193.05–206.84	1 524
Titanium alloys	4.5	103.42–114.45	1 509

The structural properties of materials are also affected by the way the material is produced and the method of fabrication. When a metal cools, crystals form in a regular array. If the metal cools slowly, the crystals grow to be quite large. When a metal deforms, one section slips with respect to other sections along planes formed by the crystals. Metals which consist of relatively large crystals are weaker than metals which consist of fine crystals. They have fewer crystalline planes along which slipping can occur, and thus for the same strain each plane has to slip further.

The size of the crystals in a metal can be changed by **heat treatment**. Common heat treatment techniques are **quenching**, **case hardening**, **annealing**, and **tempering**. Steel is quenched by heating it to red heat (850 °C) and then plunging it into water. The resultant material has small crystals, and is hard and brittle. If steel is plunged into a suitable solution other than water, the solution reacts with the outer layer of the material, changing its structural properties. Steel is case hardened by plunging it into a solution containing carbon, such as sodium cyanide. The carbon diffuses into the outer layer, forcing an irregular and small crystalline structure. Case hardening is often used on surfaces that will be subject to wear such as gear teeth.

Steel is annealed by heating it slowly to red heat and then cooling it slowly. An inert atmosphere may be used to stop oxidation. Annealing allows the crystals to reform, and is often used to reduce internal stresses produced by fabrication. After annealing the material is soft and not very springy. When steel is tempered it is first quenched, and then it is heated to 250 °C and allowed to cool in air. The reheating process allows enough recrystallization for the steel to become tough and springy.

it is thicker (being of lighter material). Resistance to bending is improved by placing more of the material further out from the axis; this is why a tube has better bending resistance than a rod. An aluminium tube has a greater wall thickness than a steel tube of the same weight, increasing its resistance to bending. Also, tubes with a greater wall thickness are easier to make and weld. Aluminium alloys resist oxidation better than steel, but in general have poorer corrosion resistance.

The **method of fabrication** will also affect the choice of material, as some materials do not have the properties required by some manufacturing processes and some manufacturing processes are not always suitable. Machining is not economical for large batches of components. Forging, pressing, and forming are easier to automate, but are limited in the range of shapes they can produce. Casting allows a greater freedom in shaping solid metal objects. Sand casting, in which a wooden mould is used to create a sand mould bound by resin is again, only economic for small batches, because of the short life of the moulds. In addition, the low accuracy of the process makes (2 mm) machining necessary. Die casting, where the mould is made of steel, is more accurate, and suited to mass production, but only certain metals can be die cast. Also, the cast object has low strength because it cools slowly. Structural properties of materials are affected by refining and fabrication so special metal treatment procedures may be needed to produce the desired properties in the material. Heat treatment for example, is used to remove the internal stresses produced by welding, and to increase the strength of a material by recrystallization.

Most aluminium alloys were developed prior to the widespread use of robots. Research into materials for specific robot applications is very limited. Dynamic response of a square aluminium tube is improved by coating the outside with a high damping vinyl elastomer (Mendelson and Rinderle, 1984). Higher frequency oscillations are damped quickly, but the fundamental frequency is not affected, because the elastomer does not dissipate the vibrational energy. Also, damping material increases the weight of the tube significantly, thereby lowering the natural frequency of the tube. One manufacturer uses specially strengthened carbon fibre to build strong lightweight arms that have high repeatability and low thermal expansion.

Materials technology in robotics is in its infancy, however, some researchers are using specialised materials, and specialised methods for testing these materials. Memory metal is used for the whisker sensors in the TITAN III walking robot because of its springiness and resistance to wear (Hirose, 1984). Fatigue life and load-carrying capacity of tendons designed for use in the UTAH/MIT hand have been measured using a specially designed testing machine (Jacobsen *et al.*, 1984).

2.9 User interface

Manually, the motion of a robot is controlled with a teach box (Figure 2.56). This hand-held box contains a display and an array of push buttons. With these buttons, the operator controls the position and orientation of the end effector in Cartesian, joint, or tool coordinates while the display indicates the current coordinate frame, and the instantaneous value of the variable being controlled. Only one variable is controlled at a time. The operator uses the teach box to move the end effector along a desired trajectory, and at the

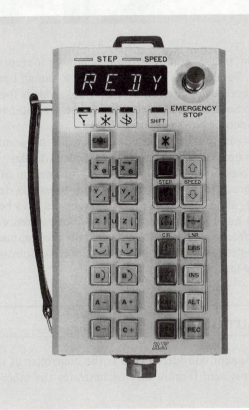

Figure 2.56
Robot teach box for Hobart
Motoman Robot.

Figure 2.57
Remote control of Prowler
robot using joy sticks and
television pictures from
Robot Defence Systems.

push of a button, requests the controlling computer to record positions along that trajectory. Some robots can be taught by a human operator physically pushing the robot through the desired motions. This is the method used in spray painting. Sophisticated teleoperators use a combination of joy stick controls and video displays (Figure 2.57).

Most robots can be programmed using a programming language. Usually, programs are entered from a video display terminal. Some researches are experimenting with automatic generation of programs from models of the processes. No robot has an easy-to-use six degree of freedom pointing device, although, some experimental ones have been built. Such a device converts hand motions into six decoupled reference signals, one for each degree of freedom. With such a device, the programmer moves the end effector to the desired position and orientation by pointing, considerably speeding up the teaching process.

2.10   Controllers

The final component considered here is the controller of the mechanisms. The control subsystem (Figure 2.1) orchestrates the other mechanisms to perform the specified task. Robot controllers typically consist of a small but powerful computer system mounted in a special cabinet near the robot. The computer executes programs to perform the following tasks:

- Maintain a model of relationships between the references to the actuators and their consequential movements using measurements made by the internal sensors.
- Maintain a model of the environment using the measurements made by external sensors.
- Plan the sequence of steps required to execute a task. This may be done on a remote host computer.
- Control the sequence of robot commands to perform the task.
- Modify the robot's actions in response to changes in the external environment.

The power of a controller and the ease with which it can be programmed are determined by the operating system, the programming language, and the programming environment. These issues are discussed in detail in Chapter 12.

2.11 Robot classification

The power of the software in the controller determines the utility and flexibility of the robot within the constraints of mechanical design and sensor availability. Robots have been classified according to their generation, their intelligence level, their level of control, and their programming language level. These classifications overlap, but they all reflect the power of the software in the controller, in particular, the sophistication of sensor interaction. The **generation** of a robot is determined by the historical order of developments in robotics. Five generations are normally assigned to industrial robots. The third generation is used in industry, the fourth is being developed in research laboratories, and the fifth generation is largely a dream. The generations are:

1. **Playback robots** which play back a sequence of recorded instructions, such as in spray painting and spot welding. These robots often have open loop control – for example, pick-and-place robots which use mechanical stops to limit travel.
2. **Sensor-controlled robots** which have closed-loop control of manipulator motions, and decision making based upon sensor inputs.
3. **Vision-controlled robots** where the robot can manipulate an object using information from a vision system.

4. **Adaptively controlled robots** where the robot can automatically reprogramme its actions on the basis of sensor inputs.

5. **Artificially intelligent robots** where the robot uses the techniques of artificial intelligence to make its own decisions and solve problems.

The Japanese robot association (JIRA) has classified robots into six classes on the basis of their **level of intelligence**:

1. **Manual handling devices** controlled by a person.

2. **Fixed sequence robots**.

3. **Variable sequence robots** where an operator can modify the sequence easily.

4. **Playback robots** where the human operator leads the robot through the task.

5. **Numerically controlled robots** where the operator supplies a movement program, rather than teaching it the task manually.

6. **Intelligent robots** which can understand and interact with changes in the environment.

The programs in a robot controller can be grouped according to the **level of control** they perform (Coiffet and Chirouze, 1982):

1. **Artificial intelligence level**, where the program will accept a command such as, 'Pick up the bearing' and decompose it into a sequence of lower level commands based on a strategic model of the task.

2. **Control mode level** where the motions of the system are modelled, including the dynamic interactions between the different mechanisms, trajectories planned, and grasp points selected. From this model a control strategy is formulated, and control commands issued to the next lower level.

3. **Servo system level** where actuators control the mechanism parameters using feedback of internal sensory data, and paths are modified on the basis of external sensory data. Also failure detection and correction mechanisms are implemented at this level.

The final classification we will consider is **programming language level**. The key to the effective application of robots to a wide variety of tasks is the development of high-level robot languages. Many robot programming systems exist, although the most advanced are currently available only in research laboratories. Existing robot programming systems fall into three broad categories (Lozano-Perez, 1983).

1. **Guiding systems**, in which the user leads the robot through the motions to be performed.

2. **Robot-level programming systems**, in which the user writes a computer program to specify motion and sensing.

3. **Task-level programming systems**, in which the user specifies operations by their actions on the objects the robot is to manipulate.

2.12 Implications for robot design

The mechanical and electrical design of robots is a complex task, involving a variety of differing mechanisms, and a host of conflicting constraints. Robot design must be guided by a thorough understanding of the underlying principles of robotics – developed in the following chapters – combined with a working knowledge of current technology. This chapter has done little more than describe the mechanisms in use, and list some of the reasons for their choice. In the following chapters on robot design, an understanding of mechanisms is assumed, and the material presented is basically a mathematical formulation of the science of robotics, with practical implications enumerated where possible.

However, good software cannot overcome poor mechanical design. While 80 per cent of all malfunctions occur in devices peripheral to the manipulator, such as the controller, a robot system can achieve only 99.5 per cent availability if the mechanical system is designed for 99.9 per cent availability. Thus, potentially weak points in mechanical design must be eliminated. Such weak points (Table 2.3) include structural deformation, gear backlash, poor bearing clearance, friction, thermal effects, and poor connection of transducers. In addition, tolerances in the processes used to manufacture the robot result in links that are not quite true to specification. Permanent deformation of the structure, and some manufacturing tolerances can be compensated for in the kinematic model of the robot. Dynamic deformation either has to be designed out or compensated for by using sophisticated controllers. A significant problem with the latter is measuring the dynamic deformation.

Backlash, bearing clearance, and friction are best solved by mechanical design. As they are non-linear, they can create severe problems for servo-control. Changes in the physical size of the robot can be compensated for by a controller, if they can be measured. Finally, measurement of any parameter is only as good as the mechanical connection of the transducer to the robot. Transducers are sensitive to environmental problems such as dust, heat, vibration, and mechanical problems in the coupling such as backlash, slope, axial forces, and springyness.

From the mathematical models of robots developed in the following chapters, a number of additional characteristics for good mechanical design are desired. When designing a robot, the mechanical designer should:

1. keep the weight toward the base to reduce the inertia and the load on the actuators,

Table 2.3 Potential weak points in mechanical design.

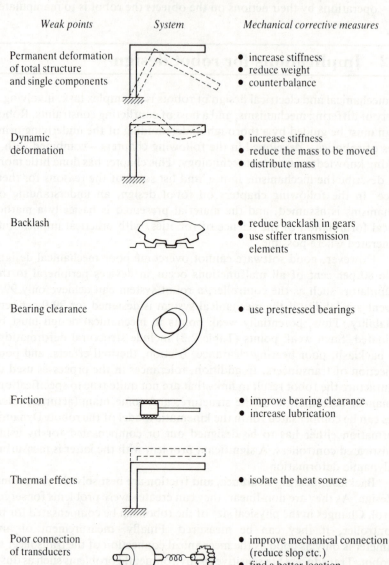

Weak points	System	Mechanical corrective measures
Permanent deformation of total structure and single components		• increase stiffness • reduce weight • counterbalance
Dynamic deformation		• increase stiffness • reduce the mass to be moved • distribute mass
Backlash		• reduce backlash in gears • use stiffer transmission elements
Bearing clearance		• use prestressed bearings
Friction		• improve bearing clearance • increase lubrication
Thermal effects		• isolate the heat source
Poor connection of transducers		• improve mechanical connection (reduce slop etc.) • find a better location • shield against environment

2. keep the geometry simple and eliminate interaction between the joints to simplify the control algorithms,

3. try to balance the forces on the joints to reduce the load on the actuators,

4. keep the structure stiff and light to keep the resonant frequency high and to reduce the load on the bearings and actuators,

5. pay attention to gear backlash, bearing play, and manufacturing tolerances to increase accuracy and repeatability.

6. provide protection for transducers, cables and hoses, and

7. design a tool plate that enables rapid change of the end effector.

Key points

- A robot can be decomposed into a set of functional subsystems: mechanical, electrical, sensor, software, process, planning and control.

- The software subsystem knits the other subsystems into an integrated robot.

- While people and many animals walk on legs, most mobile machines roll on wheels, but there are many places where wheeled vehicles cannot go.

- A vehicle is statically stable when its centre of gravity lies within a polygon formed by the points of contact between the vehicle and the ground.

- The energy efficiency of a legged vehicle is increased by recovering energy from one stride for use in the next.

- An articulated arm emulates the characteristics of a human arm but, unlike a human arm, each joint has only one degree of freedom.

- Manipulators are classified according to the geometry of their workspace, which arises out of the joints used in their construction: Cartesian, cylindrical, polar and revolute.

- The motion of a robot can be described in four different coordinate systems: motor, joint, world and tool.

- The degrees of freedom of an object is the number of independent movements it can make with respect to a coordinate frame – a maximum of six for a Cartesian system: three translational and three rotational.

- The degrees of mobility of a robot is the number of independent joints.

- During the development of a robot application, a significant amount of time is spent on the design of task specific grippers.

- A robot system can achieve only 99.5% availability if the mechanical system is designed for 99.9% availability.

- Good software cannot fix the problems caused by poor mechanical design.

Exercises

■ *Essay questions*

2.1. Tabulate the advantages and disadvantages of wheeled and legged vehicles (Section 2.1).

2.2. In a sentence or two for each one, describe the following concepts and mechanisms: synchronous drive (Section 2.1.1), static stability (Section 2.1.2), the articulated arm, SCARA (Section 2.2), and the spherical wrist (Section 2.3).

2.3. Write short definitions for the following robotics terms (Section 2.2): Cartesian geometry, cylindrical geometry, polar geometry, revolute geometry, workspace, frame of reference, motor co-ordinates, joint co-ordinates, world co-ordinates, tool co-ordinates, degrees of freedom, and degrees of mobility.

2.4. Compare and contrast electric, hydraulic, and pneumatic actuators for use in robotic applications (Section 2.5).

2.5. Discuss the issues involved when designing a 'friendly' user interface for a robot (Section 2.9).

2.6. Derive equations for the doverential (Figure 2.23), which express output rotation and translation in terms of input rotations.

2.7. Derive the equations of motion for a three-wheeled robot, where two wheels are driven (Section 2.1.1).

2.8. A lot of research has been done in developing materials for bicycles. Would the materials used in a bicycle frame be suitable for robot linkages? (Section 2.8)

2.9. Design a spherical wrist with yaw-pitch-roll axes rather than the roll-pitch-roll axes normally used. What problems have you encountered? Why do most wrists use roll-pitch-roll axes to achieve three degrees of freedom? (Section 2.3)

2.10. In what circumstances would a cylindrical robot be better than a Cartesian robot?

2.11. Discuss how the control of the robot arm on the space shuttle might be different to the control of a fixed industrial arm. Do the same for an arm on a mobile robot, and for an arm on a submersible robot.

2.12. How can the mechanical designer improve the reliability and performance of the robot (Section 2.12)?

■ *Practical questions*

Select a robot, either one used in your laboratory, or a robot used by a local company, and perform the following analysis:

2.1.   Obtain the specifications for this robot. Calculate its workspace, and its reach. Devise an experiment to measure the length of each linkage, and compare the measurements to the specification.

2.2.   List all the components of the robot under the subsystems shown in Figure 2.1.

2.3.   List each of the mechanisms used, its type and specifications. Why did the designer choose the mechanisms, actuators, transmission, and sensors that he used?

2.4.   Classify the robot according to generation, intelligence, control, and programming level using the classifications given in Section 2.11.

2.5.   Calculate the positional accuracy of the robot from the specifications of the number of pulses per revolution of the encoder and the physical dimensions of the robot. Does this match the manufacturer's specifications? (Section 2.7)

2.6.   Devise experiments to measure the backlash in each of the joints of a robot, and the stiffness of the linkages. For example, you could extend the arm horizontally and measure the deflection caused by placing known weights on it.

3 · *Object Location*

We have seen more of Neptune than we have of the ocean bottom which is, at most, only a few miles from view. Why is this?

Richard Blidberg, 1989

Objectives

In this chapter, the style of presentation changes from the descriptive style used in the first two chapters to a rigorous mathematical style for the next five chapters. Our objective is to develop tools for modelling the geometric relationships between objects using coordinate frames and homogeneous transforms. The reader is assumed to have a basic knowledge of linear algebra, coordinate geometry, and calculus. Little background in mechanics is assumed, so the reader familiar with statics and dynamics can proceed fairly quickly. This modelling includes the following topics:

- 2-D transformations and homogeneous coordinates,
- 3-D coordinate frames and transformation matrices,
- relative transformations,
- general position and orientation transforms.
- inverse transforms, and
- transform graphs.

Manipulation is the skilful handling and treating of objects: picking them up, moving them, fixing them to one another, and working on them with tools. For a robot to manipulate an object, it must move its gripper to the object. To pick an object up, the gripper must be placed around the object, and closed to grasp the object. To operate on an object with a tool, the tool must be moved into contact with the object, and then moved along the object, so that contact is maintained between the object and the tool, for example, when smoothing the edges of an object with a deburring tool. Before we can program a robot to perform these operations, we require a method of specifying where the object is relative to the robot gripper, and a way of controlling the motion of the gripper.

A walking robot has to move its foot to the object it is to stand on. Before we can program it to do this, we require a method for specifying where the object is relative to the foot of the robot, and a way of controlling the motion of the foot. Controlling the motion of arms and legs involves the same basic operations on a set of linkages; it is the application which is different. In this text, the discussion will usually concern robot arms (currently the major application), but much of the material applies to fingers and legs, too. Some animals also manipulate with trunks and wings – trunks have been implemented on some robots as highly flexible arms, but, at present, there is little use in robotics for wings.

Controlling the motion of a hand is complicated by the fact that there may be several arm configurations that will place the hand on the object. For example, if there is a pen on a table it can be picked up with the forearm parallel to the table or perpendicular to it. A hand can be placed in several positions relative to the pen, because it has flexible joints; each joint has at least two degrees of freedom. On the other hand, the joints in a robot arm usually have only one degree of freedom, but they can move over a much greater range than human joints can. Because the same hand location can often be achieved with several arm configurations, we need a method for choosing which of these redundant configurations to use.

When picking up a pen, a human hand approaches it from different directions depending upon the configuration of the person's arm. Some objects are most easily picked up from one direction – a cup of tea for example. The orientations from which a hand can approach an object depend not only on the object but also on the environment. When picking up an object, a robot may have to avoid obstacles. This limits the number of available approach paths. Due to these restrictions, the path along which a robot hand approaches an object has to be controlled, placing extra constraints on the control of the arm: constraints which help to solve the redundancy problem, but complicate the control of hand motion.

Before a robot can move its hand to an object, the object must be located relative to it. In many applications, the object may be moving, further complicating this task. For example, to pick a part up off a moving conveyor, a robot must move its hand with the object while grasping the object. For a robot to do this, it not only has to know where the object is, but also which way and how fast it is moving. People pick up moving objects with little more difficulty than they pick up stationary objects. A person relates the position of his hand to the object automatically, and unless the object is moving fast, or is in an awkward position, will not consciously think about the process. People use a combination of visual, tactile, and arm position feedback when grasping an object. There is currently no simple method for measuring the location of a robot hand – it is not practical to attach transducers to the hand, as these impede the motion of the hand (see Section 10.5.1.1) – most robots calculate the position of their hand using a kinematic model of their arm (see Chapter 4).

This chapter deals with a method of specifying where an object is located, where the base of the robot is located, the position of the hand relative to the base of the robot and, hence, the position of the hand relative to the object. To do this, both the position of the object and the direction in which it is moving must be specified. This can be described using coordinate geometry. In turtle geometry (Abelson and di Sessa, 1981), the turtle has a position on the plane and a direction of motion. The direction in which an object is moving can be described with a vector – a quantity having both magnitude and direction (see Appendix A, Section 4.7). The notation used to represent various quantities is shown in Figure 3.1.

Figure 3.1
Notation

Point vectors	p, q, x, y, z
Coordinates	x, y, z, x_i, y_j, z_k
Matrices	**A, T, R**
Frames	W, R, H
Points	x, y, z, x_i, y_i, z_i
Derivatives	$dx \; d^2x$
Increment	Δx
Transforms	$^R\mathbf{T}_N$: R = reference frame, N = new frame
	$^R\mathbf{Trans}$: translation transform
	$^N\mathbf{Rot}$: rotation transform
Vectors	^Rp_n: position
	^Nv_p: linear velocity
	$^R\omega_p$: angular velocity
	^Na_q: linear acceleration
	$^R\alpha_q$: angular acceleration
$^Rp_{n-1,n}$	position of vector from frame $n-1$ to frame n with respect to frame R
$^Rf_{n-1,n}$	force vector from frame $n-1$ to frame n with respect to frame R
^RZ_n	torque at joint n as seen from frame R.

*Fixed and sliding vectors include two subscripts: one to anchor the vector, the other to define the vector. If the vector has only one subscript, the anchor is the frame in the leading superscript.

Cross product: **x**

Dot product: .

Figure 3.2
Location of a point in a two-dimensional coordinate system, and an object in a three-dimensional coordinate system.

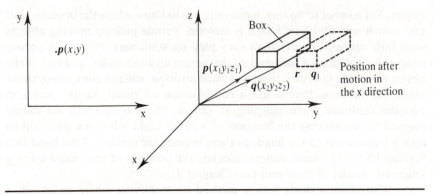

3.1 Cartesian coordinates

The position of an object in space is described with Cartesian coordinates. Coordinate axes for two- and three-dimensional systems are normally labelled as shown in Figure 3.2. Using this labelling, the two-dimensional view must be rotated to map onto the three-dimensional axes. This discrepancy is responsible for some of the inconsistencies found in robotics when applying three-dimensional conventions to two-dimensional systems. The reader should be aware that no convention exists in computer graphics, and axis labelling varies between books (Figure 3.3). This creates few, if any, problems, in graphics, where the result is a two-dimensional view of the world. However, when dealing with three-dimensional physical objects, consistent labelling is important, particularly for direction.

In robotics, the chosen coordinate frame forms a right-handed set of vectors. The positive direction of rotation is chosen in accordance with the right-hand rule illustrated in Figure 3.4. Hold your right hand open, with your thumb pointing in the direction of the axis of rotation, and your fingers pointing in the direction of a second axis. Curl your fingers through 90° until they point in the direction of the third axis – this is the direction of positive rotation. The positive directions of the axes are the directions in which your thumb, your hand, and your fingers are pointing. One way to make visualization of coordinate frames easier, particularly when rotating and translating a coordinate frame, is to use a physical model such as that shown in Figure 3.5.

Figure 3.3
Three-dimensional coordinate systems used in computer graphics.

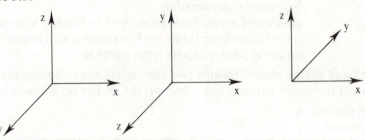

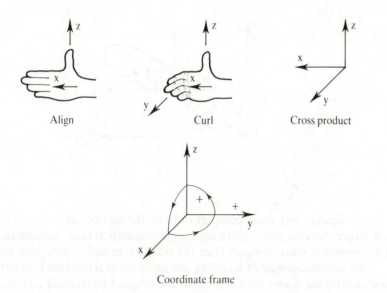

Align   Curl   Cross product

Coordinate frame

Figure 3.4
Coordinate frame showing positive directions of axes according to the right-hand rule.

We can describe the location of an object with coordinate positions relative to the origin of a coordinate frame ($x_1, y_1 z_1$), or with a point vector (p). We can define the location of a box with eight point vectors, one for each corner, on the assumption that the edges are straight-line intersections of planes (Figure 3.2). However, if the box is moved in the x direction from $p(x_1, y_1, z_1)$ to $r(x_3, y_3, z_3)$, eight new vectors must be calculated to define the new position of the box. This translation can be performed by adding the vector $r - p$ to each point vector. For example, the bottom right hand-corner is moved from q to q_1.

$$q_1 = q + r - p \tag{3.1}$$

Figure 3.5
Physical model (Tinker Toys) used to make coordinate frame visualization easier.

Figure 3.6
Object location described
with a coordinate system
located in the object.

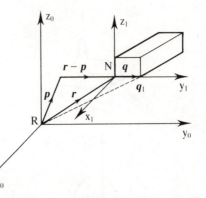

Obviously, with more complex objects, the number of vectors will be much larger. Motion will require additional calculation time, particularly if the movement is more complex than the simple translation described here.

An alternative way of handling this problem of relocation is to define a new coordinate frame with respect to the original (reference) coordinate frame (x_0, y_0, z_0). We achieve this by placing the origin of the object coordinate frame (x_1, y_1, z_1) at an appropriate point in the object (the bottom left corner of the box in Figure 3.6, for example). The position of points on the object are defined with respect to the object coordinate frame. Now, when the box is translated, all that we have to calculate is the movement of the origin from vector p to vector r:

$$r = p + (r - p) \tag{3.2}$$

Finally, to calculate the location of any point on the object with respect to the reference coordinate frame, we add the vector which describes the object with respect to the origin of the object coordinate frame ($^R q$ or q) to the vector which describes the origin of the object coordinate frame with respect to the original (reference) coordinate frame ($^R r$ or r):

$$q_1 = r + q \quad \text{or} \quad ^R q_1 = {}^R r + {}^R q \tag{3.3}$$

In this way, the problem of calculating object motion has been reduced to calculating the relationship between two coordinate frames, and then using this relationship to calculate the new positions of points of interest on the object. From now on, we are interested in the relationship between coordinate frames, and in how to relocate from one frame to another. The method described above works if the object is translated, but is inadequate if the object is rotated, because the axes of the new coordinate frame are no longer parallel to the axes of the original coordinate frame. This is illustrated in Figure 3.7. After rotation, the new coordinate frame is represented by four vectors: one representing the relocation of the origin, and the other three representing the directions of the three axes.

An object, and hence its internal coordinate frame, has six degrees of freedom, that is, six independent ways in which it can be moved. There are

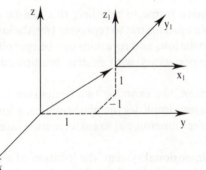

Figure 3.7
Relationship between two
coordinate frames. The new
frame has been rotated by
90 degrees around the z
axis, and then translated.

three degrees of translation: translation in the x direction, translation in the y direction, and translation in the z direction; and three degrees of rotation: rotation about the x axis, rotation about the y axis, and rotation about the z axis (Figure 3.8). Any movement of the object within a coordinate frame can be described as a sequence of translations and rotations of the object coordinate frame with respect to the reference coordinate frame. For example, the new frame in Figure 3.7 has been rotated 90° about the z axis, translated one unit in the negative x direction, translated one unit in the y direction, and translated one unit in the z direction.

3.2 Two-dimensional transformations

To describe the motion of an object, we must describe one coordinate frame with respect to another. A new coordinate frame can be described with a 4×4 matrix of vectors: one vector representing the translation of the origin, and the other vectors representing the directions of the new axes. In addition, we must describe the sequence of rotations and translations required to relocate

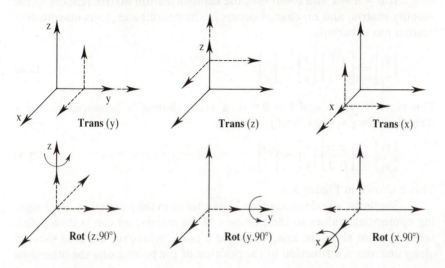

Figure 3.8
The six degrees of freedom
of a coordinate frame –
three rotations and three
translations – direction
according to right hand rule.

from one coordinate frame to another; this can be done with a transformation matrix. We use a matrix to represent translation and rotation because a sequence of translations and rotations can be combined to produce a complex relocation more easily with matrix multiplication than with vector addition.

In this section, we examine two-dimension transformations: eliminating one dimension simplifies the mathematics, allowing us to concentrate on concepts. Three-dimensional transformation are covered in the next section.

In a two-dimensional system, the location of a point is described with a two-component vector $p[x, y]$. If this point is multiplied with a general 2×2 transformation matrix a set of transformed coordinates $p_1[x_1, y_1]$ is produced.

$$\begin{bmatrix} x_1 \\ y_1 \end{bmatrix} = \begin{bmatrix} a & c \\ b & d \end{bmatrix} \begin{bmatrix} x \\ y \end{bmatrix} = \begin{bmatrix} (ax + cy) \\ (bx + dy) \end{bmatrix} = \begin{bmatrix} x_1 \\ y_1 \end{bmatrix} \tag{3.4}$$

where

$$\begin{bmatrix} a & c \\ b & d \end{bmatrix}$$

is a general 2×2 transformation matrix.

The constants in this matrix can be used to describe the various operations involved in transforming the point. Note, some computer graphics texts express the above equation using row vectors, and hence the transpose of the transformation matrix (Equation 3.5).

$$[x_1 \ y_1] = [x \ y] \begin{bmatrix} a & b \\ c & d \end{bmatrix} = [(ax + cy)(bx + dy)] \tag{3.5}$$

If $a = d = 1$ and $c = b = 0$, the transformation matrix reduces to the **identity matrix,** and no change occurs in the coordinates, thus no transformation has occurred.

$$\begin{bmatrix} x_1 \\ y_1 \end{bmatrix} = \begin{bmatrix} 1 & 0 \\ 0 & 1 \end{bmatrix} \begin{bmatrix} x \\ y \end{bmatrix} = \begin{bmatrix} x \\ y \end{bmatrix} \tag{3.6}$$

However, if $d = 1$ and $c = b = 0$, a **scale change** is produced in the x direction, since $x_1 = ax$, and $y_1 = y$.

$$\begin{bmatrix} x_1 \\ y_1 \end{bmatrix} = \begin{bmatrix} a & 0 \\ 0 & 1 \end{bmatrix} \begin{bmatrix} x \\ y \end{bmatrix} = \begin{bmatrix} ax \\ y \end{bmatrix} \tag{3.7}$$

This is shown in Figure 3.9.

Similarly, a scale change can be produced in the y direction. By assigning appropriate values to the elements of the matrix, we can scale a point, reflect a point about an axis, and shear a point, where the distance sheared along one axis is a function of the position of the point along the other axis

Figure 3.9
Effect of various terms in the
2×2 general transformation
matrix (note shear (y) is a
shear proportional to x).

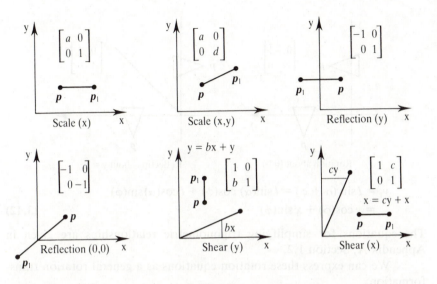

(Figure 3.9). If the point p in the above example is the origin of a coordinate frame, the frame will move within the two-dimensional space to p_1. However, if p is located at the origin, no transformation will occur, because the origin is invariant under a general 2×2 transformation. This limitation is overcome when homogeneous coordinates are introduced.

A 2×2 matrix can also be used to represent rotation. The triangle in Figure 3.10 is rotated through 90° about the origin in a counter clockwise sense by transforming each vertex:

$$\begin{bmatrix} x_1 \\ y_1 \end{bmatrix} = \begin{bmatrix} 0 & -1 \\ 1 & 0 \end{bmatrix} \begin{bmatrix} x \\ y \end{bmatrix} = \begin{bmatrix} -y \\ x \end{bmatrix} \tag{3.8}$$

where

$$\begin{bmatrix} 0 & -1 \\ 1 & 0 \end{bmatrix} = \begin{bmatrix} \cos(\phi) & -\sin(\phi) \\ \sin(\phi) & \cos(\phi) \end{bmatrix} \text{ when } \phi = 90° \tag{3.9}$$

and

$$\begin{bmatrix} \cos(\phi) & -\sin(\phi) \\ \sin(\phi) & \cos(\phi) \end{bmatrix} \tag{3.10}$$

is the 2×2 transformation matrix which produces rotation about the origin.

If both terms in the matrix were positive, a reflection would have occurred and not a rotation (Figure 3.10). This 2×2 rotation matrix can also be used to rotate vectors. Consider the vector p, which is at $\alpha°$ to the x axis and passes through the origin (Figure 3.11). If it is rotated through $\phi°$ to become p_1 the coordinates of the point p_1 are:

$$x_1 = l \cos(\alpha + \phi) = l \cos(\alpha)\cos(\phi) - l \sin(\alpha) \sin(\phi)$$
$$= x \cos(\phi) - y \sin(\phi) \tag{3.11}$$

Figure 3.10
Rotation and reflection.

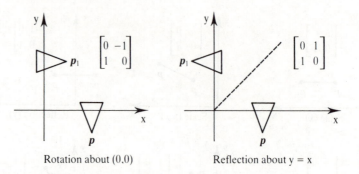

Rotation about (0,0)   Reflection about y = x

$$y_1 = l \sin(\alpha + \phi) = l \sin(\alpha) \cos(\phi) + l \cos(\alpha) \sin(\phi)$$
$$= y \cos(\phi) + x \sin(\phi) \tag{3.12}$$

The equations for simplifying trigonometric relationships are given in Appendix A, Section 1.2.

We can express these rotation equations as a general rotation transformation:

$$\begin{bmatrix} x_1 \\ y_1 \end{bmatrix} = \begin{bmatrix} \cos(\phi) & -\sin(\phi) \\ \sin(\phi) & \cos(\phi) \end{bmatrix} \begin{bmatrix} x \\ y \end{bmatrix} \tag{3.13}$$

Translation cannot be produced by assigning values to the elements of a 2×2 matrix, because it is not a function of the location of a point, but rather motion along a straight path by a constant distance. This difficulty is overcome by introducing a third component to the point vectors $p[x\ y\ 1]^T$ and $p_1[x_1\ y_1\ 1]^T$. The new coordinates are known as **homogeneous coordinates**. The transformation matrix must also be modified to become a 2×3 matrix so that the two matrices can be multiplied. As the transformation matrix is no longer square, it does not have an inverse, so a third row is added to it to make it square. Thus, the transformation equation becomes:

$$\begin{bmatrix} x_1 \\ y_1 \\ 1 \end{bmatrix} = \begin{bmatrix} \cos(\phi) & -\sin(\phi) & m \\ \sin(\phi) & \cos(\phi) & n \\ 0 & 0 & 1 \end{bmatrix} \begin{bmatrix} x \\ y \\ 1 \end{bmatrix} \tag{3.14}$$

where m and n are the translation constants in the x and y directions respectively.

Translation and rotation can be combined simply by substituting the correct values into the matrix. In the case of pure translation (where there is

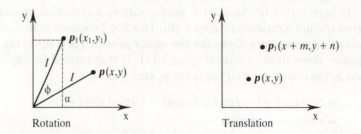

Rotation   Translation

no rotation) the angle ϕ is zero. Thus, the point p is translated to the point p_1 (Figure 3.11) by the following equations:

$$x_1 = x + m \tag{3.15}$$

$$y_1 = y + n \tag{3.16}$$

Window 3.1 Homogeneous Coordinates

Homogeneous coordinates (Forest, 1969) were introduced into computer graphics to overcome a number of problems involved in matrix calculations. The result is that an n dimensional space is represented by $n + 1$ dimensions, for example (x, y, z) becomes (hx, hy, hz, h) where h is an arbitrary number. The n dimensional space can be re-created by projecting a particular perspective in the $n + 1$ space into the n space. In robotics, h will normally be set to 1, selecting a direct mapping between spaces as the perspective projection.

The additional coordinate h can be used as a scaling factor, overcoming the limited word size of some computers by scaling large numbers down into the range of the computer, with the loss of some resolution. Other disadvantages include an increase in complexity of the calculations, and a consequent reduction in speed.

The term *homogeneous* is applied because the representation for a class of objects involves no explicit constants. For example, the equation of a 2 dimensional line $y = ax + b$ becomes the homogeneous equation $ax - y + b = 0$, which is a representation of the line in three-dimensional space.

Homogeneous coordinates can be viewed as the addition of an extra coordinate to each vector, so that the vector has the same meaning if each component, including the scale factor, is multiplied by a constant. A point vector $v = ai + bj + ck$, where i, j, and k are unit vectors along the x, y and z axes respectively, is represented in homogeneous coordinates as a column matrix:

$$v = \begin{bmatrix} x \\ y \\ z \\ w \end{bmatrix} = \begin{bmatrix} aw \\ bw \\ cw \\ w \end{bmatrix} = \begin{bmatrix} a \\ b \\ c \\ 1 \end{bmatrix}$$

where $w = 1$.

A second problem in computer graphics was also solved by the use of homogeneous coordinates. A 3×3 matrix can be used to describe the rotation, scaling, and shear of a three-dimensional object, but not the translation of that object. It is this problem that is of main interest in robotics. We can describe translation by introducing an extra column vector, but the resultant matrix is not square and thus it doesn't have an inverse. We overcome this difficulty by defining a 4×4 transformation matrix. We use this matrix to describe the rotation, translation, shear, projection, local scaling, and overall scaling transformations between two views of an object.

$$T = \begin{bmatrix} \text{rotation} & \vdots & \text{translation} \\ \text{shearing} & \vdots & \\ \text{local scaling} & \vdots & \\ \text{------------} & \vdots & \text{------------} \\ \text{projection} & \vdots & \text{scaling} \end{bmatrix} = \begin{bmatrix} 3 & \vdots & 3 \\ & * & * \\ & & \\ 3 & \vdots & 1 \\ 1*3 & \vdots & 1*1 \end{bmatrix}$$

In robotics, we are normally only interested in rotation, and translation transformations, as we are dealing with solid physical objects not computer generated images. Also, because the scale factor is 1, the 4 dimensional transformation maps directly into three dimensions. Thus, transformed homogeneous coordinates are the same as transformed ordinary coordinates.

$$T = \begin{bmatrix} \text{rotation} & \vdots & \text{translation} \\ \text{------------} & \vdots & \text{------------} \\ 0 & \vdots & 1 \end{bmatrix}$$

3.3 Three-dimensional transformation matrices

In robotics, we are normally interested in the location of objects in three-dimensional space. The transformation and rotation transforms developed in the previous section for two-dimensional space can be extended to cover three-dimensional space by introducing an extra row and column in the matrix. The general, 4×4, three-dimensional transformation matrix has the following form:

$$\mathbf{T} = \left[\begin{array}{c|c} \begin{matrix} 3 \\ * \\ 3 \end{matrix} & \begin{matrix} 3 \\ * \\ 1 \end{matrix} \\ \hline 1 * 3 & 1*1 \end{array} \right] = \left[\begin{array}{c|c} \text{rotation} & \text{translation} \\ \hline 0 & 1 \end{array} \right] \qquad (3.17)$$

In the three-dimensional transform, there are three translation components, one for each direction. The general transformation matrix, corresponding to a translation by a vector $p_x \mathbf{i} + p_y \mathbf{j} + p_z \mathbf{k}$ is:

$$\mathbf{Trans}(p_x, p_y, p_z) = \begin{bmatrix} 1 & 0 & 0 & p_x \\ 0 & 1 & 0 & p_y \\ 0 & 0 & 1 & p_z \\ 0 & 0 & 0 & 1 \end{bmatrix} \qquad (3.18)$$

Rotation is more complex, because it is possible to rotate about any one of three coordinate axes. Rotation about a general axis can be eliminated by appropriate assignment of coordinate frames to the links of the mechanism, and by decomposing a rotation about a general vector into a sequence of rotations about the coordinate axes. Consequently, there are three rotation transforms corresponding to rotation about the x, y, and z axes by an angle ϕ:

$$\mathbf{Rot}(x, \phi) = \begin{bmatrix} 1 & 0 & 0 & 0 \\ 0 & \cos(\phi) & -\sin(\phi) & 0 \\ 0 & \sin(\phi) & \cos(\phi) & 0 \\ 0 & 0 & 0 & 1 \end{bmatrix} \qquad (3.19)$$

$$\mathbf{Rot}(y, \phi) = \begin{bmatrix} \cos(\phi) & 0 & \sin(\phi) & 0 \\ 0 & 1 & 0 & 0 \\ -\sin(\phi) & 0 & \cos(\phi) & 0 \\ 0 & 0 & 0 & 1 \end{bmatrix} \qquad (3.20)$$

$$\mathbf{Rot}(z, \phi) = \begin{bmatrix} \cos(\phi) & -\sin(\phi) & 0 & 0 \\ \sin(\phi) & \cos(\phi) & 0 & 0 \\ 0 & 0 & 1 & 0 \\ 0 & 0 & 0 & 1 \end{bmatrix} \qquad (3.21)$$

A translation and a rotation can be combined by multiplying the transformation matrices (Appendix A, Section 3.3): the translation terms do not affect the rotation terms. For example:

$$\mathbf{Trans}(p_x, p_y, p_z)\mathbf{Rot}(z, \phi) = \begin{bmatrix} 1 & 0 & 0 & p_x \\ 0 & 1 & 0 & p_y \\ 0 & 0 & 1 & p_z \\ 0 & 0 & 0 & 1 \end{bmatrix} \begin{bmatrix} \cos(\phi) & -\sin(\phi) & 0 & 0 \\ \sin(\phi) & \cos(\phi) & 0 & 0 \\ 0 & 0 & 1 & 0 \\ 0 & 0 & 0 & 1 \end{bmatrix}$$

$$= \begin{bmatrix} \cos(\phi) & -\sin(\phi) & 0 & p_x \\ \sin(\phi) & \cos(\phi) & 0 & p_y \\ 0 & 0 & 1 & p_z \\ 0 & 0 & 0 & 1 \end{bmatrix} \qquad (3.22)$$

To study the combination of transformations further, we will examine a series of transformations applied to a point located at the origin of our coordinate frame (Figure 3.12). This point is translated in the y direction, rotated around the x axis, translated in the z direction, and finally rotated around the y axis. The resultant transformation is described with the following equation.

$$^R\mathbf{T}_N = \mathbf{Rot}(y, 90)\mathbf{Trans}(z, a)\mathbf{Rot}(x, 90)\mathbf{Trans}(y, a) \qquad (3.23)$$

You should trace the trajectory of the point in Figure 3.12 until you understand the result of each transformation in the sequence of transforms. As the transforms are executed from right to left, each succeeding transform premultiplies the following transforms. If the transforms are executed in reverse order, left to right, a different result is obtained (Figure 3.12). In the

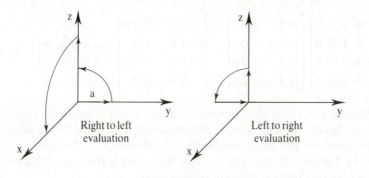

Right to left evaluation

Left to right evaluation

Figure 3.12
Combined rotations and translations (Equation 3.23) showing the effect of the order of evaluation of the transform equation.

reverse operation, the first rotation does not show up because we are only considering a point, that is, the change in position of the point vector is seen, but not the change in direction. To see the change in direction a **coordinate frame** must be attached to the point. These are discussed in the next section.

3.4   Coordinate frames

When Equation 3.23 is applied to a coordinate frame located at the origin, the coordinate frame is relocated as shown in Figure 3.13. The new frame is translated *a* units in the y direction, rotated 90° around the x axis, translated *a* units in the z direction, and finally, rotated 90° about the y axis. As the transforms have been premultiplied, all translations and rotations are with respect to the reference coordinate frame. In general, when transform are premultiplied, the transforms are executed with respect to the reference coordinate frame. The final position and orientation of the new coordinate frame is calculated by multiplying the matrices.

$${}^{R}\mathbf{T}_{N} = \mathbf{Rot}(y, 90)\mathbf{Trans}(z, a)\mathbf{Rot}(x, 90)\mathbf{Trans}(y, a)$$

$$
= \begin{bmatrix} \cos(90) & 0 & \sin(90) & 0 \\ 0 & 1 & 0 & 0 \\ -\sin(90) & 0 & \cos(90) & 0 \\ 0 & 0 & 0 & 1 \end{bmatrix} \begin{bmatrix} 1 & 0 & 0 & 0 \\ 0 & 1 & 0 & 0 \\ 0 & 0 & 1 & a \\ 0 & 0 & 0 & 1 \end{bmatrix} \begin{bmatrix} 1 & 0 & 0 & 0 \\ 0 & \cos(90) & -\sin(90) & 0 \\ 0 & \sin(90) & \cos(90) & 0 \\ 0 & 0 & 0 & 1 \end{bmatrix} \begin{bmatrix} 1 & 0 & 0 & 0 \\ 0 & 1 & 0 & a \\ 0 & 0 & 1 & 0 \\ 0 & 0 & 0 & 1 \end{bmatrix}
$$

$$
= \begin{bmatrix} 0 & 0 & 1 & 0 \\ 0 & 1 & 0 & 0 \\ -1 & 0 & 0 & 0 \\ 0 & 0 & 0 & 1 \end{bmatrix} \begin{bmatrix} 1 & 0 & 0 & 0 \\ 0 & 1 & 0 & 0 \\ 0 & 0 & 1 & a \\ 0 & 0 & 0 & 1 \end{bmatrix} \begin{bmatrix} 1 & 0 & 0 & 0 \\ 0 & 0 & -1 & 0 \\ 0 & 1 & 0 & 0 \\ 0 & 0 & 0 & 1 \end{bmatrix} \begin{bmatrix} 1 & 0 & 0 & 0 \\ 0 & 1 & 0 & a \\ 0 & 0 & 1 & 0 \\ 0 & 0 & 0 & 1 \end{bmatrix}
$$

$$
= \begin{bmatrix} 0 & 0 & 1 & 0 \\ 0 & 1 & 0 & 0 \\ -1 & 0 & 0 & 0 \\ 0 & 0 & 0 & 1 \end{bmatrix} \begin{bmatrix} 1 & 0 & 0 & 0 \\ 0 & 1 & 0 & 0 \\ 0 & 0 & 1 & a \\ 0 & 0 & 0 & 1 \end{bmatrix} \begin{bmatrix} 1 & 0 & 0 & 0 \\ 0 & 0 & -1 & 0 \\ 0 & 1 & 0 & a \\ 0 & 0 & 0 & 1 \end{bmatrix}
$$

$$
= \begin{bmatrix} 0 & 0 & 1 & 0 \\ 0 & 1 & 0 & 0 \\ -1 & 0 & 0 & 0 \\ 0 & 0 & 0 & 1 \end{bmatrix} \begin{bmatrix} 1 & 0 & 0 & 0 \\ 0 & 0 & -1 & 0 \\ 0 & 1 & 0 & 2a \\ 0 & 0 & 0 & 1 \end{bmatrix} = \begin{bmatrix} 0 & 1 & 0 & 2a \\ 0 & 0 & -1 & 0 \\ -1 & 0 & 0 & 0 \\ 0 & 0 & 0 & 1 \end{bmatrix} = \begin{bmatrix} x & y & z & p \\ 0 & 0 & 0 & 1 \end{bmatrix} \quad (3.24)
$$

In this example, the angles were deliberately chosen to make the calculations easy, so that the principles being illustrated are not clouded by mathematics. If you compare the final matrix with the drawing of the new coordinate frame in Figure 3.13 you will see that the result is the same. The resultant matrix contains some important information:

Figure 3.13
Interpreting the transform as
a coordinate frame by
evaluating the transformation
equation right to left with
respect to the reference
frame.

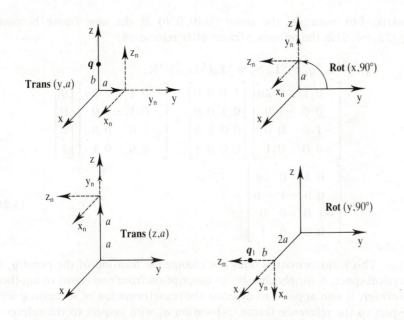

- The first column is a vector describing the direction of the new x axis: *x* is in the negative z direction.

- The second column is a vector describing the new y axis: *y* is in the positive x direction.

- The third column is a vector describing the new z axis: *z* is in the negative y direction.

- The fourth column is a vector describing the displacement of the origin of the new coordinate frame from the origin of the reference coordinate frame: *p* is a translation of 2*a* units in the positive x direction.

Thus the resultant transformation matrix effectively transforms the origin of the reference coordinate frame to the origin of the new coordinate frame. That is, it describes the position and orientation of the new coordinate frame in terms of the reference frame.

$$\begin{bmatrix} 1 & 0 & 0 & 0 \\ 0 & 1 & 0 & 0 \\ 0 & 0 & 1 & 0 \\ 0 & 0 & 0 & 1 \end{bmatrix} \begin{bmatrix} 0 & 1 & 0 & 2a \\ 0 & 0 & -1 & 0 \\ 1 & 0 & 0 & 0 \\ 0 & 0 & 0 & 1 \end{bmatrix} = \begin{bmatrix} 0 & 1 & 0 & 2a \\ 0 & 0 & -1 & 0 \\ -1 & 0 & 0 & 0 \\ 0 & 0 & 0 & 1 \end{bmatrix} = \begin{bmatrix} x & y & z & p \\ 0 & 0 & 0 & 1 \end{bmatrix} \quad (3.25)$$

In addition to transforming the new coordinate frame, we can use this transformation to transform any point that has been defined with respect to the new frame to the reference frame. We can calculate the position of this point with respect to the reference frame from its location in the new frame by pre-multiplying the vector describing the point with the transformation matrix. For example, the point ${}^N q_1(0, 0, b)$ in the new frame becomes ${}^R q_1(2a, -b, 0)$ in the reference frame after relocation.

$$
{}^R q_1 = {}^R T_N {}^N q_1 = {}^R T_N N_q = {}^R T_N ({}^R T_{\text{Nold}})^{-1} R_q
$$

$$
= \begin{bmatrix} 0 & 1 & 0 & 2a \\ 0 & 0 & -1 & 0 \\ -1 & 0 & 0 & 0 \\ 0 & 0 & 0 & 1 \end{bmatrix} \begin{bmatrix} 1 & 0 & 0 & 0 \\ 0 & 1 & 0 & 0 \\ 0 & 0 & 1 & b \\ 0 & 0 & 0 & 1 \end{bmatrix} = \begin{bmatrix} 0 & 1 & 0 & 2a \\ 0 & 1 & -1 & 0 \\ -1 & 0 & 0 & 0 \\ 0 & 0 & 0 & 1 \end{bmatrix} \begin{bmatrix} 0 \\ 0 \\ b \\ 1 \end{bmatrix}
$$

$$
= \begin{bmatrix} 0 & 1 & 0 & 2a \\ 0 & 0 & -1 & -b \\ -1 & 0 & 0 & 0 \\ 0 & 0 & 0 & 1 \end{bmatrix} \tag{3.26}
$$

This transformation does not change the location of the point q_1 in physical space, it simply changes its description from one frame to another. However, it also appears to describe the transformation of location q with respect to the reference frame to location q_1 with respect to the reference frame. This occurs because the original position of the new frame coincided with the reference frame, and the original transformation matrix was the identity matrix.

3.5 Relative transformations

In our discussion so far, we have considered translation and rotation with respect to the reference coordinate frame, known as the **absolute** or **forward transformation**. We have shown that when transformation matrices are pre-multiplied, the transformations are performed with respect to the reference frame. In contrast, when we postmultiplied the transformation matrices we obtained the wrong result. However, if each transformation is considered with respect to the new frame, postmultiplication *will* produce the correct result. When postmultiplying transforms, each transformation is executed with respect to a different coordinate frame, as the location of the new frame changes with each transformation. In general, there are two methods for processing a transformation equation:

1. Execute the transformations right to left with respect to the reference frame (premultiply).

2. Execute the transformations left to right with respect to the new frames (postmultiply).

To illustrate the difference between the two methods, consider the simple two-dimensional case of a rotation of 45° followed by a translation of a units in the x direction shown in Figure 3.14. The absolute transformation

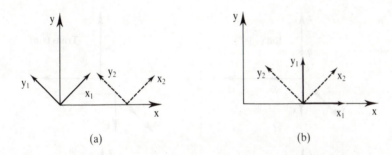

(a)   (b)

Figure 3.14
Absolute (direct) (a)
transformation versus
relative transformation for
the equation (b)
Trans(x, a)**Rot**(45).

consists of a rotation about the origin of the reference frame followed by a translation in the x direction of the reference frame. The relative transformation consists of a translation in the x direction of the reference frame followed by a rotation about the origin of the new frame. In both cases, the end result is the same.

Postmultiplication of a more complex transformation as in Equation 3.23 is illustrated in Figure 3.15. The new frame is rotated around the y axis, translated along the new z axis, rotated around the new x axis, and finally translated along the new y axis, to reach the same position and orientation with respect to the reference frame as with premultiplication illustrated in Figure 3.13.

3.6   General transformations

A transform can be thought about in a number of ways:

- as a transformation from one coordinate frame to another.
- as a description of the origin and axes of a new coordinate frame in terms of reference frame,
- as a description of the motion of an object from one location (reference frame) to another (new frame),
- as a means of calculating the location of a point on an object with respect to the reference frame from its location with respect to the new frame.

$$^{R}\mathbf{T}_{N}\,{}^{N}q = {}^{R}q \tag{3.27}$$

$^{R}\mathbf{T}_{N}$ is the transform of the new frame with respect to the reference frame. That is, it is the transformation made on frame R to get frame N. This transform is known as the **forward transform**. If $^{N}q_{1}$ is the location of a point in the new frame, $^{R}q_{1}$ is the location of the same point in the reference frame (Figure 3.16). Alternatively, given a point $^{N}q_{1}$ in the new frame, its location $^{R}q_{1}$ in the reference frame can be found by premultiplying the point vector by the transformation matrix. Before the transformation, the frames were

Figure 3.15
Interpreting the transform as a coordinate frame by evaluating the transformation matrix from left to right with respect to the new coordinate frames.

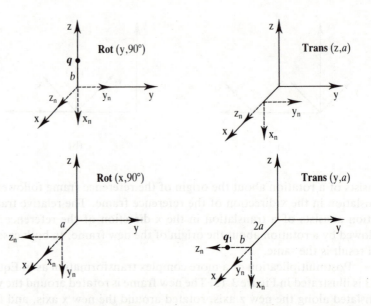

coincident and, consequently, the transformation matrix was the identity matrix. Thus, the description of the point with respect to both frames (^Rq and ^Nq) was the same. The transformation describes the relocation of the new frame and, thus, it describes the relocation of the point from ^Rq to $^Rq_1$ with respect to the reference frame.

We have also seen that the transformation matrix is a set of four vectors, three of which describe the directions of the axes of the new frame and the fourth the location of the origin of the new frame. These axes are described by the unit vectors x, y, and z, and the location of the origin is described by the vector p. We calculate the elements of the general transformation matrix by equating it to the transformation matrix which describes the relocation being performed; for example, by equating Equation 3.28 to Equation 3.24.

The **general transformation matrix** ^RT_N is:

$$^RT_N = \begin{bmatrix} x_x & y_x & z_x & p_x \\ x_y & y_y & z_y & p_y \\ x_z & y_z & z_z & p_z \\ 0 & 0 & 0 & 1 \end{bmatrix} = \begin{bmatrix} x & y & z & p \\ 0 & 0 & 0 & 1 \end{bmatrix} \quad (3.28)$$

$p = p_x i + p_y j + p_z k =$ location of the origin of the new frame   (3.29)

$x = x_x i + x_y j + x_z k =$ direction of the x axis of the new frame

(3.30)

$y = y_x i + y_y j + y_z k =$ direction of the y axis of the new frame

(3.31)

$z = z_x i + z_y j + z_z k =$ direction of the z axis of the new frame

(3.32)

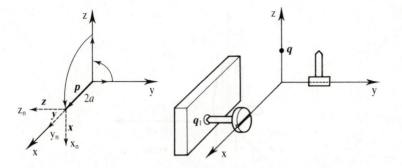

Figure 3.16
Interpreting the transform as
a coordinate frame — general
transformation, and
movement of an object.

The vectors x, y, and z form a right-handed set of vectors such that:

$$x = y \times z \quad \text{where } x \text{ is the vector cross product} \quad \text{(see Section 13.4.3)} \tag{3.33}$$

3.7 General orientation transformations

Calculating the orientation of the object from the vectors x, y, and z may involve complicated vector analysis (see Example 3.1), because the vectors are unit vectors. Calculating the vectors from the required orientation angles also involves complicated vector manipulation. Once again, we introduce a transformation as a substitute for vector analysis.

In Cartesian space, we are interested in the orientation of the object with respect to the reference frame, so it is natural to specify orientation as a sequence of rotations about the axes of the reference frame. A number of ways of doing this have been proposed. The simplest to understand is the roll–pitch–yaw transformation (see Figure 2.30). Roll, pitch, and yaw are nautical terms used to describe the rocking of a boat with respect to its three axes. To demonstrate this, stretch your arm out in front of you with your palm facing down. You can move your hand in three distinct rotations: first, rotate your hand about an axis along your arm – this is roll; second, tilt your hand up and down about your wrist joint – this is pitch; third, turn your hand side to side about your wrist joint – this is yaw (Figure 3.17). A general roll–pitch–yaw orientation transformation can be specified as a sequence of three rotations: a rotation about the x axis, a rotation about the y axis, and a rotation about the z axis. This transformation is described in Equations 3.34 and 3.35. Note, when calculating orientation transforms the order of multiplication is important: premultiplication *must* be used.

$$\mathbf{RPY}(\phi, \theta, \psi) = \mathbf{Rot}(z, \phi)\mathbf{Rot}(y, \theta)\mathbf{Rot}(x, \psi) \tag{3.34}$$

$$= \begin{bmatrix} C(\phi)C(\theta) & C(\phi)S(\theta)S(\psi)-S(\phi)C(\psi) & C(\phi)S(\theta)C(\psi)+S(\phi)S(\psi) & 0 \\ S(\phi)C(\theta) & S(\phi)S(\theta)S(\psi)+C(\phi)C(\psi) & S(\phi)S(\theta)C(\psi)-C(\phi)S(\psi) & 0 \\ -S(\theta) & C(\theta)S(\psi) & C(\theta)C(\psi) & 0 \\ 0 & 0 & 0 & 1 \end{bmatrix} \tag{3.35}$$

Figure 3.17
Roll, pitch, and yaw
orientation angles.

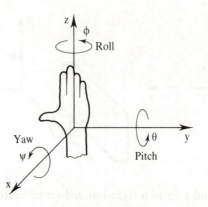

Another popular way of specifying hand orientation is **Euler angles.** Wrists which have roll–pitch–roll axes are usually described with Euler angles, because they match the mechanical structure of the wrist, for example the Puma wrist (see Figure 2.34). Euler angles describe any possible orientation of the hand in terms of a rotation about the z axis, followed by a rotation about the new y axis, and finally a rotation about the new z axis. These rotations can also be interpreted right to left with respect to the reference frame.

$$\mathbf{Euler}(\phi, \theta, \psi) = \mathbf{Rot}(z, \phi)\mathbf{Rot}(y, \theta)\mathbf{Rot}(z, \psi) \tag{3.36}$$

Again, the transformation matrices can be multiplied to form a general orientation transform.

In our discussion so far we have described the world of the robot with Cartesian coordinates. **Cylindrical coordinates** and **spherical coordinates** can also be used (Window 3.2). For robots with cylindrical or spherical geometries, equations based on one of these alternative coordinate systems may be simpler, and hence faster, to compute.

With our orientation transform, we have a second general method for specifying the position and orientation of the end of a manipulator, given in Equation 3.37.

$$
{}^{R}\mathbf{T}_{H} = \begin{bmatrix} x & y & z & p \\ 0 & 0 & 0 & 1 \end{bmatrix} = \begin{bmatrix} \text{translation} \\ \text{transform} \end{bmatrix} \begin{bmatrix} \text{orientation} \\ \text{transform} \end{bmatrix} \tag{3.37}
$$

$$
= \begin{bmatrix} 1 & 0 & 0 & p_x \\ 0 & 1 & 0 & p_y \\ 0 & 0 & 1 & p_z \\ 0 & 0 & 0 & 1 \end{bmatrix} \begin{bmatrix} \text{Orientation} \\ \text{transform.} \\ \text{Roll-pitch-yaw} \\ \text{Equation 3.35} \end{bmatrix} \tag{3.38}
$$

Transformation matrices were introduced to reduce the complexity of the mathematics, by doing matrix multiplication rather than vector addition.

Window 3.2   *Polar coordinates (Paul, 1981)*

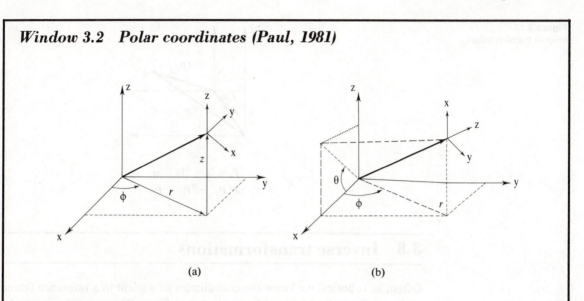

(a)   (b)

Cylindrical polar coordinates
Another coordinate system which we can use to describe a point is cylindrical coordinates Figure (a). These coordinates are a translation r along the x axis (a radial translation in the xy plane), a rotation ϕ about the z axis, and a translation z along the z axis.

$$\mathbf{Cyl}(z, \phi, r) = \mathbf{Trans}(0, 0, z)\mathbf{Rot}(z, \phi)\mathbf{Trans}(r, 0, 0)$$

Spherical polar coordinates
A third coordinate system which we can use to describe a point in space is spherical coordinates Figure (b). These coordinates are a translation r along the x axis, a rotation ϕ about the z axis, and a rotation θ about the y axis. The angles ϕ and θ can be thought of as describing the azimuth and elevation of a ray projected into space.

$$\mathbf{Sph}(\phi, \theta, r) = \mathbf{Rot}(y, \theta)\mathbf{Rot}(z, \phi)\mathbf{Trans}(0, r, 0)$$

However, we should remember that the transform of a point is equivalent to the sum of the vector from the new frame (N) to the point (frame q) with respect to the reference frame and the vector from the reference frame (R) to the new frame (Figure 3.18).

$$^{R}q = {}^{R}p_{q} = {}^{R}p_{N,q} + {}^{R}p_{N} = {}^{R}\mathbf{T}_{N}{}^{N}q = {}^{R}\mathbf{T}_{N}{}^{N}p_{q} \qquad (3.39)$$

where

p is a position vector,
$^{R}p_{N,q} = {}^{R}\mathbf{Rot}_{N}{}^{N}p_{q}$ is the vector from the origin of frame N to point q as seen from frame R,
$^{R}\mathbf{Rot}_{N}$ is the rotation transform from frame R to N.

Figure 3.18
Inverse transformation.

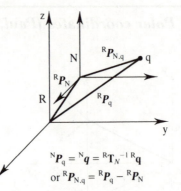

$$^{N}P_{q} = {}^{N}q = {}^{R}T_{N}^{-1}{}^{R}q$$

$$\text{or } {}^{R}P_{N.q} = {}^{R}P_{q} - {}^{R}P_{N}$$

3.8   Inverse transformations

Often, in robotics, we know the coordinates of a point in a reference frame and we want to find its coordinates in a new frame. For example, it may be necessary to calculate the position of an object relative to the hand of a robot from its position in relation to the world coordinate system. To do this, we locate a new coordinate frame in the hand and use a transformation to transform the new coordinate frame back to the reference frame, that is, an **inverse transformation**. The inverse transformation equation can be obtained by premultiplying both sides of the general transformation equation with the inverse of the forward transform:

$$^{R}T_{N}^{-1}\,{}^{R}T_{N}{}^{N}q = {}^{R}T_{N}^{-1}\,{}^{R}q \tag{3.40}$$

$$^{N}q = {}^{R}T_{N}^{-1}\,{}^{R}q \tag{3.41}$$

Thus, the inverse transform is the inverse of the **forward transformation matrix**. As with the forward transform, it is easy to become confused between the description of the transform and the action of the transform. The inverse transform is the transform of the reference frame with respect to the new frame. It calculates the description of a point with respect to the new frame from its description with respect to the reference frame. Thus, the description and the action of the inverse transform are the reverse of the description and action of the forward transform. If the forward transform is equivalent to vector addition when applied to a point on an object (Equation 3.39), the inverse transform is equivalent to vector subtraction (Figure 3.18).

$$^{R}p_{N.q} = {}^{R}p_{q} - {}^{R}p_{N} \tag{3.42}$$

The general forward transform is expressed as a matrix of four column vectors (Equation 3.28), and the general inverse transform can be expressed in a similar way (Equation 3.43), providing a simple set of equations for calculating the inverse. Using these equations is simpler than matrix inversion. The top left 3×3 sub-matrix of the inverse transform is the transpose of the top left 3×3 sub-matrix of the forward transform.

$$\mathbf{T}^{-1} = \begin{bmatrix} x_x & x_y & x_z & -\boldsymbol{p} \cdot \boldsymbol{x} \\ y_x & y_y & y_z & -\boldsymbol{p} \cdot \boldsymbol{y} \\ z_x & z_y & z_z & -\boldsymbol{p} \cdot \boldsymbol{z} \\ 0 & 0 & 0 & 1 \end{bmatrix} = \begin{bmatrix} x_x & x_y & x_z & -p_x x_x - p_y x_y - p_z x_z \\ y_x & y_y & y_z & -p_x y_x - p_y y_y - p_z y_z \\ z_x & z_y & z_z & -p_x z_x - p_y z_y - p_z z_z \\ 0 & 0 & 0 & 1 \end{bmatrix} \tag{3.43}$$

You can prove that Equation 3.43 is the inverse of the general forward transform by multiplying the two transforms together, and confirming that the result is the identity matrix. The results of the matrix multiplication are simplified using dot product relationships: the dot product of two parallel vectors is 1, and the dot product of two perpendicular vectors is 0 (see Appendix A, Section 4.1).

$$\mathbf{T}\mathbf{T}^{-1} = \begin{bmatrix} x_x & y_x & z_x & p_x \\ x_y & y_y & z_y & p_y \\ x_z & y_z & z_z & p_z \\ 0 & 0 & 0 & 1 \end{bmatrix} \begin{bmatrix} x_x & x_y & x_z & -p_x x_x - p_y x_y - p_z x_z \\ y_x & y_y & y_z & -p_x y_x - p_y y_y - p_z y_z \\ z_x & z_y & z_z & -p_x z_x - p_y z_y - p_z z_z \\ 0 & 0 & 0 & 1 \end{bmatrix} = \begin{bmatrix} 1 & 0 & 0 & 0 \\ 0 & 1 & 0 & 0 \\ 0 & 0 & 1 & 0 \\ 0 & 0 & 0 & 1 \end{bmatrix} \tag{3.44}$$

Considering our example (Equation 3.25), we can find the point $^N q$ by premultiplying the point $^R q_1$ with the inverse transformation, which can be obtained using Equation 3.43.

$$^R\mathbf{T}_N^{-1} = \begin{bmatrix} 0 & 0 & -1 & 0 \\ 1 & 0 & 0 & -2a \\ 0 & -1 & 0 & 0 \\ 0 & 0 & 0 & 1 \end{bmatrix} \tag{3.45}$$

$$^N q_1 = {}^R\mathbf{T}_N^{-1}\,{}^R q_1 = \begin{bmatrix} 0 & 0 & -1 & 0 \\ 1 & 0 & 0 & -2a \\ 0 & -1 & 0 & 0 \\ 0 & 0 & 0 & 1 \end{bmatrix} \begin{bmatrix} 2a \\ -b \\ 0 \\ 1 \end{bmatrix} = \begin{bmatrix} 0 \\ 0 \\ b \\ 1 \end{bmatrix} \tag{3.46}$$

3.9 Object location

The transformation of coordinate frames was introduced to make modelling the relocation of objects easier. An object is described with respect to a frame located in the object, and this frame is relocated with a transformation. The transformation is the result of a sequence of rotations and translations, which are recorded with a transformation equation. Throughout this chapter, we have illustrated this process with an example (Figure 3.15). In this example, the tip of a screw, represented by the point *q*, is located in the new frame (Figure 3.16). In many situations, transformation equations can be simplified by replacing the two translations with one equivalent translation, but external constraints such as the need to avoid an obstacle may make the simplification unwise.

In this example, we wish to use a robot to pick up a screw located at $(0, a, 0)$, relocate it to $(2a, 0, 0)$, and change its orientation so that it points in the negative z direction, with the slot of the screw head parallel to the x axis (Figure 3.16). The two translations serve separate purposes: the first to relocate the new frame from the origin to the base of the screw, and the second to relocate the screw to a position where it can be screwed into another object. The two rotations align the screw with the axis of the hole in the object, and align the slot in the screw with the x axis. The whole operation

---

Window 3.3   Quaternions (Taylor, 1979)

In the text, we used homogeneous transforms to represent spatial quantities, and illustrated that they are equivalent to vector analysis. Vector analysis can be used solely (Duffy, 1980), but is more complex than homogeneous transforms. In practice, homogeneous transformations are inefficient because computations on matrices require more operations than other representations, and, since their representation of rotation is highly redundant, numerical inconsistencies can be a problem. So, quaternions are often used to represent rotations.

In general a **quaternion** *Q* consists of a scalar part *s* and a vector part *v*.

$$Q = [s + v]$$

If two quaternions are multiplied, the result is a new quaternion:

$$Q_1 \times Q_2 = [s_1 s_2 - v_1 \cdot v_2 + s_2 v_1 + s_1 v_2 + v_1 \times v_2]$$

From this definition, it follows that if

$$S = \sin(\phi/2) \quad \text{and} \quad C = \cos(\phi/2)$$

Then the quaternion

$$0 + \mathbf{Rot}(n, \phi) \times u = [C + S \cdot n] \times [0 + u] \times [C + -S \cdot n]$$

$$\therefore \quad Q = \mathbf{Rot}(n, \phi) = [C + S \cdot n]$$

which corresponds to a rotation by an angle ϕ about an axis *n*, where *u* is a unit vector.

A rotation of 0° is

$$\mathbf{Rot}(n, 0) = [1 + 0 \cdot n] = [1 + 0]$$

If a rotation **R** is represented by a quaternion *Q*, then the quaternion corresponding to $\mathbf{R}^{-1}$ is obtained by negating the vector part of *Q*. Also, if rotations $\mathbf{R}_1$ and $\mathbf{R}_2$ are represented by quaternions Q_1 and Q_2, the rotation $\mathbf{R}_1 \times \mathbf{R}_2$ will be represented by the quaternion $Q_1 \times Q_2$.

can be described with a series of transformations, given the location of the screw with respect to the new frame.

A set of mathematical tools for describing the location of an object (position and orientation), and the relocation of that object have been developed in this chapter. These tools are based on Cartesian coordinate geometry, matrix algebra, and homogeneous coordinates. Other tools, based on different mathematical representations, are also available (Windows 3.3, and 3.4). Some of these tools produce more efficient solutions than those discussed here.

3.10   Transform graphs

The problem of locating an object has been decomposed into two steps: first, describe the object with respect to a coordinate frame located within it, and

---

Window 3.4   Screw theory (Ball, 1900)

In practice, robot joints are either revolute or prismatic. A revolute joint is constrained to turn around its axis, while a prismatic joint is constrained to move along its axis. In both joints, the kinematic constraints are line dependent, which implies that a geometry based on lines, rather than points, will provide an efficient description of the properties of a manipulator. Since motion and force are body dependent and not point dependent, descriptions based upon lines are intrinsic to these phenomena and have advantages over point based formulations. Screw theory provides such a geometry; an alternate way of representing spatial vector quantities.

A displacement of a rigid body in space depends on six independent parameters: three translational and three rotational. Alternately, it can be described as a translation along a unique axis combined with a rotation about that axis – that is a screw displacement along a screw axis. A **screw** is a directed line in space associated with a scalar called pitch, where pitch is the ratio of linear translation to the rotation angle. A **motor** is a screw reduced to a particular point. A force acting along a screw is called a **wrench**, and consists of a force along the screw axis coupled with a torque around the screw axis. The magnitude of the force is the magnitude of the wrench, and the ratio of the magnitudes of the force and torque is determined by the pitch. A wrench is defined as a magnitude and a screw. Also, screw displacement (twist) and screw velocity (twist velocity) can be defined as a magnitude and a screw. As a result, we have a common mathematical form for expressing all these quantities: a vector of 6 real numbers.

- A **twist** is represented with a vector of six real numbers called screw coordinates: four describing the position of the vector in space (screw axis), one describing the pitch, and one describing the rotation angle about the screw axis.
- A **wrench** can be represented as a vector of six real numbers: four describing the screw axis, one describing the pitch, and one describing the torque around the screw axis.

In both cases, we have a six-element column vector, which we can decompose into two three element column vectors: a free vector m defining the magnitude and direction of the screw axis, and a moment vector m_0 defining the position of the axis in space.

$$\text{Screw} = [m^T, m_0^T]^T$$

Roth (1984) used screw theory to develop kinematic models, and Featherstone (1983a) used it to model manipulator dynamics.

Figure 3.19
Transformation graph for
transformation Equation
3.48.

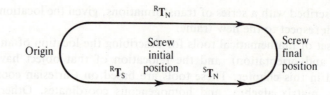

second, describe the object frame with a transformation of the reference frame. We described the relocation of this object as a series of transformations that relocate the object frame to the new location of the object. This series of transformations can be illustrated with a **transform graph**. This is a closed graph; that is, any transformation can be described in terms of the other transformations in the graph. The transform graph for our screw example is shown in Figure 3.19. From this graph, you can see that there are two descriptions of the final location of the screw: one is a direct transform from the origin to the final location of the screw; and the other decomposes this transform into two transforms: one describes the initial move to the screw, and the other the movement of the screw (Equation 3.47).

$$^{R}T_{N} = {^{R}T_{S}} {^{S}T_{N}} \tag{3.47}$$

The transform which describes the relocation of the screw ($^{S}T_{N}$) is found either by reading the transform equation (Equation 3.48) directly from the graph (Figure 3.19), or by premultiplying both sides of the above equation by the inverse of the transform which describes the screw frame with respect to the reference frame.

$$^{R}T_{S}^{-1} {^{R}T_{N}} = {^{S}T_{N}} \tag{3.48}$$

A second, more complex example is shown in Figure 3.20. In this example, we wish to grasp the box with the hand on the manipulator. To do this, the robot has to move the hand until it is positioned around the box, and

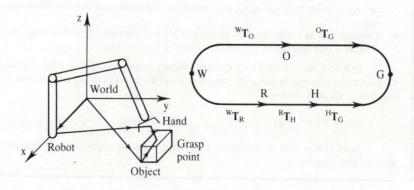

Figure 3.20
Transform graph for an
object about to be grasped
by a manipulator.

then close it to grasp the box. This situation can be described with a transformation equation as given in Equation 3.49.

$$^{W}T_{O}\,^{O}T_{G} = \,^{W}T_{R}\,^{R}T_{H}\,^{H}T_{G} \tag{3.49}$$

where

        W is the origin of the world coordinate system
        O is the origin of the coordinate frame in the object
        G is the grasp point
        H is a point half way between the fingers of the hand
        R is the base of the robot.

The aim of this grasping exercise is to make a point half way between the fingers of the hand coincide with the grasp point on the object. The above equation can be solved for the transform from the hand to the grasp point, either by premultiplication or by inspection of the transform graph to obtain Equation 3.50.

$$^{W}T_{R}^{-1}\,^{R}T_{H}^{-1}\,^{W}T_{O}\,^{O}T_{G} = \,^{H}T_{G} \tag{3.50}$$

Our goal is achieved when the transform from the hand to the grasp point ($^{H}T_{G}$) is the identity matrix – that is, the hand is in the correct position to grasp the object.

3.11   Programming

In this section, the programming concepts relevant to the ideas developed in this chapter are examined. These concepts are expressed in Modula-2 rather than a common robot programming language, to allow freedom to explore the concept without the constraints applied by many of the common industrial robot programming languages. The implementation of these concepts in a number of robot languages is discussed fully in Chapter 12.

    The concepts discussed in this chapter are implemented differently in different robot programming languages. However, the concept of a **frame** (Blume and Jakob, 1986) is common in many languages. A frame is a Cartesian space description of the location (position and orientation) of an object. A frame is a data structure which directly maps the homogeneous coordinate frame described in this chapter (Section 3.4). While mapping a concept into a data structure makes the program easy for a person to read, it can result in inefficient code if not done carefully. A frame should be defined so that it can be manipulated as a frame, or as a 4×4 array. The latter enables the implementation of functions to be as efficient as possible.

Figure 3.21
Data structures for representing vectors and coordinate frames.

```
DEFINITION MODULE RobotStruct3;
            (*The data structures and procedures for use in Chapter 3 are
            defined here*)
CONST
      SCALE = 1.0;

TYPE
      Location = (xcord, ycord, zcord, scale);
            (*indexes to the elements of a homogeneous vector*)
      Axis = (xaxis, yaxis, zaxis, pvec);
            (*the four vectors which define a frame in homogeneous
            coordinates*)
      PointVector = ARRAY [xcord..scale] OF REAL;
            (*a 4 X 1 column vector used to describe a point or line in space*)
      Frame = ARRAY[xaxis..pvec] OF PointVector;
            (*a 4 X 4 matrix used to describe a coordinate frame attached to an
            object*)
      Orientation = (xrot, yrot, zrot);
            (*indexes to rotations around the x, y, and z axes*)
      Angle = REAL;
            (*amount of rotation around an axis*)
      Distance = REAL;
            (*amount of translation along an axis*)

VAR
      xdist, ydist, zdist : Distance;
            (*distance translated along the x, y, and z axes*)
      psi, theta, phi : Angle;
            (*angle of rotation around the x, y, and z axes*)
      origin : PointVector;
            (*a vector describing the origin of a frame with respect to itself*)
      xuvec, yuvec, zuvec, puvec : PointVector;
            (*unit vectors in the x, y, z, and p directions*)
      identity4, worldframe : Frame;
            (*4 X 4 identity matrix*)
END RobotStruct3.

IMPLEMENTATION MODULE RobotStruct3;
            (*this module initializes the variables declared in the definition
            module*)
VAR
      i : Location;

BEGIN
      FOR i := xcord TO scale DO        identity4[xaxis] := xuvec;
            origin[i] := 0.0               identity4[yaxis] := yuvec;
      END;                                 identity4[zaxis] := zuvec;
      xuvec := origin;                     identity4[pvec] := puvec;
      yuvec := origin;                     worldframe := identity4;
      zuvec := origin;                     psi := 0.0;
      puvec := origin;                     theta := 0.0;
      xuvec[xcord] := 1.0;                 phi := 0.0;
      yuvec[ycord] := 1.0;                 xdist := 0.0;
      zuvec[zcord] := 1.0;                 ydist := 0.0;
      puvec[scale] := SCALE;               zdist := 0.0;
      origin := puvec;             END  RobotStruct3.
```

DEFINITION MODULE HomoVectors;
                    (*a set of general purpose vector manipulation routines are defined
                    here, for use with vectors of type PointVector – a 4 × 1 column
                    vector*)

FROM RobotStruct3 IMPORT Location, Axis, PointVector, Frame, Angle, puvec;

PROCEDURE   VectorAdd(VAR vec1 : PointVector;
                           VAR vec2 : PointVector) : PointVector;
                    (*returns the sum of two vectors*)

PROCEDURE   VectorSub(VAR vec1 : PointVector;
                           VAR vec2 : PointVector) : PointVector;
                    (*returns the difference between two vectors*)

PROCEDURE   VectorDot(VAR vec1 : PointVector;
                           VAR vec2: PointVector) : PointVector;
                    (*returns the dot product of two vectors*)

PROCEDURE VectorCross(VAR vec1 : PointVector;
                           VAR vec2 : PointVector) : PointVector;
                    (*returns the cross product of two vectors*)

PROCEDURE   VectorAng(VAR vec1 : PointVector;
                           VAR vec2 : PointVector) : Angle;
                    (*returns the angle between two vectors*)

PROCEDURE   VectorMag(VAR vec1 : PointVector) : REAL;
                    (*returns the magnitude of a vector*)

PROCEDURE VectorInit() : PointVector;
                    (*returns an initialized vector – a copy of puvec from
                    RobotStructures*)

PROCEDURE WriteVector(VAR vec1 : PointVector);
                    (*Writes the contents of a vector to a text window*)

PROCEDURE DrawVector(VAR vec1 : PointVector;
                           VAR frameref : Frame);
                    (*Draws a vector on a graphics window relative to the reference
                    frame*)

END HomoVectors.

Figure 3.22
Library of routines for vector
manipulation – definition of
procedures only.

An example of a frame data structure is given in Figure 3.21. It
consists of a set of four vectors, which define the axes and origin of the frame
with respect to a reference frame. A vector consists of a set of three spatial
coordinates, plus an additional element in order to convert it to homogeneous coordinates. Each vector, and each element in a vector can be
uniquely specified with the equations throughout this chapter because they
have been identified with specially declared enumerated types. Thus, the
frame data structure defined in Figure 3.21 is a direct mapping of the frame
developed in this chapter.

In addition to defining the data structures, we can specify initial
conditions for these structures in the implementation module (Figure 3.21).

These initialized variables can then be exported with the data types for use by procedures in other modules. An important initial data structure is a 4×4 identity matrix, as it can be used to initialize frames, and it is the world coordinate frame. In addition, unit vectors in each direction, and zero translations and rotations are defined.

These data structures are imported by three libraries of functions, each defined with a definition module. One module (Figure 3.22) defines a comprehensive set of procedures for vector manipulation, including procedures to print and draw vectors. As we have defined special data objects, procedures to display these objects must be written. A second module (Figure 3.23) is a set of matrix calculation functions, for manipulating frames. Some of the functions defined in these modules are imported by a

---

```
DEFINITION MODULE HomoFrames;
            (*a set of general purpose matrix manipulation routines are defined
            here, for use with matrices of type Frame – a 4 × 4 square matrix*)

FROM RobotStruct3 IMPORT Location, Axis, PointVector, Frame, Angle,
            identity4;

PROCEDURE     FrameAdd(VAR frame1 : Frame;
                              VAR frame2 : Frame) : Frame;
            (*returns the sum of two matrices*)

PROCEDURE     FrameSub(VAR frame1 : Frame;
                              VAR frame2 : Frame) : Frame;
            (*returns the difference between two matrices*)

PROCEDURE     FrameMult(VAR frame1 : Frame;
                              VAR frame2: Frame) : Frame;
            (*returns the product of two matrices*)

PROCEDURE   FrameTrans(VAR frame1 : Frame) : Frame;
            (*returns the transpose of a matrix*)

PROCEDURE     FrameInv(VAR frame1 : Frame) : Frame;
            (*returns the inverse of a matrix*)

PROCEDURE     FrameDet(VAR frame1 : Frame) : REAL;
            (*returns the determinant of a matrix*)

PROCEDURE FrameInit( ) : Frame;
            (*returns an initialized frame – a copy of identity4*)

PROCEDURE   WriteFrame(VAR frame1 : Frame);
            (*Writes the contents of a frame to a text window*)

PROCEDURE   DrawFrame(VAR framenew : Frame;
                              VAR frameref : Frame);
            (*Draws a frame on a graphics window relative to the reference
            frame*)

END HomoFrames.
```

Figure 3.23
Library of routines for manipulating matrices representing coordinate frames – definition of procedures only.

DEFINITION MODULE Transforms;
        (*a set of general purpose frame transformation routines are defined
        here, for use with matrices of type Frame – 4×4 square matrix, and
        vectors of type PointVector – a 4×1 column vector*)

FROM RobotStruct3 IMPORT Location, Axis, PointVector, Frame, Orientation,
Angle, Distance;

FROM HomoVectors IMPORT VectorInit;

FROM HomoFrames IMPORT FrameMult, FrameInit;

PROCEDURE Premult(VAR frame1 : Frame;
                VAR frame2 : Frame) Frame;
        (*returns the result of premultiplying frame1 by frame2*)

PROCEDURE Postmult(VAR frame1 : Frame;
                VAR frame2 : Frame) : Frame;
        (*returns the result of postmultiplying frame1 by frame2*)

PROCEDURE PointTransf(VAR frame1 : Frame;
                VAR vec1 : PointVector) : PointVector;
        (*returns the result of transforming vec1 by frame1*)

PROCEDURE ConvVec(Var vec1 : PointVector) : Frame;
        (*converts a vector into a frame by substituting the vector for pvec
        in the 4×4 identity matrix*)

PROCEDURE PositionVector(xdist: Distance;
                ydist: Distance;
                zdist: Distance) : PointVector;
        (*returns a PointVector representing the translation – xdist, ydist,
        zdist – with respect to the world frame*)

PROCEDURE Translate(xdist: Distance;
                ydist: Distance;
                zdist: Distance) : Frame;
        (*returns a frame representing the translation of an object – xdist,
        ydist, zdist*)

PROCEDURE Rotate(direction: Orientation;
                amount: Angle) : Frame;
        (*returns a frame representing the rotation of an object around a
        specified axis*)

PROCEDURE RPY(psi: Angle;
                theta: Angle;
                phi: Angle) : Frame;
        (*returns a frame representing the roll–pitch–yaw rotation*)

END Transforms.

Figure 3.24
Library of routines for
calculating transformations of
points and frames –
definition of procedures
only.

third module, which defines a set of functions for performing transformations (Figure 3.24). As defined, all these functions operate on numeric data, by substituting values into transformation matrices, or into equations derived from those transforms. Manipulation of matrix equations at the symbolic level, as we did in Section 3.7 to obtain the roll–pitch–yaw transformation, and as we will do in the kinematic analysis of manipulators in Chapter 4, will be discussed in the next chapter.

Key points

- Manipulation is the skilful handling and treating of objects.
- An object has six degrees of freedom with respect to a Cartesian coordinate frame – three degrees of translation: **Trans** (x, y, z) and three degrees of rotation: **Rot** (ϕ, θ, ψ).
- We describe the location of a point relative to a frame with a vector ${}^R q$.
- We describe the location (position and orientation) of an object with the transformation of a frame attached to the object with respect to a reference frame ${}^R \mathbf{T}_N$.

- $${}^R \mathbf{T}_N = \begin{bmatrix} x, & y, & z, & p \\ 0 & 0 & 0 & 1 \end{bmatrix} = \begin{bmatrix} \text{Rot} & \text{Trans} \\ (3 \times 3) & (3 \times 1) \\ \hline 0 & 1 \end{bmatrix} \qquad (3.28)$$

  where 1. x, y, and z are vectors describing the directions of the axes of the new frame,

  2. p is the vector from the origin of the reference frame to the origin of the new frame, and

  3. the 3×3 rotation transform is equivalent to an orientation transform, such as roll, pitch, yaw

  $$\mathbf{RPY} = \mathbf{Rot}\,(z, \phi)\,\mathbf{Rot}\,(y, \theta)\,\mathbf{Rot}\,(x, \psi) \qquad (3.34)$$

- We describe complex motion with a sequence of transforms:
- We combine these transforms in two ways:
  1. To execute the transformations right to left with respect to the reference frame, we premultiply transforms.
  2. To execute the transformations left to right with respect to successive new frames we postmultiply transforms.
- We can think of the transformations ${}^R \mathbf{T}_N$ in several ways:
  1. as a transformation from one frame to another,
  2. as a description of the origin and axes of a new frame with respect to a reference frame,

3. as a description of the motion of an object from one location (reference frame) to another (new frame), and

4. as a means of calculating the location of a point in a reference frame from the description of its location with respect to a new frame.

$$^Rq = {}^R\mathbf{T}_N\,{}^Nq \tag{3.27}$$

- The inverse transform is

$$^R\mathbf{T}_N^{-1} = {}^N\mathbf{T}_R = \begin{bmatrix} [x, y, z]^T & -p.x \\ & -p.y \\ & -p.z \\ 0 & 1 \end{bmatrix} \tag{3.43}$$

- When assigning coordinate frames to objects to model an assembly problem, we attach the frames so that they capture the motion of the objects during mating, i.e. so that the object frames align when the objects are correctly mated.

Examples

Example 3.1   End effector transform

To bring the results of this chapter into focus, we will now work a specific example. Consider that the hand on a robot is to be located at $p(a, b, c)$, pointing towards the origin (Figure 3.25(c)). What is the transformation matrix from the origin of the reference frame to the hand? For consistency with later chapters, the z axis of the hand frame will point towards the origin. Also, the y axis of the hand frame must be parallel to the xy plane.

The transformation of the axes can be done in the following sequence (Figure 3.26):

(a) translate to $p(a, b, c)$,

(b) rotate around the new z axis by $90°$,

(c) rotate around the new y axis by $-90 - \phi_1^\circ$. (The z axis of the new frame (z_3) now intersects the x axis of the reference frame),

(d) rotate around the new x axis by $-\phi_2^\circ$. (The new z axis (z_2) is pointing towards the origin, fulfilling one of our specifications) and, finally,

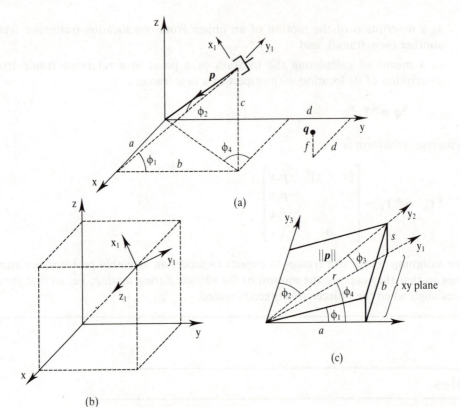

(a)

(b)

(c)

Figure 3.25
Location of the hand in
Example 3.1: (a) problem
description; (b) coordinate
frames; (c) orientation
transform.

(e) a rotation about the new z axis of $-\phi_3°$. (This orients the y axis so that it is parallel to the xy plane.)

If you are having difficulty visualizing this series of transformations, obtain two physical models of coordinate frames, such as those in Figure 3.5, and work through the sequence. The transformation equation for this problem is:

$$^R T_H = \text{Trans}(a, b, c)\text{Rot}(z, 90)\text{Rot}(y, -90-\phi_1)\text{Rot}(x, -\phi_2)$$
$$\text{Rot}(z, -\phi_3)$$
$$= {}^R T_A {}^A T_H$$
$$= T_A T_O$$
$$= \text{Approach transform} \times \text{Orientation transform} \qquad (3.51)$$

Having obtained the transformation equation, the transformation matrix must be calculated next. First, however, let us examine the impact of adding 90° or 180° degrees to a rotation. The sine and cosine curves are given in Section 13.1.1. The effect of adding π degrees to a rotation is to change sign of the result (Equations 3.52 and 3.53). The effect of adding $\pi/2$ degrees is the same as subtracting the angle from 90 degrees.

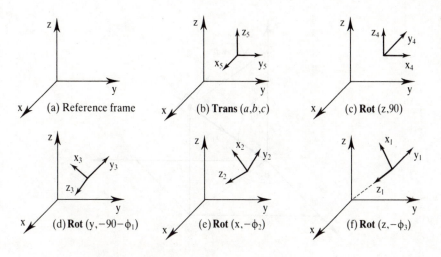

Figure 3.26
Sequence of transforms and resulting frames to solve Example 3.1.

$$\sin(\pi + \phi_1) = -\sin(\phi_1) \tag{3.52}$$

$$\cos(\pi + \phi_1) = -\cos(\phi_1) \tag{3.53}$$

The main problem when calculating the transformation matrix is to find the values of the angles ϕ_1, ϕ_2 and ϕ_3.

$$\phi_1 = \text{atan}\left(\frac{c}{b}\right) \tag{3.54}$$

$$\phi_2 = \text{atan}\left(\frac{a}{\sqrt{b^2 + c^2}}\right) \tag{3.55}$$

$$\phi_3 = \text{atan}\frac{ac}{b\sqrt{a^2+b^2}} = \text{atan}\left(\frac{s}{r}\right) \tag{3.56}$$

where

$$s = a \times \tan(\phi_1) = \frac{ac}{b},$$

and $r = \sqrt{a^2+b^2}$

We can simplify the transform calculation by constraining the y axis to remain in the xy plane during the transformation. This constraint leads to a second transformation equation (Equation 3.57) which involves one translation and two rotations (Figure 3.27).

$$^R\mathbf{T}_H = \mathbf{Trans}(a, b, c)\mathbf{Rot}(z, \theta_2)\mathbf{Rot}(y, \pi + \theta_1) \tag{3.57}$$

Note: $\mathbf{Rot}(\pi + \theta_1) = \mathbf{Rot}(\theta_1 - \pi)$

Figure 3.27
Alternative transformation
sequence which maintains
the new y axis in the correct
orientation.

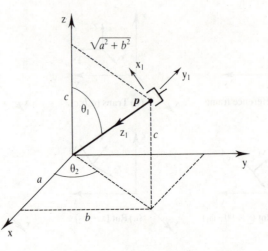

The coordinate frame is translated to the new position, rotated about the
new z axis (now the x axis of the new frame intersects the z axis of the
reference frame), and, finally, rotated about the new y axis. If we consider
the transformation sequence with respect to the reference frame, neither
rotation moves the y axis out of the xy plane, thus, correct orientation of the
y axis is maintained. In an actual robotics situation, however, the choice of a
transform sequence may well be determined by external constraints. Where
possible, choose the simplest sequence.

$$^R\mathbf{T_H} = \mathbf{Trans}(a,b,c)\mathbf{Rot}(z,\theta_2)\mathbf{Rot}(y,\pi+\theta_1)$$

$$= \begin{bmatrix} 1 & 0 & 0 & a \\ 0 & 1 & 0 & b \\ 0 & 0 & 1 & c \\ 0 & 0 & 0 & 1 \end{bmatrix} \begin{bmatrix} C_2 & -S_2 & 0 & 0 \\ S_2 & C_2 & 0 & 0 \\ 0 & 0 & 1 & 0 \\ 0 & 0 & 0 & 1 \end{bmatrix} \begin{bmatrix} -C_1 & 0 & -S_1 & 0 \\ 0 & 1 & 0 & 0 \\ S_1 & 0 & -C_1 & 0 \\ 0 & 0 & 0 & 1 \end{bmatrix}$$

$$\begin{bmatrix} -C_1C_2 & -S_2 & -S_1C_2 & a \\ -C_1S_2 & C_2 & -S_2S_1 & b \\ -S_1 & 0 & -C_1 & c \\ 0 & 0 & 0 & 1 \end{bmatrix}$$

(3.58)

This result can be confirmed using vector arithmetic, a procedure not
recommended because the algebra can be complex. However, it is included
here to show that multiplication of transformation matrices achieves the
correct result. The magnitude and direction cosines (Section 13.4.1) of a
vector $p(a, b, c)$ are:

$$\|p\| = \surd(a^2 + b^2 + c^2)$$

(3.59)

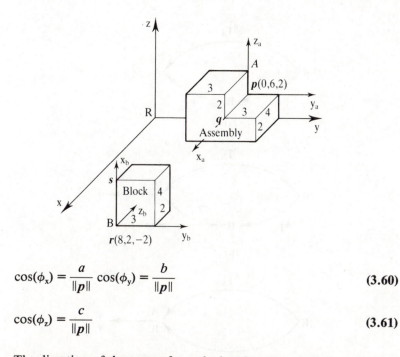

Figure 3.28
Assembly problem in
Example 3.2.

$$\cos(\phi_x) = \frac{a}{\|p\|} \quad \cos(\phi_y) = \frac{b}{\|p\|} \tag{3.60}$$

$$\cos(\phi_z) = \frac{c}{\|p\|} \tag{3.61}$$

The direction of the vector from the hand to the origin is opposite to the direction of p. This vector specifies the z axis of the hand frame. The y axis is rotated through θ_2° in the xy plane, so the direction of the vector describing the direction of the y axis of the hand is:

$$-\sin(\theta_2)i + \cos(\theta_2)j + 0k \tag{3.62}$$

Finally, the direction of the x axis of the hand can be found from the cross product of the vector in the y direction and the vector in the z direction (Section 13.4.3). The result is the following homogeneous transformation matrix, which is identical to the transformation matrix found using matrix transforms.

$$^R T_H = \begin{bmatrix} ac/(\sqrt{(a^2+b^2)}\|p\|) & -b/\sqrt{(a^2+b^2)} & -a/\|p\| & a \\ bc/(\sqrt{(a^2+b^2)}\|p\|) & -a/\sqrt{(a^2+b^2)} & -b/\|p\| & b \\ \sqrt{(a^2+b^2)}/\|p\| & 0 & -c/\|p\| & c \\ 0 & 0 & 0 & 1 \end{bmatrix} \tag{3.63}$$

Example 3.2   Assembly problem

In the simple assembly problem in Figure 3.28, the block must be placed on the assembly so that line *rs* is coincident with line *pq*. To achieve this, we first

Figure 3.29
Transform graphs for
assembly problem in Figure
3.28: (a) frame graph; (b)
original location of points; (c)
final location of points.

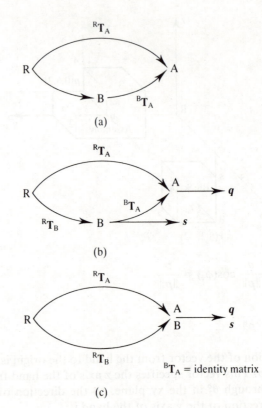

(a)

(b)

(c)

$^B\mathbf{T}_A$ = identity matrix

place frames at *r* and *p* so that they align when the assembly is complete. This
choice of frames completely describes the motion of the block. Second, we
draw the transform graph for the problem (Figure 3.29(b)). Third, we calculate the transforms.

$$^R\mathbf{T}_A = \mathbf{Trans}(0, 6, 2) = \begin{bmatrix} 1 & 0 & 0 & 0 \\ 0 & 1 & 0 & 6 \\ 0 & 0 & 1 & 2 \\ 0 & 0 & 0 & 1 \end{bmatrix} \tag{3.64}$$

$$^R\mathbf{T}_B = \mathbf{Trans}(8, 2, -2)\mathbf{Rot}(y, -90) = \begin{bmatrix} 0 & 0 & -1 & 8 \\ 0 & 1 & 0 & 2 \\ 1 & 0 & 0 & -2 \\ 0 & 0 & 0 & 1 \end{bmatrix} \tag{3.65}$$

From the transform graph we obtain an equation for the motion of the
block.

$$\mathbf{^{B}T_{A}} = \mathbf{^{R}T_{B}^{-1}} \mathbf{^{R}T_{A}} = \begin{bmatrix} 0 & 0 & 1 & 4 \\ 0 & 1 & 0 & 4 \\ -1 & 0 & 0 & 8 \\ 0 & 0 & 0 & 1 \end{bmatrix} \qquad (3.66)$$

$$\mathbf{^{A}T_{B}} = \mathbf{^{B}T_{A}^{-1}} = \begin{bmatrix} 0 & 0 & -1 & 8 \\ 0 & 1 & 0 & -4 \\ 1 & 0 & 0 & -4 \\ 0 & 0 & 0 & 1 \end{bmatrix} \qquad (3.67)$$

Equation 3.67 describes the location of the block frame relative to the assembly frame before the block is moved. Using this transform, we find the location of point s relative to the assembly frame.

$$A_{s} = \mathbf{^{A}T_{B}} B_{s} = \begin{bmatrix} 0 & 0 & -1 & 8 \\ 0 & 1 & 0 & -4 \\ 1 & 0 & 0 & -4 \\ 0 & 0 & 0 & 1 \end{bmatrix} \begin{bmatrix} 4 \\ 0 \\ 0 \\ 1 \end{bmatrix} = \begin{bmatrix} 8 \\ -4 \\ 0 \\ 1 \end{bmatrix} \qquad (3.68)$$

Finally, we wish to calculate the new location of point s with respect to the reference frame after the block has been moved (that is, point q). The relationship between the points and frames is shown in the transform graph in Figure 3.29(b). The original location of point s is:

$$\mathbf{^{R}s} = \mathbf{^{R}T_{B}} \mathbf{^{B}s} \qquad (3.69)$$

$$\therefore \mathbf{^{B}s} = \mathbf{^{R}T_{B}^{-1}} \mathbf{^{R}s} \qquad (3.70)$$

After motion, the relationship between the points and frames is shown by the transform graph in Figure 3.29(c). Point s is coincident with point q, so

$$\mathbf{^{A}q} = \mathbf{^{B}s} \text{ (after motion)} \qquad (3.71)$$

$$\therefore \quad \mathbf{^{A}q} = \mathbf{^{R}T_{B}^{-1}} \mathbf{^{R}s} \qquad (3.72)$$

$$\text{and } \mathbf{^{R}q} = \mathbf{^{R}T_{A}} \mathbf{^{A}q} = \mathbf{^{R}T_{A}} \mathbf{^{R}T_{B}^{-1}} \mathbf{^{R}s} \qquad (3.73)$$

$$= \begin{bmatrix} 1 & 0 & 0 & 0 \\ 0 & 1 & 0 & 6 \\ 0 & 0 & 1 & 2 \\ 0 & 0 & 0 & 1 \end{bmatrix} \begin{bmatrix} 0 & 0 & 1 & 2 \\ 0 & 1 & 0 & -2 \\ -1 & 0 & 0 & 8 \\ 0 & 0 & 0 & 1 \end{bmatrix} \begin{bmatrix} 8 \\ 2 \\ 2 \\ 1 \end{bmatrix} = \begin{bmatrix} 4 \\ 6 \\ 2 \\ 1 \end{bmatrix} \qquad (3.73)$$

This result can be confirmed by inspection of Figure 3.28, which validates the transform. While we can obtain this result by mental arithmetic, a computer can only solve this problem when we program the above equations.

Exercises

■ *Essay questions*

3.1 An object is moved from $p(1, 2, 3)$ or $r(1, 5, 4)$. Using vectors (Section 3.1) find the new location of a point $q(2, 6, 4)$. What is the location of q with respect to an object coordinate frame located at p? Repeat, this time using coordinate transforms. (Section 3.6)

3.2 A vector $p(4, 6)$ is rotated anticlockwise through 30°. What are the new coordinates of p?

3.3 A general two-dimensional transformation matrix is given in Equation 3.4. Substitute values into the matrix to produce the following transformations: a scale change in the y direction, stretching in the x direction, clockwise rotation, and reflection about the x axis. Draw these transforms. What is the difference between scaling and translation? What is the difference between reflection and rotation? Why can a 2×2 matrix not be used to represent translation?

3.4 Derive a general rotation transform $\mathbf{Rot}(x, \phi_1) \, \mathbf{Rot}(y, \phi_2) \, \mathbf{Rot}(z, \phi_3)$ from the three rotation transforms (Equations 3.19–3.21). If the order of the rotations is reversed, do you get the same transform?

3.5 Given the two-dimensional transformations $\mathbf{A} = \mathbf{Trans}(2, 0)$, $\mathbf{B} = \mathbf{Trans}(0, 2)$, and $\mathbf{C} = \mathbf{Rot}(45)$, draw the following transformations: **AB, AC, BC, CA, CB, ABC, CBA, ACBA, ABCA, CCA, ACCAB**.

3.6 What does each element in a three-dimensional transformation matrix represent?

3.7 Why do we use homogeneous coordinates? What are the disadvantages of homogeneous coordinates?

3.8 (a) What is the result of applying the following transform sequence to $p(1, 1, 1)$?

$$\mathbf{Rot}(z, 90)\mathbf{Trans}(x, 2)\mathbf{Trans}(y, 3)\mathbf{Rot}(x, -90)$$

   (b) If a coordinate frame is attached to that point with axes parallel to the reference frame, by premultiplying transforms, find the transformation which describes the new frame. (Section 3.4)
   (c) What does each column in the matrix represent?
   (d) Using the transformation matrix, calculate the new location of the point with respect to the reference frame. (Section 3.4)
   (e) Recalculate the transformation by postmultiplying the transforms (Section 3.5). Draw the intermediate positions of the new coordinate frame for both premultiplication and postmultiplication.

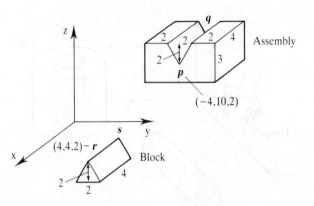

Figure 3.30
Assembly problem.

(f) Using the general orientation transform, calculate the orientation of the axes of the new coordinate frame (Section 3.7)

(g) Calculate the inverse transform using Equation 3.4.3.

3.9 Repeat question 3.8 for the transform sequence:

$$\text{Trans}(x, -5)\text{Rot}(x, -60)\text{Rot}(y, 45)\text{Trans}(z, -6)$$

3.10 What action does a transformation perform on a coordinate frame and on a point defined with respect to that frame? (Section 3.6)

3.11 Calculate the homogeneous transformation matrix for the following transform sequence

$$\text{Trans}(4, -3, 7)\text{Rot}(y, 90)\text{Rot}(z, 90)$$

What are the vectors which describe the transformed coordinate frame? Where is the origin of this frame?

3.12 Find the inverse of the transform in Example 3.1.

3.13 Simplify the transformation matrix in Example 3.1 for the case where a, b and c are equal.

3.14 Example 3.1 can be generalized by placing the hand at $p(a, b, c)$, as in Figure 3.25, and having the z axis of the hand frame point toward an arbitrary point $q(d, e, f)$. Calculate the homogeneous transform for this case. Verify your result by locating point q at the origin, and see if your matrix reduces to the one given in Example 3.1.

3.15 A robot and an object are located in the world coordinate system. Given the following transforms, find the transformation from the base of the robot to the hand of the robot, assuming that the hand is placed on the part. Start by finding the transform graph for this situation.

Figure 3.31
Pin-in-hole problem – the pin
is lying parallel to x axis and
the hole is parallel to z axis.

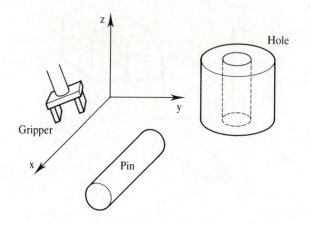

$$
{}^{W}T_{O}=\begin{bmatrix} 1 & 0 & 0 & 1 \\ 0 & 0 & -1 & 4 \\ 0.1 & 0 & 0 \\ 0 & 0 & 0 & 1 \end{bmatrix} \qquad {}^{W}T_{R}=\begin{bmatrix} 0 & -1 & 0 & 2 \\ 1 & 0 & 0 & -1 \\ 0 & 0 & 1 & 0 \\ 0 & 0 & 0 & 1 \end{bmatrix}
$$

3.16 Multiply the matrices in the general orientation transform (Equation 3.35) to verify the result in Equation 3.36.

3.17 Multiply the matrices in the Euler angle transformation (Equation 3.36) to get a single transformation matrix.

3.18 Find the transformation matrix which solves the simple assembly problem in Figure 3.30. The wedge-shaped block is to be placed on the assembly so that *p* and *r* are touching, and *s* and *q* are touching, and the final assembly is a rectangular block. Verify the transformation by transforming point *s* to point *q*. Use the following method:

    (a) Assign coordinate frames to each object.
    (b) Develop transformation matrices for each frame with respect to world coordinates.
    (c) Draw the transform graph.
    (d) Calculate the transformation matrix.
    (e) Use the matrix to transform point *s*.

3.19 For the problem of inserting a pin in a hole in Figure 3.31,

    (a) assign coordinate frames at appropriate locations to describe the motion, and the grasping location.
    (b) draw the transform graph,
    (c) define the transformation equations.

3.20 Derive the transformation equations for the grasping problem in Figure 3.32.

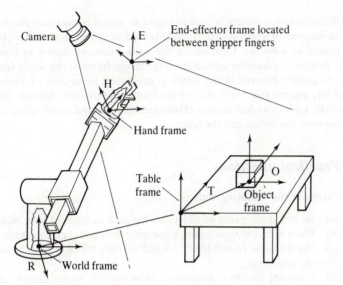

Figure 3.32
Grasping problem — move
the gripper to grasp a block.

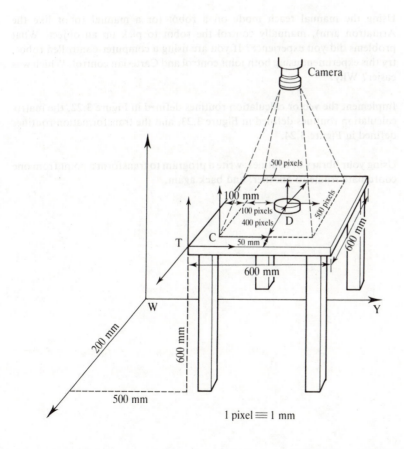

1 pixel ≡ 1 mm

Figure 3.33
Vision calibration problem.

3.21   Before a vision system is used to locate an object, image coordinates have to be mapped to world coordinates. Often a disc of known diameter (100 mm) is placed at a known location on the work table, as shown in Figure 3.33. Calculate the transformation from the image frame to the world frame when one picture element in the image is equivalent to an area of 1 mm×1 mm. First, assume that the y axes of the frames are parallel. Second, allow for a small angle (rotation around z) between the table and world coordinates, and between the image and the table.

■ *Practical questions*

3.1   Carry out the following actions:

   (a)   Sit at a desk, place an object on the desk in front of you, pick it up.
   (b)   Place it on the desk again, close your eyes and pick the object up.
   (c)   Get someone to blindfold you and to place the object on the desk. Pick the object up.
   (d)   Compare the three situations. How did you locate the object in each situation? What feedback did you use in each case?

3.2   Using the manual teach mode on a robot (or a manual robot like the Armatron arm), manually control the robot to pick up an object. What problems did you experience? If you are using a computer-controlled robot, try this experiment using both joint control and Cartesian control. Which was easier? Why?

3.3   Implement the vector calculation routines defined in Figure 3.22, the matrix calculation routines defined in Figure 3.23, and the transformation routines defined in Figure 3.24.

3.4   Using your library of routines, write a program to transform a point from one coordinate frame to another, and back again.

4 · *Kinematics: Manipulator Position*

'The whole is equal to the sum of its parts'
Euclid.

Objectives

In this chapter, we use the tools developed in the previous chapter to model the spatial relationships between the links in a manipulator arm. Our objective is to calculate the Cartesian location of the end effector from measured values of the joint angles (forward model) and to estimate the joint angles required to place the end effector at a desired location in space (inverse model). To simplify the analysis, we examine several two-link manipulators. This analysis includes the following topics:

- assignment of coordinate frames to links,
- modelling links with A matrices,
- the forward kinematics algorithm,
- the roll—pitch—yaw orientation transform,
- the inverse kinematics heuristic, and
- problems when programming kinematic models.

In Chapter 3 we defined the mathematical tools necessary to specify the location of an object in space. The location of an object can be specified with a transformation between the coordinate frame attached to the object and a reference coordinate frame. This reference frame may be located in the hand of the robot, in the base of the robot, or it may be the universal coordinate frame in which both the robot and the object are located. Each of these frames can be related to the others with a closed transformation equation, which we can draw as a transform graph.

Kinematics *is the relationships between the positions, velocities, and accelerations of the links of a manipulator*, where a manipulator is an arm, finger, or leg. In this chapter, we will develop a mathematical framework for describing these relationships, in particular position. The transformation, ($^R\mathbf{T}_H$) between a coordinate frame located in the hand of the robot (known as the **hand frame**) and a coordinate frame located in the base of the robot (known as the **base frame**) will be studied in detail. This transformation specifies the location (position and orientation) of the hand in space with respect to the base of the robot, but it does not tell us which configuration of the arm is required to achieve this location. As we will see, it is often possible to achieve the same hand position with many arm configurations.

A **serial link manipulator** is a series of links, which connects the hand to the base, with each link connected to the next by an actuated joint. If a coordinate frame is attached to each link, the relationship between two links can be described with a homogeneous transformation matrix – an **A** matrix. The first **A** matrix relates the first link to the base frame, and the last **A** matrix relates the hand frame to the last link. We use a sequence of these **A** matrices to describe the transform from the base to the hand of the manipulator, a sequence called the forward kinematic transform of the manipulator (Equation 4.1). Again, the equation is closed (Figure 4.1), so any term in it can be expressed in terms of the other terms.

$$^R\mathbf{T}_H = {}^R\mathbf{T}_1 \, {}^1\mathbf{T}_2 \cdots {}^{n-2}\mathbf{T}_{n-1} \, {}^{n-1}\mathbf{T}_H = \mathbf{A}_1 \mathbf{A}_2 \cdots \mathbf{A}_{n-1} \mathbf{A}_n \tag{4.1}$$

In the kinematic analysis of manipulator position, there are two separate problems to solve: **direct kinematics**, and **inverse kinematics**. Direct kinematics involves solving the forward transformation equation to find the location of the hand in terms of the angles and displacements between the links. The angles and displacements between the links are called **joint coordi-**

Figure 4.1
Six-link manipulator
transform graph.

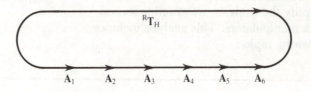

nates and are described with link variables, while the location of the hand in space is described with **Cartesian coordinates**. Inverse kinematics involves solving the inverse transformation equation to find the relationships between the links of the manipulator from the location of the hand in space. Direct kinematic analysis of manipulator position is carried out using Algorithm 4.1.

Algorithm 4.1   Direct Kinematic Algorithm

1. Move the manipulator to its zero position.
2. Assign a coordinate frame to each link.
3. Describe the rotations and translations between joints with link variables.
4. Define the **A** matrices relating the links.
5. Multiply the **A** matrices to calculate the manipulator transformation matrix $^R T_H$.
6. Equate the manipulator transformation matrix and the general transformation matrix to obtain Cartesian coordinates in terms of joint coordinates.
7. Equate the manipulator transformation matrix and the general orientation matrix to obtain the hand orientation angles.

Inverse kinematics is the more difficult problem to solve and, for some manipulators, closed form solutions cannot be found. However, constraints are usually placed on manipulator design so that the inverse solution *can* be found; without this, the robot is difficult to control in Cartesian space. The inverse kinematic solution for a manipulator is usually derived from the direct kinematic transform, so direct kinematics will be discussed first. Before we discuss the direct kinematic algorithm in detail, we will develop a method for assigning coordinate frames to links. To assign a coordinate frame to a link, the relationship between it and the previous link must be understood. This relationship comprises the rotations and translations that occur at the joints.

4.1   Joints

Two types of joints are commonly found in robots: **revolute joints**, and **prismatic joints** (Figure 4.2). Unlike the joints in the human arm, the joints in a robot are normally restricted to one degree of freedom, to simplify the mechanics, kinematics, and control of the manipulator. Revolute, or rotary,

Figure 4.2
Common joints found in
robots:
(a) Revolute joint with axis
coincident with link;
(b) Revolute joint with joint
axis perpendicular to link;
(c) Prismatic joint.

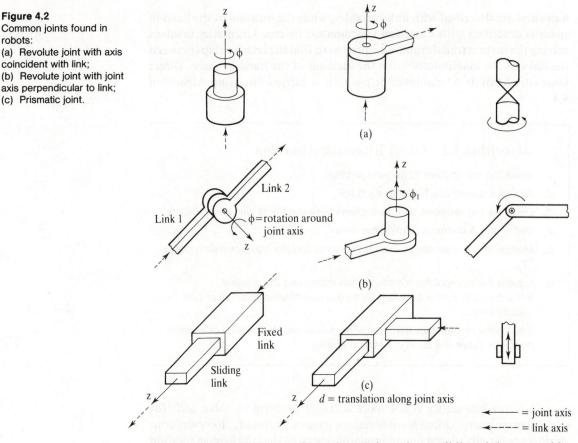

(a)

Link 2

Link 1

ϕ=rotation around
joint axis

(b)

Fixed
link

Sliding
link

(c)

d = translation along joint axis

———— = joint axis
◄----- = link axis

joints provide one degree of rotation. Prismatic, or sliding, joints, provide
one degree of translation. Joints are connected by solid links.

A revolute joint is used to join links in two basic configurations:
collinear and orthogonal. In the first (Figure 4.2(a)), the axis of the joint is
coincident with the centre line of the proximal link. In some designs it is
normal to the distal link. This joint is often used as a waist joint. In the
second (Figure 4.2(b)), the axis of the joint is normal to the proximal link.
One common use of this joint is as an elbow joint. In both cases, a revolute
joint is capable of one degree of rotation, the joint variable is the angle θ, and
the joint axis is in the z direction. Most revolute joints cannot rotate through
a full 360°, but are mechanically constrained.

A prismatic joint (Figure 4.2(c)) is a sliding joint, with the axis of the
joint coincident with the centre line of the sliding link. Since any prismatic
form can be used for the elements of a sliding pair, it does not have a specific
axis (as a turning pair does) but merely an axial direction. Nevertheless, it
is convenient to choose a centre line or axis as a basis for analysis. As with
the revolute joint, there are two basic configurations: the axis can be
collinear with the preceding (fixed) link, or orthogonal to it. A prismatic

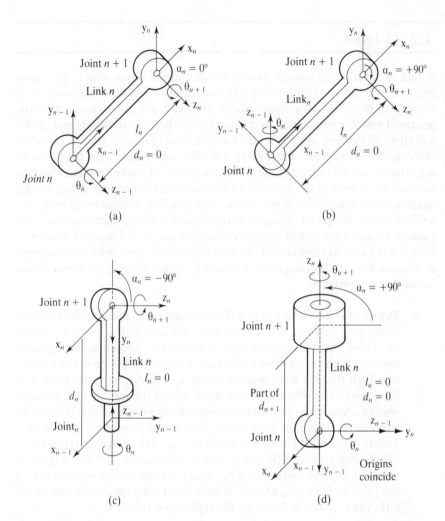

Figure 4.3
Typical link configurations connecting revolute joints.
(a) Type 1 link: parallel revolute joints with no twist between joint axes;
(b) Type 2 link: parallel revolute joints with 90 degrees twist between joint axes;
(c) Type 3 link: revolute joints with intersecting axes — axes are perpendicular;
(d) Type 4 link: revolute joints with perpendicular axes — coordinate frame origins coincide.

joint provides one degree of translation, the joint variable is the distance d, and the joint axis is in the z direction.

 With both types of joints, there are several common configurations of the joint with respect to the links attached to it. Actually, there is an infinite number of possible configurations, but for practical purposes only four will be considered here. First, the axis of the joint is collinear with the centre line of both links; in the second and third cases, the axis of the joint is orthogonal to the link with which it was aligned in the first case. The difference between the second and third cases is determined by which of the two orthogonal axes of the preceding joint the joint axis is parallel to. For example, for a revolute joint, the z axis of the preceding joint (Figure 4.3(a)) or the y axis of the preceding joint (Figure 4.3(b)). For the revolute joint, there is a fourth common case: the axis of the joint is orthogonal to both links.

4.2 Links

A link is a solid mechanical object which connects two joints. The main purpose of a link is to maintain a fixed relationship between the joints at its ends. The last link of a manipulator has only one joint, located at the **proximal end** (the end closest to the base) of the link. At the **distal end** of this link (the end furthest away from the base) instead of a joint, there is usually a place to attach a gripper: a tool plate. Initially, we will limit our discussion to a restricted set of link configurations, in order to make the relationships between the joints at the ends of a link easier to understand. Later in this chapter, we will discuss the general case. In practice, similar restrictions are applied to the design of joints to make robots easier to manufacture, and control. Eight common link configurations are shown in Figures 4.3 and 4.4. Between the axes of the joints at the ends of any link there can be two degrees of translation and two degrees of rotation. These degrees of freedom are called **link parameters**.

- **Type 1 link** The simplest link (Figure 4.3(a)) has two parallel revolute joints with no twist between the axes; the axes of the joints are parallel. These joints are separated by a distance l_n, known as the length of the link. If the centre line of the link is considered to be in the x direction then there is a translation in the x_{n-1} direction, from joint n to joint $n+1$. The whole link can rotate about the joint n by a variable angle θ_n, known as the angle between the links. This angle is the joint variable for a revolute joint. If the joint axis is considered to be in the z direction then this rotation is about the z_{n-1} axis. Thus, the type 1 link can be characterized by one degree of translation and one degree of rotation. Having assigned the z_{n-1} axis to be coincident with the axis of the joint and the x_{n-1} axis to be coincident with the centre line of the link, the y_{n-1} axis is found by the right-hand rule.

- **Type 2 link** If one of the joints in a type 1 link is twisted about the centre line of the link (axis x_{n-1}), by an angle α_n (Figure 4.3(b)), an extra degree of rotation is added. The twist angle (α_n) is the angle that would exist between the joint axes if the joints were coincident, and it can be thought of as a rotation around the x_{n-1} axis. Thus, the type 2 link has one degree of translation and two degrees of rotation.

- **Type 3 link** In this link, the second type of revolute joint in introduced. If joint n in the type 1 link is rotated 90° degrees about the y_{n-1} axis so that the z_{n-1} axis is collinear with the centre line of the link, we have the link configuration shown in Figure 4.3(c). The significant difference between this link and the previous two links is that the joint axes intersect, whereas in the type 1 and type 2 links they are parallel.

Figure 4.4
Typical link configurations
connecting prismatic joints,
and prismatic joints to
revolute joints.
(a) Type 5 link: intersecting
prismatic joints with 90
degree twist angle;
(b) Type 6 link: intersecting
revolute and prismatic joints
with 90 degree twist angle;
(c) Type 7 link: parallel
revolute and prismatic joints;
(d) Type 8 link: intersecting
prismatic and revolute joints.

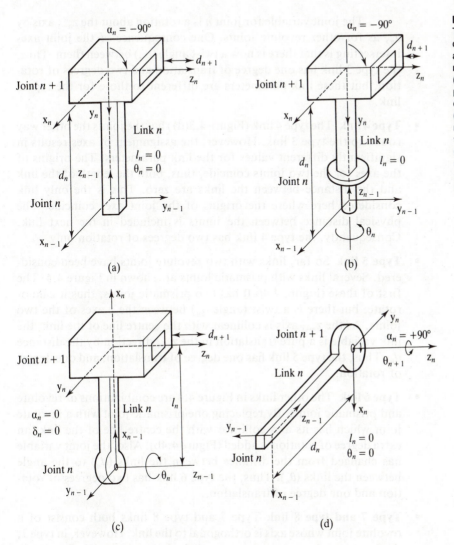

The distance between the joint axes (z_{n-1} and z_n) is therefore zero, and consequently, the length of the link (l_n) is also zero.

However, there is a translation of distance d_n between the two joints, measured between the common normals to the joint axes (usually the x_{n-1} and x_n axes). This translation in the z direction is known as the distance between the links, and it is the joint variable for a prismatic joint. The names given to the link parameters can cause confusion, even though they capture the essence of the link parameters, because the length-of-the-link parameter can be zero when, physically, the link does have length.

The joint variable for joint n is a rotation about the z_{n-1} axis by θ_n, as for other revolute joints. One consequence of the joint axes intersecting is that there is now a twist angle (α_n) between them. Thus, the type 3 link has one degree of translation and two degrees of rotation, but these link parameters are different to those for the type 2 link.

- **Type 4 link** The type 4 link (Figure 4.3(d)) has the joints the other way round to the type 3 link. However, the assignment of axes results in significantly different values for the link parameters. The origins of the axes for the two joints coincide, thus, both the length of the link and the distance between the links are zero. This is the only link considered here where the origins of the joint axes coincide. The physical distance between the joints is included in the next link. Consequently, the type 4 link has two degrees of rotation only.

- **Type 5 link** So far, links with two revolute joints have been considered. Several links with prismatic joints are shown in Figure 4.4. The first of these (Figure 4.4(a)) has two prismatic joints, thus it cannot rotate, but there is a twist (angle α_n) between the z axes of the two joints. As the z_{n-1} axis is collinear with the centre line of the link, the link variable is a pure translation in the z_{n-1} direction by the distance d_n. Thus, the type 5 link has one degree of translation, and one degree of rotation.

- **Type 6 link** The other links in Figure 4.4 are combinations of revolute and prismatic joints. By replacing one prismatic joint with a revolute joint which has its axis collinear with the centre line of the link, an extra degree of rotation is added (Figure 4.4b). Also, the joint variable has changed from the distance between the links (d_n) to the angle between the links (θ_n). Thus, the type 6 link has two degrees of rotation and one degree of translation.

- **Type 7 and type 8 link** Type 7 and type 8 links both consist of a revolute joint whose axis is orthogonal to the link. However, in type 7, the joint axes (z_{n-1} and z_n) are parallel whereas in type 8, they intersect. The type 7 link has the angle between the links as the joint variable, and has one degree of rotation and one degree of translation. The type 8 link has the distance between the links as the joint variable, and also has one degree of translation and one degree of rotation.

4.3 General links

The links studied so far have been constrained to be straight, with collinear or orthogonal joints axes. General links (Figure 4.5) do not have these

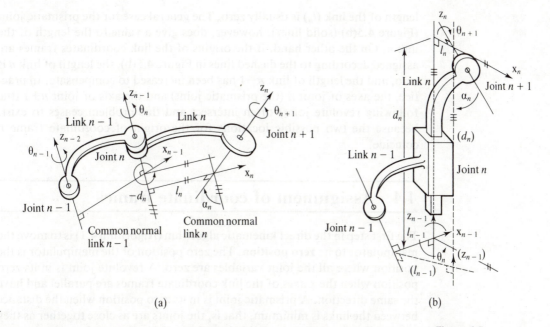

(a)   (b)

Figure 4.5
General links showing link parameters and coordinate frames.
(a) General link with revolute joints.
(b) General link with prismatic joint.

constraints. It is unusual to find the general case in a robot manipulator, however, the kinematic analysis described in this chapter applies to the general case as well. Any link can be characterized by four **link parameters**:

1. the length of the link (the distance, along the common normal, between the joint axis): l_n,
2. the twist angle between the joint axes: α_n,
3. the angle between the links: θ_n,
4. the distance between the links (the displacement, along the joint axis, between the links) d_n.

The **common normal** of a link (Figure 4.5(a)) is the shortest line which is orthogonal to the axes of the joints at the ends of the link (z_{n-1} and z_n). The **length of the link** is the length of the common normal. The **twist angle** is the angle that would exist between the joint axes if the origins of the joint frames were coincident. The **angle between the links** is the angle between the common normals of successive links (x_{n-1} and x_n). The **distance between the links** is the distance along the axis of the joint (z_{n-1}), between the intersections of the common normals of the links with the joint axis. The link parameter which can be varied is called the **joint variable**. Link parameters for the links of a manipulator are stored in tabular form (Figure 4.6(d)). For a revolute joint, the joint variable is the angle between the links, and for a prismatic joint, the joint variable is the distance between the links.

In the preceding examples, we examined a number of link configurations where some of the link parameters were zero. For a prismatic joint, the length of the link (l_n) is usually zero. The general case for the prismatic joint (Figure 4.5(b) (solid line)), however, does give a value to the length of the link n. On the other hand, if the origins of the link coordinates frames are assigned according to the dashed lines in Figure 4.5(b), the length of link n is zero, and the length of link $n-1$ has been increased to compensate. In practice, the axes of joint n (the prismatic joint) and the axis of joint $n+1$ (the following revolute joint) often intersect and this problem ceases to exist, because the two possible locations for the origin of coordinate frame n coincide.

4.4   Assignment of coordinate frames

The first step in the direct kinematic algorithm (Algorithm 4.1) is to move the manipulator to its **zero position**. The zero position of the manipulator is the position where all the joint variables are zero. A revolute joint is in its zero position when the x axes of the link coordinate frames are parallel and have the same direction. A prismatic joint is in its zero position when the distance between the links is minimum, that is, the joints are as close together as they can be. For revolute joints, this is a circular description, because the zero position depends upon the assignment of the coordinate frames, and vice versa. Thus, the assignment of frames often tends to be an iterative process. Also, some manipulators have several zero positions (see Section 4.15).

The second step in the direct kinematics algorithm is to assign a coordinate frame to each link in the manipulator. Coordinate frames are assigned in accordance with the convention developed by Denavit and Hartenberg (1955) for spatial mechanisms.

Algorithm 4.2   Algorithm for assigning coordinate frames (based on Paul, 1981)

1. Starting at the base, number the links from 0 to n, where n is the number of the links. The base is link 0 (Figures 4.6(a), 4.7(a)).

2. One coordinate system is assigned to each link, each coordinate system is orthogonal, and the axes obey the right-hand rule (see Figure 3.4).

3. The base coordinate frame (R or O) is assigned with axes parallel to the world coordinate frame. The origin of the base frame is coincident with the origin of joint 1 (see Note 1). This assumes that the axis of the first joint is normal to the xy plane.

4. Coordinate frames are attached to the link at the distal joint, (the joint farthest from the base). A frame is internal to the link it is attached to, and the succeeding link moves relative to it. Thus, coordinate frame 1 is at joint 2: the joint which connects link 1 to link 2. (see Note 2)

5. The origin of the frame is located at the intersection of the common normal (the normal to the axes of the joints) and the axis of the distal joint. If the

axes of the joints are parallel, then the position of the origin is chosen to make the distance between the links (d_n) zero, or minimum if there is an offset between the links (see Section 4.16). If the joint axes intersect, the origin is placed at the intersection of the axes. For a prismatic joint (Figure 4.5(b)), follow the procedure for revolute joints (see Note 3).

6. The z axis is coincident with the joint axis. For a prismatic joint, the direction of the z axis is in the direction of motion away from the joint. For a revolute joint, the direction of the z axis is determined from the positive direction of rotation around the z axis. This definition is ambiguous, as the designer chooses the positive direction of rotation. In this book, the direction of the z axes is choosen such that the twist angle is minimum and positive (Figure 4.7) where possible.

7. The x axis is parallel to the common normal between the joint axes of the link. In the case of parallel axes, the x axis is coincident with the centre line of the link. If the axes intersect, there is no unique common normal, and the x axis is parallel, or anti-parallel, to the vector cross product of the z axes for the preceding link and this link ($z_{n-1} \times z_n$). In many cases this results in the x axis being in the same direction as the x axis for the previous link (the direction defined by placing the manipulator in the zero position). At this point, you should check that the selected zero position is consistent with the allocation of the x axis.

8. Finally, the direction of the y axis can be found using the right-hand rule.

9. A coordinate frame is attached to the end of the final link (n), usually within the end effector or tool. If the robot has an articulated hand, or changes end effectors regularly, it may be necessary to locate this coordinate frame at the tool plate, and have a separate hand transformation (see Note 4). The z axis of this frame is in the same direction as the z axis of the frame assigned to the last joint ($n-1$).

Notes

1 Paul (1981) makes the base coordinate frame coincident with coordinate frame 1, and considers the displacement between joints 1 and 2 to be part of the transformation of the robot with respect to the world coordinate frame, on the assumption that the displacement is fixed. In practice, flexing occurs in links, due to the compliance of the arm, changes the transform. Also, when an arm is attached to a mobile robot the transformation to world coordinates is no longer constant. Including the displacement of the link in the manipulator transform decouples these effects.

2 Some books (Wolovich, 1987 and Craig, 1986) use a different convention for numbering the coordinate frames, which results in a different set of A matrices.

3 Paul (1981) uses a different method, because, for a theoretical prismatic joint the direction of the axis is defined, but its position in space is not defined. The length of the link (l_n) is set to zero. Actually, it is absorbed in l_{n-1}. In this case (dashed lines in Figure 4.5(b)), we find the location of the origin of coordinate frame n by assuming the prismatic joint is a revolute joint, with the same joint axis. Then we locate the origin of coordinate frame $n-1$ at a distance d_n from the origin of coordinate frame n, along a vector, through the origin of coordinate frame n, parallel to the axis of the prismatic joint. In many robots, the axes of joints n and $n+1$ intersect and the two cases reduce to one.

4 Paul (1981) locates frame n coincident with the frame $n-1$, not at the end of the link, because the rotation, or displacement, of the last link takes place with respect to the frame $n-1$. In this situation, an extra transformation is required to relate the hand coordinate frame to frame n.

186 · *Kinematics: Manipulator Position*

Figure 4.6
Type 1 two-link manipulator
(Horn, 1975).
(a) Manipulator in zero
position; (b) Assignment of
coordinate frames; (c)
Workspace; (d) Link
parameters; (e) 3D
representation e.g. SCARA
robot.

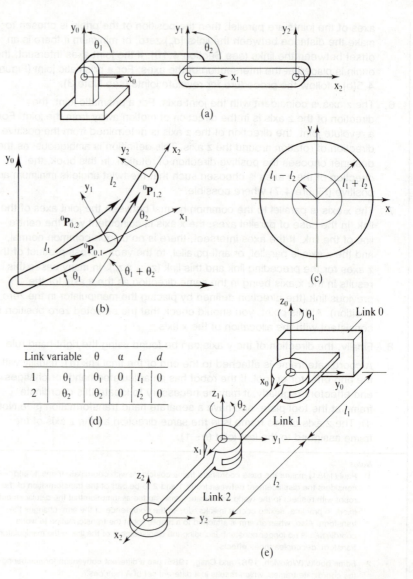

Link variable	θ	α	l	d
1	θ_1	θ_1	0	l_1	0
2	θ_2	θ_2	0	l_2	0

(d)

A number of two-link manipulator configurations are shown in
Figures 4.6 to 4.10. These configurations of linkages can be combined to
form the more complex manipulators found in industry. The type 1 two-link
manipulator (Figure 4.6) operates in two dimensions. The assignment of axes
in two dimensions (Figure 4.6(a)) is the same as for three dimensions (Figure
4.6(e)), but the different orientations of the two- and three-dimensional axes
result in different physical zero positions.

4.5 Trigonometric solution

Simple manipulators, such as the **type 1 two-link manipulator** (Figure 4.6(b)), can be analysed using simple trigonometry, rather than homogeneous transformation equations. For complex manipulators the trigonometric relationships between links are difficult to visualize, and homogeneous transforms are used. Both methods produce the same results. To demonstrate trigonometric methods, we will develop a geometric model for the type 1 two-link manipulator.

This robot can be described with a vector equation:

$$^0p_{0,2} = {}^0p_{0,1} + {}^0p_{1,2} \tag{4.2}$$

where $^0p_{i,j}$ is the vector from the origin of frame i to the origin of frame j as seen from the reference frame.

With simple trigonometry, we can find the x and y components of the vectors $^0p_{0,1}$ and $^0p_{0,2}$. When these values are substituted into Equation 4.2, we obtain the geometric model of the robot (Equation 4.5).

$$^0p_{0,1} = (l_1\cos(\theta_1),\ l_1\sin(\theta_1)) \tag{4.3}$$

$$^0p_{1,2} = (l_2\cos(\theta_1 + \theta_2),\ l_2\sin(\theta_1 + \theta_2)) \tag{4.4}$$

$$^0p_{0,2} = \begin{bmatrix} p_x \\ p_y \end{bmatrix} = \begin{bmatrix} x \\ y \end{bmatrix} = \begin{bmatrix} l_1\cos(\theta_1) + l_2\cos(\theta_1 + \theta_2) \\ l_1\sin(\theta_1) + l_2\sin(\theta_1 + \theta_2) \end{bmatrix} \tag{4.5}$$

The orientation of the second link is the sum of the joint angles. This geometric model relates the Cartesian coordinates of the end effector (Cartesian space) to the joint angles (joint space). Thus, it can be used, to calculate the Cartesian coordinates of the manipulator (position of the end of the links) from the joint coordinates (angles). The work space of this robot is a flat disc (Figure 4.6(c)), where the maximum radius equals the sum of the lengths of the linkages, and the minimum radius equals the difference between the length of the linkages. In practice, a manipulator of this type is usually constrained to less than 360° rotation, and the second link is shorter than the first.

4.6 A matrices

The third step in the direct kinematic algorithm (Algorithm 4.1) is to represent the homogeneous transformations between joints with **A** matrices. We saw that the transformation from one joint to the next can be characterized by four link parameters. A general **A** matrix (Equation 4.6) can be specified by multiplying the transformations which describe the effect of these para-

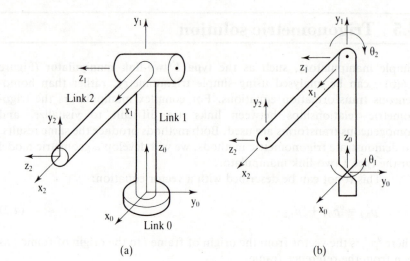

(a)   (b)

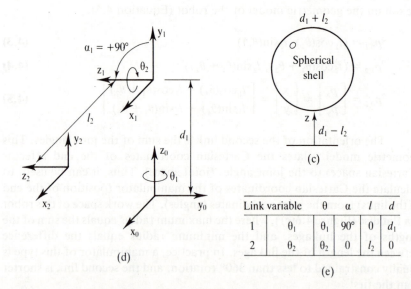

(d)

Link variable	θ	α	l	d
1	θ_1	θ_1	90°	0	d_1
2	θ_2	θ_2	0	l_2	0

(e)

meters. When we relocate from frame $n-1$ to frame n (that is, from joint n
to joint $n+1$), the following transformations occur (Figure 4.5(a)):

- a rotation about the z_{n-1} axis by the angle between the links (θ_n),
- a translation along the z_{n-1} axis of the distance between the links (d_n),
- a translation along the x_n axis (rotated x_{n-1} axis) of the length of the
  link (l_n),
- a rotation about the x_n axis of the twist angle (α_n).

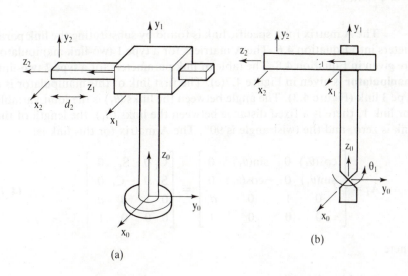

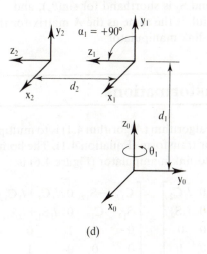

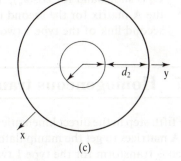

Figure 4.8
Type 3 two-link manipulator:
(a) manipulator in zero
position; (b) line diagram; (c)
workspace; (d) assignment
of coordinate frames; (e) link
parameters.

Link variable	θ	α	l	d
1	θ_1	$90°$	0	d_1
2	d_2	0	0	d_2

(e)

$$\mathbf{A}_n = \mathbf{Rot}(z,\theta)\mathbf{Trans}(0,0,d)\mathbf{Trans}(l,0,0)\mathbf{Rot}(x,\alpha)$$

$$= \begin{bmatrix} \cos(\theta) & -\sin(\theta) & 0 & 0 \\ \sin(\theta) & \cos(\theta) & 0 & 0 \\ 0 & 0 & 0 & 0 \\ 0 & 0 & 0 & 0 \end{bmatrix} \begin{bmatrix} 1 & 0 & 0 & l \\ 0 & 1 & 0 & 0 \\ 0 & 0 & 1 & d \\ 0 & 0 & 0 & 1 \end{bmatrix} \begin{bmatrix} 1 & 0 & 0 & 0 \\ 0 & \cos(\alpha) & -\sin(\alpha) & 0 \\ 0 & \sin(\alpha) & \cos(\alpha) & 0 \\ 0 & 0 & 0 & 1 \end{bmatrix}$$

$$= \begin{bmatrix} \cos(\theta) & -\sin(\theta)\cos(\alpha) & \sin(\theta)\sin(\alpha) & l\cos(\theta) \\ \sin(\theta) & \cos(\theta)\cos(\alpha) & -\cos(\theta)\sin(\alpha) & l\sin(\theta) \\ 0 & \sin(\alpha) & \cos(\alpha) & d \\ 0 & 0 & 0 & 1 \end{bmatrix} \qquad (4.6)$$

The **A** matrix for a specific link is found by substituting the link parameters into Equation 4.6. The **A** matrices for a type 1 two-link manipulator are given in Equation 4.8. The table of link parameters for a **type 2 two-link manipulator** is given in Figure 4.7(e). The first link of this manipulator is a type 3 link (Figure 4.3). The angle between the links (θ_1) is the joint variable for link 1, there is a fixed distance between the links (d_1), the length of the link is zero, and the twist angle is 90°. The **A** matrix for this link is:

$$
\mathbf{A}_1 =
\begin{bmatrix}
\cos(\theta_1) & 0 & \sin(\theta_1) & 0 \\
\sin(\theta_1) & 0 & -\cos(\theta_1) & 0 \\
0 & 1 & 0 & d_1 \\
0 & 0 & 0 & 1
\end{bmatrix}
=
\begin{bmatrix}
C_1 & 0 & S_1 & 0 \\
S_1 & 0 & -C_1 & 0 \\
0 & 1 & 0 & d_1 \\
0 & 0 & 0 & 1
\end{bmatrix}
\tag{4.7}
$$

where

C_n is shorthand for $\cos(\theta_n)$, and S_n is shorthand for $\sin(\theta_n)$, and the **A** matrix for the second link is the same as the **A** matrix for the second link of the type 1 two-link manipulator.

4.7 Homogeneous transformations

The fifth step in the direct kinematic algorithm (Algorithm 4.1) is to multiply the **A** matrices to get the manipulator transform (Equation 4.1). The homogeneous transform for the type 1 two-link manipulator (Figure 4.6) is:

$$
{}^{R}\mathbf{T}_{H} =
\begin{bmatrix}
C_1 & -S_1 & 0 & l_1 C_1 \\
S_1 & C_1 & 0 & l_1 S_1 \\
0 & 0 & 1 & 0 \\
0 & 0 & 0 & 1
\end{bmatrix}
\begin{bmatrix}
C_2 & -S_2 & 0 & l_2 C_2 \\
S_2 & C_2 & 0 & l_2 S_2 \\
0 & 0 & 0 & 0 \\
0 & 0 & 0 & 1
\end{bmatrix}
=
\begin{bmatrix}
C_{12} & -S_{12} & 0 & l_1 C_1 + l_2 C_{12} \\
S_{12} & C_{12} & 0 & l_1 S_1 + l_2 S_{12} \\
0 & 0 & 1 & 0 \\
0 & 0 & 0 & 1
\end{bmatrix}
\tag{4.8}
$$

where

S_{12} is an abbreviation for $\sin(\theta_1 + \theta_2)$, and C_{12} is an abbreviation for $\cos(\theta_1 + \theta_2)$

It will be shown later (Section 4.8) that this homogeneous transform leads to the same result as the trigonometric solution (Equation 4.4) for the type 1 two-link manipulator. For a second example, consider the **type 3 two-link manipulator** (Figure 4.8), which moves in three dimensional space, and has a prismatic joint as well as a revolute joint.

$$
{}^R\mathbf{T}_H =
\begin{bmatrix}
C_1 & 0 & S_1 & 0 \\
S_1 & 0 & -C_1 & 0 \\
0 & 1 & 0 & d_1 \\
0 & 0 & 0 & 1
\end{bmatrix}
\begin{bmatrix}
1 & 0 & 0 & 0 \\
0 & 1 & 0 & 0 \\
0 & 0 & 1 & d_2 \\
0 & 0 & 0 & 1
\end{bmatrix}
=
\begin{bmatrix}
C_1 & 0 & S_1 & d_2 S_1 \\
S_1 & 0 & -C_1 & -d_2 C_1 \\
0 & 1 & 0 & d_1 \\
0 & 0 & 0 & 1
\end{bmatrix}
\tag{4.9}
$$

4.8 Direct kinematics

So far in this chapter, we have calculated the homogeneous transform which defines the manipulator transform in terms of joint space. To complete our kinematic analysis, this joint space description of the manipulator must be related to the Cartesian space description. In joint space, the manipulator transform is a function of the joint variables, one for each link. In Cartesian space, the manipulator transform is a function of the position and orientation (location) of the tool plate. The direct kinematic model describes the Cartesian coordinates and orientation angles of the tool plate in terms of the joint variables. Conversely, the indirect kinematic model describes the joint variables in terms of the Cartesian coordinates and orientation angles of the tool plate (the inverse of the direct kinematic model).

The location of the tool plate (or hand) in Cartesian space is described by the general transformation equation (Equation 3.28). The position and orientation of the hand in joint space is described by the manipulator transformation equation (Equation 4.1). Also, the position and orientation of the manipulator in Cartesian space can be described with an orientation transform (Equation 3.35). The kinematic model of the manipulator is obtained by equating these three equations:

$$
{}^R\mathbf{T}_H =
\begin{bmatrix}
x & y & z & p \\
0 & 0 & 0 & 1
\end{bmatrix}
=
\begin{bmatrix}
x_x & y_x & z_x & p_x \\
x_y & y_y & z_y & p_y \\
x_z & y_z & z_z & p_z \\
0 & 0 & 0 & 1
\end{bmatrix}
=
\begin{bmatrix}
1 & 0 & 0 & p_x \\
0 & 1 & 0 & p_y \\
0 & 0 & 1 & p_z \\
0 & 0 & 0 & 1
\end{bmatrix}
\begin{bmatrix}
\text{Orientation} \\
\text{transform.} \\
\\
\text{Equation 3.34}
\end{bmatrix}
\tag{4.10}
$$

We find the orientation transform for the type 1 two-link manipulator (Figure 4.6) by substituting values for the orientation angles into the above transformation equation. As this manipulator can move only in the xy plane, there is a rotation about the z axis of $\phi°$, and the rotations about the x and y axes are fixed at $0°$. The orientation transformation matrix (Equation 4.11) reduces to a rotation about the z axis (Equation 3.21).

$$
\mathbf{RPY}(\phi, \theta, \psi) = \mathbf{Rot}(z, \phi)\mathbf{Rot}(y, \theta)\mathbf{Rot}(x, \psi)
\tag{4.11}
$$

$$= \mathbf{Rot}(z, \phi)\mathbf{Rot}(y, 0)\mathbf{Rot}(x, 0)$$

$$= \begin{bmatrix} C(\phi) & -S(\phi) & 0 & 0 \\ S(\phi) & C(\phi) & 0 & 0 \\ 0 & 0 & 1 & 0 \\ 0 & 0 & 0 & 1 \end{bmatrix} \tag{4.12}$$

We can enumerate the kinematic model by assigning values to the 12 components which make up the four vectors in the general transformation matrix, and by assigning values to the orientation transform. For the type 1 two-link manipulator, the following model is obtained:

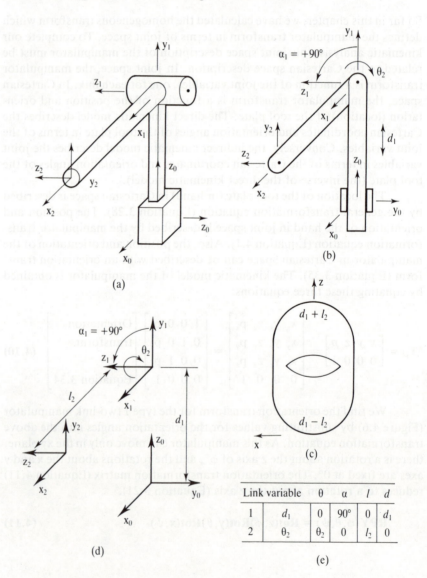

Figure 4.9
Type 4 two-link manipulator.
(a) Manipulator in zero position;
(b) Line diagram;
(c) Workspace;
(d) Assignment of coordinate frames;
(e) Link parameters.

Link variable	θ	α	l	d
1	d_1	0	90°	0	d_1
2	θ_2	θ_2	0	l_2	0

(a)

(b)

(c)

(d)

(e)

$$^R T_H = \begin{bmatrix} x_x & y_x & z_x & p_x \\ x_y & y_y & z_y & p_y \\ x_z & y_z & z_z & p_z \\ 0 & 0 & 0 & 1 \end{bmatrix} = \begin{bmatrix} C_{12} & -S_{12} & 0 & l_1 C_1 + l_2 C_{12} \\ S_{12} & C_{12} & 0 & l_1 S_1 + l_2 S_{12} \\ 0 & 0 & 1 & 0 \\ 0 & 0 & 0 & 1 \end{bmatrix}$$

$$= \begin{bmatrix} C(\phi) & -S(\phi) & 0 & p_x \\ S(\phi) & C(\phi) & 0 & p_y \\ 0 & 0 & 1 & p_z \\ 0 & 0 & 0 & 1 \end{bmatrix} \tag{4.13}$$

By equating the terms in these matrices, we obtain values for the elements of the vector $^0 p_{0,2}$, the vector which describes the location of the hand with respect to the reference frame, and for the orientation angle, ϕ. The result is the same as we obtained with the trigonometric model discussed in Section 4.5.

$$^0 p_{0,2} = \begin{bmatrix} p_x \\ p_y \end{bmatrix} = \begin{bmatrix} x \\ y \end{bmatrix} = \begin{bmatrix} l_1 \cos(\theta_1) + l_2 \cos(\theta_1 + \theta_2) \\ l_1 \sin(\theta_1) + l_2 \sin(\theta_1 + \theta_2) \end{bmatrix} \tag{4.14}$$

$$C(\phi) = \cos(\phi) = C_{12} = \cos(\theta_1 + \theta_2) \tag{4.15}$$

$$\therefore \phi = \theta_1 + \theta_2 \tag{4.16}$$

As a second example, consider the **type 4 two-link manipulator** (Figure 4.9), which contains a prismatic joint as well as a revolute joint. The transform of this manipulator differs from the transform of the type 3 two-link manipulator (Equation 4.9) because the joint configuration is different. The orientation transform includes a fixed rotation of $0°$ about the z_0 axis, a variable rotation of $-\theta$ about the y_0 axis (θ_2), and a fixed rotation of $90°$ about the x_0 axis (α_1). These rotations are more easily visualized by comparing frame 2 to frame 0. A formal method for calculating orientation angles is developed in Section 4.10.

$$\mathbf{RPY}(\phi, \theta, \psi) = \mathbf{Rot}(z, 0)\mathbf{Rot}(y, -\theta)\mathbf{Rot}(x, 90) \tag{4.17}$$

$$= \begin{bmatrix} C(\theta) & -S(\theta) & 0 & 0 \\ 0 & 0 & -1 & 0 \\ S(\theta) & C(\theta) & 0 & 0 \\ 0 & 0 & 0 & 1 \end{bmatrix} \tag{4.18}$$

$$^R T_H = \begin{bmatrix} C_2 & -S_2 & 0 & l_2 C_2 \\ 0 & 0 & -1 & 0 \\ S_2 & C_2 & 0 & d_1 + l_2 S_2 \\ 0 & 0 & 0 & 1 \end{bmatrix} = \begin{bmatrix} x_x & y_x & z_x & p_x \\ x_y & y_y & z_y & p_y \\ x_z & y_z & z_z & p_z \\ 0 & 0 & 0 & 1 \end{bmatrix}$$

$$= \begin{bmatrix} C(\theta) & -S(\theta) & 0 & p_x \\ 0 & 0 & -1 & p_y \\ S(\theta) & C(\theta) & 0 & p_z \\ 0 & 0 & 0 & 1 \end{bmatrix} \tag{4.19}$$

$$p_x = l_2 C_2 \tag{4.20}$$

$$p_z = d_1 + l_2 S_2 \tag{4.21}$$

$$\theta = -\theta_2 \tag{4.22}$$

By examining this model, you will see that we have a two dimensional manipulator, whose motion is restricted to the xz plane (Equations 4.20 and 4.21), because the value of p_y is zero, and the orientation of the hand is the same as the joint variable for link 2 (Equation 4.22).

Finally, we consider a manipulator containing solely prismatic joints: the **type 5 two-link manipulator** (Figure 4.10). When we look at the coordinate frame model of this manipulator (Figure 4.10(d)), we see that frame 2 has been rotated by 90° (α_1) around the x_0 axis, translated a distance d_1 in the z_0 direction, and translated a distance $-d_2$ in the y_0 direction. The orientation transform comprises a fixed rotation around the x axis of α_1.

$$\mathbf{RPY}(\phi, \theta, \psi) = \mathbf{Rot}(z, 0)\mathbf{Rot}(y, 0)\mathbf{Rot}(x, 90) \tag{4.23}$$

$$^R\mathbf{T}_H = \mathbf{A}_1\mathbf{A}_2 = \begin{bmatrix} 1 & 0 & 0 & 0 \\ 0 & 0 & -1 & -d_2 \\ 0 & 1 & 0 & d_1 \\ 0 & 0 & 0 & 1 \end{bmatrix} = \begin{bmatrix} x_x & y_x & z_x & p_x \\ x_y & y_y & z_y & p_y \\ x_z & y_z & z_z & p_z \\ 0 & 0 & 0 & 1 \end{bmatrix}$$

$$= \mathbf{Trans}(y, -d_2)\mathbf{Trans}(z, d_1)\mathbf{Rot}(x, 90) \tag{4.24}$$

By equating the elements in the matrices, we solve the Cartesian coordinates in terms of the link variables:

$$p_y = -d_2 \tag{4.25}$$

$$p_z = d_1 \tag{4.26}$$

$$\psi = 90° \tag{4.27}$$

A by-product of calculating the orientation transformation matrix is that it provides a cross check on the manipulator transformation matrix: the elements that have zero value must do so in both matrices; the sign of the elements must be the same in both matrices and simple elements consisting of one transcendental function must match in both matrices.

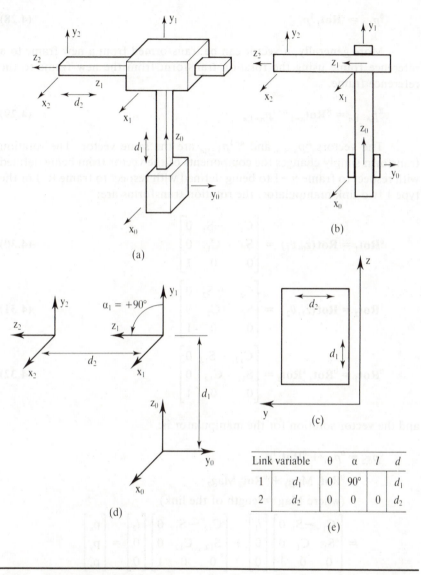

Figure 4.10
Type 5 two-link manipulator.
(a) Manipulator in zero position;
(b) Line diagram;
(c) Workspace;
(d) Assignment of coordinate frames;
(e) Link parameters.

Link variable	θ	α	l	d
1	d_1	0	90°		d_1
2	d_2	0	0	0	d_2

(e)

4.9   Vector solution

In Section 4.5, we developed a trigonometric solution for the type 1 two-link manipulator using vectors (Equation 4.2). Vectors can only be added if they are defined with respect to the same coordinate frame. The vector describing the second link can be transformed from frame 1 to frame 0 with a rotation transform. Note, though, that the physical vector does not change, just its description.

$$^0p_{1,2} = {}^0\text{Rot}_1\, {}^1p_{1,2} \tag{4.28}$$

More generally, a vector can be transformed from a new frame to a reference frame using the rotation transform from the new frame to the reference frame.

$$^Rp_{n-1,n} = {}^R\text{Rot}_{n-1}\, {}^{n-1}p_{n-1,n} \tag{4.29}$$

The vectors $^Rp_{n-1,n}$ and $^{n-1}p_{n-1,n}$ are the same vector. The rotation transform simply changes the components of the vector from being defined with respect to frame $n-1$ to being defined with respect to frame R. For the type 1 two-link manipulator, the rotation transforms are:

$$^0\text{Rot}_1 = \text{Rot}(z_0, \theta_1) = \begin{bmatrix} C_1 & -S_1 & 0 \\ S_1 & C_1 & 0 \\ 0 & 0 & 1 \end{bmatrix} \tag{4.30}$$

$$^1\text{Rot}_2 = \text{Rot}(z_1, \theta_2) = \begin{bmatrix} C_2 & -S_2 & 0 \\ S_2 & C_2 & 0 \\ 0 & 0 & 1 \end{bmatrix} \tag{4.31}$$

$$^0\text{Rot}_2 = {}^0\text{Rot}_1\, {}^1\text{Rot}_2 = \begin{bmatrix} C_{12} & -S_{12} & 0 \\ S_{12} & C_{12} & 0 \\ 0 & 0 & 1 \end{bmatrix} \tag{4.32}$$

and the vector solution for the manipulator is:

$$
\begin{aligned}
^0p_{0,2} &= {}^0p_{0,1} + {}^0\text{Rot}_1\, {}^1p_{1,2} \\
&= {}^0\text{Rot}_1\, \text{Mag}_1 + {}^0\text{Rot}_2\, \text{Mag}_2 \\
&\quad \text{(where Mag = length of the link)} \\
&= \begin{bmatrix} C_1 & -S_1 & 0 \\ S_1 & C_1 & 0 \\ 0 & 0 & 1 \end{bmatrix} \begin{bmatrix} l_1 \\ 0 \\ 0 \end{bmatrix} + \begin{bmatrix} C_{12} & -S_{12} & 0 \\ S_{12} & C_{12} & 0 \\ 0 & 0 & 1 \end{bmatrix} \begin{bmatrix} l_2 \\ 0 \\ 0 \end{bmatrix} = \begin{bmatrix} p_x \\ p_y \\ p_z \end{bmatrix} \\
&= \begin{bmatrix} l_1 C_1 \\ l_1 S_1 \\ 0 \end{bmatrix} + \begin{bmatrix} l_2 C_{12} \\ l_2 S_{12} \\ 0 \end{bmatrix} = \begin{bmatrix} l_1 C_1 + l_2 C_{12} \\ l_1 S_1 + l_2 S_{12} \\ 0 \end{bmatrix}
\end{aligned} \tag{4.33}
$$

This gives the same solution obtained by the other methods.

4.10 Solving the general orientation transform

The examples of direct kinematic analysis worked in Section 4.8 were all restricted to a plane, and thus, the orientation matrix entailed only one orientation angle. In these simple cases, the orientation angle was solved by equating matrix elements. More general manipulators move in three dimensions, and consequently, orientation angles are not as easy to evaluate, because the matrix elements contain terms with multiple angles. Also, the orientation of a general vector is not easy to visualize, and hence, the process of decomposing orientation into three distinct rotations is difficult. To overcome both these difficulties, we will solve the general roll–pitch–yaw orientation transform (Equation 3.34) to obtain equations relating the orientation angles to the elements of the general transformation matrix (Equation 3.28). The orientation elements of the general transform are dimensionless, while the translation elements have the dimension of length.

$$
{}^{R}T_{H} = \begin{bmatrix} x_x & y_x & z_x & p_x \\ x_y & y_y & z_y & p_y \\ x_z & y_z & z_z & p_z \\ 0 & 0 & 0 & 1 \end{bmatrix} = \textbf{Trans}\,(p_x, p_y, p_z)\ \textbf{RPY}\,(\phi, \theta, \psi)
$$

$$
= \textbf{Trans}\,(p_x, p_y, p_z)\ \textbf{Rot}\,(z, \phi)\ \textbf{Rot}\,(y, \theta)\ \textbf{Rot}\,(x, \psi)
$$

$$
= \begin{bmatrix} C(\phi)C(\theta) & C(\phi)S(\theta)S(\psi) - S(\phi)C(\psi) & C(\phi)S(\theta)C(\psi) + S(\phi)S(\psi) & p_x \\ S(\phi)C(\theta) & S(\phi)S(\theta)S(\psi) + C(\phi)C(\psi) & S(\phi)S(\theta)C(\psi) - C(\phi)S(\psi) & p_y \\ -S(\theta) & C(\theta)S(\psi) & C(\theta)C(\psi) & p_z \\ 0 & 0 & 0 & 1 \end{bmatrix} \quad (4.34)
$$

We solve for the orientation angles by equating terms in these two matrices, as shown below.

$$x_z = -\sin(\theta) \tag{4.35}$$

$$\theta = -\sin^{-1}(x_z) \tag{4.36}$$

$$y_z = \cos(\theta)\sin(\psi) \tag{4.37}$$

$$\psi = \sin^{-1}(y_z/\cos(\theta)) \tag{4.38}$$

$$x_y = \sin(\phi)\cos(\theta) \tag{4.39}$$

$$\phi = \sin^{-1}(x_y/\cos(\theta)) \tag{4.40}$$

Window 4.1   Problems with transcendental functions

(a) $x = \cos(\phi)$ $\phi = \cos^{-1}(x)$

   1.   Accuracy is dependent on the angle – around $0°$ the accuracy is the least.

   2. $\cos(-\phi) = \cos(\phi)$. Thus, when using the inverse cosine function, the sign of the angle is undefined, resulting in redundant solutions.

   3. $\cos(\phi)$ is zero at $+90°$ and at $-90°$. Thus, division by $\cos(\phi)$ results in inaccuracy near these angles, and indeterminacy at these angles.

(b) $x = \sin(\phi)$ $\phi = \sin^{-1}(x)$

   1.   Accuracy is dependent on the angle – around $90°$ the accuracy is the least.

   2. $\sin(\phi)$ is zero at $0°$ and at $180°$. Thus, division by $\sin(\phi)$ results in inaccuracy near these angles, and indeterminacy at these angles.

(c) $x = \tan(\phi)$ $\phi = \tan^{-1}(x)$

   1. $\tan(\phi)$ approaches infinity at $+90°$ and at $-90°$. Thus, multiplication by $\tan(\phi)$ results in indeterminacy at these angles.

   2. $\tan(\phi)$ is zero at $0°$. Thus, division by $\tan(\phi)$ results in indeterminacy at these angles.

The above solutions for the orientation angles all suffer from the inaccuracies of the sine function when the angle approaches $90°$(Window 4.1), and two of the angles are undefined when $\theta = 90°$. These problems can be overcome using the atan2 function (Window 4.2). This function returns angles in the range $-\pi < =\theta < \pi$, when passed two signed arguments which specify the length and direction of two sides of a right triangle. To obtain equations for the orientation angles in terms of the atan2 function, we look for suitable equivalence relationships by manipulating Equation 4.34. Two new matrices can be obtained by premultiplying both matrices by the inverse of the first two terms in the orientation equation (Equation 4.34).

$$^R\mathbf{T}_H = \mathbf{Trans}\,(p_x, p_y, p_z)\,\mathbf{Rot}\,(z, \phi)\,\mathbf{Rot}\,(y, \theta)\,\mathbf{Rot}\,(x, \psi) \tag{4.41}$$

$$\mathbf{Rot}^{-1}(z, \phi)\,\mathbf{Trans}^{-1}(p_x, p_y, p_z)^R\mathbf{T}_H = \mathbf{Rot}(y, \theta)\mathbf{Rot}(x, \psi) \tag{4.42}$$

The inverse of the general transformation (Equation 3.43, repeated here for convenience) was calculated in Section 3.7. Using this equation, we calculate the inverse of the two matrices (Equation 4.43).

$$\mathbf{T}^{-1} = \begin{bmatrix} x_x & x_y & x_z & -\mathbf{p} \cdot \mathbf{x} \\ y_x & y_y & y_z & -\mathbf{p} \cdot \mathbf{y} \\ z_x & z_y & z_z & -\mathbf{p} \cdot \mathbf{z} \\ 0 & 0 & 0 & 1 \end{bmatrix} = \begin{bmatrix} x_x & x_y & x_z & -p_x x_x - p_y x_y - p_z x_z \\ y_x & y_y & y_z & -p_x y_x - p_y y_y - p_z y_z \\ z_x & z_y & z_z & -p_x z_x - p_y z_y - p_z z_z \\ 0 & 0 & 0 & 1 \end{bmatrix} \tag{3.43}$$

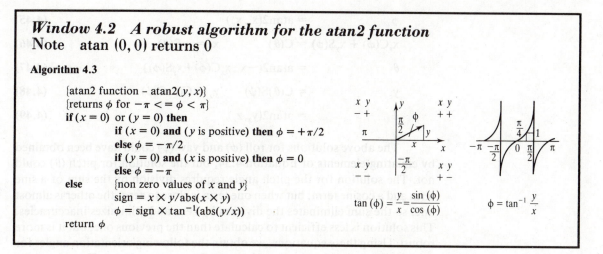

Window 4.2   A robust algorithm for the atan2 function
Note   atan (0, 0) returns 0

Algorithm 4.3

```
{atan2 function – atan2(y, x)}
{returns φ for −π <= φ < π}
if (x = 0) or (y = 0) then
        if (x = 0) and (y is positive) then φ = +π/2
        else φ = −π/2
        if (y = 0) and (x is positive) then φ = 0
        else φ = −π
else    {non zero values of x and y}
        sign = x × y/abs(x × y)
        φ = sign × tan⁻¹(abs(y/x))
return φ
```

$$\tan(\phi) = \frac{y}{x} = \frac{\sin(\phi)}{\cos(\phi)} \qquad \phi = \tan^{-1}\frac{y}{x}$$

$$
\begin{bmatrix}
C(\phi) & S(\phi) & 0 & 0 \\
-S(\phi) & C(\phi) & 0 & 0 \\
0 & 0 & 1 & 0 \\
0 & 0 & 0 & 1
\end{bmatrix}
\begin{bmatrix}
1 & 0 & 0 & -p_x \\
0 & 1 & 0 & -p_y \\
0 & 0 & 1 & -p_z \\
0 & 0 & 0 & 1
\end{bmatrix}
\begin{bmatrix}
x_x & y_x & z_x & p_x \\
x_y & y_y & z_y & p_y \\
x_z & y_z & z_z & p_z \\
0 & 0 & 0 & 1
\end{bmatrix}
$$

$$
=
\begin{bmatrix}
C(\theta) & 0 & S(\theta) & 0 \\
0 & 1 & 0 & 0 \\
-S(\theta) & 0 & C(\theta) & 0 \\
0 & 0 & 0 & 1
\end{bmatrix}
\begin{bmatrix}
1 & 0 & 0 & 0 \\
0 & C(\psi) & -S(\psi) & 0 \\
0 & S(\psi) & C(\psi) & 0 \\
0 & 0 & 0 & 1
\end{bmatrix}
$$

$$
=
\begin{bmatrix}
x_x C(\phi) + x_y S(\phi) & y_x C(\phi) + y_y S(\phi) & z_x C(\phi) + z_y S(\phi) & 0 \\
x_y C(\phi) - x_x S(\phi) & y_y C(\phi) - y_x S(\phi) & z_y C(\phi) - z_x S(\phi) & 0 \\
x_z & y_z & z_z & p_z \\
0 & 0 & 0 & 1
\end{bmatrix}
$$

$$
=
\begin{bmatrix}
C(\theta) & S(\theta)S(\psi) & S(\theta)C(\psi) & 0 \\
0 & C(\psi) & -S(\psi) & 0 \\
-S(\theta) & C(\theta)S(\psi) & C(\theta)C(\psi) & 0 \\
0 & 0 & 0 & 1
\end{bmatrix}
\tag{4.43}
$$

Again, solutions for the orientation angles are obtained by equating elements in the two matrices.

$$x_y C(\phi) - x_x S(\phi) = 0 \tag{4.44}$$

$$\phi = \text{atan2}(x_y, x_x) \tag{4.45}$$

$$x_x C(\phi) + x_y S(\phi) = C(\theta) \qquad x_z = -S(\theta) \tag{4.46}$$

$$\theta = \text{atan2}(-x_z, x_x C(\phi) + x_y S(\phi)) \tag{4.47}$$

$$y_z = C(\theta) S(\psi) \qquad z_z = C(\theta) C(\psi) \tag{4.48}$$

$$\psi = \text{atan2}(y_z, z_z) \tag{4.49}$$

The above solutions for roll (ϕ) and yaw (ψ) could have been obtained by equating elements of Equation 4.34, but the solution for pitch (θ) could not. The solution for the pitch angle requires division by the sum of a sine term and a cosine term, but when one term is close to zero, the other is almost one, so the sum eliminates the division by zero and minimizes inaccuracies. This solution is less efficient to calculate than the previous one, but it is more robust. Using these equations, we obtain the following orientation angles for the type 1 two-link manipulator from the forward transform (Equation 4.8). They agree with our previous calculations (Equation 4.13).

$$\phi = \text{atan2}(S_{12}, C_{12}) = \theta_1 + \theta_2 \tag{4.50}$$

$$\theta = \text{atan2}(-0, C_{12}C(\phi) + S_{12}S(\phi)) = 0 \tag{4.51}$$

$$\psi = \text{atan2}(0, 0) = 0 \tag{4.52}$$

The type 2 two-link manipulator (Figure 4.7) has a three-dimensional workspace, but the orientation of the end effector within that space is constrained to two degrees of freedom. By substituting components of the transformation matrix for this manipulator (Equation 4.53) into the above equations, we obtain the following orientation angles.

$$^R\mathbf{T}_H = \begin{bmatrix} C_1C_2 & -C_1S_2 & S_1 & l_2C_1C_2 \\ S_1C_2 & -S_1S_2 & -C_1 & l_2S_1C_2 \\ S_2 & C_2 & 0 & d_1+l_2S_2 \\ 0 & 0 & 0 & 1 \end{bmatrix} = \begin{bmatrix} x_x & y_x & z_x & p_x \\ x_y & y_y & z_y & p_y \\ x_z & y_z & z_z & p_z \\ 0 & 0 & 0 & 1 \end{bmatrix} \tag{4.53}$$

$$\phi = \text{atan2}(S_1C_2, C_1C_2) = \text{atan2}(S_1, C_1) = \theta_1 \tag{4.54}$$

$$\theta = \text{atan2}(-S_2, C_1C_2C(\phi)+S_1C_2S(\phi)) = \text{atan2}(-S_2, C_2C(\theta_1 - \phi)) \tag{4.55}$$

$$\psi = \text{atan2}(C_2, 0) = \pi/2 \tag{4.56}$$

This completes the direct kinematic algorithm. We have been able to define both the position and orientation of the end of the manipulator in terms of the joint coordinates. Next, we will develop the inverse solution.

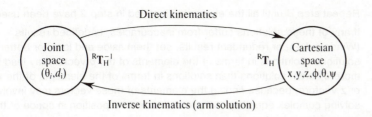

Direct kinematics

Inverse kinematics (arm solution)

Figure 4.11
Mapping from joint to
Cartesian space using a
kinematic model.

4.11   Inverse kinematics

Given a required location in Cartesian space for the end of a manipulator, we
need to find values for the joint variables which will achieve this required
position and orientation. To do this, the joint variables have to be expressed
in terms of the Cartesian space description (Figure 4.11). This is known as
inverse kinematics, and the solution is called the **arm solution.** The arm
solution can often be found from the manipulator transform using the
inverse kinematic heuristic (Algorithm 4.4). This heuristic is a method for
finding solutions, but it does not guarantee a solution. Two people using the
heuristic may end up with different solutions, and some solutions may be
redundant. The heuristic can be used to find either a general solution for a
manipulator or a solution for a particular configuration of a manipulator.

Algorithm 4.4   Inverse Kinematic Heuristic (To find equations for the joint variables in terms of the Cartesian space description)

1. Equate the general transformation matrix to the manipulator transformation
    matrix. If a particular, rather than a general, solution is required a matrix
    describing the desired position and orientation of the end of the
    manipulator is equated to the manipulator transformation matrix (similar to
    solving for the orientation angles).

2. Look at both matrices for:
    (a)   elements which contain only one joint variable;
    (b)   pairs of elements which will produce an expression in only one
          joint variable when divided. In particular look for divisions that
          result in the atan2 function;
    (c)   elements, or combinations of elements, that can be simplified
          using trigonometric identities (Appendix 1.2 and Appendix 5).

3. Having selected an element, equate it to the corresponding element in the
    other matrix to produce an equation. Solve this equation to find a
    description of one joint variable in terms of the elements of the general
    transformation matrix.

4. Repeat step 3 until all the elements identified in step 2 have been used.

5. If any of these solutions suffer from inaccuracies, undefined results (Window 4.2), or redundant results, set them aside and look for better solutions. Solutions in terms of the elements of the *p* vector may lead to more efficient solutions than solutions in terms of the elements of the *x*, *y*, or *z* vectors, because finding the elements of these vectors may involve solving complex equations, whereas the desired position in space of the manipulator is known.

6. If there are more joint angles to be found, premultiply both sides of the matrix equation by the inverse of the **A** matrix for the first link to produce a new set of equivalent matrix elements. Alternatively, you can postmultiply both sides by the *inverse* of the **A** matrix for the last link in the manipulator, if you think doing so will lead to simpler results.

7. Repeat Steps 2 to 6 until either solutions to all the joint variables have been found, or you have run out of **A** matrices to premultiply (or postmultiply).

8. If a suitable solution cannot be found for a joint variable, choose one of those discarded in step 5, taking note of regions where problems may occur.

9. If a solution cannot be found for a joint variable in terms of the elements of the manipulator transform, it may be that the manipulator cannot achieve the specified position and orientation: the position is outside the manipulator's workspace. Also, theoretical solutions may not be physically attainable because of mechanical limits on the range of joint variables.

To illustrate the use of the inverse kinematic heuristic in finding the general solution for a manipulator, we will find the arm solution for the type 2 two-link manipulator (Figure 4.7).

$$
{}^R T_H = \begin{bmatrix} C_1C_2 & -C_1S_2 & S_1 & l_2C_1C_2 \\ S_1C_2 & -S_1S_2 & -C_1 & l_2S_1C_2 \\ S_2 & C_2 & 0 & d_1+l_2S_2 \\ 0 & 0 & 0 & 1 \end{bmatrix} = \begin{bmatrix} x_x & y_x & z_x & p_x \\ x_y & y_y & z_y & p_y \\ x_z & y_z & z_z & p_z \\ 0 & 0 & 0 & 1 \end{bmatrix} \tag{4.57}
$$

We solve for θ_1 by dividing the expressions for p_y and p_x. We can also solve for θ_1 in terms of x_y and x_x, but this is less efficient if these elements have to be calculated just to find the value of θ_1.

$$
\frac{p_y}{p_x} = \frac{l_2S_1C_2}{l_2C_1C_2} \tag{4.58}
$$

$$
\therefore \theta_1 = \text{atan2}(p_y, p_x) \tag{4.59}
$$

We can solve for θ_2 using the expression for p_z, but the result includes an arcsine, and is thus inaccurate around 90°. To find a better solution for θ_2, premultiply both matrices by the inverse of the first $\mathbf{A}$ matrix. This solution (Equation 4.62) is less efficient, but more robust. It does, however, use the solution for θ_1, placing a greater accuracy requirement on θ_1.

$$\mathbf{A}_1^{-1}\,{}^R\mathbf{T}_H = \mathbf{A}_2$$

$$\begin{bmatrix} x_xC_1 + x_yS_1 & y_xC_1 + y_yS_1 & z_xC_1 + z_yS_1 & p_xC_1 + p_yS_1 \\ x_z & y_z & z_z & p_z - d_1 \\ x_xS_1 - x_yC_1 & y_xS_1 - y_yC_1 & z_xS_1 - z_yC_1 & p_xS_1 - p_yC_1 \\ 0 & 0 & 0 & 1 \end{bmatrix}$$

$$= \begin{bmatrix} C_2 & -S_2 & 0 & l_2C_2 \\ S_2 & C_2 & 0 & l_2S_2 \\ 0 & 0 & 1 & 0 \\ 0 & 0 & 0 & 1 \end{bmatrix} \tag{4.60}$$

$$p_xC_1 + p_yS_1 = l_2C_2 \qquad p_z - d_1 = l_2S_2 \tag{4.61}$$

$$\therefore \theta_2 = \operatorname{atan2}(p_z - d_1,\, p_xC_1 + p_yS_1) \tag{4.62}$$

As an example of one problem experienced when using the inverse kinematic heuristic to find the general solution for a manipulator, we will solve the type 1 two-link manipulator (Figure 4.6). As in previous examples involving this manipulator, it is easier to find the arm solution using trigonometric methods (Section 4.5).

$$^R\mathbf{T}_H = \begin{bmatrix} C_{12} & -S_{12} & 0 & l_1C_1 + l_2C_{12} \\ S_{12} & C_{12} & 0 & l_1S_1 + l_2S_{12} \\ 0 & 0 & 1 & 0 \\ 0 & 0 & 0 & 1 \end{bmatrix} = \begin{bmatrix} x_x & y_x & z_x & p_x \\ x_y & y_y & z_y & p_y \\ x_z & y_z & z_z & p_z \\ 0 & 0 & 0 & 1 \end{bmatrix} \tag{4.63}$$

In this case, there are no elements with only one joint variable, and premultiplying or postmultiplying is of no help either, so we have to take two expressions and use trigonometric identities to simplify them (see Section 13.5). By equating elements of the matrices, the following expressions are obtained:

$$p_x = l_1C_1 + l_2C_{12} \tag{4.64}$$

$$p_y = l_1S_1 + l_2S_{12} \tag{4.65}$$

$$p_z = 0 \tag{4.66}$$

Equations 4.64 and 4.65 are in the form of a Class 5 solution (Section 13.5). The square of the magnitude of a vector is equal to the sum of the

squares of the elements of the vector, and is independent of the orientation
(see Section 13.4).

$$p_x^2 + p_y^2 = (l_1C_1 + l_2C_{12})^2 + (l_1S_1 + l_2S_{12})^2 \tag{4.67}$$

$$= l_1^2C_1^2 + l_2^2C_{12}^2 + 2l_1l_2C_1C_{12} + l_1^2S_1^2 + l_2^2S_{12}^2 + 2l_1l_2S_1S_{12}$$

$$\text{(as } C_1^2 + S_1^2 = 1\text{)}$$

$$= l_1^2 + l_2^2 + 2l_1l_2(C_1C_{12} + S_1S_{12})$$

$$\text{(and } C(\theta_1 - [\theta_1 + \theta_2]) = C_1C_{12} + S_1S_{12}\text{)}$$

$$= l_1^2 + l_2^2 + 2l_1l_2C_2 \tag{4.68}$$

$$C_2 = \left(\frac{p_x^2 + p_y^2 - l_1^2 - l_2^2}{2l_1l_2}\right) \tag{4.69}$$

Now

$$S_2 = \sqrt{1 - C_2^2} \tag{4.70}$$

and $\theta_2 = \text{atan2}(S_2, C_2)$ (4.71)

The square root in the numerator indicates that the angle can be either
positive or negative. This is called a **redundancy** (Section 4.12).

Having found θ_2, we will now solve for θ_1.

$$p_x = l_1C_1 + l_2C_{12} = l_1C_1 + l_2C_1C_2 - l_2S_1S_2$$

$$= (l_1 + l_2C_2)C_1 - l_2S_2S_1 \tag{4.72}$$

$$p_y = l_1S_1 + l_2S_{12} = l_1S_1 + l_2S_1C_2 + l_2C_1S_2$$

$$= (l_1 + l_2C_2)S_1 + l_2S_2C_1 \tag{4.73}$$

$$\frac{p_y}{p_x} = \frac{(l_1 + l_2C_2)S_1 + l_2S_2C_1}{(l_1 + l_2C_2)C_1 - l_2S_2S_1} = \frac{S_1/C_1 + l_2S_2/(l_1 + l_2C_2)}{1 - (l_2S_2S_1/(l_1 + l_2C_2)C_1)}$$

$$= \frac{\tan(\theta_1) + l_2S_2/(l_1 + l_2C_2)}{1 - \tan(\theta_1)(l_2S_2/[l_1 + l_2C_2])} \tag{4.74}$$

$$\tan^{-1}(p_y/p_x) = \tan^{-1}(\tan(\theta_1)) + \tan^{-1}\left(\frac{l_2S_2}{l_1 + l_2C_2}\right) \tag{4.75}$$

$$\text{as } \tan(\phi + \theta) = \left(\frac{\tan(\phi) + \tan(\theta)}{1 - \tan(\phi)\tan(\theta)}\right)$$

$$\theta_1 = \text{atan2}(p_y, p_x) - \text{atan2}(l_2S_2, l_1 + l_2C_2) \tag{4.76}$$

An alternative way to arrive at a solution for θ_1 is to use the second
part of the Class 5 solution given in Section 13.5. Again, the result is
complex.

4.12 Redundancy and degeneracies

When a manipulator can reach a specified position with more than one configuration of the linkages, the manipulator is said to be **redundant.** Redundancy occurs when more than one solution to the inverse kinematic transform exists. The number of possible solutions is 2^n, where n is the number of redundancies. If the number of solutions is larger than the number of joint variables, the manipulator may be unsolvable using the inverse kinematic heuristic. In this case, constraints have to be placed on the manipulator before a solution can be found. Alternatively, an iterative algorithm can be used (Window 4.3). It may be possible to get equations for each of the joint variables, but these will not be independent. The occurrence of certain mathematical functions in the inverse kinematic solution indicates the existence of redundancies in a manipulator. The square root function and the cosine function both return results without defining the sign of the result. Thus, whenever a square root or cosine occurs, there are two solutions: one using the positive result of the function and one using the negative result.

The type of 1 two-link manipulator (Figure 4.12) exhibits this type of redundancy. The joint variable for the second link (θ_2) can be either positive or negative (Equation 4.69), giving two possible arm configurations: elbow down or elbow up. Which solution we choose to use depends largely upon external constraints, for example the need to reach around an object. How-

---

Window 4.3 Iterative inverse kinematic solutions

Closed-form solutions to the inverse kinematic transform can be found for only a few classes of robot. The problem of the lack of a closed-form solution is most critical with kinematically redundant robots, where the number of degrees of mobility exceeds six. The inverse kinematics of these robots can be solved using iterative procedures. Goldenberg and Lawrence (1985) use iterative procedures to solve a system of non-linear equations. Featherstone (1983b) divides the kinematic model into subsystems to obtain some joint variables iteratively and others by closed form solution. Goldenberg *et al*. (1985) consider the kinematic model as a whole and determine all the joint variables using a rapidly converging iterative procedure.

Uicker *et al*. (1964) and Oh *et al*. (1984) use iterative methods with matrix algebra. Most of the algorithms proposed to solve non-linear kinematic equations use Newton's method based on simultaneous successive linear interpolation of non-linear equations. Since these are local methods, they require a close initial estimate to the exact solution and the correct step size to avoid divergence. Goldenberg *et al*. (1985) use a modified Newton-Rapson method for solving the non-linear equations. Their algorithm requires that the Jacobian (Chapter 5) is either analytically or numerically computed. Using an analytically determined Jacobian considerably improves the rate of convergence.

Manseur and Doty (1988) developed an iterative technique for manipulators where the knowledge of one joint variable allows closed-form solutions of the remaining joint variables. This method does not use Jacobians. It uses the fact that rotation transforms are orthogonal to reduce the number of inverse equations. This work is a simplification of a homotopy map method developed by Tsai and Morgan (1984) which can be used to solve the inverse kinematics of any manipulator.

Figure 4.12
Redundant solution for the
Type 1 two-link manipulator.

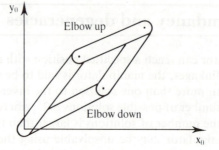

ever, once a solution (positive or negative angle) has been chosen, we must continue to use that solution, and not alternate between the two, as this will cause the manipulator to move between the two configurations unnecessarily. The only time it is valid to change the sign of this angle is when the manipulator must move from one configuration to another to follow a trajectory.

Redundancy can also occur when a manipulator has more degrees of mobility than the task requires. For example, a manipulator with three degrees of translation can reach any point in its three dimensional workspace. If an extra link, which translates in the x direction, is added to a Cartesian robot, which of the two prismatic joints which translate in the x direction is moved to achieve a desired position? Manipulators with more than six degrees of mobility (such as the human arm) are said to be **infinitely redundant**. In many respects, redundant manipulators are more able than non-redundant ones: they can reach into holes, keep away from joint limits, avoid collisions with obstacles, and avoid degenerate states where manipulators lose some degrees of freedom (Yoshikawa, 1984). It is not usually possible to solve these arms using the inverse kinematic analysis discussed in the previous section unless the manipulator is artificially constrained.

When an infinite number of configurations achieve the desired position, the manipulator has a **degeneracy**. A **degenerate configuration** is any manipulator configuration where control over one or more degrees of freedom is lost. This occurs when the solution for one of the joint angles goes to infinity, often due to the denominator of the equation going to zero. For example, if the lengths of the links of the type 1 two-link manipulator are equal the manipulator has a degeneracy at the point (0, 0). In this configuration (Figure 4.13), θ_2 is 180°, and, consequently, both terms in the equation for θ_1 are undefined (Equation 4.65).

$$\theta_1 = \operatorname{atan2}(p_y, p_x) - \operatorname{atan2}(l_2 S_2, l_1 + l_2 C_2)$$
$$= \tan^{-1}(0/0) - \tan^{-1}(0/0) \tag{4.77}$$

In practice, this degeneracy is avoided, because the mechanical design of most manipulators is such that a joint angle of 180° is physically impossible. Secondly, the atan2 function (Window 4.2) will detect a zero

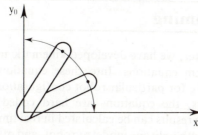

Figure 4.13
Degenerate solution for the
Type 1 two-link manipulator.

denominator and return a specific angle: a function of the sign and value of the numerator.

Another situation in which degeneracy occurs is in wrists which have joints where two axes are collinear (Figure 4.14). These joints are usually separated by a third joint whose axis is perpendicular to their axes. As a result, the degeneracy only occurs in one position, that shown in Figure 4.14. When the axes are collinear, the rotation of the end effector is the sum of the two rotations, but this, too, is degenerate. Setting the first joint to the zero position and using the last joint to control the final orientation is consistent with a design goal of having the last joint control roll and the first joint control yaw. Using both joints does extend the range of the roll angle, but only near the degenerate position.

The controllers of commercial manipulators may not handle the degenerate case very well. One manipulator, with this wrist configuration, rotates one joint by 180° in one direction, and the other by 180° degrees in the other direction, whenever the motion of the manipulator results in coincidence of these axes. The result is a 0° change in the roll angle. If the joint axes coincide, the change is smooth, but, if there is a small angle between them, the resultant motion can be quite violent, causing the manipulator and controller to crash.

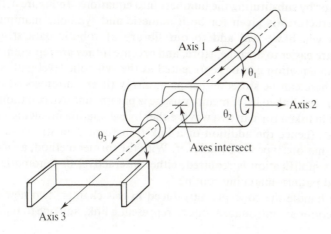

Figure 4.14
Degenerate wrist configuration.

4.13 Programming

Throughout this chapter, we have developed kinematic models by manipulating symbols to form equations. Into these equations, we substituted numeric values to solve for particular robot configurations. In most industrial robot controllers, the equations are hard coded into the control programs so that these results can be calculated in real time. However, these controllers will work with only one model of robot, and often do not have the flexibility to handle robots of the same model but different in size, or to compensate for individual robot signatures. The signature of a robot is the table of measured link parameters (see Section 10.5.1.1). To handle these situations, the code in the controllers of these robots has to be modified and recompiled. As a controller is shipped from a factory for a specific robot, it is unlikely to be used on another, but a robot's signature may change as the result of a repair, for example when a bearing is replaced. Also, the transform from the tool plate to the gripper will change every time the gripper is changed.

While practical robots require numeric calculation for efficiency, symbolic calculation is useful in a number of situations. If a robot is likely to be reconfigured regularly, symbolic manipulation provides the flexibility needed to generate new kinematic models. Some research groups are developing a modular robot which can be configured with a varying number of linkages. Computer-aided design packages for use in the design of robot applications and in off-line programming include simulation models for robots. In these applications, symbol manipulation provides the key to flexibility, but extra computational power is required to achieve adequate response.

Depending on the application, data structures are required for numeric calculation and/or symbolic calculation of manipulator transforms. Numeric calculation is achieved either by multiplying matrices of numbers, or by substituting the numbers into equations. In Figure 4.15, a set of data structures is given for both numeric and symbolic manipulation, structures which we will add to our library of robotic data structures. Symbols are easier to arrange, store, and execute if they are represented with tokens. An equation can be represented at the symbolic level with a list of tokens. These can be stored either as an array (if execution speed is paramount), or as a linked list if memory usage is paramount. An equation can be generated in token form in two ways: either by calculation involving matrices of symbols (hence the addition of a link transform data structure), or by parsing equations typed in by the user. With the former method, a method of equation simplification is required, either interactive, or automatic with a rule-based pattern-matching routine.

To handle the concepts introduced in this chapter, two new robotic data structures are introduced: one to represent a link, and one to represent a

TYPE

(*where manipulation of symbolic equations is required, the following is a list of possible tokens for storage of kinematic equations; q = joint angle, a = twist angle, j = joint variable*)

Tokens = (Cos, Sin, q1, q2, q3, q4, q5, q6, q12, q23, q123, q34, a1, a2, a3, a4, a5, a6, a12, a23, a123, a34, l1, l2, l3, l4, l5, l6, d1, d2, d3, d4, d5, d6, plus, minus, mult, divide, lbracket, rbracket, zero, one, xx, xy, xz, yx, yy, yz, zx, zy, zz, px, py, pz, roll, pitch, yaw, arcsin, arccos, arctan, j1, j2, j3, j4, j5, j6);

(*additional data structures, enumerated types and vectors*)

TokenList = ARRAY [1..40] OF Tokens;   (*used to store an equation in token form*)

LinkTransform = ARRAY [1..4],[1..4] OF Tokens;   (*A matrix in symbolic form*)

CartCoords = (posx, posy, posz, rotx, roty, rotz);

JointCoords = (joint1, joint2, joint3, joint4, joint5, joint6);

CartVector = ARRAY[posx..rotz] OF REAL;

JointVector = ARRAY[joint1..joint6] OF REAL;

Joint = (rotary, prismatic);

Link = RECORD   (*record to store numeric and symbolic data about a link*)
    linknumb : [0..6];
    linktype : [1..8];
    jointangle : Angle;
    twist : Angle;
    length : Distance;
    displacement : Distance;
    Amatrix : Frame;   (*numeric form of **A** matrix*)
    symAmat : LinkTransform;   (*symbolic form of **A** matrix*)
    CASE linkvar : Joint OF
        rotary   : minangle : Angle;
              maxangle : Angle;
     | prismatic : minrange : Distance;
              maxrange : Distance
    END;
END;

Robot = RECORD   (*record to store information about a robot arm*)
    nooflinks : [0..6];
    manipulator : ARRAY [0..6] OF Link;
        (*the size of the array is the number of links plus 1 for the base
        –link zero is the base to which the manipulator is attached*)
    RTN : Frame;   (*actual values of transform for current configuration*)
    cartspace : CartVector;   (*actual Cartesian space values*)
    jointspace : JointVector;   (*actual joint space values*)
    ForwardEqns : ARRAY[posx..rotz] OF TokenList;
        (*equations for forward kinematic transform*)
    BackwardEqns : ARRAY[joint1..joint6] OF Tokenlist;
        (*equations for backward kinematic transform*)
END;

VAR
    twolinkmanip : Robot;   (*for a two-link manipulator the array of link can be reduced to 0..2*)

Figure 4.15
Additional data structures for representing links and manipulators – to be added to library of robot structures (Figure 3.21).

Figure 4.16
Additional routines for
calculating and displaying
transformation data
structures – to be added to
transformation library (Figure
3.24).

```
PROCEDURE Atan2 (yval : REAL;
                 xval : REAL): Angle;

        (*calculate an A matrix for given configuration*)
PROCEDURE CalcAmatrix(jointangle:Angle;
                      displacement:Distance;
                      length:Distance;
                      twist:Angle):Frame;

        (*procedures to write contents of data structures to text window*)
PROCEDURE WriteTokenList(VAR list1 : TokenList);
PROCEDURE WriteLinkTrans(VAR link1 : LinkTransform);
PROCEDURE WriteCartVector(VAR vec1 : CartVector);
PROCEDURE WriteJointVector(VAR vec1 : JointVector);
PROCEDURE WriteLink(VAR link1 : Link);
PROCEDURE WriteRobot(VAR robot1 : Robot);

        (*procedures to draw a link and a robot on a graphics window*)
PROCEDURE DrawLink(VAR link1 : Link);
PROCEDURE DrawRobot(Var robot1 : Robot);
```

robot. With both, we can store numeric data, and, if desired, symbolic data. A link data structure includes all the information about a link, including the range of the link variable. As there are two types of joints, a variant record is used to handle the different range types. A robot data structure holds all the information about a robot arm, including a link data structure for each link, the forward and inverse kinematic models as equations in token form, and values for the current configuration of the robot. An expression evaluator is required to evaluate the token strings representing the equations and execute the equations to calculate the joint and Cartesian space coordinates.

A number of additional procedures are required to perform the calculations described in this chapter, and to print out the new data structures (Figure 4.16). As an **A** matrix is a clearly defined transform, we can include a procedure to calculate it. However, as the procedure in Figure 4.16 is for numeric calculation, an additional procedure is required for the symbolic level. Due to the number and complexity of the procedures required for symbolic level calculation, they have not been defined in Figure 4.16. Also, the choice of which symbolic manipulation procedures to include depends on the way in which symbolic computation is to be performed. Finally, the implementation of these procedures is left to the reader.

4.14 Accuracy of the kinematic model

A manipulator can place the tip of a tool (tool centre point) at a location in space with a certain precision. The static precision of a manipulator is described with three parameters: accuracy, repeatability, and resolution. **Accuracy** is the difference between the actual location and the commanded location. **Repeatability** is the variation in the actual location when the manipulator repeatedly moves the tool centre point to the same commanded location. **Resolution** is the minimum distance that the tool centre point can be guaranteed to move. The repeatability and resolution of most robots is better than their accuracy. A number of factors cause inaccuracy in the kinematic model.

There are two classes of model parameters: non-geometric and geometric. **Non-geometric parameters** include compliance, gear backlash, gear eccentricity, encoder resolution, gear transmission errors, temperature-related expansion, linkage wobble due to bearing slop, and cross coupling between joints due to the mechanical construction of the robot. The impact of these errors on the spatial resolution of the robot is dependent on its configuration. In a manipulator constructed with prismatic joints, the joint errors do not accumulate because the joints move in orthogonal directions. Thus, the spatial resolution in an axial direction of the manipulator is equal to the resolution of the joint which controls motion in that direction. In a manipulator constructed with revolute joints, joint errors accumulate, and thus the error in the spatial resolution increases proportionally with the number of revolute joints.

Before we can compensate for non-geometric errors, they must be measured and modelled in terms of the variables which change them. The outputs of these models can be used to correct joint-variable feedback signals. While gear and encoder errors are constant (although direction dependent), errors due to the compliance of the linkages and joints are not. These errors depend on the arm configuration and the weight of the object held by the gripper. Whitney *et al.* (1984) measured a vertical deflection at the end of a Puma 560 robot, with its arm in a horizontal position, of 1 mm when a load of 3.5 kg was held by the gripper. They also measured a backlash of 0.003° in one of the joints, an error comparable to the resolution of the encoder (Section 2.7).

Cross coupling is the rotation of joint n due to a rotation about joint $n-1$. The joints of the Mini-Mover 5 arm (Figure 4.17) are controlled by tendons driven by motors mounted in its trunk. When the elbow joint is moved, the angles of the joints in the wrist and the gripper opening are affected. The change in the angle of the elbow joint alters the length of the paths traversed by the wrist and gripper tendons. Cross coupling effects have to be compensated for by the joint controllers.

Geometric model parameters are the link parameters in the kinematic model. Errors in these parameters include joint encoder offsets, and variation in the lengths of links and the orientations of axes from the specification (axes can be up to 0.5° from the design angle). These errors are all due to manufacturing tolerances. Manufacturers of quality robots will guarantee the link parameters to be within certain limits. The consequence of these

Figure 4.17
Mini-mover 5 arm with
controller and power supply.

errors is that both forward and inverse kinematic transforms give inaccurate results. If we want accurate manipulator control from a kinematic model, we must compensate for these errors.

Absolute errors in the zero position of joints can cause errors when using different configurations to reach the same point. One way to measure the zero error in an elbow joint is to move the end effector to a known location with the elbow up (see Figure 2.23), and record the joint angles. Then move the end effector to the same location with the elbow down, read the angles, and compare them to the angles recorded in the elbow-up configuration.

Another problem is that some manipulators can control the position of the end effector accurately, but not the orientation. Also, the vector around which the last joint rolls may not coincide with the approach vector. The flange to which a gripper is attached, at the end of the last link, may not be flat, and it may not be orthogonal to the roll axis. These errors can be demonstrated by gripping a point source of light, pointing it at a target, and then rolling the last joint.

Errors in the kinematic model can be minimized by measuring the link parameters precisely, a procedure called **arm signature analysis**. Some manufacturers are planning to provide a signature with each arm they make. To measure and model the errors, it may be necessary to obtain a description of the procedure the manufacturer used to calibrate the robot. One of the driving forces behind vision research is the possibility of eliminating the impact of all the above errors by measuring the position of the end effector.

4.15   Efficiency of the kinematic solutions

Throughout this chapter, we have deliberately chosen robust solutions over efficient solutions. Robustness of a robot control system is more important than efficiency, particularly in an industrial situation where control failure can damage equipment, or, worse, injure people. However, if the robot is to be controlled in real time, the algorithms used must be efficient, or we will have to wait for faster computers before we can implement our control strategies. Many current industrial robots use a simple trigonometric model because of the time taken to build a full kinematic model. Some robots do not include a kinematic model, but replay vectors of joint angles which were recorded when an operator manually moved it through its motions.

The efficiency of the kinematic model of a manipulator is often measured as a function of the number of additions, multiplications, and transcendental function calls required to solve the model. For example, the solutions for the roll, pitch, and yaw angles derived from the general orientation transformation require one addition, two multiplications, and five transcendental function calls (see Section 4.10). Fast hardware for multiplication and addition is common in today's computers, but transcendental functions are usually evaluated with software. Thus, the speed of the algorithms is very dependent on the efficiency of the transcendental function algorithms.

Some work has been done on implementing transcendental functions in VLSI in an attempt to achieve higher speeds. Such circuits could be used to construct a transcendental co-processor for a microprocessor system. Others (Cook and Vu-Dinh, 1984) have recognized that we are trying to solve an analogue problem with digital methods, and have suggested an analogue approach. The difficulty with current analogue circuits is their low accuracy (roughly 0.5%). However, an analogue computer would provide very fast solutions for intermediate positions along the trajectory of an arm, giving the digital computer time to calculate the final position of the arm accurately.

Owing to these efficiency problems, homogeneous transforms are often used to solve the theoretical models of a manipulator, but are not implemented in the controller. Instead, the equations which result from these models are used, often in a simplified form, and more efficient mathematical representations are substituted, for example quaternions for rotation transforms (see Window 3.4).

In all areas of robotics, the selection of an appropriate mechanical design can simplify the kinematic model, and, consequently, the control algorithms. In the past, robots were often designed to realize interesting concepts, but were later found to be very difficult to control, due to complexities in the kinematic model that arose from the chosen design. As robot design matures, there is a shift to an integrated approach to design, where the kinematics, dynamics, and the required control algorithms are worked out as part of the design. Problems with the models, or the algorithms, may dictate a new mechanical or electronic design, particularly if the robot is to be controlled in real time. Also, the concept of form following function is playing a greater role in design decisions. For example, why use a six degree of freedom robot when a three degree of freedom one will do the task? Design of this maturity requires robotic engineers and scientists who are skilled in the various disciplines which make up robotics.

Key points

- Kinematics is the modelling of the relationship between the positions, velocities, and accelerations of the links of a manipulator.

- The forward transform describes the Cartesian space location (position and orientation) of the end effector as a function of the joint variables.

- The inverse transform describes the joint space coordinates as a function of the Cartesian location of the end effector.

- The angles (or displacements) at the joints are the joint coordinates in an n dimensional joint space.

- The forward transform of an n link manipulator is:

$$^R\mathbf{T}_H = \mathbf{A}_1 \times \mathbf{A}_2 \times \ldots \mathbf{A}_n \tag{4.1}$$

- A manipulator is in its zero position when all the joint variables are zero.

- Coordinate frames are fixed to the distal end of each link so that the z axes of the frames are collinear with the axes of the distal joints. The motion of succeeding links is defined with respect to these frames.

- The transformation from link $n-1$ to link n is completely described by 4 link parameters:
  - a rotation about the z_{n-1} axis by the angle between the links (θ_n),
  - a translation along the z_{n-1} axis by the distance between the links (d_n),
  - a translation along the x_n axis by the length of the link (l_n), and
  - a rotation about the x_n axis by the twist angle (α_n).

- These parameters are combined in an **A** matrix.

$$\mathbf{A}_n = \begin{bmatrix} C_\theta & -S_\theta C_\alpha & S_\theta S_\alpha & lC_\theta \\ S_\theta & C_\theta C_\alpha & -C_\theta S_\alpha & lS_\theta \\ 0 & S_\alpha & C_\alpha & d \\ 0 & 0 & 0 & 1 \end{bmatrix} \tag{4.6}$$

- The equations of the components of the end effector position vector are found by equating elements of the forward transform and the general transformation matrix.

- The orientation angles of the end effector are found by equating elements of the forward transform and the RPY orientation transform.

$$\phi = \text{atan2}(x_y, x_x) \qquad (4.45)$$

$$\theta = \text{atan2}(-x_z, x_x C_\phi + x_y S_\phi) \qquad (4.47)$$

$$\psi = \text{atan2}(y_z, z_z) \qquad (4.49)$$

- The inverse transform is found from the forward transform using a heuristic to equate elements of the forward transform and the general transform.
- When a manipulator can reach a location with more than one configuration it is redundant.
- When the axes of 2 joints align, the manipulator is in a degenerate configuration. A spherical wrist exhibits such a degeneracy.
- The static precision of a manipulator is defined with 3 parameters: accuracy, repeatability, and resolution.
- The repeatability and resolution of most robots is better than their accuracy.

Examples

Example 4.1   Trigonometric model of Mini-Mover 5

In our first example, we will solve the kinematic model for the Mini-Mover 5 arm (Figure 4.17) using trigonometric methods (Microbot, 1981). This is a five degree of freedom arm which has waist, shoulder, elbow, roll, and pitch joints. Roll and pitch are controlled with a differential pair, so the origins of the coordinate frames for these joints are coincident. The kinematic model for this manipulator is shown graphically in Figure 4.18. The end of the manipulator is located at $p\,(x, y, z)$ relative to a coordinate frame located in the base. The values of these coordinates (direct kinematic solution) are found first.

$$z = a_1 + a_2 \sin(\theta_2) + a_3 \sin(\theta_3) + a_4 \sin(\theta_4) \qquad (4.78)$$

$$r = a_2 \cos(\theta_2) + a_3 \cos(\theta_3) + a_4 \cos(\theta_4) \qquad (4.79)$$

$$x = r \cos(\theta_1) \qquad (4.80)$$

$$y = r \sin(\theta_1) \qquad (4.81)$$

Figure 4.18
Mini-mover 5 arm.
(a) Manipulator in zero
position.
(b) Kinematic model.
(c) Elbow triangle.
$a_1 = 195$ mm
$a_2 = a_3 = 177.8$ mm
$a_4 = 96.5$ mm

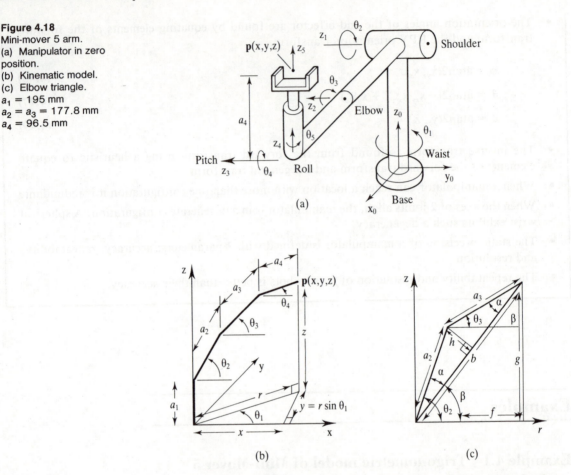

The above equations involve the angles of the links relative to the xy plane, not the actual angles between the links: these angles can be considered to be Cartesian angles. Using these angles for control is not problematic as long as the inverse solution uses them, and the manipulator is initialized correctly. If the actual angles between the links are used, the equations are more complex.

Solving for the inverse kinematic model is more difficult: equations have to be found for the five joint variables in terms of the position (x, y, z), and the orientation (roll (ϕ), pitch (θ)), of the hand. The value for the first joint angle is:

$$\theta_1 = \tan^{-1}(y/x) \tag{4.82}$$

If the manipulator arm is placed with all links in a vertical position, roll of the hand represents a rotation around the z axis, as does rotation around the waist. Thus, the value of the last joint angle is:

$$\theta_5 = \phi - \theta_1 \tag{4.83}$$

Similarly, pitch can be considered to be a rotation about the x axis, giving:

$$\theta_4 = \theta \tag{4.84}$$

If we consider the triangle formed by the second and third links (Figure 4.18(c)) we obtain the following relationships:

$$f = a_2\cos(\theta_2) + a_3\cos(\theta_3) = r - a_4\cos(\theta_4) \tag{4.85}$$

$$g = a_2\sin(\theta_2) + a_3\sin(\theta_3) = z - a_1 - a_4\sin(\theta_4) \tag{4.86}$$

$$b = \sqrt{f^2 + g^2} \tag{4.87}$$

$$h = a_3^2 - (b/2)^2 \tag{4.88}$$

$$\alpha = \tan^{-1}(h/b) \tag{4.89}$$

$$\beta = \tan^{-1}(g/f) \tag{4.90}$$

$$\theta_2 = \alpha + \beta \tag{4.91}$$

$$\theta_3 = \beta - \alpha \tag{4.92}$$

Once the solution has been found, it appears reasonably simple. However, the method leaves us with an uneasy feeling. First, someone has to find the appropriate heuristics needed to find the solution. Second, the method for finding the last joint angle is not a general solution. The method of homogeneous transforms attempts to overcome both these problems by using algorithmic methods to find general solutions (Exercise 4.15).

Example 4.2 Kinematic model of simplified Puma

In our second example, we will attempt to solve the kinematic model for simplified version of a popular industrial manipulator (Figure 4.19) using homogeneous transforms (Lee, 1982). This robot includes two type 4 links (see Figure 4.3). The axes of the two joints in these links intersect in the proximal joint, not in the distal joint like the other links in the manipulators discussed in earlier parts of the text. A consequence of this is that the two coordinate frames coincide, even though in the actual robot there is a physical distance between the two joints. In the analysis, this distance is added to the distance between the joints of the link attached to the distal joint.

The correct assignment of coordinate frames (following Algorithm 4.2) is shown in Figure 4.19(c). The zero position for kinematic analysis

Figure 4.19
Six degree of freedom Puma
Robot (simplified by
neglecting l_3).
(a) Puma manipulator;
(b) Manipulator in zero
position;
(c) Assignment of
coordinate frames.

$$d_1 = 660.4\,\text{mm}$$
$$d_2 = 149.5\,\text{mm}$$
$$d_4 = 432.0\,\text{mm}$$
$$d_6 = 56.5\,\text{mm}$$
$$l_2 = 432.0\,\text{mm}$$
$$(l_3 = 20.3\,\text{mm})$$

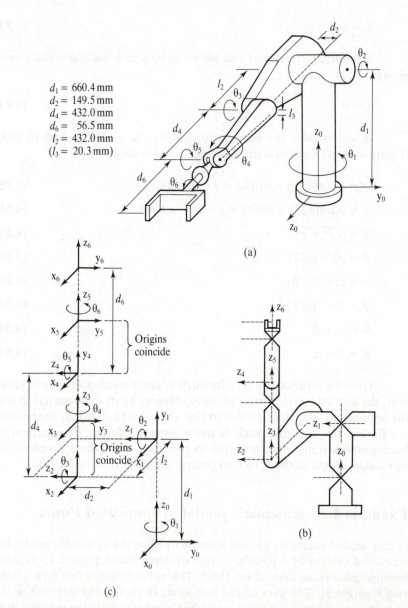

(a)

(b)

(c)

(Figure 4.19(b)) is different from the zero position used by Paul *et al.* (1981),
where the left-arm position is used, which is the zero position used by the
Unimation controller. The algorithm for assigning coordinate frames does
not include a method for selecting the direction of the axis of a revolute joint.
The choice of axis direction used here resulted in a right-arm configuration,
where the choice used by Paul *et al.* (1981) resulted in a left-arm configuration. This difference changes the sign of the twist angles between the links,

Figure 4.20
(a) Link parameters and (b)
A matrices for the simplified
puma robot arm.

Link	Joint variable	Angle θ_n	Displacement d_n	Length l_n	Twist α_n	Range
1	θ_1	θ_1	$d_1=660.4$	0	$+90°$	-160 to $+160$
2	θ_2	θ_2	$d_2=149.5$	$l_2=432.0$	$0°$	-225 to $+45$
3	θ_3	θ_3	0	0	$-90°$	-45 to $+225$
4	θ_4	θ_4	$d_4=432.0$	0	$+90°$	-110 to $+170$
5	θ_5	θ_5	0	0	$-90°$	-100 to $+100$
6	θ_6	θ_6	$d_6=56.5$	0	$0°$	-266 to $+266$

(a)

$$^0A_1 = \begin{bmatrix} C_1 & 0 & S_1 & 0 \\ S_1 & 0 & -C_1 & 0 \\ 0 & 1 & 0 & d_1 \\ 0 & 0 & 0 & 1 \end{bmatrix} \quad ^1A_2 = \begin{bmatrix} C_2 & -S_2 & 0 & l_2C_2 \\ S_2 & C_2 & 0 & l_2S_2 \\ 0 & 0 & 1 & d_2 \\ 0 & 0 & 0 & 1 \end{bmatrix} \quad ^2A_3 = \begin{bmatrix} C_3 & 0 & -S_3 & 0 \\ S_3 & 0 & +C_3 & 0 \\ 0 & -1 & 0 & 0 \\ 0 & 0 & 0 & 1 \end{bmatrix}$$

$$^3A_4 = \begin{bmatrix} C_4 & 0 & +S_4 & 0 \\ S_4 & 0 & -C_4 & 0 \\ 0 & 1 & 0 & d_4 \\ 0 & 0 & 0 & 1 \end{bmatrix} \quad ^4A_5 = \begin{bmatrix} C_5 & 0 & -S_5 & 0 \\ S_5 & 0 & +C_5 & 0 \\ 0 & -1 & 0 & 0 \\ 0 & 0 & 0 & 1 \end{bmatrix} \quad ^5A_6 = \begin{bmatrix} C_6 & -S_6 & 0 & 0 \\ S_6 & C_6 & 0 & 0 \\ 0 & 0 & 1 & d_6 \\ 0 & 0 & 0 & 1 \end{bmatrix}$$

(b)

and results in a kinematic model with the same components in the equations, but with some components having different signs. Also, the zero position for the kinematic model is different from the zero position used by the manufacturer to calibrate the robot – all links pointing in a vertical direction.

The six **A** matrices (Figure 4.20) are found by substituting the link parameters for this robot into Equation 4.6, and the manipulator transform is found by multiplying these matrices. A complete kinematic model of this robot includes an l_3 parameter of 20.32mm due to asymmetry of the forearm. The axes of joints 3 and 4 do not intersect. In the following analysis, the robot kinematics are simplified by assuming a symmetric arm.

$$^RT_H = {}^0A_1\,{}^1A_2\,{}^2A_3\,{}^3A_4\,{}^4A_5\,{}^5A_6 = \begin{bmatrix} x_x & y_x & z_x & p_x \\ x_y & y_y & z_y & p_y \\ x_z & y_z & z_z & p_z \\ 0 & 0 & 0 & 1 \end{bmatrix} \tag{4.93}$$

where the elements of the matrix are:

$$x_x = C_1[C_{23}(C_4C_5C_6 - S_4S_6) - S_{23}S_5C_6] - S_1(S_4C_5C_6 + C_4S_6) \tag{4.94}$$

$$x_y = S_1[C_{23}(C_4C_5C_6 - S_4S_6) - S_{23}S_5C_6] + C_1(S_4C_5C_6 + C_4S_6) \tag{4.95}$$

$$x_z = S_{23}(C_4C_5C_6 - S_4S_6) + C_{23}S_5C_6 \tag{4.96}$$

$$y_x = C_1[-C_{23}(C_4C_5S_6 + S_4C_6) + S_{23}S_5S_6] - S_1(-S_4C_5S_6 + C_4C_6) \tag{4.97}$$

$$y_y = S_1[-C_{23}(C_4C_5S_6 + S_4C_6) + S_{23}S_5S_6] + C_1(-S_4C_5S_6 + C_4C_6) \tag{4.98}$$

$$y_z = -S_{23}(C_4C_5S_6 + S_4C_6) - C_{23}S_5S_6 \tag{4.99}$$

$$z_x = -C_1(C_{23}C_4S_5 + S_{23}C_5) + S_1S_4S_5 \tag{4.100}$$

$$z_y = -S_1(C_{23}C_4S_5 + S_{23}C_5) - C_1S_4S_5 \tag{4.101}$$

$$z_z = -S_{23}C_4S_5 + C_{23}C_5 \tag{4.102}$$

$$p_x = C_1[-C_{23}d_6C_4S_5 - S_{23}(d_6C_5 + d_4) + l_2C_2] + S_1(d_6S_4S_5 + d_2) \tag{4.103}$$

$$p_y = S_1[-C_{23}d_6C_4S_5 - S_{23}(d_6C_5 + d_4) + l_2C_2] + C_1[d_6S_4S_5 + d_2] \tag{4.104}$$

$$p_z = -S_{23}d_6C_4S_5 + C_{23}(d_6C_5 + d_4) + l_2S_2 + d_1 \tag{4.105}$$

Using the solutions derived for the orientation transform (Section 4.9), we find the orientation of the coordinate frame located at the end of this robot (frame 6).

$$\phi = \text{atan2}(x_x, x_y)$$

$$= \tan^{-1}\left(\frac{\begin{array}{c} C_1[C_{23}(C_4C_5C_6 - S_4S_6) - S_{23}S_5C_6] \\ - S_1(S_4C_5C_6 + C_4S_6) \end{array}}{\begin{array}{c} S_1[C_{23}(C_4C_5C_6 - S_4S_6) - S_{23}S_5C_6] \\ + C_1(S_4C_5C_6 + C_4S_6) \end{array}} \right) \tag{4.106}$$

$$\theta = \text{atan2}[-x_z, x_xC(\phi) + x_yS(\phi)]$$

$$= \tan^{-1}\left(\frac{-S_{23}(C_4C_5C_6 - S_4S_6) - C_{23}S_5C_6}{\begin{array}{c} [C_1C_\phi + S_1S_\phi][C_{23}(C_4C_5C_6 - S_4S_6) - S_{23}S_5C_6] \\ + [-S_1C_\phi + C_1S_\phi](S_4C_5C_6 + C_4S_6) \end{array}} \right) \tag{4.107}$$

$$\psi = \text{atan2}(y_z, z_z) = \tan^{-1}\left(\frac{-S_{23}(C_4C_5S_6 + S_4C_6) - C_{23}S_5S_6}{-S_{23}C_4S_5 + C_{23}C_5} \right) \tag{4.108}$$

The next step is to attempt to find the inverse transform using Algorithm 4.4. The forward solution involves complex terms, and joint variables are difficult to find, so we will premultiply both sides of the transformation equation (Equation 4.93) by the inverse of the first matrix.

$$^0A_1^{-1}\ ^RT_H = {}^1A_2\ {}^2A_3\ {}^3A_4\ {}^4A_5\ {}^5A_6 = \begin{bmatrix} C_1 & S_1 & 0 & 0 \\ 0 & 0 & 1 & -d_1 \\ S_1 & -C_1 & 0 & 0 \\ 0 & 0 & 0 & 1 \end{bmatrix} \begin{bmatrix} x_x & y_x & z_x & p_x \\ x_y & y_y & z_y & p_y \\ x_z & y_z & z_z & p_z \\ 0 & 0 & 0 & 1 \end{bmatrix}$$

$$= \begin{bmatrix} C_1x_x + S_1x_y & C_1y_x + S_1y_y & C_1z_x + S_1z_y & C_1p_x + S_1p_y \\ x_z & y_z & z_z & p_z - d_1 \\ S_1x_x - C_1x_y & S_1y_x - C_1y_y & S_1z_x - C_1z_y & S_1p_x - C_1p_y \\ 0 & 0 & 0 & 1 \end{bmatrix}$$

$$
= \begin{bmatrix}
C_{23}(C_4C_5C_6 - S_4S_6) - S_{23}S_5C_6 & -C_{23}(C_4C_5S_6 + S_4C_6) + S_{23}S_5S_6 \\
S_{23}(C_4C_5C_6 - S_4S_6) + C_{23}S_5C_6 & -S_{23}(C_4C_5S_6 + S_4C_6) - C_{23}S_5C_6 \\
-S_4C_5C_6 - C_4S_6 & S_4C_5S_6 - C_4C_6 \\
0 & 0
\end{bmatrix}
$$

$$
\begin{bmatrix}
-C_{23}C_4S_5 - S_{23}C_5 & -C_{23}d_6C_4S_5 - S_{23}(d_6C_5 + d_4) + l_2C_2 \\
-S_{23}C_4S_5 + C_{23}C_5 & -S_{23}d_6C_4S_5 + C_{23}(d_6C_5 + d_4) + l_2S_2 \\
S_4S_5 & d_6S_4S_5 + d_2 \\
0 & 1
\end{bmatrix} \quad \textbf{(4.109)}
$$

If we equate matrix elements (1, 4) and (3, 4) from the two matrices, simplify the resulting equations using trigonometric identities, and divide the equations, we can solve for the first joint variable θ_1.

$$\phi = \tan^{-1}(p_y/p_x) \qquad r = +\sqrt{p_y^2 + p_x^2} \qquad \textbf{(4.110)}$$

$$\text{where } p_y = r\sin(\phi) \qquad p_x = r\cos(\phi) \qquad \textbf{(4.111)}$$

$$C_1p_x + S_1p_y = C_1r\cos(\phi) + S_1r\sin(\phi) \quad = r\cos(\theta_1 - \phi) \qquad \textbf{(4.112)}$$

$$= -C_{23}d_6C_4S_5 - S_{23}(d_6C_5 + d_4) + l_2C_2 \ \{\text{element 1, 4}\} \qquad \textbf{(4.113)}$$

$$S_1p_x - C_1p_y = S_1r\cos(\phi) - C_1r\sin(\phi) = r\sin(\theta_1 - \phi) = -d_6S_4S_5 + d_2 \qquad \textbf{(4.114)}$$

$$\frac{r\sin(\theta_1 - \phi)}{r\cos(\theta_1 - \phi)} = \tan(\theta_1 - \phi) = \frac{-d_6S_4S_5 + d_2}{-C_{23}d_6C_4S_5 - S_{23}(d_6C_5 + d_4) + l_2C_2} \qquad \textbf{(4.115)}$$

$$\theta_1 = \tan^{-1}\left(\frac{p_y}{p_x}\right) + \tan^{-1}\left(\frac{-d_6S_4S_5 + d_2}{-C_{23}d_6C_4S_5 - S_{23}(d_6C_5 + d_4) + l_2C_2}\right) \qquad \textbf{(4.116)}$$

Premultiply the transformation equation again:

$$
{}^1A_2^{-1}\,{}^0A_1^{-1}\,{}^RT_H = {}^2A_3\,{}^3A_4\,{}^4A_5\,{}^5A_6
$$

$$
= \begin{bmatrix}
C_2(C_1x_x + S_1x_y) + S_2x_z & C_2(C_1y_x + S_1y_y) + S_2y_z \\
-S_2(C_1x_x + S_1x_y) + C_2x_z & -S_2(C_1y_x + S_1y_y) + C_2y_z \\
S_1x_x - C_1x_y & S_1y_x - C_1y_y \\
0 & 0
\end{bmatrix}
$$

$$
\begin{bmatrix}
C_2(C_1z_x + S_1z_y) + S_2z_z & C_2(C_1p_x + S_1p_y) + S_2(p_z - d_1) \\
-S_2(C_1z_x + S_1z_y) + C_2z_z & -S_2(C_1p_x + S_1p_y) + C_2(p_z - d_1) \\
S_1z_x - C_1z_y & S_1p_x - C_1p_y - d_2 \\
0 & 1
\end{bmatrix}
$$

$$= \begin{bmatrix} C_3C_4C_5C_6 - C_3S_4S_6 - S_3S_5C_6 & -C_3C_4C_5S_6 - C_3S_4C_6 + S_3S_5S_6 \\ S_3C_4C_5C_6 - S_3S_4S_6 + C_3S_5C_6 & -S_3C_4C_5S_6 - S_3S_4S_6 - C_3S_5S_6 \\ -S_4C_5C_6 - C_4S_6 & S_4C_5S_6 - C_4C_6 \\ 0 & 0 \end{bmatrix}$$

$$\begin{bmatrix} -C_3C_4S_5 - S_3C_5 & -C_3d_6C_4S_5 - S_3(d_6C_5 + d_4) \\ -S_3C_4S_5 + C_3C_5 & -S_3d_6C_4S_5 + C_3(d_6C_5 + d_4) \\ S_4S_5 & d_6S_4S_5 \\ 0 & 1 \end{bmatrix} \quad \textbf{(4.117)}$$

$$C_2(C_1p_x + S_1p_y) + S_2(p_z - d_1) = -C_3d_6C_4S_5 - S_3(d_6C_5 + d_4) \quad \textbf{(4.118)}$$

$$-S_2(C_1p_x + S_1p_y) + C_2(p_z - d_1) = -S_3d_6C_4S_5 + C_3(d_6C_5 + d_4) \quad \textbf{(4.119)}$$

$$\theta_2 = \sin^{-1}\left(\frac{(p_z - d_1)[-C_3d_6C_4S_5 - S_3(d_6C_5 + d_4) }{+[S_3d_6C_4S_5 + C_3(d_6C_5 + d_4)](C_1p_x + S_1p_y)}{[(C_1p_x + S_1p_y)^2 + (p_z - d_1)]^2} \right) \quad \textbf{(4.120)}$$

Two equations involving θ_2 and θ_3, have been obtained with no obvious way of solving for either angle in terms of the atan2 function. A solution for θ_2 is calculated using the inverse sine function, and a solution for θ_3 can be found in a similar way, but it is not independent of θ_2. If we premultiply the transformation equation again, we can solve for θ_6:

$$^2A_3^{-1}{}^1A_2^{-1}{}^0A_1^{-1}{}^R T_H = {}^3A_4 {}^4A_5 {}^5A_6 \quad \textbf{(4.121)}$$

Equating elements (3, 1) and (3, 2) gets:

$$\theta_6 = \tan^{-1}\left(\frac{S_3[C_2(C_1y_x + S_1y_y) + S_2y_z] - C_3(S_1y_x - C_1y_y)}{-S_3[C_2(C_1x_x + S_1x_y) + S_2x_z] + C_3(S_1x_x - C_1x_y)} \right) \quad \textbf{(4.122)}$$

Premultiplying the transformation again, to solve for θ_4 and θ_5:

$$^3A_4^{-1}{}^2A_3^{-1}{}^1A_2^{-1}{}^0A_1^{-1}{}^R T_H = {}^4A_5 {}^5A_6 \quad \textbf{(4.123)}$$

Equating elements (1, 4) and (2, 4) to get:

$$\theta_5 = \tan^{-1}\left(\frac{\begin{matrix} -C_4[C_3(C_2(C_1p_x + S_1p_y) + S_2(p_z - d_1)] \\ + S_3(-S_2(C_1p_x + S_1p_y) + C_2(p_z - d_1))] + S_4[S_1p_x - C_1p_y - d_2] \end{matrix}}{\begin{matrix} S_3[C_2(C_1p_x + S_1p_y) + S_2(p_z - d_1)] \\ - C_3[-S_2(C_1p_x + S_1p_y) + C_2(p_z - d_1)] - d_4 \end{matrix}} \right)$$

$$\textbf{(4.124)}$$

By equating element (3, 4) we get:

$$\theta_4 = \tan^{-1}\left(\frac{S_1p_x - C_1p_y - d_2}{\begin{array}{l}C_3[C_2(C_1p_x + S_1p_y) + S_2(p_z - d_1)] \\ + S_3[-S_2(C_1p_x + S_1p_y) + C_2(p_z - d_1)]\end{array}}\right) \qquad (4.125)$$

Equations have now been found for all the joint angles, but they are of little use because all of the equations involve other joint angles. No equations have been found for any joint angle in terms of the Cartesian space description only. To find values for the joint coordinates an iterative algorithm must be used (Window 4.3). Discussion of such algorithms is beyond the scope of this book. The unsolvability of the manipulator is due to its geometric design, where a deliberate attempt was made to mimic a human. There are three places where redundant configurations can occur: the shoulder can be a left or a right shoulder, the elbow can be up or down, and the wrist pitch can be up or down (see Figure 2.23). Thus, the manipulator has eight solutions, but only six joint variables. Also the wrist configuration has a degeneracy of the type shown in Figure 4.14.

Paul *et al.* (1981) simplify the equations by shifting the first and last displacements (d_1 and d_6) out of the manipulator transform into the transforms on either side. There is some justification for doing this with d_1, because the Puma controller locates the origin of the world coordinate system at the point where the shoulder and waist axes intersect.

$$p_x = C_1(S_{23}d_4 + l_2C_2) + S_1d_2 \qquad (4.126)$$

$$p_y = S_1(S_{23}d_4 + l_2C_2) - C_1d_2 \qquad (4.127)$$

$$p_z = -C_{23}d_4 + l_2S_2 \qquad (4.128)$$

Lee (1983) calculates an inverse solution for this manipulator by dividing it into two 3 link manipulators, and solving for them separately. First, he solves a transform form the base to the wrist (end of link 3), given a vector from the wrist to the hand, to find equations for the first three joint angles, and then he uses this solution in conjunction with the transform from the wrist to the hand. His solution also handles the decisions which have to be made between different configurations. The details of this method of inverse kinematics are beyond the scope of this book. Manseur and Doty (1988) obtain a reduced set of equations by choosing the same frames as Paul *et al.* (1981) and applying rotational orthogonality. A manipulator is termed 'orthogonal' when all twist angles are 0° or 90°. They decompose the forward transform into a position vector and a rotation transform. Using the fact that dot products are invariant under rotation transforms, because rotation transforms are orthogonal, they obtain a set of four inverse equations. This method is a simplification of previous work by Tsai and Morgan (1984).

Pieper (1968) shows that one advantage of a spherical wrist (a wrist design where the three axes intersect at a point) is that it has a closed form solution. However, the above solutions only handle the case of a perfectly manufactured robot. As soon as a signature for the particular robot is used, the errors in the kinematics significantly complicate the model, again requiring the use of iterative solutions.

Example 4.3   Replacing an elbow with a prismatic joint

An alternative solution to the problem in Example 4.2 is to reduce the number of redundancies by constraining the manipulator in some way. If the third revolute joint (elbow) is replaced with a prismatic joint, the location of the end of the third link, where the wrist is attached, is the same, but the orientation is different. Consequently, to reach the same location (position and orientation), the joint angles for the last three joints are different than for the manipulator with an elbow. Also, a manipulator with an elbow can reach around behind some objects, where a manipulator with a prismatic joint cannot. To demonstrate the reduction in the complexity of the kinematic model, which results from removing one redundancy, we will replace the elbow joint with a prismatic joint. The distance between the shoulder (frame 2) and the wrist (frame 4) is a function of the joint angle (see the elbow triangle in Figure 4.21(c)).

$$\theta_3 = 2 \times \sin^{-1}\left(\frac{d}{2 \times l}\right) \tag{4.129}$$

where

d is the distance between the frames,
l is the length of the two links that form the sides of the triangle, and
θ_3 is the joint variable (note again that the sign is not defined)

This design change results in a different zero position for the manipulator, and hence a different set of coordinate frames (Figure 4.21). Changing the joint variable for the third link from an angle to a displacement changes the second, third, and fourth **A** matrices (Figure 4.22). The third matrix reduces to an identity matrix, and the displacement appears in the fourth matrix because of the coincidence of coordinate frame origins. If the **A** matrices are multiplied, we obtain the following forward transform, which is considerably simpler than that for the manipulator with an elbow joint:

$$z_x = C_1(-C_2C_4S_5 - S_2C_5) + S_1S_4S_5 \tag{4.130}$$

$$z_y = S_1(-C_2C_4S_5 - S_2C_5) - C_1S_4S_5 \tag{4.131}$$

$$z_z = -S_2C_4S_5 + C_2C_5 \tag{4.132}$$

$$p_x = d_6(-C_1C_2C_4S_5 - C_1S_2C_5 + S_1S_4S_5) - dC_1S_2 + d_2S_1 \tag{4.133}$$

$$= d_6z_x - dC_1S_2 + d_2S_1 \tag{4.134}$$

$$p_y = d_6(-S_1C_2C_4S_5 - S_1S_2C_5 - C_1S_4S_5) - dS_1S_2 - d_2C_1 \tag{4.135}$$

$$= d_6z_y - dS_1S_2 - d_2C_1 \tag{4.136}$$

$$p_z = d_6(-S_2C_4S_5 + C_2C_5) + dC_2 + d_1 \tag{4.137}$$

$$= d_6z_z + dC_2 + d_1 \tag{4.138}$$

Using the same technique as in Example 4.2, we find a value for θ_1:

$$\theta_1 = \tan^{-1}\left(\frac{p_y}{p_x}\right) + \tan^{-1}\left(\frac{d_6S_4S_5 + d_2}{d_6(C_2C_4S_5 - S_2C_5) - dS_2}\right) \tag{4.139}$$

but this value is in terms of other joint angles. If we take the equations for p_x, p_y, and p_z (Equations 4.134, 4.136 and 4.138), and manipulate these

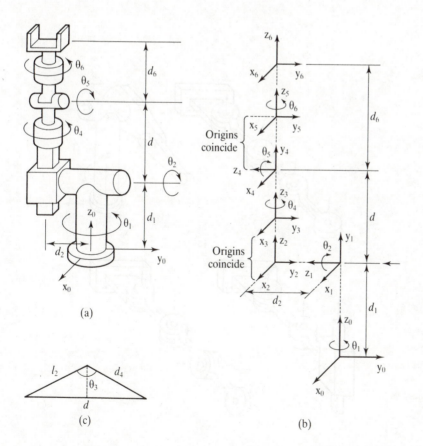

(a)

(b)

(c)

Figure 4.21
Reducing redundancy by replacing elbow joint.
(a) Manipulator in zero position;
(b) Assignment of coordinate frames;
(c) Elbow triangle.

Figure 4.22
Link parameters and **A** matrices for the modified robot arm: (a) link parameters; (b) **A** matrices

Link	Joint variable	Angle θ_n	Displacement d_n	Length l_n	Twist α_n	Range
1	θ_1	θ_1	$d_1 = 660.4$	0	$+90°$	-160 to $+160$
2	θ_2	θ_2	$d_2 = 149.5$	0	$-90°$	-225 to $+45$
3	d	θ_3	0	0	$0°$	-330 to $+864$
4	θ_4	θ_4	$d = 864.0$ max	0	$+90°$	-110 to $+170$
5	θ_5	θ_5	0	0	$-90°$	-100 to $+100$
6	θ_6	θ_6	$d_6 = 56.5$	0	$0°$	-266 to $+266$

(a)

$$
{}^0A_1 = \begin{bmatrix} C_1 & 0 & S_1 & 0 \\ S_1 & 0 & -C_1 & 0 \\ 0 & 1 & 0 & d_1 \\ 0 & 0 & 0 & 1 \end{bmatrix} \quad
{}^1A_2 = \begin{bmatrix} C_2 & 0 & -S_2 & 0 \\ S_2 & 0 & C_2 & 0 \\ 0 & -1 & 0 & d_2 \\ 0 & 0 & 0 & 1 \end{bmatrix} \quad
{}^2A_3 = \begin{bmatrix} 1 & 0 & 0 & 0 \\ 0 & 1 & 0 & 0 \\ 0 & 0 & 1 & 0 \\ 0 & 0 & 0 & 1 \end{bmatrix}
$$

$$
{}^3A_4 = \begin{bmatrix} C_4 & 0 & S_4 & 0 \\ S_4 & 0 & -C_4 & 0 \\ 0 & 1 & 0 & d \\ 0 & 0 & 0 & 1 \end{bmatrix} \quad
{}^4A_5 = \begin{bmatrix} C_5 & 0 & -S_5 & 0 \\ S_5 & 0 & C_5 & 0 \\ 0 & -1 & 0 & 0 \\ 0 & 0 & 0 & 1 \end{bmatrix} \quad
{}^5A_6 = \begin{bmatrix} C_6 & -S_6 & 0 & 0 \\ S_6 & C_6 & 0 & 0 \\ 0 & 0 & 1 & d_6 \\ 0 & 0 & 0 & 1 \end{bmatrix}
$$

(b)

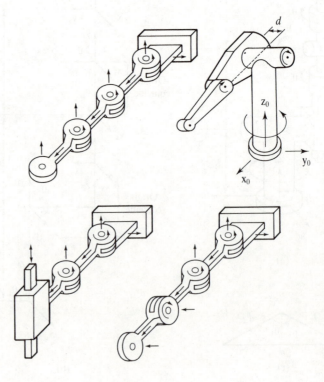

Figure 4.23
Three link manipulators.

equations we find a value for θ_1 in terms of the position and orientation of the end effector. From Equation 4.138:

$$C_2 = \frac{p_z - d_6 z_z - d_1}{d},$$

(4.140)

and thus:

$$S_2^2 = 1 - \left(\frac{p_z - d_6 z_z - d_1}{d}\right)^2$$

(4.141)

If we move terms in θ_1 to one side of Equations 4.134 and 4.136, square both sides of the equations, subtract the squared equations, add the squared equations, and use trigonometric identities the following equations are obtained:

$$(p_x - d_6 z_x)^2 - (p_y - d_6 z_y)^2 = (d^2 S_2^2 + d_2)\cos(2\theta_1)$$

(4.142)

$$(p_x - d_6 z_x)^2 + (p_y - d_6 z_y)^2 = d^2 S_2^2 + d_2^2 + 2dd_2 S_2 \sin(2\theta_1)$$

(4.143)

From these two equations a solution is obtained for θ_1 in terms of the atan2 function:

$$\theta_1 = \tfrac{1}{2}\tan^{-1}\left(\frac{[(p_x - d_6 z_x)^2 + (p_y - d_6 z_y)^2 - d^2 S_2^2 - d_2^2](d^2 S_2^2 + d_2)}{(2dd_2 S_2)[(p_x - d_6 z_x)^2 - (p_y - d_6 z_y)^2]}\right)$$

(4.144)

The final equation is fairly complex, but it does provide a solution independent of the other joint angles, when we substitute Equation 4.141 for S_2, something we were unable to do for the more complex manipulator. In addition, all the transcendental functions have been removed, improving the efficiency. The rest of the joint angles can be found using the inverse kinematic heuristic, as in Example 4.2.

Exercises

■ *Essay questions*

4.1 What is the direct kinematic algorithm?

4.2 What is the standard form for the manipulator transform? Draw it as a transform graph.

4.3 Which three types of joints are commonly found in robots?

Figure 4.24
Kinematic details of a five degree of freedom four bar linkage robot – link 2, 3 forms a pantograph mechanism (Figure 2.20(c)).

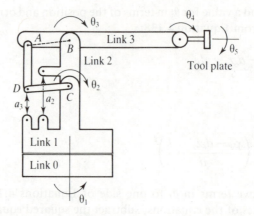

4.4 Take a type 7 link and rotate the revolute joint through 90° around the x_{n-1} axis. What are the link parameters for this new link?

4.5 Take a type 6 link and rotate the revolute joint through 90° around the x_n axis so that the joint axes are collinear. What are the link parameters for this new link?

4.6 Define the four link parameters.

4.7 Why does the type 4 link not have a degree of translation when it has physical length? How is the physical length accounted for? (Section 4.2)

4.8 Using Algorithm 4.2, assign coordinate frames to:

(a) the type 2 two-link manipulator shown in Figure 4.7, and
(b) the articulated arm in Figure 4.19, in the left arm position.

4.9 Solve the kinematic model for the type 3 two-link manipulator using trigonometry.

4.10 Define **A** matrices for each of the links in Figures 4.3 and 4.4.

4.11 Find the inverse kinematic transform for each of the two-link manipulators discussed in this chapter (Figures 4.5–4.10).

4.12 For the four three-link manipulators shown in Figure 4.23 carry out the following steps:

(a) assign coordinate frames;
(b) allocate link parameters;
(c) find the forward kinematic transform;
(d) find the orientation angles;
(e) find the inverse kinematic transform;
(f) define the work space.

4.13   Using homogeneous transforms, prove that the wrist in Figure 4.14 is degenerate.

4.14   Solve the rotation transform based on Euler angles.

4.15   Find the kinematic model of the Mini-Mover 5 manipulator, using homogeneous transforms.

4.16   If the distance d_2 on the simplified Puma robot (Equation 4.109) is reduced to zero, so that there ceases to be left and right shoulder positions, a solution for the first joint angle may be found in terms of the Cartesian space description. What is this solution?

4.17   The kinematic details of a typical five degree of freedom four bar linkage robot (Figure 1.10) are shown in Figure 4.24. Joints 2 and 3 are controlled by linear actuators a_2 and a_3. When the angle θ_2 changes, the orientation of link 3 with respect to the ground does not, as joint 3 controls the orientation of link 3 with respect to the world coordinate frame, not with respect to the frame in link 2, and ABCD forms a parallelogram. With this linkage arrangement, the structural rigidity of the linkages is increased and, hence, the robot can be positioned more precisely. These robots have a two degree of freedom wrist driven by motors mounted on link 1, usually through chains, so that actuator 4 controls wrist pitch with respect to world coordinates and actuator 5 controls wrist roll.

(a)   Find the kinematic model of this mechanism trigonometrically, and with homogeneous coordinates.

(b)   Find the kinematic model in terms of actuator positions a_2 and a_3 rather than joint angles θ_2 and θ_3.

(c)   Find the inverse kinematic equations. *Hint*: Look at the geometry of the robot and at the constraints placed on the robot by its design.

4.18   From the workspace description of the robot in Figure 4.25, calculate the link parameters and hence, the forward kinematic model.

■ *Practical questions*

4.1   Make a three-link planar manipulator (Figure 4.23) with three pieces of wood. Develop a kinematic model for this manipulator. Measure the joint angles for several Cartesian configurations, and use these to validate the model.

   Find the workspace for your manipulator. Select a point in the workspace, and find the redundant solutions for this position. What constraints can be placed on the robot to reduce the redundancies. Draw a straight line from one point in the workspace to another describing a path for the end of the manipulator to follow. Draw a graph of each joint angle as the manipulator end point traces out the path. What can you learn about trajectory planning from this experiment?

Figure 4.25
Detailed specification of a
six-axis Motoman Robot.

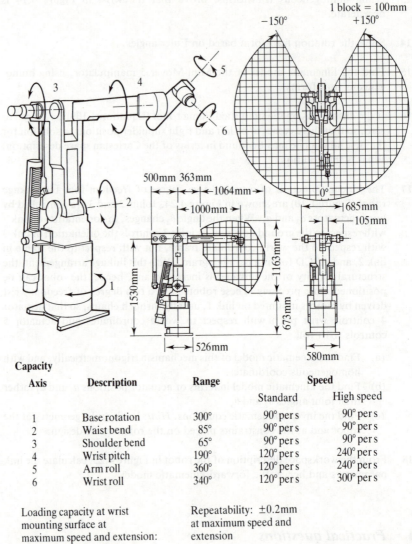

Grid scale:
1 block = 100mm

−150°   +150°

0°

500mm 363mm
←1064mm→
←1000mm→
1163mm
1530mm
673mm
526mm

685mm
105mm
580mm

Capacity

Axis	Description	Range	Speed	
			Standard	High speed
1	Base rotation	300°	90° per s	90° per s
2	Waist bend	85°	90° per s	90° per s
3	Shoulder bend	65°	90° per s	90° per s
4	Wrist pitch	190°	120° per s	240° per s
5	Arm roll	360°	120° per s	240° per s
6	Wrist roll	340°	120° per s	300° per s

Loading capacity at wrist
mounting surface at
maximum speed and extension:
Standard type: 10kg
High Speed Type: 5kg

Repeatability: ±0.2mm
at maximum speed and
extension

4.2   Implement the data structures and procedures in Figures 4.15 and 4.16, and add them to your library.

4.3   Write a set of routines to do the following:

(a)   calculate an **A** matrix given the values of the link parameters;
(b)   calculate the manipulator transformation matrix from the **A** matrices; and
(c)   calculate the orientation angles from the manipulator transform.

4.4   Using your library of routines, write a program to request the joint variables for one of the three-link manipulators in Figure 4.23, and calculate the location of the end effector. Write a second program to calculate the joint variables from the location.

4.5   Develop the kinematic model for a robot in the laboratory. Using the programs you have written so far, write a program to transform joint space coordinates to Cartesian space coordinates and vice versa for this robot. Develop a way to check the accuracy of your model, using measurements of the manipulator configuration.

4.6   Using a manipulator with an elbow joint, place the end effector at a known position using both elbow up and elbow down positions, record the angles, and calculate the zero error. Alternatively move the elbow joint to the same angle in both positions, and measure the error in the position of the end effector. Next, grip a pencil, or a light source, with the gripper (the axis of the pencil should be coincident with the roll axis), point it at a target, roll the gripper, and measure the orientation error. From these experiments, calculate the accuracy repeatability, and resolution of the robot (Section 4.14).

5 · *Kinematics: Manipulator Motion*

'There is a time for everything, and a season for every activity under heaven:

> a time to be born and a time to die.
> a time to plant and a time to uproot,
> a time to kill and a time to heal.
> a time to tear down and a time to build,. . .'

Ecclesiastes 3:1 – 3

Objectives

In this chapter, we extend the manipulator model to include time. Our objective is to study the motion of a set of linkages as the end effector traces out a trajectory in space. In this chapter and the next two, the reader is assumed to have a working knowledge of Newtonian mechanics. The modelling of motion includes the following topics:

- linear and angular velocity of manipulator links,
- linear and angular acceleration of manipulator links,
- differential motion,
- the manipulator Jacobian,
- inverse Jacobian algorithms,
- the problem of singularities.

In many robotic applications, a programmer specifies the end points of a path, and lets the robot follow an unconstrained trajectory between those points. This scheme can result in the end effector tracing out a wildly varying path. A **path** is a sequence of points in space that the end effector of a robot traverses as it moves from one end point to the next. A **trajectory** is a path with time constraints, that is, it includes velocity and acceleration as well as location at every point along the path. A common control strategy is to calculate the change in the joint variables required to achieve the final location, and to control the joint motors so that all the joints reach their final values at the same time. This strategy, which is known as **joint interpolated motion** (Section 9.3.3.2), results in smooth joint motion, but may result in a very crooked Cartesian path.

In many applications, the trajectory of the end effector; as well as the path it traces has to be specified. For example, when moving an open container of liquid, spillage can result if the acceleration is too high, or if the container is not kept in the correct orientation. Also, if the acceleration is too high, a joint motor control amplifier may saturate, and lose control of the manipulator. Arc welding, spray painting, conveyor-belt tracking, laser cutting, and gluing are some of the applications where Cartesian velocities and accelerations have to be controlled as well as location in order to achieve the desired result.

Much of the work in the design of prosthetic arms for the handicapped has involved velocity control in Cartesian space (Whitney, 1969). It seems that people control the motion of their hands when reaching for an object, and only control the absolute position when moving the hand into the final grasping position. As soon as time or path constraints are applied to the motion of the end effector, velocity and acceleration have to be controlled. We find the path traced out by the end effector by substituting the sequence of joint angles into the kinematic model. To calculate velocities and accelerations, we require kinematic models of manipulator velocity and acceleration.

Fine movement of our hands involves differential motion based on feedback information from both vision and touch senses. These motions are sometimes called **motions of accommodation**. In robotics, **differential motion** is useful in many applications. For example, when we use a vision system to monitor the location of the end effector, we can calculate the differential changes in position and orientation required to place the hand on an object from successive images. By transforming these differential changes from vision space to the Cartesian space of the robot, we can eliminate the transformation to absolute positions. To use this information, we must be able to control the differential motion of the robot.

In complex applications, a robot is often programmed by teaching. An example is spray painting where a painter guides the end effector through the desired sequence of motions. The sequence of joint angles corresponding to these motions is recorded, and, when the robot is to paint, this sequence is replayed by the joint controllers to move the robot through the same motions. Before a human teacher can be replaced with a program to generate trajectories from a CAD database, the process must be modelled and we must be able to calculate a joint trajectory from a Cartesian trajectory (location, velocity, and acceleration). Thus, inverse kinematic transforms are required to compute joint velocities and accelerations.

In this chapter, we will look at kinematic models for differential motion, velocity and acceleration. Also, we will develop transformations for these models from one coordinate frame to another. To obtain a feel for the physics of manipulator motion, we will start with vector analysis of the velocity and acceleration of a rigid body, and apply this analysis to two-link manipulators. Then we will develop descriptions of differential motion, and finally the transformation between joint and Cartesian velocities, known as the **Jacobian**.

5.1 Derivatives

Average velocity is the change in position of an object divided by the time to make the change. As the time interval approaches zero, the average velocity approaches the instantaneous velocity and is the derivative of position with respect to time (Window 5.1). Similarly, acceleration is the derivative of velocity with respect to time (Windows 5.2 and 5.3). Thus, there is a relationship between differential motion, velocity, and acceleration. This relationship will be applied to the kinematics of manipulators.

Homogeneous transformations describe the location of objects in space with respect to various coordinate frames. Given a transformation whose elements are functions of some variable, a differential transformation can be found with respect to that variable by differentiating the elements of the original transformation. For example, if the **A** matrix in Equation 5.1 represents a revolute joint, the transformation is a function of the angle θ between the links. If, on the other hand, it represents a prismatic joint, the transformation is a function of the distance d between the links.

$$\mathbf{A}_n = \begin{bmatrix} \cos(\theta) & -\sin(\theta)\cos(\alpha) & \sin(\theta)\sin(\alpha) & l\cos(\theta) \\ \sin(\theta) & \cos(\theta)\cos(\alpha) & -\cos(\theta)\sin(\alpha) & l\sin(\theta) \\ 0 & \sin(\alpha) & \cos(\alpha) & d \\ 0 & 0 & 0 & 1 \end{bmatrix} \tag{5.1}$$

In the case of a revolute joint, we obtain the differential transform by differentiating each element (Section 13.2) with respect to θ.

$$\frac{d\mathbf{A}_n}{d\theta} = \begin{bmatrix} -\sin(\theta) & -\cos(\theta)\cos(\alpha) & \cos(\theta)\sin(\alpha) & -l\sin(\theta) \\ \cos(\theta) & -\sin(\theta)\cos(\alpha) & \sin(\theta)\sin(\alpha) & l\cos(\theta) \\ 0 & 0 & 0 & 0 \\ 0 & 0 & 0 & 0 \end{bmatrix} \tag{5.2}$$

Window 5.1   Linear velocity

An object is moving if it occupies a different position in space at different times. Velocity is displacement in unit time and is therefore a vector divided by a scalar, that is, velocity is a vector. Speed is the magnitude of velocity, and thus, it is a scalar, because it has no direction.

$$v = \frac{d - d_0}{t - t_0} = \frac{\text{distance travelled}}{\text{time}} = \frac{d}{t} = \int_{t_0}^{t} \frac{v \, dt}{t - t_0} = v_{\text{average}}$$

We can calculate the average velocity of an object by dividing the distance travelled by the time period. At any instant during the period, the instantaneous velocity may differ from the average. If an object is subject to two independent velocities v_1 and v_2, the resultant velocity is the vector sum of v_1 and v_2. The two common methods of vector addition are:

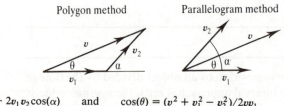

Polygon method   Parallelogram method

$$v^2 = v_1^2 + v_2^2 + 2v_1 v_2 \cos(\alpha) \quad \text{and} \quad \cos(\theta) = (v^2 + v_1^2 - v_2^2)/2vv_1$$

The principle of independence of velocities states that any velocity v may be resolved into two components v_1 and v_2, which can be combined to represent the actual velocity, and each component may be analysed independently of the others. This is a special case of the general principle of superposition. The instantaneous velocity is the rate of change of position with respect to time.

$$0 \overset{d}{\underset{t}{\rule{2cm}{0.4pt}}} \overset{d + \Delta d}{\underset{t + \Delta t}{}} > v$$

$$v_{\text{average}} = \frac{\Delta d}{\Delta t} \text{ where } \Delta \text{ represents a small change}$$

$$v_{\text{instantaneous}} = \underset{\Delta t \to 0}{\text{limit of }} \frac{\Delta d}{\Delta t} = \frac{dd}{dt}$$

If object 1 is moving with velocity v_1 and object 2 is moving with velocity v_2 then the velocity of object 2 with respect to object 1 (relative velocity) is the vector summation of vector $-v_1$ with vector v_2.

$$v_{\text{relative}}^2 = v_1^2 + v_2^2 + 2v_1 v_2 \cos(\alpha)$$

Window 5.2   Linear acceleration

Motion in which velocity changes from point to point is accelerated motion. Thus, acceleration is the time rate of change of velocity. As acceleration is the difference between two vectors, it is also a vector. Note, acceleration is not the time rate of change of speed. An object moving with constant speed in a circle is accelerating, because the velocity is changing continuously, since the direction of motion is changing.

$$a = \frac{v - v_0}{t - t_0} = \text{velocity change/time}$$

$$v = v_0 + at \quad \text{and} \quad d = \left(\frac{v_0 + v}{2}\right) t$$

where $(v_0 + v)/2$ = average velocity for uniformly accelerated motion in a straight line.

$$d = v_0 t + \frac{at^2}{2} \quad \text{and} \quad d = vt - \frac{at^2}{2}$$

$$v^2 = v_0{}^2 + 2ad$$

Instantaneous acceleration is the rate of change of velocity with respect to time.

$$a_{\text{average}} = \frac{\Delta v}{\Delta t}$$

$$a_{\text{instantaneous}} = \text{limit of } \underset{\Delta t \to 0}{} \frac{\Delta v}{\Delta t} = \frac{dv}{dt} = \frac{d^2 d}{dt^2}$$

Window 5.3   Uniform circular motion

When an object is moving in a circle with constant speed its velocity has constant magnitude, but its direction is continually changing. Thus, the object is accelerating.

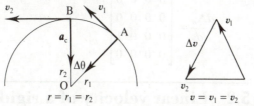

The direction of a_c is along the radius r, thus, it is called radial or normal acceleration. v_1 is perpendicular to r_1, and v_2 is perpendicular to r_2. Observe that the vector triangle is similar to the physical triangle OAB. If we consider magnitude only, then

$$\frac{\Delta v}{v} = \frac{AB}{r} = \frac{v \Delta t}{r} \qquad \text{when } \Delta t \text{ is small, AB is approximately equal to chord } AB = v \Delta t$$

$$\Delta v = \frac{v^2 \Delta t}{r}$$

$$a_{\text{average}} = \frac{\Delta v}{\Delta t} = \frac{v^2}{r}$$

$$a_c = \text{limit of } \underset{\Delta t \to 0}{} \frac{\Delta v}{\Delta t} = \frac{dv}{dt} = \frac{v^2}{r} = \text{centripetal acceleration}$$

So far we have defined velocity and acceleration linearly. We can also define them in terms of the angular velocity of the object, and the period of the cyclic motion.

$$v = 2\pi r/T = 2\pi rf = \text{distance/time}$$
$$a_c = 4\pi r^2/T^2 = 2\pi r^2 f^2$$

where $f = 1/T$ = frequency of motion, and T is the period of motion (time for one cycle).

Tangential velocity $v = \omega r$, and thus,

Centripetal acceleration $a_c = v^2/r = 4\pi r^2/T^2 = 2\pi r^2 f^2 = \omega^2 r$

where ω = angular velocity = $2\pi/T = 2\pi f$ radians/second

Figure 5.1
Modelling the position
kinematics of a rigid body
with coordinate frame.
(a) Location of a rigid body
relative to a reference frame;
(b) Location of coordinate
frames on body.

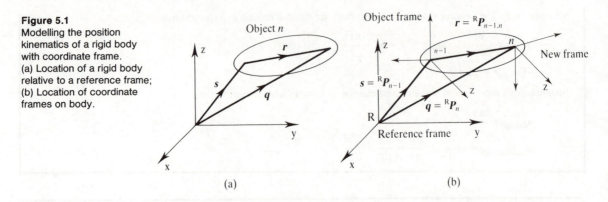

(a)   (b)

In the case of a prismatic joint, we obtain the differential transform by differentiating each element with respect to d.

$$\frac{dA_n}{dd} = \begin{bmatrix} 0 & 0 & 0 & 0 \\ 0 & 0 & 0 & 0 \\ 0 & 0 & 0 & 1 \\ 0 & 0 & 0 & 0 \end{bmatrix} \qquad (5.3)$$

5.2 Linear velocity of a rigid body

If a body is located at a point s relative to a reference frame (Figure 5.1), the position of a point q on that body located at r relative to s is described by the vector sum:

$$^Rq = {}^Rs + {}^Rr \qquad \text{or} \qquad ^Rp_n = {}^Rp_{n-1} + {}^Rp_{n-1,n} \qquad (5.4)$$

If the body is moving in space with velocity ds/dt and the point q is moving relative to s with velocity dr/dt then the velocity of q with respect to the reference frame is:

$$\frac{dq}{dt} = \frac{ds}{dt} + \frac{dr}{dt} \qquad \text{or} \qquad ^Rv_q = {}^Rv_s + {}^Rv_r \qquad (5.5)$$

As with location, we attach frames to the body. The motion of these frames describes the motion of the body (Figure 5.1), and the location of these frames is described with transformations (Section 3.3). An object frame is attached (frame $n-1$) at the point s, and the body is allowed to move within this frame. We attach a new frame (frame n) at the point q, and fix it to the body. Now the linear velocity of the point q can be described with respect to the reference frame as the velocity of the object frame with respect to the reference frame plus the velocity of the new frame with respect to the object frame as seen from the reference frame.

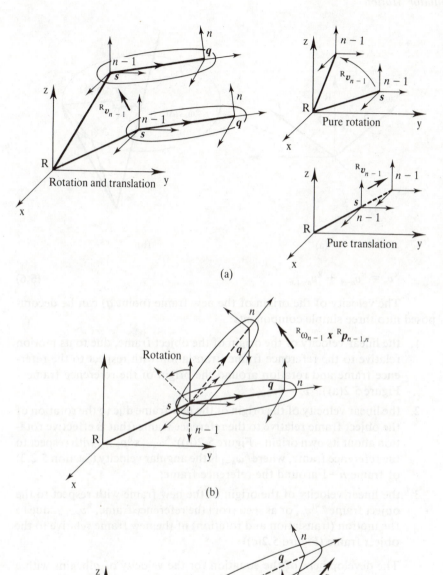

(a)

(b)

(c)

Figure 5.2
Decomposition of the velocity of a point on a moving body.
(a) First component of the velocity of q: the linear velocity of the origin of the object frame ($n-1$) due to the motion of the origin with respect to the reference frame.
(b) Second component of the velocity of q: the linear velocity of the origin of the new frame (n) due to the rotation of the object frame ($n-1$) with respect to the reference frame (around its own origin).
(c) Third component of the velocity of q: the linear velocity of the origin of the new frame (n) due to the motion of the new frame with respect to the object frame.

Figure 5.3
Velocity component due to rotating frames.
(a) Object frame rotating with respect to reference frame.
(b) Velocity of a point due to angular velocity.

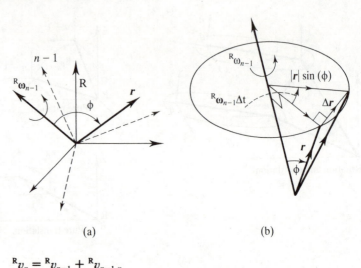

(a)   (b)

$$^R v_n = {}^R v_{n-1} + {}^R v_{n-1,n} \tag{5.6}$$

The velocity of the origin of the new frame (point q) can be decomposed into three simple components:

1. the linear velocity of the origin of the object frame, due to its motion relative to the reference frame (translation with respect to the reference frame and rotation around the origin of the reference frame – Figure 5.2(a)): $^R v_s = {}^R v_{n-1}$;

2. the linear velocity of the origin of the new frame due to the rotation of the object frame relative to the reference frame (that is effective rotation about its own origin – Figure 5.2(b)): $^R \omega_{n-1} \mathbf{x} \, ^R p_{n-1,n}$ with respect to the reference frame, where $^R \omega_{n-1}$ is the angular velocity (Section 5.2.3) of frame $n-1$ around the reference frame;

3. the linear velocity of the origin of the new frame with respect to the object frame $^{n-1} v_n$, or as seen from the reference frame, $^R v_{n-1,n}$, due to the motion (translation and rotation) of the new frame relative to the object frame (Figure 5.2(c)).

The development of the equation for the velocity of q begins with a look at each of these three components in isolation. We isolate the first component by allowing the object to translate (but not rotate) as it moves. The linear velocity of the origin of the object frame involves two elements: a translational element due to the change in magnitude of the vector between the origins, and a rotational element due to the change in direction of this vector.

$$^R v_{n-1} = {}^R vtrans_{n-1} + {}^R \omega_{n-1} \mathbf{x} \, ^R p_{n-1} = \frac{d}{dt} \, ^R p_{n-1} = {}^R v_s \tag{5.7}$$

Next, we isolate the second component of the velocity. To consider the contribution that the rotation of the object frame makes to the linear velocity of q, the origin of the object frame is made coincident with the origin of the reference frame, and the object frame allowed to rotate (but not translate)

(Figure 5.3(a)). In this special situation, vectors q and r are the same. Also, the object is fixed with respect to the object frame (Figure 5.2(b)).

To derive a general relationship between angular and linear velocity, we study the small signal case. In Figure 5.3, vector r is at an angle ϕ to angular velocity vector $^R\omega_{n-1}$ and is rotating around it. During an incremental time, Δt, vector r moves an incremental distance Δr in a direction perpendicular to both the angular velocity vector and vector r (Figure 5.3(b)). Using trigonometry (Section 13.1.1), we find the incremental distance:

$$\Delta r = (|^R p_{n-1,n}| \sin(\phi))(|^R \omega_{n-1}| \Delta t) \tag{5.8}$$

The ratio of the incremental position change of r due to the rotation of the frame to the incremental time change is:

$$\Delta r / \Delta t = [|^R p_{n-1,n}| \sin(\phi)](|^R\omega_{n-1}|) = |^R\omega_{n-1}| \, |^R p_{n-1,n}| \sin(\phi) \tag{5.9}$$

which, as Δt approaches zero, becomes the instantaneous velocity (Equation 5.10), which is expressed as the cross product of two vectors: one describing the angular velocity of the object frame, and one describing the location of the point.

$$^R v_n = {}^R\omega_{n-1} \times {}^R p_{n-1,n} = {}^R\omega_{n-1} \times {}^R\text{Rot}_{n-1}{}^{n-1} p_n \tag{5.10}$$

Note that, $^R p_{n-1,n}$ and $^{n-1} p_{n-1,n}$ are the same vector: the rotation transform simply transforms the components along the axes of frame $n-1$ to components along the axes of the reference frame. In practice, the origins of the two frames do not coincide, but it can be shown that for any motion of one frame relative to another, an angular velocity vector can be found that satisfies Equation 5.10.

We isolate the third component by fixing the object frame with respect to the reference frame and allowing the object to move in the object frame. In this situation, we have the linear velocity of the origin of the new frame n with respect to the object frame $n-1$ as seen from the reference frame. Component 3 can be expanded in a similar way to component 1 (Equation 5.7). The rotation transform is used to convert the components of the velocity of the new frame from being parallel to the object frame to being parallel to the reference frame – since velocity is a free vector (Section 13.4.2).

$$^R v_{\text{Rot}\,n} = {}^R\text{Rot}_{n-1}{}^{n-1} v_n = {}^R v\text{trans}_{n-1,n} + {}^R\omega_n \times {}^R p_{n-1,n} \tag{5.11}$$

Finally, we combine the three components to derive the general formula for the linear velocity of a point moving on an object as seen from a reference frame.

$$^R v_n = {}^R v_{n-1} + {}^R\omega_{n-1} \, {}^R p_{n-1,n} + {}^R v_{n-1,n}$$

$$= {}^R v_{n-1} + {}^R\omega_{n-1} \times {}^R\text{Rot}_{n-1}{}^{n-1} p_n + {}^R\text{Rot}_{n-1}{}^{n-1} v_n$$

$$= \frac{d}{dt} {}^R p_n = \frac{d}{dt} ({}^R p_{n-1} + {}^R p_{n-1,n}) = \frac{d}{dt} {}^R p_{n-1} + \frac{d}{dt} ({}^R\text{Rot}_{n-1}{}^{n-1} p_n) \tag{5.12}$$

This equation expresses the velocity relationship between fixed and moving axes. If we consider only the case rotating axes, the linear velocity of the origin of the object frame with respect to the reference frame ($^{R}v_{n-1}$) is zero, and we are left with components 2 and 3 of our general velocity equation. In this situation, we can generalize Equation 5.12 to establish the relation for converting first time derivatives of any free vector between fixed and rotating systems.

Consider a vector s as observed from both a reference frame and a new frame. The new frame is rotating with angular velocity ω with respect to the reference frame. The derivative of s in the reference frame is the derivative of s in the new frame plus the derivative it would have if it were at rest in the new frame (the derivative due to the rotation of the new frame).

$$^{R}ds = {}^{N}ds + \omega \mathbf{x} s \tag{5.13}$$

While s is the same vector in both frames, its components along the axes of each frame are different. In order to add vectors, the components must all be expressed with respect to the same frame. The derivative of s with respect to time is:

$$\frac{d^{R}s}{dt} = {}^{R}\mathbf{Rot}_{N} \frac{d^{N}s}{dt} + {}^{R}\omega_{N} \mathbf{x} {}^{R}\mathbf{Rot}_{N} {}^{N}s \tag{5.14}$$

where the first term is the derivative of the vector with respect to the new frame, and the second term is the result of the rotation of the new frame.

5.2.1 Linear velocity of manipulator links

To model a manipulator link (link n), we attach a link coordinate frame (frame n) at the distal joint of the link (joint $n+1$: see Section 4.4). This frame is internal to the link and is fixed to it. The link moves within the frame attached to the preceding link (link $n-1$), (the frame at joint n – the proximal joint of link n). Thus, the above description given of the velocity of a point moving on an object maps directly to the velocity of the origin of the link frame attached to the distal joint of an isolated link (Figure 5.4). In the case of a link, the first component of the velocity in Equation 5.12 is the velocity of the origin of the coordinate frame at the proximal joint of the link (frame $n-1$ at joint n). The second component is the velocity of the origin of the link coordinate frame (frame n at joint $n+1$) due to the rotation of frame $n-1$. This rotation is the result of the motion of the links between the reference frame and frame $n-1$. The third component is due to the motion of link n within frame $n-1$, as described by the velocity of the origin of frame n.

To see how the general velocity formula (Equation 5.12) applies to the special case of a manipulator, we will model a type 1 two-link manipulator (Figure 5.5). Equation 5.12 applies directly to this manipulator if we consider x_0, y_0 to be the reference frame; x_1, y_1 to be the object frame; and x_2, y_2 to be the new frame. From the geometry of the manipulator, the following observations are made about the terms in the velocity equation:

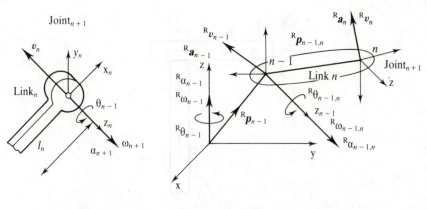

Figure 5.4
The linear velocity of link *n* is
the velocity of the origin
coordinate frame *n* at the
distal joint (joint *n*+1).

1. Frame 1 does not translate with respect to frame 0: the magnitude of $^0p_1$ is fixed. However, owing to the rotation of joint 1, the direction of $^0p_1$ changes and thus frame 1 has a linear velocity with respect to the reference frame – the first term in the velocity equation.

2. As link 1 rotates, the object frame rotates around the reference frame giving frame 2 a linear velocity with respect to the reference frame – the second term in the velocity equation.

3. Link 2 rotates around the origin of the object frame, causing the vector $^0p_{1,2}$ to change in direction, but not in magnitude. This rotation of joint 2 gives frame 2 an instantaneous linear velocity with respect to the reference frame – the third term in the velocity equation.

After substitution into Equation 5.12, the velocity of the end effector of the type 1 two-link manipulator is:

$$^0v_2 = {^0v_1} + {^0\omega_1} \times {^0}\text{Rot}_1 {^1p_2} + {^0}\text{Rot}_1 {^1v_2}$$

$$= \begin{bmatrix} -l_1S_1 - l_2S_{12} & -l_2S_{12} \\ l_1C_1 + l_2C_{12} & l_2C_{12} \end{bmatrix} \begin{bmatrix} d\theta_1 \\ d\theta_2 \end{bmatrix} \qquad \textbf{(5.15)}$$

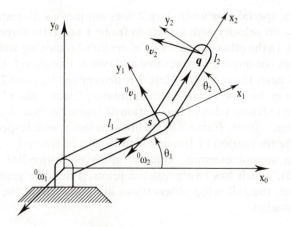

Figure 5.5
Velocity of end effector of
type 1 two-link manipulator.

Figure 5.6
Velocity of end effector of type 5 two-link manipulator.

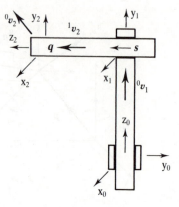

where

$$d\theta_1 = {}^0\omega_1 \qquad \text{and} \qquad d\theta_2 = {}^1\omega_2.$$

To calculate ${}^0v_1$ and ${}^1v_2$, each link is modelled separately. In this model, the object frame is the same as the reference frame, and we use the equation for the third component of the general velocity equation (Equation 5.12). For the type 1 two-link manipulator:

$$
{}^0v_1 = {}^0\omega_1 \times {}^0p_1 = \begin{bmatrix} 0 \\ 0 \\ d\theta_1 \end{bmatrix} \times \begin{bmatrix} l_1 C_1 \\ l_1 S_1 \\ 1 \end{bmatrix} = \begin{bmatrix} -l_1 S_1 \\ l_1 C_1 \end{bmatrix} d\theta_1 \qquad (5.16)
$$

and

$$
{}^1v_2 = {}^1\omega_2 \times {}^1p_2 = \begin{bmatrix} 0 \\ 0 \\ d\theta_2 \end{bmatrix} \times \begin{bmatrix} l_2 C_2 \\ l_2 S_2 \\ 1 \end{bmatrix} = \begin{bmatrix} -l_2 S_2 \\ l_2 C_2 \end{bmatrix} d\theta_2 \qquad (5.17)
$$

In the special case where link 2 does *not* move with respect to link 1, frame 2 has no velocity with respect to frame 1 and term three of Equation 5.15 is zero. In the other special case, where link 2 is moving and link 1 is not, frame 1 does not move and terms one and two of Equation 5.15 are zero. In the general case, the motion of link 2 is determined by joint 2. If joint 2 is revolute, as in the type 1 two-link manipulator, frame 2 has a linear velocity with respect to frame 1 due to the rotation of frame 2 around frame 1. If joint 2 is a prismatic joint, frame 2 has a linear velocity with respect to frame 1 owing to the translation of frame 2 with respect to frame 1.

As a second example, consider the type 5 two-link manipulator (Figure 5.6), which has two prismatic joints. From the geometry of this manipulator, the following observations are made about the terms in the velocity equation:

1. Frame 1 translates with respect to the reference frame, but does not rotate, that is the magnitude of $^0p_1$ can vary, but its direction cannot. Hence, the second term in Equation 5.12 is zero, as it is the velocity which results from the rotation of frame 1. Also, the first term in the general velocity equation is the velocity due to the change in the magnitude of $^0p_1$.

2. Frame 2 translates with respect to the frame 1, causing the magnitude of vector $^1p_2$ to change, but there is no change in its direction. This translation gives frame 2 an instantaneous linear velocity with respect to the reference frame – the third term in the velocity equation.

The equation describing the velocity of the end effector of the type 5 two-link manipulator is:

$$^0v_2 = {}^0v_1 + {}^0\mathbf{Rot}_1\,{}^1v_2 \tag{5.18}$$

where

$$^0\mathbf{Rot}_1 = \mathrm{Rot}(x, 90)$$

5.2.2 Propagation from link to link

As a manipulator is a chain of links, when one link moves, the links attached to its distal joint move too. So the motion of link n with respect to the reference frame is the sum of the motions of all the links from the reference frame to link n plus the motion of link n. Thus, to calculate both the angular and linear velocities of link n, we the sum of the angular and linear velocities of the proximal links to the angular and linear velocities of link n. Before we can sum vectors, we must express them with respect to the same coordinate frame. Sometimes that frame will be the reference frame, and sometimes it will be one of the link frames, (such as frame n, the frame at the distal joint of link n). To obtain the velocities of individual links with respect to a desired reference frame, the velocity vector has to be transferred from one frame to another.

Linear velocity is transferred from one frame to another using rotation transforms as in Equation 5.12. For example, the velocity of link n is the velocity of frame $n-1$ plus the velocity due to the motion of link n. The velocity of link n is obtained with respect to frame $n-1$ by substituting $n-1$ for R in Equation 5.12, and with respect to frame n by substituting n for R.

$$
\begin{aligned}
{}^{n-1}v_n &= {}^{n-1}\mathbf{Rot}_n({}^nv_{n-1} + {}^n\omega_{n-1}\times{}^np_{n-1,n} + {}^nv_{n-1,n}) \\
&= {}^{n-1}v_{n-1} + {}^{n-1}\omega_{n-1}\times{}^{n-1}p_{n-1,n} + {}^{n-1}v_{n-1,n}
\end{aligned} \tag{5.19}
$$

$$
\begin{aligned}
{}^nv_n &= {}^n\mathbf{Rot}_{n-1}({}^{n-1}v_{n-1} + {}^{n-1}\omega_{n-1}\times{}^{n-1}p_n + {}^{n-1}v_n) \\
&= {}^nv_{n-1} + {}^n\omega_{n-1}\times{}^n\mathbf{Rot}_{n-1}{}^{n-1}p_n + {}^n\mathbf{Rot}_{n-1}{}^{n-1}v_n
\end{aligned} \tag{5.20}
$$

In the above equations, the first term is the velocity of the proximal frame of the link due to the motion of the previous links. The other terms are a result of the motion of the link. The velocity vectors are transfered from one frame to the other by applying a rotation transform.

5.2.3 Angular velocity

In our calculation of the linear velocity of a point on a rigid body, the angular velocity of frame $n-1$ with respect to the reference frame was used. The angular velocity of a body is the rate at which the body turns about an axis. Angular velocity is described with a vector whose magnitude is the rate of turning and whose direction is along an axis determined by the right-hand rule. The angular velocity of frame n is the sum of the angular velocity of frame n with respect to frame $n-1$ and the angular velocity of frame $n-1$ with respect to the reference frame. Before we can add these vectors, they must be expressed with respect to the same frame.

$$^R\omega_n = {}^R\omega_{R,n-1} + {}^R\omega_{n-1,n} \tag{5.21}$$

Angular velocity is transformed from one frame to another, with a rotation transform.

$$^R\omega_{n-1,n} = {}^R\mathbf{Rot}_{n-1}{}^{n-1}\omega_n \tag{5.22}$$

When calculating the angular velocity of a manipulator link, the velocities are expressed with respect to the same frame, and added. The angular velocity of link n is the angular velocity of frame $n-1$ plus the angular velocity of link n relative to frame $n-1$.

$$^{n-1}\omega_n = {}^{n-1}\omega_{n-1} + {}^{n-1}\omega_{n-1,n} = {}^{n-1}\mathbf{Rot}_n({}^n\omega_{n-1} + {}^n\omega_{n-1,n}) \tag{5.23}$$

$$^n\omega_n = {}^n\omega_{n-1} + {}^n\omega_{n-1,n} = {}^n\mathbf{Rot}_{n-1}({}^{n-1}\omega_{n-1} + {}^{n-1}\omega_n) \tag{5.24}$$

In the case of a manipulator, angular velocity vectors describe the rotation of links around revolute joints. As the rotation is constrained to be around the joint axis, the angular velocity of the link with respect to the proximal frame consists of a single component.

$$^{n-1}\omega_n = \frac{d\theta_n}{dt} z_{n-1} = \begin{bmatrix} 0 \\ 0 \\ \theta_n \end{bmatrix} \tag{5.25}$$

where

z_{n-1} is a unit vector in the direction of the joint axis, and

θ_n is the joint angle.

For the type 1 two-link manipulator:

$$^0\omega_1 = d\theta_1 \qquad \text{and} \qquad {}^1\omega_2 = d\theta_2 \tag{5.26}$$

and

$$^0\omega_2 = {}^0\omega_1 + {}^0\omega_{1,2} = {}^0\omega_1 + {}^0\mathbf{Rot}_1\,{}^1\omega_2 = \begin{bmatrix} 0 \\ 0 \\ d\theta_1 \end{bmatrix} - \begin{bmatrix} C_1 & -S_1 & 0 \\ S_1 & C_1 & 0 \\ 0 & 0 & 1 \end{bmatrix} \begin{bmatrix} 0 \\ 0 \\ d\theta_2 \end{bmatrix}$$

$$= \begin{bmatrix} 0 \\ 0 \\ d\theta_1 + d\theta_2 \end{bmatrix} = {}^0\omega_1 + {}^1\omega_2 \tag{5.27}$$

because the axes of the two joints are parallel.

5.3   Acceleration of a rigid body

When an object is stationary, its position remains constant with time. In contrast, when an object is moving, its velocity is unlikely to remain constant with time. Variation in velocity with respect to time is called **acceleration**. At any instant, the derivative of a linear velocity vector is linear acceleration (Window 5.2), and the derivative of an angular velocity vector is angular acceleration (Window 5.3). If we differentiate the general velocity formula, a general formula for linear acceleration is obtained:

$$^R a_n = {}^R a_{n-1} + {}^R\alpha_{n-1} \times {}^R\mathbf{Rot}_{n-1}{}^{n-1}p_n + {}^R\omega_{n-1} \times \frac{d}{dt}({}^R\mathbf{Rot}_{n-1}{}^{n-1}p_n)$$

$$+ \frac{d}{dt}({}^R\mathbf{Rot}_{n-1}{}^{n-1}v_n) \tag{5.28}$$

where

$^R a_{n-1}$ is the linear acceleration of the origin of the object frame, and

$^R\alpha_{n-1}$ is the angular acceleration of the object frame, around the reference frame.

Terms three and four require further expansion. For term three, we derive an expression for the derivative of ${}^R\mathbf{Rot}_{n-1}{}^{n-1}p_n$ from Equation 5.12. The fourth term is the acceleration of the origin of the new frame with respect to the object frame. Using the general form of the derivative of a vector in a rotating frame (Equation 5.14), we express this acceleration as an acceleration due to the angular velocity of the object frame, plus an acceleration due to the motion of the object relative to the object frame.

$$\frac{d}{dt}{}^R v_{n-1,n} = \frac{d}{dt}({}^R\mathbf{Rot}_{n-1}{}^{n-1}v_n)$$

$$= {}^R\omega_{n-1} \times {}^R\mathbf{Rot}_{n-1}{}^{n-1}v_n + {}^R\mathbf{Rot}_{n-1}\frac{d}{dt}{}^{n-1}v_n$$

$$= {}^R\omega_{n-1} \times {}^R v_{n-1,n} + {}^R\mathbf{Rot}_{n-1}{}^{n-1}a_n$$

$$= {}^R\omega_{n-1} \times {}^R v_{n-1,n} + {}^R a_{n-1,n} \tag{5.29}$$

By substituting Equations 5.12 and 5.29 into Equation 5.28, we obtain the general formula for the linear acceleration of a point on an object with respect to the reference frame.

$${}^R a_n = {}^R a_{n-1} + {}^R\alpha_{n-1} \times {}^R p_{n-1,n} + {}^R\omega_{n-1} \times ({}^R\omega_{n-1} \times {}^R p_{n-1,n})$$

$$+ 2{}^R\omega_{n-1} \times {}^R v_{n-1,n} + {}^R a_{n-1,n}$$

$$= {}^R a_{n-1} + {}^R\alpha_{n-1} \times {}^R\mathbf{Rot}_{n-1}{}^{n-1}p_n$$

$$+ {}^R\omega_{n-1} \times ({}^R\omega_{n-1} \times {}^R\mathbf{Rot}_{n-1}{}^{n-1}p_n)$$

$$+ 2{}^R\omega_{n-1} \times {}^R\mathbf{Rot}_{n-1}{}^{n-1}v_n + {}^R\mathbf{Rot}_{n-1}{}^{n-1}a_n \tag{5.30}$$

Physically, Equation 5.30 represents the sum of four accelerations. The first term is the linear acceleration of the origin of the object frame with respect to the reference frame. The second and third terms are the tangential and normal components of the acceleration of the origin of the new frame with respect to the object frame as seen from the reference frame. The second term is the acceleration of the origin of frame n due to changes in the angular velocity of frame $n-1$. In the case of a revolute joint, this is the acceleration of the joint variable. The third term is the centripetal acceleration due to the uniform circular motion of the origin of frame n, which results from the rotation of frame $n-1$. The fourth term is the Coriolis acceleration, and represents the difference between the acceleration measured from the reference frame and the relative acceleration measured from the object frame. Finally, the fifth term is the acceleration of the origin of frame n with respect to the frame $n-1$ due to the motion of frame n relative to frame $n-1$.

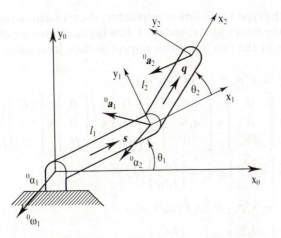

Figure 5.7
Acceleration of the end effector of a type 1 two-link manipulator.

5.3.1 Linear acceleration of manipulator links

Applying Equation 5.30 directly to the type 1 two-link manipulator, we obtain:

$$^0a_2 = {}^0a_1 + {}^0\alpha_1 \times {}^0\mathbf{Rot}_1{}^1p_2 + {}^0\omega_1 \times ({}^0\omega_1 \times {}^0\mathbf{Rot}_1{}^1p_2)$$
$$+ 2{}^0\omega_1 \times {}^0\mathbf{Rot}_1{}^1v_2 + {}^0\mathbf{Rot}_1{}^1a_2 \qquad (5.31)$$

Term one is the acceleration due to the circular motion of frame 1 around joint 1, and term five is the acceleration of frame 2 relative to frame 1 (Figure 5.7). This acceleration is determined by the nature of joint 2. If joint 2 is revolute, as for the type 1 two-link manipulator, frame 2 rotates around frame 1, and thus, it has a linear velocity with respect to frame 1 of $^1\omega_2 \times {}^1p_2$, and a linear acceleration with respect to frame 1 of $^1\omega_2 \times {}^1v_2$. If joint 2 is a prismatic joint, frame 2 translates with respect to frame 1, and thus, has a linear velocity with respect to frame 1 of $^1v_2$, and a linear acceleration with respect to frame 1 of $^1a_2$.

To find the linear acceleration of a link with respect to the axis at the proximal joint of that link, we differentiate the equation for the velocity of that link (Equation 5.11):

$$\frac{d}{dt}{}^Rv_{n-1,n} = \frac{d}{dt}{}^Rvtrans_{n-1,n} + \frac{d}{dt}({}^R\omega_n \times {}^Rp_{n-1,n}) \qquad (5.32)$$

$$^Ra_{n-1,n} = {}^Ratrans_{n-1,n} + {}^R\alpha_n \times {}^Rp_{n-1,n} + {}^R\omega_n \times \frac{d}{dt}{}^Rp_{n-1,n}$$

$$= {}^Ratrans_{n-1,n} + {}^R\alpha_n \times {}^Rp_{n-1,n} + {}^R\omega_n \times ({}^R\omega_n \times {}^Rp_{n-1,n}) \qquad (5.33)$$

For the type 1 two-link manipulator, the translation term disappears, because of the rotary joints, and the following equations are obtained for the acceleration of the two links with respect to their joint axes:

$$^0\mathbf{a}_1 = {}^1\alpha_1 \times {}^0p_1 + {}^0\omega_1 \times ({}^0\omega_1 \times {}^0p_1)$$

$$= \begin{bmatrix} 0 \\ 0 \\ d^2\theta_1 \end{bmatrix} \times \begin{bmatrix} l_1C_1 \\ l_1S_1 \\ 0 \end{bmatrix} + \begin{bmatrix} 0 \\ 0 \\ d\theta_1 \end{bmatrix} \times \left(\begin{bmatrix} 0 \\ 0 \\ d\theta_1 \end{bmatrix} \times \begin{bmatrix} l_1C_1 \\ l_1S_1 \\ 0 \end{bmatrix} \right)$$

$$= \begin{bmatrix} -l_1S_1 \\ l_1C_1 \end{bmatrix} d^2\theta_1 - \begin{bmatrix} l_1C_1 \\ l_1S_1 \end{bmatrix} (d\theta_1)^2 \qquad (5.34)$$

$$^1\mathbf{a}_2 = {}^1\alpha_2 \times {}^1p_{1,2} + {}^1\omega_2 \times ({}^1\omega_2 \times {}^1p_{1,2})$$

$$= \begin{bmatrix} -l_2S_2 \\ l_2C_2 \end{bmatrix} d^2\theta_2 - \begin{bmatrix} l_2C_2 \\ l_2S_2 \end{bmatrix} (d\theta_2)^2 \qquad (5.35)$$

where

$$^0\alpha_1 = d^2\theta_1 \quad ^0\omega_1 = d\theta_1 \quad ^1\alpha_2 = d^2\theta_2 \quad \text{and} \quad ^1\omega_2 = d\theta_2$$

Finally, the acceleration equations (Equations 5.34–35), the velocity equations (Equation 5.16–17), and the translation vectors and rotation transforms (Equation 4.8) are substituted into Equation 5.31 to obtain the acceleration of the end effector in Cartesian space.

$$^0\mathbf{a}_2 = \begin{bmatrix} -l_1S_1 \\ l_1C_1 \end{bmatrix} d^2\theta_1 - \begin{bmatrix} l_1C_1 \\ l_1S_1 \end{bmatrix} (d\theta_1)^2 + \begin{bmatrix} 0 \\ 0 \\ d^2\theta_1 \end{bmatrix} \times \begin{bmatrix} l_2C_{12} \\ l_2S_{12} \\ 1 \end{bmatrix}$$

$$+ \begin{bmatrix} 0 \\ 0 \\ d\theta_1 \end{bmatrix} \times \left(\begin{bmatrix} 0 \\ 0 \\ d\theta_1 \end{bmatrix} \times \begin{bmatrix} l_2C_{12} \\ l_2S_{12} \\ 1 \end{bmatrix} \right) + 2 \begin{bmatrix} 0 \\ 0 \\ d\theta_1 \end{bmatrix} \times \begin{bmatrix} C_1 & -S_1 & 0 \\ S_1 & C_1 & 0 \\ 0 & 0 & 1 \end{bmatrix} \begin{bmatrix} -l_2S_2 \\ l_2C_2 \\ 1 \end{bmatrix} d\theta_2$$

$$+ \begin{bmatrix} C_1 & -S_1 & 0 \\ S_1 & C_1 & 0 \\ 0 & 0 & 1 \end{bmatrix} \left(\begin{bmatrix} -l_2S_2 \\ l_2C_2 \end{bmatrix} d^2\theta_2 - \begin{bmatrix} l_2C_2 \\ l_2S_2 \end{bmatrix} (d\theta_2)^2 \right)$$

$$= \begin{bmatrix} -l_1S_1 \\ l_1C_1 \end{bmatrix} d^2\theta_1 - \begin{bmatrix} l_1C_1 \\ l_1S_1 \end{bmatrix} (d\theta_1)^2 + \begin{bmatrix} -l_2S_{12} \\ l_2C_{12} \end{bmatrix} d^2\theta_1 - \begin{bmatrix} l_2C_{12} \\ l_2S_{12} \end{bmatrix} (d\theta_1)^2$$

$$- 2 \begin{bmatrix} l_2C_{12} \\ l_2S_{12} \end{bmatrix} d\theta_1 d\theta_2 + \begin{bmatrix} -l_2S_{12} \\ l_2C_{12} \end{bmatrix} d^2\theta_2 - \begin{bmatrix} l_2C_{12} \\ l_2S_{12} \end{bmatrix} (d\theta_2)^2$$

$$= \begin{bmatrix} -l_1S_1 & -l_2S_{12} \\ l_1C_1 & l_2C_{12} \end{bmatrix} \begin{bmatrix} d^2\theta_1 \\ d^2\theta_1 + d^2\theta_2 \end{bmatrix} - \begin{bmatrix} l_1C_1 & l_2C_{12} \\ l_1S_1 & l_2S_{12} \end{bmatrix} \begin{bmatrix} (d\theta_1)^2 \\ (d\theta_1 + d\theta_2)^2 \end{bmatrix} \qquad (5.36)$$

Look at the type 5 two-link manipulator (Equation 5.18), which contains two prismatic joints, and you will see that the third term in the general velocity equation (Equation 5.12) is zero, because the orientation of the object frame is fixed with respect to the reference frame. For this manipulator, the linear acceleration equation reduces to:

$$^0a_2 = {}^0a_1 + {}^0\mathbf{Rot}_1\,{}^1a_2 \tag{5.37}$$

The calculation of the acceleration of the end effector, by substitution of link parameters into Equation 5.37 is left as an exercise for the reader.

5.3.2 Angular acceleration

When one body rotates around another at constant velocity, it is subject to angular acceleration (Window 5.3). By differentiating the angular velocity equation (Equation 5.21), and applying the expression for converting the first derivative of a free vector between fixed and rotating frames (Equation 5.14), we obtain an equation for angular acceleration.

$$^R\alpha_n = {}^R\alpha_{n-1} + \frac{d}{dt}({}^R\mathbf{Rot}_{n-1}\,{}^{n-1}\omega_n)$$

$$= {}^R\alpha_{n-1} + {}^R\omega_{n-1} \times {}^R\omega_{n-1,n} + {}^R\alpha_{n-1,n} \tag{5.38}$$

In the case of the type 1 two-link manipulator, $^R\alpha_{n-1}$ is the acceleration of joint 1, and $^R\alpha_{n-1,n}$ is the acceleration of joint 2, and the middle term in the equation is the Coriolis acceleration.

The angular acceleration of frame 2 with respect to frame 1 is:

$$^0\alpha_2 = {}^0\alpha_1 + {}^0\omega_1 \times {}^0\omega_{1,2} + {}^0\alpha_{1,2} \tag{5.39}$$

The calculation of the angular acceleration of the second link, by substitution of link parameters into the above equations is left as an exercise for the reader. What happens to the Coriolis term, and why?

5.4 Differential motion

An object is moving if it occupies a different position in space at different times. It has a constant velocity if the change in position is constant during successive units of time, and it is accelerating if the change in position is not constant during successive units of time. Velocity is displacement per unit time, and is therefore a vector having both magnitude (speed) and direction

Figure 5.8
Differential motions.
(a) Differential translation.
(b) Differential rotation.

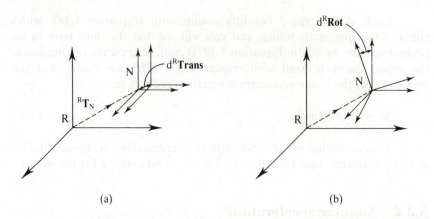

(a)　　　　　　　　　　　　　　　(b)

(Window 5.1). When a computer is used to control motion, the feedback signals are read at discrete intervals in time. If an analogue velocity signal is read, it is accurate at the instant of reading, and assumed to remain constant until the next reading. If a digital value for position or displacement is read, then the average velocity is the displacement during the sampling interval. Thus the measurement and control of differential motion is analogous to the measurement and control of velocity.

In many robot systems, an optical encoder (see Figure 10.9) is mounted on the motor shaft, or on the joint shaft. These encoders produce a train of pulses proportional to the distance moved by the joint. The measurement at the end of each sampling interval is a measurement of the distance moved by the joint during the sampling interval. Consequently, in purely digital control systems, the accurate measurement of both displacements during sampling intervals and the length of the sampling interval is important in the calculation of velocity and acceleration.

In our discussion of object location, we found that we could resolve a three-dimensional vector describing the location of an object into components along the coordinate axes. This is a special case of the general principle of superposition. The principle of independence of velocities states that any velocity v may be resolved into two components v_1 and v_2, which can be combined to represent the actual velocity, and each component may be analysed independently of the others. Again, this is a special case of the general principle of superposition, which also applies to displacements, accelerations, and forces.

5.4.1 Differential translations and rotations

In our discussion of robotic kinematics, we considered only translation and rotation transformations. Consequently, we will consider only differential translation and differential rotation transforms (Figure 5.8). A **differential**

translation transform (Equation 5.40) describes a small translation of an object in space, and a **differential rotation transform** describes a small rotation of an object in space (Equation 5.41) . In both cases, differential motion is defined with respect to a coordinate frame (indicated by the leading superscript).

$$d^R\text{Trans} = \text{Trans}(d_x, d_y, d_z) \qquad (5.40)$$

$$d^R\text{Rot} = \text{Rot}(x, \delta_x)\text{Rot}(y, \delta_y)\text{Rot}(z, \delta_z) \qquad (5.41)$$

An object is located in space by attaching a coordinate frame to it. This object frame is described with respect to a reference frame with a transformation matrix – $^R\mathbf{T}_N$. After a differential change in the location of an object, we find its new location with respect to the reference frame by premultiplying the transformation matrix by the differential transforms.

$$\text{New location} = d^R\text{Trans}\, d^R\text{Rot}\, {}^R\mathbf{T}_N \qquad (5.42)$$

A **differential location transform** is the transform which, when added to the original transformation of the coordinate frame, results in the transformation which describes the new location of the object.

$${}^R\mathbf{T}_N + d^R\mathbf{T}_N = d^R\text{Trans}\, d^R\text{Rot}\, {}^R\mathbf{T}_N \qquad (5.43)$$

where the differential location transform is:

$$d^R\mathbf{T}_N = \begin{bmatrix} dx_x & dy_x & dz_x & dp_x \\ dx_y & dy_y & dz_y & dp_y \\ dx_z & dy_z & dz_z & dp_z \\ 0 & 0 & 0 & 1 \end{bmatrix} \qquad (5.44)$$

Thus, the effect of moving the object by a small amount is described by adding a differential location transform to the coordinate frame transform of the object, and by premultiplying the coordinate frame transform of the object by a differential rotation transform followed by a differential translation transform. We are interested in the differential location transform because it defines the change in the position and orientation of the object in terms of differential changes in the elements of the vectors which describe the coordinate frame of the object. The differential location transform is equivalent to a velocity transform if the motion takes place in a small time interval δt. By manipulating Equation 5.43, we obtain an equation for the differential location transform.

$$d^R\mathbf{T}_N = (d^R\text{Trans}\, d^R\text{Rot} - \mathbf{I})^R\mathbf{T}_N = {}^R\Delta\, {}^R\mathbf{T}_N \qquad (5.45)$$

where

$${}^{R}\Delta = d^{R}\text{Trans}\, d^{R}\text{Rot} - I \tag{5.46}$$

Alternatively, the differential change can be expressed in terms of a differential translation and a differential rotation with respect to the new coordinate frame, in which case the transforms are postmultiplied.

$${}^{R}T_{N} + d^{R}T_{N} = {}^{R}T_{N}d^{N}\text{Trans}\, d^{N}\text{Rot} \tag{5.47}$$

$$d^{R}T_{N} = {}^{R}T_{N}(d^{N}\text{Trans}\, d^{N}\text{Rot} - I) = {}^{R}T_{N}{}^{N}\Delta \tag{5.48}$$

where

$${}^{N}\Delta = d^{N}\text{Trans}\, d^{N}\text{Rot} - I \tag{5.49}$$

In the above equations, a common sub-expression can be identified (Equation 5.50). This sub-expression represents a differential translation and rotation transformation, which we will call a **differential motion transform.**

$$\Delta = d\text{Trans}\, d\text{Rot} - I \tag{5.50}$$

A general 3-dimensional transformation matrix (Section 3.3) is the product of three translation transformation matrices and three rotation transformation matrices. We derive expressions for the differential translation transform and the differential rotation transform by linearizing these matrices for small signal conditions. In the case of translation, we replace the values in the translation transformation with the differential translations, as both represent translations.

$$d\text{Trans} = \text{Trans}(d_{x}, d_{y}, d_{z}) = \begin{bmatrix} 1 & 0 & 0 & d_{x} \\ 0 & 1 & 0 & d_{y} \\ 0 & 0 & 1 & d_{z} \\ 0 & 0 & 0 & 1 \end{bmatrix} \tag{5.51}$$

In the case of differential rotations, we make use of the fact that $\sin(\theta)$ approaches $\delta\theta$ and $\cos(\theta)$ approaches 1 when θ approaches zero, and we replace $\sin(\theta)$ with $\delta\theta$ and $\cos(\theta)$ with 1. For angles less than 0.1 radians (5.7°) the error is less than 0.02% for sine functions and 0.5% for cosine functions (Snyder, 1985). The following equations cannot be used in iterative algorithms because the errors accumulate. Also, since the sine of these angles is small (sine of 5° is 0.0872) the result of multiplying two differential rotations is negligible (0.0076 for two 5° rotations). Consequently, the results of multiplying the rotation transformation matrices can be simplified further by neglecting second and higher order terms. One consequence of neglecting these terms is that the final differential rotation matrix is independent of the order in which the rotations are performed.

$$d\mathbf{Rot} = \mathbf{Rot}(x, \delta_x)\mathbf{Rot}(y, \delta_y)\mathbf{Rot}(z, \delta_z)$$

$$= \begin{bmatrix} 1 & 0 & 0 & 0 \\ 0 & 1 & -\delta_x & 0 \\ 0 & \delta_x & 1 & 0 \\ 0 & 0 & 0 & 1 \end{bmatrix} \begin{bmatrix} 1 & 0 & \delta_y & 0 \\ 0 & 1 & 0 & 0 \\ -\delta_y & 0 & 1 & 0 \\ 0 & 0 & 0 & 1 \end{bmatrix} \begin{bmatrix} 1 & -\delta_z & 0 & 0 \\ \delta_z & 1 & 0 & 0 \\ 0 & 0 & 1 & 0 \\ 0 & 0 & 0 & 1 \end{bmatrix}$$

$$= \begin{bmatrix} 1 & -\delta_z & \delta_y & 0 \\ \delta_z & 1 & -\delta_x & 0 \\ -\delta_y & \delta_x & 1 & 0 \\ 0 & 0 & 0 & 1 \end{bmatrix} \tag{5.52}$$

$$\Delta = d\mathbf{Trans}\,d\mathbf{Rot} - \mathbf{I} = \begin{bmatrix} 1 & 0 & 0 & d_x \\ 0 & 1 & 0 & d_y \\ 0 & 0 & 1 & d_z \\ 0 & 0 & 0 & 1 \end{bmatrix} \begin{bmatrix} 1 & -\delta_z & \delta_y & 0 \\ \delta_z & 1 & -\delta_x & 0 \\ -\delta_y & \delta_x & 1 & 0 \\ 0 & 0 & 0 & 1 \end{bmatrix} - \begin{bmatrix} 1 & 0 & 0 & 0 \\ 0 & 1 & 0 & 0 \\ 0 & 0 & 1 & 0 \\ 0 & 0 & 0 & 1 \end{bmatrix}$$

$$= \begin{bmatrix} 0 & -\delta_z & \delta_y & d_x \\ \delta_z & 0 & -\delta_x & d_y \\ -\delta_y & \delta_x & 0 & d_z \\ 0 & 0 & 0 & 0 \end{bmatrix} \tag{5.53}$$

This equation is simpler than the absolute transformation (Equation 4.34), but it applies only to differential motion relative to the current object position. The differential motion transform Δ is considered to be composed of two vectors d and δ, known as the differential translation and the differential rotation vectors respectively.

$$d = d_x \mathbf{i} + d_y \mathbf{j} + d_z \mathbf{k} \tag{5.54}$$
$$\delta = \delta_x \mathbf{i} + \delta_y \mathbf{j} + \delta_z \mathbf{k} \tag{5.55}$$

These two vectors are combined to form a row matrix known as the **differential motion vector(D)**.

$$D = [d_x\, d_y\, d_z\, \delta_x\, \delta_y\, \delta_z]^{\mathrm{T}} \tag{5.56}$$

In Section 3.9, we examined the transformations required to pick up a screw and place it in position ready for insertion into a hole in a block (Figure 3.16). This example relied on the accurate placement of the block, through the use of special fixturing, to guarantee correct position and orientation. If a vision system is used to measure the errors in the placement of the block, the control program can apply a differential motion correction to the position and orientation of the screw before insertion (Section 11.7).

As before the manipulator moves the tip of the screw to $q_1(2, a-b, 0)$ with respect to the reference frame, so that it lies parallel to the y axis. The vision system indicates that the screw has to be rotated by -0.1 radians around the new x axis, and translated $+0.05a$ units in the new y direction, and $+0.1b$ units in the new z direction, with respect to the object coordinate frame. Other motions of the block are constrained by placing it on a table whose top surface is in the xy plane, with respect to the reference coordinate frame. The coordinate frame of the screw is:

$$^R\mathbf{T}_N = \begin{bmatrix} 0 & 1 & 0 & 2a \\ 0 & 0 & -1 & 0 \\ -1 & 0 & 0 & 0 \\ 0 & 0 & 0 & 1 \end{bmatrix} \tag{5.57}$$

The differential motion vector is:

$$^N\mathbf{D} = [d_x\ d_y\ d_z\ \delta_x\ \delta_y\ \delta_z]^T$$
$$= [0\ 0.05a\ 0.1b - 0.1\ 0\ 0]^T \tag{5.58}$$

giving a differential motion transform of:

$$^N\Delta = \begin{bmatrix} 0 & 0 & 0 & 0 \\ 0 & 0 & 0.1 & 0.05a \\ 0 & -0.1 & 0 & 0.1b \\ 0 & 0 & 0 & 0 \end{bmatrix} \tag{5.59}$$

To calculate the differential location transform of the screw with respect to the coordinate frame of the screws, substitute these values into Equation 5.48:

$$d^R\mathbf{T}_N = {}^R\mathbf{T}_N{}^N\Delta = \begin{bmatrix} 0 & 1 & 0 & 2a \\ 0 & 0 & -1 & 0 \\ -1 & 0 & 0 & 0 \\ 0 & 0 & 0 & 1 \end{bmatrix} \begin{bmatrix} 0 & 0 & 0 & 0 \\ 0 & 0 & 0.1 & 0.15a \\ 0 & -1 & 0 & 0.1b \\ 0 & 0 & 0 & 0 \end{bmatrix}$$

$$= \begin{bmatrix} 0 & 0 & 0.1 & 0.05a \\ 0 & 0.1 & 0 & -0.1b \\ 0 & 0 & 0 & 0 \\ 0 & 0 & 0 & 0 \end{bmatrix} = \begin{bmatrix} dx_x & dy_x & dz_x & dp_x \\ dx_y & dy_y & dz_y & dp_y \\ dx_z & dy_z & dz_z & dp_z \\ 0 & 0 & 0 & 1 \end{bmatrix} \tag{5.60}$$

5.4.2 Transformation differential motion between coordinates frames

In the above example, we assumed that the differential transforms calculated by the vision system were in the coordinate frame of the object. In practice, the control program has to transform these differential motions from the coordinate frame of the vision system to the coordinate frame of the object. Also, it often has to transform differential motion from Cartesian space to joint space before it can command the robot to move. In this section, we will look at how to transform differential changes between coordinate frames. That is, given $^R\Delta$, find $^N\Delta$. Considering our example again, we find the differential motion transformation with respect to the reference frame from the differential location transform, by manipulating Equation 5.45.

$$d^R\mathbf{T_N}{}^R\mathbf{T_N^{-1}} = {}^R\Delta \tag{5.61}$$

$$
^R\Delta =
\begin{bmatrix}
0 & 0 & 0.1 & 0.05a \\
0 & 0.1 & 0 & -0.1b \\
0 & 0 & 0 & 0 \\
0 & 0 & 0 & 0
\end{bmatrix}
\begin{bmatrix}
0 & 0 & -1 & 0 \\
1 & 0 & 0 & -2a \\
0 & -1 & 0 & 0 \\
0 & 0 & 0 & 1
\end{bmatrix}
$$

$$
=
\begin{bmatrix}
0 & -0.1 & 0 & 0.05a \\
0.1 & 0 & 0 & -0.2a-0.1b \\
0 & 0 & 0 & 0 \\
0 & 0 & 0 & 0
\end{bmatrix}
\tag{5.62}
$$

If we equate this matrix to Equation 5.53, we obtain the differential motion vector:

$$^R D = [d_x \ d_y \ d_z \ \delta_x \ \delta_y \ \delta_z]^T$$
$$= [0.05a \ -0.2a \ -0.1b \ 0 \ 0 \ 0.1]^T \tag{5.63}$$

When we compare these differential motions to Figure 3.16, we see that they are the rotation and translations we would expect, given the constraint of the block sitting on a table. This example illustrates a particular case of a general method. Instead of working through the equations, we can define a **general motion transformation** between coordinate frames. In Equations 5.45 and 5.48, there are two expressions for the differential location transform $d^R\mathbf{T_N}$. By equating these equations, we obtain an expression for transforming a differential transformation from one coordinate frame to another. In this situation, the general transform ($^R\mathbf{T_N}$) is a **differential coordinate transform**.

$$d^R\mathbf{T_N} = {}^R\mathbf{T_N}{}^N\Delta = {}^R\Delta\ {}^R\mathbf{T_N} \tag{5.64}$$

$$^R\Delta = {}^R\mathbf{T_N}{}^N\Delta\ {}^R\mathbf{T_N^{-1}} \tag{5.65}$$

$$
\begin{aligned}
{}^{N}\Delta &= {}^{R}T_{N}^{-1}\,{}^{R}\Delta\,{}^{R}T_{N} \\[4pt]
&=
\begin{bmatrix}
x_x & x_y & x_z & -p\cdot x \\
y_x & y_y & y_z & -p\cdot y \\
z_x & z_y & z_z & -p\cdot z \\
0 & 0 & 0 & 1
\end{bmatrix}
\begin{bmatrix}
0 & -\delta_z & \delta_y & d_x \\
\delta_z & 0 & -\delta_x & d_y \\
-\delta_y & \delta_x & 0 & d_z \\
0 & 0 & 0 & 0
\end{bmatrix}
\begin{bmatrix}
x_x & y_x & z_x & p_x \\
x_y & y_y & z_y & p_y \\
x_z & y_z & z_z & p_z \\
0 & 0 & 0 & 1
\end{bmatrix} \\[4pt]
&=
\begin{bmatrix}
x_x & x_y & x_z & -p\cdot x \\
y_x & y_y & y_z & -p\cdot y \\
z_x & z_y & z_z & -p\cdot z \\
0 & 0 & 0 & 1
\end{bmatrix}
\begin{bmatrix}
(\delta x x)_x & (\delta x y)_x & (\delta x z)_x & [(\delta x p)+d]_x \\
(\delta x x)_y & (\delta x y)_y & (\delta x z)_y & [(\delta x p)+d]_y \\
(\delta x x)_z & (\delta x y)_z & (\delta x z)_z & [(\delta x p)+d]_z \\
0 & 0 & 0 & 0
\end{bmatrix}
\end{aligned}
\tag{5.66}
$$

where $(\delta x x)_x = \delta_y x_z - \delta_z x_y$, which is the x element of the expansion of the determinant formed from the cross product of the two vectors (Section 13.4.3), that is, the magnitude of the x component of the resultant vector. δ and d are the differential rotation and differential translation vectors, respectively (Equations 5.54 and 5.55).

$$
{}^{N}\Delta =
\begin{bmatrix}
x\cdot(\delta x x) & x\cdot(\delta x y) & x\cdot(\delta x z) & x\cdot[(\delta x p)+d] \\
y\cdot(\delta x x) & y\cdot(\delta x y) & y\cdot(\delta x z) & y\cdot[(\delta x p)+d] \\
z\cdot(\delta x x) & z\cdot(\delta x y) & z\cdot(\delta x z) & z\cdot[(\delta x p)+d] \\
0 & 0 & 0 & 0
\end{bmatrix}
\tag{5.67}
$$

The elements of the matrix in Equation 5.67 are triple scalar products of vectors (Section 13.4.4). If any two elements in the triple product are the same, the value of the triple product is zero. In these products, pairs of vectors may be interchanged if the sign of the triple product is changed after each interchange. For example:

$$
a\cdot(b x c) = -b\cdot(a x c) = b\cdot(c x a)
\tag{5.68}
$$

Also, by definition, x, y, and z form an orthogonal set of vectors, and thus, any one of these vectors is the cross product of the other two (see Equation 3.33). By rearranging the elements of the matrix (Equation 5.67), substituting zero where terms in triple products occur twice, and replacing the cross product of two vectors with their orthogonal vector, the matrix reduces to:

$$
{}^{N}\Delta =
\begin{bmatrix}
0 & -\delta\cdot z & \delta\cdot y & \delta\cdot(p x x) + d\cdot x \\
\delta\cdot z & 0 & -\delta\cdot x & \delta\cdot(p x y) + d\cdot y \\
-\delta\cdot y & \delta\cdot x & 0 & \delta\cdot(p x z) + d\cdot z \\
0 & 0 & 0 & 0
\end{bmatrix}
\tag{5.69}
$$

${}^N\Delta$ and ND have been previously defined as:

$$
{}^N\Delta = \begin{bmatrix} 0 & -{}^N\delta_z & {}^N\delta_y & {}^Nd_x \\ {}^N\delta_z & 0 & -{}^N\delta_x & {}^Nd_y \\ -{}^N\delta_y & {}^N\delta_x & 0 & {}^Nd_z \\ 0 & 0 & 0 & 0 \end{bmatrix} \tag{5.70}
$$

$$
{}^ND = [{}^Nd_x \; {}^Nd_y \; {}^Nd_z \; {}^N\delta_x \; {}^N\delta_y \; {}^N\delta_z]^T \tag{5.71}
$$

By equating the elements of the matrices in Equations 5.69 and 5.70, we obtain expressions for the elements of the differential motion vector with respect to reference coordinates.

$$
{}^Nd_x = \delta \cdot (p \times x) + d \cdot x = x \cdot [(\delta \times p) + d] \tag{5.72}
$$

$$
{}^Nd_y = \delta \cdot (p \times y) + d \cdot y = y \cdot [(\delta \times p) + d] \tag{5.73}
$$

$$
{}^Nd_z = \delta \cdot (p \times z) + d \cdot z = z \cdot [(\delta \times p) + d] \tag{5.74}
$$

$$
{}^N\delta_x = \delta \cdot x \tag{5.75}
$$

$$
{}^N\delta_y = \delta \cdot y \tag{5.76}
$$

$$
{}^N\delta_z = \delta \cdot z \tag{5.77}
$$

The above transformation of differential motion from one coordinate frame to another can be expressed as a 6×6 matrix.

$$
\begin{bmatrix} {}^Nd_x \\ {}^Nd_y \\ {}^Nd_z \\ {}^N\delta_x \\ {}^N\delta_y \\ {}^N\delta_z \end{bmatrix} \begin{bmatrix} x_x & x_y & x_z & (p \times x)_x & (p \times x)_y & (p \times x)_z \\ y_x & y_y & y_z & (p \times y)_x & (p \times y)_y & (p \times y)_z \\ z_x & z_y & z_z & (p \times z)_x & (p \times z)_y & (p \times z)_z \\ 0 & 0 & 0 & x_x & x_y & x_z \\ 0 & 0 & 0 & y_x & y_y & y_z \\ 0 & 0 & 0 & z_x & z_y & z_z \end{bmatrix} \begin{bmatrix} {}^Rd_x \\ {}^Rd_y \\ {}^Rd_z \\ {}^R\delta_x \\ {}^R\delta_y \\ {}^R\delta_z \end{bmatrix} \tag{5.78}
$$

$$
{}^ND = {}^NM_R \, {}^RD \tag{5.79}
$$

where ${}^NM_R$ is the **general motion transform**, used to transform differential motion from the reference frame to the new frame.

In the example at the start of this section, we calculated a value for ${}^R\Delta$ (Equation 5.62). If this value is substituted into Equation 5.78, the original value for ${}^N\Delta$ (Equation 5.59) should result.

$$
x = (0 \; 0 \; -1) \quad y = (1 \; 0 \; 0) \quad z = (0 \; -1 \; 0) \tag{5.80}
$$

$$p = (2a \quad 0 \quad 0) \quad d = (0.05a \quad -0.2a-0.1b \quad 0) \quad \delta = (0 \quad 0 \quad 0.1)$$

(5.81)

$$\delta \cdot x = 0 \times 0 + 0 \times 0 + 0.1 \times -1 = -0.1 \quad \delta \cdot y = 0 \quad \delta \cdot z = 0$$

(5.82)

$$\delta \mathbf{x} p = \begin{bmatrix} i & j & k \\ 0 & 0 & 0.1 \\ 2a & 0 & 0 \end{bmatrix} = 0i + 0.2aj + 0k$$

(5.83)

$$(\delta \mathbf{x} p) + d = 0.05ai - 0.2aj - 0.1bj + 0k + 0.2aj$$
$$= 0.05ai - 0.1bj + 0k$$

(5.84)

$$x \cdot [(\delta \mathbf{x} p) + d] = 0 \quad y \cdot [(\delta \mathbf{x} p) + d] = 0.05a \quad z \cdot [(\delta \mathbf{x} p) + d] = 0.1b \quad (5.85)$$

$$^N\Delta = \begin{bmatrix} 0 & -\delta \cdot z & \delta \cdot y & x \cdot [(\delta \mathbf{x} p) + d] \\ \delta \cdot z & 0 & -\delta \cdot x & y \cdot [(\delta \mathbf{x} p) + d] \\ -\delta \cdot y & \delta \cdot x & 0 & z \cdot [(\delta \mathbf{x} p) + d] \\ 0 & 0 & 0 & 0 \end{bmatrix} = \begin{bmatrix} 0 & 0 & 0 & 0 \\ 0 & 0 & 0.1 & 0.05a \\ 0 & -0.1 & 0 & 0.1b \\ 0 & 0 & 0 & 0 \end{bmatrix}$$

(5.86)

which is the same as Equation 5.59.

Using Equation 5.79 we can transform a differential motion vector from the reference frame to the new frame. There are three ways to carry out the transformation in the reverse direction, from new frame to reference frame:

1. calculate a new 6×6 differential transformation matrix from Equation 5.65;
2. calculate the inverse of the 6×6 differential transformation matrix in Equation 5.78,
3. modify Equation 5.65 to the same format as Equation 5.66, by inverting the transformation matrix. Equations 5.73–5.77 can then be used as they are. As we often calculate the inverse of the transformation matrix anyway, and it is a 4×4 matrix, this last solution makes some sense.

$$^R\Delta = {}^R\mathbf{T}_N {}^N\Delta {}^R\mathbf{T}_N^{-1} = ({}^R\mathbf{T}_N^{-1})^{-1} {}^N\Delta({}^R\mathbf{T}_N^{-1})$$

(5.87)

Throughout this chapter, we have discussed reference and new coordinate frames. The techniques we have developed are general, and, thus, will transform motion between any two coordinate frames, provided the transformation matrix between these coordinate frames is known. The easiest way to identify the transformation between two coordinate frames is with a transform graph (Section 3.10).

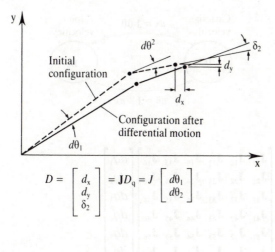

Figure 5.9
Differential motion vectors
for a type 1 two-link
manipulator.

$$D = \begin{bmatrix} d_x \\ d_y \\ \delta_2 \end{bmatrix} = JD_q = J \begin{bmatrix} d\theta_1 \\ d\theta_2 \end{bmatrix}$$

5.5 The manipulator Jacobian

A **Jacobian** is a matrix of differentials. In the case of a manipulator, differential changes in the location of the tool plate are caused by differential changes in joint variables (Figure 5.9). The differential displacement of the tool plate in world coordinates is described with a differential motion vector (Equation 5.56). Similarly, the differential displacement of the tool plate in joint coordinates can be described with a differential motion vector (a six-element vector for a six-joint manipulator).

$$D_q = [dq_1 \, dq_2 \, dq_3 \, dq_4 \, dq_5 \, dq_6]^T \tag{5.88}$$

where dq_n is a differential rotation ($d\theta_n$) or a differential translation (dd_n) at joint n.

For a manipulator with six joints, these two vectors are related by a 6×6 matrix of differentials called the manipulator Jacobian **J**.

$$D = JD_q = (J_1, J_2, J_3, J_4, J_5, J_6)D_q \tag{5.89}$$

$$\begin{bmatrix} d_x \\ d_y \\ d_z \\ \delta_x \\ \delta_y \\ \delta_z \end{bmatrix} = \begin{bmatrix} d_{x1} & d_{x2} & d_{x3} & d_{x4} & d_{x5} & d_{x6} \\ d_{y1} & d_{y2} & d_{y3} & d_{y4} & d_{y5} & d_{y6} \\ d_{z1} & d_{z2} & d_{z3} & d_{z4} & d_{z5} & d_{z6} \\ \delta_{x1} & \delta_{x2} & \delta_{x3} & \delta_{x4} & \delta_{x5} & \delta_{x6} \\ \delta_{y1} & \delta_{y2} & \delta_{y3} & \delta_{y4} & \delta_{y5} & \delta_{y6} \\ \delta_{z1} & \delta_{z1} & \delta_{z3} & \delta_{z4} & \delta_{z5} & \delta_{z6} \end{bmatrix} \begin{bmatrix} dq_1 \\ dq_2 \\ dq_3 \\ dq_4 \\ dq_5 \\ dq_6 \end{bmatrix} \tag{5.89}$$

Figure 5.10
Jacobian – relationship
between joint and Cartesian
velocities.

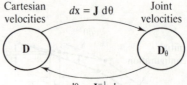

Cartesian velocities — $dx = \mathbf{J}\,d\theta$ — Joint velocities

$\mathbf{D}$ $\mathbf{D}_\theta$

$d\theta = \mathbf{J}^{-1}\,dx$

$$= \begin{bmatrix} J_{11} & J_{12} & J_{13} & J_{14} & J_{15} & J_{16} \\ J_{21} & J_{22} & J_{23} & J_{24} & J_{25} & J_{26} \\ J_{31} & J_{32} & J_{33} & J_{34} & J_{35} & J_{36} \\ J_{41} & J_{42} & J_{43} & J_{44} & J_{45} & J_{46} \\ J_{51} & J_{52} & J_{53} & J_{54} & J_{55} & J_{56} \\ J_{61} & J_{62} & J_{63} & J_{64} & J_{65} & J_{66} \end{bmatrix} \begin{bmatrix} dq_1 \\ dq_2 \\ dq_3 \\ dq_4 \\ dq_5 \\ dq_6 \end{bmatrix} \qquad (5.90)$$

where

$$d_x = d_{x1}dq_1 + d_{x2}dq_2 + d_{x3}dq_3 + d_{x4}dq_4 + d_{x5}dq_5 + d_{x6}dq_6 \qquad (5.91)$$

is the x component of the differential motion of the tool plate as a function of the differential motion of the joints,

δ_y is the y component of the angular motion of the tool plate as a function of the differential motion of the joints,

$d_{x1} = J_{11} = \partial x/\partial q_1$ is the partial derivative of the x component of the position of the tool plate with respect to the joint variable of joint 1, and

$\delta_{y6} = J_{56}$ is the partial derivative of the y component of the orientation of the tool plate with respect to the joint variable of joint 6.

The manipulator Jacobian relates the velocity of the joints in joint space to the velocity of the tool plate in Cartesian space. The inverse Jacobian relates the velocity of the tool plate in Cartesian space to the joint velocities (Figure 5.10).

$$D_q = \mathbf{J}^{-1}D \qquad (5.92)$$

The number of rows in a Jacobian is determined by the number of degrees of freedom in Cartesian space required by the task which is in turn determined by the degrees of mobility of the manipulator and task constraints. For example, a planar manipulator can have three degrees of freedom. However, the type 1 two-link manipulator has only two because the orientation of the end effector cannot be controlled independently of

Figure 5.11
Calculation of end effector
velocity from joint velocities
by recursive application of
the velocity formula.

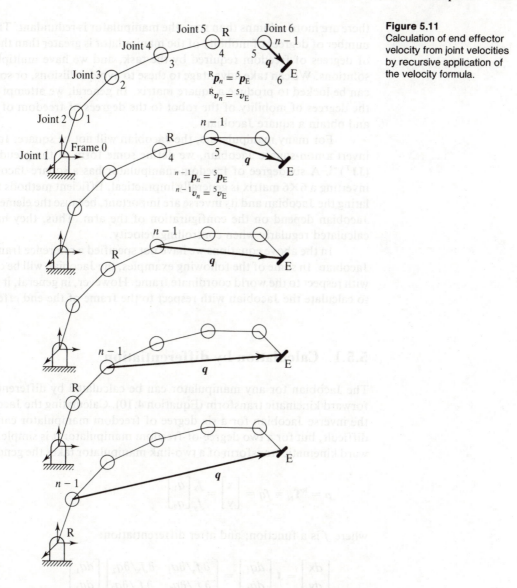

position. In contrast, orientation can be controlled independently with a three-link planar manipulator (see Figure 5.14).

Task constraints may result in some degrees of freedom being redundant. If necessary, these redundant degrees of freedom can be left out of the Jacobian to make it square. For example, the control of an arc-welding torch is a five degree-of-freedom task because the torch is symmetric about its centre line. Consequently, there is no need to control roll.

The number of columns in the Jacobian is determined by the number of joints in the manipulator, that is, the degrees of mobility in joint space. If there are more columns than rows the manipulator is redundant. That is, the number of degrees of mobility of the manipulator is greater than the number of degrees of freedom required by the task, and we have multiple inverse solutions. We can take advantage to these to avoid collisions, or some joints can be locked to produce a square matrix. In general, we attempt to match the degrees of mobility of the robot to the degrees of freedom of the task, and obtain a square Jacobian.

For many manipulators, the Jacobian will not be square. In order to invert a non-square Jacobian, we define some form of the pseudo inverse $(\mathbf{J}\mathbf{J}^T)^{-1}$. A six degree of freedom manipulator has a square Jacobian, but inverting a 6×6 matrix is generally impractical. Efficient methods for calculating the Jacobian and its inverse are important, because the elements of the Jacobian depend on the configuration of the arm. Thus, they have to be calculated regularly when controlling velocity.

In the above equations we have not specified a reference frame for the Jacobian. In some of the following examples, the Jacobian will be calculated with respect to the world coordinate frame. However, in general, it is simpler to calculate the Jacobian with respect to the frame of the end effector.

5.5.1 Calculation by differentiation

The Jacobian for any manipulator can be calculated by differentiating its forward kinematic transform (Equation 4.10). Calculating the Jacobian and the inverse Jacobian for a six degree of freedom manipulator can be quite difficult, but for a two degree-of-freedom manipulator it is simple. The forward kinematic transform of a two-link manipulator takes the general form:

$$p = {}^R\mathbf{T}_N = fq = \begin{bmatrix} x \\ y \end{bmatrix} = \begin{bmatrix} f_x \\ f_y \end{bmatrix}\begin{bmatrix} q_1 \\ q_2 \end{bmatrix} \tag{5.93}$$

where f is a function; and after differentiation:

$$\begin{bmatrix} dx \\ dy \end{bmatrix} = \mathbf{J}\begin{bmatrix} dq_1 \\ dq_2 \end{bmatrix} = \begin{bmatrix} \partial f_x/\partial q_1 & \partial f_x/\partial q_2 \\ \partial f_y/\partial q_1 & \partial f_y/\partial q_2 \end{bmatrix}\begin{bmatrix} dq_1 \\ dq_2 \end{bmatrix} \tag{5.94}$$

For example, we will calculate the Jacobian for the type 1 two-link manipulator by differentiating its forward kinematic transform (Equation 4.4).

$$\begin{bmatrix} x \\ y \end{bmatrix} = \begin{bmatrix} l_1 C_1 + l_2 C_{12} \\ l_1 S_1 + l_2 S_{12} \end{bmatrix} \tag{5.95}$$

$$\begin{bmatrix} dx \\ dy \end{bmatrix} = \begin{bmatrix} -l_1 S_1 - l_2 S_{12} & -l_2 S_{12} \\ l_1 C_1 + l_2 C_{12} & l_2 C_{12} \end{bmatrix}\begin{bmatrix} d\theta_1 \\ d\theta_2 \end{bmatrix} \tag{5.96}$$

The above Jacobian is defined with respect to the reference frame (frame 0). We transform the Jacobian with respect to the end effector (frame 2) to the Jacobian with respect to the reference frame (frame 0), using the rotation transform (Equation 4.8). We transform velocity with a rotation transform because velocity is a free vector (Section 13.4.1).

$$^0\mathbf{J} = {}^0\mathbf{Rot}_3 {}^3\mathbf{J} = \begin{bmatrix} C_{12} & -S_{12} \\ S_{12} & C_{12} \end{bmatrix} \begin{bmatrix} l_1 S_2 & 0 \\ l_1 C_2 + l_2 & l_2 \end{bmatrix} = \begin{bmatrix} -l_1 S_1 - l_2 S_{12} & -l_2 S_{12} \\ l_1 C_1 + l_2 C_{12} & l_2 C_{12} \end{bmatrix} \quad (5.97)$$

Now, we can find the acceleration transform by differentiating the velocity equations with respect to θ_1 and $\theta_1 + \theta_2$, and the joint variables with respect to the world frame.

$$\begin{bmatrix} d^2 x \\ d^2 y \end{bmatrix} = \begin{bmatrix} -l_1 S_1 & -l_2 S_{12} \\ l_1 C_1 & l_2 C_{12} \end{bmatrix} \begin{bmatrix} d^2 \theta_1 \\ d^2 \theta_1 + d^2 \theta_2 \end{bmatrix} - \begin{bmatrix} l_1 C_1 & l_2 C_{12} \\ l_1 S_1 & l_2 S_{12} \end{bmatrix} \begin{bmatrix} (d\theta_1)^2 \\ (d\theta_1 + d\theta_2)^2 \end{bmatrix} \quad (5.98)$$

Next, we find the inverse Jacobian (Section 13.3.4):

$$\mathbf{J}^{-1} = \frac{\begin{bmatrix} \mathbf{J}_{22} & -\mathbf{J}_{12} \\ -\mathbf{J}_{21} & \mathbf{J}_{11} \end{bmatrix}}{|\mathbf{J}|} \quad (5.99)$$

where

$$\begin{aligned} |\mathbf{J}| &= \mathbf{J}_{11}\mathbf{J}_{22} - \mathbf{J}_{12}\mathbf{J}_{21} \\ &= (-l_1 S_1 - l_2 S_{12})(l_2 C_{12}) + (l_2 S_{12})(l_1 C_1 + l_2 C_{12}) \\ &= -l_1 l_2 C_{12} S_1 - l_2 l_2 C_{12} S_{12} + l_1 l_2 S_{12} C_1 + l_2 l_2 S_{12} C_{12} \\ &= l_1 l_2 (C_1 S_{12} - S_{12} C_{12}) = l_1 l_2 \sin \theta_2 \end{aligned} \quad (5.100)$$

$$\begin{bmatrix} d\theta_1 \\ d\theta_2 \end{bmatrix} = \frac{1}{l_1 l_2 S_2} \begin{bmatrix} l_2 C_{12} & l_2 S_{12} \\ -l_1 C_1 - l_2 C_{12} & -l_1 S_1 - l_2 S_{12} \end{bmatrix} \begin{bmatrix} dx \\ dy \end{bmatrix} \quad (5.101)$$

Last, we derive the joint accelerations from Equation 5.98, also by matrix inversion:

$$\begin{aligned} \begin{bmatrix} d^2 \theta_1 \\ d^2 \theta_1 + d^2 \theta_2 \end{bmatrix} &= \frac{1}{l_1 l_2 S_2} \begin{bmatrix} l_2 C_{12} & l_2 S_{12} \\ -l_1 C_1 & -l_1 S_{12} \end{bmatrix} \begin{bmatrix} d^2 x \\ d^2 y \end{bmatrix} \\ &\quad + \frac{1}{l_1 l_2 S_2} \begin{bmatrix} l_1 l_2 C & l_2^2 \\ -l_1^2 & -l_1 l_2 C_2 \end{bmatrix} \begin{bmatrix} (d\theta_1)^2 \\ (d\theta_1 + d\theta_2)^2 \end{bmatrix} \end{aligned} \quad (5.102)$$

5.5.2 Calculation with vectors

In Section 5.2.1 the velocity vector for the type 1 two-link manipulator (see Equation 5.15) was derived by applying the general formula for the linear velocity of a point moving on an object as seen from a reference frame. Using this equation, and the **A** matrices for this manipulator (see Equation 4.8), we can derive the Jacobian for the type 1 two-link manipulator. Note, the angular velocity due to the rotation of the joints contains only a z component, because the axes of the joints are aligned with the z axis of each frame.

$$ {}^0v_2 = {}^0\omega_1 \times ({}^0p_1 + {}^0\mathbf{Rot}_1\,{}^1p_2) + {}^0\mathbf{Rot}_1({}^1\omega_2 \times {}^1p_2) \tag{5.103} $$

where

$$ {}^0p_1 + {}^0\mathbf{Rot}_1\,{}^1p_2 = \begin{bmatrix} l_1C_1 \\ l_1S_1 \\ 1 \end{bmatrix} + \begin{bmatrix} C_1 & -S_1 & 0 \\ S_1 & C_1 & 0 \\ 0 & 0 & 1 \end{bmatrix} \begin{bmatrix} l_2C_2 \\ l_2S_2 \\ 1 \end{bmatrix} $$

$$ = \begin{bmatrix} l_1C_1 + l_2C_{12} \\ l_1S_1 + l_2S_{12} \\ 1 \end{bmatrix} \tag{5.104} $$

This result could have been obtained directly from the forward transform (Equation 4.8), and

$$ {}^1v_1 = {}^1\omega_2 \times {}^1p_2 = \begin{bmatrix} 0 \\ 0 \\ d\theta_2 \end{bmatrix} \times \begin{bmatrix} l_2C_2 \\ l_2S_2 \\ 1 \end{bmatrix} = \begin{bmatrix} -l_2S_2 \\ l_2C_2 \end{bmatrix} d\theta_2 \tag{5.105} $$

$$ {}^0v_2 = \begin{bmatrix} 0 \\ 0 \\ d\theta_1 \end{bmatrix} \times \begin{bmatrix} l_1C_1 + l_2C_{12} \\ l_1S_1 + l_2S_{12} \\ 1 \end{bmatrix} + \begin{bmatrix} C_1 & -S_1 & 0 \\ S_1 & C_1 & 0 \\ 0 & 0 & 1 \end{bmatrix} \begin{bmatrix} -l_2S_2 \\ l_2C_2 \\ 1 \end{bmatrix} d\theta_2 $$

$$ = \begin{bmatrix} -l_1S_1 - l_2S_{12} & -l_2S_{12} \\ l_1C_1 + l_2C_{12} & l_2C_{12} \end{bmatrix} \begin{bmatrix} d\theta_1 \\ d\theta_2 \end{bmatrix} \tag{5.106} $$

As expected, this is the same as the Jacobian calculated by differentiation. The acceleration transform can be calculated in a similar way. However, this method of calculation is complex for multi-link manipulators.

If we rewrite the general velocity equation to express velocities with respect to link $n-1$ rather than to the reference frame (Equation 5.107), we can derive a recursive algorithm (Algorithm 5.1) for finding the velocity of the end effector of an n link manipulator. As we move from the base of the manipulator to the distal joint, each preceding link contributes to the velocity of the current link. Eventually the end effector is reached, where there are no more velocities to add. The velocity of link n is the velocity of link $n-1$ plus the velocity due to the motion of link n.

Algorithm 5.1 Algorithm for finding the velocity of the end effector using vectors

1. Place the three frames R, n, and E at joints 1, 2, and the end effector respectively (Figure 5.11), (that is, n is 1).

2. Calculate the velocity of the end effector with respect to the base using Equation 5.107

$$^{n-1}v_E = {}^{n-1}v_n + {}^{n-1}\omega_n \times {}^{n-1}\text{Rot}_n \, {}^n p_E + {}^{n-1}\text{Rot}_n \, {}^n v_E \qquad (5.107)$$

3. The vector $^n p_E$ is obtained from the forward kinematic transform.

4. The vector $^n v_E$ is obtained by a recursive call to solve Equation 5.107 with $n = n + 1$.

5. The recursion terminates when n equals the number of degrees of mobility of the manipulator — when frame $n - 1$ is located at the last joint — $n = E$.

Alternatively, if the algorithm moves in the other direction, from the distal joint to the base, we obtain an iterative solution for an n link manipulator. Eventually a stationary reference frame is reached where the velocity of link 0 is zero, and the iteration terminates – in the case of a mobile robot this frame may not be the base frame. In the iterative algorithm, the results of one calculation $^R p_n$ and $^R v_n$ become $^{n-1}p_n$ and $^{n-1}v_n$ in the next calculation. The process is repeated until frame R is the base frame of the robot.

These algorithms calculate the Cartesian velocities from the joint velocities. If required, the Cartesian velocity can be expressed with an equation, rather than with the numbers as in the above algorithms. For two-link manipulators, such as the two-link manipulator in the example above, the final equation is simple, and we obtain a Jacobian matrix. For multi-link manipulators, the final equation is complex, and manipulating it into the form of a Jacobian is difficult. In Section 5.8.3, we will simplify Algorithm 5.1 for the case of revolute joints.

A number of alternative algorithms exist for velocity and Jacobian calculations using vectors (Whitney, 1972; Duffy, 1980; Wang and Ravani, 1985; Craig, 1986). In general, the elements of the Jacobian are found by transforming the linear and angular velocity vectors of each joint to end effector coordinates. This transformation is achieved by pre-multiplying these vectors with the rotation transform of the coordinate frame of the end effector with respect to the coordinate frame of the joint (Algorithm 5.2). In practice, efficiency is achieved by calculating the velocities directly, and not using the Jacobian matrix. These techniques are also used for calculating end effector accelerations, and for finding acceleration transformations.

5.5.3 Calculation with homogeneous coordinates

A number of algorithms for calculating the Jacobian and its inverse have been published. Several Jacobian algorithms are compared by Orin and Schrader (1984). Others have developed highly efficient algorithms for specific manipulator configurations, for example, a six degree of freedom articulated manipulator with a spherical wrist (Featherstone, 1983; Hollerbach and Sahar 1984). One way to achieve efficiency is to calculate the inverse kinematic velocities directly without inverting the Jacobian matrix. We will study the algorithm developed by Paul (1981), not because it is the most efficient, but, as it uses homogeneous transforms, it is consistent with the mathematical formulations developed so far. Some of the other algorithms are based on different mathematical formulations, and are beyond the scope of this book. For example, LaBrooy (1987) published algorithms for calculating the Jacobian and its inverse using screw transforms. They are part of an advanced course in kinematics.

Paul's algorithm can be used to calculate the Jacobian of a six degree of freedom manipulator, where each degree of freedom corresponds to one joint. It can also be used with manipulators with less than six joints. Paul's algorithm is derived by defining manipulator motion in such a way that the differential motion vector (Equation 5.56) can be used to calculate the elements of the Jacobian. Looking closely at the columns of the matrix in Equation 5.90 we can see that they are in the form of differential motion vectors. Thus, each column in the Jacobian is a differential motion vector, which describes the differential motion of one joint. Using Equations 5.72 to 5.77, we can calculate the components of this vector with respect to the new frame, and then transform them into the reference frame with Equation 5.78, but first manipulator motion must be described with differential motion vectors.

In a manipulator, differential changes in the position and orientation of the tool plate $d^R T_E$ are caused by differential changes in joint coordinates dq_n. From Equation 5.48, a differential change in the location of the tool plate is a function of the differential motion transform with respect to the tool plate:

$$d^R T_E = {}^R T_E {}^E \Delta \qquad (5.108)$$

The differential motion of the tool plate is a result of the differential motion of the joint variables, and the differential motion transform is the cumulative effect of those joint differential motions. To simplify this analysis, we consider differential motion at only one joint. First, the differential motion transform $({}^E \Delta)$ is split into two parts (Equation 5.109): a differential motion in joint coordinates (dq_n) multiplied by a differential transformation from joint n to the end effector frame $({}^E \Delta_n)$.

$$^E\Delta = {}^E\Delta_n dq_n \tag{5.109}$$

In Section 5.4.2, we derived an expression for transforming differential motion from one frame to another (Equation 5.66). To transform joint motion from the frame of the joint (frame $n-1$) to the frame of the tool plate (E) we rewrite this equation as:

$$^E\Delta_n = {}^{n-1}T_E^{-1}\,{}^{n-1}\Delta_n\,{}^{n-1}T_E \tag{5.110}$$

where $^{n-1}\Delta_n$ is a differential motion transform, which corresponds to a unit differential rotation about the z axis, if joint n is revolute, and a unit differential translation along the z axis, if joint n is prismatic.

Substituting Equations 5.109 and 5.110 into Equation 5.108, we get:

$$
\begin{aligned}
d^R T_E &= {}^R T_E\,{}^{n-1}T_E^{-1}\,{}^{n-1}\Delta_n\,{}^{n-1}T_E\, dq_n \\
&= {}^R T_{n-1}\,{}^{n-1}\Delta_n\,{}^{n-1}T_E\, dq_n \\
&= A_1 \cdots A_{n-1}\,{}^{n-1}\Delta_n A_n \cdots A_E\, dq_n
\end{aligned} \tag{5.111}
$$

This equation describes the Cartesian motion of the end effector as a function of the differential motion of joint n. Thus, it is in the form of the Jacobian, with Equation 5.110 describing the column vector for joint n. The components of this column vector, with respect to the new frame can be calculated using Equations 5.72 to 5.77. A problem with this approach is that Paul (1981) does not explain how to measure or verify differential motion transforms.

Algorithm 5.2   Paul's algorithm for finding the manipulator Jacobian with respect to the frame of the end effector (Paul, 1981)

1. Start at joint 1, where $n = 1$,

$$^E\Delta_1 = {}^R T_E^1\,{}^0\Delta_1\,{}^R T_E \tag{5.112}$$

$$
\begin{aligned}
d^0 T_E &= {}^R T_{n-1}\,{}^{n-1}\Delta_n\,{}^{n-1}T_E\, dq_n = {}^R T_R\,{}^0\Delta_1\,{}^R T_E\, dq_1 \\
&= {}^0\Delta_1 A_1 \cdots A_E\, dq_n
\end{aligned} \tag{5.113}
$$

and

$$^{n-1}T_E = {}^R T_E = A_1 \cdots A_E \tag{5.114}$$

2. Apply Equations 5.72 to 5.77 to get the first column of the Jacobian – the differential motion vector for joint 1, $(n=1)$; the elements of $^0\Delta_1$.

A revolute joint has a differential rotation around the z axis:

$$\mathbf{J}_1 = [\mathbf{x} \cdot \delta \mathbf{x} \mathbf{p} \quad \mathbf{y} \cdot \delta \mathbf{x} \mathbf{p} \quad \mathbf{z} \cdot \delta \mathbf{x} \mathbf{p} \quad \delta \cdot \mathbf{x} \quad \delta \cdot \mathbf{y} \quad \delta \cdot \mathbf{z}] \tag{5.115}$$

where, because $\delta_x = \delta_y = 0$,

$$\mathbf{x} \cdot \delta \mathbf{x} \mathbf{p} = \frac{{}^E \partial x}{\partial \theta_n} = \mathbf{J}_{1n} = {}^{n-1}x_y \, {}^{n-1}p_x - {}^{n-1}x_x \, {}^{n-1}p_y = {}^0 x_y \, {}^0 p_x - {}^0 x_x \, {}^0 p_y \tag{5.116}$$

$$\mathbf{y} \cdot \delta \mathbf{x} \mathbf{p} = \frac{{}^E \partial y}{\partial \theta_n} = \mathbf{J}_{2n} = {}^{n-1}y_y \, {}^{n-1}p_x - {}^{n-1}y_x \, {}^{n-1}p_y = {}^0 y_y \, {}^0 p_x - {}^0 y_x \, {}^0 p_y \tag{5.117}$$

$$\mathbf{z} \cdot \delta \mathbf{x} \mathbf{p} = \frac{{}^E \partial z}{\partial \theta_n} = \mathbf{J}_{3n} = {}^{n-1}z_y \, {}^{n-1}p_x - {}^{n-1}z_x \, {}^{n-1}p_y = {}^0 z_y \, {}^0 p_x - {}^0 z_x \, {}^0 p_y \tag{5.118}$$

$$\delta \cdot \mathbf{x} = \frac{{}^E \partial \delta_x}{\partial \theta_n} \mathbf{J}_{4n} = {}^{n-1}x_z \tag{5.119}$$

$$\delta \cdot \mathbf{y} = \frac{{}^E \partial \delta_y}{\partial \theta_n} = \mathbf{J}_{5n} = {}^{n-1}y_z \tag{5.120}$$

$$\delta \cdot \mathbf{z} = \frac{{}^E \partial \delta_z}{\partial \theta_n} = \mathbf{J}_{6n} = {}^{n-1}z_z \tag{5.121}$$

A prismatic joint has a differential translation along the z axis:

$$\mathbf{J}_1 = [\mathbf{d} \cdot \mathbf{x} \quad \mathbf{d} \cdot \mathbf{y} \quad \mathbf{d} \cdot \mathbf{z} \quad 0 \quad 0 \quad 0] \tag{5.122}$$

where, because $d_x = d_y = 0$, and the angles between the axes are fixed,

$$\mathbf{d} \cdot \mathbf{x} = \frac{{}^E \partial x}{\partial d_n} = \mathbf{J}_{1n} = {}^{n-1}x_z = {}^0 x_z \tag{5.123}$$

$$\mathbf{d} \cdot \mathbf{y} = \frac{{}^E \partial y}{\partial d_n} = \mathbf{J}_{2n} = {}^{n-1}y_z = {}^0 y_z \tag{5.124}$$

$$\mathbf{d} \cdot \mathbf{z} = \frac{{}^E \partial z}{\partial d_n} = \mathbf{J}_{3n} = {}^{n-1}z_z = {}^0 z_z \tag{5.125}$$

$$\frac{{}^E \partial \delta_x}{\partial d_n} = \frac{{}^E \partial \delta_y}{\partial d_n} = \frac{{}^E \partial \delta_z}{\partial d_n} = 0 = \mathbf{J}_{4n} = \mathbf{J}_{5n} = \mathbf{J}_{6n} \tag{5.126}$$

3. Next, to calculate the differential motion vector for joint 2, ($n=2$) obtain the differential coordinate transform for joint n, by premultiplying the differential coordinate transform for joint $n-1$ (the previous joint – Equation 5.114) by the inverse of the **A** matrix of joint $n-1$.

$$^{n-1}\mathbf{T}_E = \mathbf{A}_{n-1}^{-1} \, {}^{n-2}\mathbf{T}_E = \mathbf{A}_n \cdots \mathbf{A}_E \tag{5.127}$$

$$^1\mathbf{T}_E = \mathbf{A}_1^{-1} \, {}^0\mathbf{T}_E \quad = \mathbf{A}_2 \cdots \mathbf{A}_E \tag{5.128}$$

Now, calculate the second column of the Jacobian by substituting the elements of the differential coordinate transform into Equations 5.116 to 5.121, if the joint is revolute, or into Equations 5.123 to 5.126, if the joint is prismatic.

4. Repeat step 3 until all the columns in the Jacobian are calculated, one for each joint.

As an example, we calculate the Jacobian of the type 1 two-link manipulator again, this time using Paul's algorithm.

From the forward kinematic transform (Equation 4.8):

$$^0T_E = \begin{bmatrix} C_{12} & -S_{12} & l_1C_1 + l_2C_{12} \\ S_{12} & C_{12} & l_1S_1 + l_2S_{12} \\ 0 & 0 & 1 \end{bmatrix} \tag{5.129}$$

$$^1T_E = \begin{bmatrix} C_2 & -S_2 & l_2C_2 \\ S_2 & C_2 & l_2S_2 \\ 0 & 0 & 1 \end{bmatrix} \tag{5.130}$$

$$^EJ = \begin{bmatrix} ^0x_y\,^0p_x - \,^0x_x\,^0p_y & ^1x_y\,^1p_x - \,^1x_x\,^1p_y \\ ^0y_y\,^0p_x - \,^0y_x\,^0p_y & ^1y_y\,^1p_x - \,^1y_x\,^1p_y \end{bmatrix}$$

$$= \begin{bmatrix} S_{12}(l_1C_1 + l_2C_{12}) - C_{12}(l_1S_1 + l_2S_{12}) & S_2l_2C_2 - C_2l_2S_2 \\ C_{12}(l_1C_1 + l_2C_{12}) - S_{12}(l_1S_1 + l_2S_{12}) & C_2l_2C_2 - S_2l_2S_2 \end{bmatrix}$$

$$= \begin{bmatrix} l_1S_2 & 0 \\ l_1C_2 + l_2 & l_2 \end{bmatrix} \tag{5.131}$$

The result is the same as the Jacobian with respect to the end effector given in Equation 5.97. As a second example, we calculate the Jacobian for a manipulator with prismatic joints, the type 5 two-link manipulator. From the forward kinematic transform (Equation 4.24):

$$^0T_E = \begin{bmatrix} 1 & 0 & 0 & 0 \\ 0 & 0 & -1 & -d_2 \\ 0 & 1 & 0 & d_1 \\ 0 & 0 & 0 & 1 \end{bmatrix} \qquad ^1T_E = \begin{bmatrix} 1 & 0 & 0 & 0 \\ 0 & 1 & 0 & 0 \\ 0 & 0 & 1 & d_2 \\ 0 & 0 & 0 & 1 \end{bmatrix} \tag{5.132}$$

$$^EJ = \begin{bmatrix} ^0x_z & ^1x_z \\ ^0y_z & ^1y_z \\ ^0z_z & ^1z_z \end{bmatrix} = \begin{bmatrix} 0 & 0 \\ 1 & 0 \\ 0 & 1 \end{bmatrix} \tag{5.133}$$

5.5.4 Inverse Jacobian algorithms

In Equations 5.99 – 5.101, we calculated the inverse Jacobian for the type 1 two-link manipulator using matrix inversion. For a multi-link manipulator, the equations in the Jacobian may be far more complex, and consequently, **symbolic inversion** is both difficult and time consuming. Renaud (1980, 1981) developed a systematic approach to symbolic inversion in terms of an intermediate coordinate frame, which Paul *et al.* (1984) have extended to apply to recursive manipulators. The details of these techniques are beyond the scope of this book, as they belong in a high-level kinematics course.

A second technique for Jacobian inversion is **numerical inversion**, where the numerical value of the elements of the Jacobian at an instant in time are found, and this matrix of numbers is inverted. However, the Jacobian changes as the manipulator moves, and consequently, this process of Jacobian calculation and inversion has to be repeated regularly, which makes it computationally expensive. One way to reduce this expense, and hence to obtain the inverse Jacobian in real time as the manipulator moves, is to precompute inverse Jacobians for various manipulator configurations along the planned trajectory and interpolate between these (Whitney, 1972). Because of rapid changes in the Jacobian, interpolation is valid over only a limited range of joint variables around the precomputed configuration. A second problem with numerical inversion is the use of floating point arithmetic to maintain precision, with a consequent increase in computing time.

One approach to this problem, which offers both precision and speed, is to use Gaussian elimination to simplify the inverse Jacobian to a set of linear equations which can be solved numerically (Snyder, 1985). Angeles (1986) developed a kinematic model of a manipulator as a set of nonlinear displacement equations. His inverse kinematic solution calculates the Jacobian as a set of linear displacement equations, from which the inverse Jacobian is found, again as a set of linear equations. These equations are solved numerically to obtain instantaneous joint velocities from Cartesian velocities.

A third, technique for Jacobian inversion is to calculate the inverse Jacobian directly by differentiating the inverse kinematic transform, starting with the proximal joint and moving along the manipulator to the distal joint. If a joint is at a limit and not able to move in the desired direction, its velocity is set to zero, and following joints compensate. This approach assumes the existence of an arm solution, and can result in very complex equations. A fourth technique is to use screw transforms (La Brooy, 1987).

5.6 Singularities

Most manipulators have configurations where the Jacobian is singular, that is, it has no inverse. Near a singularity, matrix inversion becomes ill-conditioned. When a manipulator is in a singular configuration it has lost one or more degrees of mobility, which for a manipulator with six or less degrees of mobility corresponds to a loss of degrees of freedom. This means that it is physically impossible for the manipulator to move its end effector in some Cartesian directions. An obvious position where this occurs is at the boundary of the workspace of the robot.

Singularities commonly fall into two categories (Gorla and Renaud, 1984): workspace internal singularities, and workspace boundary singularities. A **workspace internal singularity** occurs within the workspace of the manipulator, often when two or more joint axes line-up. A **workspace boundary singularity** occurs when the manipulator is fully extended to the outer boundary of its workspace or fully retracted to the inner boundary of its workspace. In this situation, the end effector can move along the boundary, and into the workspace, but it cannot move out of the workspace.

For example, the type 1 two-link manipulator exhibits two workspace boundary singularities: one when the arm is fully retracted (the angle between the links is zero), and one when it is fully extended (180°). In both cases, the determinant of the Jacobian (Equation 5.100) is zero. As a result, a small Cartesian velocity in some directions requires an infinite joint velocity, a physical impossibility for the manipulator.

$$|J| = l_1 l_2 \sin\theta_2 = 0 \qquad (5.134)$$

when

$$\theta_2 = 0 \text{ or } \pi$$

At the singular configuration, Equation 5.96 becomes

$$
\begin{bmatrix} dx \\ dy \end{bmatrix} = \begin{bmatrix} -l_1 S_1 - l_2 S_1 & -l_2 S_1 \\ l_1 C_1 - l_2 C_1 & l_2 C_1 \end{bmatrix} \begin{bmatrix} d\theta_1 \\ d\theta_2 \end{bmatrix}
$$

$$
= \begin{bmatrix} -2lS_1 & -lS_1 \\ 2lC_1 & lC_1 \end{bmatrix} \begin{bmatrix} d\theta_1 \\ d\theta_2 \end{bmatrix} = \begin{bmatrix} -S_1 \\ C_1 \end{bmatrix} [2l\,d\theta_1 + l\,d\theta_2] \qquad (5.135)
$$

when

$$l_1 = l_2 = l$$

The two column vectors in the Jacobian are parallel. Consequently, the end point can be moved in a direction perpendicular to the arm links, but not in any other direction. As the singularity involves joint 2 only, motion of joint 1 can be controlled to move the end effector along the boundary of the workspace. Also, joint 2 can be controlled to move the end effector back into the workspace, but, near the singularity, the inverse Jacobian is undefined, and some other method of joint velocity calculation is required.

Figure 5.12
Type 1 two-link manipulator
tracking a straight line
trajectory past a singularity.
Dotted lines show the result
of extending the trajectory
towards the work space
boundaries.
(a) 7-link configurations
along the trajectory.
(b) Joint angles and joint
velocities calculated with the
inverse Jacobian.

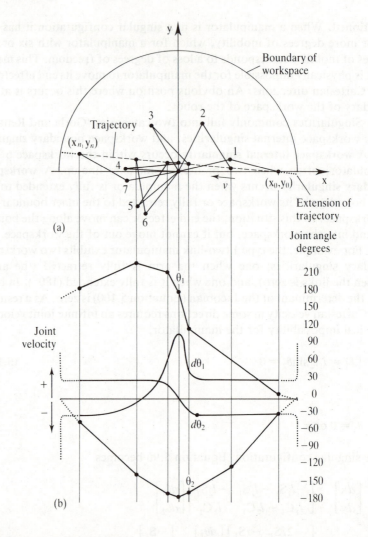

Singularities can cause problems when tracking a trajectory. To find the profile of joint velocities for a trajectory, we calculate the joint angles for each Cartesian point on the trajectory. Then we calculate the required joint velocities using Equation 5.101. When such a profile is plotted (Figure 5.12), the calculated joint velocities are excessively large near the singularities. At the outer bounds of the workspace, no joint motion can move the end effector further along a radial trajectory. This condition must be avoided, as the calculated velocity will not achieve the desired result. Near the singularity at the centre of the trajectory, the velocity of joint 1 is large because link 1 must rotate rapidly to keep the end effector on the trajectory. If the path is too close to the singularity, the calculated velocity will be greater than the joint can achieve and control will be lost.

For any manipulator, every configuration that places the end effector at the extremities of the workspace is a workspace degeneracy. In these configurations, the number of degrees of freedom of the manipulator is reduced by the workspace constraints, since motion in directions outside the workspace is not possible. However, singularities do not always occur at such degeneracies. In contrast, singularities always occur at degenerate configurations inside the workspace (Section 4.12).

Many robot wrists have singularities. Any spherical wrist is singular when two axes are collinear. For a roll-pitch-yaw wrist, singularities occur when the roll and pitch axes align or the roll and yaw axes align. This occurs at a pitch of 90° in either direction, or a yaw of 90° in either direction, respectively. This results in a circular region of singularities in a plane at right angles to the roll axis. In practice, the singularity is not a point but extends either side of the singular point. For a roll–pitch–roll wrist (Figure 2.36) a singularity occurs when the two roll axes line up. This results in a singular region, or cone, around the roll axis. At a workspace internal singularity, one axis will often flip through 180° in one direction while the collinear axis flips through 180° in the other direction. The location of the end effector doesn't change, but the flipping action can be quite violent. In many applications, this is undesirable.

Singularities are best overcome by avoiding them during the design of the wrist. For example, the 'Elephant Trunk' wrist used on the Australian sheep-sheering robot (Trevelyan *et al.*, 1986) was designed to remove all singularities out of the desired work space. In some applications, singularities are avoided by using a manipulator with more than six joints: the extra joints allow the arm to be configured to avoid singular configurations. Unfortunately, the extra degrees of mobility introduce redundancy to the kinematic model, and the Jacobian is no longer square. This means that a consistent strategy for joint control is required both to avoid the singular configurations and to handle redundancy. Control can be achieved by adding extra equations to the Jacobian to make it square (Whitney, 1972). If these are appropriately selected, the joints which provide the additional degrees of mobility will be stationary when the end effector is away from a singularity, and will move at increasing speeds as the end effector approaches a singularity, in order to avoid the singular configuration. Whitney (1972) proposes equations that calculate minimum or maximum joint rotations as a function of joint velocities.

When we have a manipulator with singularities in the desired workspace, where only some degrees of freedom are lost, we can minimize the effect of these singularities. First, identify the degrees of freedom that are lost, and the joints involved. Then remove those rows in the Jacobian which correspond to the lost degrees of freedom and the columns which correspond to the offending joints. The result is a new limited Jacobian which is not singular, which can be used to calculate the joint velocities of the remaining joints from the remaining Cartesian degrees of freedom. Normally, the offending joints are held still while the other joints move the manipulator through the region of the singularity.

5.7 Programming

In most industrial robot controllers, velocity is set at the start of a motion, and is fixed for that motion (see Figure 12.4). In some languages, velocity is set as a global parameter, and the speed for each motion is set as a percentage of the global velocity. In these systems trajectories are followed by calculating new Cartesian and/or joint space values at fixed intervals along the path, and the rate of recalculation is automatically determined from the preset speed. However, for some tasks this method of fixed velocity control is inadequate, as the velocity must vary during the motion. Acceleration is often controlled by setting fixed acceleration and deceleration rates. Again, this may be inadequate.

Most robot controllers currently in use do not calculate either the Jacobian or the inverse Jacobian, as their calculation is time consuming, and early applications of robots did not require this sophistication. However, new robot controllers, and robot control languages will include velocity calculation and control based on regular calculation of the Jacobian and its inverse. Real-time performance can be achieved by calculating the Jacobian at intervals along the path and linearly interpolating between these calculation points. These issues are discussed further under trajectory planning in Section 9.3.4.2.

In order to achieve adequate execution speed, with existing microprocessors, equations derived from the Jacobians will be hard coded into robot controllers. However, in controllers built with parallel processors, equations stored in symbolic form will be executable in real time, which will provide greater flexibility.

Most of the calculations in this chapter involve variables of the data types defined in previous chapters, such as frames and point vectors. In Chapter 4, a Cartesian space vector and a joint space vector were introduced as storage elements in a robot data structure. These six-element vectors are heavily used in this chapter and the next. Also, they are used in kinematics of position when six degree of freedom transformations are used.

In this chapter, we introduce a new data structure, a six-by-six matrix for storing six degree of freedom transformations such as motion transforms and Jacobians (Figure 5.13). As this is a large matrix, which is used for several different transformations, and appropriate names for elements are hard to conceive, data abstraction as used with the frame structure has not been used in defining the elements. But, as the elements of the Jacobian are referenced by row and column, we have data abstraction for Jacobians. An initialized variable of this type should be included in the implementation module.

```
TYPE
    SixDofTransf=ARRAY[1..6],[1..6] of REAL;        (*used for differential
    motion transforms and Jacobians*)

    Robot=RECORD         (*record to store information about a robot arm*)
        nooflinks : [1..6];
        manipulator : ARRAY [0..6] OF Link;
        (*the size of the array is the number of links plus 1 for the base
        -link zero is the base to which the manipulator is attached*)
        RTN : Frame;       (*actual values of transform for current
        configuration*)
        invRTN : Frame;        (*actual values of inverse transform for current
        configuration*)
        cartspace : CartVector;       (*actual Cartesian space values*)
        jointspace : JointVector;        (*actual joint space values*)
        cartvel : CartVector;      (*actual Cartesian space velocities*)
        jointvel : JointVector;       (*actual joint space velocities*)
        cartaccel : CartVector;       (*actual Cartesian space accelerations*)
        jointaccel : JointVector;       (*actual joint space accelerations*)
        jacobian : SixDofTransf;       (*actual Jacobian values*)
        invjacobian : SixDofTransf;        (*actual inverse Jacobian values*)
        fwdaccel : SixDofTransf;       (*actual acceleration transform values*)
        invaccel : SixDofTransf;       (*actual inverse acceleration transform
        values*)
        ForwardEqns : ARRAY[posx..rotz] OF TokenList;
            (*equations for forward kinematic transform in symbolic
            form*)
        BackwardEqns : ARRAY[joint1..joint6] OF TokenList;
            (*equations for backward kinematic transform in symbolic
            form*)
        Determinant : TokenList;
            (*determinant of velocity Jacobian in symbolic form for finding
            singularities*)
        Veljacobian : ARRAY[posx..rotz] OF TokenList;
            (*equations for velocity Jacobian in symbolic form*)
        Invveljacobian : ARRAY[joint1..joint6] OF TokenList;
            (*equations for inverse velocity Jacobian in symbolic form*)
        Acceljacobian : ARRAY[posx..rotz] OF TokenList;
            (*equations for acceleration transform in symbolic form*)
        Invacceljacobian : ARRAY[joint1..joint6] OF TokenList;
            (*equations for inverse acceleration transform in symbolic
            form*)

    End;
```

Figure 5.13
Additional data structure and modified robot data structure for representing manipulator motion – to be added to the library of robot structures (Figure 3.21).

In Figure 5.13, the robot data structure has been extended to include numeric values and symbolic equations for both velocity and acceleration calculations. This data structure is quite large: a reflection of the volume of information required to model a manipulator. Also, the equation for the determinant of the velocity Jacobian has been added to the robot data structure, for use in detecting when the manipulator is in the vicinity of a singularity.

In the text of this chapter, we have defined a number of algorithms for calculating velocity, acceleration, Jacobians and differential motion transforms. Each of these should be implemented as a procedure. The calculation of these algorithms will require the declaration of many new variables, of type frame, vector, and six degree of freedom frame. For compatibility, and ease of calculation, the derivatives of vectors are of the same type as the vectors themselves. Also the differential motion transforms are of type frame, for the same reasons.

Key points

- A path is a sequence of points in space.
- A trajectory is a path with time constraints.
- The linear velocity of a point (frame n) moving on an object ($n-1$) as seen from a reference frame (R) is:

$$^{R}v_n = {}^{R}v_{n-1} + {}^{R}\omega_{n-1} \times {}^{R}\text{Rot}_{n-1} {}^{n-1}p_n + {}^{R}\text{Rot}_{n-1} {}^{n-1}v_n \qquad (5.12)$$

- The first time derivative of a free vector (s) can be transformed from a rotating frame (N) to a fixed frame (R)

$$\frac{d^{R}s}{dt} = {}^{R}\text{Rot}_{N} \frac{d^{N}s}{dt} + {}^{R}\omega_{N} \times {}^{R}\text{Rot}_{N} {}^{N}s \qquad (5.14)$$

- Linear velocity can be transformed from frame n to frame $n-1$

$$^{n-1}v_n = {}^{n-1}\text{Rot}_n({}^{n}v_{n-1} + {}^{n}\omega_{n-1} \times {}^{n}p_{n-1,n} + {}^{n}v_{n-1,n}) \qquad (5.19)$$

- Angular velocities can be added when expressed with respect to the same frame.
- Angular velocity is transformed from one frame to another with a rotation transform.

$$^{R}\omega_{n-1,n} = {}^{R}\text{Rot}_{n-1} {}^{n-1}\omega_n \qquad (5.22)$$

- The linear acceleration of a point (n) moving on an object ($n-1$) as seen from a reference frame (R) is

$$^{R}a_n = {}^{R}a_{n-1} + {}^{R}\alpha_{n-1} \times {}^{R}\text{Rot}_{n-1} {}^{n-1}p_n + {}^{R}\omega_{n-1} \times ({}^{R}\omega_{n-1} \times {}^{R}\text{Rot}_{n-1} {}^{n-1}p_n)$$
$$+ 2{}^{R}\omega_{n-1} \times {}^{R}\text{Rot}_{n-1} {}^{n-1}v_n + {}^{R}\text{Rot}_{n-1} {}^{n-1}a_n \qquad (5.30)$$

- When one body rotates around another it is subject to angular acceleration.

$$^R\alpha_n = {}^R\alpha_{n-1} + {}^R\omega_{n-1} \times {}^R\omega_{n-1,n} + {}^R\alpha_{n-1,n} \qquad (5.38)$$

- A differential motion transform (Δ) describes a small change in location.

$$d^R\mathbf{T}_N = {}^R\Delta \, {}^R\mathbf{T}_N = {}^R\mathbf{T}_N \, {}^N\Delta \qquad (5.45)$$

- Differential motions (*D*) are transformed from one frame to another using a general motion transform (**M**).

$$^N D = {}^N\mathbf{M}_R \, {}^R D \qquad (5.79)$$

- The manipulator Jacobian is a matrix of differentials used to transform velocities from joint space to Cartesian space.

$$D = \mathbf{J}D_q \qquad (5.89)$$

- When the determinant of a Jacobian is zero, the Jacobian has no inverse, and the manipulator is in a singular configuration.

- At a singularity, control of motion in some Cartesian directions is physically impossible. Singularities occur when joint axes align, and at workspace boundaries.

Examples

Example 5.1   Type 2 two-link manipulator Jacobian

In this example, we calculate the Jacobian and the inverse Jacobian for the type 2 two-link manipulator (Figure 4.7) using differentiation. The forward kinematic transform for this manipulator is:

$$^0\mathbf{T}_2 = \begin{bmatrix} C_1C_2 & -C_1S_2 & S_1 & l_2C_1C_2 \\ S_1C_2 & -S_1S_2 & -C_1 & l_2S_1C_2 \\ S_2 & C_2 & 0 & d_1 + l_2S_2 \\ 0 & 0 & 0 & 1 \end{bmatrix} = \begin{bmatrix} x_x & y_x & z_x & p_x \\ x_y & y_y & z_y & p_y \\ x_z & y_z & z_z & p_z \\ 0 & 0 & 0 & 1 \end{bmatrix} \qquad (4.53)$$

$$p_x = l_2C_1C_2 \qquad p_y = l_2S_1C_2 \qquad p_z = d_1 + l_2S_2 \qquad (5.136)$$

$$\frac{\partial p_x}{\partial \theta_1} = -l_2S_1C_2 \qquad \frac{\partial p_y}{\partial \theta_1} = l_2C_1C_2 \qquad \frac{\partial p_z}{\partial \theta_1} = 0 \qquad (5.137)$$

$$\frac{\partial p_x}{\partial \theta_2} = -l_2 C_1 S_2 \quad \frac{\partial p_y}{\partial \theta_2} = -l_2 S_1 S_2 \quad \frac{\partial p_z}{\partial \theta_2} = l_2 C_2 \tag{5.138}$$

$$\begin{bmatrix} dx \\ dy \\ dz \end{bmatrix} = \begin{bmatrix} -l_2 S_1 C_2 & -l_2 C_1 S_2 \\ l_2 C_1 C_2 & -l_2 S_1 S_2 \\ 0 & l_2 C_2 \end{bmatrix} \begin{bmatrix} d\theta_1 \\ d\theta_2 \end{bmatrix} \tag{5.139}$$

The inverse kinematic transform is:

$$\theta_1 = \text{atan2}(p_y, p_x) \text{ and } \theta_2 = \text{atan2}(p_z - d_1, p_x C_1 + p_y S_1) \tag{4.59,62}$$

From Equation 4.59, rewrite the solution for θ_1 as:

$$p_x \sin \theta_1 = p_y \cos \theta_1 \tag{5.140}$$

Differentiate Equation 5.140 with respect to time, to get:

$$(p_x \cos \theta_1 + p_y \sin \theta_1) d\theta_1 = \cos \theta_1 dp_y - \sin \theta_1 dp_x \tag{5.141}$$

$$d\theta_1 = \frac{1}{C_1 p_x + S_1 p_y}(C_1 dp_y - S_1 dp_x) \tag{5.142}$$

From Equations 4.53 and 4.59, the solution for θ_2 is rewritten as:

$$(p_z - d_1) \cos \theta_2 = (p_x C_1 + p_y S_1) \sin \theta_2 \tag{5.143}$$

$$p_z C_2 - d_1 C_2 = (l_2 C_1 C_2 C_1 + l_2 S_1 C_2 S_1) S_2 = l_2 C_2 S_2 \tag{5.144}$$

Differentiate Equation 5.144 with respect to time, to get:

$$dp_z C_2 - p_z S_2 d\theta_2 + d_1 S_2 d\theta_2 = l_2 C_2^2 d\theta_2 - l_2 S_2^2 d\theta_2 \tag{5.145}$$

$$d\theta_2 (l_2 C_2^2 - l_2 S_2^2 + (p_z - d_1) S_2) = d\theta_2 (l_2 C_2^2) = dp_z C_2 \tag{5.146}$$

$$d\theta_2 = \frac{-1}{l_2 C_2} dp_z = \frac{-1}{(p_x C_1 + p_y S_1)} dp_z \tag{5.147}$$

and the inverse Jacobian is:

$$\mathbf{J}^{-1} = \frac{1}{l_2 C_2} \begin{bmatrix} -S_1 & C_1 & 0 \\ 0 & 0 & -1 \end{bmatrix} \tag{5.148}$$

This manipulator has a singularity when θ_2 is at 90°, that is, when link 2 is vertical. Paul (1981) developed a standard form from the derivative of the arctangent. In this example, the standard form requires as much work as straight differentiation, but in more complex problems it can save considerable effort. If equations for the elements of the atan2 function can be found in the form

$$\tan\theta_i = \frac{N\sin\theta_i}{N\cos\theta_i} \tag{5.149}$$

then, using the formula for the derivative of u/v (Section 13.2)

$$d\tan\theta_i = \sec^2\theta_i d\theta_i = (\tan^2\theta_i + 1)d\theta_i = \frac{(\sin^2\theta_i + \cos^2\theta_i)d\theta_i}{\cos^2\theta_i}$$

$$= \frac{N\cos\theta_i d(N\sin\theta_i) - N\sin\theta_i d(N\cos\theta_i)}{(N\cos\theta_i)^2} \tag{5.150}$$

$$d\theta_i = \frac{N\cos\theta_i d(N\sin\theta_i) - N\sin\theta_i d(N\cos\theta_i)}{(N\sin\theta_i)^2 + (N\cos\theta_i)^2} \tag{5.151}$$

From Equation 4.61, we obtain equations for the elements of the atan2 function in the correct form, and differentiate them.

$$N\sin\theta_2 = p_z - d_1 = l_2 S_2 \text{ and } N\cos\theta_2 = p_x C_1 + p_y S_1 = l_2 C_2 \tag{5.152}$$

$$dN\sin\theta_2 = dp_z \text{ and } dN\cos\theta_2 = -l_2 S_2 d\theta_2 \tag{5.153}$$

Substitute these values in Equation 5.151 to obtain a solution for $d\theta_2$. The parameters in the final result depend on which of the equivalent expressions are substituted, a choice which can have a considerable impact on the computation time.

$$d\theta_2 = \frac{1}{l_2^2(S_2^2 + C_2^2)} [l_2 C_2 dp_z - l_2 S_2(-l_2 S_2 d\theta_2)] \tag{5.154}$$

$$l_2^2 S_2^2 d\theta_2 + l_2^2 C_2^2 d\theta_2 = l_2 C_2 dp_z + l_2^2 S_2^2 d\theta_2 \tag{5.155}$$

$$d\theta_2 = \frac{-1}{l_2 C_2} dp_z = \frac{-1}{(p_x C_1 + p_y S_1)} dp_z \tag{5.147}$$

Example 5.2   Planar three-link manipulator Jacobian

As a second example, we calculate the Jacobian will for a planar three-link manipulator (Figure 5.14) using Paul's algorithm (Equations 5.116–121), and the inverse Jacobian using matrix inversion. In this example, equations are simplified using trigonometric relationships (Section 13.1.2). From the forward kinematic transform for this manipulator, we get:

$$^0T_3 = \begin{bmatrix} C_{123} & -S_{123} & 0 & l_3 C_{123} + l_2 C_{12} + l_1 C_1 \\ S_{123} & C_{123} & 0 & l_3 S_{123} + l_2 S_{12} + l_1 S_1 \\ 0 & 0 & 1 & 0 \\ 0 & 0 & 0 & 1 \end{bmatrix} \tag{5.156}$$

$$^1T_3 = \begin{bmatrix} C_{23} & -S_{23} & 0 & l_3C_{23} + l_2C_2 \\ S_{23} & C_{23} & 0 & l_3S_{23} + l_2S_2 \\ 0 & 0 & 1 & 0 \\ 0 & 0 & 0 & 1 \end{bmatrix} \qquad (5.157)$$

$$^2T_3 = \begin{bmatrix} C_3 & -S_3 & 0 & l_3C_3 \\ S_3 & C_3 & 0 & l_3S_3 \\ 0 & 0 & 1 & 0 \\ 0 & 0 & 0 & 0 \end{bmatrix} \qquad (5.158)$$

$$\begin{aligned} J_{11} &= {}^0x_y{}^0p_x - {}^0x_x{}^0p_y = S_{123}(l_3C_{123} + l_2C_{12} + l_1C_1) \\ &\quad - C_{123}(l_3S_{123} + l_2S_{12} + l_1S_1) \\ &= l_2S_3 + l_1S_{23} \end{aligned} \qquad (5.159)$$

$$\begin{aligned} J_{12} &= {}^1x_y{}^1p_x - {}^1x_x{}^1p_y = S_{23}(l_3C_{23} + l_2C_2) - C_{23}(l_3S_{23} + l_2S_2) \\ &= l_2S_3 \end{aligned} \qquad (5.160)$$

$$J_{13} = {}^2x_y{}^2p_x - {}^2x_x{}^2p_y = S_3 l_3 C_3 - C_3 l_3 S_3 = 0 \qquad (5.161)$$

$$\begin{aligned} J_{21} &= {}^0y_y{}^0p_x - {}^0y_x{}^0p_y = C_{123}(l_3C_{123} + l_2C_{12} + l_1C_1) \\ &\quad + S_{123}(l_3S_{123} + l_2S_{12} + l_1S_1) \\ &= l_3 + l_2C_1 + l_1C_{23} \end{aligned} \qquad (5.162)$$

$$\begin{aligned} J_{22} &= {}^1y_y{}^1p_x - {}^1y_x{}^1p_y = C_{23}(l_3C_{23} + l_2C_2) + S_{23}(l_3S_{23} + l_2S_2) \\ &= l_3 + l_2C_3 \end{aligned} \qquad (5.163)$$

$$J_{23} = {}^2y_y{}^2p_x - {}^2y_x{}^2p_y = C_3 l_3 C_3 + S_3 l_3 S_3 = l_3 \qquad (5.164)$$

$$J_{31} = {}^0z_y{}^0p_x - {}^0z_x{}^0p_y = 0 = J_{32} = J_{33} \qquad (5.165)$$

$$J_{41} = {}^0x_z = 0 \qquad (5.166)$$

$$J_{51} = {}^0y_z = 0 \qquad (5.167)$$

$$J_{61} = {}^0z_z = 1 \qquad (5.168)$$

$$\begin{bmatrix} dx \\ dy \\ dz \end{bmatrix} = \begin{bmatrix} l_2S_3 + l_1S_{23} & l_2S_3 & 0 \\ l_3 + l_2C_1 + l_1C_{23} & l_3 + l_2C_3 & l_3 \\ 1 & 1 & 1 \end{bmatrix} \begin{bmatrix} d\theta_1 \\ d\theta_2 \\ d\theta_3 \end{bmatrix} \qquad (5.169)$$

Now, find the inverse Jacobian using matrix inversion (Section 13.3.4).

$$J^{-1} = \frac{1}{|J|} [ADJ(J)]^T \qquad \text{(where ADJ(J) is the matrix of cofactors)}$$

$$= \frac{1}{l_1 l_2 S_3} \begin{bmatrix} l_2C_3 & -l_2S_3 - l_1S_{23} & l_2l_3S_3 \\ -l_2C_3 - l_1C_{23} & l_2S_3 + l_1S_{23} & -l_2l_3S_3 - l_1l_3S_{23} \\ l_1C_{23} & -l_1S_{23} & l_1l_3S_{23} + l_1l_2S_2 \end{bmatrix} \qquad (5.170)$$

This manipulator has a singularities when θ_3 is 0° or 180°.

Example 5.3   End effector velocity

For a third example, we calculate the Jacobian for the same planar three-link manipulator (Figure 5.14) using Algorithm 5.1. This algorithm uses repetitive calls to Equation 5.107 to solve for the velocity of the end effector with respect to the base. As there are three links, the calculation recurses (or iterates) three times – that is $n=1\ldots3$.

$$^0v_3 = {}^0v_1 + {}^0\omega_1 \times {}^0\text{Rot}_1 {}^1p_3 + {}^0\text{Rot}_1 {}^1v_3 \qquad (5.171)$$

$$^1v_3 = {}^1v_2 + {}^1\omega_2 \times {}^1\text{Rot}_2 {}^2p_3 + {}^1\text{Rot}_2 {}^2v_3 \qquad (5.172)$$

$$^2v_3 = {}^2v_{\text{trans3}} + {}^2\omega_3 \times {}^2\text{Rot}_3 {}^3p_3 + {}^2\text{Rot}_3 {}^3v_3 \qquad (5.173)$$

As all the joints are revolute, the length of the linkages is constant, frame 0 is stationary and nothing moves with respect to frame 3, we can simplify the above equations.

$$^0v_3 = {}^0\omega_1 \times {}^0p_1 + {}^0\omega_1 \times {}^0\text{Rot}_1 {}^1p_3 + {}^0\text{Rot}_1 {}^1v_3 \qquad (5.174)$$

$$^1v_3 = {}^1\omega_2 \times {}^1p_2 + {}^1\omega_2 \times {}^1\text{Rot}_2 {}^2p_3 + {}^1\text{Rot}_2 {}^2v_3 \qquad (5.175)$$

$$^2v_3 = {}^2\omega_3 \times {}^2p_3 \qquad (5.176)$$

At this point, we could substitute values and find the Cartesian velocities of the link coordinate frames as a function of the joint velocities. Instead, we will manipulate the equations further, and see a standard form emerge. Substitute Equation 5.176 into Equation 5.175, and Equation 5.175 into 5.174.

$$^0v_3 = {}^0\omega_1 \times {}^0p_1 + {}^0\omega_1 \times {}^0\text{Rot}_1 {}^1p_3$$
$$+ {}^0\text{Rot}_1[{}^1\omega_2 \times {}^1p_2 + {}^1\omega_2 \times {}^1\text{Rot}_2 {}^2p_3 + {}^1\text{Rot}_2({}^2\omega_3 \times {}^2p_3)] \qquad (5.177)$$

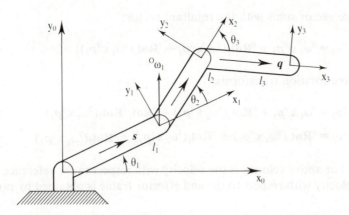

Figure 5.14
Planar three-link manipulator.

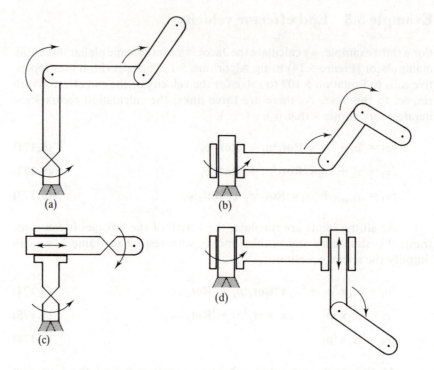

Now apply the relation $a \times b + a \times c = a \times (b + c)$ (Section 13.3.3):

$$^0v_3 = {}^0\omega_1 \times ({}^0p_1 + {}^0\text{Rot}_1\,{}^1p_3)$$
$$+ {}^0\text{Rot}_1[{}^1\omega_2 \times ({}^1p_2 + {}^1\text{Rot}_2\,{}^2p_3) + {}^1\text{Rot}_2({}^2\omega_3 \times {}^2p_3)] \qquad (5.178)$$

Replace vector sums with the resultant vector:

$$^0v_3 = {}^0\omega_1 \times {}^0p_3 + {}^0\text{Rot}_2[{}^1\omega_2 \times {}^1p_3 + {}^1\text{Rot}_2({}^2\omega_3 \times {}^2p_3)] \qquad (5.179)$$

Combine rotation transforms:

$$^0v_3 = {}^0\omega_1 \times {}^0p_3 + {}^0\text{Rot}_1({}^1\omega_2 \times {}^1p_3) + {}^0\text{Rot}_1\,{}^1\text{Rot}_2({}^2\omega_3 \times {}^2p_3) \qquad (5.180)$$

$$^0v_3 = {}^0\text{Rot}_0({}^0\omega_1 \times {}^0p_3) + {}^0\text{Rot}_1({}^1\omega_2 \times {}^1p_3) + {}^0\text{Rot}_2({}^2\omega_3 \times {}^2p_3) \qquad (5.181)$$

The above velocity is the velocity with respect to the reference frame. The velocity with respect to the end effector frame is obtained by premultiplying by the inverse rotation transform. We use the rotation transform to transform velocity because velocity is a free vector.

$$^0v_3 = \,^0\mathbf{Rot}_3\,^3v_3 \tag{5.182}$$

$$^3v_3 = \,^0\mathbf{Rot}_3^{-1}\,^0v_3 = \,^2\mathbf{Rot}_3^{-1}\,^1\mathbf{Rot}_2^{-1}\,^0\mathbf{Rot}_1^{-1}\,^0v_3 \tag{5.183}$$

$$^3v_3 = \,^0\mathbf{Rot}_3^{-1}(^0\omega_1 \times \,^0p_3) + \,^1\mathbf{Rot}_3^{-1}(^1\omega_2 \times \,^1p_3) \\ + \,^2\mathbf{Rot}_3^{-1}(^2\omega_3 \times \,^2p_3) \tag{5.184}$$

Substituting values into Equation 5.181, from the forward kinematic transform (Equations 5.156–158), to calculate the velocity and the Jacobian.

$$^0v_3 = \begin{bmatrix} 0 \\ 0 \\ d\theta_1 \end{bmatrix} \times \begin{bmatrix} l_3C_{123} + l_2C_{12} + l_1C_1 \\ l_3S_{123} + l_2S_{12} + l_1S_1 \\ 0 \end{bmatrix}$$
$$+ \begin{bmatrix} C_1 & -S_1 & 0 \\ S_1 & C_1 & 0 \\ 0 & 0 & 1 \end{bmatrix} \left(\begin{bmatrix} 0 \\ 0 \\ d\theta_2 \end{bmatrix} \times \begin{bmatrix} l_3C_{23} + l_2C_2 \\ l_3S_{23} + l_2S_2 \\ 0 \end{bmatrix} \right)$$
$$+ \begin{bmatrix} C_{12} & -S_{12} & 0 \\ S_{12} & C_{12} & 0 \\ 0 & 0 & 1 \end{bmatrix} \left(\begin{bmatrix} 0 \\ 0 \\ d\theta_3 \end{bmatrix} \times \begin{bmatrix} l_3C_3 \\ l_3S_3 \\ 0 \end{bmatrix} \right) \tag{5.185}$$

$$^0v_3 = \begin{bmatrix} -l_3S_{123} - l_2S_{12} - l_1S_1 \\ l_3C_{123} + l_2C_{12} + l_1C_1 \\ 0 \end{bmatrix} d\theta_1 + \begin{bmatrix} C_1 & -S_1 & 0 \\ S_1 & C_1 & 0 \\ 0 & 0 & 1 \end{bmatrix} \begin{bmatrix} -l_3S_{23} + l_2S_2 \\ l_3C_{23} + l_2C_2 \\ 0 \end{bmatrix} d\theta_2$$
$$+ \begin{bmatrix} C_{12} & -S_{12} & 0 \\ S_{12} & C_{12} & 0 \\ 0 & 0 & 1 \end{bmatrix} \begin{bmatrix} -l_3S_3 \\ l_3C_3 \\ 0 \end{bmatrix} d\theta_3 \tag{5.186}$$

$$^0v_3 = \begin{bmatrix} -l_3S_{123} - l_2S_{12} - l_1S_1 \\ l_3C_{123} + l_2C_{12} + l_1C_1 \end{bmatrix} d\theta_1 + \begin{bmatrix} -l_3S_{123} - l_2S_{12} \\ l_3C_{123} + l_2C_{12} \end{bmatrix} d\theta_2$$
$$+ \begin{bmatrix} -l_3S_{123} \\ l_3C_{123} \end{bmatrix} d\theta_3 \tag{5.187}$$

$$^0\mathbf{J} = \begin{bmatrix} -l_3S_{123} - l_2S_{12} - l_1S_1 & -l_3S_{123} - l_2S_{12} & -l_3S_{123} \\ l_3C_{123} + l_2C_{12} + l_1C_1 & l_3C_{123} + l_2C_{12} & l_3C_{123} \\ 1 & 1 & 1 \end{bmatrix} \tag{5.188}$$

The third row of the Jacobian is the sum of the rotations around the z axis, and can be found using angular velocity vectors. The calculation of the Jacobian with respect to frame 3 is left as an exercise for the reader. By

---

Algorithm 5.3 **Algorithm for finding the velocity of the end effector of a multi-link articulated manipulator using vectors**

1. The reference frame R is located at joint 1 (frame 0).

2. The end effector frame (E) is placed at the tool plate (frame N), where N is the number of joints.

3. Initialize the velocity to zero.

$$^R v_N = 0 \text{ and } ^N v_N = 0$$

4. Calculate the velocity of the end effector with a loop:
For $n=1$ to N do

$$^R v_N = {}^R v_N + {}^R\mathbf{Rot}_{n-1}({}^{n-1}\omega_n \times {}^{n-1}\boldsymbol{p}_N) \tag{5.189}$$

$$^N v_N = {}^N v_N + {}^{n-1}\mathbf{Rot}_N^{-1}({}^{n-1}\omega_n \times {}^{n-1}\boldsymbol{p}_N) \tag{5.190}$$

5. The vector $^{n-1}\boldsymbol{p}_N$ is obtained from the forward kinematic transform.

6. The iteration terminates when n is equal to the number of joints in the manipulator.

---

recognizing that there is a repeating pattern in Equations 5.181 and 5.184, a simple iterative algorithm is obtained for calculating the velocity of a multi-link manipulator with revolute joints. A similar exercise for a prismatic robot is left for the reader.

Exercises

Essay questions

5.1. Calculate the differential transformation of the **A** matrix for a revolute joint.

5.2. For each of the five two-link manipulators, derive equations for:
(a) the linear velocity of frame 2.
(b) the linear acceleration of frame 2.
(c) the angular velocity and the acceleration of frame 2.

5.3. Prove that the differential rotation transform is independent of the order in which the rotations are performed.

5.4. If the small signal assumption for differential motion is applied to the **A** matrix, what is the error in the result for differential joint angles of 1°, 5°, and 10°?

5.5. Verify the correctness of Equation 5.69 by working through the calculation of this matrix.

5.6. The robot which moves the screw in Figure 3.16 is not very accurate. Assume the block is inaccurately placed. A vision system indicates that the screw has to be moved $0.05a$ units in the new x direction, rotated 0.2 radians around the new y axis, and rotated -0.1 radian around the new z axis to correct for this inaccuracy. Calculate ${}^N D$, ${}^N \Delta$, $d^R T_N$, ${}^R D$, ${}^R \Delta$, and ${}^N M_R$ for the required differential motion (Sections 5.4.1).

5.7. Repeat Exercise 5.6, but, this time, assume that the errors in the placement of the block given in Equation 5.59 exist.

5.8. Find the Jacobian and inverse Jacobian for each of the five two-link manipulators by differentiation, with vectors, and with Paul's algorithm.

5.9. Find the Jacobian and inverse Jacobian for each of the three-link manipulators in Figure 4.23 and Figure 5.15. Identify the locations of their singularities.

5.10. Using vectors, calculate the Jacobian with respect to frame 3 for the three-link planar manipulator in Example 5.3. Verify the correctness of your solution by pre-multiplying it by the rotation transformation to obtain the Jacobian with respect to frame 0.

5.11. Draw a graph of the workspace internal singularities of the planar three-link manipulator in Example 5.2. Can their locations be described geometrically? Can this result be generalized to all three-link manipulators with revolute joints?

5.12. Design a three-link three-dimensional manipulator with a Jacobian equal to the identity matrix.

5.13. Derive a simple iterative algorithm for calculating the velocity of a multi-link manipulator with prismatic joints similar to Algorithm 5.3.

5.14. The end effector (frame 2) of a type 1 two-link manipulator is moving from $(0, l_1 + 0.5l_2)$ to $(l_1 + 0.5l_2, 0)$ at constant velocity. For the case where $l_1 = 300$mm, $l_2 = 200$mm, and $v_2 = 100$mm/s, graph the joint angles, velocities, and accelarations at ten points along the path. (*Hint.* Write a program.)

5.15. Repeat Exercise 5.14 for the planar three-link manipulator, with $l_3 = 100$mm. If the sequence of manipulator configurations is such that either joint angle, velocity, or acceleration reverses rapidly, redesign the sequence of configurations so that this does not happen by taking advantage of the redundancy of the manipulator. What can you learn about manipulator control from this example?

5.16. Manipulators can have configurations where the columns of the Jacobian become orthogonal and of equal magnitude. These are known as **isotropic points**. For the type 1 two-link manipulator, and for the planar three-link manipulator, determine if any isotropic points exist. (**Hint.** What effect does the length of the links have on this?)

5.17. An object is sitting on a conveyor belt, which is moving in the $-x_0$ direction towards the three-link planar manipulator (Figure 5.14) at a velocity of 200mm/s. The surface of the conveyor belt is at the same height as the axis of joint 1, and the conyeyor stops 150mm from the manipulator (from the origin of frame 0). Using the dimensions given in Exercises 5.15, graph the joint angles and velocities required for the manipulator to track the object from 400mm from the manipulator, grasp the object, and lift the object off the conveyor belt 200mm from the manipulator, to a height of 20mm.

■ *Practical questions*

5.1. Set up a vision system in the laboratory, so that the camera views the gripper of a robot and an object lying on a flat surface (Figure 3.32). If you do not have a robotics laboratory, build a cardboard model.

    (a) Assign coordinate frames to the world, the flat surface, the robot, the object, and the vision system.

    (b) Measure the physical distances and orientations between these frames and calculate the position transformations.

    (c) Derive the equations to transform the error in the gripper position relative to the object, as seen by the vision system, into end effector coordinates, and then into joint coordinates.

    (d) Write a program to calculate the joint differential motion required to overcome this error.

    (e) Move the joints of the robot by the calculated amount and see if the error is eliminated.

5.2. Determine the location of the workspace internal singularities of the robot in the laboratory. Program the robot to pass through these singularities. What happens to the joints involved in the singularity when the arm passes through the singularity. From your observations, comment on the control algorithms used in the controller of the robot (Chapter 11).

5.3. Implement procedures for calculating velocity, acceleration, and differential motion transforms, and add these to the library of transforms.

5.4. Implement and compare various algorithms for calculating manipulator velocity and manipulator Jacobians.

5.5. Select a three-link manipulator, and write a program to calculate the symbolic equations for position, velocity, and acceleration. Include procedures to find the location of singularities, and the location of isotropic points in the workspace of the manipulator.

6 · *Statics*

It appears that pure position and pure force control are dual concepts, and that the historical emphasis on position control is the natural result of applications which involve very little physical contact.

Matthew Mason, 1981.

Objectives

In this chapter, we turn from a study of position and motion to examine the forces and torques involved in manipulation. Our objective is to model the forces set up within a manipulator when it touches an object. Force analysis is divided into two related sections: task forces, and the resultant joint forces. The analysis of task forces is less mature than the analysis of the static force balance within a manipulator. The modelling of forces and torques includes the following topics:

- compliance,
- configuration space and surfaces,
- inserting a peg into a hole,
- static balance in a manipulator, and
- programming force control.

Mechanics is the physical science which deals with the state of rest or motion of bodies under the action of forces (Meriam, 1966). Mechanics can be logically divided into two parts: statics, which we cover in this chapter; and dynamics, which we will cover in the next chapter. **Statics** concerns the equilibrium of bodies under the action of forces. Force is the action of one body on another. A force tends to translate a body in the direction in which it acts upon the body, and to rotate a body around a moment axis (Window 6.1). When that motion is resisted, reaction forces are set up in the body, and in any object in contact with it, reaction forces that can distort the body. **Compliance** is the tendency of the body to distort due to these reaction forces.

In statics, an equilibrium analysis is normally performed while holding the manipulator still. It is done by equating the sums of the external forces and torques acting on the links to zero. As there is no motion, these external forces and torques must balance. External forces and torques are produced by the weight of the links, the weight of the object grasped by the end effector, and interaction between the end effector and the workpiece. Interactions between sections of the manipulator (other than the end effector) and the environment are usually due to error conditions, for example a collision with an object. However, mobile robots do interact with the ground through their wheels or feet, and underwater robots interact with the water that surrounds them. On the other hand, space robots have special problems due to the lack of gravity. The analysis of these two applications is outside the scope of this chapter, although many of the principles discussed here apply.

Static analysis is important in grasping, where we do not want to damage the object being grasped; in assembly, where we want to join parts without damaging them; in force control, where we wish to control the forces generated by the interaction of the end effector with the environment; and in compliance, where we use controlled distortion of the manipulator or workpiece to achieve fine manipulation. In each of these situations, it is often easiest to start with a static analysis of a stationary, though possibly stressed, manipulator. Static analysis can also be generalized to situations where the manipulator is not at rest using d'Alembert's Principle (Section 7.1), which reduces dynamics to statics through the formulation of a force of inertia (Brady *et al.*, 1982). In the treatment of statics here, we will add the forces and torques acting on the manipulator to calculate the net forces and torques, which are, in fact, d'Alembert forces and torques.

6.1 Compliance

The material discussed in this section was originally developed by Mason (1982).

Window 6.1   Force and torque vectors

Force is the action of one body on another. A force tends to move a body in the direction of its action on the body. Since the effect of a frame depends on its direction of action as well as its magnitude, a force is a vector which is completely specified by its magnitude, direction, and point of action. Force is applied either by direct mechanical contact, or by remote action, for example gravitational and electromagnetic forces. The action of a force on a body can be separated into two effects, internal and external. The effects of a force internal to a body are the resulting internal movements and forces distributed throughout the material of the body. **Compliance** is the tendency of a body to move due to the internal effects of the force applied to it, for example bending and twisting, and due to the slop in the joints between sections of the body, or between it and another body.

External effects are the force applied to a body and any reactive forces which are applied to the body by other bodies in opposition to the applied force. When considering only the external effects, as in the analysis of forces on rigid bodies (non compliant bodies), force is a sliding vector. The **principle of transmissibility** states that a force may be applied at any point on its line of action without altering the external effect of the force on the rigid body on which it acts, i.e the reaction forces. Force is distributed over a contact area, but for the sake of analysis, force vectors are usually constrained to act on a point. Like velocity vectors, force vectors in the same plane can be added (see Window 5.1).

Our analysis of forces is based on Newton's Laws (1687):

1. A particle remains at rest or continues to move in a straight line with a uniform velocity if there is no unbalanced force acting on it.

2. The acceleration of a particle is proportional to the resultant force acting on it and is in the direction of the force.

   $$f = ma$$

   where

   f is the resultant force acting on the particle,

   m is the mass of the particle, and

   a is the resulting acceleration.

3. The forces of action and reaction between interacting bodies are equal in magnitude, opposite in direction, and collinear.

His first law contains the principle of equilibrium of forces, a topic of major concern in manipulator statics. His second law forms the basis of most of our analysis of manipulator dynamics. His third law is also important in statics, as it states that forces always occur in pairs, which are equal and opposite. When an object is unable to sustain the reactionary force, it deforms and, unless it is designed to be compliant, may be damaged. Analysis of pairs of forces is fundamental to robotic grasping and assembly operations.

In addition to moving a body in the direction of the force vector, a force may also cause the body to rotate around an axis. For rotation to occur, the force vector must not intersect the axis of rotation, and the body must be free to rotate. For example a manipulator link will rotate around a revolute joint when a force that does not intersect the joint axis is applied to it. If a body is not free to rotate, a reaction force in the body opposes the applied moment. The tendency of a force to cause rotation about an axis is called the **moment** of the force about the axis (or **torque**). Only, the component of the force which lies in a plane perpendicular to the axis produces a moment. Torque is a sliding vector, with line of action coincident with the moment axis, and with direction determined by the right hand rule. Curl your fingers in the direction of the tendency to rotate around the axis, and your thumb points in the direction of the moment vector.

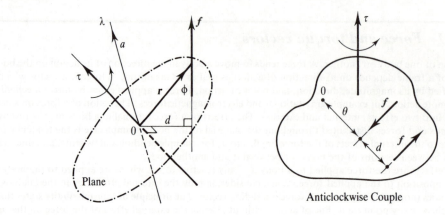

Plane

Anticlockwise Couple

$$M = \tau = fd$$

where

> $M = \tau$ is the resultant torque,
>
> d is the length of the common normal between the force vector and the axis, and is known as the moment arm, and
>
> f is the component of the force in a plane perpendicular to the axis.

The above formula can be generalized, for analysing three dimensional force systems.

$$\tau_\lambda = (r \, x \, f \cdot n)n$$

where

> n is a unit vector in the direction of the axis λ,
>
> r is a vector from the point O where the axis cuts the plane to any point on the force vector,
>
> $d = r \sin(\phi)$ where ϕ is the angle between r and the force vector f, and
>
> $\tau \cdot n = r \, x \, f \cdot n$ is the scalar magnitude of the component of τ in the λ direction.

If several forces are acting on an object, their moments around a common axis can be summed to obtain a resultant torque. This resultant torque is with respect to the axis except in the special case of a **couple**. Consider the action of two equal and opposite forces a distance d apart. These forces sum to zero, and thus, produce no resultant force, but they do produce a torque.

$$\tau = f(d + a) - fa = fd \text{ and is in an anticlockwise direction for the couple in the above diagram.}$$

This expression for the magnitude of the couple does not contain any reference to the distance a which positions the forces with respect to the axis. Hence a couple has the same magnitude for all moment centres on the object. Consequently, a couple is a free vector, with direction normal to the plane of the couple, and the sense of the vector determined by the right hand rule. Couples acting in nonparallel planes may be added by the ordinary rules of vector addition.

As a force on an object usually tends to produce both translation and rotation of that object, it is often convenient to replace the applied force by an equivalent parallel force, which acts through the moment axis, and a couple, which is the moment around the axis produced by the applied force. As the equivalent force vector intersects the moment axis, it produces no torque, and is considered to be a pure force. This decomposition allows us to analyse forces and torques separately.

Compliant motion occurs when the location of the end effector is constrained by the task, and is required in an enormous variety of manipulation tasks. Examples of compliant motion are wiping a pane of glass, stirring a fluid, opening a door, turning a crank, inserting a peg in a hole, placing an object on a table, grasping an object, driving a screw, and feeling an object. In all these tasks, the trajectory of the end effector is modified by the contact forces or tactile stimuli which occur as the end effector is moved to carry out the task. In robotics, we encounter two classes of compliance: passive compliance, and active compliance. **Passive compliance** is the tendency of a body to move due to the internal effects of the forces applied to it. Examples are bending and twisting. **Active compliance** is the controlled movement of a body in response to force or tactile stimuli, in order to minimize the magnitude of those stimuli. For some time, there has been a debate about the relative merits of active versus passive compliance in robotic manipulation (force control versus remote-centre-compliance devices – Whitney, 1982).

People find all the tasks listed above easy, as compliant motion comes naturally to people, but, generally, these tasks are very difficult for robot manipulators. For a manipulator to perform a compliant motion, it either has to rely on the natural passive compliance of both the manipulator and the object being manipulated or it has to measure the forces produced by noncompliant interactions and respond compliantly in accordance with preprogrammed control strategies. Compliance is a key element when joining two parts, operating on one part with another, or mating parts to build an assembly (Rebman, 1982). It is that forgiving factor which makes many tasks possible, because it overcomes the minor imprecisions in the parts that would otherwise impede sliding motion between them.

In many situations, compliance provides a simple means of adapting trajectories during motion. Active compliance lies at the heart of one of the key problems in manipulation: the intergration of sensing into robot programming and control systems. Force and tactile sensing are paramount in applications where the locations of objects are known only approximately. For example, inserting a pin in a hole is a highly precise operation, but the actual position of the hole may be imprecise in comparison. The tolerance between the diameter of the pin and the diameter of the hole may be tens of micrometres, while the placement of the hole may vary by hundreds of micrometres.

These problems are best overcome as the assembly proceeds. There are several way of doing this: by measuring the precise location of the hole; by measuring the forces during insertion and modifying the motion to respond to these forces; or by building passive compliance into the manipulator system, so that part of it moves to correct for the variation. Measuring the precise location of the hole and calculating a trajectory to suit may not achieve an effective insertion, as compliance plays another significant role in manipulation – it overcomes the inaccuracies in the manipulator and allows a manipulator to execute tasks that require a higher precision than the resolution of the manipulator.

One application that depends on structural compliance is the task of placing an object on a surface (Will and Grossman, 1975). It is almost impossible to program the trajectory so that the object is just touching the surface when it is released. Either the object is dropped from a small height or it is forced into the surface. In the latter case, damage to the object is prevented only by the compliance of the manipulator and the surface. Precise placement of objects on to surfaces is not a well-understood task. Note that we have not considered how to detect the surface, nor how to control the robot to avoid dropping the object, nor how to model and control impact forces. In practice, we place heavy reliance on compliance in robotic applications.

Two other tasks that rely heavily on compliant motion are the coordination of multiple manipulators, and the stable grasping of objects with a multifingered gripper. When grasping an object with multiple fingers, the forces applied by the fingers should balance for a stable grasp (Hanafusa and Asada, 1977). When two manipulators are handling the same object, their motions have to be carefully coordinated to avoid applying excessive forces to the object (Section 6.6.1). The passive compliance of the mechanisms will compensate for forces due to minor errors in finger placement, but active control of compliant motion is usually required to minimise forces resulting from major errors. However, with proper modeling of both the task and the compliances involved, passive compliance mechanisms can often be used to achieve the desired control (Hogan, 1980). As a consequence, the complexity of the active controllers is reduced, leading to improved performance.

6.1.1 Sources of compliance

Every element in a robot is compliant to some extent. Even though manufacturers have concentrated on building very stiff structures, so that robot motions are repeatable, manipulator links still flex under load. Also, motors are not perfect position sources, as their position, velocity, and acceleration are not independent of the forces applied to them. In contrast, some researchers are experimenting with highly flexible lightweight manipulators in an attempt to achieve fast dynamic response. These manipulators are very compliant, and require special control algorithms to achieve repeatability, and, sometimes, stability.

In all robots, there is usually one element whose compliance is dominant. For example, in manipulators, the dominant compliance occurs in the structure, due to the deformation of links and slop in gears. Generally, this structural compliance can be relied on to overcome minor positioning errors. However, with a very stiff manipulator, structural compliance may be insufficient and damage may occur. Sometimes, this problem is overcome by increasing the compliance of the end effector, or by using a compliant wrist. Again, we have conflicting goals: very stiff manipulators to achieve high positioning accuracy versus compliant manipulators to correct for position errors automatically.

This conflict can be overcome only by programming the compliance to suit the task, either passively by using compliant tools or actively by force control. Devices with passive compliance – for example, the remote-centre-compliance devices used in insertion tasks (Section 6.3.7) – are specially programmed during their design for one task only. Consequently, systems based on passive compliance are only effective in limited task domains. In many practical situations, compliance can be varied only by active control of force.

6.1.2 Centre of compliance

The centre of compliance is the point at which an applied force will produce pure translation in the direction of the force, and a pure moment applied about a line through the point will produce a pure rotation about that line. A force applied at a point other than the centre of compliance will produce both translation of the body and rotation about the centre of compliance. When a centre of compliance exists, it is a useful way of characterizing the behaviour of compliant motion. We determine the location of the centre of compliance from the location and characteristics of the individual compliance elements.

Physically, the centre of compliance is the point at which the entire compliance of the system is considered to be concentrated and acting. In many ways, this concept is analogous to the concept of centre of gravity. It is the point at which the compliant behaviour appears to reside. With certain body shapes the center of gravity lies outside the body itself – for example, the centre of gravity of a cup is located in the air space inside the cup. Similarly, the centre of compliance can lie outside the compliant body. In Section 6.3.7, we will investigate the design of a remote-centre-compliance device, where the problems associated with inserting a peg in a hole are solved by placing the centre of compliance away from the compliant elements.

6.1.3 Compliance frame

An object located in space has six degrees of freedom: three of translation, and three of rotation. When that object is constrained, some of its degrees of freedom are lost. For example, a sphere sitting on a flat surface has two degrees of translation and three of rotation. Technically, the sphere can be considered to have 5½ degrees of freedom as the translation constraint applies to one direction only – motion away from the surface will restore the sixth degree. Also, the number of degrees of freedom may be further reduced by the physical shape of the object. A cylinder lying on a flat surface has one less degree of rotation than a sphere, and a cube one less again. These freedoms and constraints are described with a **compliance frame**: an orthogonal coordinate system whose axes specify task freedoms for compliant motion (Paul and Shimano, 1976; Raibert and Craig, 1981). A compliance frame is similar to a Cartesian coordinate system, with three degrees of translation along frame axes, and three degrees of rotation about those axes, but some degrees are free and some are constrained.

Generally, the origin of the compliance frame is placed at the centre of compliance and the the axes are oriented so that the state of the degrees of motion (free or constrained) do not change during the execution of the task unless the physical situation changes. In the examples below (Figures 6.1 and 6.2), this permanence of the constraints is achieved for different tasks by fixing compliance frames with respect to the gripper, the object, world coordinates, and frames that have not been predefined. As a consequence,

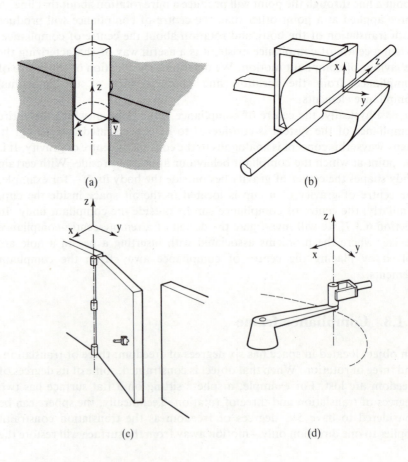

Figure 6.1
Placement of compliance frames (Mason, 1982).
(a) Peg in a hole: frame is located at the tip of the peg.
(b) Bead on a wire: frame is fixed with respect to the gripper.
(c) Door on hinge: frame is fixed in world coordinates.
(d) Turning a crank: frame is fixed with respect to crank.

the trajectory of the compliance frame and the trajectory of the end effector are often different.

The location of the compliance frame and the motion constraints are determined from the physics of the task. When inserting a peg into a hole (Figure 6.1(a)), the origin of the compliance frame is located at the tip of the peg, and the z axis coincides with the axis of the peg. Once in the hole, the peg is free to move in the z direction and to rotate about the z axis. All other degrees of motion are constrained. We express these constraints with the diagonal elements of a six-by-six compliance matrix. Each element represents one degree of constraint. The compliance matrix for a peg moving in a hole is:

$$
\begin{bmatrix}
x_{trans} & 0 & 0 & 0 & 0 & 0 \\
0 & y_{trans} & 0 & 0 & 0 & 0 \\
0 & 0 & z_{trans} & 0 & 0 & 0 \\
0 & 0 & 0 & x_{rot} & 0 & 0 \\
0 & 0 & 0 & 0 & y_{rot} & 0 \\
0 & 0 & 0 & 0 & 0 & z_{rot}
\end{bmatrix}
=
\begin{bmatrix}
cons & 0 & 0 & 0 & 0 & 0 \\
0 & cons & 0 & 0 & 0 & 0 \\
0 & 0 & free & 0 & 0 & 0 \\
0 & 0 & 0 & cons & 0 & 0 \\
0 & 0 & 0 & 0 & cons & 0 \\
0 & 0 & 0 & 0 & 0 & free
\end{bmatrix}
= \mathbf{C}
$$

(6.1)

When moving a bead along a wire (Figure 6.1(b)), the compliance frame is located at the centre of the bead, with the z axis coincident with the tangent to the wire, and the frame fixed with respect to the gripper. As the wire may be bent, the direction of the tangent changes as the bead slides along the wire, and, therefore, the compliance frame also changes. This change is automatically accommodated by fixing the compliance frame with respect to the gripper.

When closing a door (Figure 6.1(c)), the compliance frame is fixed with respect to the world frame, and located so that the z axis coincides with the axis of the hinge. Only one degree of motion is free: rotation around the z axis. An example which involves more complex motion is that of the turning of a crank (Figure 6.1(d)). In this case, the compliance frame is placed at the

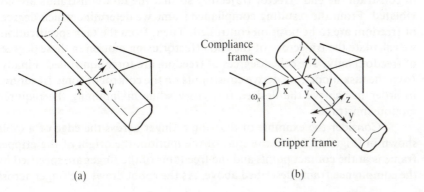

Compliance frame

Gripper frame

(a) (b)

Figure 6.2
Drawing a finger across the edge of a table (Mason, 1982).
(a) Compliance frame is not fixed with respect to any predefined frame.
(b) Effective compliance centre is at the contact point.

crank handle, with the z axis coincident with the handle axis, and the x axis pointing towards the centre of the crank. In this case, the compliance frame is fixed to the crank, and thus, it rotates around the crank axis with the x axis always pointing to the crank axis. As a result of this placement, rotation about the z axis and translation along the y axis are free, and all other degrees of motion are constrained.

A situation where there are few constraints is drawing the finger of a gripper across the edge of a table (Figure 6.2). If the motion freedoms are not to change during this motion, then the compliance frame must be placed at the point of contact between the finger and the table, with the x axis aligned with the edge of the table, and the y axis tangential to the direction of motion of the finger. With this compliance frame, the only motion which is constrained is motion in the z direction. This motion is constrained in the −z direction by the table, and in the +z direction by the task requirement of keeping the finger in contact with the table.

From the task constraints, we can determine which degrees of motion of the end effector should be position controlled and which should be force controlled. In general, if a degree is constrained, it should be force controlled, because it is physically impossible to control position without deforming the object being manipulated. In contrast, if a degree of freedom is unconstrained, it should be position controlled, because the reaction force used in force feedback control exists only when the robot is pushing against an object. If a free degree is force controlled, the manipulator will accelerate away in the direction of the desired force until it reaches the limit of its workspace or it collides with another object. For example, when moving a peg in a hole (Figure 6.1(a)), the free degrees of motion are translation in the negative z direction and rotation around the z axis, and hence, they are position controlled, while all other degrees of freedom are force controlled because they are constrained.

Because the compliance frame may not coincide with the end effector frame, their trajectories may be different. We can handle this problem by specifying independent trajectories, which are related through a model of the task kinematics. Alternatively, when a task model is available, we can use it to constrain the end effector trajectory so that the task constraints are not violated. From the resulting compliance frame we determine which degrees of freedom are to be position controlled. Then, from the task specification, we calculate the trajectory of the end effector using motion in these degrees of freedom only. The other degrees of freedom are force controlled. Finally, from the task model, we derive constraints on the control of some freedoms, in order to achieve the desired trajectory while maintaining the required motion constraints.

Consider the example of drawing a finger across the edge of a table shown in (Figure 6.2). At the start of the motion, the origin of the gripper frame is at the contact point, and the freedoms of the finger are specified by the compliance frame described above. As the robot draws the finger across the edge, the gripper frame moves away from the table (Figure 6.2(b)). When the two frames were coincident, translation in the z direction was not possible, but now that the gripper frame is away from the table, the gripper can translate in the z direction and still maintain the same task freedoms at the contact point. However, to maintain contact between the finger and the table while translating in the z direction, the translation velocity in the z direction must be the product of the normal distance between the two frames and the angular velocity about the x axis.

$$v_{ztrans} = l_n \omega_x \qquad\qquad (6.2)$$

If the finger does not rotate around the z axis, the frames remain parallel and the normal distance between the frames is the distance between origins (l). However, if the finger does rotate around the z axis, the normal distance is the y component of the distance between the origins. If the end effector trajectory includes translation in the z direction, this can be achieved, while controlling force in the z direction, by controlling the velocity of rotation around the x axis to conform with the above relation. Thus, from this model of the task, we have inferred that force in the z direction can be controlled directly, and translation in the z direction controlled indirectly, while at the same time maintaining the motion constrains at the compliance frame.

To specify the compliant motion of an object, five sets of information are required:

1. the location of the compliance frame,
2. the degrees of motion which are free and the degrees which are constrained,
3. the degrees of motion which are position controlled, and the degrees which are force controlled,
4. the position, orientation, force, and torque goals of the planned motion, and
5. a model of the task kinematics.

In the peg-in-the-hole problem, the goal is to move the peg to the bottom of the hole without damage. When the peg is in the hole, the compliance frame is located at the tip of the peg; the z degrees are free, and consequently position controlled; while the other degrees are constrained, and consequently force controlled. In contrast, when the peg is above the hole, the hole does not place any physical constraints on motion so all degrees of freedom are free, and should be position controlled. However, the model of the task of inserting a peg into a hole must constrain the location of the peg prior to entry into the hole if it is to be inserted successfully. The peg should be located with the axis of the peg coincident with the axis of the hole before insertion starts. Passive compliance or force control can compensate for minor errors in the location of the axis of the peg with respect to the axis of the hole, but not for major ones. This change in the compliance matrix during the execution of the task requires a compensating change in control strategy.

6.2   Configuration space

As defined above, the compliance frame specifies the motion freedoms at a point: the origin of the frame. However, the compliance frame moves during manipulation. The region over which a specific compliance frame is valid is called a **surface-in-configuration space**. Configuration space is a rectangular coordinate space where each axis represents one degree of motion freedom. In this section, we deal with Cartesian configuration space, where the motion freedoms map to Cartesian degrees of freedom. (Joint configuration space, where each axis represents one joint parameter, will be dealt with in Section 9.3.3.1.)

The dimension of the configuration space (0 to 6) is determined by the number of degrees of motion freedom in the compliance frame. An ideal configuration-space surface is a smooth surface consisting of all the possible locations of an ideal end effector. When a hand is required to move in order to perform a task, we obtain a set of linear equations for end effector velocity and force, one equation for each of the six degrees of freedom. We calculate these equations by combining the compliance frame and the configuration space surface to model the natural constraints of the task. That is, natural constraints are modelled by integrating compliance frame freedoms with compliance frame motions.

If an end effector is grasping an immobile, stiff, solid object, it has no positional freedom, as it is constrained in all six degrees of mobility. In this situation, configuration space has a dimension of zero, as the manipulator is immobile in solid space. Owing to these constraints, the manipulator has complete force freedom, that is, it can apply a force in any of the six degrees of the compliance frame (actually force in three degrees and torque in the other three). Now consider the opposite extreme, the end effector in free space where configuration space has a dimension of six. The state of the compliance matrix is completely reversed, and the manipulator has complete position freedom. There is no force freedom, because the end effector is not in contact with any object.

Between the extremes of solid space and free space are surfaces in configuration space – **C surfaces** (Mason, 1981). A C surface is a task configuration which allows only partial positional freedom. Freedom of motion occurs along C surface tangents, while freedom of force occurs along C surface normals. These freedoms are completely specified by the compliance frame. The C surface is the region where we either rely on the inherent compliances of the task to eliminate problems, or we actively control force to overcome problems. On the C surface, neither pure position nor pure force control is appropriate, but rather hybrid control, where force is controlled along C surface normals, and position along C surface tangents.

During the execution of a task, a manipulator may move from free space on to one C surface, frequently on to another C surface, possibly to solid space, and finally back to free space. While on a C surface, the freedoms of the manipulator are specified by the compliance frame. One of the criteria when selecting a compliance frame is that it is constant for the desired C surface. When a manipulator moves from one C surface to another, the compliance frame changes to reflect the new physical constraints. In effect, for tasks where some degrees of motion are constrained, configuration space specifies the domain of a compliance frame for control purposes.

In our analysis, the end effector of a manipulator was modelled using a coordinate frame. This describes a point in position space with a six element location vector. Also, force can be described as a point in force space and velocity as a point in velocity space. Thus, we used an ideal manipulator. Similarly, our analysis is simplified by using an ideal C surface – a smooth hypersurface consisting of all the possible positions of the ideal end effector. This surface is assumed to be connected and smooth, with a dimension between zero and six. When a curve is differentiated the slope of the curve is obtained. At each point along the curve, this slope is the tangent to the curve. An ideal C surface has a unique tangent space at each point on the surface – a vector subspace with the same dimensions as the ideal C surface but tangential to it. This is the velocity subspace, and is described with equivalent velocity coordinates.

A complex C surface is often difficult to visualize, so we will illustrate the properties of ideal C surfaces with a few examples. A point in space is an ideal C surface with a dimension of 0, because it lacks any freedom of motion. Similarly, if a gripper is grasping an immobile, stiff, solid object, it has an ideal C surface with a dimension of 0. In contrast, an end effector in free space has a C surface with a dimension of 6, because it is free to move in any direction. By comparison, a hand holding the end of a spring with the other end fixed to a solid object has a C surface of dimension 6, because, while the spring opposes motion, the hand can move in any direction within the limits of the elasticity of the spring.

To ease the task of constructing a C surface, we construct rectangular coordinate frames to describe regions of configuration space, with each axis representing a motion freedom in the compliance frame. This decomposes C space into three-dimensional subspaces, which are easier to visualize. Then, we draw lines to represent the motion freedoms, and calculate their Cartesian product to obtain the C surface. As we saw previously, a peg in a hole has only two motion freedoms: translation in the z direction, and rotation about the z axis. To calculate the C surface for this task, we draw a line for the translational freedom in the z direction in one subspace, and a line for the rotational freedom around the z axis in the second subspace (Figure 6.3(a)). The ideal C surface is the plane equal to the Cartesian product of these two lines. Physically, the ideal C surface is a line collinear with the axis of the peg, along which the end effector can translate, and about which it can rotate.

For the more complex task of turning a crank, the C surface is harder to construct (Figure 6.3(b)). The compliance frame has already been fixed with respect to the crank (Figure 6.1(d)), with the result that there are two motion freedoms: rotation about the z axis, and translation along the y axis. However, the origin of this frame moves in the instantaneous y direction and, with respect to world coordinates, traces a circular path in a plane parallel to the xy plane. By combining this circular path with the motion freedom of rotation about the z axis, we obtain a spiral in one subspace. As this representation also accounts for the motion freedom of translation in the y direction, translation in the y direction can be represented by a fixed point in the second subspace. The ideal C surface for turning the crank is the Cartesian product of the spiral and the point. Physically, it is the circular path traced out by the handle of the crank.

Note, that, in these two examples, the coordinate axes in the subspaces represent different freedoms of six-dimensional Cartesian configuration space, hence the physical representations of the same concept may be different in different subspaces. For example, in Figure 6.3(a), a rotation about the z axis is represented by a straight line, whereas in Figure 6.3(b), it is

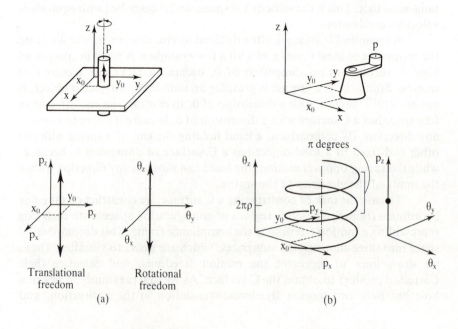

Figure 6.3
Ideal C-surfaces (Mason, 1982).
(a) Peg moving in a hole.
(b) Turning a crank.

Translational freedom

Rotational freedom

(a)

(b)

represented by a spiral. The reasons for choosing the axes of a particular subspace may not be immediately obvious; they have to do with relating the motion of the compliance frame to world coordinates, modelling any constraints that are placed on the motion of the compliance frame, obtaining a physical representation that can be visualized, and developing a control strategy that can be accomplished with a real manipulator. Also, when the subspaces are multiplied, the resultant C surface is defined with respect to world coordinates.

Since the ideal location of the end effector lies in the ideal C surface, the ideal velocity of the end effector will lie in a vector subspace parallel to the tangent space. For the crank example (Figure 6.4), the tangent space is the product of the broken line and the point in the right subspace, and the velocity vector is the product of the solid line and the point. These constraints on velocity can be expressed as a set of linear equations. Similarly, if tangential forces are neglected, then effector force is restricted to be normal to the tangent space, a constraint which can be expressed as a set of linear equations. These ideal equations in end effector force and velocity are called **natural constraints**, and are derived from the compliance frame and the motion of the compliance frame. Control strategies are called **artificial constraints**, and are the components of end effector force and velocity required to conform to the natural constraints during manipulation.

For example, the natural constraints for the peg in the hole problem are:

$$v_x = 0 \quad v_y = 0 \quad f_z = 0 \quad \omega_x = 0 \quad \omega_y = 0 \quad \tau_z = 0 \tag{6.3}$$

and the artificial constraints for the control system are:

$$f_x = 0 \quad f_y = 0 \quad v_z = c_1 \quad \tau_x = 0 \quad \tau_y = 0 \quad \omega_z = c_2 \tag{6.4}$$

where c_1 and c_2 are reference values for velocity control.

As the motion of the compliance frame is linear with respect to world coordinates, and hence the C surface is a plane, these constraints were obtained directly from the compliance matrix (Equation 6.1). In more

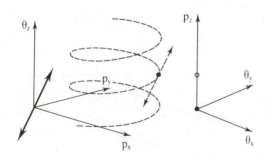

Figure 6.4
Tangent and velocity spaces for the crank surface. The tangent space is the Cartesian product of the broken line on the left with the point on the right. The velocity space is the Cartesian product of the solid line with the point.

complex examples, such as the crank example, the model of the natural constraints is not so simple.

6.2.1 Nonhomogeneous C surfaces

The C surfaces discussed so far have been **homogeneous C surfaces**. They have a consistent set of homogeneous linear equations in the components of end effector velocity, and an orthogonal set of homogeneous linear equations in the components of end effector force. This orthogonality arises from the original specification of the compliance frames, where velocity and force constraints were defined to be along mutually exclusive orthogonal axes. A homogeneous C surface can become nonhomogeneous when additional external constraints are applied, often due to a new element in the environment of the task.

For example, the homogeneous C surface for the motion of a peg in a hole becomes nonhomogeneous if the object containing the hole is placed on a moving conveyor belt (Figure 6.5). The requirement for the gripper to track the conveyor belt adds a velocity constraint in the x direction, a direction which, according to the compliance frame, has no motion freedom. Both constraints can be achieved by active force control, as the force applied to the gripper by the motion of the peg results in compliant motion of the gripper at the required velocity. The natural constraints for moving a peg in a moving hole are:

$$v_x = v_{belt} \quad v_y = 0 \quad f_z = 0 \quad \omega_x = 0 \quad \omega_y = 0 \quad \tau_z = 0 \tag{6.5}$$

with the only change being due to the motion of the belt. As this motion is accommodated by the compliance of the manipulator under force control, the artificial constraints have not changed.

The above example illustrates a useful strategy for handling nonhomogeneous C surfaces. When nonhomogeneity occurs, there are natural constraints that call for both force and velocity control in the same direction; but it is physically impossible for a manipulator actively to control both velocity and force in the same direction. However, the required control

Figure 6.5
Nonhomogeneous C-surface
due to velocity of the
conveyor belt.

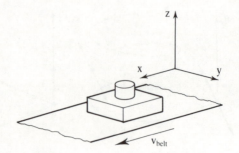

can often be achieved with the same artificial constraints as for the homogeneous case, if the additional constraint can be satisfied by compliant motion, as in the above example. If this is not possible, it may be possible to achieve the required control by active control of another freedom, in accordance with a new constraint. The example of drawing a finger across the edge of a table (Equation 6.1) illustrates the modelling of a constraint in terms of a motion freedom in another direction.

6.2.2   Unilateral C surfaces

So far, unilateral constraints – constraints which prevent motion in one direction but not in the opposite direction – have been ignored. For example, when a peg reaches the bottom of a hole, it can no longer move down, but it can move up. As our compliance matrix does not differentiate the direction of motion on an axis, it is unable to specify unilateral constraints, and hence, this situation cannot be modelled with an ideal C surface. In practice, when motion along a C surface ends in a unilateral constraint, an artificial constraint is placed on the control scheme in the form of a guard on the motion in that direction. For example, when inserting a peg in a hole, a force guard is placed on motion along the axis of the peg into the hole. This guard stops motion when a specified force is exceeded in the z direction, and indicates that the insertion is complete.

The next action of the manipulator, depends on the task specification. The gripper could move back along the C surface and withdraw the peg, it could release the peg and immediately move into free space; or it could turn the peg in the hole while applying a small bias force in the $-z$ direction to overcome any errors in the control system caused by holding the peg against the bottom of the hole. The task of turning an inserted peg adds a task constraint to the compliance matrix: motion in the z direction is no longer allowed. As a result, the manipulator has moved on to a new C surface. The translational subspace in Figure 6.3(a) has been reduced to a point, and the resultant C surface is a line in the θ_z direction. Also, to comply with the new compliance matrix, a new artificial constraint is required, that of zero velocity in the z direction, which can be actively controlled by a bias force in the $-z$ direction. While the natural constraints are homogeneous, the artificial constraints are nonhomogeneous, reflecting the fact that, physically, the natural constraints are nonhomogeneous, and homogeneity is a result of the task constraints.

6.2.3   Forces tangential to C surfaces

When specifying the elements of the compliance matrix, we allowed motion freedom along C surface tangents and force freedom along C surface normals. In real applications, this ideal model is inadequate. The example of moving a peg in the hole of an object on a moving conveyor belt illustrates the real possibility of a task requiring motion along a C surface normal. However, we found that this motion was accommodated by the compliance of an active force control system, without invalidating the basic model. Now we will look at the possibility of force constraints along C surface tangents.

Three physical phenomena give rise to forces along C surface tangents: friction, mass, and springs. Both dry and viscous friction oppose the motion of a body sliding along a surface (Window 6.2). When a body is accelerated, an inertial force proportional to the mass of the body opposes the acceleration (Window 6.1). A spring will apply a force proportional to the extension (or compression) of the spring. This spring force will increase until the spring reaches its elastic limit, where further extension or compression will damage the spring. Thus, spring force imposes a natural constraint on position; viscous friction (or damping) imposes a natural constraint on velocity; dry friction imposes a natural constraint on both velocity and acceleration as it limits the force available to produce motion; and inertia imposes a natural constraint on acceleration.

The natural constraints which result from these tangential forces can be extremely complicated. However, a robot position controller will call for increasing force while there is a positional error, until the control amplifier is saturated and the limit of applied force is reached. Once sliding starts, tangential frictional forces are compenated for by a fixed force in the direction of motion, after an initially higher force to overcome static friction (Window 6.2). Inertial forces are compensated for by temporary increases in applied force during acceleration. However, spring force increases as extension increases, and if the manipulator is capable of applying forces greater than the spring can handle, a force guard must be placed on the motion freedom in the direction of the tangential force. If the spring is stronger than the manipulator the spring will stop the motion of the manipulator.

In all these situations, we can model the task using a compliance frame and a C surface. The controller will accommodate the tangential forces, provided a force guard is imposed on motion against spring forces. Again, the natural compliance of the system is used to accommodate for nonhomogeneous constraints, except this time compliance accommodates for force problems with position errors, whereas previously it accommodated for position problems with force errors. For example, consider the task of sliding a bead along a wire (see Figure 6.1(b)). The motion freedoms are in the z direction for both translation and rotation, with force freedoms in all other directions. As the bead is symmetrical about the wire, the components of force in the x and y direction will be replaced by a normal force orthogonal to the z axis and passing through the centre of compliance. The C surface for this task is identical to the C surface for the peg moving in the hole, provided the wire is straight, except that it defines the region of motion of the bead, not the wire, and the centre of compliance is at a different place. The natural constraints are:

$$v_x = 0 \quad v_y = 0 \quad \omega_x = 0 \quad \omega_y = 0 \quad f_z = ma_x + \mu f_n \quad \tau_z = m\omega_z + \mu f_n \quad \textbf{(6.6)}$$

where

m is the mass of the bead,

μ is the coefficient of friction,

the force constraints are nonhomogeneous and tangential to the C surface, and

there are no force constraints along normals to the C surface.

The artificial constraints are:

$$f_x = 0 \quad f_y = 0 \quad \tau_x = 0 \quad \tau_y = 0 \quad v_z = c_1 \quad \omega_z = c_2 \qquad \textbf{(6.7)}$$

6.2.4 Other constraints

In practice, a further set of constraints can arise. There are limits to the motions of a manipulator along C surface tangents, and limits to the force a manipulator can apply along C surface normals. In the above analysis, we have assumed that we were working within these limits. Workspace limits can only be accommodated by relocating the task inside the manipulator's workspace, or by increasing the workspace of the manipulator. The limits to applied force can only be changed by using a stronger manipulator or by redesigning the task.

However, constraints to normal force freedoms and tangential motion freedoms can arise owing to the nature of the task. For example, when moving an open container of liquid, motion constraints are required to stop spillage. Control of force freedoms usually differs from control of motion freedoms in that, for most tasks, zero force is often required along force normals, but zero motion is rarely needed. Thus, when controlling force freedoms, force constraints normal to the C surface do not usually have to be considered. One application where we do have to consider them is pulling a knife through butter, where we want to cut the butter to a certain depth, but not right through. Another interesting example is a spinning top, where a force along one axis is transformed into a velocity along an orthogonal axis. In these special cases, we attempt to resolve constraint conflicts by modelling the task to see if the control requirements can be decoupled with natural compliance, or with active control of another freedom. If this fails, the task must be redefined. Finally, our analysis is based around the motion of a point, but end effectors have physical volume, which can further interfere with motion.

6.3 Inserting a peg into a hole

Many problems in parts mating are similar to the problem of inserting a peg into a hole, a task which is a common assembly operation. Usually, the tolerance between the outside diameter of the peg and the inside diameter of the hole is very fine. However, when parts arrive at an assembly station there may be significant errors in their position and orientation. These gross errors can be measured, the location of the hole determined, and a revised trajectory calculated. Even then, the task of inserting the peg in the hole might not proceed smoothly. There could still be minor errors in both the task model and the kinematic model which will cause the trajectory of the end effector to be far enough away from the axis of the hole for the peg to jam, or even, not enter the hole. The fine motions required to accommodate these errors, known as **motions of accommodation**, are achieved either by the passive compliance of the system or by active force control.

In previous sections, we analysed the forces involved in moving the peg once it is in the hole. In this section, we will analyse the forces involved while inserting the peg into the hole. This analysis was first performed by Simunovic (1975) and Ohwovoriole and Roth (1980), and reformulated by Whitney (1982).

When inserting a peg into a hole, the mating event proceeds through several clearly defined stages (Figure 6.6): approach, chamfer crossing, one-point contact, and two-point contact. After the two-point contact stage, the axes of the peg and hole are assumed to be parallel, and insertion can proceed along the C surface as discussed previously. In this situation, one-point (or line) contact can recur. Also, if the peg is correctly aligned as it approaches the hole, two-point contact may not occur during insertion.

To improve the chance of the peg entering the hole either the hole or the peg is chamfered. The situation where the face of the peg lands on the flat surface, and consequently cannot enter the hole, can be avoided by accurately positioning the part by locating the hole with a vision system, or

Figure 6.6
Four stages in part mating during assembly (Whitney, 1982): (a) approach; (b) chamfer crossing; (c) one-point contact; (d) two point contact.

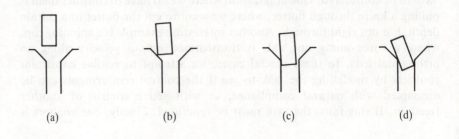

(a)   (b)   (c)   (d)

by employing search strategies (Section 9.3.4.1). In general, to achieve insertion, the part must rotate and translate during mating to correct for initial lateral and angular errors. This re-orientation of the part can occur passively, through the use of a remote centre compliance device, or actively, through force control (Section 11.8). In both cases, the gripper must provide angular and lateral compliance for the peg (Figure 6.7).

We model the required compliance with a lateral spring of stiffness K_x, and an angular spring of stiffness K_θ, acting at the centre of compliance. As we are considering symmetrical objects, a cylindrical peg and a circular hole, their interaction can be analysed in two dimensions. This reduces the problem to three degrees of freedom: translation in the x and z directions, and rotation around the y axis. Extensions of this work to non-symmetrical three-dimensional objects is a matter for continuing research (Sturges, 1988).

6.3.1 Compliance frames and C surfaces

The centre of compliance of the gripper is located at a distance l_g from the tip of the peg, and the z axis of the compliance frame is collinear with the axis of the peg (Figure 6.7(a)). The gripper is assumed to grip the part at this point, and the compliance of the gripper is represented mathematically by a compliance frame located at this point. The smaller the value of l_g, the fewer the problems during insertion. Ideally l_g should be zero, with the centre of compliance located at the tip of the peg. Placing the centre of compliance at the tip of the peg is the major function of remote-centre-compliance devices. The forces and torques applied by the gripper are expressed in peg tip coordinates (Figure 6.7(a)). Successful insertion depends on maintaining certain relationships between these applied forces and torques during two-point contact.

The event of mating these two parts can be represented by the paths of the peg and of the gripper, and, as these deviate, the forces and torques applied to the peg by contact and friction. As contact between the objects is difficult to avoid, the typical path for the peg is considered to be the path of the origin of the compliance frame along the C surface for each stage. During the approach stage, the forces are zero, the compliances relaxed, and the C surface has no motion constraints. The initial errors in the position (lateral distance ϵ_0) and orientation (θ_0) of the peg combine to place the centre of compliance a small distance d_0 to one side of the axis of the hole (Figure 6.7(b)). The analysis in the following sections assumes that these errors are small.

During chamfer crossing (Figure 6.8(a)), translation in the z direction is impeded by the chamfer and translation in the x direction and rotation around the y axis, are constrained by the object. These two constraints complement the artificial constraints provided by the spring model of

Figure 6.7
Parts for inserting a peg in a hole.
(a) Rigid peg supported by compliant gripper.
(b) Hole in object and initial errors in peg alignment.

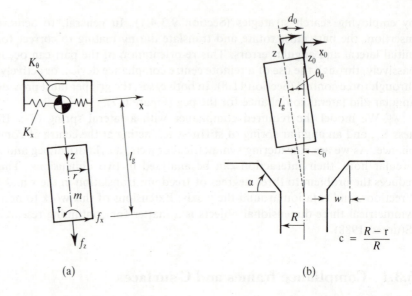

(a)   (b)

gripper compliance. As the gripper can translate away from the object into free space, or rotate around the point of contact, these physical constraints are unilateral. However, when combined with a task constraint of sliding along the chamfer, they cease to be unilateral. The task requires translation in the z direction, which is achieved indirectly by compliant translation in the x direction, and compliant rotation around the y axis, in reaction to the combined action of the applied force and the chamfer. For the peg to slide along the chamfer, the applied force must be outside the friction cone at the contact point (Window 6.2). The chamfer has to be very shallow to stop sliding.

The z axis of the compliance frame lies in the C surface, but may not be parallel to the chamfer. If the peg contacts the chamfer on the side it is approaching from, the z axis of the compliance frame can lie in a triangle defined by the axis of the hole and the chamfer, and still maintain one-point contact with the chamfer. For a completely stiff system, the C surface is a point, because the peg hits the chamfer and stops. However, we are considering compliant motion, and consequently, the point C surfaces combine to form a line as the peg slides down the chamfer. This line is curved, because both rotation and translation of the compliance frame occur as translation along the z axis proceeds. Only pure translation in the x direction is required, and if the compliance frame is located at the tip of the peg, only pure translation will occur. During both chamfer crossing and one-point contact, the natural constraints tend to rotate the peg to increase the orientation error, and thus, the difficulty of insertion. A second C surface exists for the opposite chamfer.

After the peg crosses the chamfer, it enters the one-point contact stage, where the edge of the chamfer rubs against the side of the peg (Figure

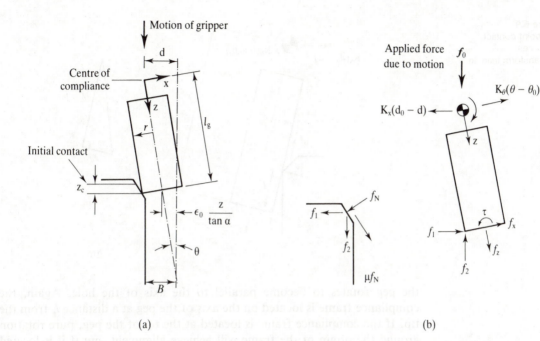

(a)

(b)

Figure 6.8
Chamfer crossing:
(a) Geometry;
(b) Force balance.

6.9). This is similar to drawing a finger across the edge of a table, which we discussed earlier. In that example, the compliance frame was located at the point of contact. In this situation, the origin of the compliance frame is located on the axis of the peg at a distance l_g from the tip, to be consistent with the other stages. We can describe the transform between these two locations with a simple geometric relation: a right-angle triangle, with one side being the radius of the peg, and the other the distance l_g minus the insertion depth l (Figure 6.9(b)). Hence, the different location does not significantly complicate our analysis. The motion freedoms are the same as for chamfer crossing, with translation in the z direction achieved by the force freedoms in the other two directions allowing compliant motion in those directions. The C surface is defined as the area in which the tip of the peg can move without either breaking contact or entering the two-point contact stage. In this area, rotation about the point of contact is not constrained by the objects.

One-point contact can occur in a second mode: the corner of the peg furthest from the insertion side can rub against the far wall of the hole. The only physical difference is that the reaction force is in the wall of the hole, not in the surface of the peg. As a force balance yields the same equations, we will regard these modes of one-point contact as equivalent, and only analyse one of them.

As soon as two-point contact occurs, rotation about the first point of contact must occur for the insertion to proceed. During this stage, the axis of

Figure 6.9
One-point contact.
(a) Forces;
(b) Transform triangle.

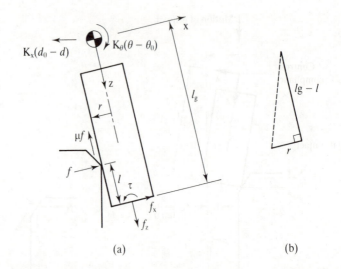

(a)   (b)

the peg rotates to become parallel to the axis of the hole. Again, the compliance frame is located on the axis of the peg at a distance l_g from the tip. If the compliance frame is located at the tip of the peg, pure rotation around the origin of the frame will achieve alignment, but if it is located away from the tip, translation in the x direction is also required. The motion freedoms are now the same as those for the peg moving in the hole, and the force constraints are no longer unilateral. The C surface is the area between the curved path which the tip of the peg must follow to maintain two-point contact while being aligned, and the axis of the hole (Figure 6.10(b)). Again, a symmetrical C surface exists for insertion from the other direction. Once the peg is in the hole, it has attained the state of a peg moving in a hole, as discussed in a previous section.

6.3.2 Chamfer crossing

When the edge of the peg comes in contact with the chamfer, the second stage is entered, and motion is constrained by the chamfer (Figure 6.8). The compliance of the gripper allows the peg to translate and rotate. The geometry of the task at this stage is described by:

$$d_0 = \epsilon_0 + l_g \theta_0 \tag{6.8}$$

$$d = l_g \theta - \frac{z_c}{\tan(\alpha)} + \epsilon_0 \tag{6.9}$$

where

> d is the distance from the centre of compliance to the axis of the hole,

ϵ is the distance between the axis of the peg and the axis of the hole at the tip of the peg, and the subscript 0 represents initial values before contact,

θ is the angle between the axis of the peg and the axis of the hole,

z_c is the distance the edge of the peg has slid along the chamfer, and

α is the angle of the chamfer.

At the bottom of the chamfer, when chamfer crossing is complete and one-point contact commences, the peg has slid a distance:

$$z_c = \epsilon \tan(\alpha) \tag{6.10}$$

where

$$\epsilon = \epsilon_0 - cR \tag{6.11}$$

and

$$c = \frac{R - r}{R} \tag{6.12}$$

where

c is the clearance ratio (Figure 6.7(b)),

R is the radius of the hole, and

r is the radius of the peg.

During chamfer crossing a static force balance yields:

$$f_1 = f_N[\sin(\alpha) - \mu\cos(\alpha)] \quad \text{and} \quad f_2 = f_N[\cos(\alpha) + \mu\sin(\alpha)] \tag{6.13}$$

where

f_N is the component of the applied force f_a which is normal to the chamfer, and the applied force results from opposition to motion in the z direction,

f_1 is the component of the reaction force parallel to the surface of the object,

f_2 is the component of the reaction force normal to the surface of the object, and

μ is the coefficient of friction.

The force balance between contact and support forces at the tip of the peg is:

$$f_x = -f_1 = -K_x(d_0 - d) \tag{6.14}$$

$$f_z = f_2 \tag{6.15}$$

$$\tau = f_2 r = K_x l_g (d_0 - d) - K_\theta(\theta - \theta_0) \tag{6.16}$$

where K_x and K_θ are the equivalent spring constants of the compliant support.

By combining Equations 6.8–16, we obtain expressions for the position and orientation of the compliance frame, relative to the axis of the hole, during chamfer crossing.

$$\theta = \theta_0 + \frac{(K_x(z/\tan(\alpha)\{l_g[\sin(\alpha) - \mu\cos(\alpha)] - r[\cos(\alpha) + \mu\sin(\alpha)]\}}{(K_x l_g{}^2 + K_\theta)[\sin(\alpha) - \mu\cos(\alpha)] - K_x l_g r[\cos(\alpha) + \mu\sin(\alpha)]} \tag{6.17}$$

$$d = d_0 - \frac{K_\theta(z/\tan(\alpha)[\sin(\alpha) - \mu\cos(\alpha)]}{(K_x l_g{}^2 + K_\theta)[\sin(\alpha) - \mu\cos(\alpha)] - K_x l_g r[\cos(\alpha) + \mu\sin(\alpha)]} \tag{6.18}$$

6.3.3 One-point contact

Once the peg has crossed the chamfer, it enters the region of one-point contact where the edge of the hole contacts the side of the peg (Figure 6.9). In this region, the peg can continue to slide without changing the angle between the axis of the peg and the axis of the hole. That is, pure translation of the compliance frame is possible. However, the torque applied to the centre of compliance by the force interaction at the contact point may cause the axis of the peg to rotate away from the axis of the hole. This rotation is in the opposite direction to the required rotation. Starting with an equation describing the geometric constraint (Equation 6.19), and using an algorithm analogous to the one for solving chamfer crossing, we derive the following expressions for one-point contact.

$$d = R - r + l_g\theta - l\theta \qquad \text{is the geometric constraint} \tag{6.19}$$

$$C = K_x(l_g - l - \mu r) \qquad \text{is a convenient sub-expression} \tag{6.20}$$

$$\theta = \frac{C(\epsilon + l_g\theta_0) + K_\theta\theta_0}{C(l_g - l) + K_\theta} \tag{6.21}$$

$$d = d_0 - \frac{K_\theta(\epsilon + l\theta_0)}{C(l_g - l) + K_\theta} \tag{6.22}$$

The insertion depth (l) is the distance from the contact point to the tip of the peg, and is zero when the peg is at the bottom of the chamfer. When the insertion depth is zero, the angle between the axes is:

$$\theta_1 = \theta_0 + \frac{K_x(l_g - \mu r)\epsilon}{K_x l_g(l_g - \mu r) + K_\theta} \tag{6.23}$$

6.3.4 Two-point contact

The next stage is two-point contact, where the corner of the hole on the insertion side contacts the peg, and the corner of the peg opposite to the insertion side contacts the side of the hole (Figure 6.10). This second contact establishes reaction forces which tend to align the axis of the peg with that of the hole. If this rotation is sucessful, the whole insertion task will succeed. However, during two-point contact, the peg can jam or wedge, and, if this happens, the insertion will fail. Two-point contact is initiated by errors in either the location ($\pm\epsilon$) or the orientation ($\pm\theta$) of the peg. Thus, there are four possible error conditions which will initiate two-point contact, but, as they are similar, we will only analyse one of them. During two-point contact, geometric compatability between the peg and the hole is constrained by:

$$2R = l\tan(\theta) + 2r\cos(\theta) \tag{6.24}$$

which, when θ is small, becomes:

$$l\theta = 2cR = 2(R - r) \qquad (\text{= a constant}) \tag{6.25}$$

and θ must be less than $\sqrt{2c}$

To determine where two-point contact begins, rewrite the geometric constraint for one-point contact (Equation 6.26) and substitute Equation 6.24 into it:

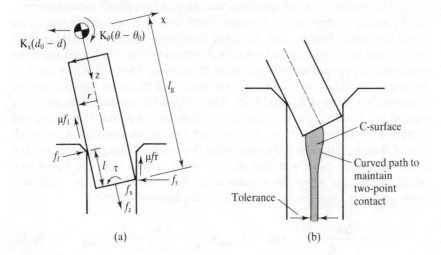

Figure 6.10
Two-point contact.
(a) Forces;
(b) C-surface.

$$d_0 - d = \epsilon + l_g(\theta_0 - \theta) + l\theta \tag{6.26}$$

$$d_0 - d = \epsilon_0 + R - r + l_g(\theta_0 - \theta) \tag{6.27}$$

Using Equation 6.27 in conjunction with a force balance similar to that for chamfer crossing, the position and orientation of the peg at the onset of two-point contact is:

$$\theta_2 = \theta_0 + \frac{K_x(\epsilon_0 + R - r)(l_g - l_2 - \mu r)}{K_x l_g^2 + K_\theta - K_x l_g(l_2 + \mu r)} \tag{6.28}$$

$$d_2 = d_0 - \frac{K_\theta(\epsilon_0 + R - r)}{K_x l_g^2 + K_\theta - K_x l_g(l_2 + \mu r)} \tag{6.29}$$

where the subscript 2 indicates the precise values for the start of a two-point contact.

The insertion depth at which two-point contact begins (l_2) is found by substituting Equation 6.25 into Equation 6.29, and solving for the roots of the resultant quadratic equation:

$$A l_2^2 - B l_2 + K = 0 \tag{6.30}$$

where

$$
\begin{aligned}
A &= K_x(\epsilon_0 + R - r + l_g \theta_0) \\
B &= (l_g - \mu r) A + 2 K_x l_g(R - r) + K_\theta \theta_0, \text{ and} \\
K &= 2(R - r)(K_x l_g^2 + K_\theta - K_x l_g \mu r)
\end{aligned}
\tag{6.31}
$$

The existence of two solutions for the insertion depth shows that two-point contact is confined to a region, with one insertion depth specifying where the region begins, and the other specifying where two-point contact finishes and one-point contact resumes. Once one-point contact resumes, the insertion can proceed without jamming or wedging. In addition, we can find the angles at which two-point contact starts and stops by substituting the insertion depths into Equation 6.25. Also, if l_g and θ_0 are small enough, there will be no solution for the quadratic equation, implying that two-point contact will not occur. If we assume that the spring constant K_θ is much greater than $K_x l_g^2$ (which is the case when the centre of compliance is located at the tip of the peg), and that $K_\theta \theta_0$ is much greater than $\mu K_x(\epsilon_0 + R - r)r$ (which is the case when the angular error θ_0 is greater than the positional error $\epsilon_0 + R - r$), then the insertion depths are approximately:

$$l_{2\text{start}} = \frac{2(R - r)}{\theta_0} \quad \text{and} \quad l_{2\text{finish}} = \frac{K_\theta \theta_0}{K_x(\epsilon_0 + R - r)} - l_{2\text{start}} \tag{6.32}$$

Window 6.2 Frictional forces

When one body moves across the surface of another, its motion is opposed by frictional forces. Several distinct types of frictional forces are encountered: dry friction, fluid friction, rolling friction, and internal friction. **Dry friction** (or **Coulomb friction**) occurs when one body slides or attempts to slide over another, and there is no lubrication between the contacting surfaces. **Fluid friction** occurs when adjacent layers in a fluid are moving at different velocities. **Rolling friction** is the resistance encountered when a circular body is rolled, and is associated with the deformation of both the circular body and the supporting surface. **Internal friction** occurs in solid objects that are subject to cyclic loads, and is associated with the deformation of the body produced by the load.

Dry friction is described by **Coulomb's law**:

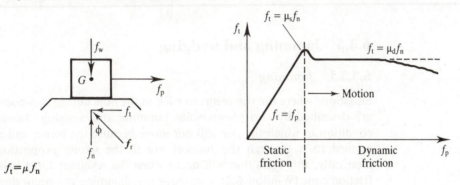

$$f_t = \mu f_n$$

where

f_t is the frictional force opposing motion,

f_n is the normal force, due to the weight of the body or an applied force,

μ is the coefficient of friction.

The **weight** of a body is the force of gravity distributed over its volume, however, for analysis, the gravitational force is constrained to be a force vector acting through the centre of gravity of the body. The position of the centre of gravity is usually obvious from considerations of symmetry. The weight of the body is counteracted by a normal force (f_n). When a force f_p is applied to a body, the body tends to slide along the supporting surface. The tendency to slide is opposed by the frictional force (f_t). If the tangent of the angle of the resultant force (the vector sum of the frictional and normal forces) with respect to the normal force is greater than the coefficient of friction, the body slides. The coefficient of static friction is higher than the coefficient of dynamic friction, thus, it takes a larger force to initiate sliding than to maintain it.

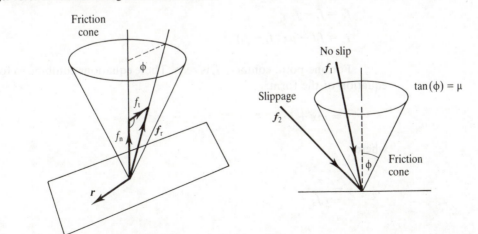

A geometric interpretation of Coulomb's law that is of importance in robotics is the concept of a friction cone (Moseley, 1839).

$f_t = \mu f_n$ and $\phi = \tan^{-1}(f_t/f_n) =$ angle of the sides of the friction cone to the normal.

The friction angle ϕ is the angle of the resultant force to the normal. When $\tan(\phi)$ is equal to the coefficient of friction, the object applying the force is on the verge of slipping. A set of vectors at this angle to the normal defines the friction cone. If the vector defining the force applied to the surface (in the case of an object sitting on the surface this is the reaction force f_r) is inside the friction cone, no slippage will occur. In contrast, if the force vector is outside the friction cone, slippage will occur.

6.3.5 Jamming and wedging

6.3.5.1 *Jamming*

Situations where the peg seems to stick in the hole during two-point contact are described by two phenomena: jamming and wedging. **Jamming** is a condition in which the peg will not move because the forces and moments applied to it through the support are in the wrong proportions. Geometrically, this condition will occur when the resultant force is inside the friction cone (Window 6.2). Consequently, jamming can occur during both one-and two-point contact. As the resultant force is inside the friction cone, increasing the applied force will not cause the peg to slide. Therefore, jamming can be overcome only by changing the direction of the applied force so that the resultant force lies outside the friction cone. This is best achieved by removing the peg from the hole and changing the orientation of the peg before attempting to insert it again.

A condition of force equilibrium exists when the resultant force lies at the edge of the friction cone. When the resultant force is outside the friction cone, the peg slides or falls into the hole. The force balance when a peg is sliding in a hole (Figure 6.10) is described by the following equations:

$$f_z = \mu(f_l + f_r) \tag{6.33}$$

$$f_x = f_r - f_l \tag{6.34}$$

$$\tau = f_l l - \mu r(f_r - f_l) \tag{6.35}$$

For one-point contact, f_r is zero. These equations combine to form an equation of the form:

$$y = mx + b \tag{6.36}$$

where

$$y = \frac{\tau}{r f_z}$$

$$x = \frac{f_x}{f_z}$$

$$\tau = \frac{l}{2r\mu}$$

$m = -\mu(1 + \lambda)$, and $b = \lambda$ for the peg leaning one way, and $b = -\lambda$ for the peg leaning the other way.

The results of this analysis are summarized with the parallelogram in Figure 6.11. The corners of the parallellogram are specified by the four possible one-point contact configurations. The diagonal lines represent equilibrium conditions for two-point contact, and the vertical dotted lines represent equilibrium conditions for one-point contact, that is, the resultant force lies in the sides of the friction cone, and sliding can just occur. Thus, combinations of f_x, f_z, and τ which fall on the edges of the parallelogram describe equilibrium sliding in. Outside the parallelogram lie combinations which jam the peg. Inside the parallelogram, the peg is falling in.

As λ approaches zero, that is, the insertion depth is small compared to the radius of the peg, the parallelogram collapses to a line from $(1/\mu, -1)$ on the right to $(-1/\mu, 1)$ on the left. Thus, at the initiation of two-point contact, the no-jam region is quite small, and the possibility of jamming is high. Jamming is most likely to occur during insertion tasks with very small tolerances, because the smaller the tolerances, the smaller the insertion depth at which two-point contact occurs. When the peg is deep in the hole, λ approaches infinity, and the parallelogram expands to be a vertical strip lying between $-1/\mu$ and $1/\mu$, implying that one-point contact jamming is possible, but two-point contact jams are difficult to achieve.

We can see from the jamming parallelogram, that jamming can be avoided when the following two conditions are satisfied:

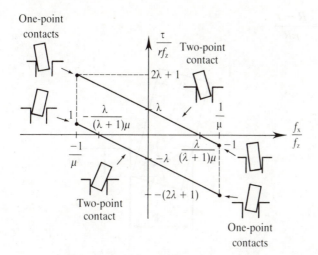

Figure 6.11
Jamming parallelogram
(Whitney, 1982).

$$-\lambda < \frac{\tau}{rf_z} + \mu(1+\lambda)\frac{f_x}{f_z} < \lambda \qquad \text{from the horizontal sides} \qquad \textbf{(6.37)}$$

$$\frac{-1}{\mu} < \frac{f_x}{f_z} < \frac{1}{\mu} \qquad \text{from the vertical sides} \qquad \textbf{(6.38)}$$

6.3.5.2 *Wedging*

Wedging is a worse condition than jamming, because removal of the applied force will not remove the reaction forces. Wedging occurs when the two contact forces f_1 and f_2 are both inside their friction cones, and act along the same line (Figure 6.12). Unlike jamming the cause is geometric rather than ill-proportioned forces. Wedging can become so severe that the force required to move the peg, either into or out of the hole, will damage the parts at the contact points. Wedging is often difficult to visualize. To make it easier, imagine a similar situation when a peg which fits snugly in a hole is heated, while the object containing the hole is not. As the temperature of the peg rises, the peg expands and applies forces to the sides of the hole. These contact forces are absorbed by elastic deformation and oppose the sliding motion of the peg. While the physical phenomena causing the forces in this case are different from those at work in wedging, the effect of the forces is the same.

Wedging occurs if two-point contact starts when the insertion depth is smaller than the coefficient of friction times the diameter of the peg.

$$l_{2\text{start}} = 2r\mu \qquad \textbf{(6.39)}$$

At depths less than this, the friction cones at the contact points intersect, and the parts elastically deform. From Equation 6.32, this maximum depth corresponds to a maximum error in the orientation of the peg of:

$$\theta = \frac{R-r}{\mu R} \qquad \textbf{(6.40)}$$

Figure 6.12
Geometry of wedging condition showing the intersection of the left and right side friction cones (drawn for the case of the largest insertion depth for which wedging can occur) (Whitney, 1982).

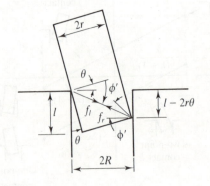

In the example given in Figure 6.12, the right side force is inside the friction cone indicating that relative motion between the parts on the right side has ceased. The left side contact force lies in the lower edge of the friction cone, indicating that the left side of the peg is attempting to move out of the hole. This situation could occur if the peg had been pushed counter-clockwise, elastically deformed at the contact points, and then released.

6.3.6 Remote-centre-compliance devices

In summary, to insert a peg into a hole successfully, the following conditions must be met.

- The initial error in the lateral position must be less than the width of the chamfer for chamfer crossing to start.
- At the start of the two-point contact, the error in the orientation must be less than $(R - r)/\mu R$, to avoid wedging.
- The combination of f_x, f_z, and τ must lie inside the jamming parallelogram to avoid jamming.

A remote-centre-compliance device placed between the toolplate and the gripper (Whitney and Nevins, 1979) overcomes minor errors in the location of the peg by using passive compliance (Figure 6.13). The essential characteristic of remote-centre compliance is that lateral and angular errors are absorbed independently. This decoupling is achieved by placing the centre of compliance at the tip of the peg ($l_g = 0$) where forces produce pure translation, and torques produce pure rotation. A typical remote-centre compliance device (Figure 6.13(a)) contains two sets of flexing members. The rotational springs allow the gripper to rotate about the tip of the peg

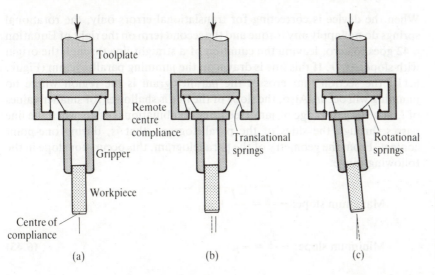

Toolplate

Remote centre compliance

Gripper

Workpiece

Translational springs

Rotational springs

Centre of compliance

(a)   (b)   (c)

Figure 6.13
A remote-centre-compliance device: (a) relaxed; (b) translational accommodation; (c) rotational accommodation.

(Figure 6.13(c)), while the translational springs allow the gripper to translate without rotation (Figure 6.13(b)).

Remote-centre-compliance devices are designed to permit lateral motion in response to laterally directed contact forces (such as those produced during chamfer crossing) without any accompanying angular motion. We saw earlier that, during chamfer crossing and one-point contact, the task constraints tend to cause the peg to rotate in order to increase the orientation error. Increasing the orientation error is undesirable, as it increases the chance of wedging. The closer the centre of compliance is to the tip of the peg, the smaller the change in the orientation angle during chamfer crossing (Equation 6.17), and during one-point contact (Equation 6.23).

In contrast, during two-point contact, the peg is required to rotate without translating. The closer the centre of compliance is to the tip of the peg during two-point contact, the smaller is the change in lateral position due to the torque produced by the contact forces. The force balance during two-point contact can be modelled by applying the geometric constraint for two-point contact (Equation 6.25) to the spring model in Equations 6.14–16.

$$\tau = -f_x l_g - K_\theta \left[\frac{2(R - r)}{l} - \theta_0 \right] \tag{6.41}$$

Equation 6.41 describes the support forces of the remote-centre-compliance device in peg tip coordinates (Figure 6.7(a)). To map this model onto the jamming parallelogram, divide Equation 6.41 by $r f_z$:

$$\frac{\tau}{r f_z} = -\frac{f_x l_g}{r f_z} - \frac{K_\theta}{r f_z} \left[\frac{2(R - r)}{l} - \theta_0 \right] \tag{6.42}$$

When the device is correcting for translational errors only, the rotational springs do not apply any torque and the second term on the right of Equation 6.42 goes to zero, leaving the equation of a straight line through the origin with slope $-l_g/r$. If this line is drawn on the jamming parallelogram (Figure 6.11), the section that crosses the parallelogram is the region where no jamming will occur. Also, the slope of the line is shallower for smaller values of l_g. The largest range of jam-free force combinations occurs when the line passes through the sides of the parallelogram, that is, during one-point contact. From the geometry of the parallelogram, this occurs for slope in the following range:

Maximum slope: $-\dfrac{l_g}{r} = \dfrac{-l}{r} + \mu$

Minimum slope: $-\dfrac{l_g}{r} = -\mu$ \hfill (6.43)

The range of l_g for this condition is μr to $l + \mu r$. Within this range, two-point contact cannot occur. But, as the insertion proceeds, l increases, and thus, the deeper the peg is in the hole, the greater the range of l_g for one-point contact. If l_g is outside this range, two-point contact will occur, if the force conditions lie on the edge of the parallelogram in Figure 6.12. Interestingly, if l_g is zero, the line described by Equation 6.40 becomes the horizontal axis, and the peg will not jam while the ratio of f_x to f_z is less than $\lambda / [\mu(\lambda + 1)]$.

This analysis confirms that the best placement of the centre of compliance is at a distance $l + \mu r$ from the tip of the peg. That is, it should move away from the tip as the insertion proceeds. However, as this is difficult to achieve in practice, a safe working range for l_g is from the tip of the peg to a distance $l + \mu r$ from the tip of the peg. In fact, it can be larger and still avoid jamming.

In the more general case, where both translational and rotational errors are present, the second term on the right of Equation 6.42 displaces the line in a negative direction, and thus, it no longer passes through the origin. If we examine the rotational term, we can see that it is inversely proportional to the insertion depth l and the applied force in the z direction f_z. Thus, increasing the applied force will reduce the value of this offset, and, hence, decrease the possibility of jamming, as one would expect from Equation 6.38. Also, as the insertion depth increases, this offset will decrease, and accordingly decrease the possibility of jamming. As this term is a pure moment, it is independent of the centre of compliance. Hence, the placement of the centre of compliance is determined by lateral considerations only.

Most remote-centre-compliance devices place the centre of compliance at a fixed distance from the tool plate (Figure 6.13). As the location of the remote centre is determined by a complex function of the stiffness of

Figure 6.14
Automatically adjustable
remote centre compliance
device built by CMU
Robotics Institute.

the springs, remote-centre-compliance devices are suited to pegs whose lengths lie within a small range. One way to increase the range of peg lengths that a remote centre compliance device can accommodate is to have springs with variable stiffness. Such a device (Figure 6.14) has been built at Carnegie–Mellon University using stiff elastomeric spheres as the springs. These hollow spheres are made from a composite of rubber and Kevlar. Their stiffness is adjusted by altering the pressure of the fluid inside them, effectively changing the location of the remote centre of compliance.

6.4   Manipulator statics

In the previous sections, we investigated the forces applied to the end effector as a result of its interaction with the environment. Before we can control the force a manipulator applies to an object, or hold a manipulator stationary while it is subjected to applied forces, we must relate the forces applied to the end effector to the forces at the joints. At a revolute joint, the actuator applies a torque around the axis of the joint, and at a prismatic joint, the actuator applies a force along the axis of the joint. As each actuator supplies some of the end effector force and torque, a way of sharing the torque among the actuators must be found. As with position, we calculate the contribution made by each joint with a transformation from Cartesian force space to joint torque space.

6.4.1   Force balance on an isolated link

Before analysing a manipulator, we will derive the net force and net torque acting on a single link due to external forces (Figure 6.15). A link can be isolated from the links on either side of it by considering that the neighbouring links apply external forces and torques to this link. These arise from three

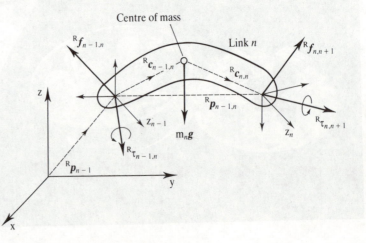

Figure 6.15
Static force-torque balance for an isolated link.

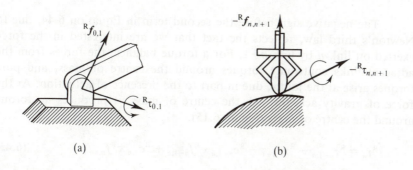

Figure 6.16
Forces and torques at the
extremities of a manipulator.
(a) At the base;
(b) At the end effector.

(a)　　　　　　　　　　(b)

sources: the mass of the neighbour link, external force inherited from contact between the manipulator tip and an object (Figure 6.16), and, if the neighbour link is accelerating, the d'Alembert force of the neighbour link. As the link is isolated and stationary, the net force and net torque must be balanced by actuator force and torque. Obviously, an actuator for a revolute joint can apply only pure torque (Figure 6.17) and an actuator for a prismatic joint can apply only pure force.

Three external forces are applied to link n: link $n-1$ applies a force through joint n, link $n+1$ applies a force through joint $n+1$, and the force of gravity acting through the centre of gravity. The force balance is:

$$^{R}f_{n} = {}^{R}f_{n-1,n} - {}^{R}f_{n,n+1} + m_{n}\,{}^{R}g \qquad (6.44)$$

$$= 0 \quad \text{for static balance.}$$

where

m_{n} is the mass of link n,

^{R}g is the gravity vector,

$^{R}f_{n}$ is the net force applied to link n,

$^{R}f_{n-1,n}$ is the force applied to link n by link $n-1$,

$^{R}f_{n,n+1}$ is the force applied to link $n+1$ by link n,

(All forces are expressed with respect to the reference frame.)

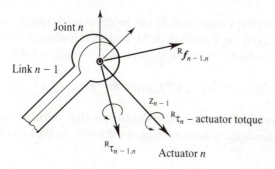

Figure 6.17
Force and torque applied by
one link to the next across
joint n.

The negative sign before the second term in Equation 6.44, due to Newton's third law, reflects the fact that we are interested in the force exerted on link n by link $n+1$. For a torque balance, the forces from the adjacent links contribute torques around the centre of mass, and pure torques arise at the joints, due in part to the presence of actuation. As the force of gravity acts through the centre of mass, it produces no torque around the centre of mass (Figure 6.15).

$$^R\tau_n = {}^R\tau_{n-1,n} - {}^R\tau_{n,n+1} - {}^Rc_{n-1,n} \times {}^Rf_{n-1,n} + {}^Rc_{n,n} \times {}^Rf_{n,n+1} \tag{6.45}$$

$$= 0 \quad \text{for static balance.}$$

where

$^Rc_{n-1,n}$ is the position vector from the origin of frame $n-1$ at joint n to the centre of gravity of link n, as seen from the the reference frame, and

$^R\tau_{n-1,n}$ is the torque applied to link n by link $n-1$, as seen from the reference frame.

6.4.2 Torque balance at a revolute joint

Of more interest, in the case of a revolute joint, is the torque applied to the joint (Figure 6.17). For a static torque balance, the left-hand side of Equation 6.45 is set to zero, and, by manipulating the terms, the torque around the axis of joint n is obtained.

$$^R\tau_{n-1,n} = {}^R\tau_{n,n+1} + {}^Rc_{n-1,n} \times {}^Rf_{n-1,n} - {}^Rc_{n,n} \times {}^Rf_{n,n+1} \tag{6.46}$$

However, from basic physics, the force applied by link $n-1$ produces no torque as it passes through the joint axis, the moment arm of the force applied by link n is the length of the link, and the force due to gravity does produce torque, as the centre of gravity rarely coincides with the joint axis.

$$^R\tau_{n-1,n} = {}^R\tau_{n,n+1} + {}^Rp_{n-1,n} \times {}^Rf_{n,n+1} + {}^Rc_{n-1,n} \times m_n {}^Rg \tag{6.47}$$

Alternatively, Equation 6.47 can be developed from Equation 6.46 by setting ^Rf_n to zero in Equation 6.44 and manipulating terms to obtain Equation 6.48, which is then substituted into Equation 6.46.

$$^Rc_{n-1,n} \times {}^Rf_{n-1,n} = {}^Rc_{n-1,n} \times ({}^Rf_{n,n+1} + m_n {}^Rg) \tag{6.48}$$

The final step is to calculate the torque that must be supplied by the actuator to balance the torque applied to the joint. As the axis of the actuator is aligned with the joint axis, which is aligned with the z axis of the joint frame, the actuator torque is the z component of the joint torque.

$$^R\tau_{n\,act} = {}^R\tau_{n-1,n}^T \cdot {}^Rz_{n-1} \tag{6.49}$$

where $^Rz_{n-1}$ is the unit vector describing the joint axis, and positive joint torque tends to increase the joint angle.

As the actuator at a revolute joint can supply only torque, the forces applied to the manipulator must be balanced either by torque through a moment arm or by reaction forces internal to the manipulator links. From Equation 6.44, the force balance at joint n is

$$^Rf_{n-1,n} = {}^Rf_{n,n+1} - m_n\,{}^Rg \tag{6.50}$$

6.4.3 Static force-torque balance on a manipulator

Using the above equations, we can calculate the static force and torque balance on a manipulator. For example, consider the type 1 two-link manipulator with an external force applied to the end of the second link, and no external torque applied to the end of that link (Figure 6.18). From Equation 6.47, the equations for the torques at the joints are:

$$^0f_{2,3} = \text{external force,} \quad {}^0\tau_{2,3} = 0 \text{ and } {}^0f_{1,2} = {}^0f_{2,3} - m_2\,{}^0g \tag{6.51}$$

$$^0\tau_{1,2} = {}^0p_{1,2}\,\mathbf{x}\,{}^0f_{2,3} + {}^0c_{1,2}\,\mathbf{x}\,m_2\,{}^0g \tag{6.52}$$

$$^0\tau_{0,1} = {}^0\tau_{1,2} + {}^0p_1\,\mathbf{x}\,({}^0f_{2,3} - m_2\,{}^0g) + {}^0c_1\,\mathbf{x}\,m_1\,{}^0g \tag{6.53}$$

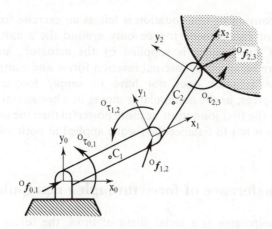

Figure 6.18
Force and torque balance for a type 1 two-link manipulator.

Due to the symmetry of the links, the distance from a joint to the centre of gravity of a link is half the length of the link (l_n). Thus, these torque equations (Equations 6.52 and 6.53) can be simplified by substituting for the distance to the centre of gravity (Equation 6.54). Also, as the manipulator is restricted to motion within the xy plane, the vector describing the force applied by the manipulator to an object is restricted to the xy plane, but the force applied by the object to the manipulator is not. For example, if the object is at an angle to the xy plane, the reaction force will tend to cause the manipulator to bend.

$$^0p_1 = 2 \times {^0c_1} = \begin{bmatrix} l_1 C_1 \\ l_1 S_1 \end{bmatrix} \quad \text{and} \quad ^0p_{1,2} = 2 \times {^0c_{1,2}} = \begin{bmatrix} l_2 C_{12} \\ l_2 S_{12} \end{bmatrix} \tag{6.54}$$

$$^0\tau_{1,2} = \begin{bmatrix} l_2 C_{12} \\ l_2 S_{12} \\ 0 \end{bmatrix} \times \begin{bmatrix} ^0f_{2,3x} \\ ^0f_{2,3y} \\ ^0f_{2,3z} \end{bmatrix} + 0.5 \times \begin{bmatrix} l_2 C_{12} \\ l_2 S_{12} \\ 0 \end{bmatrix} \times m_2 \begin{bmatrix} 0 \\ 0 \\ g \end{bmatrix}$$

$$= (l_2 S_{12} {^0f_{2,3z}})i - (l_2 C_{12} {^0f_{2,3z}})j + (l_2 C_{12} 0f_{2,3y} - l_2 S_{12} 0f_{2,3x})k$$
$$+ (0.5 \times m_2 l_2 S_{12}g)i - (0.5 \times m_2 l_2 C_{12}g)j$$

$$= \begin{bmatrix} l_2 S_{12} {^0f_{2,3z}} + 0.5g\, m_2 l_2 S_{12} \\ -l_2 C_{12} {^0f_{2,3z}} - 0.5g\, m_2 l_2 C_{12} \\ l_2 C_{12} {^0f_{2,3y}} - l_2 S_{12} {^0f_{2,3x}} \end{bmatrix} \begin{bmatrix} i \\ j \\ k \end{bmatrix}$$

$$= l_2 C_{12} {^0f_{2,3y}} - l_2 S_{12} {^0f_{2,3x}} \text{ around the joint axis} \tag{6.55}$$

$$^0\tau_{0,1} = {^0\tau_{1,2}} = {^0\tau_{1,2}} + {^0p_1} \times ({^0f_{2,3}} - m_2 {^R}g) + {^0c_1} \times m_1 {^R}g$$

$$= {^0\tau_{1,2}} + \begin{bmatrix} l_1 C_1 \\ l_1 S_1 \\ 0 \end{bmatrix} \times \begin{bmatrix} ^0f_{2,3x} \\ ^0f_{2,3y} \\ ^0f_{2,3y} - m_2 g \end{bmatrix} + 0.5 \times \begin{bmatrix} l_1 C_1 \\ l_1 S_1 \\ 0 \end{bmatrix} \times m_l \begin{bmatrix} 0 \\ 0 \\ g \end{bmatrix} \tag{6.56}$$

The expansion of this equation is left as an exercise for the reader. As the actuator can provide torque only around the z axis, only the z component of the torques is supplied by the actuator, and the other components are balanced by internal reaction forces and compliant forces. Note that the actuator does not have to supply torque to balance gravitational forces, as the manipulator moves in a horizontal plane. Also, the actuator at the first joint must be more powerful than the actuator at the second joint as it has to balance the torque applied to both joints.

6.4.4 Transference of force through a manipulator

Because a manipulator is a serial chain of links, the forces and torques applied to the end effector propagate from one link to the next, through to the base. In this section, we are interested in the joint torques, in the case of revolute joints, and the joint forces, in the case of prismatic joints, required to balance the externally applied force. The external force can be a reaction force resulting from the manipulator pushing on an object or an applied force due to the weight of an object held by the gripper. This force changes from task to task, and from C surface to C surface, where the mass of the manipulator links is constant. The forces and torques required to balance the mass of the links vary with the configuration of the manipulator, and the forces and torques required to balance the forces and torques due to interaction with the environment vary with the task.

We wish to derive a standard method for solving the set of joint torques and/or forces needed to support a static load acting at the end effector. As we are interested in the transference of forces due to environmental interaction, mass will be neglected. First, all the joints are locked, so that the manipulator becomes a rigid structure. Then, we consider each link in this structure, and write equations for the force and torque balance for each link with respect to the coordinate frame for that link (Equations 6.57 and 6.58). From the analysis of the torque balance at a revolute joint in Section 6.4.2, we derive the equations for static balance by using the joint frame as the reference frame (Equations 6.47, 6.50). Also, a rotation transform is introduced so that all forces are specified in their own coordinate frames.

$$^{n-1}f_{n-1,n} = \,^{n-1}f_{n,n+1} = \,^{n-1}\mathbf{Rot}_n\,^{n}f_{n,n+1} \tag{6.57}$$

$$^{n-1}\tau_{n-1,n} = \,^{n-1}\mathbf{Rot}_n\,^{n}\tau_{n,n+1} + \,^{n-1}p_{n-1,n}\,\mathbf{x}\,^{n-1}\mathbf{Rot}_n\,^{n}f_{n,n+1} \tag{6.58}$$

This equation is simplified further by substituting Equation 6.57 into it:

$$^{n-1}\tau_{n-1,n} = \,^{n-1}\mathbf{Rot}_n\,^{n}\tau_{n,n+1} + \,^{n-1}p_{n-1,n}\,\mathbf{x}\,^{n-1}f_{n-1,n} \tag{6.59}$$

Using Equation 6.57 and 6.59, we can solve the static balance for a manipulator by starting with the forces and torques applied to the gripper and iterating link by link to the base. Alternatively, we can start at the base and recursively move link by link to the gripper, until the static balance for the entire robot is solved.

From these equations, we can compute the static torque or force that must be supplied by each actuator to maintain static equilibrium in response to external forces and torques. These actuation forces and torques maintain the rigidity of the structure, assumed in our analysis. The force and torque vectors are six degree of freedom vectors, but a typical robot joint has only one degree of freedom, and hence, the actuator can supply reaction force or torque only in that degree – reaction forces and torques in all other degrees are provided by the mechanism itself. Consequently, the actuator torque or force is the component of the joint force or torque in the direction of the actuator freedom. That component is found by calculating the dot product of the vector which describes the joint axis with the force or torque vector acting on the link. For a revolute joint, the actuation torque is:

$$^{n-1}\tau_{\text{act}} = {^{n-1}\tau_{n-1,n}^{\text{T}}} \cdot {^{n-1}z_{n-1}} \tag{6.60}$$

where $^{n-1}z_{n-1}$ is the vector describing the joint axis, and positive joint torque tends to increase the joint angle.

For a prismatic joint, the actuation force is:

$$^{n-1}f_{\text{act}} = {^{n-1}f_{n-1,n}} \cdot {^{n-1}z_{n-1}} \tag{6.61}$$

From the above equations, a simple iterative algorithm (Algorithm 6.1) is obtained for calculating the static balance of external forces and torques, and the required actuator forces and torques to balance the external load.

Algorithm 6.1 Iterative algorithm for static force balance

1. Obtain values for the forces and torques acting on the gripper.

2. Starting at the gripper and working towards the base
   For each link
   1. Solve Equation 6.57 to find the reaction force.
   2. Solve Equation 6.59 to find the reaction torque.
   3. **If** the joint is revolute **Then**
      solve Equation 6.60 to find the required actuator torque
      Else   {the joint is prismatic}
      solve Equation 6.61 to find the required actuator force.

3. The iteration terminates when the link attached to the base has been solved.

6.4.5 Static force balance on a type 1 two-link manipulator

To illustrate the use of this algorithm, we will solve the static balance for the type 1 two-link manipulator shown in Figure 6.18. The required rotation transforms and translation vectors are obtained from the **A** matrices for this manipulator (See Equation 4.8). A force $^2f_3$ is applied to the end effector, acting at the origin of frame 2 and lying in the xy plane.

$$^2f_{2,3} = \begin{bmatrix} f_x \\ f_y \\ 0 \end{bmatrix} \quad {^2\tau_{2,3}} = 0 \tag{6.62}$$

From this force we calculate the force and torque on link 2 and the actuator torque for joint 2:

$$^1f_{1,2} = {}^1\mathbf{Rot}_2\,{}^2f_{2,3} = \begin{bmatrix} C_2 & -S_2 & 0 \\ S_2 & C_2 & 0 \\ 0 & 0 & 1 \end{bmatrix} \begin{bmatrix} f_x \\ f_y \\ 0 \end{bmatrix} = \begin{bmatrix} f_xC_2 - f_yS_2 \\ f_xS_2 + f_yC_2 \\ 0 \end{bmatrix} \quad (6.63)$$

$$^1\tau_{1,2} = {}^1\mathbf{Rot}_2\,{}^2\tau_{2,3} + {}^1p_2 \times {}^1f_{1,2} = \begin{bmatrix} l_2C_2 \\ l_2S_2 \\ 0 \end{bmatrix} \times \begin{bmatrix} f_xC_2 - f_yS_2 \\ f_xS_2 + f_yC_2 \\ 0 \end{bmatrix} = \begin{bmatrix} 0 \\ 0 \\ l_2f_y \end{bmatrix} (6.64)$$

$$^1\tau_{act2} = {}^1\tau_{1,2}^T \cdot {}^1z_1 = l_2f_y \quad (6.65)$$

Next, we calculate the force and torque on link 1 and the actuator torque for joint 1:

$$^0f_{0,1} = {}^0\mathbf{Rot}_1\,{}^1f_{1,2} = \begin{bmatrix} C_1 & -S_1 & 0 \\ S_1 & C_1 & 0 \\ 0 & 0 & 1 \end{bmatrix} \begin{bmatrix} f_xC_2 - f_yS_2 \\ f_xS_2 + f_yC_2 \\ 0 \end{bmatrix} = \begin{bmatrix} f_xC_{12} - f_yS_{12} \\ f_xS_{12} + f_yC_{12} \\ 0 \end{bmatrix} (6.66)$$

$$^0\tau_{0,1} = {}^0\mathbf{Rot}_1\,{}^1\tau_{1,2} + {}^0p_1 \times {}^0f_{0,1}$$

$$= \begin{bmatrix} C_1 & -S_1 & 0 \\ S_1 & C_1 & 0 \\ 0 & 0 & 1 \end{bmatrix} \begin{bmatrix} 0 \\ 0 \\ l_2f_y \end{bmatrix} + \begin{bmatrix} l_1C_1 \\ l_1S_1 \\ 0 \end{bmatrix} \times \begin{bmatrix} f_xC_{12} - f_yS_{12} \\ f_xS_{12} + f_yC_{12} \\ 0 \end{bmatrix}$$

$$= \begin{bmatrix} 0 \\ 0 \\ l_2f_y \end{bmatrix} + \begin{bmatrix} 0 \\ 0 \\ l_1C_2f_y + l_1S_2f_x \end{bmatrix} = \begin{bmatrix} 0 \\ 0 \\ l_1C_2f_y + l_1S_2f_x + l_2f_y \end{bmatrix} \quad (6.67)$$

$$^0\tau_{act1} = {}^0\tau_{0,1}^T \cdot {}^0z_0 = l_1C_2f_y + l_1S_2f_x + l_2f_y \quad (6.68)$$

The equations for actuator torque (Equations 6.65, 6.68) can be rewritten to obtain a transformation from Cartesian force space to joint torque space for this manipulator. An important observation is that this transformation matrix (Equation 6.69) is the transpose of the Jacobian with respect to the end effector frame (Equation 5.97).

$$\begin{bmatrix} ^0\tau_{joint1} \\ ^1\tau_{joint2} \end{bmatrix} = \begin{bmatrix} l_1S_2 & l_1C_2 + l_2 \\ 0 & l_2 \end{bmatrix} \begin{bmatrix} f_x \\ f_y \end{bmatrix} = {}^3\mathbf{J}^T\,{}^2f_{2,3} \quad (6.69)$$

6.4.6 Force transformation

In the above example, we saw that the transformation from Cartesian force space to joint torque space for the type 1 two-link manipulator is the same as the transpose of the velocity Jacobian. In this section, we prove that the force transformation between any two coordinate frames is the same as the transpose of the Jacobian for those two coordinate frames.

When force is applied to a mechanism, work is done if the mechanism moves by a small amount. In statics, where the allowable displacement is infinitesimally small, there is the concept of virtual work; a mechanical variant of small signal analysis. Work is measured in units of energy, and is invariant with respect to multiple coordinate frames. When a manipulator is loaded, the end effector moves slightly in Cartesian space, and a corresponding motion occurs at the joints in joint space. Thus, the work done in Cartesian space is identical to the work done in joint space. This is not two different types of work, but two descriptions of the same work. The work done when moving an object is the product of the applied force and the distance moved, which for multi-dimensional systems is the dot product of the force vector and the displacement vector.

$$\text{Virtual work} = f \cdot \delta p \text{ in Cartesian space, and}$$

$$= \tau \cdot \delta\theta \text{ in joint space.} \qquad (6.70)$$

where

f is a force vector in cartesian space $= [f_x f_y f_z \tau_x \tau_y \tau_z]^T$

δp is a differential position vector in Cartesian space,

τ is a force vector in joint space – joint torques for revolute joints and joint forces for prismatic joints, and

$\delta\theta$ is a differential position vector in joint space, that is, differential changes in the joint variables.

As the dot product of two vectors is the same as the product of the transpose of the first vector with the second vector, Equation 6.70 can be rewritten as:

$$\text{Virtual work} = f^T \delta p = \tau^T \delta\theta \qquad (6.71)$$

In Section 5.5, a Jacobian was defined as:

$$\delta p = \mathbf{J}\delta\theta \qquad (6.72)$$

So substituting Equation 6.72 into Equation 6.71 gives:

$$f^T \mathbf{J}\delta\theta = \tau^T \delta\theta \qquad (6.73)$$

As this relationship must hold for any virtual displacement, the following relationship holds between Cartesian space forces and joint space torques.

$$f^\mathsf{T}\mathbf{J} = \tau^\mathsf{T} \qquad\qquad (6.74)$$

or, after transposing both sides:

$$\tau = \mathbf{J}^\mathsf{T}f \qquad\qquad (6.75)$$

This equation verifies that the result for the type 1 two-link manipulator is a particular case of a general relationship. While we have developed a transformation from Cartesian space to joint space, it is simple to show that this relationship can be used to transform a force vector from one coordinate frame to another. In the above example, we started with a Cartesian force defined with respect to the end effector coordinate frame and obtained a Jacobian with respect to the end effector coordinates. However, if the force is defined in the frame of the base of the robot, the Jacobian is defined with respect to the same frame, and the above equation holds. This equation has the interesting quality of performing an inverse transformation from Cartesian space to joint space, without inverting a transformation matrix.

This relationship can be extended to include the joint forces or torques required to balance the gravitational forces due to the mass of the links. If τ_m is the vector of joint torques due to gravity, Equation 6.71 can be rewritten as:

$$\text{Virtual work} = \tau^\mathsf{T}\delta p = (\tau - \tau_m)^\mathsf{T}\delta\theta \qquad\qquad (6.76)$$

and, following the same analysis as above the transform is:

$$\tau - \tau_m = \mathbf{J}^\mathsf{T}f \qquad\qquad (6.77)$$

The negative sign for the torques due to gravitational forces indicates that the forces due to the mass of the link are in the negative z direction with respect to world coordinates. When the robot lifts an object, it has to lift the links as well, but when the robot applies a downward force to an object, the gravitational forces increase the applied force and the sign should be positive.

6.4.7 Singularities in the force domain

In Section 5.6, we saw that, matrix inversion becomes ill-conditioned near a singularity. As a result it may be physically impossible for the manipulator to move its gripper in some Cartesian directions near a singular position. As the Jacobian is also used in the force domain, singularities cause problems for force control as well. However, the transpose of the Jacobian is used in the inverse force transform (Equation 6.75) and not the inverse Jacobian as in the inverse velocity transform (Equation 5.92). The inverse Jacobian is used in the forward force transform. The forward force transform is obtained are by premultiplying both sides of Equation 6.75 by the inverse of the transpose of the Jacobian.

$$f = (\mathbf{J}^{-1})^{\mathrm{T}} \tau \tag{6.78}$$

Near a singular position, the applied force in the singular directions can vary greatly with no effect on the torque. For example, if the type two-link manipulator is fully extended to the outer limit of its workspace (θ_2 is zero – see Figure 4.6), a force vector in the x_2 direction passes through the axes of both joints, and there is no applied torque. Also, when the manipulator is in this configuration, the joint actuators cannot produce a force in the x_2 direction. However, in the y_2 direction, the manipulator can generate large forces, with small actuator torques, because of the increased mechanical advantage of this configuration in the y_2 direction.

6.4.8 Calculating mass from joint torques

When a stationary manipulator is holding an object in space, the force applied to the end effector is the force of gravity due to the mass of the object. This force acts in the $-z$ direction with respect to the world coordinate frame. If a force sensor is mounted in the wrist, the forces can be measured with respect to the coordinate frame of the sensor, and transformed to another frame, such as the world frame, for analysis. Under these conditions, the force in the $-z$ direction with respect to world coordinates is the force due to gravity. This force is the sum of the gravitational forces due to the mass of the object and the mass of the gripper.

If we do not have a force sensor, we may be able to measure the torque at the actuators. The torque supplied by a direct-current electric motor is proportional to the armature current (Equation 2.3), and can be calculated from a measurement of the current. Once we have obtained the torques in joint space, they can be transformed to forces in Cartesian space, and the force due to gravity calculated. This force is the sum of the mass of the object and the masses of the manipulator links.

The force due to the mass of the object can be separated from the other forces if the measurements are made twice: first with an empty gripper, and second with the manipulator holding the object. In the first instance, the sensors measure the static forces on an unloaded manipulator due to the masses of the links. The force due to the mass of the object is calculated by subtracting these link forces from the second measurement. In theory, this measurement should be configuration independent, because we have assumed that the gravitational force vector acts through the centre of gravity. In practice, the mass distribution with in a link is not uniform, and the link torques vary with configuration. Making both measurements with the same manipulator configuration should minimize this problem.

In practice, there are simpler ways to measure the mass of an object. However, the technique described above is used to calibrate force and torque sensors by lifting objects with known masses. Several objects each with a different mass are lifted and the reaction torques are measured and plotted to obtain a mass/torque curve for each joint. As part of the calibration procedure, the static torques for an unloaded manipulator are measured in a variety of configurations to determine the variation in the link torques with manipulator configuration. All this assumes that the forces produced by loading the manipulator are significantly greater than the torque required to overcome the static friction of the drive mechanisms.

Once the torque sensors are calibrated, they can be used to measure the mass of the object. As the mass of the object affects the dynamic response of the manipulator, such measurements are required when the control system compensates for manipulator dynamics. Paul (1981) discusses the measurement of object mass while moving the joints at constant velocity, for use in setting the gains of the control loops.

6.4.9 Implications for robot design

The preceding analysis of static forces should be carried out when selecting a manipulator for an application, to ensure that the manipulator is powerful enough to lift the objects in the desired task configurations. Usually, the robot manufacturer specifies the lift capacity of the manipulator at full extension (see Figure 2.27). This value is obtained both by calculation during design and by measurement of the actual robot. When designing a robot, the designer should consider the following factors. First, friction in the actuators, gear boxes, and transmissions, which was not considered in the above analysis, must be taken into account. Also, if these constitute a large percentage of the load on the actuator, most of the energy of the actuator will be expended in frictional losses and in overcoming link gravitational forces, leaving little energy for moving external loads. High frictional loading minimizes the effect of external forces, and reduces the need to control manipulator dynamics, but it increases the response time and reduces the lifting capacity of the manipulator.

Second, a significant portion of the torque applied to a revolute joint is used to balance the mass of the link. For the joint about which the link rotates, this torsional load can be reduced by balancing the mass of the link around the axis to place the centre of gravity of the link as close as possible to the joint axis. For this reason, the actuator for the next joint in the kinematic chain is often placed in the current link on the side of the current joint away from the next joint, so that the mass of the actuator tends to balance the mass of the succeeding links (Figure 6.19).

Figure 6.19
Balancing the mass of a link around a joint axis to reduce the gravitational torque.

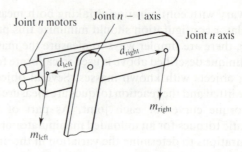

$$\tau_{\text{gravity}} = d_{\text{left}} \, m_{\text{left}} - d_{\text{right}} \, m_{\text{right}} = 0 \text{ (when centre of gravity coincides with joint axis)}$$

Third, the actuators and other heavy components are placed as close to the base of the robot as possible, to reduce both the inertia of the links, and the torsional loading placed on the actuators of the links close to the base. Typically, the shoulder joint of an articulated manipulator has to support the mass of the upper arm, the forearm, the wrist, the gripper, and the payload, where as the wrist joints only have to support the gripper and the payload. If the weight of the links can be reduced, the torques required for static balance and in overcoming inertia are reduced, and consequently, smaller actuators can be used, which further reduces the mass of the links the actuators are housed in.

Fourth, the lighter the material the links are constructed from, the lighter the load on the actuators. A second criterion in material selection is stiffness, as the resonant frequency of a link is a function of both the mass and the stiffness of the link. A light stiff structure is desirable to keep the resonant frequency high, and hence, to increase the velocity and acceleration of the manipulator at which non-linear dynamic effects occur due to resonance.

6.5 Programming

In the sections on programming in previous chapters, we attempted to look at concepts of robot programming in isolation. With force, this is not easy to do, not because the problems are peculiar to statics, but rather that they have been ignored in previous chapters. The programming of force is usually discussed in terms of force control. However, we look at programming issues here because a large section of this chapter is devoted to modelling the force, position, and velocity constraints of tasks, from which formalized strategies for control are developed.

As our models cannot work in isolation, real world data must be measured to validate them, and to use them in control schemes. Here, we are faced with the major difference between robot programming languages and other programming languages. Robots must monitor conditions in their environment and respond to changes in those conditions in real time. To achieve the required level of perception, robot languages include facilities for sensor integration. First, they must access measured data directly using variables defined in the language, variables which are bound to specific sensor signals. Second, they must specify the reference frame in which the values of the signals are defined. For example, force may be defined with respect to the gripper frame or the base frame. One way of doing this is to define force with respect to a force frame, which we then equate to the gripper frame or the base frame. If the force is not measured with respect to the equated frame, the language construct must perform the required transformations automatically.

To facilitate sensor integration, the programming language must include language constructs that enable the control of actuators based on feedback from sensors, that enable algorithms to terminate when task goals are achieved, that enable the flow of control of the program to change in response to sensed conditions, and that enable the robot to adapt to changing conditions in the environment by altering trajectories during motions. In this chapter, we defined control strategies in terms of artificial constraints. These constraints require the control of force, position, and velocity in accordance with constraint equations. Also, we saw the need for guarded commands with guards based on sensor signals both to detect the completion of an operation, and to protect objects from damage. Typical language constructs facilitate the following actions:

- **On** these force conditions **do** this action,
- **If** these force conditions exist **then** perform this action,
- **While** these force conditions exist **perform** this action,
- **Repeat** this action **until** the following force conditions occur,
- **Move** along this path **until** this location is reached **or** these force conditions exist,
- **Move** along this path **with** the following force conditions along these axes,
- **If** this force is exceeded during this motion **then** abort the motion, and
- **If** this interrupt (state) occurs during this motion **then** react with this response.

Individually, many of these constructs exist in normal programming languages, but the ability to combine several of them into one program construct is a special requirement of robot programming languages. For example, the task of inserting a peg into a hole requires the control of position along several axes, with force guards on those axes; the control of force along other axes, with position guards on those axes; the detection of task completions and error conditions such as jamming and wedging; and the initiation of appropriate recovery actions. These requirements introduce the whole area of parallelism in the language, parallelism that must occur in real time. This parallelism is a dual parallelism which operates at two levels. At one level there is the parallel operation of the linkages within the robot, and at another level there is the parallel operation of the robot and other equipment in its environment, such as sensors, conveyors, and other robots.

No new data structures are required to perform the calculations in this chapter, but extensive use is made of the existing data structures. Four vectors are required: point vectors for force and torque, a Cartesian force vector, and a joint torque vector. Compliance frames, natural constraint frames, task constraint frames, and artificial constraint frames are all variables of type six degree of freedom transforms. The equations defining these constraints are stored in symbolic form as lists of tokens, as are the equations which define C-surfaces. Elements are added to the robot data structure to store force vectors. A constraint data structure is required for each task, but, as this is task dependent it cannot be completely specified, although it does include the constraint frames and equations. Several additional procedures can be added to our transformation library to implement the peg in the hole equations and the force balance algorithms discussed in the text.

Key points

- **Statics** concerns the equilibrium of bodies under the action of forces.
- **Compliance** is the tendency of reaction forces to distort a body.
- The centre of compliance is the point at which an applied force will produce pure translation in the direction of the force, and a pure moment applied about a line through the point will produce pure rotation about the line.
- A compliance frame is an orthogonal coordinate system whose axes specify task freedoms for compliant motion, and whose origin is at the centre of compliance.
- The location of the compliance frame and the motion constraints are determined from the physics of the task.
- Problems caused by the end effector frame and the compliance frame following different trajectories are overcome with a model of the kinematics of the task.
- The following information specifies complaint motion:
  - the location of the compliance frame,
  - the degrees of motion which are free and the degrees of motion which are constrained,
  - the degrees which are position controlled and the degrees which are force controlled,
  - the position, orientation, force and torque goals of the planned motion, and
  - a model of the kinematics of the task.

- Configuration space is an *n* dimensional rectangular coordinate space where each axis represents a degree of motion freedom
- Surfaces in configuration space represent task configurations which allow partial motion freedom.
- Force is controlled along C-surface normals in opposition to motion constraints, and position along C-surface tangents in opposition to motion freedoms.
- Unilateral constraints prevent motion in one direction only, and usually require a force guard on the motion freedom.
- When inserting a peg into a hole, the mating event proceeds through the following stages: approach, chamfer crossing, one point contact, and two-point contact.
- During two-point contact a peg can become jammed or wedged in the hole.
- Jamming occurs when the forces and torques applied to the peg are in the wrong proportions.
- Wedging occurs when the two contact forces are within their friction cones and act along the same line.
- A remote-centre-compliance device uses a network of springs to produce passive compliance to correct for minor errors in peg location.
- the force balance on link *n* is

$$^R f_n = {}^R f_{n-1,n} - {}^R f_{n,n+1} + m_n {}^R g = 0 \text{ for static balance} \tag{6.44}$$

- The torque balance at a revolute joint is

$$^R \tau_{n-1,n} = {}^R \tau_{n,n+1} + {}^R p_{n-1,n} \times {}^R f_{n,n+1} + {}^R c_{n-1,n} \times m_n {}^R g \tag{6.47}$$

- Force and torque can be transferred from one frame to another

$$^{n-1} f_{n-1,n} = {}^{n-1}\mathbf{Rot}_n {}^n f_{n,n+1} \tag{6.57}$$

$$^{n-1} \tau_{n-1,n} = {}^{n-1}\mathbf{Rot}_n {}^n \tau_{n,n+1} + {}^{n-1} p_{n-1,n} \times {}^{n-1} f_{n-1,n} \tag{6.59}$$

- Joint space torque is transformed to Cartesian space force using the Jacobian

$$f = (\mathbf{J}^{-1})^T \tag{6.78}$$

Examples

Example 6.1   Multiple robot interaction

In this example, we develop a set of artificial constraints for the interaction
of two manipulators holding the same object from the natural and geometric

constraints (Mason, 1981). The manipulators are planar manipulators, both rigidly grasping the object, one at A and the other at B (Figure 6.20). Consequently, the problem is confined to three degrees of freedom translation in the x and y directions, and rotation around the z axis.

First, we formulate a control strategy using the notion of orthogonal complement. A C surface in six-dimensional space can be decomposed into a set of orthogonal-complementary subspaces where their direct sum is the original six-dimensional space, and they are mutually orthogonal. The control of two manipulators can be coordinated by choosing artificial constraints so that, together with the natural constraints, they form an orthogonal-complementary set.

If we examine the task from the perspective of manipulator A, and assume that the object imposes no natural velocity constraints, the subspace spanned by the three axes (x, y, and **Rot** z) is the subspace of all possible velocities. As there are no natural constraints, the artificial constraints on gripper A can be chosen to be three velocity constraints. Now, the set of natural velocity constraints for gripper B is the set of natural constraints of the object plus the artificial constraints of gripper A. Consequently, the artificial constraints of gripper B are the three force constraints. Hence, manipulator A is velocity controlled and manipulator B is force controlled.

If we choose one artificial velocity constraint and two force constraints for A, then the artificial constraints of B are one force constraint, and two velocity constraints. The subspaces are made orthogonally complementary by ensuring that if a degree of freedom has a velocity constraint for one manipulator, it has a force constraint for the other and vice versa. Any mixture of constraints is possible, and all choices produce asymmetry in the behaviour of the manipulators, with the final choice determined by other task constraints.

Second, we will formulate a control strategy that is symmetric with respect to the roles of the two manipulators. As the grippers are rigidly attached to each other through the object, the following natural velocity constraints occur assuming that rotation is produced by the difference between the y components of end effector velocities.

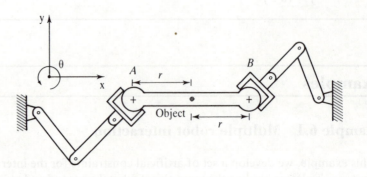

Figure 6.20
Two planar grippers grasping an object.

$$v_{Ax} = v_{Ox} = v_{Bx} \quad \text{and} \quad \omega_{Az} = \omega_{Oz} = \omega_{Bz} \tag{6.79}$$

$$v_{Oy} = \frac{v_{Ay} + v_{By}}{2} \quad \text{and} \quad \omega_{Oz} = \frac{v_{By} - v_{Ay}}{2\rho} \tag{6.80}$$

where

O is the object, and
ρ is the instantaneous radius of rotation.

When the only forces acting on grippers A and B are the contact forces, then by a static balance of forces and torques, the following natural force constraints apply:

$$f_{Ax} + f_{Bx} = f_{Ox} \quad \text{and} \quad f_{Ay} + f_{By} = f_{Oy} \tag{6.81}$$

$$\tau_{Az} + \tau_{Bz} + \rho(f_{By} - f_{Ay}) = \tau_{Oz} \tag{6.82}$$

Using the above equations, we can transform the velocity and force of the object to the velocity and force of the gripper pair. The above natural constraints assume total freedom of motion of the object. However, more natural constraints can be introduced by applying task constraints to the motion of the object. For example, if the object is pinned at the centre so that only rotations are possible, the additional natural constraints due to the geometry of the task constraints are:

$$v_{Ox} = 0 \quad v_{Oy} = 0 \quad \text{and} \quad \tau_{Oz} = 0 \tag{6.83}$$

Using the equations for the natural constraints for an unconstrained object to transform these task constraints into natural constraints for the gripper pair, gives the following natural constraints:

$$v_{Ax} = 0 \quad \frac{v_{Ay} + v_{By}}{2} = 0 \quad \text{and} \quad \tau_{Az} + \tau_{Bz} + \rho(f_{By} - f_{Ay}) = 0 \tag{6.84}$$

and the corresponding artificial constraints are:

$$f_{Ax} = 0 \quad \frac{f_{Ay} + f_{By}}{2} = 0 \quad \text{and} \quad (v_{By} - v_{Ay})\rho + \omega_{Az} + \omega_{Bz} = k \tag{6.85}$$

where

k is a constant determined by the goal trajectory, and
in the pinned case $\rho = r$.

In addition, the task has three artificial constraints which are independent of the external constraints on the object. Again, these are derived by transformation of the free space constraints on the object to constraints on the gripper pair.

$$f_{Ax} - f_{Bx} = 0 \quad \tau_{Az} - \tau_{Bz} = 0 \quad \text{and} \quad \rho(f_{By} - f_{Ay}) - \tau_{Oz} = 0 \qquad (6.86)$$

These constraints prevent compression or torsion of the object and prevent force being applied to the pin in the xy plane. They also provide for compliant rotation about the pin. Just as important, they prevent the manipulators entering into a tug of war, or pushing against each other, or flying away in one direction, all of which could cause serious damage, as well as failure to accomplish the task.

Example 6.2 Static balance in a type 3 two-link manipulator

In this example, we analyse the static force balance for the type 3 two-link manipulator (Figure 4.8). The required rotation transforms and translation vectors are obtained from the **A** matrices for this manipulator (Equation 4.9). A force $^2f_3$ is applied to the end effector (acting at the origin of coordinate frame 2). By examining the physical structure of this manipulator, we can make some intuitive comments about the components of the force vector. The component in the x_2 direction is balanced by joint 1 actuator torque, the component in the z_2 direction is balanced by joint 2 actuator force, and the component in the y_2 direction is balanced by the structure. The following analysis validates these comments. Consequently, the gravitational force due to the mass of an object held by the end effector is balanced by the structure, and not by an actuator.

$$^2f_{2,3} = \begin{bmatrix} f_x \\ f_y \\ f_z \end{bmatrix} \qquad ^2\tau_{2,3} = 0 \qquad (6.87)$$

Next, we calculate the force and torque on link 2, and the actuator force for joint 2:

$$^1f_{1,2} = {}^1\text{Rot}_2\, {}^2f_{2,3} = \begin{bmatrix} 1 & 0 & 0 & 0 \\ 0 & 1 & 0 & 0 \\ 0 & 0 & 1 & 0 \\ 0 & 0 & 0 & 1 \end{bmatrix} \begin{bmatrix} f_x \\ f_y \\ f_z \\ 0 \end{bmatrix} = \begin{bmatrix} f_x \\ f_y \\ f_z \\ 0 \end{bmatrix} \qquad (6.88)$$

$$^1\tau_{1,2} = {}^1\mathbf{Rot}_2\,{}^2\tau_{2,3} + {}^1p_2 \mathbf{x}\,{}^1f_{1,2} = \begin{bmatrix} 0 \\ 0 \\ d_2 \end{bmatrix} \mathbf{x} \begin{bmatrix} f_x \\ f_y \\ f_z \end{bmatrix} = \begin{bmatrix} -d_2 f_y \\ d_2 f_x \\ 0 \end{bmatrix} \tag{6.89}$$

$$^1f_{\text{act2}} = {}^1f_{1,2} \cdot {}^1z_1 = f_z \tag{6.90}$$

Next, we calculate the force and torque on link 1, and the actuator torque for joint 1:

$$^0f_{0,1} = {}^0\mathbf{Rot}_1\,{}^1f_{1,2} = \begin{bmatrix} C_1 & 0 & S_1 \\ S_1 & 0 & -C_1 \\ 0 & 1 & 0 \end{bmatrix} \begin{bmatrix} f_x \\ f_y \\ f_z \end{bmatrix} = \begin{bmatrix} f_x C_1 + f_z S_1 \\ f_x S_1 - f_z C_1 \\ f_y \end{bmatrix} \tag{6.91}$$

$$^0\tau_{0,1} = {}^0\mathbf{Rot}_1\,{}^1\tau_{1,2} + {}^0p_1 \mathbf{x}\,{}^0f_{0,1}$$

$$= \begin{bmatrix} C_1 & 0 & S_1 \\ S_1 & 0 & -C_1 \\ 0 & 1 & 0 \end{bmatrix} \begin{bmatrix} -d_2 f_y \\ d_2 f_x \\ 0 \end{bmatrix} + \begin{bmatrix} 0 \\ 0 \\ d_1 \end{bmatrix} \mathbf{x} \begin{bmatrix} f_x C_1 + f_z S_1 \\ f_x S_1 - f_z C_1 \\ f_y \end{bmatrix}$$

$$= \begin{bmatrix} -d_1 f_x S_1 + d_1 f_z C_1 - d_2 C_1 f_y \\ d_1 f_x C_1 + d_1 f_z S_1 - d_2 S_1 f_y \\ d_2 f_x \end{bmatrix} \tag{6.92}$$

$$^0\tau_{\text{act1}} = {}^0\tau^T_{0,1} \cdot {}^0z_0 = d_2 f_x \tag{6.93}$$

Rewriting the equations for actuator torque in matrix form gives a transformation from Cartesian force space to joint torque space for this manipulator.

$$\begin{bmatrix} {}^0\tau_{\text{joint1}} \\ {}^0f_{\text{joint2}} \end{bmatrix} = \begin{bmatrix} d_2 & 0 & 0 \\ 0 & 0 & 1 \end{bmatrix} \begin{bmatrix} f_x \\ f_y \\ f_z \end{bmatrix} = {}^2\mathbf{J}^{T\,2}f_{2,3} \tag{6.94}$$

$$^2\mathbf{J} = \begin{bmatrix} d_2 & 0 \\ 0 & 0 \\ 0 & 1 \end{bmatrix} \text{ and } {}^0\mathbf{J} = {}^0\mathbf{Rot}_2\,{}^2\mathbf{J} = \begin{bmatrix} C_1 & 0 & S_1 \\ S_1 & 0 & -C_1 \\ 0 & 1 & 0 \end{bmatrix} \begin{bmatrix} d_2 & 0 & 0 \\ 0 & 0 & 0 \\ 0 & 1 & 0 \end{bmatrix}$$

$$= \begin{bmatrix} d_2 C_1 & 0 & S_1 \\ d_2 S_1 & 0 & -C_1 \\ 0 & 0 & 0 \end{bmatrix} \tag{6.95}$$

The above force transform can be validated by calculating the Jacobian by differentiation of the forward transform (Equation 4.9) with respect to the joint variables. This is left as an exercise for the reader.

Exercises

■ *Essay questions*

6.1. Define the following terms:

> statics,
> compliance,
> active compliance,
> static compliance,
> centre of compliance,
> compliance matrix,
> degrees of motion freedom.

6.2. Find the compliance frame for the following tasks:

   (a) writing on a flat surface with a sharp pencil,
   (b) writing on a sphere with a ball-point pen,
   (c) painting on a flat surface with a rectangular brush,
   (d) opening a drawer,
   (e) turning a screw with a screwdriver,
   (f) threading a needle,
   (g) turning a nut on a bolt with an open-ended spanner,
   (h) cutting cheese with a knife.

6.3. What five items of information are required to specify the compliant motion of an object?

6.4. From the compliance matrix for each of the examples in Exercise 6.2, determine which freedoms should be force controlled and which should be position controlled.

6.5. For the examples in Exercise 6.2, when the physics of the task changes, how does the compliance frame change, and hence, how should the control strategy change? For example, when lifting the pencil off the surface, or when the nut reaches the end of the thread.

6.6. In the examples in Exercise 6.2, do the trajectories of the compliance frame and the end effector frame coincide? If not, develop a mathematical model of the task and derive appropriate additional freedom constraints.

6.7. Determine the C-surfaces for each of the examples in Exercise 6.2. From these C surfaces, determine the natural constraints, and the artificial constraints, and from these develop a control strategy. Do these strategies match the strategies developed in Exercise 6.4?

6.8 Determine the ideal C surfaces for:

   (a) moving a bead on a wire,
   (b) drawing a finger across a table,

    (c) moving a two degree-of-freedom joystick,

    (d) pressing a key on a piano, and

    (e) rubbing a cylinder with a polishing cloth.

6.9.   For each task in Exercise 6.8, determine the tangent space and the velocity constraints.

6.10.   For each task in Exercise 6.8, develop a set of equations to describe the natural constraints and the artificial constraints.

6.11.   The task of moving a bead on a wire is modified by attaching a spring to the bead. What changes must be made to the control strategy?

6.12.   Describe the four stages of inserting a peg in a hole.

6.13.   Define the terms

        chamfer crossing,
        two-point contact,
        wedging,
        jamming.

6.14.   A 10mm diameter peg is to be inserted into a 10.02mm diameter hole, with a 0.5mm wide, 45° chamfer. The spring constants are: $K_x=7\text{N/mm}$ and $K_\theta=53\,000N/\text{rad}$, and the coefficient of friction is 0.1. Using the equations in Section 6.3, for the following sets of conditions: $l_g=1\text{mm}$ and 50mm, initial lateral errors of 0.1mm and 0.5mm, and initial orientation errors of 0.1° and 1°, calculate the following:

    (a) the displacement and orientation of the peg during chamfer crossing,

    (b) the insertion depths at which two-point contact starts and ends.

    Is the insertion successful? If not, why not?

6.15.   Calculate the static balance for the types 2, 4, and 5 two-link manipulators. Verify these equations by comparing them to the Jacobian for these manipulators.

6.16.   Repeat Exercise 6.15 for the three-link manipulators in Figure 5.15.

6.17.   What implications does statics have for the design of robots?

6.18.   A 1kg mass is lifted by a 3-link planar manipulator to a position where the joint angles are 60°, −60°, and 30° degrees. The lengths of the links are 200, 120, and 50mm. Calculate the joint torques due to this load.

■   *Practical questions*

6.1.   Write a program to perform the calculations which model the process of inserting a peg in a hole.

6.2. Program your lab robot to perform the task of drawing a thin rod across the edge of a table.

6.3. Model the static equilibrium for your lab robot.

6.4. Pick up a known mass with your lab robot, and measure the joint torques. Also, measure these torques for the robot in the same configuration, but without a load. Compare the measured values to your model.

6.5. If your lab robot has a wrist force sensor, repeat Practical question 6.4, and obtain the force transformations between the sensor and the joint torques.

6.6. Write a program to implement Algorithm 6.1.

6.7. Examine several robot languages, and compare their features for sensor integration.

7 · *Dynamics*

'Since one of the goals in robotics is to make manipulators move as fast as possible, it can be expected that dynamics will become increasingly important for the lightweight stronger manipulators of the future.'

John Hollerbach (in Brady et al., 1982)

Objectives

In this chapter, we combine the motion and force models developed in previous chapters. Our objective is to model the complete non-linear dynamics of a manipulator, so that we can control it to follow a rapidly varying trajectory with minimum error. As the mathematics is extremely complex, we restrict our analysis to two-link manipulators. The analysis of dynamics includes the following topics:

- virtual work and D'Alembert force,
- Newton—Euler formulation of dynamics,
- Lagrange formulation of dynamics,
- closed form and recursive algorithms, and
- parameter estimation for dynamics models.

347

Dynamics concerns the motion of bodies. This includes **kinematics**, which is the study of the motion of bodies without reference to the forces* that cause the motion (Chapters 4 and 5), and **kinetics**, which relates these forces to the resulting motions. When a force is applied to a body, it tends to accelerate in accordance with Newton's laws (Window 6.1). Thus, dynamics is the branch of mechanics which deals with the motion of bodies under the action of forces. On the basis of this definition, the dynamic behaviour of a robot is described in terms of the time rate of change of the arm configuration in relation to the torques exerted by its actuators.

To control the motion of a set of linkages so that the end effector traces a desired trajectory the control system has to produce torques at the joints to balance the forces on the links. When a link is accelerated, the actuator must provide torque to overcome inertia. If the robot uses pure feedback control of position or velocity, the dynamics of the system will cause the end effector to lag behind the desired trajectory during acceleration, and possibly to overshoot the end point of the trajectory (see Section 9.3.3.2). With a feedback control system, an error in trajectory following is required before the controller will call for more torque to overcome inertia. To minimize this sort of error, most industrial robots operate at reduced speed.

The problem of **inverse dynamics** is: given a vector of joint positions, velocities, and accelerations, calculate the required vector of joint torques. If the inverse dynamics is modelled accurately, the controller can predict the additional torque required to follow a trajectory during acceleration and deceleration and can use feedforward control to overcome the errors in trajectory following (Section 11.5). With such a controller, the robot can increase the velocity of its end effector and, hence, reduce the time to perform a task. A second problem, of importance in simulation studies of manipulators, is the problem of **forward dynamics**: given a vector of applied joint torques, calculate the resultant manipulator motions.

An actuator has to balance torques from four sources: dynamic torques, which arise from motion; static torques, which arise from friction in the mechanism; gravity torques, which arise from the force of gravity acting on the link; and external forces and torques acting on the end effector, which arise from the task. Three types of **dynamics torques** arise from the motion of the manipulator: inertial, centripetal, and Coriolis torques. **Inertial torques** are proportional to joint acceleration in accordance with Newton's second law. Inertia is the property of matter causing resistance to change in motion, and mass is the quantitative measure of inertia (Window 7.1). **Centripetal torques** arise from the centripetal forces which constrain a body to rotate about a point. They are directed towards the centre of the uniform

---

* In this section, we use the word *force* to mean a vector of forces and torques in Cartesian space and *torque* to mean a vector of forces and torques in joint space, unless indicated otherwise in the text.

circular motion, and are proportional to the square of the joint velocity. **Coriolis torques** arise from vortical forces derived from the interaction of two rotating links. They are similar to the forces that cause whirlpools, and are proportional to the product of the joint velocities of those links.

We can formulate the basic laws of dynamics from first principles in several ways, including Newton's laws together with the concept of virtual work, D'Alembert's principle, Lagrange's equations, Hamilton's equations, and Hamilton's principle. All these formulations are equivalent, and they can all be derived from Newton's laws and the principle of virtual work. In robotics, the two common formulations of dynamics are derived from the Newton–Euler equations and Lagrange's equations. In this chapter, we examine both these formulations of dynamics, together with their application to robots, and methods of solving the resulting equations. In forward dynamics, *n* second order, coupled, nonlinear differential equations describe the dynamics of an *n* link manipulator, equations which are difficult to solve analytically. Many topics in dynamics are beyond the scope of this book, but as in previous chapters, the principles upon which robot dynamics based are covered in detail.

We can express the equations describing the dynamics of a robot in several forms, depending on the chosen method of solution. With each method, the equations have to be solved for every point along the trajectory. Common forms of the equations are iterative, closed, and recursive. With iterative form equations, general equations for the dynamics of a robot are solved numerically. This method of solution is slow because the iteration may take a while to converge. To obtain **closed form** equations, the general equations of dynamics are solved for a particular robot to produce a set of analytical expressions for that robot. Thus, the dependence of joint torques on movements of all joints is made explicit, and, as the calculations are noniterative, they are faster. Closed form equations are preferred to iterative form equations because a solution is guaranteed.

However, because we are dealing with a serial link manipulator, when a force is applied to one link it may produce motion in several links. This interaction between links results in closed form solutions that include considerable duplication of calculation. If the closed form expressions can be expressed in a **recursive form**, this duplication of calculation can be avoided, and hence, the calculation can be made more efficient. Recursive algorithms have been developed for both the Newton–Euler and the Lagrangian formulations of dynamics. They are efficient enough for inverse dynamics to be calculated in real time with an array processor.

7.1 Virtual work and the D'Alembert force

In the development of analytical dynamics, virtual displacements and virtual work play a very important part, but, once the formulations are developed,

Window 7.1 Inertia

Inertia is the tendency of a body to remain in a state of rest or uniform motion. From Newton's first law, we see that an external force is required to change that state. The reference frame in which the state is measured is called the inertial reference frame (i.e. a frame at rest or moving with constant velocity with respect to the fixed stars).

- *Inertial forces* are introduced when classical mechanics are applied to a noninertial frame (a frame that is accelerating with respect to an inertial frame such as a rotating frame). Usually the reference frame is set up as an inertial frame, and the frame attached to an object is a noninertial frame. These are forces, which cannot be associated to a body, but are due to the motion of the noninertial frame with respect to an inertial frame. If the two frames coincide, the inertial force is zero.

- *Inertial mass* is the mass which opposes a force as it accelerates a body when no gravity or friction applies – the mass in the formula for Newton's second law ($f = ma$). This occurs for example, when the mass of a body is accelerating on a frictionless horizontal surface. When a body accelerates due to the force of gravity, the mass in Newton's second law is the gravitational mass.

- *Moment of inertia* is the rotational inertia of a body with respect to an axis of rotation. It depends upon the particular axis about which the body is rotating, the shape of the body, and the manner in which mass is distributed. The rotational inertia is the sum of the product of the masses of the particles which make up the body and the squares of their distances from the axis of rotation.

$$\mathbf{I} = \sum_1^i m_i r_i^2$$

where

m_i is the mass of particle i, and

r_i is the distance to particle i.

For a rigid body – that is, one not composed of discrete point masses, but rather a continuous distribution of matter – this summation becomes an integration over the whole body. If we consider the body to be subdivided into infinitesimal elements of mass dm, each at distance r from the axis of rotation, then the inertia is:

$$\mathbf{I} = \int r^2 \, dm$$

For bodies with irregular shape, the integral may be difficult to evaluate, but for bodies with a simple geometric shape, the integrals are relatively easy to evaluate when an axis of symmetry is the rotational axis. For example, to calculate the inertia of a cylinder, of length l and mass M, about its axis, we first consider it to be made of an infinite number of thin cylinders of thickness dr, at radius r, of mass dm, and volume dV. If the density of the material is ρ, then

$$dm = \rho \, dV = 2\pi l \rho r \, dr$$

where $dV = 2\pi r \, dr \, l$

and the rotational inertia about the axis of the cylinder is

$$\mathbf{I} = \int r^2 \, dm = 2\pi l \int \rho \, r^3 \, dr \text{ (integrated from } r_1, \text{ the inner radius of the cylinder, to } r_2, \text{ the outer radius)}$$

$$= 2\pi l \rho \frac{(r_2^4 - r_1^4)}{4} = \rho \, \pi (r_2^2 - r_1^2) l \frac{(r_2^2 + r_1^2)}{2} = M \frac{(r_1^2 + r_2^2)}{2}$$

- *Parallel axis theorem*. There is a simple and useful relation between the rotational inertia of a body about any axis ($\mathbf{I}$) and its rotational inertia about a parallel axis through the centre of mass ($\mathbf{I}_{cm}$), where h is the distance between the two axes.

$$\mathbf{I} = \mathbf{I}_{cm} + Mh^2$$

The inertias of several common shapes are shown in Figure 7.4.

---

they fade from the picture. In a full development of these concepts, we would develop the equations for a single particle first, and then generalize them for a system of particles. The object that we will consider is a system of particles with uniform mass distribution. The details of this development are covered in most introductory text books on dynamics (see, for example, Symon, 1963). Here, we are concerned with the results, and their implications for robotics.

Consider an object of mass m which is constrained to move in contact with a rough surface, which itself is moving with respect to inertial coordinates x, y, and z (Figure 7.1). The object moves along a definite path, and traces a line on the surface in response to a resultant force f (vector sum of applied force, frictional force, and force of constraint). During any interval of time dt, the object is displaced by a distance ds relative to the stationary inertial reference frame. This displacement ds is referred to as the **actual displacement**.

If the object moves by an arbitrary infinitesimal displacement δs in any direction, including against a constraint, then the virtual work δW done by the resultant force, where the object consists of p particles is:

$$\delta W = \sum_{1}^{p} (f_{xi}\delta x_i + f_{yi}\delta y_i + f_{zi}\delta z_i) \tag{7.1}$$

$$= \sum_{1}^{p} f_i \cdot \delta s$$

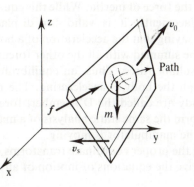

Figure 7.1
Object moving on a rough surface which itself is moving relative to an inertial frame (Window 7.1).

and for a solid object:

$$\delta W = f_x \delta x + f_y \delta y + f_z \delta_z \qquad (7.2)$$

If the surface is regarded as stationary by holding time fixed, work is done when the applied forces cause a displacement in any direction on the surface. But, it can be shown that the virtual displacement is in conformity with the constraints, and consequently the work done by the forces of constraint is zero, because they produce no displacement (Window 7.4). **Forces of constraint** are the forces that maintain certain fixed position relationships between objects in the system. In effect, forces of constraint (Section 6.2) have been eliminated from Equation 7.1. (For a detailed discussion of virtual work see Wells, 1967.) While frictional forces do work, which is dissipated as heat, they are not forces of constraint, but depend upon them.

Because the object is moving on a surface, it has two degrees of translational freedom and one degree of translational constraint. For simplicity, assume that no frictional force is acting. The resultant force acting on the object is the vector sum of all the forces which may be acting on the particle: applied force, spring force, gravitational force, and forces of constraint. For an object of mass m moving in an inertial frame, the Newtonian equations of motion are:

$$f_x = ma_x \qquad f_y = ma_y \qquad \text{and} \qquad f_z = ma_z \qquad (7.3)$$

If the object undergoes an arbitrary virtual displacement, the virtual work done by the resultant force is:

$$\delta W = f_x \delta x + f_y \delta y + f_z \delta z \qquad (7.4)$$

Combining Equations 7.3 and 7.4, gives D'Alembert's equation:

$$\delta W = f_x \delta x + f_y \delta y + f_z \delta z = m(a_x \delta x + a_y \delta y + a_z \delta_z) \qquad (7.5)$$

D'Alembert's equation includes statics as a special case of dynamics, through the use of the force of inertia. While this equation was derived using infinitesimal displacements, it is valid for displacements of any size. Physically, we are saying that the acceleration of a body generates a force of inertia which can be summed with all the other forces acting on the body to obtain a single resultant force. Thus, an equilibrium analysis can be performed even though the body is accelerating. The net forces and torques which act on a body are called the D'Alembert forces and torques. Using these, we can perform the same static analysis of a manipulator as in Section 6.4, even though the manipulator is moving.

By applying the proper coordinate transforms, and equations of constraint, we can derive the equations of motion of any system in any coordi-

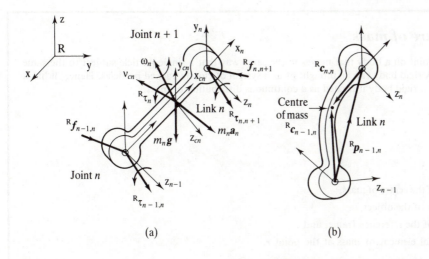

Figure 7.2
Dynamic force-torque
balance on a single link.
(a) Forces and moments;
(b) Vectors used in force
balance.

(a)   (b)

nate frame from D'Alembert's equation. Lagrange's equations (Section 7.3)
are merely a more convenient form of D'Alembert's equation. Also, the
D'Alembert force and torque on a link are related to the acceleration of the
link by the Newton–Euler equations.

7.2   Newton–Euler formulation

In order to move an end effector to perform a task, the control program
plans a trajectory by converting the desired hand movement into a time
sequence of joint motions. For this trajectory plan, it finds the net forces and
torques acting on each link using the Newton–Euler formulations. From
these, the control program formulates the required joint torques using the
static balance equations derived in Chapter 6. The Newton–Euler equations
relate forces and torques to the velocities and accelerations of the centroids
of the links by taking into account the masses, lengths, positions and inertias
of the links.

Consider an isolated link (link n) with forces and torques acting upon
it (Figure 7.2). A centroidal frame is placed at the centre of mass (Window
7.2), a frame which is fixed to the link and moves with respect to a stationary
(inertial) reference frame. The forces and torques acting on the link cause it
to move, in accordance with the following relations.

$$f_n = \frac{d\mathbf{P}_n}{dt} = \text{force applied to link } n \tag{7.6}$$

$$\tau_n = \frac{d\mathbf{L}_n}{dt} = \text{torque about the centroid of link } n \tag{7.7}$$

Window 7.2   Centre of mass

The **centre of mass** is the point on a body that moves in the same way that a single particle subject to the same external forces will move. A rigid body can be thought of as a system of closely packed particles. Hence, it has a centre of mass. In practice, a rigid body it treated as a continuous distribution of mass.

$$r_{cm} = \frac{1}{\mathbf{M}} \int r \, dm$$

where

r_{cm} is the location of the centre of mass,

$\mathbf{M}$ is the total mass of the object,

r is the location of the reference frame, and

dm is the differential element of mass at the point r.

If the origin of the reference frame is at the centre of mass then

$$r_{cm} = 0 \qquad \text{and} \qquad \int r \, dm = 0$$

Also, the first moment of mass of the system is

$$\int r \, dm = \sum_{1}^{i} m_i r_i$$

From the above equation, for homogeneous objects which have a point, a line, or a plane of symmetry, the centre of mass lies at the point, on the line, or in the plane of symmetry. For example, the centre of mass of a sphere is the centre of the sphere, the centre of mass of a cylinder lies on the axis of the cylinder.

Motion of the centre of mass

The centre of mass of a system of particles moves as though all the mass of the system is concentrated at the centre of mass and all the external forces are applied at that point. The motion of the centre of mass is the translational motion of the body because if the body is moving in pure translation every point will experience the same displacement as the centre of mass, and if the body is rotating, as it translates, the centre of mass experiences translation only.

Linear momentum

$$\mathbf{P} = mv$$

where

$\mathbf{P}$ is the linear momentum,

m is the mass, and

v is the velocity.

Thus, the total momentum of a body is equal to the product of the mass of the body and the velocity of its centre of mass. When a resultant force acts on a body, it produces a rate of change of momentum in accordance with Newton's second law.

$$f = \frac{d\mathbf{P}}{dt} = ma$$

where

$d\mathbf{P}$ is the rate of change of momentum,

f is the resultant force acting on the body, and

a is the acceleration.

Angular momentum

$$\mathbf{L} = r \times \mathbf{P}$$

$$= r \times mv$$

where

$\mathbf{L}$ is the angular momentum, and

r is the position relative to the origin of the inertial reference frame, and

$r \times v = \omega$, the angular velocity.

The time rate of change of the total angular momentum of a body about the origin of an inertial reference frame is equal to the resultant torque acting on the body.

$$\tau = \frac{d\mathbf{L}}{dt}$$

Also, if we measure the vectors with respect to the centre of mass, the equation for torque is correct. Thus, we can separate the general motion of a body into translational motion of its centre of mass and rotational motion around its centre of mass.

where the momenta of the link are a function of the velocities of the centroid.

$$\mathbf{P}_n = m_n {}^R v_n = \text{linear momentum of link } n \qquad (7.8)$$

$$\mathbf{L}_n = {}^C \mathbf{I}_n {}^R \omega_n = \text{angular momentum of link } n \qquad (7.9)$$

where

${}^R v_n$ is the linear velocity of the centroid with respect to the reference frame,

m_n is the mass of link n,

${}^R \omega_n$ is the angular velocity of link n, and

${}^C \mathbf{I}_n$ is the centroidal inertia tensor of link n with respect to the centroidal frame C.

The inertia tensor is a matrix containing the moments of inertia for rotations about the axes of the centroidal frame and their products (Window 7.3). It is the transform from angular velocity to angular momentum. The inertia tensor is fixed with respect to any frame that is fixed to the link, such as the centroidal frame, where it can be thought of as moving with the link. In contrast, the inertia tensor with respect to the stationary reference frame changes as the orientation of the link changes. To calculate the inertial torque at any instant, angular momentum is differentiated with respect to time (Equation 5.14).

$$\tau = \frac{dL_n}{dt} = \frac{d}{dt}(^C\mathbf{I}_n{}^R\omega_n) = {}^C\mathbf{I}_n{}^R\alpha_n + {}^R\omega_n \times (^C\mathbf{I}_n \cdot {}^R\omega_n) \tag{7.10}$$

where $^R\alpha_n$ is the angular acceleration of link n.

The resultant equation is the general form of Euler's equation of motion, and contains two terms. The first is the inertial torque due to angular acceleration, and the second is the gyroscopic torque resulting from changes in the inertia tensor as the orientation of the link changes. The inertia tensor at the centroid is used because the torque balance equation (Equation 7.17) balances torques around the centroid. Later (Section 7.2.3), it will be shown that, when the torque at the joint is calculated from the Newton–Euler equations, the inertia tensor is transformed from the centroidal axis to the joint axis.

In the case of a symmetrical link, the axes of the centroidal frame are parallel to the principal axes to the link. Euler's equations for the torque about the centroidal axes are:

$$\tau_x = {}^C\mathbf{I}_x{}^R\alpha_x + (^C\mathbf{I}_z - {}^C\mathbf{I}_y){}^R\omega_y{}^R\omega_z \tag{7.11}$$

$$\tau_y = {}^C\mathbf{I}_y{}^R\alpha_y + (^C\mathbf{I}_x - {}^C\mathbf{I}_z){}^R\omega_x{}^R\omega_z \tag{7.12}$$

$$\tau_z = {}^C\mathbf{I}_z{}^R\alpha_z + (^C\mathbf{I}_y - {}^C\mathbf{I}_x){}^R\omega_y{}^R\omega_x \tag{7.13}$$

Newton's equation (Equation 7.14) relates the linear acceleration of the centre of mass of the body to the d'Alembert force acting on the body, and Euler's equation (Equation 7.15) relates the angular velocity and acceleration to the net torque acting on the body. The net force acts through the centre of mass, and the net torque acts around an axis through the centre of mass.

$$^R f_n = m_n{}^R a_n \tag{7.14}$$

$$^R \tau_n = {}^C\mathbf{I}_n{}^R\alpha_n + {}^R\omega_n \times {}^C\mathbf{I}_n{}^R\omega_n \tag{7.15}$$

In Section 6.4.1, we developed the static balance for both force and torque on an isolated link. Here, we extend these static equations (Equations

Window 7.3   Inertia tensor

A rigid body, which is free to move in space has an infinite number of possible rotation axes. The **inertia tensor**, or inertia matrix **I**, is the analog, for general rotations, of the moment of inertia for rotation about a single axis. It is a way of characterizing the mass distribution of the body, as it rotates about an arbitrary axis.

Consider a rigid body moving in space, with coordinate axes x_1, y_1, z_1 located at its centre of mass. The angular velocity of the body ω is the angular velocity of the frame $O(x_1, y_1, z_1)$ with respect to the reference frame $R(x, y, z)$. The angular momentum of the body **H** about its centre of mass is the vector sum of the angular momenta of all the particles in the body. Note, by comparison, the linear momentum **P** of the body is the linear sum of the linear momenta of the particles. Hence, the angular momentum is:

$$\mathbf{H} = \int_0^i \mathbf{r}_i \, \mathbf{x} \, (\omega \, \mathbf{x} \, \mathbf{r}_i) \, dm$$

where

$\mathbf{r}_i$ is the distance to particle i from the origin of x_1, y_1, $z_1 = i x + j y + k z$

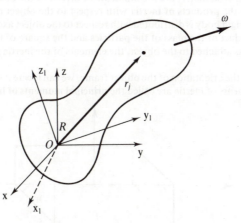

This equation also holds true if the body is rotating about a fixed point, which is not the centre of mass, and the origin of the object frame and the reference frame coincide, as in the above figure. For the rest of this discussion, we will use this second case. Next, we expand the integrand. Note that the components of angular velocity are invariant with respect to integrals over the body, and hence are treated as constants.

$$\mathbf{H} = \begin{bmatrix} \mathbf{H}_x \\ \mathbf{H}_y \\ \mathbf{H}_z \end{bmatrix} = \int \begin{bmatrix} y^2+z^2 & -xy & -xz \\ -yx & z^2+x^2 & -yz \\ -zx & -zy & x^2+y^2 \end{bmatrix} \begin{bmatrix} \omega_x \\ \omega_y \\ \omega_z \end{bmatrix} dm$$

$$= \begin{bmatrix} \mathbf{I}_{xx} & -\mathbf{I}_{xy} & -\mathbf{I}_{xz} \\ -\mathbf{I}_{yx} & \mathbf{I}_{yy} & -\mathbf{I}_{yz} \\ -\mathbf{I}_{zx} & -\mathbf{I}_{zy} & \mathbf{I}_{zz} \end{bmatrix} \begin{bmatrix} \omega_x \\ \omega_y \\ \omega_z \end{bmatrix} = \mathbf{I} \cdot \omega$$

where

$$\mathbf{I}_{xx} = \int (y^2 + z^2)dm = \int (y^2 + z^2)\rho dV = \iiint (y^2 + z^2)\rho \, dx \, dy \, dz$$

= moment of inertia of the body with respect to the x axis of a Cartesian frame,

$$\mathbf{I}_{xy} = \int xy \, dm = \text{the product of inertia with respect to the x coordinate axis, and}$$

$$\mathbf{I}_{xy} = \mathbf{I}_{yx} - \text{the inertia matrix } \mathbf{I} \text{ is symmetric around the diagonal.}$$

The triple integral can be evaluated in any order, but one order will often be easier. These equations are for objects described in Cartesian coordinates. We determine limits of integration by projecting the equations for the surfaces on to the planes defined by the coordinates axes. The determination of these limits is the principal difficulty in calculating an inertia matrix. Wilson and Deb (1989) present a Fortion program for calculating the moments of inertia for solids of revolution. For circular objects, it is often easier to use polar coordinates, in which case:

$$\mathbf{I}_{zz} = \int (x^2 + y^2)dm = \int (x^2 + y^2)\rho dV = \iiint (y^2 + z^2)\rho \, dz \, r \, dr \, d\theta$$

The diagonal quantities in the inertia matrix are the **moments of inertia** of the body about the respective axes, and the off diagonal quantities are the **products of inertia** with respect to the object axes. These quantities define the manner in which the mass of a rigid body is distributed with respect to the object axes. When calculating the moment of inertia, we integrate the product of the mass of the particles and the square of the perpendicular distance to the axis. Because the frame x, y, z is attached to the object, the elements of the inertia matrix are invariant with respect to time.

If we are free to choose the orientation of the object frame, we can locate it so that the off-diagonal terms are zero. In this situation, the moments of inertia are called the **principal moments of inertia**, and the axes are called the **principal axes**.

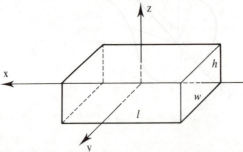

Consider the object above, with a reference frame located at the centre of mass and parallel to the sides of the object, so that the object is symmetrical with respect to each axis. When two axes of a reference frame form a plane of symmetry for the mass distribution of the body, the products of inertia which have as an index the coordinate which is normal to the plane are zero. In this case, all the pairs of axes form planes of symmetry, so all the off diagonal terms in the inertia matrix are zero. The moments of inertia can be calculated or obtained directly from Figure 7.4. The resulting inertia matrix with respect to the object frame is:

$$^{0}\mathbf{I} = \begin{bmatrix} \dfrac{m(h^2 + w^2)}{12} & 0 & 0 \\ 0 & \dfrac{m(l^2 + h^2)}{12} & 0 \\ 0 & 0 & \dfrac{m(w^2 + l^2)}{12} \end{bmatrix}$$

As in the above example, moments of inertia are always positive, and their sum is constant for different orientations of the reference frame. Unfortunately, the shape of the linkages of most manipulators is more complex, and the inertia matrix is not easy to evaluate.

From the inertia tensor, defined with respect to a frame located in the body, we can calculate the moment of inertia of the body about any vector through the origin of the frame.

$$\mathbf{I}_m = l^2\mathbf{I}_{xx} + m^2\mathbf{I}_{yy} + n^2\mathbf{I}_{zz} - 2lm\,\mathbf{I}_{xy} - 2ln\,\mathbf{I}_{xz} - 2mn\,\mathbf{I}_{yz}$$

where l, m, n are the direction cosines of the vector, and are the coordinates of a point located at a distance $\sqrt{\mathbf{I}_m}$ along the vector from the origin of the frame.

This is equivalent to applying a rotation transform between two frames, with the same origin, one fixed to the body (F), and one stationary (S).

$$^S\mathbf{I} = {}^F\mathbf{Rot}_S^T\,{}^F\mathbf{I}\,{}^F\mathbf{Rot}_S$$

where $^F\mathbf{Rot}_S^T\,{}^F\mathbf{Rot}_S$ = identity matrix.

As in the above example, we usually try to simplify the calculation of the inertia tensor. First, we locate a frame at the centre of mass, and orient the axes so that the z axis is parallel to the desired axis of rotation, that is, the joint axis. Then we orient the other two axes so that they are principal axes, if possible. The more principal axes we have, the less off-diagonal terms. If all axes are oriented so that the mass of the body is distributed symmetrically around them, all the off-diagonal terms go to zero. Once we have calculated the inertia tensor at the centre of mass, the **parallel axis theorem** is used to translate the inertia tensor to the frame at the axis of rotation. The two frames must be parallel.

$$\text{new}\mathbf{I}_{xx} = cm\mathbf{I}_{xx} + m(d_y^2 + d_z^2) \qquad \text{and} \qquad \text{new}\mathbf{I}_{yz} = cm\mathbf{I}_{yx} + md_y d_x$$

where $d_x d_y$ and d_z are the displacements between the origins.

If the axis of rotation of a link is parallel to a symetrical axis, we obtain a simple equation for the inertia of the link.

6.44 and 6.45) to include dynamics by adding the dynamic terms for the forces and torques due to motion.

$$^R f_n = {}^R f_{n-1,n} - {}^R f_{n,n+1} + m_n\,{}^R g = m_n\,{}^R a_n \tag{7.16}$$

$= 0$ when the forces are balanced.

$$^R \tau_n = {}^R \tau_{n-1,n} - {}^R \tau_{n,n+1} - {}^R c_{n-1,n} \times {}^R f_{n-1,n} + {}^R c_{n,n} \times {}^R f_{n,n+1}$$

$$= \mathbf{I}_n\,{}^R \alpha_n + {}^R \omega_n \times \mathbf{I}_n\,{}^R \omega_n \tag{7.17}$$

$= 0$ when the torques are balanced.

where $^R c_{n,n}$ is the distance from frame n to the centroid of link n as seen from the reference frame.

As in the static case, the net force and torque are zero when the forces and torques on the link are balanced. For example, a robot moving in free space has a torque balance when the actuator torques match the torques due to inertia and gravitation. If an external force or torque is applied to the tip of the robot, additional actuator torques are required to regain torque

Figure 7.3
Dynamics of Type 1 two-link
manipulator.

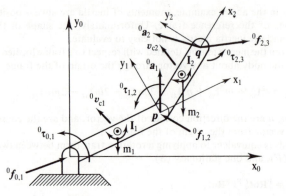

Figure 7.3
Dynamics of Type 1 two-link
manipulator.

balance. In the case of a revolute joint, the z axis component of the torque at
the joint is the torque the actuator has to supply, and, in the case of a prismatic joint, the z axis force at the joint is the force the actuator has to supply.
By rearranging Equations 7.16 and 7.17, we obtain equations for the situation where the actuator torque and force balances all the applied torques and
forces. Equation 7.18 describes the force at the joint with respect to the
reference frame.

$$^{R}f_{n-1,n} = m_n\,^{R}a_n + {}^{R}f_{n,n+1} - m_n\,^{R}g \tag{7.18}$$

$$^{R}\tau_{n-1,n} = {}^{R}\tau_{n,n+1} + {}^{R}c_{n-1,n} \times {}^{R}f_{n-1,n} - {}^{R}c_{n,n} \times {}^{R}f_{n,n+1}$$
$$+ \mathbf{I}_n\,^{R}\alpha_n + {}^{R}\omega_n \times \mathbf{I}_n\,^{R}\omega_n \tag{7.19}$$

By substituting Equation 7.18 into 7.19, we obtain the equation for
the torque at the joint with respect to the reference frame, in terms of the
centroidal velocities and accelerations (Figure 7.8).

$$^{R}\tau_{n-1,n} = {}^{R}\tau_{n,n+1} + {}^{R}c_{n-1,n} \times m_n\,^{R}a_n + {}^{R}p_{n-1,n} \times {}^{R}f_{n,n+1}$$
$$- {}^{R}c_{n-1,n} \times m_n\,^{R}g + \mathbf{I}_n\,^{R}\alpha_n + {}^{R}\omega_{\mathrm{n}} \times \mathbf{I}_n\,^{R}\omega_n \tag{7.20}$$

7.2.1 Inverse dynamics of the type 1 two-link manipulator

In Chapter 5, we developed equations for the velocities and accelerations of
manipulator links. By combining these with the force and torque equations,
we can solve the Newton–Euler equations to obtain the inverse dynamics of a
manipulator. To illustrate this process, we will solve the inverse dynamics for
the type 1 two-link manipulator (Figure 7.3).

First, the dynamic forces and torques must be found. The net dynamic
forces acting at the centre of mass of the links are expressed with Newton's
equation (Equation 7.14).

$$^0f_1 = m_1\,^0a_1 \qquad \text{and} \qquad ^0f_2 = m_2\,^0a_2 \tag{7.21}$$

The net dynamic torques acting around the centre of mass of the links are related to the angular velocities and accelerations of the links by Euler's equation (Equation 7.15)

$$^0\tau_1 = \mathbf{I}_1\,^0\alpha_1 + ^0\omega_1\,\mathbf{x}\,\mathbf{I}_1\,^0\omega_1 \qquad \text{and} \qquad ^0\tau_2 = \mathbf{I}_2\,^0\alpha_2 + ^0\omega_2\,\mathbf{x}\,\mathbf{I}_2\,^0\omega_2 \tag{7.22}$$

To combine the net dynamic torques with the static torques, substitute for n in Equation 7.20 to derive the following equations for the torques at the joints.

$$^0\tau_{1,2} = ^0\tau_{2,3} + ^0c_{1,2}\,\mathbf{x}\,m_2\,^0a_2 + ^0\mathbf{p}_{1,2}\,\mathbf{x}\,^0f_{2,3} - ^0c_{1,2}\,\mathbf{x}\,m_2\,^0g$$
$$+ \mathbf{I}_2\,^0\alpha_2 + ^0\omega_2\,\mathbf{x}\,\mathbf{I}_2\,^0\omega_2 \tag{7.23}$$
$$^0\tau_{0,1} = ^0\tau_{1,2} + ^0c_{0,1}\,\mathbf{x}\,m_1\,^0a_1 + ^0\mathbf{p}_{0,1}\,\mathbf{x}\,^0f_{1,2} - ^0c_{0,1}\,\mathbf{x}\,m_1\,^0g$$
$$+ \mathbf{I}_1\,^0\alpha_1 + ^0\omega_1\,\mathbf{x}\,\mathbf{I}_1\,^0\omega_1 \tag{7.24}$$

The externally applied force $^0f_{2,3}$ is transferred through the manipulator to link 1 using Equation 7.18 to obtain an expression for $^0f_{1,2}$ (Equation 7.25), which is then substituted into Equation 7.24.

$$^0f_{1,2} = m_2\,^0a_2 + ^0f_{2,3} - m_2\,^0g \tag{7.25}$$
$$^0\tau_{0,1} = ^0\tau_{1,2} + ^0c_{0,1}\,\mathbf{x}\,m_1\,^0a_1 + ^0\mathbf{p}_{0,1}\,\mathbf{x}\,(m_2\,^0a_2 + ^0f_{2,3} - m_2\,^0g)$$
$$- ^0c_{0,1}\,\mathbf{x}\,m_1\,^0g + \mathbf{I}_1\,^0\alpha_1 + ^0\omega_1\,\mathbf{x}\,\mathbf{I}_1\,^0\omega_1$$
$$= ^0\tau_{1,2} + ^0c_{0,1}\,\mathbf{x}\,m_1\,^0a_1 + ^0\mathbf{p}_{0,1}\,\mathbf{x}\,m_2\,^0a_2 + ^0\mathbf{p}_{0,1}\,\mathbf{x}\,^0f_{2,3}$$
$$- ^0\mathbf{p}_{0,1}\,\mathbf{x}\,m_2\,^0g - ^0c_{0,1}\,\mathbf{x}\,m_1\,^0g + \mathbf{I}_1\,^0\alpha_1 + ^0\omega_1\,\mathbf{x}\,\mathbf{I}_1\,^0\omega_1 \tag{7.26}$$

In this manipulator, the axis of rotation does not vary, reducing the inertia tensor to a scalar moment of inertia. Hence, the final term in both of these equations can be eliminated, because the cross product of a vector with itself is zero (Section 13.4.3). As this is a planar manipulator, the torque is normal to the xy plane (the plane in which the manipulator moves), and hence, the vectors normal to the plane can be replaced with their scalar magnitudes. Also, as the gravity vector acts in the negative z direction, that is, normal to the plane in which the manipulator moves, it can produce no torque around the joint axes, so the gravity term disappears. Finally, assuming the manipulator links are made from sections of uniform mass such that the centre of mass coincides with the centre of the link, the distance to the centre of mass is half the length of the link (Equation 6.54).

$$^0\mathbf{p}_{0,1} = 2 \times ^0c_{0,1} = \begin{bmatrix} l_2C_1 \\ l_1S_1 \end{bmatrix} \qquad \text{and} \qquad ^0\mathbf{p}_{1,2} = 2 \times ^0c_{1,2} = \begin{bmatrix} l_1C_{12} \\ l_2S_{12} \end{bmatrix} \tag{7.27}$$

$$
{}^0\tau_{1,2} = {}^0\tau_{2,3} + \begin{bmatrix} \dfrac{l_2 C_{12}}{2} \\[2mm] \dfrac{l_2 S_{12}}{2} \end{bmatrix} \times m_2 \, {}^0a_2 + \begin{bmatrix} l_2 C_{12} \\[1mm] l_2 S_{12} \end{bmatrix} \times {}^0f_{2,3} + \mathbf{I}_2 \, {}^0\alpha_2 \tag{7.28}
$$

$$
{}^0\tau_{0,1} = {}^0\tau_{1,2} + \begin{bmatrix} \dfrac{l_1 C_1}{2} \\[2mm] \dfrac{l_1 S_1}{2} \end{bmatrix} \times m_1 \, {}^0a_1 + \begin{bmatrix} l_1 C_1 \\[1mm] l_1 S_1 \end{bmatrix} \times m_2 \, {}^0a_2
$$

$$
+ \begin{bmatrix} l_1 C_1 \\[1mm] l_1 S_1 \end{bmatrix} \times {}^0f_{2,3} + \mathbf{I}_1 \, {}^0\alpha_1 \tag{7.29}
$$

The linear accelerations of the links of the type 1 two-link manipulator are given in Equations 5.34 and 5.36. To calculate the acceleration of the centre of mass of link *n* from the equation for the acceleration of frame *n*, we substitute the distance from the proximal joint to the centre of mass of link *n* for the length of link *n*.

$$
{}^0a_1 = \begin{bmatrix} \dfrac{-l_1 S_1}{2} \\[2mm] \dfrac{l_1 C_1}{2} \end{bmatrix} {}^0\alpha_1 - \begin{bmatrix} \dfrac{l_1 C_1}{2} \\[2mm] \dfrac{l_1 S_1}{2} \end{bmatrix} ({}^0\omega_1)^2 \tag{7.30}
$$

$$
\begin{bmatrix} {}^0a_{1x} \\[1mm] {}^0a_{1y} \end{bmatrix} = \begin{bmatrix} \dfrac{-l_1 S_1}{2} d^2\theta_1 - \dfrac{l_1 C_1}{2} (d\theta_1)^2 \\[3mm] \dfrac{l_1 C_1}{2} d^2\theta_1 - \dfrac{l_1 S_1}{2} (d\theta_1)^2 \end{bmatrix} \tag{7.31}
$$

$$
{}^0a_2 = \begin{bmatrix} -l_1 S_1 & -\dfrac{l_2 S_{12}}{2} \\[2mm] l_1 C_1 & \dfrac{l_2 C_{12}}{2} \end{bmatrix} \begin{bmatrix} {}^0\alpha_1 \\[1mm] {}^0\alpha_2 \end{bmatrix} - \begin{bmatrix} l_1 C_1 & \dfrac{l_2 C_{12}}{2} \\[2mm] l_1 S_1 & \dfrac{l_2 S_{12}}{2} \end{bmatrix} \begin{bmatrix} ({}^0\omega_1)^2 \\[1mm] ({}^0\omega_2)^2 \end{bmatrix} \tag{7.32}
$$

$$
\begin{bmatrix} {}^0a_{2x} \\[1mm] {}^0a_{2y} \end{bmatrix} = \begin{bmatrix} -l_1 S_1 d^2\theta_1 - \dfrac{l_2 S_{12}}{2} (d^2\theta_1 + d^2\theta_2) - l_1 C_1 (d\theta_1)^2 \\[3mm] l_1 C_1 d^2\theta_1 + \dfrac{l_2 C_{12}}{2} (d^2\theta_1 + d^2\theta_2) - l_1 S_1 (d\theta_1)^2 \\[3mm] - \dfrac{l_2 C_{12}}{2} (d\theta_1 + d\theta_2)^2 \\[3mm] - \dfrac{l_2 S_{12}}{2} (d\theta_1 + d\theta_2)^2 \end{bmatrix} \tag{7.33}
$$

Now we substitute these equations for the accelerations of the centre of mass into the joint torque equations (Equations 7.28 and 7.29) to calculate equations for the joint torques. As the equations for the centroidal accelerations are expressed in terms of joint parameters, the resultant torque equations are in closed from. First, calculate the torque required at joint 2:

$$
{}^0\tau_{1,2} = {}^0\tau_{2,3} + \begin{bmatrix} l_2C_{12} \\ l_2S_{12} \end{bmatrix} \times \begin{bmatrix} {}^0f_{2,3x} \\ {}^0f_{2,3y} \end{bmatrix} + I_2(d^2\theta_1 + d^2\theta_2)
$$

$$
+ m_2 \begin{bmatrix} \dfrac{l_2C_{12}}{2} \\ \dfrac{l_2S_{12}}{2} \end{bmatrix} \times \begin{bmatrix} -l_1S_1d^2\theta_1 - \dfrac{l_2S_{12}}{2}(d^2\theta_1 + d^2\theta_2) \\[2mm] l_1C_1d^2\theta_1 + \dfrac{l_2C_{12}}{2}(d^2\theta_1 + d^2\theta_2) \\[2mm] -l_1C_1(d\theta_1)^2 - \dfrac{l_2C_{12}}{2}(d\theta_1 + d\theta_2)^2 \\[2mm] -l_1S_1(d\theta_1)^2 - \dfrac{l_2S_{12}}{2}(d\theta_1 + d\theta_2)^2 \end{bmatrix}
$$

$$
= {}^0\tau_{2,3} + l_2C_{12}{}^0f_{2,3y} - l_2S_{12}{}^0f_{2,3x} + I_2(d^2\theta_1 + d^2\theta_2)
$$

$$
+ \frac{m_2l_2C_{12}l_1C_1}{2}d^2\theta_1 - \frac{m_2l_2C_{12}l_1S_1}{2}(d\theta_1)^2
$$

$$
+ \frac{m_2l_2S_{12}l_1C_1}{2}(d\theta_1)^2 + \frac{m_2l_2S_{12}l_1S_1}{2}d^2\theta_1
$$

$$
+ \frac{m_2l_2^2S_{12}^2}{4}(d^2\theta_1 + d^2\theta_2) + \frac{m_2l_2^2C_{12}^2}{4}(d^2\theta_1 + d^2\theta_2)
$$

$$
+ \frac{m_2l_2^2S_{12}C_{12}}{4}(d\theta_1 + d\theta_2)^2 - \frac{m_2l_2^2C_{12}S_{12}}{4}(d\theta_1 + d\theta_2)^2
$$

$$
= {}^0\tau_{2,3} + l_2C_{12}{}^0f_{2,3y} - l_2S_{12}{}^0f_{2,3x} + \frac{m_2l_1l_2S_2}{2}(d\theta_1)^2
$$

$$
+ \left(\frac{m_2l_1l_2C_2}{2} + \frac{m_2l_2^2}{4} + I_2 \right)d^2\theta_1
$$

$$
+ \left(\frac{m_2l_2^2}{4} + I_2 \right)d^2\theta_2 \tag{7.34}
$$

Second, calculate the torque required at joint 1:

$$
^{0}\tau_{0,1} = {}^{0}\tau_{1,2} + \begin{bmatrix} \dfrac{l_1 C_1}{2} \\ \dfrac{l_1 S_1}{2} \end{bmatrix} \times m_1 {}^{0}a_1 + \begin{bmatrix} l_1 C_1 \\ l_1 S_1 \end{bmatrix} \times m_2 {}^{0}a_2
$$

$$
+ \begin{bmatrix} l_1 C_1 \\ l_1 S_1 \end{bmatrix} \times {}^{0}f_{2,3} + \mathbf{I}_1 {}^{0}\alpha_1
$$

$$
= {}^{0}\tau_{1,2} + \begin{bmatrix} \dfrac{l_1 C_1}{2} \\ \dfrac{l_1 S_1}{2} \end{bmatrix} \times m_1 \begin{bmatrix} -\dfrac{l_1 S_1}{2} d^2\theta_1 - \dfrac{l_1 C_1}{2}(d\theta_1)^2 \\ \dfrac{l_1 C_1}{2} d^2\theta_1 - \dfrac{l_1 S_1}{2}(d\theta_1)^2 \end{bmatrix}
$$

$$
+ \begin{bmatrix} l_1 C_1 \\ l_1 S_1 \end{bmatrix} \times m_2 \begin{bmatrix} -l_1 S_1 d^2\theta_1 - \dfrac{l_2 S_{12}}{2}(d^2\theta_1 + d^2\theta_2) \\ l_1 C_1 d^2\theta_1 + \dfrac{l_2 C_{12}}{2}(d^2\theta_1 + d^2\theta_2) \\ \\ -l_1 C_1 (d\theta_1)^2 - \dfrac{l_2 C_{12}}{2}(d\theta_1 + d\theta_2)^2 \\ \\ -l_1 S_1 (d\theta_1)^2 - \dfrac{l_2 S_{12}}{2}(d\theta_1 + d\theta_2)^2 \end{bmatrix}
$$

$$
+ \begin{bmatrix} l_1 C_1 \\ l_1 S_1 \end{bmatrix} \times \begin{bmatrix} {}^{0}f_{2,3x} \\ {}^{0}f_{2,3y} \end{bmatrix} + \mathbf{I}_1 d^2\theta_1
$$

$$
= {}^{0}\tau_{1,2} + \left[\frac{l_1^2 m_1}{4} + m_2 l_2^2 + \frac{m_2 l_1 l_2 C_2}{2} + \mathbf{I}_1 \right] d^2\theta_1
$$

$$
+ \frac{m_2 l_1 C_2 l_2}{2} d^2\theta_2 - \frac{m_2 l_1 l_2 S_2}{2}(d\theta_1)^2 - \frac{m_2 l_1 l_2 S_2}{2}(d\theta_2)^2
$$

$$
- m_2 l_1 l_2 S_2\, d\theta_1\, d\theta_2 + l_1 C_1 {}^{0}f_{2,3y} - l_1 S_1 {}^{0}f_{2,3x} \tag{7.35}
$$

The torque at joint 1 (Equation 7.35) appears to be a simple expression until we realize that the first term is the torque at joint 2. To obtain the full equation for the torque at joint 1, substitute for the joint 2 torque (Equation 7.34).

$$
^{0}\tau_{0,1} = {}^{0}\tau_{2,3} + \left(\frac{m_2 l_2^2}{4} + \mathbf{I}_2 + \frac{m_2 l_1 l_2 C_2}{2} \right) d^2\theta_2 - \frac{m_2 l_1 l_2 S_2}{2}(d\theta_2)^2
$$

$$
+ \left(m_2 l_1 l_2 C_2 + \frac{m_1 l_1^2}{4} + \frac{m_2 l_2^2}{4} + m_2 l_1^2 + \mathbf{I}_2 + \mathbf{I}_1 \right) d^2\theta_1
$$

$$
- m_2 l_1 l_2 S_2\, d\theta_1\, d\theta_2 + (l_1 C_1 + l_2 C_{12}) {}^{0}f_{2,3y} - (l_1 S_1 + l_2 S_{12}) {}^{0}f_{2,3x} \tag{7.36}
$$

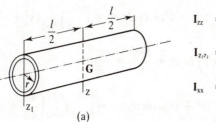

$$I_{zz} = \frac{mr^2}{2} + \frac{ml^2}{12}$$

$$I_{z_1z_1} = \frac{mr^2}{2} + \frac{ml^2}{3}$$

$$I_{xx} = mr^2$$

(a)

Figure 7.4
Moments of inertia of geometric shapes used to represent links.
(a) Thin-walled cylinder;
(b) Solid cylinder;
(c) Thin-walled rectangular section;
(d) Solid rectangular section.

$$I_{zz} = \frac{mr^2}{4} + \frac{ml^2}{12}$$

$$I_{z_1z_1} = \frac{mr^2}{4} + \frac{ml^2}{3}$$

$$I_{xx} = \frac{mr^2}{2}$$

(b)

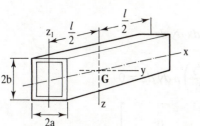

$$I_{zz} = \frac{ma^2}{6} + \frac{ml^2}{12}$$

$$I_{yy} = \frac{mb^2}{6} + \frac{ml^2}{12}$$

$$I_{z_1z_1} = \frac{ma^2}{6} + \frac{ml^2}{3}$$

$$I_{xx} = \frac{ma^2}{6} + \frac{mb^2}{6}$$

(c)

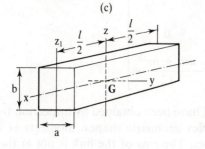

$$I_{zz} = \frac{ml^2}{12} + \frac{ma^2}{12}$$

$$I_{yy} = \frac{mb^2}{12} + \frac{ml^2}{12}$$

$$I_{z_1z_1} = \frac{ma^2}{12} + \frac{ml^2}{3}$$

$$I_{xx} = \frac{ma^2}{12} + \frac{mb^2}{12}$$

(d)

7.2.2 Inertia tensor

Before we can solve these torque equations, we must calculate the moments of inertia for the links. These moments are the elements of the inertia tensor for each link (Window 7.3). These elements depend upon the shape and mass distribution of the links. For example, when we model the links as solid square sections (Figure 7.4(d)) of length *l* and width *r*, the following elements are obtained for a symmetric frame located at the centre of mass of the link.

$$\mathbf{I}_{xx} = \int_{-r/2}^{r/2} \int_{-r/2}^{r/2} \int_{-l/2}^{l/2} (y^2 + z^2)\rho \, dx \, dy \, dz = \int_{-r/2}^{r/2} \int_{-r/2}^{r/2} (y^2 + z^2)l\rho \, dy \, dz$$

$$= \int_{-r/2}^{r/2} \left(\frac{r^3}{12} + z^2 r\right) l\rho \, dz = \frac{l\rho r^4}{6} = \frac{mr^2}{6} \tag{7.37}$$

$$\mathbf{I}_{zz} = \int_{-r/2}^{r/2} \int_{-r/2}^{r/2} \int_{-l/2}^{l/2} (x^2 + y^2)\rho \, dx \, dy \, dz = \int_{-r/2}^{r/2} \int_{-r/2}^{r/2} \left(\frac{l^3}{12} + y^2 l\right) \rho \, dy \, dz$$

$$= \int_{-r/2}^{r/2} \left(\frac{l^3 r}{12} + \frac{lr^3}{12}\right) \rho \, dz$$

$$= \frac{\rho l r^2}{12}(l^2 + r^2) = \frac{ml^2}{12} + \frac{mr^2}{12} = \mathbf{I}_{yy} \tag{7.38}$$

As the mass distribution is symmetrical about the axes, the off-diagonal terms are zero.

$$\mathbf{I}_{xy} = \int_{-r/2}^{r/2} \int_{-r/2}^{r/2} \int_{-r/2}^{l/2} xy \, \rho \, dx \, dy \, dz$$

$$= \int_{-r/2}^{r/2} \int_{-r/2}^{r/2} \left(\frac{l^2 y}{8} - \frac{l^2 y}{8}\right) \rho \, dy \, dz = 0 \tag{7.39}$$

$$\mathbf{I} = \begin{bmatrix} \dfrac{m^2 r}{6} & 0 & 0 \\[2mm] 0 & \dfrac{ml^2 + mr^2}{12} & 0 \\[2mm] 0 & 0 & \dfrac{ml^2 + mr^2}{12} \end{bmatrix} \tag{7.40}$$

These equations could have been obtained by inspection from Figure 7.4. In fact, for more complex geometric shapes, moments of inertia are obtained by looking up tables. The axis of the link is not at the centre of mass, but is displaced by a distance $l/2$. The inertia at the joint axes can be calculated from the inertia at the centre of mass using the parallel axis theorem (Window 7.3), but that is not necessary. In the next section, we will see that this has already been done during the calculations (Equations 7.45 and 46). As the links of the type 1 two-link manipulator are constrained to rotate around the z axis, the inertia in the joint torque equations is equal to $\mathbf{I}_{zz}$.

7.2.3 Closed form equations

The Newton–Euler equations (Equations 7.18 and 7.20) describe the force and torque to be applied to a joint by an actuator as functions of all the other

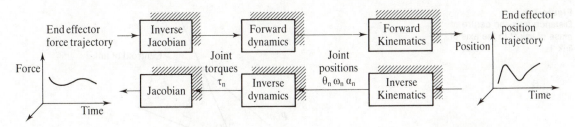

Figure 7.5
Dynamics and inverse dynamics.

forces and torques acting on that joint. These equations express the joint torques and forces in terms of the velocities and accelerations of the centroids of the links. But, as the motions of the centroids are constrained by the kinematic structure of the manipulator they are not independent and, consequently, they are not suitable as output variables.

To obtain equations suitable for use in controlling the motion of the manipulator, these equations are reorganized so that they express explicit input–output relationships in terms of independent variables. A suitable set of generalized independent position variables is the set of joint angles. For dynamics, the inputs are the joint torques and the outputs are the joint-position variables. For inverse dynamics, the inputs are the joint-position variables and the outputs are the joint torques (Figure 7.5). The closed form of the Newton–Euler dynamic equation is:

$$\tau_n = \sum_{j=1}^{i} \mathbf{H}_{nj} d^2\theta_j + \sum_{j=1}^{i} \sum_{k=1}^{i} \mathbf{C}_{njk} d\theta_j d\theta_k + \mathbf{G}_n + \mathbf{F}_n + \tau_e \qquad (7.41)$$

where

$\mathbf{H}_{nj}$ is the matrix specifying the moments of inertia of links j to i reflected to joint n, and $\mathbf{H}$ is the manipulator inertia tensor matrix,

$\mathbf{C}_{njk}$ is the matrix specifying the centrifugal effect when $j = k$, and the Coriolis effect when $j \neq k$ at joint n,

$\mathbf{G}_n$ is the effect of gravity on link n,

$\mathbf{F}_n$ is the end effector force as seen from joint n coordinates, and

τ_e is the end effector torque as seen from joint n coordinates.

For the type 1 two-link manipulator, the above equation expands to:

$$\tau_1 = \mathbf{H}_{11} d^2\theta_1 + \mathbf{H}_{12} d^2\theta_2 + (\mathbf{C}_{112} + \mathbf{C}_{121}) d\theta_1 d\theta_2$$
$$+ \mathbf{C}_{122}(d\theta_2)^2 + \mathbf{F}_1 \qquad (7.42)$$

$$\tau_2 = \mathbf{H}_{22} d^2\theta_2 + \mathbf{H}_{12} d^2\theta_1 + \mathbf{C}_{211}(d\theta_1)^2 + \mathbf{F}_2 \qquad (7.43)$$

Figure 7.6
Distance from the centre of
mass of link 2 to the axis of
link 1.

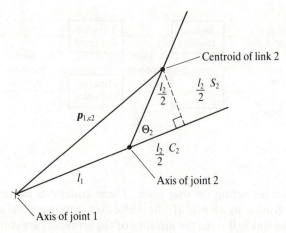

When the terms in Equations 7.34 and 7.36 are rearranged and equated to the above closed form equations, we obtain expressions for the coefficients. For example:

$$\mathbf{H}_{11} = m_2 l_1 l_2 C_2 + \frac{m_1 l_1^2}{4} + \frac{m_2 l_2^2}{4} + m_2 l_1^2 + \mathbf{I}_2 + \mathbf{I}_1 = \mathbf{I}_{1,1} + \mathbf{I}_{1,2} \qquad (7.44)$$

The coefficient $\mathbf{H}_{11}$ in Equation 7.42 is the total moment of inertia of both links as seen from the axis of the first joint. This term can be isolated by fixing the second joint so that it cannot move. Then all terms in Equation 7.42 but the first and last thus go to zero. As the last is the externally applied force, it can be eliminated by setting it to zero. Thus, the first term is due to the motion of the links caused by the acceleration of joint 1. By the parallel axis theorem, the inertia of link 1 as seen by joint 1 is:

$$\mathbf{I}_{1,1} = \mathbf{I}_1 + \frac{m_1 l_1^2}{4} \qquad (7.45)$$

For the second link, the distance ($p_{1,c2}$) from the centre of mass of the link to the axis of joint 1 is found using trigonometry (Figure 7.6). By the parallel axis theorem, the inertia of link 2 as seen by joint 1 is:

$$\mathbf{I}_{1,2} = \mathbf{I}_2 + m_2 (p_{1,c2})^2 = \mathbf{I}_2 + m_2 \left(l_1^2 + l_1 l_2 C_2 + \frac{l_2^2}{4} \right) \qquad (7.46)$$

We add these two inertias to calculate the coefficient $\mathbf{H}_{11}$ (Equation 7.44). Also, the inertia reflected from link 2 to joint 1 is a function of the configuration of the arm. The inertia is greatest when the arm is straight, (when the cosine of θ_2 is 1).

The second term in Equation 7.42 is the effect of the acceleration of the second link on the first. This term can be isolated by locking the first joint so that it cannot move and setting the velocity of the second joint to zero. At the instant that the second joint commences to accelerate, the only non-zero term in Equation 7.42 is the second term. To accelerate link 2, the actuator applies a torque to joint 2 and an equal and opposite reaction torque to link 1. The value of this torque can be found from the equation for the torque at joint 1 (Equation 7.35). Under these conditions, what is left is the contribution of coupling force and torque across joint 2 on to link 1.

$$
{}^0\tau_{0,1} = {}^0\tau_{1,2} + {}^0p_{0,1} \times {}^0f_{1,2} = \mathbf{H}_{12}d^2\theta_2
$$
$$
= \left(\frac{m_2 l_2^2}{4} + \mathbf{I}_2 + \frac{m_2 l_1 C_2 l_2}{2} \right) d^2\theta_2 \tag{7.47}
$$

The third and fourth terms in Equation 7.42 are due to joint velocities, and can be isolated by setting the joint accelerations to zero. The fourth term is the torque due to the centrifugal effect on joint 1 of link 2 rotating at constant velocity.

$$
\tau_{cent} = {}^0p_{1,c2} \times f_{cent} = \mathbf{C}_{122}(d\theta_2)^2 = - \frac{m_2 l_1 l_2\, S_2(d\theta_2)^2}{2} \tag{7.48}
$$

where f_{cent} is the centrifugal force.

The third term is the torque due to the Coriolis force, which results from the interaction of two rotating frames.

$$
\tau_{cor} = {}^0p_{1,c2} \times f_{cor} = (\mathbf{C}_{112} + \mathbf{C}_{121})d\theta_1 d\theta_2 = -m_2 l_1 l_2 S_2 d\theta_1 d\theta_2 \tag{7.49}
$$

where f_{cor} is the Coriolis force.

In the above equations, the centrifical force and the Coriolis force both act through the centre of mass of the second link, and hence produce a torque around the second joint, which is reflected to the first joint. The terms in the equation for the torque at the second joint (Equation 7.43) have similar physical meanings. Thus, the dynamic torque at the joint is the sum of several torques, each of which is dependent on the configuration of the manipulator arm. Consequently, the inverse dynamics have to be calculated in real time if they are used in the control of the manipulator.

7.2.4 Algorithms and computational efficiency

A major topic of research has been the search for efficient algorithms for calculating the dynamic equations. From the torque and force balance equations (Equations 7.18 and 7.20), we can develop an iterative algorithm for computing the dynamics of a manipulator as we did for statics (Algorithm 6.1). This algorithm provides a general means for computing the dynamics of any manipulator. However, it is not useful for control because it does not explicitly express joint torque as a function of joint-position variables. To overcome this problem, we rearranged the equation into closed form.

Closed-form equations for a particular manipulator are usually more efficient than the general iterative form. In Section 7.2.1, we solved the general torque balance equations for a particular manipulator and ended up with equations in closed form (Equations 7.34 and 7.36). In the process, some terms were eliminated and others combined, resulting in more compact equations.

The last step in the expansion of the torque balance equation for joint 1 (Equation 7.36) was the substitution of an expression for the torque balance at joint 2 (Equation 7.34). The efficiency of the iterative solution can be increased by calculating the torque balance for joint 2 and then substituting a number into the equation for joint 1. However, with the closed-form derivation (Equation 7.42), the expressions are already combined and common expressions must thus be re-evaluated for every point. Also, many sub-expressions are common to the equations for both joints (Equations 7.34 and 7.36), and occur in several terms within the one equation. For example, the expression $l_1 l_2 m_2$ occurs five times in Equation 7.36 and twice in Equation 7.34. This expression is also often multiplied by the sine or cosine of the second joint angle.

This observation has led to the simplification of dynamic equations by tabularization, where portions of the dynamic equations are precomputed and stored in look-up tables. By combining look-up tables with simple analytical expressions, dynamics can be computed in real time.

This approach usually results in a compromise between computational efficiency and table size. Some researchers have reduced the size of the tables by eliminating some terms in the equations as discussed below. Usually table entries are calculated off line, although some work has been done on automatic identification of table values (for example Raibert, 1978). This method suffers from changes in the parameters of the robot as a result of picking up an object. If there is no way to change the table to compensate for changes in length, inertia and centre of gravity during manipulation, the dynamic calculations will be exact only when the manipulator is not grasping anything.

Recursive forms of the dynamic equations have been developed to reduce this duplication in calculation, and hence, they are more efficient. Before we look at a recursive Newton–Euler algorithm, we will look at another method of simplifying the dynamic equations: eliminating the less significant terms.

There has been some controversy over the significance of exact dynamics computation in the control of manipulators. In some manipulators, static forces due to gravity and friction (particularly in harmonic drives) are so large that by comparison inertial forces, centridugal forces, and Coriolis forces are insignificant. However, as the dynamic terms are a function of velocity, the faster the manipulator moves the more significant the dynamic terms become. Thus, a controller with feedforward compensation for gravity and friction only will be adequate for slow motions but not for fast motions. Hollerbach (in Brady *et al.*, 1982) showed that, for type 1 two-link manipulator operating in a vertical plane along a trajectory requiring an end effector movement of 0.6 metres, the inertia terms are larger than the gravity terms for movement periods less than 0.5 seconds. (The links of the robot were of equal length and mass.) Hollerbach also demonstrated a trajectory where the gravity torque is comparable to the centrifugal and Coriolis torques.

In other manipulators, the inertial terms may be significant due to high acceleration rates, but, as the velocities are small, the Coriolis and centrifugal torques are insignificant. Again, Hollerbach has demonstrated that there are trajectories where all the dynamic torques are significant. Also, for many trajectories when the velocity is constant for a period, the inertial terms are zero, because the joints are not accelerating.

7.2.5 Recursive formulation

One advantage of closed-form equations is that, when parameter changes can be estimated, such changes do not affect the accuracy of the computation. If the change in length, centre of mass, and inertia of the final link that

---

Algorithm 7.1 Recursive Newton—Euler algorithm

1. Compute the inertia tensors (I_n), link position vectors ($p_{n+1,n}$) and joint axis vectors (z_n) with respect to the frames attached to the links, as then they do not change when the manipulator configuration changes.

2. Working from the base to the end effector, recursively calculate the velocities (Equations 5.20 and 5.23) and accelerations (Equations 5.28 and 5.38) of the centroids of the manipulator links with respect to link coordinates.

3. Working from the end effector to the base of the robot, recursively calculate the forces (Equation 7.50) and torques (Equation 7.51) at the actuators with respect to link coordinates.

$$^{n-1}f_{n-1,n} = m_n{}^{n-1}a_n + {}^{n-1}f_{n,n+1} + m_n{}^{n-1}g \tag{7.50}$$

$$^{n-1}\tau_{n-1,n} = {}^{n-1}\tau_{n,n+1} + {}^{n-1}c_n \times m_n{}^{n-1}a_n + {}^{n-1}p_n \times {}^{n-1}f_{n,n+1}$$
$$+ {}^{n-1}c_n \times m_n{}^{n-1}g + I_n{}^{n-1}\alpha_n + {}^{n-1}\omega_n \times I_n{}^{n-1}\omega_n \tag{7.51}$$

occurs when an object is grasped by the end effector is modelled, then the calculation of the required joint torques is reasonably accurate.

We wish to retain the accuracy of the closed form, but eliminate the inefficiency caused by duplication. A recursive algorithm (Algorithm 7.1) that achieves this aim falls fairly naturally out of the torque and force balance equations (Luh, Walker and Paul, 1980). This algorithm is more efficient if the dynamics are calculated with respect to link parameters rather than with respect to the world reference frame.

7.2.6 Dynamics in three dimensions

The example used throughout this text was chosen because it is simple. Much of its simplicity arises because the type 1 two-link manipulator operates in two dimensions. The expansion of the torque balance equation for a three–dimensional manipulator results in far more complex expressions.

First, in this example we eliminated gravity by having the manipulator operate in a horizontal plane. Second, the Euler equation was reduced to a scalar because all rotations were about axes perpendicular to the plane of the robot. Also, the second term in the equation, the gyroscopic torque, is zero in two dimensions, because the inertia tensor is reduced to a scalar moment of inertia, and the gyroscopic torque becomes the cross product of a vector with itself. In three dimensions, the inertia tensor is represented by the dot product of two three-component vectors (Window 7.3).

Third, in three dimensions, linear position, velocity and acceleration are three component vectors, not two, increasing the complexity of Newton's equations. Fourth, angular position, velocity and acceleration are three component vectors, not scalars, and must be transformed from frame to frame using rotation transforms, because joint axes might not be parallel. This, coupled with the inertia tensor, considerably increases the complexity of the calculation. Also, rotations in three dimensions are not commutative and have to be handled with care.

7.3 Lagrange formulation

In the Newton–Euler formulation, dynamic equations were derived in terms of forces and motions. The forces of constraint were eliminated through the use of the principle of virtual work, and the effect of acceleration as a force of inertia was described with D'Alembert's equation. The resulting torque balance equation was manipulated to obtain a closed-form equation for actuator torque.

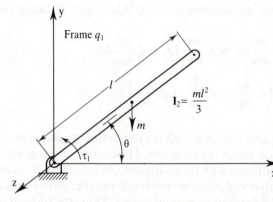

Frame q_1

l

$I_2 = \dfrac{ml^2}{3}$

m

θ

τ_1

Figure 7.7
Uniform slender rod rotating
about a joint.

The Lagrangian formulation describes the dynamic behaviour of a robot in terms of the work done by, and energy stored in, the system. The robot is treated as a black box that has an energy balance. The constraint forces are eliminated during the formulation of the equations. As with Newton–Euler dynamics, the closed-form equations can be derived in any coordinate system.

7.3.1 A single link

Lagrange's equations can be obtained from D'Alembert's equation (Equation 7.5). To illustrate the development of Lagrange's equation, we will derive it for a uniform slender rod rotating about a fixed axis (Figure 7.7). As the axis is perpendicular to the earth's surface, gravity does not come into these calculations and, hence, the potential energy does not change. As this system has only one degree of freedom, there is only one equation, expressed in terms of a single generalized coordinate, q_1, such that Cartesian coordinates are expressed as functions of q_1.

$$x = x(q_1), y = y(q_1), \quad \text{and} \quad z = z(q_1) \tag{7.52}$$

If the equations were expressed in terms of *two* generalized coordinates, q_1 and q_2, the resulting function would be $x = x(q_1, q_2)$. In this section, we restrict the discussion to one generalized coordinate for simplicity, and partial derivations are used for completeness. This means the equations easily extend to systems involving more than one generalized coordinate.

Virtual displacements in Cartesian coordinates can be described in terms of virtual displacements of the generalized coordinates.

$$\delta x = \frac{\partial x}{\partial q_1} \delta q_1, \ \delta y = \frac{\partial y}{\partial q_1} \delta q_1 \text{ and } \delta z = \frac{\partial z}{\partial q_1} \delta q_1 \tag{7.53}$$

Substituting these displacements into D'Alembert's equation gives:

$$\delta W = f_x \frac{\partial x}{\partial q_1} \delta q_1 + f_y \frac{\partial y}{\partial q_1} \delta q_1 + f_z \frac{\partial z}{\partial q_1} \delta q_1$$

$$= m \left(a_x \frac{\partial x}{\partial q_1} + a_y \frac{\partial y}{\partial q_1} + a_z \frac{\partial z}{\partial q_1} \right) \delta q_1 \qquad (7.54)$$

These displacements conform with the constraint of motion in one degree of freedom: rotation about the joint axis. Hence, the virtual work for a virtual displacement conforms with the constraint. As δq_1 can be given an arbitrarily small value without violating the constraint and the constraint is smooth, the work done by the force of constraint is zero. Thus, the force of constraint is eliminated from the equation.

To derive a relationship between virtual work and kinetic energy, we start by obtaining expressions to relate the derivative of the Cartesian coordinates to the generalized coordinates. First, differentiate Equation 7.52 with respect to time.

$$\frac{dx}{dt} = v_x = \frac{\partial x}{\partial q_1} \dot{q}_1 \qquad (7.55)$$

The equations for v_y and v_z are similar. Now, partially differentiate with respect to q_1.

$$\frac{\partial v_x}{\partial q_1} = \frac{\partial}{\partial q_1} \left(\frac{\partial x}{\partial q_1} \right) \dot{q}_1 \qquad (7.56)$$

As second derivatives are commutative, the result is the same if the order of differentiation is reversed

$$\therefore \frac{d}{dt} \left(\frac{\partial x}{\partial q_1} \right) = \frac{\partial v_x}{\partial q_1} = \frac{\partial}{\partial q_1} \left(\frac{\partial x}{\partial q_1} \right) \dot{q}_1 \qquad (7.57)$$

Next, partially differentiate Equation 7.55 with respect to $\dot{q}_1$:

$$\frac{\partial v_x}{\partial \dot{q}_1} = \frac{\partial x}{\partial q_1} = \frac{\partial \dot{x}}{\partial \dot{q}_1} \qquad (7.58)$$

Second, calculate an acceleration equation.

$$\frac{d}{dt} \left(v_x \frac{dx}{dq_1} \right) = a_x \frac{dx}{dq_1} + v_x \frac{d}{dt} \left(\frac{dx}{dq_1} \right) \qquad (7.59)$$

Rearrange Equation 7.59:

$$a_x \frac{dx}{dq_1} = \frac{d}{dt}\left(v_x \frac{dx}{dq_1}\right) - v_x \frac{d}{dt}\left(\frac{\partial x}{\partial q_1}\right) \tag{7.60}$$

Substitute Equations 7.57 and 7.58 into Equation 7.60.

$$a_x \frac{dx}{dq_1} = \frac{d}{dt}\left(v_x \frac{\partial v_x}{d\dot{q}_1}\right) - v_x \frac{\partial v_x}{dq_1} = \frac{d}{dt}\left[\frac{\partial\left(\frac{v_x^2}{2}\right)}{d\dot{q}_1}\right] - \frac{\partial\left(\frac{v_x^2}{2}\right)}{dq_1} \tag{7.61}$$

Finally, substitute Equation 7.61 into Equation 7.54, to obtain a relationship between virtual work and kinetic energy.

$$\delta W_{q1} = \left\{\frac{d}{dt}\left[\frac{\partial}{\partial\dot{q}_1} m \frac{(v_x^2 + v_y^2 + v_z^2)}{2}\right] - \frac{\partial}{\partial q_1} m \frac{(v_x^2 + v_y^2 + v_z^2)}{2}\right\} \delta q_1$$

$$= \left[\frac{d}{dt}\left(\frac{\partial K}{\partial\dot{q}_1}\right) - \frac{\partial K}{\partial q_1}\right] \delta q_1 = \left(f_x \frac{\partial x}{\partial q_1} + f_y \frac{\partial y}{\partial q_1} + f_z \frac{\partial z}{\partial q_1}\right) \delta q_1 \tag{7.62}$$

where

$$K = \frac{1}{2} m(v_x^2 + v_y^2 + v_z^2) \text{ is the kinetic energy of the link.}$$

In this example, a single rotating link, the generalized coordinate is the joint angle θ, and Equation 7.62 reduces to the Lagrange equation.

$$\frac{d}{dt}\left(\frac{\partial K}{\partial\omega}\right) - \frac{\partial K}{\partial\theta} = f_x \frac{\partial x}{\partial\theta} + f_y \frac{\partial y}{\partial\theta} + f_z \frac{\partial z}{\partial\theta} = F \tag{7.63}$$

where ω is the angular velocity, and F is the generalized force.

The kinetic energy (Window 7.4) of a body moving with both translation and rotation is:

$$K = \frac{1}{2} m v^2 + \frac{1}{2} {}^c I \omega^2 \tag{7.64}$$

where

    v is the linear velocity of the centre of mass,

    ω is the angular velocity of the body, and

    ${}^c I$ is the moment of inertia of the body about the centre of mass.

Window 7.4   Energy

When a force is applied to an object, the **work** done by the force on the object is the product of the magnitude of the force and the distance moved by the object. If the motion is in a different direction to the force, the work is done by the component of the force in the direction of motion.

$$W = Fd\cos\phi = f \cdot d$$

where

F is the magnitude of the force,

d is the distance the object moves, and

ϕ is the angle between the force and motion vectors.

If the force is varying with respect to time, the work done is:

$$W_{0,1} = \int_{r_0}^{r_1} f \cdot dr$$

where

f is the force that produced the change in potential energy, and

r is the position vector of the body with respect to a reference frame.

$\mathbf{r}_0$ is the starting point of motion and $\mathbf{r}_1$ is the terminating point of motion.

When a force is applied to a body to accelerate that body, the work done by the force on the body is equal to the **kinetic energy** imparted to that body. That is the work done to overcome the inertia of the body, neglecting friction. The kinetic energy of a moving body is the equal to the work required to bring the body to rest.

The kinetic energy of a translating body is:

$$K = \frac{Mv^2}{2}$$

where

M is the mass of the body, and

v is the linear velocity of the body.

The kinetic energy of a rotating body is:

$$K = \frac{I\omega^2}{2}$$

where

$\mathbf{I}$ is the rotational inertia of the body, and

ω is the angular velocity of the body.

The work done on a body by a resultant force is always equal to the change in kinetic energy of the body – known as the **work energy theorem**. When an applied force does not change the speed of a body, no work is done. For example, no work is done by the centripetal force which maintains a body in uniform circular motion, because only the direction of the velocity is changing not the magnitude.

$$W = \Delta K = -\Delta U$$

where U is the potential energy.

Potential energy is energy due to the removal of an object from the origin of its reference frame. For example the potential energy of a body due to gravitational force is a function of its height above the ground.

$$U = mgh$$

where

      h is the height of the body above the ground,
      m is the mass of the body, and
      g is the acceleration due to gravity.

Potential energy is a function of position, whose negative derivative is force.

$$\Delta U = - \int_{r_0}^{r_1} f(r) \cdot dr$$

Mechanical energy is the total energy in the body, and is the sum of the kinetic energy and the potential energy of the body. Any change in the kinetic energy of a body is compensated for by an equal and opposite change in the potential energy of the body. The total mechanical energy of a body remains constant unless acted upon by dissipative forces, such as friction which converts mechanical energy into heat energy.

$$E = K + U$$

Power is the time rate at which work is done.

$$P = \frac{W}{t} = \text{average power}, \quad \text{and,} \quad P_i = \frac{dW}{dt} = \text{instantaneous power.}$$

For a uniform slender rod, rotating about a joint (Figure 7.7), these vectors all become scalars, with reference to the generalized coordinate q_1, and the centroidal inertia is:

$$^c\mathbf{I} = \frac{ml^2}{12} \tag{7.65}$$

So, the total kinetic energy of the rod is:

$$K = \frac{m}{2}\left(\frac{l}{2}\omega\right)^2 + \frac{1}{2}\left(\frac{ml^2}{12}\right)\omega^2 = \frac{1}{6}ml^2\omega^2 \tag{7.66}$$

If friction and internal stresses are ignored, the generalized force in the Lagrange equation is the torque at the joint (τ). To find the Lagrange equation, the partial derivatives of the kinetic energy must first be found and substituted in Equation 7.63. When finding the partial derivatives, we assume that θ and ω are independent variables.

$$\frac{\partial K}{\partial \omega} = \frac{1}{3} ml^2 \omega \quad \text{and} \quad \frac{\partial K}{\partial \theta} = 0 \tag{7.67}$$

$$\tau = \frac{d}{dt}\left(\frac{1}{3} ml^2 \omega\right) = \frac{1}{3} ml^2 \alpha \tag{7.68}$$

where α is the angular acceleration.

From this equation, the second order, non-linear equation that describes the dynamics of the system is:

$$\frac{1}{3} ml^2 \alpha(t) = \tau(t) \tag{7.69}$$

7.3.2 Generalized dynamics

The above example is a specific case of the generalized Lagrange equation. When applying it to robotics, the n independent generalized coordinates $q_1 \ldots q_n$ are the joint coordinates as they completely locate the dynamics of a robot.

$$L(q_n, \dot{q}_n) = K - U \tag{7.70}$$

where L is the Lagrangian, K is kinetic energy, and U is potential energy.

Using the Lagrangian, the n non-linear, coupled, equations of motion which describe the dynamics of an n link robot are

$$\frac{d}{dt}\left(\frac{\partial L}{\partial \dot{q}_n}\right) - \frac{\partial L}{\partial q_n} = F_n \tag{7.71}$$

where $n = 1..$ number of links and F_n is the generalized force corresponding to coordinate q_n (the generalized force acting on link n in joint n coordinates).

The generalized force acts on link n in the direction of permissible link motion, and is a scalar quantity. It is composed of a torque vector, in the case of a revolute joint, or a force vector, in the case of a prismatic joint, gravitational forces, frictional forces, and other nonlinear forces due to dead zones and hysteresis. As potential energy is position dependent only,

$$F_n = \frac{d}{dt}\left(\frac{\partial K}{\partial \dot{q}_n}\right) - \frac{\partial K}{\partial q_n} + \frac{\partial U}{\partial q_n} \tag{7.72}$$

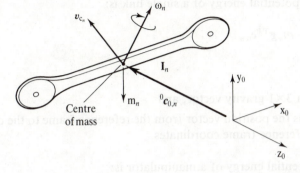

Figure 7.8
Velocity at centroid of link *n*.

The total kinetic energy of a manipulator is the sum of the kinetic energy of the links.

$$K = \sum_{1}^{n} K_n \qquad (7.73)$$

The kinetic energy of a single link (Figure 7.8) in three-dimensional space is a scalar quantity.

$$K_n = \frac{1}{2} m_n {}^R v_n^{T\ R} v_n + \frac{1}{2} \omega_n^T \mathbf{I}_n \omega_n \qquad (7.74)$$

where

m_n is the mass of link *n*,

${}^R v_n$ is the linear velocity of the centroid of link *n* with respect to the reference frame – a 3×1 vector,

ω_n is the angular velocity of link *n* relative to the reference frame – a 3×1 vector,

$\mathbf{I}_n$ is the inertia tensor of link *n* at the centroid – a 3×3 matrix.

As the kinetic energy due to angular velocity is independent of which coordinate frame it is calculated in, it can be calculated in either the reference frame or a frame fixed to the link, provided both the angular velocity vector and the inertia tensor are expressed with respect to the same frame. The advantage of calculating kinetic energy with respect to the centroidal frame is that we do not have to transform inertia to another frame. If kinetic energy is calculated with respect to the link frame (frame *n* at the distal joint) the parallel axis theorem is used to calculate the inertia from the centroidal inertia. If kinetic energy is calculated with respect to the reference frame, the inertia tensor matrix changes with respect to the reference frame as the link rotates and, hence, can be complex to calculate.

The potential energy of a single link is:

$$U_n = m_n g^{\mathrm{T}} {}^0c_{0,n} \tag{7.75}$$

where

g is a 3×1 gravity vector, and

${}^0c_{0,n}$ is the position vector from the reference frame to the centroid of link n in reference frame coordinates.

and the potential energy of a manipulator is:

$$U = \sum_{n=1}^{n} U_n \tag{7.76}$$

So the contribution of potential energy to Lagrangian dynamics is

$$\frac{\partial U}{\partial q_n} = -\sum_{n=1}^{n} m_n g^{\mathrm{T}} \frac{\partial}{\partial q_n} ({}^0\mathrm{T}_n) {}^0c_{0,n} \tag{7.77}$$

7.3.3 Closed form equations and recursive algorithms

The Lagrange equation (Equation 7.72) can be reworked into the same form as the closed-form Newton–Euler equation (Equation 7.41) by rewriting the equation for kinetic energy (Equation 7.74) in terms of joint displacements, and using the Jacobian to relate the Cartesian linear velocities of the link centroid to joint velocities. Asada and Slotine (1986) derived the Lagrangian dynamics in this way, to demonstrate that the Lagrangian formulation provides the closed-form dynamic equations directly.

Equation 7.72 is a closed-form expression, in the sense that the dependence of a joint torque on the movement of all joints is explicit. Expanding

---

Algorithm 7.2   Recursive Lagrangian

1. Calculate the velocities and accelerations with a backward recursion working from the base towards the end effector. If the base is stationary, the velocities and accelerations of the base are zero.

2. Calculate the forces and torques with a forward recursion by reflecting them from the end effector to the base.

this equation by substituting for the partial derivatives results in a very complex equation, and, in this form, most terms are re-evaluated many times. Hollerbach (1980) improved the efficiency of Lagrangian dynamics by reformulating the equations into a recursive form (Algorithm 7.2).

A considerable improvement in efficiency is obtained by using 3×3 rotation matrices instead of homogeneous coordinates. With this algorithm, the computational complexity of calculating Lagrangian dynamics is reduced from order n^4 for the closed-form equations to order n.

7.3.4 Type 1 two-link manipulator dynamics

We write the equations for the type 1 two-link manipulator in terms of two generalized coordinates – the joint angles. As the manipulator moves in a horizontal plane, the potential energy is constant and can be ignored. When we model the linkages as slender cylindrical rods of uniform mass (Figure 7.3), the scalar moment of inertia of each rod about its centre of mass is:

$$I_1 = \frac{m_1 l_1^2}{12} \quad \text{and} \quad I_2 = \frac{m_2 l_2^2}{12} \tag{7.78}$$

The kinetic energy for link 1 is

$$K_1 = \frac{1}{2} m_1 \, {}^0v_{0,1}^T \, {}^0v_{0,1} + \frac{1}{2} \, {}^{c1}\omega_{0,1}^T \, {}^{c1}I_1 \, {}^{c1}\omega_{0,1} \tag{7.79}$$

where ${}^{c1}\omega_{0,1} = -\omega_1$, and the angular velocity component is calculated in the centroidal frame.

For link 2 the kinetic energy is

$$K_2 = \frac{1}{2} m_2 \, {}^0v_{0,2}^T \, {}^0v_{0,2} + \frac{1}{2} \, {}^{c2}\omega_{0,2}^T \, {}^{c2}I_2 \, {}^{c2}\omega_{0,2} \tag{7.80}$$

where ${}^{c2}\omega_{0,2} = -(\omega_1 + \omega_2)$

From Equations 5.16 and 5.17 the linear velocities of the centroids are:

$$^0v_{0,1} = \frac{1}{2} \begin{bmatrix} -l_1 S_1 \\ l_1 C_1 \end{bmatrix} \omega_1 \tag{7.81}$$

$$^0v_{0,2} = \begin{bmatrix} -l_1 S_1 - \dfrac{l_2}{2} S_{12} & -\dfrac{l_2}{2} S_{12} \\[2mm] l_1 C_1 + \dfrac{l_2}{2} C_{12} & +\dfrac{l_2}{2} C_{12} \end{bmatrix} \begin{bmatrix} \omega_1 \\ \omega_2 \end{bmatrix} \tag{7.82}$$

As the robot is planar, and the joint axes are perpendicular to the plane, the angular velocities can be represented as scalars, considerably simplifying the equations. The velocity products are:

$$^0v_{0,1}^T \, ^0v_{0,1} = \frac{\omega_1^2}{4}[-l_1 S_1 \, l_1 C_1]\begin{bmatrix} -l_1 S_1 \\ l_1 C_1 \end{bmatrix} = \frac{l_1^2 \omega_1^2}{4} \tag{7.83}$$

$$^0v_{0,2}^T \, ^0v_{0,2} = \left(l_1^2 + \frac{l_2^2}{4} + l_1 l_2 C_2\right)\omega_1^2 + \frac{l_2^2 \omega_2^2}{4}$$

$$+ \left(\frac{l_2^2}{2} + l_1 l_2 C_2\right)\omega_1 \omega_2 \tag{7.84}$$

The total kinetic energy is

$$K = K_1 + K_2 = \frac{1}{8} m_1 l_1^2 \omega_1^2 + \frac{1}{24} m_1 l_1^2 \omega_1^2 + \frac{1}{24} m_2 l_2^2 (\omega_1 + \omega_2)^2$$

$$+ \frac{1}{2} m_2 \left(l_1^2 + \frac{l_2^2}{4} + l_1 l_2 C_2\right)\omega_1^2 + \frac{1}{8} m_2 l_2^2 \omega_2^2$$

$$+ \frac{1}{2} m_2\left(\frac{l_2^2}{2} + l_1 l_2 C_2\right)\omega_1 \omega_2$$

$$= \left(\frac{m_1 l_1^2}{6} + \frac{m_2 l_1^2}{2} + \frac{m_2 l_2^2}{6} + \frac{m_2 l_1 l_2 C_2}{2}\right)\omega_1^2 + \frac{m_2 l_2^2}{6}\omega_2^2$$

$$+ \left(\frac{m_2 l_2^2}{3} + \frac{m_2 l_1 l_2 C_2}{2}\right)\omega_1 \omega_2 \tag{7.85}$$

Next, we differentiate the equation for kinetic energy with respect to the generalized coordinates and their derivatives.

$$\frac{\partial K}{\partial \theta_1} = 0 \tag{7.86}$$

$$\frac{\partial K}{\partial \omega_1} = \left(\frac{m_1 l_1^2}{3} + m_2 l_1^2 + \frac{m_2 l_2^2}{3} + m_2 l_1 l_2 C_2\right)\omega_1$$

$$+ \left(\frac{m_2 l_2^2}{3} + \frac{m_2 l_1 l_2 C_2}{2}\right)\omega_2 \tag{7.87}$$

$$\frac{\partial K}{\partial \theta_2} = -\frac{m_2 l_1 l_2 S_2}{2}\omega_1^2 - \frac{m_2 l_1 l_2 S_2}{2}\omega_1 \omega_2 \tag{7.88}$$

$$\frac{\partial K}{\partial \omega_2} = \frac{m_2 l_2^2 \omega_2}{3} + \left(\frac{m_2 l_2^2}{3} + \frac{m_2 l_1 l_2 C_2}{2}\right)\omega_1 \tag{7.89}$$

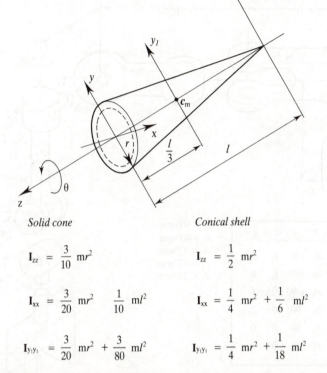

Figure 7.9
Modelling a link as a conical
shell or a solid cone.

Solid cone

$$I_{zz} = \frac{3}{10} mr^2$$

$$I_{xx} = \frac{3}{20} mr^2 \qquad \frac{1}{10} ml^2$$

$$I_{y_l y_l} = \frac{3}{20} mr^2 + \frac{3}{80} ml^2$$

Conical shell

$$I_{zz} = \frac{1}{2} mr^2$$

$$I_{xx} = \frac{1}{4} mr^2 + \frac{1}{6} ml^2$$

$$I_{y_l y_l} = \frac{1}{4} mr^2 + \frac{1}{18} ml^2$$

To obtain the dynamic equations for the joint torques, substitute these equations into the Lagrangian

$$
\begin{aligned}
\tau_2 &= \frac{d}{dt}\left(\frac{\partial K}{\partial \omega_2}\right) - \frac{\partial K}{\partial \theta_2} = \frac{m_2 l_2^2 \alpha_2}{3} + \frac{m_2 l_2^2 \alpha_1}{3} + \frac{m_2 l_1 l_2 C_2 \alpha_1}{2} \\
&\quad - \frac{m_2 l_1 l_2 S_2}{2} \omega_1 \omega_2 + \frac{m_2 l_1 l_2 S_2}{2} \omega_1^2 + \frac{m_2 l_1 l_2 S_2}{2} \omega_1 \omega_2 \\
&= \frac{m_2 l_2^2 \alpha_2}{3} + \left(\frac{m_2 l_2^2}{3} + \frac{m_2 l_1 l_2 C_2}{2}\right) \alpha_1 + \frac{m_2 l_1 l_2 S_2}{2} \omega_1^2 \qquad \textbf{(7.90)}
\end{aligned}
$$

$$
\begin{aligned}
\tau_1 &= \frac{d}{dt}\left(\frac{\partial K}{\partial \omega_1}\right) - \frac{\partial K}{\partial \theta_1} = \left(\frac{m_1 l_1^2}{3} + m_2 l_1^2 + \frac{m_2 l_2^2}{3} + m_2 l_1 l_2 C_2\right) \alpha_1 \\
&\quad - m_2 l_1 l_2 S_2 \omega_1 \omega_2 + \left(\frac{m_2 l_2^2}{3} + \frac{m_2 l_1 l_2 C_2}{2}\right) \alpha_2 - \frac{m_2 l_1 l_2 S_2}{2} \omega_2^2 \qquad \textbf{(7.91)}
\end{aligned}
$$

These equations for joint torque are the same as the equations that were obtained using the Newton–Euler formulation of dynamics (Equations 7.34 and 7.36). This example clearly illustrates the equivalence of the two methods.

Figure 7.10
Kinematic model of the CMU
direct-drive arm.

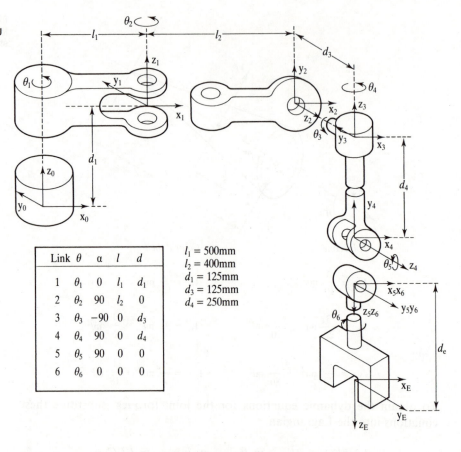

Link	θ	α	l	d
1	θ_1	0	l_1	d_1
2	θ_2	90	l_2	0
3	θ_3	−90	0	d_3
4	θ_4	90	0	d_4
5	θ_5	90	0	0
6	θ_6	0	0	0

$l_1 = 500$mm
$l_2 = 400$mm
$d_1 = 125$mm
$d_3 = 125$mm
$d_4 = 250$mm

7.4 Parameter estimation

While the derivation of the dynamic equations is tedious, owing to the complexity of the mathematics, the process is reasonably straightforward. In practice, estimating the moments of inertia accurately is much more difficult than this (Window 7.3). So far we have assumed that links are of uniform shape and mass distribution. Real robots, however, tend to have their mass concentrated at the joints. For this reason, links are often modelled as point masses at the joints. Sometimes, arm links are modelled as cones or conical shells, to reflect concentration of mass around the joint (Figure 7.9).

To calculate the inertia tensors for the CMU direct-drive arm (see Figure 2.53), the designers modelled each link as a composite of hollow cylinders, solid cylinders, prisms and rectangular parallelepipeds (Figure 7.10, see also Figure 9.10) (Khosla, 1986). Then, they obtained the location and mass of every component from the design database. Finally, they used a dynamic

Inertia elements (kg m^2)		
$I_{1xx} = 0.135283$	$I_{1xz} = 0.048943$	$I_{1yy} = 1.225357$
$I_{1zz} = 1.193645$	$I_{2xx} = 0.033108$	$I_{2xy} = -0.027993$
$I_{2xz} = -0.001146$	$I_{2yy} = 0.264736$	$I_{2yz} = -0.000115$
$I_{2zz} = 0.286647$	$I_{3xx} = 0.014622$	$I_{3yy} = 0.006615$
$I_{3yz} = 0.001269$	$I_{3zz} = 0.012432$	$I_{4xx} = 0.023775$
$I_{4yy} = 0.004055$	$I_{4yz} = 0.003083$	$I_{4zz} = 0.021652$
$I_{5xx} = 0.002018$	$I_{5yy} = 0.001049$	$I_{5yz} = -0.000092$
$I_{5zz} = 0.001396$	$I_{6xx} = 0.000426$	$I_{6yy} = 0.000421$
	$I_{6zz} = 0.000047$	

Centres of Gravity (m)		
$s_{1x} = -0.300000$	$s_{1z} = 0.100399$	$s_{2x} = -0.131742$
$s_{2y} = -0.013219$	$s_{2z} = 0.001105$	$s_{3y} = -0.039703$
$s_{3z} = -0.012487$	$s_{4y} = 0.071645$	$s_{4z} = 0.022866$
$s_{5y} = 0.005481$	$s_{5z} = -0.017932$	$s_{6z} = 0.008176$

Link masses (kg)		
$m_1 = 19.753$	$m_2 = 7.894$	$m_3 = 2.801$
$m_4 = 1.881$	$m_5 = 0.936$	$m_6 = 0.269$

Figure 7.11
Numerical values for the inertial parameters of the CMU direct-drive arm.

simulation package to compute the inertia tensor, and the vector to the centre of gravity of each link (Figure 7.11), (Swartz, 1984).

In the control of a direct-drive arm, the manipulator dynamics must be modelled accurately for precise control. As there is no gearbox, the friction at each joint is very small, and dynamic terms dominate the control equations. In practice, it is also necessary to identify the mass and inertial characteristics of the payload in order to achieve accurate control. This must be done on-line during manipulator motion.

Each link of a robot is characterized by a maximum of ten dynamic parameters: link mass, a three-element vector to the centre of mass, and the six values in the inertia tensor (Window 7.3). When all these parameters are significant for every link, the dynamic model is incredibly complex. In practice, careful robot design significantly reduces the number of parameters and, hence, the complexity of the equations. We are interested only in the dynamic parameters that affect the joint torque. For example, when modelling a waist joint, the only inertial parameter of interest is the moment of inertia about the joint axis.

Khosla and Kanade (1985) presented an algorithm for the on-line identification of the parameters involved in robot dynamics (Algorithm 7.3).

Figure 7.12
On-line adaption of inverse
dynamic model.

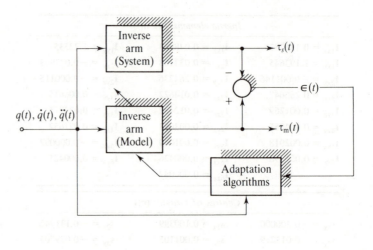

$q(t), \dot{q}(t), \ddot{q}(t)$

Algorithm 7.3   Parameter estimation algorithm

1. Model the links and estimate the centres of mass and inertia tensors.
2. Develop the dynamic equations for the robot in closed form.
3. If a Newton–Euler model is used, convert these to equations involving the inertia around the link frames, so that the model is linear in the centre of mass vectors. The Lagrangian model is already linear in the dynamic parameters.
4. With the actual manipulator, and no payload, repeat the following steps starting at the distal joint and moving in to the joint closest to the base.

    (a) Freeze all other joints to simplify the equations.
    (b) Accelerate this joint and measure the inputs (joint torque/force) and outputs (joint position, velocity and acceleration).
    (c) Calculate values for the inertia tensor for this link based on these measurements. Alternatively, the adaption system in step 5 can be used.
    (d) Modify the equations to include these new inertia parameters.

5. Once the parameters of the robot are modelled with sufficient accuracy, this model can be compared to measured values during motion to estimate the inertial parameters of the payload. An on-line model adaption system is used to do this (Figure 7.12). Adaption is based on equations which model the relationship between the torque error at a joint and the dynamic parameters of each link, given that the mass and kinematic parameters of each link have been measured.

7.5   Implications for robot design

A number of design considerations arise out of our study of dynamics. First, the further an object is from a joint and the larger its mass, the greater will be the resultant inertial torques. Such torques are transferred inwards towards the base of the robot resulting in increasing joint torques as we approach the base. Consequently, reducing the mass of the links, and shifting the mass towards the base by relocating actuators into the base, will reduce the torques required to overcome inertia. Locating a motor close to the axis of a joint will reduce the inertial load on that joint, and hence, the load transferred to preceeding joints.

Second, the significance of inertial torque is inversely proportional to the friction in the joint gear boxes. For example, harmonic drives have high friction, which swamps inertial loads, except at high speeds, whereas direct-drive robots have very low joint friction, and consequently, require velocity and acceleration control based on inverse dynamics.

Third, dynamically simple robot design leads to diagonal inertia tensors. Eliminating the off-diagonal terms in the tensors considerably reduces the complexity of the equations. A second reason for using physically simple shapes is that they are easier to model and hence, estimates of moments of inertia are more accurate.

Finally, the stiffness of the linkages is important, as flexing of the links will cause errors in trajectory following. Modelling flexible link structures is a subject of continuing research.

7.6   Programming

The complexity of the dynamic equations necessitates the use of parallel processing to calculate the inverse dynamics in real time. Simplifying the equations by neglecting terms will reduce their calculation time but also their accuracy (Section 7.2.4). Dynamics programs use all the data structure variables from previous chapters: position, velocity, acceleration, torque and force vectors. Additional data structures are required to store the centre of mass vectors and the inertia tensors.

As efficient algorithms for the calculation of manipulator dynamics use recursion, a language that either supports recursion or parallel processing is required. These tend to be available for specialized research robots only. When dynamic models are included in industrial robots, they will be hard coded for efficiency and probably not accessible to the user. Although, the model parameters will have to be stored in data structures if on-line adaption of the model is included.

Examples

Example 7.1 Lagrangian dynamics of the type 2 two-link manipulator

In this example, we move out of the plane into three-dimensional space (see Figure 4.7). The most important consequence is that when adding angular velocity vectors, the rotation transforms from one frame to the next become significant because the joint axes are no longer parallel. The type 2 two-link manipulator forms the first two links of an articulated robot: waist and upper arm. The waist link is a cylindrical link with a collinear axis and, as a consequence, the centre of mass does not move. The linear velocity term in the kinetic energy equation is therefore zero, and the potential energy of link 1 is fixed.

In this example, we will model the links as a point mass (m) at the distal end. As the kinetic energy is independent of the frame it is calculated in, we will calculate the kinetic energy due to angular velocity in the link frame, so that the inertia tensors do not have to be transformed to the base frame. The kinematic model for this manipulator is given in Equations 4.7, 4.53, and 5.139.

$$^0v_{0,1} = 0 \tag{7.92}$$

$$^0v_{0,2} = \begin{bmatrix} -l_2 S_1 C_2 & -l_2 C_1 S_2 \\ l_2 C_1 C_2 & -l_2 S_1 S_2 \\ 0 & l_2 C_2 \end{bmatrix} \begin{bmatrix} \dot{\theta}_1 \\ \dot{\theta}_2 \end{bmatrix} = \begin{bmatrix} -S_1 C_2 \dot{\theta}_1 - C_1 S_2 \dot{\theta}_2 \\ C_1 C_2 \dot{\theta}_1 - S_1 S_2 \dot{\theta}_2 \\ C_2 \dot{\theta}_2 \end{bmatrix} l_2 \tag{7.93}$$

$$^1\omega_0 = \begin{bmatrix} 0 \\ \dot{\theta}_1 \\ 0 \end{bmatrix} = \dot{\theta}_1 \tag{7.94}$$

$$^2\omega_0 = {}^2\omega_1 + {}^2\mathbf{R}_1\,{}^1\omega_0$$

$$= \begin{bmatrix} 0 \\ 0 \\ \dot{\theta}_2 \end{bmatrix} + \begin{bmatrix} C_2 & S_2 & 0 \\ -S_2 & C_2 & 0 \\ 0 & 0 & 1 \end{bmatrix} \begin{bmatrix} 0 \\ \dot{\theta}_1 \\ 0 \end{bmatrix} = \begin{bmatrix} S_2 \dot{\theta}_1 \\ C_2 \dot{\theta}_1 \\ \dot{\theta}_2 \end{bmatrix} \tag{7.95}$$

First, we calculate the kinetic energy of each link:

$$K_1 = \frac{1}{2} m \dot{\theta}_1^2 = 0 \tag{7.96}$$

because the axis of rotation is through a point mass, and

$$K_2 = \frac{1}{2} m \ {}^0v_{0,2}^2 + \frac{1}{2} m \ {}^2\omega_0^2 \tag{7.97}$$

$${}^2\omega_0^2 = [S_2\dot{\theta}_1 \ C_2\dot{\theta}_1 \ \dot{\theta}_2] \begin{bmatrix} S_2\dot{\theta}_1 \\ C_2\dot{\theta}_1 \\ \dot{\theta}_2 \end{bmatrix}$$

$$= S_2^2\dot{\theta}_1^2 + C_2^2\dot{\theta}_1^2 + \dot{\theta}_2^2 = \dot{\theta}_1^2 + \dot{\theta}_2^2 \tag{7.98}$$

But, because the axis of rotation is through the point mass (the angular velocity was transformed to the link frame), the inertia makes no contribution to the kinetic energy.

$$\begin{aligned}
{}^0v_{0,2}^2 &= l_2^2[(-S_1C_2\dot{\theta}_1 - C_1S_2\dot{\theta}_2)^2 + (C_1C_2\dot{\theta}_1 - S_1S_2\dot{\theta}_2)^2 + C_2^2\dot{\theta}_2^2] \\
&= l_2^2[S_1^2C_2^2 + C_1^2C_2^2]\dot{\theta}_1^2 + l_2^2[C_1^2S_2^2 + S_1^2S_2^2 + C_2^2]\dot{\theta}_2^2 \\
&= l_2^2C_2^2\dot{\theta}_1^2 + l_2^2\dot{\theta}_2^2
\end{aligned} \tag{7.99}$$

$$K_2 = \frac{1}{2} m l_2^2 (C_2^2\dot{\theta}_1^2 + \dot{\theta}_2^2) \tag{7.100}$$

Second, calculate the potential energy of each link.

$$U_1 = mgl_1 \tag{7.101}$$

$$U_2 = mgl_2(S_2 + 1) \tag{7.102}$$

Third, add the energies to obtain the total energy.

$$\begin{aligned}
L &= K_1 + K_2 - U_1 - U_2 \\
&= 0 + \frac{1}{2} m l_2^2 (C_2^2\dot{\theta}_1^2 + \dot{\theta}_2^2) - mgl - mgl_2(1+S_2)
\end{aligned} \tag{7.103}$$

Fourth, we calculate the components of the Lagrangian.

$$\frac{\partial L}{\partial \dot{\theta}_1} = m l_2^2 C_2^2 \dot{\theta}_1^2 \tag{7.104}$$

$$\frac{\partial L}{\partial \theta_1} = 0 \tag{7.105}$$

$$\frac{d}{dt}\left(\frac{\partial L}{\partial \dot{\theta}_1}\right) = m l_2^2 (C_2^2\ddot{\theta}_1 - 2C_2S_2\dot{\theta}_1\dot{\theta}_2) \tag{7.106}$$

$$\frac{\partial L}{\partial \theta_2} = -m l_2^2 S_2 C_2 \dot{\theta}_1^2 - mgl_2 C_2 \tag{7.107}$$

Figure 7.13
Modelling the type 2 two-link
robot.

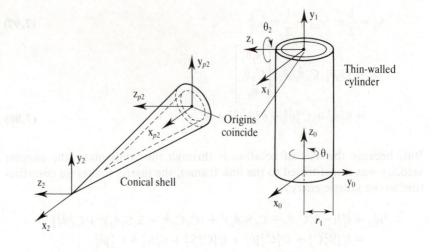

$$\frac{\partial L}{\partial \dot\theta_2} = ml_2^2 \dot\theta_2 \tag{7.108}$$

$$\frac{d}{dt}\left(\frac{\partial L}{\partial \dot\theta_2}\right) = ml_2 \ddot\theta_2 \tag{7.109}$$

Finally, derive the equations for the control of joint torques.

$$\tau_1 = ml_2^2(C_2^2\ddot\theta_1 - 2C_2S_2\dot\theta_1\dot\theta_2) \tag{7.110}$$

$$\tau_2 = ml_2^2\ddot\theta_2 + ml_2^2 S_2 C_2 \dot\theta_1 + mgl_2 C_2 \tag{7.111}$$

$$\begin{bmatrix} \tau_1 \\ \tau_2 \end{bmatrix} = ml_2^2 \begin{bmatrix} C_2^2 & 0 \\ 0 & 1 \end{bmatrix} \ddot\theta_1 + ml_2^2 \begin{bmatrix} 0 \\ S_2 C_2 \end{bmatrix} \dot\theta_1^2$$

$$- 2ml_2^2 \begin{bmatrix} S_2 C_2 \\ 0 \end{bmatrix} \dot\theta_1 \dot\theta_2 + \begin{bmatrix} 0 \\ mgl_2 C_2 \end{bmatrix} \tag{7.112}$$

From our discussion of the closed-form equations in Section 7.2.3, we can attribute physical meaning to the terms in the above torque equation. The first term is the contribution due to inertia, the second is the centrifugal torque, the third is the Coriolis torque and the fourth is the effect of gravity.

Example 7.2 Lagrangian dynamics with distributed mass

To achieve more accurate dynamic equations for the type 2 two-link manipulator, the linkages can be modelled as sections with distributed mass. Here, we will model the first link with a thin walled cylinder, and the second link as a conical shell (Figure 7.13). The first step in calculating the Lagrangian is to calculate the kinetic energy of the links. Again, the centroid of link 1 does not move, so its potential energy is constant, and the kinetic energy is due to angular velocity. Also, the orgin of frame 1 does not move, so the kinetic energy is expressed relative to frame 1, and the parallel axis theorem is used to transform the inertia tensor. Recognizing that a link has a point which is fixed in space and calculating the energy with respect to that point simplifies the calculations.

$$K_1 = \frac{1}{2} \omega_1^T \mathbf{I}_1 \, \omega_1 \tag{7.113}$$

where $\mathbf{I}_1$ and ω_1 are measured with respect to frame 1.

$$\omega_1 = - \begin{bmatrix} 0 \\ 0 \\ \dot{\theta}_1 \end{bmatrix} \tag{7.114}$$

$$\mathbf{I}_1 = \begin{bmatrix} \dfrac{m_1 r_1^2}{2} + \dfrac{m_1 l_1^2}{3} & 0 & 0 \\ 0 & \dfrac{m_1 r_1^2}{2} + \dfrac{m_1 l_1^2}{3} & 0 \\ 0 & 0 & m_1 r_1^2 \end{bmatrix} \tag{7.115}$$

where r_1 is the radius of the cylinder.

By substituting these equations into Equation 7.113, we obtain the kinetic energy for link 1.

$$K_1 = \frac{1}{2} m_1 r_1^2 \dot{\theta}_1^2 \tag{7.116}$$

In the case of link 2, which rotates around the origin of frame 1, the only point that is fixed in space is this origin (Figure 7.13). But link 2 moves with respect to frame 1 and, consequently, the inertia tensor with respect to frame 1 varies. However, if we fix a new frame (frame $p2$) to link 2 with its origin coincident with the origin of frame 1, we have a frame in which the inertia tensor is fixed.

The new frame $p2$ is called $p2$ because it is fixed to link 2 at the proximal joint, and is parallel to frame 2, the link frame at the distal joint. To calculate the kinetic energy relative to frame $p2$, we have to calculate the angular velocity of link 2 relative to the reference frame with respect to frame $p2$.

$$^{p2}\omega_{0,2} = {}^2\omega_{0,2} = {}^{-0}\omega_{0,2} = - \begin{bmatrix} S_2 \dot{\theta}_1 \\ C_2 \dot{\theta}_1 \\ \dot{\theta}_2 \end{bmatrix} \tag{7.117}$$

From Figure 7.9, the inertia matrix relative to frame $p2$ is

$$
^{p2}\mathbf{I}_2 =
\begin{bmatrix}
\dfrac{m_2 r_2^2}{2} & 0 & 0 \\[2ex]
0 & \dfrac{m_2 r_2^2}{4} + \dfrac{m_2 l_2^2}{6} & 0 \\[2ex]
0 & 0 & \dfrac{m_2 r_2^2}{4} + \dfrac{m_2 l_2^2}{6}
\end{bmatrix}
\tag{7.118}
$$

As frame $p2$ is fixed in space, the linear velocity component of the kinetic energy is zero, and the total kinetic energy is

$$
\begin{aligned}
K_2 &= \frac{^{p2}\omega_{0,2}^{\mathrm{T}}\, ^{p2}\mathbf{I}_2\, ^{p2}\omega_{0,2}}{2} \\[2ex]
&= \frac{m_2 (r_2 S_2 \dot{\theta}_1)^2}{2} + \left(\frac{m_2 r_2^2}{8} + \frac{m_2 l_2^2}{12} \right) (C_2^2 \dot{\theta}_1^2 + \dot{\theta}_2^2)
\end{aligned}
\tag{7.119}
$$

The potential energy of the links is the same as for the previous example (Equations 7.101, 102) except that the lengths are the distances to the centroid ($l_1/2$ and $l_2/3$). The total energy is the sum of the potential and kinetic energies of the links, and the joint torques are found by solving the Lagrangian. These two steps are left as an exercise for the reader.

In the case of a link where no point is fixed in space, the kinetic energy is calculated with respect to a frame located at the centroid. For example, the forearm of an articulated manipulator has no fixed point. In this situation, the linear velocity of the centroid must also be calculated with respect to the reference frame, as the linear velocity also contributes to kinetic energy.

Key points

- Dynamics is the study of the motion of bodies under the action of forces.
- The dynamic behaviour of a robot is the time rate of change of manipulator configuration as a function of actuator torque.
- The inverse dynamic problem is to calculate the joint torques required to follow a trajectory.
- An actuator has to balance torques from four sources: motion, friction, gravity, and the manipulation task.
- Manipulator motion produces three types of dynamic torque: inertial, centripetal, and Coriolis.
- D'Alembert's equation includes statics as a special case of dynamics.

$$\delta W = f_x \delta x + f_y \delta y + f_z \delta z = m(a_x \delta x + a_y \delta y + a_z \delta z) \tag{7.5}$$

- Newton's equation expresses force as a function of linear acceleration

$$^R f_n = m_n \,^R a_n \tag{7.14}$$

- Euler's equation expresses torque as a function of angular acceleration

$$^R \tau_n = {}^C I_n \,^R \alpha_n + {}^R \omega_n \times {}^C I_n \cdot {}^R \omega_n \tag{7.15}$$

- The force at a joint is

$$^R f_{n-1,n} = m_n \,^R a_n + {}^R f_{n,n+1} - m_n \,^R g \tag{7.18}$$

- The torque at a joint is

$$^R \tau_{n-1,n} = {}^R \tau_{n,n+1} + {}^R c_{n-1,n} \times m_n \,^R a_n + {}^R p_{n-1,n} \times {}^R f_{n,n+1}$$
$$- {}^R c_{n-1,n} \times m_n \,^R g + I_n \,^R \alpha_n + {}^R \omega_n \times I_n \,^R \omega_n \tag{7.20}$$

- The centroidal inertia tensor is a matrix of the moments of inertia for rotations about the axes of the centroidal frame and their products.
- The closed form of the Newton–Euler dynamic equations is:

$$\tau_n = \sum_{j=1}^{i} H_{nj} d^2 \theta_j + \sum_{j=1}^{i} \sum_{k=1}^{i} C_{njk} d\theta_j d\theta_k + G_n + F_n + \tau_e \tag{7.41}$$

- The generalized Lagrange equation for a manipulator with n independent joint coordinates is

$$L(q_n, \dot{q}_n) = K - U \tag{7.70}$$

- Using the Langrangian, the n non-linear, coupled equations for the dynamics of an n link robot are:

$$F_n = \frac{d}{dt}\left(\frac{\partial K}{\partial \dot{q}_n}\right) - \frac{\partial K}{\partial q_n} + \frac{\partial U}{\partial q_n} \tag{7.72}$$

- The kinetic energy is:

$$K = \sum_{1}^{n} K_n = \sum_{1}^{n} \left(\frac{m_n \,^R v_n^{T \, R} v_n}{2} + \frac{\omega_n^T I_n \omega_n}{2} \right) \tag{7.74}$$

- The potential energy is:

$$U = \sum_1^n U_n = \sum_1^n m_n g^{T0} c_{0,n} \tag{7.75}$$

- Correct estimation of the moments of inertia of the links is a significant problem in the control of dynamic behaviour.
- To simplify their dynamics, robots are designed to have diagonal inertia tensors.

Exercises

■ *Essay questions*

7.1. Calculate the joint torques for the type 1 two-link manipulator using Newton–Euler dynamics and Lagrangian dynamics (Section 7.3.4) for links made of a solid square sections.

7.2. Calculate the Newton–Euler dynamics for the single link manipulator shown in Figure 7.7. Verify that the closed form equation is the same as that obtained using Lagrangian dynamics.

7.3. Verify that the equations for joint torque for a type 1 two-link manipulator obtained using Lagrangian dynamics in Section 7.3.4 are the same as those obtained using Newton–Euler dynamics in Section 7.2.1.

7.4. Find the equations for the torques at the joints of a type 1 two-link manipulator when the links are modelled as point masses at the distal end of each link.

7.5. Complete the calculation of the Lagrangian dynamics for the type 2 two-link manipulator in Section 7.7.2.

7.6. Repeat the calculation of the Lagrangian dynamics for the type 2 two-link manipulator by referring inertias and angular velocities to frames fixed at the centroids of the links.

7.7. Calculate the dynamics of the type 2 two-link manipulator using Newton–Euler dynamics for both the point mass model and the distributed mass model (Figure 7.13).

7.8. Calculate the Lagrangian dynamics for the planar two-link manipulator in Figure 7.14, using thin-walled square sections to model the links.

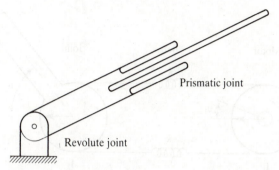

Figure 7.14
Two-link manipulator.

Prismatic joint

Revolute joint

7.9. Calculate the Newton–Euler dynamics for the first two links of the CMU direct-drive arm. Parameters are given in Figures 7.10 and 11.

7.10. The closed-form dynamic equation is given in Equation 7.41. For the type 2 two-link manipulator find the components of the closed form equation. Also, find the manipulator inertia tensor matrix.

7.11. The single-link robot in Figure 7.15, is modelled as a thin-walled cylinder, and a spherical tool of mass m_t is fixed to the end. Calculate the location of the centroid and the centroidal inertia tensor for this robot.

7.12. A tool is placed at the end of the type 1 two-link manipulator. The manipulator is modelled with slender cylindrical rods (Section 7.3.4) and the tool with a point mass. What change does the mass of the tool make to the dynamics?

7.13. Repeat Exercise 7.11, but this time, model the links with thin-walled square sections and the tool with a cube of mass m.

7.14. When the type 1 two-link manipulator is perpendicular to the earth's surface, its potential energy changes with configuration. Calculate the Newton–Euler dynamic equations and the Lagrange dynamic equations for the robot in this configuration. What is the effect of gravity on the dynamics of this robot?

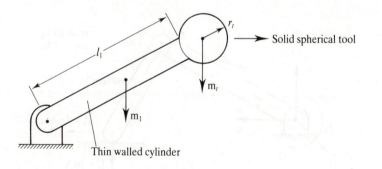

r_t

Solid spherical tool

l_1

m_t

m_1

Thin walled cylinder

Figure 7.15
Single-link robot with spherical tool.

Figure 7.16
Motor coupled to a joint with
a belt.

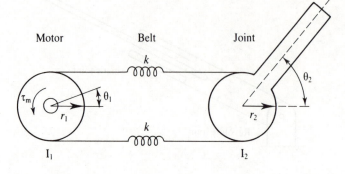

7.15. In some robots, the motor is coupled to the joint by a belt drive. The belt is under tension and may be considered to be a spring in series with the inertia of the link (Figure 7.16). Find the Lagrangian for this system and find the dynamic equations relating the input motor torque τ_m to the angles θ_1 and θ_2. Assume small differences between θ_1 and θ_2.

7.16. A type 1 two-link manipulator, in contact with a smooth surface, applies a normal force to that surface while the tool centre point slides along the surface. Calculate the required joint torques for the situation in the Figure 7.17. Model the links with solid cylinders.

7.17. A type 1 two-link manipulator is moving an object in free space (Figure 7.18). A force sensor is mounted between the end of the second link and the gripper. This sensor measures the x and y components of force and the z component of torque at the wrist. Model the links with thin-walled cylinders, and the gripper/object with a solid sphere. Derive an equation for the mass of the object/gripper from:

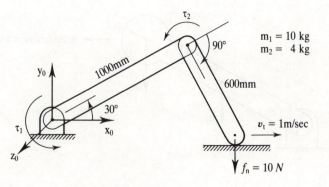

Figure 7.17
Type 1 two-link planar
manipulator pushing on an
object.

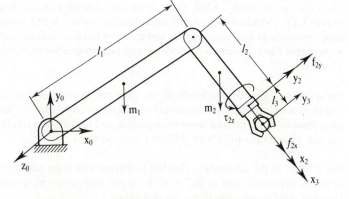

Figure 7.18
Type 1 two-link manipulator
moving an object.

(a) the data measured by the force sensor, and

(b) the torques at the joints.

7.18. Wilson and Deb (1989) present a Fortran program for computing the volume, first moments and inertia moments for bodies formed by revolving polygonal shapes using line integrals. Implement this program and calculate the moments of inertia for a cone and a conical shell (Figure 7.9).

■ *Practical questions*

7.1. Construct a motor-sensor-linkage system as shown in Figure 7.19. The motor is a direct current motor with an electronic controller to enable control of the angular position, velocity, or acceleration of the shaft. The armature current (A) and the back EMF(E) of the motor should be measured. These can be used in Equations 2.1 to 2.3 to calculate angular velocity (ω) and shaft torque (τ). The other parameters to be sensed are shaft torque, angular position, angular velocity, and angular acceleration using the sensors in Figure 7.19.

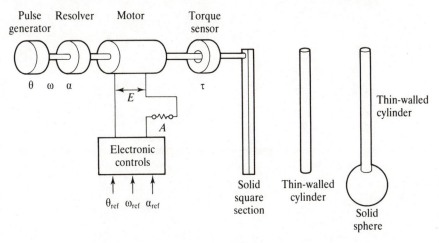

Figure 7.19
Laboratory set up for
measuring the inertia of
links.

7.2. Fix a link to the shaft – a link made from a solid square section is shown in Figure 7.19. Calculate the dynamic equation for this single link manipulator. Run the motor at constant velocity and measure the acceleration and torque. Repeat this for a number of velocities and plot torque verses velocity, and acceleration.

7.3. For a range of angular accelerations, measure the torque and plot the results. Use these measurements to calculate the inertial parameters for the link. Compare these to those in your dynamic equation and identify the errors. Repeat the experiments for links with different cross sections.

7.4. For a robot in the laboratory, find the kinematic and mass parameters of all linkages, actuators, and so on, either from the manuals or by measurement. Develop the dynamic equations for this robot.

8 · *Mobile Robots*

Despite excellence in using our own legs for locomotion, we are still at a primitive stage in understanding the control principles that underlie walking and running.

Marc Raibert, 1986.

Objectives

In this chapter, the style of presentation changes from the rigorous mathematical style of the previous five chapters to a descriptive algorithmic style for the rest of the book. Our objective is to understand the algorithms used in solving robotics problems so that we are better able to program robotics systems. Thus, this chapter is a significant turning point in the book.

The material in this chapter is not as mature as that in previous chapters and, consequently, is the subject of vigorous research. Our objective is to model the mechanics of mobility, and to study the algorithms and data structures used in navigation. As many of these algorithms use techniques from computational geometry (Guibas and Stolfi, 1988), the reader is

assumed to have studied the programming of data structures at first year university computer science level. The study of mobility includes the following topics:

- kinematic modelling of wheeled robots,
- models of walking robots,
- a model of dynamic stability,
- navigation of mobile robots,
- dead reckoning,
- guidance systems,
- beacons and landmarks,
- environment mapping,
- path planning, and
- collision avoidance.

A robot can manipulate objects only that it can reach. As most industrial robots are fixed in place, their workspace is limited by the maximum extension of their linkages (see Figure 2.27). Components are brought to the robot and taken away again by conveyors and other mechanical feed devices. To overcome the problems caused by the limited reach of robot arms, two approaches are under investigation. One is the flexible manufacturing cell, where the robot is fixed in place and the machines that it services are placed around it. As the robot can reach several machines, it can service one while the others are performing their tasks, and it can transfer components from one machine to the next. This approach works best when the machines are small enough to fit close to the robot, when all machines are carrying out the same task or all are working on different stages of the same task, and when no machine is idle waiting for the robot to service it.

A second approach is to mobilize the robot – for example, by mounting it on rails – so that it can move from one machine to another. While this restricts the motion of the robot to a known path, it is simple to model and control and is adequate for large flexible manufacturing cells.

Owing to the nature of the processes involved, many manufacturing operations cannot be restricted in space and rely heavily on material transfer between work cells. In the car manufacturing industry for example, manipulator arms are fixed in place in work cells (for welding, painting, glueing, sealing, and so on) and the car chassis is moved from cell to cell using AGVs (Automated Guided Vehicles). The motion of these vehicles is restricted to certain predefined paths, and once the guidance mechanism is installed, it is expensive to alter.

In the past, a manufacturer set up his plant on the basis of an expected long product run. Such a factory changed little from day to day and in order to achieve continuous throughput, the manufacturer kept large stocks of raw materials and parts. With the advent of design for manufacture and computer-controlled inventory systems all this has changed. Now customers expect a variety of options, and fast delivery. The rising cost of keeping large inventories has stimulated the development of just-in-time manufacturing. One of the most serious problems in this environment is the transport of parts and sub-assemblies (work in process) between manufacturing cells. Often individual parts must be quickly transferred from one cell to another to keep production going. In this environment, traditional AGVs are too cumbersome and inflexible. Smaller, more flexible mobile robots are needed.

Robots with the flexibility to move in less constrained environments are starting to appear in industry (Figure 8.1), but their motion is still restricted. Before a general-purpose mobile robot can move freely in a factory, home, farm, or military environment, we have to achieve an 'intelligent' connection between perception (sensing and understanding the environment) and action (control of robot motion within the environment).

Figure 8.1
Flexible manufacturing
systems (FMS) mobile robot
carrying silicon wafers
between work stations.

This is the emphasis of most of the research into ALVs (Autonomous Land Vehicles) (Thorpe and Kanade, 1987).

In this chapter, we will look at the issues relating to action in two-dimensional space, (while a mobile robot is a three dimensional entity it moves along paths described in two dimension). Some of these topics will be extended in Chapter 9 to the more complex problems of moving a manipulator in three dimensional space. In Chapter 10, issues relating to perception will be examined.

In Chapter 2, we examined the mechanical construction of both wheeled and legged vehicles. In this chapter, we discuss the modelling, programming and control of robot motion, starting with the kinematics of robot motion. Many of the topics covered here are subject to continuing research, so this chapter is intended as an introduction only.

This chapter is divided into three major sections: the kinematics of wheeled robots, the dynamics of walking robots, and navigation. In the first section, we develop a kinematic modelling technique for wheeled robots by modelling the robot as a multiple closed-link chain, first proposed by Muir and Newman (1986). However, the complete development of mobile robot kinematics is extensive and, hence, beyond the scope of this book.

In the second section, we examine the problems of walking robots. Many robots are designed to be statically stable, that is, they maintain their centre of gravity within a triangle defined by the contact points between three feet and the ground. However, these robots can be slow and cumbersome. To improve the speed and dexterity of walking robots, several researchers are formulating dynamic models of walking. We will examine the dynamic model developed by Marc Raibert (1986).

In the third section, we investigate the problems of navigation: environment mapping, path planning and collision avoidance. For a mobile robot to be autonomous it must be able to plan and traverse paths through its environment. A variety of mapping methods are used by researchers. The ideal data structure for navigation is suitable for storing maps of the environment and for searching for paths. Most data structures are a compromise between these two desires. Once a path is planned, the robot must traverse it without colliding into anything. To achieve this goal, information from sensors must be integrated into the control algorithms.

8.1 Kinematic modelling of wheeled robots

Muir and Newman (1986) formulated the kinematic equations of motion for a variety of wheeled mobile robots. Their development parallels the development of kinematics for manipulator arms in Chapters 4 and 5 and draws heavily upon the concepts of manipulator kinematics. However, the kinematic modelling of wheeled robots differs from the modelling of manipulators because the wheels are always in contact with the ground forming a multiple closed-link chain, whereas a manipulator is a single, open link chain. They decompose kinematics into two sections: internal and external kinematics.

Internal kinematics describes the relationships between the linkages within the robot. These relationships are important when steering the robot. **External kinematics** describes the relationships between the robot and the rest of the world, – the trajectory of the robot.

There are several inherent differences between a mobile robot and a manipulator arm:

1. A wheeled mobile robot always has more than one wheel in contact with the surface it is travelling over and, consequently, is modelled as a multiple closed-link chain. In constrast, a manipulator is modelled as a single open-link chain when in free space, and is modelled only as a closed-link chain when in contact with a workpiece. A legged robot can be modelled with a chain for each leg, which opens and closes as the foot is lifted off the ground and placed back on the ground.

2. All the joints of a manipulator arm are restricted to one degree of freedom, and the degrees of freedom of the end effector are constrained by the task. In contrast, the wheel of a mobile robot can both turn and translate with respect to the contact point between it and the floor. This pseudo joint is described as a **higher order pair**. A higher order pair is constrained by a point or line contact, where a lower-order pair is constrained by a common surface of contact, such as a prismatic joint.

3. On a manipulator arm, all joints are actuated and are used to control the motion of the end effector. On a mobile robot, some wheels are not actuated at all and some degrees of freedom are not actuated on some wheels.

4. To control the trajectory of the end effector of a manipulator, the position, velocity and acceleration of each joint must be measured. In contrast, when controlling the trajectory of a mobile robot, there is no need to measure the position, velocity and acceleration of each degree of freedom of each wheel.

8.1.1 Definitions and assumptions

To provide a framework within which to develop their kinematic models, Muir and Newman defined a **wheeled mobile robot** as:

> A robot capable of locomotion on a surface solely through the actuation of wheel assemblies mounted on the robot and in contact with the surface. A **wheel assembly** is a device which provides or allows relative motion between its mount and a surface on which it is intended to have a single point of rolling contact.
>
> Muir and Newman, 1986.

Further, to obtain tractable equations, they assumed that:

1. the robot is built from rigid mechanisms,
2. the robot contains a maximum of one steering link per wheel,
3. all steering axes are perpendicular to the floor,
4. the surface is a smooth plane,
5. no translational slip occurs between the wheel and the floor,
6. the rotational friction at the point of contact is small enough for the wheel to turn about a vertical axis through that point.

8.1.2 Assignment of coordinate frames

In a multiple closed-link chain, the Denavit-Hartenberg convention for coordinate frame assignment leads to ambiguous transformation matrices because the joint ordering is not obvious. To overcome this problem, Muir and Newman used the Sheth-Uicker (1971) convention to assign coordinate frames, and modelled each wheel as a planar pair at the point of contact. A planar pair has two degrees of translation and one of rotation (Figure 8.2(a)). With this representation, the multiple degrees of freedom of wheel motion can be modelled without ambiguities in the transformation matrices. A conventional wheel (Figure 8.2(b)) has only two degrees of freedom,

Figure 8.2
Planar pair model of a wheel
with two degrees of
translators and one of
rotation.
(a) Planar pair;
(b) conventional wheel.

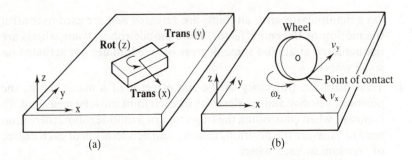

(a)　　　　　　　(b)

because the third degree of freedom in the planar pair model is eliminated
when we set the x component of wheel velocity to zero to eliminate sideways
slip, and the y component of wheel velocity to the angular velocity times the
radius.

　　　In the Sheth-Uicker convention, coordinate frames are assigned at
both ends of each link. Consequently, there are two coordinate frames at
each joint. When these frames coincide, the joint variable is zero. The links
of a wheeled mobile robot are the floor, the robot body and the steering links
(Figure 8.3). These three links are connected by three joints: the wheel, the
steering axis, and the mid-point of the robot. This last joint is not a physical
joint, but the relationship between the body of the robot and the floor is
modelled as a planar pair located at the centre of the robot. The wheel is also
modelled as a planar pair located at the point of contact between the wheel
and the floor. The steering axis may be an actual joint or some other

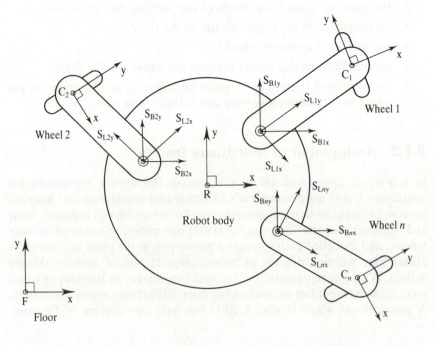

Figure 8.3
Assignment of coordinate
frames for a wheeled mobile
robot. Instantaneously
coincident frames are not
shown as they are coincided
with frames R and $C_2 \ldots C_n$
(Muir and Newman, 1986)

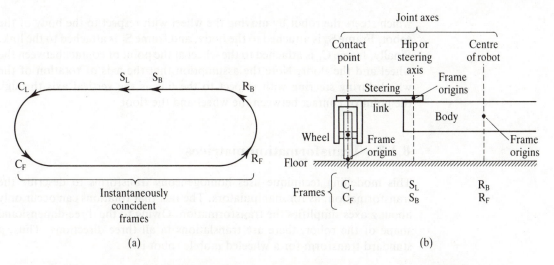

Figure 8.4
Assignment of coordinate
frames for an isolated wheel.
(a) Transform diagram;
(b) coordinate frame
location.

mechanical arrangement, and is modelled as a revolute pair. The z axis of all these frames is vertical, and is neglected in two-dimensional analysis.

If a wheel is considered in isolation (Figure 8.4), it has three links, three joints, and six coordinate frames. Two of these coordinate frames were not shown on Figure 8.3 (frames C_F and R_F), as they are **instantaneously coincident coordinate systems**. This is a stationary coordinate frame that is located at the same point as a moving coordinate frame at the instant of observation. It is equivalent to instantaneously placing a floor coordinate frame at the same location as the moving frame. Thus, the position transform between the two frames is zero, but the velocity and acceleration transforms are not. They are not the same as the velocity and acceleration transforms of the moving frame with respect to the floor frame, because setting the distance transform to zero eliminates the contribution of the angular velocity of the moving frame to the linear velocity. Instantaneously coincident coordinate frames are introduced to enable the velocities and accelerations of this multi-dimensional moving coordinate system to be calculated independently of the location of the vehicle.

They use the instantaneous robot frame R_F to specify the velocities and accelerations of the robot independently of robot position at the instant of observation and they use the instantaneous contact frame C_F to calculate wheel velocities and accelerations because the position of the wheel contact point is not measured with sensors. These frames are instantaneously fixed with respect to the floor not the robot. At the instant these frames are considered, they are coincident with the frames attached to the robot. Frame R_F coincides with frame R_B and frame C_F coincides with frame C_L.

The floor coordinate frame F is stationary, and serves as a reference frame for the motion of the robot. The robot frame R_B is located at the centre of the robot, and serves to define the location of the robot with respect to the floor frame for external kinematics. Two frames are located at the hip joint, which steers the robot by moving the wheel with respect to the body of the robot. Frame S_B is attached to the body, and frame S_L is attached to the link. Finally, frame C_L is attached to the wheel at the point of contact between the wheel and the floor. Note the assumption that the axis of rotation of the wheel during steering with respect to the link is the vertical axis through the point of contact between the wheel and the floor.

8.1.3 Transformation matrices

This modelling technique uses homogeneous transforms to describe the transformation, as for manipulators. The fact that rotations can occur only about z axes simplifies the transformation. Owing to the three-dimensional shape of the robot, there are translations in all three directions. Thus, a standard transform for a wheeled mobile robot is:

$$
{}^{R}T_{N} = \begin{bmatrix} C_\theta & -S_\theta & 0 & p_X \\ S_\theta & C_\theta & 0 & p_Y \\ 0 & 0 & 1 & p_Z \\ 0 & 0 & 0 & 1 \end{bmatrix} \tag{8.1}
$$

where $\theta = {}^{R}\theta_{N}$ is the rotation angle between two frames.

The inverse transform is obtained as before (see Section 3.8), and the velocity transform and acceleration transform are calculated by differentiation.

$$
{}^{R}v_{N} = \begin{bmatrix} -\omega S & -\omega C & 0 & v_x \\ \omega C & -\omega S & 0 & v_y \\ 0 & 0 & 0 & 0 \\ 0 & 0 & 0 & 0 \end{bmatrix} \tag{8.2}
$$

$$
{}^{R}a_{N} = \begin{bmatrix} -\alpha S - \omega^2 C & -\alpha C + \omega^2 S & 0 & a_x \\ \alpha C - \omega^2 S & -\alpha S - \omega^2 C & 0 & a_y \\ 0 & 0 & 0 & 0 \\ 0 & 0 & 0 & 0 \end{bmatrix} \tag{8.3}
$$

where

$\omega = {}^{R}\omega_{N}$ = angular velocity.

$\alpha = {}^{R}\alpha_{N}$ = angular acceleration.

$v_x = {}^{R}v_{NX}$ = x component of linear velocity,

$a_x = {}^{R}a_{NX}$ = x component of linear acceleration.

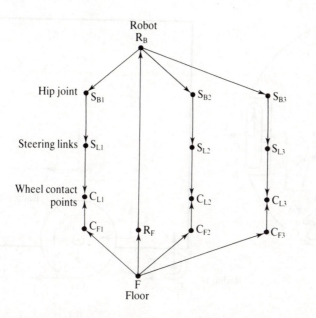

Figure 8.5
Transform graph for three-wheeled robot.

The transformation between any two coordinate frames is simply the multiplication of the intermediate frames as before. Thus, for an isolated link (Figure 8.4) the transformation from the centre of the robot to the point of contact of the wheel is:

$$^{RB}\mathbf{T}_{CF} = {}^{RB}\mathbf{T}_{SB}\,{}^{SB}\mathbf{T}_{SL}\,{}^{SL}\mathbf{T}_{CL}\,{}^{CL}\mathbf{T}_{CF} = {}^{CF}\mathbf{T}_{RF}\,{}^{RF}\mathbf{T}_{RB} \qquad (8.4)$$

Many robots do not have steering links, as shown in Figure 8.3. For these robots, the steering axis and the contact point axis coincide and the transforms between these axes reduce to identity matrices. Thus the equations are simplified to match the simpler robot configuration. As the two instantaneously coincident coordinate frames coincide with two other frames, the transform between the instantaneously coincident frames and the frames they coincide with is the identify matrix, as far as position is concerned, simplifying the position transform equation.

$$^{RB}\mathbf{T}_{CF} = {}^{RB}\mathbf{T}_{SB}\,{}^{SB}\mathbf{T}_{SL}\,{}^{SL}\mathbf{T}_{CL} = {}^{CF}\mathbf{T}_{RF} \qquad (8.5)$$

With this equation, the position of any point p on the robot defined with respect to one frame (new frame) can be found with respect to any other frame (reference frame).

$$^{R}p = {}^{R}\mathbf{T}_{N}\,{}^{N}p \qquad (8.6)$$

For a robot, with three wheels, as shown in Figure 8.3, the kinematic model is illustrated with a parallel transform graph (Figure 8.5) with four

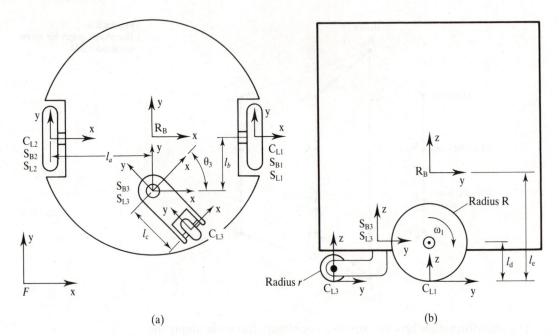

(a)

(b)

Figure 8.6
Coordinate frames for Newt robot which has diametrically opposed drive wheels and a free-wheeling castor (Hollis, 1977): (a) top view – z axes point out of page; (b) Side view – y axes point out of page

paths: one for each wheel, and a common return path. This is the parallel transform graph of a multiple closed-link chain, and completely describes the internal kinematics of a three-wheeled robot. The transform equations for this robot are:

$$^{RF}\mathbf{T}_{RB} = {}^{RB}\mathbf{T}_{SB1}\,{}^{SB1}\mathbf{T}_{SL1}\,{}^{SL1}\mathbf{T}_{CL1}\,{}^{CL1}\mathbf{T}_{CF1}\,{}^{CF1}\mathbf{T}_{F}\,{}^{F}\mathbf{T}_{RF} \qquad (8.7)$$

$$= {}^{RB}\mathbf{T}_{SB2}\,{}^{SB2}\mathbf{T}_{SL2}\,{}^{SL2}\mathbf{T}_{CL2}\,{}^{CL2}\mathbf{T}_{CF2}\,{}^{CF2}\mathbf{T}_{F}\,{}^{F}\mathbf{T}_{RF} \qquad (8.8)$$

$$= {}^{RB}\mathbf{T}_{SB3}\,{}^{SB3}\mathbf{T}_{SL3}\,{}^{SL3}\mathbf{T}_{CL3}\,{}^{CL3}\mathbf{T}_{CF3}\,{}^{CF3}\mathbf{T}_{F}\,{}^{F}\mathbf{T}_{RF} \qquad (8.9)$$

As an example of this modelling technique, consider the Newt mobile robot in Figure 8.6. Newt (Hollis, 1977) has diametrically opposed drive wheels, which are used for motion and steering, and a free-wheeling castor. As the drive wheels are fixed to the body, the steering frames do not move with respect to either the robot body frame or the wheel contact frame. If they are placed coincident with the wheel contact frames, the transform between the steering frame and the contact frame is the identity matrix.

$$^{SB1}\mathbf{T}_{SL1} = {}^{SL1}\mathbf{T}_{CL1} = {}^{SB2}\mathbf{T}_{SL2} = {}^{SL2}\mathbf{T}_{CL2} = \mathbf{I} \qquad (8.10)$$

Thus, the transforms between the centre of the robot and the driven wheel contact points are:

$$^{RB}T_{CL1} = {}^{RB}T_{SL1} = \begin{bmatrix} 1 & 0 & 0 & l_a \\ 0 & 1 & 0 & 0 \\ 0 & 0 & 1 & -l_e \\ 0 & 0 & 0 & 1 \end{bmatrix} \tag{8.11}$$

$$^{RB}T_{CL2} = \begin{bmatrix} 1 & 0 & 0 & l_a \\ 0 & 1 & 0 & 0 \\ 0 & 0 & 1 & -l_e \\ 0 & 0 & 0 & 1 \end{bmatrix} \tag{8.12}$$

In contrast, the castor moves with respect to the robot, and its transform is:

$$^{RB}T_{CL3} = {}^{RB}T_{SB3} \, {}^{SB3}T_{SL3} \, {}^{SL3}T_{CL3}$$

$$= \begin{bmatrix} 1 & 0 & 0 & 0 \\ 0 & 1 & 0 & -l_b \\ 0 & 0 & 1 & -l_e + l_d \\ 0 & 0 & 0 & 1 \end{bmatrix} \begin{bmatrix} C_3 & -S_3 & 0 & 0 \\ S_3 & C_3 & 0 & 0 \\ 0 & 0 & 1 & 0 \\ 0 & 0 & 0 & 1 \end{bmatrix} \begin{bmatrix} 1 & 0 & 0 & 0 \\ 0 & 1 & 0 & -l_c \\ 0 & 0 & 1 & -l_d \\ 0 & 0 & 0 & 1 \end{bmatrix}$$

$$= \begin{bmatrix} C_3 & -S_3 & 0 & l_c S_3 \\ S_3 & C_3 & 0 & -l_b - l_c C_3 \\ 0 & 0 & 1 & -l_e \\ 0 & 0 & 0 & 1 \end{bmatrix} \tag{8.13}$$

8.1.4 Velocity and Jacobian

We can calculate the velocity v_p of a point p on a robot with respect to a reference frame from its location with respect to a new frame by differentiating the position transform in Equation 8.6. Since the point p is fixed with respect to the new frame, its velocity with respect to the new frame is zero.

$$^{R}v_p = \frac{d}{dt} \, {}^{R}T_N \, {}^{N}p \tag{8.14}$$

For example, from the position of a point located on a steering link (Figure 8.7) relative to the link frame (S_L), we will calculate the velocity of this point relative to the floor (frame F). The position transform of the point is:

$$^{F}p = {}^{F}T_{RF} \, {}^{RF}T_{RB} \, {}^{RB}T_{SB} \, {}^{SB}T_{SL} \, {}^{SL}p \tag{8.15}$$

and the velocity transform is:

Figure 8.7
Velocity of a point on the
steering link.

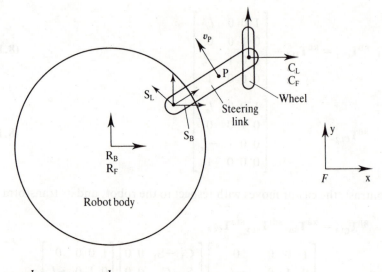

$$\frac{d}{dt}\,^{F}p = \,^{F}v_{p} = \frac{d}{dt}(\,^{F}\mathbf{T}_{RF}\,^{RF}\mathbf{T}_{RB}\,^{RB}\mathbf{T}_{SB}\,^{SB}\mathbf{T}_{SL})\,^{SL}p \tag{8.16}$$

where

$$\frac{d}{dt}(\,^{F}\mathbf{T}_{RF}\,^{RF}\mathbf{T}_{RB}\,^{RB}\mathbf{T}_{SB}\,^{SB}\mathbf{T}_{SL}) + \frac{d}{dt}(\,^{F}\mathbf{T}_{RF})\,^{RF}\mathbf{T}_{SL}$$

$$+ \,^{F}\mathbf{T}_{RF}\frac{d}{dt}(\,^{RF}\mathbf{T}_{RB})\,^{RB}\mathbf{T}_{SL} + \,^{F}\mathbf{T}_{RB}\frac{d}{dt}(\,^{RB}\mathbf{T}_{SB})\,^{SB}\mathbf{T}_{SL}$$

$$+ \,^{F}\mathbf{T}_{SB}\frac{d}{dt}(\,^{SB}\mathbf{T}_{SL}) \tag{8.17}$$

Note, while it was possible to differentiate transformation equations for mechanisms containing lower pairs (manipulator arms), differentiation is not allowable for transformation equations of higher pair mechanisms. To overcome this problem, Muir and Newman (1986) introduce a velocity cascade algorithm to express velocities in terms of the multiplication of transforms, from which the above equation was derived. The reader will observe that the result is identical to that which we would have obtained from the standard differentiation of a product (*uv* – Section 13.2).

Some of the terms in Equation 8.17 can be eliminated. First, the velocity of the frame R_F, located on the floor and instantaneously coincident with the frame R_B, is zero with respect to the floor frame, so the first term in Equation 8.17 is eliminated. Second, the third term contains the velocity of frame S_B with respect to R_B. As these are both attached to the robot, and S_B is fixed with respect to R_B, this term is also eliminated. The resulting equation is:

$$\frac{d}{dt}\,{}^{F}\mathbf{T}_{SL} = {}^{F}\mathbf{T}_{RF}\frac{d}{dt}\left({}^{RF}\mathbf{T}_{RB}\right){}^{RB}\mathbf{T}_{SB}\,{}^{SB}\mathbf{T}_{SL}$$

$$+\,{}^{F}\mathbf{T}_{RB}\,{}^{RB}\mathbf{T}_{SB}\frac{d}{dt}\left({}^{SB}\mathbf{T}_{SL}\right) \tag{8.18}$$

where

$$\frac{d}{dt}\left({}^{RF}\mathbf{T}_{RB}\right) = {}^{F}v_{\text{robot}} \text{ is the velocity of the robot,}$$

${}^{SB}\mathbf{T}_{SL}$ is the steering position and its derivative is the steering velocity.

${}^{F}\mathbf{T}_{RB} = {}^{F}p_{\text{robot}}$ is the position of the robot, and

${}^{RB}\mathbf{T}_{SB}$ is the robot-to-hip transformation.

To solve the above equation for the velocity of point p with respect to the floor, we have to assign values to the terms. The robot-to-hip transform is a function of the design of the robot and does not usually change. The steering position and velocity are measured with sensors. The robot velocity is calculated from the measurements of wheel velocity, and the position of the robot is calculated by dead reckoning from wheel motions or by the integration of sensor data with a map. For example, the instantaneous velocity of the contact point between the free-wheeling castor on Newt (Figure 8.6) and the floor is:

$$^{F}v_{CL3} = {}^{F}p_{\text{robot}}\,{}^{F}v_{\text{robot}}\,{}^{RB}\mathbf{T}_{SL} + {}^{F}p_{\text{robot}}\,{}^{RB}\mathbf{T}_{RB}\,{}^{B}v_{\text{steering}} \tag{8.19}$$

The two transformations in Equation 8.19 are obtained from Equation 8.13 and the value of the steering angle θ_3 is measured. The other parameters are measured. Alternatively, the velocity of the robot can be calculated from measurements of wheel position and wheel velocity. If we consider one of the drive wheels on Newt, Equation 8.7 for the position of the robot reduces to:

$$^{RF}\mathbf{T}_{RB} = {}^{RB}\mathbf{T}_{SB1}\,\mathbf{I}\,\mathbf{I}\,{}^{CL1}\mathbf{T}_{CF1}\,{}^{CF1}\mathbf{T}_{F}\,{}^{F}\mathbf{T}_{RF} \tag{8.20}$$

By differentiating this equation, we obtain an equation for the velocity of the robot

$$\frac{d}{dt}\,{}^{RF}\mathbf{T}_{RB} = v_{\text{robot}} = {}^{RB}\mathbf{T}_{SB1}\frac{d}{dt}\,{}^{CL1}\mathbf{T}_{CF1}\,{}^{CF1}\mathbf{T}_{F}\,{}^{F}\mathbf{T}_{RF}$$

$$= {}^{RB}\mathbf{T}_{SB1}\,{}^{F}v_{\text{wheel}}\,{}^{F}p_{\text{wheel}}^{-1}\,{}^{F}p_{\text{robot}} \tag{8.21}$$

When the robot is travelling in a straight line, the velocity of the robot is the linear velocity of the wheel ($^R v_{1y}$), and the position of the wheel is the distance moved ($^R v_{1y} t$); both of which can be measured with a pulse generator (see Section 10.5.1.2). When the robot is turning, the velocity of both wheels has to be taken into account when robot velocity is calculated.

This example demonstrates the calculation of the position and velocity of a robot from wheel motions for dead reckoning control. Muir and Newman (1986) developed a wheel Jacobian to express this relationship.

$$^{RF} v_{RB} = \mathbf{J}_{n\,pseudo}\, v_n \tag{8.22}$$

$$= \text{instantaneous velocity of the robot with respect to the coincident floor frame}$$

$$= (v_x, v_y, \omega_z)^T$$

where $\mathbf{J}_{n\,pseudo}$ is the pseudo Jacobian matrix for wheel n, and v_n is the pseudo velocity vector for wheel n.

The Jacobian is developed by differentiating the transform equation (Equation 8.7) of the robot. Once the velocity transform is simplified, the expressions for the transforms (Equations 8.1 and 8.2) are substituted, taking note that some transforms contain only translations and others only rotations. The resulting Jacobian is

$$\mathbf{J}_{n\,pseudo} = \begin{bmatrix} \cos{}^{RB}\theta_{CLn} & -\sin{}^{RB}\theta_{CLn} & {}^{RB}p_{CLny} & -{}^{RB}p_{SBny} \\ \sin{}^{RB}\theta_{CLn} & \cos{}^{RB}\theta_{CLn} & -{}^{RB}p_{CLnx} & {}^{RB}p_{SBnx} \\ 0 & 0 & 1 & -1 \end{bmatrix} \tag{8.23}$$

where

$$^R\theta_N = \text{sum of the angles between the two frames, for example}$$

$$^{RB}\theta_{CL} = {}^{RB}\theta_{SB} + {}^{SB}\theta_{SL} + {}^{SL}\theta_{CL} \tag{8.24}$$

$$^{RB}p_{CL} = \text{vector from the origin of one frame to the other}$$

$$= \begin{bmatrix} {}^{RB}p_{SBx} + {}^{SL}p_{CLx}\cos{}^{RB}\theta_{SL} - {}^{SL}p_{CLx}\sin{}^{RB}\theta_{SL} \\ {}^{RB}p_{SBy} + {}^{SL}p_{CLx}\sin{}^{RB}\theta_{SL} - {}^{SL}p_{CLy}\cos{}^{RB}\theta_{SL} \end{bmatrix} \tag{8.25}$$

The pseudo-velocity vector of a wheel contains four components.

$$v_{n\,pseudo} = \begin{bmatrix} {}^{CF}v_{CLnx} \\ {}^{CF}v_{CLny} \\ {}^{CF}\omega_{CLn} \\ {}^{SB}\omega_{CLn} \end{bmatrix} \tag{8.26}$$

where

> $^{CF}v_{CLn}$ is the instantaneous linear velocity of wheel n with respect to the floor.

> $^{CF}\omega_{CLn}$ is the instantaneous velocity of wheel n around the contact point.

> $^{SB}\omega_{SLn}$ is the angular velocity of the steering link around the hip joint.

The physical velocity vector (v_n) of a typical wheel does not contain all four components of the pseudo-velocity vector, because typical wheels have less than four wheel variables. For example, a conventional wheel has no linear velocity in the x direction (Figure 8.2(b)). Also, a conventional wheel rotates about an axis, and the linear velocity is calculated from the angular velocity of the wheel, which can be measured. The pseudo velocity vector (size 4×1) can be related to the physical velocity vector (size $w_n\times1$) by a wheel matrix (size $4\times w_n$).

$$v_{n\,\text{pseudo}} = \mathbf{W}_n\, v_{n\,\text{physical}} \tag{8.27}$$

and the physical wheel Jacobian ($3\times w_n$) is derived in a similar way.

$$\mathbf{J}_{n\,\text{physical}} = \mathbf{J}_{n\,\text{pseudo}}\mathbf{W}_n \tag{8.28}$$

From the rank of this Jacobian, we determine the number of degrees of freedom of the wheel (where the rank is the number of independent row or column vectors). If the number of degrees of freedom is less than the number of wheel variables, the wheel is redundant. As an example, we will calculate the Jacobian of a conventional nonsteered wheel often used as the drive wheel in robots. This wheel has two degrees of freedom: motion in the direction the wheel is pointing due to rotation of the wheel about its axis, and rotational slip about the contact point.

$$v_{n\,\text{pseudo}} = \begin{bmatrix} ^{CF}v_{CLny} \\ ^{CF}\omega_{CLn} \end{bmatrix} \quad \text{and} \quad v_{n\,\text{physical}} = \begin{bmatrix} ^{CF}\omega_{wnx} \\ ^{CF}\omega_{wnz} \end{bmatrix} \tag{8.29}$$

where

> ω_{wx} = angular velocity of wheel about its axis, and

> ω_{wz} = angular velocity of rotational slip.

The wheel matrix $\mathbf{W}$ is

$$\mathbf{W} = \begin{bmatrix} 0 & 0 \\ r & 0 \\ 0 & 1 \\ 0 & 0 \end{bmatrix} \text{ where } r \text{ is the radius of the wheel} \qquad (8.30)$$

and the physical Jacobian is (Equations 8.23 and 8.28).

$$\mathbf{J} = \begin{bmatrix} -r\sin{}^{RB}\theta_{CLn} & {}^{RB}p_{CLny} \\ r\cos{}^{RB}\theta_{CLn} & -{}^{RB}p_{CLnx} \\ 0 & 1 \end{bmatrix} \qquad (8.31)$$

This wheel is considered to be degenerate because the Jacobian does not have an inverse. Thus, while the robot velocity can be calculated from the wheel velocity, the wheel cannot always be calculated from the robot velocity. Hence, a wheeled mobile robot that has nonsteered conventional wheels cannot be controlled in three degrees of freedom, that is, it cannot move sideways.

From Equation 8.31, the Jacobians for the two nonsteered wheels in Newt (Figure 8.6) are obtained:

$$^{RF}v_{robot} = {}^{RF}v_{RB} = \begin{bmatrix} v_{RX} \\ v_{RY} \\ \omega_{RZ} \end{bmatrix} = \begin{bmatrix} 0 & 0 \\ R & -l_a \\ 0 & 1 \end{bmatrix} \begin{bmatrix} \omega_{w1x} \\ \omega_{w1z} \end{bmatrix} = \mathbf{J}_1 v_{1\,physical} \qquad (8.32)$$

$$\mathbf{J}_2 = \begin{bmatrix} 0 & 0 \\ R & -l_a \\ 0 & 1 \end{bmatrix} \qquad (8.33)$$

The Jacobian for the free-wheeling castor is derived in Section 8.4.1.

8.1.5 Acceleration and transformation between frames

Again, Muir and Newman (1986) use an algorithm to cascade transformation matrices to obtain an acceleration transform. Using a parallel development to the previous section, they obtain the following equations. These equations are rarely calculated in practice because of the difficulty of measuring acceleration accurately.

$$^{R}a_n = \frac{d^2}{dt}({}^{R}\mathbf{T}_N)^{N}p \qquad (8.34)$$

$$
\begin{bmatrix} {}^{RF}a_{RBnx} \\ {}^{RF}a_{RBny} \\ {}^{RF}\alpha_{RBn} \end{bmatrix} = \begin{bmatrix} {}^{RB}p_{CLx} & {}^{RB}p_{SBx} & {}^{RB}p_{SBx} \\ {}^{RB}p_{CLy} & {}^{RB}p_{SBy} & {}^{RB}p_{SBy} \\ 0 & 0 & 0 \end{bmatrix} \begin{bmatrix} {}^{CF}\omega_{CLn}^2 \\ -2\,{}^{CF}\omega_{CLn}\,{}^{SB}\omega_{SLn} \\ {}^{SB}\omega_{SLn}^2 \end{bmatrix}
$$

$$
+ \, \mathbf{J}_{n\,\text{pseudo}} \begin{bmatrix} {}^{CF}a_{CLxn} \\ {}^{CF}a_{CLny} \\ {}^{CF}\alpha_{CLn} \\ {}^{SB}\alpha_{SLn} \end{bmatrix} \tag{8.35}
$$

We have calculated the velocity and acceleration of the robot with respect to the floor frame instantaneously coincident with the robot. In practice, we wish to know these velocities and accelerations with respect to the fixed floor frame. It turns out that a single motion matrix $\mathbf{V}$ transforms both velocity and acceleration.

$$
{}^{F}v_{RB} = \mathbf{V}\,{}^{RF}v_{RB} \tag{8.36}
$$

and

$$
{}^{F}a_{RB} = \mathbf{V}\,{}^{RF}a_{RB} \tag{8.37}
$$

where

$$
\mathbf{V} = \begin{bmatrix} \cos{}^{F}\theta_{RB} & -\sin{}^{F}\theta_{RB} & 0 \\ \sin{}^{F}\theta_{RB} & \cos{}^{F}\theta_{RB} & 0 \\ 0 & 0 & 1 \end{bmatrix} \tag{8.38}
$$

The angular velocities and angular accelerations are the same in both frames, whereas the linear velocities and accelerations are a function of the orientation of the robot.

8.1.6 Composite robot equation

In Section 8.1.3, we developed the set of equations (Equations 8.7 to 8.9) which defines the location of the robot as a function of the location of each wheel. Any one of these is sufficient to determine the location of the robot. In contrast, the velocity equations for the wheels must be combined to determine the resultant robot velocity.

The velocity contribution of a single wheel is

$$
{}^{RF}v_{RBn} = \mathbf{J}_n v_n = v_{\text{robot}\,n} \tag{8.39}
$$

For an *n* wheeled robot, we must solve *n* of these equations simultaneously to calculate the motion of the robot.

$$v_{\text{robot}} = \begin{bmatrix} \mathbf{J}_1 & 0 & \cdot & 0 \\ \cdot & \mathbf{J}_2 & \cdot & \cdot \\ \cdot & \cdot & \cdot & \cdot \\ 0 & \cdot & 0 & \mathbf{J}_n \end{bmatrix} \begin{bmatrix} v_1 \\ v_2 \\ \cdot \\ v_n \end{bmatrix} \tag{8.40}$$

This equation expresses the velocity of the robot as a function of the velocities of the individual wheels. These wheel velocities can be measured, and hence, the equation is referred to as the **sensed forward solution** for the robot. The inverse equation, known as the **actuated inverse solution**, is used to calculate the wheel velocities from the desired robot velocity. In practice, the fact that only some of the wheels are actuated and/or sensed has to be accounted for.

The mobility, actuation and sensing characteristics of a wheeled mobile robot can be determined by reformulating the above equation and examining the properties of the solutions to that equation. The composite robot equation is rewritten as:

$$\begin{bmatrix} \mathbf{I}_1 \\ \mathbf{I}_2 \\ \cdot \\ \mathbf{I}_n \end{bmatrix} v_{\text{robot}} = \begin{bmatrix} \mathbf{J}_1 & 0 & \cdot & 0 \\ \cdot & \mathbf{J}_2 & \cdot & \cdot \\ \cdot & \cdot & \cdot & \cdot \\ 0 & \cdot & 0 & \mathbf{J}_n \end{bmatrix} \begin{bmatrix} v_1 \\ v_2 \\ \cdot \\ v_n \end{bmatrix} \tag{8.41}$$

or

$$\mathbf{A}\, v_{\text{robot}} = \mathbf{B}\, v_{\text{wheels}} \tag{8.42}$$

where

v_{robot} is the of robot velocity vector,

v_{wheels} is the composite wheel velocity vector (up to four components for each wheel),

$\mathbf{A}$ is a matrix of *n* (3×3) identity matrices, and

$\mathbf{B}$ is a ($3n \times w$) block diagonal matrix, where *w* is the total number of wheel variables.

To find the mobility characteristics of the robot (Figure 8.8), we compare the number of degrees of freedom of the robot (three possible) to the rank of matrix $\mathbf{A}$ and the rank of the augmented matrix $\mathbf{A}, \mathbf{B}$. Muir and Newman (1986) validate this method by calculating the least-squares error of the vector of robot velocities for all wheel velocities.

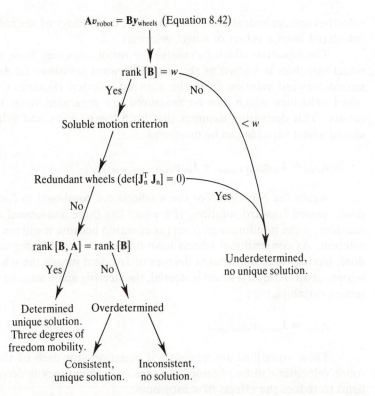

Figure 8.8
Mobility characterization tree for determining the degrees of mobility of a robot

If the system of equations has fewer independent equations than independent variables, it is underdetermined, and there is no unique solution. As the rank of matrix **A** is three, and there are three independent variables in the robot velocity vector (Equation 8.22), the model of a wheeled mobile robot cannot be underdetermined. Hence, the motion of the robot is completely specified by the motion of the wheels.

If the system has the same number of independent equations as independent variables, it is determined. The rank of the augmented matrix **A,B** is greater than three when there is more than one wheel. Thus, a one-wheeled robot is determined, and there is a unique solution to the equations.

If the system has more·independent equations than independent variables, it is overdetermined, which is the case for all multiwheeled robots. This is a consequence of the closed-link kinematic structure of a multi-wheeled robot.

The robot has a unique solution if the robot equations are consistent. If the equations are inconsistent there is no solution. As we have assumed that there is no translational slip at the wheels, the motion of the robot is consistent with the motion of the wheels and a solution is possible. However, this solution depends on being able to measure all the actual wheel velocities. The rotational slip between the wheel and the floor is difficult to measure. Since there are several wheels, each forming a closed-link chain, many wheel velocities are dependent and, consequently, the velocity of the robot can be calculated from a subset of wheel velocities.

The equation which calculates the robot velocities from the sensed wheel velocities is known as the **sensed forward solution**. To develop the sensed forward solution from the forward solution (Equation 8.39), the wheel velocities which can be measured are separated from those that cannot. This derivation assumes that both the position and velocity of a sensed wheel variable can be measured.

$$v_{\text{robot}} = \mathbf{J}_{ns} \, v_{\text{wheel } n \text{ sensed}} + \mathbf{J}_{nn} \, v_{\text{wheel } n \text{ nonsensed}} \qquad (8.43)$$

Again the equations for the n wheels are combined to form a composite sensed forward solution. If a wheel has three non-sensed degrees of freedom, it can be eliminated from the equation because it will not affect the solution. As conventional wheels have only three possible degrees of freedom, having three non-sensed degrees of freedom means the wheel has no sensing at all. Also, if a wheel is steered, the steering angle must be one of the sensed variables.

$$v_{\text{robot}} = \mathbf{J}_{\text{sensed}} \, v_{\text{wheel sensed}} \qquad (8.44)$$

These equations are adequate if equations for each of the possible robot velocities can be obtained. In sensing, redundancy is desirable as it helps to reduce the effects of sensor noise.

Newt (Figure 8.6) has position and velocity sensors on the two drive wheels and no sensors on the castor. These sensors provide sufficient information to measure the velocity of the robot accurately, but the result is not robust because the sensed wheel variables and the actuated ones are identical: that is, there are no redundant measurements to reduce errors. The sensed forward solution for Newt is:

$$\begin{bmatrix} v_{\text{RBx}} \\ v_{\text{RBy}} \\ \omega_{\text{RB}} \end{bmatrix} = \frac{R}{2l_a} \begin{bmatrix} 0 & 0 \\ l_a & -l_a \\ 0 & 1 \end{bmatrix} \begin{bmatrix} \omega_{\text{w1x}} \\ \omega_{\text{w1z}} \end{bmatrix} \qquad (8.45)$$

The x component of the robot's velocity is independent of sensor measurements. The y component is proportional to the sum of the wheel velocities, and the θ_z component is proportional to the difference in wheel velocities.

8.1.7 Actuated inverse solution

With the forward solution, we can calculate the velocity and location of the robot, but we gain little physical insight into the operation or control of the robot. To understand the operation of the robot, we must study the inverse solution as we did for manipulators. An essential step in the design of a wheeled robot is to ensure that the robot can be controlled. If the wheel Jacobians cannot be inverted, control equations cannot be derived. We can determine the mobility of a robot by looking at the matrices in Equation 8.42, in a similar manner to our analysis of the forward solution. Whether the inverse solution is underdetermined, determined, or overdetermined depends upon the kinematic design of the robot, which is modelled by matrices **A** and **B**.

If the rank of the matrix **B** is less than the total number of wheel variables (w), the system is underdetermined and the robot has no solution (Section 8.4.2). If the rank of matrix **B** is equal to the total number of wheel variables, the design satisfies the **soluble motion criterion** and a unique solution exists for some robot velocity vectors (Figure 8.8). The rank of **B** is equal to the sum of the ranks of the wheel Jacobian matrices when there is no coupling between the wheels.

The soluble motion criterion corresponds to the determinant of $\mathbf{J}_n{}^T\mathbf{J}_n$ being nonzero for all wheels. If the determinant for a wheel is zero, the wheel is redundant. A wheeled robot which has redundant wheels and no coupling between wheels is underdetermined and the inverse is not soluble (Section 8.4.2).

Having determined that the robot satisfies the soluble motion criterion, we must ascertain next if the solution is determined or over-determined by comparing the rank of the augmented matrix **B**, **A** to the rank of matrix **B**. If the ranks are equal, the system is determined and a unique solution exists for all robot trajectories. Physically, this situation occurs only when all wheels are nonredundant and possess three degrees of freedom. Thus, for a robot to be able to move in any of the three possible degrees of freedom (x translation, y translation, and rotation about the z axis) all wheels must have three degrees of freedom. A robot with three Stanford wheels (see Figure 2.11) satisfies this criterion.

Useful robots can be built which cannot move in all three degrees of freedom, because a robot can reach any location (position and orientation) on a plane with one degree of translation and one degree of rotation. For example, Newt can translate in the direction of wheel orientation, and rotate about its axis, but it cannot move perpendicular to the wheel orientation. Robots of this type, which satisfy the soluble motion criterion, are overdeter-mined (Figure 8.8), because some degrees of freedom are dependent. The robot has an inverse solution if the equations are consistent, otherwise the robot is not controllable, in the sense that we cannot calculate wheel veloci-ties for desired trajectories.

When we examined the rank of the matrices for Newt (Figure 8.6), we find that the rank of **B** is 3 and, thus, the robot can be solved (Figure 8.8). However, the rank of **A**, **B** is less than the rank of **B**, since two wheels have only two degrees of freedom. Consequently, Newt has only two degrees of freedom: translation in the y direction and rotation about the z axis. Also, none of the wheels is redundant, because the determinant of the Jacobian product is nonzero.

Having determined that an inverse solution is available, the next step is to derive the inverse equations in order to calculate actuator references. In contrast to an arm, we do not derive inverse solutions for all wheels because not all wheels are actuated, and for wheels that are actuated, not all wheel variables are actuated. To derive the inverse equation, the actuated and unactuated wheel variables in Equation 8.39 must be separated.

$$v_{\text{robot } n} = \mathbf{J}_{na} \, v_{\text{wheel a}} + \mathbf{J}_{ua} \, v_{\text{wheel u}} \tag{8.46}$$

Then these equations for the n wheels which are actuated, are combined to form a composite actuated inverse equation

$$v_{\text{wheel a}} = \mathbf{J}_a \, v_{\text{robot}} \tag{8.47}$$

However, $\mathbf{J}_a$ is a very complex matrix. Study of this matrix has revealed that the inverse solution for each wheel is independent of the kinematic equations of the other wheels (Muir and Newman, 1986). When a wheel is non-redundant, with three degrees of freedom, and all three wheel variables are actuated, a simple relationship exists for that wheel.

$$v_{na} = \mathbf{J}_n^{-1} \, v_{\text{RB}n} = v_{\text{wheel a}} = (\mathbf{J}_{\text{wheel}}^{-1}) \, v_{\text{robot}} \tag{8.48}$$

In practice, the above conditions are assumed to apply to all actuated wheels when calculating the required actuator references. However, we must check that there are enough actuators to control the robot in all the degrees of freedom allowed by the design of the robot, and that actuators do not conflict. If actuation is overdetermined, some actuator motions are dependent. For robot motion to occur without wheel slippage or internal stress to the robot structure, these actuator motions must be consistent.

The two drive wheels on Newt are actuated, providing robust two degree of freedom actuation with no actuator conflict. The actuated inverse solution for Newt is

$$\begin{bmatrix} \omega_{\text{w1x}} \\ \omega_{\text{w1z}} \end{bmatrix} = \frac{1}{R} \begin{bmatrix} 0 & 1 & l_a \\ 0 & 1 & -l_a \end{bmatrix} \begin{bmatrix} v_{\text{RBx}} \\ v_{\text{RBy}} \\ \omega_{\text{RB}} \end{bmatrix} \tag{8.49}$$

As expected, motion in the x direction is not controllable.

8.1.8 Implications for design

The preceding analysis indicates that it is very easy to design a robot that cannot be controlled (see Section 8.4.2 for a classic robot design that doesn't meet the soluble motion criterion). As with all engineering design, a wheeled mobile robot must be able to perform the desired task, must be robust, must include sufficient sensors and actuators, and must be controllable.

A general purpose mobile robot can follow an xy path in any direction θ over a plane. Such a robot is omnidirectional and, is usually capable of controlled motion in all three degrees of freedom. Two degree of freedom robots have singularities in their workspace. At a singularity, a robot cannot move in one of the three possible degrees of freedom. Many tasks do not require omnidirectional mobility and, for these tasks, a robot with one degree of translation and one degree of rotation is adequate. Such a robot can also follow a path in any direction but first it must rotate around its axis to face that direction. These robots usually have two diametrically opposed drive wheels, for example, a turtle. Because of the simplicity of their mechanical design, and consequently simple kinematics, this is the recommended design for two degree of freedom robots.

A robot with two degrees of translation can reach any point on a plane and follow any path to that point but the orientation of the robot is fixed. For example, the pen on an xy plotter. A robot that can turn as it moves, but cannot rotate around an axis through its centre can follow some curved paths. A motor car is an example of this.

For a robot to be robust, its motion must be insensitive to actuator tracking errors. This is usually achieved by feedback control of wheel variables using sensor measurements. Also, the calculation of robot position and velocity from sensor data must be insensitive to noise and wheel slippage. Finally, actuators must not conflict. Muir and Newman (1986) extend this work to analyse a variety of robot configurations, their actuation characteristics, sensing characteristics, and their control using dead reckoning. These topics are beyond the scope of this book. A simple robot is analysed in the examples at the end of this chapter.

8.2 Models of walking

Wheeled mobile robots are designed to maintain their wheels in contact with the floor at all times. Consequently, stability is designed into the robot and only becomes a problem when the robot is on a steep slope. By contrast, legged robots lift their feet off the ground to walk. The motion of walking dynamically changes the stability of the robot.

A robot is **statically stable** if the centre of gravity of the robot always lies within a triangle defined by the contact points between three feet and the ground, assuming that each foot contacts the ground at only one point, unlike human feet which contact the ground in seven regions (heel, sole and toes). If the centre of gravity lies outside this triangle, the robot is no longer stable and tends to fall over. For statically stable walking, a robot must have four or more legs in order to have three feet in contact with the ground at all

Figure 8.9
Repetitive nature of a regular
gait.

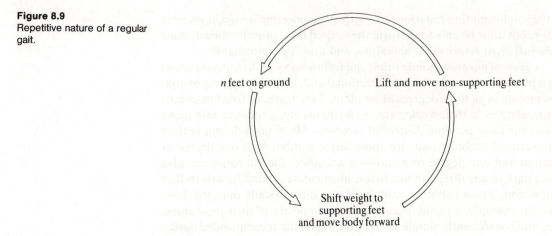

n feet on ground   Lift and move non-supporting feet

Shift weight to
supporting feet
and move body forward

times. If less than three feet are on the ground, then the triangle reduces to a
line (two on the ground) or a point (one foot on the ground) and the robot
tends to fall over. In these situations, the robot is **dynamically stable** if it
doesn't fall over.

8.2.1 Gait

The repetitive pattern of foot placement when walking is called a **regular
gait**. And irregular gait is used only to solve specific problems, for example, a
shuffle to get out of a tight corner. A gait can be expressed in a cyclic form
(Figure 8.9). Starting with *n* feet on the ground, the weight of the body is
shifted to the supporting feet, and the nonsupporting feet are lifted and
moved. Once these feet are placed on the ground, they become the supporting feet, and the weight of the body is transferred to them during the next
cycle.

A statically stable gait always maintains at least three feet on the
ground and keeps the centre of gravity within the triangle defined by the
points of contact between the feet and the ground. A dynamic gait has less
than three feet on the ground at some point during the cycle, and can have all
feet off the ground for short periods.

An important part of the study of walking is the classification and
recording of gaits. We usually start by recording a gait during straight line
motion. From this recording, the stability of the gait can be analysed, the
effect of varying the foot placement studied, and the change in foot
placement required to follow a curved path determined. In the control of a
walking robot, it is important that legs do not collide, so the chosen gait must
avoid tangling the legs while maintaining the desired compromise between
speed and stability.

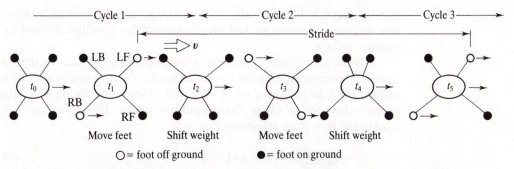

Figure 8.10
Four-legged trot gait moving alternate diagonal pairs of feet.

Most gait classifications treat a foot as a two-state device: it is either on or off the ground. A gait can be recorded as a function of distance or time. Gaits are usually recorded with diagrams. Two cycles of a trot gait (or diagonal gait) are shown in Figure 8.10. In the first cycle, the weight of the body is supported by the right-front and left-back feet (right diagonal pair) while the left diagonal pair are moved forward. When all feet are on the ground, the body is moved forward and the weight transferred to the left diagonal pair. The right diagonal pair is then moved forward.

In Figure 8.11 this motion is recorded with a gait diagram and a footfall diagram. A gait diagram is a bar graph where the length of the bar represents the time the foot is on the ground. The footfall diagram shows which feet are on the ground after a foot changes state. Both these diagrams show a regular straight-line gait on a smooth surface. If the surface is rough, the gait will not be so regular. For example, if it slopes upwards, the feet will touch the ground early. If the ground is very rough, foot placement for comfort and stability may be more important than maintaining a regular gait.

More complex gait analysis requires a quantitative description of gait. The basic cycle of any gait is called a **stride** (Todd, 1985). Technically, a stride is the complete cycle of leg movement from one occurence of a leg movement to its repetition. For example, in the trotting gait in Figure 8.10, a stride starts when the left-front foot leaves the ground (t_1) and finishes when the left-front foot leaves the ground again (t_5).

$$v = lf \qquad\qquad (8.50)$$

where

v = mean speed of the robot

l = length of the stride, and

f = stride frequency.

The **duty factor** (β) of a foot is the fraction of the stride during which the foot is on the ground. For the trotting gait in Figure 8.10, the duty factor is slightly over 0.5. For statically stable walking, the minimum duty factor is 3 (the minimum number of feet on the ground for stability) divided by the number of legs.

During the action of walking, a leg propels the body during part of the stride and recovers during the rest of the stride, so that it can propel the body again during the following stride. The part of the stride during which the leg propels the body is called the **propulsion stroke**. During the propulsion stroke, the foot is on the ground.

$$T = t_{prop} + t_{rec} = \beta T + (1 - \beta)T \tag{8.51}$$

where

T is the period of the stride,

t_{prop} is the duration of the propulsion stroke, and

t_{rec} is the duration of the recovery stroke.

$$v = \frac{s}{t_{prop}} = \frac{s}{t_{rec}}\left(\frac{1 - \beta}{\beta}\right) \tag{8.52}$$

where $s =$ length of the propulsion stroke.

Waldron *et al.*, (1984) formulated the mean speed equation in this form because the major limit on speed, in most legged systems, is the time taken to move the leg through the air to its new starting position (the recovery time). Thus, the maximum speed of a robot is determined by the minimum recovery time. For a given leg design, the speed of the robot can be increased by increasing the number of legs ($v = 0.333s/t_{rec}$ for four legs, $1.0s/t_{rec}$ for six legs, and $1.67s/t_{rec}$ for eight legs). Thus, increasing the number of legs can improve the speed as well as the stability, but at the cost of increased mechanical and computational complexity.

The above equations describe the proportion of time the feet are on or off the ground, but say nothing about the sequence in which they are placed on the ground. The gait diagram and footfall diagrams show the sequence in which the feet are placed on the ground but, as drawn, show both feet of a pair moving in unison. It is not uncommon for one foot of a pair to touch the ground before the other. The proportion of the stride between the two feet touching the ground is called the **relative phase** of the pair of legs (Alexander, 1984).

A gait can be completely specified by making one foot the reference foot and recording the stage of the stride at which each subsequent foot is set down as a fraction of the stride. Thus, the reference foot has a relative phase of 0.0 and the others have relative phases in the range 0.0–1.0. For a trot gait, the left diagonal pair have a relative phase of 0.0 and the right diagonal pair a relative phase of 0.5.

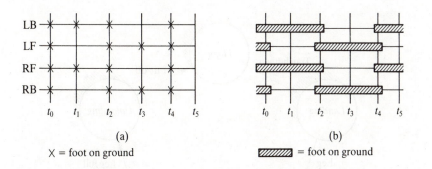

Figure 8.11
Diagrametric representations
of four-legged trot gait.
(a) Footfall diagram.
(b) Gait diagram.

A **symmetrical gait** is one in which the feet of a pair (one foot on each side of the robot) have equal duty factors and a relative phase of less than half a stride. Much work has been done in classifying the common gaits for animals and machines with up to eight legs. Robots with six or more legs can move with a wave gait, where a forward wave or stepping action occurs on each side of the body, with a half-cycle phase difference between the two members of any left-right pair. As a child, I often watched with fascination the waves moving along the sides of a centipede as it walked.

The trot gait (Figure 8.11) is classed as a walking gait because the duty factor is greater than 0.5. If the legs are kept off the ground for a little longer so that the duty factor is less than 0.5, there are periods when all feet are off the ground, and we have a running gait. Both these gaits are dynamically stable gaits as there are periods with less than three feet on the ground. Before we can control a machine with a dynamic gait, we need a dynamic model of locomotion.

8.2.2 A model of dynamic stability

The mechanical construction of a one-legged hopping machine was described in Section 2.1.2. This robot was used to test a simple model of dynamic locomotion (Raibert, 1986). Tests have shown that Raibert's model is adequate for a one-legged hopping machine, a two-legged machine running with a one-legged gait while attached to a boom for stability, and a four-legged machine walking with a trotting gait. While Raibert has demonstrated the feasibility of his model, he sees these machines as purely experimental laboratory devices for exploring ideas about legged locomotion, not as prototypes of useful vehicles.

Raibert (1986) decomposed the problem of controlling the motion of a one-legged hopping machine into three independent, time-related subsystems. These are control of hopping height, forward speed, and body attitude. His model includes a differential equation for each of these independent variables and a state diagram to track the hopping cycle. This state machine synchronises the three parts of the control system. With controllers based on this model, he has achieved the dynamic balance of a

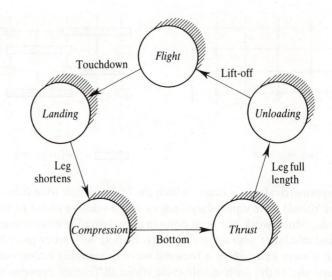

one-legged machine. In the next sections, we will look at his model for one-legged planar machines.

8.2.2.1 *State machine*

The state machine (Figure 8.12) models the action of hopping as five independent states and five transitions between those states. The transition from one state to the next is triggered by information from sensors as the robot moves from one phase in its cycle to the next. Each state specifies which of the three independent variables is to be controlled.

The state machine starts in the thrust state with the robot on the ground and the leg compressed. In this state, the foot is in contact with the ground allowing the robot to apply thrust to the ground and torque around the hip joint. Hopping height is controlled with vertical thrust, and body attitude is controlled with torque around the hip. As the foot is fixed firmly on the ground, this hip torque causes the body to rotate around the hip joint.

At the end of the thrust phase, the leg is fully extended and the state machine moves to the unloading state. The control system reduces both the vertical thrust and hip torque to zero. As the foot of the robot leaves the ground, the robot enters the flight phase. In effect, the air cylinder shoots the robot off the ground like a bullet from a gun. During the flight state, the hip joint swings the leg into place for landing. The placement of the foot on landing determines the length of the stride, and the length of the stride controls the forward speed. The leg remains at full length and the thrust cylinder is exhausted to atmosphere.

At the end of the flight phase, the foot of the robot touches the ground, the robot enters the landing phase, and the state machine moves to the landing state. At this point, hip torque is reduced to zero, as the foot is in place, and the leg thrust cylinder is no longer allowed to exhaust to atmosphere. As the robot settles, the leg shortens, and the state machine moves to the compression state. During this state, the leg continues to compress storing energy in the air spring, and the hip joint is used to control body attitude. In effect, this is an elastic collision. When the leg bottoms out, the state machine moves to the thrust state, and the cycle is repeated.

From the above description, we can see that the transition from one state to the next is controlled by three sensors. One detects when the foot is touching the floor, one detects when the leg is near full extension, and one detects when the leg is near full compression. The leg sensors are a short distance from the ends of the cylinders to allow time for thrust to be stopped so that the piston does not slam into the end of the cylinder. Also, it is easier to detect that the piston is in the region of the end of the cylinder than to detect it is exactly at the end, due to noise and variations in sensor signals over time.

8.2.2.2 *Hopping height*

For a hopping machine to move across the ground, each leg must spend some time supporting the body and some time with its foot off the ground. The overall hopping behaviour can be modelled as an oscillation of a mass (body)-spring (air spring in leg)-damper (gravity) system with the air cylinder injecting sufficient energy during the thrust phase of each hop to maintain the amplitude of the oscillation.

This model decomposes the control of hopping into two parts: the basic hopping motion is determined by mechanical oscillation, and the amplitude of the hop is determined by the thrust. In theory, the operator could select a hopping height, and the control system calculate the thrust to reach that height either from a model which includes losses or using feedback of hopping height. The sensing of hopping height is an interesting problem. In practice, the operator sets a fixed thrust and the robot settles at the hopping height determined by the equilibrium between energy input (thrust) and energy expenditure (acceleration and losses).

8.2.2.3 *Body attitude*

During flight, any torque about the hip causes both the leg and the body to turn in order a conserve angular momentum. As the leg is much lighter than the body, it swings through a greater angle, and effectively, the torque controls the angle of the leg with respect to the ground, but the attitude of the body is altered (Figure 8.13). We can only change the angular momentum of the whole robot, and hence the body attitude, while the foot of the robot is firmly placed on the ground (during the compression and thrust states). The frictional force between the foot and the ground is relied upon to balance the

Figure 8.13
Diagram of a planar one-legged machine showing the variables used for control (Raibert, 1986).

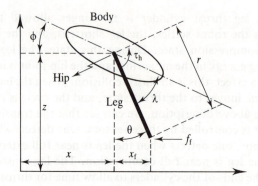

force due to the torque at the actuator hip. Provided the foot does not slip, the body rotates about the hip joint when torque is applied at the hip.

The control system maintains an upright body attitude by exerting torque about the hip while the robot is on the ground. The control system does this with a linear control law.

$$\tau_h = -k_p(\phi - \phi_d) - k_v\omega_\phi \tag{8.53}$$

where

τ_h = torque at the hip to correct attitude,

ϕ = pitch angle of the body (Figure 8.12),

ϕ_d = desired pitch angle,

$\omega_\phi = \dot{\phi}$ = rate of change of the pitch angle, and k_p, k_v are position and velocity feedback gains.

The angle between the leg and the ground changes while the robot is on the ground because the body continues to move forward with constant velocity while the foot is fixed in place (Figure 8.14). The control system must allow this change in leg-to-body angle to happen while controlling the attitude of the body. The frictional force between the foot and the ground sets up a torque in the leg which causes the leg to rotate about the contact point. As the body cannot supply a reaction torque, the leg torque tends to cause the body to pitch. Any pitch in the body is detected by the hip torque servo and this servo automatically supplies a reaction torque at the hip to balance the leg torque and to maintain the attitude of the body.

8.2.2.4 *Forward speed*

Forward speed is controlled by the placement of the foot when it first touches the ground. During flight, the control system swings the leg around the hip to

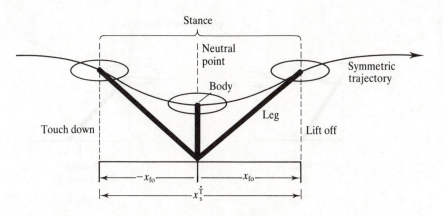

Figure 8.14
Neutral point at which the
net acceleration is zero
(Raibert, 1986).

position the foot with respect to the body and so, determine its placement on landing. Once the foot is firmly on the ground and the stance phase (compression and thrust states) of motion begins, the control system takes no further action, as the dynamics of the mechanical system govern what happens.

The net forward acceleration during the stance phase is the difference between the forward speed at touchdown and the forward speed at lift off.

$$\Delta \dot{x} = \dot{x}_{lo} - \dot{x}_{td} \qquad (8.54)$$

Where $\dot{x}$ is the forward speed

For each forward speed, there is a unique foot position that results in zero net acceleration. This position (Figure 8.14) is called the neutral point. When the foot is placed at this point, the robot body follows a symmetric trajectory with respect to the foot. Time and position are defined to be zero when the body is directly over the neutral point, (halfway through the stance phase). Thus, the body is at $-x_{fo}$ when it lands and at $+x_{fo}$ when it lifts off.

$$x_{fo} = \frac{\dot{x} T_s}{2} \qquad (8.55)$$

where

T_s = duration of the stance phase, and

x_{fo} = forward displacement of the foot with respect to the centre of mass on landing.

For the robot to run at constant speed, the control system swings the leg forward during flight until the foot is at a distance x_{fo} in front of the hip. During the stance phase, the centre of mass of the body spends the same amount of time in front of the foot as it spends behind the foot, so the

Figure 8.15
(a) Placing the foot before the neutral point causes it to accelerate.
(b) Placing it after the neutral point causes the robot to decelerate (Raibert, 1986).

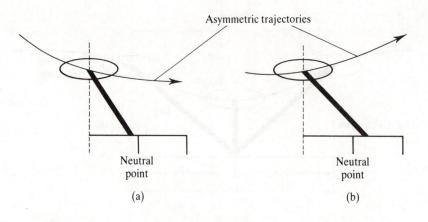

Asymmetric trajectories

Neutral point

Neutral point

(a)

(b)

forward tipping that occurs during the second half of the stance precisely compensates the backward tipping that occurs during the first half of the stance. When the foot is located under the centre of mass, the leg is at maximum compression. As a result, the horizontal components of the axial leg force before the body is over the neutral point balance the horizontal components of the axial leg force after the body is over the neutral point. Consequently, the horizontal forces acting on the body during the stance phase balance to zero and no acceleration occurs.

If the foot is not placed at the neutral point, the body trajectory is no longer symmetrical and a resultant net applied force causes a net acceleration of the body. If the foot is placed before the neutral point (Figure 8.15), the robot accelerates and if it is placed after the neutral point, the robot slows down. The control system uses a linear function of the error in the forward speed to find the displacement of the foot from the neutral point.

$$\Delta x_{\text{fo}} = k_x(\dot{x} - \dot{x}_d) \tag{8.56}$$

where

Δx_{fo} is the displacement from the neutral point,

$\dot{x}_d$ is the desired forward speed, and

k_x is the feedback gain.

By combining Equations 8.55 and 8.56, an equation is obtained for calculating the placement of the foot with respect to the hip.

$$x_f = \frac{\dot{x}T_s}{2} + k_x(\dot{x} - x_d) \tag{8.57}$$

Because the period of oscillation of a spring-mass system is independent of amplitude, we can use the measurement of the period from the previous stance phase in the above equation. The required hip angle (Figure 8.13) to achieve correct foot placement is calculated using kinematics.

$$\lambda_d = \phi - \arcsin\left(\frac{x_f}{r}\right) \tag{8.58}$$

This angle is used by the servo system to control hip torque during the flight phase in accordance with the following control law.

$$\tau_h = k_p(\lambda - \lambda_h) - k_v \omega_\lambda \tag{8.59}$$

where $\omega_\lambda = \dot{\lambda}$ = the rate of change of the angle between the body and the leg.

In summary, the problem of controlling the dynamic balance of a one-legged hopping robot has been decomposed into the control of hopping height, forward speed, and body attitude. Each of these has been modeled and simple linear control laws designed. Raibert and his colleagues have implemented both two- and three-dimensional hopping machines using this model.

8.3 Navigation

Navigation is the science (or art) of directing the course of a mobile robot as it traverses the environment (land, sea, or air). Inherent in any navigation scheme is the desire to reach a destination without getting lost or crashing into anything. Navigation involves three tasks: mapping, planning, and driving. A higher-level process, called a task planner, specifies the destination and any constraints on the course, such as time.

Many problems have to be solved before the sophisticated navigation abilities of people will be matched by robots. Most mobile robot algorithms (like Algorithm 8.1) abort when they encounter situations that make navigation difficult.

Algorithm 8.1 commences by checking to see if the robot has a map of the terrain. If it does not, the robot has to proceed cautiously and search the terrain for a path to the goal. The learning algorithm used in Algorithm 8.1 will work if the terrain is simple, but the robot may run around in circles if the terrain is complex. If the robot does have a map, it searches the map for possible paths, chooses an appropriate path, and traverses that path, assuming that such a path exists. While traversing the path, the robot must

Algorithm 8.1   Simple navigation algorithm for travelling from Start to Goal

If there is a map **then**
    Search map for paths
    Select a path using an optimizing function
    If path is complex **then** decompose path into subgoals
    Sense environment
    While not at goal **do**
        Traverse path {move in direction indicated by path plan}
        If at a subgoal **then** obtain next subgoal
        Sense environment
        If object on path **then**
        Halt robot
        If object is stationary **then**
          Update map
          Search for alternate path to sub-goal
          If an alternate path exists **then**
            Follow alternate path
          Else {no alternate path}
            Abort and replan task
        Else {object is moving}
          Halt till path clears
    End {of while loop}
    {robot at goal}
Else {no map – Initiate learning strategy}
    While not at goal **do**
        sense environment
        If clear in direction of goal **then**
        Move toward goal
        Else {object in the way}
        If clear in other directions **then**
          Select a direction using a heuristic
          Move in that direction
        Else {robot is trapped}
          Abort and replan task
    End {of while loop}
    {robot at goal}
End {of navigation task}

examine it with sensors for objects on the path that were not shown on the map. If an object is detected, the robot must take evasive action.

Put simply, the navigation problem is to find a path from start (S) to goal (G) and traverse it without collision. We have decomposed navigation into three sub-tasks: mapping and modelling the environment; path planning

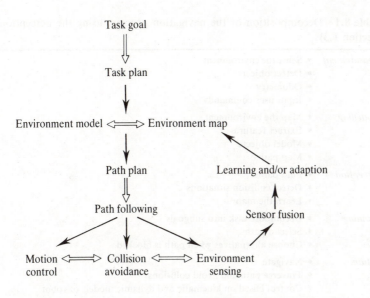

Figure 8.16
Mobile robot control
hierarchy, showing
information flow.

and selection; and path traversal and collision avoidance. The relationship
between these tasks is shown in Figure 8.16.

Using the perception model of robotics (Section 1.3), we solve these
sub-problems with interrelated information transformation processes (Table
8.1). The measurement process includes all the sensors. Measurement is used
by the modelling process and by the action process. Maps of the terrain are
stored in a map data structure. They are either digitized from existing maps
or 'learned' by the robot from sensory data as it traverses the terrain. The
modelling process analyses the sensory data to construct and modify maps.

The second task of navigation is path planning. The perception process searches the map for possible paths. If no map exists, it perceives paths
between objects from the model under construction by the modelling
process. The planning process selects a suitable path from the alternatives to
meet the constraints imposed by the task.

Once the path is planned, the third task is to drive the robot as it
traverses the path. The action process controls the motion of the robot using
kinematic and dynamic models of the robot. During motion, the perception
process continuously examines the sensory data and compares the sensor
model of the environment to the map to detect potential collisions. When a
collision is possible, the perception process initiates evasive action, which is
executed by the action process. In all mobile robots, the final level of safety is
collision detection using contact sensors (Section 10.6.1). This level of safety
is implemented by the action process.

In all current applications of mobile robots, a person specifies the task
goal and, usually, the task plan. The concept of a robot that can generate its

Table 8.1 Decomposition of the navigation process, using the perception model (Section 1.3).

Measurement	• Sense the environment • Detect objects • Odometry • Input user commands
Modelling	• Map the environment • Extract features • Model objects • Map paths
Perception	• Find paths • Detect collision situations • Learn the map
Planning	• Decompose task into subgoals • Select a path • Choose alternatives when path is blocked
Action	• Navigate • Traverse path and avoid collisions • Control based on kinematic and dynamic models of robot

own goals and plan its own tasks is interesting philosophically but is a long way from reality (Brooks, 1986). In this section, we concentrate on a lower level problem: having been given a goal, how do we navigate the robot to achieve that goal?

Some researchers are developing heuristics to decide how to handle the unexpected while negotiating a path. An expert system is used in the HERMIES IIB robot to diagnose unexpected occurrences and decide what the robot should do (Burks et al., 1987). Also, a neural network is used to represent a sensor derived graph of the space in a room for path planning (Jorgensen, 1987). Crowley (1987) has proposed the use of a rule-based system to control twin hierarchies for navigation and perception. The research teams working on ALVs (Autonomous Land Vehicles) are making extensive use of rule-based systems (McTamaney, 1987) in an attempt to solve perception problems.

Navigation based on guidance systems is in common use in industry and navigation using the detection of landmarks to correct errors in following predefined paths is just entering into practical use. Navigation based on autonomous path planning will continue to be a research issue for many years to come.

In the rest of this section, we examine techniques for implementing the sub-tasks of mapping, planning, and driving. Underlying all these sub-tasks is a map data structure. The requirement to store maps in a way that they can be searched efficiently often conflicts with the requirement of storing a path in a way that it can be retrieved efficiently. The choice of data structure determines the algorithms used for path planning (Table 8.2).

Environment maps fall into four broad groups: path maps, free-space maps, object-oriented maps, and composite-space maps (Table 8.2). The characteristics of each group determine the type of data structure used and the path-planning algorithms. As the path-planning algorithms are data structure dependent, most papers present data structures and path-planning algorithms together (the columns in Table 8.2). In this book, we look at data structures and path-planning separately (the rows in Table 8.2).

8.3.1 Guidance systems

We start with systems that use maps of predetermined paths. Some of these systems store the network of paths as a graph, and others record a sequence of 'taught' motions. AGVs (Automated Guided Vehicles) in the car industry follow guide wires buried in the floor of the factory (see Figure 1.7). These wires are detected using induction, and the AGV is commanded by a remote computer over a radio link. Some AGVs use other physical methods to define the path including painted stripes, rows of magnets, invisible fluorescent lines, and laser beams.

Table 8.2 Mobile robot data structures. (a) Data structure usage; (b) relationship between map type and planning method.

(a)

Data Storage	Data Manipulation
Maps	Record and display
Features	Extract features
Object models	Identify objects
Paths	Search for paths
Sensor data	Update and learn maps

(b)

Map type	Paths	Free space	Object-oriented	Composite space

Data Structures	• None
	• List of paths
	• Recorded motion
	• Graph of path
		• Graphs
		  – Voronoi Diagrams
		  – free ways
		  – connectively
		• Trees
		  – places
			• Vertex graphs
			• Trees – landmarks
				• Grids
				• Quadtrees
				• Rules

Planning	• Teaching • Tree search • Graph search	• Teaching • Learning • Graph theory • Tree search • Delaunay triangulation	• Teaching • Learning • Graph search • Tree search	• Teaching • Learning • Graph search • Distance transform • Tree search
Navigation	• Guide wires • Dead reckoning • Beacons • Replay of recorded motions	• Dead reckoning • Beacons • Sensor feedback	• Dead reckoning • Beacons • Sensor feedback	• Dead reckoning • Beacons • Sensor feedback

All AGVs are limited to following a fixed number of physically defined paths. They cannot wander from these paths, and if an object is placed on a path they cannot continue until it is removed. All have a collision detection system which shuts them down when they collide with another object. While this level of navigation is sufficient for a plant that doesn't change, it is expensive to install, more expensive to change, and totally inflexible. For capital intensive industries like the car industry, these problems are acceptable, but in many others they are not.

A third problem is that breaks in the physical guidance system can be difficult to find, expensive to fix, and may cause significant delays in production. In some buildings, mail delivery robots follow a magnetic stripe from one office to the next. It has been reported, that in one building a hard working cleaner removed sections of the magnetic stripe with a floor polisher. When the mail robot entered this area, it could not detect the stripe, lost its way, and failed to deliver the mail. Mimicking of tracks can also be a problem. Robots guided by fluorescent stripes have been known to follow the salt tracks created when salt drops off peoples' shoes during the winter months. For those who live in warm climates, salt is placed on footpaths and roads in many North American and European cities to melt snow during the winter months, leaving the path free of ice and snow.

8.3.1.1 *Dead reckoning*

To reduce the expense of following a physical path, although at the cost of increased computing power on the robot, some robots follow a pre-programmed path by dead reckoning, using landmarks or beacons to correct errors in position. Some use laser beams to lay a guide path from one beacon to the next. Dead reckoning is the calculation of the robot's position and orientation from measurements of wheel motion, also called odometry. Dead reckoning control suffers from several sources of inaccuracy: poor mechanical alignment of wheels, slop in gears, noise in sensor signals, errors in sensor signals, wheel slippage, and trajectory variations due to surface unevenness.

Consider a turtle type robot with two parallel drive wheels. The wheels are driven at the same angular velocity, and hence at the same circumferential speed. If one wheel rolls over an obstacle and the other doesn't, the robot will turn slightly towards the obstacle because the wheel which rolls over the obstacle will travel a shorter distance in the direction of motion (Figure 8.17(a)).

Consider a second robot which has a non-driven sensing wheel (Figure 8.17(b)). If this wheel rolls over an object, it travels farther than the other wheel does. If the wheel is on the side of the robot, the control system will interpret the resultant increase in sensed velocity and position as a small turn and correct for it, driving the robot away from the preplanned trajectory. If the sensing wheel is on the centre line of the robot, the sensing system will calculate the distance travelled incorrectly. To minimize the effect of these

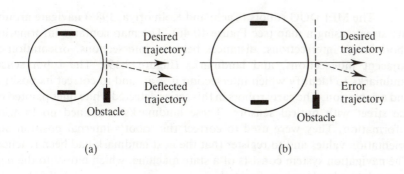

(a)

(b)

Figure 8.17
Effect of a wheel rolling over an obstacle on dead reckoning control.
(a) Driven wheel rolls over obstacle, robot doesn't realize it is off course;
(b) non-actuated sensing wheel rolls over obstacle, robot thinks it is off course and incorrectly changes course.

measurement errors, some robots have an inertial guidance system on board (gyroscope) with which they detect whether the actual trajectory of the robot has changed.

8.3.1.2 *Beacons*

To reduce the problems with dead reckoning, some robots detect beacons located along the path. They calculate their location by sensing these beacons, and correct either their trajectory or modify their planned trajectory to compensate for the errors. The Sencar AGV (Rathbone *et al.*, 1986) uses infrared beacons mounted on the ceiling. These beacons are connected to a host computer with a two wire bus, which carries power and data.

To 'teach' the vehicle the path, the operator drives it along the route, and specifies stops and docking manoeuvres along the way. The robot records its path and records the location of any beacons it passes. It can then repeatedly follow that path using the beacons to rectify tracking errors. If a path is to be modified or a branch added, the robot is stopped at the required point and manually driven over the revised or branching path.

The beacons are similar to television remote controls, and operate in the near infrared (880–950 mm wavelength) range. Infrared signals in this range are attenuated less by smoke and airborne dust. Also, at these frequencies semiconductor transmitters and receivers are most efficient. Each beacon transmits a pulse train. When operating in 'beacon mode', the train contains a beacon identification number and check bits. In 'communications mode', the beacon becomes an infrared transceiver passing data between the robot and the host computer.

The beacons are detected with a sensor mounted on top of the robot. In this sensor, a 180° fish-eye lens focuses light onto an array of detectors. This lens effectively maps a hemispherical space on to a two dimensional plane. Thus, the light from a beacon will be detected by a small region of the array, clearly identifying the location of the beacon relative to the robot. Using the fisheye lens eliminates moving parts but, because the lens introduces substantial light loss, the detection circuitry has to be very sensitive.

The MELDOG robots (Tachi and Kolmoriya, 1985) navigate around city streets using a map (see Figure 10.46). The map contains information about street intersections, distances between intersections, orientation to adjacent intersections, and landmarks (Figure 8.19). The robot senses landmarks to identify which intersection it is at, and to correct its position and orientation. The early robots in this series detected white lines painted on the street with optical sensors. These landmarks contained no location information. They were used to correct the robot's internal position and orientation values and to register that the next landmark had been reached. The navigation system consists of a state machine, which moves to the next state when a landmark is detected.

This system has two problems. First, the landmarks had to be installed in the environment. Second, if the robot missed a landmark or made a wrong turn it became lost because the next landmark detected did not contain location information. To overcome these problems, the research team at the Mechanical Engineering Laboratory (MEL) in Tsukuba City are attempting to locate and identify natural landmarks with ultrasonic transducers (Komoriya *et al.*, 1986).

8.3.2 Environment maps, models and data structures

Fundamental to the development of flexible mobile robots is the design of data structures to store maps of the environment, and algorithms to search and manipulate those data structures. The supervisory computer which controls the AGVs in a car factory has a map of all the physical paths, their intersections and branches, and the docking points along those paths. This map is used to plan paths for the AGVs to travel along from one stage in the process to the next. While most of the paths in a continuous process like this are preplanned, AGVs have to be rerouted when a breakdown occurs. In addition, the map is used to keep track of the AGVs as they carry car chassis through the process.

Robots which use beacons or landmarks for navigation rely heavily on a map to navigate from one beacon to the next and to determine their location. The more flexible the navigation system used by a robot, the more dependent it is on its mapping system. Future mobile robots will use vision, ultrasonics, laser rangefinders, and other sensors to determine their location (see Section 10.6.8). This sensory information must be combined with a map to determine the location of the robot accurately. It is also used to adapt maps to account for changes in the environment, and to construct maps of unknown environments.

8.3.2.1 *Ideal data structures*

To store a map efficiently, it is broken up into small regions (tesselated), such as squares or polygons. Each region is represented with one element in the data structure, and is considered to be homogeneous (all object or all empty space). The relationship between the regions is captured by the relationship between the elements in the data structure. In this type of map, a path is a list of connected regions.

An ideal data structure for environment mapping has the following characteristics.

- It suits the chosen method of path planning.
- It minimizes the amount of nonhomogeneous or ambiguous space: areas that contain both objects and empty space.
- It maps the complex shape of the environment as closely as possible, or as required by the task.
- It does not rely on the assumption that the environment is true to .square, as invariably it is not.
- It stores complex shapes with a small number of data structure elements.
- It stores large areas of space, and large objects, with a minimum of data structure elements. It is most important in path planning to avoid excess detail on parts of the space that do not affect the planning operation (Lozano-Perez, 1981).
- It can handle both local and global maps – for example, room and building.
- It stores information about the state of mapped areas.
- It facilitates easy movement from any element in the structure to the elements which represent adjacent areas in space.
- It includes a data structure for storing paths that complements the map data structure.
- It has efficient algorithms for locating the robot, path searching, and navigation.
- It enables the easy integration of sensor data with simple algorithms for map construction, adaption and extension.

No data structure has yet been found that meets all these criteria. Hence data structure design is an exercise in trading off task requirements against implementation efficiency. The most detailed data structure is a **pixel** map, such as a digitized survey photograph. However, the volume of data is so large that very powerful computers are required to analyse it in reasonable time. When the problem of generating a map from a photograph is solved, many of the problems in computer vision will also be solved.

Geographical and survey maps of the physical world are often stored as line segments, either with the coordinates of the points at both ends or in a compacted form. A drawing of the map can be produced easily from this data structure, but dividing it up into regions, and determining the state of those regions, is a computationally difficult task.

Figure 8.18
Linked list of path segments
used to store taught paths,
including branching paths.

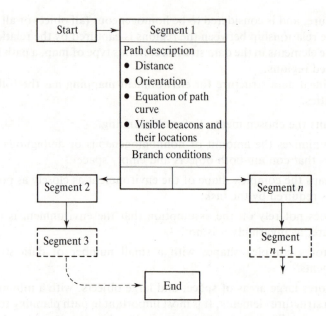

In the control of robot motion, the state of a region that the robot is
about to enter is important. State can include such information as: empty
space, object, restricted area, rising slope, stairwell, lift bay, docking area,
danger zone, and people zone. Most data structures used in mobile robots
divide the environment up into regions. The result is a coarse data structure
that is efficient to search, but may have ambiguous regions.

8.3.2.2 *Landmark navigation*

Robots like the Sencar AGV, which traverse recorded paths, store these
paths as linked lists of path segments (Figure 8.18). As the robot traverses
each path segment, the path following program picks up the next segment
descriptor from the list. This information can be stored more compactly in
arrays, but arrays are fixed in size and less efficient to modify. Manufacturing processes change regularly, and, as a consequence, path segments may
have to be inserted or deleted. For maximum efficiency, this is done by
reteaching the affected sections of the path, not the whole path.

The MELDOG robots, which are experimental guide dogs for blind
people, store their street maps as directed graphs of landmarks (Figure 8.19).
A landmark identifier is allocated to each street that enters an intersection.
This graph can be interpreted as a tree for path planning, and is used as
a state machine to control the robot during path execution. Landmarks
are represented by nodes in the graph, and the streets connecting these
landmarks by arcs. A node stores the landmark number, pointers to other
landmarks connected by streets (arcs), the location of these other landmarks

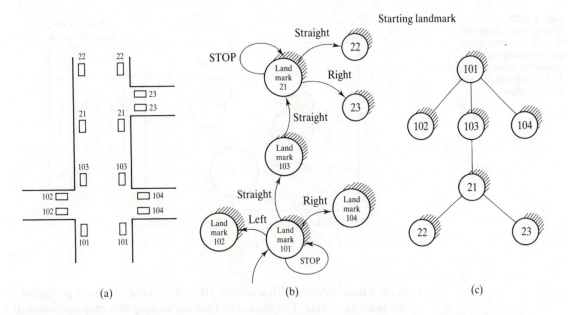

(a) (b) (c)

(distance and direction – left, right, etc.), and a landmark code. The land-mark code stores information about the landmark: intersection identifier, intersection type (crossing, fork, etc.), and whether or not the robot should stop at the intersection.

This data structure is reasonably efficient, maps to the task, and eliminates unwanted geographical data. An area of 500 metres by 500 metres with 276 landmarks uses 2kbyte of storage. This type of data structure is suitable for tasks which have a small number of clearly defined paths.

Figure 8.19
Data structure for storing a street map in MELDOG robots where nodes represent landmarks and arcs represent the connecting streets (Tachi and Komoriya, 1985).
(a) Streets with numbered landmarks;
(b) directed graph of landmarks;
(c) tree form of graph.

8.3.2.3 *Sensor data*

Attempts to construct maps from sensor data have lead to the development of data structures that aid in the interpretation of that data. Hans Moravec (1983) based his vision system for the control of the Stanford cart on the detection and tracking of features. A feature is a high contrast point in the scene which can be located unambiguously from different views. (Section 10.8.8.3.)

Once a feature was chosen, and had been identified from several camera positions, the location of the feature was determined using triangulation (see Section 10.6.3). The feature was stored as a point, or, more correctly, the centre of a circle. The system modelled the world as clusters of points. If enough points were found to define each object adequately, this model was sufficient for planning a collision-free path, if one existed.

As the cart moved, all visible objects became modelled as spheres. The radius of the sphere was a function of the uncertainty of the location of the

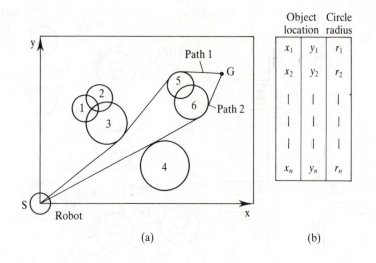

(a)   (b)

feature. Those spheres with a similar elevation to the cart were projected on to the floor as circles. The data structure for storing this map consisted of a three-element array containing the x and y positions and radii for each feature (Figure 8.20). Thompson (1977) and Giralt *et al.* (1979) took their visual models further and mapped the world as a set of nontraversable walls built out of curves represented by short lines, and objects modeled with polyhedra.

In contrast to vision systems, which have to calculate the distance to objects by comparing multiple images, range finders (Section 10.6.3) measure this distance directly. James Crowley (1984) used a rotating ultrasonic sensor to measure the distance to objects (Figure 8.21). Each sonar reading gave the distance to a surface in space relative to the robot. From these readings, he modelled the room as a two-dimensional sequence of line segments oriented in a counter-clockwise order around the robot. In some experiments, he used a prerecorded map to determine the location of the robot by comparing the range information to the map.

One scan of the sensor only provided enough data to identify some line segments. As the robot moved around the room, the sensor could see previously occluded surfaces of objects, and more line segments were added to the map. To store this information, a doubly linked circular list (Figure 8.22) was used, so that segments could be inserted, combined and deleted easily. Each node in the list stored the end points of the line, line length, line orientation, and the relationship between this line and the next: convex, concave or disconnected.

Alberto Elfes (1986) used a Denning sonar ring: a ring of 24 sonar sensors placed 15° apart (Figure 2.5). The area around the robot was divided into squares with a grid, where each square represented an area 150 mm by 150 mm. The range reading from each sonar sensor was used to determine

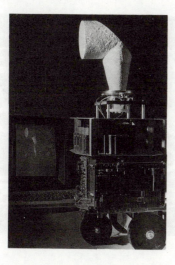

Figure 8.21
Hero robot with a rotating
sonar sensor, with a line
segment map on the video
display, used by Jim
Crowley at CMU Robotics
Institute.

the probability of the squares covered by the beams being occupied (Figure
8.23). Overlapping readings from multiple sensors and from multiple sensing
locations were integrated. The map was stored in a two-dimensional array
with a value between -1 and $+1$ for the state of each square. A value less
than zero represented a probably empty region, a value of zero represented
unknown occupancy, and a value greater than zero implied a probably
occupied space. The closer the value was to 1 the greater the probability of
occupancy.

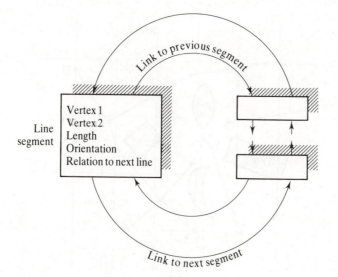

Figure 8.22
Doubly-linked circular list
used to store room modelled
as a sequence of line
segments.

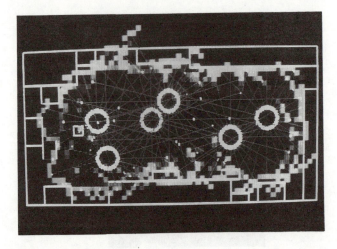

In the following sections, we discuss map data structures from the perspective of how they describe the environment, rather than from the perspective of sensing. Each map can be constructed from sensor information, and all have been used when learning a map (Section 8.3.5).

8.3.2.4 Free-space maps

A robot can traverse an unknown environment without a detailed map by using sensors. As the robot moves, the paths it travels can be recorded as a spatial graph (Figure 8.24). The nodes on the graph are stop points where the

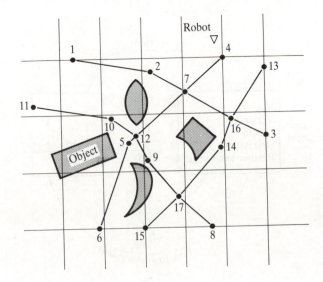

Figure 8.24
Spatial graph showing four
paths taken by a robot.
Sensors were used to detect
and avoid the objects. The
nodes are points where
sensor readings were taken
and the arcs record the
motion of the robot between
these points. (Jorgensen *et
al.*, 1986; Iyengar *et al.*,
1986).

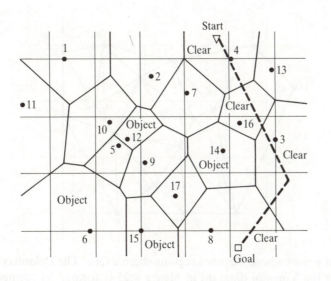

Figure 8.25
Voronoi diagram of
environment from the spatial
graph in Figure 8.24. An
optimal path produced by a
path planner is shown by the
broken line. (Jorgensen *et
al.*, 1986).

robot halted to sense the environment. The arcs record the straight line motions of the robot between stop points. Intersections occur at the nodes where paths cross. Any region that is bounded by arcs may contain an object (Jorgensen *et al.*, 1986). The more paths recorded the more complex the data structure and the more accurate the map.

From the spatial graph, a Voronoi diagram can be drawn to divide the environment into regions (O'Dunlaing and Yap, 1985). A Voronoi diagram is formed by partitioning a plane into polygonal regions, each of which is associated with a given point (Lee and Drysdale, 1981). The region associated with a point is the locus of points closer to that point than to any other given point. The edge separating two regions is composed of points equidistant from the given points.

The Voronoi diagram in Figure 8.25 was constructed by selecting the stop points of the spatial graph as the given points. The convex polygonal regions enclose the points that are closest to the given points. All the regions in the diagram are convex hulls (Window 8.2). By comparing the regions with the spatial graph, we can see that some regions are clear, some have objects in them, and most are ambiguous. Ambiguity can be reduced by traversing the robot to more stop points in the environment.

When a map has been obtained an alternative Voronoi diagram can be generated. This Voronoi diagram (sometimes called the **generalized Voronoi diagram**) is the locus of points which are equidistant from object boundaries (Takahashi and Schilling, 1989). When navigating a robot, a natural strategy is to keep the robot as far away from objects as possible. Thus, the robot moves down the centre of space corridors. The graph of all such centre lines is the Voronoi diagram of the obstacles (O'Rourke, 1984). One way of generating this Voronoi diagram is by Delaunay triangulation. The Delaunay triangulation is the dual graph of the Voronoi diagram. It connects

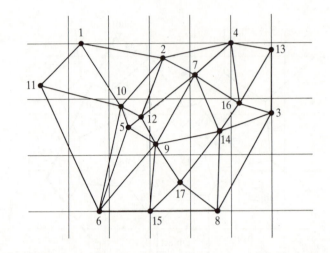

the given points whose Voronoi regions share a face. The Delaunay triangulation of the Voronoi diagram in Figure 8.25 is formed by connecting the stop points whose Voronoi regions share a face. Normally, the outer boundary of the Delaunay triangulation coincides with the convex hull of the points. In Figure 8.26 it does not because the total space has not been explored. When we have a map, the Delaunay triangulation of the objects, can be obtained by placing a given point at the centre of each object. The triangles are formed by connecting these points (Figure 8.27). To obtain the Voronoi regions, the edges of the triangles are bisected with orthogonal lines. These lines correspond to the centre lines between the objects and form the edges of the Voronoi regions.

Unfortunately, the centre of the edge of a triangle may not be the centre of the corridor between the objects. To overcome this, some systems bisect the section of the edge of the triangle which lies in the space between the objects. Other systems simulate Delaunay triangulation by finding the shortest line between each pair of objects and bisecting it with an orthogonal line to find the edge of the Voronoi region (Parodi, 1985). All these techniques assume that the objects are convex.

Voronoi diagrams are one of a number of free-space data structures where the spaces between objects are more important that the objects themselves. Brooks (1985) represents free space as freeways: elongated regions of free space which naturally describe a large class of collision-free straight-line motions. Freeways can be described with generalized cones (Brooks, 1982). They can overlap, and cross. Some areas of space are better described as meadows: convex regions. Freeways can be found by drawing tangents to the objects parallel to the edges of the Voronoi regions. They are represented by a length and minimum width, and meadows are represented by circles. The map is represented as a graph, where nodes are meadows, and arcs are freeways. As well as size and connectivity, the relative positions and orientations of the meadows and freeways are stored in the data structure.

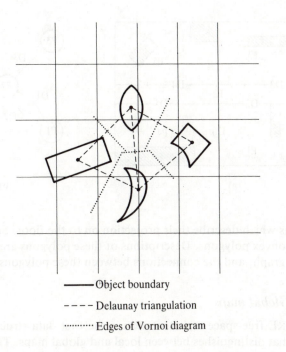

Figure 8.27
Finding the edges of the
object Voronoi diagram using
Delaunay triangulation. The
regions will enclose the
objects when the walls of
the room are added to the
map.

——— Object boundary

– – – – Delaunay triangulation

·········· Edges of Vornoi diagram

Meadows and freeways are derived from visual information similar to the
features discussed earlier.

This map has a number of problems. There are degenerate meadows
where collinear freeways meet. There are degenerate freeways where meadows overlap. The same point in physical space can occur in several freeways
as the roving robot builds up its map. As a result, the map contains
considerable redundancy, and an algorithm is required to reduce this over-
mapping by recognizing that some points occur in several freeways or
meadows.

The HILARE robot (Giralt *et al.*, 1985; Chatilla, 1985) uses a free-
space representation where space is decomposed recursively into places
(rooms, hallways) and connectors between these spaces (doors, gates). A
place is a region of space that serves a functional (for example, a docking
bay) or a topological function (for example, a hallway). In this system, space
is represented at two levels: topological and geometric. At the topological
level, places are the nodes and connectors are the arcs in a connectivity graph
(Figure 8.28(b)). At the geometric level, dimensions of the elements of the
connectivity graph are stored: width for the connectors and boundary
dimensions for the spaces.

Each place has an internal frame of reference. Also, places can contain specific locations, such as landmarks and workstations, locations which
can be used as reference points. The structure of each space is further refined
with a graph of the contents of that space. Objects and walls are represented

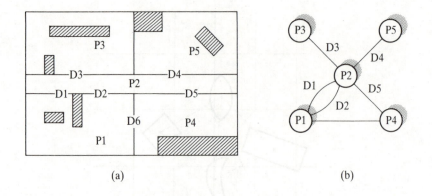

(a)   (b)

by polygons which describe their projection on to the floor. Space is represented by convex polygons. Descriptions of these polygons are stored in the nodes of a graph, and the connections between these polygons are the arcs.

8.3.2.5 *Global maps*

The HILARE free-space representation is the first data structure we have examined that distinguishes between local and global maps. The street map used by the MELDOG robots is a global map showing the connections between regions of interest. All the other maps have been local maps: detailed maps of the robot's immediate environment.

In real-world applications of mobile robots, both global and local maps are used. Global maps should decompose hierarchically into local maps to allow easy movement between the two. One obvious advantage of this structure is a reduction in the use of local memory without loss of detail, because the computer in the robot has to store only the global map and a detailed local map for the area it is in, not a detailed map of its whole universe. This assumes that local maps can be retrieved from secondary storage, or a host computer, at any time.

8.3.2.6 *Object-oriented maps*

In situations where the environment is well known, objects are often mapped with vertex graphs (Lozano-Perez, 1983). A vertex graph is an object oriented map which explicitly records the location of objects, implying that areas not occupied by objects are free space. Vertex graphs are not restricted to known environments. Vertex graphs can be stored as linked lists of objects, where each record in the list describes the position and orientation of the object (Figure 8.29). Each object can be described with an array of vertices – absolute *x*, *y* coordinates.

If the objects are moveable, this description is too limited. A more flexible alternative is the transformation developed in Chapter 3. The posi-

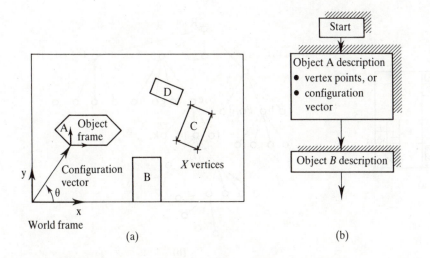

Figure 8.29
Vertex graph of a set of objects stored as a linked list.
(a) Objects projected on to plane;
(b) linked list.

tion and orientation of a reference point on the object can be described with a configuration vector: a 3 degree of freedom vector in 2 dimensional space, and a description of the object relative to the frame located at the reference point.

8.3.2.7 *Composite-space maps*

Free-space and object-oriented descriptions have the limitation that they only partially map the environment. Either free space is coarsely mapped and everything else is ignored, or objects are mapped and free space is found by implication. Many problems in mobile robotics require a knowledge of both free space and objects. While the robot travels through free space, it must avoid collisions with objects, and it may have to approach objects as part of its task (for example, during docking operations).

The most common method of composite space mapping is the area-grid method, where a grid is laid over the space and grid squares are given a state descriptor which specifies the occupancy of that square. A typical example is the sonar map developed by Elfes (1986), shown in Figure 8.23, which is stored as an array.

As an alternative to an area grid, a point grid can be used to model the world. To construct a point grid, the world is covered with a regular grid of points. Each point is connected to its neighbours by the arcs of a graph. A four-connected grid connects to either the orthogonal (vertical and horizontal) neighbours or to the diagonal neighbours. An eight-connected grid connects to all neighbouring grid points. The only information stored at the nodes is whether the point is on an object or in free space. The advantage of grids is that they use a compact, geographically related data structure that is easy to search: either a graph or an array.

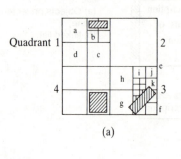

Quadrant 1

(a)

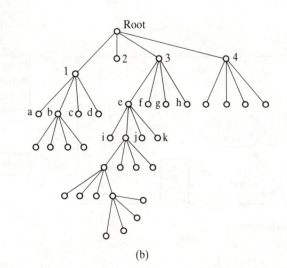

(b)

Figure 8.30
Quadtree data structure
stores a multi-resolution
representation of composite
space.
(a) Geometric
representation;
(b) tree data structure –
each node contains a
quadrant descriptor.

Their main disadvantage is that the resolution of the map is determined by the coarseness of the grid. If the grid is too coarse, grid points will not occur in free space areas that the robot can fit into, and an area grid may include large areas of uncertainty: squares that are part object and part space. Decreasing the grid size increases the cost of computation. Also, large uniform areas take many grid squares to cover them, and global maps consume large amounts of memory.

One approach to a composite-space map that tries to minimize these problems is a **quadtree** (Kambhampati and Davis, 1986). A quadtree recursively divides space into equal area quadrants (Figure 8.30). The recursion terminates when either all quadrants are homogeneous or the minimum quadrant size is reached. A quadrant is homogeneous when all the area covered by the quadrant has the same state. A quadtree is stored as a tree, with quadrant descriptors stored at the nodes. If the quadrant covers an area of uniform space, it is not subdivided any further. Thus, large areas of the same state are covered by a small number of quadrants. This works well for edges between objects and spaces that are parallel to the edges of the quadrants. Edges that are at an angle (see the object in quadrant 3 of Figure 8.30) require smaller and smaller quadrants to reduce the area of uncertain space to a minimum. The minimum quadrant size determines the depth of the tree and the accuracy of the mapping (Sammet, 1987).

One of the motives for research into the use of multiresolution hierarchical data structures like quadtrees is the desire to achieve a compromise between methods which use the map as it is for path planning (regular grid, vertex graph) and methods that make elaborate representation changes to convert the map to a form suitable for path planning (free-space methods). The quadtree has been proposed as such a compromise (Zelinsky, 1988).

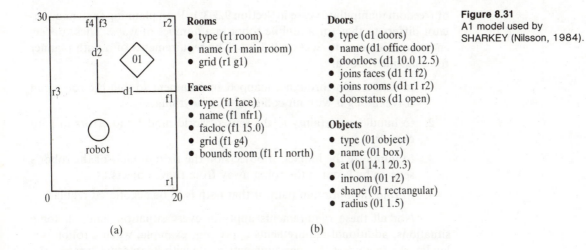

Figure 8.31
A1 model used by
SHARKEY (Nilsson, 1984).

Rooms
- type (r1 room)
- name (r1 main room)
- grid (r1 g1)

Faces
- type (f1 face)
- name (f1 nfr1)
- facloc (f1 15.0)
- grid (f1 g4)
- bounds room (f1 r1 north)

Doors
- type (d1 doors)
- name (d1 office door)
- doorlocs (d1 10.0 12.5)
- joins faces (d1 f1 f2)
- joins rooms (d1 r1 r2)
- doorstatus (d1 open)

Objects
- type (01 object)
- name (01 box)
- at (01 14.1 20.3)
- inroom (01 r2)
- shape (01 rectangular)
- radius (01 1.5)

(a)

(b)

8.3.2.8 *Rule-based maps*

The last environment description that we will consider is the rule-based model used by SHAKEY (Nilsson, 1984). This model is a collection of predicate calculus statements stored as prenexed clauses in an indexed data structure. This model can be used as the axiom set for the STRIPS (Fikes and Nilsson, 1971) planning system.

The model was defined for five classes of entities: doors, wall faces, rooms, objects and robots (Figure 8.31). For each of these classes, a set of primitive predicates was defined. These predicates described these entities and the relationship of these entities to other entities in the model. This type of model is not in common use in mobile robots, as most current research is dealing with the lower-level problems of sensing and control.

8.3.3 Path planning

Maps are used for two main purposes: to record where a robot has been, and to plan paths for it to follow. In this section, we will examine algorithms for planning paths through a mapped environment. Path planning in partially known and unknown environments is discussed briefly in Section 8.3.5.

Much of the work in path planning for mobile robots is derived from earlier work in path planning for manipulators, where it is often referred to as the find-path problem of spatial planning. In the context of mobile robots, path planning is simplified by restricting the robot to three degrees of freedom on a plane. The concept of a robot passing under an object (for example, a table) is beyond current path planners.

The algorithms discussed in this section are extended to the six degree of freedom manipulator case in Section 9.3.3.1. Path planning for a manipulator differs to that for a mobile robot in a number of ways. These differences are discussed in Section 9.3.3.1. The requirements of a path planner for a mobile robot are:

1. to find a path through a mapped environment so that the robot can travel along it without colliding with anything,
2. to handle uncertainty in the sensed world model and errors in path execution,
3. to minimize the impact of objects on the field of view of the robot's sensors by keeping the robot away from those objects,
4. to find the optimum path, if that path is to be negotiated regularly.

Not all these requirements apply in every situation, and, in some situations, additional requirements apply. For example, when a robot uses landmarks to correct the measurements made with its internal sensors, the path must pass the landmark in such a way that the robot can detect it easily, for example, to avoid occlusion of the landmark.

8.3.3.1 *Teaching routes*

Paths for AGV systems are usually planned by people. When the paths are clearly defined by guide wires in the floor, a person with a map carefully plans the paths to be followed by the vehicles to achieve the efficient transfer of materials through the factory. Operations research techniques may be used to optimize the use of the robots or the transfer of material. The paths are stored in the control computer, which moves the robots from process to process in response to the completion of production steps.

The Sencar AGV (Section 8.3.1.2) is designed to be installed quickly, and to have its path through a factory modified easily. The path is planned by a person who understands the production requirements. An operator then drives the robot along the path and the robot records the path as it travels. As the operator drives the robot, docking points are indicated, and the robot records the location of beacons and branches. This system describes the paths as a series of curved trajectories, as operators find it easier to drive the robot along curved paths then along straight ones.

8.3.3.2 *Automatic path planning*

If there are a few well-known paths, the simplest map is the graph of paths used in the MELDOG robots (Tachi and Komoriya, 1985). For path planning, the graph of nodes is treated as a tree with the root at the starting node. By using common artificial intelligence techniques, a program searches the tree to see if a route to the destination node exists. This route is extracted as a subgraph.

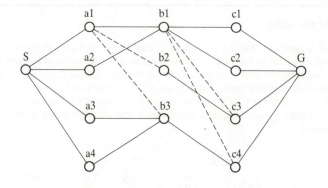

Figure 8.32
Multiple path graph formed
by connecting subgraphs
representing valid routes.
(Tachi and Komoriya, 1985).

If multiple routes exist, the subgraphs are connected to form a multiple path graph (Figure 8.32). The route with the minimum length is found using dynamic programming (Window 8.1). Other optimization criteria can also be used.

The paths used in this system are called virtual paths, because they are defined using landmarks, in contrast to physical paths such as the guidewires followed by AGVs or the taught paths used by the Sencar robot. For a well-defined task in a small environment, there will be a small number of clearly defined paths, and the MELDOG data structure is suitable.

In a less structured, complex, or partly unknown environment, the number of possible paths may be extremely large. In these circumstances, it may be more efficient to store a map of the environment and plan paths through the environment than to search a large number of known paths. If the environment is only partial known or constantly changing, there may be few paths that exist over a long period of time, and a path planner has to be used.

Most path planners abstract the search space to a graph of possible paths. This graph is then searched to find the shortest path. This approach arises naturally in a learning environment, where a robot may have traversed several paths to map the world. An example of this is the spatial graph shown in Figure 8.24.

8.3.3.3 *Free-space planners*

In general, path planners can be categorized according to their mapping structure. Free-space path planners explicitly deal with the free space rather than the space occupied by obstacles. All free-space planners reduce the find path problem to graph search techniques (Gouzenes, 1984). In the learned Voronoi diagram in Figure 8.25, paths pass through the midpoints of the faces of connecting clear regions. The boundaries of an object Voronoi diagram (see Figure 8.27) form a network of possible paths. Optimal paths

Window 8.1 *A* search algorithm*

Selecting the best path from a graph of several possible paths is one of a number of problems that use artificial intelligence search techniques. A number of search techniques are modifications of the **branch and bounds search**. This search starts by expanding the root node by one step to form a tree of depth two. The cost (length) of each path from root to subnodes is calculated. These costs are compared and the path with the lowest cost chosen. The node at the end of this path is expanded by one step and the cost of the set of new paths is calculated. The cost of all paths (the old one-step paths and the new two-step paths) are compared and the path with the lowest cost is chosen. This process is repeated until the goal is reached.

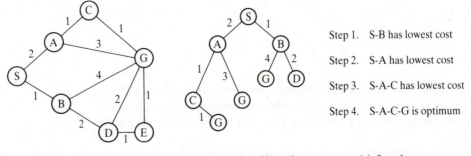

Step 1.   S-B has lowest cost

Step 2.   S-A has lowest cost

Step 3.   S-A-C has lowest cost

Step 4.   S-A-C-G is optimum

(a) Graph of paths   (b) Branch and bounds search tree   (c) Search steps

      The **A* search** is a refinement of the branch and bounds search. The search space is reduced by deleting multiple paths to a subnode, and leaving only the lowest cost path. This is known as the use of a **dynamic programming principle**. The choice of the lowest cost path for expansion at each stage is improved by adding an estimated cost for the remaining path to the actual cost of the path so far. This estimated cost is different for each node. If this estimated cost is a lower bound on the actual cost, the A* search produces an optimal solution. A typical lower bound estimate in path planning is the straight-line distance between the position represented by the current node and the goal position.

A * Algorithm   (Winston, 1984)

1. Use a queue to store all the partially expanded paths.

2. Initialize the queue by adding to the queue a zero length path from the root node to nowhere.

3. **Repeat**
    Examine the first path on the queue.
    If it reaches the goal node **then** success.
    Else {continue search}
    Remove the first path from the queue.
    Expand the last node on this path by one step.
    Calculate the cost of these new paths.
    Add these new paths to the queue.
    Sort the queue in ascending order according to the sum of the cost of the expanded path and the estimated cost of the remaining path for each path.
    If more than one path reaches a subnode
      Then delete all but the minimum cost path
    Until the goal has been found or the queue is empty.

4. If the goal has been found return success and the path, otherwise return failure.

are found with techniques from graph theory. Paths that contain corridors between objects that are too narrow for the robot to pass through must be detected and eliminated.

When free space is represented by regular geometric shapes with links between those geometric shapes, possible paths are found by connecting the axes of the geometric shapes using a technique known as **medial axis transforms**. Again, the paths that are too narrow must be eliminated, and an optimum path selected.

Many path planners simplify the calculations involved in path planning by treating the robot as a point, and determining the trajectory of that point. In free-space methods, the free-space corridors must be made narrower by the width of the robot plus clearances. In object-oriented methods, the objects must be expanded by the dimensions of the robot.

Free-space algorithms suffer from two problems, both of which result from a data abstraction that throws away too much information (Thorpe, 1984). The first problem is that paths always run down the centre of space corridors. In a narrow corridor, this is desirable, because it minimizes the chance of collision due to robot tracking errors. In an open space, on the other hand, it may cause the robot to travel a much greater distance than necessary. The second problem is the difficulty of selecting paths that allow enough clearance for the robot to pass through without tracking errors causing collisions. This problem occurs in all planners.

8.3.3.4 *Piano-mover's problem*

Many path planners assume that the robot does not rotate when tracking a path; that is, when a robot turns the orientation of the body does not change, as in a synchronous-drive robot (see Figure 2.7). If the robot has a circular cross-section, this assumption is valid. However, if the robot is rectangular this assumption will eliminate paths that the robot can negotiate if it rotates as it turns. The problems which occur when planning paths through complex narrow corridors that require the robot to rotate are known as the piano-mover's problem (Schwartz and Sharir, 1983).

In practice, many robots are not cylindrical and must turn to go through doors, or travel along hallways. Allowing for the irregular shape of a robot increases the complexity of path planning, because now we have to plan a trajectory that is subject to geometric constraints, so that no part of the robot contacts an obstacle while turning (Figure 8.33)

This problem can be simplified by restricting the robot to maintain a single orientation during path traversal, or by allowing rotation only when the robot is in a large area of free space. These restrictions eliminate many of the paths that give rise to the piano mover's problem.

To solve this problem, we place several axes on the robot around which it can rotate. The placement of these axes is dependent on the manoeuvrability of the robot, but typical points are the centre of the robot,

Figure 8.33
Piano-mover's problem. A
path that the rectangular
robot can negotiate only if it
rotates around A as it turns
the corner C.

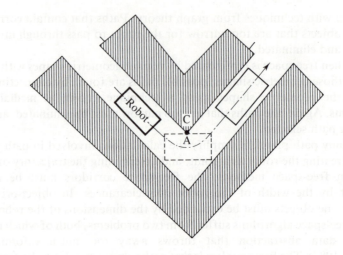

the wheel-to-floor control points, and the corners of the robot. Considering the example, in Figure 8.33, each axis is placed at the inside intersection of the walls in turn, that is, point C. The robot is then rotated about this axis and the trajectories of the other axes are drawn. This process is continued until an axis of rotation is found where the trajectories of all the axes are within the free space area.

In this example, if the robot rotates around axis A, it can negotiate the elbow without collision. If several possible paths exist, the best one can be selected based on criteria such as greatest clearance from walls or least number of motion steps. In some situations, a combination of rotations and translations may be required to negotiate a bend. Current mobile robots do not have this level of sophistication, as the solution of other problems is more pressing.

8.3.3.5 *Vertex graphs*

In object-oriented models, paths are planned as a series of vectors connecting the vertices of objects. When the objects are modelled as circles (Figure 8.20), the robot is shrunk to a point and the circles are expanded by the diameter of the robot. A path is either a straight line from start to goal or a sequence of tangential segments between the circles and arcs around segments of the circles. The path can be visualized as a rubber band stretched from start to goal so that it curves around the circles and follows tangential paths between the circles.

In this planning method, the optimization problem is to find the shortest graph of connected vertices. This is more complex than it first appears. There are four possible paths tangential to any pair of circles. Obstacles cover area, so the point at which one tangent arrives and the point

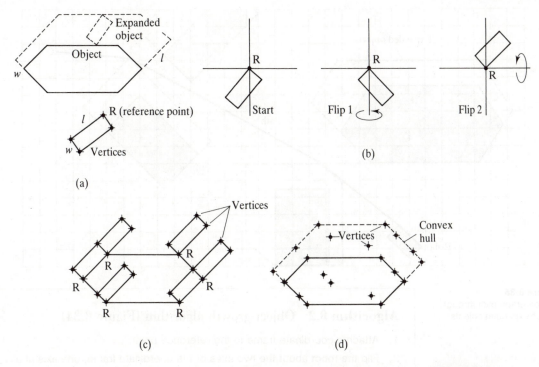

Figure 8.34

Figure 8.34
Expanding objects for vextex graph path planning. (a) distance expansion; (b) to (d) same result with object growth algorithm.
(a) Distance expansion of object to compensate for shrinking robot to a point, R. Note if robot orientation changes then a different expansion occurs;
(b) flipping robot around two orthogonal axes through point that robot will shrink to;
(c) placing flipped robot at object vertices to obtain the vertices of the expanded object;
(d) Finding the convex hull of the resultant vertices to obtain the expanded object.

at which the next leaves is not the same. The length of the arc between these contact points has to be added to the path length.

A complete path search requires every tangential path between every pair of circles to be generated and, if it is not blocked by another obstacle, added to the graph of possible paths. This graph then has to be searched to find sequences of tangential segments that connect the start to the goal. Finally, this multipath graph is searched to find the optimum path. (Window 8.1).

If the world is modelled as a vertex graph of polygonal objects the problem is to find a sequence of vectors between vertices that connect the start to the goal. The length of the path is the sum of the lengths of these vectors, as the vectors connect at vertex points. The robot is modelled as a point located at a reference vertex of the robot, and the objects are expanded by the distances from this point to the other verticles of the robot (Figure 8.34(a)). Each face of the object is moved by the distance from the reference point of the robot to the vertex on the robot which would contact that face if the robot approached the object with its current orientation.

While this is conceptually simple, the calculations can be messy in practice. Jarvis (1983) developed a simple algorithm for finding the vertices of the expanded object.

Through this process of expansion, the problem of path planning has been reduced to the problem of finding a path for the reference point on the

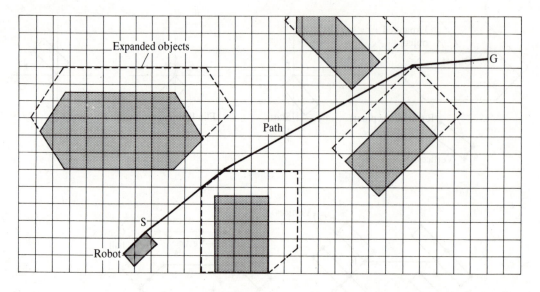

Figure 8.35
Vertex graph path through a
set of expanded objects.

Algorithm 8.2   Object-growth algorithm (Figure 8.34)

1. Attach a coordinate frame to the reference point,

2. Flip the robot about the two axes of the coordinate frame, one axis at a
    time (Figure 8.34(b)),

3. Place the reference point of the flipped robot at each of the vertices of the
    object and calculate the positions of the vertices of the robot
    (Figure 8.34(c)),

4. Find the convex hull (Window 8.2) of the vertices (Figure 8.34(d)). The
    convex hull is the convex polygon formed by stretching a rubber band
    around the vertices.

robot through the expanded objects (Figure 8.35). Because the actual shape
of the robot is used, this algorithm is not restricted to robots with a circular
cross-section. The search space for paths is the set of visibility vectors
between vertices. Visibility vectors are the vectors from one vertex to all the
vertices that are visible from that vertex. A path graph is built by following
all the vectors from the start point to the visible vertices around it. From
these vertices another set of vectors is followed. This process is repeated until
the goal is reached. At which point, the search is terminated if only one path
is required. If several paths are required for optimization, the search is
continued until the required number of paths has been found or all paths
exhaustively searched. Any paths that do not reach the goal are pruned from
the graph (Window 8.1). The optimum path is the shortest one.

   A modified version of this algorithm can handle paths that require the
robot to rotate. The solution for one orientation is called a **slice**. Slices are
generated for a range of robot orientations. By overlaying these slices, paths

Window 8.2 Convex hull algorithms

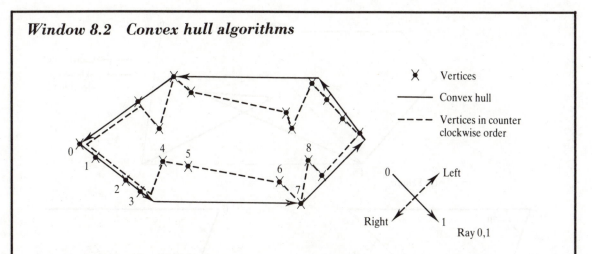

The convex hull of a set of vertices is the shortest bounding polygon that has all the vertices within its boundaries. It is the shape that results if a nail is driven into each vertex and a rubber band stretched around the nails so that all the nails are inside the area prescribed by the rubber band.

A simple convex hull algorithm was described by Sklansky (1972). This algorithm assumes that the vertices are ordered in a counter-clockwise order to form a closed nonintersecting chain, a chain that describes a polygon on a plane. The vertices are numbered from 0 to $n-1$, with vertex n being identical to vertex 0. Vertex 0 is on the convex hull and is the vertex with the most negative x coordinate.

Shansky's algorithm considers sets of three vertices. The vertices are held in an ordered list. The first two vertices (0 and 1) are removed from the list and pushed on to a stack. These top two vertices define a straight line or ray. The first vertex in the list (next counter-clockwise vertex on the polygon) is compared to the ray. If this vertex is to the right of the ray, then the ray is inside the polygon. The vertex at the top of the stack is popped and discarded, and the vertex at the start of the list is removed from the list and pushed on to the stack. If the first vertex on the list is to the left of the ray, the ray is considered to be on the convex hull, and the vertex is removed from the list and pushed on to the stack. A new ray is formed by the two vertices at the top of the stack. This process is repeated until all vertices have been removed from the list. The stack contains the vertices that describe the convex hull.

Sklansky's Algorithm

1. Place vertices into a counter-clockwise ordered list
2. Allocate a stack
3. Push vertex 0 onto stack
4. Push vertex 1 onto stack
5. **For** $i=2$ **to** n **do**
   {compare vertex i to ray formed by the 2 vertices at the top of the stack}
   If vertex i is to the right of the ray (stacktop-1, stacktop) **then**
       pop {discard top element of stack}
   End
   push vertex i {put vertex i onto stack}
   End

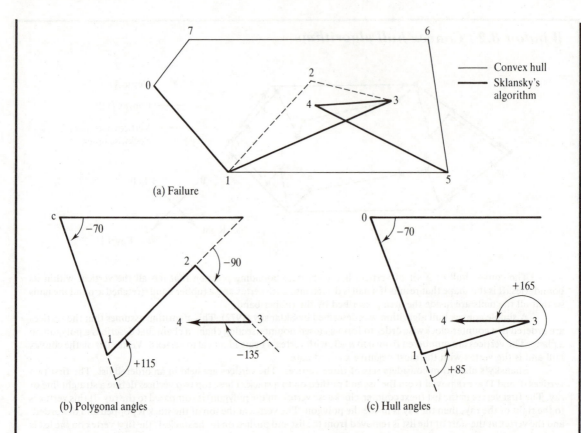

(a) Failure

(b) Polygonal angles

(c) Hull angles

This algorithm works if the vertices are in counter-clockwise order and the next vertex is always in the direction of the convex hull. However, in circumstances where the next vertex is not in the direction of the convex hull, the algorithm may fail. In the example above, vertex 3 is to the right of ray 1, 2, so vertex 2 is discarded. But vertex 4 is to the left of ray 1, 3, so vertex 3 is kept when it should have been discarded.

This situation can be detected by calculating the cumulative angle for the vector from the end of the ray to the vertex under consideration. This angle is calculated for the polygon, from the list of vertices, and for the partial hull from the stack of vertices. If these differ (always by a multiple of 360°) then the vertex should be discarded. In the above diagram, the accumulated angle for ray 3, 4 is −180° for the polygon and +180° for the hull. Hence, vertex 4 should be discarded. Peshkin and Sanderson (1985) extend Sklansky's Algorithm to include this test.

This class of algorithm assumes that the vertices are known in counter-clockwise order, with no sides of the polygon intersecting. In situations where this is not the case, other algorithms have to be used (Green and Silverman, 1979).

Convex hull algorithm – when vertices are not in order

1. Find the vertices with the maximum and minimum *x* and *y* values (4 vertices)

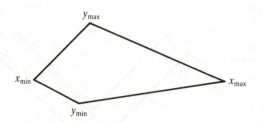

2. Sort the vertices into ascending x order {if not already done}
3. Start at the x_{min} vertex – push it onto a stack.
   (a) Find the slope of all rays starting at the vertex at the top of the stack and going to vertices to the left of the y_{min} vertex and to the right of and below the top of stack vertex.
   (b) Select the vertex at the end of the ray with the greatest negative slope – push this vertex onto the stack.
4. Repeat Step 3 with the new top of the stack vertex until the y_{min} vertex is pushed onto the stack.
5. Repeat Steps 3 and 4 to find the rays between the y_{min} vertex and the x_{max} vertex, for vertices to right of y_{min} and below x_{max} with the smallest positive slope.
6. Repeat Steps 3 and 4 to find rays between x_{max} and y_{max}, for vertices above x_{max} and to the right of y_{max}, with the greatest positive slope.
7. Repeat Steps 3 and 4 to find rays between y_{max} and x_{min}, for vertices above x_{min} and to the left of y_{max}, with the smallest negative slope.

that require rotation of the robot can be found. For example, to solve the piano mover's problem in Figure 8.33, the robot follows a path with one orientation until it intersects a path with another orientation (Figure 8.36). In the region of this intersection, the robot rotates to the new orientation and follows the new path. This algorithm for finding paths through small corridors with bends in them can be used if several slices are generated for the region of the bend. Lozano-Perez (1981, 83) specified this algorithm formally in terms of configuration-space vectors.

Vertex graphs suffer from the problem that paths pass too close to the corners of objects and may run along the edges of some objects (Thorpe, 1984). Any slight error in trajectory following will result in a collision. This problem can be minimized by expanding the size of the robot to include clearances, but that requires a method of calculating clearances. Also, close proximity to objects can interfere with sensor systems. A better, but computationally more expensive, approach is to plan the path using vertex methods, and then shift the path to the centre of the free space between the objects.

Kant and Zucker (1986) describe the free space that the vertex path traverses with a sequence of triangles whose vertices are defined by the

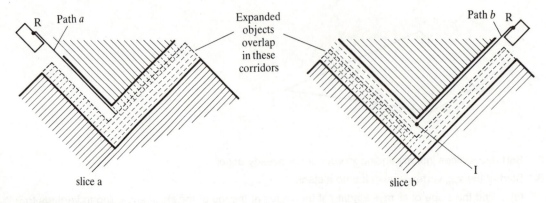

slice a   slice b

Figure 8.36
Finding a path using two
slices. The robot follows
path *a* on entry and path *b*
on exit. It rotates and
changes paths at the
intersection I as shown in
Figure 8.33.

Figure 8.37
Free space path developed
from the vertex path of
Figure 8.35 using triangle
representation. Note the
extra length near source, the
shift to the centre between
objects, and the jaggedness
of the path.

vertices of the expanded objects on the faces near the path. The new free-space path is formed from the sequences of vectors which traverse the midpoints of the sides of the triangles which cross the old vertex path (Figure 8.37). This method has the disadvantage that path length and complexity are often increased.

8.3.3.6 *Composite-space path planners*

The simplest composite space path planners are based on regular grid data structures. Planners which use area grids plan paths from the centre of one

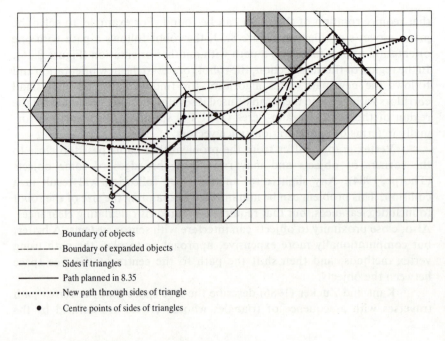

———————— Boundary of objects

- - - - - - - - Boundary of expanded objects

— — — — Sides if triangles

———————— Path planned in 8.35

· · · · · · · · · · · New path through sides of triangle

•   Centre points of sides of triangles

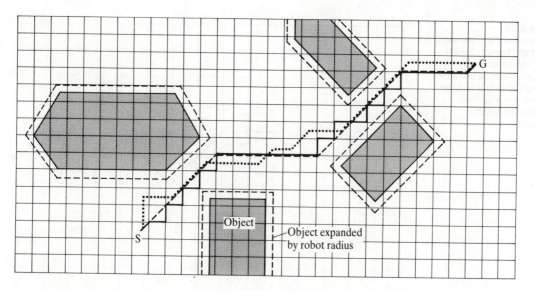

free-space grid square to the centre of connected free-space grid squares. These planners suffer from the same problems as free-space planners, although not to the same extent. Because many grid squares cover a typical free space polygon, planned paths tend to be closer to objects, and hence, closer to optimal (Figure 8.38). The area of the robot is usually taken into account by shrinking the robot and expanding the objects.

Figure 8.38
Paths for a cylindrical robot, with diameter equal to grid width, planned using grid data structures.
· · · Area grid;
--- 8-connected grid;
——— orthogonal 4-connected grid.

Planners which use connected grids search the graph for the shortest path. A straightforward grid search has the same problems as a vertex graph in that the paths can be too close to objects (Figure 8.38). More sophisticated grid maps assign weights to the free space nodes: weights which are a function of the distance from the point to the nearest object.

All grid planners suffer from two significant problems: missed paths and crooked paths. If an area grid is too coarse, it may include large areas of uncertainty and permissible paths may not be found. If a connected grid is too coarse, some permissible corridors may not have grid points in them. Any point on a grid has four orthogonal neighbours and four diagonal ones (Figure 8.44(c)). In an eight-connected grid, the point is connected to all eight neighbours. The concept of connectivity is explored further in Section 10.8.7.1. In an eight-connected grid, a grid spacing the size of the robot will guarantee that all corridors that the robot can fit through will have a grid point in them (Thorpe, 1984). To allow for clearance problems this size can be increased slightly depending on the precision of the robot. In an orthogonal four-connected grid, where the point is connected to its four orthogonal neighbours, the spacing has to be $\sqrt{2}/2$ times the diameter of the robot to guarantee that grid points occur in valid diagonal paths.

At first sight, it may appear that selecting the grid size according to the above criteria will eliminate the need to reduce the robot to a point and expand the objects. However, connected grids have the problem that a grid

Figure 8.39
Operation of path relaxation
algorithm (Thorpe, 1984).
—— Original grid path
through cylindrical obstacles;
—·— path after first iteration
of relaxation algorithm;
--- path after second
iteration.

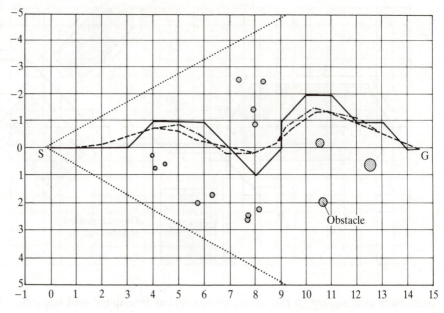

point can occur in a corridor that is much too narrow for the robot. If the objects are expanded to eliminate this problem, the above criteria are no longer valid.

As the path is a sequence of vectors from grid point to grid point, or centre to centre in the case of area grids, it can be quite crooked (Figure 8.38). A number of algorithms have been suggested for path smoothing (Mitchell and Keirsey, 1984). One is path relaxation (Thorpe, 1984). **Path relaxation** attempts to overcome all the above problems by calculating a cost function for each path. An eight-connected grid, with grid spacing the size of the robot, is used because the paths produced by grid search are smoother than with a four-connected grid (Figure 8.39). Also, the grid size is coarser reducing the amount of storage and computation time.

Once the grid data structure has been established, it is searched for paths that connect the start point to the goal point. As the start and goal points usually do not coincide with the grid points, they have to be included as special nodes. Then a cost function is calculated for each path and the best one selected. This is a global cost function for the whole path with the intent of finding the globally optimal path, which at some points may not be locally optimal.

The cost function balances three conflicting requirements: short path length, maximum margin away from obstacles, and minimum distance in unmapped areas. The cost of a path is the sum of the products of the cost of each node through which it passes and the distance to adjacent nodes. In eight-connected graphs, orthogonal and diagonal distances differ. The node cost consists of three parameters.

1. A cost of one unit for path length.

2. An object cost that is an inverse function of the distances to nearby objects. The slope of this cost function depends on the accuracy of the robot (a precise robot can pass near objects) and its speed (a faster robot must slow down to turn sharp corners).

3. A cost for being in an unmapped, restricted or dangerous region. This is a function of the task goal.

If the cost function is set up correctly, paths which include corridors that are too narrow for the robot should be high-cost paths. The lowest cost path should not only be the best path, but also be a passable path. The best path may not be optimal for two reasons. First, it follows grid lines, so it is crooked. Second, a grid point in a narrow corridor may be near enough to the side of the corridor to cause a collision.

The second stage of path relaxation is to allow the path to move off the grid to overcome these problems. This relaxation process involves moving one node at a time in a direction perpendicular to the line connecting the preceding and following nodes in order to minimize the cost of that node. Since moving a node may affect the cost of its neighbours, the entire procedure is repeated until no node moves more than a small amount.

As the node moves, all three parameters of the cost function are affected. Owing to the difficulty of calculating the position with minimum cost directly, a binary search is used to find the position. The relaxation process turns jagged lines into straight ones, finds the 'saddle' in the cost function between objects, and curves the path around isolated objects. A grid path and two smoothing iterations are shown in Figure 8.39.

Conceptually, the cost function can be pictured as the height of the terrain, where high-cost points – hills with sloping sides – represent obstacles, and low cost points – valleys between those hills – represent free space. The height of the hill is a function of the probability of an object being there, and the slope is a function of the precision of the robot. Path relaxation tries to find the path to the goal with the lowest integral of height, where the grid search finds the best valley and the relaxation step finds the bottom of the valley.

Path relaxation can be used with area maps, such as the map developed by Elfes (1986) with a sonar ring (Figure 8.23). An area grid map can be turned into a connected grid map by locating the grid points at the centre of the squares and assigning the probability value to them. This probability value is then included in the calculation of the cost function.

A planning method that uses an area grid data structure is the **distance transform method** (Kang and Jarvis, 1986). In this method, the planner starts at the goal cell and propagates distances through free space. Like

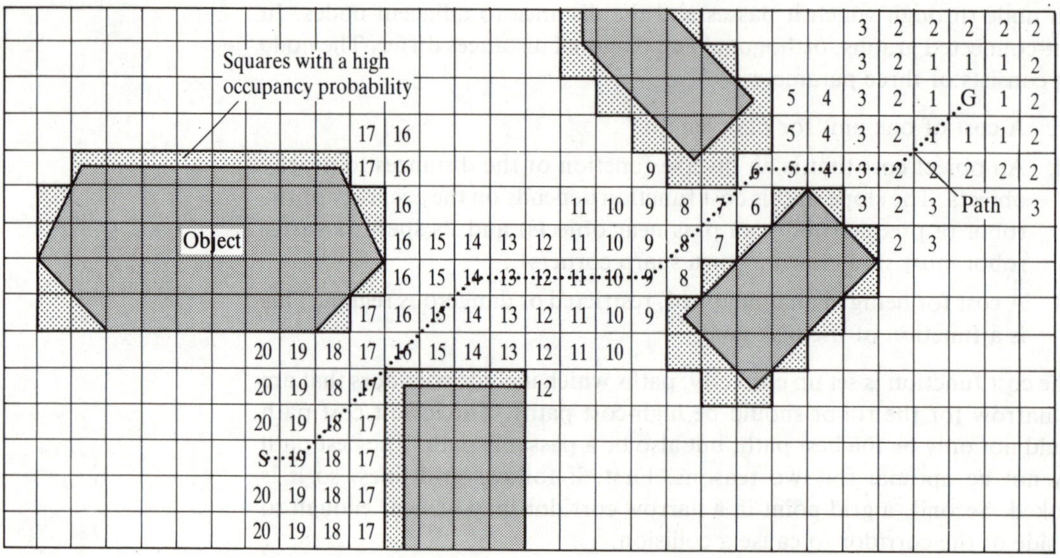

Squares with a high occupancy probability

Object

G

Path

S

Figure 8.40
8-connected distance transform applied to an area grid, showing considerable ambiguity due to both orthogonal and diagonal distances having a value of 1.

dropping a stone in a pond, the ripples radiate out, bouncing off objects in their path, with the first ripple to reach a designated point taking the shortest path. A distance transform value is calculated for each grid square, and stored in its data record. The transform can be calculated simply by adding one for each grid square crossed, as in the eight-connected transform in Figure 8.40, or by actually adding the distance between centres of the grid squares, as in the eight-connected transform in Figure 8.41.

Algorithm 8.3 tests for the presence of objects and does not calculate the transform for squares with objects in them. So that the path-finding algorithm does not have to test whether or not a square contains an object, objects are given high values so that paths will naturally flow away from them. A simple way to do this is to multiply the value we calculate for a square by an occupancy probability factor. If we set this factor to be 1 for a square known to be free space and 3 for a square known to be an object, the objects will have much higher values. The larger the object factor, the steeper the slopes around the objects. If the factor is too large, numeric overflow may occur if there are a large number of object squares on a grid line. Grey areas – areas that contain both space and object – have a factor somewhere between empty and full depending on the probability of occupancy. The factor for unmapped regions can be set low if the robot is on a mapping run, or high if it is not to go into unmapped areas. With this scheme neither the distance-transform algorithm nor the path-planning algorithm has to look explicitly for objects. Both work over the whole grid.

The algorithm for propagating distance transforms (Jarvis, 1985) is computationally expensive on a large grid. A graph of a grid data structure

Algorithm 8.3 Distance transform propagation (Jarvis and Byrne, 1983)

1. Set factor for all grid squares: empty=1, object=n, $1 <$ grey $< n$.

2. Store the map in a two-dimensional array 1 . . xmax, 1 . . ymax . .

3. Allocate a two-dimensional array 0 . . xmax+1, 0 . . ymax+1 to store the distance transforms. The outer rows and columns form an enclosing box (sentinel rectangle) one grid square thick.

4. Initialize the distance transform array by setting the goal cell to zero and all other cells to a large number (xmax×ymax).

5. Calculate the distance transform by repeated forward and reverse scans across the array.

Repeat {Forward Scan}
    For the rows of the map (1 . . ymax)**do**
        For the columns of the map (1 : . xmax)**do**
            If map cell does not contain an object **Then**
                Calculate transform with an 8-connected algorithm
                For each of 4 neighbours
                    (3 below and 1 to left – Figure 8.42a)
                    Calculate the distance transform for this cell
                        =(neighbour value+distance)×factor.
                If any of these transforms is less than the current value of
                the cell **then** assign the minimum to the cell.
            (Note: the first **if** statement leaves all object squares untouched. If
            we want to propagate the transform across objects using a scale
            factor (Figure 8.42) then we leave the test out. When the **if**
            statement is used, the scale factor can be left out)
    {Reverse Scan}
    For the rows of the map (ymax . . 1)**do**
        For the columns of the map (xmax . . 1) **do**
            If map cell does not contain an object **then**
                Calculate transform with the 3 cells above and one to the right –
                Figure 8.42(a).
Until the distance transform array settles.

includes multiple loops, making an efficient graph following algorithm difficult to find, so scanning algorithms are used (Algorithm 8.3). Surprisingly, this algorithm converges fairly quickly. The example in Figure 8.42 converges with two forward scans and one reverse scan. If each scan is monitored for changes, the fourth scan (second reverse scan) will indicate no change and the algorithm will terminate after the second execution of the repeat loop. After the first execution of the repeat loop, the transform is correct, except for the concave region of the object, and could be used for path planning. The worst case is a spiral with the goal at the centre. It

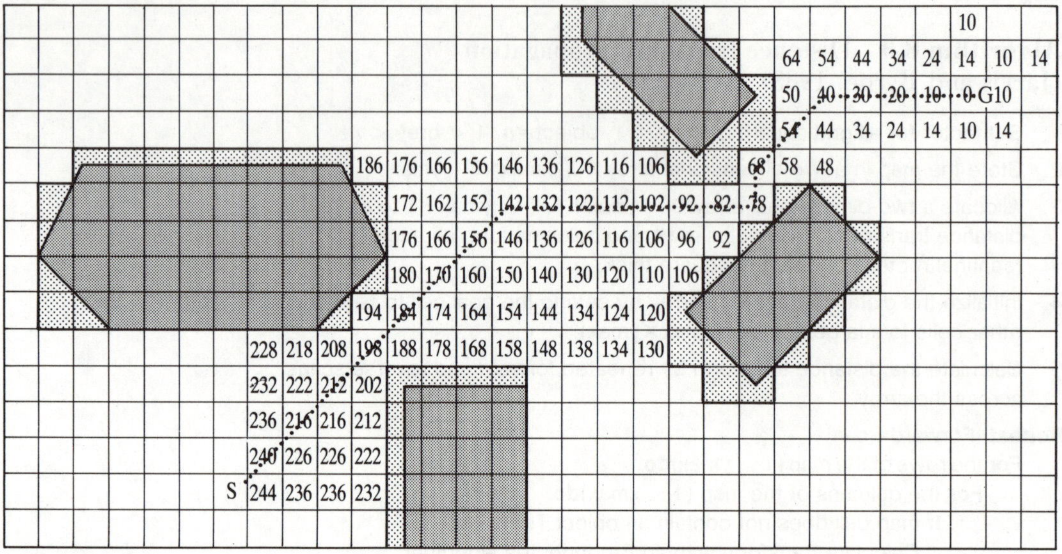

														10		
										64	54	44	34	24	14	10	14
										50	40··30··20··10··0·G10						
										54	44	34	24	14	10	14
186	176	166	156	146	136	126	116	106		68	58	48				
172	162	152	142	132	122	112	102	92	82	78						
176	166	156	146	136	126	116	106	96	92							
180	170	160	150	140	130	120	110	106								
194	184	174	164	154	144	134	124	120								
228	218	208	198	188	178	168	158	148	138	134	130					
232	222	212	202													
236	216	216	212													
240	226	226	222													
S 244	236	236	232													

Figure 8.41
8-connected distance transform based on actual distance between centres $(10 \times \sqrt{2} = 14)$ generates a non-ambiguous path using an 8-connected path finding algorithm.

typically takes two to five iterations to obtain a solution with ten to twenty convex and simple concave objects.

Once the distance transforms are generated, the path is planned from start to goal. Algorithm 8.4 is simple: if the cells around the start cell do not have a lower value than it does, ripples in the distance transform did not reach it and, thus, there is no path. If they do have a lower value, the ripples did reach the start cell and there is a path. To find it, follow the valley (lowest values) to the goal. In this way, a path can be found from any start point to the goal.

Algorithm 8.4   Distance transform path planning

Move to start cell
Scan all neighbours to see if a cell has a lower value
If no lower value cell is found **then** terminate {because there is no path}
Else {there is a path}
    Add start cell identifier to list
    Repeat
        Scan neighbouring cells to find cell with lowest value
        {4- or 8-connected}
        Move to this cell
        Add cell identifier to list
    Until at goal cell
End
Return path found flag and cell identifier list

Columns

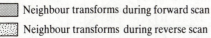

Neighbour transform
= (neighbourvalue + Distance) × factor

New value = Minimum (current value,
4 neighbour transforms)

Rows

Neighbour transforms during forward scan

Neighbour transforms during reverse scan

(a)

55	55	55	55	55	55	55	55	55	55	55
55	55	55	55	55	55	55	55	55	0	55
55	55	55	55	55	55	55	55	55	55	55
55	55	55	55	55	55	55	55	55	55	55
55	55	55	55	55	55	55	55	55	55	55

(b)

55	55	55	55	55	55	55	55	1.4	1	1.4
55	55	55	55	55	55	55	55	55	0	1
55	55	55	55	55	55	55	55	55	55	1.4
55	55	55	55	55	55	55	55	55	55	55
55	55	55	55	55	55	55	55	55	55	55

$\sqrt{2} \approx 1.4$
Factor = 3 for object

(c)

9.4	8.4	7.4	6.4	5.4	4.4	3.4	2.4	1.4	1	1.4
9.8	26.4	23.4	20.4	5.8	4.8	11.4	6	1	0	1
10.8	11.2	21.8	21.6	6.2	5.2	21.6	7.2	1.4	1	1.4
11.2	36.6	37.8	20.4	5.8	4.8	3.8	2.8	2.4	2	2.4
10.2	9.2	8.2	7.2	6.2	5.2	4.2	3.8	3.4	3	3.4

(d)

Figure 8.42
Distance transform propagation algorithm, using 8-connected transform and object weighting factors.
(a) 8-connected distance calculation;
(b) distance transform after initialization step;
(c) distance transform after forward scan;
(d) distance transform after reverse scan (one more forward scan and the transform will settle).

Simple distance transforms that are calculated by adding one for each square crossed create ambiguity problems for the path planner. Consider the path in Figure 8.40. When the path is at distance 14, it can go to three squares with a distance value 13. There are no obvious criteria for solving the ambiguity. If a square is selected randomly, the path can become crooked. If the ratio of the x and y distances to the goal is used, the complexity of the algorithm is increased. In this figure, a valley of low values exists, but it is very broad.

One solution is to use a four-connected distance transform (Figure 8.43). If a four-connected path planning algorithm is used, the ambiguity still exists, but to a lesser extent, and a zigzag path is generated. If an eight-connected path planning algorithm is used with four-connected distance transforms, the same path is found as with an eight-connected transform based on actual distances (Figure 8.41). However, there are situations when four-connected algorithms are known to fail (Figure 8.44).

Consequently, the eight-connected transform based on actual distances with an eight-connected path planner should be used, despite the additional calculation cost. The final path (Figure 8.41) is not optimal and requires smoothing. Also, the path may clip the edges of objects. The main disadvantages of this approach are the inefficiencies of grid maps and the cost of calculating the distance transforms.

[Figure 8.43: Orthogonal 4-connected distance transform grid with numbered cells and obstacles, showing a path from S to G]

														7	6	5	4	3	2	1
														5	4	3	2	1	G
														6	5	4	3	2	1
		21	20	19	18	17	16	15	14	13		8	7	6	5	4	3	2
		19	18	17	16	15	14	13	12	11	10	9		6	5	4	3
		20	19	18	17	16	15	14	13	12	11
		21	20	19	18	17	16	15	14	13
		23	22	21	20	19	18	17	16	15
27	26	25	24	23	22	21	20	19
28	27	26	25
29	28	27	26
S	29	28	27
31	30	29	28

Figure 8.43
Orthogonal 4-connected distance transform with (a) orthogonal 4-connected path planning algorithm giving an ambiguous path —·—. (b) 8-connected path planning algorithm giving an unambiguous path ······.

Figure 8.44
(a) Pinch point: 8-connected and diagonal 4-connected algorithms will find the path but orthogonal 4-connected will not; (b) narrow corridor: 8-connected and orthogonal 4-connected algorithms will find path but diagonal 4-connected will not. (c) connectivity of a point to its neighbour.

Distance transforms can be used to plan paths to multiple goals, either by using separate transform grids for each goal or by setting the additional goal squares to zero during the initialization step in Algorithm 8.3. The piano mover's problem can also be handled with multiple grids of distance transforms (slices) similar to the multiple vertex graphs. In this case, the grid is rectangular with length equal to the length of the robot and width equal to the width of the robot. Different orientations of the robot are handled by rotating the grid parallel to the robot before calculating the distance transform for that slice.

The final group of composite-space path planners are the **multiresolution planners**. Quadtree data structures are used in an attempt to obtain a multiresolution composite-space map that can be used for path planning. In a typical planner (Kambhampati and Davis, 1986), the robot is shrunk to a point, objects are expanded, and the world is mapped with a

(a)

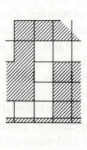

(b)

8 connected   orthogonal 4 connected   diagonal 4 connected

(c)

quadtree. (Figure 8.30). First, we find the leaf nodes in the tree that contain the start and goal positions. Then we find a minimum cost path between these nodes in the subtree formed by the free-space quadrants using an A* search (Window 8.1). The cost of a path (C_p) is a function of both the distance travelled and the clearance of the path from obstacles. At any node n on the path, the cost of the path is:

$$C_p = C_{s,n} + C_{n,g} \tag{8.60}$$

where

$\quad\quad$ $C_{s,n}$ is the cost of the path from the start to node n, and

$\quad\quad$ $C_{n,g}$ is a heuristic estimate of the cost of the path from node n to the goal.

and

$$C_{s,n} = C_{s,n-1} + C_{n-1,n} \tag{8.61}$$

$\quad\quad$ The cost of the path is a function of the distance travelled and the clearance of the path from obstacles. The clearance cost function ($C_{n-1,n}$) is a linear function based on relative distances from free-space nodes to obstacle nodes.

$$C_{n-1,n} = d_{n-1,n} + \alpha(d_{o,f} - d_{n,o}) \tag{8.62}$$

where

$\quad\quad$ $d_{n-1,n} = \frac{1}{2}$ (size node $n - 1$ + size node n)
$\quad\quad\quad\quad$ = distance from node $n - 1$ to node n

$\quad\quad$ $d_{n,o}$ $\quad$ = distance of node n from the nearest obstacle.

$\quad\quad$ $d_{o,f}$ $\quad$ = maximum distance from the obstacle to any node in the quadtree, and

$\quad\quad$ α $\quad\quad$ is a positive constant which determines how far the path will be away from obstacles.

$\quad\quad$ The second part of the cost of a path, as seen from node n, is calculated with a heuristic. A simple heuristic is the Euclidean distance between the midpoint of node n and the goal mode. This heuristic gives the minimum cost of the remaining path. If the actual path deviates greatly from a straight line, due to the presence of obstacles, this heuristic is inaccurate, but meets the requirements of an A* search.

$\quad\quad$ The path search must be broader than the paths in the quadtree graphs. These simply show the decompositions of the space, and not the connectedness of one region to another. At each node, a node expansion process searches the tree for all the non-obstacle leaf nodes that are physically adjacent to the node of interest. Thus, the graph of paths is different from the quadtree graph. The cost of these neighbour finding algorithms (Samet, 1982) is a significant disadvantage of the quadtree data structure for path planning. Zelinsky (1988) has developed algorithms for propagating distance transforms across a quadtree and planning paths by following the valleys in the transform.

8.3.3.7 *Rule-based maps*

In Section 8.3.2.8, we discussed a map based on predicate calculus statements. This map forms the knowledge base for the STRIPS planning system (Fikes and Nilsson, 1971). STRIPS is a problem-solving system developed in the early 1970s. Problem solving is seen as decomposing a task into a chain of intermediate-level actions.

Intermediate-level actions are a set of subroutines that carry out simple tasks. These tasks are a sequence of low-level actions, typically robot motions. One of the problems of high-level task planners is that they assume a set of robust and accurate intermediate-level actions. The most difficult problems in the design of immediate-level routines are the handling of errors and uncertainty. None of the immediate-level routines used by STRIPS has been implemented (Nilsson, 1984). Proponents of a behavioural decomposition of robot-control architectures (See Brooks and Flynn, 1989, for a detailed description of this approach) claim that rule-based systems are too slow for real-time control and are not used in human navigation.

The intermediate-level action of interest to us in this section is the proposed FINDPATH routine. This routine is passed a starting position, a goal position, and a journey type: either roll, where the robot simply moves along the path, or push, where the robot pushes a box along the path. The routine returns a path as a series of x, y coordinates.

The algorithm builds a tree from the goal position towards the start position from the information contained in the knowledge base. At each node, it tests for a direct-line path from that node to the start position. If one exists the path is returned. Otherwise the tree is grown one level deeper and the test repeated. This process is repeated until a path is found.

8.3.4 Path following and collision avoidance

A global path may consist of a list of places to visit or rooms to pass through as the robot travels from start to goal. In each room, a local path specifies how the robot is to get from one side of the room to the other. In theory, once the path is planned, the robot should follow it as instructed and that is that.

In practice, however, obstacles have a habit of suddenly appearing across a path: often carefully placed there by a person carrying out another task, or even the person himself may be the obstacle. At the lowest level, the robot must have a way of detecting the object and avoiding a collision with it. Many robots have 'bump' detectors (a ring of touch switches around the periphery of the robot) as the last line of defence, detectors which require a minor collision to operate.

More sophisticated robots also have noncontact sensors which they use to detect objects in their path. Both ultrasonic and vision sensors are used, and occasionally laser rangefinders. At a higher level, robots often have to locate precisely docking points where they put down and pick up parts. A range of specialized sensors are used for this.

When a robot is moving, it keeps track of its location by dead reckoning. Even with the most precise robot, errors quickly accumulate in dead reckoning measurements. So the robot requires a method of correcting its internal position and orientation measurements based on an external reference. Three methods of obtaining an external reference are in common use: inertial reference frames with gyroscopes and compasses, detection of coded beacons, and detection of objects with sensors.

Also, many of the paths produced by path planners are not smooth – some are quite jagged – and they often clip the corners of objects. A robot may be physically incapable of following a path that changes direction by a large amount at a single point, partly due to the degrees of mobility of the robot and partly due to the inability of motors to achieve infinite acceleration (Section 9.3.3.2).

Paths that are not smooth are usually not optimal, because they require the robot to turn more than is necessary and, as dynamics are ignored by the path planners, cause the motion of the robot to be jerky. One method of local path planning, that can be used to smooth paths, to avoid collisions, and to move paths away from objects is the **potential field method** (Krogh, 1984).

This method has the disadvantage that it can run into a dead end, that is, a local minimum – a valley in the potential field that has only one way out and that is the way the robot came in. Special algorithms are required to solve this problem. However, this approach allows sensory measurements of obstacles to be used as feedback during the execution of paths planned with another planning algorithm. This feedback can be used to steer the robot towards the centre of a corridor between two obstacles, to smooth a jagged path, to shift the path away from obstacles, to avoid clipping corners, to avoid collisions with unknown objects, and as position feedback by the path navigation system.

Conceptually, the robot can be visualized as a marble on a floor that slopes toward the goal and the obstacles are hills with sloping sides (similar to distance transforms). As the marble rolls towards the goal, it is deflected by the hills into the valleys. Sophisticated algorithms even give the marble

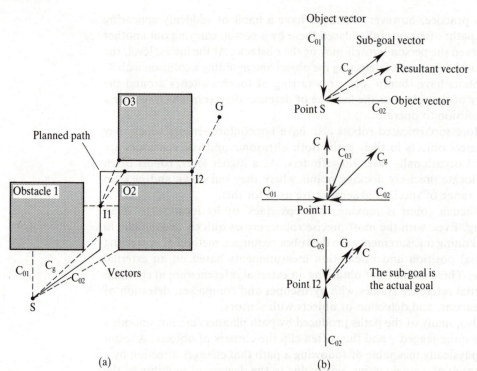

Figure 8.45
Potential field method of
trajectory following
(a) Planned path through
obstacles;
(b) attraction and avoidance
vectors at various points
along the path.

momentum, taking into account the energy needed to accelerate, decelerate, and turn. With its sensors, map, and the planned trajectory the robot determines:

(a) the direction and distance to the goal,

(b) the direction and distance to visible objects – objects that can be detected by its sensors from its current location,

(c) the direction and distance to the furthest point on the planned path that is visible from its present location (Figure 8.45).

From this information, the robot controller first determines a subgoal, namely the furthest point that it can see on the planned path, and then calculates an acceleration vector.

$$C = C_0 + \alpha C_g \tag{8.63}$$

where

C is the acceleration direction vector,

C_0 is the avoidance vector resulting from the obstacles,

C_g is the attraction vector resulting from the subgoal and,

α is a goal factor.

At each instant, the system is accelerated in the best direction, in order to navigate towards the goal while avoiding obstacles. The avoidance vector is the sum of the avoidance vectors from the visible obstacles.

$$C_0 = \beta C_{01} + \beta C_{02} \ldots + \beta C_{0n} \qquad (8.64)$$

where β is an avoidance function.

The closer the robot is to an object, the greater the magnitude of the avoidance vector. A hyperbolic function (β) relating vector magnitude to distance is ideal, as it gives high repulsion when the robot is close to the object, and as the robot moves away from the object, the repulsion rapidly falls to a minimum. Also, the position of the vertical asymtote can be a function of the clearances required to guarantee collision avoidance.

The effect of the potential field equation (Equation 8.63) is to accelerate the robot away from obstacles, to track the robot centrally between obstacles, and to cause the robot to follow curved paths around obstacles. An example is shown in Figure 8.45. The goal factor α provides an extra degree of control by varying the preference given to the conflicting objectives of obstacle avoidance and reaching the goal. In practice, the higher the value of α, the closer the robot tracks to obstacles: it determines how close the robot goes to clipping corners. In a sense, it is the gain of the path-following control system.

While the vector sum provides feedback for the control of path following by indicating the direction in which the robot should accelerate, it does not give the magnitude of that acceleration. This magnitude can be determined from the direction vector, but it is probably better to obtain it another way. Conceptually, if the robot can see only a short distance, it should travel slowly, but if it can see a long distance it can travel faster. Also, the robot must be able to decelerate as well as accelerate, otherwise it will overshoot on corners and run into obstacles. Finally, it must stop when it reaches the goal. More formally, the desired velocity is a function of the distance to the subgoal and the maximum velocity specified by the task or the limitations of the robot.

$$\text{desired velocity} = \gamma(d_g, v_{\max}) \qquad (8.65)$$

where

d_g is the distance to the subgoal,

$v_{\max}$ is the maximum speed of the robot, and

γ is a function.

This system will decelerate the robot automatically as it approaches a corner, and accelerate it as it leaves a corner. When the robot can see the goal, the goal becomes the subgoal and the robot slows to stop at the goal. The rate of acceleration is determined by the characteristics of the robot within the bounds of task constraints, and is a function of the velocity error.

$$\text{Acceleration} = \eta\,(\text{Desired velocity} - \text{Actual velocity}) \qquad \textbf{(8.66)}$$

where η is a function.

The function η can be used as the gain of a velocity control loop, and has an effect on path following. If the system is overdamped (η small), the robot will track too wide around corners, and if it is underdamped (η large), the robot will oscillate as it tracks around corners.

This path-following control scheme guarantees that the robot will reach its goal along a smoothed version of the planned trajectory without collision. Also, the robot can navigate through localized areas of unknown (or changed) environments successfully. The dynamics of the robot are taken into account, and the calculations can be done in real time. The main problem is finding adequate sensors (Chapter 10).

8.3.5   Learning

Most of this topic was covered in previous sections. 'Learning' and map building from sensor data are nearly the same, except it is possible to navigate a robot through an unknown environment without storing a map. The potential field algorithm will achieve this. When a robot detects and avoids an obstacle on a planned path through a known environment, it has 'learned' a path around the obstacle. Should that obstacle be added to the map? The robot has no knowledge of how long the obstacle will be there.

A number of researchers have been looking at heuristics (Chattergy, 1985) and algorithms (Zelinsky, 1988) for mobile robot navigation with 'learning'. The most common learning problem presented to robots is the maze-solving problem, for example the micromouse competition (Problem 8.4 in Section 8.6). Maze-solving systems range from simple heuristics for square mazes (move towards goal until wall detected, then turn and follow the wall) to complex heuristics for mazes of any shape. (Sutherland, 1969).

The HERMIES project (Iyengar *et al.*, 1986) has developed one of the most advanced learning systems. The robot is placed in an unknown room and starts learning by characterising room information with spatial graphs (Figure 8.24). As the robot traverses the terrain, new paths are added to the graph. As learning proceeds, the objects are enclosed by bounding polygons. Basically, the 'learning' consists of adding new nodes for stop points and arcs for the paths to the spatial graph. As the system learns, the spatial ambiguity decreases.

The major problem with any learning system is the collection and analysis of sensor data. The problems of perception will be discussed in greater detail in Chapter 10. The time has come for you to do some learning by studying the examples and completing the exercises in the next sections.

Key points

- Mobility is a key issue in the development of intelligent antonomous systems.

- A wheeled mobile robot is capable of locomotion on a surface solely through the actuation of wheel assemblies mounted on the robot and in contact with the surface.

- A wheeled mobile robot is modelled as a multiple-closed-link chain; where the links are the floor, the body, and the steering linkages; and the joints are the wheels, the steering axes, and the centre axis of the robot.

- Each joint is modelled as a planar pair with two degrees of translation and one degree of rotation.

- As coordinate frames are attached to both ends of a link, each joint has two frames.

- An instantaneously coincident coordinate system is a stationary coordinate frame at the same location as a moving frame at the instant of observation.

- The general transform for a wheeled mobile robot is

$$^R T_N = \begin{bmatrix} C_\theta & -S_\theta & 0 & p_x \\ S_\theta & C_\theta & 0 & p_y \\ 0 & 0 & 1 & p_z \\ 0 & 0 & 0 & 1 \end{bmatrix} \qquad (8.1)$$

- The transform equation for one wheel is:

$$^{RB}T_{CF} = {}^{RB}T_{SB}\,{}^{SB}T_{SL}\,{}^{SL}T_{CL} = {}^{CF}T_{RF} \qquad (8.5)$$

- The velocity of a wheeled mobile robot is calculated from measurements of wheel motion using the sensed forward solution.

$$v_{robot} = \begin{bmatrix} J_1 & \cdot & \cdot & 0 \\ \cdot & & & \cdot \\ \cdot & & & \cdot \\ 0 & \cdot & \cdot & J_n \end{bmatrix} \begin{bmatrix} v_1 \\ \cdot \\ \cdot \\ v_n \end{bmatrix} \qquad (8.40)$$

- The mobility actuation and sensing characteristics of a wheeled mobile robot can be determined from the properties of the sensed forward solution.

- When the wheel Jacobians cannot be inverted, we cannot obtain an actuated inverse solution and, consequently, we are unable to derive control equations.

- A robot is statically stable when its centre of gravity lies within a polygon defined by the surface contact points.
- At least three feet are on the ground during a statically stable gait.
- There may be periods when no feet are on the ground during a dynamically stable gait.
- The control of a one-legged hopping machine can be decomposed into the control of three independent, but time related parameters: hopping height, forward speed, and body attitude.
- Hopping height is a function of the thrust applied to extend the leg.
- Body altitude is controlled by the hip torque actuator during the stance phase.

$$\tau_h = -k_p(\phi - \phi_d) - k_v\omega_\phi \tag{8.53}$$

- Forward speed is controlled by selecting the placement of the foot with the high torque actuator during the flight phase.

$$\tau_h = -k_p(\lambda - \lambda_h) - k_v\omega_\lambda \tag{8.59}$$

- Navigation is the science of directing the course of a mobile robot as it traverses the environment.
- Navigation involves three tasks: environment mapping, path planning, and driving.
- Dead reckoning is the calculation of the location of the robot from odometry.
- Sensor based navigation is desired because navigation using guide wires or beacons lacks the flexibility required by many tasks.
- The choice of a map data structure is usually a trade-off between efficient representation of the environment and efficient representation of paths through the environment.
- Maps fall into four broad groups: path maps, free space maps, object maps, and composite maps.
- The path planning algorithms and the method of sensor integrations are determined by the data structure.
- Distance transform algorithms will find the shortest path in a known environment.
- Potential field methods can be used for collision avoidance when traversing a planned path.

Examples

Example 8.1   Kinematics of a steered wheel

In Section 8.1.4, we found the Jacobian of a conventional nonsteered wheel. In this example the analysis is extended to include steering (Muir and

Newman, 1986). As this wheel can be steered, it has an additional degree of freedom: the angular velocity $^{SB}\omega_{SL}$ around the steering axis. The physical steering velocity and the pseudosteering velocity are the same.

$$v_{n\,pseudo} = \begin{bmatrix} ^{CF}v_{CLny} \\ ^{CF}\omega_{CLn} \\ ^{SB}\omega_{SL} \end{bmatrix} \quad \text{and} \quad v_{n\,physical} = \begin{bmatrix} ^{CF}\omega_{W3x} \\ ^{CF}\omega_{W3z} \\ ^{SB}\omega_{SL3z} \end{bmatrix} \text{ for Newt.}$$

$$W = \begin{bmatrix} 0 & 0 & 0 \\ R & 0 & 0 \\ 0 & 1 & 0 \\ 0 & 0 & 1 \end{bmatrix} = \begin{bmatrix} 0 & 0 & 0 \\ r & 0 & 0 \\ 0 & 1 & 0 \\ 0 & 0 & 1 \end{bmatrix} \text{ for Newt.}$$

$$J_n = \begin{bmatrix} -r\sin {}^{RB}\theta_{CLn} & {}^{RB}p_{CLny} & -{}^{RB}p_{SBny} \\ r\cos {}^{RB}\theta_{CLn} & -{}^{RB}p_{CLnx} & {}^{RB}p_{SBnx} \\ 0 & 1 & -1 \end{bmatrix}$$

$$= \begin{bmatrix} -rs_3 & -l_cC_3-l_b & l_b \\ rc_3 & -l_3S_3 & 0 \\ 0 & 0 & -1 \end{bmatrix} \text{ for Newt.}$$

The wheel can operate in all three degrees of freedom, and the Jacobian can be inverted if its determinant is non zero. The determinant is zero under two conditions:

1. the steering axis passes through the contact point, and
2. the wheel is perpendicular to the steering link.

Example 8.2 Kinematics of a tricycle robot

In a tricycle robot (Figure 8.46), wheel 1 is driven and steered, and the other two wheels are parallel, nonsteered, and nondriven.

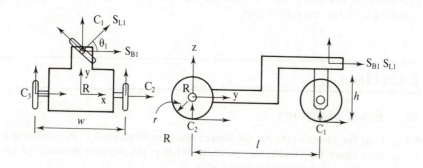

Figure 8.46
Tricycle robot.

The position transformation matrices are:

$$^{R}\mathbf{T}_{SB1} = \begin{bmatrix} 1 & 0 & 0 & 0 \\ 0 & 1 & 0 & l \\ 0 & 0 & 1 & h-r \\ 0 & 0 & 0 & 1 \end{bmatrix} \quad ^{SB1}\mathbf{T}_{SL1} = \begin{bmatrix} C_1 & -S_1 & 0 & 0 \\ S_1 & C_1 & 0 & 0 \\ 0 & 0 & 1 & 0 \\ 0 & 0 & 0 & 1 \end{bmatrix}$$

$$^{L1}\mathbf{T}_{C1} = \begin{bmatrix} 1 & 0 & 0 & 0 \\ 0 & 1 & 0 & 0 \\ 0 & 0 & 1 & l-h \\ 0 & 0 & 0 & 1 \end{bmatrix} \quad ^{R}\mathbf{T}_{C2} = \begin{bmatrix} 1 & 0 & 0 & w/2 \\ 0 & 1 & 0 & 0 \\ 0 & 0 & 1 & -r \\ 0 & 0 & 0 & 1 \end{bmatrix} = -^{R}\mathbf{T}_{C3}$$

The wheel Jacobian matrices are:

$$\mathbf{J}_1 = \begin{bmatrix} -rS_1 & l & -l \\ rC_1 & 0 & 0 \\ 0 & 1 & -1 \end{bmatrix}$$

$$\mathbf{J}_2 = \begin{bmatrix} 0 & 0 \\ r & -w/2 \\ 0 & 0 \end{bmatrix} = -\mathbf{J}_3$$

If we examine the Jacobian for wheel 1, we can see that two columns are linearly dependent, which indicates that wheel 1 is redundant, that is, it has fewer degrees of freedom (two) than wheel variables (three). Consequently, the actuated inverse equations for this robot cannot be computed, making control difficult.

Physically, wheels 2 and 3 serve the same purpose. They are separated by a distance w to make the robot statically stable. They differ from a single wheel of length w in that they can rotate at different speeds. However, these wheels can be modelled with a virtual wheel at the centre of the robot which has low resistance to rotational slip around the contact point. By modelling the tricycle as a bicycle one wheel is eliminated. Neglecting the stability problems of a bicycle, as an exercise calculate its kinematic model and compare it to the tricycle model.

Exercises

■ *Essay questions*

8.1. Find the determinant for the steered wheel in Example 8.1. Prove that it is zero under the conditions specified. What is the physical meaning of the positions where the determinant is zero?

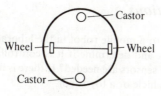

Figure 8.47
Turtle robot.

8.2. A turtle robot (Figure 8.47) has two parallel non-steered drive wheels on a diagonal axis, and two free wheeling castors, or skids, on a perpendicular axis.

      The robot is steered by turning the drive wheels at different speeds. Solve the kinematics for this robot. What observations can you make about its controllability?

8.3. Solve the kinematics for the bicycle model of a tricycle discussed in Example 8.2. Compare is controllability to that of the tricycle. Physically what does the lack of an actuated inverse solution mean? Can you get around it and produce a set of equations which define the velocity of the drive/steering wheel as a function of the velocity of the robot?

8.4. A six-legged robot can walk with an alternating tripod gait where three legs support the robot while three legs move. Design a stable alternating tripod gait, and draw the gait diagram and the footfall diagram for it. If this robot has a stroke of 0.5 m and a recovery time of 1 second, what is its maximum speed with this gait?

8.5. Compare and contrast the various mapping data structures discussed in Section 8.3.2. Does any approach the ideal?

8.6. Compare and contrast the various path planners discussed in Section 8.4.

8.7. Draw a map of a room showing the obstacles and free space. Choose a suitable data structure. Choose a suitable path planner. Plan the path by hand. What did you learn about path planning from this exercise?

8.8. Write a program to store your map and plan a path through it using the data structure and path planner you chose in Exercise 8.7.

8.9. Explain the differences between free-space, object-oriented, and composite-space path planners.

8.10. List the problems that a robot control system has to handle to avoid collisions when following a planned path.

8.11. How does using beacons and landmarks simplify the path following problem?

■ *Practical questions*

8.1. If you have access to a mobile robot in the laboratory, develop a kinematic model of the robot and determine if it is controllable. If it is controllable, what actuators and sensors are needed? If there is no robot in the laboratory, model a wheeled vehicle or a toy robot.

8.2. Watch a horse while walking, trotting, cantering and running. Analyse and record its gait.

8.3. Record the walking gaits of several four legged animals? How to they differ?

8.4. Build a Micromouse. Every year the IEEE runs a competition where a small robot called a mouse has to traverse a maze. On the first run, it has to map and solve the maze. On the subsequent runs, it has to plan a path through the maze and follow that path. Rules for entering the competition can be obtained from:

> IEEE Micromouse Competition,
> 10662 Los Vaqueros Circle,
> Los Alamitos,
> CA 90720,
> USA

8.5. Design and code a data structure for mapping a maze.

8.6. Using the data structure in Practical Exercise 8.5, design and code a path planning algorithm.

8.7. Write a simulator to test your map data structure, and path planning algorithms.

9 · *Task Planning*

'Robotics severely challenges artificial intelligence (AI) by forcing it to deal with real objects in the real world. Techniques and representations developed for purely cognitive problems often do not extend to meet the challenge.'

Michael Brady (1985)

Objectives

In this chapter, we study the problems of planning robot motion sequences to execute tasks. Our objective is to tackle the problem of task planning by decomposing a task into actions and then decompose these actions into robot commands which can be implemented in a standard robot programming language. Some of the algorithms for 6-dimensional path planning presented in this chapter are extensions of those developed in the previous chapter for planning the three-dimensional motions of mobile robots. Little background in artificial intelligence is assumed, so the reader who has studied planning and search strategies will find much of the material familiar.

Robots exist to perform tasks. We use them instead of other machines because they are flexible. The potential offered by flexibility will only be fully realized when industrial robots can be reprogrammed easily. Even for simple tasks, the cost of programming a robot can be very high; often approaching the cost of the robot. Consequently, reducing this cost will improve the economic viability of using robots in industry.

This high cost occurs in current robot programming systems (teach boxes and languages), because the position and orientation (location) of every object in the system has to be specified exactly, in painful detail. Any variation from one of these locations will cause the system to fail. One key to handling the problems caused by this uncertainty is improved sensing. Another is the parameterization of robot control procedures so that they are independent of physical assumptions. A third key is the development of multifingered general-purpose grippers coupled with a theory of grasping. For any robotic assembly operation, the largest proportion of mechanical design time is spent on the design of specialized grippers. A fourth key is the development of tools for task planning, and for converting task plans into robot programs. In this chapter, we examine issues relating to task planning.

9.1 Robot language hierarchy

When we design computer programs we use the tools of hierarchical decomposition, stepwise refinement, and program modularization to break complex tasks into intellectually manageable subtasks. As research in software engineering has developed, we have progressed from low-level machine-code programming to higher levels of abstraction as we strive for the goal of task-level programming. The lower levels of programming continue in parallel with high-level programming activities, and tools such as compilers have been developed to transfer from one level to the next. For a discussion of the hierarchical decomposition of computer systems see McKerrow (1988).

A similar hierarchical decomposition is emerging in robot programming systems (Figure 9.1). This decomposition reflects the nature of robotic tasks and the nature of robots themselves. The use of existing robot languages to implement tasks once they have been planned is discussed in Chapter 12. Here, we look at robot programming from the point of view of planning a task. The robot programming/control/planning hierarchy is:

- **System level** The user buys robots to perform one or more tasks in a production process, or another application environment. The robots are a means to achieving the production goals.
- **Task level** The user specifies, in detail, what he wants the robot to do. This is done within the framework of the user's conceptual model of

Level	Planning steps	Program	Model/sensing
System	Production process	Set of parallel tasks.	User's view of the world.
⇓			⇓
Task	What is to be done?	Specification of individual tasks	Process model.
⇓			⇓
Action	Decompose task into a sequence of actions.	Sequence of actions	Task model. Perception.
⇓			⇕
Robot	Decompose actions into a sequence of robot motions in Cartesian space.	Sequence of robot operation primitives.	Geometric model. Sensor fusion.
⇓			⇕
Joint	Decompose robot motions into parallel joint space motions.	Parallel joint motions.	Kinematic model of robot. Physical model of sensors.
⇓			⇑
Physical	⇒ Control of linkages.	⇒ Actuators.	⇒ Sensors.

Figure 9.1
Hierarchical decomposition of robot planning, programming, sensing and control systems.

the production process. Robot tasks can be classified by domain; including pick and place, material transfer, assembly, and welding.

- **Action level** Tasks in each domain can be decomposed into a sequence of primitive actions. For example, primitives for an assembly task include slide, place, rotate, and insert. Thus, the action-level planner deals with the movement of objects. Action-level planning requires a model of the world in the domain of the task, that is, a task model that is constructed from task-oriented descriptions. At this level, the perception system attempts to understand the sensor data and 'interpret' it in the task domain.

- **Robot level** A robot can execute a set of primitive operations. Each action must be mapped into a sequence of these operations. For example, 'pick up part A' decomposes into 'open gripper, move gripper to grasping position, grasp part, and raise part to position C.' Thus, the robot-level planner deals with the motion of the end effector. From the perspective of the programmer, these operational primitives define the robot in the same way as machine code defines a computer. For this reason, the set of such operations is sometimes referred to as **robot machine code**. Robot-level planning requires a mapping between the task domain model and a geometric model of the world. The robot is modelled in Cartesian space and sensor data is fused with the kinematic model of the robot and its environment to form the geometric world model.

- **Joint level** A robot is a set of linkages connected by joints. At this level, position, velocity, and force control systems regulate the actuators to control the joint parameters. Each robot-level operation

Figure 9.2
Simple pick and place task –
picking up parts off a
conveyor and packing them
into a box.

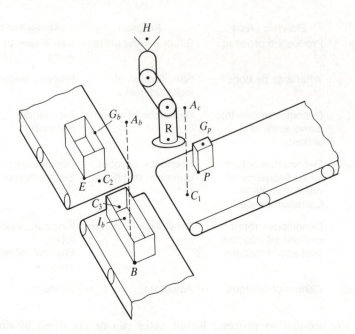

primitive is based on the kinematic model of the robot, and decomposes into parallel control of the linkages. Joint-level planners include the kinematic, static and dynamic models of the robot.

- **Physical level** At the lowest level, a robot is a collection of linkages, transmissions, grippers, actuators and sensors. The actuators control the location of the mechanisms, and the sensors measure their location relative to each other and the world. The computer interface and measurement software converts sensor signals from electrical voltages and currents into values representing physical quantities.

While this hierarchy looks simple, an example demonstrates the complexity of planning a task, and the difficulty of executing that plan. Consider the pick-and-place example in Figure 9.2.

- **Task level description** A robot is to pick parts up off the end of a conveyor and pack them into boxes. This task decomposes into six actions.

- **Action level description**
  1. Place an empty box at the packing location,
  2. Continually,
     (a) When a part is at the end of the conveyor
         (i) Pick the part up and place it in the box
     (b) When the box is full
         (i) Remove the full box
         (ii) Get a new empty box and place it at the packing location.

Next, each action is decomposed into a sequence of robot operations. But, the actions must first be related to a geometric model of the world. We will use a simple model where each location of interest is represented with frames and the transforms from one frame to another are described by homogeneous coordinates.

- **Geometric model**: Frames and their locations.

  A_b above the box

  A_c above the part conveyor

  B position of box during packing on full box conveyor

  C_n mid point of end of conveyor belt n

  E position of empty box on empty box conveyor

  G_b grasping point on box

  G_p grasping point on part

  H. robot hand grasping point

  I_b position of part inside box

  P. position of part on conveyor

  R. world reference frame at base of robot

- **Robot level description**

  1. (a) Move H to EG_b (move end effector to empty box)
     (b) Grasp (t_p) (t_p is the thickness of the wall of the box)
     (c) Move H to BG_b (move box to packing position)
     (d) Ungrasp
     (e) Move H to A_c
     (f) Index empty box conveyor
     (g) Reset part counter $c_p=0$

  2. **Loop**   {forever}

     If s_p **Then**   {part present signal}

     Move H to PG_p

     Grasp (w_p) {w_p is thickness of part}

     If grasp error **Exit** (Error Flag)

     Move H to A_c {part conveyor starts to move}

     Move H to A_b

     PlacePart $(I_b, full)$ {calculate where to put part and set flag when box is full}

     Move H to I_b

     If collision **exit** (Error Flag)

     Ungrasp

     Move H to A_b

     End

     IF *full* **Then**   . . .

Considerable insight into the problems of task planning can be gained from this simple example. First, as we go down the hierarchy the volume of code required to describe the plan expands very rapidly. Second, the decomposition of action primitives into operation primitives can be very complex and is dependent both on the nature of the task and the capability of the robot. As yet, this decomposition is an unsolved problem in many task domains.

The 'PlacePart' procedure is a very task-specific geometric procedure. Given the sizes of the parts and the box, it calculates where to place the next part and determines when the box is full. In contrast to packing groceries, where the parts are all shapes and sizes, most industrial packaging operations pack only one size and shape of part. This considerably reduces the geometric complexity of the 'PlacePart' procedure, but the gripper must be able to get into the box, release the part, and retract without disturbing the other parts. The complexity of this problem is a function of the design of the gripper. Usually, grippers are designed to minimize this problem, but clearances may place severe constraints on the motion of the end effector.

A related problem is deciding when the gripper should ungrasp the part. The simple answer is when the part is in the right place. But how does the robot know it is in the right place? Simple geometric calculations are adequate in a perfect world, but if a part is slightly oversize, the manipulator may push it into the part beneath. If a part is undersize, the manipulator drop it a small distance.

Coping with errors of this kind is possibly the most difficult problem of all in task planning. What errors should be tested for? How should they be handled? The initialization section of the above program assumes everything is in the right place, and ignores the possibility of errors. The packing section tests for errors in two places: when grasping the part, and when inserting it into the box. How are these errors detected? If a piece of the box that includes the grasp point is broken away, what then? Does the robot pack a nonexistent box? Three sources of uncertainty of particular importance in this task are the orientation of the parts, the tolerances of the parts, and the force required to ensure an adequate grasp. To improve the ability of the robot to handle uncertainty we often add sensors. Should the sensor information be used to adapt the model of the task, or just used by joint-level controllers to modify their references?

At a higher level, 'Where does the geometric model come from?' and 'how are the grasp points determined?'. At a lower level, 'should the end effector follow a special trajectory?' and 'should the part be grasped from above or from one side? These decisions require a knowledge of task-level information when decomposing the action primitives into operation primitives.

Most of the above issues will be examined in later sections of this chapter. Many will continue to be research topics for some time. Robotics challenges computer science and artifical intelligence by forcing them to deal with real objects in the real world. In the mean time engineers will continue to program robots by teaching, and to devise ways of handling or enunciating uncertainty – such as by physically forcing parts to be in the correct orientation – but this can be very expensive.

In this chapter, we discuss action-level planning (the generation of action sequences), and robot-level planning (the generation of robot operations). In Chapter 10, we will examine sensing and how it fits within this hierarchy. In Chapter 11, we will deal with joint-level control, and in Chapter 12, with robot-level programming.

9.2   Action-level planning

Tasks to be performed by robots are planned in four stages. First, at the task level, the task is specified clearly. Then, at the action level, it is decomposed into a sequence of actions. Sometimes actions can be performed in parallel. These actions are ordered in a way that will allow efficient execution of the task while avoiding dead end situations. Third, a process is designed to carry out these actions. This step involves merging the operations of the tools with the task actions. At the action level, a robot can perform only one operation at a time and parallelism is achieved by employing more than one machine. Fourth, at the robot level, a control program is designed and coded.

Most action-level planning is done manually. However, researchers are currently working on tools to assist in the process of action-level planning and rule-based systems to plan sequences of actions. In this section, we examine two related areas of action-level planning: programming systems that automatically generate plans and task modelling. Attempts to develop high-level teaching are also looked at.

9.2.1   Programming systems

The automatic generation of action sequences from task specifications and models is of interest to researchers. STRIPS (Fikes, *et al.*, 1972) and BUILD (Fahlman, 1974) were developed as part of this work. However, these programming systems are unlikely to see practical use until many lower-level problems are solved. They represent an early attempt to apply rule-based systems to action-level planning. Rule-based programming has been proposed as the solution to many robotics problems, including the perception of the environment from sensor data (Michie, 1985).

STRIPS (Stanford Research Institute Problem Solver) is the planner used with the mobile robot SHAKEY (Figure 1.4). This planning system links together action-level primitives to accomplish a specific goal (Section 8.3.3.7). Nilsson (1984) comments that more recent hierarchical planning systems are more appropriate for robot planning, such as NOAH (Sacredoti, 1977) and SIPE (Wilkins, 1984).

In STRIPS, the primitive actions that can be performed by the mobile robot are precoded in a set of action routines. For example, execution of the routine GOTHRU (d1, r1, r2) causes the robot to go through the doorway

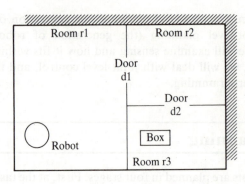

Model

INROOM (ROBOT,r1)
INROOM (BOX,r3)
CONNECTS (d1,r1,r2)
CONNECTS (d2,r2,r3)

Goal

INROOM (BOX,r2)

Task decomposition into actions

Move from r1 to r3
Find Box
Push Box into r2 through d2

d1 from room r1 to room r2. The task and geometric models for STRIPS are discussed in Sections 8.3.2.8 and 8.3.3.7.

Tasks are specified in the form of a predicate calculus well-formed formula. The planning system then attempts to find a sequence of actions that change the world model to make the well-formed formula true. If the model is accurate, the execution of these actions by the robot should achieve the goal. In order to generate the plan, STRIPS must model the effect of each action. If the STRIPS operator correctly models the action, the resulting world model will correctly model the world.

As the world model is a set of clauses (Figure 9.3), the STRIPS operators model the actions by changing (adding to or deleting from) the set of clauses. Each operator contains a precondition well-formed formula, an add function, and a delete function. If the precondition formula is satisfied by the current world model, the operator can be applied to that model: the robot can perform that action. To update the model, the operator deletes the clauses specified by the delete function from the model and adds the clauses specified by the add function.

STRIPS starts its search for a plan by testing to see if the goal well-formed formula is satisfied by the current model. If it is, the goal has already been achieved, no action is required, and the planner terminates. If it is not satisfied, the list of operators is searched for an operator whose precondition is satisfied, and which, when applied to the model, will produce a new model in which the goal formula is more nearly satisfied. If the goal formula is not satisfied in the new model, the process is repeated until a model is found where the goal formula is true. In effect, this planner executes a tree search of possible actions. An action is chosen that will move the process closer to the goal. The execution of the operator associated with this action moves the search to a new node of the tree, with a new world model and a new list of possible actions. When the goal is reached, the search is terminated and the branches of the tree define the sequence of actions required to achieve the goal. The preconditions for the operators which model this action sequence are the subgoals.

The difficult problem in this search is testing to see if an operator will produce a model in which the goal formula is more near satisfied. Consider the situation in Figure 9.3. The robot is in room r1, and a box is in room r3. The planner is given the goal INROOM (BOX, r2), which means the robot is to find the box and put it in room r2. The goal is not satisfied by the model, so a subgoal has to be selected. Selection of subgoals is based on a knowledge of the environment and an understanding of that knowledge. To achieve the goal, the robot must first move to the room the box is in. But, how does the planner know this? Either the planner includes a set of rules describing what to do to perform a task, or it tries various operations to see which one moves the system closer to the goal. In the first case, action planning has been done manually and is stored as a set of rules. In the second case, how does the planner test that the system is closer to the goal? One way is to build all possible subtrees until one achieves the goal. The larger the task domain, the more expensive the search. This approach can be very expensive unless an effective branch-pruning technique is included, again requiring task-specific knowledge.

This example clearly illustrates that any action-planning system must use a database of task-specific knowledge: typically a list of rules in a rule-based system. The rules can either be entered manually from a manual decomposition of the task or the robot can be stepped through a task and the steps recorded. A problem with the latter is that teaching is usually done at a lower level and it may be difficult to infer task actions from robot operations. Action-level teaching is discussed in Section 9.2.3. An important part of learning research is the generalization of these steps so that they can be automatically applied in similar situations.

BUILD (Fahlman, 1974) is a computer programm which generates plans for building structures with toy blocks. A good problem solver must be able to recognize and classify problems, select the right method to deal with each situation, recover from failure, and anticipate the constraints that one action will place on subsequent actions. Consider, for example, the simple construction problem in Figure 9.4. The action-level plan is simply the sequence in which the blocks are placed on top of each other. The task model specifies the relationship between the blocks in the completed construction, and the geometric model the size and relative position of the blocks. But, is it that simple?

A typical heuristic is to place the blocks on top of each other vertically in ascending order. This heuristic makes sense, because it is easier to place an object on top of another than it is to place an object underneath another, particularly when using a robot with only one gripper. This heuristic produces a plan with block placement in the order A, B, C, D. This plan fails as soon as block C is placed on block B, because the weight of block C causes block B to tilt and slide off block A (Figure 9.4(b) and (c)).

This simple example – which is not unusual in assembly situations –

Figure 9.4
Simple blocks construction
problem (Fahlman, 1974).
(a) Goal;
(b) failure situation;
(c) failure mode;
(d) using a subassembly.

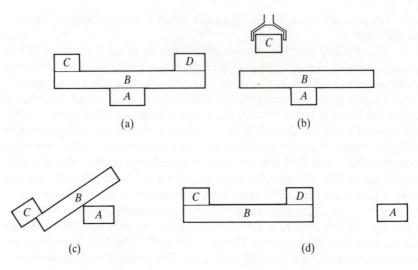

(a)

(b)

(c)

(d)

requires a more powerful heuristic. The planner has to recognize the failure situation and solve it using a subassembly (Figure 9.4(d)). Fahlman (1974) discusses other solutions to this and similar problems, and the techniques used to analyse and solve construction problems. However, he does not tackle difficult lower level problems of finding an identifying the blocks, of detecting when a block is in place and can be released by the gripper, of detecting failure during construction, and of avoiding collisions between the manipulator and the partially built structure. After all, this is an action-level planning system and lower level problems should be handled by lower level planners. However, problems can arise at lower levels that require a change in higher level plans, for example, the construction is unstable and falls over or a block cannot be put in place without the manipulator colliding with the structure.

9.2.2 Task modelling

One important lesson that was learnt from these early attempts at automatic action-level planning is that before a sequence of actions can be planned, the task must be understood. The BUILD system, for example, consisted largely of strategies for handling unusual situations. Unfortunately, for many tasks, most situations are unusual and few are straightforward.

The aim of task modelling is to understand the task and all its complexities, often by studying specific examples, and then to generalize from these examples to produce an abstract model of the task. As with any abstraction, this model captures a very limited set of knowledge, but it must capture the essence of the task in a form that is easy to manipulate with a computer program.

From this model, it should be possible to generate plans for a range of similar tasks with an action-level planning program. The instantiation of the specific geometric details of the parts from a geometric model is left to the robot-level planner. If the robot-level planner finds a situation for which it cannot produce a robust (correct and reliable) sequence of robot operations to achieve a desired action, it must pass the information back to the action-level planner with a request for a modified plan. The occurence of such a problem may indicate that the task model is inadequate.

9.2.2.1 *Assembly process models*

People assemble objects from plans. A man looks at the plan, and visualizes the shapes of the parts and the final assembly, if three-dimensional views are not included. If the plan does not include a set of assembly instructions, the man works out the assembly sequence from an understanding of the plan. Then he examines the parts and matches them to the plan. Finally, he puts the parts together to complete the assembly. During the course of the assembly, he may revise the assembly plan as his understanding of the task increases.

Ejiri *et al.* (1972) sought to duplicate this process with a robot. The robot used one camera to examine the plan and another to examine the parts. The objects were constructed from simple polyhedral parts – toy blocks. The plan was an orthographic projection showing three sides of the required assemblage, and was composed of straight solid lines only. A drawing-recognition algorithm generated a three-dimensional model of the object and separated out the individual parts. First, the vertices were identified from the intersection of lines, and their Cartesian space coordinates calculated. Second, lines between the vertices were identified, and the vertices defining their end points were stored. Third, the planes which defined the surfaces of the blocks were determined. From this information, the parts which made up the object were identified. Then the vision system located and identified the blocks. Finally, an assembly plan was generated and the robot built the object. If the robot could not reach the assembly position, the process stopped pending human instructions.

As the final objects were simple, and contained no unusual situations, task planning was a simple matter of placing blocks on top of or next to one another. The planning algorithm determined the assembly sequence by disassembling the object into parts. The assembly order was the reverse of the disassembly order, for the set of simple objects they were working with. The alogrithm then checked that the parts could be removed from the assembly.

A part can be removed from an assembly if it is free to move in the positive z direction, for objects that are assembled from above. To determine the freedom of a block, a set of line vectors were placed on the object, one perpendicular to each surface and all pointing out of the object. If a vector passed through the surface of another block, the block under consideration was constrained in that direction. Once the algorithm determined that a part

Figure 9.5
CAD model of the components of a valve (left) and size details (right), produced on the McDonnell Douglas CAD system.

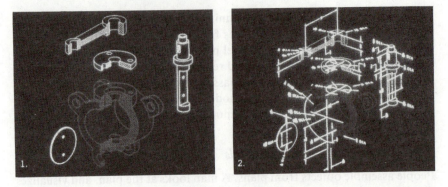

was free to move, it checked to see if the part could be grasped. To do this, it looked for two parallel surfaces on an object that were not constrained. Like many research projects, this system works in a very limited domain. Today, much design is done using CAD systems which automatically generate three-dimensional views, so work on visual reading of plans is of less interest to researchers.

CAD models, like plans, are geometric models of the parts and their relationships but, normally, they do not contain any information about the sequence in which assembly is to occur (Figure 9.5). Somehow, the assembly process has to be inferred from the geometric model, or it has to be defined by the designer. But what tools does the designer have to design and record the assembly process? A list of instructions in English is difficult for a computer to understand or manipulate.

One approach to task modelling is the **discrete action (operation) model** (Krough and Sanderson, 1986). In this model, an assembly process is described in terms of discrete actions on components, and precedence relations among actions are stored in a graph. This model is used as a framework for designing an assembly process, and for selecting tools (such as fixtures and grippers) to handle the parts during the actions. Consider, for example, a torch which can be assembled in a number of steps. First, each component is labelled (Figure 9.6(a)) and the component-to-component assembly actions are defined (Figure 9.6(b)). Then, the assembly process is defined with a precedence graph (Figure 9.6(c)). Only one action-precedence graph is shown in Figure 9.6(c), but several are possible. This graph exhibits considerable parallelism. If the assembly cell cannot execute these operations is parallel, an action precedence graph, where the actions proceed in serial, may be a better choice. So far, we have only described the actions required to join the components into an assembly, we have not assigned tools to each action or implemented a control algorithm to sequence and synchronize the actions. Thus, the task has been modelled at the action level. To model the task at the robot level, we must expand the graph to include the tools that manipulate the parts and form an operation precedence graph (Figure 9.6(e)). Then, we expand the graph further to include the sequence of robot

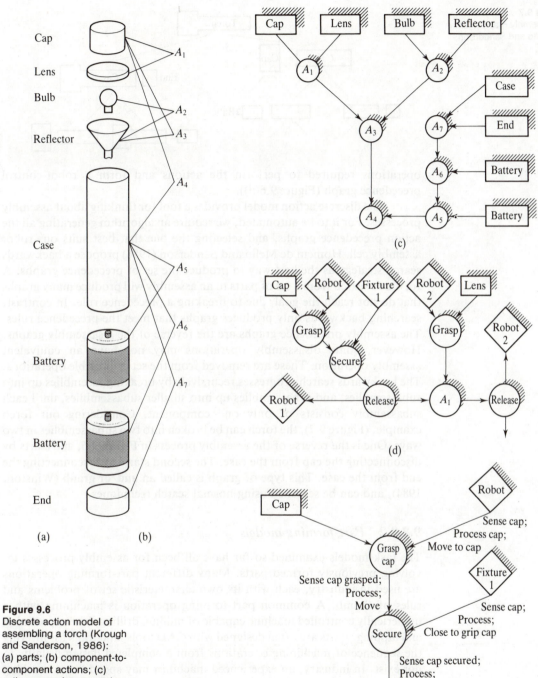

Figure 9.6
Discrete action model of
assembling a torch (Krough
and Sanderson, 1986):
(a) parts; (b) component-to-
component actions; (c)
action-precedence graph;
(d) operation-precedence
graph; (e) robot-control-
precedence graph.

Figure 9.7
Disassembly graph (Homan
de Mello and Sanderson,
1986).

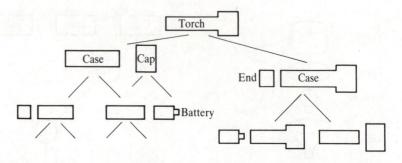

operations required to perform the actions and form a robot-control
precedence graph (Figure 9.6(d)).

The discrete action model provides a tool for thinking about assembly
processes. For it to be automated, we require an algorithm generating all the
action precedence graphs, and selecting the one that best suits our robot
assembly cell. Homem de Mello and Sanderson (1986) propose a backwards
search strategy as the best way to produce the set of precedence graphs. A
forwards search from a set of parts to an assembly will produce many graphs
that do not reach the goal, due to breaking a precedence rule. In contrast,
searching backwards only produces graphs that meet the precedence rules.
The assembly-precedence graphs are the reverse of the disassembly graphs.
However, some disassembly operations may not have an equivalent
assembly operation. These are removed from the set of possible operations.
The backwards search progresses recursively by breaking assemblies up into
subassemblies, and subassemblies up into smaller subassemblies, until each
subassembly consists of only one component. Considering our torch
example, (Figure 9.7), the torch can be broken into two subassemblies in two
ways. One is the reverse of the assembly process in Figure 9.6, and starts by
disconnecting the cap from the case. The second starts by disconnecting the
end from the case. This type of graph is called an **and/or graph** (Winston,
1984), and can be searched using normal search techniques.

9.2.2.2 *Part-forming models*

The task models examined so far have all been for assembly processes involving previously formed parts. Many different part-forming operations
are used in industry, each with its own characteristic set of problems and
rules of thumb. A common part-forming operation is machining with a
numerically controlled machine capable of milling, drilling, boring, reaming
and tapping. Parts are often designed with CAD tools, and tools for infering
the sequence of machining operations from a completed design usually do
not exist. In industry, an experienced machinist may spend hours working
out the correct machining sequence.

Recent research into machining has produced a rule-based system for
planning the machining of single parts out of prismatic blocks of material
(Hayes, 1987). The program contains 180 OPS5 rules, and makes plans that

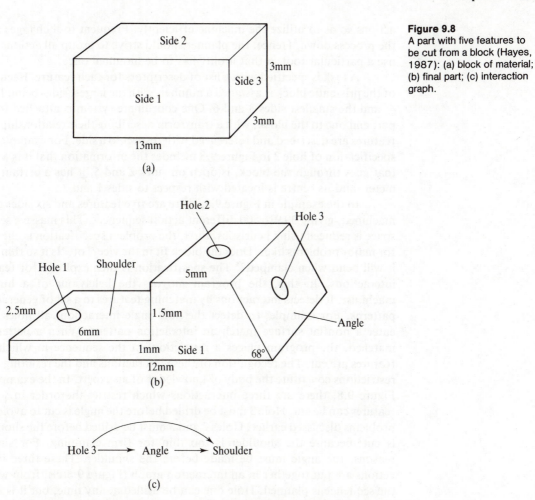

Figure 9.8
A part with five features to
be cut from a block (Hayes,
1987): (a) block of material;
(b) final part; (c) interaction
graph.

are equivalent to those made by an experienced machinist, for this limited task domain. To produce a part, the machinist must cut a set of features into the block. (Figure 9.7). The block can be aluminium , steel, copper, or plastic with the finish of individual surfaces being either smooth or rough. The planning task is to describe the order in which features are cut. A major problem is that cutting one feature may make it difficult or impossible to cut subsequent ones. The interaction between task actions is the most significant problem in planning. One common interaction is that producing one feature removes the clamping surfaces needed to grip the workpiece while cutting another feature. This is an interaction between a task action and subsequent tooling. Other interactions occur between task actions. For example, in Figure 9.8, if the angle is cut first, the drill will slide when it starts to drill hole 3. Consequently, the hole must be drilled before the angle is cut, provided the hole doesn't interact with the milling process.

In addition to handling interactions, the planner should sequence the actions so as to utilize the machine efficiently. Frequent tool changes slow the process down. Hence, the planner should strive to group all actions that use a particular tool so that it only has to be mounted once.

A task is specified with a list of descriptors for each feature. Each side of the prismatic block is assigned a number, with the largest sides being 1 and 4, and the smallest sides 3 and 6. One coordinate system is attached to the part and one to the block, with a transform describing their relationship. All features are described and referenced with respect to a side. For example, the specification of hole 2 in Figure 9.8 includes the information that it is a hole that goes through the block, is open on sides 2 and 5, it has a certain diameter, and its centre is located with respect to sides 1 and 3.

In the example in Figure 9.8, there are five features and six sides to be machined, giving 39 916 800 different action sequences. This massive search space is reduced using heuristics. First, the problem specification is checked for major problems like, 'Does the block fit in the vice?' or, 'Is it so thin that it will bend when clamped?' The specification is then explored for feature interactions. In this, the program mirrors the behaviour of a human machinist. It detects interactions by matching features to a set of generalized patterns. For example, to detect the hole-angle interaction, all holes that enter a nonflat surface match an interaction pattern. When a pattern is matched, the program places a restriction on the sequence in which the features are cut. The recognition of these interactions and the resulting plan restrictions constitute the body of knowledge of an expert. In the example in Figure 9.8, there are three interactions which restrict the order in which features can be cut. Hole 3 must be drilled before the angle is cut to avoid the problems discussed earlier. Holes 2 and 3 must be drilled before the shoulder is cut, because the shoulder is too thin for firm clamping. For similar reasons, the angle must be made before the shoulder. These three interactions are put together in an interaction graph (Figure 9.8(c)), from which the sequence is planned. Hole one can be drilled at any time, but it is most efficient in drilling time to drill it after the shoulder is cut, and most efficient in tooling time to drill it at the same time as the other two.

The problem of machining the sides of the block is handled with a squaring graph. A squaring graph outlines all the methods for getting the block into a square and accurate shape with minimum waste of material. For high-accuracy parts, the majority of shapes and sizes can be squared up using only nine squaring graphs. These are stored in memory, and an appropriate graph is chosen based on the block's size, shape and surface finish. Finally, the two graphs are merged to form a machining plan. In a typical sequence, squaring and feature-cutting actions that require the same fixturing of the block are combined. However, to ensure accuracy the sides between the clamps of the vice must be squared first. Once the plan is generated it can either be executed by a human machinist or automatically. In the latter case, further planning is required to incorporate a robot to position the block in the vice and a sensor system to detect its position and orientation.

The techniques described in the discrete action model of task planning

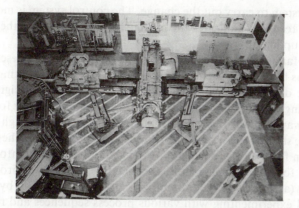

Figure 9.9
Westinghouse turbine blade
manufacturing cell.

can be used to integrate the robot operations into the plan. One step is still to be done: the plan has to be verified, either by simulation or by machining a part and seeing if there are any problems.

9.2.3 Teaching

Teaching has the advantage that it can be done by manufacturing personnel who are skilled in the production process, while programming requires skill in computer programming as well. At the robot and joint levels, many robots are programmed by moving the robot through the motions required to perform the task and recording those motions. Some researchers are asking, 'Can we teach at a higher level?' and a few people are looking at enhancing robot-level teaching to include sensor strategies (Section 12.4.3), while others are looking at action-level teaching.

One approach to action-level teaching is used in the supervisory control of a turbine blade manufacturing cell (Figure 9.9). The cell includes two robots: one to pick up billets from a furnace and place them into a forge, the other to pick up the finished blades from the output side of the forge and either place them in an automatic inspection gauge or stack them on a pallet. The robots are controlled with a rule-based system. When the cell enters a new state, some of the rules fire (Boolean expression for rule is true). These rules determine the subsequent actions of the robots and other equipment in the cell. Cell state is a combination of current robot position, stage of process just completed, and sensor data.

The rules can be programmed in an English-like action-oriented language (Bourne, 1982). The values assigned to the parameters which describe the low-level details of the task are stored in relational tables. The rows and columns of these tables all have symbolic names which correspond with the words in the rule set. When a rule fires, it triggers a set of relational operations that make the appropriate changes in the tables in the database. If, for example, the rule called for the set point of a control system to be changed, the database is updated to reflect this and a request is sent to the control system to carry out the change. The control system is monitored and when the feedback indicates the change has been effected, the state of the system is updated.

So far an action-level programming system has been described, where the actions to perform the task are coded as a set of rules sitting on top of a geometric database which models the world. When the designers came to determining the rules and the numbers for the database, they found that the simplest way of doing this was to manually run the cell through the task and record the state of the system prior to each action. The state then formed the expression for the rule for the following action. Numerical information was recorded for the database at the same time. In this environment, task planning (action-level programming) can be carried out by production personnel experimenting with various process sequences and recording the ones which produce the desired result.

One problem with this approach to teaching is that every state parameter occurs in every rule. In a large system, with many states this results in a lot of redundant information being stored in the rules. A second problem is that the system has rules only for the states it has seen – typically states in a correct production run. Consequently, rules to handle error conditions either have to be hand coded, which the system allows, or error conditions have to be simulated so the system can generate a rule from the record of the state and the subsequent action. Unforeseen circumstances are handled by the system coming to a halt when it enters a state for which there is no rule. In this system, rules for preventative maintenance also can be hand coded.

Before high-level teaching systems can be developed, the communication protocols involved in teaching must be understood. Barber and Agin (1986) conducted a series of experiments where an 'expert' guided an 'apprentice' through a complex assembly task (the IBM Proprinter – Figure 1.19) using spoken language but no visual communication. When they analysed the dialogue, they found that certain protocols facilitate communication, and that communication breaks down when these protocols are not observed. They classified these protocols into five classes: focusing, validators, referencing, descriptors and dialogue structure.

Focusing statements directed the apprentice's attention to the dialogue that followed by telling him what was to come next. In assembly tasks, four types of focusing statements were prevalent: goal statements to indicate the purpose of the next instructions; statements to specify which parts were to be used; statements to specify the location either of parts or where they were to go; and statements to specify the orientation of a part. Validators are feedback statements used to check that an instruction was understood. During an assembly, the apprentice would ask the expert to clarify an instruction and the expert would ask questions to verify that the instructions had been performed correctly. Referencing is the process of recalling knowledge that both expert and apprentice know. For example, referring to a previously learned assembly sequence, or a subassembly that has been built and set aside. Descriptors are words and phrases that are used to describe specific characteristics of a part, action or location. Dialogue structure refers to regularity within the dialogue. For example, new subtasks are often introduced by the word 'next'.

This work represents an initial step toward high-level teaching. Before it can be applied in robotics, much more research has to be done. Actions that are common among a variety of tasks have to be isolated and classified. The parameters of the common actions have to be identified, and non-ambiguous descriptors found. Then all of this has to be built on top of robot-level commands that can achieve the desired actions.

9.3   Robot-level planning

Research into action-level planning has highlighted many robot-level problems. Often, well-constructed plans fail hopelessly because the robot is incapable of performing the required operation. For this reason, a large amount of research effort has concentrated on the problems of robot-level planning. At this level, plans must be transformed from the ideal task domain into the inaccurate real-world domain of the robot.

Robot-level planning involves decomposing every action in an action-level plan into a set of robot motions. The expansion of an action-precedence graph into a robot-control-precedence graph in Figure 9.6 is an example of this. Research has been concentrated in two broad areas: the derivation of sequences of robot motions, and the modelling of robot operations.

Sequences of robot motions to perform task actions are generated in three ways: automatically, by using programs; interactively, by using off-line programming languages and simulation; and by teaching. The modelling of robot operations divides into two areas: gross-motion planning and fine-motion planning.

All robot-level planners rely heavily on accurate geometric models of the robot, the task, and the environment. These models can be coordinate frame models, as used in Chapter 3, feature models, wire frame models, solid models or mathematical models of physical processes.

9.3.1   Geometric modelling

A world model for a task contains:

- a task model,
- a physical description of all objects in the environment of the task – including mass, inertia, colour, object name, and other relevant physical properties,
- a geometric description of all objects – parts and their tolerances, tools, grippers, robots and their workspace,

Figure 9.10
Solid model of the CMU
direct-drive robot (Figure
2.44) in a work cell (Herbert
and Hoffman, 1985),
derived from constructive
solid geometry primitives —
block, wedge, cylinder and
cone.

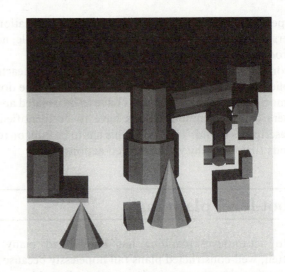

- a geometric description of the relationship between all objects with reference to a world coordinate system,
- a description of the characteristics of the tools, grippers, and robots – maximum opening, maximum grasp force, acceleration bounds, kinematics, and so on,
- a description of all sensors, their characteristics, and their position and time relationships.

The development of modelling techniques and algorithms is essential to the development of computer-aided task planning. Task models have to be combined with geometric models, before we can expand task actions into sequences of robot operations. During the expansion process, the state of the task (the location of all objects and the configuration of the robot) has to be modelled to check for possible collisions and for possible action failure due to uncertainty caused by tolerance mismatches.

The principal component of the world model is the geometric description of the objects involved in the task. In the examples throughout this chapter, we will examine systems that use feature models, line models, surface models and solid models. The simpler models lead to move efficient algorithms, but, as they contain less information, they are inadequate for some calculations.

Objects in the workspace should be represented with solid models (Figure 9.10) rather than with wire-frame models (Figure 9.11). A wire-frame model is a list of edge descriptions and is not sufficient to describe a unique polyhedron (Requicha and Voelekar, 1982). When we use a solid modelling system, we can check for interference between objects, we can remove hidden lines and surfaces, and we can calculate mass properties automatically. Due to the development of parallel graphics processors, solid modelling is approaching the speed of conventional wire-frame modelling (Herbert and Hoffman, 1985).

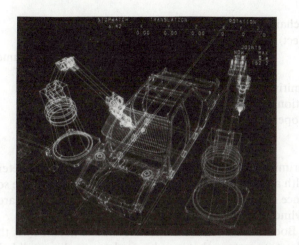

Figure 9.11
Wire frame model used in
the McDonnell Douglas off-
line programming system.

Six of the known solid-modelling schemes produce unambiguous object representations (Requicha, 1980). Of these six methods, constructive solid geometry (CSG) and boundary representation (BR) are the best understood and the most commonly used. Many solid-modelling systems receive input from engineers in CSG format, because it is easier for the user to handle, and internally convert it to boundary representation format, because BR is easier for display processors to handle. Also, the CSG representation with a recursively defined tree structure, and the BR model consisting of an abstraction hierarchy, are the most promising modelling schemes for storing solid objects in a computer-aided manufacturing (CAM) database (Kemper and Wallrath, 1987). However, traditional data models (such as the relational database model) do not adequately support technical applications because they lack object orientation – that is, technical models do not map naturally into database structures. Consequently, researchers are working on structural object-oriented databases and behavioural object-oriented databases. A second problem is that (CSG) data is easier to manipulate recursively, but recursive language features are not included in current object-oriented databases.

9.3.1.1 *Constructive solid geometry*

As its name implies, CSG refers to the construction of solid objects from a set of solid geometric shapes. A solid object is constructed by combining a few primitive shapes using motional and combinatorial operators. Motional operators include *rotate*, *translate* and *scale*. Combinatorial operators are the Boolean operators *union*, *intersection* and *difference* applied to two solid shapes, as defined in a Boolean algebra for constructive solid geometry.

A particular constructive solid geometry scheme is defined by its set of primitive shapes and its set of operators. These can be specified with a context-free grammar. For example:

$$\langle\text{mechanical part}\rangle ::= \langle\text{object}\rangle$$
$$\langle\text{object}\rangle \quad\quad ::= \langle\text{primitive}\rangle\,|$$
$$\langle\text{object}\rangle\langle\text{motion op}\rangle\langle\text{motion arguments}\rangle\,|$$
$$\langle\text{object}\rangle\langle\text{set operator}\rangle\langle\text{object}\rangle$$
$$\langle\text{primitive}\rangle \quad ::= \text{cube}\,|\,\text{wedge}\,|\,\text{cone}\,|\,\text{cylinder}\,|\ldots$$
$$\langle\text{motion op}\rangle \quad ::= \text{rotate}\,|\,\text{translate}\,|\,\text{scale}\,|\ldots$$
$$\langle\text{set operator}\rangle \quad ::= \text{union}\,|\,\text{intersection}\,|\,\text{difference}\,|$$
$$\text{complement}\,|\ldots$$

A primitive solid is described by volumetric parameters (such as length, width and height for a cuboid), and the position of the solid relative to a reference frame. The volumetric parameters of a sphere are its radius, and of a cylinder are its radius and length.

The Boolean algebra for constructive solid geometry is the group of regularized set operators that can be used to combine solid shapes. The universe of solid geometry W has a topology T, that is, a collection of all open subsets of W. In the topological space (W, T), a subset X of W (a set of primitive shapes) is a regular (closed) set if it equals the closure of its interior.

$$X = ki\,X \tag{9.1}$$

where

k denotes closure,

i denotes interior.

In this space, the regularized set union, intersection, difference and complement of two subsets X and Y of W are defined as:

Union $\quad\quad X \cup {}^* Y = ki(X \cup Y) \tag{9.2}$

Intersection $\quad X \cap {}^* Y = ki(X \cap Y) \tag{9.3}$

Difference $\quad X - {}^* Y = ki(X - Y) \tag{9.4}$

Complement $\quad C^* X \quad = kiCX \tag{9.5}$

where * represents the regularized operator.

The regular subsets of W, together with the regularized set operators form a Boolean algebra for constructive solid geometry (Requicha, 1980).

From the grammar for constructive solid geometry, we see that construction is defined recursively as an ordered binary tree. Primitive shapes and motion arguments are stored in the leaf nodes, and operators are stored in the nonterminal nodes (Figure 9.12). As only a few primitive shapes are used, the tree can become quite deep, which can lead to inefficient data retrieval. One advantage of this tree structure, however, is that it is easy to

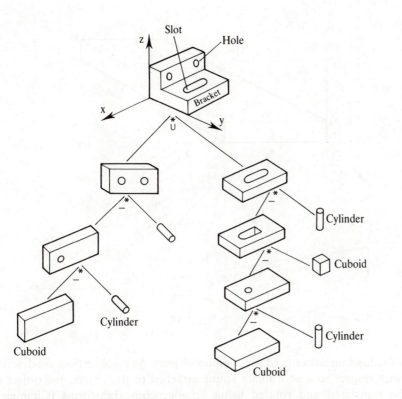

Figure 9.12
Constructive solid geometry
description of a bracket with
two holes and a slot
(Requicha, 1980).

represent subassemblies. An object can be described as a tree of subassemblies, where each subassembly is itself described as a tree.

9.3.1.2 *Boundary representation*

Constructive solid geometry representations are not efficient sources of
geometric data for producing line drawings on a display. Also, some types of
graphic interactions, such as pick and edge, are difficult to support directly
from constructive solid geometry while others, such as 'pick a face', require
parallel processing. For this reason, many systems produce a boundary
representation of the object (Figure 9.13) from the constructive solid geometry data.

In boundary representation, a solid is segmented into its nonover-
lapping faces (or patches) which are, in turn, modelled by their bounding
edges and vertices. The resulting data structure is a directed graph containing
object, face, edge and vertex nodes. As the complexity of the object
increases, the tree gets wider but not deeper.

Vertices are stored as Cartesian coordinates, edges are stored as vertex
tuples, and faces as a variable number of edges. To create a unique description of the cuboid in Figure 9.13, the only data that is stored in the tree is the
coordinates of the eight vertices. Various schemes exist to reduce the amount

Figure 9.13
Boundary representation of a
cuboid (Requicha, 1980).

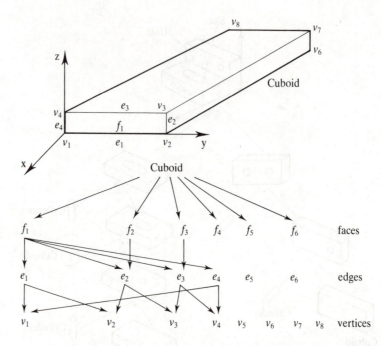

Figure 9.13
Boundary representation of a
cuboid (Requicha, 1980).

of redundant data stored for complex objects. As these vertices are described with respect to a coordinate frame attached to the object, the object can be translated and rotated using homogeneous transforms (Chapter 3). To display an object, we may also want to use scaling and projection transforms.

The major difficulty in using boundary representation is covering the surface with faces. For example, it is not intuitively obvious what the faces on a curved object are. Part of the design of a boundary representation is the definition of the term 'face'. One advantage of using constructive solid geometry primitives for input, is that the set of possible faces is clearly defined.

Given that there is a limited set of primitive shapes, faces should satisfy the following conditions (Requicha, 1980).

- A face of an object is a subset of the object's boundary.
- The union of all faces of an object equals the boundary of the object.
- Each face is a subset of a primitive surface.
- A face must have area and must not have dangling edges or isolated points – it must be a closed 2-D polyhedron.

For a boundary representation to be unambiguous, faces must be represented unambiguously. Faces on planes can be represented by their bounding edges, but faces on curves have to be represented by primitive surfaces. For example, the cylinders in Figure 9.10 are represented with decahedron.

9.3.1.3 *Extensions for robot applications*

Conventional solid modelling systems are concerned with static objects. In contrast, robotic applications involve moving parts around and bringing them into contact with each other. Consequently, robot planning systems require additional information from the solid modelling system (Ambler, 1985). The additional information falls into three categories: constraints on the motion of objects, features not included in the descriptions of the object, and geometric tolerances.

The essence of robotics is motion: parts are moved around, manipulator linkages move from one configuration to another, and grippers open and close as they manipulate objects. Manipulator links are constrained by their joints, so this information must be included in the model of the manipulator. While performing a task, a manipulator must not collide with any object in its environment. During an assembly operation, such as fitting a bearing on a shaft, the motion of the gripper is constrained by the task.

The solid model of a part must include the grasp points, information which may not be included in the object description. One way of defining the final configuration of the parts is to specify the relationship between surface features on the parts. Thus, solid modelling systems for robotics require the ability to specify surface features which do not contribute to the shape of the body. An example of such a feature is the axis of the shaft on to which a bearing is to be fitted.

Most parts are manufactured to certain tolerances. Tolerancing and surface-finish data must be included in the model if it is to be used for automatic planning of the manufacture, inspection, and robotic assembly of mechanical components. Requicha (1983) developed a theory of tolerancing that states that an object satisfies a tolerance specification if the bounding surfaces of the object lie within regions of space called tolerance zones. The tolerances that constrain the features of an object to lie within a tolerance zone are size, surface form, curve form, position, surface orientation, surface runout, and curve runout. The variation of each of these tolerances associated with a solid shape can be stored in a graph called a variational graph. This graph can be incorporated into a constructive solid geometry based model easily (Requicha and Chan, 1986).

Modelling motion introduces other problems to the modelling system. First, all the objects can be moved, and after moving must be in the correct relationship. Thus, all model data must be capable of being transformed, without the model of an object coming unstuck. When a gripper grasps a part, or parts are assembled into an object, the parts are affixed – connections are established between them. When one part in an affixment moves, the rest move with it. Second, data on the size and shape of parts should be automatically scalable so that a model for the assembly of a valve, for example, can be used to model the assembly of a larger valve. Third, is the problem of uncertainty. If the uncertainty in the location or relative position of objects is large, data from sensors has to be introduced. During planning

Figure 9.14
Model of the right-hand side
of a sheep consisting of
front leg, side and rear leg
patches.

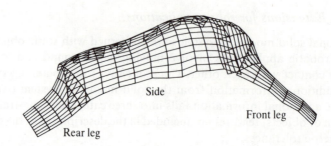

Figure 9.14
Model of the right-hand side
of a sheep consisting of
front leg, side and rear leg
patches.

with a simulator, we must be able to use simulated sense data to reorient parts. Finally, when we use a model for real-time planning, we must be able to adapt the model in response to changes in the workspace. The sheep-shearing robot (see Figure 1.20) models the surface of the sheep with a number of patches, such as sides, belly, back, and so on (Owens, 1984). Each patch is described by a number of equally spaced parallel curves (Figure 9.14). Before shearing starts, the weight, shoulder to rump distance, hip width and maximum belly width are measured. These measurements are used by a surface-prediction algorithm to predict a surface model for the sheep. During the shearing of a patch, measurement of the actual surface of the sheep's skin is used to adapt the model for that patch. Real-time variations in the location of the sheep's skin occur due to breathing and small movements of the sheep. The sheep is constrained to eliminate gross motions. Also, very few sheep are the ideal shape.

9.3.2 Off-line programming

Off-line programming is the development of robot programs without using the robot. Curently, no general-purpose off-line programming system is commercially available, but continued research is expected to quickly lead to their development. Since the mid-1980s, a number of companies have offered simulation systems for use in developing robot operation sequences.

Research into off-line programming is stimulated by a number of considerations. Current robot teaching methods are time consuming, and the robot is unproductive while it is being taught. Simple changes to taught programs may require the robot to be removed from production, and teach systems lack the flexibility of programming. In a batch-production environment, where the robot has to be reprogrammed regularly, the time overhead in teaching a robot may make it uneconomical. In contrast, if off-line programming is used, the program for the next batch can be developed while the current batch is being processed. Finally, the integration of robots with computer-aided design (CAD) databases requires programs that can automatically generate robot-level programs.

Off-line programming provides an essential link between (CAD) and

CAM (computer-aided manufacture). The development of off-line programming systems will result in greater use of robots and accelerate the implementation of flexible manufacturing systems (FMS). A successful off-line programming system will include (Yong *et al.*, 1985):

- knowledge of the process or task to be programmed,
- a three-dimensional world model,
- kinematic and dynamic models of the robot,
- a graphical or textual robot programming system,
- methods for verifying the correctness of the programs,
- interfaces to the robots for downline loading of programs and upline transfer of process data,
- a user-friendly programming environment.

Problems that slow the development of off-line programming systems occur in three areas. First is the difficulty of developing a modelling and programming system that is independent of both the robot and the application. These problems are compounded by the lack of facilities for easily entering precise geometric data. Second, there is no standard for the interface between robots, sensors, and computers. Third is the difficulty of simulating the inaccuracies that occur in the real world.

9.3.2.1 *Simulation*

From the user's point of view, the easiest method of robot-level planning is interactive simulation. The simulator provides immediate (user-time not real-time) feedback of manipulator motions by displaying the model of the world on a graphical display. Wire frame models (Figure 9.11) are usually used because they are faster to draw. However, many systems will also display a solid model on request (Figure 9.10). To simulate the behaviour of a robot successfully, the simulator must include theoretical models of both the robot and the task.

The programmer moves the simulated robot through its paces with keyboard or mouse commands. The simulator records the sequence of motions, and a sophisticated simulator will check for collisions, workspace, violations, and singular positions. When the programmer is happy with the sequence of motions, the system converts the recording into a robot-level program.

A typical simulator package includes models of robots from several manufacturers, and models of conveyors, boxes, and other common components. A facility is included to enter the model of a part either manually or from a CAD database. The programmer can specify features, such as grasp points and select trajectories with one of a number of motion strategies.

Figure 9.15
Industrial assembly sheet
description of the task
'screw the bracket and
interlock together'
(Lieberman and Wesley,
1977).

```
 9  1. ASM SUPPORT BRACKET
10  P/U AND POSITION THE NUT IN THE NEST OF THE FIXTURE.
11  1090037 NUT, CAR RET TAB      QTY 01
12  P/U. ORIENT AND POSITION THE BRACKET INTO THE FIXTURE WITH ITS TAB OVER
    THE NUT.
13  1115191 BRKT ASM, RAIL SUPPORT      QTY 01
14  P/U SCREW AND LOAD DRIVER.
15  1107379 STUD, CR TAB INTLK      QTY 01
16  P/U, ORIENT AND POSITION THE INTERLOCK OVER THE BRACKET HOLE, WITH
    THE NOTCHED LUG UP.
17  1117637 INTERLOCK, CR + TAB      QTY 01
18  P/U AIR DRIVER.
19  DRIVE SCREW TIGHT.
20  TORQUE 12.0 IN/LBS.
21  ASIDE AIR GUN.
```

In addition to off-line programming, simulators can be used to evaluate various robot-based task solutions. One stimulation to the development of off-line programming by simulation is that robot-level languages require a programmer with specialized knowledge, and hence, cannot be used by production personnel. A second stimulation is that programming systems are still a research topic, where simulation can rely on the user to solve difficult problems. The visual feedback provided by the graphics system enables the operator to identify and fix bugs quickly.

9.3.2.2 *Programming systems*

A number of researchers have developed moded-based, formal task-specification languages. Programs in these languages specify the task as a sequence of task actions, which are then compiled into robot operations. Examples of these languages are AUTOPASS (Lieberman and Wesley, 1977), LAMA (Lozano-Perez and Winston, 1977), and RAPT (Popplestone, Ambler and Bellas, 1978). The decomposition of the task into actions resides with the programmer, while the language provides a tool for describing that decomposition, and the underlying model supplies a method for handling details.

So that the researchers developing these languages can concentrate on robotics problems rather than language design issues, most of these languages are embedded in a host language. For example, AUTOPASS programs are embedded in a pseudo PL/1 language, and LAMA is LISP based.

The AUTOPASS (AUTOmated Parts ASSembly) system attempted to generate a robot command sequence from an English-like description of the assembly actions (Lieberman and Wesley, 1977). Unfortunately, they have not reported how much of this system was implemented and tested. The concept was to take an existing industrial assembly instruction sheet (Figure 9.15) and convert it into a program (Figure 9.16) which could be compiled into a sequence of robot actions.

1. OPERATE *nutfeeder* WITH *car-ret-tab-nut* AT *fixture.nest*
2. PLACE *bracket* IN *fixture* SUCH THAT *bracket.bottom*
     CONTACTS *car-ret-tab-nut.top*
     AND *bracket.hole* IS ALIGNED WITH *fixture.nest*
3. PLACE *interlock* ON *bracket* SUCH THAT
       interlock.hole IS ALIGNED WITH *bracket.hole*
       AND *interlock.base* CONTACTS *bracket.top*
4. DRIVE IN *car-ret-intlk-stud* INTO *car-ret-tab-nut*
     AT *interlock.hole*
     SUCH THAT TORQUE IS EQ 12.0 IN-LBS USING *air-driver*
     ATTACHING *bracket* AND *interlock*
5. NAME *bracket interlock car-ret-intlk-stud car-ret-tab-nut*
     ASSEMBLY *support-bracket*

Figure 9.16
AUTOPASS program for the task 'screw the bracket and interlock together' (Lieberman and Wesley, 1977).

The instruction sheet in Figure 9.15 details the set of steps required to screw a bracket and an interlock together. These instructions assume that the user can recognize the parts, work out how to place the bracket on the fixture (line 12), decide which hole to put the screw in (line 16), and understand how to drive the screw tight (line 19). All this information has to be modelled and expressed in a form that can readily be compiled before a robot control program can be generated.

The AUTOPASS language was designed to allow the programmer to specify the sequence of assembly actions in pseudoEnglish. AUTOPASS supported miscellaneous statements for flow of control and variable assignment, and assembly statements for specifying the assembly sequence. The latter were divided into three groups: state change, tool, and fastener. Miscellaneous statements were supported by the PL/1 host language. State-change statements were used to describe assembly operations such as placement of parts, adjustment of parts, and the motion of the manipulator. State changes were described with a single PLACE statement. The PLACE statement on line 2 in Figure 9.16 specifies that the robot is to place the bracket into the fixture so that the bottom of the bracket contacts the top of the nut and the hole in the bracket is aligned with the nest in the fixture. The tool statement was used to select a tool and define how to use it. A general purpose OPERATE statement (line 1 Figure 9.16) was used for this purpose. The characteristics of each tool were hard coded into the compiler. The final group of statements were the fastener statements such as ATTACH and DRIVE IN (line 4 in Figure 9.16). These were used to describe the attachment of one object to another, and the appropriate tool to use.

Once the AUTOPASS program was written, it was compiled. During compilation, the compiler obtained geometric information from a world model database. The world model consisted of a graph in which each vertex represented a part or an assembly (Figure 9.17). The edges represented four possible interobject relationships: part-of, attachment, constraint, and assembly-component. Each object was represented internally as a polyhedron, with lists of vertices, edges and surfaces. Objects were constructed by combining these primitive volumes.

Figure 9.17
AUTOPASS world model for the task 'screw the bracket and interlock together' (Lieberman and Wesley, 1977).

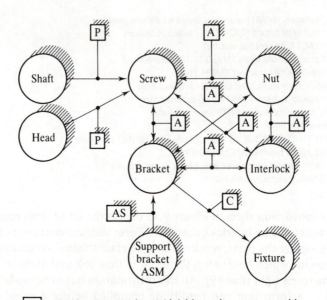

A	**Attachment:** may be *rigid* (objects do not move with respect to each other), *non-rigid* (objects are attached, but have limited relative movement (a joint), or *conditional* (objects are attached only under certain conditions).
C	**Constraint:** may be *translational* or *rotating*; described by direction or axis vector and force threshold.
AS	**Assembly:** indicates that an object (and each object attached to it) is a component of an assembly.
P	**Part-of:** indicates a component of a rigid part. (Not all components and part-of relationships are shown above.)

The fixed set of verbs and qualifiers in AUTOPASS was too restricted for use on a wide range of assembly tasks. Also, there was no facility to sense changes in the environment and update the world model.

LAMA (Language for Automatic Mechanical Assembly) was a program that converted action-level descriptions of an assembly task into a robot-level description of the operations to be performed by the robot to achieve the task (Lozano–Perez, 1976). The programmer described the assembly sequence in terms of the desired effects on the parts being assembled, and LAMA provided a tool for describing the assembly sequence and decomposing it into robot operations.

The compilation of assembly actions into robot motions was modelled as a three-stage process: assembly planning, pick and place, and feedback planning.

1. In the assembly planning phase, the programmer's description of an assembly was combined with a description of the available assembly operations. A plan for the assembly of a piston (Figure 9.18) is shown in Figure 9.19. The significant problems of this stage were, modelling

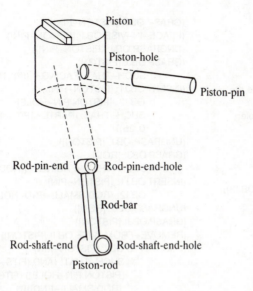

Figure 9.18
Piston subassembly from
model aircraft engine
(Lozano-Perez, 1976).

of the parts both individually and assembled, and modelling the position and orientation constraints placed on the parts during assembly actions.

2. In the pick-and-place phase, the assembly plan was converted into a program that assumed ideal position information and no position uncertainty. The task model and the geometric model were combined to produce manipulator motions defined in Cartesian space. The significant problems at this stage were determining how and where to grasp the parts, and planning collision free paths. These issues are discussed in Sections 9.3.3.1 and 9.3.4.3.

3. In the feedback phase, the assumptions of an ideal world used in the pick and place phase were recognised as being untenable. The feedback planner expanded the program to handle manipulator position control errors and uncertainty in part location, shape, and size. A significant problem at this stage was the prediction and modelling of such errors. A continuing debate between researchers is whether error handling should be carried out at robot level by programmed instructions or at the joint level by passive compliance or active feedback loops.

LAMA was only partially implemented, although the assembly of the piston subassembly (Figure 9.18) was demonstrated. It was the first system to attempt to deal with the significant problems of spatial planning: selection of grasp points, collision avoidance during manipulator motion, and uncertainty in the location of both the manipulator and the parts.

RAPT is a language for describing an assembly process (Popplestone *et al.*, 1978) and is based on the numerical control language APT. RAPT uses a partial body model, where objects are described in terms of their features.

(1) Insert the piston pin partway into the piston.
(2) Place the rod's pin end on the piston pin inside the piston.
(3) Push the pin through the rod and the piston hole.

(a)

```
(INSERT OBJ1: [PISTON–PIN]
        OBJ2: [PISTON PIN–HOLE]
        SUCH–THAT: (PARTLY (FITS–IN OBJ1 OBJ2)))
(INSERT OBJ1: [PISTON–PIN]
        OBJ2: [ROD SMALL–END–HOLE])
(PUSH–INTO OBJ1: [PISTON–PIN]
        OBJ2: (AND [PISTON PIN–HOLE]
                [ROD SMALL–END]))
```

(b)

```
(GRASP OBJ: [PISTON–PIN])
(PLACE–IN–VISE OBJ: [PISTON–PIN])
(UNGRASP OBJ: [PISTON–PIN])
(GRASP OBJ: [PISTON]
        SUCH–THAT (FACING+ ([PISTON] TOP) DOWN))
(INSERT OBJ1: [PISTON–PIN]
        OBJ2: [PISTON PIN–HOLE]
        SUCH–THAT: (PARTLY (FITS–IN OBJ1 OBJ2)
        0.25))
(UNGRASP OBJ: [PISTON])
(GRASP OBJ: [ROD]
        SUCH–THAT: (FACING+ ([ROD–BAR] TOP) UP))
(INSERT OBJ1: [PISTON–PIN]
        OBJ2: [ROD SMALL–END–HOLE])
(UNGRASP OBJ: [ROD])
(GRASP OBJ: [PISTON])
(REMOVE–FROM–VISE OBJ: [PISTON])
(PUSH–INTO OBJ: [PISTON–PIN]
        SUCH–THAT: (AND (FITS–IN [PISTON–PIN]
        [PISTON PIN–HOLE]) (FITS–IN [PISTON–PIN]
        [ROD SMALL–END])))
(UNGRASP OBJ: [PISTON])
```

(c)

Figure 9.19
LAMA assembly plan for piston subassembly. (Lozano-Perez, 1976): (a) English description of assemble process; (b) input to LAMA – user program; (c) assembly plan – output from LAMA.

A feature is a plane face, a cylindrical shaft, a cylindrical hole, an edge, a vertex, or a spherical face. Object descriptions are brief as they only describe those features which are relevant to the handling and placing of objects.

An obvious advantage of a partial model is the simplicity of describing objects with complex geometrical forms involving curved surfaces. In contrast, the specification of complete object descriptions can be tedious. Partial models have the disadvantage that they cannot be used for checking assemble plans, or for planning collision-free trajectories.

An assembly process consists of a series of actions in which objects are picked up, moved around, fitted into other objects and fixed into special positions. In RAPT, the interactions between parts are described with three spatial relationships: *against*, *fits* and *coplanar*. With these relationships, the state of all the parts in an assembly can be described. When two parts are assembled, they must stay together. Affixment is specified with the notion of a rigid tie: an instruction that states that one part is tied to another. Also, when a manipulator grasps a part tightly, the part is tied to the gripper. Immovable bodies are tied to the world.

This geometric model is combined with a task model by two action descriptors: *move* (translation) and *turn* (rotation). These actions can be qualified: a move can be parallel or perpendicular to an object, and a turn can be about a feature. Naturally, the qualifiers are constrained to refer to certain features. For example, a move cannot be perpendicular to a hole, or a turn about a face.

These actions transform the geometric model from one state to another. For example, from the action 'move the rod perpendicular to the face of the block', a RAFT program can construct an expression for the position of the rod after it has been moved in terms of its position before being moved, the position of the block, and a single variable representing the magnitude of the movement.

The relationship between the parts at any stage during an assembly is the state of the task. Actions transform the task from one state to another. A subassembly is a set of bodies tied together with a set of spatial relationships that exists over a set of states. Once the assembly task is programmed, this action-level program has to be converted into a robot-level program. The design of an interpreter or compiler to do this is not a simple task (Popplestone *et al.*, 1980). A translator converts statements about bodies, situations, and actions into a knowledge tree, a tree which specifies the state of the assembly after each robot operation. Each path through the tree specifies a solution to the assembly task. Ideally, a properly written program will produce only one solution, but any turn involving three independent rotations will have at least two distinct solutions and therefore the tree will branch. A strategy function scans the tree forward and backward to choose the 'best' motion sequence. This sequence is the robot-level program.

9.3.3 Gross motion planning

Gross motions are robot movements in free space, where the only constraint is that the robot does not collide with anything. In the example at the start of this chapter, the command to move the gripper to above the conveyor is a gross motion command, as is the command to move the gripper to the grasping position. Gross motion planning deals with planning collision-free paths through the environment, paths which the manipulator can follow. It decomposes into two planning steps: path planning and trajectory planning.

In path planning, we are concerned with finding paths through free space from start to goal. We are also interested in finding the optimum path. In trajectory planning, we are concerned with the details of robot motion along the planned path.

9.3.3.1 *Path planning*

Sometimes end-effector paths have task constraints. For example, in arc welding the torch may have to follow a complex three-dimensional path during the welding process. Because manually specifying such a path can be time consuming and tedious, some researchers are developing methods for automatic path generation. Once the path is generated, the robot motions required to follow that path have to be examined for collision, and avoidance motions planned. Task specific motion planning is beyond the scope of this book. In this section, however, we examine the more general problem of planning collision-free paths for pick-and-place operations.

In Section 8.3.3, we discussed path planning for mobile robots. That planning was simplified by the fact that the motion of a mobile robot is restricted to a plane. Path planning for manipulators differs from path planning for mobile robots owing to fundamental differences in their nature.

- A manipulator is required to move its end effector (and anything it is grasping) from the start to the goal, in contrast to a mobile robot where the whole robot moves.

- As well as the base being tied to one spot, the linkages of a manipulator change configuration with respect to one another as the manipulator moves. Consequently, the physical structure of the volume occupied by the manipulator is continually changing, where a mobile robot can usually be treated as a solid body that occupies a fixed volume.

- A manipulator can move its end effector in six degrees of freedom, whereas a planar mobile robot is limited to three.

- The exact location of all objects in the workspace of a manipulator must be known for a manipulator to execute a given task but, often, mobile robots only have an incomplete model of their environment.

- The sensors for a manipulator are positioned to give the best view of the manipulation process without occlusion, but the sensors on a mobile robot are often restricted by the environment. Consequently, the field of view of sensors has to be considered during planning for mobile robots.

- A manipulator will negotiate a given path many more times than a mobile robot will. So path optimization is more important with manipulators.

- Manipulator planning relies very heavily on the accuracy and repeatability of joint motions. In contrast, the dead-reckoning control of a mobile robot is subject to significant errors which accumulate.

These differences result in path planning for manipulators being a more complex process than path planning for mobile robots, hence the order of their treatment in this book. However, the differences are differences of purpose and complexity, not differences in the basic problems of path planning or in algorithms to solve those problems.

Algorithms for planning paths that avoid obstacles fall into three broad groups: hypothesize-and-test, penalty function, and free space. Hypothesize-and-test algorithms involve three steps. In the first step, a candidate path from start to goal is hypothesized, where start and goal specify manipulator configurations to achieve desired end-effector locations. In the second step, immediate positions along the path are tested for possible collisions. If a solid geometry model is used, collision detection amounts to detecting intersections between solids. Most geometric modelling systems have facilities for detecting intersections. If a collision is found, the third step is to propose an avoidance motion by examining the obstacles involved in the collision. Steps two and three are repeated until a collision-free path is found. The third step is the most difficult. A typical heuristic is to define a new intermediate configuration by moving the colliding objects apart. In a sparse environment, this works well, but, in a cluttered environment, the new path will often cause a collision with another obstacle.

In the second group of algorithms, a penalty function that encodes the presence of objects is calculated for each manipulator configuration. A good penalty function gives an infinite value for configurations that cause collisions, with the value dropping off sharply as the manipulator moves away from obstacles. A typical penalty function is the sum of the penalties for individual obstacles and a penalty for deviation from the shortest path.

The first decision is, 'For which configurations do we calculate the penalty function?', as calculating it for all possible configurations is computationally expensive. The number of configurations can be reduced to a manageable size by overlaying the workspace with a three-dimensional grid and calculating the penalty function at each grid point. A path from start to goal is found by following the valleys in the penalty function values. This path is the sequence of manipulator configurations defined by the grid points. Penalty functions provide a simple way to combine constraints from multiple objects, but the cost of calculating the penalty function is prohibitive when the shape of the objects is complex. The more realistic the model, the greater the computation cost. Another problem with penalty functions is that a path search can lead to a local minimum and not be able to get out. However, they can be used for automatic smoothing and feedback control when following a path planned with another method. Penalty functions have similar properties to potential field planners (Section 8.3.4) and can be defined in the same way.

The third group of algorithms is free-space algorithms. These are all extensions of the path-planning algorithms discussed for mobile robots (Section 8.3.3.3). These algorithms build an explicit representation of free space: subsets of robot configurations that are free of collisions. These methods guarantee to find a path if one exists, within the known subset of free space but 'as they only compute subsets of the free space' they miss paths in the space that has not been mapped. In cluttered space, they are computationally expensive, but will find a path where other methods won't.

The first problem in multidimensional path planning is to find a representation of the problem that is mathematically tractable. In Cartesian space, a manipulator is easy to visualize but its description is very complex.

Also, regions of free space are easy to find and model, but planning paths through them is inherently difficult.

Configuration space (C space) is a representation where the description of a manipulator is simple, but it is difficult to visualize. Also, planning paths is relatively easy, but modelling the regions of free space is complex. A configuration of a moving object is a set of parameters that completely specify every point on the object. The kinematic model of a manipulator specifies the location of each link, hence the joint parameters are a configuration, but the Cartesian parameters of the end effector are not, because of multiple inverse kinematic solutions. Configuration space is a rectangular coordinate space in which each axis represents one joint parameter. Hence, a six-jointed manipulator is described with a point in a six degree of freedom configuration space. In configuration space, each point represents a distinct manipulator configuration, and a line represents a manipulator trajectory. Configuration space can be divided into volumes that represent groups of configurations. Some volumes represent configuration space, that is, manipulator configurations that do not collide with objects, and some volumes represent configuration objects, that is manipulator configurations that involve collisions.

In configuration space, path planning is reduced to planning the path of a point through intersecting configuration space volumes. But there is one drawback: the mapping of Cartesian space configurations to volumes in configuration space is difficult and computationally expensive. Testing every manipulator configuration for the possibility of a collision can take an excessive amount of time.

The generation of configuration space representations can be simplified by quantizing the space, by only considering a subset of configuration space, and by projecting configuration space on to slices with fewer dimensions. In the vertex-graph method of path planning for mobile robots (Section 8.3.3.5), we initially dealt with robots with fixed orientation and configuration space was simply a plane. Cartesian space objects were mapped into configuration space objects by shrinking the robot to a point and expanding the objects. To handle the fact that rotation of the robot introduced a third degree of freedom which changed the shape of the configuration space objects, we introduced slices, with one slice for each orientation.

In two dimensions, we found a path from start to goal by searching the graph connecting all vertices. This method fails in three dimensions because, typically, the shortest paths do not traverse the vertices of the configuration-space objects, and there may be no paths via vertices.

Lozano–Perez (1981, 1983) developed an algorithm for representing multidimensional configuration space with a set of three-dimensional slices. Each slice represents a swept volume in Cartesian space, and is described with a plane and a sweep angle. The sweep angle can be within the plane, or the plane can rotate with that angle. The result is a slice with areas represent-

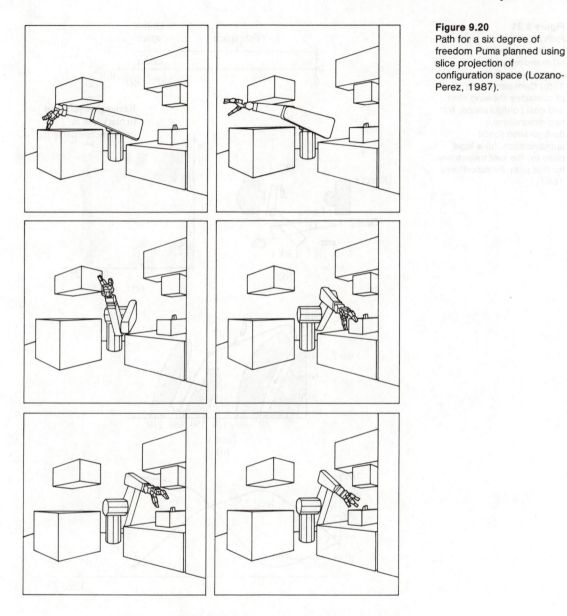

Figure 9.20
Path for a six degree of
freedom Puma planned using
slice projection of
configuration space (Lozano-
Perez, 1987).

ing free space and the swept volume of objects. This approach to free-space
mapping is very complex and has been replaced by simpler, more general,
algorithms.

Jarvis (1986), for example, applies the distance transform method of
path planning (Section 8.3.3.6) to configuration-space planning. As six-
dimensional configuration space is computationally difficult to handle, he
models only the waist, shoulder and elbow joints. The wrist and end effector

Figure 9.21
Path planning for a type one
two-link manipulator.
(a) one-dimensional
configuration space for link
1; (b) Cartesian space view
of obstacles showing start
and goal configurations; (c)
two-dimensional
configuration space
approximation; (d) a legal
path; (e) the joint trajectories
for that path. (Lozano-Perez,
1987).

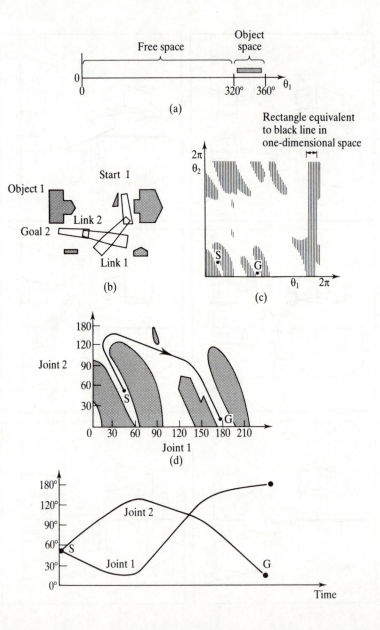

are treated as a fixed extension to the lower arm. Configuration space is
quantized with a three-dimensional grid. This reduces configuration space to
a three-dimensional volume of cubes, where each cube represents a set of
manipulator configurations. If a 10° quantization is used for each angle, the
whole space is represented by 36×36×36 cells. To calculate the state of each
cell (empty or collision), a manipulator model is moved into this configuration and tested for collision. If the upper arm is checked first, and testing
stops as soon as a collision is detected, the expense of this operation is

reduced. However, this method of planning is so expensive that it can be justified only in very cluttered environments.

Once all the cells have been tested, and their state set to indicate collision or free space, distance transforms are propagated out from the goal configuration. Path finding is simply a matter of following the transform values downhill from start to goal, as for mobile robot planning (Section 8.3.3.6).

Lozano–Perez (1987) approximates an n dimensional configuration space with sets of n one-dimensional slices. His algorithm uses quantization of joint angles, but no attempt is made to characterize the surface of obstacles in configuration space, instead, the obstacles are approximated by a series of ranges for each joint variable. Quantization leads to efficient solutions by approximating objects. Figure 9.20 shows a path planned for a six degree of freedom Puma robot using this algorithm. The hand does not change configuration during motion, but its shape is considered during planning. This motion took three minutes to plan on a Symbolics 3600 with a joint angle quantization of 3°. The computer took less time to plan the path than it took to compute the hidden surface displays in this figure.

To study this planning process we will consider the type one two-link manipulator example in Figure 9.21. In this example, both Cartesian and configuration space are two-dimensional. Even in this simple example, the correct path is not easy to visualize. The configuration-space representation of the obstacles is a list of one-dimensional slice projections. These are shown as black lines in Figure 9.21(c) and represent configurations that will cause collisions, while the white areas represent configurations in free space. Note, the path is restricted to a very narrow corridor at the start of the path (position S in Figure 9.21(d)).

The configuration-space description is generated with the following algorithm:

Algorithm 9.1   Configuration space slice calculation

1. Start with link 1, which is connected to link 0, a fixed base, by joint 1,

2. **While** n < number of links **Do**
    - (a)   Ignore all links beyond link n
    - (b)   **For** each value in the legal joint ranges of joints 1 to $n-1$.
        - (i)   Calculate the legal ranges of values for joint n by rotating link n around joint n.
        - (ii)   Calculate a 1-dimensional slice for joint n by quantizing the legal ranges.

For the type one two-link manipulator, we start with link 1 and ignore link 2. Link 1 is rotated around joint 1 to find the ranges of angles through which it is free to move. In our example (Figure 9.21), joint 1 has only one free space angle range from a joint angle of 0° to 320°. At both these angles, it contacts the object at the bottom right. The one-dimensional slice for this link (Figure 9.21(a)) is a line, with white representing free space and black representing object space. This forbidden region for link 1 becomes a rectangle in two-dimensional configuration space (Figure 9.21(c)).

Next, link 1 is positioned at the first quantization point in its legal range, and link 2 is rotated about joint 2 to find the legal ranges for the angle of joint 2. Then a slice is generated by quantizing these legal ranges. Having computed the first slice (left hand vertical line in Figure 9.21(c)), the program moves to the next quantization point for link 1 and calculates its slice. This process is repeated for the legal range of joint 1.

Consider the start configuration of the manipulator. If link 2 is rotated, it will collide with the two objects at the top right of the figure. Thus, the slice will have two regions of empty space (white) and two regions of object (black), as shown by the slice through point 5 in Figure 9.21(c).

In this example, there is a path from the start configuration to the goal configuration which avoids collisions. Starting from the start position (Figure 9.21(d)) the path moves up a narrow corridor into a large area of free spaces, traverses this space, and then moves down a wider corridor to the goal position. The joint angle trajectories for this path (Figure 9.21(e)) are read directly off the two-dimensional configuration space diagram.

The complexity of this process increases rapidly as the number of degrees of freedom of the configuration space increases. However, the algorithm remains the same, as it is recursive. The recursive nature of the algorithm calls for a recursive data structure to store the configuration space slices: an n-level tree whose leaves represent legal ranges of configurations for the manipulator. This data structure has the advantage of simple and efficient algorithms which deal with linear ranges. It has the disadvantage that the breadth of the tree increases rapidly, and hence the storage and processing time, with the number of objects in the environment and the number of dimensions in the configuration space.

In order to reduce the complexity of searching for paths in this data structure, a more compact representation, called regions, that captures some of the coherence between adjacent slices is used. A region is a rectangle made up of sections of free space in parallel slices. In this way, a two-dimensional configuration space made up of slices, such as that in Figure 9.21(c), is reduced to a set of rectangular regions of free space (Figure 9.22). From this set, a region graph is constructed with nodes representing free space and links indicating overlap between regions.

To handle three-dimensional configuration space, links are made between regions that overlap in the third direction. Thus, a set of two-dimensional region graphs (one for each two-dimensional slice) is connected into a three-dimensional region graph for the whole volume. This process is repeated for higher dimensions, resulting in an n dimensional graph of regions.

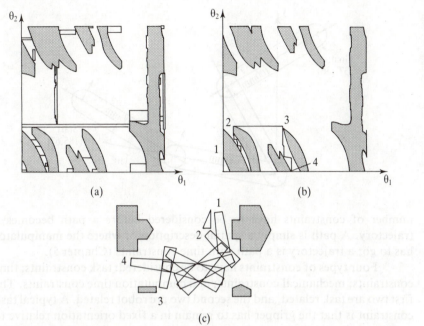

Figure 9.22
(a) Regions for example in Figure 9.21; (b) path found between start (1) and goal configuration (4); (c) some intermediate configurations (Lozano-Perez, 1987).

In this representation, a path is a sequence of links and nodes that connect the start node to the goal node. An A* search is used to find the optimum path. At each node in the path graph, an entry point is stored. This point is the point on the boundary between this region and the previous region that is closest to the entry point of the previous region. The result is a rather jagged path (Figure 9.22(b)) that tends to pass close to objects. Algorithms to smooth the path are the subject of continuing research.

Path searching can be speeded up by searching only subsets of the configuration space. The path in Figure 9.20 was planned using two simple heuristics to choose subsets of the configuration space (Lozano–Perez, 1987). First, link 3 was extended to include a simple approximation of the wrist, gripper and load. This reduced the configuration space to three-dimensions. A path was planned from a start to goal in this three-dimensional space.

As the start and goal in three-dimensional configuration space may differ slightly from the start and goal in six-dimensional space, two short paths are planned in six-dimensional configuration space, one at each end of the three-dimensional path. Thus the problem has been neatly decoupled into three-dimensional path planning for gross motions, and six-dimensional path planning for small motions near the start and goal.

9.3.3.2 *Trajectory planning*

It may seem that once we have found a path from start to goal, all the manipulator has to do is follow it. But that is not as easy as it sounds as a

Figure 9.23
Start and goal configurations
for a Type 1 two-link
manipulator.

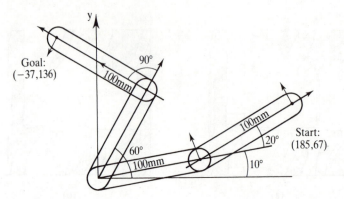

number of constraints have to be considered before a path becomes a trajectory. A path is simply a spatial description of where the manipulator has to go; a trajectory is a path with time constraints (Chapter 5).

Four types of constraints have to be considered: task constraints; time constraints; mechanical constraints; and computation time constraints. The first two are task related, and the second two are robot related. A typical task constraint is that the gripper has to remain in a fixed orientation relative to world coordinates during motion – if the robot is grasping a flask of liquid, it must not spill any. A typical time constraint is that an action must be executed within a certain time. For example, a casting must be removed from a mould before it cools and sticks to it, or a billet must be placed in a forge before it cools. A second area of time constraint is maximum utilization of equipment. A machine should not be idle waiting for the robot. These constraints are generally considered during task planning, and should have little impact on trajectory planning. The robot-related constraints often conflict with the task constraints. If a task requires the robot to follow a straight-line trajectory, the velocity of the robot may have to be reduced to enable the continuous calculation of inverse kinematics. Additionally, a robot may be physically incapable of following the planned path, and the path has to be smoothed.

Consider the type 1 two-link manipulator in Figure 9.23. The task action planner has generated the robot motion command move from start to goal. The path planner has planned a straight-line path as there are no obstacles in the way. The task of the trajectory planner is to convert this path description into a time sequence of manipulator configurations. To do this, the trajectory planner first has to choose a path-following strategy. Available strategies are unconstrained joint motion, joint-by-joint control, linear interpolated joint motion, polynomial trajectories, knot point trajectories, straight line trajectories and resolved motion rate control. In unconstrained joint motion, the joints are moved, in parallel, from the start configuration to the goal configuration at maximum joint speed. For the manipulator in Figure 9.23, joint 1 has to move by 50° and joint 2 by 70°. If they move at the

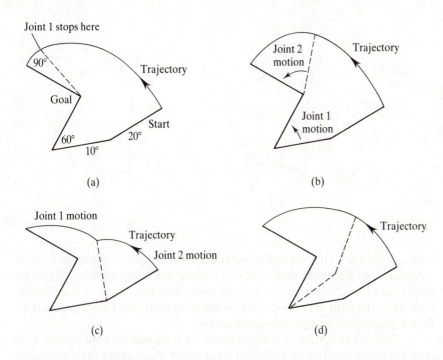

Figure 9.24
Joint space trajectory
control.
(a) Unconstrained joint
control;
(b) joint by joint (joint 1 first);
(c) joint by joint (joint 2 first);
(d) Linear interpolated joint
motion.

same rate, joint 2 will take 1.4 times as long to reach the goal. The resulting trajectory is quite complex (Figure 9.24(a)), and consists of two distinct curves.

Joint-by-joint control gives trajectories that are simpler to model: two circular arcs (Figure 9.24(b) and (c)). However, the trajectory where joint 2 is moved first has a discontinuity at the point where one joint stops and the other starts. To follow this trajectory, the end effector must come to rest at the end of joint 2 motion before joint 1 motion starts. When joint angles have to change in opposite directions, the end effector may move away from the goal at the start (Figure 9.25(a)) which is undesirable. Also, moving joint 2 faster than joint 1 can cause trajectory reversal (Figure 9.25(b)).

Linear interpolated motion achieves a smooth trajectory, described by a single, more complex curve, without any discontinuities. Consequently, it usually results in the fastest and smoothest motion, because the end effector does not have to come to rest half way through the motion. Also, when the first link is longer than the second, the end effector will not move away from the goal when joint angles change in opposite directions (Figure 9.25(c)). Linear interpolated motion is achieved by controlling the velocities of the joints so that they take the same time to reach the goal configuration. Consequently, the joint with the smallest angle to traverse travels the slowest.

Trajectory control in joint space has the advantage of simplicity, and consequent low calculation cost. The system simply calculates joint position set points and joint velocities, and the joint controllers do the rest. However,

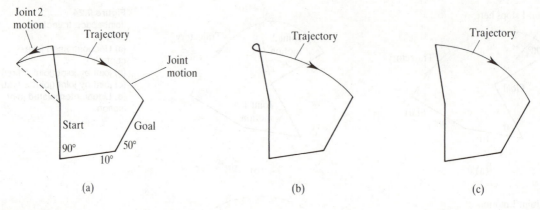

Figure 9.25
Joint space trajectories when joint angles are changing in different directions: (a) Effect of joints moving in opposite directions – joint 2 moves then joint 1; (b) Joint 2 moving at three times the speed of joint 1 – joints moving in parallel; (c) linear interpolated motion.

its disadvantage is that the end effector does not follow a straight path. If an automatic path planner was used to generate the initial path, it has to be called again to check that the curved path does not result in a collision, otherwise, the path of the end effector has to be controlled more precisely to follow predefined straight lines and curves.

Due to the nature of revolute joints, a manipulator constructed with resolute joints can follow a circular path much more easily than a straight path. In contrast, a manipulator constructed with prismatic joints can follow a straight path much more easily than a curved path. The simplest method of obtaining straight-line Cartesian motion is to control the manipulator in Cartesian space by continually calculating the inverse transform to obtain joint controller set points and the forward transform to obtain Cartesian space feedback (Figure 9.26(a)). However, this method suffers from a number of drawbacks. First, the computation of inverse kinematics may be too slow for real-time control. Second, it is not always possible to pick which of several redundant configurations to use. Third, the inverse kinematics of the manipulator may be intractable except by numeric methods. Fourth, position control alone is not enough, velocity control and sometimes acceleration control is required as well.

The problems of inverse kinematics, computation efficiency in particular, led to the concept of bounded deviation paths for straight-line segments (Taylor, 1979), where a trade off is made between implementation efficiency and accuracy of path tracking. As we have seen, linear interpolation between joint angles is very efficient to implement, but the resultant path deviates from the planned path. Taylor (1979) recognized that this deviation is small for short paths, and that for many common manipulators, the maximum deviation occurs near the middle of the trajectory. His algorithm proceeds as follows:

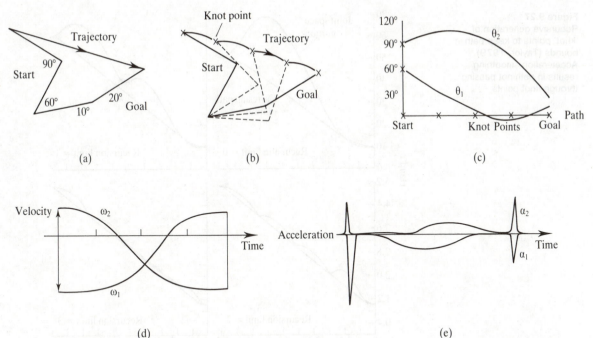

(a)   (b)   (c)

(d)   (e)

Figure 9.26
Straight-line motion.
(a) Straight-line trajectory;
(b) almost straight line using linear joint interpolation between knot joints. Dashed lines show intermediate configurations;
(c) joint trajectories for straight-line Cartesian trajectory;
(d) joint velocities;
(e) joint acceleration.

Algorithm 9.2   Taylor's bounded deviation algorithm

1. Compute the joint-space configuration for the start and goal configurations.
2. Compute the joint space mid point, and the Cartesian position for this configuration.
3. **If** the error in the path is greater than the allowed deviation **then**
    (a)   Place a knot point at the mid point of the straight-line Cartesian path.
    (b)   Split the path into two around the knot point.
    (c)   Recursively call this algorithm for the left half of the path.
    (d)   Recursively call this algorithm for the right half of the path.
          Else terminate this call to the algorithm.
4. Return the sequence of knot points.

This algorithm converts a straight-line trajectory into a sequence of knot points between which the trajectory is linearly interpolated in joint space (Figure 9.26(b)). An example of the application of this algorithm is given in Figure 9.27. In this example, three levels of recursion are required to bring the joint interpolated path within the required deviation from the

Figure 9.27
Recursive generation of
'knot' points to keep path in
bounds (Taylor, 1979).
Acceleration smoothing
results in path not passing
through knot points.

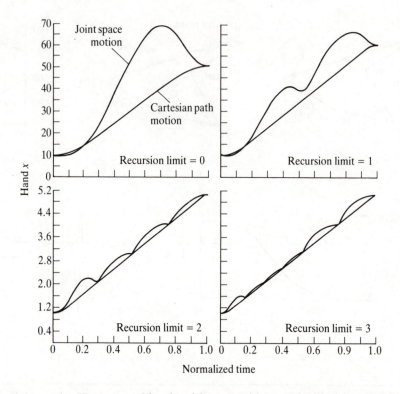

Figure 9.27
Recursive generation of
'knot' points to keep path in
bounds (Taylor, 1979).
Acceleration smoothing
results in path not passing
through knot points.

straight path. However, this algorithm provides no facility for choosing between redundant manipulator configurations. If the required start and goal configurations differ, the manipulator must change configuration during the motion. If the joint that changes configuration is close to zero (full extension of the two links), the transition is smooth, but if the joint angle is large, a violent joint motion can occur as the configuration changes while moving between knot points. Manipulator configurations near singularities and near workspace boundaries can also cause problems. In these regions, small joint motions can cause large Cartesian motions, and hence the algorithm will cluster knot points in an attempt to achieve a bounded path.

Finally, as the changes in joint angles in one path segment are different to the changes in another path segment, the angular velocities of the joints must change at knot points. As the manipulator is incapable of infinite acceleration, the actual path will deviate from the planned path. Consequently, the path must be modified to enable smooth transition in the trajectory at knot points. The variation in velocity at the knot point is calcuated for each joint. From this variation, the time period required to achieve the change is calculated, and the joint trajectory is modified to start accelerating the joint half this period before the knot point. Provided the transition period is less than the time between knot points, a smooth path is produced, at the cost of a deviation from the planned path (Figure 9.27).

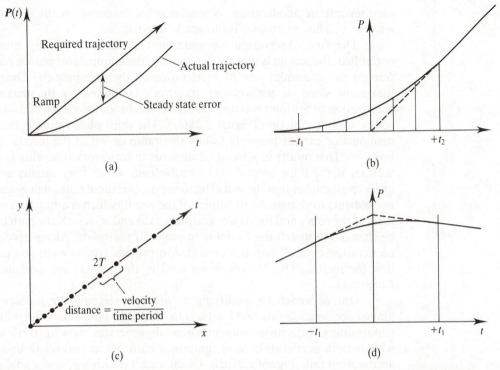

(a)

(b)

(c)

(d)

Figure 9.28
Polynomial trajectories.
(a) Steady state error in
trajectory following;
(b) start up trajectory to
minimize steady-state error;
(c) path for a Type 1 two-link
manipulator – distance
travelled per time period
increases as velocity
increases;
(d) smoothing at corners.

Having obtained a path (a sequence of points in space), we now have
to convert it to a trajectory (a sequence of spatial points in time). For the end
effector to move along a straight line path from start to goal, it must
accelerate smoothly to the desired velocity, travel along the path at the
desired velocity and decelerate smoothly to arrive at the goal. Thus, a linear
path (points separated by a fixed amount of space) becomes a nonlinear
trajectory (points separated by varying time periods) (Figure 9.28). Only
when the end effector is moving at constant velocity is the trajectory linear.
However, a linear end effector trajectory may require a highly nonlinear
joint trajectory.

To achieve the straight-line trajectory in Figure 9.26(a), both joints
have to move, first in one direction and then in the other (Figure 9.26(c)). In
this example, straight-line control requires a much greater change in joint
angles than joint control does. Also, with joint control each joint moves in
only one direction, but to achieve straight line control the joints have to
change direction in the middle of their motion (Figure 9.26(c)). Thus each
joint motor must accelerate to a maximum velocity in one direction, then
decelerate through zero velocity, accelerate to a maximum velocity in the
reverse direction, and finally decelerate to a halt when the goal is reached
(Figure 9.26(d) and (e)). However, the trajectory as designed calls for
instantaneous transfer from zero to maximum velocity at the start, which

requires infinite acceleration. A similar situation occurs at the end of the trajectory. This, of course, is physically impossible.

The first observation we make here is that the velocity must be controlled; the second is that the dynamics of the manipulator place a restriction on the maximum rate of acceleration of the manipulator. Thus, the maximum slope of the velocity trajectory is limited by the maximum acceleration of the joint motors, and the reference for the velocity servo must follow a ramp function (Figure 9.28(a)). The third observation is that the manipulator cannot precisely follow this ramp owing to the inertia of the linkages. This results in a steady state error in trajectory following (Figure 9.28(a)) if the joint controls are overdamped, which they usually are, in order to guarantee that the end effector never overshoots the goal. Since it is not possible to change the dynamics of the robot (which is a function of the mass of the robot and the object grasped by the end effector), the path has to be changed to match the dynamic response of the robot. Alternatively, an acceleration control loop can be added to provide feedforward compensation for inertia. The control terms used in this section are explained in Chapter 11.

One approach to modifying a path to overcome the problems of limited acceleration rate and inertia is to model the path with a polynomial. Constraining trajectories with polynomials generates start up trajectories with smooth acceleration, and smooths a path out at corners to limit the acceleration rate (Figure 9.28(d)). Given a start position p_s and a goal position p_g, a general trajectory can be defined as:

$$p(t) = f(t)p_g + [1 - f(t)]p_s \qquad (9.6)$$

where $f(t)$ is a continuous function that converts the path to a trajectory, such that $f(0) = 0$ and $f(1) = 1$. The simplest case is $f(t) = t$. The resultant trajectory is a linear combination of the end points, and velocity is fixed.

$$p(t) = tp_g + (1 - t)p_s \qquad (9.7)$$

$$v = p_g - p_s \qquad (9.8)$$

This is the ramp trajectory in Figure 9.28(a), which has a steady state error, and requires infinite acceleration. The steady state error is removed by adding velocity and acceleration constraints to the function. We achieve this by specifying start and goal velocities. There are now four constraints on the function: start and goal positions and start and goal velocities. For this simple example, the resulting trajectory is a third-order polynomial.

$$p(t) = (1 - t^2)[p_s + (2p_s + v_s)t] + t^2[p_g + (2p_2 - v_g)(1 - t)] \qquad (9.9)$$

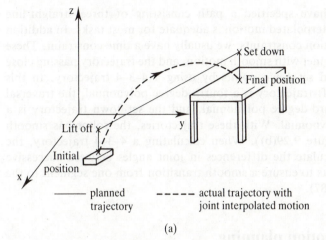

(a)

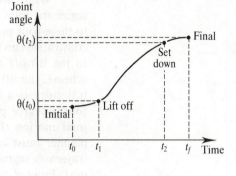

(b)

Figure 9.29
Trajectories of a pick and place task.
(a) Cartesian trajectories.
(b) Joint trajectory of one joint.

This equation does not take into account the fact that there is a maximum velocity. If we add acceleration constraints at the start and goal, we end up with a fifth order polynomial.

$$p(t) = (1 - t)^3 \left[p_s + (3p_s + v_s)t + (a_s + 6v_s + 12p_s)\frac{t^2}{2} \right]$$

$$+ t^3 \left[p_g + (3p_g - v_g)(1 - t) + (a_g - 6v_g + 12p_g)\frac{(1 - t^2)}{2} \right] (9.10)$$

The result is a complex trajectory for a very simple path. More complex paths with more constraints will result in a more complex trajectory description. In practice, it may be simpler to specify a maximum velocity and acceleration rate for each section of the path, and calculate a trajectory from the path to give smooth acceleration. If accurate path following is important, steady-state errors in the trajectory can be neglected, providing the manipulator stays on the path. In contrast, an application that requires accurate velocity control necessitates the elimination of errors in trajectory following.

When planning the trajectory for a pick-and-place task, the path is defined with four points: initial, lift-off, set-down and final (Figure 9.29). The object is picked up at the initial point and set down at the final point. The lift-off-point is a small distance from the initial point along a vector normal to the supporting surface. When picking an object up, the end effector must move away from the supporting surface. The set-down point is a small distance from the final point along a vector normal to the final supporting surface. This distance is known as the approach distance.

While we have specified a path consisting of three straight-line segments, joint-interpolated motion is adequate for most tasks. In addition to these four position constraints, we usually have a time constraint. These constraints can be met with smooth motion, and the trajectory passing close to the lift-off and set-down points by using a 4–3–4 trajectory. In this scheme, the lift-off trajectory is a fourth-degree polynomial, the traversal trajectory is a third-degree polynomial, and the set-down trajectory is a fourth-degree polynomial. With these trajectories, the robot has smooth joint motion (Figure 9.29(b)). When calculating a 4–3–4 trajectory, the planner must calculate the differences in joint angles between successive trajectory segments to ensure a smooth transition from one segment to the next (Fu *et al.*, 1987).

9.3.4 Fine-motion planning

Fine motions are robot movements that include the possibility of contact between the robot and the object it is manipulating. In these situations, slight errors in the motion of a robot can damage the objects being manipulated. For example, if a robot forces one object into another, or if the object slips within the gripper, serious damage can occur to the object.

In the presence of objects, uncertainty in the world model and inaccuracies in the kinematic model result in motions that are potentially dangerous. Fine-motion planning deals with strategies to make manipulation safe in the presence of uncertainties. As our models are never completely accurate representations of the real world, pure position control is not enough for fine manipulation. Guarded motions are required when approaching a surface, and complaint motions are required when in contact with a surface.

Research in fine motion planning has concentrated on three issues: physical modelling of manipulation, sensor-based strategies, and complaint motion (Section 6.1). We will study these issues with reference to insertion, grasping, touching and pushing. We discussed insertion in Section 6.3, so, in this section, we will examine only the prior problem of finding the hole.

9.3.4.1 *Touching*

A number of researchers have developed fine motion planners based on the assumption that all fine motions are characterized by a basic set of operations, such as 'insert the peg in the hole', and 'place the block in the corner'. The geometric structure of these operations is predefined and modelled with reasonable accuracy. In these planners, fine-motion synthesis is reduced to selecting the correct operation for the task at hand, choosing an appropriate order for the steps in that operation, and assigning values to the model parameters. Unfortunately, the world of assembly is not quite that regular,

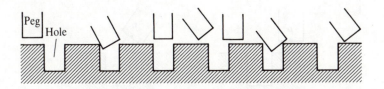

Figure 9.30
When finding a hole with
touch, a peg can approach
from a variety of directions,
with a variety of orientations.

and small changes in part geometry can require significant changes in a fine-motion strategy.

An alternative approach is based on the view that the structure of a fine motion strategy for a task is determined by the set of geometric interactions that can occur during the execution of the task (Lozano–Perez, Mason and Taylor, 1984). For example, a different strategy is needed when the surface around a hole is sloping, to that required when the surface is flat. In this view, geometric constraints should guide parts to their destination, eliminating the requirement for accurate geometric models of the relationships between the parts.

Before a robot can insert a peg in a hole, it must find the hole. A number of strategies have been developed to solve this problem, all of which rely on the sensing of touch. A peg can approach a hole from a variety of directions (Figure 9.30). The resultant position uncertainty is so large that geometric constraints cannot be determined unambiguously. In these circumstances, a combined touch-motion strategy has to be used to find the hole. Such a strategy is called a fine-motion strategy.

Four strategies have been considered: chamfers, search, biased search, and tilting the peg. Chamfering the hole or the peg increases the range of relative positions where the peg can fall into the hole, by increasing the region of constraint unambiguity. This technique works well with passive compliance devices (Section 6.3.7). Tilting the peg has almost the same geometric effect as chamfering.

The simplest strategy for finding the hole is to slide the peg along the surface until it falls into the hole. In general, the search algorithm moves in one direction until either the hole is found or the limit of the search area is reached. If the hole is not found, the algorithm changes direction and searches again. A biased search introduces a bias into the start position so that the peg is guaranteed to be on one side of the hole. This strategy reduces the chance of the peg entering the hole without a search.

Lozano–Perez, Mason and Wesley (1984) synthesize fine-motion strategies for both finding the hole and inserting the peg by transforming the problem into configuration space and computing a sequence of pre-images that lead to the goal. The transformation to configuration space is the same as that used in mobile robot path planning (Section 8.3.3.5), the peg is shrunk to a point, and the obstacles are expanded by the dimensions of the peg (Figure 9.31(b)); in the case of a hole, the diameter of the hole is shrunk by the effective diameter of the peg. If the peg is tilted, the bottom of the hole

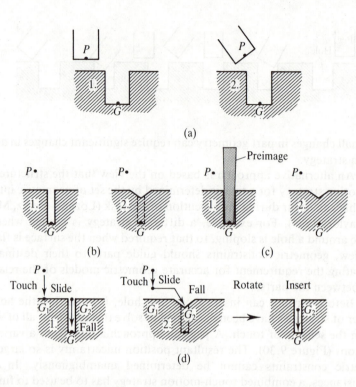

is inside the configuration space object. Thus, the transformation makes the constraints on motion explicit.

A pre-image is simply the range of positions of the peg from which it can reach the goal by a single motion. In configuration space, the pre-image is the area of free space defined by the vectors radiating out from the goal. This area is determined by task constraints, such as jambing, as well as geometric constraints. If the peg (point P) is not in this area, it cannot reach the goal in a single motion, as shown in the first example in Figure 9.31(c). If the goal is not in free space, as in the second example in Figure 9.31(c), the peg has to be rotated as well as translated. This example shows the effect of tilting the peg on the search. The point P is moved so that it falls toward the bottom of the **V** in the configuration space hole. When the point can proceed no further, the peg is rotated and falls in. If the point cannot reach the goal by a single motion, a subgoal within the pre-image has to be established, and a pre-image for that subgoal generated. This process is repeated until a sequence of pre-images connects the goal to the start position. For the first example in Figure 9.31, the point is moved towards the surface until it touches the surface, and then slid along the surface until it falls into the hole. In the second example, the same sequence is followed, except that, once the peg has found the hole, it must be rotated before it will fall in.

This strategy can be generalized for planning motions in any situation involving touch. When used with a biased search strategy, the initial motion

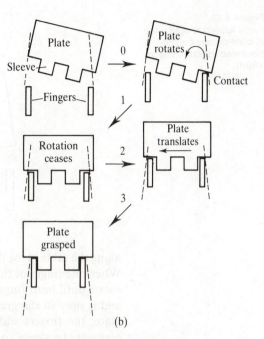

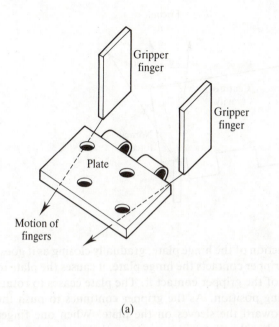

(a)

(b)

Figure 9.32
Using pushing to resolve
uncertainties while grasping
a hinge plate (Mason,
1986).
(a) The hinge is grasped by
moving the fingers toward
the hinge while slowly
closing them;
(b) Pushing the hinge causes
it to turn into the grasp.

from the bias position along the surface can be used to identify the type of surface and hence the geometric constraints. A significant advantage of this approach is that the effects of uncertainty are directly incorporated into the planning process, and not left to the sensing system to change the plan to handle errors during execution. The main problem with this approach, however, is that as yet there is no effective procedure for computing pre-images. Erdman (1986) presents a method for computing a simple class of pre-images, known as **back projections**: regions where the goal is reachable and recognizable with sensors. By reachable, he means that the point is guaranteed to reach the goal, because all points at which sticking might occur during sliding motion have been removed. These points are detected by comparing the motion vector to a friction cone model (Window 6.2).

9.3.4.2 *Pushing*

Many fine motion operations involve pushing. Mason (1986) is exploring the mechanics of pushing. Pushing can be observed in almost every mechanical assembly task, and can be used to resolve the uncertainty in the loction of objects before they are grasped. Unfortunately, the resultant motion of an object being pushed is partially indeterminate in many practical situations. This motion is determined by a complex balance between applied, reaction and friction forces.

The benefits that acrue from pushing are illustrated by the classic example of grasping a hinge plate shown in Figure 9.32. The gripper moves

Figure 9.33
Force applied to right edge
of plate causes counter
clockwise rotation (Mason,
1986).

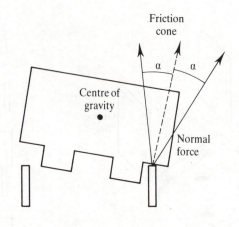

along the table in the direction of the hinge plate, gradually closing as it goes. When one finger of the gripper contacts the hinge plate, it causes the plate to rotate until both fingers of the gripper contact it. The plate ceases to rotate and is now in the grasping position. As the gripper continues to push the plate, the fingers slide toward the sleeves on the plate. When one finger contacts the sleeve, it pushes the plate sideways toward the second finger. When both fingers contact sleeves, the grasping operation is complete. During this process, the hinge plate has been located, and initial variations in the location have been eliminated without the use of sensors. Pushing relies on frictional forces to orient the object into the location required for grasping. However, the same forces can also cause an object to rotate out of the gripper.

When the first finger touches the plate, it applies a force to it (Figure 9.33) at the point of contact, and within the friction cone (Window 6.2). If the force is outside the friction cone, the finger will slide along the plate. The plate will rotate in a counter-clockwise direction if the friction cone is entirely to the right of the centre of gravity, as in Figure 9.33. To guarantee that pushing the plate results in a firm grasp, we also have to confirm that the finger cannot slip off the edge of the plate, and that rotation is complete before the fingers close. This analysis is based on the assumption that frictional forces dominate the inertial forces arising from accelerating the plate. Above a certain pushing velocity, inertia will dominate and the results may be completely different.

These pushing motions can be used to orient a wide range of objects. Many parts-orienting devices rely on pushing. For example, objects on a conveyor are pushed into an angled plate by the motion of the conveyor to align them. Mason's (1986) analysis of pushing answers the questions, 'Does the object rotate, and in what direction?'. To answer the more complex question, 'What is the motion of the object?' requires knowledge of the location and magnitude of the forces supporting the object.

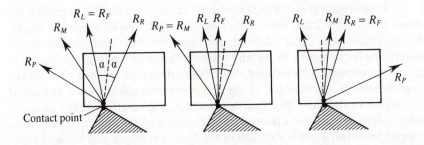

Figure 9.34
Finding the motion of the
object using rays. These
three cases cover all
possibilities (Mason, 1986).

The motion of the object being pushed can be described with a motion ray R_M (Figure 9.34). Ray R_F is the ray of force, and is parallel to the force applied to the object by the pushing contact. Both these rays dictate the sense of rotation, but they are often indeterminate. The three rays R_L, R_R and R_P vote on the direction of rotation. Rays R_R and R_L delimit the friction cone. Ray R_P is the ray of pushing, and is parallel to the pusher velocity. If two of these three rays pass to the left of the centre of mass, the object will rotate clockwise, – the centre of mass and centre of friction are assumed to coincide. If two rays pass to the right of the centre of mass, the object will rotate counter-clockwise. If one ray passes through the centre of mass with a ray on either side, the object may translate, but could also rotate in either direction.

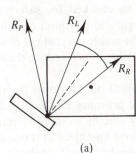

(a)

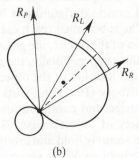

(b)

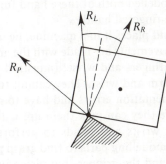

(c)

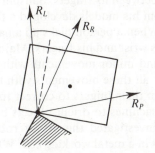

(d)

Figure 9.35
Typical pushing
configuration, all of which
produce clockwise rotation
(Mason, 1986).

Several examples of configurations that result in clockwise motion are shown in Figure 9.35. If the small rectangle in the first example is a finger, the rotation of the object depends on the orientation and motion of the finger. The friction cone varies with the orientation of the finger, whereas, in the other examples, it is independent of the orientation of the finger. In the second example, the rotation of the object depends solely on the motion of the finger. In the third and fourth examples, the rotation of the object is independent of both the orientation and motion of the finger. It may seem counter intuitive, but the rotation in the fourth example will be clockwise.

9.3.4.3 *Grasping*

Grasping involves all the problems of robotics in miniature. First, we select a gripper suitable to the task. Then, we specify locations where the gripper can grasp the object (known as grasp points). These can be specified by teaching, by analysis of models, and by analysis of sensor data. Finally, we plan the motion of the fingers so they grasp the object without colliding with other parts of the object.

Gripping surfaces are the surfaces on the gripper used for grasping, such as the inside and outside of fingers. The initial grasp configuration is the manipulator configuration at the point when the object is grasped, and the final grasp configuration is the manipulator configuration when the object is released. When planning the overall motion of the manipulator, the initial and final grasp configurations have to be checked for safety and reachability. The robot must reach each configuration without collision. During the motion of the object, the grasp must be stable, so that the object doesn't move in the gripper. Finally, the grasp motions must reduce the uncertainty in the initial location of the object.

Salisbury (1985) and Cutkosky (1985) have studied the problem of gripper design and configuration for the grasping and manipulation of a wide variety of object shapes. Salisbury sought to identify hand designs which can securely hold and arbitrarily move an object. It is one thing to get a robot to hold an object securely, it is another to get a robot to rotate the object between its fingers. Salisbury modelled both of these hand functions and from his models developed a three-fingered hand.

When a person picks up a part and places it in a machine, he uses his arm, his wrist and his fingers. Major movements are made with the arm and wrist, and minor movements with the fingers and wrist. Industrial robots attempt all these movements with the arm and wrist. They cannot turn the object in their fingers to correct for orientation errors and have to rely on other machines to orient objects before they can pick them up. Cutkosky (1985) investigated the use of robotic wrists and hands to perform fine motions in a metal working cell. When modelling parts to find grasp points, we not only have to consider the part and the gripper, but also any other object that the part interacts with. If the part is to be slotted into a

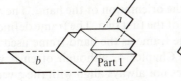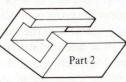

Figure 9.36
Grasp point selection. If part
1 is grasped at point a, the
gripper will collide with part
2, but if it is grasped at point
b, the robot will be able to
insert part 1 some of the
way into part 2.

subassembly, we have to make sure that the gripper can be withdrawn from the subassembly after releasing the part (Figure 9.36).

For two-fingered grippers, grasp points consist of two parallel surfaces that are not obstructed by other features of the part. Peskin and Sanderson (1986) developed an algorithm (convex rope algorithm) for finding grasp points from vertex models of parts. Jarvis (1988) applied the distance transform methodology to finding grasp points from visual images of parts. Mason (1985) extended the work on pushing, discussed in Section 9.3.4.2 to model grasping. Brost (1985) extended this work further to a method for automatic planning of grasping motions when the location of objects is uncertain. Brost models objects as polygons between the parallel jaws of a gripper. He analyses the motion of an object as the jaws close, and determines the range of final configurations of the object and the jaws that guarantee stable grasps. Finally, the grasping process has to be included in our kinematic model. When discussing the task at the beginning of this chapter, we stated that the object is grasped when the grasp point and the end effector frame coincide. This is a purely kinematic description, and does not include grasp forces or gripper opening.

The end effector frame is described with three vectors: *a*, *o* and *n* (Figure 9.37). The *a* (approach) vector is normal to the palm of the hand and is the direction in which the gripper will normally approach an object. The *o* (orientation) vector is the vector orthogonal to the gripping surfaces of a

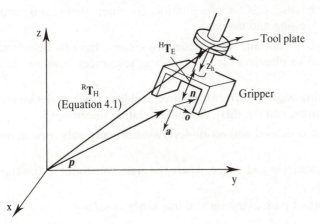

Figure 9.37
Kinematic description of grasping.

parallel-jaw gripper and defines the orientation of the hand. The *n* (normal) vector is simply the cross product of the first two. The frame defined by these vectors is not necessarily the same frame as the hand frame used in the $^R T_H$ description of a manipulator in Chapter 4, although often it will be. In practice, the approach vector does not always align with the *z* vector in the last frame of the kinematic model of the manipulator, and an end-effector transform is needed to complete the model. Also, this description of the end effector frame is designed for parallel jaw grippers, and may have to be redefined for multifinger grippers.

Key points

- One approach to planning is to decompose a robot system into the following levels: system, task, action, robot, joint and physical.

- At each level we use different planning tools, programming languages, and symbolic representations of the world.

- The most difficult problem is task planning is the handling of uncertainties and errors.

- Action-level planning involves decomposing a task into parallel sequences of actions to be executed by the robot and associated tools.

- Most action-level planners do not generate usable plans because they assume a perfect world.

- Much research is devoted to task modelling because we must understand the task before we can generate effective plans.

- A discrete-action model describes an assembly process with a precedence graph of discrete actions on components.

- Robot-level planning involves the decomposition of actions into sequences of robot motions.

- Robot-level planners rely heavily on accurate geometric models.

- Many solid modelling systems use CSG representation for user input and boundary representation for internal processing and display.

- Because the essence of robotics is motion, solid modelling systems have to be extended to provide additional information to planners such as features, tolerances, graph points, and motion constraints.

- In general, off-line programming systems suffer from three problems: lack of device independence, lack of interface standards, and the difficulty of simulating uncertainty.

- Languages for programming at task level and action level are normally only used in research laboratories.

- Gross motions are robot movements in free space, where the main constraint is that the robot does not collide with anything.

- Gross motion planning consists of path planning and trajectory planning.

- The best path planning algorithms for six-dimensional motion quantize configuration space to achieve efficiency.
- Four types of constraints have to be considered when planning a trajectory: task constraints, time constraints, mechanical constraints, and computation time constraints.
- Linear interpolated motion often achieves the best compromise between smooth trajectory following and computation time.
- Fine motions are robot movements that involve contact between the robot and the object it is manipulating.
- Fine-motion planning deals with strategies for safe manipulation in the presence of uncertainties during touching, pushing and grasping.
- The structure of a fine motion strategy is determined by the geometric interactions that occur during the execution of the task.
- Many objects can be moved into the correct orientation for grasping without the use of sensors by pushing them.

Exercises

■ *Essay questions*

9.1. Obtain several simple items from a hardware store, for example, a hinge, a window latch, a light switch, or a water tap. Disassemble these objects and develop an assembly plan using the discrete-action model techniques described in Section 9.2.2.1. Design a robotic cell to assemble one of these items.

9.2. For the example in Figure 9.3, plan the sequences of actions required for the robot to move the box into room $R1$.

9.3. Design assembly sequences, and strategies involving supports and balancing weights to build the blocks model in Figure 9.38.

9.4. Describe the assemblies in Figure 9.38 in terms of vertices, lines, planes and objects.

9.5. Obtain a part that has been formed in some way – machining, sawing, moulding, etching, forging, welding – and plan the sequence in which the forming operations must occur to avoid interaction.

9.6. Develop a constructive solid geometry model and a boundary model of the block assemblies in Figure 9.38.

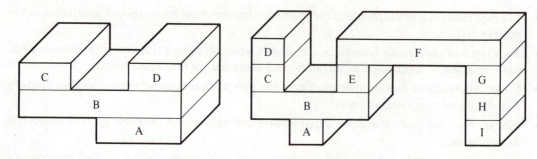

Figure 9.38
Assemblies of blocks.

9.7. Calculate the two-dimensional configuration space using slice projections (Algorithm 9.1) for the planar two-link manipulators in Figure 9.39. Having obtained the configuration space description, plan a path for the manipulator using two-dimensional slice projections, and distance transforms. Note, a link with a prismatic joint occupies volumes on both sides of the joint.

9.8. For each of the paths planned in Exercise 9.7, determine which type of joint control gives the 'best' trajectory.

■ *Practical questions*

9.1. Design a simple pick and place task, preferably involving a conveyor. Decompose the task into a sequence of actions, and then decompose the actions into a sequence of robot motions. Set up the equipment for the task in the laboratory and program the robot to execute the task. What is the effect of uncertainty on the execution of the task?

9.2. Define a path for the robot in the laboratory between two configurations. A suitable task is to draw a line on a table with a pen. Convert this path into a trajectory. Program the robot to follow this path using joint-by-joint motion, joint-interpolated motion, straight-line motion, and bounded straight-line motion using knot points. How well does the robot track the path? What happens to the joint variables? What is the effect of the limits on the velocity and acceleration on path tracking.

9.3. Use the robot to pick up objects of several different shapes by pushing them along a flat surface. What do you observe about the motion of these objects?

Elevation   Plan

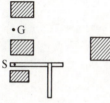

Start

Object

•Goal

(a)

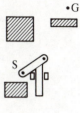

•G

S

(b)

•G

S

(c)

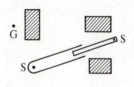

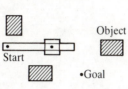

•G

S

S

(d)

•G

S

(e)

Figure 9.39
Two-link manipulator
configurations for path
planning task in Exercise 7.
(a) Type 3 two-link
manipulator;
(b) type 4 two-link
manipulator;
(c) type 5 two-link
manipulator;
(d) type 6 two-link
manipulator;
(e) type 7 two link
manipulator.

10 · *Sensors, Measurement and Perception*

'I will make justice the measuring line and righteousness the plumb line'

Isaiah 28:17.

Objectives

In this chapter, the first of three on the low-level issues, we describe the significant sensors used in robotics. Our objective is to understand the physical principles of sensing, the devices used to measure parameters, and the algorithms for interpreting sensor data. Robot sensing divides naturally into two categories: measuring the parameters internal to the robot, and perceiving the environment external to the robot. The reader is assumed to be familiar with analog and digital electronics at the level taught in service courses to nonelectronic-engineering students. Sensing includes the following topics:

- computer interfaces,
- fusion of data from several sensors,
- position, motion, and acceleration sensing,
- force and torque sensing,
- contact and touch sensing,
- proximity sensing,
- range finding,
- binary and grey-level vision.

545

Measurement of robot and environment parameters is fundamental to the successful application of robots. Today, most industrial robots are severely restricted by their lack of sensing capabilities. Many of these robots can only measure joint position, plus a few interlocks and timing signals. These robots are taught the exact location of the object to be manipulated by manually moving the end effector to that location and recording the joint angles. If, during operation, the object is not in that exact location, the whole process fails.

To ensure that parts are in the correct orientation requires either the use of parts-handling equipment or manual positioning of work pieces. However, the former is expensive and the latter can be very tedious. To free robots from these restrictions, researchers are developing an array of sensors; some general purpose and some application specific. Increasing the sensory capabilities of robots will increase their flexibility by reducing their dependence on parts-feeding machines and, hence, reduce the cost of production by eliminating these machines. Also, increasing the sensory capabilities of robots will increase productivity by saving time. Reprogramming a robot for a new or modified task takes time. Sensors make the task of locating components easier, and hence, save time. Time can also be saved by eliminating delays in the production process. Consider an application where the object the robot is manipulating is on a conveyor line, being spot welded for example. The addition of a sensor to detect the object and a sensor to measure the speed of the line will enable the robot to weld the object while it is moving. This will increase the productivity of the line because it no longer has to stop every time a weld is made.

In robotics, sensors are used for:

1. measuring robot parameters for control loops,
2. finding the location of objects,
3. correcting for errors in the robot's models of itself and of the world,
4. detecting and avoiding failure situations,
5. detecting and avoiding collisions,
6. monitoring interaction with the environment such as forces during compliant motion,
7. monitoring the environment for changes (such as temperature) that may affect the task,
8. inspecting the results of processes.

Sensory capability in each of these areas is essential for a robot to work in an unstructured environment, where it has to respond to changes in that environment.

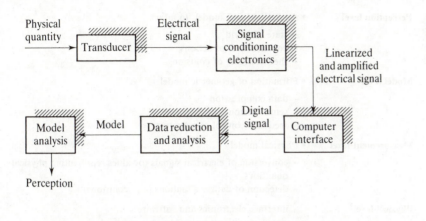

Figure 10.1
The sensing process (measurement and modelling).

10.1 Sensing hierarchy

In Chapter 1, robotics was defined as the intelligent connection of perception to action. That definition was then decomposed into a perception model of robotics to describe the information processing required to perceive the current state of the environment and respond to it (see Section 1.3). This perception model consists of five processes; measurement, modelling, perception, planning and action. To perceive is to understand the data we have about a problem. It includes measurement and modelling. In the measurement process, data is collected with sensors, and with this data the modelling process develops a model of the problem. In the perception process, the consequences of current and proposed actions are inferred from the model. Based on this information, the planning process plans the action of the robot and the action process executes the plan. Here, the measurement and modelling processes are examined.

A sensor (Figure 10.1) consists of a transducer and an electronic circuit. A transducer is a device that converts a physical or chemical quantity to an electrical signal. For example, a strain gauge converts the strain applied to a linkage to an electrical signal, a solar cell converts incident light energy to an electrical signal, and the motion of a toothed wheel past a magnetic pick-up produces a train of electrical pulses. The electrical signal may be a voltage, a current, a frequency, a train of pulses, or a phase shift. Usually, the signal from the transducer is small and has to be amplified before it can be used. Also, many transducers are nonlinear and the signal has to be linearized. For example, the signal from a thermocouple has to be linearized to obtain a voltage proportional to temperature.

The output from the signal conditioning electronics is an electrical signal (analogue, digital, frequency, or pulse) that is proportional to the quantity being measured. For a simple sensor, this signal may be a simple

Figure 10.2
The sensing hierarchy: measurement, modelling and perception.

Perception level	• Analysis of task model, to infer
	– state of world
	– consequences of actions
	– the possibility of collisions
Model level	• Formation of geometric model
	– data compression
	– sensor fusion
	– feedback control of actuators
Measurement level	• Physical model
	– conversion of electrical signals to values representing physical quantities
	– detection of danger situations (e.g. collisions)
Physical level	– interface electronics and software
	– signal conditioning electronics
	– transducers

value, for example a tachometer produces a voltage proportional to the speed of a rotating shaft. For a complex sensor, on the other hand, this signal may be a matrix of digital values such as a tactile array, or a time multiplexed sequence of analogue values such as a video signal.

The signal proportional to the sensed value is read into a computer through interface electronics for further processing. Sensing can be decomposed into a hierarchy (see Figure 9.1), with the sensor at the bottom or physical level of that hierarchy (Figure 10.2). Further up the hierarchy is the model level, where the sensed data is analysed, reduced, and combined with other data to form a model of the world. The top level is the perception level, where the model is analysed to infer the state of the world and the consequences of actions.

A common use of sensor data is in feedback control loops. For example, the loop controlling joint angles controls the actuators to move the joint to the desired angle by measuring the angle. More complex perception tasks, such as the interpretation of visual images, are currently a major topic of research.

10.2 Computer interfaces

To get the information from the sensor into a computer for analysis, we use a computer interface. The type of interface depends upon the characteristics of the signal. Once the interface type has been resolved, we must select an electronic circuit that will produce the required range, resolution, linearity and speed.

For digital signals, we are simply concerned with range and speed. The range is the number of bits in the signal, and the speed is the time it takes to

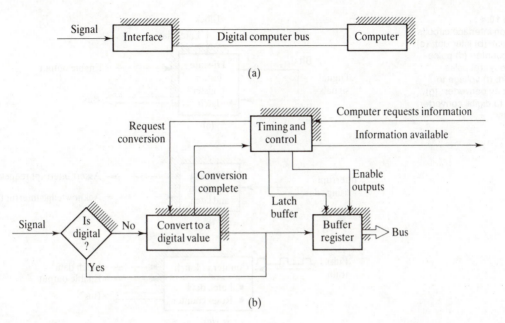

Figure 10.3
Sections of a computer interface: (a) connection to computer; (b) block diagram.

read the digital value. Usually, this is one processor read cycle. However, in industrial applications digital inputs may be latched into registers by a much slower clock to filter out electrical noise on the signals. Analog signals have to be converted to digital values before they can be stored in a computer. The range of the interface is the number of digital bits used to represent a full scale analog value. The resolution is the voltage (or current) per bit, and linearity is a measure of the relationship between the analog input value and the digital output value.

A typical interface circuit (Figure 10.3) consists of a timing and control section, a converter section, and a buffer register. The timing and control section monitors the address bus of the computer to determine when the interface is being read, and handles the bus handshake. Also, if conversion is required, it controls the timing of the conversion. The converter section maps the incoming signal into a digital value, and the buffer register stores the result.

The simplest interface is the interface for digitals signals. This often consists of a tristate buffer which is enabled on to the bus during the computer's read cycle (Figure 10.4(a)). An interrupt is a single-bit digital signal that requests immediate attention by the computer to some condition. The interrupt pulse sets a latch which asserts the interrupt request line. When the computer services the interrupt, the latch is reset pending another interrupt.

Digital signals can be levels as above, or pulse trains. We can count pulses, measure pulse frequency, measure pulse length, measure the time between successive pulses, and measure the phase relationship between

Figure 10.4
Common interface circuits.
(a) Digital; (b) interrupt; (c)
pulse counter; (d) pulse
frequency; (e) pulse
duration; (f) voltage to
frequency converter; (g)
analog to digital converter;
(h) phase.

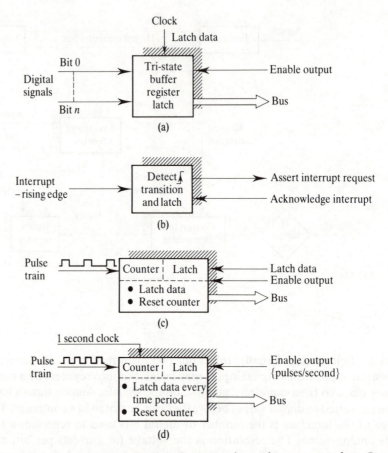

(a)

(b)

(c)

(d)

pulses in two pulse trains. A digital counter is used to count pulses. It rolls over to zero when it reaches the maximum. When the counter is read, it is reset to zero. To measure frequency, the counter is simply reset once per time period, after latching the count. To measure the duration of the pulse, clock ticks are counted while the pulse is high or low depending upon whether the mark or the space is to be measured. Given the clock frequency, the pulse time can be calculated from the count. The count must be latched at the end of the pulse, and the counter reset, ready to measure the next pulse.

Analog signals, both voltage and current, can be interfaced with a pulse frequency counter, by using a voltage-controlled oscillator to convert voltage into a train of pulses whose frequency is proportional to the voltage. If we are measuring current, we simply pass it through a precise resistor and use the voltage developed across the resistor as input. This type of analog input is usually used when the signal has to travel a long distance from sensor to interface. The pulse train is less susceptible to errors caused by earthing problems.

There are a number of methods for analog-to-digital conversion. Successive approximation (Figure 10.4(g)) is a common technique. As this

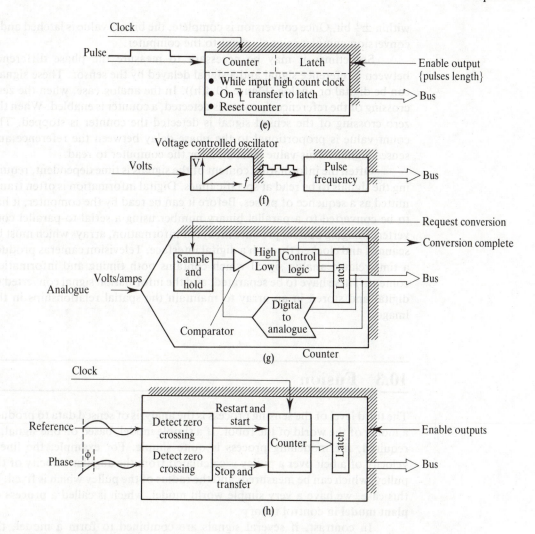

Figure 10.4
Cont.

method takes a finite amount of time, the computer must request a conversion and wait for it to complete, or respond to a completion interrupt. When the computer requests conversion, the analog input is sampled and stored, usually in a capacitor. The output of the converter (digital) is converted to analog and compared to the sampled input in a comparitor. The output of the comparitor indicates if the current digital value is high or low.

The control logic uses a sucessive approximation technique similar to binary search to set the bits in the output register. First, the most significant bit is set. The comparitor output indicates if this is high or low. If it is high, the most significant bit is reset and the next most significant bit is set. If it is low, the most significant bit is left set and the next most significant bit is set. This process continues on successive bits until the least significant bit is reached. At this point, the binary value is proportional to the analog input within $\pm \frac{1}{2}$ bit. Once conversion is complete, the binary value is latched and a conversion complete signal is sent to the computer.

Sometimes it may be necessary to measure the phase difference between a reference signal and a signal delayed by the sensor. These signals can be digital or analog (Figure 10.4(h)). In the analog case, when the zero crossing of the reference sinewave is detected, a counter is enabled. When the zero crossing of the sensed signal is detected the counter is stopped. The count value is proportional to the phase delay between the reference and sensed signals. This value is latched for the computer to read.

Often the information content of the signals is time dependent, requiring the signals to be read at specific times. Digital information is often transmitted as a sequence of pulses. Before it can be read by the computer, it has to be converted to a parallel binary number using a serial-to-parallel converter. Imaging devices produce arrays of information, arrays which must be scanned and clocked through a digital interface. Television cameras produce a time-related analog signal which contains both timing and information content. These have to be separated, and the information signal converted to digital and stored in an array to maintain the spatial relationships in the image.

10.3 Fusion

The third level of the sensing process is the analysis of sensed data to produce a model of the world of the robot. If a simple model, based on one signal, is required, the modelling process is quite simple. For example, the linear velocity of a belt over a pulley is calculated from the angular velocity of the pulley, which can be measured, and the radius of the pulley which is fixed. In this case, we have a very simple world model, which is called a **process** or **plant model** in control theory.

In contrast, if several signals are combined to form a model, the modelling process can be quite complex. A major task for the systems engineer is to develop these process models. These models usually consist of a set of differential equations. For example, the model used for sensor fusion in the pick-and-place task in Section 1.3 (Equation 1.1). In robotics, the models are even more complex, for example, a map of all the objects in the workspace of a manipulator. Also, data structures for storing these models can be complex. Criteria for designing these data structures are an important research topic.

Combining signals from several sensors to form a world model is known as **sensor fusion**. Fusing data from multiple sensors into a robust, consistent model is fraught with difficulty. First, the sensors measure different features of the environment. For example, visual, range and thermal images of the same environment measure different physical parameters: light reflection, distance, and thermal radiation. Consequently, different features will dominate in each image, making image alignment difficult. With vision, it is often difficult to align successive images from the same camera, because motion of the camera changes the relative spacing of features in a two-dimensional image. Second, the sensors are often located in different physical locations. Before their data can be fused, it has to be transformed to a single reference frame. This task is complicated by the field of view (width and height) and the depth of field (range of distances in focus) of each sensor. Consequently, the images not only have to be translated and rotated, they also have to be scaled and their perspective changed. In addition, when these transformed images are merged, true fusion occurs only in the regions of overlap. Third, the sensors may have a different time base. That is some sensors will update their images more quickly than others. If all objects are stationary during the period of time required for all sensors to update their images, differences in time bases are irrelevant, but if objects are moving, or if the robot is moving, the sensor data has to be transformed to a single time base. Fourth, noise and incompleteness of sensor data further complicates the process. If one image has ten times the resolution of another, how do you sensibly combine them?

Research into these problems is focusing on two areas. One area is the design of a range of sensors with the same resolution, time base, field of view, and depth of field. This will reduce the problems, but the perspective problem which arises from different physical location of the sensors remains. The second area is the development of transforms which map each sensor into a similar field of view, and then at specific time instants combine the images. This is like overlaying several drawings on a blackboard.

10.4 Classification

The range of sensors is so large that they are usually classified according to a desirable characteristic. Which characteristic is desirable differs from one field of technology to another. The user of a sensor is normally interested in the function it performs. That is, what does it measure, and to what resolution and accuracy? The designer of a sensor may be more interested in the technology it uses, for example, piezo-electric, magnetic, silicon and fibre optic.

Common sensor classifications include:

- the physical or chemical quantity the sensor is to measure such as, velocity, viscosity, colour;
- the physical principle the sensor is based on such as, magnetostriction, memory metal, Hall effect;
- the technology that is used such as silicon, electro-mechanical, fibre optic;

- the type of energy involved such as electrical, mechanical, solar,
- the spatial relationship between the sensor and the object it is sensing such as, contact, non-contact, remote.

In recent years, people have attempted to develop 'smart' sensors – sensors that include a lot of electronic processing at the sensing element. Often the sensing element and a processing unit are integrated into a silicon chip. For example, the integration of computing circuitry with silicon based gas sensors enables these sensors to correct for temperature changes, as well as to perform linearization and statistical analysis.

In robotics, sensors are classified into two groups: internal and external. Internal sensors are used to measure robot parameters relative to the reference frame of the robot such as joint angle, linkage deflection, and grip force. External sensors are used to measure the environment and the position of the robot relative to the environment.

10.5 Internal sensors

To model and control a robot, position, motion, force and mass must be measured. All of these are measured relative to coordinate frames attached to the robot; frames which are located relative to a reference frame. Kinematic modelling and control requires the measurement of position and motion. Static modelling and control requires the measurement of force and of the mass of the object grasped by the end effector.

The mass and dimensions of the linkages, which are fixed parameters, are measured manually and entered into the robot model as constants. Parameters which affect the gain of control loops are either ignored by using overdamped loops or, in some research robots, adapted for. These include temperature, gear-box backlash, joint friction and transmission springiness. The mass of the object grasped by the end effector is obtained from a database, measured with a set of scales, or calculated form force errors.

10.5.1 Position and motion

As we have modelled robots in both joint and Cartesian space, we require measurements of position, velocity and acceleration in both spaces. Normally, position and motion parameters are measured in joint space and a kinematic model is used to calculate Cartesian space parameters.

10.5.1.1 *Cartesian space*

Some researchers have attempted to directly measure the position and orientation of the end effector in Cartesian space. Cartesian space measurements

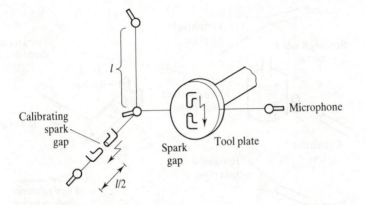

Figure 10.5
Measuring the location of an end effector with a spark gap.

eliminate the effect of errors in the kinematic model due to joint misalignment and the dynamic flexing of links under load.

In kinematic signature analysis the location of the end effector must be measured accurately. One way to do this is to mount a spark gap on the tool plate (Stone, 1987). The spark is generated by an electronic pulse and is recorded with microphones. The microphones are placed in a known fixed relationship to each other (Figure 10.5). The times from spark generation to spark recording at each microphone are measured. Also, the speed of sound, in the current environment, is measured using a spark gap located at a fixed position relative to the microphones. Using the times of flight from the spark gap to the microphones and the speed of sound, the distances from the spark gap to the microphones are calculated. Next, a sphere is constructed at each microphone, with centre at the microphone and radius equal to the distance from the microphone to the spark gap. The spark gap is located at the intersection of these spheres. Finally, the Cartesian space values of this intersection are calculated, and compared to the kinematic model. Errors in the model due to misalignment of individual joints and linkages can be measured by placing the spark gap on each linkage, and measuring its position over a range of joint angles.

An alternative method for measuring end effector location has been developed by MacFarlane and Donath (1984). They use a scanning laser to track the end effector of a robot as it moves. An experimental system can track motion of up to 1 metre/second with a resolution better than 1 in 2 000. A moving light curtain is produced using a cylindrical lens to focus the laser beam into a plane and a rotating mirror to sweep the beam through the volume of interest (Figure 10.6). As the beam sweeps, it is detected with photo diodes. Some diodes are mounted in fixed locations to provide reference values and others are mounted on the linkages of the robot. The diodes are mounted to minimize occlusion by other linkages. Situations where occlusion can occur can be eliminated either by placing additional diodes on the links or by using additional lasers. As the sweep velocity of the light plane is fixed (a function of the angular velocity of the mirror), the time

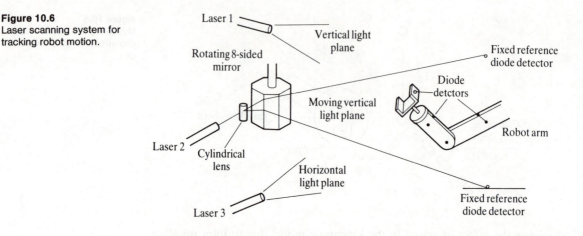

Figure 10.6
Laser scanning system for tracking robot motion.

between when the beam is detected by a reference diode and when it is detected by a diode on a linkage is proportional to the distance between the two diodes, in the swept direction. By sweeping several lasers through the volume, in different directions, at different times (that is, out of phase), several measurements of distance are obtained. From these measurements, and the known fixed relationship between the reference diodes, the system calculates the Cartesian location of a diode on a linkage. Once the locations of three diodes on a linkage are known, the system determines the orientation of that linkage. These measures of the position and orientation of the linkages can be used in feedback control of the robot.

10.5.1.2 *Joint space*

In joint space, we have two types of joints: revolute and prismatic, and hence two types of motion: rotary and linear. To measure rotary motion we use rotary potentiometers, tachometers, pulse generators, shaft encoders, and synchro resolvers. To measure linear motion, we use linear potentiometers, linear variable differential transformers and linear optical grids. Other, more sophisticated methods exist such as detecting the torsion in a wire when a current pulse passes a magnet (Section 2.5), but these are used less often.

A **potentiometer** is a resistance element with a voltage across it and a sliding contact (Figure 10.5), known as a wiper. The resistance element can be a coil of nichrome wire, a carbon rod or a resistive plastic. In the case of a linear potentiometer, the element is straight but in the case of a rotary potentiometer, it is circular in a single turn potentiometer and a circular spiral in a multi-turn potentiometer. For most industrial applications, the resistance of the element is linear. The wiper is physically connected to the joint whose motion is to be measured, such that, when the joint moves, the wiper moves proportionally. The voltage on the wiper is determined by its

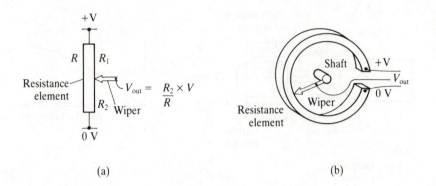

Figure 10.7
Potentiometer.
(a) Linear;
(b) rotary.

position on the resistance element and is thus proportional to the position of the joint. During sensing, this voltage has to be converted to millimeters for linear position and angle for rotary position.

Potentiometers measure position to an accuracy of approximately ± 0.5 per cent, which is typical for analog signals. For accurate measurement, the voltage source must be stable. During installation, the potentiometer must be zeroed, usually by recording the voltage at a known point and subtracting that value from the input, and the scale must be determined, usually by measuring the voltage at the zero and maximum positions.

We can calculate velocity by differentiating the potentiometer voltage, but the resulting signal may be noisy. Differentiation accentuates any electrical noise on the original signal. Noise is rapid variations in the value for a very short period (often called spikes), where stability is the lack of slow variations over longer periods (often called drift). The angular velocity of a direct current electric motor can be calculated from measurements of the armature voltage and current (Equations 2.1 and 2.2). This calculation is subject to changes in frictional loading on the motor, and the motor parameters must be measured.

Angular velocity is usually measured using a direct current (d.c.) **tachogenerator** (Figure 2.47). A tachogenerator is a d.c. motor in reverse: it converts rotational energy to electrical energy. The tachometer shaft is coupled to the rotating shaft (motor or gear-box) whose angular velocity we wish to measure. A tacho consists of a wire-wound armature which rotates inside a magnetic field generated by permanent magnets fixed in the stator (Figure 10.8). When a wire moves in a magnetic field, an electromotive force (voltage) is generated. The magnitude of the voltage generated by a tachogenerator is proportional to the speed of rotation of the armature (Equation 2.2), and its polarity is dependent on the direction of rotation.

The output d.c. voltage has two signals superimposed on it: a modulation at shaft rotation frequency and a high frequency ripple. The modulation is due to slight eccentricity of the armature, and is usually small. The ripple is caused by slot and commutation effects, and can be filtered out. The armature consists of a set of wire coils, connected to segments in the commutator

Figure 10.8
Tachogenerator used to measure angular velocity.
(a) Tachogenerator;
(b) output voltage as a function of velocity;
(c) ripple on output voltage.

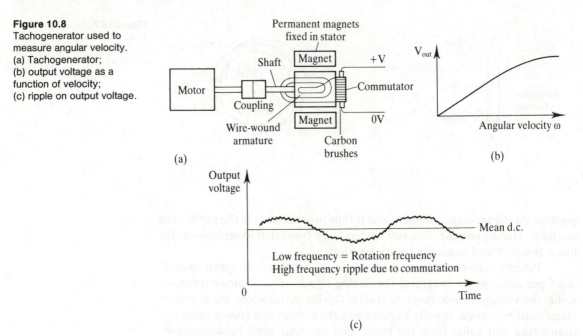

(see Figure 2.48). These segments are connected to the output through carbon brushes. As the armature rotates, the coil connected to the output is changed to maintain a d.c. voltage at the output terminals. Switching from one coil to the next is called commutation and is responsible for the ripple. The output voltage is a function of the angular velocity of the shaft and the strength of the magnetic field. When a tachogenerator is dismantled, the magnetic field can decay, changing the relationship between output voltage and angular velocity. To avoid this, pieces of steel, called keepers, are placed over the magnets when the armature is not present. A typical tachogenerator produces 5 volts per 1000 rpm, with a linearity of 1 per cent and a root mean squared ripple voltage of 5 per cent of the mean d.c. level. Like potentiometers, tachogenerators usually have an accuracy of ±0.5 per cent.

In many industrial applications, particularly robotics, greater accuracy, repeatability and resolution are required. Pulse generators and synchro resolvers are used to achieve these characteristics. A **pulse generator** produces an electrical pulse every time a shaft turns through a fixed angle or a slide moves a fixed distance. Pulse generators can be used to measure distance (or angle of rotation) by counting pulses and for measuring velocity (or angular velocity) by measuring the frequency of the pulse train. As the principles of linear and rotary pulse generators are the same, only rotary pulse generators (Figure 10.9) will be discussed here.

A pulse generator consists of a light beam, a light detector, and a rotating disc with a radial grating on its surface. The grating consists of black lines separated by clear spaces. The width of the lines and spaces is the same, ensuring the resultant pulse train has a one-to-one mark-space ratio. As the disc rotates, the beam is either cut by a line or allowed to pass through by a clear space. The beam is detected with a silicon solar cell, which produces a current proportional to the amount of incident light. As the disc rotates, the light beam is alternately cut and allowed to pass through by the grating. The frequency of the modulation of the light falling on the detector is proportional to the rotational speed of the shaft and the number of lines in the grating. The output of the detector is a sine wave: electronic circuits are used to shape this signal into a square wave.

The size of the lamp producing the beam determines the width of the beam and places a minimum limit on the width of the lines. For a line to cut the beam, it must be as wide as the beam. To overcome this limit, and hence, increase the number of pulses per revolution, a fixed index grating is placed in the path of the beam. When the two gratings align, the beam can pass through; when they are 180° out of phase the beam is cut.

From a train of pulses, the magnitude of the angular velocity can be measured but not the direction. To measure the direction, a second grating is placed on the index, and a second detector is used to detect the beam which passes through this grating. This second index grating is 90° out of phase with the first index grating and hence, two pulse trains, which are 90° out of phase, are produced by the pulse generator. The direction of rotation is determined by which pulse comes first.

The resolution of a pulse generator is proportional to the number of lines in the radial grating on the disc. For a 1° resolution, 360 lines are required. Low-cost pulse generators typically have 300 to 2 000 lines in the grating. Very precise, and very expensive, pulse generators have up to 36 000 lines on the grating, or a resolution of 0.01°.

The resolution of a pulse generator can be increased mechanically and electronically. Mechanically, a gear box is used to step up the angular velocity of the shaft to be measured to a higher angular velocity on the shaft to which the pulse generator is attached. A step-up gear ratio of 1:10 will increase the resolution by a factor of 10. Using a gearbox works only when the angle resolved by one line is greater than the error due to backlash.

Two electronic techniques are used to increase the resolution: evaluation and interpolation. Evaluation is the simpler of the two, and involves detecting the edges (rising and falling) of the two pulse trains (Figure 10.9). During one cycle, there are four edges. At each edge, a pulse a generated, with pulse width equal to half the distance between edges, to form a new pulse train. The frequency of this pulse train is four times that of the original train. Interpolation is carried out by measuring the length of the previous cycle and generating an integral number of cycles (n) to fit in that period to replace the next cycle. At the end of each cycle, the interpolation pulses are synchronized with the incoming signal to correct for changes in the frequency of the incoming signal. For example, in five-fold interpolation, each incoming cycle is replaced by five cycles of one fifth the length of the incom-

Figure 10.9
Heidenhain rotary pulse generator.

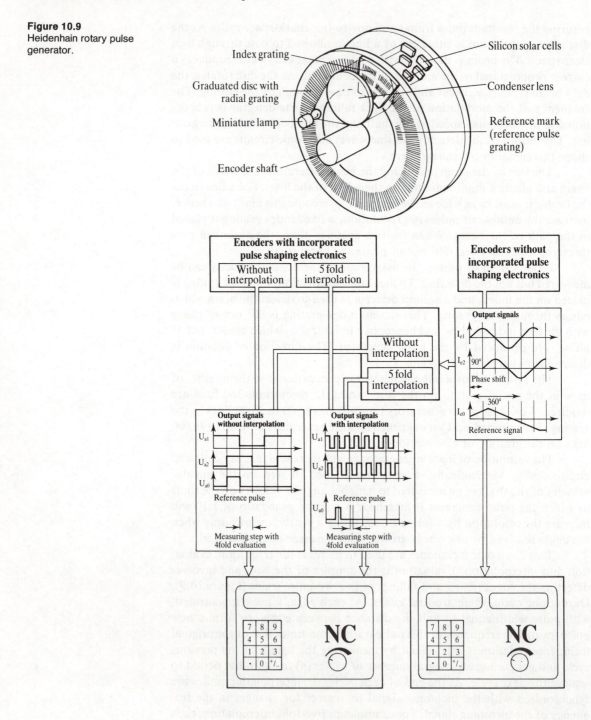

-ing cycle is replaced by five cycles of one fifth the length of the incoming cycle. A 36 000 lines pulse generator with 25 times interpolation followed by 4 times evaluation has a resolution of 0.0001°, or 3 600 000 pulses per revolution. To achieve this resolution, the shaft must be directly coupled to the shaft of interest as gear box backlash is much greater than 0.0001°.

The Heidenhain pulse generator shown in Figure 10.9 also includes a reference grating on the disc. This grating is used to identify the zero degree position of the pulse generator. This pulse generator is called in incremental encoder as the count of pulses gives a relative measure. To obtain an absolute measure of angle, the shaft has to be moved to a reference position, and the pulse counters set at zero. In addition to counting pulses, the electronic circuit should count the number of turns of the shaft.

Some encoders produce an absolute output by having several radial gratings on the disc, with lines of different widths. The grating closest of the centre has only one line with length equal to 180°. Each successive grating towards the periphery has twice the number of lines. By combining the outputs from the detectors for each grating, a binary value proportional to the absolute angle of the shaft is obtained. Some absolute encoders use grey-scale encoding on the gratings to minimize measurement errors. The resolution of these encoders is low compared to that of incremental encoders. Also, if more than one revolution of the shaft is involved, electronic circuitry must be included to count the number of turns of the shaft, and this counter has to be initialized to a reference position on power up.

Velocity can be measured with incremental encoders in three ways: frequency to voltage conversion, pulse frequency measurement, and pulse duration measurement. A frequency-to-voltage converter produces an analogue voltage proportional to the incoming frequency. Normally, velocity is measured by counting the number of pulses during fixed units of time. For rapid angular velocities, the pulse frequency is high and precise, accurate measurements can be made. As the angular velocity decreases, the number of pulses during a unit of time decreases. For very low velocities, the duration of individual pulses in measured and the velocity calculated from that.

For highly accurate measurement of angular position, we can also use a **synchro**. A synchro produces a precise sine wave with a cycle length exactly equal to one shaft revolution making it, in effect, a synchronous motor in reverse (Figure 10.10). Synchros are used in direct-drive arms (see Figure 2.53), where high resolution is required because the shaft turns less than 360°. The rotor of the synchro is excited with an alternating current (a.c.), with frequency in the range of 400 Hz to 10 kHz, via slip rings. The stator consists of three coils, placed at an angle of 120° to each other, connected in star or delta (Figure 10.11). The three-wire output of the synchro is connected to a T transformer, in the synchro-to-digital converter. Two voltages are obtained from this transformer: one proportional to the sine of the angle of the rotor (θ), and one proportional to the cosine of the angle of the rotor. By using the ratio of the sine and cosine values in the conversion process, the

Figure 10.10
Direct drive motor in CMU
direct drive arm II with a
pancake synchro sitting on
top of it.

Figure 10.11
Functional diagram of an
analog device's synchro to
binary converter.

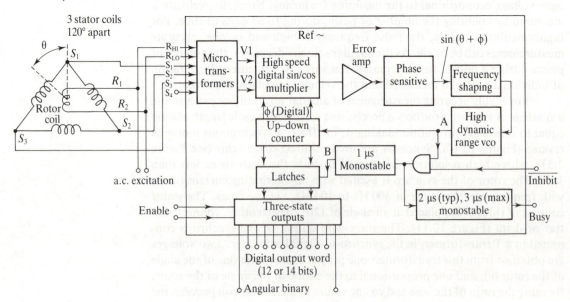

Digital output word
(12 or 14 bits)
Angular binary

measurement is insensitive to variations in the magnitude and frequency of the reference voltage. The output of the converter is in angular binary, where the most significant bit represents 180°, the next represents 90°, etc. A 16-bit converter has a resolution of 0.00549 degrees. The converter continuously tracks the a.c. input and a conversion typically takes 1 to 3 microseconds.

A practical advantage of synchros is that a.c. signals can be transmitted over long distances to remote electronic cabinets in the presence of noise. A second advantage is that they have fixed a zero point. However, multiple revolutions have to be counted with external electronics. Velocity can be calculated by differentiating the position signal.

Linear displacement and rotary displacement within ±40° can be measured with **variable differential transformers**. A linear variable differential transformer (LVDT) (Figure 10.12) consists of a magnetic core which moves inside three cylindrical coils. The central or primary coil is energized with an alterating current. The secondary coils are wound in opposite directions so their output voltages are opposite in polarity. When the coils are connected in series, the output voltage is the difference between the two secondary voltages. The rod-shaped iron core provides a path for magnetic flux to link the primary and secondary coils. When the rod is at the centre null position, the flux linking the secondary coils is equal and the differential output voltage is zero. As the core moves away from the centre, the core overlaps one secondary coil more than the other, increasing the flux linkage to one coil and decreasing it to the other. The induced voltage in the coil in the direction of motion increases, while the induced voltage in the other coil decreases.

The output differential voltage is proportional to the distance the core moves, and, over the nominal range, has a linearity of 0.25 per cent of full range. At 150 per cent of the nominal range, the linearity decreases to 0.5 per cent. LVDTs are available from Schaevitz with nominal ranges of ±1.25 mm to ±250 mm. The phase of the output voltage changes abruptly by 180° as the core moves past the null position. The sensitivity of an LVDT is rated in millivolts our per input volt per millimetre, and ranges from 250 for an LVDT with ±1.25 mm nominal range down to 3 for an LVDT with a ±250 mm nominal range. The nominal input voltage is 3V RMS. While the resolution of an LVDT is fixed, the absolute accuracy is a function of the stability of the input voltage. If a stable a.c. supply is not available, then a d.c. LVDT, which generates its own a.c. supply and includes an output amplifier, can be used.

A rotary differential transformer works on the same principle, except the output varies linearly with shaft rotation. A specially shaped ferromagnetic rotor simulates the linear displacement of the straight cylindrical core of the LVDT.

Schaevitz also manufacture **linear velocity transducers** (LVTs). An LVT consists of a rod-shaped permanent magnetic core which slides inside a cylinder containing two coils (Figure 10.13). No primary coil is needed as the

Figure 10.12
Schaevitz linear variable
differential transformer
(LVDT).
(a) Cutaway view;
(b) electrical connection;
(c) voltage output as a
function of core position.

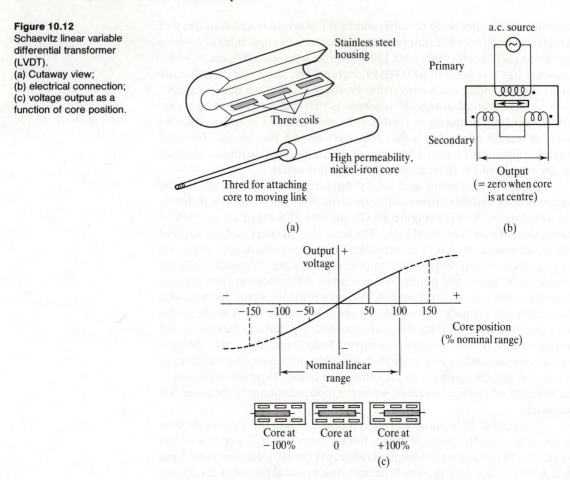

magnet provides the flux. By Faraday's law of induction, a voltage proportional to the rate of change of magnetic flux is developed in each coil as the end of the magnet moves through it. Because the flux of the permanent magnet is constant, the rate of flux change in each coil is linearly proportional to the velocity of the core. As the polarity of the magnetic field is different at each end of the core (north at one end south at the other), the voltages in the two coils are equal and opposite. To alleviate this problem, the coils are wound in opposite directions, so the voltages have the same polarity. The coils are connected in series and the output is the sum of the two voltages. As the core moves, deviations in the output voltage occur because of variations in the winding of the coils. This deviation in output at a constant velocity is known as LVT linearity, and, for quality LVTs, is ±1 per cent of output. An LVT with a nominal linear operating range of 100 mm has a typical sensitivity of 18 millivolts d.c. per millimetre per second.

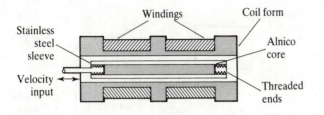

Figure 10.13
Simplified cross-section of a
Schaevitz LVT.

10.5.2 Limits and references

Many position sensors are relative sensors. When they are powered up they have to be moved to a reference position and initialized before they can be used for absolute measurement. Also, there are limits to the motion of most joints. The approach of a joint to a limit has to be detected so that the motion of the joint can be halted before the robot damages itself. On power up, a robot moves to its reference position and initializes all its joint position values. The reference position is detected either with a limit switch or with a low-resolution absolute position sensor. Some robots include a second sensor on each joint, such as a single turn potentiometer attached to the shaft of a rotary joint.

Detecting joint limits can be done in three ways. Once the joint sensors are initialized, they can be used to measure joint position and detect limits. The secondary sensors can be used in the same way in case of a fault in the primary sensor. Thirdly, physical limit switches can be mounted at the extremities of travel as a final level of protection.

10.5.3 Acceleration

We can calculate acceleration by differentiating velocity, although the resulting signal may be noisy. Sensors for measuring acceleration exploit Newton's second law (Window 6.1) to measure acceleration by measuring the force required to produce the acceleration of a known mass. In this section, we look at an angular servo accelerometer and a linear piezo-resistive accelerometer.

A **servo accelerometer** (Figure 10.14) is a closed-loop torque balance system, where a pendulous mass develops a torque proportional to the product of its mass unbalance and the applied acceleration. The motion of the mass is detected with a position sensor. This position signal is compared to a fixed reference by a servo amplifier, which drives a torque motor to balance the torque due to acceleration. The applied torque stops the motion of the mass at a position proportional to the acceleration. Thus, the current through the torque motor is proportional to the error in the position of the

Figure 10.14
Block diagram of Schaevitz
angular accelerometer.

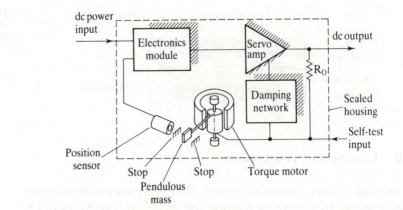

mass and, hence, the acceleration applied to the mass. This current produces
a voltage across the output resistor (R_0) proportional to the acceleration. The
sensor can be tested by injecting a current into the torque motor through the
self-test input. Also, the operating characteristics of the accelerometer can be
changed by adjusting the parameters of the servo amplifier and related electronic networks. In a typical sensor, the electronics are placed in a sealed
enclosure with the torque motor. Jewel pivots are used to minimize friction.
Accelerometers are available with a range ±200 through to ±1500
radians/second². They have a linearity of ±0.05 per cent of full scale, a
resolution of 0.0005 per cent of full scale, and a hysteresis of 0.02 per cent of
full scale.

A **piezo-resistive accelerometer** is constructed by placing strain gauges
on a cantilevered beam (Figure 10.15). When acceleration is applied to the
sensor, inertial forces cause the beam to bend. This deflection sets up strain
forces in the beam, forces that are measured with strain gauges. Two gauges
are attached to the beam; one to measure tension and one to measure compression. The gauges are placed across a slit in the beam. The outboard end
of the beam forms a rigid mass, and the narrow slit forms a flexing member.
Hence, the bending motion is concentrated in the slit, with the strain forces
across the slit. These strain gauges form two arms of a Wheatstone bridge

Figure 10.15
Piezo-resistive strain gauges
used in linear accelerometer
from Endevco.
(a) Accelerometer design
using cantilever beam with
overload stops;
(b) semiconductor strain
gauge with large mounting
pads and narrow active
neck.

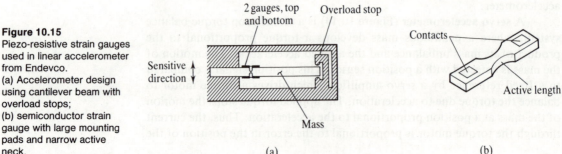

(a)   (b)

circuit. As the transducer is accelerated, one gauge is under tension and the other under compression, causing an imbalance in the bridge. This imbalance causes an output voltage proportional to the acceleration. Piezo-resistive accelerometers have the advantages of small size, low output impedance, zero phase shift, and wide frequency response – 0.1 Hz to 5000 Hz. They are available with ranges from 10 g to 50 kg. The accelerometer in Figure 10.15 measures acceleration in one direction only. Triaxial models are also available. Stops are used to protect the cantilevered mass from damage if it is dropped and the natural resonance frequence is excited.

10.5.4   Force and torque

Force sensors fall into both sensor categories: internal and external, depending upon the application. Wrist-mounted force sensors are usually used to measure the external forces and torques applied to the end effector as it interacts with the environment – hence they are usually classified as external sensors. In contrast, joint torques are sensed with internal sensors. Rather than artificially divide force and torque sensing, both internal and external sensing will be covered here.

There are two common methods of sensing force: deflection of an elastic element, and resistance change of an elastic element or spring which deflects, expands or contracts linearly when a force is applied to it. This deflection can be measured with an LVDT.

10.5.4.1   *Strain gauges*

Most force sensors found in robots use strain gauges as the basic sensing element. When a force is applied to a body, the body deforms. **Strain** is the deformation per unit length, and is measured in millimeters/millimetre.

$$\epsilon = \frac{\Delta l}{l} = \text{Strain} \tag{10.1}$$

For most metals, the strains we measure are less than 0.005 mm/mm. Since practical strain values are so small, they are often expressed in *micro-strain* ($\mu\epsilon = \epsilon \times 10^{-6}$). Because strain is a fractional change in length, it is directly measurable. Strain is measured with a **bonded resistance strain gauge**. The resistance element can be a semiconductor section (Figure 10.15(b)) or a metallic foil (Figure 10.16). Two factors are important in strain gauge design. First, the sensitivity of the gauge increases as the active gauge area decreases. Second, the area of the gauge bonded to the force-producing structure must be maximized to produce an inelastic bond. Hence, the dumbell shape of the semiconductor gauge in Figure 10.15(b). The choice of bonding adhesive is important because of the requirement of matching thermal coefficients of expansion. Semiconductor gauges have a strain limit

Figure 10.16
Standard patterns for metal
foil strain gauges.
(a) Linear;
(b) rosette;
(c) torque;
(d) diaphragm.

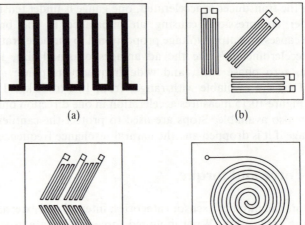

(a)

(b)

(c)

(d)

around 3000 $\mu\epsilon$. Metal foil strain gauges consist of a grid of thin metallic
film bonded to a thin insulating backing called a carrier matrix (Figure
10.17). Gauge resistances vary from 30Ω to 3kΩ, with 120Ω and 350Ω being
the most common; lengths vary from 3 μm to 100 mm.

Strain gauge elements are chosen so that the resistance change is linear
over the operating force range. Also, we try to match the thermal coefficient
of the gauge to the thermal coefficient of the force-producing structure to
eliminate temperature-induced strain. Unfortunately, the element's resistance also changes with temperature, often nonlinearly. This nonlinearity
has to be corrected either by mounting the resistors in the other arms of the
bridge in the same environment and making them from the same material, or
by linearizing the signal in software.

To convert the change in resistance due to strain to a voltage proportional to strain a Wheatstone bridge circuit is used (Figure 10.18). This

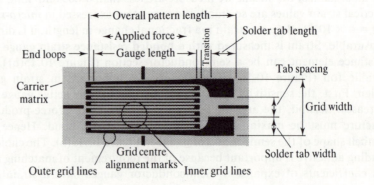

Figure 10.17
Typical metal-foil-bonded
strain gauge.

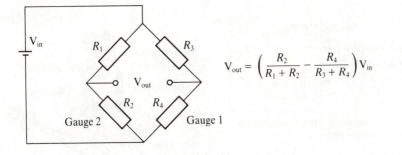

Figure 10.18
Wheatstone bridge circuit.

$$V_{out} = \left(\frac{R_2}{R_1 + R_2} - \frac{R_4}{R_3 + R_4} \right) V_{in}$$

bridge is extremely sensitive to resistance changes, and works as a resistive divider. In the piezo-resistive accelerometer, one gauge is in tension and increases in resistance, while the other is under compression and decreases in resistance, effectively doubling the sensitivity. As the two gauges are mounted together, they experience the same temperature changes. Wiring the bridge as shown effectively cancels out changes due to temperature variations.

10.5.4.2 *Shaft torque*

We can calculate the torque on the shaft of a d.c. motor from the armature current and the torque on the shaft of a hydraulic motor from the back pressure. These calculations are subject to errors which change over time, for example, varying frictional load as bearing grease hardens.

Shaft torque is measured with a strain gauge bridge (Figure 10.19) mounted on a shaft with a specially designed cross-section. The hollow cruciform section has high torsional sensitivity with good bending strength in comparison to a circular shaft. The bars in the hollow cruciform are subjected to a combination of torsion and bending when twisted, hence the hollow cruciform is only used for low capacity transducers (Lebow, 1979). For high-capacity transducers, a square shaft is used because of its increased bending strength.

The torque transducer is inserted in the shaft between the motor and the load. The type of coupling is very important. If rapid changes in torque are to be measured, they must be transferred to the shaft of the torque sensor without damping or deformation. The coupling should be installed so that no radial forces, other than coupling weight, are applied to the sensor. The force applied to the measurement shaft causes it to deform in a predictable way. The deformation causes the resistance of the strain gauges to changes in proportion to the torsional load. The strain gauges are physically placed to cancel out non-torsional forces and cross coupling between gauges, and are electrically connected in a Wheatstone bridge to compensate for temperature

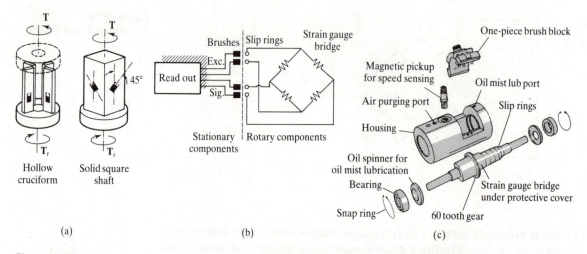

Figure 10.19
Lebow shaft torque sensor.
(a) General structure of
torque transducer;
(b) slip ring rotating shaft
torque measuring system.
(c) disassembled view of a
typical Lebow torque sensor.

effects and cancel signals caused by non-torsional loads.

As the shaft rotates, the strain gauge bridge must be connected to the stationary housing with slip rings. Silver slip rings and silver graphite brushes are used to provide a zero-resistance electrical path. The rings and brushes must be cleaned periodically to maintain a satisfactory signal-to-noise ratio. The bridge can be excited with either a.c. or d.c., and the output is in millivolts. External electronics are used to amplify and calibrate this signal.

10.5.4.3 *Wrist force*

A wrist force sensor measures the force and torque between the tool plate and the end effector (Figure 10.20). This force and torque must be resolved into a six degree of freedom force-torque vector with respect to the hand coordinate frame. Mechanically decoupling the six components is very difficult, so most sensors are designed to produce signals that can be easily decoupled electronically.

In every sensor, the input shaft is coupled to the output shaft with beams. Strain gauges are mounted on these beams in Wheatstone bridge configurations. The mechanical placement of the gauges coupled with the mechanical location of the beam determines the combination of forces in a bridge output signal. A sensor developed at SRI (Rozen and Nitzan, 1977) had eight beams milled into an aluminium tube: four parallel to the z axis (axis of the cylinder) and four in a plane parallel to the z axis. Each group of four was spaced at 90° intervals around the cylinder.

The sensor in Figure 10.20 uses three radial beams (like spokes 120° apart), with each beam instrumented with two strain gauge bridges. The signals from these bridges are combined by an on-board microprocessor (Figure 10.21) to produce a six degree of freedom force vector.

Four beam wrist sensors (Figure 10.22), based on a design by Bejczy (1980), are relatively easy to decouple. A strain gauge pair is mounted at the end of each beam. The gauges at opposite ends of the beams are wired

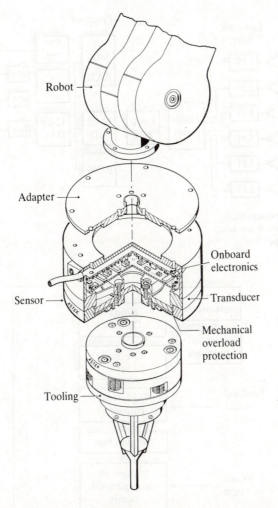

Figure 10.20
Astek 6-axis force sensor
with on board
microprocessor from Barry
Wright Corporation.

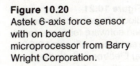

Robot

Adapter

Onboard
electronics

Sensor

Transducer

Mechanical
overload
protection

Tooling

differentially to form a potentiometer circuit, whose output voltage is
proportional to the component of force normal to the plane of the strain
gauge. This sensor produces eight signals ($w_1 \ldots w_8$) proportional to the
force applied to the beams, in the directions shown in Figure 10.22. The
transformation from these eight sensed signals to a six-axis force vector is
known as the **resolved force matrix**.

$$
\begin{bmatrix} f_x \\ f_y \\ f_z \\ \tau_x \\ \tau_y \\ \tau_z \end{bmatrix} = \begin{bmatrix} 0 & 0 & k_{13} & 0 & 0 & 0 & k_{17} & 0 \\ k_{21} & 0 & 0 & 0 & k_{25} & 0 & 0 & 0 \\ 0 & k_{32} & 0 & k_{34} & 0 & k_{36} & 0 & k_{38} \\ 0 & 0 & 0 & k_{44} & 0 & 0 & 0 & k_{48} \\ 0 & k_{52} & 0 & 0 & 0 & k_{56} & 0 & 0 \\ k_{61} & 0 & k_{63} & 0 & k_{65} & 0 & k_{67} & 0 \end{bmatrix} \begin{bmatrix} w_1 \\ w_2 \\ w_3 \\ w_4 \\ w_5 \\ w_6 \\ w_7 \\ w_8 \end{bmatrix}
\qquad \textbf{(10.2)}
$$

Figure 10.21
Block diagrams of hardware
and software for 6-axis force
transducer in Figure 10.20.
(a) Electronic block diagram;
(b) software flow chart.

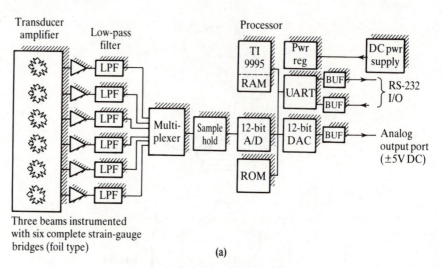

Transducer amplifier

Low-pass filter

Processor

Three beams instrumented
with six complete strain-gauge
bridges (foil type)

(a)

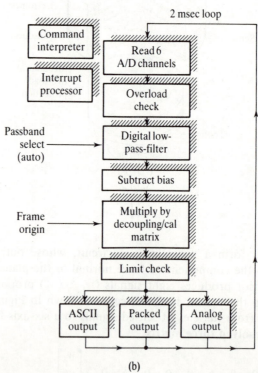

2 msec loop

Command interpreter

Interrupt processor

Passband select (auto)

Frame origin

Read 6 A/D channels

Overload check

Digital low-pass-filter

Subtract bias

Multiply by decoupling/cal matrix

Limit check

ASCII output

Packed output

Analog output

(b)

The components of the matrix are the factors required to convert the sensed signals into force values. If we assume that the coupling effects between the signals are zero, the above equation can be obtained by inspection from Figure 10.22. However, the coupling that exists in practical sensors can produce up to 5 per cent error in the force calculation. Hence, commer-

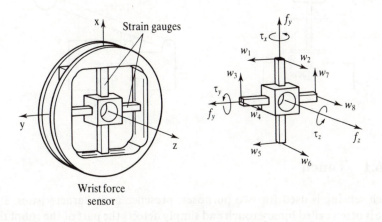

Deflection beams

Figure 10.22
Bejczy's four beam wrist
force sensor.

cial sensors must be calibrated during manufacture to obtain accurate values for all 48 parameters in the matrix (Shimano and Roth, 1979).

Typical sensors are about 120 mm in diameter, 60 mm thick, weigh about 1 kg, with a range of 100 to 600 Newtons force and 2 to 12 Newton metres of torque. They have a resolution of 0.1 Newtons force and 0.002 Newton metres torque, with a measurement rate of 480 Hz maximum. So that the distortions of the beams in the force sensor do not affect the positioning accuracy of the manipulator, the sensor must be stiff. To achieve high stiffness, low hysteresis and good linearity, the sensor is usually machined from a solid piece of aluminium. High stiffness also ensures that the natural frequency of the sensor is high, and impact forces are quickly dampened.

10.6 External sensors

External sensors measure the interaction of a robot with its environment. They are used to locate the robot with respect to the environment and to locate objects in the environment with respect to the robot. Under this definition, the Cartesian-space position sensors (Section 10.5.1.1) and the wrist-force sensor (Section 10.5.4.3) are both classified as external sensors. Some sensors do not fit clearly within any one classification, but overlap several.

The range of external sensors is very large, so only those sensors that measure touch, proximity, range and location are examined here. Measurement of speech, sound, humidity, gas mixture, pressure and temperature are not covered, due to space restrictions. Vision is possibly the single most important external sensor and, as it is used for measurement of both range and location as well as inspection, we will deal with it separately.

Figure 10.23
Mechanically operated switches.
(a) Push switch;
(b) lever operated microswitch.

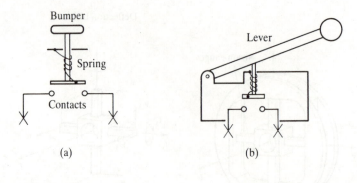

Bumper

Spring

Contacts

Lever

(a)　　　　　　　　　　(b)

10.6.1 Touch

Touch sensing is used for two purposes: presence and characteristics. Presence is often called binary touch and simply detects the part of the robot that is touching an object. The simplest binary touch sensor is the mechanically operated switch (Figure 10.23). When the switch is depressed the circuit is closed and current flows, and when it is released the circuit is open and no current flows. Thus, the output of the sensor is a binary value. Switches can be used as push buttons to enable operator input, or as limit switches to detect collision.

Another binary touch sensor is the whisker sensor (Russell 1984). A whisker sensor emulates human hair and detects the presence of an object before collision occurs. The whisker contacts the object but, as it is flexible, it does not damage the object. The motion of the whisker is detected at its base, either by closing a switch, or, in the case of hair, by pressure. The Titan III walking robot (see Figure 2.19) uses whisker sensors on its feet to detect steps (Figure 10.24).

More sophisticated touch sensors measure the characteristics of the object being touched as well as its presence (Harmon, 1982). The most

Figure 10.24
Wisker sensors on a foot of the Titan III robot. (Figure 2.19) built by Shigeo Hirose, at the Tokyo Institute of Technology.

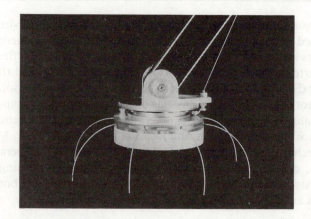

Figure 10.25
Tactile sensor from Tactile
Robotic Systems mounted
on a gripper and grasping an
open-ended spanner.

sophisticated touch sensor is the human finger, and considerable research effort is expended in trying to emulate the finger. The sensing of a range of parameters with our fingers allows us to carry out fine manipulation with our eyes closed. Object characteristics that we can detect with our fingers include object shape, object temperature, grasp force and torque, slip of the object through our fingers, fluid viscosity, wetness, surface texture and surface roughness. These characteristics are detected with receptors in our skin. Some skin receptors can detect static parameters like pressure and tempera-ture, but most can sense only rapidly varying parameters (Dario and De Rossi, 1985). These receptors generate electrical signals which are sent to the brain for processing. The brain periodically recalibrates the skin receptors, but pays little attention to the static signals. The skin converts mechanical signals to electrical signals, like piezo-electric material, and converts thermal signals to electrical signals, like pyro-electric material. These properties have been found in dead skin, indicating that skin tissue has energy conversion characteristics.

A material that is both piezo-electric and pyro-electric is called ferro-electric. Some synthetic polymers exhibit ferro-electric properties, such as polyvinylidene flouride (PVF2). PVF2 is available in thin flexible sheets, making it ideal for use in mechanical fingers. Other materials used in experi-mental sensors are carbon-impregnated rubbers and conductive elastomers which exhibit piezo-resistive behaviour – that is, they change resistance under pressure.

Tactile sensing is the ability to detect an object and recognize its shape. To do this, the sensor must have multiple sensing points. The apparent spatial resolution of a human finger seems to vary with the shape of the object. If two sharp points are pressed against the skin, for example, they have to be 2–3 mm apart to be recognized as separate points. Yet a set of parallel grooves or raised lines with a spacing as narrow as 0.8 mm can be

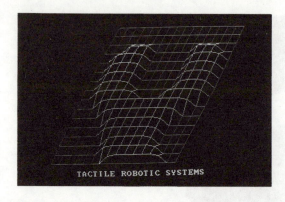

Figure 10.26
Force pattern produced on a computer display of an open-ended spanner resting on a tactile sensor.

resolved. It appears that when a larger area is touched, the receptors obtain more information, which allows a finer resolution to be perceived. Commercially available tactile sensors are flat square pads (Figure 10.25). These sensors detect the force applied to the sensor when an object is pushed against the sensor (Figure 10.26). From this force image, a program can recognize the object and determine its orientation. Typical sensors have a 16 by 16 array of force transducers at 1–2 mm spacing.

The force sensors are made in a number of ways. For example, Lord Corporation use a plastic pin connected to an elastomeric pad (Figure 10.27). The end of the pin blocks part of a light beam. When force is applied to the sensor, the pin moves in proportion to the applied force, cutting off more of the light beam. Thus, the light reaching the photo detector is inversely proportional to the force. Other groups have used pressure-sensitive conductive rubber laid over an array of sensing electrodes (Figure 10.28). The most sophisticated of these uses a sensor constructed from a

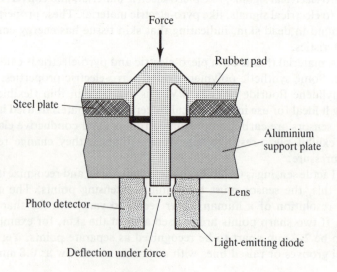

Figure 10.27
Force sensing transducer used in Lord Corporation tactile sensors.

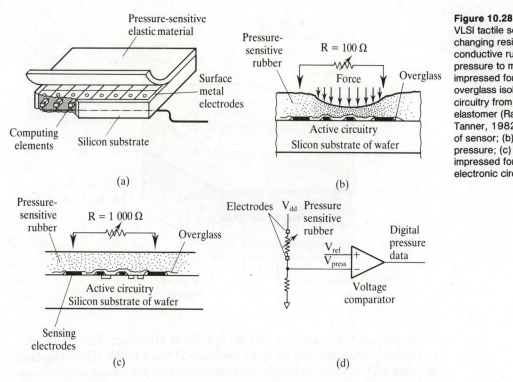

Figure 10.28
VLSI tactile sensor using changing resistance of conductive rubber under pressure to measure impressed force. The overglass isolates the active circuitry from the conductive elastomer (Raibert and Tanner, 1982): (a) structure of sensor; (b) sensor under pressure; (c) sensor with no impressed force; (d) electronic circuitry.

VLSI wafer (Raibert and Tanner, 1982). This sensor includes local processing to amplify, decouple and multiplex sensor signals. The conductive rubber forms a resistive path between the electrodes in each cell of the sensor array. When pressure is applied to the rubber, it compresses and the resistance decreases nonlinearly after a threshold pressure establishes electrical conductivity between the electrodes and the rubber (Snyder and St Clair, 1978). Conductive elastomers are a homogeneous dispersion of electrically

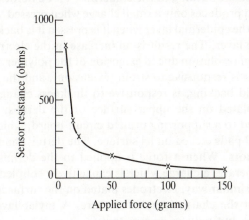

Figure 10.29
Resistance versus applied force for a typical conductive elastomer (Courtesy of A. Russell).

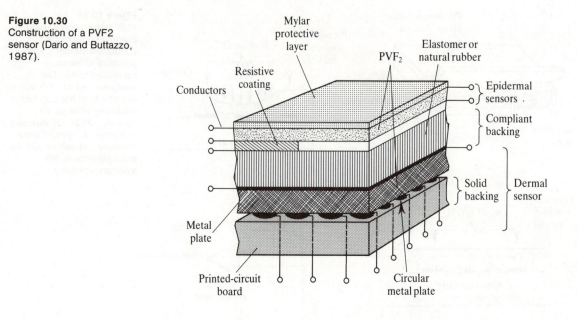

conducting particles, silver or carbon, in a silicon elastomer. Their resistance to pressure characteristics are quite nonlinear (Figure 10.29). The advantage of using a VLSI wafer as the electrode matrix is that processing elements can be integrated into the same wafer, and the output signals can be multiplexed to reduce the number of connecting wires. The disadvantage is that they are flat, inflexible and susceptible to damage.

A more flexible tactile sensing array can be made with ferro-electric polymers (Dario and Buttazzo, 1987). A flat sensor (Figure 10.30) consists of a 100 μmeter thick layer of PVF2 to simulate the human dermis, or inner layer of the skin, and a 40 μmeter thick layer to represent the epidermis or outer layer of skin. These are separated by an elastomer layer, which provides a compliant backing to the epidermis. PVF2 deforms only slightly under stress, and produces only a small charge when pressed. To increase the deformation of the epidermal layer when it is pressed it is backed with a compliant elastomer layer. The result is an increase in the electric signal at the expense of spatial resolution due to extension of the polymer. As a result, the epidermal sensor is responsive to strain (extension), and the dermal sensor, which has a solid backing, is responsive to thickness changes. Thin metal electrodes are plated on the upper surface of the dermis, and the lower surface is bonded to a supporting printed circuit board, which has an array of circular metal pads etched on its surface. The dermis sandwich forms an array of capacitors. When a force is applied to the dermis, the resulting deformation generates a charge which is capacitively coupled to the circular electrodes. In a similar way, electrodes plated on the surfaces of the epidermal layer collect the charges generated there. A mylar layer protects the epidermal sensor, but reduces its sensitivity.

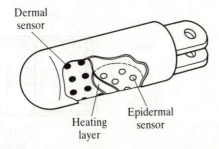

Dermal
sensor

Heating
layer

Epidermal
sensor

Figure 10.31
PVF2 sensor mounted on a
finger tip (Dario and
Buttazzo, 1987).

A 21 mm diameter fingertip sensor constructed in this way (Figure 10.31) has a 5 by 7 matrix of sensors. As the charges produced during deformation are small, signal processing electronics has to be located nearby. A major headache in the design of tactile sensors is getting the analogue signals from the sensor array to the electronic circuits. The larger the array, the greater the physical wiring problem, particularly as coaxial cables are used to shield noise. Integration of electronic circuitry into the sensing sites allows the individual charges to be transferred out of the sensor using a shift register, in a similar way to charge-coupled video chips (Section 10.8.1). To measure the temperature of objects, the epidermal sensing element is backed by a thin layer of resistive paint. A current flowing through this layer raises the sensor's temperature to about 37 °C. When the sensor touches an object, heat flows through the epidermal sensor to the object, generating an electrical charge in the epidermal sensor. The flow of heat depends upon the temperature and thermal conductivity of the object. This can be used to discriminate between objects made of different materials or between objects made of the same material with different temperatures.

To obtain both force and thermal information from the sensor, the two signals have to be decoupled. The elastomer layer introduces a time lag of about one second between the detection of thermal signals at the epidermal and dermal layers. Also, the sensitivity of the dermal layer to temperature changes is lower. The greater thickness, and solid backing, of the dermal layer means that it produces charges due to thickness changes only, charges that are due primarily to the geometric features of the object – edges, corners, depressions. By comparing the signals generated in the two layers, when an object is grasped and released, a program can calculate the hardness of the object. While the epidermal layer is extremely sensitive to deformations and temperature variations, it provides only gross information on contact location. When gently rubbed against an object, the signal from the epidermal layer is proportional to surface roughness. It can also be used to detect slippage, as the grasping forces across the sensor change. Its response is fast enough to detect the microvibrations caused by the variable contact between the object and the sensor. The algorithms, used to decouple the thermal and force data and to interpret the data are quite complex (Dario and Buttazzo, 1987). From this one sensor, information about the shape, texture, hardness and thermal qualities of an object can be obtained.

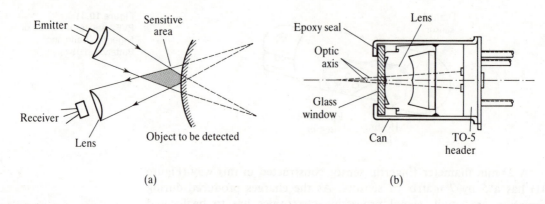

(a)

(b)

Figure 10.32
Optical proximity sensor.
(a) Principle of operation.
(b) Hewlett-Packard HEDS
1000 high resolution optical
reflective scanner used in
bar code readers.

We have discussed touch sensors that respond to static signals to produce an image of an object (Figure 10.26) and sensors that ignore static signals and respond to dynamic signals to produce skin-like signals (Figure 10.30). The interpretation of data from tactile sensors is complex and is subject to continuing research.

In comparison to vision, touch sensors produce little data, but data that is more directly related to the variable being measured – shape, position, orientation. With touch, these can be measured directly, whereas with vision, they have to be deduced from optical images. Also, images can be obtained only when the sensor has an unobstructed view of the object. As the tactile sensor is mounted in the gripper, this is always the case, whereas a camera has to be placed remote from a gripper.

To recognize objects using touch, we must define a number of characteristics of objects that we can sense with a tactile array. The characteristics represent the 'feel' of an object, and they fall into four broad categories: shape, bumps, stability and texture (Hills, 1982). Shape can be categorized with geometric descriptions such as long, short, square, rectangular, round and pointed. Bumps are the locations of local pressure anomalities. These may be due to holes, grooves and raised studs, and are described in relation to an image coordinate frame. Stability is the tendency of an object to roll or rotate as the sensor slides over it. Texture sensing requires the measurement of the bulk effects of the many tiny surface features. When a touch sensor produces a static image, such as the image of the spanner in Figure 10.26, the techniques used in the analysis of visual images can be used (Section 10.8.6).

10.6.2 Proximity

A proximity sensor detects that an object is near the sensor but without physically touching it. Two principles are used in the design of proximity detectors: modification of an emitted signal and disturbance in the environ-

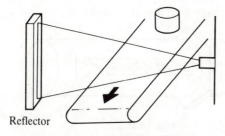

Figure 10.33
Light barrier.

Reflector

ment. Modification of an emitted signal can occur by blocking the path of the signal to a receptor or by reflecting the signal to a receptor. Optical sensors typically fall into this class.

Optical proximity sensors consist of a light emitter and receiver (Figure 10.32). They detect the presence of an object by reflection. If the object is in the sensitive range, it will reflect the emitted beam back to a receptor. Typical sensors have a beam angle of 10° and an adjustable detection range between 0 and 500 mm. Optical sensors suffer from four problems: dirty lenses, ambient light, poor surface reflectance, and incorrect object orientation. Problems due to dirty lenses can be reduced by regular cleaning, protective covers, and mounting the sensor face down so that dust cannot settle on the sensing elements. Noise from ambient light can be minimized by modulating or pulsing the beam. An object with a smooth surface will reflect the beam, as described by the law of reflection, but if the orientation of the object is away from perpendicular, the reflected beam may not hit the detector. As the roughness of the surface increases, this problem decreases.

Surface reflectance characteristics can be used to advantage. If we just want to detect the object, a highly reflective surface is required. Bar codes, for instance, can be read with an optical sensor because the white lines reflect light and the black ones do not. We can determine the colour of an object by shining varying coloured lights on the object and detecting the reflected beam. One robot has three light emitting diodes (red, blue and green) and a detector mounted in a finger of the gripper. By pulsing the leads in sequence and measuring the reflected beam, it can determine the colour of the object it is grasping.

Members of the second group of optical sensors locate a reflecting mirror opposite the sensor to form a **light barrier**, for example, across a conveyor (Figure 10.33). The mirror reflects the light beam back to the sensor. When an object cuts the light curtain, no light is reflected back to the sensor, and the sensor signals the presence of an object.

A group of proximity sensors use **electro-magnetic induction**. They sense metal objects, typically iron and steel, by inducing a current in them. The sensor includes an oscillator. The object provides a magnetic path between the oscillator coils. When no object is present, the coupling between the two coils is minimal (Figure 10.34). The gain of the circuit is increased

Figure 10.34
Inductive proximity sensor.
(a) Physical construction.
(b) simplified circuit.

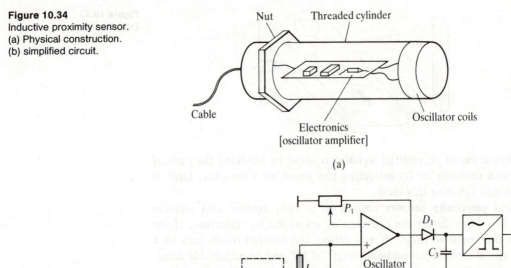

(a)

(b)

until the circuit oscillates, by adjusting the potentiometer. The output of the oscillator is rectified and converted into an impulse which is suitable for switching a thyristor, triac or relay. When a metal object approaches the coils, eddy currents are induced in the object. These eddy currents remove the energy from the coils, the oscillator stops, and the output falls to zero.

Inductive proximity sensors can be used in very rugged environments. They are enlcosed in threaded stainless steel cylinders for easy mounting, and are encapsulated in epoxy resin for environmental protection. Typical sensors have a range from 1 to 20 mm.

Other sensors based on the principle of modifying or coupling an emitted signal include fibre optic sensors and air-flow sensors. An air-flow sensor emits a stream of air. When an object is present, the flow is restricted causing a back pressure to build up in the orifice. A second class of sensors detect disturbances in the environment, such as a change in the magnetic field or a change in capacitance. Magnetic field sensors detect changes in a magnetic field and include reed relays, Hall-effect devices, wiegand wire, eddy-current sensors and magneto–restrictive sensors.

10.6.3 Range

Range is the distance from a sensor to an object, and is also referred to as **depth**. Range perception is important in object recognition and in the control of robot motion. Range-finding sensors are often used in conjunction with

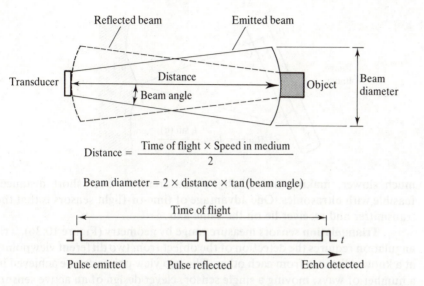

Figure 10.35
Two-dimensional view of
time of flight range
measurement.

$$\text{Distance} = \frac{\text{Time of flight} \times \text{Speed in medium}}{2}$$

$$\text{Beam diameter} = 2 \times \text{distance} \times \tan(\text{beam angle})$$

vision to restore the third dimension. A visual image is a two-dimensional representation of a three-dimensional scene, with. the third dimension, depth, lost. Many researchers are currently working on algorithms to perceive depth from scene characteristics such as shadowing and occlusion of background objects by foreground objects.

There are many simple situations where the expense of vision cannot be justified, but where a simple range finder will do the job. For example, ultrasonic range finders are used for collision avoidance. Also, range information can be used to determine an object's shape for grasping. The Bell Laboratories controlled-impedance gripper (Figure 2.40) includes a near-field ultrasonic sensor in its palm for this purpose.

Range sensors are based on two physical principles: the time of flight of a pulse and triangulation. **Time-of-flight sensors** emit a pulse and measure the time between when the pulse is emitted and when the return echo is detected. Half this time is multiplied by the speed of the pulse in the medium (air or water) to calculate the distance to the object. The direction in which the pulse was transmitted coupled with the beam angle gives the general direction of the object. By combining distance and direction, a segment of a three-dimensional spherical shell is obtained. The object is located in that shell (Figure 10.35).

Radar is the most common example of time-of-flight range measurement. Owing to the large distances covered, the narrow beam angle and the short pulse length (a consequence of the high frequency), radar can be used to measure characteristics of the object as well as its location. By using a short pulse length, echoes from the nose and tail of an aeroplane can be separated to measure its length. To use radar or any other electromagnetic signal for the short distances typical of robots in indoor environments, the phase shift of the reflected signal must be measured, because the time between emission and detection is so short. In contrast, the speed of sound is

Figure 10.36
Principle of operation of a
triangulation range finder.

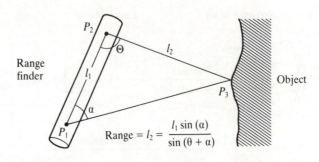

Range
finder

P_2

Θ

l_2

l_1

P_3

Object

α

P_1

$$\text{Range} = l_2 = \frac{l_1 \sin(\alpha)}{\sin(\theta + \alpha)}$$

much slower, making time-of-flight measurements over short distances feasible with ultrasonics. One advantage of time-of-flight sensors is that the transmitter and receiver lie on the same axis.

Triangulation sensors measure range by geometry (Figure 10.36). Triangulation requires the detection of the object from two different viewpoints at a known distance from each other. The two view points can be achieved in a number of ways: moving a single sensor, clever design of an active sensor, and multiple sensors. An active sensor detects an emitted beam, and a passive sensor simply records ambient signals, such as a camera recording light. Mobile robots tend to use single sensors and rely on the measurable motion of the robot to provide the alternate view. Some scanning laser sensors slowly sweep the field of view with a thin a sheet of light (Pipitone and Marshall, 1983) which is detected by a rotating scanner which sweeps the field at a much faster rate. When the light reflected from an object is detected, the angles of the emitter and detector are recorded, and the range is calculated.

Stereo vision – a passive form of triangulation – uses two cameras with a known spatial separation to obtain images of a well-lit scene (Thorpe, 1984). Features (for example, points of high reflection) are identified in one image and a match is sought for these in a second image. For each match, the location of the feature is calculated with respect to the coordinate frame of the image. Perspective transforms are used to transform the two images to a common reference frame, where the distances between features are calculated. These distances are called disparities and are inversely proportional to the range. From the disparities, the ranges to the features are calculated by triangulation (Kak, 1985). All passive triangulation range finders must make a trade-off between accuracy and disparity between the two views. The greater the distance between the two cameras, the higher the accuracy, but, as the separation increases, the difficulty of matching features increases (Jarvis, 1983).

10.6.3.1 *Laser range finders*

A simple **short-range**-finding sensor, which has no moving parts (Figure 10.37), was developed by Okada (1982). The sensor uses a laser diode as a

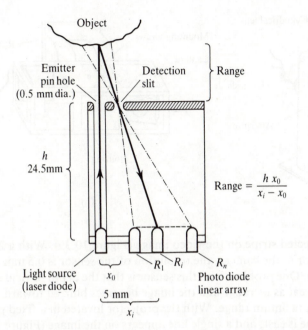

Figure 10.37
Okada's optical short-range-finding sensor.

light source, and a linear photo-diode array as a detector. The light path connecting the light source and the emitter pin-hole is enclosed to prevent light reflecting from the inside of the sensor on to the array. The light beam is reflected off an object, and part of the reflected beam passes through the detection slit on to the diode array. Rough surfaces scatter the reflected beam and reduce the effect of surface orientation. The range from the sensor to the object is a function of the position along the array where the maximum reflected light is detected. The effect of ambient light can be minimized by comparing successive readings of the array with the laser on and then with it off. Because of the use of pin-holes or narrow slits, the influence of surface orientation, roughness and reflectivity is negligible. This sensor has an active range of 5 to 60 mm with reasonable accuracy. It is a monocular sensor, but can be made binocular by mounting a second light source on the other side of the array.

Another sensor that uses an array of photo detectors, known as a line-scan array, is the weld seam detector shown in Figure 1.14. The position at which the beam strikes the array is proportional to the distance to the object. This sensor uses a pair of rotating mirrors to sweep the beam so that distances are measured to a line across the object, not just to a single point as in Okada's sensor.

Agin (1985) produced a sheet of light from a laser diode using a cylindrical lens (Figure 10.38). This system projects a stripe of light about 200 mm long and 1 mm wide at a distance of 300 mm. A camera is mounted in a housing with the projector so that range can be determined from the position

Figure 10.38
Agin's light-stripe projector used for three-dimensional range measurements.
(a) Light-stripe projector;
(b) camera and projector in housing mounted on robot tool plate.

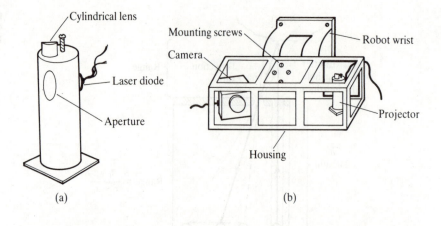

(a)   (b)

of the reflected stripe on the video image (Figure 10.39). With a 256 by 256 array sensor in the camera, the resolution of the sensor is 0.5 mm at a range of 300 mm. One problem with this sensor is that the depth of field of the lens is not as great as its range and the image becomes blurred towards the minimum and maximum range. With the projector located in a fixed position, a single stripe is cast, and a single line appears on the image (Figure 10.39(b)). By moving the sensor in one direction and recording several stripes, a range image of a scene can be constructed. The image of a cup with a spoon resting on it in Figure 10.39(c) was generated by recording a stripe every 10 mm. As the sensor is mounted on the tool plate of a robot, the accuracy of the range data is dependent on the accuracy of the kinematic model of the robot. Once the errors due to the model have been eliminated, the sensor can be used to measure the position and orientation of objects accurately. For example, it can be used to find the top bolt in a box of bolts, where the bolts are lying over one another at various angles.

The Environmental Research Institute of Michigan (ERIM) has developed a range sensor that measures the distances to all objects in the area in front of the sensor. This sensor was designed for use in autonomous land vehicle research (Herbert and Kanade, 1986). A sophisticated optical system (Figure 10.40) sweeps a modulated laser beam over the scene from left to right and bottom to top. The horizontal scan is achieved with a rotating polygonal mirror, and the vertical scan with a flat nodding mirror. Because the transmitter and receiver apertures are 33 mm apart, the folding mirrors are adjusted to make the axes of the transmitter and receiver intersect 18 metres in front of the sensor, resulting in a parallax angle of 0.414°. The net effect of the parallax error is a small reduction in the reflected energy reaching the sensor at close range.

Distance to an object is measured by comparing the phase of the transmitted beam to the phase of the reflected beam. At the modulation frequency used in the sensor, one complete phase shift is equal to 19.2 metres. Consequently, the eight-bit values in the image repeat every 19.2 metres, causing an

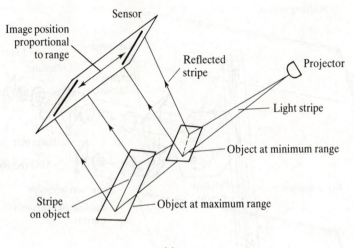

Sensor

Image position
proportional
to range

Reflected
stripe

Projector

Light stripe

Object at minimum range

Stripe
on object

Object at maximum range

(a)

Figure 10.39
Measuring the distances to a
line across an object using a
light-stripe range finder.
(a) Sensing the range of an
object using a light-stripe;
(b) image of a single stripe
crossing a pipe; (c)
perspective view of a cup
and spoon.

Projector

Beam

Stripe

Pipe

Image

Range

Width

(b)

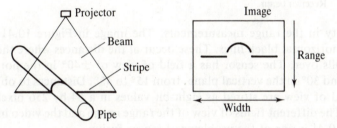

(c)

Figure 10.40
Optics of the ERIM laser
range finder.

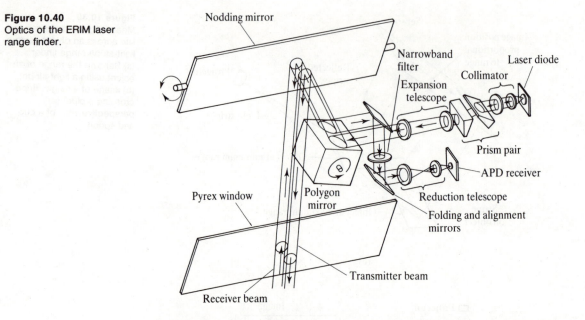

ambiguity in the range measurements. The image in Figure 10.41 shows
several horizontal black lines. These occur at the distances where the range
value rolls over. The sensor has a field of view of ±40° in the horizontal
plane, and 30° in the vertical plane, from 15° to 45°. Distances to objects in
this field of view are stored as eight-bit values in a 64 by 256 pixel range
image. The different fields of view of the range image and the video image in
Figure 10.41 is one of the problems of sensor fusion.

The first step in processing the range image is to remove the ambiguity
caused by the repeating values. Next, the image is processed to extract
features relevant to navigation: three-dimensional edges, smooth regions
and obstacles. These features are extracted by computing low-level attributes

Figure 10.41
Video image (top) and laser
range finder image (bottom)
of the same scene, showing
the differences in format and
field of view of these
sensors.

from the image (edges, surface normals, curvatures), and merging the segmentations derived from these attributes into a connectivity graph of features. From these features, a three-dimensional model of the scene is constructed (Herbert and Kanade, 1986).

10.6.3.2 *Ultrasonic echolocation*

Echolocation using sound waves is found in two groups of animals in nature. In water, dolphins use ultrasonic pulses to locate and track fish, to navigate and to communicate. In many underwater situations, vision is restricted due to low light levels and sediment in the water. In contrast, sound waves travel great distances, and are not affected by the visual clarity of the water. In the air, bats use ultrasonic echolocation to navigate, locate and track moths, and to track mice through wheat stubble. They also use echolocation to navigate in dark caves. By using sound waves to locate objects, bats can hunt at night, when the low light level makes vision difficult. Other animals have some ability to locate objects with sound, and some build auditory maps of their environment, which they fuse with visual maps.

The variety of sonar (sound **n**avigation **a**nd **r**anging) beams used by bats is quite large. Some bats produce narrow beams with which they sweep the environment, others produce wide angle beams with very short pulses. Some use fixed frequency chirps, others vary the frequency of their chirp. One species varies the frequency of their chirp so that the returning echoes off stationary objects are at a fixed frequency (Busnel and Fish, 1980). While the sonar beams generated by man-made ultrasonic transducers are similar in frequency and beam angle to those of bats, man-made sensors have nowhere near their ability to locate objects. We have a long way to go before our sensors will even approach the echolocation ability of a bat.

Sound waves differ from electromagnetic radiation in three important physical characteristics: medium, velocity and wavelength. Sound requires a medium for transmission, such as air. The velocity of sound ($331.6 + 0.6 \times$ °C metres/second) in air is much slower than the velocity of light, so we can use time of flight to measure short distances. The wavelength of a 50 kHz sonar beam is 6.872 mm, which is much larger than the roughness of most indoor surfaces. As a result, the reflection of ultrasonic beams off smooth surfaces forms a well-defined reflected beam. This mirror-like reflection is called **specular reflection**. In contrast, when the beam falls on a rough surface it is reflected in all directions. This omnidirectional reflection is called **diffuse reflection**. Owing to the scattering of sound waves by diffuse reflection, other objects in the environment become visible to the transducer. As the surfaces of natural environments are much rougher than the surfaces of man-made environments, ultrasonic range finding in natural environments can make use of diffuse reflection, while in man-made environments it must be able to handle specular reflection. Whether reflection is diffuse or specular is a function of the surface roughness. Specular reflection will occur

Figure 10.42
Construction of polaroid
ultrasonic transducer.

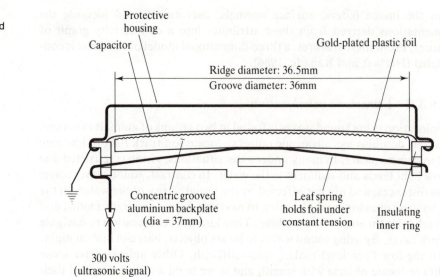

only if the average depth of the surface irregularities is substantially less than the wavelength of the incident beam. Also, the transverse dimensions of the reflecting surface must be substantially larger than the wavelength of the incident beam. For this reason, a smooth round pole will produce diffuse reflection, particularly when the diameter of the pole is less than the beam width.

While there are significant differences between sound waves and electromagnetic waves, the modelling of them is similar. Most ultrasonic range finders used in robotics have a transducer similar to the one used in Polaroid cameras (Biber *et al.*, 1980). These transducers are modelled as radiating plane pistons (Kinsler and Frey, 1962). By varying the ratio of the ultrasonic wavelength to the diameter of the transducer, we can change from a transducer that produces spherical waves to one which produces a conical beam with side lobes, similar to a radio beam.

The Polaroid transducer (Figure 10.42) acts as both a transmitter and receiver. In receiver mode, it functions as an electrostatic microphone. The radius is roughly three times the wavelength, and determines the acoustical lobe pattern. The angular beam width (polar angle from axis) is approximately 15° (Figure 10.43). The moving element of the transducer is a plastic foil (Kapton) with a conductive coating (gold) on the front surface. The motion of this foil converts electrical energy into sound waves and vice versa. The grooved plate and foil form a capacitor. When this capacitor is charged, it exerts an electrostatic force on the foil, causing the pliable foil to move like a loudspeaker. When used in the microphone mode, sound pressure moves the foil and changes the capacitance of the capacitor.

In normal operation, the Polaroid system produces a 1 millisecond chirp every 200 milliseconds. The chirp contains 56 pulses: 8 at 60 kHz, 8 at

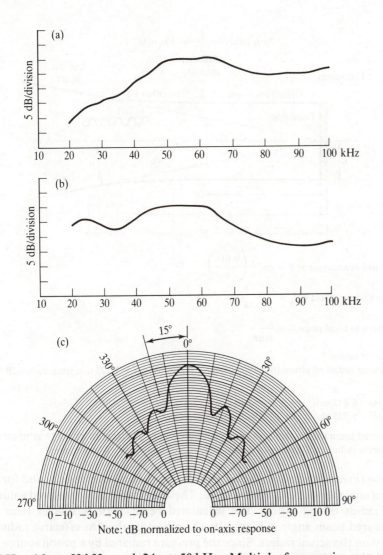

Figure 10.43
Characteristics of the
polaroid ultrasonic
transducer: (a) typical
transmit response; (b) typical
free field receive response;
(c) typical beam pattern at
50 kHz.

Note: dB normalized to on-axis response

57 kHz, 16 at 53 kHz and 24 at 50 kHz. Multiple frequencies are used because some materials absorb acoustic energy and no echo is reflected. Also, a textured surface can produce sufficient phase shift for some parts of the reflected signal to interfere with other parts and cancel out the echo. Usually, time of flight to the first echo is recorded and all other echoes discarded, wasting a lot of valuable range information. The beam is formed by the main lobe, which can be thought of as a 24° cone radiating out from the transducer (Figure 10.44). In the near field, the beam intensity fluctuates rapidly, and peaks at a distance of l_1 from the transducer (Figure 10.44). In this region, the beam is cylindrical. For distances greater than $2l_1$, the intensity decreases inversely with the square of distance and the beam is conical. The theoretical calculations for the point of transition from the near field

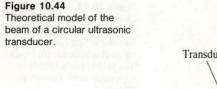

Figure 10.44
Theoretical model of the
beam of a circular ultrasonic
transducer.

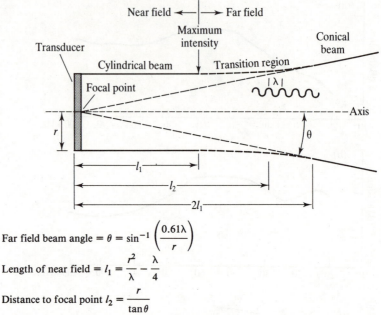

Far field beam angle $= \theta = \sin^{-1}\left(\dfrac{0.61\lambda}{r}\right)$

Length of near field $= l_1 = \dfrac{r^2}{\lambda} - \dfrac{\lambda}{4}$

Distance to focal point $l_2 = \dfrac{r}{\tan\theta}$

Polaroid sensor
Measured radius of piston (outermost ridge – Figure 10.42) = 18.25 mm temperature 20 °C

f	λ	θ	l_1	l_2
50 kHz	6.872 mm	13.3°	50.18 mm	77.2 mm
60 kHz	5.723 mm	11.02°	56.77 mm	93.71 mm

Measured beam angle − between lowest intensity points on Figure 10.43 = 15° at 50 kHz
Apparent radius at 50 kHz = 16.2 mm l_1 = 36.5 mm   and l_2 = 60.5 mm

region (Fresnel region) to the far field region (Fraunhofer region) and for the
beam angle are given in Figure 10.42. These are based on a measured value of
the radius of the piston. The calculated beam angle is smaller than the
measured beam angle in Figure 10.42, indicating that the effective radius is
less than the actual radius. Since the pressure radiated by a piston source is a
function of polar angle (with respect to the beam axis), as well as a function
of distance from the source, the pressure of the wave front is highest on the
axis and drops off toward the sides of the cone. Also, the phase of the pressure on the wavefront is the same at all points within the cone.

A number of apparent measurement errors can occur with ultrasonic
range finders. When the axis of the beam is perpendicular to a flat object, the
measured range is accurate (Figure 10.45(a)). If a small object is placed in
front of the wall, the measured range is correct, but the lateral position of the
object is only known to be within a certain range. (Figure 10.45(b)). The
lateral resolution is a function of beam angle. If the transducer is rotated so
that the axis of the beam is at an angle to the wall (beam angle in Figure
10.45(c)) the measured range is the distance along the edge of the beam to the
wall, not the distance along the axis of the beam. Thus, the apparent range is

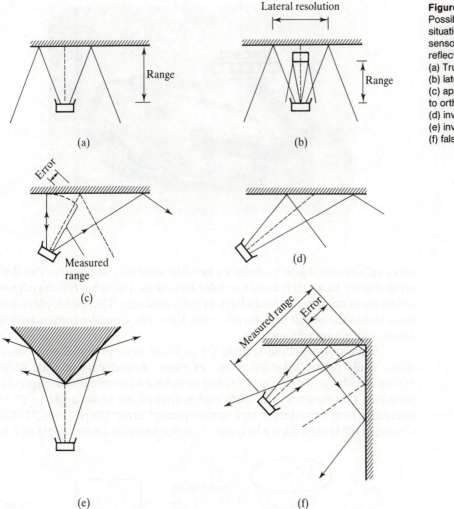

Figure 10.45
Possible range error
situations with an ultrasonic
sensor, and specular
reflection.
(a) True range measurement;
(b) lateral resolution problem;
(c) apparent range error due
to orthogonal reflection;
(d) invisible wall;
(e) invisible corner;
(f) false reflection.

shorter than the axial range, resulting in range uncertainty, that is a function of transducer rotation and beam angle.

These errors can be reduced by using a transducer with a narrower beam. Decreasing the beam angle will, however, increase the possibility of the following errors. These errors are a consequence of the specular reflection of sonar beams off smooth surfaces. They can be reduced by increasing the roughness of the surface, which increases the scattering of the reflected beam. If the rotation of the transducer is greater than the beam angle (the amount by which it is greater is a function of the roughness) the beam will be reflected away from the transducer, and the wall will be invisible (Figure 10.45(d)). Worse still is the situation depicted in Figure 10.45(e), where a corner is invisible and a collision could result. Fortunately, only a small curvature is required for the corner to become visible. The polaroid sensor

Figure 10.46
Meldog guide dog robot uses ultrasonic sensors to locate and identify objects built by Susumu Tachi at the Ministry of International Trade and Industry, Tsukuba Science City.

picks up a reasonable echo from a 1 mm diameter wire at 1 metre. The final error (Figure 10.45(f)) is known as **false reflection**. The beam reflects off one object on to another, and then back to the transducer. These multiple reflections makes the object look further away than it is. Concave corners tend to bloom out in range images.

Some range-finding systems try to avoid these potential error situations, while others take advantage of them. Researchers at Oak Ridge National Laboratory wrapped objects in bubble wrap to eliminate specular reflection (Jorgensen *et al.*, 1986) and narrowed the beam angle to 6° by operating four transducers in a square-phased array (Burks *et al.*, 1987). Crowley (1984) used a horn to focus the sonar beam to a beam angle of 1.5°

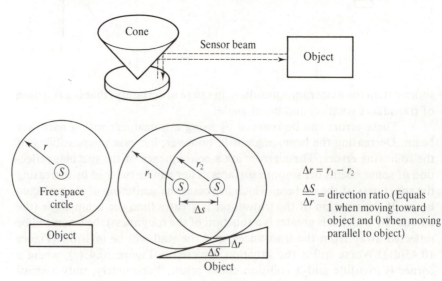

Figure 10.47
Omnidirectional ultrasonic sensor when combined with motion can measure object orientation.

in a rotating sensor (see Figure 8.21). Denning used a ring of sensors to rapidly obtain measurements in all directions around the robot (see Figure 2.5). The Meldog guide dog robot (Figure 10.46) uses a linear array of sensors to locate objects precisely (Komoriya *et al.*, 1986).

Considerable information can be obtained from simple ultrasonic sensing systems, particularly when combined with motion. For example, a simple omni-directional sensor (Figure 10.47), made by placing a 45° cone at the centre of an ultrasonic transducer, can be used to measure the orientation of an object (Kuc, 1984). The distance measured by the sensor is the distance to the closest object. As the sensor is omnidirectional, this distance is the radius of a circle of free space around the sensor. If a measurement is made (r_1), the sensor moved by a distance Δs, and the radius measured again (r_2), the ratio of the distance moved by the sensor to the change in radius indicates the orientation of the object. Also, the general direction in which the object is located can be determined. If the robot is moving towards an object, the radius will decrease: if it is moving away, the radius will increase until a second object is closer.

10.7   Location

Location is defined with a six degree-of-freedom vector describing the position and orientation of an object in space. We can measure position by dead reckoning from odometry, by range finding, and by detecting beacons. All of these have been covered in previous sections. Orientation can be measured using a compass, a gyroscope or an inclinometer. These will be covered briefly here.

A **compass** gives an absolute measure of orientation in a horizontal plane, by aligning a magnetic needle with the earth's magnetic field. However, local disturbances in the earth's magnetic field due to large bodies of iron ore, or steel girders in a building will cause inaccurate orientation measurements.

A more commonly used orientation transducer is a **gyroscope**, which measures an object's attitude relative to an inertial frame of reference. Attitude is the relative orientation of an object represented by its angles of inclination to the axes of a reference frame. Attitude rate is the time rate of change of attitude. The inertial reference system is provided by a rapidly revolving rotor, which turns about a spin axis (Figure 10.48). As long as the rotor continues turning, inertial forces will keep the spin axis fixed in space. The ends of the shaft on which the rotor is mounted are supported by a gimbal frame, which is free to pivot about a gymbal axis. The housing of the gyro is attached to the object whose attitude is to be measured. When the object turns about the gymbal axis, the gymbal frame turns in the opposite direction, and the axis of the rotor remains in a fixed direction. A two degree of freedom gyro has two gymbal axes. The orientation of the spin axis, and

Figure 10.48
Principle of operation of
gyroscopes.
(a) Single-degree-of-freedom
gyro;
(b) two-degree-of-freedom
gyro;
(c) rate gyro.

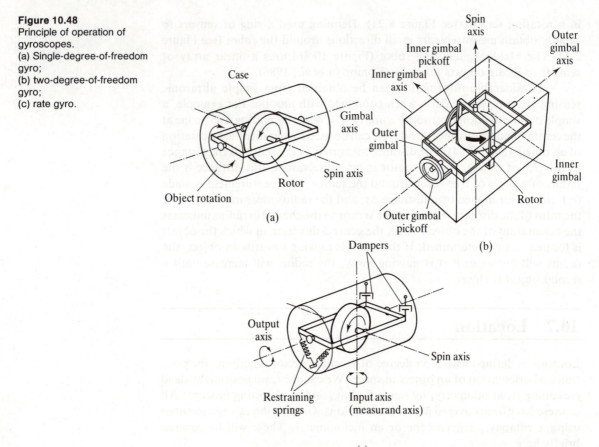

(a)

(b)

(c)

hence the inertial frame, is the orientation of the rotor when it is accelerated
up to speed. Angular displacement transducers are used to measure the
angles of the gymbal frames relative to the inertial frame. The rotor is driven
by an electric motor.

An accurate gyroscope is a complex and precise piece of mechanical
equipment. Two degree-of-freedom gyros include a caging mechanism to
hold the inner gymbal in place while the rotor is accelerated up to speed. Rate
gyros operate on the same principle, except that the gymbal is elastically
restrained and motion is damped. The deflection of the gymbal about its axis
is proportional to rate. A number of companies are developing ring laser
gyroscopes to replace mechanical gyroscopes (Martin, 1986).

Inclinometers, tilt sensors, or level sensors measure the angle of an
object to a horizontal axis. Spectron electrolytic level sensors (Figure 10.49)
use gravity to provide a reference. An electrolyte (electrically conducting
fluid) is placed in a sealed glass vial with three platinum electrodes. The void,
or bubble, in the vial performs the function of a gravity-controlled wiper arm

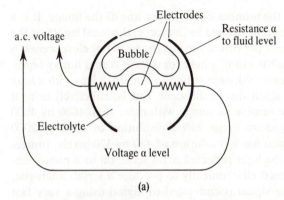

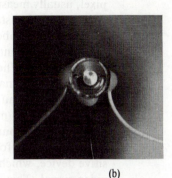

(a)

(b)

Figure 10.49
Spectron electrolytic level
sensor. (a) Principle of
operation; (b) actual sensor.

for the potentiometer element, which is made up of the conducting electrolyte. When the sensor is level, the volume of the fluid between the centre electrode and each of the two outer electrodes is equal, and the resistances are the same. As the sensor tilts, the volume of fluid on one side increases, while the volume on the other decreases, resulting in a resistance imbalance proportional to the tilt angle. The sensor is an alternating current device, because direct current will cause an electroplating action between the electrodes and a precipitation of the conducting salts in the electrolyte. A typical level sensor has a range of ±30°, and an output of 7 millivolts per degree per volt input. Capacitive effects due to the a.c. excitation cause 0.3 seconds time delay in the response of the sensor to a change in tilt.

10.8 Vision

Vision is the ability to see and recognize objects by collecting the light reflected off those objects into an image and processing that image. The human eye focuses light on to the retina, where the rods and cones record the intensity and wavelength of the light. This information is then passed to the brain, which interprets it as a scene and identifies objects in that scene. Robot vision makes use of computers or other electronic hardware to analyse visual images – and recognize objects of importance in the current application of the robot.

An electronic image is an array of pixels that has been digitized into the memory of a computer. A pixel or a picture element is the smallest element in that image. A binary number is stored in each pixel to represent the intensity and possibly the wavelength of the light falling on that part of the image. In a binary image, a pixel can have a value of 0 or 1 representing black and white. In a grey scale image, a binary number represents an intensity level between black and white. In a colour image, information about colour is stored as well as intensity information.

The spatial resolution of an image is the area represented by each pixel, usually measured as the number of pixels per line of the image. It is a function of the distance from the camera to the scene, the focal length of the lens, and the number of pixels per row in the image array. For close scenes, a pixel may represent $0.1\,mm \times 0.1\,mm$, where for distant scenes it may represent $1\,m \times 1\,m$. When the scene is distant from the camera, a lens with a long focal length will magnify a small area of the scene, that is, effectively bring it closer. The human eye can resolve an image with more than 4000 by 4000 pixels. A 35 mm motion picture image has a resolution of 2000 by 2000 pixels, and a colour television has a resolution of 480 by 320 pixels. Images are produced by focusing the light reflected off a scene on to a photo sensitive device, which is scanned electronically to produce a serial, analogue, video signal. This analogue signal is converted to digital using a very fast analogue-to-digital converter, called a flash converter, and stored in the memory of the computer.

10.8.1 Cameras

A camera consists of a lens, a photo sensitive target, and electronic circuitry. The lens focuses the scene on to the target. The electronic circuit controls the scanning of the target and produces a composite video signal. This signal contains both timing and scene illumination information.

Colour images are produced by optically filtering the light into red, green and blue wavelengths. The optical elements project three images on to three imaging devices, one for each primary colour. These three video signals are added in a matrix to form a composite video signal. A colour signal has three characteristics: **hue** – light wavelength; **saturation** – amount of white light mixed with the colour; and **brightness** – grey-scale level.

Two types of light-sensitive devices are used in robot video cameras: vidicons and charged coupled arrays. A **vidicon** camera tube (Figure 10.50) is a cylindrical glass tube with a photosensitive target at one end and an electron gun at the other. When an optical image is focused on to the target, it produces a charge image. The target consists of two layers: a transparent film of conducting material (signal plate), and a layer of photosensitive material (selenium or antimony compounds). This layer has a resistance of 20 megohms in the dark. When light strikes the sensitive layer, the resistance drops to as low as 2 megohms in the area where the light rays fall. The signal plate is connected to a positive voltage via a load resistor. At the point where the electron beam strikes the back of the target, an electrical circuit is produced from the positive supply, through the target, through the electron beam ($\approx$ 90 megohms resistance) to ground. Electrons flow from the gun to the target to neutralise the charge which has built up on the target and return the target to its dark resistance. The current which flows is determined by the resistance of the target, which is in turn determined by the intensity of the light falling on it. The more intense the light, the lower the target resistance, and the higher the current. This flow of current produces a voltage drop

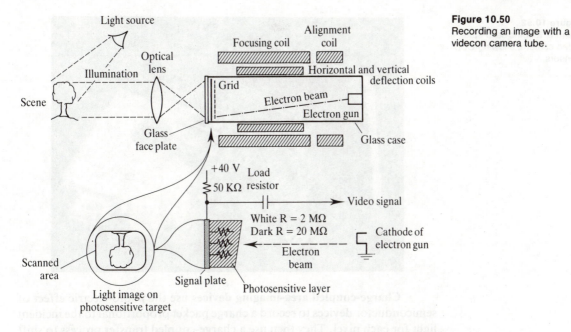

Figure 10.50
Recording an image with a videcon camera tube.

across the load resistor proportional to the intensity of the light illuminating this region of the target. The video signal is picked off from this point and amplified. The electron beam is scanned from right to left and from bottom to top (as the image is the optical inverse). During the scan, the charge on a pixel area builds up. During the few microseconds that the electron beam contacts the pixel area the charge is discharged. The output is a signal proportional to the light intensity on the pixel area. Scanning the beam along a row of pixels produces a sequential analogue output voltage proportional to the intensity of the light falling on the pixels across the screen. So that this voltage is aligned with its position on the screen, special timing signals are electronically inserted into the sequential analogue signal during horizontal and vertical retrace. The resultant signal is called composite video (Figure 10.51). The frequency of the synchronization pulses is determined by the television system in use in a particular country.

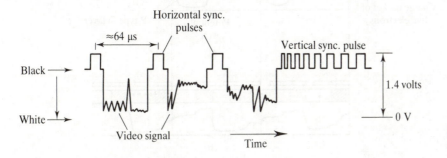

Figure 10.51
Composite video signal.

Figure 10.52
General Electric solid state video camera, showing CCD sensors.

Charge-coupled area-imaging devices use the photo-electric effect of semiconductor devices to record a charge packet proportional to the incident light for each pixel. They then use a charge-coupled transfer process to shift the information in each row of the array along the lines of storage elements on to an output bus, or into a circuit which generates a composite video signal. A charged coupled device (CCD) is a semiconductor array of area-imaging photosensitive elements (Figure 10.52). Each pixel is sensed by a small area of silicon semiconductor. The light falling on that area creates free electrons in the area. The number of electrons is proportional to the intensity

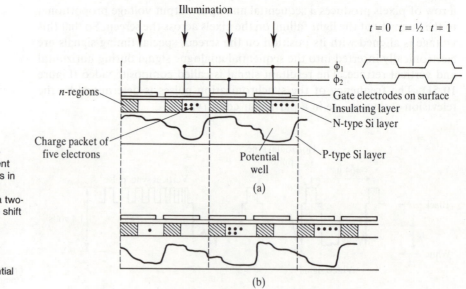

Figure 10.53
Operation of a charged-coupled device – incident light generates electrons in charge packets – after desired exposure time a two-phased clock is used to shift these packets out.
(a) Position of charge packets at $t = \phi$;
(b) position of charge packets at $t = \frac{1}{2}$ – potential well shifted to right.

of the illumination and the exposure time. The area of the pixel, or storage element, is defined by the field of a pair of gate electrodes very close to the surface of the silicon. This field holds the electrons in what is called a charge packet (Figure 10.53). A positive voltage on an electrode forms a deep potential well in the substrate, and the electrons fall into it. To form an array, these storage elements are placed close to each other in lines. The pairs of electrodes, one pair for each storage element, along a line are connected to a two-phase clock – one member of each pair to one phase and the other member of the other phase (Figure 10.53). This causes the voltages on adjacent electrodes to be alternatively raised and lowered. The resultant field change moves the charge packets from one storage element to the next. The result is a simple analogue shift register.

10.8.2 Lighting

As vision images are a record of the light reflected by a scene, the lighting of the scene is important. In television drama productions, lighting is controlled both to illuminate the scene clearly and to produce dramatic effect. For example, shadows produce a spooky or sinister-looking room. In computer vision, the type of lighting and the way it is used depends on the type of image we require and the information we want to extract from that image. Adequate lighting is crucial to the success of any computer-vision application. The principle of lighting for computer vision is to ensure that the information to be extracted is as prominent in the picture as possible. Special lighting will often be required to achieve this.

A binary image consists of pixels that are either black or white. To obtain a good binary image, we must have a high contrast between the object and its background. Also, the object should be in the centre of the camera's field of view with background all around it. Most systems require that the object is isolated from all other objects. If the object is on a conveyor belt, for example, it is essential that the colour of the object be such that it contrasts with the conveyor belt. A shiny machined steel part on a black conveyor belt is easy to see, but a dull grey casting might not be. A light coloured conveyor is better for a dark object. The camera is usually placed so that it points straight down to get the best view of the object. High contrast silhouettes are ideal for binary vision (see Figure 1.15), and can be created using backlighting. An object is backlit by placing it on a transparent, or translucent background and a light is shone through the background towards the camera. The object stops light reaching the camera and so forms a silhouette. Backlighting is used in printed circuit board inspection systems, where cracks in the copper track are detected by light leaking through the track.

For objects with smooth regular surfaces, which cannot be backlit, diffuse lighting should be used, as it reduces the depth of shadows. For grey scale vision, diffuse lighting provides an even scene illumination, with grey level proportional to surface reflectance and not due to shadows. Shadows

Figure 10.54
Consight vision system used
two light sheets which
overlapped to form a line
across the conveyor. When
an object passed the stripes
separated: (a) sensor
arrangement; (b) object
separates stripes.

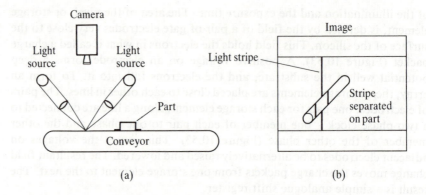

Camera

Light
source

Light
source

Image

Light stripe

Part

Stripe
separated
on part

Conveyor

(a)   (b)

Figure 10.54
Consight vision system used
two light sheets which
overlapped to form a line
across the conveyor. When
an object passed the stripes
separated: (a) sensor
arrangement; (b) object
separates stripes.

can result in an incorrect interpretation of a scene by distorting the perceived silhouette or by hiding detail.

In three-dimensional vision, where we are trying to estimate the distance to objects as well as their shape, shadows can provide cues as to which
object is closer to the camera. In this situation, highly directional lighting
may be used to produce shadows and to emphasize the edges of objects.
Specular reflection off objects can cause loss of detail in the image, but small
areas of specular reflection are easily identifiable features. Spatially modulated lighting is often used to extract three-dimensional information. In this
lighting technique, points, stripes or grids are projected on to the scene. Surface irregularities, such as curves are easily detected by the distortion in the
light pattern. Agin's light stripe ranging system (Section 10.6.3.1) is a typical
example. A second example is the Consight system (Holland *et al.*, 1979).
This system focused two sheets of light into a single light stripe across a conveyor (Figure 10.54). A camera pointed directly down at the conveyor. As
the light sheets were at an angle, they separated into two light stripes when an
object passed between them and the conveyor. The distance between the
stripes was proportional to the height of the object, and the position of the
object across the conveyor could be obtained from the point where the
stripes separated.

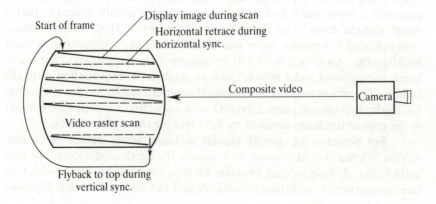

Start of frame

Display image during scan

Horizontal retrace during
horizontal sync.

Composite video

Camera

Video raster scan

Flyback to top during
vertical sync.

Figure 10.55
Video raster generated from
composite video to display
information on a monitor.

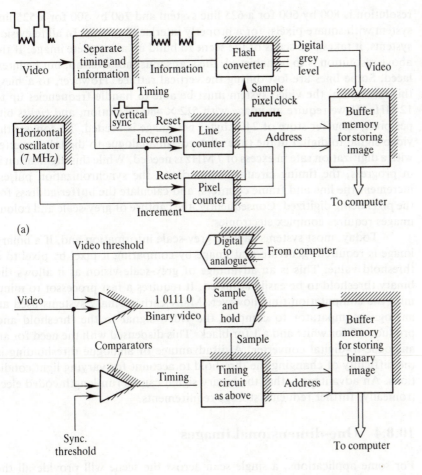

Figure 10.56
Typical vision interface circuits.
(a) Block diagram of a frame grabber circuit for capturing greyscale images;
(b) block diagram of analogue thresholding.

(a)

(b)

10.8.3 Interfaces

A television signal consists of 25 frames per second with 625 lines per frame in Australia and the UK or 30 frames per second with 525 lines per frame in the USA (Figure 10.55). The vertical synchronization pulse occurs 50 (or 60 in USA) times a second, and the horizontal synchronization pulse 15 625 (or 15 750 in USA) times a second. The video information ranges from less than 10 kHz for slowly varying background up to 7 MHz for fine detail.

To extract the video information from the composite video signal and store it in a pixel array, the interface hardware performs the functions of timing, digitization and buffering (Figure 10.56). The conversion of one complete image must be done in 40 (or 33 in USA) milliseconds. As the aspect ratio (in width to height) of a standard television image is 4:3, the maximum resolution is 800 by 600 for a 625 line system and 760 by 500 for a 525 line system with square pixels, for a properly interlaced system. In all television systems, it takes two scans of the scene to build up a complete image. If the above resolution is to be achieved, the scans must not overlap, but be interlaced. Some lines are lost during the vertical retrace. However, to achieve this resolution, the video system must be able to handle frequencies up to 12 MHz. If we require an image with 512×480 resolution, and eights bits per pixel, a buffer store of 240 kbytes per image is needed. To convert the video signal to digital in the time allowed, an analogue-to-digital converter with a digitization rate in excess of 7 MHz is needed. While this digitization is in progress, the timing circuitry must detect the synchronization pulses, increment the line and frame counters, and calculate the buffer address for the pixel being digitized. Consequently, the capture of grey-scale and colour images requires complex electronics.

Today, most systems capture grey-scale information and, if a binary image is required, generate that image by comparing it pixel by pixel to a threshold value. This is an advantage of grey-scale vision as it allows the binary threshold to be easily adjusted. It requires a fast processor to minimize the computation time however. Many earlier binary systems used an analogue comparator to compare the video signal to the threshold and produce a 0 for white and a 1 for black. This dispensed with the need for an analogue-to-digital converter. A disadvantage of analogue thresholding is the difficulty of changing the threshold to account for varying light conditions. An advantage is that the binary signal can be run-length-coded electronically, further reducing storage requirements.

10.8.4 One-dimensional images

For some applications, a single scan across the scene will provide all the information needed. For example, line scan cameras can be used to detect holes in continuously moving material, such as steel strip. The hole may be a flaw or it may indicate the presence of a join in the strip. Another application is bar-code reading, where a single scan across the code is sufficient to read it. Usually the object is translated or rotated past a fixed camera. Successive scans are either compared for a change, as in the hole detection example, or combined to build up a two-dimensional image. The main advantage of single-line scanning is that it greatly reduces the volume of information that has to be processed. The major disadvantage, particularly with a linear-array camera, is that lining up the camera is difficult in comparison to lining up a camera which produces a two dimensional image. A second approach to linear scanning is to use a laser beam to sweep across the area of interest, and single detectors to pick up the reflected light. Several detectors can be used to obtain several views of the beam.

Both types of linear-scan systems usually produce a binary image. Thus, lighting control and thresholding control are important elements in these systems. As the output of the devices is a time-varying analogue wave form, it can be averaged to obtain a thresholding level that will compensate for light variations. If the characteristics of the object produce a known pattern of light and dark, the object can be detected by comparing successive scans to this pattern, in a simple form of template matching.

10.8.5   Template matching

Template matching is a process of object recognition where the image is compared to stored masks or templates. If a match is sufficiently close then the object is recognized. Templates are generated by placing the objects under the camera, one at a time, and recording their images. Template matching can be used with one-dimensional images, two-dimensional binary images, and two-dimensional grey-scale images.

The major problem with template matching is that slight errors in the orientation or position of the object can result in a failure to match. Also, with grey-scale images, the lighting has to be exactly the same for recognition to occur. Errors in the position of the object can be fixed by translating the mask with respect to the image: this process takes time. Rotating the mask to overcome orientation errors in a very computer-intensive process, and can lead to distortions which result in a failure to match. In some systems, the object is centred on a backlit rotating table, and the table turned while successive images are compared to the template. When the object is recognized, it has been turned into a known orientation.

Direct matching involves a pixel-by-pixel comparison of part or all of the image to the template. Because of the above problems, direct matching is usually used only for inspection of objects in known orientations, and for locating a small feature of interest. Two parameters are evaluated when testing for a match: the sum of the differences, and the sum of the squares of the differences. To speed up processing, some systems compare only partial templates. For example, an unusual feature is identified in the template, and a search is made for that feature in the image. Another approach is to break the template up into pieces, and look for matches to those pieces. Both these matching approaches can result in incorrect identification. Some researchers have experimented with rubber mask templates which can be stretched and distorted until a match is achieved.

10.8.6   Run-length coding

While a binary image can be stored compactly as an array of bits, storage can be further reduced by using coding techniques. As pixels in a binary image can have only one of two values, most rows in an image contain runs of consecutive 1s or 0s. In a typical application, one object, which takes up a large amount of the image area, is surrounded by background. The area of the object is all 1s while the backgound is all 0s (Figure 10.57).

Figure 10.57
Run-length coding of a
binary image. (a) Image. (b)
Pixel array. (c) Run-length
code.

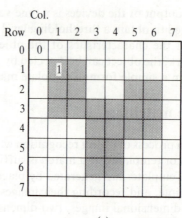

(a)

	Column							
Row	0	1	2	3	4	5	6	7
0	0	0	0	0	0	0	0	0
1	0	1	1	0	0	0	0	0
2	0	1	1	0	0	1	1	0
3	0	1	1	1	1	1	1	0
4	0	0	0	1	1	1	1	0
5	0	0	0	1	1	0	0	0
6	0	0	0	1	1	0	0	0
7	0	0	0	0	0	0	0	0

(b)

Row	Triplet	
0	0	→ [0,8,0]
1	1	→ [0,1,0] [1,2,1] [3,5,0]
2	4	→ [0,1,0] [1,2,1] [3,2,0] [5,2,1] [7,1,0]
3	9	→ [0,1,0] [1,6,1] [7,1,0]
4	12	→ [0,3,0] [3,4,1] [7,1,0]
5	15	→ [0,3,0] [3,2,1] [5,3,0]
6	18	→ [0,3,0] [3,2,1] [5,3,0]
7	21	→ [0,8,0]

(c)

Run-length coding takes advantage of this spatial coherence. Instead of storing a row of pixels, the column numbers at which transitions take place are stored. We use a three-element data structure to store information about each transition. The data structure contains the column number of the start of the run of consecutive values, the length of the run, and the number of the shape these pixels belong to. For a raw image, the shape number is 0 and 1. After the image is processed, each blob (object silhouette) has a different shape number if there is more than one object in the image.

The triplet data structure contains redundant information and can be reduced to a tuple containing the run length and shape number. As it is assumed that the first run starts in column 0, the start position of successive runs can be calculated from the run-lengths. Which data structure is used depends on a compromise between storage and computation efficiency. In the example in Figure 10.57, the run-length code takes more space than the original binary image. A typical vision system with an image of 256 by 256 pixels requires 8 192 bytes to store the image.

With run-length coding, an image of a circle 126 pixels in diameter can be stored in as little as 512 bytes. Reducing the volume of data considerably reduces the processing time. The most efficient algorithms for processing binary images depend to a great extent on the fact that only transitions are significant, and hence, only transitions need to be processed. Run-length encoding reduces the data to a sequence of transitions, making it an ideal input to these algorithms.

Algorithm 10.1   Run-length coding

Allocate an array to store triplets in sequence.
Allocate a second array, indexed by row number, to store the number of the
        first triplet in each row.
Set next_triplet number to zero.
For each row in the image **do**
        Set triplet index for this row to next_triplet number
        Set pixel_sequence counter to 1.
        Set current_shape number to shape number of column 0.
        For each column starting at column 1 **do**
                Compare column_shape number to current_shape number
                If the same **then**
                        Increment pixel counter.
                Else
                        Save triplet for run just completed.
                        Increment next_triplet number.
                        Set pixel_sequence counter to 1.
                        Set current_shape number to column_shape number.
                End
        End
        Save triplet for last run of row.
        Increment next_triplet number.
End

A simple algorithm for converting a binary image to run-length coding format is given in Algorithm 10.1. This algorithm scans the image one row at a time, from left to right, counting the number of pixels in each sequence, and saving the triplets in a linear array. A second array is used to index into the triplet array. It contains the number of the start triplet for each row.

10.8.7   Connectivity analysis

In order to recognize an object in a binary image, the image must be converted into a form that allows us to separate objects, select the portion of the

Figure 10.58
Connectivity – definitions and paradox: (a) 1s connected, 0s connected – 2 blobs; (b) 1s not connected, 0s not connected – 3 blobs; (c) 1s connected, 0s not connected – 3 blobs; (d) 1s connected, 0s connected (paradox) – not obvious how many blobs; (e) 4 connected; (f) 6 connected; (g) 8 connected.

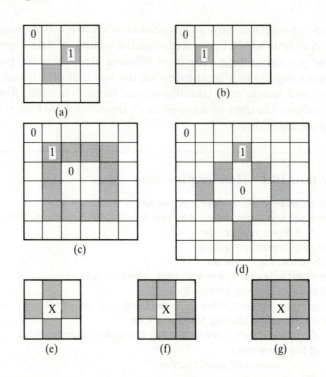

image that represents an object, and calculate parameters representative of the object. Connectivity analysis (Agin, 1985) is a series of steps that allows us to do that in a robust and repeatable way.

The first step in connectivity analysis is to segment the image into groups of connected pixels. Each object silhouette forms a group, as does the background. This process is called **blob growing**. Holes in objects are also represented by blobs. Once the blobs are grown, parameters can be calculated for each blob, such as area, centre of area and circumference. Object overlap and noisy signals play havoc with this process.

10.8.7.1 *Connectivity*

The concepts of connectivity were introduced in Chapter 8 during the discussion of distance transforms (Section 8.3.3.6). A blob is a connected cluster of pixels which are all the same colour. Two pixels are connected if they are adjacent (Figure 10.58). They can be orthogonally and/or diagonally adjacent depending on the description of connectivity.

A 4-connected algorithm looks at the four pixels that are orthogonally adjacent or the four pixels that are diagonally adjacent, but not both. An 8-connected algorithm examines all the eight pixels that surround the current pixel for connectivity. A 6-connected algorithm looks at six of the neighbouring pixels in a positive or negative sloping hexagonal pattern. In most situations, these algorithms produce the same results. However, a paradox

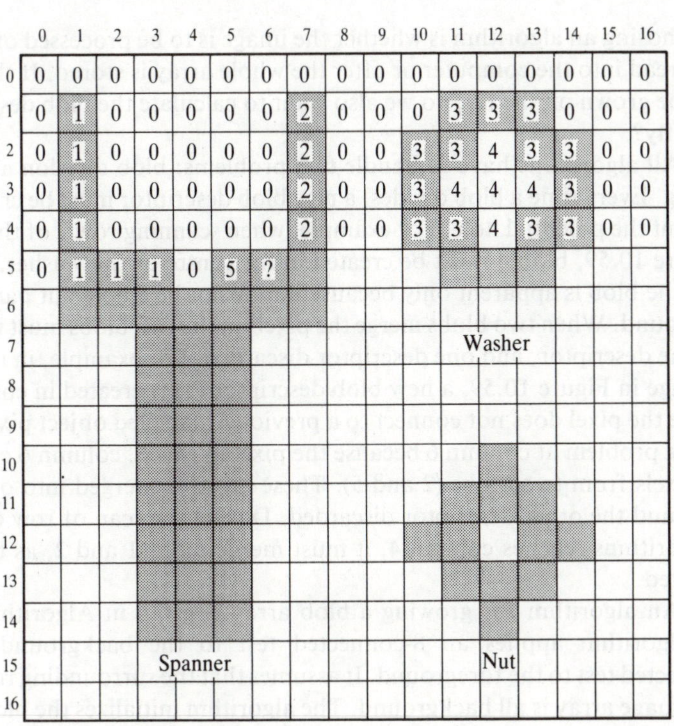

Figure 10.59
Blob array – scanning has reached the point where blobs 2 and 5 have to be combined.

	0	1	2	3	4	5	6	7	8	9	10	11	12	13	14	15	16
0	0	0	0	0	0	0	0	0	0	0	0	0	0	0	0	0	0
1	0	1	0	0	0	0	0	2	0	0	0	3	3	3	0	0	0
2	0	1	0	0	0	0	0	2	0	0	3	3	4	3	3	0	0
3	0	1	0	0	0	0	0	2	0	0	3	4	4	4	3	0	0
4	0	1	0	0	0	0	0	2	0	0	3	3	4	3	3	0	0
5	0	1	1	1	0	5	?										

Washer

Spanner   Nut

arises with a one-pixel-wide line of diagonal pixels (Figure 10.58(d)). Do the dark pixels represent a thin square hollow object, or several small square objects arranged in a hollow square? An orthogonal 4-connected algorithm will produce two background blobs and eight object blobs. An 8-connected algorithm will produce one background blob, merging the hole into the background, and one object blob. A negative sloping 6-connected algorithm will produce one background blob and four object blobs. Thus, the six-connected algorithm solves the paradox in one direction only. Also, we want connectivity to have the property that each blob (except the background) is totally surrounded by another blob of the opposite colour. We can achieve this by treating the 1s as 8-connected and the 0s as 4-connected or vice versa. We can also achieve it with a 6-connected algorithm. Neither algorithm totally solves the paradox, but they do produce consistent results. The advantage of the 6-connected algorithm is that it is independent of the colour of the blob.

10.8.7.2   *Blob growing*

A blob is a connected cluster of pixels of the same colour. The algorithm used to grow blobs is chosen on the basis of the definition of connectivity and the data structures used. Intuitively, the simplest algorithm operates on an image array and produces a blob array (Figure 10.59). Another decision to be made when chosing an algorithm is whether the image is to be processed on the fly as it is read into the computer or after the whole array is stored. If the blobs are to be grown on the fly, do we also want to calculate the blob descriptors on the fly?

All algorithms have to handle two problems: blob division and blob merging. Every time a blob divides, a new blob descriptor must be created to represent the potential hole. For example, when scanning row 2 of the image in Figure 10.59, blob 4 must be created in the centre of the washer. At this point, the blob is apparent only because it may not be a hole but part of the background. When two blobs merge the pixels in the two blobs must be given the same descriptor, and one descriptor discarded. For example, in row 5 of the image in Figure 10.59, a new blob descriptor (5) is created in column 5, because the pixel does not connect to a previously labelled object pixel. This causes a problem at column 6 because the pixel in row 5, column 6 connects with pixels from two blobs (2 and 5). These must be merged into one blob (say 2) and the other descriptor discarded. During the scan of row 6, when the algorithms reaches column 4, it must merge blobs 1 and 2, as they are connected.

An algorithm for growing a blob array is given in Algorithm 10.2. This algorithm applies an 8-connected test to the background and a 4-connected test to the foreground. It assumes that the surrounding rectangle in the image array is all background. The algorithm initializes the blob array to blob 0, and scans the image array one row at a time from left to right looking for objects. Every pixel in the array is scanned, except the pixels in a one pixel-wide bounding rectangle. At each pixel, a four pixel square window is selected with the target pixel at the bottom right. From the values stored in the pixels in this window, a window state value is calculated (Figure 10.60). By applying a binary weighting to the pixels in the window, we obtain a binary value between 0 and 15 for the state. As there is a distinct state value for each window pattern (Figure 10.61), this value is used to index into a pattern table. The pattern table specifies the actions that are to be performed to update the blob array. These actions are selected on the basis of the chosen connectivity algorithm.

As an example of the operation of this algorithm, we will apply it to the divide and merge situations (Figure 10.62). During the scan of row 1, the left arm of object 1 is labelled as blob 1 and the right arm is labelled as blob 2,

$$
\begin{array}{|c|c|}
\hline
P_3 & P_2 \\
\hline
P_4 & P_1 \\
\hline
\end{array}
\qquad P_1 = \text{Target pixel}
$$

Raster scan window

Window state $= w = 2^0 P_1 + 2^1 P_2 + 2^2 P_3 + 2^3 P_4$

$= P_1 + 2P_2 + 4P_3 + 8P_4$

Figure 10.60
Raster scan window state.

Window state	Window pattern	Action
0		1 Connect to background blob
1		2 Start new object blob
2		1 Connect to background blob
3		3 Connect to object blob
4		4 End of object blob, connect to background blob, and merge background blobs
5		5 Start a new object blob and end old object blob
6		1 Connect to background blob
7		3 Connect to object blob
8		1 Connect to background blob
9		3 Connect to background blob
10		1 Connect to background blob
11		6 End of background blob, connect to object blob and merge object blobs
12		1 Connect to background blob
13		3 Connect to object blob
14		7 Start a new background blob
15		3 Connect to object blob

Figure 10.61
Pattern look up table for eight-connected background and four-connected objects, used in Algorithm 10.2.

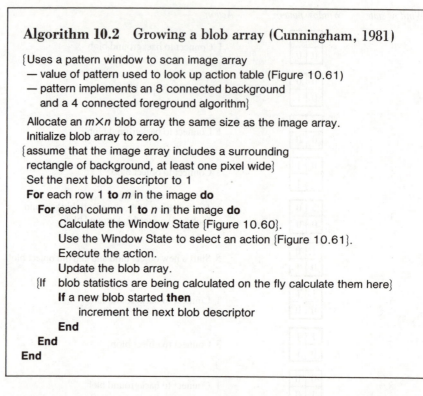

Algorithm 10.2   Growing a blob array (Cunningham, 1981)

{Uses a pattern window to scan image array
— value of pattern used to look up action table (Figure 10.61)
— pattern implements an 8 connected background
    and a 4 connected foreground algorithm}

Allocate an $m \times n$ blob array the same size as the image array.
Initialize blob array to zero.
{assume that the image array includes a surrounding
rectangle of background, at least one pixel wide}
Set the next blob descriptor to 1
For each row 1 **to** m in the image **do**
  For each column 1 **to** n in the image **do**
    Calculate the Window State {Figure 10.60}.
    Use the Window State to select an action {Figure 10.61}.
    Execute the action.
    Update the blob array.
  {If blob statistics are being calculated on the fly calculate them here}
    If a new blob started **then**
      increment the next blob descriptor
    End
  End
End

because these arms are separated by background. During the scan of row 2, these two blobs have to be merged during the scan of the pixel in column 3. Blob 3 shows the divide situation. During the scan of row 2, the left leg of blob 3 is labelled correctly. The next image pixel is a background pixel, but we don't know whether it is part of the background or a hole in the object, so it is labelled as a new blob (blob 4). During the scan of row 3, we identify that blob 4 is connected to the background and merge it with the background.

Merge is usually more complex than in this simple example. The blob whose identifier is to be changed may be quite large, requiring extensive searching of the previous rows. In this example, two situations arise where a merge action is requested but, as the pixels are already correctly labelled as part of the background blob, no relabelling is required.

Algorithm 10.2 is simple, but computationally expensive. Every pixel, except those in the bounding rectangle, has to be examined, and every pixel is used four times in calculations. Thus, for an n element image, we calculate n window states, requiring $4n$ array references. In Section 10.8.6, we pointed out that run-length coding of the image will normally lead to a reduction in processing. An algorithm for growing blob descriptors from run-length coded image data examines a row of the image at a time, comparing each new row to the previous row (Algorithm 10.3). First a copy of the raw image is

Pixel	Image	Window State	Action	Blob Descriptor
1,1	1	1	2	1
1,2	0	8	1	0
1,3	1	1	2	2
1,4	0	8	1	0
1,5	1	1	2	3
1,6	1	9	3	3
1,7	1	9	3	3
1,8	0	8	1	0
2,1	1	3	3	1
2,2	1	13	3	1
2,3	1	11	6	1 {merge}
2,4	0	12	1	0
2,5	1	3	3	3
2,6	0	14	7	4 {divide}
2,7	1	7	3	3
2,8	1	12	1	0
3,1	0	2	1	0
3,2	0	6	1	0
3,3	0	6	1	0
3,4	0	4	4	0 {merge done but not required}
3,5	0	2	1	0
3,6	0	4	4	0 {merge}
3,7	0	2	1	0 {merge done but
3,8	0	4	4	0 {not required}

(a)

	0	1	2	3	4	5	6	7	8
0	0	0	0	0	0	0	0	0	0
1	0	1	0	1	0	3	3	3	0
2	0	1	1	1	0	3	0	3	0
3	0	0	0	0	0	0	0	0	0

Merge   Divide

(b)

Figure 10.62
Blob array growing example. (a) Step-by-step execution of Algorithm 10.2 on image in (b).

made. The algorithm examines the raw image for connectivity and inserts blob descriptors into the copy or blob image. The algorithm uses a positive-sloping 6-connected pixel match (Figure 10.63).

In the previous algorithm, every pixel was matched to a pattern. In contrast, in this algorithm, a match is only done at the transitions. Thus for the image in Figures 10.62 and 10.65, the number of matches is reduced from 24 to 12, but the algorithms are considerably more complex. For a realistic image, the saving in execution can be considerable.

At the start of each row, the *Merge* procedure is called to see if any blobs from the previous row have to be merged with the background. Blob 4 in the image in Figure 10.62 has to be merged with blob 0 (the background) during the processing of row 3. Again, we assume that the objects in the image are surrounded by background. Next, the algorithm scans across the row performing a match at each transition. A special procedure is used to find the colour of the four pixels from the run-length-coded data in the raw image (Algorithm 10.4). As we are interested only in transitions, half of the window states are redundant (Figure 10.63). The other states fall into two groups: obvious overlap and possible overlap. If there is an obvious overlap the current run is added to the blob it overlaps with. If there is not an obvious overlap, the whole run must be scanned for an overlap (Algorithm 10.6). The variables used in these algorithms are described in Figure 10.64.

Figure 10.63
Pattern look up table for positive sloping 6-connected run-length coded data used in algorithm 10.5: (a) 6-connected foreground and background with positive slope; (b) examples of overlap with 6-connected algorithm; (c) patterns and action table.

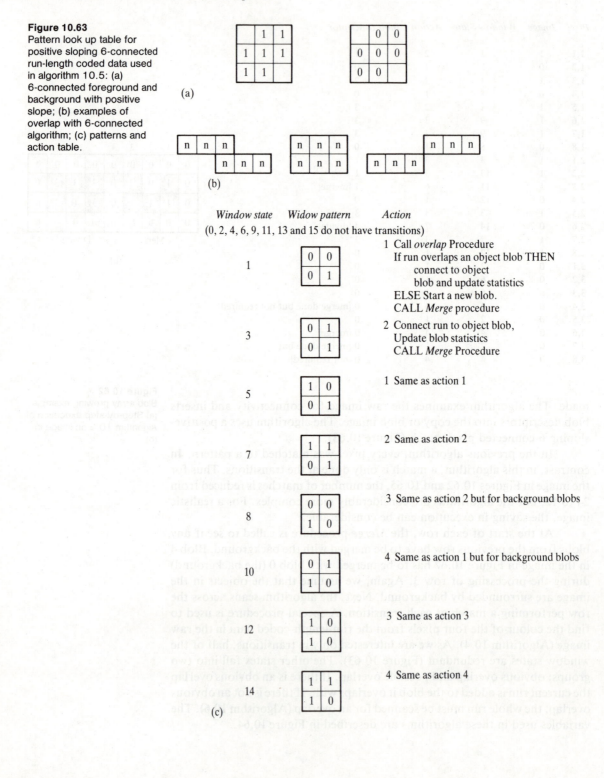

Window state   Widow pattern   Action
(0, 2, 4, 6, 9, 11, 13 and 15 do not have transitions)

1

1 Call *overlap* Procedure
    If run overlaps an object blob THEN
        connect to object
        blob and update statistics
    ELSE Start a new blob.
    CALL *Merge* procedure

3

2 Connect run to object blob,
    Update blob statistics
    CALL *Merge* Procedure

5

1 Same as action 1

7

2 Same as action 2

8

3 Same as action 2 but for background blobs

10

4 Same as action 1 but for background blobs

12

3 Same as action 3

14

4 Same as action 4

(c)

Algorithm 10.3   Blob growing of a run-length coded image

       {Image already in run-length coded from (Figure 10.65)
       and stored in an index array and a triplet array.
       Blob descriptor 0 is the background.
       Assumes row 0 is already set to descriptor 0.}
Copy *raw-image* data structure to *blob_image* data structure
For *rows* 1 to *max_row* **do**
       {first triplet already set to descriptor 0}
       Set *triplet_count* to index of first triplet in row
       Set *previous_run* to index of first triplet in previous row
       {May have to do a merge to first triplet eg. row 3 in Figure 10.65}
       Call *Merge* procedure
       Assign *start column+length*-1 to *column* {last column in run}
       While *column* < *max_column* **do**
              Increment *triplet_count* {moves to next run}
              Assign *start_column* to *column* {first column in new run}
              Call *State* procedure to calculate
                       window state for pixel at *row, column*
              Perform action based on state (Algorithm 10.5)
       End
End

If an overlap is found, the run is connected to an existing blob (Algorithm 10.5). If not, a new blob is created. The final step in processing a run is to scan along the run to see if any blobs have to be merged (Algorithm 10.7). The fact that we scan runs rather than look at single pixels makes the algorithms for blob growing from run-length coded data more complex. Again, with a slightly different algorithm, the generation of the blob image can be done on the fly, as the image is read into the computer. Also, the blob statistics can be calculated as the blob is constructed. A more sophisticated algorithm for connectivity analysis using dynamic data structures is given by Agin (1985).

So far, we have studied algorithms that convert a raw-image into a blob image. Before we can calculate features for blob identification, we must obtain a description of each blob. This can be done as the blobs are constructed. For a run-length coded image, we obtain a list of runs for each blob (Figure 10.65(d)). We can calculate blob statistics directly from this list. For

Figure 10.64
Variables used in algorithms
10.3–7.

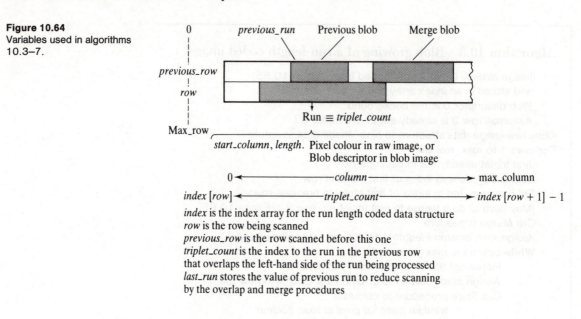

index is the index array for the run length coded data structure
row is the row being scanned
previous_row is the row scanned before this one
triplet_count is the index to the run in the previous row
that overlaps the left-hand side of the run being processed
last_run stores the value of previous run to reduce scanning
by the overlap and merge procedures

Algorithm 10.4   State procedure

{Calculates the window state of a pixel from a raw run-length coded image.
Pass in *pixel_colour*, *previous_run*, *row* and *column* – Algorithm 10.3
Row, *column* specifies position of target pixel P1 – Figure 10.60}

Assign *pixel_colour* to P1
Assign **Not** pixel_colour to P4
Assign *row*-1 to *previous_row*
Assign *previous_start_column*+*previous_length*-1 to *count*
    {last column in run on previous row}
While count < column-1 **do** {find run in previous row with P3 in it}
    Increment *previous_run*
    Assign *previous_start_column*+*previous_length*-1 to count
End
    {P3 is in run *previous_triplet_count*}
Assign *previous_colour* to P3 {*previous_run*}
Assign *previous_run* to *previous_triplet_count*
    {Get colour of P2}
    {P2 is not in run *previous_triplet_count*}
If count < column **then**
    Increment *previous_triplet_count* {P2 is in next run}
End
Assign *previous-colour* to P2 {*previous_triplet_count*}
Calculate window state (Figure 10.60)
{Return window state, *previous_run*}

	0	1	2	3	4	5	6	7	8
0	0	0	0	0	0	0	0	0	0
1	0	1	0	1	0	3	3	3	0
2	0	1	1	1	0	3	0	3	0
3	0	0	0	0	0	0	0	0	0

(a)

Row	*Index array*	*Triplet array*
0	→	[0,9,0]
1	→	[0,1,0] [1,1,1] [2,1,0] [3,1,1] [4,1,0] [5,3,3] [8,1,0]
2	→	[0,1,0] [1,3,1] [4,1,0] [5,1,3] [6,1,0] [7,1,3] [8,1,0]
3	→	[0,9,0]

(c)

Row	*Index array*	*Triplet array*
0	→	[0,9,0]
1	→	[0,1,0] [1,1,1] [2,1,0] [3,1,1] [4,1,0] [5,3,1] [8,1,0]
2	→	[0,1,0] [1,3,1] [4,1,0] [5,1,1] [6,1,0] [7,1,1] [8,1,0]
3	→	[0,9,0]

(b)

Blob No		*Row No*		*Runs*
1	→	1	→	[1,1,1] [3,1,1]
		2		[1,3,1]
3	→	1	→	[5,3,3]
		2		[5,1,3] [7,1,3]

(d)

Figure 10.65
Blob growing from run-length. (a) Image as a pixel array. (b) Run-length coded raw image. (c) Run-length coded blob data. (d) Blob list.

Algorithm 10.5 Action procedure

{Executes an action on the run_length_coded blob image to update it in response to the change in window state at the start of a new run – Figure 10.63
Pass in State, *triplet_count*, *previous_run* and *row*}

States 1 and 5
  Call *Overlap* procedure
  If run overlaps an object blob **then**
    Connect run to object blob
    Update blob statistics
  Else
    Start a new blob
  End
  Call *Merge* procedure
State 3
  {State procedure left *previous_run* indexing a background blob
  Thus object blob is in *previous_run*+1}
  Connect run to object blob
  Update Blob statistics
  Call *Merge* procedure
State 7
  Same as State 3 except *previous_run* indexes correct blob
State 10, 14
  Same as States 1 and 5 except for a background blob
State 8
  Same as State 7 except for a background blob
State 12
  Same as State 3 except for a background blob
{Return *previous_run*}

a blob array, we use a boundary-tracking algorithm (Cunningham, 1981) to find the pixels in the boundary of the blob. The boundary is stored as a chain code (Wilf, 1981), which is a sequence of digits, one for each pixel in the boundary. The digit has a value in the range 0 to 3, which indicates the direction in which the boundary is moving at this pixel: 0 = right, 1 = down, 2 = left, and 3 = up.

10.8.7.3 *Blob features*

In binary vision, an object can be recognized either by matching the blob to a template (Section 10.8.5) or by calculating features. The latter is more general. We can calculate these features during blob growing, or from the blob lists after the blob is grown. In practical systems, features are calculated during blob growing. In order to illustrate each step in connectivity analysis, we have broken it up into several discrete steps: run-length coding, blob growing and feature calculation:

To calculate features from a blob array, the boundary of the blob

---

Algorithm 10.6 Overlap procedure

{Tests for overlap between current run and a previous blob by comparing runs in the raw image
Pass in the *triplet_count*, *previous_run*, *row*}

    Assign *start_column* to *start*
    Assign *start+current_length* to *end* {actually start of next run}
        {satisfies 6-connected overlap – Figure 10.63(b)}
    Assign *previous_run* to *previous_triplet_count*
    {Scan *previous_row* for a triplet that begins between start and end}
    While *previous_start_column+previous_length* < *start+1* **do**
        increment *previous_triplet_count*
    End
        {Found triplet in previous row that starts left of triplet in this row
        Note: the state check means that this procedure is only called for
            states 1, 5, 10, 14 which guarantees that the colour of this
            triplet in the previous row is opposite the colour of the triplet in
            this row.}
    If *previous_start_column+previous_length* < =end **Then**
        {found an overlap}
        Set *overlap* flag
        Assign *previous_triplet_counter* to *previous_run*
        increment *previous_triplet_count* {overlapping triplet}
        assign *previous_triplet_blob_descriptor* to *descriptor*
    End
    {return *blob descriptor*, *overlap flag*, *previous_run*}

---

must be found as above, and each pixel must be manipulated. Run-length coded blob lists have the advantage that pixels are already aggregated into lines, which considerably reduces the number of calculations. Features can be divided into two categories: those that are independent of location and those that are not. Location-dependent features include the centroid and angular orientation. Location-independent features include area, perimeter length, and the number of holes in the blob. As features are calculated, they are added to the blob descriptor data structure.

The simplest feature to calculate is **colour**, as it is stored in the run-

---

Algorithm 10.7   Merge procedure

{Tests for blobs of same colour in raw image that overlap current run, and
  updates the blob if required
  Pass in *last_run*, *triplet_count*, *row*}
{Note: this algorithm assumes that the current run is connected to a previous
  blob}
Assign *start_column+length* to *end*
Assign *previous_run* to *previous_triplet_count*
Increment *previous_triplet_count* {to overlapping triplet}
If *previous_start_column+previous_length* < *end* **then**
    {Previous run finishes before new run so possibility of a merge
     Skip over this triplet as it is the known blob}
    Increment *previous_triplet_counter* {to start of triplet of opposite colour}
    While *previous_start_column+previous_length* < =*end* **do**
        Increment *previous_triplet_count*
        If *previous_colour=colour* THEN
            {Found a blob to merge, * Update blob statistics * }
            Assign *previous_triplet_blob descriptor* to *update*
            {Scan blob image and update}
            Assign *row* to *update_row*
            Repeat
                Decrement *update_row*
                {Scan and update row}
                Assign *count* to index of first triplet in update row
                While *count_start_column+count_length* < =*max_column* **do**
                    If *count_blob_descriptor=update* **Then**
                        count_blob_descriptor=descriptor
                        set *update_flag*
                    End
                    Increment *count*
                End
            Until *update_flag* not set
        End
    End
End

Figure 10.66
Parameters for feature
calculation.

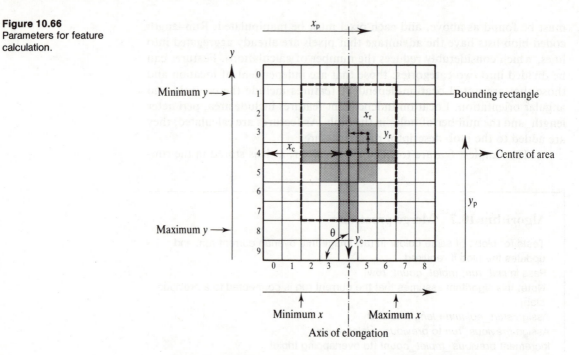

length code. **Inclusion relationships**, such as holes in objects, are found by searching the run-length coded blob image, and building a blob tree. The root of the tree is the background, and its branches are the blobs it surrounds. The **bounding rectangle** is described with four values: minimum x, maximum x, minimum y, and maximum y (Figure 10.66). The y values are the first and last rows in the blob. The x values are found by comparing the start columns of the first run in every row, and the end columns of the last run in every row. From the bounding rectangle values, we can calculate the position of the **centroid** (x_c, y_c) and the **height** and **width**.

$$x_c = \frac{1}{2}(\text{minimum } x + \text{maximum } x) \tag{10.3}$$

$$y_c = \frac{1}{2}(\text{minimum } y + \text{maximum } y) \tag{10.4}$$

While the bounding rectangle gives us a measure of its **largeness**, it tells us very little about the shape, apart from whether the rectangle is square or elongated. A measure which does capture information about the complexity of the shape of the object is the shape and length of the perimeter of the blob. The perimeter is the boundary between the pixels of the blob and the pixels of the surrounding blob. The **perimeter length** of a blob is the length of the boundary, that is the number of pixels in the boundary of the blob. The number of boundary pixels can be accumulated as the blob is grown (Agin, 1985), or a boundary-tracking algorithm (Cunningham, 1981)

can be used to find the boundary of a blob. One problem with using perimeter length in object recognition is that the number of pixels in the boundary varies with object orientation.

We want to recognize objects of known shape in any position and
orientation in the image. Also, in addition to recognizing the object, we want
to obtain its position and orientation. Features that capture this information
are the **moments** of **area**. Such moments are defined as area equivalents of
mass moments. The zeroth moment of area is the **physical area** of the object
(A). If we describe the object with the characteristic function $f(x, y)$, where
the value of $f(x, y)$ at pixel x, y is 1 if the pixel is in an object and 0 otherwise,
then the area is:

$$A = \iint f(x, y)dx\, dy = \sum_{y\,\min}^{y\,\max} \sum_{x\,\min}^{x\,\max} 1 = \text{the number of pixels in blob} \qquad \textbf{(10.5)}$$

where the integration is over the area of the image which contains the blob.
For a discrete binary image, area is the total number of pixels in the blob.
With run-length coded data, we calculate area by adding the lengths of the
runs in the blob.

The **centre of area** (centroid) is the area equivalent of the centre of
mass of a thin sheet with the same shape and uniform mass distribution
(Window 7.2). If all the mass is concentrated at the centre of mass, rotation
about any axis through that point will produce no torque. That is the first
moment of the object doesn't change. The centre of area of a homogeneous
object lies on the point, line or plane of symmetry of that object, just as the
centre of mass does. The first moment about an axis is zero if the axis lies
along a line of symmetry. Consequently, the first moments capture **position
information.**

$$M_x = \iint x f(x, y)dx\, dy = x_c A \qquad \textbf{(10.6)}$$

$$M_y = \iint y f(x, y)dx\, dy = y_c A \qquad \textbf{(10.7)}$$

As we are analysing discrete-blob images, we replace the integrations
in the equations for continuous-binary images with summations. For a blob
array, the first moments are the sum of the coordinates of the pixels in the
blob.

$$M_x = x_c A = \sum_1^p x \qquad \textbf{(10.8)}$$

$$M_y = x_c A = \sum_1^p y \qquad \textbf{(10.9)}$$

where there are p pixels in the blob.

When the blob image is run-length coded, we use the formula for the sum of x over a range, to add the x coordinates of the pixels in a run.

$$\sum_{m}^{n-1} x = \sum_{1}^{n-1} x - \sum_{1}^{m-1} x = \frac{n^2 - n}{2} - \frac{m^2 - m}{2} = \frac{1(n-m)(m+n-1)}{2} \quad \textbf{(10.10)}$$

where m is the column number at the start of the run and
n is the column number at the start of the next run
$= m + $ length of this run.

For the whole blob,

$$M_x = \sum_{1}^{\text{runs}} \frac{(n-m)(m+n-1)}{2} = \sum_{1}^{\text{rows}} \sum_{1}^{r} \frac{(n-m)(m+n-1)}{2} \quad \textbf{(10.11)}$$

where r is the number of runs in the row.

The sum of the y coordinates of the pixels in a run is the product of the length of the run and the row number. For the whole blob,

$$M_y = \sum_{1}^{\text{runs}} y(n-m) = \sum_{1}^{\text{rows}} \sum_{1}^{r} y(n-m) \quad \textbf{(10.12)}$$

From the two first moments of area, we can calculate the position of the centroid (x_c, y_c) using Equations 10.8 and 10.9.

When an object rotates, inertial forces are generated (Window 7.3). These forces are a function of the orientation of the body relative to the axis of rotation and the shape of the body – roundness, slenderness, and so on. The manner in which the mass of the body is distributed with respect to the axes is defined by the moments of inertia. The second moments of area are the area equivalents of moments of inertia. As there is an axis of rotation where the inertia is least, so there is an axis of elongation where the second moments of area are least. The axis of elongation is the line through the blob for which the integral of the square of the distance to the pixels in the blob is minimum (Horn, 1986). For a continuous binary image, the integral is

$$E = \iint d^2 f(x, y) dx \, dy \quad \textbf{(10.13)}$$

where d is the perpendicular distance from the axis of the elongation to the pixels (x_p, y_p). A second property of this axis is that it passes through the centre of area (x_c, y_c).

We calculate the second moments of area with respect to axes (x_d, y_d) located at the centre of area and parallel to the reference axes. We obtain three equations which capture information about the **orientation** and **shape** of the blob.

$$x_d = x_p - x_c \text{ and } y_d = y_p - y_c \tag{10.14}$$

where x_p, y_p is the position of the pixel relative to the reference frame.

$$M_{x^2} = \iint x_d^2 f(x, y)\, dx_d\, dy_d = \sum_1^p x_d^2 A \tag{10.15}$$

$$M_{xy} = 2\iint x_d y_d f(x, y)\, dx_d\, dy_d = 2\sum_1^p x_d y_d A \tag{10.16}$$

$$M_{y^2} = \iint y_d^2 f(x, y)\, dx_d\, dy_d = \sum_1^p y_d^2 A \tag{10.17}$$

For a blob array, the second moments are the sums of products of the distances from the centre of area to each pixel. As we have calculated the coordinates of the centroid with Equations 10.8 and 10.9, we can calculate the second moments by summation. For example, for the second moments about the x axis are:

$$\sum_1^p (x_p - x_c)^2 = M_{x^2} = \sum_1^p x_d^2 A \tag{10.18}$$

When the blob image is run-length coded, we use the formula for the sum of x^2 over a range, to sum the squares of the x coordinates in a run.

$$\sum_m^{n-1} x^2 = \sum_1^{n-1} x^2 - \sum_1^{m-1} x^2 \frac{2n^3 - 3n^2 + n}{6} - \frac{2m^3 - 3m^2 + m}{6}$$

$$= \frac{1}{12}\left[3(n - m)(n + m - 1)^2 + (n - m)^3 - (n - m)\right] \tag{10.19}$$

For the whole blob,

$$\sum_1^{\text{runs}} x^2 = \sum_1^{\text{rows}} \sum_1^r \frac{1}{12}\left[3(n - m)(n + m - 1)^2 + (n - m)^3 - (n - m)\right] \tag{10.20}$$

The sum of the squares of the y coordinates of the pixels in a run is the product of the length of the run and the row numer squared. For the whole blob,

$$\sum_1^{\text{runs}} y^2 = \sum_1^{\text{rows}} \sum_1^{r} y^2(n-m) \tag{10.21}$$

The product of the x and y coordinates of the pixels in the runs in the blob is

$$\sum_1^{\text{runs}} xy = \sum_1^{\text{rows}} \sum_1^{r} \frac{y(n-m)(m+n-1)}{2} \tag{10.22}$$

From these summations, we calculate the second moments of area, but first we need an algorithm to accumulate these summations in one pass over the run-length coded data structure.

Algorithm 10.8   Accumulating moments of area parameters

Initialize accumulators to zero: A, $\sum x$, $\sum y$, $\sum xy$, $\sum y^2$, $\sum x^2$
{y is the row number and x is the column number}
For the rows in the blob **do**
    For the runs in the row **do**
        {accumulate values}
        $A = A + n - m$

$$\sum x = \sum x + \frac{(n-m)(m+n-1)}{2}$$

$$\sum y = \sum y + y(n-m)$$

$$\sum xy = \sum xy + \frac{y(n-m)(m+n-1)}{2}$$

$$\sum y^2 = \sum y^2 + y^2(n-m)$$

$$\sum x^2 = \sum x^2 + \frac{1}{12}[3(n-m)(n+m-1)^2 + (n-m)^3 - (n-m)]$$

Note the values in the accumulators can become large, and cause arithmetic overflow. For an n by n image, $\sum x^2$ has a maximum value of $\frac{1}{3}n^4$. The body of this algorithm can be included in the connectivity analysis of the image (Algorithm 10.5) to generate these values while building the blobs. Once we have these values, we can calculate the second moments of area. From Equation 10.13:

$$M_{x2} = \sum (x - x_c)^2 \equiv \sum x^2 - 2x_c \sum x + x_c^2 A \tag{10.23}$$

where $\sum x$ and so on are the variables in Algorithm 10.8

$$M_{y2} = \sum (y - y_c)^2 \equiv \sum y^2 - 2y_c \sum y + y_c^2 A \qquad (10.24)$$

$$M_{xy} = \sum (x - x_c)(y - y_c) \equiv \sum xy - y_c \sum x - x_c \sum y + x_c y_c A \qquad (10.25)$$

From the three second moments of area, we calculate the orientation (θ) of the axis of elongation.

$$\sin 2\theta = \pm \frac{M_{xy}}{\sqrt{M_{xy}^2 + (M_{x2} - M_{y2})^2}} \qquad (10.26)$$

$$\cos 2\theta = \pm \frac{M_{x2} - M_{y2}}{\sqrt{M_{xy}^2 + (M_{x2} - M_{y2})^2}} \qquad (10.27)$$

The derivation of these equations is found in Horn (1986). Of the two solutions, the one with the plus signs in Equations 10. 26 and 10.27 leads to the minimum value in Equation 10.13. However, while the above equations give a value for the orientation, they do not tell us whether the slope of the axis of elongation is positive or negative. Also, for a symmetrical object (like a disk), the numerator of Equations 10.26 and 10.27 will be zero because all axes through the centroid, are axes of symmetry.

A unique set of features that describe the object, including its position and orientation, are the parameters of the approximating ellipse (Agin, 1985). Given a blob with its six moments of area, we can find the parameters of the ideal ellipse with identical moments. These parameters are major axis length, minor axis length (size and shape), centroid x coordinate, centroid y coordinate (position), orientation (rotation) and density. We calculate these parameters from the accumulated values. First, we introduce scale factors s_x and s_y, the width and height of the pixels, so that we are working in true area.

$$\text{Area} = s_x s_y A \qquad (10.28)$$

$$\text{Centroid } x = s_x \frac{\sum x}{A} \qquad (10.29)$$

$$\text{Centroid } y = s_y \frac{\sum y}{A} \qquad (10.30)$$

$$\text{Major axis} = \sqrt{\frac{a + b + e}{2f}} \qquad (10.31)$$

$$\text{Minor axis} = \sqrt{\frac{a + b - e}{2f}} \qquad (10.32)$$

$$\text{Rotation} = \frac{1}{2}\,\text{atan2}(2c, a - b) \tag{10.33}$$

$$\text{Density} = \frac{4}{\pi}\,\frac{s_x s_y A}{2f} \tag{10.34}$$

where

$$a = \frac{4}{\pi}s_x^3 s_y\left(\sum x^2 - \frac{\left(\sum x\right)^2}{A}\right) \tag{10.35}$$

$$b = \frac{4}{\pi}s_x s_y^3\left(\sum y^2 - \frac{\left(\sum y\right)^2}{A}\right) \tag{10.36}$$

$$c = \frac{4}{\pi}s_x^2 s_y^2\left(\sum xy - \frac{\sum x \sum y}{A}\right) \tag{10.37}$$

$$e = \sqrt{(a - b)^2 + \frac{4}{\pi}c^2} \tag{10.38}$$

$$f = \sqrt[4]{ab - c^2} \tag{10.39}$$

Figure 10.67
Features for the object in the above image using the equations in the text. Note the ambiguity in the orientation angle.

We can use these features to generate a unique object description (Figure 10.67), which we match to the features of other blobs in order to recognize the object and determine its location. We select m location

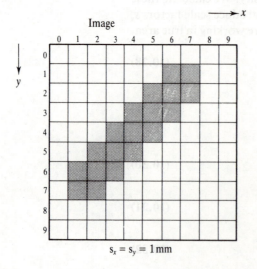

Image

$s_x = s_y = 1\text{mm}$

Bounding rectangle

min $x = 1$	max $x = 7$	x_c 4
min $y = 1$	max $y = 7$	y_c 4

Circumference

14 pixels

$\Sigma 1$	19 pixels	Area	19		
Σx	76	M_x	76	x_c	4
Σy	76	M_y	76	y_c	4
Σxy	244	M_{xy}	−60	$\sin 2\theta$	∓1
Σx^2	370	M_{x2}	66	$\cos 2\theta$	±0
Σy^2	370	M_{y2}	66		

a	84.03	Major axis length 4.61
b	84.03	Minor axis length 2.62
c	−76.39	Rotation = $\frac{1}{2}\tan^{-1}(-\infty)$ as $a = b$
e	86.20	= $\frac{1}{2}$ x −90° = 45°
f	5.97	Density 2.03

independent features of interest and generate an *m* dimensional feature space, where each feature is represented by one dimension. In this space, the object is represented as a point, and each object that the system can recognise is stored as a point in that space. When an image of an object is recorded, the feature vector (point in feature space) is calculated, and compared to the pre-recorded vectors. The nearest match defines which object it is. After, we have recognised the object, we can calculate its position and orientation from the other parameters.

10.8.8 Grey-scale vision

Grey-scale images contain much more information than binary images. In robotic applications, the processing of grey-scale images has the potential to provide greater generality and flexibility. These images depend less on controlled lighting, and background clutter is less of a problem. Provided there is reasonable contrast between the objects of interest and the background, we can threshold to separate them. However, the processing of grey-scale images requires much more time.

Typical grey-scale vision systems (Figure 10.68) use sophisticated array processors to obtain real-time image analysis (Figure 10.69). A number of techniques are available for image analysis, but they tend to produce ambiguous results. To overcome these problems, decision thresholds must be fine tuned for a specific application. While grey-scale systems are increasingly used in industry, many of the processing techniques lack robustness and, hence, only a few techniques are in common use.

Figure 10.69
Block diagram of International Robomation/Intelligence P256 grey-scale vision system. The iconic processor can histogram a 256×256×256 grey level image in 17 μs. The iconic processor and array processor execute a range of grey-scale image functions.

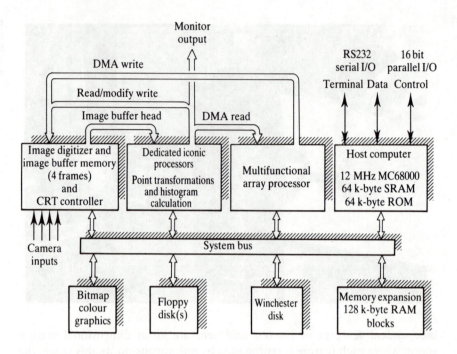

10.8.8.1 *Threshold setting*

A common use of grey-scale images is to convert them to binary images, and use binary processing to analyse the image. The advantage of this technique is that the threshold level can be set to discriminate between the object in the foreground and the background. If the criteria for calculating the threshold are based upon image characteristics, the threshold will automatically change in response to changes in overall light levels. Also, specific features on objects can be isolated from the rest of the image, for example, those which cause specular reflection, such as machined surfaces.

A **histogram** of an image is a plot of the number of pixels in the image at each grey-scale level (Figure 10.70). Threshold selection is made considerably easier if the histogram has a bimodal distribution, that is, it peaks at two grey-scale levels that are separated by several intermediate levels. Such a distribution occurs when the background scene is uniform in colour and contrasts with the object, which is also uniform in colour. To separate the object from the background, the threshold is set at the bottom of the valley between the two peaks. At this grey-scale level, the image is least sensitive to lighting changes. As the threshold is moved toward the background grey level, the object blobs increase in size, and, as the threshold is moved toward the object grey level, the object blobs decrease in size. Placing the threshold in the valley produces the closest match to binary vision with good lighting. One way to select the threshold level, is to place an object of known size under the camera and adjust the threshold until the blob is the correct size.

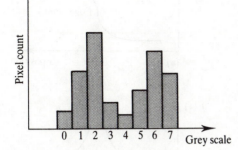

Figure 10.70
Histogram of a grey-scale
image. This plot is bimodel
as it has two peaks.

A histogram generated from a real grey-scale image (with 256 levels), will be ragged with many local maxima and minima. To find the major peaks and valleys, we must consider a range of brightness levels at one time. A major peak occurs when the number of pixels at a grey level is higher than those for $\pm k$ grey levels on either side, where k is half the expected distance between peaks and valleys. When the threshold is incorrect, the resulting binary image tends to have ragged edges. As a consequence, connectivity analysis will produce a feature vector that will not match any points in the prerecorded feature space. The threshold can be adjusted until the feature vector approaches a match. Again, this process is enhanced if we know beforehand what object is in the image.

10.8.8.2 *Edge finding*

One approach to identifying objects in grey-scale images is to find the edges in the image, and thus, reduce the image to a series of lines, like a wire frame model. Edge finding is the process of locating the boundaries between regions of an image. If we assume that regions of near uniform intensity in the image are surfaces of objects, then an edge is a boundary between such regions.

In practice, most images do not show that uniformity. However, edges found by this method will still be useful in identifying objects. One consequence of the fact that surfaces do not reflect uniformly, and that adjacent surfaces may have the same intensity in the image, is that we do not obtain all the edges. Shadows can result in false edges, or in spaces between objects appearing to be part of the objects.

Edge finding is a two-step process. First, we find pixels in the image that are likely to be on an edge. Second, we join those points together into a coherent line. The first step is straightforward, but the second can be tricky. Whenever a discontinuity in brightness occurs, we have a possible edge. We can identify such candidate edge points by estimating the **image gradient** at that point. The image gradient is the spatial derivative of image brightness, and can be characterized by a vector with magnitude and direction (or x and y

Figure 10.71
Finding the edge point in an image by taking the first and second derivatives of the intensity function in the x direction. (a) Original image – change in intensity corresponds to an edge; (b) first derivative – peak corresponds to edge; (c) second derivative – zero crossing corresponds to edge.

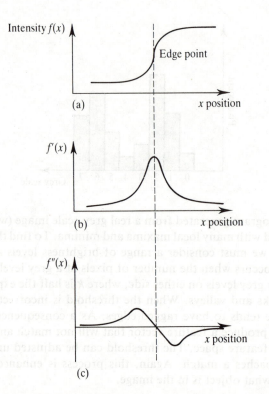

components). Normally, we estimate the x and y derivatives directly and convert them into magnitude and direction.

Mathematically, we can regard an image as a function of two variables (Hildreth, 1981). Every location (x, y) in an image has an intensity $(I(x, y))$. While the image is stored as an array of discrete pixels, we can consider the intensity to be a continuous function over the image space. If we consider that function along one row of pixels, we get a curve (Figure 10.71). An edge point exists where the intensity function is at its maximum slope between two intensity levels. If we differentiate this intensity function, the derivative peaks at each edge point (Figure 10.71(b)). If the intensity function is differentiated again to obtain the second derivative, a zero crossing occurs in the second derivative at each edge point (Figure 10.71(c)).

A practical system computes the gradient within a window containing several pixels. As the window size increases, the sensitivity to pixel noise and digitization error decreases, but the computation cost increases and sharply defined edges are blurred. Thus, the selection of window size is a compromise. For each window size, a specific gradient operator gives the best estimate. A gradient opeator calculates the gradient in x and y directions by summing the pixels according to a specified weighting. A Sobel operator is used with a 3 by 3 window (Figure 10.72). This operator gives the following derivatives based upon the weightings in Figure 10.72.

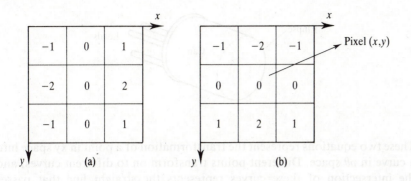

Figure 10.72
Sobel operator derives
image gradient from
directional derivatives across
a 3×3 window. (a) Vertical
edge equivalent to gradient
change in horizontal
direction; (b) horizontal edge
equivalent to gradient
change in vertical direction.

$$dx = (p_{y-1,x+1} + 2p_{y,x+1} + p_{y+1,x+1}) - (p_{y-1,x-1} + 2p_{y,x-1} + p_{y+1,x-1}) \quad \text{(10.40)}$$

$$dy = (p_{y+1,x-1} + 2p_{y+1,x} + p_{y+1,x+1}) - (p_{y-1,x-1} + 2p_{y-1,x} + p_{y-1,x+1}) \quad \text{(10.41)}$$

$$\text{Gradient magnitude} = \sqrt{dx^2 + dy^2} \quad \text{(10.42)}$$

$$\text{Gradient direction} = \tan^{-1}\left(\frac{dy}{dy}\right) \quad \text{(10.43)}$$

Sobel gradients can be calculated quickly with parallel processors, or special hardware. The output of this operation is a gradient image containing the magnitude and direction of each pixel. This image is thresholded to separate candidate edge points from nonedge points. The result is a binary image of edge points. Choosing the threshold level is usually not easy, as there is noise mixed with the edge points. To detect the edges, we must separate the signal from the noise by using sophisticated techniques to identify edges. One approach is to choose a point with a high gradient magnitude, an obvious edge, and search for nearby points in the orthogonal direction to the gradient direction. This process is continued from point to point, chaining the points together to form an edge, until an end point is reached. This strategy works in simple cases, but fails in complex cases.

Edge-finding algorithms can be improved if we know what type of edge we are looking for: straight, curved, and so on. For example, gradient directions will be similar at all points on a straight line. Histogramming the gradient directions of all edge points in a region can identify prominent edge directions. An alternative approach is to use a Hough transform. If we represent a straight line by an equation of the form:

$$x\sin\theta + y\cos\theta - \rho = 0 \quad \text{(10.44)}$$

all the lines that pass through the point (x_i, y_i) are represented by the values of θ and ρ that satisfy the equation

$$\rho = x_i\sin\theta + y_i\cos\theta \quad \text{(10.45)}$$

Figure 10.73
Edges of a transistor can be obtained from a grey-scale image using the Sobel edge operator. The orientation of the transistor can be calculated from the shape of the ellipse.

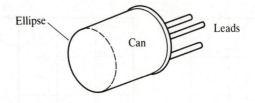

These two equations represent the transformation of a point in xy space into a curve in $\rho\theta$ space. Different points transform on to different curves, and the intersection of these curves represents the straight line that passes through the points. The values of ρ and θ at the point of intersection specify the equation of the line. Agin (1985) gives an algorithm for finding all the lines in an image. The Hough transform technique can be generalized to locate any curve which can be characterized with two parameters, for example, circles.

10.8.8.3 *Features*

Once equations have been fitted to the edges, we can look for features that will enable us to recognize the object. As with binary images, a feature space of objects can be built by imaging the objects in known locations. For constrained environments, such as recognizing parts on a conveyor, this provides a powerful recognition technique. But for unstructured environments, such as the environment of a mobile robot, a higher level strategy is required for perception.

In constrained environments, numerical features that do not change with orientation provide a straightforward way of recognizing objects. Features such as edge length, region perimeter length and region area can easily be found. Again, a feature vector can be constructed and compared to points in a prerecorded feature space. More sophisticated techniques of object recognition based on pattern matching are beyond the scope of this book. To pursue these further, the reader is referred to Horn (1986), and Gonzalez and Wintz (1987).

An interesting example of object recognition using grey-scale vision is the recognition of a transistor (Foster and Sanderson, 1984). By applying the Sobel edge operator to the image, a set of edges showing the outline of the transistor is obtained (Figure 10.73). The top surface of the transistor appears in the two dimensional image as an ellipse. By fitting an ellipse to this curved edge, the orientation of the transistor can be calculated. Foster and Sanderson (1984) found that they could calculate the orientation of the transistor with reasonable accuracy, except at orientations where the elliptical shape is difficult to discern.

A second example is separating the images of objects that overlap or lie together in a bin. Kelly *et al.* (1983) present three algorithms for recogniz-

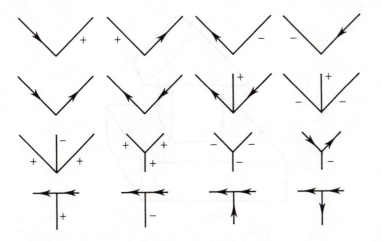

Figure 10.74
Junction dictionary for solids
in which three surfaces
intersect at a point.

ing sections of objects which can be grasped by a vacuum cup or parallel jaw gripper. These algorithms look for hold sites rather than the position and orientation of the parts. They postulate that if they can identify a grasp point, then the robot can remove the part from the bin, and once it is isolated from other parts, normal object recognition techniques can be used.

One way of enhancing the description of an object is to label the edges to show whether the junctions are concave or convex, and hence obtain a three-dimensional description of the object. A convex line (labelled+) is formed when two surfaces of a convex solid intersect, for example, the edges of a cube. A concave line (labelled −) is formed by the intersection of two surfaces belonging to two different solids, for example, the corner of a room. An occluding line (labelled with an arrow) is the edge of a surface which obscures another surface. The line separates the two surfaces. If you look along the line in the direction of the arrow, the occluded surface is on the left.

For solids where only two or three plane surfaces can intersect at a point, such as a cube, all the possible junctions are described in the junction dictionary in Figure 10.74. Physical constraints allow only a few combinations of line labels at a junction. Also, a line cannot change its label between junctions. After the lines in a scene have been labelled, their junctions provide clues about the nature of the 3D solids in the scene (Figure 10.75). For example, when three convex lines join, we have a convex vertex, such as the vertex of a cube. Usually, a set of heuristics is used to map these labelled lines into solids. For example, the object in Figure 10.75 is made of three solids. This object has a boundary that is occluding except for two lines, where it touches the table. As these lines are both concave, we know there is nothing in front of the object. The vertex with three convex lines (three+'s) indicates that is object is a rectangular solid. While the description of this process appears simple, in practice it involves very complex algorithms.

Figure 10.75
Labelling edges in a scene
gives a feel for three
dimensional shape.

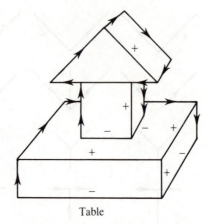

Table

Key points

- Accurate measurement is fundamental to the successful application of robots.

- To perceive is to understand the data we have about a problem.

- A transducer is a device that converts a physical quantity into an electrical signal: a voltage, current, frequency, phase shift, or train of pulses.

- A computer interface contains timing and control circuits (including a bus interface), a converter circuit to convert an electrical signal into a digital value, and a buffer to store the result of the conversion.

- Sensor fusion is the process of combining information from several sensors into a coherent world model.

- Robot sensors are classified into two classes: internal and external sensors.

- Internal sensors measure the position, motion and torque at the joints; from which Cartesian space values are calculated using kinematic models.

- Position and motion are measured with potentiometers, tachogenerators, pulse generators, synchros, linear variable differential transformers, and linear velocity transducers.

- Acceleration is calculated from the motion of a mass due to the force of inertia as described by Newton's second law.

- Shaft torque and wrist force are measured with strain gauge bridges.

- External sensors include contact, touch, proximity, range, orientation, inclination, and vision sensors.

- Simple touch sensors detect the presence of objects, and array touch sensors measure characteristics, such as shape, bumps, stability, and texture.

- With their fingers, humans can detect presence, shape, temperature, grasp force, slip, fluid viscosity, wetness, texture and surface roughness.

- Proximity is detected by the object cutting a light beam and, in the case of ferromagnetic objects, by electromagnetic induction.
- Range sensors measure the distance to objects using either time of flight or triangulation.
- Optical range sensors have fewer problems with specular reflection than ultrasonic sensors.
- Orientation is measured with compasses, gyroscopes, and inclinometers.
- A camera consists of a lens, a photo-sensitive target (vidicon or CCD), and electronic amplification and scanning circuits.
- As a video image is a record of the light reflected by a scene, correct scene lighting is critical to robot vision.
- Newer binary vision systems capture a grey-scale image and threshold it to binary, because the computer can calculate a threshold from a histogram of the image to correct for lighting changes.
- By taking advantage of the spatial coherence of images, run-length coding reduces the storage requirement and, as a result, reduces the computation time for image analysis.
- A blob is a cluster of connected pixels of the same colour.
- Blob features used in object recognition include colour, inclusion relationships, bounding rectangle dimensions, centroid, perimeter length, physical area, moments of area, and the approximating ellipse.
- Grey-scale image processing includes smoothing to reduce noise, sharpening to increase edge contrast, edge finding by gradient detection, fitting lines to edges, combining edges to form surface patches, combining surfaces to form objects, and object recognition.

Exercises

■ *Essay questions*

10.1 Explain the levels of the sensing hierarchy with an example.

10.2 Describe the electrical signals that are used to represent physical quantities.

10.3 Describe the common computer interfaces for sensors.

10.4 List some of the problems in sensor fusion and develop possible solutions.

10.5 Explain the sensor classifications: *external* and *internal*.

10.6 Why is it difficult to measure the location of an end effector in Cartesian space?

10.7 Explain how to measure velocity from a pulse generator when it is turning rapidly and when it is turning slowly.

10.8 Compare sensors for measuring joint angle and joint velocity.

10.9 For an articulated robot with a reach of two metres, what resolution in angle measurement is required at the shoulder joint for a Cartesian resolution of 0.1 mm.

10.10 How can the resolution of a pulse generator be increased?

10.11 Why are limits on the travel of joints important?

10.12 Describe the operation of an accelerometer.

10.13 Describe the operation of a Wheatstone strain-gauge bridge with equations.

10.14 How can strain gauges be used to measure shaft torque?

10.15 From Figure 10.22, derive Equation 10.2 for the Bejczy force-sensing wrist.

10.16 What problems must be considered when using strain gauges?

10.17 Describe the operation of a proximity sensor.

10.18 Describe the operation of a tactile sensor.

10.19 What features of human touch are useful in a robotic gripper? Why?

10.20 Describe the operation of a laser range sensor.

10.21 What two techniques are used for measuring range? Explain how they work.

10.22 Discuss the problems that specular reflection causes for ultrasonic range finders.

10.23 Explain how a television camera captures an image.

10.24 What is composite video?

10.25 What is a frame grabber and what does it do?

10.26 What are the problems with template matching?

10.27 For the image in Figure 10.59:
   (a) derive the run-length code;
   (b) derive the chain code;
   (c) calculate the circumference of each object;
   (d) calculate the bounding rectangle, area and centre of area of each object;
   What features would you use to recognize the objects?

10.28 Explain the ambiguity problem in connectivity analysis.

10.29 Why are run-length coded images used in preference to blob arrays?

10.30 Program the algorithms for analysing an image using arrays and using run-length coding.

10.31 Explain Algorithm 10.2 for growing a blob array. Develop an algorithm for merging two blobs when using a blob array.

10.32 What is the physical meaning of moments of area?

10.33 Calculate the features for the image in Figure 10.67 by hand and compare your results to those in the figure.

10.34 Develop an algorithm for finding the histogram of an n by m grey-scale image.

10.35 Develop an algorithm for finding the bottom of the valley in a bi-modal histogram.

10.36 Explain the operation of the Sobel operator in edge finding.

10.37 Search the literature for an application of grey-scale vision. What grey-scale algorithms are used?

■ *Practical questions*

10.1. Examine the sensors on a robot in the laboratory.
   (a) Clarify them as being either internal and external.
   (b) Record their range, resolution and accuracy.
   (c) Determine what interfaces are used to read them into the computer.
   (d) Determine what processing is done upon the signals to obtain measurements of robot parameters and models of the world.

10.2. Study the vision system on the robot, and program (teach) it to recognize several objects such as nuts and bolts.

10.3. Set up a vision system in a personal computer with a frame grabber and a camera. Program the system to capture an image, grow blobs, calculate features and recognise objects using either blob arrays or run-length coding and the algorithms in this chapter.

10.4. Set up an ultrasonic range finder on a mobile robot and use it to map a room.

10.5. If you don't have a vision system, write a program to read a 16 by 16 array from the keyboard, grow blobs, and calculate features. Display the results on the screen.

11 · *Control*

'If anyone can control his tongue, it proves that he has perfect control over himself in every other way.'

James 3:2 (Living Bible)

Objectives

In this chapter, we discuss the control systems used in robots. Our objective is to understand the control laws used to stabilize position, motion and force control loops. Hence, control laws are analysed in the context of specific control problems. While many control concepts are explained, the reader who wants to master this chapter will need to have studied classical control systems at the level taught in undergraduate engineering courses. When teaching students without this background, the lecturer may have to expand on the introductory explanation

given here. The analysis of control systems includes the following topics:

- transfer functions,
- feedback, feedforward, and adaptive control,
- control laws and stability,
- joint position control,
- compensation of link dynamics,
- visual servoing,
- force and torque control, and
- direct digital-control.

The task of a control system is to execute the planned sequence of motions and forces correctly in the presence of unforeseen errors. Errors can arise from inaccuracies in the model of the robot, tolerances in the workpiece, static friction in joints, mechanical compliance in linkages, electrical noise on transducer signals, and limitations in the precision of computation. Often, computational precision is sacrificed to obtain calculation results in real-time.

At the robot level in the task-planning hierarchy (Figure 9.1), an action is decomposed into a sequence of robot motions and forces in Cartesian space. At the joint level, these motions and forces are decomposed into parallel joint motions and joint torques. In both Cartesian and joint spaces, we require precise control of position, velocity, force and torque. To obtain this control, we use feedback and control laws.

11.1 Basic concepts

In Cartesian space, we use the inverse kinematic model to calculate the joint angles that will place the gripper at the required location in space. The joints are moved to these angles and the robot is assumed to be in the correct Cartesian location, as, generally, there is no way of measuring whether it is or not. This is called **open-loop control**. Open-loop control is as accurate as the model of the process (in this case the inverse kinematic model), provided there are no disturbances to cause errors. Mechanical and environmental variations cause errors in the final location, which the control system can neither detect nor correct. In open-loop control, the desired change in a parameter is calculated, the actuator energy needed to achieve that change is determined using a model of the process, and that amount of energy is applied to the actuator. If the model is correct and there are no disturbances, the desired change is achieved. Once the energy is applied there is no control over what happens.

For example, in lawn bowls, the bowler decides where he wants the ball to go, estimates the amount of energy, swings his arm and releases the ball. Once the ball leaves his hand, he has no control over it and external disturbances (a wet patch, or a pebble) cause errors in the trajectory of the ball. Having bowled one ball, he uses the information about its trajectory to estimate the amount of energy needed to place the next ball in the correct position. This is one use of feedback: to update the model of the process based upon the results of previous actions. This approach is used in model reference **adaptive control**, where the measurements of the results of previous actions are used to adapt the process model to correct for changes in the process and errors in the model. This type of adaption corrects for errors in the model due to long-term variations in the environment but it cannot correct for dynamic changes in the trajectory of the ball caused by local disturbances.

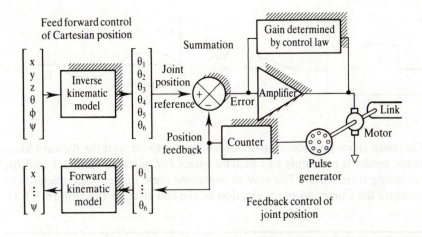

Feed forward control
of Cartesian position

Summation

Gain determined
by control law

$$\begin{bmatrix} x \\ y \\ z \\ \theta \\ \phi \\ \psi \end{bmatrix}$$

Inverse
kinematic
model

$$\begin{bmatrix} \theta_1 \\ \theta_2 \\ \theta_3 \\ \theta_4 \\ \theta_5 \\ \theta_6 \end{bmatrix}$$

Joint
position
reference

Error

Amplifier

Link

Motor

Position
feedback

Counter

Pulse
generator

$$\begin{bmatrix} x \\ \vdots \\ \psi \end{bmatrix}$$

Forward
kinematic
model

$$\begin{bmatrix} \theta_1 \\ \vdots \\ \theta_6 \end{bmatrix}$$

Feedback control of
joint position

Figure 11.1
Basic structure of a robot
position control loop.

The use of a model to predict how much action to take, or the amount of energy to use, is called **feedforward control**. Feedforward control is used to predict actuator settings for processes where feedback signals are delayed (in the above example the bowler has to wait until the ball stops) and in processes where the dynamic effects of disturbances must be reduced. Consider the situation of an acrobat holding a glass of water while standing on the shoulders of a second acrobat. If the bottom acrobat moves without telling the top acrobat, then, due to inertia and gravity, the top acrobat starts to fall backwards. He detects this disturbance through his legs (a change in reference) and through the motion of his body (feedback). He then reacts to overcome the disturbance, but by this time the water may have spilled. To reduce the disturbance, the bottom acrobat tells the top one that he is about to move, (feedforward), and the top one braces his legs to compensate for the expected disturbance.

To obtain accurate control of a process during the execution of an action, we use **feedback control**. In feedback control, the parameter that is being controlled is continually measured (feedback), compared to a reference (error calculation), and the action modified according to a control law to overcome the error. For example, when threading a needle, you watch the end of the thread (feedback), compare it to the hole in the needle (reference), and adjust the motion of your hand to feed the thread through the hole. When controlling a robotic manipulator, feedforward control is used to calculate references for the joints from the Cartesian space references using the inverse kinematic model. To control an individual joint, feedback control (Figure 11.1) is used to compare the measured joint angle to the reference angle. Any error between the feedback signal and the reference is amplified to provide power to the actuator.

While the Cartesian space location can be calculated from measurements of the joint angle, and these calculations used for feedback control during motion, the accuracy of the control is only as good as the kinematic model, so little is gained over feedforward control. Consequently, the

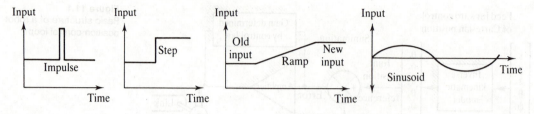

Figure 11.2
Changes in the input to a
control system.

Cartesian space position-control loop is rarely closed, and the forward kinematic model is used only to calculate values for operator feedback and for
recording trajectories. The way to overcome these model inaccuracies is to
measure the Cartesian space location of the end effector (Section 10.5.1.1).

11.2   Transfer functions

The first step when designing a control system is to find the transfer
function, or plant model, of the process we are trying to control. A static
plant model describes the output as a function of the input, excluding
dynamic effects. For a linear system, a static model is the ratio of the output
to the input. For example, the ratio of the output revolutions to the input
revolutions of a gear box (Section 2.6) is constant. Most physical systems are
linear within only a limited range of the variables. Control system designers
try to design the system so that it will work in that linear range. When that
cannot be achieved, we have to control a nonlinear system: a system whose
static model is a nonlinear function of one or more variables.

Transfer functions are plant models which include dynamic effects as
well as the static relationship between output and input. These dynamic
effects cause the relationship between output and input to vary during the
transition from one output state to the next. The main dynamic effect of
concern in control is the time delay between when the input is changed and
when the output responds. For example, when mixing hot and cold water to
obtain the desired water temperature in a shower, there is a delay between
when you turn the taps and when the water temperature changes.

The input to a system can be changed in a number of ways (Figure
11.2). An impulse input is usually the result of some unwanted disturbance.
A step input is an instantaneous change from one reference value to another,
and is usually only used during control loop tuning. A continuously varying
input, like a sinusoid, is used to measure the transfer function, or is the result
of continuous changes in the task. Most inputs are ramps: inputs that vary at
a fixed rate.

Dynamic effects are frequency dependent and not only delay the
change of the output in response to the input but limit the rate at which the
output can change as well. This limit is called the **slew rate** (Figure 11.3) of

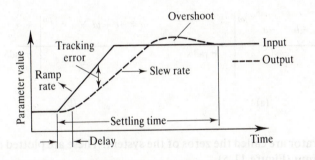

Figure 11.3
Tracking error due to
dynamic effects.

the system. If the ramp is faster than the slew rate, the output cannot catch
the input and a tracking error results. A tracking error is the difference
between input and output at any instant in time. One of the uses of feedforward control is to cause the input to change early to reduce the tracking
error. Transfer functions for linear systems are expressed in the time domain
as differential equations, and in the Laplace domain as Laplace transforms.
Consider a block of mass (m) being pulled along a surface with friction (f)
with a cable with spring constant (k) (Figure 11.4). A model for this system
can be derived from Newton's laws. When a force $F(t)$ is applied, a
reactionary force is established composed of an inertial force proportional to
the acceleration of the mass, a frictional force proportional to the velocity of
the mass, and a spring force proportional to the stretch of the cable.

$$m\ddot{x} + f\dot{x} + kx = F(t) \tag{11.1}$$

The transfer function is the ratio of the Laplace transform of the
output to the Laplace transform of the input.

$$\frac{\text{output}}{\text{input}} = G(s) = \frac{1}{mS^2 + fS + k} = \frac{1}{(S+a)(S+b)} \tag{11.2}$$

The polynomial in the denominator, when equated to zero, is called
the **characteristic equation**, since the roots of this equation determine the
character of the time response of the system. The roots of this equation are
called the poles or singularities of the system. The roots of the polynomial in

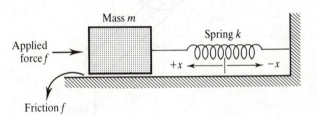

Figure 11.4
Mass-spring damper system.

Figure 11.5
5-plane pole-zero diagram:
(a) simple poles;
(b) complex poles.

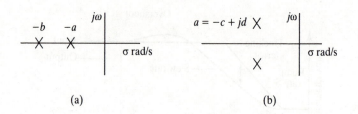

(a)   (b)

the numerator are called the zeros of the system. These are plotted on **a pole-zero diagram** (Figure 11.5).

In robotics, transfer functions are required for both the links and the actuators. For example, a link can be modelled as a pendulum (Figure 11.6) with all the mass concentrated at a point (Section 7.7.1). The torque applied to the shaft of the joint is a function of the inertia, the joint friction, and gravity.

$$\tau = m\ddot{\theta} + f\dot{\theta} + mgl\theta \tag{11.3}$$

where θ in the gravity term is a linear approximation to $\sin\theta$ in the range $\pm 45°$.

11.2.1 Actuator models

In Chapter 2, we described the common actuators used for controlling robots: d.c. motors, hydraulic motors and cylinders, and pneumatic cylinders. Each actuator type has a standard transfer function. The parameters of the transfer function for an individual actuator are determined by the characteristics of that actuator, characteristics such as power, torque and acceleration rate.

11.2.1.1 *Hydraulic servo valve*

The transfer function for a linear hydraulic servovalve (Figure 2.43) is the ratio of the displacement of the actuator (y) to the current (i) applied to the

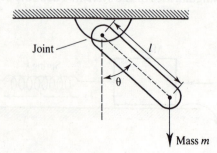

Figure 11.6
Modelling a link as a
pendulum.

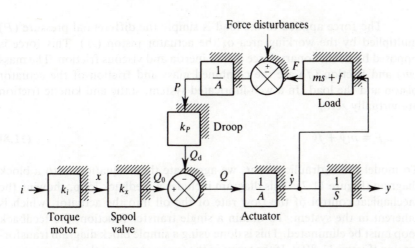

Figure 11.7
Block diagram of linear
hydraulic motor. (i = torque
motor current; x = spool
displacement; y = actuator
displacement; P = pressure
across actuator piston; Q =
flow rate of oil into actuator;
F = force due to load; m =
load mass; f = viscous
friction; k_i = torque motor
gain; k_x = spool valve gain;
k_p = servo valve droop; A =
working area of piston.)

torque motor (Figure 11.7). The current applied to the torque motor causes
the spool valve to move a distance x. If we consider that the dynamic
response of the actuator and load is much slower than the response of the
spool valve and the torque motor (by at least a factor of 10), the dynamics of
both the torque motor and the servovalve can be neglected.

We discussed the feedback control of spool valve position by mechanical means in Section 2.5. The result of that feedback loop is a linear relationship between spool-valve position (x) and input current (i)

$$x = k_i i \tag{11.4}$$

With constant supply pressure, the volumetric flow rate (Q_0) of oil into the
actuator cylinder is proportional to the displacement of the spool valve.

$$Q_0 = k_x x \tag{11.5}$$

However, the differential pressure (P) across the actuator piston causes the
spool valve to shift slightly. This shift in spool-valve position as a result of
load is known as the **droop** of the servovalve. Droop causes a slight drop in
the volumetric flow rate (Q_d).

$$Q_d = k_p P \tag{11.6}$$

The flow of oil into the cylinder causes the actuator piston to move with
velocity $\dot{y}$.

$$\dot{y} = \frac{Q}{A} = \frac{Q_0 - Q_d}{A} \tag{11.7}$$

The force applied to the load is simply the differential pressure (P) multiplied by the working area of the actuator piston (A). This force is opposed by a reactionary force due to inertia and viscous friction. The mass (m) and friction (f) are the combined mass and friction of the actuator piston and the load. In a well-lubricated system, static and kinetic friction are virtually zero.

$$F = m\ddot{y} + f\dot{y} \qquad (11.8)$$

To model the hydraulic motor, we aggregate these equations into a block diagram (Figure 11.7). This diagram includes a feedback loop, showing the mechanical control of the flow rate of the oil into the actuator, which is inherent in the system. To obtain a single transfer function, the feedback loop must be eliminated. This is done using a simple block diagram transformation (Figure 11.8(f)). If the terms in the forward part of the loop are represented by G, and the feedback terms by H, then the transfer function of the feedback loop is

$$\frac{\text{output}}{\text{input}} = \frac{G}{1 \pm GH} = \frac{1/A}{1 \pm \dfrac{k_p}{A^2}(mS + f)} = \frac{\dot{y}}{Q} \qquad (11.9)$$

When we multiply this transfer function by the transfer functions in series with it in the block diagram (Figure 11.7), we obtain the transfer function for a linear hydraulic servomotor

$$\frac{y}{i} = \frac{\dfrac{A\, k_x k_i}{k_p}}{S\left(mS + f + \dfrac{A^2}{k_p}\right)} \qquad (11.10)$$

11.2.1.2 *Direct current motor*

The output velocity of a direct current motor can be controlled either by varying the armature voltage or the field current. We will develop the block diagram for an armature controlled motor. The steady state equations for this motor are given in Section 2.5 (Equations 2.1–2.3). In the dynamic situation, we must consider the effects of armature inductance, load inertia (includes armature inertia) and friction. As the field current is constant, there are no dynamic effects of the field. The armature current (I) is a function of the applied voltage (V), the armature resistance (R_a), the armature inductance (L), and the back-electromotive-force voltage (E).

$$V(s) = (R_a + LS)I(s) + E(s) \qquad (11.11)$$

Original diagram   Equivalent diagram

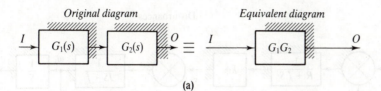

(a)

Figure 11.8
Block diagram
transformations.
(a) Cascading two blocks;
(b) moving a summing point
behind a block; (c) moving a
pick-off point ahead of a
block; (d) moving a pick-off
point behind a block; (e)
moving a summing point
ahead of a block; (f)
eliminating a feedback loop.

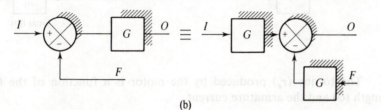

(b)

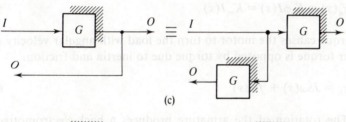

(c)

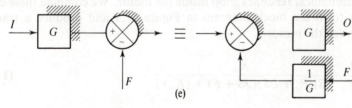

(d)

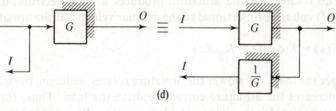

(e)

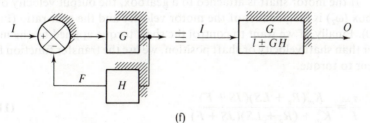

(f)

Figure 11.9
Block diagram of an armature
controlled direct current
motor.

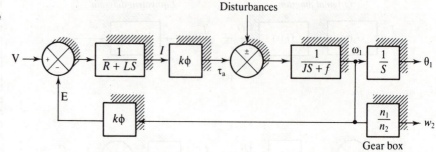

The torque (τ_a) produced by the motor is a function of the field strength (ϕ) and the armature current.

$$\tau_a(s) = K_a\phi I(s) = K_m I(s) \tag{11.12}$$

This torque causes the motor to turn the load with angular velocity ω. The actuator torque is opposed by torque due to inertia and friction.

$$\tau_L = JS\omega(s) + f\omega(s) \tag{11.13}$$

The rotation of the armature produces a back-electromotive-force (back emf) voltage proportional to the angular velocity of the armature (ω).

$$E(s) = K_a\phi\omega(s) = K_m\omega(s) \tag{11.14}$$

The larger the load, the slower the armature rotates, reducing the back emf, which increases the armature current to drive the load. Thus, there is an electromechanical feedback loop inside the motor. We combine these equations to form the block diagram in Figure 11.9 and produce a transfer function for the motor.

$$\frac{\theta_1}{V} = \frac{K_m}{S[(R_a + LS)(JS + F) + (K_m)^2]} \tag{11.15}$$

If the motor shaft is attached to a gearbox, the output velocity of the gearbox (ω_2) is the product of the motor velocity and the gear ratio (Figure 11.10). Finally, if we want to control the shaft torque applied by the motor rather than shaft velocity or shaft position, we use the transfer function from current to torque.

$$\frac{\tau}{I} = \frac{K_m(R_a + LS)(JS + F)}{K_m^2 + (R_a + LS)(JS + F)} \tag{11.16}$$

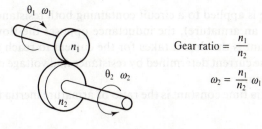

Gear ratio = $\dfrac{n_1}{n_2}$

$\omega_2 = \dfrac{n_1}{n_2}\,\omega_1$

Figure 11.10
Transfer function of a
gearbox is the gear ratio.

Consider the low-inertia micromotor in Table 11.1. The back emf constant and the torque constant are the same when expressed in metre-kilogram-second (MKS) units.

$$K_m = 3.5 \text{ volts}/1000\text{rpm} = \frac{3.5 \times 60}{1000 \times 2\pi}$$

$$= 33 \times 10^{-3} \text{ volt seconds/radian} \qquad (11.17)$$

and

$$K_m = 33 \times 10^{-3} \text{ newton metres/amp.}$$

The electrical time constant is the ratio of the armature inductance to the armature resistance.

$$T_e = \frac{L}{R_a} = \frac{0.6 \times 10^{-3}}{4.5} = 0.13 \times 10^{-3} \text{ s} \qquad (11.18)$$

Table 11.1 Parameters for four d.c. motors.

Quantity	Units	High speed micromotor	Low inertia micromotor	High torque direct drive motor	Ordinary motor
V	volts	4	15	–	36
No-load speed	rpm	20 300	4300	487	3250
No-load current	Amps	16×10^{-3}	20×10^{-3}	–	–
Stall torque	Newton metres	318×10^{-6}	110×10^{-3}	1.356	53×10^{-3}
Power	watts	0.2	12	70	–
Back-EMF-constant	volts/1000 rpm	0.181	3.5	–	11
Inductance	Henry	0.18×10^{-3}	0.6×10^{-3}	–	2.9×10^{-3}
Resistance	ohm	20	4.5	–	0.8
Torque constant	Newton metres/amp	1.73×10^{-3}	33×10^{-3}	163×10^{-3}	176×10^{-3}
Inertia	kg.m²	11.3×10^{-9}	32×10^{-7}	749×10^{-6}	233×10^{-6}
Friction	Newton metres/radian/s	13.3×10^{-9}	1×10^{-6}	–	67×10^{-6}
Motor time constant	s	75×10^{-3}	13×10^{-3}	–	17×10^{-3}
Electrical time constant	s	–	–	0.7×10^{-3}	3.7×10^{-3}

When a voltage is applied to a circuit containing both resistance and inductances (such as an armature), the inductance opposes the flow of current. The time constant is the time it takes for the current to reach 63.2% of the final current (the current determined by resistance and voltage only), as it is a first order system.

The inertia time constant is the ratio of armature inertia to the viscous friction

$$T_i = \frac{J}{F} = \frac{32 \times 10^{-7}}{1 \times 10^{-6}} = 2.183 \text{ s} \tag{11.19}$$

Thus, for this motor, the position (in radians) to voltage transfer function is:

$$\frac{\theta}{V} = \frac{K_m/FR_a}{S\left[(1 + 0.13 \times 10^{-3}S)(1 + 2.183S) + \frac{K_m^2}{FR_a} \right]} \tag{11.20}$$

As the electrical time constant is much smaller than the inertia time constant, the mechanical dynamics dominate, and we can neglect the effect of armature inductance in our transfer function.

$$\frac{\theta}{V} = \frac{K_m}{S(R_a(F + JS) + K_m^2)} = \frac{K_m/R_a J}{S\left(S + \frac{R_a F + K_m^2}{R_a J}\right)} = \frac{K_0}{S(S + \alpha)} \tag{11.21}$$

Where $K_0 = K_m/R_a J$ is the open loop gain constant and $\tau = 1/\alpha$ is the motor time constant (sometimes called the mechanical time constant).

$$\tau = \frac{R_a J}{R_a F + K_m^2} = \frac{32 \times 10^{-7} \times 4.5}{4.5 \times 10^{-6} + (33 \times 10^{-3})^2} = 13.17 \text{ ms} \tag{11.22}$$

The friction term has negligible effect (reduces the time constant by $50\,\mu s$) and can be neglected for this motor, resulting in a transfer function of

$$\frac{\theta}{V} = \frac{K_m}{R_a J} \times \frac{1}{S\left(S + \frac{K_m^2}{R_a J}\right)} = \frac{1/K_m}{S\left(1 + \frac{R_a JS}{K_m^2}\right)}$$

$$= \frac{30.303}{S(1 + 13.22 \times 10^{-3}S)} = \frac{2292.2}{S(S + 75.63)} \tag{11.23}$$

This motor is a micromotor, with a specially wound rotor that minimizes the inertia by using as little iron as possible in it, which means that it has a very rapid acceleration.

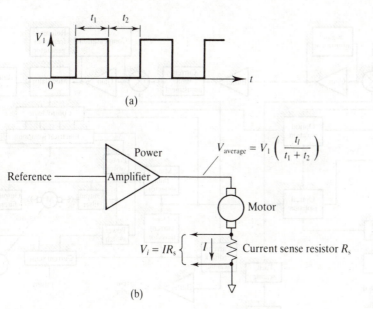

Figure 11.11
Pulse-width modulation:
(a) pulse train reference;
(b) power circuit.

11.2.2 Amplifiers

A direct-current motor is driven by an amplifier, as is the torque motor in a hydraulic servovalve. The amplifier controls the voltage on the motor's terminals and, hence, the speed of the motor. Two types of amplifiers are in common use: d.c. power amplifiers, and pulse-width modulation amplifiers.

A d.c. power amplifier converts a low power voltage signal into a high power drive current. Both input and output are analog values. The voltage gain is usually small, but the power gain can be quite high. The output current is a function of the load resistance. These amplifiers usually include internal feedback, so that they have a linear voltage transfer function. As a result, they can simply be modelled as a gain constant. While they have some internal delays, their time constants are much smaller than the motor time constants.

$$\frac{V_0}{V_i} = K_a = \text{amplifier voltage gain} \tag{11.24}$$

The second type of amplifier is the pulse-width modulated amplifier. This amplifier supplies a train of pulses to the motor (Figure 11.11). The voltage at the motor is the average d.c. value.

$$V_{\text{average}} = V_1 \left(\frac{t_1}{t_1 + t_2} \right) \tag{11.25}$$

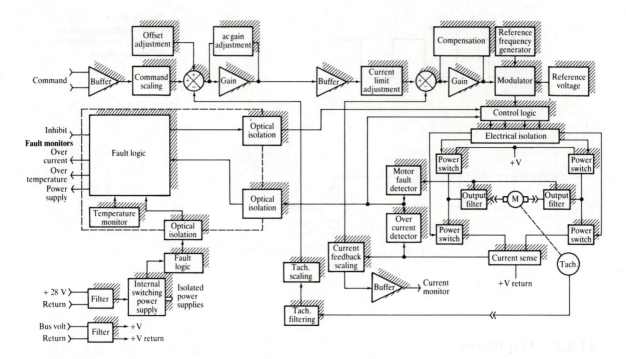

Figure 11.12
Inland Motor pulse width modulated drive electronics.

This type of amplifier has two advantages: simple drive electronics and good low voltage operation. The drive electronics can be simplified to power switches (transistors) with the timing done by software. At low speeds, the voltage applied by a d.c. amplifier may not be sufficient to break down the contact resistance between the brushes and the commutator of the motor, or to overcome static friction. As the pulse-width modulated amplifier always applies a high voltage, these problems do not occur, but as the pulses get farther apart, the motion can become jerky. To minimize this problem, the modulation frequency is very high, so the armature becomes a resistance-inductance filter, and averages out the pulses. For example, a 2 kilowatt controller from Inland Motor (Figure 11.12) operates at 20 kHz. To achieve this frequency, and bidirectional operation, fast-switching field-effect transistors are used in a bridge configuration. This controller also includes analogue electronics for closed loop control of velocity and current. The current loop minimises the effect of armature inductance and linearizes the system as seen by the velocity loop.

As the voltage and current gains are similar to those of the d.c. amplifier, we also model this amplifier with a linear gain. However, if simple drive electronics are used, a voltage control loop in software may be required to linearize the voltage control, although a current loop can usually achieve the linearization by itself.

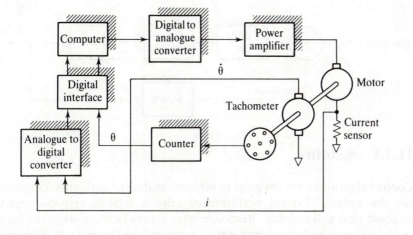

Figure 11.13
Typical digital controller.

11.3 Closing the loop

In feedback control, the parameter we want to control is measured, compared to a reference, and the error used to determine what action to take. This is known as **closing the feedback loop**. A robot controller usually closes the loop inside a digital computer, although many controllers close the inner (or fastest) loop in analogue electronics. The controller in Figure 11.12 closes the inner current loop using analogue electronics in all modes of operation. The outer velocity loop can be closed in analogue electronics or bypassed for digital control.

A typical digital controller (Figure 11.13) sends a reference voltage to a power amplifier via a digital-to-analogue converter. It reads the parameters of interest for control (for example, current, velocity and position) via a digital interface. Analogue signals, such as velocity from a tachometer, must first be converted to digital using an analogue-to-digital converter. The reference for the control loop is calculated by higher-level software. For example, the reference for a joint-position control loop is calculated by the joint-level planner (see Figure 9.1) from the trajectory plan. This reference (θ_R) is compared to the measured angle (θ_m) to obtain a position error.

$$\text{Error} = \theta_R - \theta_m = \text{reference} - \text{feedback} \qquad (11.26)$$

This error is then multiplied by a control function to obtain the output to drive the power amplifier (Figure 11.14)

$$\text{Amplifier input} = \text{control output} = \text{function (error)} \qquad (11.27)$$

The control function is known as the control law, or control algorithm, and is effectively the gain of the feedback controller.

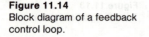

Figure 11.14
Block diagram of a feedback
control loop.

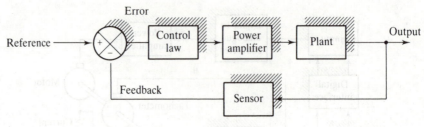

11.3.1 Stability

Control algorithms are designed to achieve the desired performance criteria for the system. Typical performance criteria include response delay, response time and stability. Response delay is time between when the input starts to change and the output starts to change (see Figure 11.3). Response time of 10–90 per cent is the time the system takes to go from 10–90 per cent of the desired change in response to a small step input. It is a measure of the maximum slew rate of the system. These times depend on the dynamics of the system, and may have to be compromised to achieve stability.

A control system is stable when the feedback matches the reference within a desired error without hunting. For example, on a multilane highway a car that stays within a lane is considered to be stable, while one that continually wanders from lane to lane is unstable. Hunting is the condition where the feedback continually varies above and below the reference by a small amount, usually in a cyclical manner (Figure 11.15). In this situation, the error oscillates about zero. In some systems this is adequate for stability, for example in the temperature control of an oven, but for others it is not, for example when scribing a straight line. Hunting is one of the possible 'stable' responses to a change in input.

The transient reponse to a small step input (10 per cent) is a measure of the damping of the system. If the system is critically damped (Figure 11.15) the controlled variable moves quickly to the new value with minimum delay and no overshoot. For lower gains of the feedback controller, the response is slower and is overdamped. At higher gains, the response is underdamped and the controlled variable overshoots the reference and must be brought back. At still higher gains, ringing, hunting and instability occur.

When deriving the control law for an inner loop, the loop gain is normally set to the gain for critical damping, as an outer loop can inject a step input into the inner loop. When deriving the control law for an outer loop, the loop gain may be set to obtain one overshoot (as in Figure 11.15) to improve the ability of the system to track a ramped input. If the gain is too high, a large error can force an amplifier into saturation, or a digital calculation to full range, at which point, control is effectively lost until the error is reduced. This is not a desirable situation, as it may result in considerable overshoot. In many robotic applications, overshoot is undesirable as it might

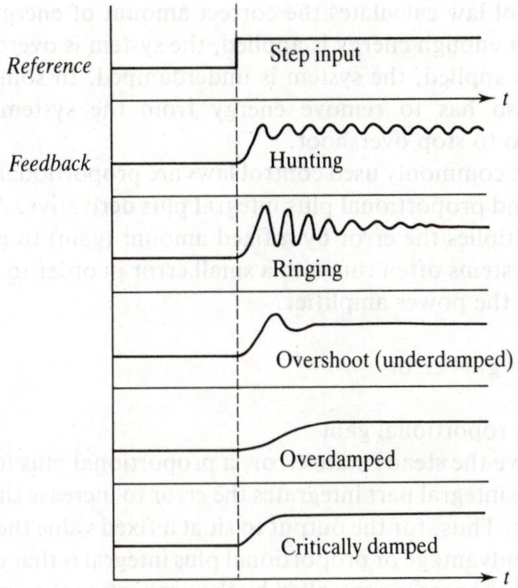

Figure 11.15
Transient responses to a
step input.

Reference

Step input

Feedback

Hunting

Ringing

Overshoot (underdamped)

Overdamped

Critically damped

cause damage, for example, when placing a glass on a table, overshoot could cause the glass to collide with the table with considerable force.

A second problem is linearity. If the system is linear over the full range, the damping will remain constant over the full range. However, if the system is nonlinear, the damping will change. In a robot, the inertia of a link with respect to a proximal joint is a function of the angle of the link with respect to the proximal link. Thus, a robot at full stretch has much higher inertia than when the arm is folded in upon itself. As most robot control systems do not include dynamics, the control loops are overdamped to avoid regions of instability caused by the non-linear dynamics.

A third problem is changes in parameters over time. For example, grease in bearings and gear boxes gets dirty and stiff with age causing the coefficient of friction to change. In robots that use tendons, the spring constant of the tendons change with use. Finally, the load applied to the motors is a function of the mass (and hence intertia) of the object held by the gripper.

11.3.2 Control laws

When an error occurs between reference and feedback, the control law calculates the energy that has to be applied to the system to eliminate the error. The control law in the feedback controller must be matched to the dynamics of the plant to achieve critical damping. Critical damping occurs when the control law calculates the correct amount of energy to overcome the error. If not enough energy is applied, the system is overdamped; if too much energy is applied, the system is underdamped. In some systems, the control law also has to remove energy from the system as the error approaches zero to stop overshoot.

The most commonly used control laws are proportional, proportional plus integral, and proportional plus integral plus derivative. A proportional law simply multiplies the error by a fixed amount (gain) to get the output. Proportional systems often run with a small error in order to have a control output to drive the power amplifier.

$$\text{Output} = g_1 \times \text{error} \tag{11.28}$$

where g_1 is the proportional gain

To remove the steady state error, a proportional plus integral control law is used. The integral part integrates the error to increase the output when there is an error. Thus, for the output to sit at a fixed value the error must be zero. A second advantage of proportional plus integral is that the response of the law to rapid changes is controlled by the proportional gain, which can be quite low to minimize the effect of disturbances. The output of this law in response to a step input is a step followed by a ramp.

$$\text{Output} = g_1 \times \text{error} + g_2 \int \text{error} \, dt \tag{11.29}$$

Sometimes, the delay between input and output has to be reduced, for example to track a trajectory. Also, it might be necessary to reduce the overshoot while maintaining a fast rise time. To get the system to respond more quickly, we add a derivative function to the control law. This causes the output to change as a function of the rate of change of the error. Derivative control is a type of feedforward control. Its main disadvantage is that it is subject to disturbances (electrical noise).

$$\text{Output} = g_1 \times \text{error} + g_2 \int \text{error} \, dt + g_3 \frac{d \, \text{error}}{dt} \tag{11.30}$$

11.3.3 Tuning

Tuning is the process of adjusting the gains in the control law to achieve the desired response. Many control systems have been carefully studied and are well understood. These systems are often tuned in the field using rules of thumb. The type of control law is chosen based on experience.

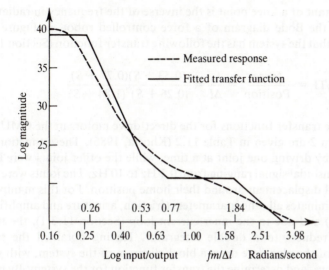

Figure 11.16
Bode plot of a Puma 560
robot and force sensor
(courtesy Stephen Young).

The gain is set up by injecting a small step (10 per cent) on to the reference and recording the feedback. After each step, the gain is increased if the response is overdamped and decreased if the response is underdamped. Usually, proportional gain is set, then integral, then derivative. However, these gains can interact, and they are adjusted relative to one another to achieve the desired response based upon experience.

Rules of thumb don't always work, and a more scientific approach is often needed. To design a control law, the transfer function of the plant must be combined with the transfer functions of the control law, the power amplifier, and the feedback transducers. The response of the system can then be calculated.

In Section 11.2.1, we developed the general transfer function for a linear hydraulic actuator and for a d.c. motor. The parameters for the d.c. motor (Table 11.1) were obtained from manufacturers' data. If such data is not available, the transfer function has to be measured. When the actuator drives a load, the load modifies these parameters, particularly inertia and friction. The parameters for the load have to be obtained as well, either from CAD models (Section 7.4) or by measurement.

Parameters for an open-loop transfer function are measured by injecting a small sinusoidal signal on to the reference and measuring the open-loop response (that is, the feedback signal). The sinusoid is small enough to maintain operation in the linear region without saturation. The frequency of the sinusoid is varied over the dynamic range of the system, usually from 0.01 Hz to 100 Hz. The logarithm of the open-loop gain (ratio of output to input) is plotted against the logarithm of frequency on a Bode plot. The knees in the plot (Figure 11.16) occur at the poles and zeros in the transfer function, and the gain constant is the gain at the flat part of the curve. The time constant of a knee point is the inverse of the frequency in radians. For example, the Bode diagram of a force controlled robot, in Figure 11.16, indicates that the system has the following transfer function (Section 11.8.2).

$$\text{OLTF} = \frac{\text{force}}{\text{Position}} = \frac{f_m}{\Delta l} = \frac{(0.53 + S)(0.77 + S)}{(0.26 + S)^2(1.84 + S)} \qquad (11.31)$$

The transfer functions for the direct-drive motors in the CMU-Direct Drive Arm 2 are given in Table 11.2 (Khosla, 1986). These functions were obtained by driving one joint at a time, while the other joints were locked, with a sinusoidal signal ranging from 0.1 Hz to 10 Hz. The joints were moved by a small displacement around their home position. For this manipulator, inertia dominates all other parameters (friction, armature and amplifier time constants) and due to the inner current loop (Section 11.3.1), the transfer function reduces to a double integrator. Having obtained the transfer function of the plant, we draw a block diagram of the system, with various control laws, and determine the transfer function for the system. By plotting the poles and zeros of the transfer function on a pole-zero diagram for various gains we can study the response of the system.

From the transfer function for the low-inertia micromotor (Equation 11.23) we see that there is a pole at 0 and a pole at -75.6 radians/s and the motor has a gain of 2,292 radians per volt (Figure 11.17). The consequence

Table 11.2 Transfer functions and gains of the six joint controllers in the CMU direct-drive arm II (Khosla, 1986). Note that these controllers include pulse-width modulated amplifiers and inner current loops.

Joint	Open loop Transfer Function $\left(\dfrac{1}{JS^2}\right)$	g_1	g_3
1	$\dfrac{1}{12.3\,S^2}$	40.0	12.6
2	$\dfrac{1}{2\,S^2}$	58.0	15.2
3	$\dfrac{1}{0.251\,S^2}$	400	40.0
4	$\dfrac{1}{0.007\,S^2}$	2800.0	106.0
5	$\dfrac{1}{0.006\,S^2}$	1200.0	69.3
6	$\dfrac{1}{0.0003\,S^2}$	3000.0	110.0

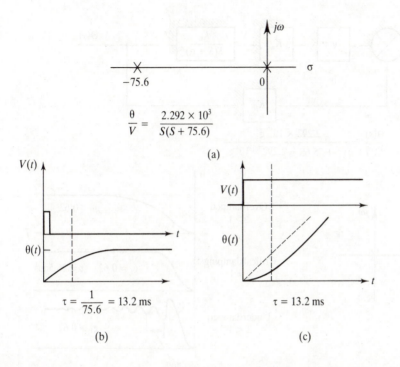

$$\frac{\theta}{V} = \frac{2.292 \times 10^3}{S(S + 75.6)}$$

(a)

$$\tau = \frac{1}{75.6} = 13.2 \text{ ms}$$

(b)

$$\tau = 13.2 \text{ ms}$$

(c)

Figure 11.17
Open loop pole-zero plot and
response of a low inertia
micromotor.
(a) Pole-zero diagram;
(b) Impulse response;
(c) Step response.

of the pole at 0 (a pure integrator) is that a constant input voltage gives a steady-state constant angular velocity, and the angular position increases at a constant rate. The time constant of the motor determines the response of the motor to various inputs.

In the following analysis, we use the parameters for the motor only and assume that it includes the load. The load changes the values of the parameters in the model, not the model itself. The effect of adding a gearbox to the motor is to increase the friction and reduce the output velocity. The effect of the manipulator linkages is to increase the inertia of the system. The result is a shift in the open-loop poles and hence a change in the closed-loop gains for critical damping. The numbers are different, but the analysis is the same.

11.4 Position control

To examine the use of feedback, we will develop a control scheme for joint position using proportional feedback. To simplify this development, we assume that the power amplifier and the feedback transducer both have unity gain (K_a and K_{fb}). From the block diagram (Figure 11.18), we calculate the closed-loop transfer function for proportional-feedback control of the low-inertia micromotor.

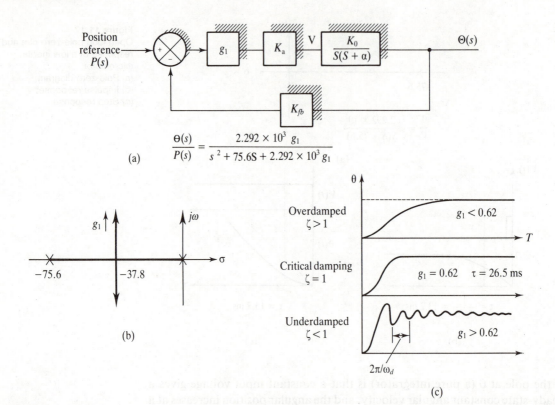

$$\frac{\Theta(s)}{P(s)} = \frac{2.292 \times 10^3 \, g_1}{s^2 + 75.6S + 2.292 \times 10^3 \, g_1}$$

(a)

(b)

(c)

Figure 11.18
Closed loop proportional
feedback control of a direct
current motor.
(a) Block diagram;
(b) pole-zero diagram;
(c) step response.

$$\frac{\Theta(s)}{P(s)} = \frac{g_1 K_a K_o}{S^2 + \alpha S + g_1 K_a K_o K_{fb}} = \frac{2292 g_1}{S^2 + 75.6S + 2292 g_1} \tag{11.32}$$

To study the closed-loop response, we examine the pole-zero diagram of this transfer function. The arcs of the root-locus plot start at the open-loop poles and move toward the open-loop zeros. There are as many zeros as poles, with the unspecified zeros at infinity. For low gains, the poles are on the σ axis and the control is overdamped. As the gain increases, the poles reach the midpoint between the open-loop poles and the control is critically damped. Increasing the gain further moves the poles parallel to the $j\omega$ axis, and the control is underdamped. For critical damping of the low-inertia micromotor, Equation 11.32 becomes

$$\frac{\Theta(s)}{P(s)} = \frac{1428.84}{(S + 37.8)^2} \tag{11.33}$$

so the gain g_1 is 0.6234 $\tag{11.34}$

While a stable closed-loop control (poles to the left of the imaginary axis) has been achieved, the response is poor. An equation for the time response can be derived from the transfer function

$$\frac{\Theta(s)}{P(s)} = \frac{2292g_1}{S^2 + 75.6S + 2292g_1} = \frac{\omega_n^2}{S^2 + 2\zeta\omega_n S + \omega_n^2} \qquad (11.35)$$

The undamped natural frequency (ω_n) is the frequency of oscillation of the system in radians per second in the undamped case, when the damping ratio (ζ) is zero. We find the poles of the transfer function by finding the roots of the denominator, using the equation for finding the roots of a quadratic.

$$\sigma_{1,2} = -\zeta\omega_n \pm \omega_n\sqrt{\zeta^2 - 1} = -\sigma \pm j\omega_d \qquad (11.36)$$

where $\omega_d = \omega_n\sqrt{1 - \zeta^2} =$ damped natural frequency $\qquad (11.37)$

For any second order system (system with two poles), there are three forms of the characteristic equation (the denominator of the transfer function): the overdamped case, the critically damped case, and the under-damped case (Figure 11.19). In the overdamped case, the roots are real, and the damping ratio is greater than 1. In the critically damped case, the roots are real and equal, and the damping ratio is 1. In the underdamped case, the roots are complex with equal real parts, and the damping ratio is less than 1.

If an input $I(s)$ is applied to a system, the output is

$$O(s) = T(s)I(s) = \frac{\Theta(s)}{P(s)} \times T(s) \qquad (11.38)$$

For most systems, a unit step input $(1/S)$ gives a good feel for the response of the system. The time response is found by taking the inverse transform. The exact derivation of these equations is covered in most good control textbooks. The step response consists of a steady component (the desired output) and a transient component.

$$\Theta(t) = \Theta_1(t) + A_1 e^{\sigma_1 t} + A_2 e^{\sigma_2 t} \qquad (11.39)$$

The transient component is the summation of an exponential curve for each pole. The further a pole is from the imaginary axis, the faster are the exponential decays. Thus, poles close to the imaginary axis dominate the time response. For this reason, a first approximation to the response of a complex multipole system can be obtained by studying the two poles closest to the origin. Hence, while the following analysis applies to second order system, it is often used to study higher-order systems. For a critically damped system, the time response is:

Figure 11.19
Step response of a second
order system for different
damping conditions:
(a) overdamped; (b) critically
damped; (c) underdamped.

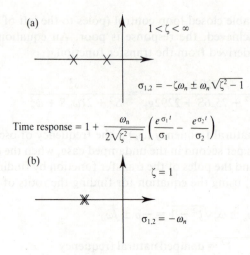

(a)

$$1 < \zeta < \infty$$

$$\sigma_{1,2} = -\zeta\omega_n \pm \omega_n\sqrt{\zeta^2 - 1}$$

$$\text{Time response} = 1 + \frac{\omega_n}{2\sqrt{\zeta^2 - 1}}\left(\frac{e^{\sigma_1 t}}{\sigma_1} - \frac{e^{\sigma_2 t}}{\sigma_2}\right)$$

(b)

$$\zeta = 1$$

$$\sigma_{1,2} = -\omega_n$$

$$\text{Time response} = 1 - e^{-\omega_n t}(1 + \omega_n t)$$

(c)

$$0 < \zeta < 1$$

$$\sigma_{12} = -\zeta\omega_n \pm j\omega_d$$

$$\text{Time response} = 1 + \frac{\omega_n e^{-\zeta\omega_n t}}{\omega_d}\left(\sin \omega_d T + \tan^{-1}\left(\frac{\omega_n}{\omega_n \zeta}\right)\right)$$

$$\text{10 to 90\% rise time} \approx \frac{1 + 1.1\zeta + 1.4\zeta^2}{\omega_n}$$

$$\Theta_t = 1 - e^{-\omega_n t}(1 + \omega_n t) \tag{11.40}$$

The equations for the overdamped and underdamped cases are given in
Figure 11.19. By plotting these equations, for a specific control system, we
obtain the time response of the system for various gains. The time response
of the proportional feedback control of the low-inertia micromotor at
critical damping is shown in Figure 11.20.

$$\Theta(t) = 1 - e^{-37.8t}(1 + 37.8t) \tag{11.41}$$

where $\omega_d = \omega_n = 37.8$ radians/s.

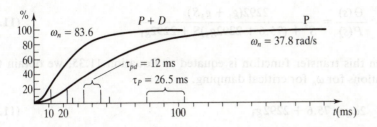

Figure 11.20
Step response for
proportional and
proportioned plus derivative
feedback control of the low-
inertia micromotor, with
critical damping.

11.4.1 Proportional plus derivative control law

While stable closed-loop control has been achieved, the response is slow. The rise time can be decreased by increasing the gain but at the cost of overshoot – or a different control law can be tried. We can improve the response significantly with a proportional plus derivative law (PD).

$$\text{Proportional plus derivative law} = g_1 + g_3 S \qquad (11.42)$$

and the closed-loop transfer function is

$$\frac{\Theta(s)}{P(s)} = \frac{(g_1 + g_3 S) K_o K_a}{S^2 + S(\alpha + g_3 K_a K_o K_{fb}) + g_1 K_a K_o K_{fb}} \qquad (11.43)$$

The derivative gain results in a zero to the left of both poles in the pole-zero diagram (Figure 11.21). This zero causes the root locus to circle back to the real axis, and hence results in critically damped control with a much faster response. For the low-inertia micromotor, the transfer function is:

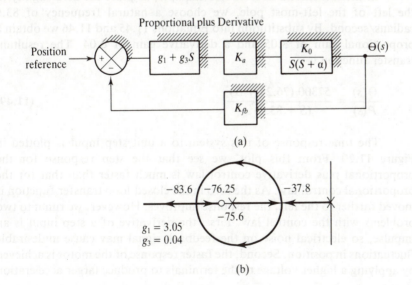

(a)

(b)

Figure 11.21
Proportional plus derivative
control law results in a zero
in the pole-zero diagram.
(a) Block diagram;
(b) pole-zero diagram.

$$\frac{\Theta(s)}{P(s)} = \frac{2292(g_1 + g_3 S)}{S^2 + (75.6 + 2292g_3)S + 2292g_1} \qquad \textbf{(11.44)}$$

When this transfer function is equated to Equation 11.35, we obtain two equations for ω_n for critical damping.

$$2\omega_n = 75.6 + 2292g_3 \qquad \textbf{(11.45)}$$

$$(\omega_n)^2 = 2292g_1 \qquad \textbf{(11.46)}$$

Within certain practical constraints, we can choose a desired undamped natural frequency for the critical damped case. Paul (1981) suggests that the undamped natural frequency must be less than half the resonant frequency of the joint and link structure in order not to excite structural oscillation and resonance of the joint. The stiffer the material the higher the resonant frequency. The stiffness produces a restoring torque which opposes the inertial torque of the motor, like a spring.

The resultant mass-spring system has a characteristic equation of

$$JS^2 + k_{\text{stiff}} = 0 \qquad \textbf{(11.47)}$$

From this equation, we derive an equation for the resonant frequency of the system (Fu *et al.*, 1987).

$$W_r = \sqrt{\frac{k_{\text{stiff}}}{J}} \qquad \textbf{(11.48)}$$

In the low-inertia micromotor example, to place the zero slightly to the left of the left-most pole, we choose a natural frequency of 83.6 radians/second. By substitution into Equations 11.45 and 11.46 we obtain a proportional gain of 3.05 and a derivative gain of 0.04. The resultant transfer function is

$$\frac{\Theta(s)}{P(s)} = \frac{57300\,(76.25 + S)}{(S + 83.6)^2} \qquad \textbf{(11.49)}$$

The time response of this system to a unit step input is plotted in Figure 11.20. From this plot, we see that the step response for the proportional plus derivative control law is much faster than that for the proportional control law. As the zero in the closed-loop transfer function is moved farther to the left, the response improves. However, we run into two problems with the control law. First, the derivative of a step input is an impulse, so electrical noise on the feedback signal may cause undesirable fluctuations in position. Second, the faster response of the motor is achieved by applying a higher voltage to the terminals to produce larger acceleration

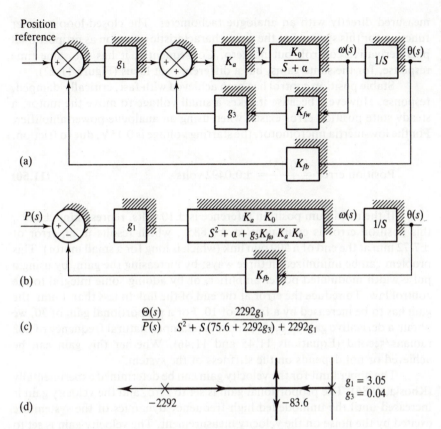

Figure 11.22
Using velocity feedback
rather than derivative of
position.
(a) Block diagram;
(b) reduced block diagram;
(c) transfer function;
(d) pole-zero diagram.

and deceleration torques. Some industrial systems apply up to twice nominal voltage to motors for short periods of time. This is known as **forcing**. However, there is a limit to the amount of forcing which can be applied to a motor without damaging it. In most robot controllers, the speed of response to position errors is limited by the maximum velocity of the joint. Often, the nominal operating velocity is restricted to be much less than the maximum in order to minimize the effect of the dynamics of the link. Also, once the forcing limit is reached, the tracking error increases and the controller may saturate. In an analogue controller, saturation occurs when the output of an amplifier is driven to its maximum, or minimum, value. In a digital controller, saturation occurs when the calculations overflow (or reach a limit). While the controller is saturated, it has lost control of the system.

11.4.2 Proportional plus velocity control law

The problems caused by the derivative law amplifying electrical noise can be eliminated by using velocity feedback (Figure 11.22). Velocity can be measured directly with an analogue tachometer. The closed-loop transfer function for this system has the same characteristic equation as proportional plus derivative control, but no zero. Consequently, it has the same time response, for the same gains, but a different root locus (Figure 11.22).

Stable position control has been achieved with fast, critically-damped, response. However, because it takes a small voltage to move the motor, a steady state position error exists, when using an analogue power amplifier. For the low-inertia micromotor, the starting voltage is 0.15V, due to friction.

$$\text{Position error} = \frac{0.15}{g_1} = \pm 0.0492 \text{ volts} \qquad (11.50)$$

If the maximum position reference is ±10 volts, representing ±180°, this position error is equivalent to ±0.885°, which results in an error of ±7.72 mm at the end of a 500 mm link (which is long for a small motor). This problem can be minimized in three ways: by increasing the gain, by using a pulse-width modulated power amplifier, or by adding some integral to the control law. To reduce the error at the end of the link to less than 1 mm, the gain has to be increased by a factor of 10. For a proportional gain of 30, we obtain a derivative gain of 0.195, and an undamped natural frequency of 262 radians/second (Equations 11.45 and 11.46). Whether this gain can be achieved or not depends on the stiffness of the system.

The upper limit for the velocity gain can be determined experimentally (Khosla, 1986). The proportional gain is set to zero, and the velocity gain is increased until the unmodelled high-frequency dynamics of the system are excited by the noise on the velocity measurement. The velocity gain is set to 80 per cent of this value and the proportional gain for critical damping calculated. The gains for the six independent joint controllers of the CMU Direct-Drive Arm 2 (Khosla, 1986) were determined this way (Table 11.2). These gains are quite high, indicating a stiff system. The transfer functions have been simplified by assuming negligible friction, which is valid for a direct-drive actuator, but not for a harmonic drive. They confirmed that the system was critically damped by injecting a 0.1 radian step into individual controllers, while the other joints were locked.

The second approach is to use a pulse-width modulated power amplifier to drive the motor. By applying a short-duration full-voltage pulse to the motor, the pulse width modulated system eliminates the zero error due to static friction. This is the main advantage of pulse-width modulated control. It results in a proportional plus voltage controller with zero position error.

11.4.3 Proportional plus velocity plus integral control law

The third approach to reducing the zero error is to add an integral component to the control law (Figure 11.23). The integral component adds both

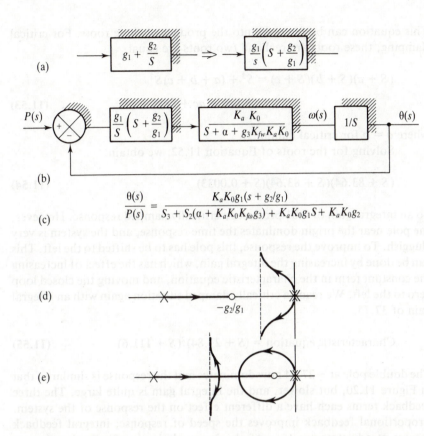

Figure 11.23
Adding integral control law to reduce zero error.
(a) Proportional plus integral control law; (b) block diagram; (c) closed loop transfer function; (d) root locus; (e) shifting pole towards origin.

(a)

(b)

$P(s)$ $\dfrac{g_1}{S}\left(S + \dfrac{g_2}{g_1}\right)$ $\dfrac{K_a K_0}{S + \alpha + g_3 K_{fw} K_a K_0}$ $\omega(s)$ $1/S$ $\theta(s)$

(c)
$$\frac{\theta(s)}{P(s)} = \frac{K_a K_0 g_1(s + g_2/g_1)}{S_3 + S_2(\alpha + K_a K_0 K_{fw} g_3) + K_a K_0 g_1 S + K_a K_0 g_2}$$

(d)

(e)

a pole at the origin and a zero on the real axis to the forward part of the loop. The additional pole results in a double pole at the origin which causes the root loci to move out along the imaginary axis. Thus, the system is unstable. However, the zero can be used to stabilize the system. The zero has the effect of pulling the loci back into the left half of the plane.

If the integral gain is too large or too small, the response is under-damped, and the position control overshoots. A midrange integral gain places the pole close to the origin $(-g_2/g_1)$, and the loci are bent down on to the real axis eliminating the overshoot. In the limit, when the integral gain is zero, the transfer function reverts to the proportional plus velocity control transfer function (Figure 11.22). The characteristic equation of the closed loop system is cubic.

$$S^3 + (\alpha + K_a K_0 K_{fw} g_3) + K_a K_0 g_1 S + K_a K_0 g_2 \tag{11.51}$$

If the proportional and derivative gains are used for the proportional plus derivative control, and an integral gain of 0.01 chosen, the equation for the low-inertia micromotor is

$$S^3 + 167.3 S^2 + 6991.2 S + 22.92 \tag{11.52}$$

This equation can be factored into the product of three roots. For critical damping, these roots are real and two roots are equal.

$$(S + a)(S + b)(S + c) = S^3 + (a + b + c)S^2$$

$$+ (ab + ac + bc)S + abc \qquad (11.53)$$

where $a = b$ for critical damping.

Solving for the roots of Equation 11.52, we obtain

$$(S + 83.64)(S + 83.64)(S + 0.0033) \qquad (11.54)$$

So an integral gain of 0.01 produces a critically damped response. However, the pole near the origin dominates the time response, and the system is very sluggish. To improve the response, this pole has to be shifted to the left. This can be done by increasing the integral gain, which has the effect of increasing the constant term in the characteristic equation, and moving the closed loop zero to the left. We reach a critically damped situation again with an integral gain of 37.75.

$$\text{Characteristic equation} = (S + 27.84)^2(S + 111.6) \qquad (11.55)$$

The double pole at -27.84 now dominates and the response is similar to that in Figure 11.20, but slower, and the integral gain is quite large. The three feedback terms each have a different effect on the response of the system. Proportional feedback improves the speed of response; integral feedback assures steady-state tracking of the input; derivative feedback enhances stability by increasing the damping of the system. However, when one is varied, the others also have to be varied to achieve critical gain.

By looking at the characteristic equation, we can see that each coefficient can be adjusted by adjusting one gain term only. First, we will increase the derivative gain to 0.1 and see what happens to the roots for critical gain. Critical gain is obtained with a lower integral gain (18.24) but the dominant poles shift to the right slowing the time response. At these gains, the loci just touch the real axis, and the characteristic equation is

$$(S + 12.22)^2(S + 279.9) \qquad (11.56)$$

To investigate the effect of increasing the proportional gain, we will calculate the proportional gain for the above derivative gain (0.1) for the proportional plus derivative controller (Equations 11.45, 11.46). The proportional gain is 10.09 and the undamped natural frequency is 151.42. Critical damping of this system occurs at an integral gain of 228.9, with a time response approaching that of the original proportional plus derivative control

$$(S + 50.81)^2(S + 203.16) \qquad (11.57)$$

Due to the difficulty of factorizing a third order polynomial, particularly to find coefficients that have two identical real roots, the roots and integral gains of the above systems were found using a computer program. The above designs were based on motor inertia only. Normally, a fixed inertia representing the load is added to the motor inertia, which increases the motor time constant and slows the response. Due to this complexity, and the poorer response when using integral control, proportional plus velocity control with a pulse-width modulated amplifier is the best choice for robot joint-position control systems.

11.5   Dynamic effects

Most commercial robots use fixed gain controllers as described above. However, the robot's transfer function (motor + linkages) continually changes due to the nonlinearities in the robot. These nonlinearities include changing inertial loads, coupling between joints, changes in gravitational torque, gear backlash, shaft eccentricity, mass imbalance, inherent vibrations and friction. Friction changes occur slowly as bearing grease dries up and, consequently, result in long-term drift in robot characteristics.

The coupling between joints (Figure 11.24(d)) is a consequence of the mechanical design, and can be modelled easily. Usually, compensation is included in joint control loops to overcome the effect of one joint upon another. However, differences in the speed of response of joint controls can result in disturbances in Cartesian space tracking. Backlash in gears and slop in control linkages also introduce undersirable disturbances.

The dynamic effects which have the most impact on control loop stability are due to changing mass or configuration. The torque required to balance gravitational load changes as the configuration of the manipulator changes (Figure 11.24(e)). The inertias of the robot linkages, as seen by an actuator, change rapidly as the configuration changes. Also, the inertia changes whenever an object is picked up or put down. When the inertia changes, the transfer function of the robot (actuator plus linkages) changes (Equation 11.21).

$$K_0 = \frac{K_m}{R_a J} \tag{11.58}$$

$$\alpha = \frac{R_a F + K_m^2}{R_a J} \tag{11.59}$$

Increasing the inertia, reduces the open-loop gain (K_0) and shifts the left pole ($-\alpha$) towards the origin with the result that a critically damped system becomes underdamped. The two poles that were located together on the real

Figure 11.24
Major dynamic non-linearities
in robot control.
(a) Inertia changes with
configuration; (b) inertia
changes when robot picks
upon object; (c) open loop
pole moves causing
underdamped response;
(d) coupling between joints –
length of tendon to joint 2
changes with angle of joint
1; (e) gravitational
component of joint torque
changes with configuration.

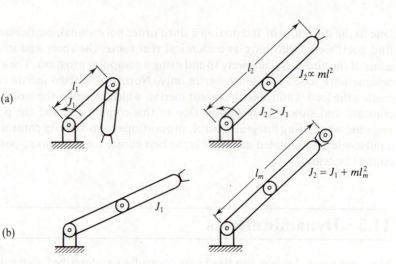

(a)

$J_2 \propto ml^2$

$J_2 > J_1$

$J_2 = J_1 + ml_m^2$

(b)

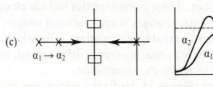

(c)

$\alpha_1 \to \alpha_2$

α_2

α_1

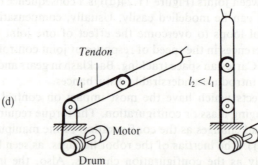

Tendon

l_1

(d)

$l_2 < l_1$

Motor

Drum

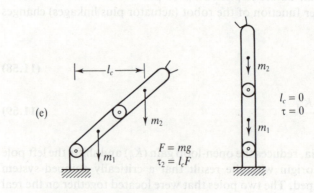

(e)

l_c

m_2

m_1

$F = mg$

$\tau_2 = l_c F$

m_2

m_1

$l_c = 0$
$\tau = 0$

axis, in the closed-loop transfer function, move apart and become complex. Increasing the friction (Equation 11.59) moves the open-loop pole away from the origin, and the closed-loop response is overdamped.

Most commercially available robots use fixed-gain proportional plus velocity control or proportional plus integral plus velocity control. Because of the rapidly changing inertial load, the damping ratios and, hence, the responses of the control loops, change considerably during operation. As a result, control can shift from overdamped to underdamped while following a single trajectory. However, underdamped control is undesirable in an industrial robot, as overshoot can cause damage to the objects the robot is manipulating. Most controllers are tuned to give near critically damped response at normal operating speeds. High speeds are avoided because of the rapid changes in inertial loads. At low speeds, some robots move with noticeable vibration.

All these dynamic effects generate disturbances which cause errors in trajectory following. To minimize the effect of these disturbances, robot designers try to keep the loop gains as high as possible. The higher the gain of a feedback loop and the higher the damped natural frequency of the closed-loop system, the faster it can respond to errors caused by disturbances. For this reason, some controllers use high-gain proportional plus velocity controllers, and rely on the high proportional gain and pulse-width modulation to minimize zero errors.

By rearranging the block diagram of the proportional plus velocity control loop for zero position reference (Figure 11.25), we obtain the transfer function for disturbances.

$$\frac{\Theta(s)}{\tau(s)} = \frac{1}{JS^2 + S\left(F + \dfrac{K_m^2}{R + LS} + \dfrac{K_m K_a K_{fw} g_3}{R + LS}\right) + \dfrac{K_m K_a K_{fb} g_1}{R + LS}} \tag{11.60}$$

This transfer function can be simplified by assuming the effects of friction and armature inductance to be negligible.

$$\frac{\Theta(s)}{\tau_d(s)} = \frac{1/J}{S^2 + S(\alpha + K_o K_a K_{fw} g_3) + K_o K_a K_{fb} g_1} \tag{11.61}$$

The result is a transfer function with the same characteristic equation as the closed-loop transfer function. Consequently, the higher the gain, the faster the control system responds to disturbances. This is known as the stiffness of the system.

11.5.1 Dynamics compensation

So far we have developed a simple, linear, control law with the intention that a separate controller is used for each joint. While the damping of each

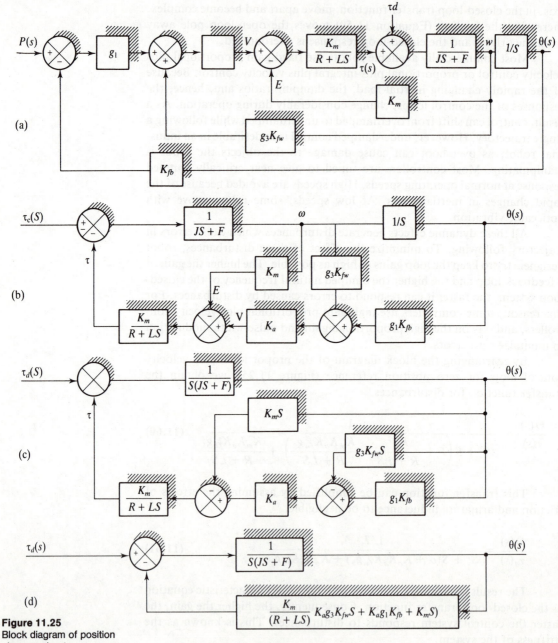

Figure 11.25
Block diagram of position changes due to disturbances. (a) Block diagram of proportional plus velocity position control; (b) block diagram of zero input controller with disturbance; (c) reorganizing block diagram; (d) transfer function.

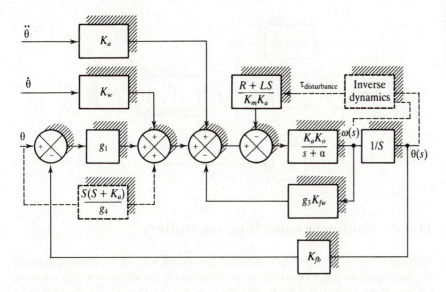

Figure 11.26
Simple linear controller with
nonlinear compensation
shown in broken lines.

control loop varies with manipulator configuration, the system is basically
stable. This type of control is known as independent-joint control, because it
is based on the assumption that the coupling torque between the joints is
small. We have demonstrated that systems with high gain have good disturbance rejection qualities. However, independent-joint control is limited to
speeds and trajectories which have small coupling torques. Most industrial
robots use independent-joint control.

The basic problem in robot control is to calculate the actuating
torques required to cause the manipulator to follow a desired trajectory. As
we have seen (Chapter 7), the dynamics of a robot manipulator is a set of
highly nonlinear and coupled differential equations. As more rapid and
precise motion will be required of future robots, simple linear controllers will
not surface, and more sophisticated controllers will be required.

The dynamic terms in the manipulator equations tend to dominate in
direct drive robots. While the reduction in friction due to the lack of gear
boxes, reduces the natural damping of these systems, it also reduces the
problems caused by the difficulty of accurately modelling static and dynamic
friction. Khosla (1986) has demonstrated that Coriolis forces, centrifugal
forces, and off-diagonal elements of the inertia matrix are all significant in a
direct-drive arm and must be compensated for.

Researchers are taking three approaches to improving the control of
manipulators under dynamics conditions: nonlinear cancelling, adaptive
control and model-based control schemes. All three approaches make use of
models, but the third requires accurate models. At this point, we should
point out that a dynamic controller requires position, velocity and acceleration references (Figure 11.26) for each joint from the trajectory planner
(Section 9.3.3.2) for accurate trajectory following. Also, we assume that
joint position, velocity and acceleration are all measurable.

Figure 11.27
Feedforward nonlinear
cancelling.

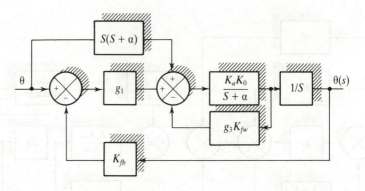

11.5.2 Nonlinear cancelling controllers

Nonlinear cancelling methods increase the complexity of the control laws of the independent-joint controllers to compensate for dynamics and account for non-linearities. Effectively, these methods cancel out the nonlinear terms that characterize the dynamics, so that the resulting behaviour resembles that of a linear system. Basically, a vector of joint torques (motor voltages) is computed from the accelerations.

Feedforward cancelling attempts to achieve accurate trajectory following by modifying the position reference to compensate for the dynamics of the joint plus link. Compensation is derived from the calculated acceleration and velocity reference values (Figure 11.27). The feedforward path has a transfer function of $S^2 + \alpha S$, which is the characteristic equation of the open-loop transfer function of the joint. Thus, changes in the reference (θ) are multiplied by the characteristic equation and then by its inverse. Provided the controller does not saturate, the output $\theta(s)$ follows the change in the input exactly with no time delay.

The feedforward transfer function $S(S+\alpha)$ is equivalent to $\ddot{\theta} + \alpha\dot{\theta}$, the sum of the acceleration reference plus the velocity reference divided by the mechanical time constant. Using the references calculated by the trajectory planner eliminates having to doubly integrate the position reference. As the controller includes a velocity-feedback loop, some systems use feedforward of the acceleration reference ($\ddot{\theta} = S^2$) only. Experimental work has shown that feeding the reference acceleration and velocity forward results in noticeable improvement in trajectory tracking with independent-joint-control schemes. In making this change to the standard proportional plus velocity controller, the gain of the feedback control has not been changed at all. So this change has an impact on trajectory tracking only, and when the system is critically damped, trajectory tracking is very good. When the configuration of the robot changes causing the inertia to change, the characteristic equation changes, but feedforward compensation does not: the tracking is inaccurate, but better than with no compensation at all. Thus, a model that is accurate

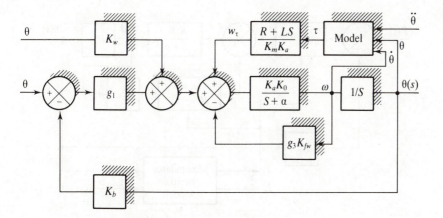

Figure 11.28
Feedback nonlinear
cancelling.

only at normal operating speeds and for a restricted range of configurations
can be used to improve tracking performance.

Feedback cancelling attempts to achieve accurate trajectory following
by modifying the velocity reference to compensate for the dynamics of the
system using measured acceleration values (Figure 11.28). Again, the basic
proportional plus velocity position-control loop is not changed. A model is
used to calculate the additional torque needed to be applied by each actuator
to overcome the dynamic effect of interest, from measured values of
position, velocity and acceleration. This torque is then multiplied by the
inverse of the voltage-to-torque transfer function to obtain a voltage
reference.

Over most of its range, the voltage-to-torque transfer function is
linear, as shown in the block diagram in Figure 11.28. However, at low
voltages, static friction produces a considerable nonlinearity in the function,
and, at high torques, saturation of the motor windings causes considerable
nonlinearity. To minimize the effect of these nonlinearities, particularly the
low-voltage one, some systems use a lookup table when calculating voltage
from torque. This table is constructed from measurements of the motor-link
system.

The feedforward cancelling controller will cancel nonlinearities and
dynamics due to inertia but not due to gravity, because it is based on joint
acceleration. If a feedforward cancelling function is used, the feedback
function only has to cancel gravitational effects. Thus, the model used to
convert measured position to torque is a gravitational model only; if we wish
to compensate for Coriolis and centrifugal effects, we need to include these
terms in the model also, and measure the velocity. If we are not using
feedforward cancelling, we can use the full inverse dynamic model (Chapter
7) in the feedback calculation. As calculation of inverse dynamics takes a
long time, many experimental systems have used feedforward cancellation of
inertia and feedback cancellation of gravity. These systems may use a highly
accurate model where the inertias are updated with configuration or load

Figure 11.29
Adaptive control using inertia
calculations.

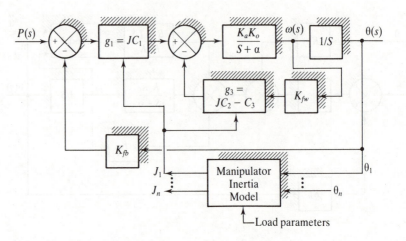

changes, or assume fixed inertia and load. In the latter case, they are set up
for best performance at normal operating speeds.

11.5.3 Adaptive control

Unlike compensation systems, adaptive control systems adjust the gains of
the control loops in order to maintain critical damping over a range of
operating velocities, and a range of manipulator configurations. As they
perform a different function to nonlinear compensation, adaptive control
can be used with nonlinear compensation to achieve critical damping and
good tracking over a wide range of operating conditions. Adaptive systems
achieve the best results with accurate models, but can improve performance
with poor models.

The closed loop transfer function for the proportional plus velocity
position controller (Figure 11.22) is

$$T(s) = \cfrac{\dfrac{g_1\,K_a}{J\,R_a}(R_aF + K_m^2)}{S^2 + \dfrac{S}{JR_a}[K_m + g_3K_{fw}K_a(R_aF + K_m^2)] + \dfrac{g_1\,K_a}{J\,R_a}(R_aF + K_m^2)} \qquad (11.62)$$

The parameter in the transfer function which changes with configuration is inertia. To maintain critical damping over a range of configurations, the gains have to be adjusted to keep the roots of the characteristic
equation $S^2 + aS + b$ constant.

$$b = \frac{g_1}{J}\frac{K_a}{R_a}(R_aF + K_m^2) \qquad (11.63)$$

therefore

$$g_1 = J \times C_1 \tag{11.64}$$

where

$$C_1 = \frac{bR_a}{K_a(R_aF + K_m^2)} = \text{constant}$$

and

$$a = \frac{K_m}{JR_a} + \frac{g_3 K_{fw} K_a}{JR_a}(R_aF + K_m^2) \tag{11.65}$$

therefore

$$g_3 = JC_2 - C_3 \tag{11.66}$$

where

$$C_2 = \frac{aR_a}{K_{fw}K_a(R_aF + K_m^2)} = \text{constant}$$

and

$$C_3 = \frac{K_m}{K_{fw}K_a(R_aF + K_m^2)} = \text{constant}$$

By continuously calculating the inertia as seen by each joint, the controller can continually change the loop gains while the manipulator is moving and, hence, maintain critical damping. In a computer-based control system, continuous means at regular intervals (Section 11.9). The main problems with this system are the difficulty of modelling inertia, and that dynamic effects other than inertia have to be compensated for by other methods. Performance can be improved by adapting the manipulator inertia model to account for changes in the load.

While this approach to adaptive control can ensure that the independent joint controllers remain at or near critical gain, it does not ensure zero tracking error. In many applications, minimizing the tracking error is more important than maintaining critical gain. Several researchers have investigated systems to adapt the parameters of the control law and/or model to achieve zero tracking errors.

Slotine and Li (1987) define the controller design problem as:

Figure 11.30
Adaption of unknown
dynamics parameters.

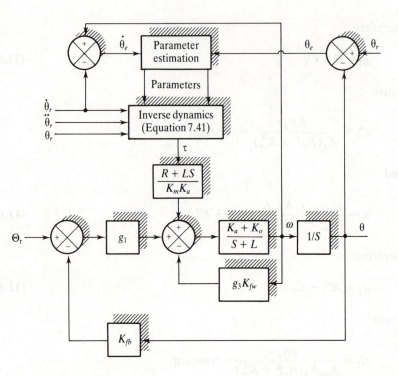

Given the desired trajectory $q_d(t)$, and with some or all the manipulator
parameters being unknown, derive a control law for the actuator torques
and an estimation law for the unknown parameters such that the
manipulator output $q(t)$ tracks the desired trajectories after an initial
adaption process.

Slotine and Li (1987) plan to adapt a feedforward compensation controller
on line, by using the tracking errors to adapt the unknown parameters in
the inverse dynamic model (Figure 11.30). In such a system, the load is
considered to be part of the last link and the estimated parameters compensate for it. In this type of adaptive control, initial errors are used to obtain
better model parameters, so when the load changes, tracking errors occur
until the estimation process settles.

A number of approaches to automatic parameter estimation have
been proposed including model-reference adaptive control (Dubowsky and
Des Forges, 1979), autoregressive models (Koiuo and Guo, 1983), and
recursive least-squares identification based on perturbation theory (Lee
and Chung, 1985). Resolved-motion adaptive control is an extension of
adaptive perturbation control into Cartesian space (Fu *et al.*, 1987). Much
work still needs to be done before any of these will be used in industrial
robots.

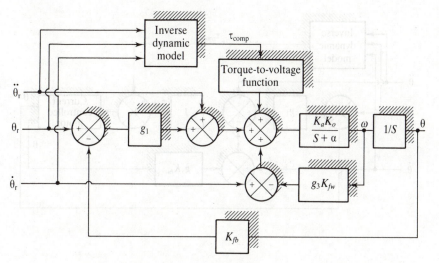

Figure 11.31
Feedforward compensation
control scheme.

11.5.4 Model-bassed schemes

Model-based control schemes assume knowledge of the full inverse dynamic
model when designing the controller. By accounting for the nonlinearities
and dynamic coupling with a model, we can use a simple linear control law –
the proportional plus voltage law. The aim is to compensate for the dynamics
by calculating the actuating torques required to cause the manipulator to
follow the desired trajectory. Three problems make model based schemes
difficult to implement.

(1) Real-time computation of inverse dynamics requires the use of a high-
speed parallel processor, and a customised model.

(2) They assume that the model is accurate, but the estimation of dynamic
parameters is difficult (Section 7.4).

(3) With nondirect-drive manipulators, static and dynamic friction are
difficult to estimate and have a large effect on control.

The feedback nonlinear cancelling controller in Figure 11.28 is a
model-based controller when the complete inverse dynamic model is used. If
reference trajectory values are used in the model instead of feedback values,
it is a feedforward, model-based, control system (Figure 11.31). In this
scheme, we use the inverse dynamic model to calculate the torque required to
correct for dynamic nonlinearities and coupling. This torque is transformed
to an equivalent velocity and added to the velocity reference.

In systems that use an inner current loop (Section 11.8.1), the output
of the proportional plus voltage control law is transformed to a torque
reference. The torque compensation value from the inverse dynamic model is

Figure 11.32
Feedforward compensation control with an inner current loop.

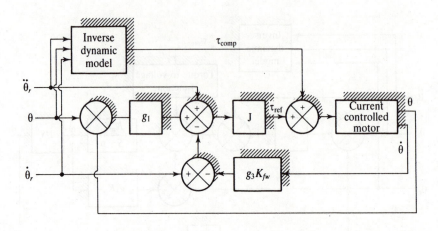

added to this torque reference to compensate for the dynamics which cause tracking errors. The main disadvantage of model-based feedforward compensation of dynamics is that friction and other external disturbances are not modelled, and consequently might not be handled well.

The basic idea of model-based control is to use the full inverse dynamic model to achieve dynamic decoupling of the joints. By moving the inverse dynamic model into the main control loop, the computed-torque control scheme does just that (Figure 11.33). The proportional plus velocity control law computes a commanded acceleration signal, which the nonlinear model transforms into a torque reference for the inner current loop. Effectively, an accurate inverse dynamic model exactly compensates for the dynamics of the manipulator. As a result, the proportional plus velocity control laws have decoupled linear actuators to control. Extending this

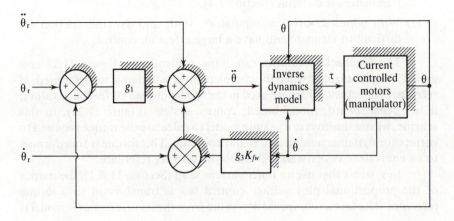

Figure 11.33
Computed torque control scheme.

system to operate in Cartesian space, by including kinematics is called resolved-acceleration control (Luh *et at.*, 1980).

Controlling the manipulator in Cartesian space is known as resolved control, because the joint positions, velocities and accelerations are combined and resolved into separately controllable hand motions along the world coordinate axes. Combination and resolution are effected using the kinematic models of the manipulator (Chapters 4 and 5). The position reference in Cartesian space is the homogeneous transform which describes the location of the end effector. Thus, the joint feedback values must be transformed into a feedback matrix using the forward kinematic transform.

$$\text{Reference} = {}^{R}T_{H} = [x\,y\,z\,p] \tag{11.67}$$

$$\text{Feedback} = {}^{R}T_{Hm} = [x_m\,y_m\,z_m\,p_m] \tag{11.68}$$

where the subscript m means measured and r means reference.

$$\text{Position error } e_p(t) = p_r(t) - p_m(t) \tag{11.69}$$

$$\text{Orientation error } e_o(t) = \frac{1}{2}(x_r(t) \times x_m + y_r(t) \times y_m$$

$$+ z_r(t) \times z_m) \tag{11.70}$$

These are combined to form a six-element location error

$$e_1(t) = l_r(t) - l_m(t) \tag{11.71}$$

From the trajectory planner, we obtain the six degree of freedom Cartesian location $l_r(t)$, velocity $v_r(t)$ and acceleration $a_r(t)$ references for the hand with respect to the base coordinate frame. Velocities are transformed from joint space to Cartesian space using the Jacobian (Chapter 5).

$$v = \mathbf{J}\dot{\theta} \tag{11.72}$$

$$a = \mathbf{J}\ddot{\theta} + \dot{\mathbf{J}}\dot{\theta} \tag{11.73}$$

The purpose of closed-loop control is to apply sufficient torque to the joints to reduce the errors in location, velocity and acceleration to zero.

$$g_4[a_r(t) - a_m(t)] + g_3[v_r(t) - v_m(t)] + g_1[l_r(t) - l_m(t)]$$

$$= g_4\ddot{e}_1(t) + g_3\dot{e}_1(t) + g_1 e_1(t) = 0 \tag{11.74}$$

where g_1, g_3 and g_4 are gain constants and $g_4 = 1$.

Figure 11.34
Resolved acceleration
control.

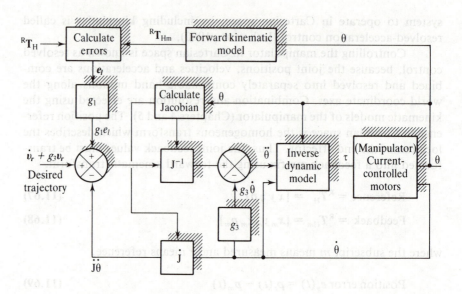

To reduce the tracking errors to zero using resolved-acceleration control, Equation 11.74 is reorganized to obtain an equation for commanded acceleration.

$$a_c(t) = a_r(t) + g_3(v_r(t) - v_m(t)) + g_1 e_1(t) \qquad (11.75)$$

Equating Equations 11.73 and 11.75.

$$J\ddot{\theta} + \dot{J}\dot{\theta} = \dot{v}_r + g_3(v_r - v_m) + g_1 e_1 \qquad (11.76)$$

By rearranging this equation, and substituting Equation 11.72, we obtain an equation for the commanded joint acceleration vector.

$$\ddot{\theta} = -g_3\dot{\theta} + J^{-1}(\dot{v}_r + g_3 v_r + g_1 e_1 - \dot{J}\dot{\theta}) \qquad (11.77)$$

Equation 11.77 is the control law for resolved-acceleration control (Figure 11.34). Again, gains g_1 and g_3 are selected to achieve critical damping with the desired time response. The control scheme is effectively a Cartesian space version of the proportional plus voltage controller, with the inverse dynamic model used to compensate for the dynamics. In addition to the extensive calculation of inverse dynamics required by the other model-based systems, this system also requires calculation of the inverse Jacobian and the derivative of the Jacobian. The difficulty of calculating the inverse Jacobian near singularities causes significant problems for this control scheme.

11.6 Control of type 1 two-link manipulator

The Newton-Euler dynamic equations for a type 1 two-link manipulator were derived in Section 7.2.1. For simplicity, we will assume that the links are solid square sections (Section 7.2.2) of length 1, thickness 1/10, and mass m. The closed form of the dynamic equations (Equation 7.41) expresses the vector of actuating torques in terms of the dynamic torques.

$$\tau_{\text{actuator}} = \tau_{\text{inertia}} + \tau_{\text{coupling}} + \tau_{\text{Coriolis}} + \tau_{\text{centrifugal}} + \tau_{\text{gravity}} + \tau_{\text{friction}} \quad \text{(11.78)}$$

For a type 1 two-link manipulator operating in a horizontal plane, the gravitational torque is zero. The actuation torque required a joint 2 (Equation 7.43) is

$$\tau_2 = \text{Inertia}\,\ddot{\theta}_2 + \text{Coupling}\,\ddot{\theta}_1 + \text{Centrifugal}\,(\dot{\theta}_1)^2 + \tau_{\text{friction}} \quad \text{(11.79)}$$

where

$$\text{Inertia} = 0.3342\,ml^2 \quad \text{(11.80)}$$

$$\text{Coupling} = \left(0.3342 + \frac{C_2}{2}\right)ml^2 \quad \text{(11.81)}$$

$$\text{Centrifugal} = \frac{ml^2}{2}S_2 \quad \text{(11.82)}$$

From these equations, we observe that the inertia is constant, hence the proportional plus velocity joint controller is critically damped in all configurations. However, the coupling and centrifugal torques vary significantly with configuration. The effect of these torques on trajectory tracking depends upon how much frictional torque is required.

The actuation torque required at joint 1 (Equation 7.42) is

$$\tau_1 = \text{Inertia}\,\ddot{\theta}_1 + \text{Coupling}\,\ddot{\theta}_2 + \text{Coriolis}\,\theta_1\theta_2$$
$$+ \text{Centrifugal}\,(\dot{\theta}_2)^2 + \tau_{\text{friction}} \quad \text{(11.83)}$$

where

$$\text{Inertia} = (1.6683 + C_2)ml^2 \quad \text{(11.84)}$$

$$\text{Coupling} = \left(0.3342 + \frac{C_2}{2}\right)ml^2 \quad \text{(11.85)}$$

$$\text{Coriolis} = ml^2 S_2 \quad \text{(11.86)}$$

$$\text{Centrifugal} = -\frac{ml^2}{2}S_2 \quad \text{(11.87)}$$

Figure 11.35
Robot acquiring an object
using visual feedback.

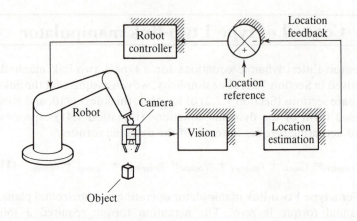

For both joints, the magnitudes of the multiplying constants for coupling and centrifugal torques are the same, although the centrifugal torques have opposite sign. The first joint has a Coriolis torque, where the second does not. The other significant difference is that the inertia at the first joint varies with the configuration of the second link. Thus, the damping of the proportional plus velocity controller for the first joint changes with configuration. The inertia varies by up to 37.5 per cent below the maximum as the configuration changes. The impact of the second link on the dynamics of the first joint can be reduced either by mechanical design or control system design. Mechanically, the impact is reduced by reducing the mass or the length of the second link. From the control system's point of view, one of the controllers discussed in the previous section can be used. The controller used will depend on the significance of the dynamic terms at normal operating velocities, the accuracy with which the dynamic parameters can be modelled, and the available computing power.

11.7   Visual servoing

While resolved-acceleration control appears to close the position-control loop in Cartesian space, the accuracy of the control is limited by the accuracy of the forward kinematic model. The Cartesian-space feedback signal is calculated from the joint-space parameters using the model, not measured. To overcome the difficulties caused by model uncertainties and to cope with unknown environments, we must measure the parameters to be controlled using external sensors. For example, the measurement of weld-bead position in arc welding with through-the-arc sensors (Section 1.5.1.1). External sensors are also used to obtain the location of objects. From this location information, a position control reference vector is calculated. For example, the measurement of seam position in arc welding with a laser scanner (Figure 1.14).

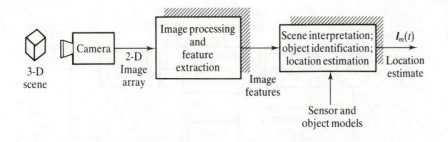

Figure 11.36
Using vision to obtain a location feedback vector.

The use of vision to acquire the location of objects (Figure 11.35) requires extensive computing power, and robust recognition algorithms. The camera captures a two-dimensional image (Figure 11.36), from which the vision processing software must extract image features. These features are compared to models of the objects to identify the object of interest, and the location of grasp points. The location (position and orientation) of the object relative to the hand, and/or relative to world coordinates is then estimated to produce an object location signal.

The most commonly used control system is the static look and move system (Figure 11.37). Control is achieved by a sequence of independent steps. In Step 1, the task planner generates a position reference using visual information as described in the previous paragraph. In Step 2, the vision system estimates the location of the hand relative to world coordinates. In Step 3, the task computer calculates the Cartesian motions required to move the hand to the desired location. In Step 4, the robot controller moves the hand. The steps are repeated until the robot hand is in the correct position to grasp the object.

This control scheme is based upon a hierarchy of three, independent, sensing activities. At the top level, a vision system is used to identify the object, estimate the location of the grasp point, and calculate a location-reference vector relative to world coordinates (Figure 11.36). This vision system may be the one attached to the hand of the robot, or a stationary camera placed to view the whole scene. At the intermediate level, a vision

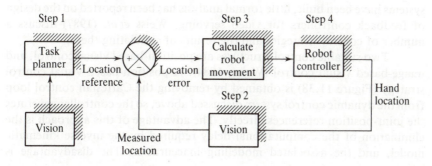

Figure 11.37
Static look and move control.

Figure 11.38
Position-based visual
servoing.

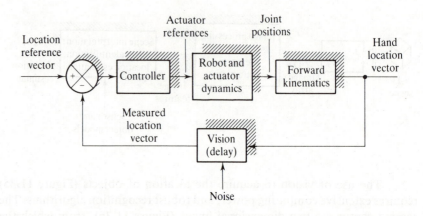

system calculates the position of the hand relative to world coordinates
(Figure 11.37) for use as a feedback signal. At the bottom-level, the internal
sensors measure the joint parameters for use in calculating the kinematic and
dynamic models. If the kinematic models of the vision system and the robot
are reasonably accurate, the static look-and-move steps are executed once
only.

If greater accuracy is required, or there are external disturbances, or
the object is moving, the whole process has to be repeated until the object is
grasped. As structured, the system is static because the four steps are
executed independently and in sequence, and consequently the internal
dynamics of each step do not affect the overall stability of the system. In
contrast, when the four steps are executed in parallel, we have a dynamic
control system, where the dynamic interactions between levels in the control
hierarchy are critical. For example, if the location error is updated to
produce a new controller reference before the last motion has completed, the
system may overshoot, or, worse, become unstable. Thus, to achieve
dynamic closed-loop control of position, we must include a gain block in the
location controller.

The control law used in this servo loop has to account for the nonlinearity, noise, coupling and computational delays involved in measuring
the location of the hand with vision. While a number of visual control
systems have been built, little formal analysis has been reported on the design
of feedback controllers for video servoing. Weiss *et al.* (1987) discuss a
number of control strategies and the results of simulating them.

Two suitable control structures are position-based visual control, and
image-based visual control (Weiss, 1984). A position-based visual control
strategy (Figure 11.38) is obtained by removing the Cartesian control loop
from the dynamic control system discussed above, so the controller generates
the joint-position references directly. The advantage of this approach is the
elimination of the computational delay required by the inverse kinematic
model, and the associated modelling inaccuracies. The disadvantage is

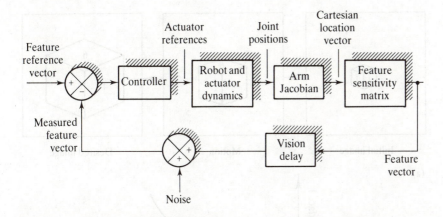

Figure 11.39
Image-based visual servoing.

that the controller must compensate for any nonlinear and coupled robot dynamics and kinematics, as well as measurement delays and noise.

In position-based control, the vision system measures the location of the hand, either relative to world coordinates, or relative to an object is a known position. If an object in a known position is located within the view of the camera, it can be used as a reference frame for hand location reference and feedback. This reduces the time taken by the vision system to calculate the feedback vector because it eliminates the transformation from the vision frame to the world frame. It also minimizes the errors caused by incorrect mapping between distances in the image and actual distances, as both reference and feedback are in image dimensions.

The measurement of hand location with vision can be decomposed into two nonlinear transformations: image to feature space, and feature space to location. The control loop can be sped up by eliminating the visual transformation, and using a feature vector as reference. The result is the image-based visual servoing control structure of Figure 11.39.

We can model feature extraction as

$$f = \mathbf{I}^{-1} l_{\text{rel}} \tag{11.88}$$

where

f is the feature vector,

l_{rel} is the actual location of the hand in vision space, and

$\mathbf{I}$ is the ideal interpreter.

The ideal interpreter, $\mathbf{I}$, is the feature to location transformation based on an exact model of the object and image transducer. The feature space to location transformation is modelled as

$$l_m = \mathbf{I}_n f \tag{11.89}$$

Figure 11.40
Relationship between feature
(area of side 1) and motion
of the camera: (a) image
sequence; (b) area of
surface 1 relative to camera
position.

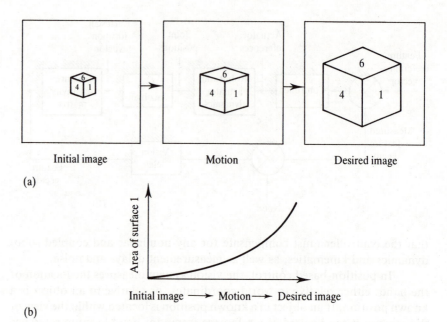

Initial image   Motion   Desired image

(a)

(b)

where

l_m is the measured location of the hand in vision space and

$\mathbf{I}_n$ is the interpreter subject to noise.

Unfortunately, in practical systems, modelling inaccuracies and transducer noise result in less than the ideal interpretation function $\mathbf{I}_n$. If the practical interpretation function has a unique inverse mapping, such that Equation 11.89 produces a unique location vector for every feature vector, the system can be controlled using features directly as reference and feedback signals. This is the basis of image-based video servoing.

The unique inverse mapping required for feature-based feedback relies on the systematic variation of image features with relative object position. For example, when the image contains a single object, as the camera moves towards the object, the object fills an increasingly large area of the image (Figure 11.40). Consequently, features such as the area of a surface, and sums and ratios of areas of surfaces, vary according to nonlinear functions of camera motion. This technique can be enhanced by marking special features on objects, for example, the pattern of dots placed on satelite grasp points (Section 1.5.5).

A set of functions is unique when their partial derivatives are continuous, and the Jacobian of the ideal inverse interpretation is nonsingular (Weiss, *et al.*, 1987). This Jacobian is the feature sensitivity matrix in Figure

11.39. When multiplied by the manipulator Jacobian, it transforms the joint-space vector describing the hand into the feature vector.

The design of a control law to compensate for the non-linearities and coupling of this system is a formidable task. Weiss (1984) found that a model-reference adaptive controller simplified the design. The results of simulations of this controller for one, two, and three degree of freedom manipulators are reported in Weiss *et al.*, (1987). Such a scheme should achieve real-time control based on local features, while global scene interpretation occurs at a much slower rate.

11.8 Force control

In many applications, a robot must explicitly control the force it applies to the object it is manipulating. Often, task constraints require control of position in some Cartesian degrees of freedom and control of force in others. In Chapter 6, we examined ways of partitioning the Cartesian degrees of freedom of the end effector into 2 orthogonal sets; one that must be position controlled and one that must be force controlled. In this section, we are interested in how to control the actuators to achieve the desired forces.

11.8.1 Joint torque control

We control force (a vector of three forces and three torques) in Cartesian space by controlling torques in joint space. In Chapter 6, we found that the transformation between joint space torques and Cartesian space force is the transpose of the manipulator Jacobian (Equation 6.75).

$$\tau = J^T f \tag{11.90}$$

Torque in joint space is controlled by controlling the torque applied by each actuator. Torque can be measured using a sensor (Section 10.5.4.2), or calculated from armature current (Equation 11.12). As motor torque is used to overcome friction and windage, the shaft torque applied to the load will be less than the torque calculated from armature current. Hence, direct measurement of shaft torque results in more accurate control. The simplest torque control is an armature-current control loop, which is often called an inner current loop. The complete block diagram for this control is shown in Figure 11.41. Again, we simplify the block diagram by neglecting armature inductance and manipulating the blocks. To obtain a controller with fast exponential response, we choose a proportional plus integral control law, with a zero to compensate for the motor pole.

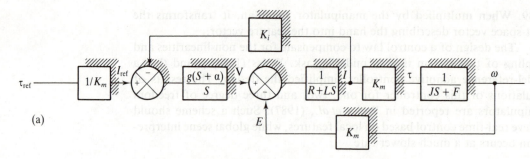

(a)

(b)

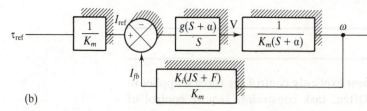

(c)

$$\text{CLTF} = \frac{G}{I+GH} = \frac{g}{S\left(K_m + g\dfrac{J}{K_m}\right) + F}$$

(d)

$$\frac{g}{(33 \times 10^{-3} + 97 \times 10^{-6}g)S + 1 \times 10^{-6}}$$

Figure 11.41
Joint torque control based
upon closed-loop current
control. (a) Block diagram;
(b) modified block diagram;
(c) closed loop transfer
function; (d) closed loop
transfer function for low-
inertia micromotor.

$$\text{Control law} = g + \frac{g\alpha}{S} = \frac{g(S+\alpha)}{S} \tag{11.91}$$

The closed loop transfer function for this controller is

$$\text{CLTF} = \frac{g}{S\left(K_m + \dfrac{gJ}{K_m}\right) + F} \tag{11.92}$$

When the friction is small in comparison to the torque constant, it can be neglected and the transfer function becomes a pure integrator, as shown for the low-inertia micromotor in Figure 11.41. The time response is a ramp, with the gain determining the slope of the ramp. As a result, the motor velocity will continue to increase until the system saturates, unless an external force is applied to stop it. Fundamental to force (or torque) control is Newton's third law: to every action there is an equal and opposite reaction.

To control actuator torque, we must have a load that will apply reactive torque. Also, we have assumed that the load is very stiff. In practice, the compliance of the load increases the damping of the system, enabling still faster response.

When an inner current loop is used in a position controller, the motor transfer function is a double integrator (Table 11.2). Calculating the impact of this upon the proportional plus voltage position controller is left as an exercise for the reader. Using an inner torque loop, based upon shaft torque measurements reduces the effect of nonlinearities like static friction (Luh, *et al.*, 1983). When the friction is large, such as when a harmonic drive is used, the pole moves to the left along the real axis. When the armature inductance is significant, as in many large industrial motors, the zero in the control law is used to cancel the pole due to armature inductance, leaving a complex transfer function with 3 poles and one zero (Exercise 11.18).

Force control using feedback of joint torques is limited by the accuracy of the static model of the manipulator (Section 6.4). To obtain accurate control of the force vector at the end effector, we place a wrist force sensor between the tool plate and the end effector (Section 10.5.4.3) to measure end effector force. The force transform from the sensor to the end effector is usually simple.

11.8.2 Add-on force control

A number of schemes have been proposed for force control (Whitney, 1985). Some schemes control force directly, while others control it indirectly by modifying position references. The latter occurs because most industrial robots are supplied with position control loops which cannot be modified easily. These loops are implemented in software, and, as the manufacturers do not supply source code, are inaccessible to the user.

To oversome these problems, Hendy and Holzer (1984) developed an add-on force controller (Figure 11.42). This controller uses the supplied joint position controllers, and modifies the Cartesian position controllers. When a Cartesian degree of freedom is to be force controlled, the Cartesian space reference is modified by a force control loop. The VAL-II ALTER command is used to alter the path during the motion dynamically (Figure 12.22). This loop calculates a Cartesian position feedback vector using a stiffness matrix.

$$f = \mathbf{K}\,\delta l \tag{11.93}$$

The stiffness matrix ($\mathbf{K}$) is a 6 by 6 matrix which relates the displacement (δl) of the end effector to the applied forces (f). The stiffness matrix is dependent on manipulator configuration and is diagonal when there is no cross-coupling between the components of the force vector and the

Figure 11.42
Add-on force controller.

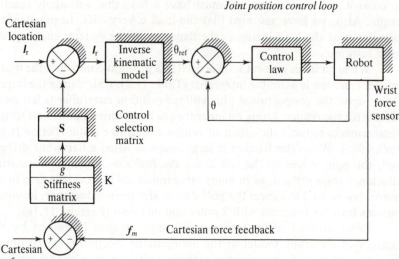

components of the displacement vector. Such coupling is usually small. Setting the nondiagonal components of the matrix to zero considerably reduces the computations to be performed during each servo cycle.

For a particular manipulator, the stiffness matrix is measured experimentally by fixing the end effector, incrementing the Cartesian position in each degree of freedom, and measuring the resultant forces with the wrist sensor. With this method, we obtain the total stiffness of the robot including base, arm, wrist sensor, end effector, and position controllers. Coupling can be measured by comparing the forces measured when the position is incremented in individual degrees of freedom to when it is incremented in several degrees of freedom.

When a Cartesian degree of freedom is to be force controlled (for example, in the x direction), its position reference is,

$$x = x_r + g \left(\frac{{}^f r_x - {}^f m_x}{K_x} \right) S_x \tag{11.94}$$

where g is the proportional gain of the force loop. Thus, a variation in the position reference is calculated which will result in the desired force, provided the motion of the end effector is constrained in that direction. The parameter S_x is an element of a diagonal matrix which is used to represent which Cartesian directions are to be force controlled, and which ones are to be position controlled (see discussion on hybrid control in Section 11.8.7). In this example, it has a value of 1. If the force control software is implemented on the computer in the robot controller, the system works well and at

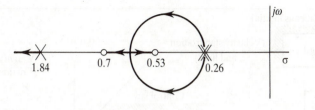

Figure 11.43
Pole-zero plot of proportional
gain control law for an add-
on force controller using a
wrist-force sensor.

reasonable speed. However, if it is implemented on a separate computer, the
time to transfer data between the computers may make real-time control
impossible. Hendy and Holzer found that they could easily calculate the new
location vector 40 times a second in the supervisory computer. However, the
vectors could only be transferred to the robot at a rate of two per second
using a serial link, and four per second using the controller's parallel interface. As a consequence, the system was painfully slow.

Similar delays in communication were found by Young (1985), as he
researched the ability of add-on force control to follow a contour (Section
12.4.6). To investigate the stability of the system, he plotted the open-loop
transfer function of the robot (Puma 560) plus force sensing wrist (Figure
11.16). The open-loop transfer function is given in Equation 11.31. To do
this, he wrote a set of programs to command the robot to track a sinusoidal
trajectory in the z direction, and to record its response. To filter out the large
proportion of harmonics and noise on the feedback signals from the wrist
force sensor, Young used discrete-time Fourier series analysis when calculating the points on the Bode plot.

From the pole-zero diagram of the open-loop transfer function
(Figure 11.43), we can see that closing the loop using proportional gain will
result in a stable system. As the gain increases, the system moves from being
underdamped to overdamped. Young demonstrated good contour following
with this system. He also demonstrated that the system could be used to
record an ideal force/motion trajectory for a particular task, for example,
inserting a pin into a circuit board. This recorded trajectory could then be
used as a reference for subsequent insertions. Thus, he designed a means of
teaching tasks to force controlled systems.

11.8.3   Stiffness control

When force can be controlled directly, a number of strategies are possible.
Salisbury (1980) developed a system to control actively the apparent stiffness
of a manipulator. Stiffness is the rate at which the forces (and torques) on the
end effector increase as it is deflected from its nominal position (Equation
11.93). Stiffness is the inverse of compliance. The structural stiffness of the
robot is fixed, as is the elasticity of the gripper. So, to control the apparent

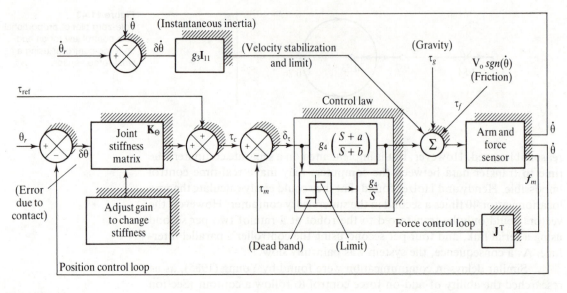

Figure 11.44
Stiffness control.

stiffness of the manipulator, we must adjust the gain of the position-control loops (Figure 11.44).

In effect, reducing the gains of the position-control loops increases the compliance of the system to position errors. Where a remote-centre-compliance device achieves this by allowing the end effector to move relative to a fixed wrist, stiffness control achieves this by allowing errors in position control. The stiffness of the system determines the magnitude of the force generated in opposition to this error. If the stiffness is high, the force is high, and little position error is tolerated. If the stiffness is low, only a small opposing force is generated, and large position errors are tolerated. Thus, the controller acts like a spring, where stiffness is the spring constant. Thus, the stiffness matrix can be thought of as a six-dimensional spring matrix.

When generating the control strategy for a task (Section 6.2), we determined that some degrees of freedom should be force controlled and others position controlled. This can be achieved with high stiffness for the position controlled degrees of freedom and low stiffness for the force controlled degrees of freedom.

The stiffness control scheme (Figure 11.44) calculates a commanded torque from the desired position and torque trajectories.

$$\tau_c = \tau_{ref} + \mathbf{K}\delta\theta \qquad (11.95)$$

where $\delta\theta$ is a six degree of freedom incremental displacement in joint angles. This joint displacement is related to the Cartesian displacement by the Jacobian (Chapter 5).

$$\delta l = \mathbf{J} \delta \theta \qquad\qquad (11.96)$$

Thus, the torque required for the hand to behave as a six-dimensional spring is

$$\tau = \mathbf{J}^{\mathsf{T}} f = \mathbf{J}^{\mathsf{T}} \mathbf{K} \delta l = \mathbf{J}^{\mathsf{T}} \mathbf{K} \mathbf{J} \delta \theta = \mathbf{K}_{\theta} \delta \theta \qquad\qquad (11.97)$$

by substitution of Equations 11.90 and 11.93. The joint stiffness matrix $(\mathbf{K}_{\theta})$ is related to the Cartesian stiffness matrix by the Jacobian.

$$\mathbf{K}_{\theta} = \mathbf{J}^{\mathsf{T}} \mathbf{K} \mathbf{J} \qquad\qquad (11.98)$$

The joint stiffness matrix is nondiagonal and symmetrical, indicating that joint stiffnesses are highly coupled. Consequently, position errors in one joint will affect torque in others. Because of this coupling, we can control the location of the stiffness centre – the point at which the application of pure forces results in pure translation and the application of pure torque results in pure rotation. This is a desirable feature for tasks like insertion.

This system allows us to control the Cartesian stiffness of the hand. In order to make the arm behave with the desired stiffness, we must be able to control the forces at the end effector directly. We achieve this with an inner force control loop (Figure 11.44). While these control loops control joint torque, the torque feedback signal is derived from force measurement at the wrist. Consequently, the forces at the end effector are controlled and disturbance torques, such as gravity and friction, are automatically accounted for.

When a joint is under pure torque control, that is, the stiffness is zero, it will accelerate away if it is not restrained by an external object. To stop the joint reaching velocities that could cause damage, a parallel velocity control loop is included in the controller. This controller also improves stability, as discussed in Section 11.4.2, particularly with changing inertia. As designed, this controller accounts only for dynamic effects by feedback of force and position errors caused by these effects.

When the end effector is in contact with an object, the transfer function of the whole system (base, robot, force sensor, end effector, and object which is attached to the base) is a lighlty-damped second-order oscillatory function. Open loop impact tests can be used to determine the natural frequency of the structural resonances. These can vary from 20Hz for an articulated manipulator to 100Hz for a Cartesian manipulator when in contact with a stiff object. These structural resonances will cause a high-gain force servo to chatter when the end effector is in contact with a low compliance object, such as an aluminium block. Thus, the gain of the force-control loops is limited by the compliance of the object being manipulated. Consequently, tuning the force controller is difficult. Salisbury (1980) tuned the loop for the worst case using a zero and a pole (lead-lag law), and a

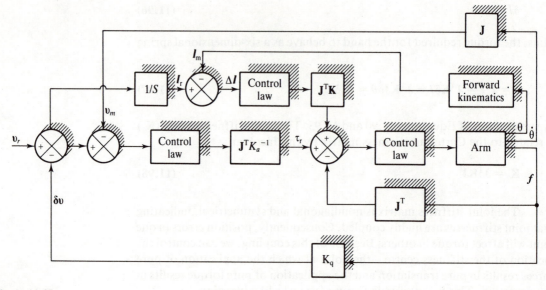

Figure 11.45
Damping control.

parallel integrator to remove zero errors. The integrator is preceded by a deadband to reduce limit cycling (small oscillations about the reference) and a limiter to reduce the integral gain for large force errors.

11.8.4 Damping control

A second direct force-control strategy is damping control, sometimes called accommodation (Whitney, 1977). In damping control, the controller calculates velocity feedback from measured forces. When the end effector is pushed, the control system generates an opposing force proportional to the impressed velocity. Thus, damping control acts like a six degree of freedom dashpot, where small motions are created to null forces, or small forces are created to null motions. The ratio of velocity to force is called admittance, giving rise to a 6 by 6 admittance matrix for a manipulator.

$$\mathbf{K}_a = \text{admittance matrix} = \frac{v}{f} \tag{11.99}$$

Damping control is based on resolved-motion rate control, where the controller calculates the rates of change of the joint angles required to achieve the desired Cartesian velocities of the end effector.

$$i = v = \mathbf{J}\dot{\theta} = \mathbf{K}_a f \tag{11.100}$$

We will discuss a Cartesian-space controller (Figure 11.45) rather than a joint-space controller with transforms on the references, as we did for the stiffness controller. The outer loop is the velocity control loop.

$$v_{error} = v_{ref} - v_{fb} - \delta v \tag{11.101}$$

To transform this Cartesian velocity error to a joint torque reference for the inner loop, we derive a transform from the above equations.

$$\tau_r = \mathbf{J}^T f = \mathbf{J}^T \mathbf{K}_a^{-1} \mathbf{J} \dot{\theta} = \mathbf{J}^T \mathbf{K}_a^{-1} v_{error} \tag{11.102}$$

To obtain a position reference, the controller integrates the velocity reference. When there is no force, we have a velocity controller, with the position-control loop holding the robot in the position where motion stopped. As the admittance matrix is in the force-feedback path, changing it changes the damping of the system.

11.8.5 Impedance control

A third direct-force control strategy is impedance control (Hogan, 1980). If a joint is driven by opposing actuators then the torque about the joint is the difference between the two actuation torques.

$$\tau_j = \tau_1 - \tau_2 \tag{11.103}$$

$$\tau_{stiff} = \text{smaller of } \tau_1 \text{ and } \tau_2 \tag{11.104}$$

If the actuators apply equal and opposite torques, there is no torque about the joint, but the joint is much stiffer than when the actuators apply no torque. That is the tendency of the joint to drift in response to disturbances is diminished, as the joint opposes forces that try to move it. This rotational stiffness is called impedance. When two actuators are in opposition, the impedance of the joint and the torque about the joint can be controlled independently.

Impedance control is equivalent to stiffness plus damping, that is, impedance is equivalent to a six degree of freedom spring-damper system. With a single actuator, impedance control is implemented by combining a stiffness controller with a damping controller. We can change the damping control in Figure 11.45 into an impedance control by removing the velocity integrator and using a position reference generated by a path planner.

Impedance control is often used to control the fingers on grippers (Section 2.4), where the hand is to grasp and object with a certain force, but the fingers are to be springy enough to deform and not damage the object. Also, the fingers are to be stiff enough to hold the object when subject to

Figure 11.46
Explicit force control.

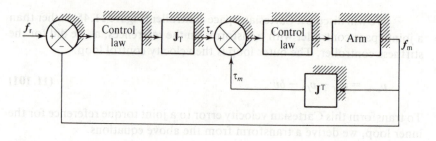

disturbances caused by contact with other objects, for example, during assembly.

11.8.6 Explicit force control

A fourth direct-force control strategy is explicit force control (Nevins and Whitney, 1973). An explicit force controller consists of two loops: an inner loop to control torque in joint space and an outer loop to control force in Cartesian space (Figure 11.46). Position and velocity are determined completely by the constraints applied by the object being manipulated. When this controller is used, the task planner generates a force trajectory. Elements of stiffness, damping and impedance can all be achieved by appropriate adjustment of the proportional, integral and derivative gain terms of the outer force-control loop. However, the only time we can have explicit force control in all degrees of freedom is when the gripper is firmly grasping an immovable object. When motion is possible in any degree of freedom, explicit force control will accelerate the gripper in that direction, resulting in damage to either the manipulator or the object. We analysed the decomposition of task requirements into force control in some degrees of freedom and position control in other degrees of freedom in Section 6.2. The question is, How do we achieve that segregation of control?

11.8.7 Hybrid control

We observed that it is not possible to control the torque and position of a joint independently due to conflicting constraint requirements. Control of torque depends on the joint position being constrained. Control of position depends on there being no constraints to motion. This raises a problem for Cartesian control. While control in Cartesian space can be decomposed into orthogonal components of either force or position, it is not instinctively obvious that such a decomposition transfers to joint space. That is, can we guarantee that each joint controller is required to control torque or motion only, not torque and motion?

It is known that independent Cartesian space motions result in coupled joint space motions. By coupled, we mean that motion of more than one joint is required to achieve Cartesian motion in one direction. The same is true for force. So how can we generate a joint-space control strategy that requires joints to be either torque- or motion-controlled from a Cartesian-space task strategy that specifies orthogonal position and force control. In general, this is an unsolved problem.

Raibert and Craig (1981) proposed a hybrid position/force controller as a way to solve this problem. Using the methodology of Chapter 6, they derived a constraint frame located in the hand that specifies which Cartesian degrees of freedom are to be force controlled and which are to be position controlled. This frame is represented by a diagonal constraint matrix (**S**), whose components are 1 for a degree of freedom that is force controlled, and 0 for a degree of freedom that is position controlled.

$$\mathbf{S} = \text{diag}(c) = \begin{bmatrix} S_1 & 0 & .. & 0 \\ 0 & S_2 & .. & 0 \\ : & .. & & : \\ 0 & .. & & S_n \end{bmatrix} = \text{Constraint matrix} \tag{11.105}$$

This matrix is included in the six degree-of-freedom manipulator controller (Figure 11.47). When the appropriate matrix element is 1, the control loop is closed, and when the matrix element is 0, the control loop is open. In the position control loops the constraint matrix is substracted from the identity matrix to reverse the values. As the constraint matrix can be changed at any time, the control loops can be dynamically reconfigured to handle changing task constraints. The force reference is fed directly into the torque references, via a transform, as a feedforward control and to keep the integrator output near zero. It also enables proportional control with reduced gains, as the torque reference is not a function of the force error. A clamp is placed on the input of the integrator to reduce the gain for large force errors. The integral gain overcomes the frictional damping of the system. In hybrid control, the actuator drive signal for each joint is the instantaneous contribution of that joint to satisfying each Cartesian position or force constraint. The actuator command signal for the ith joint has n components, one for each degree of freedom in the constraint frame.

$$\tau_i = \sum_{j=1}^{n} (\text{Force gain}_{ij} \times S_j \times \text{force error}_j + \text{Position gain}_{ij}$$
$$\times (1 - S_j) \text{ position error}_j) \tag{11.106}$$

Hybrid control relies on the kinematics of the manipulator to sort out the transform from independent Cartesian control to independent joint

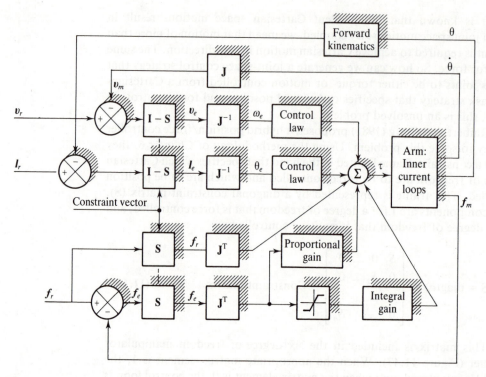

Figure 11.47
Hybrid position/force control.

control. The result of the outer loops is a vector of joint torque references. Thus, each joint is commanded to achieve a desired torque, and any conflict between force and motion control is resolved in the outer loops. A rigorous mathematical proof of this control strategy is still to be formulated, and a general six degree of freedom practical system has not been built.

11.9 Programming

In this chapter, we have discussed control systems as if the signals and calculations were continuous functions of time. When implemented in analogue electronics they are. Inner current loops are so fast that they are usually analogue and, hence, are continuous. Although, the speed of microprocessors has increased to the point where direct digital-control of current loops is used in some controllers. Direct digital-control is the closing of a control loop inside a computer. As the computer has to read the feed-back signal, often via an analogue to digital converter; calculate the error between the feedback and the reference; calculate the actuator command from the error, using the control law; and output the actuator command to the power amplifier, via a digital to analogue converter; one iteration of the control loop takes a finite amount of time.

The process of sampling the feedback signal and calculating the output at regular intervals is called sampled-data control. A whole theory has been developed to analyse sampled-data systems. For our purposes, we simply recognize that the sampling rate must be fast enough for the system to appear continuous. As a rule of thumb, the sampling and calculation process must occur 10 to 100 times during a period equal to the loop time constant for smooth control.

Direct digital-control loops have to be carefully programmed so that they are fast and robust. A typical industrial robot trajectory execution program will update the joint position references every 30 ms. The joint position controllers sample, calculate, and output every 2 ms. Any error that occurs during these calculations can cause significant problems. Even an error in sampling a feedback signal can cause unpredicted motion of the manipulator. Errors that can cause a program crash, such as divide by zero and arithmetic overflow, must either be guarded against or detected and corrected for. A program crash will result in loss of control of the manipulator and possible damage.

The calculations inside the control loops fall into three groups – manipulator models, signal processing and control laws. To calculate the inverse dynamic model for the computed torque control (Figure 11.33) of the CMU Direct Drive Arm 2 in less than two ms a special array processor was used. When models are used in controllers, the general model is customised to a set of equations for the particular manipulator. These equations are hard coded, often with common sub-expressions calculated separately.

When an optical encoder is used for joint feedback, joint position, velocity and direction have to be calculated from the train of pulses. Often, a hardware up/down counter is used to count the pulses, which the computer reads on every iteration of the control loop. Any other sensor values used in the control loop have to be read and converted to suitable units also.

Most control laws use a combination of proportional, integral and derivative gains.

$$\text{Output} = g_1 e + g_2 \int e \, dt + g_3 \frac{de}{dt} \tag{11.107}$$

where e is the error.

At each iteration of a sampled-data system, the control program adds the integral for the current period to the total integral and calculates the derivative for the current period. Integration is reduced to a simple summation and differentiation is reduced to subtraction. Thus, the control law becomes:

$$\text{Output} = g_1 e_t + g_2 (e_t + I_{t-1}) + g_3 (e_t - e_{t-1}) \tag{11.108}$$

where e_t is the error at time t, and I_{t-1} is the running sum of the errors.

If we assume unit time between samples then I_t is the area under the curve or the integral.

$$I_t = e_t + I_{t-1} = \sum_1^t e_t = \int e\, dt \qquad (11.109)$$

In addition to calculating the output value, the control program may have to check for maximum and minimum limits. Closed loop control involves a lot of processing in a very short time. Often these loops are coded in assembler, but with modern high-speed processors languages such as C++ and Modula-2 are being used. The programming of direct-digital control software is a highly specialized task. We will look at programming in greater depth in Chapter 12.

Key points

- The task of a control system is to execute the planned sequence of motions and forces in the presence of unforeseen errors.

- In feedback control, the error between the desired and measured values of a parameter is amplified to drive the actuator.

- The amount of amplification is determined by a control law:

  output = control law (error) $\qquad (11.27)$

- The transfer function of a plant is a model of the relationship of the output to the input including dynamic effects.

- A control system is stable when the feedback matches the reference without hunting.

- Control laws use proportional, integral and derivative functions:

$$\text{Output} = g_1 \times \text{error} + g_2 \int \text{error}\, dt + g_3 \frac{d\,\text{error}}{dt} \qquad (11.30)$$

$$= g_1 e_t + g_2(e_t + I_{t-1}) + g_3(e_t - e_{t-1}) \qquad (11.108)$$

- Tuning is the process of adjusting the gains of the control law to achieve stability and the desired step response.

- When controlling joint position with a d.c. motor, a proportional plus velocity control law achieves fast, stable response with minimum error.

- The transfer function of a robot joint/linkage system changes with configuration due to varying inertial and gravitational loads.

- Unless the control system corrects for these non-linear dynamics, the response and stability of the joint controllers change with configuration.
- Three classes of controller are used to compensate for dynamics: non-linear cancelling, adaptive, and model-based controllers.
- Three problems make accurate compensation for dynamics complex:
  — inverse dynamic models can be solved in real-time only with specialized parallel processors,
  — estimating the dynamic parameters accurately is difficult, and
  — estimating friction is difficult.
- The unique inverse mapping required for feature based visual servoing relies on systematic variation of image features with relative object position.
- Force and torque in Cartesian space is controlled by controlling force or torque in joint space.
- Motor shaft torque is often controlled with an inner current loop, whose closed-loop transfer function is a double integrator.
- Strategies used for force control include stiffness, damping, impedance, explicit force, and add-on force control schemes.
- Add-on force controllers control force by modifying position references.
- Stiffness control acts like a six-degree of freedom spring, where stiffness is the rate at which forces on the end effector increase as it is deflected – that is, the spring constant.
- Damping control acts like a six degree of freedom dashpot, where the control system generates opposing forces proportional to the impressed velocity.
- When opposing actuators act on a joint, the opposing torques increase the impedance (rotational stiffness) of the joint.
- Hybrid control addresses the problem of mapping force and position control in independent degrees of freedom in Cartesian space into decoupled torque and position controllers in joint space.

Exercises

■ *Essay questions*

11.1. Define the following control terms:

> open-loop, closed-loop, feedforward, feedback, adaptive, transfer function, plant model, control law, linear system, step, impulse, ramp, root locus, slew rate, tracking error, overshoot and settling time.

11.2. What is a pole-zero diagram used for?

11.3. Draw the block diagram of the mass-spring-damper system in Figure 11.4 and devise a control law.

11.4. Obtain the transfer function for the linear hydraulic motor (Equation 11.10) by transformation of the block diagram in Figure 11.7 using the transformations in Figure 11.8.

11.5. Calculate the transfer function (Equation 11.21) for each motor in Table 11.1. Find the electrical time constant, the motor time constant, the open loop gain, and the undamped natural frequency for each motor.

11.6. Using the proportional plus velocity control law in Section 11.4.2, calculate the gains for critical damping for each motor in Exercise 11.5.

11.7. Compare and contrast d.c. power amplifiers and pulse-width modulated amplifiers (Section 11.2.2).

11.8. What is meant by the following terms: stability, hunting, ringing, critical damping, and overshoot?

11.9. What is the purpose of a control law? (Section 11.3.2).

11.10. What is the effect of changing the proportional, integral, and derivative gains when tuning a joint-position-control loop?

11.11. What impact does an inner current loop have on the motor transfer function?

11.12. What dynamic effects occur in a manipulator, and what is their impact on the damping of the controllers?

11.13. Compare and contrast the various methods of dynamics compensation.

11.14. How does an adaptive control law improve the response of a control system?

11.15. How could visual servoing be used to control the motion of the space shuttle arm when grasping a satellite? What features can be used, and how do they change as the camera moves towards them? Develop a model of the change in feature parameters with camera position.

11.16. Compare and contrast the various methods of force control.

11.17. How is integration and differentiation performed in real time in a digital computer?

11.18. What impact does increasing the friction or the inductance of the motor have on the control of an inner current loop?.

■ *Practical questions*

11.1. Examine the robot in the lab and determine what control loops are used. Draw a block diagram for the control system. If you have access to the actuator data and the control system gains, model the control loops and investigate their level of damping.

11.2. Write a program to simulate proportional plus velocity control of a single link.

11.3. Develop joint position and joint-velocity control systems for the motor-sensor-linkage system in Practical question 7.1. What effect does changing the shape of the link have on the damping?

11.4. Construct a type 1 two-link manipulator driven by d.c. motors with joint position and joint velocity sensing. Develop joint-position and joint-force control loops for this robot. What effect does the inertia of the second link have on the damping of the controller of the first joint?

11.5. Could an add-on force controller (Section 11.8.2) be used with the robot in the laboratory?

12 · *Programming*

Objectives

In this chapter, we divide robot programmers into three distinct classes: users, applications programmers, and systems programmers. Our objective is to examine the problems faced by each class of programmer and to elucidate the language constructs and system features required to program solutions to these problems. In the first third of the chapter, which deals with systems programming, the reader is assumed to understand operating systems at the level taught in undergraduate computer science courses. When teaching a class without this background, the lecturer will have to explain unfamiliar concepts. In the rest of the chapter, the reader is assumed to be able to program in a structured language, such as Pascal. Programming of robots includes the following topics:

- special requirements of robot languages,
- real-time operating systems,
- user programming by teaching,
- world modelling,
- motion control,
- reading sensor data,
- conveyor belt tracking,
- force control, and
- error detection and recovery.

While the correct operation of all subsystems (see Figure 2.1) is critical to the performance of a robot, the correct operation of the software subsystem is the most critical. Language limitations, poor algorithms, and code with errors in it all result in frustrating performance problems. Without software, a robot is a collection of mechanisms, sensors, and actuators with no common purpose. Computer programs tie these components together into an integrated robot: a robot with the flexibility to perform a variety of tasks because it can be rapidly reprogrammed.

The economic viability of a robot system is often determined by the time required to program the robot to perform the desired tasks. Programming time is a function of the features supported by the language, the ease or difficulty of coding in that language, and the support for program development, testing, and debugging provided by the programming environment.

Robot programming is concerned with observing and manipulating three-dimensional objects in space. This requirement to deal directly with physical objects is where robot programming differs from engineering and scientific programming. In scientific programming especially, programs deal with variables which only exist inside the computer, and execution time is a matter of convenience. It does not matter if the user has to wait a while for the results. In contrast, a robot program deals with variables whose parameters are determined by events external to the computer, and execution time is critical.

Robot programming languages are used for two purposes: to define the task the robot is to perform, and to control the robot as it performs that task. These requirements lead to a conflict in language design: should the programming environment be designed to enhance programmer productivity or program performance? Obviously, we want both, but that is not always easy to achieve. One approach to handling this conflict is to use different languages at different levels in the task hierarchy (see Figure 9.1). Each language can be tailored to meet the productivity/performance trade-off at that level. As we move down the hierarchy, performance increases in importance. Programming systems for the higher levels of the hierarchy were discussed in Chapter 9; in this chapter, we focus on robot-level and joint-level programming. A second approach is to separate the time-critical control software from the task-planning software (Figure 12.1). As most robot computer systems use several processors connected by a network, a processor can be allocated for task planning. Often this processor will have disk storage and a graphical user interface. When programs can be developed on this processor, while the other processors in the network control the robot, we have an off-line programming system (Section 9.3.2).

A second source of conflict in robot language design is that there are three classes of robot programmers (Cox *et al*, 1988), each with different requirements, expectations and abilities. These classes are the users, the applications programmers, and the systems programmers. The **user**, or operator, responsible for the control of the robot on the factory floor, normally has no training in programming. Consequently, the operator inter-

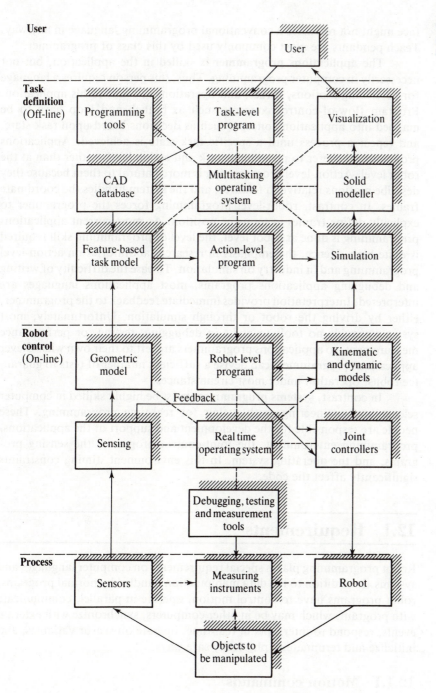

Figure 12.1
Elements of a robot programming environment.

face might not resemble a conventional programming language in any way. Teach pendants are most commonly used by this class of programmer.

The **applications programmer** is skilled in the application, but not necessarily in computer programming. Thus, this person requires a language for describing motions, forces, and operations relevant to his application. Program flow-of-control concepts such as branch and loop have to be mapped into application concepts such as decisions based upon task state, and repeat a process until a specific task state is achieved. Applications programmers prefer to program at task and action levels rather than at the robot level. Action-level programming is more natural to them because they describe motions relative to features, and the system handles the coordinate frames. In contrast, robot-level programming forces the programmer to explicitly define frames in terms of position. As most current applications programming is done at robot level, the level of programming skill required is quite high. Hence, the emphasis in research laboratories on action-level programming and in industry on simulation. To ease the difficulty of writing and debugging applications programs, most applications languages are interpreted. Interpretation provides immediate feedback to the programmer, either by driving the robot or through simulation. Unfortunately, most systems provide no tools to assist in debugging, testing, or performance measurement, so applications programmers are left to their own wits. Clever applications programmers can devise a sufficient number of tests to guarantee robust operation under most circumstances.

In contrast, **systems programmers** must be highly skilled in computer science and engineering, with a flair for real-time programming. These people are responsible for the development and support of the applications-programming environment, the joint-control programs, the sensing programs, and the operating system. In this environment, timing constraints significantly affect the code.

12.1 Requirements

Robot programming places special requirements on computer languages and systems. In addition to the data manipulation handled by normal programs, robot programs have to control motion, operate in parallel, communicate with programs which may be in other computers, synchronize with external events, respond to interrupts in real-time, operate on sensor variables, and initialize and terminate in physically safe ways.

12.1.1 Motion commands

The control of motion requires the addition of move commands to the robot-level language, and the control of force requires the addition of force commands. Move commands must not terminate until the motion has ceased, but program execution may pause during execution of the motion so that other programs can execute. In contrast, force commands set a reference for a control loop, and then terminate. The control loop maintains the force until commanded otherwise. When we say that 'program execution may pause during robot motion', we mean the robot-level program, not the joint-level control program which executes the motion. However, if we are using sensor input to modify the trajectory we must have a way of modifying the motion command to effect the change in trajectory. This may be done by resuming the robot-level program or by overriding it. If it is overriden the motion command terminates when the modified motion completes and the process is transparent to the robot-level program. If the robot-level program is resumed, it must reissue the motion command with a new set of references. In effect, this is an abnormal termination of the motion command followed by a motion modification routine which calculates the modified motion references and restarts the motion command. Thus, the termination of motion commands differs from the termination of normal program constructs.

12.1.2 Concurrency

Two distinct levels of parallelism exist within a robot. At a low level, the programs must concurrently control the joint motions to achieve the desired Cartesian motion of the end effector. These control programs must meet very tight timing constraints. Once a motion is finished, the sequential robot-level program moves on to execute the next instruction. At a higher level, the robot operates in parallel with other robots and the external sensors. Data from external sensors is required by the robot-level programs for making decisions. Concurrency can be achieved in three ways: parallel processing, multitasking operating systems, and concurrent language constructs. The latter two are actually pseudoconcurrent as they rely on time slicing to give the appearance of concurrency. **Time slicing** is a scheduling process that allocates a small amount of cpu time to each program according to a scheduling criterion. Typical criteria are round robin, where each program gets an equal amount of time, and priority, where higher priority programs get more time.

The timing requirements of the software at various levels in the task hierarchy are so varied that we cannot control a robot with a single large program. The system must be broken up into processes according to these timing requirements. At the joint level, the timing constraints are so tight that a separate process may be needed for each joint controller. Also, modularization into processes makes the system easier to design, debug and test.

12.1.3 Interprocess communication

To achieve the desired integration of all robot subsystems, concurrent processes cannot run in isolation: they must communicate with other processes, which may be executing on other computers, or other robots. To achieve ease of programming, a process-to-process communication model that is independent of the physical location of the processes is required. Such a model allows the programmer to concentrate on information transfer without getting bogged down in the physical details of the underlying communication protocol.

Three models of interprocess communication are in common use: shared memory, remote-procedure call, and message passing. In the shared memory model, an area of memory is set aside for the storage of common data. This area must be accessible by several processes for both read and write operations. From the programming point of view, the use of shared memory is simplified by systems that support independent compilation. The shared-memory data structure can be defined in a module that is imported by all processes using it. The additional requirement that common memory places on the language is the ability to lock the common-memory data structure into a segment of memory which is accessible to all processes, without violating memory-protection mechanisms.

Problems can occur if more than one process can write to a particular variable. Usually, these problems are minimized by allowing only one process to update a variable. If more than one process must write to a variable, they should call a common write procedure. This procedure must terminate before it can be called again. Further problems occur when a process reads a variable before another process writes a value into that variable. Synchronization of programs using shared memory is a major headache for the system designer. Also, if a program can access shared memory, it can corrupt the data in that memory, causing other programs to produce unpredictable results.

One way of minimizing these problems is to use procedure calls to obtain information from another process. These procedures are provided by the other process and should support reading and writing of the data structures maintained by that process. These procedures are often called with operating system traps, and the calling process waits for their termination. If the data is on another computer, the networking software issues a remote procedure call to execute the process on that computer. Some systems provide task libraries to support this method of communication.

A simpler and safer model is the message-passing model, where processes send messages to other processes. One design problem with this method is that when a new process requires data from another process, the sending process has to be modified also. One way of overcoming this problem is to have a common-data-handling process that handles all common data structures. Processes that generate data send it to this common data handling process, and processes that consume data receive it from this process. Often, small intermediary processes (called gofors) are used to generalize this mechanism. The designer still has to specify the synchronization sequence, but this can be done in a well-defined and protected environment, as message-passing primitives (send, receive, wait, and, so on) are provided by the programming system. Also, the same primitives are easily extended to interprocess communication across a network, in a way that is transparent to the programmer.

To achieve synchronization, the rendezvous method of message passing is often used. In this method, process A sends a message to process B and pauses until process B reads and acknowledges the message. Then process A resumes execution. If process B reaches the rendezvous point first, it pauses and waits for the message from process A. After process B reads and acknowledges the message it resumes execution. In the extended rendezvous method, information can be transferred in both directions during the rendezvous. Both processes wait until the data is transferred. While extended rendezvous provide more services (data transfer in both directions), they can be more complex to program, and to support.

12.1.4 Event synchronization

Because robots manipulate physical objects, the programs controlling the robot must be synchronized with events external to the computer. These events fall into three categories: initiation events, termination events, and error events. A typical initiation event is the arrival of a workpiece on a conveyor. This event must be detected and, in response, processes in the control computers of the robot must be launched to deal with the event. For example, when a part is detected, the robot is commanded to pick it up and place it into a fixing. Termination events occur when a commanded action completes, such as when the part is correctly placed in the fixing. Another example is the completion of a motion command. Regularly, a robot program must wait until the termination of the action required to execute the current instruction before moving on to the next instruction.

In a computer program, instructions at all levels take time, and the next instruction is not executed until the current one is complete, unless the processor is pipelined or includes parallel-execution features. However, as instruction sequencing is handled by the hardware, it is transparent to the programmer. In contrast, a robot work cell is not so well defined, and the programmer must concern himself with termination events. Also, the programmer must ensure that the process pauses and releases computing resources to other processes while waiting for the termination event. In addition, when the termination event occurs, the program must check that the robot-level instruction was executed successfully. For example, when commanded to grasp an object, the robot program should check that the object is grasped before proceeding (Figure 12.21). If the grasp action failed, an alternative course of action must be taken, such as calling an error-recovery routine.

In general, error recovery should be handled at the level in the task hierarchy at which the error occurs. If the failure to grasp was due to slippage of the object because insufficient force was applied, the joint-level grasp routine should handle the error. On the other hand, if the failure to grasp was because the gripper was not in the correct grasping position, the joint-level routine should abort, and a higher-level program command the robot to move to the correct position. Analysing and recovering from errors is not easy (Section 12.4.7). Error events are the most difficult to define, and are potentially disastrous. When moving a part into a fixer, the robot must check that the fixer is open and empty before placing the part in it. If the fixer is closed or holding a part, the robot must take evasive action. One problem with some low-cost robot controllers is that, once started, a motion cannot be aborted. To avoid collisions with unexpected objects, a robot must be able to terminate any motion or action before it is complete.

12.1.5   Polling or interrupts

Two methods of event detection are commonly used in computing: polling and interrupts. In polling, a program continually checks the state of a sensor input. When certain predefined conditions occur, the polling program either sets a flag to indicate the occurence of the event, or executes a procedure to handle the event. When a polling loop sets a flag to indicate the occurence of an event, it usually launches another process to handle the event. This keeps the polling code to a minimum and, hence, reduces the polling overhead.

Polling processes can be either continuous or synchronous. A continuous polling process sits in a continuous loop reading the external inputs while no other process is executing. The disadvantage of this mechanism is that the execution of a large process to handle an event can cause a considerable delay before the inputs are read again. A synchronous polling process reads the external inputs once every time period in response to an interrupt from a clock. The advantage of synchronous polling is that polling continues during the execution of other processes.

The second method of event detection is interrupts. When an event occurs, an electrical pulse causes the processor to halt execution and vector to an interrupt-handling routine. As with polling, the interrupt routine can either set a flag or execute a procedure to handle the event. Interrupts have the advantage that asynchronous events can be detected when they occur without continuously using processing resources. However, in applications where the interrupts occur rapidly and regularly, the time taken to save and restore registers (interrupt latency) when switching to the interrupt handler may be excessive.

With both types of event detection, we have the choice of setting a flag

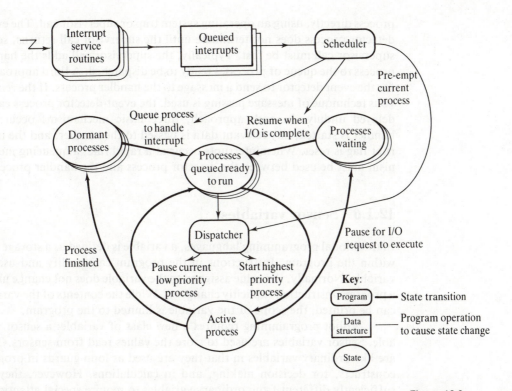

Figure 12.2
Process states and the actions which cause state transitions in a real-time operating system.

and launching another process or handling the event directly. The disadvantage of the latter is that no more events can be detected before the current one has been processed. The advantage of the former is that the event detection code is small. In the case of interrupts, all interrupts of the same or lower priority have to be disabled while an interrupt is acknowledged. So that no interrupts are missed, we must minimize the time interrupts are disabled. When interrupts are likely to occur faster than we can handle them, the interrupt request, plus any data that must be read immediately, is added to a queue. The handling program takes the interrupt requests off the queue one at a time. It catches up with the backlog during periods when there are long delays between interrupts. When handling interrupts, we often have to guarantee that the interrupt routine will execute within a certain time frame, for example, before the data the program is to read has gone away, or before a subsequent event occurs. For these reasons, all real-time systems do the absolute minimum of processing in the event-detection processes.

The detected event can be passed to the handler process in a number of ways. Some systems maintain an event vector, and, when a process pauses or terminates, the controlling process (or scheduler, in an operating system kernel) adds the handler process to the queue of processes ready to be dispatched (Figure 12.2). The scheduler may also clear the vector and buffer any data. In other systems, the event-detector process launches the handler process directly, using an operating system trap or supervisor call. The event-detector process does not terminate until the supervisor call returns, so the supervisor call must be fast. Typically, the supervisor call adds the handler process to the queue of processes ready to be dispatched. A third approach is for the event detector to send a message to the handler process. If the rendezvous technique of message passing is used, the event-detector process can be delayed unduly. In each approach, three basic mechanisms occur: the handler is started, any relevant data is passed to the handler; and the interrupt flag is reset. When interrupts occur at a rapid rate, a queueing mechanism must be used between the detector process and the handler process.

12.1.6 Sensor variables

In traditional programming languages, a variable is defined as a storage area within the program. Instructions in the program can modify and use the variable. Normally, the value assigned to the variable does not change unless a program instruction explicitly changes it. While the contents of the variable can be printed, the scope of the variable is limited to the program.

Robot programming requires a new class of variable: a sensor variable. Sensor variables are used to store the values read from sensors. They are like ordinary variables in that they are used as loop guards in program constructs, for decision making, and in calculations. However, they are sufficiently different from ordinary variables to require special attention in the language. Each sensor produces an electrical signal which may be a single bit, a binary number, or an array of binary numbers. Thus, the type of the sensor variable is determined by the data structure required to store the sensed information.

Many programming languages require that a variable is explicitly initialized before it is used, with either a read statement or an assignment statement. While a default value can be assigned to a sensor variable, it is preferable to obtain the actual value from the sensor. If a default value is used in a calculation, such as in a control loop, a dangerous condition could arise. The scope of a sensor variable is not restricted to the program in which it is used. Action by the robot and events in the environment of the robot cause the value of the sensed parameter to change. Consequently, when a sensor variable is referenced in a program it must be updated to match the sensed value before it is used. Updating the value assigned to a sensor variable is done in two ways: on request or by regular sampling. If the variable is updated on request, a function is called to read the sensor and process the input every time the sensor variable is referenced. In effect, the compiler replaces the sensor variable with a call to a user-defined function. As more than one process may want to use the information from that sensor, the function is stored in a run-time library of common procedures. These procedures are called either directly or via a supervisor trap. Obtaining the sensor value upon request has the advantage that the data is up-to-date, but the program must wait for the function to execute. Also, if several processes require the information about the same time, the function can be executed several times unnecessarily.

In contrast, with the regular sampling method the program simply uses the value currently assigned to the sensor variable. This speeds up the execution of the program, but the value stored in the sensor variable may be out-of-date. The accuracy of this value is a function of the rate of change of the sensor output and the sampling period. The sampling period is determined by the requirements of the process and the speed of response of the sensor. When a sensor takes a period of time to respond to changes in the physical quantity it represents, or it calculates a value by integration, the sampling period is limited by the sensor. Often, integrating and statistically averaging sensors generate an interrupt when the output is available. The response of the sensor places a minimum limit on the updating of sensor variables, and a maximum limit on the execution frequency of processes that use the sensed values. When the response of the sensors is fast, the sampling period is determined by the requirements of the process. A feedback value for a joint controller must be sampled at a much faster rate than a sensor input used to modify a task plan. As control loops are usually executed synchronously, the first operation in the control software is to read the feedback sensors and update the sensor variables.

Which method we use to update sensor variables is determined by timing considerations and by the interprocess communications mechanisms supported by the system (Section 12.1.3). A crucial question for the programmer is, Do you store sensor variables in a common-memory area that is accessible to all processes, or do you pass them to each process as required using messages? A common-memory area guarantees that there is only one copy of the variable in the system, but is open to corruption. Message passing requires the sensor program to explicitly send the data to the processes that use it, or to a common-data-handler process.

Some researchers are currently experimenting with the object-oriented approach to programming as a means of solving these problems (Section 12.5). In this approach, a new class of object-representing sensors is defined. A sensor is an object (variable with a data structure) of this class. Associated with the class is a set of methods (procedures) for initializing and updating sensor variables. When an object is referenced in a program, the data structures, values and methods are automatically inherited by the program. The handling of low-level processes like sampling, in an object-oriented environment is an area of continuing research. As we have seen, there are different types of sensor variables. Each type is defined as a new object class based upon the generic object class. For example, the class image may be an object with a 256 by 256 array as a data structure. It will have methods to read and store the image, and methods to pass the image to other processes, such as message-passing send and receive. The input from a specific camera will be an instance of this object. When this sensor variable is referenced by a program, the underlying support mechanisms for object-oriented programming make both the data and methods available to the program.

12.1.7 Initialization and termination

When writing a scientific program, our main concern at the start of the program is to initialize the variables to a known state. Failure to correctly initialize the variables can result in incorrect results. The same is true in a robot program, except incorrect initialization can result in physical damage to the environment.

To reduce the problems of initializing a robot, we normally place it in a known home position. If it was not left in that position at the completion of the previous task, it may have to be placed there manually. Some robots include low-resolution, absolute, joint encoders, such as potentiometers, to enable the software to measure where the robot is and move it to the home position.

Once it is in the home position, the incremental joint encoders can be zeroed. Then each joint can be moved by a known amount and sensor calibration checked. If on-line identification of model parameters or on-line adaption of control-loop gains is used, the robot must be driven through a sequence of motions to allow these parameters to be calculated.

Finally, all subsystems should be run through a self-test sequence. Self-test is important: it improves the safety of the system by detecting malfunctions, and improves the maintenance by reporting on variations from expected behaviour. Once the robot has passed the self-test, it is fully functional and safe to use.

When we write scientific programs, we usually do so in the context of a running system, having relied on the operating system to handle initialization on power up. When powering up a robot, the operating system may well initialize all the internal variables, but we have to go further and ensure that the robot is unable to move. To do this, brakes must be applied to all joints, the outputs of controllers zeroed and controller set points set to actual joint positions. Robots that have brakes on joints use fail-safe brakes, that is, spring-loaded brakes that apply when the power fails, and have to be energized to allow motion.

When a scientific program terminates or aborts, we rely on the operating system to deallocate the memory the program used. When a robot program terminates, it should move the robot to the home position, apply the brakes, and zero all controller outputs. Controller outputs are zeroed by reducing the gain of the control loops to zero. This process is called 'suiciding', as no combination of inputs can produce an output: the controller is dead.

When a robot program aborts, a potentially dangerous situation occurs. Applying the brakes can cause an object to fly out of the gripper and failure to apply the brakes can allow the robot to crash into other objects. Some commercial robots abort when passing near a singularity due to the violence of the motion about the singular point. If such a robot has no brakes, it will collapse in a heap on to the objects it is manipulating.

Robot programs should detect possible failure situations and abort gracefully. A failure that causes the control computer to enter into a computer debug routine or monitor can be catastrophic. We need to develop the equivalent robot programs: a robot debug routine and a robot monitor. These programs will allow us to examine the execution of the robot program that led to failure and give us simple manual control over the robot.

Finally, the robot control system requires watchdog timers to detect when operations have failed. For example, if a motion command is issued, but the robot is unable to move because it is pushing against an object, the control loops will apply increasing torques in an attempt to move the robot. The resultant excessive torques can damage both the robot and the object it is pushing against. Because the robot is not moving, the move command fails to terminate and the robot sits in that destructive situation. Timing out the command allows the program to abort gracefully so that the problem can be corrected manually.

12.2   Operating systems

In the past, the timing constraints posed by robot control have often been met by carefully crafted assembler programs. The productivity of assembler programming is very low due to the tedium of handling low-level detail that has more to do with the operation of the computer than with the requirements of the application. As a result, the number of features supported by an assembler program is usually small. Also, robustness is hard to achieve due to the sheer difficulty of assembler programming.

Programmer productivity can be greatly increased by using high-level languages. However, high-level languages are not as efficient as assembler, and many do not support the low-level features required for control programming, such as bit manipulation. Also, should the designer choose a language that supports everything, and hence, is large, such as Ada, or a much smaller language that supports the application with specialized libraries, such as Modula-2? Further, should the designer choose a language that protects the programmer from himself, while providing special constructs for potentially dangerous operations, such as Modula-2, or a language that gives the programmer complete freedom at the cost of increased debugging problems, such as C? Of more importance, should all the requirements for robot programming, discussed in the previous section, be supported by the language, or should an operating system be used? Many of the handcrafted assembler systems operate in a stand-alone environment, that is, the control program is the only program running on the computer. Consequently, it must handle all the operations required by the task. Using an operating system increases programmer productivity by providing the programmer with an integrated set of resources. These resources include input/output handlers, interrupt handlers, process scheduling and dispatching, multi-tasking, inter-process-communication routines, and an environment for program development and debugging. However, there are overheads associated with using an operating system that increase the execution time of the programs, as operating system designers achieve generality at the cost of efficiency.

Due to the development of high-speed 32-bit microprocessors, and research into real-time operating systems, the modern designer has the flexibility to use high-level languages and operating systems. When the task imposes very tight timing constraints, the programmer can use an array of measurement tools (McKerrow, 1988) to pinpoint modules with poor performance. However, the use of high-speed processors does not solve all the problems in real-time computing (Stankovic, 1988) and much more research into good software design is required, particularly as the demands upon real-time systems are increasing.

As all serious robot software systems use multiprocessors, the conflicting requirements of programmer productivity and program efficiency can be met by using different operating systems in different processors. In the host processor, the operating system is tailored to support program development, off-line programming, applications programming, simulation and dubugging. The other processors use an operating system that is tailored for real-time efficiency. Often, one is a cut down version of the other (Cox *et al*., 1987). Programs developed on the host are down-line loaded into the control processors.

As processors become cheaper, there are applications where it will be easier to meet the timing constraints with several interconnected processors, each running a single program, than with several processes running on one processor. To speed up software development, routines from the operating system should be available in a library for use in stand-alone programs. These routines will handle input/output and communication between processors. Also, the designer must be able to separate the code from the data so that the code can be permanently stored in read-only memory. Thus, the ideal systems programming environment must support a wide range of programming activities, over a network of computers. The applications programming environment can reside on a single computer, but must be supported by software that allows execution of the applications program by several computers. To the users, all this must be transparent.

Real-time computing is more than fast computing. The speed of execution of software in response to external events must be predictable in absolute terms, otherwise we cannot guarantee correct operation of the system. To achieve this predictability, real-time operating systems must meet very stringent timing criteria (Stankovic, 1988). First, they must respond to external events within a certain time. Second, they must guarantee that certain modules are executed within specified maximum times.

One way to guarantee that a program executes within a defined period after the occurrence of an external event is to place the program in the interrupt-handling routine. However, this conflicts with the goal of keeping the time that interrupts are disabled to a minimum. The loss of an interrupt in a real-time system can cause a serious malfunction. To guarantee that a software module will execute within an absolute time period after an event, the operating system must support priority-based pre-emptive scheduling. Pre-emptive scheduling is a mechanism that halts the execution of the current process (pre-emption), saves its state and starts the execution of another process (Figure 12.2). 'Priority based' means that the process started is of higher priority than the one stopped. Thus, we have the situation where a high-priority process can take the central processor from a low priority-process upon demand. To meet the predictability criteria, the demand mechanism which allows one process to pre-empt another must be of higher priority than all other processes, including the interrupt.

The interrupt service routines must be small and fast. The process switch algorithm must be fast, typically less than $100\,\mu s$. Finally, we may have to disable some low-priority interrupts during the execution of time-critical modules. To achieve fast interrupt service times a common interrupt-service routine cannot be used. Special code must be written to service each interrupt. This code must acknowledge the interrupt, read any fleeting data, queue both the interrupt and data, signal the scheduler if it is a priority interrupt, and re-enable interrupts. This requirement of specially crafted interrupt-service routines conflicts with the more general requirement of extendability. To capitalize on the flexibility of robots, we must be able to add additional actuators and sensors easily. To support these, we require a mechanism that enables the easy extension of the software. Flexibility necessitates access to source code by the systems programmer.

The timing requirements of real-time systems introduce a range of debugging problems that are not found in scientific programming (Glass, 1980). In real-time systems, correctness includes time, and problems are often caused by incorrect synchronization between processes and external events, and between processes and other processes. Because the operating system is cut down to achieve efficiency, it often does not support debugging tools. The inclusion of additional code in a process for debugging purposes will change the execution time of that process and may cause or mask a timing bug. The only easy way to find timing bugs that occur during real-time execution is to use a hybrid-monitoring tool, where small, fast, probe modules write debugging information to an external instrument, such as a logic-state analyser (McKerrow, 1988). The interference of the probe modules is so small that often key probes can be left in the system for use in analysing subsequent faults.

Figure 12.3
Simple pick-and-place task.

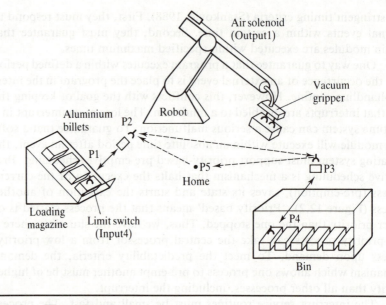

12.3 Teaching

An applications programmer can program a task with a robot-level language. Many commercial robots provide on-line facilities for coding and debugging these programs, often interactively. In these languages, motions are described in terms of variables representing end-effector positions. While coding the program may be simple, teaching the positions can be painful, even with a six degree of freedom pointing device.

Consider the simple task indicated in Figure 12.3. Rectangular aluminium billets are placed into a loading magazine by a manufacturing process. The task of the robot is to pick these billets up and stack them in a bin, one at a time. For simplicity here, we will allow the robot to drop the billets in the bin. The robot has finished the task when the magazine is empty, and should return to the safe home position. The presence of billets on the loading magazine is indicated by a limit switch, and a vacuum gripper is used to pick up the billets. The limit switch is connected to input 4 and the air solenoid is operated by output 1 on the robot controller.

A KAREL program for this task is shown in Figure 12.4. The five positions (P1...P5) that define the point-to-point path of the pick-and-place motion are declared as variables of type POSITION. These variables are six element Cartesian vectors: x, y, z, roll, pitch, yaw. Sensor input (DIN[4]) and actuator output (DOUT[1]) are referred to by general interface functions, not by sensor variable labels. These functions will read a single bit (DIN) from the interface, or write a single bit (DOUT) to the interface. The sensor input is used as a loop guard in the WHILE loop. Every time the WHILE statement is executed, the DIN function is called to read the state of

Figure 12.4
KAREL program to control a
GMF S100 robot to execute
task in Figure 12.3
(courtesy Brian Moore).

```
Program CHUTE
VAR
        P1, P2, P3, P4, P5: POSITION  define variables
BEGIN
        $TERMTYPE = FINE              system variable
        WHILE DIN [4] = ON DO         check magazine full limit switch
                MOVE to P2            magazine stand off position
                $SPEED = 100         slowdown
                MOVE TO P1           magazine load position
                DOUT [1] = ON        vacuum on
                MOVE TO P2           retract
                $SPEED = 1500        transfer speed
                MOVE TO P3           bin stand off position
                $SPEED = 100         slow down
                MOVE TO P4           unload position
                DOUT [1] = OFF       vacuum off
                MOVE TO P3
                $SPEED = 1500
        END WHILE
        MOVE TO P5                    magazine empty return to safe home position
END CHUTE
```

the limit switch. Note, this program relies on the action of the robot in moving billets to set the loop-termination condition: an empty magazine. If the robot fails to change its environment, as indicated by the limit switch, the robot will be in an infinite loop. Two other instructions are of importance in this program: $SPEED and MOVETO. $SPEED sets the maximum Cartesian velocity of the robot during point-to-point motion. MOVETO commands the robot to move to a point. The program does not transfer to the next instruction until the move is complete.

Apart from the diffferences stated above, this program is similar to a scientific program written in a high-level language like Pascal. The only thing left to do before the program can be executed is to initialize the position variables. These cannot be initialized in the program, but must be initialized by teaching.

To 'teach' the robot a point, the programmer moves the robot to the point, and records the vector describing the position and orientation of the end effector. First, the teach menu is selected from the terminal (Figure 12.5). The menu items are selected using function keys, and the position of the robot along with the name of the position variable is displayed on the screen. Using either the teach box, or keyboard commands the robot is jogged (moved) to the first position (P1).

To assign the parameters of the end effector vector to variable P1, the programmer pushes the RECORD (F4) key and the SHIFT key. Two keys are used in the record operation to prevent recording a position by mistake. Once the values are recorded, a prompt appears on the screen asking the programmer to press the DONE (F4 alone) key. When DONE is pressed, the screen display is updated ready for recording the next point. This process is repeated until all points are recorded.

Figure 12.5
Teach menu and soft keys
for GMF S100 robot.

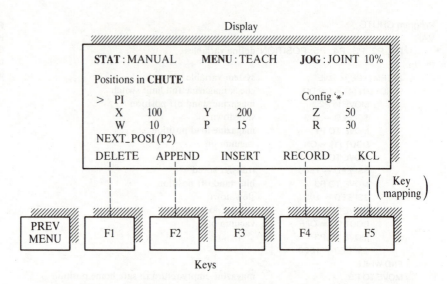

The points are recorded in relation to the world reference frame. However, when jogging the robot, it is sometimes easier to move the robot with respect to a hand frame than with respect to the world frame. For example, at position P1, the two cups on the vacuum gripper must be placed on the billet and be parallel to the billet. The robot can be jogged near the billet using motions with respect to world coordinates, then for the final approach, it is easier to jog the robot with respect to hand coordinates. Similarly, to move the robot from position P1 to P2, the gripper is translated along the z axis of the hand frame. This is much easier than trying to specify motion with respect to the world frame.

As well as teaching the location of objects, we may have to teach the tool transform when the dimensions of a tool are unknown. The tool transform is the transformation from the tool plate to the tip of the tool, that is, the part which acts on the object. For example, the blade of a screwdriver, or the grasping point of a gripper. A VAL-II program for teaching tool transforms is given in Figure 12.6. With this program, the user moves the tool plate to a reference point, records that point, fixes the tool to the tool plate, moves the tip of the tool to the reference point, records that point, and then the program calculates the tool transform. VAL-II has a parameter called the **null tool**. The null-tool is the location of the frame whose origin is at the centre of the tool plate and whose axes are parallel to the axes of the frame at the last joint of the robot. When executed, this program displays a heading on the terminal with the TYPE command, and then enables the teach pendant with the ATTACH command. Each physical device in the system (robot, teach pendant, disk, terminal, serial line) is given a logical unit number. This number is used as a parameter in the ATTACH and DETACH commands. The attach command enables the physical device for use by the program.

This program uses the null-tool location as a reference value. The code inside the IF statement puts the robot into manual control so the user can

```
PROGRAM def. tool()
   TYPE/C1, "PROGRAMME TO DEFINE TOOL TRANSFORM", /C
   ATTACH (1)                              ; enable teach pendant
   PROMPT "Have you previously set the reference location (Y/N)?" $answer
   IF $answer () "Y" THEN
      TYPE /C1, "MOVE The tool plate to the selected reference", /S
      TYPE "location", /C1, "This is the null tool location", /C2,
      TYPE "Press the COMP button on the pendant when ready to continue", /S
      DETACH (0)                           ; robot under manual control
      WAIT PENDANT (22)                    ; wait for user to press MPN button and then
                                             take control of robot
      HERE ref. loc                        ; record the reference location
   END
   TYPE /C1, "fix tool to tool plate and move its tip", /S
   Type "to the reference location", /C2, "Press COMP when", /S
   Type "Robot is in position", /S
   DETACH (0)                              ; robot under manual control
   WAIT PENDANT (22)
   ATTACH (0)                              ; compute the tool transformation new.tool
   SET new tool – INVERSE (HERE): ref.loc
   TOOL new tool                           ; apply the tool transformation
   TYPE /C2, "The tool transformation is 'new tool'.", /C1,
   DETACH (1)                              ; disable teach pendant
END
```

Figure 12.6
VAL-2 program to teach tool transform – from Adept VAL-2 reference guide.

move the null-tool location to the reference point. The user returns the robot to computer control by pressing the COMP button. The current position of the robot (frame of the null-tool location calculated from the joint-encoder values) is assigned to the variable ref.loc with the HERE statement. Once the reference has been taught, the tool is attached to the tool plate, and the process is repeated. Except this time the tip of the tool is moved to the reference point. The frame read by the HERE statement is calculated from the joint-encoder values for this new configuration. The SET statement is used to assign the result of the transformation equation to the tool transform (Figure 12.7). The variables used to store the values representing a location (Cartesian values calculated from joint-encoder signals) are called location-values.

At a higher level, the LM language (Latombe *et al.*, 1985) supports programming by showing (Figure 12.8). This simple example program can be operated by a user with no knowledge of LM to generate an LM program. First, the current location of the end effector (frame ROBOT) is saved in the

tool . loc × new . tool = ref . loc

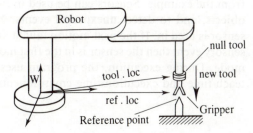

Figure 12.7
Relationship between transforms when using the program in Figure 12.6 to teach a tool transform.

Figure 12.8
LM program used to program
a robot by showing.

```
PROGRAM utility;
  BOOLEAN move; FRAME pos; FILE prog;
  BEGIN
    WRITE "PROGRAM play-back;" IN prog;
    WRITE "BEGIN," IN prog;
    move := TRUE;
    WHILE move DO
      pos := ROBOT:
      TEACH;
      IF DISTANCE (ROBOT, pos) /= 0   OR ANGLE (ROBOT, pos) /= 0
        THEN WRITE "MOVE ROBOT TO (", ROBOT,");"IN prog;
        ELSE move := FALSE;
      ENDIF;
      WRITE "END;" IN prog;
    ENDDO;
END;
```

variable pos. Then, the TEACH statement gives control of the robot to the
user. When the user returns control to the program, the new position and
orientation of the end effector are compared to the old ones (IF statement).
If there is any difference, an LM MOVE statement is written to the program
file (prog).

At the end of the teaching session, an LM program to execute the same
motion sequence is stored in a file. This program can be executed to drive the
robot through the same sequence of motions. More importantly, it can be
edited. This allows the applications programmer to add control, sensor
interaction, and error handling statements. The final program can be compiled to produce an efficient robot-control program.

The XPROBE (**EX**perimental system for **P**rogramming **RO**bots **B**y
Example) takes the idea of teaching a text program by showing a step further
to include the teaching of sensor strategies (Summars and Grossman, 1984).
With XPROBE, the user guides the robot through the desired motion
sequence, and then XPROBE automatically writes an AML (**A M**anufac-
turing **L**anguage – Section 12.4.7) text program that includes sensory
decision making as a generalization of the taught task.

The main idea behind XPROBE is that teaching is considered to be the
user's opportunity to show the system one example of the desired behaviour;
from which the system will automatically produce a program that is a
generalization of the example: a program which detects gross deviations
from the example, and includes simple sensing strategies that are inferred
from the example. Sensors can be used in two modes: to find and examine
objects, and to detect unexpected events. XPROBE infers which mode a
sensor is used in. If the next motion taught after a sensor is enabled causes a
sensory event then the sensor is in the first mode. Otherwise it is in the second
mode. During execution, the program uses sensory feedback to compare
teach-time and execution-time environments. Based on this comparison it

reports gross variations as errors, and automatically compensates for minor variations from the taught example. XPROBE has been implemented for a few applications to test this design concept. A typical XPROBE programming/teach session proceeds as follows:

(1) In the first stage, each object in the workspace is located with a frame. After the name of a frame is entered by the user, XPROBE tells the user to locate the robot at the frame using the teach box. The user moves the robot into position and pushes the define point button on the teach box. Then XPROBE requests the name of the next frame. This process is repeated until all frames have been defined, at which stage, XPROBE produces the AML code for the frame declarations.

(2) In the second stage, subroutines are defined. First, the programmer enters context information including the name of the subroutine, the object frames used, the speed of the robot and the state of sensors. Then XPROBE asks the user to define the motions that the robot is to execute during this procedure. If the robot is to move to a point, he simply enters the name of the point and, when instructed, moves the robot to the point and records it.

If the move is to be terminated by a sensor, he changes the context to enable the sensor, and to stop the motion within a specified distance after the sensing event occurs. The motion is then taught by moving the robot into a position where the sensor is tripped. Then the system asks the user to define the subroutine to be executed if the sensor event does not occur. At each stage, AML code is generated. Quite complex motion, search, and grasping strategies can be taught in this way.

(3) Once the library of subroutines required by the task is defined, the user writes a mainline to call these in a sequence or in a loop as desired.

The result is an AML program to perform the task using a set of subprograms. The program includes the location of all objects in the tasks, sensor strategies for guarded motions, and state information for each stage of the process. State information is used to detect gross errors.

While these approaches do not remove the pain of teaching points precisely, they do allow a noncomputer person to produce a working program. In addition, they can be used by an experienced programmer to speed up the programming of motion sequences. Thus, LM and XPROBE have combined manual teaching with textual programming to produce powerful programming environments. Finally, teaching often requires the programmer to work in close proximity to the robot. This can be quite dangerous, as a robot moving at reasonable speed can injure a human. So the programmer must take care not to get in the path of the robot. Once the points are taught, the robot program can be executed. The programmer should stand well clear of the robot in case something goes wrong.

12.4 Languages

Most robot programmers are concerned with programming applications in a robot-level language. The features provided by the language will determine how easy it is to program a particular application. Whether the features are supported by the operating system or the language is of little concern to the application programmer. In this section, we will look specifically at examples of applications programmed in robot-level languages.

For a comprehensive description of these languages, the reader should consult a manufacturer's programming manual or the book *Programming Languages for Industrial Robots* by Blume and Jakob (1986). Some examples of task-level and action-level languages are included in Chapter 9.

Three distinct approaches have been taken to the design of robot programming languages: design from scratch, modify an existing computer language, and modify a numerical-control language. A number of languages for example, LM (Latombe, *et al.*, 1985), WAVE (Paul, 1976) and VAL (Shimano, 1979) have been designed specifically as robot programming languages. Most of these have evolved during the development of a robot, and tend only to support the facilities required by that robot. Consequently, they often have to be modified when the robot is improved.

The United States Air Force has invested a lot of money in standardizing the language APT for numerical control of metal-cutting machines. This standardization enables tools from many manufacturers to machine the same components. As the USAF considers a robot to be just another part of a manufacturing process, they have sought to extend APT to robot control (Hollingshead, 1985). RAPT (Section 9.3.2.2) and MCL (Manufacturing Control Language) are both based on APT. APT has facilities for defining both geometry and motion. MCL includes extensions to APT to handle robot control based on sensor information.

The third approach is to take an existing computer programming language and extend it to include features to support robot control. This approach is generally favoured by computer scientists as it takes advantage of existing software libraries and recent research into programming languages. Also, there are more similarities between robot and computer programming than differences. Hence, most of the features used in modern high-level languages can be used to advantage in robot programming. Many commonly used robot languages fall into this category.

Computer programs manipulate data. Robot programs manipulate objects in three-dimensional space. By representing the objects as data, whose values are updated in real time, a robot program is transformed into a computer program. This transformation is achieved with sensor variables and actuator commands. A computer programming language provides three facilities for the programmer to use when implementing an algorithm. These are data storage, data manipulation, and flow of control of data manipula-

Figure 12.9
Declaration of geometric
data types in PASRO.

```
TYPE
      vector  =        RECORD
                            x,y,z : REAL
                       END;
      distance type =  RECORD
                            startpoint, direction : vector;
                            length : INTEGER
                       END;
      rotomatrix =     RECORD
                            t, o, a : vector
                       END;
      rotation =       RECORD
                            axis : vector;
                            angle : REAL;
                            matrix : rotmatrix
                       END;
      frame =          RECORD
                            rot : rotation
                            transl : vector
                       END;
```

tion. Data storage can be as simple as a single variable or as complex as a tree
data structure. Associated with each data structure (variable) is a data type.
The type of a variable determines the amount of storage it uses, the range of
values that can be assigned to it, the mapping of those values into a binary
code, the methods for accessing the values, and the allowable operations on
the variable, including calculation, comparison and input/output. Several
data types have been introduced into computer languages to support robot
programming. These include event, vector, distancetype, rotmatrix, rotation, frame and aggregate. A variable of type event is a special counter used
for program synchronization. These variables are called semophore variables, and are used to control the state of a process. Setting the semaphore
associated with a process activates the process, and resetting the semaphore
deactivates the process. Semaphores can also be incremented and
decremented.

In robot programming languages, events are used for two purposes:
synchronization with external events and synchronization between processes. The languages SRL and AL include two event handling statements:
SIGNAL (event-variable) and WAIT (event-variable). SIGNAL increments
the event variable (semaphore), and if it is greater than zero the process state
is set to ready (Figure 12.2). WAIT decrements the semaphore, and when it is
not positive the process goes to the wait state.

The languages VAL and ROBEX do not support process synchronization, but use the SIGNAL (SWITCH) and WAIT operations to handle I/O.
WAIT causes the program to wait for a change of state on an input, and
SIGNAL causes as output to change state. If this input and output are
connected, we can use these event synchronization commands to achieve
process synchronization.

The other data types in the above list are geometric data types (Figure
12.9). We discussed the data types needed to support kinematic models of

objects in Section 3.11. The concept of a frame is found in nearly all robot languages. A frame is simply the homogeneous coordinate representation of the location of the object or end effector. To calculate transforms, the language must support frame multiplication, frame transpose, and frame inversion. Also, it should be possible to extract the position of the origin and orientation of the frame axes from the frame data structure.

While vectors, rotations, and frames are reasonably familiar, an aggregate is an entirely new data structure found in the language AML. Like a record, an aggregate is the collection of data of different types into a new data structure, but, like an array, access to the components of an aggregate is achieved using indexes. Aggregates are not declared as new data types, but are defined in the variable declaration statement using the AML reserved word NEW. Aggregates are used to collect variables together for common operations, such that the action of an operator on an aggregate is achieved by applying that operator to the elements of the aggregate.

The third facility provided by a computer language is flow of control. Flow of control statements specify the sequence in which the manipulation of the data is performed. They support the block structure constructs of module, procedure, recursion, iteration, selection, and sequence. All standard flow of control constructs are suitable for robot programming. The only additional constructs are actuator commands, which are sequential statements which terminate when the commanded action is complete.

12.4.1 World modelling

In most robot-level languages, world models are constructed with coordinate frames. Feature based models usually only occur at higher levels. The relationship between the frames is described with transformation equations. In a static environment, where the number of objects is constant, we can assign a frame variable to each object and hard code the transformation equations. In a dynamic environment, where the number of objects can change, or objects can be physically affixed to one another, we require a dynamic way of storing frames.

In some languages, we must allocate an array of frames large enough to hold the maximum expected number of objects. SRL, PASRO and AML all support dynamic data structures with records and pointers (Figure 12.10). As each object is added to the environment, a record is added to the list. The record can include other information such as the size of the object, the grasp position, the contents of the object, and its relationship to other objects, such as on top of, beside, and affixed.

Consider the task of fixing a bracket on to a post (Figure 12.11). The sequence of positions defining the task is defined as a sequence of transformation equations. First, the robot picks up the bracket

$$^{W}T_{E} = {^{W}T_{R}}{^{R}T_{E}} = {^{W}T_{B}}{^{B}T_{G}} \tag{12.1}$$

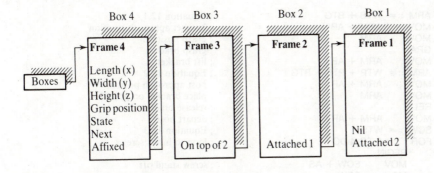

Figure 12.10
Dynamic data structure for modelling boxes.

where G is the grasp point on the bracket.

Then the robot moves the bracket to the top of the post such that frames F (fixing position) and B (bracket) align.

$$^{W}T_E = {}^{W}T_P\,{}^{P}T_F\,{}^{B}T_G \qquad (12.2)$$

Next, the robot releases the bracket and picks up a screw from the dispenser.

$$^{W}T_E = {}^{W}T_S \qquad (12.3)$$

Finally, the robot moves the screw to a hole and screws it in. The equation for hole 1 is:

$$^{W}T_E = {}^{W}T_P\,{}^{P}T_F\,{}^{B}T_{H[1]}\,{}^{S}T_T^{-1} \qquad (12.4)$$

Using the inverse kinematic model of the robot, we can calculate the joint angles required to achieve the new location of the end effector. First,

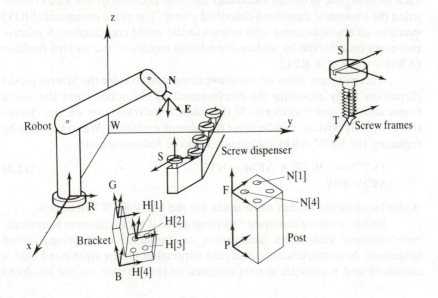

Figure 12.11
Fixing a bracket on to a post with screws.

Figure 12.12
Program for task in Figure 12.11, with all motions relative to the world frame, using a PAL-like syntax.

```
ARM ::= WTB + BTG                         ; Equation 12.1
MOV      ARM + AB                          ; bracket approach position
MOV      ARM                               ; grasp position
GRA                                        ; grasp bracket
MOV      ARM + AB                          ; lift bracket
ARM ::= WTP + PTF + BTG                    ; Equation 12.2
MOV      ARM + AP                          ; post approach position
MOV      ARM                               ; place bracket on post
REL                                        ; release bracket
MOV      ARM + AP                          ; depart post
SCW ::= WTS                                ; Equation 12.3
FOR I ::= 1 TO 4 DO                        ; loop to insert screws
    BEGIN
    MOV      SCW + AS                       ; screw stand off
    MOV      SCW
    GRA                                      ; grasp screw
    MOV      SCW + AS                        ; lift screw
    ARM ::= WTP + PTF + BTH[1] − STT         ; Equation 12.4
    MOV      ARM + HS                         ; hole stand off
    MOV      ARM                              ; place screw in hole
    SCR                                       ; turn screw
    REL                                       ; release screw
    MOV      ARM + HS
    END
ARM ::= HOME                               ; safe home position
MOV      ARM
```

obtain the inverse matrix from the transform of the end effector with respect to the world frame

$$^{R}T_{N} = {}^{W}T_{R}^{-1}\,{}^{W}T_{E}\,{}^{N}T_{E}^{1} \tag{12.5}$$

where $^{N}T_{E}$ is the tool transform.

A program to perform this task is given in Figure 12.12. In this program, the plus sign indicates matrix multiplication, and the minus sign indicates multiplication by the inverse of the matrix. Two variables ARM and SCW are used to store the results of the kinematic equations. Before each motion, the program calculates the next position of the end effector using the kinematic equations described above. The move command (MOV) executes an absolute move with respect to the world coordinates. A relative move can be achieved by adding the relative motion to the current position (ARM ::= ARM + REL).

This program relies on the move command to solve the inverse model (Equation 12.5) including the displacement of the robot from the world frame and the tool transform. If the robot is on tracks, or we can change tools, we may wish to handle these transforms explicitly. We can do this by replacing the MOV ARM statements with the following code.

$$INV ::= -WTR + ARM - NTE \tag{12.6}$$
MOV INV.

A similar substitution has to be made for the MOV SCW statements.

So far, we have discussed this program as if the assignment statements were numeric assignment statements, as found in most programming languages. In numeric assignment, the expression on the right-hand side is evaluated and a numeric matrix assigned to the variable on the left-hand side. If, instead, we use symbolic assignment, the variable on the left hand side is replaced by the symbolic expression on the right whenever it occurs in subsequent statements.

Consequently, the move statement is now passed an expression rather than a value. As a result, all expression evaluation is done by the move statement. The main advantage of this is that any changes in the matrices during the execution of the program are automatically accounted for. This facility enables the system to respond to changes in the physical environment without having to be reprogrammed. A second advantage is that the expression for INV (Equation 12.6), has to be included only once, not prior to every MOV statement. Unfortunately, this can make the program harder to read. A second disadvantage is that symbolic manipulation is computationally expensive. However, symbolic manipulation gives us the flexibility to handle sensor variables, tool changes, and changes in object size on the fly without reprogramming. For example, if the location of a post is determined with a vision system, when the post arrives on a conveyor, the post transform matrix is modified by the vision system. As the task control program evaluates the complete transform expression before commanding the motion, the calculaion is based on the latest sensor values and, as a result, errors due to inaccurate post positioning are eliminated. Similarly, a tool change during the execution of the task can be accommodated transparently to the task-control program, by modifying the tool transform. Also, the change in the length of the screw outside the hole, as it is inserted, can be modelled. The result of the model calculations can be assigned to a screw transform (STT). When the transform reaches a minimum value the screwing operation is complete. Finally, if compliance can be modelled or forces measured, compliant motion can be handled in a similar way.

In PAL (Takase *et al.*, 1981), motion is handled differently. Rather than moving the end effector to an absolute position with respect to the world frame, the end effector is moved to satisfy an equation describing a closed kinematic chain. Thus, the move statement (MOV 'expression') moves the arm to satisfy the equation

$$\text{ARM} + \text{TOL} = \text{'expression'} \qquad (12.7)$$

where ARM is a variable holding the transformation equation for the desired location of the tool plate, and TOL is a variable holding the tool transform equation.

A PAL program for placing the bracket on the post (Figure 12.11) is given in Figure 12.13. This program differs from the previous program in several ways. First, the expression assigned to the variable ARM is not the desired end effector position, but rather the location of the workpiece relative to the tool plate. Second, the variable TOL is used to describe the transform of the end effector plus any object it is holding. Third, the expression in the move statement is the location of the feature of interest (grasping position, hole, and so on) on the workpiece with respect to the workpiece frame.

Figure 12.13
PAL program for first part of
task in Figure 12.11 – PAL
identifiers are limited to 3
characters (Takase et al,
1981).

```
ARM  ::= −WTB + WTR + RTN          ; NTB transform
TOL  ::= NTE                        ; tool transform
MOV      BTG + AB                   ; move to stand off
MOV      BTG                        ; move so as to close kinematic chain
                                          = ARM + TOOL
GRA                                 ; grasp
TOL  ::= NTE − BTG + BTH[1]         ; tool includes bracket and hole
MOV BTH[1] + AH                     ; stand off hole
ARM  :=  −PTF = WTP + WTR + RTN     ; NTF transform
MOV      ARM + AP                   ; stand off post
MOV      FTN[1]                     ; align holes
REL                                 ; release bracket
TOL  ::= NTE                        ; reset tool transform
MOV      ARM + AP                   ; stand off
```

Another difference is that this program aligns the frames defining the location of hole 1 in the bracket and the post, rather than the bracket and post frames. Often, we achieve more accurate operation by aligning features than by aligning workpieces, as the location of features on a workpiece can vary from one workpiece to the next. Writing the rest of this program to put the four screws in the bracket is left as an exercise for the reader (Exercise 12.17).

In both these programs, additional matrices (**A**n), called approach matrices, are used. These matrices define a stand-off point close to the object, but far enough from it to avoid collision. Also, these matrices specify the direction from which the gripper will approach each object. Specifying the approach direction in the stand-off matrix means that the gripper will rotate to the correct orientation during the move to the stand-off point. The gripper must be oriented before the approach motion to avoid collision during the approach motion.

12.4.2   Motion control

In the examples looked at so far, we have simply commanded motion from one frame to another without considering the type of motion, or the transfer from one motion to the next (Section 9.3.3.2). A comprehensive robot-programming language includes instructions for specifying the type of motion, for defining complex paths, for control of the robot during trajectory following, and for aborting motion.

Most languages have move instructions for straight-line motion and for joint-interpolated motion. A VAL II program for the pick-and-place example in Figure 12.3 is given in Figure 12.14. The MOVE command specifies joint-interpolated motion to the point, and the MOVES command specifies a straight-line motion.

VAL II makes a distinction between frames (homogeneous matrices) and precision points (vectors of joint values). The latter is used when the robot has to move to a point with the same configuration as when the point

```
PROGRAM Chute
   LEFTY                          ; left arm configuration
   ABOVE                          ; point elbow up
   WHILE      SIG[4] DO           ; while signal 4 is true
     MOVE     P2                  ; continuous path operation
     APPROS   #P1                 ; precision point
     BREAK                        ; pause program until motion complete
     SIGNAL   +1                  ; turn vacuum on
     DEPART   20                  ; lift block
     MOVE     P3
     APPROS   P4
     BREAK
     SIGNAL   -1                  ; turn vacuum off
     DEPART   20                  ; retract along negative z axis
   END                            ; while
END
```

Figure 12.14
VAL-II program for pick and place task in Figure 12.3.

was taught. In Figure 12.14, point P1 is defined as a precision point. The APPROS statement commands the robot to approach the point with straight-line motion along the z axis of the end-effector frame. VAL II treats a sequence of motion commands (MOVE, APPROS in Figure 12.15) as a continuous-path operation, and produces a smooth change in motion, near the location specified in the first move command, when transferring from one motion command to the next. To achieve continuous-path control, VAL II does not wait until a move command is complete but the flow of control transfers to the next program statement as soon as the motion is initiated. Thus, MOVE means start moving. However, this can cause problems when a motion must be completed before the next instruction is executed. For example, we want the vacuum gripper to release the billet when the end effector has reached the release point (P4) and not before. To eliminate this problem, a BREAK command is included in the language. Flow of control pauses at the BREAK command until the previously commanded motions have finished.

A second requirement with continuous-path control is that sometimes the motion needs to be aborted before it is complete, for example, to avoid collision, or when a sensor input indicates that a motion has reached its goal.

```
FOR   index = 0 TO LAST (path [3])
        MOVES path [index]
END
```

(a)

```
FOR   angle = start TO last+start STEP angle.step
        x = radius * COS (angle) + x.centre
        y = radius * SIN (angle) + y.centre
        MOVE TRANS (x,y,0,0,180,0)
END
```

(b)

Figure 12.15
VAL-II program for following a path. (a) Store path in an array 'path'; (b) calculating a path from equations – circular arc.

Figure 12.16
RAIL program to control a
welding robot. (Hollingshead,
1985).

```
OUTPUT  PORT  CLAMP  3                          ; output signal to operate clamp
INPUT   PORT  PART__READY  4                     ; signal to indicate part in position
FUNCTION SEAM
        GLOBAL FIXTURE, SEAM1
        BEGIN
        ; SEAM is a function in which a robot welds
        ; a seam that is defined relative to a fixture
        REPEAT
            MOVE SLEW HOME                       ; coordinated axis-by-axis motion
            WAIT UNTIL PART__READY = = ON
            CLAMP = ON
            APPROACH 50 FROM FIXTURE: SEAM1
            WELD FIXTURE: SEAM1 WITH SPEEDSCHED [2],
                                        WELDSHED [2]
            ; controlled path motion
            DEPART 50
            CLAMP = OFF
        UNTIL CYCLESTOP = = ON
END
```

The BREAK command (Figure 12.22) causes the manipulator to halt in mid motion. A third requirement with continuous-path control is choosing how the transfer from one motion to the next should be achieved. The operation discussed above treats the smooth transition from one motion to the next as being more important than passing through the points specified in the motions. Consequently, during continuous-path control, the end effector passes near these points.

Sometimes the task requires that the robot must pass through specific points. This can be achieved in three ways: coming to a halt at each point, using a smoothing algorithm that modifies the motion between points, or devising a more precise specification of the path. Bringing the robot to a halt at each point is point-to-point control rather than continuous-path control, and increases the time required to perform the motion. However, if straight-line motion is required between points, this may be the only option available to the programmer. SRL has a motion command (LANEMOVE) which calculates the path so that the end effector passes through the points defined in the path with the specified orientations. These paths are evaluated with polynomials to specify the interpolated locations between points.

The third approach is to specify the path more precisely by calculating the intermediate points along a continuous path. Then the changes in direction, velocity, and orientation from one segment of the path to the next amount to a small fraction of a continuous trajectory. The path can be pre-taught and stored in an array (Figure 12.15(a)), or it can be calculated from an equation (Figure 12.15(b)). For example, a seam-welding system has either to follow a pretaught path or use a sensor to track the seam and modify the trajectory (Section 1.5.1.1). The RAIL program, in Figure 12.16, is an example of a program that achieves continuous-path motion during welding by obtaining trajectory information from a pre-taught motion schedule.

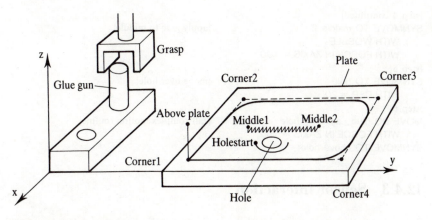

Figure 12.17
SRL program for complex
motion control with sensor
introduction when applying
glue to a plate.

```
MOVEDEF glue__around__hole
BEGIN__MOVEDEF                              {define a complex move instruction}
    PTPMOVE TO abovehole ;                  {joint motion}
    SMOVE TO holestart                      {straight line move to left of hole}
        WITH CONSTORIENT;
    CIRCLEMOVE CP = hole  DEG = 180         {describe an arc of 180° centred on Hole}
        WITH V = 150;                       {velocity-cms/sec}
END__MOVEDEF;
{step 1}
SYNMOVE TO grasp                            {joint interpolated motion}
    WITH V = 25
    WITH APPRO = 50                         {move above then down}
    WITH SMOOTHFAC = 3;
CLOSE UPTO GRIPFORCE >50                    {grasp glue gun}
    WITH VELOCITY = 0.5;
SMOVE TO aboveplate                         {above plate}
{step 2}
WHEN SENSOR z__force > = 100                {move glue gun on to plate}
    MONITORED EVERY 75 MS                   {until sufficient force is applied}
DURING
    SMOVE TO corner1
        WITH VELOCITY = 5
END__DURING
DO STOP;                                    {stop motion}
{step 3}
SMOVE TO corner1                            {apply glue around plate}
    WITH V = 150
    WITH ACC = 20
    WITH CONSTORIENT
    WITH SMOOTHFAC = 0.5
    WITH VIAFRAMES (corner 2, corner 3, corner 4)
    WITH FORCE IN ZAXIS = 100;
{step 4}
SMOVE TO middle1                            {move to middle of plate}
    WITH APPRO = 20
    WITH DEP = 20
    WITH SMOOTHFAC = 3;
```

Figure 12.17
Cont.

```
{step 4 continued}
SYNMOVE TO middle 2                    {apply glue to middle}
    WITH WOBBLE
    WITH FORCE IN ZAXIS = 100;
{step 5}
SYNMOVE TO hole                        {move over hole}
    WITH DEP = 20;
{step 6}
MOVE DO glue__around__hole             {call complex motion routine}
    WITH FORCE IN ZAXIS = 100;
SYNMOVE TO above hole;
```

12.4.3 Sensor interaction

Several of the programs in the previous section rely on simple sensor information to determine when to proceed to the next program statement. The RAIL welding program (Figure 12.16) waits until the part is in place and then applies a clamp before commencing the welding operation. Both pick-and-place programs (KAREL – Figure 12.4 and VAL II – Figure 12.15) use a sensor input as a loop guard. The pick-and-place operation continues while the sensor input indicates that there are billets in the feeder. In both programs, sensor inputs and actuator outputs are single-bit signals, which are referenced by their physical position in the input/output hardware. Thus, as with the RAIL program, the programmer is required to know the details of the input/output connections. In contrast, a language that allows an input to be bound to a label (such as billet-in-chute) frees the programmer from low-level detail to work on the task.

When more complex tasks are programmed, we often find that single-bit input signals are inadequate, and analogue input of a continuously varying signal is required. Many applications combine complex motion control with force measurement. Consider the application of glue to a plate (Figure 12.17). To ensure contact between the glue gun and the plate, and to aid glue flow, the force between the gun and the plate must be controlled while moving the gun over the plate.

The SRL program in Figure 12.17 was written to achieve this goal. The first section of the program defines a complex move instruction to move the end effector in a 180° arc around a hole. During execution, this trajectory is calculated and saved. At Step 6, the MOVEDO statement commands the robot to execute the calculated trajectory. This separation of trajectory calculation and trajectory execution can achieve considerable performance improvement in a system that supports parallel execution of code modules.

To simplify design and debugging, the task is divided into several steps. In Step 1, the robot picks up the glue gun and moves into position ready to start applying glue. A joint-interpolated move followed by an approach move places the gripper around the gun. Here the WITH statement is used to modify the commanded motion significantly. First by specifying an intermediate approach frame, and second by smoothing the resultant continuous-path motion. The SMOOTHFAC statement controls the allowable variation from the pre-defined path when smoothing the transition from one motion to the next in order to achieve continuous-path control. When the gripper is in place, it is closed until a specified gripping force is applied to the gun. This force is measured with a sensor in the jaws of the gripper, and mapped into the variable GRIPFORCE. This sensor variable is then used in comparison statements like any other variable.

In Step 2, the gun is moved down on to the plate until the force in the z direction is greater than a certain value. The WHEN construct starts a program to monitor the sensed value every 75 milliseconds, during the downward motion. When the force threshold is exceeded the DO STOP statement stops the motion of the robot. In Step 3, glue is applied around the outside of the plate. The WITH VIAFRAMES statement specifies a sequence of intermediate points, and motion is smoothed for continuous-path control. The WITH FORCE statement maintains a constant force in the downward direction. In Step 4, the WITH WOBBLE statement causes the end effector to execute a weaving pattern while moving along the path. This example illustrates the combination of complex motion control with sensor input.

12.4.4 Conveyor belt tracking

An application that requires the motion of the gripper to be controlled in response to sensor input is picking objects off a moving conveyor (Figure 12.18). VAL II supports both sensor inputs and special program statements to enable a gripper to move with a conveyor while grasping an object.

To pick an object off a moving conveyor, the robot must detect and track the object, move the gripper to the object, move the gripper with the object while the gripper closes to grasp the object, and then lift the object off the conveyor (see Section 1.3). Each stage relies on accurate sensor input. Also, we observe that a robot can only move its end effector at constant velocity along a straight line for a limited distance. This distance is called the robot's window on the conveyor. When the object is outside the window, the robot cannot pick it up.

An optical light barrier (Figure 10.33) detects the object, and a digital encoder (Figure 10.9) measures the velocity of the conveyor. In this example, we will assume that the object is located in the centre of the conveyor in the correct orientation for grasping. To obtain a reference frame for the gripper, we must fuse the information from the sensors to obtain a model of the motion of the object.

First, we locate a nominal belt frame at the centre of the window and an object location frame at the light barrier. The distance between these two frames is fixed (d_1). We assume that the conveyor moves in a straight line,

Figure 12.18
VAL-II conveyor belt tracking
program. (a) Physical
arrangement; (b) program.

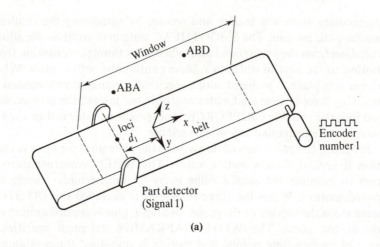

(a)

```
; set up belt mode and window
DEFBELT   %conveyor = belt, 1, velocity scale   ; initialize nominal belt transforms
MOVE      ABA                                    ; above belt approach position
OPENI                                            ; open gripper
WAIT      1                                      ; wait for object to be detected
SETBELT   %object = BELT(%conveyor)              ; initialize instantaneous
MOVES     %object:loc1                           ; move to object – straight line motion
DELAY     2.0                                    ; track object for 2 seconds
CLOSEI                                           ; grasp object
MOVE      ABD                                    ; lift object off conveyor
```

(b)

and specify that the x axis of all frames is parallel to the direction of motion of the conveyor. Consequently, motion is calculated in the x direction only. Thus, when the object is detected, it is at distance $-d_1$ relative to the nominal belt frame. This distance includes the distance from the detection point to the grasp point on the object. We attach an instantaneous belt frame to the object. When the object is detected,

$$\text{Instantaneous frame} = \text{Object location frame}$$
$$\times \text{ nominal belt frame} \qquad (12.8)$$
$$p_x = -d_1 \qquad \text{at time t=0} \qquad (12.9)$$

As the object moves with the belt, the instantaneous frame moves relative to the nominal belt frame

$$p_x = -d_1 + v_x t \qquad (12.10)$$

where v_x = belt velocity

Equation 12.10 is correct for a constant velocity system. To handle variations in the velocity of the belt, the distance the belt has moved is calculated by counting encoder pulses, rather than calculating velocity by counting pulses per unit time.

$$p_x = -d_1 + \int v_x dt = -d_1 + \sum \text{pulses} \qquad\qquad \textbf{(12.11)}$$

By moving the gripper to the instantaneous frame, which varies as p_x varies, the gripper moves to the object and then tracks the object. In VAL II, the instantaneous frame is called a belt variable (%object in Figure 12.18). VAL II has predefined inputs for two encoders as well as single-bit inputs. The encoder pulses are continuously counted in a signed 24-bit counter, which automatically rolls over.

The command DEFBELT defines a belt variable (%conveyor) and assigns the nominal belt frame (belt) to it. The second parameter in the DEFBELT statement specifies encoder 1, the third parameter specifies smoothing of encoder data when calculating velocity, and the fourth parameter is the distance the belt travels (in millimetres) for each encoder pulse. This statement initialises belt tracking. Next, the gripper is moved above the belt and opened.

When the object is detected, the SETBELT statement attaches the instantaneous frame (%object) to the belt at the position of the nominal frame. To achieve this, the program stores the current encoder count in the belt variable (%conveyor). Then, as the belt moves, the difference between the encoder count and the value in the belt variable is a measure of the motion of the instantaneous frame. This difference is used to calculate the object variable (%object). The object variable is a moving reference frame for the gripper.

The MOVES statement commands the robot to move the gripper to the location specified by the instantaneous frame plus the offset between the nominal frame and the light barrier. As the instantaneous frame is a belt variable, the command does not terminate until the next move statement is executed. Thus, the gripper tracks the object after it reaches it. The DELAY statement delays the execution of the next statement to allow the gripper's motion to settle. In effect, it overrides the continuous-path control feature of VAL II. The close-immediate instruction causes the gripper to close while moving. Finally, the grasped object is lifted off the conveyor, before the end of the window is reached.

From the above discussion, it is obvious that special features have been built into VAL II to handle conveyor tracking. One of the difficulties faced by the designer of a robot language is that the special requirements of some applications are not obvious until someone tries to program the application. Even so, the ability to specify a mobile frame and track it with an end effector is a facility that all languages should support.

12.4.5 Vision

In many robot applications, lack of sensor information is overcome by carefully placing objects in known locations and assuming that everything is correct geometrically. In the above conveyor tracking example, we assumed that the object was in the centre of the conveyor and in the correct

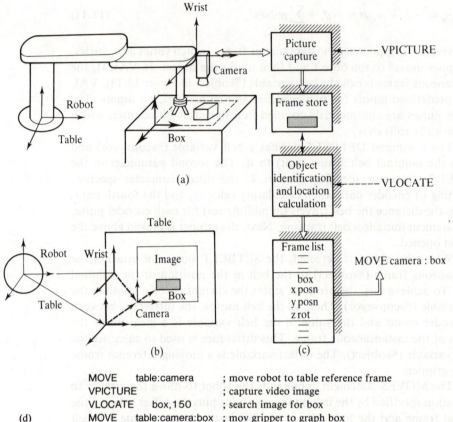

Figure 12.19
VAL-II vision program.
(Blume and Jakob, 1986):
(a) work cell; (b) coordinate
frames; (c) data flow;
(d) program.

orientation for grasping. The equipment required to place objects in precise orientations is expensive, and can be eliminated if we use vision (Section 10.8) to locate the object. Vision can also be used to recognize different objects, considerably increasing the flexibility of the system. Thus, vision gives us several important pieces of information, which can be fused with the motion model (Equation 12.11) to increase the flexibility of our control system. First, the robot can detect the presence of the object with vision, and compare it with the signal from the light barrier detector for error checking and recovery. A major use of redundant sensing is error handling (Section 12.4.7). Second, a vision system can determine the position and orientation of the object. The robot program uses this position information to update the y component of the instantaneous frame, and orientation to specify the orientation of the gripper. Third, the transformation from the detection point to the grasp point will differ from one object class to another. When the vision system recognizes an object, it selects the appropriate grasp transform for that object.

VAL II has statements for capturing and analysing video images (Figure 12.19). RAIL has functions for identifying 45 different vision

```
FUNCTION BOOLEAN INSERT(FRAME PIN, HOLE; REAL FZMAX, EPS; INTEGER NMAX);
INTEGER N; VECTOR LATF; FRAME HOLE1;
BEGIN
    N := 0;
    HOLE1 := HOLE*TRANSLATION(-VZ,10);
    WHILE N < NMAX DO
        MOVE PIN BY TRANSF(PIN,HOLE1) UNTIL FZ > FZMAX;
        IF DISTANCE (PIN, HOLE) < 1 THEN
            RETURN (TRUE)
        ELSE
            LATF := VECTOR(FX,FY,O);
            MOVE PIN BY TRANSLATION(LATF,EPS);
            EPS := EPS/2;
            N := N+1;
        END IF;
    ENDDO;
    WRITE "INSERTION FAILED";
    RETURN (FALSE);
END;
```

Figure 12.20
LM program for inserting a
pin in a hole (Latcombe,
1983).

features. In addition to analysing the image to recognize objects, a vision system has to relate the location of the blobs in the image to the physical location of the objects relative to the robot (world frame or hand frame). Before we can use a vision system, we have to 'teach' it these transforms and determine the mapping from the image to physical space.

During the teaching phase, one or more discs of known diameter are placed in known locations in the field of view of the camera. The image is analysed, and a set of object transforms relative to the bottom left corner of the image (camera frame) are calculated. These transforms are then combined with the transforms describing the known physical locations of the discs to calibrate the vision system. During calibration, we calculate the location of the camera frame, the orientation of the image, and the horizontal and vertical scales which relate image dimensions to physical dimensions. Then, the objects that are to be recognized are 'taught' to the system by showing.

In the example in Figure 12.19, the camera is attached to the wrist of the robot, and the camera frame is defined relative to the wrist frame, such that the location of the camera frame relative to world coordinates is the product of the wrist transform and the camera transform. Thus, the first statement in the program in Figure 12.19(d) will move the camera to the work area of the table.

The VPICTURE statement captures the image, and the VLOCATE statement searches the image for a box. Once a box is found, its location is calculated. The gripper is then moved to the grasping position. Again, these statements have been included in the language to handle a special situation. One of the tasks facing language designers is to develop a generalized set of vision processing functions that are applicable to a variety of situations. We also need a standard interface between robot controller software and vision processing software, so that robots and vision systems from different manufacturers can be combined.

Figure 12.21
AL program for grasping a
peg and inserting it into a
hole (Lozano-Perez, 1983).

```
BEGIN "insert peg into hole"
FRAME peg, grasp, bottom, top
        {peg = bottom of peg, grasp = grasp point, bottom and top are bottom and top of
        hole – each is a frame representing actual position of the feature}
peg←FRAME(nilrot, VECTOR(20,30,0)*mm);
bottom←FRAME(nilrot, VECTOR(25,35,0)*mm);
{define grasping position relative to bottom of peg}
grasp←FRAME(ROT(xhat,180*degrees),3*zhat*mm);
tries←2
grasped←FALSE;
{top of hole is defined to have a fixed relation to the bottom}
AFFIX top TO bottom RIGIDLY
        AT TRANS(nilrot,3*zhat*mm);
OPEN hand TO diameter +20*mm;   {diameter of peg}
{pick up peg}
MOVE arm TO bottom * grasp {move hand to grasp point}
WHILE NOT grasped AND i<tries DO
        BEGIN   {attempt grasp}
        CLOSE hand TO 0*mm;
        IF      hand < diameter/2 THEN
                BEGIN "failed to grasp peg"
                OPEN hand TO diameter +20*mm
                MOVE arm to ⊗ −20*mm;   {⊗ is current location}
                END
        ELSE    grasped←TRUE;
        i←      i + 1;
END
IF NOT grasped THEN ABORT ("Failed to grasp peg");
{define relationship between arm and peg}
AFFIX peg TO arm RIGIDLY;   {arm transform includes peg}
MOVE peg TO top;   {move peg bottom to top of hole}
{test if peg is above hole}
MOVE arm to ⊗ −20*mm
        ON FORCE (zhat) > 100*grams DO ABORT ("No Hole");
        {Found hole – move peg into hole with downward force while complying to side forces}
MOVE peg TO bottom DIRECTLY
        WITH FORCE__FRAME = station IN WORLD
        WITH FORCE (zhat) = −100*grams
        WITH FORCE (xhat) = 0*grams
        WITH FORCE (yhat) = 0*grams
        SLOWLY;
END "insert peg in hole"
```

12.4.6   Force control

The insertion of a pin in a hole requires the use of either passive compliance
(Section 6.3.7) or active force control (Section 11.8). Active force control is
achieved either by guarded moves, where motion is terminated when a
specified force is reached, or with force-control loops. In the latter case, the
control program must calculate force references for some degrees of freedom
and motion references for others.

The LM program in Figure 12.20 uses a guarded move statement to insert a pin in a hole. The pin is moved towards the bottom of the hole until a force threshold is exceeded. An IF statement tests for correct insertion, by comparing the pin frame to the hole frame. If the pin was not inserted then it was pushing against the top of the block. The pin is moved and insertion is attempted again. If the robot is unable to insert the pin after *n* tries, the search for the hole has failed, and the program gives up.

An AL program for the same task is given in Figure 12.21. First, the task is modelled with frames, and fixed relationships are defined by affixment. The robot is then commanded to grasp the peg – the grasping routine includes an error detection and recovery sequence. The peg is then moved towards the hole. If it enters the hole, the opposing force will be small and the motion will complete. If the peg runs into an obstacle the ON command will abort the motion when the opposing force exceeds a threshold of 100 grams.

If the hole is found, the program then proceeds to insert the peg. Again, the WITH statement is used to modify motion, only this time, motion is modified to achieve desired force constraints. This type of construct requires a robot that can be force- or position-controlled in independent Cartesian degrees of freedom.

The MOVE statement commands the robot to move so that the frames 'peg' (bottom of peg) and 'bottom' (of hole) align. As the success of peg insertion is dependent upon keeping the forces within bounds, the program defines a force frame (station) relative to world coordinates. Note, the frames 'top' and 'bottom' are also parallel to the world frame.

The program specifies forces references for each Cartesian direction. The downward force in the z direction is sufficient to push the peg into the hole. If a force is measured in the x or y directions, the peg is moved to reduce the force to zero. That is, force measuremens are used to effect compliant motion. If the peg jams, the motion will halt because the force in the z direction is controlled at 100 grams. As written, this program will hang because there is no code to detect such an error and initiate corrective action.

AL was an ambitious attempt to develop a language that provided all the capabilities required by robot programming in the context of a modern, high-level, structured language (Finkel *et al.*, 1975). Newer languages, such as SRL and LM make considerable use of concepts pioneered in AL. SRL uses the frame concepts of AL, and LM adopted most of its concepts, apart from parallel processing. AL ran on two computers. One computer supported program development and compilation of AL code into a lower-level language. The other computer interpreted the lower-level code in real time to control the robot.

Unfortunately, many robot controllers do not include force-control loops, and languages designed for these robots do not include force-control statements. In these systems, it might be possible to implement an add-on force controller (Figure 11.42). However, the required code may have to include low-level constructs to overcome language deficiencies.

Figure 12.22
VAL-II force control program
(courtesy Stephen Young):
(a) physical set up;
(b) program.

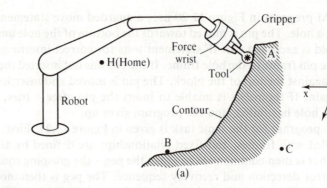

(a)

```
PROGRAM go                      ; robot control program
; code to initialize force sensing wrist goes here
MOVE A                          ; move to top of contour
continue = TRUE                 ; loop variable for process control program
PCEXECUTE bg                    ; start parallel process control program
ALTER (−1,18,1)                 ; receive setpoint increments from process control program
MOVES C                         ; move down contour in -z direction
WHILE  DX(HERE) < DX(B)         ; loop until tool reaches B
    END
continue = FALSE                ; stop process control program
BRAKE                           ; abort MOVES C command
MOVE H                          ; go to home position
. END


. PROGRAM bg                    ; process control program
WHILE continue DO
    zpoke ↑404 = 1              ; set force array index to 1
    ioput ↑176636 = 24         ; request input from force wrist
20  ptr = zpeek (↑404)         ; look at array index
    IF ptr < 13 THEN
        GOTO 20                 ; loop until 13 characters have been read
    END                        ; if
    x force = zpeek (↑412)     ; array starts at 410
    z force = zpeek (↑416)     ; want force in x and z directions
; using x and z direction forces calculate change in x (dx) for contour following
    ALTOUT 0,dx,0,0,0,0,0      ; send dx to robot control program
END                            ; while
. END
```

(b)

VAL II provides no support for force control, but an add-on force controller can be implemented (Figure 12.22). This program is actually two programs which execute in parallel. One is a high-priority robot-control program, which directly controls the motion of the robot. The other is a background process-control program which reads the force sensor information and calculates the motion changes required for force control. These changes are communicated to the robot-control program using the ALTOUT and ALTER commands.

The robot-control program (go) initializes the force-sensing wrist (code not included), and commands the robot to move to the top of the contour. The variable 'continue' is shared by both programs and is used by the robot-control program to terminate the execution of the process-control program. Next, the robot-control program launches the process-control program (bg) with the PCEXECUTE instruction, and enables input from the process-control program to modify the trajectory of the robot (ALTER statement). Having established interprocess communication, the robot-control program now executes the task. The task is to move the tool down the contour. To achieve this motion, and apply force to the contour in the $-z$ direction, the robot is commanded to move to a target frame in the $-z$ direction; that is, into the object. As a result of this attempted motion, the contour applies force to the tool in the x direction.

The process-control program reads the string of 13 characters from the force sensor, over a serial link, into an array, using some very crude code. Once the 8 degree of freedom force vector has been read, the program calculates an incremental motion in the x direction to reduce the force to a desired value. This calculation implements a control law for active force control in the x direction. Then the incremental-motion vector is sent to the robot-control program using the ALTOUT command.

The ALTER command in the robot-control program reads the incremental-motion vector and modifies the target frame for the motion command. This process continues until the bottom of the contour is reached, where the robot-control program resets the continue flag to halt the process-control program, and aborts the motion of the robot with the BRAKE statement. The main limitation on the performance of this system is the time taken to transmit the force vector over the serial link.

12.4.7 Error detection and recovery

The most tedious, difficult and time consuming code to design, write and debug is error detection and recovery code. Many of the programs we have discussed have very little error handling code in them. This lack of error handling is a major fault in all robot programming, and regularly results in a robot stalling in mid motion (for example, when the peg jams in Figure 12.21), or causing damage (for example, failure to grasp the object in Figure 12.18), or failure to complete the task (for example, failure of glue to flow in Figure 12.17).

An essential use of sensor information is the detection of error conditions. However, before errors can be detected, we must define all the possible errors which could conceivably occur during the execution of a task. It is at this point that most program designs fail. There is no easy way to identify all possible error situations. Even a programmer with years of experience can overlook error situations during design. Worse, the error may not occur for months when everyone with knowledge of the program has moved on.

Having identified possible error situations, their causes, and how to

Figure 12.23
AML subroutine to pick up
an object of type slug.
Includes extensive error
handling. (Taylor and
Grossman, 1983).

```
pick__up__slug : SUBR (fdr,tries);
cc  :NEW STRING(8);
    :NEW O;

step__1                                              – move to grasping position
    CMOVE(<feeder__loc(fdr), feeder__orient,12>);  {approach position}
    IF DCMOVE (<<0,0,20, ANY__FORCE (20 × GMS), <12>>) THEN
       BEGIN                                         – hit something on way in
       DCMOVE (<<0,0,2>>);                           – back out
       RETURN('jammed');                             – return error

step__2;                                             – attempt to grasp slug
    cc = GRASP(2.5,<0.1,0.1>,PINCH__FORCE(0.5 × KGS));
    IF cc NE 'ok' THEN
       BEGIN                                         – hit something on way in
       MOVE(GRIPPER,0.5);                            – readjust gripper
       DCMOVE(<<0,0,25>>);                           – back out
       RETURN(IF cc EQ 'too small' THEN 'empty'
                 ELSE IF cc EQ 'too big' THEN 'jammed'
                 ELSE cc);
       END;

step__3;                                             – update feed location
    fy = HAND__GOAL(Y,1.2);                          – 'Y' position at grasp
    IF ABS (fy-feeder__loc(fdr,2)) GT 0.1 THEN
         feeder__loc(f,2) = fy;

step__4:                                             – pull out slug and reverify hold
    DCMOVE(<0,0,25>);
    IF ABS(SENSIO(<LPINCH,RPINCH>)) LT 150*GMS THEN
       BEGIN                                         – dropped part
       IF tries GE t = t + 1 THEN                    – if not too many
            BRANCH(step__1);                         – then try again
       ELSE
            RETURN('dropped');                       – give up
    END;

    RETURN('ok');
    END;
```

detect them (not an easy task), the next step is to decide on recovery action. Unfortunately, it is not always obvious what to do to recover from an error, and even when it is, the solution may not be technically feasible. The simplest action is to halt the operation and call for manual intervention. Initially, all errors should be handled this way.

As errors occur, recovery strategies can be designed and tested. As halting the execution of the task causes expensive delays, the more frequent errors must either be eliminated by redesign of the system or handled automatically. Less frequent errors, and errors where the recovery strategy is complex or not feasible, are to be handled manually. If an error occurs once a year, the cost of manual recovery is probably less than the cost of sophisticated automatic recovery hardware.

The AML subroutine in Figure 12.23 includes extensive error detection code. The task is to pick up an object of type slug from a feeder. This task is a subtask of the much larger task to assemble a printer chain. The actual program used in this application handled more error situations and carried out more bookkeeping than the simplified program shown here (Taylor and Grossman, 1983).

In Step 1 of the program, the robot is commanded to move the gripper to the approach position, open it, and then approach the feeder. If the gripper hits anything, the program assumes a part is jammed in the feeder, and an error message is returned to the calling program. The structure of the DCMOVE statement is different to any move command seen in previous examples. It is implemented as a subroutine using lower-level AML statements. DCMOVE (offset, tests, cntl) causes the robot to be displaced relative to its current Cartesian position by the amount defined in the aggregate offset (in millimetres). In contrast, CMOVE (goal, tests, cntl) causes the robot to move to the frame specified by the goal aggregate. The optional parameter 'tests' describes sensor monitoring to be performed during the motion. If any of the specified sensor thresholds is exceeded, the motion is terminated. The optimal parameter 'cntl' specifies the velocity and acceleration to be used during the motion.

After the completion, or termination, of motion an aggregate of TRUE and FALSE values, one for each test, is returned by the move command, to indicate which sensor thresholds were exceeded during the motion. In Step 1, this aggregate is used by the IF statement to determine if a collision error occurred. Once the gripper is in place, it is commanded to close (Step 2). The GRASP (size, tolerance, force) command returns the string 'OK' to indicate the success of the grasp in the grasped object is within tolerance of the nominal size. Otherwise, it returns the string 'too big' or 'too small' to indicate the error in the size of the object. The details of the GRASP subroutine are described in Taylor *et al.* (1982).

The grasp routine causes the robot to move so as to centre the jaws of the gripper on the slug, using force information from the touch sensors mounted on the jaws. Any motion of the robot during grasping indicates that the world model is inaccurate, and the purpose of Step 3 in the program is to update the feeder location in the world model. Thus, this system detects and corrects for errors in the world model, such as drift in robot calibration, and changes in part presentation.

In Step 4, the slug is pulled out of the feeder ready for transfer to the chain. At the completion of the extraction motion, the program tests to see if the gripper is still holding the slug. If the slug were to be dropped, the program would attempt to pick up the next slug in the feeder. If the slug is stuck in the feeder, the program will eventually given up. This example illustrates the close attention to detail required when programming error handling sequences.

12.5   Future directions

Glass (1980) described real-time programming as, 'the lost-world of software debugging and testing', in comparison to the 'civilization' in other areas of software development. Unfortunately, for many robot programmers, this scenario is still true. They continue to test real-time robot-control programs on computers with no operating system and to program in languages that resemble high-level computer languages of two decades ago. Since Glass wrote his indictment of real-time programming, considerable research has been reported into the design of real-time systems (Steusloff, 1984), the development of robot programming languages (Lozano-Perez, 1983; Latombe, 1983), new techniques for teaching points (Hirzinger, 1984) and world models (Gini and Gini, 1985), improved programming environments (Cox, *et al*, 1987), and tools for measuring the execution of programs (McKerrow, 1988). Yet, many problems still remain (Stankovic, 1988). The examples in the previous section indicate the widely differing facilities offered by various robot languages, and the problems they have when applied to new applications.

Two computer science trends that are already affecting robot programming are object-oriented languages and parallel processing. AML/X supports object-oriented programming, where an object is described with a data structure called a class and permissible operations on the data structure are described with procedures called methods. When a new class is constructed from an existing class, the methods for the existing class are inherited by the new class. This inheritance mechanism enables the programmer to develop application-specific classes without having to reinvent the underlying procedures every time. The result is a considerable increase in programmer productivity.

The code fragments from an AML/X program (Anderson, 1988) in Figure 12.24 implement the forward kinematic model for a simplified Puma robot (Figure 4.19). The robot Puma is defined to be of type six-link robot (Figure 12.24(a)) where six-link robot is a class (Figure 12.24(b)) which is defined as an aggregate of six links. The six attributes of Puma specify the specific instance of the class six-link robot that we call Puma.

A link (Figure 12.24(c)) is an object of type **A** matrix, where an **A** matrix is a class used to represent homogeneous coordinates. The values of specific instances of objects of type **A** matrix are evaluated during the execution of the program using predefined methods. For example, the method INIT (Figure 12.24(d)) calculates the elements of an **A** matrix using the standard equation (Equation 4.6). Other methods exist for updating existing **A** matrices. The advantage of run-time evaluation is that the elements of the **A** matrix are correct for the current value of the joint variable.

Our definition of the robot Puma includes six attributes, one for each link. Each attribute is an aggregate of an **A** matrix, a joint description, and joint limits for that link (Figure 12.24(e)). The joint description specifies

PUMA: new six__link__robot(attr1,attr2,attr3,attr4,attr5,attr6);

(a)

six__link__robot:CLASS(lnk__1,lnk__2,lnk__3,lnk__4,lnk__5,lnk__6);
ivars
robot:new ⟨lnk__1,lnk__2,lnk__3,lnk__4,lnk__5,lnk__6⟩;
end;

(b)

link__1:new A__matrix.init(theta__1,disp__1,ling__1,twist__1);

(c)

INIT: CLASS__METH(theta DEFAULT 0.0 MUSTBE ⟨REAL⟩,
                  disp DEFAULT 0.0, long DEFAULT 0.0, alpha DEFAULT 0.0)
RETURN
A__MATRIX(⟨⟨COS(theta), -sin(theta)∗cos(alpha), sin(theta)∗sin(alpha), cos(theta)∗leng⟩,
          ⟨sin(theta), cos(theta)∗cos(alpha), -cos(theta)∗sin(alpha), sin(theta)∗leng⟩,
          ⟨0.0, sin(alpha), cos(alpha), disp⟩,
          ⟨0.0, 0.0, 0.0, 1.0⟩⟩);
END;

(d)

standard equations for A__matrix elements; and
attr1: new ⟨link__1, 'revolute', ⟨−260.0, 160.0⟩⟩;

(e)

theta__1: new real (0.0);   /*link variable θ in degrees*/
disp__1: new real (660.4);   /*link displacement d in mm*/
leng__1: new real (0.0);   /*link length l in mm*/
twist__1: new real (90.0);   /*link twist α in degrees*/

(f)

joint__variables: bind⟨theta__1, theta__2, theta__3, theta__4, theta__5, theta__6⟩;

(g)

forward solution: method (link__vars)
i: new,0
a: new while (++i le 6) do collect
            if (robot(i,2) eq 'revolute') then
               robot (i,1).theta (lnk__vars(i));
            else
               robot (i,1).disp(lnk__vars(i));
     return   (a(1) + a(2) + a(3) + a(4) + a(5) + a(6));
     end

(h)

Figure 12.24
AML/X object-oriented program for calculating the forward transform of a simplified PUMA robot – sections of code only. (Anderson, 1988).
(a) Declare PUMA to be an object of the type six__link__robot;
(b) a six-link robot is a class which is defined as an aggregate of sixlinks;
(c) a link is an object of type A__matrix, which is a 4 × 4 matrix;
(d) values are evaluated at run time using a method based on the standard equation for A__matrix elements;
(e) each attribute of PUMA is an aggregate of an **A** matrix, a joint description and joint limits;
(f) the link parameters for links;
(g) the joint variables for the PUMA are bound to the joint variables of type six__link__robot;
(h) a method to calculate the forward transform of a six-link robot when passed the attributes for the robot.

whether the joint is revolute or prismatic and is used to determine which method to use when evaluating the **A** matrix for that link. To reduce execution time, the **A** matrix equations are pre-solved for the fixed link parameters (Figure 12.24(f)). The joint limits are used for error detection by the inverse kinematic method.

To solve the forward kinematic model, a general method for solving six-link robot models is passed the attributes of the specific robot (Figure 12.24(h)). This method reads the joint variable and calls a method to evaluate the **A** matrix for each link, based upon the joint descriptor. Then the six **A** matrices are multiplied, and a numeric **A** matrix is returned, which defines the current end-effector frame.

Object-oriented programming requires a different way of thinking from conventional structured programming and, hence, may take some time to learn. However, current research indicates that programmer productivity increases considerably. An object-oriented implementation of a kinematic model is more flexible than a hard coded one, but is not as efficient.

Research in parallel processing is aimed at decreasing the execution time of robot software so that more complex tasks can be tackled using more sophisticated control algorithms. One popular approach to parallel processing for robot applications is the transputer network programmed in occam. A pipelined architecture for forward kinematics is shown in Figure 12.25(a)).

The problem of solving the kinematic model is broken up into six identical smaller problems (Figure 12.25(a)): one problem for each joint and associated link. Each smaller problem consists of reading a joint variable, calculating a numeric matrix from the symbolic **A** matrix, and multiplying the numeric matrix by the product of the matrices of the distal links. Each of the six smaller problems is implemented by an occam process called a joint process. These six joint processes can execute on one processor or on a network of processors.

Occam processes communicate using message passing. When one joint process finishes its calculation it sends the resultant matrix in a message to the next joint process in the pipeline. As each joint process executes, a transformation matrix flows down the pipeline to appear at the end as the forward transform. Occam processes are synchronized using the rendezvous technique, where both processes wait until the message has been passed. Once the message has been passed, the process continued execution. When the processes are started, the calculation of the first forward transform takes a reasonable time. However, after process 6 passes its results to process 5, it immediately commences recalculating **A**, matrix 6. The same occurs all along the pipe, and subsequent forward transforms appear at the end of the pipe in 20 to 30 per cent of the time taken to calculate the first transform.

The six processes are identical. The main line (Figure 12.25(b)) established the links between the processes in the pipeline and the links to the joint sensor processes with the CHAN command. A description of these links is stored in the channel array, referenced by the parameters in the command. The first PAR (parallel) statement starts the process which feeds an identity matrix into the pipeline and, in parallel, starts the process which reads the joint sensors.

As the six joint processes are identical, the program spawns six joint processes using the PAR(allel) FOR loop construct. The occam keyword PAR starts the processes in its block in parallel. Finally, an output process is started to display the results of the calculations.

A joint process (Figure 12.25(c)) calculates the numeric **A** matrix for the joint, multiplies this matrix by the matrix which is passed to it by the previous process in the pipeline, and then passes the resultant matrix to the

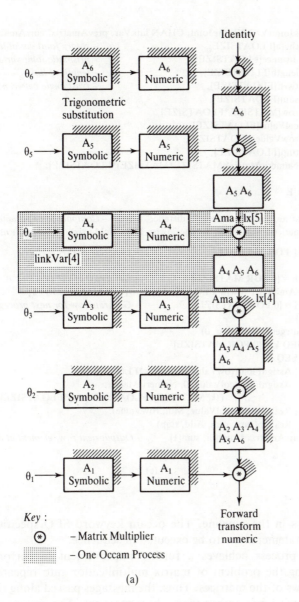

Identity

θ_6 → | A_6 Symbolic | | A_6 Numeric | → ⊛

Trigonometric substitution

A_6

θ_5 → | A_5 Symbolic | | A_5 Numeric | → ⊛

$A_5 A_6$

Amatrix[5]

θ_4 → | A_4 Symbolic | | A_4 Numeric | → ⊛

linkVar[4]

$A_4 A_5 A_6$

Amatrix[4]

θ_3 → | A_3 Symbolic | | A_3 Numeric | → ⊛

$A_3 A_4 A_5 A_6$

θ_2 → | A_2 Symbolic | | A_2 Numeric | → ⊛

$A_2 A_3 A_4 A_5 A_6$

θ_1 → | A_1 Symbolic | | A_1 Numeric | → ⊛

Forward transform numeric

Key :
⊛ – Matrix Multiplier
▓ – One Occam Process

(a)

Figure 12.25
Occam program to implement forward kinematics calculations using six parallel processes in a pipeline architecture.
(a) Architecture for a pipeline calculation of forward kinematics using homogeneous transforms;
(b) occam mainline;
(c) process for calculating joint A matrix and multiplying it by proximal matrices.

```
- main() - Main program
CHAN link Var[NUMJOINTS], Amatrix[NUMJOINTS+1]:
PAR
    FeedIdentity(Amatrix[START])              - Input initial identity matrix
    FeedTheta(linkVar)                        - Simulate reading sensors

    PAR joint = [0 FOR NUMJOINTS]             - Start up joint processes
    ProcessJoint(joint,linkVar[joint], Amatrix[joint+1], Amatrix[joint])

    ShowTransform(Amatrix[FINAL])             - Output Final Transform
```

(b)

Figure 12.25
Cont.

```
PROC ProcessJoint(VALUE theJoint, CHAN linkVar, prevAmatrix, currAmatrix) =
  VAR      theta[FLOATSIZE],                    – rotary joint variable
           distance[FLOATSIZE],                 – prismatic joint variable
           length[FLOATSIZE],                   – length of link
           twist[FLOATSIZE],                    – twist angle between joint axes
           sum[FLOATSIZE],
           row[MATSIZE*FLOATSIZE],
           colValue[FLOATSIZE],
           rowValue[FLOATSIZE],
           tmp[FLOATSIZE],
           NumericMatrix[(MATSIZE*MATSIZE)*FLOATSIZE]:
  SEQ
    WHILE TRUE
      SEQ
        JointData(theJoint, theta, length, distance, twist)   – Compute joint parameters for joint
        BuildNumeric(theta, length, distance, twist, NumericMatrix)   – Compute numeric matrix

        SEQ i = [1 FOR MATSIZE]                – Generate next A__Matrix
          SEQ
            SEQ n = [0 FOR MATSIZE]            – Get a row of the previous A__Matrix
            prevAmatrix ? row[n*FLOATSIZE]; row[(n*FLOATSIZE)+1]
            SEQ j = [0 FOR MATSIZE]            – Generate row for next process
            SEQ
              IntegerToReal(sum, 0)
              SEQ k = [0 FOR MATSIZE]
              SEQ
                AssignFloat(rowValue, 0, row, k*FLOATSIZE)
                AssignFloat(colValue, 0, NumericMatrix,
                            ((k*MATSIZE)*FLOATSIZE)+(j*FLOATSIZE))
                RealOp(tmp, colValue, Mul, rowValue)
                RealOp(sum, sum, Add, tmp)
              currAmatrix ! sum[0]; sum[1]      – Output next row, element at a time
  SKIP:
```

(c)

next process in the pipeline. The occam keyword SEQ specifies that the
following statements are to be executed in sequence.

The process achieves a further improvement in performance by
decomposing the problem of matrix multiplication into repeated calculations on rows of the matrices. Thus, the messages passed along the pipeline
contain matrix rows rather than whole matrices. The command 'prev **A**
matrix?' reads a row of a matrix from the previous process in the pipeline.
Then, the equivalent row is calculated by multiplying the received row by the
joint **A** matrix. Finally, the resultant row is passed to the next process in the
pipeline using the 'curr **A** matrix!' statement.

While these last two example programs may be somewhat esoteric in
comparison to programs currently controlling industrial robots, they are
indicative of trends in programming. Research into all areas of robot

programming is crucial to the advancement of robotics. During the next decade, specific attention must be given to world modelling, system integration, sensor processing, human interface design, and standardization of crucial interface software.

The development of action-level and task-level languages hinges upon our ability to solve the problems of modelling the task while it is executing. This includes task description techniques, methods for modelling three-dimensional objects, and algorithms and heuristics for reasoning about relationships between objects and for inferring the results of actions on those objects.

At a lower-level, considerable work remains in the development of flexible robot-level languages, languages that are easily extendable to new applications. The problems of sensor integration, including the handling of sensor variables, and of interprocess communication, particularly between sensors and robot controllers, continue to limit the performance of robots.

We started this chapter with a quotation from Peter Davey (1983). The examples we have discussed clearly indicate the current problems in robot programming, and emphasize that the future of robotics is heavily dependent upon the development of better robot programming languages and environments.

Key points

- Robot programming is concerned with observing and manipulating objects in three dimensional space.

- There are three classes of robot programmer: user, applications programmers, and systems programmers; each with different abilities and requirements.

- In addition to the data manipulation handled by computer programs, robot programs control physical motion, operate in parallel, communicate with other programs, synchronize with external events, respond to interrupts in real-time, operate on sensor variables, and initialize and terminate in physically safe ways.

- The control of motion and force requires the addition of keywords to the language that result in physical action.

- Two distinct levels of parellelism exist within a robot: internal parallelism between joint controllers, and external parellelism between robot actions and sensing.

- Three methods of interprocess communication are shared memory, remote-procedure call, and message passing.

- Events are detected by polling and with interrupts.

- Sensor variables store the values read by sensors, thus their contents are updated independently of the programs that use them.

- When a robot program aborts, we have a potentially dangerous situation.

- Using an operating system increases programmer productivity by providing the programmer with an integrated set of resources, but can reduce program performance.

- When using a robot-level language, teaching the location of frames often takes much longer than writing the program.

- Three approaches to the design of robot-level languages have been taken: design from scratch, modification of a numerical-control language, and modification of a computer programming language.

- By representing objects as data, which is independently updated in real-time, we transform a robot program into a computer program. We achieve this transformation with sensor variables and actuator command statements.

- A computer programming language provides three facilities: data storage, data manipulation, and flow of control of data manipulation.

- The data types introduced into computer languages to support robot programming include event, vector, distance type, rotmatrix, frame and aggregate.

- World models are usually constructed with coordinate frames and transformation equations.

- When programmed in a language that uses symbolic assignment rather than numeric assignment, a system can adapt to changes without reprogramming, at the cost of increased execution time.

- Specifying the approach direction in a stand-off frame causes the gripper to rotate into the correct orientation during the free-space move to the stand-off point.

- A comprehensive robot language includes instructions for specifying the type of motion, for defining complex paths, for control of trajectory following, and for aborting motion.

- Many robot languages do not support force control.

- The most tedious, difficult, and time consuming software to design, write, and debug is error detection and recovery code.

Exercises

■ *Essay questions*

12.1 Compare and contrast the three classes of robot programmer.

12.2 Discuss the trade-offs between programmer productivity and program performance that often occurs in robot language design.

12.3 Robot programming languages are used for two purposes: task definition and robot control. Explain.

12.4 What requirements must be met by a robot programming language, that are not normally supported by high-level computer languages?

12.5 In what ways do 'move' statements differ from other program statements?

12.6 Describe the three ways of achieving concurrency mentioned in Section 12.1.2.

12.7 Describe the three models of interprocess communication mentioned in Section 12.1.3.

12.8 Discuss methods for handling event synchronization.

12.9 How does a sensor variable differ from a variable in an ordinary program?

12.10 What are the advantages of using an operating system in robot control computers?

12.11 How can utility programs make teaching easier? List the range of frames, features, and so on that can be taught, and design algorithms for the teaching process.

12.12 Discuss the implications of the following statement,

> 'By representing objects as data, whose values are updated in real-time, we transform a robot program into a computer program'.

12.13 What is the data type frame? How is it implemented?

12.14 How do robot programming languages handle event synchronization and process synchronization?

12.15 How do robot programming languages support world modelling? Is this adequate? Why? Why not? (Section 12.4.1).

12.16 Compare and contrast numeric and symbolic assignment?

12.17 Complete the program in Figure 12.13, by writing the code to put four screws into the bracket.

12.18 What features does a robot programming language need to support point-to-point motion, continuous-path motion, complex trajectory following, and guarded motion?

12.19 List the examples of sensor interaction in the programs in Section 12.4, and develop classifications for the various types of sensor interaction.

12.20 Examine the use of the WITH construct in some of the examples in Section 12.4. What is it used for? Can you think of a better way of carrying out this function?

12.21 How do you test that a gripper has grasped an object?

12.22 Why is error detection and correction important?

12.23 From the example programs in this chapter categorize some typical error situations and work out appropriate strategies for recovery.

12.24 In Section 12.4.4, we discussed picking an object off a moving conveyor. A similar task is to pick an object off a rotating turntable. Develop a model of this task suitable for sensor fusion. What language features are needed to support this task?

12.25 Develop a model for the calibration of a vision system (Section 12.4.5). What language features are required to (a) calibrate the vision system, and (b) recognize objects?

12.26 What error conditions should be tested for during the insertion of a pin in a hole? (Sections 12.4.6, 11.8, 6.3.7).

■ *Practical questions*

12.1 Program the robot in the laboratory to execute the simple pick and place task in Figure 12.3.

12.2 Write a program for the robot to enable the manual teaching of tool transforms, similar to the program in Figure 12.6.

12.3 A program for teaching textual programs by showing is given in Figure 12.8. Can a similar program be written in the language of the robot in the laboratory? If so, write it.

12.4 Develop a world model (Section 12.4.1) for the problem in Figure 12.11, and implement in the language of the robot in the lab.

12.5 Does the laboratory robot cell include a conveyor? If so, write a program to pick an object off a moving conveyor, similar to the program in Figure 12.18.

12.6 A number of example programs for a variety of tasks are discussed in Section 12.4. Write equivalent programs in the language of the robot in the laboratory. If the hardware is available execute these programs.

12.7 Search conference proceedings for examples of other tasks that you can program the robot to execute in the laboratory.

12.8 A programming language supports data storage, data manipulation, and flow of control of data manipulation (Section 12.4). Classify the statements in the language of the robot in the laboratory in these three categories.

Appendix A · *Mathematics*

A.1 Trigonometry

A.1.1 Basic trigonometry

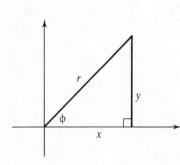
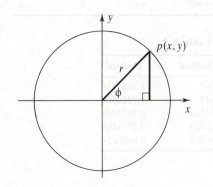

Figure A.1

$\sin(\phi) = y/r$ $\qquad\qquad$ $\csc(\phi) = 1/\sin(\phi)$

$\cos(\phi) = x/r$ $\qquad\qquad$ $\sec(\phi) = 1/\cos(\phi)$

$\tan(\phi) = y/x = \sin(\phi)/\cos(\phi)$ $\qquad$ $\cot(\phi) = 1/\tan(\phi)$

$x^2 + y^2 = r^2$ $\quad$ Pythagoras' Theorem

$\cos(\phi) = \sin(90 - \phi)$

arc = radius $\times$ ϕ, where ϕ is in radians, and 1 radian = 57° 18′
π radians in 180°, where $\pi = 3.14159$

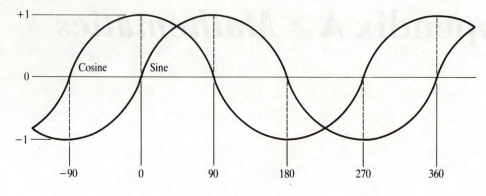

Figure A.2

Table A.1

Angle	sin	cos	tan
+90°	1	0	∞
+60°	√3/2	1/2	√3
+45°	√2/2	√2/2	1
+30°	1/2	√3/2	1/√3
0°	0	1	0
−90°	−1	0	−∞

Table A.2

Radical	Decimal
√2	1.4142136
√3	1.7320508
√2/2	0.7071068
1/√3	0.5773503
√3/2	0.8660254

A.1.2 Trigonometric relationships

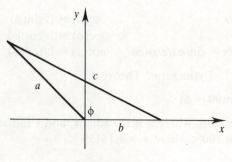

Figure A.3

$$c^2 = a^2 + b^2 - 2ab\cos(\phi)$$

$$\sin(-\phi) = -\sin(\phi) \qquad \cos(-\phi) = \cos(\phi)$$

$$\cos^2(\phi) + \sin^2(\phi) = 1 \qquad \cos(2\phi) = \cos^2(\phi) - \sin^2(\phi)$$

$$\tan^2(\phi) + 1 = \sec^2(\phi) \qquad \sin(2\phi) = 2\cos(\phi)\sin(\phi)$$

$$\sin(\theta + \phi) = \sin(\theta)\cos(\phi) + \cos(\theta)\sin(\phi)$$
$$\cos(\theta + \phi) = \cos(\theta)\cos(\phi) - \sin(\theta)\sin(\phi)$$
$$\sin(\theta - \phi) = \sin(\theta)\cos(\phi) - \cos(\theta)\sin(\phi)$$
$$\cos(\theta - \phi) = \cos(\theta)\cos(\phi) + \sin(\theta)\sin(\phi)$$

$$\tan(2\phi) = \frac{2\tan(\phi)}{1 - \tan^2(\phi)}$$

$$\tan(\phi - \theta) = \frac{\tan(\phi) - \tan(\theta)}{1 + \tan(\phi)\tan(\theta)}$$

$$\tan(\phi + q) = \frac{\tan(\phi) + \tan(q)}{1 - \tan(\phi)\tan(q)}$$

If $\alpha = \phi + \theta$, and $\beta = \phi - \theta$ then:

$$\sin(\alpha) - \sin(\beta) = 2\cos(\phi)\sin(\theta) = 2\cos\left(\frac{\alpha + \beta}{2}\right)\sin\left(\frac{\alpha - \beta}{2}\right)$$

A.2 Derivatives

$$\frac{dc}{dx} = 0 \qquad\qquad \frac{d(cu)}{dx} = \frac{cdu}{dx} = c, \text{ when } x = u$$

$$\frac{du^n}{dx} = nu^{n-1}\frac{du}{dx} \qquad \frac{d(cu^n)}{dx} = cnu^{n-1}\frac{du}{dx} = cnx^{n-1} \text{ where } x = u.$$

$$\frac{d(uv)}{dx} = u\frac{dv}{dx} + v\frac{du}{dx} \qquad \frac{d(u + v)}{dx} = \frac{du}{dx} + \frac{dv}{dx}$$

$$\frac{d(u/v)}{dx} = \frac{v\dfrac{du}{dx} - u\dfrac{dv}{dx}}{v^2}$$

Limit as $\phi \to 0$ $\dfrac{\sin(\phi)}{\phi} = 1$

$$\frac{d(\sin(\phi))}{dx} = \cos(\phi)\frac{d\phi}{dx} \qquad \frac{d(\cos(\phi))}{dx} = -\sin(\phi)\frac{d\phi}{dx}$$

$$\frac{d(\tan(\phi))}{dx} = \sec^2(\phi)\frac{d\phi}{dx} \qquad \frac{d(\sec(\phi))}{dx} = \sec(\phi)\tan(\phi)\frac{d\phi}{dx}$$

A.3   Matrix algebra

A.3.1   The matrix transpose

The transpose $\mathbf{A}^T$ of an $m \times n$ matrix $\mathbf{A}$ is obtained by writing the rows of $\mathbf{A}$, in order, as columns. In a square matrix, the transpose swaps the terms across the right-to-left diagonal.

$$\mathbf{A} = \begin{bmatrix} x \\ y \\ z \\ 1 \end{bmatrix} \qquad \mathbf{A}^T = [x \ y \ z \ 1]$$

$$\mathbf{A} = \begin{bmatrix} a_{11} & a_{12} & a_{13} & a_{14} \\ a_{21} & a_{22} & a_{23} & a_{24} \\ a_{31} & a_{32} & a_{33} & a_{34} \\ a_{41} & a_{42} & a_{43} & a_{44} \end{bmatrix} \qquad \mathbf{A}^T = \begin{bmatrix} a_{11} & a_{21} & a_{31} & a_{41} \\ a_{12} & a_{22} & a_{32} & a_{42} \\ a_{13} & a_{23} & a_{33} & a_{43} \\ a_{14} & a_{24} & a_{34} & a_{44} \end{bmatrix}$$

Thus, the transpose transforms element (row, column) to element (column, row).

Note: Most work in robotics will be done with square matrices (4×4) and vectors (4×1). Occasionally 2×2 matrices will be used in this book for simplicity of presentation, because the techniques are the same as for 4×4 matrices.

A.3.2   Identity (unity) matrix

$\mathbf{I}_n$ is an $n \times n$ unity matrix, where:

$$a_{ij} = 0, \qquad i \neq j$$
$$a_{ji} = 1, \qquad i = j$$

$$\mathbf{I}_n = \begin{bmatrix} 1 & 0 & 0 & 0 \\ 0 & 1 & 0 & 0 \\ 0 & 0 & 1 & 0 \\ 0 & 0 & 0 & 1 \end{bmatrix}$$

The right-to-left diagonal is one and all other elements are zero. Also, the transpose of a unity matrix is a unity matrix.

$$\mathbf{I}_n^T = \mathbf{I}_n$$

A.3.3   Matrix multiplication

Two matrices of the same order can be added, or subtracted, by adding, or subtracting, the corresponding elements.

$$\begin{bmatrix} a_{11} & a_{12} \\ a_{21} & a_{22} \end{bmatrix} + \begin{bmatrix} b_{11} & b_{12} \\ b_{21} & b_{22} \end{bmatrix} = \begin{bmatrix} a_{11} + b_{11} & a_{12} + b_{12} \\ a_{21} + b_{21} & a_{22} + b_{22} \end{bmatrix}$$

If a matrix is multiplied by a scalar, every element of the matrix is multiplied by that scalar.

$$k \times \mathbf{A} = [ka_{ij}]$$

$$k \times \begin{bmatrix} a_{11} & a_{12} \\ a_{21} & a_{22} \end{bmatrix} = \begin{bmatrix} ka_{11} & ka_{12} \\ ka_{21} & ka_{22} \end{bmatrix}$$

Two matrices (**A** and **B**) can be multiplied (**C**=**A** x **B**, where x is called the *cross product*) if the number of rows in **B** is equal to the number of columns in **A**. If this is satisfied then:

$$c_{ij} = a_{i1}b_{1j} + a_{i2}b_{2j} + \ldots + a_{in}b_{nj}$$

This equation is the inner product of the ith row of matrix **A** and the jth column of matrix **B**.

$$\mathbf{C} = \mathbf{A} \times \mathbf{B} = \begin{bmatrix} a_{11} & a_{12} \\ a_{21} & a_{22} \end{bmatrix} \times \begin{bmatrix} b_{11} & b_{12} \\ b_{21} & b_{22} \end{bmatrix}$$

$$= \begin{bmatrix} a_{11}b_{11} + a_{12}b_{21} & a_{11}b_{12} + a_{12}b_{22} \\ a_{21}b_{11} + a_{22}b_{21} & a_{21}b_{12} + a_{22}b_{22} \end{bmatrix}$$

In general $\mathbf{A} \times \mathbf{B} \neq \mathbf{B} \times \mathbf{A}$.

A.3.4   Matrix inversion

In matrix algebra, division is not defined, and the reciprocal of a matrix does not exist. However, an inverse matrix $\mathbf{A}^{-1}$, where $\mathbf{A}\mathbf{A}^{-1} = \mathbf{I}$, will exist if matrix **A** is square and it is regular (nonsingular) – that is, the column vectors or the row vectors are linearly independent.

Given the equations of two intersecting straight lines, solve for x and y.

$$a_1x + b_1y = c_1 \qquad a_2x + b_2y = c_2$$

Multiply the first equation by b_2, multiply the second equation by $-b_1$, and add the two equations to solve for x (we can solve for y in a similar way).

$$(a_1 b_2 - a_2 b_1)x = c_1 b_2 - c_2 b_1$$

$$x = \frac{c_1 b_2 - c_2 b_1}{a_1 b_2 - a_2 b_1} \quad \text{and} \quad y = \frac{c_2 a_1 - c_1 a_2}{a_1 b_2 - a_2 b_1}$$

Note: If the denominator is zero then we have parallel lines, and we either have an infinite number of solutions (redundancy) in the case where the lines coincide, or we have no solution (a singularity).

The above equations for two straight lines can be expressed in matrix form:

$$\begin{bmatrix} a_1 & b_1 \\ a_2 & b_2 \end{bmatrix} \begin{bmatrix} x \\ y \end{bmatrix} = \begin{bmatrix} c_1 \\ c_2 \end{bmatrix}$$

if we premultiply both sides by

$$\begin{bmatrix} a_1 & b_1 \\ a_2 & b_2 \end{bmatrix}^{-1}$$

then

$$\begin{bmatrix} x \\ y \end{bmatrix} = \begin{bmatrix} a_1 & b_1 \\ a_2 & b_2 \end{bmatrix}^{-1} \begin{bmatrix} c_1 \\ c_2 \end{bmatrix}$$

and from the above solutions

$$\begin{bmatrix} x \\ y \end{bmatrix} = \frac{1}{a_1 b_2 - a_2 b_1} \begin{bmatrix} b_2 & -b_1 \\ -a_2 & a_1 \end{bmatrix} \begin{bmatrix} c_1 \\ c_2 \end{bmatrix}$$

$$= \frac{1}{\text{determinant}} \begin{bmatrix} \text{matrix of} \\ \text{cofactors} \end{bmatrix}^{\text{T}} \begin{bmatrix} c_1 \\ c_2 \end{bmatrix}$$

Thus $\mathbf{A}^{-1}$ is

$$\frac{1}{\text{determinant}} \begin{bmatrix} \text{matrix of} \\ \text{cofactors} \end{bmatrix}^{\text{T}} = \frac{1}{|\mathbf{A}|} \begin{bmatrix} \Delta_{11} & \Delta_{12} \\ \Delta_{21} & \Delta_{22} \end{bmatrix} = \begin{bmatrix} a_{11}^{-1} & a_{12}^{-1} \\ a_{21}^{-1} & a_{22}^{-1} \end{bmatrix}$$

where

$$a_{ij}^{-1} = \frac{\Delta_{ij}}{|\mathbf{A}|}$$

and

$$\Delta_{ij} = \text{the cofactor of element } a_{ij} = (-1)^{i+j}|\mathbf{A}_{ij}|$$

where $|\mathbf{A}|$ is the determinant of $\mathbf{A}$ and $\mathbf{A}_{ij}$ is the submatrix which results when the ith row and the jth column are removed from the matrix $\mathbf{A}$.

Matrix inversion of a 4×4 matrix (the case of interest in robotics) involves the calculation of the determinant of the matrix and the cofactors.

$$\mathbf{A}^{-1} = \frac{1}{|\mathbf{A}|}\begin{bmatrix} \Delta_{11} & \Delta_{12} & \Delta_{13} & \Delta_{14} \\ \Delta_{21} & \Delta_{22} & \Delta_{23} & \Delta_{24} \\ \Delta_{31} & \Delta_{32} & \Delta_{33} & \Delta_{34} \\ \Delta_{41} & \Delta_{42} & \Delta_{43} & \Delta_{44} \end{bmatrix}^T = \frac{1}{|\mathbf{A}|}\begin{bmatrix} \Delta_{11} & \Delta_{21} & \Delta_{31} & \Delta_{41} \\ \Delta_{12} & \Delta_{22} & \Delta_{32} & \Delta_{42} \\ \Delta_{13} & \Delta_{23} & \Delta_{33} & \Delta_{43} \\ \Delta_{14} & \Delta_{24} & \Delta_{34} & \Delta_{44} \end{bmatrix}$$

$$|\mathbf{A}| = a_{i1}\Delta_{i1} + a_{i2}\Delta_{i2} + a_{i3}\Delta_{i3} + a_{i4}\Delta_{i4} = \text{sum of 24 products } (!n$$
where $n = 4$)

$$\mathbf{A}_{11} = \begin{bmatrix} x & x & x & x \\ x & a_{22} & a_{23} & a_{24} \\ x & a_{32} & a_{33} & a_{34} \\ x & a_{42} & a_{43} & a_{44} \end{bmatrix} = \begin{bmatrix} a_{22} & a_{23} & a_{24} \\ a_{32} & a_{33} & a_{34} \\ a_{42} & a_{43} & a_{44} \end{bmatrix}$$

$$\Delta_{11} = (-1)^2|\mathbf{A}_{11}| = a_{22}\Delta_{22} + a_{23}\Delta_{23} + a_{24}\Delta_{24}$$

$$\Delta_{22} = \begin{bmatrix} a_{33} & a_{34} \\ a_{43} & a_{44} \end{bmatrix} = a_{33}\Delta_{33} + a_{34}\Delta_{34} = a_{33}a_{43} - a_{34}a_{44}$$

There are a number of algorithms for calculating the inverse of a matrix. In one example, discussed in the text, the presence of zero elements in the 4×4 matrix reduces the number of product terms, and hence, simplifies the calculation. Gaussian elimination is even more efficient.

A.4 Vectors

A vector is defined geometrically as a physical quantity characterized by a magnitude and a direction in space. In drawings, a vector is represented as an arrow whose length and direction represent the magnitude and direction of the vector as in Figure A.4.

The equation of a line joining points $A(x_1, y_1)$ and $B(x_2, y_2)$ is:

$$\frac{x - x_1}{x_2 - x_1} = \frac{y - y_1}{y_2 - y_1}$$

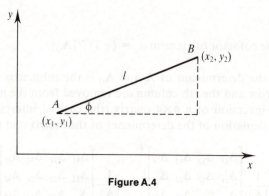

Figure A.4

The line, of length l, has x and y components:

$$x_2 - x_1 = l \sin(\phi) \quad \text{and} \quad y_2 - y_1 = l \cos(\phi)$$

This line has a direction from A to B at an angle ϕ to the x axis. If we consider the directed segment (AB) to be a displacement, or carrier, of the point A to the point B, it is appropriate to call the line a vector. Physically, a vector is a quantity having both magnitude and direction. A point vector is the displacement of a point from the origin to the position of the point in space (also referred to as a localized vector).

$$v = ai + bj + ck$$

where i, j, and k are unit vectors (of length 1) along the x, y, and z coordinate axes. These vectors can be represented as column matrices:

$$v = [i, j, k][a, b, c]^{\text{T}} = \begin{bmatrix} 1 & 0 & 0 \\ 0 & 1 & 0 \\ 0 & 0 & 1 \end{bmatrix} \begin{bmatrix} a \\ b \\ c \end{bmatrix}$$

where T = transpose of a matrix. This is shown in Figure A.5.

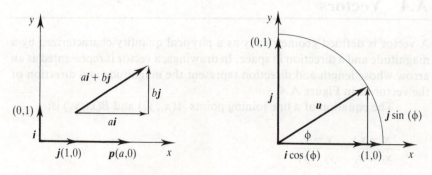

Figure A.5

If u is a unit vector obtained by rotating the unit vector i through an angle ϕ in the positive direction, then:

$$u_x = i\cos(\phi) = \cos(\phi), \text{ and } u_y = j\sin(\phi) = \sin(\phi)$$

The vector at the origin is the null vector $[0\ \ 0\ \ 0]^T$.

A.4.1 Vectors in three dimensions

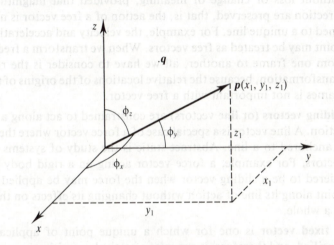

Figure A.6

Two vectors $p(x_1, y_1, z_1)$ and $q(x_2, y_2, z_2)$ may be added to form a new vector $r(x_1 + x_2, y_1 + y_2, z_1 + z_2)$, and may be subtracted to form a new vector $s(x_1 - x_2, y_1 - y_2, z_1 - z_2)$. The angle between these vectors can be found from their *inner* (or *dot*) *product*.

$$\|a\|\|b\|\cos(\phi) = x_1x_2 + y_1y_2 + z_1z_2 = p \cdot q$$

where the magnitude of $a = \|a\| = \sqrt{x_1^2 + y_1^2 + z_1^2}$, and

$$\cos(\phi) = \frac{x_1x_2 + y_1y_2 + z_1z_2}{\sqrt{(x_1^2 + y_1^2 + z_1^2)(x_2^2 + y_2^2 + z_2^2)}}$$

If the vectors p and q are parallel then $\phi = 0°$, and $p \cdot q = 1$. If the vectors p and q are perpendicular then $\phi = 90°$, and $p \cdot q = 0$. The angles between the vector and the positive direction of the axes can be found from the direction cosines of the vector:

$$\cos(\phi_x) = \frac{x_1}{\|p\|} \qquad \cos(\phi_y) = \frac{p_1}{\|p\|} \qquad \cos(\phi_z) = \frac{z_1}{\|p\|}$$

A.4.2   Classes of vectors

Vectors can be characterized with four parameters: magnitude, direction, resultant effect, and line of action. Two vectors are *equal* if they have the same magnitude and direction. Two vectors are *equivalent* in a certain capacity if they produce the same effect in that capacity. Physically, there are three classes of vectors: free vectors, sliding vectors, and fixed vectors:

- **Free vectors** are vectors which can be positioned anywhere in space without loss or change of meaning, provided that magnitude and direction are preserved, that is, the action of a free vector is not confined to a unique line. For example, the velocity and acceleration of a point may be treated as free vectors. When we transform a free vector from one frame to another, all we have to consider is the rotation transformation, because the relative locations of the origins of the two frames is not important with a free vector.

- **Sliding vectors** (or **line** vectors) are constrained to act along a line of action. A line vector is a special case of a force vector where the vector is anchored to a line. Abstract static is the study of systems of line vectors. For example, a force vector acting on a rigid body is considered to be a sliding vector when the force may be applied at any point along its line of action without changing its effects on the body as a whole.

- A **fixed vector** is one for which a unique point of application is specified, and therefore, it occupies a particular position in space. For example, a position vector is fixed in space and, hence, its components depend on the frame of reference.

  A position vector is a special case of a free vector where the origin of the vector is anchored to a fixed point. Cartesian co-ordinate geometry is the study of systems of vectors having a common reference point or origin. When we transform a fixed vector from one frame to another, both the translation between the origins must be included as well as the rotations between the frames.

A.4.3   Vector cross product

The product (*a x b*) of two vectors *a* and *b* is called the **vector cross product**. Vectors *a* and *b* determine a plane, and *n* is defined to be a unit vector perpendicular to the plane, whose direction is determined according to the right-hand rule: hold your right hand open and vertical, point your fingers in the direction of vector *a*, close your fingers by rotating them in the direction from vector *a* to vector *b*. Now your thumb points in the direction of the normal vector *n*.

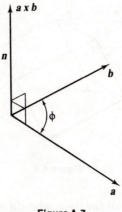

Figure A.7

Magnitude of $n = \|a \times b\| = \|a\| \, \|b\| \, \sin(\phi)$

$\qquad\qquad$ = area of the parallelogram defined by a and b.

where

$\qquad \|\mathbf{a}\|$ = magnitude of **a**

$\qquad\qquad = \sqrt{a_1^2 + a_2^2 + a_3^2}$

Thus, the vector cross product of a and b is the vector $a \times b$ with direction n and magnitude $\|a \times b\|$, and $b \times a = -a \times b$. Also, $a \times (b + c) = a \times b + a \times c$ and $a \times a = \phi$.

$\quad$ If $a = a_1 i + a_2 j + a_3 k$ and $b = b_1 i + b_2 j + b_3 k$ where i, j, and k are unit vectors then

$$a \times b = \begin{bmatrix} i & j & k \\ a_1 & a_2 & a_3 \\ b_1 & b_2 & b_3 \end{bmatrix} = a_2 b_3 i + a_3 b_1 j + a_1 b_2 k - a_2 b_1 k - a_3 b_2 i - a_1 b_3 j$$

$$= (a_2 b_3 - a_3 b_2)i + (a_3 b_1 - a_1 b_3)j + (a_1 b_2 - a_2 b_1)k$$

That is, by expanding the determinant, we get the vector cross product.

A.4.4 Product of three or more vectors

The product $(a \times b) \cdot c$ is called the **triple scalar product**. Geometrically, the triple scalar product is the volume of the parallelepiped determined by the vectors a, b, and c.

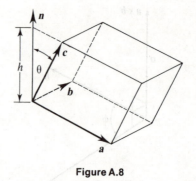

Figure A.8

$|n| = |a \times b|$ = area of the base, where $n = a \times b$ = normal to the base of the box.

$|c|\cos(\theta) = h$ = altitude of the box ($+$ or $-$).

Thus, $(a \times b) \cdot c = n \cdot c = |n| \, |c| \cos(\theta)$ = area of the box.

If c is a unit vector then $(a \times b) \cdot c$ is the area of the orthogonal projection of the parallelogram determined by a and b onto a plane whose unit normal is c.

$$(a \times b) \cdot c = (b \times c) \cdot a = (c \times a) \cdot b$$

$$(b \times c) \cdot a = a \cdot (b \times c) \text{ – dot product is commutative.}$$

Thus, $(a \times b) \cdot c = a \cdot (b \times c)$

$$a \cdot (b \times c) = \begin{bmatrix} a_1 & a_2 & a_3 \\ b_1 & b_2 & b_3 \\ c_1 & c_2 & c_3 \end{bmatrix} = a_1(b_2 c_3 - c_2 b_3) + a_2(b_3 c_1 - c_3 b_1) + a_3(b_1 c_2 - c_1 b_2)$$

The product $(a \times b) \times c$ is called the **triple vector product**, and produces a resultant vector r which lies in the plane defined by a and b.

$(a \times b) \times c$ is not generally equal to $a \times (b \times c)$.

$(a \times b) \times c = (a \cdot c) - a(b \cdot c) = r$

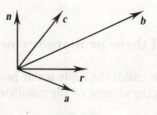

Figure A.9

$n = a \times b$ is a vector perpendicular to the plane containing *an* and *b*. The resultant vector $r = n \times c$, and, as *r* is perpendicular to *n*, it must lie in the plane defined by *a* and *b*.

$$a \cdot c = |a|\,|c|\,\cos\phi, \qquad \text{where } \phi_1 = \text{angle between } a \text{ and } c.$$

$$b \cdot c = |b|\,|c|\,\cos\phi, \qquad \text{where } \phi_2 = \text{angle between } b \text{ and } c.$$

$$r = (a \times b) \times c = |a|\,|c|\,\cos\phi_1 b = |b|\,|c|\,\cos\phi_2 a.$$

A.5 Typical equations encountered in inverse kinematic solutions

These are taken from La Brooy, 1986.

- *Class 1* When sine and cosine are both uniquely defined in the equations:

    If $aS = f$ and $bC = g$ then $\phi = \text{atan2}(fb, ga)$

    where S = sine, C = cosine, and *f* and *g* are expressions that do not include other angles. Note, if $a = 0$, we have a singularity.

- *Class 2* When sine and cosine are not uniquely defined in the equations (they can not be moved to one side of the equations):

    If $-aS + bC = 0$ then

    - add aS to both sides and divide by aC to get $\phi = \text{atan2}(b, a)$, or
    - subtract bC from both sides and divide by aC to get $\phi = \text{atan2}(-b, -a)$.

    Note: We have two valid solutions 180° apart, a redundancy.

- *Class 3* When sine and cosine are not uniquely defined in the equations, and we have the general case of class 2:

    If $aC_\theta + bS_\theta = d$ then:

    1. divide both sides by $\sqrt{a^2 + b^2}$ to get:

    $$[a/\sqrt{(a^2 + b^2)}]C_\theta + [b/\sqrt{(a^2 + b^2)}]S_\theta = d/\sqrt{(a^2 + b^2)}$$

    2. The coefficients of C_θ and S_θ may be considered to form a right-angled triangle whose sides are *a* and *b* and whose hypotenuse is $\sqrt{a^2+b^2}$.

    3. If the angle between side *a* and the hypotenuse is ϕ then

        (a) $C_\phi = a/\sqrt{(a^2 + b^2)}$, and
        (b) $S_\phi = b/\sqrt{(a^2 + b^2)}$

4. If we substitute these into our equation, we get

$$C_\phi C_\theta + S_\phi S_\theta = \frac{d}{\sqrt{a^2 + b^2}} = \cos(\theta - \phi)$$

5. Using the trigonometric identities:

$$S^2 + C^2 = 1 \quad \text{and} \quad \sin(\theta - \phi) = \sin(\theta)\cos(\phi) - \cos(\theta)\sin(\phi)$$

and substituting for $\cos(\theta - \phi)$ we get:

$$\sin(\theta - \phi) = \pm \sqrt{1 - \cos^2(\theta - \phi)} = \pm \sqrt{(1 - d^2/(a^2 + b^2)})$$

which on simplification, becomes:

$$\sin(\theta - \phi) = \pm \sqrt{(a^2 + b^2 - d^2)}/\sqrt{(a^2 + b^2)}$$

6. Using the trigonometric identities:

$$\theta = (\theta - \phi) + \phi \text{ and}$$
$$\cos(\theta + \phi) = \cos(\theta)\cos(\phi) - \sin(\theta)\sin(\phi)$$

and taking the cosine of both sides of the first identity, we get:

$$\cos(\theta) = \cos(\theta - \phi)\cos(\phi) - \sin(\theta - \phi)\sin(\phi)$$

Now, if we substitute for $\cos(\phi)$, $\sin(\phi)$, $\cos(\theta - \phi)$ and $\sin(\theta - \phi)$, we get:

$$C_\theta = ad/(a^2 + b^2) - \pm \sqrt{(b(a^2 + b^2 - d^2)/(a^2 + b^2))}$$

7. By reorganizing our original equation to form

$$S_\theta = (d - aC_\theta)/b$$

and substituting for $\cos(\theta)$, we get

$$S_\theta = db \pm a\sqrt{(a^2 + b^2 - d^2)}/(a^2 + b^2)$$

8. Finally

$$\theta = \text{atan2}(S_\theta, C_\theta)$$

where if $a = b = 0$ then θ is indeterminate, and
if $\tan^{-1}(\theta)$ is greater than 1, then $\theta = \pi/2 - \text{atan2}(C_\theta, S_\theta)$.

- *Class 4* When we have a pair of equations involving two angles of the form:

$$a\,S_{23} + b\,C_{23} + d\,C_2 = f$$
$$-a\,C_{23} + b\,S_{23} + d\,S_2 = g$$

If we square and add these two equations we get an equation of the form:

$$h = l\,S_3 + m\,C_3$$

and then we can proceed as in class 3.

- *Class 5* When we have a pair of equations involving two angles of the form:

$$a\,C_{23} + b\,C_2 = f$$
$$a\,S_{23} + b\,S_2 = g$$

We can solve them for both θ_3 and θ_2:

1. If we square and add these two equations we get an equation of the form:

    $$f^2 + g^2 = a^2 + b^2 + 2ab\,C_3$$

    from which C_3 can be obtained, and S_3 can be found using the trigonometric identity: $S^2 + C^2 = 1$ and $\theta_3 = \text{atan2}(S_3, C_3)$
    Note: problem of $f = p_x$ and $g = p_y$ (type 1 two link) that sign disappears on square.
    To select which quadrant:

    (a) carry signs along,
    (b) plug values back into equation.

2. We can solve for θ_2 by expanding C_{23} and S_{23} and eliminating S_2 and C_2 in turn, leaving us with unique expressions in S_2 and C_2, which are in class 1 form.

- *Class 6* When we have a pair of equations involving two angles of the form:

$$a\,C_{23} - b\,S_{23} = f$$
$$a\,S_{23} + b\,C_{23} = g$$

They may be solved simultaneously to obtain:

$$S_{23} = (ag - bf)/(a^2 - b^2)$$
$$C_{23} = (af + bg)/(a^2 - b^2)$$

giving

$$\theta_{23} = \text{atan2}(S_{23}, C_{23}).$$

References and Further Reading

Robotics books

Abelson, H. and di Sessa, A. A. (1981). *Turtle Geometry – The Computer as a Medium for Exploring Mathematics*. Massachusetts: MIT Press.

Andreasen, M. M. *et al.* (1983). *Design for Assembly*. Berlin: Springer-Verlag.

Andersson, R. L. (1988). *A Robot Ping-Pong Player*. Massachusetts: MIT Press.

Angeles, J. (1982). *Spatial Kinematic Chains*. Berlin: Springer-Verlag.

Arbib, M. A. and Hanson, A. R. (eds) (1987). *Vision, Brain and Cooperative Computation*. Massachusetts: MIT Press.

Asada, H. and Slotline, J. J. E. (1985). *Robot Analysis and Control*. Chichester: John Wiley and Sons.

Asada, H. and Youcef-Toumi, K. (1986). *Direct-Drive Robot*. Massachusetts: MIT Press.

Asimov, I. and Frenkel, K. A. (1985). *Robots: Machines in Man's Image*. Harmony Books.

Ayres, R. U. and Miller, S. M. (1984). *Robotics: Applications and Social Implications*. Ballinger Publishing Co.

Ball, R. S. (1900). *A Treatise on the Theory of Screws*. Cambridge: Cambridge University Press.

Beggs, J. S. (1983). *Kinematics*. Berlin: Springer-Verlag.

Benni, G. and Hackwood, S. (eds) (1985). *Recent Advances in Robotics*. Chichester: John Wiley and Sons.

Besl, P. J. (1988). *Surfaces in Range Image Understanding*. Berlin: Springer-Verlag.

Blume, C. and Jakob, W. (1986). *Programming Languages for Industrial Robots*. Berlin: Springer-Verlag.

Bonnett, K. *et al. The Everyone Can Build a Robot Book*. Englewood Cliffs: Simon and Schuster.

Boothroyd, G., Poli, C. and Murch, L. E. (1982). *Automatic Assembly*. New York: Marcel Dekker.

Brady, M., Hollerbach, J. M., Johnson, T. L., Lozano-Perez, T. and Mason, M. T. (eds) (1982). *Robot Motion Planning and Control*. Massachusetts: MIT Press.

Brady, M. and Paul, R. (eds) (1984). *Robotics Research, The First International Symposium*. Massachusetts: MIT Press.

Chiyokura, H. (1988). *Solid Modelling with Designbase: Theory and Implementation*. Reading MA: Addison-Wesley.

Coiffet, P. and Chirouze, M. (1983). *An Introduction to Robot Technology*. London: Kogan Page.

Coiffet, P. (1983). *Robot Technology Volume 1: Modelling and Control*. London: Kogan Page.

Craig, J. J. (1986). *Introduction to Robotics: Mechanics and Control*. Reading MA: Addison-Wesley.

Critchlow, A. J. (1985). *Introduction to Robotics*. New York: Macmillan.

Cutkosky, M. R. (1985). *Robotic Grasping and Fine Manipulation*. Boston: Kluwer Academic Publishers.

Dorf, R. C. (1983). *Robots and Automated Manufacture*. Reston, VA: Reston Publishing Co.

Duffy, J. (1980). *Analysis of Mechanisms and Robot Manipulators*. London: Edward Arnold.

Fu, K. S., Gonzalez, R. C. and Lee, C. S. G. (1987). *Robotics: Control, Sensors, Vision and Intelligence*. New York: McGraw-Hill.

Gevarter, W. B. (1985). *Intelligent Machines: An Introductory Perspective of Artificial Intelligence and Robotics*. Englewood Cliffs NJ: Prentice-Hall.

Gorla, B. and Renaud, M. (1984). *Robot Manipulateurs*. Toulouse: Cepadues-Editions.

Hartley, J. (1983). *Robots at Work: A Practical Guide for Engineers and Managers*. London: IFS Publications.

Hawk, G. L. and Strimaitis, J. (1984). *Advances in Laboratory Automation – Robotics*. Hopkinton, MA: Zymark.

Henson, H. (1981). *Robots*. Kingfisher.

Hoekstra, R. L. (1986). *Robotics and Automated Systems*. Rotterdam: North-Holland.

Holland, J. M. (1983). *Basic Robotic Concepts*. Howard Sams.

Horn, B. K. P. (1986). *Robot Vision*. Boston: MIT Press.

Kapur, D. and Mundy, J. L. (eds) (1989). *Geometric Reasoning*. Boston: MIT Press.

Kato, I. (1982). *Mechanical Hands Illustrated*. Berlin: Springer-Verlag.

Khatib, O., Craig, J. J. and Lozano-Perez, T. (eds) (1988). *The Robotics Review 1*. Boston: MIT Press.

Lee, C. S. G., Gonzalez, R. C. and Fu, K. S. (1983). *Tutorial on Robotics*. (First edition) New York: IEEE Computer Society.

Malone, R. (1978). *The Robot Book*. New York: Harcourt, Brace and Jovanovich.

Marsh, P. (1985). *Robots*. London: Salamander Books.

Mason, M. T. and Salisbury, J. K. (1985). *Robot Hands and the Mechanics of Manipulation*. Boston: MIT Press.

Mayhew, J. E. W. and Frisby, J. P. (1989). *3D Model Recognition from Stereoscopic Cues*. Boston: MIT Press.

Minsky, M. (ed) (1985). *Robotics*. Omni Press.

Morris, B. (1985). *The World of Robots*. New York: Gallery Books.

Nagle, R. (1984). *First World Conference on Robotics Research – The Next Five Years and Beyond*. SME.

Nof, S. Y. (ed) (1985). *Handbook of Industrial Robotics*. Chichester: John Wiley and Sons.

Paul, R. P. (1981). *Robot Manipulators – Mathematics, Programming, and Control*. Boston: MIT Press.

Popov, E. (ed) (1982). *Modern Robot Engineering*. Moscow: MIR Publishers.

Pugh, A. (1983). *Robotic Technology*. Peter Peregrinus Ltd.

Raibert, M. H. (1986). *Legged Robots that Balance*.

Boston: MIT Press.

Scott, P. B. (1986). *The Robotics Revolution*. Oxford: Basil Blackwell.

Snyder, W. E. (1985). *Industrial Robots: Computer Interfacing and Control*. Englewood Cliffs NJ: Prentice-Hall.

Song, S.-M. and Waldron, K. J. (1988). *Machines that Walk*. Boston: MIT Press.

Stone, H. W. (1987). *Kinematic Modelling, Identification and Control of Robotic Manipulators*. Boston: Kluwer.

Todd, D. J. (1985). *Walking Machines – An Introduction to Legged Robots*. New York: Chapman and Hall.

Usher, M. (1986). *Sensors and Transducers*. London: Macmillan.

Wolovich, W. A. (1987). *Robotics: Basic Analysis and Design*. New York: Holt, Rinehart and Winston.

Preface

McKerrow, P. J. and Zelinski, A. (1985). 'Developing a Robotics Educational-Laboratory', *Australian Computer Science Communications*, **7**, 1, pp. 3.1–3.10.

McKerrow, P. J. (1986). 'Robotics, An Academic Discipline?', *Robotics*, **2**, 3, pp. 267–274.

Chapter 1

Adams, J. A. (1985). Probing beneath the sea. *IEEE Spectrum*. **22**, 4, pp. 55–64.

Adler, J. and Carey, J. (1982). Enigmas of Evolution. *Newsweek*, March 29, pp. 42–47.

Anderson, J. K. and Coffin, H. G. (1977). *Fossils in Focus, Earth Science Series*, Christian Free University Curriculum, Zondervan.

Bejczy, A. K. (1980). Sensors, Controls, and Man-Machine Interface for Advanced Teleoperation. *Science*. **208**, 4450, pp. 1327–1335.

Bell, T. E. (1985). Robots in the Home: Promises, Promises. *IEEE Spectrum*. **22**, 5, pp. 51–55.

Bortz, A. B. (1985). Joseph Engelberger: The father of Industrial Robots reflects on his Progeny, *Robotics Age*, **7**, 4, pp. 15–22.

Broad, and Wade (1982). *Betrayers of the Truth*, New York: Simon and Schuster.

Brady, M. (1985). Artificial Intelligence and Robotics, *Artificial Intelligence*. **26**, pp. 79–121.

Clapp, N. W. (1982). Three Laws of Industrial Robotics. *Robotics Today*, 1982 Annual Edition, SME, pp. 16–19.

Clarke, P. T. (1985). Automatic Break up of Pork Carcasses. *Proceedings of AgriMation* **1**, ASAE, pp. 183–189.

Cook, G. E. (1983). Robotic Arc Welding: Research in Sensory Feedback Control, *IEEE Transactions on Industrial Electronics*, **IE-30**, 3, pp. 252–268.

Cooley, M. J. (1981). Some Social Aspects of CAD, *Computers in Industry*, North-Holland, **12**, pp. 209–215.

Cichowicz, R. (1985). Pittman's Executive Perspective. *ROBOT/X News*, **4**, 5, p. 13.

Cutkosky, M. R., Fussell, P. S. and Milligan, R. (1984). *Precision Flexible Manufacturing Cells Within a Manufacturing System*, CMU-RI-TR-84-12, 42 pages.

Darwin, C. (1859). *On The Origin of Species*. (A Facsimile of the First Edition) Cambridge MA: Harvard University Press, 1966.

D'Esnon, A. G. (1985). Robotic Harvesting of Apples, *Proceedings of AgriMation* **1**, ASAE, pp. 210–214.

Deutch, S. and Heer, E. (1972). Manipulator Systems Extend Man's Capabilities in Space. *Astronautics and Aeronautics*, June, pp. 30–41.

Dewdney, A. K. (1985). Computer Recreations – A circuitous odyssey from Robotropolis to the electronic gates of Silicon Valley. *Scientific American*, July, **253**, 1.

Drucker, P. (1984). quoted in: The Logical Location. *IEEE Spectrum*, **21**, 18, p. 80B.

Ernst, H. A. (1961). *MH-1, A Computer-operated Mechanical Hand*. Doctor of Science Thesis, MIT.

Feirer, J. L. and Tatro, E. E. (1961). *Machine Tool Metalworking*. Maidenhead: McGraw-Hill.

Fulsang, E. J. (1985). AI and Autonomous Military Robots. *Unmanned Systems*, **3**, 4, pp. 8–16.

Graham, W. B. (1972). RMVs in Aerial Warfare. *Astronautics and Aeronautics*, **10**, 5, pp. 36–43.

de Garis, H. (1989). What if AI Succeeds? The Rise of the Twenty-First Century Artilect, *AI Magazine*, **10**, 2, pp. 16–22.

Hanright, J. (1984). Selecting Your First Arc Welding Robot – A Guide to Equipment and Features. *Welding Journal*, **63**, 11, pp. 41–45.

Hillier, M. (1988). *Automata and Mechanical Toys*, London: Bloomsbury.

Hofstadter, D. R. (1979). *Godel, Escher, Bach: An Eternal Golden Braid*. New York: Basic Books.

Hoyle, F. and Wickramasinghe, C. (1981). *Space Tra-*

vellers: The Bringers of Life. Cardiff: University College Cardiff Press.

Hwang, H. and Sistler, F. E. (1985). The Implementation of a Robotic Manipulator on a Mechanical Transplanting Machine. *Proceedings of AgriMation* **1**, ASAE, pp. 173–182.

Jarvis, R. (1987). Robots on Hold. *The Australian Computer Magazine*, September 8th, pp. 30–32.

Jurgen, R. K. (1986). MAP and TOP combine forces in an awesome display at Autofact. *The Institute*, IEEE, January, p. 9.

Kehoe, E. J. (1984). Robots and Lasers: A perfect Match. *Robotics Today*. June, pp. 63–66.

Khosla, P. K., Neuman, C. P. and Prinz, F. B. (1984). *An Algorithm for Seam Tracking Applications*. CMU-RI-TR-84-6.

Livingston, D. (1985). Sensors Guide the Way for Machine Tools, *High Technology*, June, p. 49.

Lozano-Perez, T. (1976). *The Design of a Mechanical Assembly System*. MIT, AI Memo 397.

Lund, T. and Kahler, S. (1984). Product Design for Automatic Assembly. In Heginbotham W. B. (ed) *Programmable Assembly*. London: IFS Publications, pp. 127–141.

Lyons, Sir H., F.R.S. (1968). *The Royal Society 1660–1940: A History of its Administration and its Charters*, Greenwood Press, NY.

Martin, H. L. and Hamel, W. R. (1984). Joining Teleoperation with Robotics for Remote Manipulation in Hostile Environments, *Proceedings of ROBOTS 8*, SME, pp. 9.1–9.17.

Minsky, M. (1985). Our Roboticized Future. In: Minsky M. (ed) *Robotics*, Omni Press, pp. 287–307.

Moore, J. W. (1972). Toward Remotely Controlled Planetary Rovers. *Astronautics and Aeronautics*, June, pp. 42–48.

Moore, T. (1984). Robots Join the Nuclear Workforce. *EPRI Journal*, **9**, 9, pp. 6–17.

Moravec, H. (1985). The Rovers. In: Minsky M. (ed) *Robotics*, Omni Press, pp. 123–145.

Needham, J. and Pagel, W. (eds) (1940). *Background to Modern Science*. London: Macmillan.

Needham, J. (1969). *The Grand Titration, Science and Society in East and West*. London: Allen and Unwin.

Nevins, J. L. and Whitney, D. E. (1977). Research on Advanced Assembly Automation. *IEEE Computer*, December, pp. 551–565.

Nilsson, N. J. (1984). *Shakey the Robot*. SRI International, Technical Note 323.

Oomen, G. L. and Verbeek, W. J. P. A. (1983). A Real-Time Optical Profile Sensor for Robot Arc Welding. *SPIE*, **449**, pp. 62–71.

Oppenheimer, J. R. (1962). On Science and Culture, *Encounter*, **19**, 4, pp. 3–10.

Papert, S. (1980). *Mindstorms – Children, Computers, and Powerful Ideas*. Brighton: Harvester Press.

Pattis, R. E. (1981). *KAREL the ROBOT: A Gentle Introduction to the Art of Programming*. Chichester: John Wiley and Sons.

Pierson, R. A. (1985). IBM's Automated Material Handling System, *Robotics World*, **3**, 2, pp. 20–23.

Prinz, F. B. and Gunnarsson, K. T. (1984). *Robotic Seam Tracking*. CMU-RI-TR-84-10.

Punnett, R. C. (1938). Forty Years of Evolution Theory. In: Needham J. and Pagel W. (eds) *Background to Modern Science*, London: Macmillan.

Purver, M. (1967). *The Royal Society: Concept and Creation*, MIT Press.

Raia, E. (1985). Helping Machine Tools Help Themselves. *High Technology*, June, pp. 45–48.

Raphael, B. (1976). *The Thinking Computer – Mind Inside Matter*. San Francisco: W. H. Freeman.

Rhodes, F. H. T. (1965). Christianity in a Mechanistic Universe. In: MacKay D. M. (ed) *Christianity in a Mechanistic Universe and other Essays*, Inter-Varsity Press, pp. 11–48.

Rogers M. (1984). Birth of the Killer Robots. *Newsweek*, June 25, p. 51.

Sanderson, A. C. and Perry, G. (1983). Sensor-Based Robotic Assembly Systems: Research and Applications in Electronic Manufacturing, *Proc of the IEEE*, **71**, 7, pp. 856–871.

Schaeffer, F. A. (1968). The God who is there. In: *The Complete Works of Francis A. Schaeffer: A Christian Worldview*, Vol. 1: *A Christian view of Philosophy and Culture*, (1982). Westchester, Illinois: Crossway Books.

Schaeffer, F. A. (1976). How Should We Then Live. In: *The Complete Works of Francis A. Schaeffer: A Christian Worldview*. Vol. 5: *A Christian view of the West*. (1982), Westchester, Illinois: Crossway Books.

Scheckley, R. (1985). Scenes from the Twenty-first Century, in: Minsky M. (ed) *Robotics*, New York: Omni Press, pp. 265–285.

Schlussel, K. (1983). Robotics and Artificial Intelligence Across the Atlantic and Pacific. *IEEE Transactions on Industrial Electronics*. **IE-30**, 3, pp. 244–251.

Sevila, F. (1985). A Robot to Prune the Grapevine, *Proceedings of AgriMation* 1, ASAE, pp. 190–199.

Shaiken, H. (1986). The Human Impact of Automation. *IEEE Control Systems Magazine*, **6**, 6, pp. 3–6.

Simon, H. A. (1983). Perspectives on Computer Science. *Computing Reviews*, **24**, 6, (front cover).

Soska, G. V. (1985). Third Generation Robots: Their Definition, Characteristics, and Applications, *Robotics Age*. **7**, 5, pp. 14–16.

Stebbins, G. L. and Ayala, F. J. (1985). The Evolution of Darwinism. *Scientific American*, **253**, 1, pp. 72–82.

Stelzer, E. H. and Moss, R. H. (1985). A Microcomputer-based Control System for a Three-Joint Robot Arm. *IEEE Micro*, **5**, 3, pp. 22–40.

Tomizuka, M., Dornfeld, D. and Purceli, M. (1980). Application of Microcomputers to Automatic Weld Quality Control. *ASME Journal of Dynamic Systems, Measurement and Control*, **102**, June, pp. 62–68.

Townsend, J. J. (1985). Future Military Applications of Unmanned Systems. *Unmanned Systems*, **3**, 4, pp. 21–30.

Trevelyan, G. M. (1942). *English Social History*.

Trevelyan, J. P., Kovesi, P. D. and Ong, M. C. H. (1984). Motion Control for a Sheep-Shearing Robot, *Proceedings 1st ISRR*, MIT Press, pp. 175–190.

Walter, W. G. (1953). *The Living Brain*. New York: W. W. Norton.

Weizenbaum, J. (1983). Once More: The Computer Revolution. *Computing Reviews*, **24**, 5, (front cover).

Whitehead, A. N. (1925). *Science and the Modern World*. New York: Macmillan.

Whitney, D. E. (1969). Resolved Motion Rate Control of Manipulators and Human Prostheses. *IEEE Transactions on Man-Machine Systems*. **MMS-10**, 2, pp. 47–53.

Williams, J. A. (1978). Antique Mechanical Computers. *Byte*, **3** part series, July–September.

Winter, D. (1985). Assembly: Let the Revolution Begin. *Ward's Auto World*, **21**, 6, pp. 42–53.

Chapter 2

Acarnley, P. P. (1987). *Stepping Motors: A Guide to Modern Theory and Practice*. Peter Peregrinis Ltd.

Asada, H. and Youcef-Tomi, K. (1984). Analysis and Design of a Direct Drive Arm with Five-Bar-Link Parallel Drive Mechanism. *Journal of Dynamic Systems, Measurement and Control*, ASME, **106**, 3, pp. 225–230.

Asada, H. and Kanade, T. (1981). *Design of Direct-Drive Mechanical Arms*. CMU Robotics Institute, Technical Report 81-1.

Brown, M. K. (1984). A Controlled Impedance Robot Gripper. *AT&T Technical Journal*, **64**, 4, pp. 937–969.

Carlisle, B. (1983). An Omni-Directional Mobile Robot. In: Rooks, B. (ed) *Developments in Robotics 1983*, IFS, pp. 79–87.

Clark, D. C. (1969). *Selection and Performance Criteria for Electrohydraulic Servodrives*. Moog Technical Bulletin 122.

Dragone, R. V. (1984). Failsafe Brakes Keep Robot Arms in Position. *Robotics World*, December, pp. 20–22.

Hirose, S. (1984). A Study of Design and Control of a Quadruped Walking Vehicle. *The International Journal of Robotics Research*, **3**, 2, pp. 113–133.

Hoekstra, R. L. (1986). *Robotics and Automated Systems*. Rotterdam: North-Holland.

Holland, J. M. (1986). A Mobile Platform for Industrial Research, *Robotics Research Conference*. Scottsdale, Arizona, SME Technical Paper, No. MS86-786, 13 pages.

Jacobsen, S., Wood, J., Knutti, D. F. and Biggers, K. B. (1984). The Utah/M.I.T. Dextrous Hand: Work in Progress, *The International Journal of Robotics Research*, **3**, 4, pp. 21–50.

Kanade, T. and Schmitz, D. (1985). *Development of CMU Direct-Drive Arm II*. CMU Robotics Institute, Technical Report 85-5.

Kuo, B. C. (1978). *Proceedings of the Seventh Annual Symposium Incremental Motion Control Systems and Devices*. Incremental Motion Control Systems Society.

Kuribayashi, K. (1986). A new Actuator of a Joint Using TiNi Alloy Wire. *The International Journal of Robotics Research*, **4**, 4, pp. 47–58.

Lansky, Z. J. and Schrader, L. F. (1986). *Industrial Pneumatic Control*. Fluid Power and Control Series No. 6. New York: Marcel Dekker.

Maskrey, R. H. and Thayer, W. J. (1978). A Brief History of Electrohydraulic Servomechanisms. *ASME Journal of Dynamic Systems Measurement and Control*, June.

Madsen, E. (1980). Stepper Motors convert pulses to accurate mechanical steps. *Electronic Design*, **9**, April 26, pp. 205–209.

Mendelson, J. J. and Rinderle, J. R. (1984). Design of a Compliant Robotic Manipulator. *Robotics Research – The Next Five Years and Beyond*, SME.

Metals Handbook (1984). Ninth Edition, New York: American Society for Metals.

Miura, H. and Shimoyama, I. (1984). Dynamic Walk of a Biped, *The International Journal of Robotics Research*, **3**, 2, pp. 60–74.

Muir, P. F. and Neuman, C. P. (1985). Pulsewidth Modulation Control of Brushless d.c. Motors for Robotic Applications. *IEEE Transactions on Industrial Electronics*, **IE-32**, 3, pp. 222–229.

Nakano, Y. *et al.* (1984). Hitachi's Robot Hand. *Robotics Age*, **6**, 7, pp. 18–20.

Prokes, J. (1977). *Hydraulic Mechanisms in Automation*. Dordrecht: Elsevier.

Raibert, M. H., Brown, H. B. and Chepponis, M. (1984). Experiments in Balance with a 3D One-Legged Hopping Machine. *The International Journal of Robotics Research*, **3**, 2, pp. 75–92.

Rosheim, M. E. (1982). Robot Wrist Actuators. *Robotics Age*, Nov/Dec, pp. 15–22.

Savage, M. (1984). A Tooth for a Tooth, The Designing of Gears. *Perspectives in Computing*, **4**, 1.

Schetky, L. McD. (1984). Shape-Memory Effect Alloys for Robotic Devices. *Robotics Age*, **6**, 7, pp. 13–17.

Scott, P. B. (1985). The 'Omnigripper': A Form of Robot Universal Gripper. *Robotica*, **3**, pp. 153–158.

Sutherland, I. E. and Ullner, M. K. (1984). Footprints in the Asphalt. *The International Journal of Robotics Research*, **3**, 2, pp. 29–36.

Thompson, D. E. (1981). Biomechanics of the Hand. *Perspectives in Computing*, **1**, 3.

Walker, P. (1978). Getting Serious about EV Motors. *Machine Design*, May 11, pp. 108–112.

Yeaple, F. (1984). *Fluid Power Design Handbook*, New York: Marcel Dekker.

Zoebl, T. H. (1970). *Fundamentals of Hydraulic Circuitry*. Iliffe Books.

Chapter 3

Bowyer, A. and Woodwork, J. (1983). *A Programmer's Geometry*. Guildford: Butterworth.

Chasen, S. H. (1978). *Geometric Principles and Procedures for Computer Graphic Applications*. Englewood Cliffs: Prentice-Hall.

Featherstone, R. (1983(a)). The calculation of robot dynamics using articulated-body inertias. *The International Journal of Robotics Research*, **2**, 1, pp. 13–30.

Featherstone, R. (1983(b)). Position and velocity transformations between robot end effector coordinates and joint angles. *The International Journal of Robotics Research*, **3**, 2, pp. 35–45.

Forest, A. R. (1969). *Coordinates, Transformations, and Visualization Techniques*, CAD Group Document No. 23, Cambridge University.

Newman, W. M. and Sproull, R. F. (1979). *Principles of Interactive Computer Graphics* (Second edition). Maidenhead: McGraw-Hill.

Pedoe, D. (1963). *A Geometric Introduction to Linear Algebra*. New York: John Wiley and Sons.

Roberts, A. W. (1985). *Elementary Linear Algebra* (Second edition). Reading, MA: Benjamin/Cummings.

Roth, B. (1984). Screws, Motors and Wrenches that Cannot be Bought in a Hardware Store. In: Brady, M. and Paul, R. (eds) *Robotics Research: The First International Symposium*, Boston: MIT Press, pp. 679–693.

Rogers, D. F. and Adams, J. A. (1976). *Mathematical Elements for Computer Graphics*, Maidenhead: McGraw-Hill.

Taylor, R. H. (1979). Planning and executing straight-line manipulator trajectories, *IBM Journal of Research and Development*, **23**, 4, pp. 253–260.

Thomas, G. B. (1960). *Calculus and Analytic Geometry*. Reading MA: Addison-Wesley.

Chapter 4

Cook, C. D. and Vu-Dinh, T. (1984). A New General Algorithm for Describing Manipulator Kinematics. *National Conference and Exhibition on Robotics*, Australian Robot Association, pp. 95–101.

Denavit, J. and Hartenberg, R. S. (1955). A Kinematic Notation for Lower-Pair Mechanisms Based on Matrices, *Journal of Applied Mechanics*, ASME, **22**, pp. 215–221.

Goldenberg, A.A., Benhabib, B. and Fenton, R. G. (1985). A complete generalized solution to the inverse kinematics of robots, *IEEE Journal of Robotics and Automation*, **RA-1**, 1, pp. 14–20.

Goldenberg, A. A. and Lawrence, D. L. (1985). A generalized solution to the inverse kinematics of redundant manipulators, *Journal of Dynamic Systems, Measurement and Control*, ASME, **107**, pp. 102–106.

Hartenberg, R. S. and Denavit, J. (1964), *Kinematic Synthesis of Linkages*. New York: McGraw-Hill.

Horn, B. K. P. (1975). *Kinematics, Statics and Dynamics of two-dimensional Manipulators*, MIT Artificial Intelligence Laboratory, Working Paper 99.

Huang, B. and Milenkovic, V. (1984). Kinematics of Minor Robot Linkage. *Robotics Research – The Next Five Years and Beyond*. SME.

La Brooy, R. C. (1986). On the determination of an inverse kinematic analysis solution to a 5 degree of freedom, serially-linked, industrial research robot. *Proceedings of Robots in Australia's Future Conference*, ARA, Perth, pp. 220–232.

Lee, C. S. G. (1982). Robot Arm Kinematics, Dynamics, and Control. *IEEE Computer*, **15**, 12, pp. 62–82.

Manseur, R. and Doty, K. L. (1988). A Fast Algorithm for Inverse Kinematic Analysis of Robot Manipulators, *IJRR*, **7**, 3, pp. 52–63.

Microbot (1981). *Mini-Mover 5 Reference Manual*.

Oh, S. Y., Orin, D. and Beth (1984). An inverse kinematic solution for kinematically redundant manipulators. *Journal of Robot Systems*, **1**, 3, pp. 235–249.

Paul, R. P., Shimano, B. and Mayer, G. E. (1981). Kinematic Control Equations for Simple Manipulators. *IEEE Transactions on Systems, Man and Cybernetics*, **SMC-11**, 6, pp. 449–455.

Pieper, D. L. (1968). *The Kinematics of Manipulators under Computer Control*. Computer Science Department, Stanford University, Artificial Intelligence Report, Memo AI-72.

Sturges, R. H. (1973). *Singularities and Redundancies of the PaP-3000 Jacobian*. Charles Stark Draper Laboratory, MAT Memo No 80A.

Sturges, R. H. (1973). *Optimization of Arm Geometry (one example)*. Charles Stark Draper Laboratory, MAT Memo No 145 and 145A.

Tsai, L. W. and Morgan, A. P. (1984). Solving the kinematics of the most general six- and five-degree-of-freedom manipulators by continuation methods. *ASME Paper* 84-DET-20 ASME Design Engineering Technical Conference.

Uicker, J. J., Denavit, J. and Hartenberg, R. S. (1984). An interactive method for the displacement analysis of spatial mechanisms. *Journal of Applied Mechanics*, ASME, pp. 309–314.

Wampler, C. W. (1989). Inverse Kinematic Functions for Redundant Sperical Wrists. *IEEE Transactions on Robotics and Automation*, **5**, 1, pp. 106–111.

Whitney, D. E., Lozinski, C. A. and Rouke, J. M. (1984). *Industrial Robot Calibration Method and Results*. Charles Stark Draper Laboratory, Report No. CSDL-P-1879.

Winslow, T. (1984). Personal Computer Software for Robot Applications. *Robots 8 Proceedings*, SME, pp. 13.1–13.27.

Winston, P. H. (1984). *Artificial Intelligence* (Second edition). Reading MA: Addison-Wesley.

Yoskikawa, T. (1984). Analysis and Control of Robot Manipulators with Redundancy. In: Brady, M. and Paul, P. (eds). *Robotics Research – The First International Symposium*, MIT Press, pp. 735–748.

Zelinsky, A. (1984). *Robotic Software for the Mini-Mover 5 Robot Arm*. Department of Computer Science, The University of Wollongong, Preprint 84-6.

Chapter 5

Angeles, J. (1986). Iterative kinematic inversion of general five-axis robot manipulator. *The International Journal of Robotics Research*, **4**, 4, pp. 59–70.

Featherstone, R. (1983). Position and Velocity Transformations Between Robot End-Effector Coordinates and Joint Angles. *The International Journal of Robotics Research*, **2**, 2, pp. 35–45.

Ference, M., Lemon, H. B. and Stephenson, R. J. (1956). *Analytical Experimental Physics*. Chicago: University of Chicago Press.

Hollerbach, J. and Sahar, G. (1984). Wrist-Partitioned Inverse Kinematic Accelerations and Manipulator Dynamics. *IEEE Conference on Robotics*.

Horn, B. K. P. (1975). *Kinematics, Statics and Dynamics of two-d Manipulators*. MIT Artificial Intelligence Laboratory, Working Paper 99.

La Brooy, R. C. (1987). Screw/Line Transforms for the Rapid Determination of Jacobians. *Proceedings of Robots 11*, 17th ISIR, SME, pp. 6.55–6.71.

Lu, J. Y. S., Walker, M. W. and Paul, R. P. (1980) Resolved Acceleration Control of Mechanical Manipulators. *IEEE Trans on Automatic Control*, **25**, 3, pp. 468–474.

Meriam, J. L. (1966). *Dynamics*, Chichester: John Wiley.

Orin, D. E. and Schrader, W. W. (1984). Efficient Jacobian Determination for Robot Manipulators. In: Brady, M. and Paul, R. (eds) *Robotics Research – The First International Symposium*, MIT Press, pp. 727–734.

Paul, R. P., Renaud, M. and Stevenson, C. N. (1984). A systematic approach for obtaining the kinematics of recursive manipulators based on homogeneous transformations. In: Brady, M. and Paul, P. (eds) *Robotics Research – The First International Symposium*, MIT Press, pp. 707–726.

Paul, R. P., Shimano, B. and Mayer, G. E. (1981). Differential Kinematic Control Equations for Simple Manipulators. *IEEE Transactions on Systems Man and Cybernetics*, **SMC-11**, 6, pp. 456–460.

Renaud, M. (1980). *Contribution a la modelisation et a la commande dynamique des robot manipulators*, Ph.D. Thesis, L'Universite Paul Sabatier de Toulouse.

Renaud, M. (1981). Geometric and Kinematic Models of a Robot Manipulator: Calculation of the Jacobian Matrix and its Inverse, *Proc 11th ISIR*, Tokyo, Japan.

Sturges, R. H. (1973). *Singularities and Redundancies of the PaP-3000 Jacobian*, Charles Stark Draper Laboratory, MAT Memo No 80A.

Trevelyan, J. P., Kovesi, P. D., Ong, M. and Elford, D. (1986). ET: A Wrist Mechanism Without Singular Positions, *The International Journal of Robotics Research*, **4**, 2, pp. 71–85.

Wang, L. T. and Ravani, B. (1985). Recursive Computations of Kinematic and Dynamic Equations for Mechanical Manipulators, *IEEE Journal of Robotics and Automation*, **RA-1**, 3, pp. 124–131.

Whitney, D. E. (1969). Resolved Motion Rate Control of Manipulators and Human Prostheses. *IEEE Trans on Man-Machine Systems*, **MMS-10**, 2, pp. 47–53.

Whitney, D. E. (1972). The Mathematics of Coordinated Control of Prosthetic Arms and Manipulators. *Journal of Dynamic Systems, Measurement and Control*, ASME, pp. 784–791.

Chapter 6

Cutkosky, M. R. and Kao, I. (1989). Computing and Controlling the Compliance of a Robotic Hand. *IEEE Transactions on Robotics and Automation*, **5**, 2, pp. 151–165.

Hogan, N. (1980). Mechanical Impedance Control in Assistive Devices and Manipulators. *Proceedings of Joint Automatic Control Conference*, American Automatic Control Council, pp. TA10–13.

Holzer, A. J. (1981). Some Critical Areas in Robotics Research. In: *Computers in Industry*. Rotterdam: North-Holland, pp. 199–207.

Horn, B. K. P. (1975). *Kinematics, Statics and Dynamics of Two-dimensional Manipulators*. MIT Artificial Intelligence Laboratory, Working Paper 99.

Lane, J. D. (1982). Applying the Remote Center Compliance Device in Assembly. *Robotics Today*, 1982 Annual Edition, SME, pp. 160–164.

Mason, T. M. (1981). Compliance and Force Control for Computer Controlled Manipulators. *IEEE Transactions on Systems, Man and Cybernetics*, **SMC-11**, 6, pp. 418–432.

Mason, T. M. (982). Compliant Motion. In: Brady, M., Hollerbach, J. M. Johnson, T. L. Lozano-Perez, T. and Mason, M. T. (eds), *Robot Motion Planning and Control*, MIT Press, pp. 305–322.

Meriam, J. L. (1966). *Statics*. Chichester: John Wiley.

Mosley, H. (1839). *Illustrations of Mechanics*. London.

Newton, Sir I. (1687). *Principia*. (Revised by Cajori, F. 1934, University of California Press.)

Ohwovoriole, M. S. and Roth, B. (1981). A theory of parts mating for assembly automation. *Proc Ro-Man. Sys.*, Warsaw, Poland.

Okada, T. (1985). *Optimization of Mechanisms for Force Generation by Using Pulleys and Spring*. Carnegie-Mellon University, Robotics Institute, Technical Report, CMU-RI-TR-85-14.

Paul, R. P. and Shimano, B. (1976). Compliance and Control. *Proceedings Joint Automatic Control Conference*, San Francisco, pp. 694–699.

Raibert, M. H. and Craig, J. J. (1981). Hybrid position/force control of manipulators, *Journal of Dynamic Systems, Measurement and Control*, ASME, **102**, June, pp. 126–133.

Rebman, J. (1982). Compliance: The Forgiving Factor, *Robotics Today*, 1982 Annual Edition, SME, pp. 151–156.

Simunovic, S. (1975). Force Information in Assembly Process. *Proc 5th International Symposium on Industrial Robots*, pp. 415–431.

Sturges, R. H. (1988). A Three-Dimensional Assembly Task Quantification with Application to Machine Dexterity. *IJRR*, **7**, 4, pp. 34–78.

Whitney, D. E. (1982). Quasi-Static Assembly of Compliantly Support Rigid Parts. *Journal of Dynamic Systems, Measurement and Control*, ASME, **104**, 1, pp. 65–77.

Whitney, D. E. and Nevins, J. L. (1982). The Remote Center Compliance: What Can it do? *Robotics Today*, 1982 Annual Edition, SME, pp. 135–139.

Will, P. M. and Grossman, D. D. (1975). An experimental system for computer-controlled mechanical assembly. *IEEE Transactions on Computers*, **C-24**, 9, pp. 879–888.

Chapter 7

Featherstone, R. (1983). The calculation of robot dynamics using articulated-body inertias. *The International Journal of Robotics Research*, **2**, 1, pp. 13–30.

Hillis, D. (1983). Dynamics of Manipulators with Less Than One Degree of Freedom. MIT AI Laboratory, AI Memo 241.

Hollerbach, J. M. (1980). A Recursive Lagrangian Formulation of Manipulator Dynamics and a Comparative Study of Dynamics Formulation Complexity. *IEEE Transactions on Systems, Man and Cybernetics*, **SMC-10**, 11, pp. 730–736.

Hollerbach, J. M. and Sahar, G. (1983). Wrist-Partitioned Inverse Kinematic Accelerations and Manipulator Dynamics. MIT AI Laboratory, AI Memo 717.

Horn, B. K. P., Hirokawa, K. and Vazirani, V. V. (1977). Dynamics of a Three Degree of Freedom Kinetic Chain. MIT AI Laboratory, AI Memo 478.

Hou, F., DeSiilva, C. and Wright, P. (1980). Mechanical Structural Analysis and Design Optimization of Industrial Robots. *The Robotics Institute*, Carnegie-Mellon, Technical Report No. CMU-RI-TR-4.

Kazerounian, K. and Gupta, K. C. (1986). Manipulator Dynamics Using Extended Zero Reference Position Description. *IEEE Journal of Robotics and Automation*, **RA-2**, 4, pp. 221–224.

Khosla, P. K. and Kanade, T. (1985). Parameter Identification of Robot Dynamics. *Proceedings of the 24th conference on Decision and Control*, IEEE, December, pp. 1754–1760.

Khosla, P. K. (1986). *Real-Time Control and Identification of Direct-Drive Manipulators*, PhD Thesis, Department of Mechanical Engineering, Carnegie-Mellon University.

Kittel, C., Knight, W. D., Ruderman, M. A., Helmholz, A. C. and Moyer, B. J. (1973). *Mechanics*. Berkeley Physics Course, Volume 1, (second edition), New York: McGraw-Hill.

Lathrop, R. H. (1983). Parallelism in Manipulator Dynamics. MIT AI Laboratory, Technical Report 754.

Luh, J. Y. S., Walker, M. W. and Paul, R. P. C. (1980). On-Line Computational Scheme for Mechanical Manipulators. *Journal of Dynamic Systems, Measurement, and Control*, **102**, June, pp. 69–76.

McInnis, B. C. and Liu, C. K. (1986). Kinematics and Dynamics in Robotics: A Tutorial Based Upon Classical Concepts of Vectorial Mechanics. *IEEE Journal of Robotics and Automation*, **RA-2**, 4, pp. 181–187.

Meriam, J. L. (1966). *Dynamics*. Chichester: John Wiley.

Paul, R., Rong, M. and Zhang, H. (1984). The Dynamics of the PUMA Manipulator. School of Electrical Engineering, Purdue, Technical Report No. TR-EE 84–19.

Resnick, R. and Halliday, D. (1960). *Physics*. John Wiley and Sons.

Silver, W. M. (1981). On the Representation of Angular Velocity and its Effect on the Efficiency of Manipulator Dynamics Computation. MIT AI Laboratory, AI Memo 622.

Swartz, N. M. (1984). Arm Dynamics Simulation. *Journal of Robotic Systems*, **1**, 1, pp. 83–100.

Symon, K. R. (1963). *Mechanics*. (Second edition), Reading MA: Addison-Wesley.

Wang, L. T. and Ravani, B. (1985). Recursive Computations of Kinematic and Dynamic Equations for Mechanical Manipulators. *IEEE Journal of Robotics and Automation*, **RA-1**, 3, pp. 124–131.

Wells, D. A. (1967). *Theory and Problems of Lagrangian Dynamics*. Schaum.

Wilson, H. and Deb, K. (1989). Inertial properties of tapered cylinders and partial volumes of revolution. *Computer-Aided Design*, **21**, 7, pp. 456–462.

Chapter 8

Briot, M. (1985). Mobile Robots Architecture. *Laboratoire d'Automatique et d'Analyse des Systems du C.N.R.S.*, Publication 85.119.

Brooks, R. A. (1982). Solving the Final-Path Problem by Representing Free Space as Generalized Cones. MIT AI Lab, A.I. Memo No. 674.

Brooks, R. A. (1985(a)). A Mobile Robot Project, MIT AI Lab, Working paper 265.

Brooks, R. A. (1985(b)). Aspects of Mobile Robot Visual Map Making. In: Hanafusa, H. and Inoue, H. (eds) *Robotics Research: The Second International Symposium*, MIT Press, pp. 369–375.

Brooks, R. A. (1986). A Robust Layered Control System for a Mobile Robot, *IEEE Journal of Robotics and Automation*, **RA-2**, 1, pp. 14–23.

Brooks, R. A. and Connell, J. H. (1986). Asynchronous Distributed Control System for a Mobile Robot, *SPIE Cambridge Symposium on Optical and Optoelectronic Engineering*.

Brooks, R. A. and Flynn, A. M. (1989). Robot Beings. *Proceedings IEEE International Workshop on Intelligent Robots and Systems*, pp. 2–10.

Burks, B. L., de Saussure, G., Weisbin, C. R., Jones, J. P. and Hamel, W. R. (1987). Autonomous Navigation, Exploration and Recognition Using the Hermies-IIB Robot. *IEEE Expert*, **2**, 4, pp. 18–27.

Cahn, D. E. and Phillips, S. R. (1975). ROBNAV: A Range-Based Robot Navigation and Obstacle Avoidance System. *IEEE Transaction on Systems, Man and Cybernetics*, September, pp. 544–551.

Chatila, R. (1985). Mobile Robot Navigation: Space Modelling and Decisional Processes. *3rd ISRR*, Gouvieux, France.

Chattergy, R. (1985). Some Heuristics for the Navigation of a Robot. *IJRR*, **4**, 1, pp. 59–66.

Crisman, J. (1985). A Survey of Path Planning for Mobile Robot Navigation Systems. Carnegie-Mellon University, student assignment.

Crowley, J. L. (1984(a)). Navigation for an Intelligent Mobile Robot. CMU-RI, TR-84-18.

Crowley, J. L. (1984(b)). Dynamic World Modelling for an Intelligent Mobile Robot. *IEEE 7th International Conference on Pattern Recognition*, pp. 207–210.

Crowley, J. L. (1987). Coordination of Action and Perception in a Surveillance Robot. *IEEE Expert*, **2**, 4, pp. 32–43.

Doyle, R. J. (1982). Aspects of the Rover Problem. MIT AI Lab, Working paper 231.

Drake, K. C., McVey, E. S. and Inigo, R. M. (1987). Experimental Position and Renging Results for a Mobile Robot. *IEEE Journal of Robotics and Automation*, **RA-3**, 1, pp. 31–42.

Drumheller, M. (1985). Mobile Robot Localization Using Sonar. *IEEE Transaction on Pattern Analysis and Machine Intelligence*, **PAMI-9**, 2, pp. 325–332.

Elfes, A. (1986). A Sonar-Based Mapping and Navigation System. *Proceedings of IEEE International Conference on Robotics and Automation*.

Elfes, A. (1987). Sonar-based Real-World Mapping and Navigation. *IEEE Journal of Robotics and Automation*, **RA-3**, 3, pp. 249–265.

Fikes, R. E. and Nilsson, N. J. (1971). STRIPS. *Artificial Intelligence*, **2**, pp. 189–208.

Ghallab, M. (1985). Task Execution Monitoring by Compiled Production Rules in an Advanced Multi-Sensor Robot. *The Second International Symposium on Robotics Research*, MIT Press, pp. 393–401.

Giralt, G., Chatila, R. and Vaisset, M. (1984). An Integrated Navigation and Motion Control System for Autonomous Multisensory Mobile Robots. *Robotics Research: The First International Symposium*, MIT Press, pp. 191–214.

Giralt, G., Sobek, R. and Chatila, R. (1979). A Multilevel Planning and Navigation System for a Mobile Robot. *Proc. 6th Int. Joint Conference AI*, pp. 335–338.

Goto, Y. and Stentz, A. (1987). Mobile Robot Navigation: The CMU System. *IEEE Expert*, **2**, 4 pp. 44–54.

Gouzenes, L. (1984). Strategies for Solving Collision-Free Trajectories Problems for Mobile and Manipulator Robots. *IJRR*, **3**, 4, pp. 51–65.

Green, P. J. and Silverman, B. W. (1979). Constructing the Convex Hull of a set of points in the plane. *Computer Journal*, **22**, 3, pp. 262–266.

Guibas, L. J. and Stolfi, J. (1988). Ruler, Compass and Computer: The Design and Analysis of Geometric Algorithms. In: Earnshaw R. A. (ed.) *Theoretical Foundation of Computer Graphs and CAD*. NATO ASI series Vol F4D, pp. 111–165. Berlin: Springer-Verlag.

Harmon, S. Y. (1987). The Ground Surveillance Robot (GSR): An Autonomous Vehicle Designed to Transit Unknown Terrain. *IEEE Journal of Robotics and Automation*, **RA-3**, 3, pp. 266–279.

Holland, J. M. (1985). Agile Autonomous Vehicles in the Just in Time Environment. *Robotics Age*, December, pp. 4–8.

Hollis, R. (1977). Newt: A Mobile, Cognitive Robot. *Byte*, **2**, 6, June, pp. 30–45.

Hongo, T., Arakawa, H., Sugimoto, G., Tange, K. and Yamamoto, Y. (1987). An Automatic Guidance System of a Self-controlled Vehicle. *IEEE Transactions on Industrial Electronics*, **IE-34**, 1, pp. 5–10.

Iyengar, S. S., Jorgenson, C. C., Rao, S. V. N. and Weisbin, C. R. (1986). Robot Navigation Algorithms Using Learned Spatial Graphs. *Robotica*, **4** pp. 93–100.

Jarvis, R. A. (1983). Growing Polyhedral Obstacles for Planning Collision-free Paths. *The Australian Computer Journal*, **15**, 3, pp. 103–111.

Jarvis, R. A. (1985). Collision-free Trajectory Planning Using Distance Transforms, *Mech Eng Trans of the I E Aust.*, **ME10**, 3, pp. 187–191.

Jarvis, R. A. (1987). Configuration Space Collision-free Path Planning for Robotic Manipulators. *Australian Computer Science Communications*, **9**, 1, pp. 193–204.

Jarvis, R. A. and Byrne, J. C. (1986). Robot Navigation: Touching, Seeing and Knowing. *Proceedings of 1st Australian Conference on Artificial Intelligence*.

Jarvis, R. and Kang, K. (1986). A New Approach to Robot Collision-Free Path Planning. *Robots in Australia's Future Conference*, pp. 71–79.

Jorgensen, C., Hamel, W. and Weisbin, C. (1986). Autonomous Robot Navigation. *Byte*, January, 223–235.

Kambhampati, S. K. and Davis, L. S. (1986). Multiresolution Path Planning for Mobile Robots. *IEEE Journal of Robotics and Automation*, **RA-2**, 3, pp. 135–145.

Kant, K. and Zucker, S. W. (1986). Toward Efficient Trajectory Planning: The Path-Velocity Decomposition. *IJRR*, **5**, 3, pp. 72–89.

Komoriya, K., Tachi, S. and Tanie, K. (1986). A

Method of Autonomous Locomotion for Mobile Robots. *Advanced Robotics*, **1**, 1, pp. 3–19.

Krogh, B. H. (1983). Feedback Obstacle Avoidance Control. *21st Allerton Conference on Communication, Control and Computing*, Urbana, IL, pp. 325–334.

Krogh, B. H. (1984). A Generalized Potential Field Approach to Obstacle Avoidance Control. *First World Conference on Robotics Research*, RIA.

Kuc, R. and Siegel, M. W. (1987). Efficient Representation of Reflecting Structures for a Sonar Navigation Model. *IEEE International Conference on Robotics and Automation*, pp. 1916–1923.

Lee, D. T. and Drysdale, R. L. (1981). Generalized Voronoi Diagrams in the Plane. *SIAM Journal of Computing*, **10**, 1, pp. 73–87.

Lozano-Perez, T. (1981). Automatic Planning of Manipulator Transfer Movements. *IEEE Transactions on Systems, Man and Cybernetics*, **SMC-11**, 10, pp. 681–698.

Lozano-Perez, T. (1983). Spatial Planning: A Configuration Space Approach. *IEEE Transactions on Computers*, **C-32**, 2, pp. 108–120.

Lozano-Perez, T. and Wesley, M. A. (1979). An Algorithm for Planning Collision-free Paths Among Polyhedral Obstacles. *CACM*, **22**, pp. 560–570, October.

McTamaney, L. S. (1987). Mobile Robots: Real-Time Intelligent Control. *IEEE Expert*, **2**, 4, pp. 55–68.

Mitchell, J. S. B. (1984). An Autonomous Vehicle Navigation Algorithm. In: J. F. Gilmore (ed) *Proceedings of SPIE*, **485**: *Applications of AI*, May.

Mitchell, J. S. B. and Keirsey, D. M. (1984). Planning Strategic Paths through Variable Terrain Data. In: J. F. Gilmore (ed), *Proceedings of SPIE*, **485**: *Applications of AI*, May.

Moravec, H. P. (1980). Obstacle Avoidance and Navigation in the Real World by a Seeing Robot Rover. CMU-RI, TR-3.

Moravec, H. P. (1983). The Stanford Cart and the CMU Rover. *Proceedings of the IEEE*, **71**, 7, pp. 872–884.

Moravec, H. P. (ed) (1986). Autonomous Mobile Robots Annual Report 1985, CMU-RI, TR-86-4.

Moravec, H. P. and Elfes, A. (1985). High Resolution Maps from Wide Angle Sonar. *Proceedings of IEEE International Conference on Robotics and Automation*, pp. 116–121.

Muir, P. F. and Neuman, C. P. (1986). Kinematic Modelling of Wheeled Mobile Robots. CMU-RI, TR-86-12.

Nilsson, N. J. (1984). Shakey the Robot, SRI International, Technical Note 323.

Nitao, J. J. and Parodi, A. M. (1986). A Real-Time Reflexive Pilot for an Autonomous Land Vehicle. *IEEE Control Systems Magazine*, **6**, February, pp. 14–23.

O'Durlaing and Yap, C. K. (1983). The Voronoi Method for Motion-Planning 1: The Case of A Disk, Technical Report 53, Courant Institute, March 1983.

O'Durlaing and Yap, C. K. (1985). A retraction method for planning the motion of a disk. *J. Algorithms*, **6**, pp. 104–111.

Parodi, A. M. (1984). A Route Planning System for an Autonomous Vehicle. *First Conference on Artificial Intelligence Applications*, IEEE Computer Society, pp. 51–66.

Peshkin, M. A. and Sanderson, A. C. (1985). A Modeless Convex Hull Algorithm for Simple Polygons. CMU-RI, TR 85-8.

Rathbone, R. R., Valley, R. A. and Kindlmann, P. J. (1986). Beacon-Referenced Dead Reckoning: A Versatile Guidance System. *Robotics Engineering*, **8**, 12, pp. 11–16.

Raibert, M. H. (1984) (Guest Editor). Special Issue on Legged Locomotion. *IJRR*, **3**, 2.

Reif, J. H. and Storer, J. A. (1987). Minimizing Turns for Discrete Movement in the Interior of a Polygon. *IEEE Journal of Robotics and Automation*. **RA-3**, 3, pp. 182–193.

Samet, H. (1982). Neighbour-finding Techniques for Images Represented by Quadtrees. *Computer Graphics and Image Processing*, **18**, pp. 35–37.

Samet, H. (1989a). *Applications of Spatial Data Structures*. Reading MA: Addison-Wesley.

Samet, H. (1989b). *The Design and Analysis of Spatial Data Structures*. Reading MA: Addison-Wesley.

Schwartz, J. T. and Sharir, M. (1983(a)). On the Piano Movers' Problem I: The special case of a rigid polygonal body moving amidst polygonal barriers. *Commun. Pure Appl. Math.*, **36**, pp. 345–398.

Schwartz, J. T. and Sharir, M. (1983(b)). On the Piano Movers' Problem II: General techniques for computing topological properties of real algebraic manifolds. *Adv. Appl. Math.*, **4**, pp. 298–351.

Schwartz, J. T. and Sharir, M. (1983(c)). On the Piano Movers' Problem III: Coordinating the Motion of Several Independent Bodies: The Special Case of

Circular Bodies Moving Amidst Polygonal Barriers. *IJRR*, **2**, 3, pp. 46–75.

Sheth, P. N. and Uicker, J. J. (1971). A Generalized Symbolic Notation for Mechanisms. *Journal of Engineering for Industry*, Series B, **93**, 70-Mech-19, pp. 102–112.

Singh, J. S. and Wagh, M. D. (1987). Robot Path Planning using Intersecting Convex Shapes: Analysis and Simulation. *IEEE Journal of Robotics and Automation*, **RA-3**, 2, pp. 101–108.

Sklansky, J. (1972). Measuring Concavity on a Rectangular Mosaic. *IEEE Transactions on Computers*, **C-21**, 12, pp. 1355–1364.

Sutherland, I. E. (1969). A Method for Solving Arbitrary-Wall Mazes by Computer. *IEEE Transactions on Computers*, **C-18**, 12, pp. 1092–1097.

Tachi, S. and Komoriya, K. (1985). Guide Dog Robot. In: Hanafusa, H. and Inoue, H. (eds) *Robotics Research: The Second International Symposium*. MIT Press, pp. 333–340.

Takahashi, O. and Schilling, R. J. (1989). Motion Planning in a Plane Using Generalized Voronoi Diagrams. *IEEE Transactions on Robotics and Automation*, **5**, 2, pp. 143–150.

Thompson, A. M. (1977). The Navigation System of the JPL Robot. *Proc. 5th Int. Joint Conference AI*, pp. 749–757.

Thorpe, C. and Kanade, T. (1987). 1986 Year End Report for Road Following at Carnegie Mellon. CMU-RI-TR-87–11.

Thorpe, C. E. (1984). Path Relaxation: Path Planning for a Mobile Robot. CMU-RI, TR-84–5.

Thorpe, C. E. (1984). F100: Vision and Navigation for a Robot Rover. CMU-CS, pp. 84–186.

Waldron, K. J., Vohnout, V. J., Perry, A. and McGhee, R. B. (1984). Configuration Design of the Adaptive Suspension Vehicle. *IJRR*, **3**, 2, pp. 37–48.

Waxman, A. M., LeMoigne, J. J., Davis, L. S., Srinivasan, B., Kushner, T. R., Liang, E. and Siddalingaiah, T. (1987). A Visual Navigation System for Autonomous Land Vehicles. *IEEE Journal of Robotics and Automation*, **RA-3**, 2, pp. 124–141.

Winston, P. H. (1984). *Artificial Intelligence*. Addison-Wesley.

Zelinsky, A. (1988). Robot Navigation with Learning. *Australian Computer Journal*, **20**, 2, pp. 85–93.

Zelinsky, A. and Cook, C. (1986). Environment Mapping for Mobile Robots. *Robots in Australia's Future Conference*, pp. 80–82.

Chapter 9

Ambler, P. A. (1985). Robotics and Solid Modelling: A Discussion of the Requirements Robotic Applications put on Solid Modelling Systems. *The Second International Symposium on Robotics Research*, MIT Press, pp. 361–367.

Barber, K. S. and Agin, J. (1986). Analysis of Human Communication During Assembly Tasks. CMU RI, TR 86–13.

Bourne, D. A. (1982). A Numberless, Tensed Language for Action Oriented Tasks. CMU-RI, TR 82–12.

Brady, M. (1985). Artificial Intelligence and Robotics. *Artificial Intelligence*, **26**, pp. 79–121.

Brost, R. C. (1985). Planning Robot Grasping Motions in the Presence of Uncertainty. CMU-RI, TR 85–12.

Chester, C. (1983). Robotic Software Reaches Out for Task-Oriented Languages. The Goal: To remove all human supervision. *Electronic Design*, May 12, pp. 119–129.

Craig, J. J. (1985). Anatomy of an Off-line Programming System. *Robotics Today*, February.

Ejiri, H., Uno, T., Yoda, H., Goto, T. and Takeyasu, K. (1972). A Prototype Intelligent Robot that Assembles Objects from Plan Drawings. *IEEE Transactions on Computers*, **C-21**, 2, pp. 161–170.

Erdman, M. (1986). Using Backprojections for Fine Motion Planning with Uncertainty. *IJRR*, **5**, 1, pp. 19–45.

Fahlman, S. E. (1974). A Planning System for Robot Construction Tasks. *Artificial Intelligence*, **5**, pp. 1–49.

Fikes, R. E., Hart, P. E. and Nilsson, N. J. (1972). Learning and Executing Generalized Robot Plans. *Artificial Intelligence*, **3**, pp. 251–288.

Hayes, C. (1987). Using Goal Internations to Guide Planning: The Program Model. CMU RI, TR 87–10.

Henderson, T. C., Hansen, C. D. and Fai, W. S. (1985). Organizing Spatial Data for Robotics Systems. *Computers in Industry*, **6**, pp. 331–344.

Herbert, M. and Hoffman, R. (1985). Real-Time Graphic Simulation of Robotic Manipulation Using Solid Models. *IEEE Proceedings Trends and Applications in 1985 Utilizing Computer Graphics*, pp. 141–145.

Homem de Mello, L. S. and Sanderson, A. C. (1986). AND/OR Graph Representation of Assembly Plans. CMU RI, TR 86–8.

Jarvis, R. A. (1986). Configuration Space Collision-Free Path Planning for Robotic Manipulators. *Robots in Australia's Future Conference*, ARA, pp. 194–204.

Jarvis, R. A. (1988). Automatic Grip Site Detection for Robotics Manipulators. *Australian Computer Science Communications*, **10**, 1, pp. 346–356.

Kemper, A. and Wallrath, M. (1987). An Analysis of Geometric Modelling in Database Systems. *Computing Surveys*, **19**, 1, pp. 47–91.

Krough, B. H. and Sanderson, A. C. (1986). Modelling and Control of Assembly Tasks and Systems. CMU RI, TR 86-1.

Latombe, J. C., Laugier, C., Lefebure, J. M. and Mazer, E. (1985). The LM Robot Programming System, *The Second International Symposium on Robotics Research*, MIT Press, pp. 377–391.

Lieberman, L. and Wesley, M. (1977). AUTOPASS: An automatic programming system for computer controlled mechanical assembly. *IBM Journal of Research and Development*, **21**, p. 321.

Liegeois, A., Borrel, P. and Dombre, E. (1985). Programming, Simulating and Evaluating Robot Actions. *The Second International Symposium on Robotics Research*, MIT Press, pp. 412–418.

Lozano-Perez, T. (1976). The Design of a Mechanical Assembly System. MIT AI Lab, Technical Report 397.

Lozano-Perez, T. (1981). Automatic Planning of Manipulator Transfer Movements. *IEEE Transactions on Systems, Man and Cybernetics*, **SMC-11**, 10, pp. 681–698.

Lozano-Perez, T. (1983). Spatial Planning: A Configuration Space Approach. *IEEE Transactions on Computers*, **C-32**, 2, pp. 108–120.

Lozano-Perez, T. (1987). A Simple Motion-Planning Algorithm for General Robot Manipulators. *IEEE Journal of Robotics and Automation*, **RA-3**, 3, pp. 224–238.

Lozano-Perez, T. and Brooks, R. A. (1985). Task-Level Manipulator Programming. In: Nof, S. Y. (ed.) *Handbook of Industrial Robotics*. Chichester: John Wiley, pp. 404–418.

Lozano-Perez, T. and Winston, P. (1977). LAMA: A language for automatic mechanical assembly. *Proceedings Fifth International Joint Conference on Artificial Intelligence*.

Lozano-Perez, T., Mason, M. T. and Taylor, R. H. (1984). Automatic Synthesis of Fine-Motion Strategies for Robots. *IJRR*, **3**, 1, pp. 3–24.

Mason, M. T. (1986). Mechanics and Planning of Manipulator Pushing Operations. *IJRR*, **5**, 3, pp. 53–71.

McKerrow, P. J. (1988). *Performance Measurement of Computer Systems*. Wokingham: Addison-Wesley.

Michie, D. (1985). Expert systems and Robotics. In: Nof, S. Y. (ed.) *Handbook of Industrial Robotics*, Chichester: John Wiley, pp. 419–436.

Nagurka, M. L. and Yen, V. (1987). Optimal Design of Robotic Manipulator Trajectories: A Non-linear Programming Approach, CMU-RI, TR 87-12.

Nilsson, N. J. (1984). SHAKEY the Robot. *SRI International*, Technical Note 323.

Owens, R. A. (1984). Surface Prediction and Adaption in a Robot's Workplace. *National Conference and Exhibition on Robotics*, Melbourne.

Paul, R. P. C. (1979). Manipulator Cartesian path Control. *IEEE Transactions on Systems, Man and Cybernetics*, **SMC-9**, pp. 702–711.

Peshkin, M. A. and Sanderson, A. C. (1986). Reachable Grasps on a Polygon: The Convex Rope Algorithm. *IEEE Journal of Robotics and Automation*, **RA-2**, 1, pp. 53–58.

Pfeiffer, F. and Johanni, R. (1987). A Concept for Manipulator Trajectory Planning. *IEEE Journal of Robotics and Automation*, **RA-3**, 3, pp. 115–123.

Popplestone, R. J., Ambler, A. P. and Bellos, I. M. (1978). RAPT: A language for describing assemblies. *Industrial Robot*, **5**, 3, p. 131.

Popplestone, R. J., Ambler, A. P. and Bellos, I. M. (1980). An Interpreter for a Language Describing Assemblies. *Artificial Intelligence*, **14**, 1, pp. 79–107.

Requicha, A. A. (1980). Representations for Rigid Solids: Theory, Methods, and Systems. *Computing Surveys*, **12**, 4, pp. 437–464.

Requicha, A. A. G. (1983). Toward a Theory of Geometric Tolerancing. *IJRR*, **2**, 4, pp. 45–60.

Requicha, A. A. G. and Chan, S. C. (1986). Representation of Geometric Features, Tolerances and Attributes in Solid Modelers Based on Constructive Geometry. *IEEE Journal of Robotics and Automation*, **RA-2**, 3, pp. 156–166.

Requicha, A. A. G. and Voelcker, H. B. (1982). Solid Modelling: A Historical Summary and Contemporary Assessment. *IEEE Computer Graphics* (Special Issue on solid Modelling), **2**, 2, pp. 9–25.

Sacerdoti, E. D. (1977). *A Structure for Plans and Behaviour*. Elsevier.

Stevenson, C. N. (1987). Model-based Programming and Control of Robot Manipulators. *Computer*, **20**, 8, pp. 76–84.

Summers, P. D. and Grossman, D. D. (1984). XPROBE: An Experimental System for Programming Robots by Example. *IJRR*, **3**, 1, pp. 25–39.

Taylor, R. H. (1979). Planning and Execution of Straight Line Manipulator Trajectories. *IBM Journal of Research and Development*, 23, pp. 424–436.

Wilkins, D. (1984). Domain-independent Planning: Representation and Plan Generation, *Artificial Intelligence*, **22**, 3, pp. 269–301.

Winston, P. H. (1984). *Artificial Intelligence*. Reading MA: Addison-Wesley.

Witney, D. E. (1972). The Mathematics of Co-ordinated Control of Prosthetic Arms and Manipulator. *Journal of Dynamic Systems, Measurement and Control*, ASME, pp. 303–309.

Wong, E. K. and Fu, K. S. (1986). A Hierarchical Orthogonal Space Approach to Three-Dimensional Path Planning, *IEEE Journal of Robotics and Automation*, **RA-2**, 1, pp. 42–53.

Yong, Y. F., Gleave, J. A., Green, J. L. and Bonney, M. C. (1985). Off-Line Programming of Robots. In: Nof, S. Y. (ed.) *Handbook of Industrial Robotics*, Chichester: John Wiley, pp. 366–380.

Chapter 10

Adam, J. A. (1988). How To Design An 'Invisible' Aircraft. *IEEE Spectrum*, April, pp. 24–31.

Agin, G. J. (1980). Computer Vision Systems for Industrial Inspection and Assembly. *IEEE Computer*, **13**, 5.

Agin, G. J. (1985). Calibration and Use of a Light Stripe Range Sensor Mounted on the Hand of a Robot. *IEEE Conference on Robotics and Automation*.

Agin, G. J. (1985). Vision Systems. In: Nof, S. Y. (ed.) *Handbook of Industrial Robotics*, Chichester: John Wiley, pp. 231–261.

Agin, G. J., Uram, M. J. and Highnam, P. T. (1985). Three-Dimensional Sensing and Interpretation. CMU-RI-TR-85-1.

Anderson, R. L. (1988). Building Fast, Intelligent Robot Systems. *AT&T Technical Journal*, **67**, 2, pp. 73–86.

Anderson, R. L. *A Robot Ping-Pong Player*. MIT Press.

Angell, J. B., Terry, S. C. and Bath, P. W. (1983). Silicon Micro Mechanical Devices. *Scientific American*, **248**, 4, pp. 36–47.

Arbib, M. A., Overton, K. J. and Lawton, D. T. (1983). Perceptual Systems for Robots. *Australian Computer Bulletin*, October, pp. 8–25.

Bejczy, K. (1980). Smart Sensors for Smart Hands. *Progress in Astronautics and Aeronautics*, p. 67.

Biber, C., Ellin, S., Shenk, E. and Stempeck, J. (1980). The Polaroid Ultrasonic Ranging System, *67th Convention, Audio Engineering Society*.

Borenstein, J. and Koren, Y. (1988). Obstacle Avoidance with Ultrasonic Sensors. *IEEE Journal of Robotics and Automation*, **4**, 2, pp. 213–218.

Bower, F. H. (1984). CCD Fundamentals. *Fairchild CCD data book*.

Boyes, G. (ed.) (1980). *Synchro and Resolver Conversion*. Analog Devices.

Boyle, R. D. and Thomas, R. C. (1988). Computer Vision, A First Course. Oxford: Blackwell Scientific.

Burdic, W. S. (1984). *Underwater Acoustic System Analysis*. Englewood Cliffs: Prentice-Hall.

Burks, B. L., de Saussure, G., Weisbin, C. R., Jones, J. P. and Hamel, W. R. (1987). Autonomous Navigation, Exploration, and Recognition Using the HERMIES-IIB Robot. *IEEE Expert*, **2**, 4, pp. 18–27.

Busnel, R. G. and Fish, J. F. (eds) (1979). Animal Sonar Systems. *NATO ASI Series*, New York: Plenum Press.

Cederberg, R. L. T. (1979). Chain-Link Coding and Segmentation for Raster Scan Devices. *Computer Graphics and Image Processing*, **10**, pp. 224–234.

Cohen, P. R. and Feigenbaum, E. A. (1982). *The Handbook of Artificial Intelligence*. Vol. 3, Chap. 8, San Francisco: William Kaufman Inc.

Conrad, M. (1986). The Lure of Molecular Computing. *IEEE Spectrum*, October, pp. 55–60.

Corby, N. R. (1983). Machine Vision for Robotics. *IEEE Transactions on Industrial Electronics*, **IE-30**, 3, August, pp. 282–290.

Coren, S., Porec, C. and Word, L. M. (1984). *Sensation and Perception*. (Second edition), New York: Academic Press.

Crowley, J. L. (1984). Dynamic World Modelling for an Intelligent Mobile Robot. *IEEE 7th Conference in Pattern Recognition*, pp. 207–210.

Cunningham, R. (1981). Segmenting Binary Images. *Robotics Age*, July/August, pp. 4–19.

Dario, P. and Buttazzo, G. (1987). An Anthropomorphic Robot Finger for Investigating Artificial Tactile Perception. *IJRR*, **6**, 3, pp. 25–48.

Dario, P. and De Rossi, D. (1985). Tactile Sensors and the Gripping Challenge. *IEEE Spectrum*, August, pp. 46–52.

Davis, L. S. (1975). A Survey of Edge Detection Technique. *Computer Graphics and Image Processing*, 4, pp. 248–270.

Drumheller, M. (1987). Mobile Robot Localization Using Sonar. *PAMI-9*, 2, pp. 325–332.

Downer, J. (1988). *Supersense: Perception in the Animal World*. London: BBC Books.

Ejiri, M. *et al.* (1979). An Industrial Eye That Recognizes Hole Positions in a Water Pump Testing Process. In: Dodd and Rossol (eds), *Computer Vision and Sensor Based Robots*, New York: Plenum Press.

Eleccion, M. (1986). Sensors Tap IC Technology To Add More Functions. *Electronics*, June 2, pp. 26–30.

Everett, H. R. (1985). A Multielement Ultrasonic Ranging Array. *Robotics Age*, **7**, 7, pp. 13–20.

Fairhurst, M. C. (1988). *Computer Vision for Robotic Systems: An Introduction*. Englewood Cliffs: Prentice-Hall.

Fischetti, M. A. (1983). Probing the Human Body. *IEEE Spectrum*, January, pp. 75–78.

Fleisher, W. A. (1988). How To Select d.c. Motors. *Machine Design*, **60**, 26, pp. 99–103.

Flynn, A. M. (1985). Redundant Sensors for Mobile Robot Navigation. MIT AI Lab, TR-859.

Foster, N. J. and Sanderson, A. C. (1984). Determining Object Orientation from a Single Image Using Multiple Information Sources, CMU-RI-TR-84–15.

Freeman, H. (1974). Computer Processing of Line-Drawing Images. *Computing Surveys*, **6**, 1, pp. 57–93.

Fu, K. (1980). Pattern Recognition for Automatic Visual Inspection. *IEEE Computer*, **13**, 5.

Gamow, R. I. and Harris, J. F. (1972). What Engineers Can Learn From Nature. *IEEE Spectrum*, August, pp. 36–42.

Gonzalez, R. C. and Safabakhsh, R. (1982). Computer Vision Techniques for Industrial Applications and Robot Control. *IEEE Computer*, December, pp. 17–28.

Gonzalez, R. C. and Wintz, P. (1987). *Digital Image Processing*. (Second edition), Reading MA: Addison-Wesley.

Gooberman, G. L. (1968). *Ultrasonics*. The English University Press.

Griffin, D. R. (1954). Bird Sonar. *Scientific American*, **190**, 3, March, pp. 78–83.

Griffin, D. R. (ed.) (1974). *Animal Engineering: Readings from Scientific American*. New York: W. H. Freeman and Co.

Hall, D. J. (1984). Robotic Sensing Devices. CMU-RI-TR-84-3.

Harmon, L. D. (1982). Automated Tactile Sensing. *IJRR*, **1**, 2, pp. 3–32.

Harris, W. A. (1986). Learned Topography: The Eye Instructs The Ear. *TINS*, March, pp. 97–99.

Herbert, M. and Kanade, T. (1986). Outdoor Scene Analysis Using Range Data. *Proceedings IEEE Conference on Robotics and Automation*.

Hewlett-Packard Company. Practical Strain Gauge Measurements. Application Note 290–1.

Hildreth, E. C. (1981). Edge Detection in Man and Machine. *Robotics Age*, Sept/Oct, pp. 8–14.

Hillis, W. D. (1982). A High-Resolution Image Touch Sensor. *IJRR*, **1**, 2, pp. 33–44.

Hoffman, D. D. (1983). The Interpretation of Visual Illusion. *Scientific American*, **249**, 6, pp. 137–144.

Holland, S. W., Rossol, L. and Ward, M. R. (1979). Consight-1: A Vision-Controlled Robot System for Transferring Parts from Belt Conveyors. In: Dodd, G. G. and Rossol, L. (eds) *Computer Vision and Sensor-Based Robots*, pp. 81–97, New York: Plenum Press.

Horgan, J. (1986). Roboticists Aim to Ape Nature. *IEEE Computer*, February, pp. 66–71.

Hubel, D. H. and Wiesel, T. N. (1979). Brain Mechanisms of Vision. *Scientific American*, **241**, 3, pp. 130–144.

Jacobsen, S. C., McCammon, I. P., Biggers, K. B. and Phillips, R. P. (1988). Design of Tactile Sensing Systems for Dextrous Manipulators. *IEEE Control Systems Magazine*, **8**, 1, pp. 3–13.

Jarvis, R. A. (1982). A Computer Vision and Robotics Library. *IEEE Computer*, June, pp. 8–24.

Jarvis, R. A. (1983). A Perspective on Range Finding Techniques for Computer Vision. *PAMI-5*, 2, pp. 122–139.

Jorgensen, C. J., Hamel, W. and Weisbin, C. (1986). Autonomous Robot Navigation. *Byte*, January, pp. 223–235.

Kak, A. C. and Albus, J. S. (1985). Sensors for Intelligent Robots. In: Nof, S. Y. (ed.) *Handbook of Industrial Robotics*, Chichester: John Wiley, pp. 214–220.

Kak, A. C. (1985). Depth Perception for Robots. In: Nof, S. Y. (ed.) *Handbook of Industrial Robotics*, Chichester: John Wiley, pp. 272–319.

Kelley, R. B., Martins, H. A. S., Birk, J. R. and Dessimoz, J. D. (1983). Three Vision Algorithms for Acquiring Workpieces from Bins. *Proceedings of the IEEE*, **71**, 7, pp. 803–820.

Kent, E. W. and Shneier, M. O. (1986). Eyes for Automation. *IEEE Spectrum*, March, pp. 37–45.

Khol, R. (ed.) (1988). Sensors and Transducers. *Machine Design*, May 19, pp. 149–178.

Kinsler, L. E. and Frey, A. R. (1962). *Fundamentals of Acoustics*. New York: John Wiley.

Komoriya, K., Tachi, S. and Tanic, K. (1986). A Method of Autonomous Locomotion for Mobile Robots. *Advances in Robotics*, **1**, 1, pp. 3–19.

Kuc, R. and Siegel, M. W. (1987). Physically Based Simulation Model for Acoustic Sensor Robot Navigation. *PAMI-9*, 6, pp. 766–778.

Kuc, R. (1985). Resolution Capabilities of Ultrasound Sensors, Seminar, CMU-RI.

Laming, D. (1988). Precis of Sensory Analysis. *Behavioural and Brain Sciences*. **11**, pp. 275–339.

Lavin, M. A. and Lieberman, L. I. (1982). AML/V: An Industrial Machine Vision Programming System. *The International Journal of Robot Research*, **1**, 3, pp. 42–56.

Lebow Associates Inc. (1979). *Torque Sensor and Dynamometer Catalog*, No. 250A, Troy, Michigan.

MacFarlane, J. and Donath, M. (1984). Tracking Robot Motion in Three-Dimensional Space: A Laser Scanning Approach. *Robotics and Artificial Intelligence*, (NATO ASI Series) **F11**.

Martin, G. J. (1986). Gyroscopes May Cease Spinning. *IEEE Spectrum*, February, pp. 48–53.

Midlelhock, S., Angell, J. B. and Noorlag, D. J. W. (1980). Microprocessors Get Integrated Sensors. *IEEE Spectrum*, **17**, 2, pp. 42–46.

Myers, W. (1980). Industry Begins to Use Visual Pattern Recognition. *IEEE Computer*, **13**, 5, pp. 21–30.

Okada, T. (1982). Development of an Optical Distance Sensor for Robots. *IJRR*, **1**, 4, pp. 3–14.

Pennywitt, K. E. (1986). Robotics Tactile Sensing. *Byte*, January, pp. 177–200.

Pipitone, F. J. and Marshall, T. G. (1983). A Wide-Field Scanning Triangulation Rangefinder for Machine Vision. *IJRR*, **2**, 1, pp. 39–49.

Poggio, T. (1984). Vision by Man and Machine. *Scientific American*, **250**, 4, pp. 68–78.

Porter, G. B. and Mundy, J. L. (1980). Visual Inspection System Design. *IEEE Computer*, May, pp. 40–48.

Potter, J. L. (1983). Image Processing On the Massively Parallel Processor. *IEEE Computer*, **16**, 1.

Raibert, M. H. and Tanner, J. E. (1982). Design and Implementation of a VLSI Tactile Sensing Computer. *IJRR*, **1**, 3, pp. 3–18.

Rebman, J. and Trull, M. W. (1983). A Robust Tactile Sensor for Robot Application, Lord Corporation Report LL-2142.

Rembold, U. and Blume, C. (1985). Interfacing a Vision System with a Robot. In: Nof, S. Y. (ed.) *Handbook of Industrial Robotics*, Chichester: John Wiley, pp. 262–271.

Rembold, U., Dillman, R. and Levi, P. (1985). The Role of Computer in Robot Intelligence. In: Nof, S. Y. (ed.) *Handbook of Industrial Robotics*, Chichester: John Wiley, pp. 272–319.

Rosenfield, A. (1983). Parallel Image Processing Using Cellular Arrays. *IEEE Computer*, **16**, 1.

Russell, A. (1984). Closing the Sensor – Robot Control Loop. *Robotics Age*, **6**, 4, pp. 15–20.

Saburo, T. and Yachida, M. (1980). Industrial Computer Vision in Japan. *IEEE Computer*, **13**, 5.

Seippel, R. G. (1983). *Transducers, Sensors and Detectors*. Reston Va: Reston Publishing Co.

Shackil, A. F. (1980). An Electronic 'Human Eye'. *IEEE Spectrum*, September, pp. 89–91.

Shimano, B. E. and Roth, B. (1979). On Force Sensing Information and Its Use in Controlling Manipulators. *Proceedings of the 9th International Symposium on Industrial Robots*, pp. 119–126.

Snyder, W. E. and St. Clair, J. (1978). Conductive Elastomers as Sensors for Industrial Parts Handling Equipment. *IEEE Transaction on Instrumentation and Measurement*, **IM27**, 1, pp. 94–99.

Thompson, A. M. (1979). Introduction to Robot Vision. *Robotics Age*, **1**, 1, pp. 22–34.

Thorpe, C. E. (1984). FIDO: Vision and Navigation for a Robot Rover. CMU-CS-84-168.

Truxal, C. (1983). Watching The Brain At Work. *IEEE Spectrum*, March, pp. 52–57.

Ullmann, J. R. (1974). Binarization using Associative Addressing. *Pattern Recognition*, **6**, pp. 127–135.

Usher, M. J. (1985). *Sensors and Transducers*, New York: Macmillan.

Weszka, J. S. *et al.* (1974). A Threshold Selection Technique. *IEEE Transactions on Computers*, December, pp. 1322–1326.

Weszka, J. S. (1978). A Survey of Threshold Selection Techniques. *Computer Graphics and Image Processing*, **7**, pp. 259–265.

Wilf, J. M. (1981). Chain Code, *Robotics Age*, **3**, 2, pp. 12–19.

Wilf, J. M. (1981). Video Signal Input, *Robotics Age*, **3**, 2.

Wilson, J. F. (1984). Robotic Mechanics and Animal Morphology. In: Brady, M. *et al.* (eds) *Robotics and Artificial Intelligence*, p. 419.

Yachida, M. and Tsuji, S. (1980). Industrial Computer Vision in Japan. *IEEE Computer*, May, pp. 50–62.

Chapter 11

Asada, H. and Youcef-Toumi, K. (1987). *Direct-Drive Robots: Theory and Practice*, Boston: MIT Press.

Auslander, D. J., Takahashi, Y. and Tomizuka, M. (1978). Direct Digital Process Control: Practice and Algorithms for Microprocessor Application. *Proceedings of the IEEE*, **66**, 2, pp. 199–208.

Bennett, S. (1988). *Real-Time Computer Control: An Introduction*. Englewood Cliffs: Prentice-Hall.

Briot, M. (1985). Control System Architecture for Robot Manipulators. *LAAS*, Report No. 85, 118.

Craig, J. J. (1988). *Adaptive Control of Mechanical Manipulators*. Reading, MA: Addison-Wesley.

Dorf, R. C. (1974). *Modern Control Systems*, (Second edition), Reading, MA: Addison-Wesley.

Dransfield, P. and Haber, F. (1973). *Introducing Root Locus*, Cambridge: Cambridge University Press.

Dransfield, P., Orr, S. and Tan, E. S. P. (1988). Comparable Electric, Pneumatic, and Hydraulic Servo drives. *Proceedings 19th ISIR*, R. A. Jarvis, (ed.) Springer-Verlag, pp. 795–803.

Dubowsky, S. and Des Forges, D. T. (1979). The Application of Model Referenced Adaptive Control to Robotic Manipulators. *Transactions of ASME Journal of Dynamic Systems, Measurement and Control*, **101**, pp. 193–200.

Fleisher, W. A. (1988). How to Select d.c. Motors. *Machine Design*, **60**, 26, pp. 99–103.

Hendy, B. G. and Holzer, A. J. (1984). Force Compliant Motion in a Position Controlled Manipulator. *Proceedings, National Conference and Exhibition on Robotics*, ARA, Melbourne.

House, C. H. (1980). Perspectives on Dedicated and Control Processing. *Computer*, December, pp. 35–49.

Khosla, P. K. (1986). *Real-Time Control and Identification of Direct-Drive Manipulators*, PhD Thesis, Department of Electrical and Computer Engineering, CMU.

Koivo, A. J. and Guo, T. H. (1983). Adaptive Linear Control for Robotic Manipulators. *IEEE Transactions on Automatic Control*, **AC-28**, 1, pp. 162–171.

Kusko, A. (1969). *Solid-State d.c. Motor Drives*. MIT Press.

Lee, C. S. G. (1982). Robot Arm Kinematics, Dynamics and Control. *IEEE Computer*, December, pp. 62–80.

Lee, C. S. G. and Chung, M. J. (1985). Adaptive Perturbation Control with Feedback Compensation for Robot Manipulators. *Simulation*, **44**, 3, pp. 27–57.

Luh, J. Y. S. (1983). An Anatomy of Industrial Robots and Their Controls. *IEEE Transaction on Automatic Control*, **AC-28**, 2, pp. 133–151.

Luh, J. Y. S., Fisher, W. D. and Paul, R. P. C. (1983). Joint Torque Control by a Direct Feedback for Industrial Robots. *IEEE Transactions on Automatic Control*, **AC-28**, 2, pp. 153–161.

Luh, J. Y. S., Walker, M. W. and Paul, R. P. (1980). Resolved-Acceleration Control of Mechanical Manipulators. *IEEE Transactions on Automatic Control*, **AC-25**, 3, pp. 468–474.

Muir, P. F. and Neumann, C. P. (1985). Pulsewidth Modulation Control of Brushless d.c. Motors for Robotic Applications. *IEEE Transactions on Industrial Electronics*, **IE-32**, 3, pp. 222–229.

Neal, T. P. (1974). Performance Estimation for Electrohydraulic Control Systems. MOOG, Technical Bulletin No. 126.

Pike, H. E. (1970). Process Control Software. *Proceedings of the IEEE*, **58**, 1, pp. 87–103.

Raibert, M. H. and Craig, J. J. (1981). Hybrid Position/force Control of Manipulators, *Journal of Dynamic Systems Measurement and Control*, **102**, pp. 126–133.

Salisbury, J. K. (1980). Active Stiffness Control of a Manipulator in Cartesian Coordinates. *Proceedings, IEEE Conference on Decision and Control*. November, pp. 95–100.

Shinskey, F. G. (1967). *Process Control Systems*. Maidenhead: McGraw-Hill.

Slotine, J. J. E. (1988). Putting Physics into Control – The Example of Robotics. *IEEE Control Systems Magazine*, **8**, 6, pp. 12–17.

Slotine, J. J. E. and Li, W. (1987). On the Adaptive Control of Robot Manipulators. *IJRR*, **6**, 3, pp. 49–59.

Smith, C. L. (1970). Digital Control of Industrial Processes. *Computing Surveys*, **2**, 3, September, pp. 211–239.

Smith, C. L. (1972). *Digital Computer Process Control*. Intext Education Publishers.

Smith, L. C. (1978). Servo Control Through Software, *Machine Design*, May 25, pp. 70–75.

Steusloff, H. U. (1984). Advanced Real-Time Languages for Distributed Industrial Process Control. **17**, 2, pp. 37–46.

Tal, J. and Bacon, W. (1984). Motion Control for Automation and Robotics. *Robotics Age*, **6**, 12, pp. 8–11.

Weiss, L. E. (1984). Dynamic Visual Servo Control of Robots: An Adaptive Image-Based Approach. CMU-RI-TR-84-16.

Weiss, L. E., Sanderson, A. C. and Neuman, C. P. (1987). Dynamic Sensor-Based Control of Robots with Visual Feedback. *IEEE Journal of Robotics and Automation*, **RA-3**, 5, pp. 404–417.

Whitney, D. E. (1985). Historical Perspective and State of the Art in Robot Force Control. *IEEE Conference on Robots and Automation*, pp. 262–268.

Young, S. (1985). Sensor-based Force Control as an Alternative to Mechanical Compliance. CMU-RI, personal communication.

Chapter 12

Allworth, S. T. (1981). *Introduction to Real-Time Software Design*. London: Macmillan.

Anderson, R. (1988). AML/X – The Use of Advanced Computer Science Concepts to Solve Robot Language Problems. Department of Computer Science, The University of Wollongong, Preprint No. 88/4.

Arai, T., Takashima, S. and Sata, T. (1985). Standardisation of Robot Software in Japan. *15th International Symposium on Industrial Robots*, **2**, Tokyo, Japan, pp. 995–1002.

Ambler, A. P. (1984). Languages for Programming Robots. In: Brady, Gerhardt and Davidson, (eds) *Robotics and Artificial Intelligence*. Berlin: Springer-Verlag, pp. 219–227.

Blume, C. and Jackob, W. (1986). *Programming Languages for Industrial Robots*. Berlin: Springer-Verlag.

Bolles, R. and Paul, R. (1973). The Use of Sensory Feedback in a Programmable Assembly System, Stanford University AI Laboratory, AIM-220.

Brady, M. (1985). Artificial Intelligence and Robotics. *Artificial Intelligence*, **26**, pp. 79–121.

Buckley, S. J. and Collins, G. F. (1985). A Standard Programming Robot Language. In: Nof, S. Y. (ed.) *Handbook of Industrial Robotics*. Chichester: John Wiley, pp. 381–403.

Burckhardt, C. W. and Marchiando, C. (1984). A Multi-Robot High Level Programming System for Assembly. In: Danthine, A. and Geradin, M. (eds) *Advanced Software in Robotics*, Oxford: Elsevier Science Publishers, pp. 301–310.

Chester, M. (1983). Robotic Software Reaches Out for Task Oriented Languages. The Goal: To remove all Human Supervision. *Electronic Design*, pp. 119–129.

Cox, I. J., Kapilow, D. A., Kropfl, W. J. and Shopiro, J. E. (1988). Real-Time Software for Robotics. *AT&T Technical Journal*, **67**, 2, pp. 61–72.

Davey, P. (1983). It's The Language That Decides How Will The Robot Perform. In *Decade of Robotics*, London: IFS, pp. 26–28.

Deisenroth, M. P. (1985). Robot Teaching. In: Nof, S. Y. (ed.) *Handbook of Industrial Robotics*, Chichester: John Wiley, pp. 352–365.

Finkel, R. *et al.* (1975). An Overview of AL, a Programming System for Automation. *Proceedings of the Fourth International Joint Conference on Artificial Intelligence*, pp. 758–765.

Foster, C. C. (1981). *Real-Time Programming – Neglected Topics*. Reading MA, Addison-Wesley.

Frederickson, D. H. (1986). Dynamic Loading of C Subroutines from AML/2-X under PC-DOS. IBM T. J. Watson Research Center, N.Y.

Geschke, C. C. (1983). A System for Programming and Controlling Sensor Based Robot Manipulators. *IEEE Transaction Pattern Analysis and Machine Intelligence*, **PAMI-5**, 1, pp. 1–7.

Gini, G. C. and Gini, M. L. (1985). Dealing with World-Model-Based Programs. *ACM Transactions on Programming Languages and Systems*, **7**, 2, pp. 334–347.

Glass, R. L. (1980). Real-Time: The 'Lost World' of Software Debugging and Testing. *Communications of the ACM*, **23**, 5, pp. 264–271.

Goldman, R. (1985). *Design of an Interactive Manipulator Programming Environment*. Ann Arbor MI: UMI Research Press.

Grossman, D. (1977). Programming a Computer Controlled Manipulator by Guiding through the Motions. IBM T. J. Watson Research Center, Report RL-6393.

Grossman, D. D. and Taylor, R. H. (1978). Interactive Generation of Object Models with a Manipulator. *IEEE Transaction Systems Man. & Cybernetics*, **SMC-8**, 9, pp. 667–679.

Grossman, D. D. and Taylor, R. H. (1983). An Integrated Robot System Architecture. *Proceedings of IEEE*, **71**, 7, pp. 842–855.

Hirzinger, G. (1984). Sensor Programming – A New Way For Teaching Robot Paths and Sensory Patterns Simultaneously. In: Brady *et al.* (eds) *Robotics and Artificial Intelligence*, (NATO ASI series), **F11**, pp. 395–410.

Hollingshead, L. I. (1985). Elements of Industrial Robot Software. In: Nof, S. Y. (ed.) *Handbook of Industrial Robotics*. Chichester: John Wiley, pp. 337–351.

Kawabe, S. *et al.* (1985). Interactive Graphic Programming for Industrial Robots. *15th International Symposium on Industrial Robots*, **2**, Tokyo, Japan, pp. 699–706.

Kuwahara, H. (1985). Design Concept and Architecture of a Distributed Robot System Using A High Level Robot Language. *15th International Symposium on Industrial Robots*, **2**, Tokyo, Japan, pp. 707–714.

Latombe, J. C. (1983). Survey of Advanced General-Purpose Software for Robot Manipulators. *Computers in Industry*, **4**, pp. 227–242.

Latombe, J. C., Laugier, C., Lefebure, J. M., Mazer, E. and Miribel, J. F. (1985). The LM Robot Programming System. In: Hanafusa, H. and Inoue, H. (eds) *Robotics Research The Second International Symposium*. Boston: MIT Press, pp. 377–391.

Lieberman, L. I. and Wesley, M. A. (1977). AUTOPASS: An Automatic Programming System for Computer Controlled Mechanical Assembly. *IBM Journal of Research and Development*, **21**, 4, pp. 321–333.

Lozano-Perez, T. (1981). Automatic Planning of Manipulator Transfer Movements. *IEEE Transaction System Man. & Cybernetics*, **SMC-11**, 10.

Lozano-Perez, T. (1983). Robot Programming. *Proceedings of the IEEE*, **71**, 7, pp. 821–841.

Lozano-Perez, T. (1985). An Approach to Automatic Robot Programming. A.I. Memo No. 842, MIT.

Mazer, E. (1984). LM-GEO Geometric Programming of Assembly Robots. In: Danthine, A. and Geradin, M. (eds) *Advanced Software in Robotics*, Elsevier Science Publishers.

McKerrow, P. (1988). *Performance Measurement of Computer Systems*. Wokingham: Addison-Wesley.

McLaughlin, J. R. (1982). Trig: An Interactive Robotic Teach System. MIT AI Lab, Working paper 234.

McLellan, E. (1983). Robot Languages – The Current Position. In: Pugh, A. (ed.) *Robotic Technology*. New York: Peter Pereginus Ltd.

Nackman, L. R. *et al.* (1986). AML/X: A Programming Language for Design and Manufacturing. IBM Research Report, RC 11992.

Nackman, L. R., Lavin, M. A., Taylor, R. H. and Walter, C. D. (1986). AML/X: User's Manual. IBM Research Report, RA 175.

Parent, M. and Laurgeau, C. (1985). Logic and Programming. *Robot Technology*, **5**, Prentice Hall.

Paul, R. P. (1983). WAVE: A Model Based Language for Manipulator Control. IEEE Catalog No. EH0207-1, ISBN 0-8186-0515-4, pp. 350–365.

Paul, R. P. and Hayward, V. (1984). Robot Control and Computer Languages. *Proceedings of Romansy, The fifth CISM-IFTOMM Symposium*, pp. 187–193.

Ranky, P. G. and Ho, C. Y. (1985). *Robot Modelling*. London: IFS Publications Ltd.

Rembold, U., Dillmann, R. and Levi, P. (1985). The Role of the Computer in Robot Intelligence. In: Nof, S. Y. (ed.) *Handbook of Industrial Robotics*, Chichester: John Wiley, pp. 437–463.

Shimano, B. (1983). VAL: A Versatile Robot Programming and Control Language. IEEE Catalog No. EH0207-1, ISBN 0-8186-0515-4, pp. 366–371.

Sluzek, A. and Zielinski, C. (1985). New Data Types for 4/5 Degree of Freedom Robot Manipulators. *15th International Symposium on Industrial Robots*, **2**, Tokyo, Japan, pp. 1067–1073.

Stankovic, J. A. (1988). Misconceptions About Real-Time Computing: A Serious Problem for Next Generation Systems. *IEEE Computer*, **21**, 10, pp. 10–19.

Steusloff, A. U. (1984). Advanced Real-Time Languages for Distributed Industrial Process Control. *IEEE Computer*, **17**, 2, pp. 37–46.

Summers, P. D. and Grossman, D. D. (1984). XPROBE: An Experimental System for Programming Robots by Example. *IJRR*, **3**, 1, pp. 25–39.

Takanashi, N. *et al.* (1985). Hierarchical Robot Sensors Application in Assembly Tasks. *15th International Symposium on Industrial Robots*, **2**, Tokyo, Japan, pp. 829–836.

Takase, K., Paul, R. P. and Berg, E. J. (1981). A Structured Approach to Robot Programming and Teaching. *IEEE Transaction Systems Man. & Cybernetics*, **SMC-11**, 4, pp. 274–289.

Tan, H. and Chang, F. (1985). A Flexible Robot Programming System, UROCS. *15th International Symposium on Industrial Robots*, **2**, Tokyo, Japan, pp. 725–740.

Taskase, K., Paul, R. and Berg, E. (1979). A Structured Approach to Robot Programming and Teaching. *Proceedings of Compsac 79*, IEEE, pp. 452–457.

Taylor, R. H., Summers, P. and Meyer, J. (1982). AML: A Manufacturing Language. *IJRR*, **1**, 3, p. 19.

Taylor, R. H. and Grossman, D. D. (1983). An Integrated Robot System Architecture, *Proceedings of the IEEE*, **71**, 7, pp. 842–855.

Unimation, Inc. (1979). *User's Guide to VAL, a robot programming and control system*.

Walter, C. (1984). Control Software Specification and Design: An Overview. *IEEE Computer*, **17**, 2, pp. 20–23.

Weck, *et al.* (1984). Requirements for Robot Off-Line Programming shown at the example ROBEX. In: Danthine, A. and Geradin, M. (eds) *Advanced Software in Robotics*. Elsevier Science Publishers, pp. 321–330.

Yong, Y. F., Gleave, J. A., Green, J. L. and Bonney, M. C. (1985). Off-Line Programming of Robots. In: Nof, S. Y. (ed.) *Handbook of Industrial Robotics*, Chichester: John Wiley, pp. 366–380.

Zielinski, C. (1985). Semantics of the Low Level Robot Language Instructions. *15th International Symposium on Industrial Robots*, **2**, Tokyo, Japan, pp. 985–993.

Appendix

La Brooy, R. C. (1986). On the Determination of An Inverse Kinematic Analysis Solution to a 5 Degree-of-Freedom, Serially-linked, Industrial Research Robot. *Proceedings of Robots in Australia's Future Conference*, ARA, Perth, pp. 220–232.

Index